James L. Ginter

STRATEGIC BRAND

MANAGEMENT
BUILDING, MEASURING, AND MANAGING BRAND EQUITY

Kevin Lane Keller

The Fuqua School of Business
Duke University

Prentice Hall
Upper Saddle River, New Jersey 07458

Acquisitions Editor: Whitney Blake
Associate Editor: John Larkin
Editorial Assistant: Rachel Falk
Vice President/Editorial Director: Jim Boyd
Marketing Manager: John Chillingworth
Production Editor/Liaison: Michelle Rich
Project Management: Pine Tree Composition
Production Coordinator: Carol Samet
Permissions Coordinator: Jennifer Rella
Managing Editor: Dee Josephson
Associate Managing Editor: Linda DeLorenzo
Manufacturing Buyer: Kenneth J. Clinton
Manufacturing Supervisor: Arnold Vila
Manufacturing Manager: Vincent Scelta
Design Manager: Patricia Smythe
Cover Design: Lorraine Castellano
Illustrator (Interior): Pine Tree Composition
Composition: Pine Tree Composition
Cover Art/Photo: George Abe

> *This book is dedicated to my mother and father*
> *with much love, respect, and admiration.*

Credits and acknowledgments for materials borrowed from other sources and reproduced, with permission, in this textbook appear on pages CR-1–CR-2.

 Copyright © 1998 by Prentice-Hall, Inc.
A Simon & Schuster Company
Upper Saddle River, New Jersey 07458

Library of Congress Cataloging-in-Publication Data

Keller, Kevin Lane
   Strategic brand management : building, measuring, and managing brand equity /
Kevin Lane Keller.
     p.   cm.
   Includes bibliographical references and index.
   ISBN 0–13–120115–8
   1. Brand name products—Management. I Title.
HD69.B7K45 1998
658.8'27—dc21   97–23327
                                                                    CIP

Prentice-Hall International (UK) Limited, London
Prentice-Hall of Australia Pty. Limited, Sydney
Prentice-Hall Canada, Inc., Toronto
Prentice-Hall Hispanoamericana, S.A., Mexico
Prentice-Hall of India Private Limited, New Delhi
Prentice-Hall of Japan, Inc., Tokyo
Simon & Schuster Asia Pte. Ltd., Singapore
Editora Prentice-Hall do Brasil, Ltda., Rio de Janeiro

Printed in the United States of America

10 9 8 7 6 5 4

Contents

Prologue: Branding Is Not Rocket Science

Although the challenges in branding can be immense and difficult, branding is not necessarily rocket science. I should know. I am not a rocket scientist—but my dad is. He was a physicist in the Air Force for twenty years, working on various rocket fuels. Always interested in what I do, he once asked what the book was all about. I explained the concept of brand equity and how the book addressed how to build, measure, and manage it. He listened, paused, and remarked, "That's very interesting but, uh, that's not *exactly* rocket science."

He's right. Branding is not rocket science. It is just as much an art as a science. There is always a creativity and originality component involved with branding. Even if someone were to faithfully follow all the guidelines in the book—and all the guidelines were completely and properly specified—the success or failure of a brand strategy would still depend largely on how exactly these guidelines were translated to make up the strategy and how this strategy was then implemented. Nevertheless, good marketing is all about improving the odds for success. The hope is that this book adds to the scientific aspect of branding, illuminating the subject and providing guidance to those who make brand-related decisions.

Preface

It is useful to answer a few questions to provide the reader and instructor with some background as to what this book is about, how it is different from other books about branding, who should read it, how a reader can get the most out of using the book, and how the rest of the book is organized.

What Is the Book About?

This book deals with brands—why they are important, what they represent to consumers, and what should be done by firms to manage them properly. As many business executives now recognize, perhaps one of the most valuable of a firm's assets are the brands that they have invested in and developed over time. Although manufacturing processes and factory designs often can be duplicated, strongly held beliefs and attitudes established in the minds of consumers often cannot be so easily reproduced. The difficulty and expense of introducing new products, however, puts more pressure than ever on firms to skillfully launch their new products as well as manage their existing brands.

Although brands may represent invaluable tangible assets, creating and nurturing a strong brand poses considerable challenges. Fortunately, the concept of *brand equity*—which is the main focus of this book—can provide marketers valuable perspective and a "common denominator" to interpret the potential effects and trade-offs of various brand strategies and tactics. Fundamentally, the brand equity concept stresses the important role of the brand in marketing strategies. Brand equity relates to the fact that different outcomes result in the marketing of a product or service because of its brand name or some other brand element, as compared to what happens if that same product or service did not have that brand identification. In other words, brand equity can be thought of as the marketing effects uniquely attributable to the brand. In a practical sense, brand equity represents the added value endowed to a product as a result of past investments in the marketing activity for a brand. Brand equity serves as the bridge between what happened to the brand in the past and what should happen to the brand in the future.

The chief purpose of this book is to provide a comprehensive and up-to-date treatment of the subjects of brands, brand equity, and strategic brand management. *Strategic brand management* involves the design and implementation of marketing programs and activities to build, measure, and manage brand equity. An important goal of the book is to provide managers with concepts and techniques to improve the long-term profitability of their brand strategies. The book incorporates current thinking and developments on these topics from both academics and industry participants. The book combines a comprehensive theoretical foundation with numerous practical insights to assist managerial decision-making in day-to-day and long-term brand decisions. Illustrative examples and case studies are based on brands marketed in the United States and all over the world.

Specifically, the book provides insights into how profitable brand strategies can be created by building, measuring, and managing brand equity. It addresses three important questions:

1. How can brand equity be created?
2. How can brand equity be measured?
3. How can brand equity be used to expand business opportunities?

In addressing these questions, the book is written to deliver a number of benefits. Readers will learn:

1. The role of brands, the concept of brand equity, and the advantages of creating strong brands.
2. The three main ways to build brand equity by properly choosing brand elements, designing supporting marketing programs, and leveraging secondary associations.
3. Different approaches to measure brand equity and how to implement a brand equity measurement system.
4. Alternative branding strategies and how to devise brand hierarchies and brand portfolios.
5. The role of corporate brands, family brands, individual brands, modifiers, and how they can be combined into sub-brands.
6. How to adjust branding strategies over time and geographic boundaries to maximize brand equity.

What Is Different About This Book?

In writing this book, the objective was to satisfy three key criteria by which any marketing text can be judged:

Depth: The material in the book had to be presented in the context of a conceptual framework that was comprehensive, internally consistent and cohesive, and well-grounded in the academic and practitioner literature.

Breadth: The book had to cover all those topics that practicing managers and students of brand management find interesting and/or important.

Relevance: The book had to be well-grounded in practice and easily related to past and present marketing activities, events, and case studies.

Although a number of excellent books have been written about brands, no book has really maximized those three dimensions to the extent possible. Accordingly, this book set out to fill that gap by accomplishing three things. First, the book develops a comprehensive framework that provides a definition of brand equity, identifies sources and outcomes of brand equity, and provides tactical guidelines as to how to build, measure, and manage brand equity. Recognizing the general importance of consumers and customers to marketing—understanding and satisfying their needs and wants—this framework approaches branding from the perspective of the consumer and is referred to as *customer-based brand equity*. Second, besides these broad, fundamentally important branding topics, for completeness, a number of specific, related branding topics are covered all through the book, such as legal issues, brand crises, and corporate name changes. Finally, to maximize relevance, numerous examples are included to illuminate the discussion on virtually every topic, and over 75 Branding Briefs are included to provide more in-depth examination of certain topics or brands.

In short, this book can help readers understand the important issues in planning and evaluating brand strategies, as well as provide appropriate concepts, theories, and other tools to make better branding decisions. The book identifies successful and unsuccessful brand marketers—and why they have been so. Readers will have a greater appreciation of the range of issues covered in branding as well as a means to organize their thoughts about those issues.

Who Should Read the Book?

A wide range of people can benefit from reading this book:

- Students interested in increasing both their understanding of basic branding principles and their exposure to classic and contemporary branding applications and case studies.
- Managers and analysts concerned with the effects of their day-to-day marketing decisions on brand performance.
- Senior executives concerned with the longer-term prosperity of their brand franchises and product or service portfolios.
- All marketers interested in new ideas with implications for marketing strategies and tactics.

The perspective adopted in the book is relevant to any type of organization (public or private, large or small), and the examples provided cover a wide range of industries and geographies. To facilitate understanding of branding concepts across different settings, specific applications to industrial, high-tech, service, retailer, and small-business are reviewed in both chapters 1 and 15.

How Is the Book Organized?

The book is divided into five major parts, adhering to the "three-exposure opportunity" approach to learning. Part I introduces branding concepts, Parts II, III, and IV provide all the specific details of those concepts, and Part V summarizes and applies the concepts in various contexts. The specific chapters for each part and their contents are as follows.

Part I sets the stage for the book by providing the "big picture" in terms of what strategic brand management is all about. The goal of these chapters is to provide a sense for the content and context of strategic brand management by identifying key branding decisions and suggesting some of the important considerations for those decisions. Specifically, chapter 1 introduces some basic notions about brands and the role that they have played and are playing in marketing strategies. Chapter 1 defines what a brand is, why brands matter, how anything can be branded, and provides a historical review of branding. Chapter 2 introduces the concept of customer-based brand equity, outlines the customer-based brand equity framework, and summarizes guidelines for building, measuring, and managing customer-based brand equity. The two chapters provide a useful overview of the scope of and topics covered in the book. As such they provide an excellent "top-line summary" for readers who want a flavor for the book or when it is not possible to read all of the chapters.

Part II examines the three major ways to build customer-based brand equity, taking more of a "single product–single brand" perspective. As background, chapter 3 develops a conceptual model of brand knowledge and considers how it may impact consumer response to marketing actions. Chapter 4 addresses the first way to build customer-based brand equity and how to choose brand elements (e.g., brand names, logos, symbols, slogans) and the role they play in contributing to brand equity. Chapters 5 and 6 are concerned with the second way to build brand equity and how to optimize the marketing mix to create customer-based brand equity. Chapter 5 is concerned with product, pricing, or distribution strategies; chapter 6 is devoted to the topic of creating integrated marketing communication programs to build brand equity. Although most readers are probably familiar with these "4 Ps" of marketing, it can be illuminating to consider them from the standpoint of brand equity and the effects of brand knowledge on consumer response to marketing mix activity and vice versa. Finally, chapter 7 examines the third major way to build brand equity—leveraging secondary associations from other entities (e.g., company, geographical region, person, other brands).

Part III looks at how to measure customer-based brand equity. These chapters take a detailed look at what consumers know about brands, what marketers want them to know, and how marketers can develop measurement procedures to assess how well they are doing. Chapter 8 examines approaches to measure customers' brand knowledge structures in order to be able to identify and quantify potential sources of brand equity. Chapter 9 examines how to measure potential outcomes of brand equity in terms of the major benefits a firm accrues from these sources of brand equity. Chapter 10 puts all of these ideas together to consider how to develop and implement a brand equity measurement system.

Part IV addresses how to manage brand equity, taking a broader, "multiple product–multiple brand" perspective as well as a longer-term, multiple market perspective to brands. Chapter 11 considers issues related to branding strategies—which brand elements a firm chooses to apply across the various products it sells—and how brand equity can be maximized across all the different brands and products that might be sold by a firm. Chapter 11 describes two important tools to help formulate branding strategies—the brand-product matrix and the brand hierarchy. Chapter 12 outlines the pros and cons of brand extensions and develops guidelines to facilitate the introduction and naming of new products and brand extensions. Chapter 13 considers how to reinforce, revitalize, and retire brands, examining a number of specific topics in managing brands over time such as the advantages of maintaining brand consistency, the importance of protecting sources of brand equity, and trade-offs in fortifying versus leveraging brands. Chapter 14 examines the implications of differences in consumer behavior and the existence of different types of market segments on managing brand equity. Particular attention is paid to international issues and global branding strategies.

Finally, Part V considers some implications and applications of the customer-based brand equity framework. Chapter 15 highlights managerial guidelines and key themes that emerged in earlier chapters of the book. The chapter also summarizes success factors for branding, applies the customer-based brand equity framework to address specific strategic brand management issues for different types of products (i.e., industrial goods, high-tech products, services, retailers, and small businesses) and relates the framework to several other popular views of brand equity. The appendices that follow provide five detailed case studies on specific brand management topics.

How Can a Reader Get the Most Out of the Book?

Branding is a fascinating topic that has received much attention in the popular press. The ideas presented in the book will help readers interpret current branding developments. One obvious way to better understand branding and the customer-based brand equity framework is to apply the concepts and ideas presented in the book. These applications could involve current events or any of the more detailed branding issues or case studies presented in the Branding Briefs. The Discussion Questions from the first fifteen chapters often ask readers to pick a brand and apply one or more concepts from that chapter. Focusing on one brand across all of the questions—perhaps as part of a class or work project—permits some cumulative and integrated learning and is an excellent way to become more comfortable and facile with the book material.

Finally, although trite to say, this book truly belongs to the reader. As with most marketing, branding does not involve "right or wrong" answers, and readers should question things they do understand or do not believe. This book is designed to facilitate your understanding of what is involved with strategic brand management and present some "best practice guidelines." At the end of the day, however, what you get out of the book will be what you put into it, and how you blend the ideas contained in these pages with what you already know or believe.

Kevin Lane Keller

Acknowledgments

This book took longer to write than I might have liked, but it would have taken even longer—and perhaps may not have been finished—without the help and guidance of many people. I want to recognize and thank those and others who made valuable contributions to the writing of this book.

At Prentice Hall, Sandy Steiner, David Borkowsky, and Jim Boyd were enthusiastic supporters from start to finish. They exhibited great patience and persistence throughout the entire process. Paul Feyn helped to "seal the deal," Rachel Falk helped to coordinate, and Michelle Rich and Valerie Lentz helped in production. As editor, Whitney Blake played an invaluable role in helping me finish the book and bring it to market. Pine Tree Composition provided prompt, careful, and considerate attention all through the production process.

I have learned much about branding in my work with industry participants who have unique perspectives on what seem to be working and what sees to *not* be working (and why) in the marketplace. Our discussions have enriched my appreciation for the challenges in building, measuring, and managing brand equity and the factors affecting the success and failure of brand strategies. I particularly want to thank the following individuals and others from their respective organizations: Scott Bedbury and Jerome Conlan (Starbucks), Liz Dolan and Bill Zeitz (Nike), Meera Buck (Shell), Jamie Murray (DuPont), Dennis Carter, Sally Fundakowski, Karen Alter, Ann Lewnes, and Ellen Konar (Intel), Norbert Krapp and Ann-Christin Wagemann (Beiersdorf), Steve Goldstein (Levi-Strauss), Patrick Tickle (Silicon Graphics), Laurie Lang (Disney), Jack Kowiak (Kodak), Jay Dean (Young & Rubicam), and David Sherbon (Communication Development Consultants).

I have also learned much about branding from the many academics who are now working in the area. Their thoughtful ideas and research can be found throughout the book. I have also benefited from the wisdom of my colleagues from the institutions where I have held an academic position: Duke University, the University of California at Berkeley, Stanford University, the Australian Graduate School of Management, and the University of North Carolina at Chapel Hill. Several individuals deserve special recognition. First and foremost, University of California, Berkeley's David Aaker has been a research colleague, sounding board, and good friend for as long as I have been working in the branding area. I have learned much from him, and although it is tempting to say that he taught me all I know, that wouldn't explain my backhand (Dave, check the Epilogue—I'm still counting), Northwestern University's Brian Sternthal and Harvard University's Stephen Greyser, John Quelch, and Al Silk have been remarkably helpful to me over the years in all my teaching efforts. Katherine Jocz and Paul Root at the Marketing Science Institute have been tireless supporters of the branding area and provided me with access to numerous people and materials. John Roberts from the Australian Graduate School of Management at the University of New South Wales has broadened my perspective on branding in a number of different, important ways. Stanford University's Jim Lattin has been a resource on just about anything I could ever think of—he's as good a colleague as anyone could hope for. Finally, Duke University's Richard Staelin and Jim Bettman helped me get my academic career started and continue to serve as role models in every sense of the word.

Over the years, the doctoral students that I advised have helped in a variety of useful ways in my branding pursuits, including Sheri Bridges (Wake Forest University), Meg Campbell (U.C.L.A.), Christie Brown (N.Y.U.), Jennifer Aaker (U.C.L.A.), and Sanjay Sood (U.C.-Berkeley). Leslie Kimerling (Town Sports International) went above and beyond the call of duty in helping me reach closure on some case studies. A set of talented reviewers provided insightful feedback to earlier versions of the manuscript:

Rajeev Batra	University of Michigan
Subodh Bhat	San Francisco State University
Gerri Henderson	Duke University
Vicki Lane	University of Colorado, Colorado Springs
Mary Sullivan	University of Chicago
Bonghee Yoo	Georgia State University

Finally, special thanks go to my wife, Punam Anand Keller, and two daughters, Carolyn and Allison, for understanding why, far too many times, there was a long delay between their questions and my answers. I look forward to being able to devote more attention to them—that is my chief reward for finishing this book.

About the Author

Kevin Lane Keller is acknowledged as one of the international leaders in the study of integrated marketing communications and strategic brand management. Currently a visiting professor at the Fuqua School of Business at Duke University, Professor Keller also has been a tenured member of the faculty at the Stanford Business School, where he also served as the head of the marketing group. Additionally, Professor Keller has been on the faculty at the University of California at Berkeley and the University of North Carolina at Chapel Hill, been a visiting professor at the Australian Graduate School of Management, and has two years of industry experience with Bank of America. He received his B.A. in Mathematics and Economics from Cornell University, his M.S.I.A. from Carnegie-Mellon University, and his Ph.D. in marketing from Duke University.

Professor Keller's general area of expertise lies in consumer marketing. His specific research interest is in how understanding theories and concepts related to consumer behavior can improve advertising and branding strategies. His research has been widely cited and has received awards from numerous organizations. His advertising and branding research has been published in three of the major marketing journals—the *Journal of Marketing,* the *Journal of Marketing Research,* and the *Journal of Consumer Research*. He sits on the Editorial Review Boards of those journals. He is currently conducting a variety of studies that address strategies to build, measure, and manage brand equity.

At Duke, he teaches MBA electives on advertising and communication management and strategic brand management. He has conducted marketing seminars on those topics to top executives in a variety of forums. Actively involved with industry, he has worked on projects with marketing managers for companies such as Broderbund, CSR Australia, Jose Cuervo, Disney, Glaxo Welcome, Intel, Intuit, Kodak, Levi-Strauss, Nielsen Research, Nordstrom, Shell Oil, Silicon Graphics, and Starbucks.

Professor Keller lives in Chapel Hill with his wife, Punam, and his two daughters, Carolyn and Allison.

CHAPTER ## Introduction

Preview

More and more firms have come to the realization that one of their most valuable assets is the brand names associated with their products or services. Despite this recognition, relatively little attention has been paid to the subject of branding in management education, especially in MBA programs. An observation by Larry Light, marketing consultant and chairman of the Coalition for Brand Equity, suggests the severity of the problem: "The MBA should stand for 'Murderer of Brand Assets.'" To address this oversight, this book is an advanced MBA-level text that addresses the important branding decisions faced by individuals and organizations in their marketing. Its basic objective is:

1. To increase understanding of the important issues in planning, implementing, and evaluating brand strategies.
2. To provide the appropriate theories, models, and other tools to make better branding decisions.

Particular emphasis is placed on understanding psychological principles at the customer or consumer level so as to improve managerial decision making with respect to brands. Our objective is that this book be relevant for any type of organization regardless of size, nature of business, or profit orientation.

With this goal in mind, in this first chapter, we define what a brand is and trace some of the historical origins of branding. We consider the functions of a brand from the perspective of both consumers and firms and why brands are important to both. We consider what can and cannot be branded and identify some strong brands. The chapter concludes with more specific description of the purpose behind the book and an introduction to the important concept of brand equity, which is covered in detail in chapter 2.

What Is a Brand?

Branding has been around for centuries as a means to distinguish the goods of one producer from those of another. In fact, the word "brand" is derived from the Old Norse word "brandr," which means "to burn," as brands were and still are the means by which owners of livestock mark their animals to identify them.[1] According to the American Marketing Association, a *brand* is a "name, term, sign, symbol, or design, or a combination of them intended to identify the goods and services of one seller or group of sellers and to differentiate them from those of competition." Thus, the key to creating a brand, according to this definition, is to choose a name, logo, symbol, package design, or other attribute that identifies a product and distinguishes it from others. We can call these different components of a brand, which identify and differentiate it, *brand elements*.

These brand elements come in many different forms. For example, consider the variety of brand name strategies that exist. In some cases, the company name is essentially used for all products (e.g., General Electric and Hewlett-Packard). In other cases, manufacturers assign individual brand names to new products that are unrelated to the company name (e.g., as with Unilever and Procter & Gamble). Retailers create their own brands based on their store name or other factor (e.g., Macy's has its own Christopher Hayes, I.N.C., and Club Room brands).

The names given to products also come in many different forms.[2] Brand names can be based on people (e.g., Estee Lauder cosmetics, Porsche automobiles, and Orville Redenbacher popcorn), places (e.g., Sante Fe cologne, Chrysler's New Yorker automobile, and British Airways), animals or birds (e.g., Mustang automobiles, Dove soap, and Greyhound buses), or other things or objects (e.g., Apple computers, Shell gasoline, and Carnation evaporated milk). Some brand names use words with inherent product meaning (e.g., Lean Cuisine, JustJuice, and Ticketron) or suggest important attributes or benefits (e.g., DieHard auto batteries, Mop'n Glow floor cleaner, and Beautyrest mattresses). Some brand names are invented and include prefixes and suffixes that sound scientific, natural, or prestigious (e.g., Intel microprocessors, Lexus automobiles, or Compaq computers). Like brand names, other brand elements such as brand logos and symbols may be based on people, places, and things, abstract images, and so on in different ways. In sum, in creating a brand, marketers have many choices in the number and nature of the brand elements to identify their products.

BRANDS VERSUS PRODUCTS

It is important to contrast a brand and a product. According to Phillip Kotler, a well-regarded marketing academic, a *product* is anything that can be offered to a market for attention, acquisition, use, or consumption that might satisfy a need or want. Thus, a product may be a physical good (e.g., a cereal, tennis racquet, or automobile), service (e.g., an airline, bank, or insurance company), retail store (e.g., a department store, specialty store, or supermarket), person (e.g., a political figure, entertainer, or professional athlete), organization (e.g., a nonprofit, trade organization, or arts group), place (e.g., a city, state, or country), or idea (e.g., a political or social cause). We adopt this broad definition for our book. We will discuss the role of brands in some of these different categories in more detail later in this chapter and in much more detail in chapter 15.

Kotler defines five levels of a product:[3]

1. The *core benefit level* is the fundamental need or want that consumers satisfy by consuming the product or service.

2. The *generic product level* is a basic version of the product containing only those attributes or characteristics absolutely necessary for its functioning but with no distinguishing features. This is basically a stripped-down, "no-frills" version of the product that adequately performs the product function.

3. The *expected product level* is a set of attributes or characteristics that buyers normally expect and agree to when they purchase a product.

4. The *augmented product level* includes additional product attributes, benefits, or related services that distinguish the product from competitors.

5. The *potential product level* includes all of the augmentations and transformations that a product might ultimately undergo in the future.

Figure 1–1 illustrates these different levels in the context of air conditioners and videocassette recorders. Kotler notes that competition within many markets essen-

Level	Air Conditioner
1. Core Benefit	Cooling and comfort.
2. Generic Product	Sufficient cooling capacity (Btu per hour), an acceptable energy efficiency rating, adequate air intakes and exhausts, and so on.
3. Expected Product	*Consumer Reports* states that for a typical large air conditioner, consumers should expect at least two cooling speeds, expandable plastic side panels, adjustable louvers, removable air filter, vent for exhausting air, power cord at least 60 inches long, R–22 HCFC refrigerant (less harmful to the earth's ozone layer than other types), one-year parts-and-labor warranty on the entire unit, and a five-year parts-and-labor warranty on the refrigeration system.[a]
4. Augmented Product	Optional features might include electric touchpad controls, a display to show indoor and outdoor temperatures and the thermostat setting, an auto mode to adjust fan speed based on the thermostat setting and room temperature, a toll-free 800 number for customer service, and so on.
5. Potential Product	Silently running, completely balanced throughout the room, and energy self-sufficient.

Level	Videocassette Recorder
1. Core Benefit	Convenient entertainment.
2. Generic Product	Ability to record and play back television or video programs with adequate picture quality; programmable.
3. Expected Product	*Consumer Reports* states that for a typical VCR, consumers should expect a digital quartz tuner that receives 125 cable channels; ability to record at—and play tapes recorded at—SP, LP, and EP speeds; on-screen programming of eight events up to one year in advance with options for daily and weekly recording; power on when tape is inserted and auto rewind at end of tape; and one year warranty on tape heads and other parts, three months on labor.[b]
4. Augmented Product	Optional features might include hi-fi stereo sound, VCR Plus, and shuttle controls for easy backward and forward scanning.
5. Potential Product	Voice controlled programming; ability to edit out commercials.

[a]*Consumer Reports* 59(6) (June 1994): 400–3.

[b]*Consumer Reports* 59(3) (March 1994): 164–5.

FIGURE 1–1 Examples of Different Product Levels

tially takes place at the product augmentation level, because most firms can successfully build satisfactory products at the expected product level. Another well-respected marketing academic, Harvard's Ted Levitt, concurs and argues that: "The new competition is not between what companies produce in their factories but between what they add to their factory output in the form of packaging, services, advertising, customer advice, financing, delivery arrangements, warehousing, and other things that people value."[4]

A brand is a product, then, but one that adds other dimensions to differentiate it in some way from other products designed to satisfy the same need. These differences may be rational and tangible—related to product performance of the brand—or more symbolic, emotional, and intangible—related to what the brand represents. Marketing guru Alvin Achenbaum puts it this way:

More specifically, what distinguishes a brand from its unbranded commodity counterpart and gives it equity is the sum total of consumers' perceptions and feelings about the product's attributes and how they perform, about the brand name and what it stands for, and about the company associated with the brand.[5]

Extending our example from above, a branded product may be a physical good (e.g., Kellogg's Corn Flakes cereal, Prince tennis racquets, or Ford Taurus automobiles), a service (e.g., United Airlines, Bank of America, or Transamerica insurance), a store (e.g., Bloomingdale's department store, Body Shop specialty store, or Safeway supermarket), a person (e.g., Bill Clinton, Tom Hanks, or Michael Jordan), place (e.g., the city of Paris, state of California, or country of Australia), organization (e.g., the Red Cross, American Automobile Association, or Rolling Stones), or idea (e.g., abortion rights, free trade, or freedom of speech).

Some brands create competitive advantages with product performance. For example, brands such as Kodak, Gillette, Sony, 3M, and others have been leaders in their product categories for decades, due, in part, to continual innovation. Steady investments in research and development have produced leading-edge products, and sophisticated mass marketing practices have ensured rapid adoption of new technologies in the consumer market. Other brands create competitive advantages through non-product-related means. For example, Coca-Cola, Calvin Klein, Chanel No. 5, Marlboro, and other brands have become leaders in their product categories by understanding consumer motivations and desires and creating relevant and appealing images surrounding their products. Often these intangible image associations may be the only way to distinguish different brands in a product category.

Brands, especially strong ones, have a number of different types of associations, and marketers must account for all of them in making marketing decisions. The marketers behind some brands have learned this lesson the hard way. Branding Brief 1–1 describes the problems Coca-Cola encountered in the introduction of "New Coke" when they failed to account for all of the different aspects of the Coca-Cola brand image.

Not only are there many different types of associations to link to the brand, there are many different means to create them. The entire marketing program can contribute to consumer's understanding of the brand and how they value it. As Interbrand's John Murphy puts it:

> Creating a successful brand entails blending all these various elements together in a unique way—the product or service has to be of high quality and appropriate to consumer needs, the brand name must be appealing and in tune with the consumer's perceptions of the product, the packaging, promotion, pricing and all other elements must similarly meet the tests of appropriateness, appeal, and differentiation.[6]

By creating perceived differences among products through branding and developing loyal consumer franchises, marketers create value, which can translate to financial profits for the firm. The reality is that the most valuable assets that many firms have may not be tangible assets, such as plants, equipment, and real estate, but *intangible* assets such as management skills; marketing, financial, and operations expertise; and, most importantly, the brands themselves. Thus, a brand is a valued intangible

---

BRANDING BRIEF 1-1

Coca-Cola's Marketing Fiasco

One of the classic marketing mistakes occurred in April 1985 when Coca-Cola replaced its flagship cola brand with a new formula.[a] The motivation behind the change was primarily a competitive one. Pepsi-Cola's "Pepsi Challenge" promotion had posed a strong challenge to Coke's supremacy over the cola market. Starting initially in Texas, the promotion involved advertising and in-store sampling showcasing consumer blind taste tests between Coca-Cola and Pepsi-Cola. Invariably, Pepsi won these tests. Fearful that the promotion, if taken nationally, could take a big bite out of Coke's sales, especially among younger cola drinkers, Coca-Cola felt compelled to act.

Coke's strategy was to change the formulation of Coke to more closely match the slightly sweeter taste of Pepsi. To arrive at a new formulation, Coke conducted taste tests with an astounding number of consumers—190,000! The findings from this research clearly indicated that consumers "overwhelmingly" preferred the *taste* of the new formulation to the old one. Brimming with confidence, Coca-Cola announced the formulation change with much fanfare. Consumer reaction was swift but, unfortunately for Coke, negative. In Seattle, retired real estate investor Gay Mullins founded the "Old Cola Drinkers of America" and set up a hot line for angry consumers. A Beverly Hills wine merchant bought 500 cases of "Vintage Coke" and sold them at a premium. Meanwhile, back at Coca-Cola headquarters, roughly 1500 calls a day and literally truckloads of mail poured in, virtually all condemning Coke's actions. Finally, after several months of slumping sales, Coca-Cola announced that the old formulation would return as "Coca-Cola Classic" and join "new" Coke in the marketplace.

The new Coke debacle taught Coca-Cola a very important, albeit painful and public, lesson about its brand. Coke clearly is not just seen as a beverage or thirst-quenching refreshment by consumers. Rather, it seems to be viewed as more of an American icon, and much of its appeal lies not only in its ingredients but also in what it represents in terms of Americana, nostalgia, and its heritage and relationship with consumers. Coke's brand image certainly has emotional components, and consumers have a great deal of strong feelings for the brand. Although Coke made a number of other mistakes in introducing new Coke (e.g., both their advertising and packaging probably failed to clearly differentiate the brand and communicate its sweeter quality), their biggest slip was losing sight of what the brand meant to consumers in all of its totality. The *psychological* response to a brand can be as important as the *physiological* response to the product. At the same time, the American consumer also learned a lesson—just how much the Coke brand really meant to them. As a result of Coke's marketing fiasco, it is doubtful that either side will take the other for granted from now on.

---

[a]Patricia Winters, "For New Coke, 'What Price Success?'," *Advertising Age* (March 20, 1989): S-1–S-2.

asset that needs to be handled carefully. We next turn to some of the reasons why brands are so valuable.

Why Do Brands Matter?

An obvious question is, Why are brands important? What functions do they perform that make them so valuable to marketers? Several perspectives uncover the value of brands to both customers and firms themselves. Figure 1–2 provides an overview of the different roles that brands play to these two parties.

CONSUMERS

To consumers, brands identify the source or maker of a product and allow consumers to assign responsibility as to which particular manufacturer or distributor should be held accountable. Most importantly, brands take on special meaning to consumers. Because of past experiences with the product and its marketing program over the years, consumers learn about brands. They find out which brands satisfy their needs and which do not. As a result, brands provide a shorthand device or means of simplification for their product decisions.[7]

If consumers recognize a brand and have some knowledge about it, then they do not have to engage in a lot of additional thought or processing of information to make a product decision. Thus, from an economic perspective, brands allow consumers to lower search costs for products both internally (in terms of how much they have to think) and externally (in terms of how much they have to look around). Based on what they already know about the brand—its quality, product characteristics, and so on—consumers can make assumptions and form reasonable expectations about what they may *not* know about the brand.

CONSUMERS

    Identification of source of product
    Assignment of responsibility to product maker
    Risk reducer
    Search cost reducer
    Promise, bond, or pact with maker of product
    Symbolic device
    Signal of quality

MANUFACTURERS

    Means of identification to simplify handling or tracing
    Means of legally protecting unique features
    Signal of quality level to satisfied customers
    Means of endowing products with unique associations
    Source of competitive advantage
    Source of financial returns

FIGURE 1–2 Roles That Brands Play

The meaning embedded in brands can be quite profound. The relationship between a brand and the consumer can be seen as a type of bond or pact. Consumers offer their trust and loyalty with the implicit understanding that the brand will behave in certain ways and provide them utility through consistent product performance and appropriate pricing, promotion, and distribution programs and actions. To the extent that consumers realize advantages and benefits from purchasing the brand, and as long as they derive satisfaction from product consumption, consumers are likely to continue to buy it.

These benefits may not be purely functional in nature. Brands can serve as symbolic devices, allowing consumers to project their own self-images. Certain brands are associated with being used by certain types of people and thus reflect different values or traits. Consuming such products is a means by which consumers can communicate to others—or even to themselves—the type of person they are or would like to be. As Harvard's Susan Fournier notes:

> Relationships with mass brands can soothe the "empty selves" left behind by society's abandonment of tradition and community and provide stable anchors in an otherwise changing world. The formation and maintenance of brand-product relationships serve many culturally-supported roles within postmodern society.[8]

Pulitzer-Prize winning author Daniel Boorstein asserts that, for many people, brands serve the function that fraternal, religious, and service organization used to serve—to help people define who they are and then help them communicate that definition to others.

Brands can also play an especially significant role in signaling certain product characteristics to consumers. Researchers have classified products and their associated attributes or benefits into three major categories: search goods, experience goods, and credence goods.[9] With *search goods*, product attributes can be evaluated by visual inspection (e.g., the sturdiness, size, color, style, weight, and ingredient composition of a product). With *experience goods*, product attributes—potentially equally important—cannot be assessed so easily by inspection, and actual product trial and experience is necessary (e.g., as with durability, service quality, safety, ease of handling or use). With *credence goods*, product attributes may be rarely learned (e.g., insurance coverage). Because of the difficulty in assessing and interpreting product attributes and benefits with experience and credence goods, brands may be particularly important signals of quality and other characteristics to consumers for these types of products.[10]

Brands can reduce the risks in product decisions.[11] There are many different types of risks that consumers may perceive in buying and consuming a product:

1. *Functional risk:* The product does not perform up to expectations
2. *Physical risk:* The product poses a threat to the physical well-being or health of the user or others
3. *Financial risk:* The product is not worth the price paid
4. *Social risk:* The product results in embarrassment from others

5. *Psychological risk:* The product affects the mental well-being of the user
6. *Time risk:* The failure of the product results in an opportunity cost of finding another satisfactory product

Although there are a number of different means by which consumers handle these risks, certainly one way by which consumers cope is to only buy well-known brands, especially those brands with which consumers have had favorable past experiences. Thus, brands can be a very important risk-handling device.

In summary, to consumers, the special meanings that brands take on can change their perceptions and experiences with the products. The identical product may be evaluated differently by consumers depending on the brand identification or attribution it is given. Brands take on unique, personal meanings to consumers that facilitate their day-to-day activities and enrich their lives.

FIRMS

Brands also provide a number of valuable functions to firms.[12] Fundamentally, they serve an identification purpose to simplify product handling or tracing for the firm. Operationally, brands help to organize inventory, accounting, and other records. A brand also offers the firm legal protection for unique features or aspects of the product. A brand can retain intellectual property rights, giving legal title to the brand owner.[13] The brand name can be protected through registered trademarks, manufacturing processes can be protected through patents, and packaging can be protected through copyrights and designs. These intellectual property rights insure that the firm can safely invest in the brand and reap the benefits of a valuable asset.

As noted above, these investments in the brand can endow a product with unique associations and meanings that differentiate it from other products. Brands can signal a certain level of quality so that satisfied buyers can easily choose the product again.[14] This brand loyalty provides predictability and security of demand for the firm and creates barriers of entry that make it difficult for other firms to enter the market. Although manufacturing processes and product designs may be easily duplicated, lasting impressions in the minds of consumers from years of marketing activity and product experience may not be so easily reproduced. In this sense, branding can be seen as a powerful means to secure a competitive advantage. In its annual review of "America's Most Admired Companies," *Fortune* magazine in 1996 proclaimed that, "The Brand's the Thing," noting how companies such as Coke, Microsoft, and Disney were "... proving that having a strong name may be the ultimate weapon."[15]

Thus, to firms, brands represent enormously valuable pieces of legal property, capable of influencing consumer behavior, being bought and sold, and providing the security of sustained future revenues to their owners.[16] For these reasons, large earning multiples have been paid for brands in mergers or acquisitions, especially in the boom years of the mid-1980s. For example, one top marketing executive at Cadbury Schweppes noted that of the $220 million his firm paid to acquire Hires and Crush soft drink business from Procter & Gamble, roughly $20 million was for the physical assets—the rest was for brand value. Thus, much of the recent interest in brands from senior management has been a result of these bottom-line financial considerations.

Can Anything Be Branded?

Brands clearly provide important benefits to both consumers and firms. An obvious question then is, How are brands created? How do you "brand" a product? Although firms provide the impetus to brand creation through their marketing programs and other activities, ultimately *a brand is something that resides in the minds of consumers.* A brand is a perceptual entity, rooted in reality, but also reflecting the perceptions and perhaps even the idiosyncrasies of consumers.

To brand a product it is necessary to teach consumers "who" the product is—by giving it a name and using other brand elements to help identify it—as well as "what" the product does and "why" consumers should care. In other words, to brand a product or service, it is necessary to give consumers a *label* for the product (i.e., "Here's how you can identify the product.") and to provide *meaning* for the brand to consumers (i.e., "Here's what this particular product can do for you and why it is special and different from other brand name products."). Branding involves creating mental structures and helping consumers organize their knowledge about products and services in a way that clarifies their decision making and, in the process, provides value to the firm. *The key to branding is that consumers perceive differences among brands in a product category.* As noted above, brand differences often are related to attributes or benefits of the product itself. In other cases, however, brand differences may be related to more intangible image considerations.

The universality of branding can be recognized by looking at some different product applications. As noted above, products can be defined broadly to include physical goods, services, retail stores, people, organizations, places, or ideas. For each of these different types of products, we will review some basic considerations and provide illustrations. We will consider some of these special cases in more detail in chapter 15.

PHYSICAL GOODS

Physical goods are traditionally associated with brands and include many of the best-known and highly regarded consumer products (e.g., Coca-Cola, Kellogg's, Kodak, Marlboro, Sony, Mercedes-Benz, and Nescafe). As more and more different kinds of products are being sold or at least promoted directly to consumers, the adoption of modern marketing practices and branding has spread further.

In the pharmaceutical industry, for example, prescription drugs are increasingly being branded and sold to consumers with traditional marketing tactics such as advertising and promotion.[17] In recent years a number of prescription drugs have become available over the counter and are backed by sizable marketing budgets (e.g., Pepcid, Tagamet, and Zantac heartburn remedies; Actron and Orudis KT analgesics; and Nicorette smoking cessation aid).[18] Upjohn's anti-baldness drug Rogain—which had already been advertised heavily when it was only available by prescription to tell potential customers how to get a free, private hair-loss consultation—spent $75 million in advertising and promotions in 1996 to announce the fact that the drug was now available over the counter.

More and more companies selling industrial or durable products to other companies are recognizing the benefits of developing strong brands. Brands have begun to emerge with certain types of physical goods that heretofore did not support brands. In the remainder of this section, we will consider the role of branding with commodities and technologically intensive or "high-tech" products.

Commodities

Recent years have seen numerous branded commodities. A *commodity* is a product presumably so basic that it cannot be physically differentiated in the minds of consumers. Over the years, a number of products that at one time were seen essentially as commodities have become highly differentiated as strong brands.[19] Some notable examples (with brand pioneers in parentheses) are: coffee (Maxwell House), bath soap (Ivory), flour (Gold Medal), beer (Budweiser), salt (Morton), oatmeal (Quaker), pickles (Vlasic), bananas (Chiquita), chickens (Perdue), pineapples (Dole), and even water (Perrier).

These former commodity products have become branded in various ways. The key success factor in each case, however, was that consumers became convinced that all the product offerings in the category were not the same and that meaningful differences existed. In some instances, such as with produce, marketers convinced consumers that a product was *not* a commodity and actually could vary appreciably in quality. In these cases, the brand was seen as assuring uniformly high quality in the product category on which consumers could depend. A recent example of this approach is Intel, who has spent vast sums of money on its "Intel Inside" promotion to brand its microprocessors or computer chips as delivering the highest level of performance (e.g., power) and safety (e.g., upgradability) possible.

In other cases, because product differences were virtually nonexistent, brands have been created by image or other non-product-related considerations (e.g., as with Perrier bottled mineral water). One of the best examples of branding a commodity in this fashion was the California Raisin Advisory Board, which created some badly needed brand personality and image for its product on the basis of some highly creative advertising (see Branding Brief 1–2).

High-Tech Products

Another example of the increasing realization of the important role that brands play in the marketing equation is with technologically intensive or high-tech products (e.g., computer-related products). In many of these product markets, financial success is no longer driven by product innovation alone or by offering the "latest and greatest" product specifications and features. Marketing skills are playing an increasingly important role in the adoption and success of high-tech products.

For example, in discussing the origins of his company, Scott Cook, founder and chairman of Intuit, makers of the highly successful Quicken personal-finance software package, comments:[20] "We started with the belief that it is a consumer market, not a technology market. We'd run it like Procter & Gamble." Applying classic package-goods marketing techniques, Intuit first conducted extensive research with consumers and then designed a product to satisfy the unmet needs and wants of the market. Because its research revealed that most consumers did not like doing financial management and found it a necessary evil, Intuit designed the Quicken software package to offer two key benefits, ease of use and speed, not currently offered by other products in the market.

Making Raisins One of the "In" Crowd

In the mid-1980s California raisin growers faced a difficult branding challenge to increase their sales. Their advertising campaign at that time focused on the many different uses of the product as reflected by their advertising tag line, "Raisins Add a Little Magic." Strategically, the difficulty with the campaign was that it was attempting to increase sales primarily by targeting current users of raisins and helping them see new ways to use the product. Unfortunately, most consumers were not eating raisins, because, in part, raisins had a bad image as an undesirable, boring, and "wimpy" food. The product had low top-of-mind awareness and faced stiff competition.

With these problems as a focus, a new ad campaign was launched in 1986 to make the product more acceptable and interesting. The ads featured the California Raisins—raisin characters brought to life with a new "stop-motion" animation technique called claymation—singing and dancing in sunglasses and white gloves to songs like the Motown favorite "I Heard It through the Grapevine." The intention of the campaign was to make raisins seem hip, different, and cool. Subsequent ads introduced claymation versions of Ray Charles and his backup band, the Raylettes. The ad campaign was enormously successful, appearing for a number of years on Video Storyboard's Top 10 list of the most memorable ad campaigns of the year as chosen by consumers. As it turned out, although the California Raisins campaign reportedly did ultimately boost sales by 20 percent, perhaps its greatest value came in licensing opportunities! The characters' likeness appeared on a host of products, such as toys and shirts. In fact, according to *Harper's Magazine,* sales of licensed California Raisin merchandise in North America in 1988 was 10 times greater than sales of the actual California raisins ($450 million vs. $40 million).[a]

---

[a]1988 Harper's Index, *Harper's Magazine* (April 1989).

Adoption of package-goods marketing techniques by companies selling high-tech products has resulted in increased expenditures on mass market advertising. In the 1994–1995 television season, IBM, Intel, and Microsoft each spent about $100 million on new campaigns. Branding Brief 1–3 describes some of the branding history at IBM. Smaller companies are also getting into the act. For example, Applied Microsystems, manufacturers of emulators that help engineers to debug programs embedded in computer microprocessors, developed a print campaign featuring "nature's debuggers"—frogs! In one ad, the "Rocket Frog" symbolizes a fast-performing emulator. In another ad, the "Rambo Frog" represents an emulator that goes on "search and destroy missions." By bringing some personality to a company in a traditionally staid, technical business, Applied Microsystems hopes that it will able to stand out from the crowd.[21]

BRANDING BRIEF 1-3

IBM Learns How to Brand

IBM's experiences illustrate how important marketing and branding have become in the personal computer industry.[a] IBM introduced its first PC in 1981 and built its market share to 41 percent by 1985. Three years later, however, their market share had dropped to 28 percent, and they have struggled since. Observers blamed much of IBM's lost sales on an unfocused marketing strategy that made the brand vulnerable to appeals from low-priced clone makers. One problem suggested by many critics was the complexity of IBM's branding strategy—there were too many brands and too many names were technical and consumer "unfriendly." To improve its branding efforts, IBM established a centralized naming unit in 1988. As evidence of the transformation in branding that occurred at that time, a new touch-sensitive screen was named InfoWindows, a new desktop image-capturing device was named PageScanner, and the company's new customer-service unit was named IBM Link. The same products and services might have previously been named by engineers as the 4055 Display Unit, the 3119DICB, and the INFO/MVS, respectively.

To upgrade its image and become closer to customers, IBM conducted extensive consumer research, seeking input on issues from product design and features to appropriate brand names. A big part of their market-driven strategy was a need for catchy, persuasive advertising, a challenge for IBM given its advertising woes over the years. IBM first introduced its PC in print and TV advertising in the early 1980s using the Charlie Chaplin "Little Tramp" character. This campaign ran for over five years and attempted to use a lighter touch and put a more human face on a company seen by many at that time as cold and aloof.

To emphasize work groups and computer networks, IBM next introduced a new campaign for their PS/2 computer system featuring the cast of the popular TV series M*A*S*H. Partly because of internal complications (e.g., computer networks wouldn't catch on for four years and IBM's ad agency, Lord Geller Federico Einstein, was rocked by defections), the campaign was canned. A new agency, Lintas, was hired, but its first effort, using an embarrassing rap-like jingle, was widely panned by critics. Subsequent advertising by IBM's other new agency, Wells Rich Greene, attempted to portray IBM as helpful problem solvers. IBM had turned to another agency, Merkley Newman Harty, when in a dramatic about-face, they fired almost 40 agencies worldwide and assigned Ogilvy & Mather the $400 million to $500 million account in May 1994.

Ogilvy & Mather was chosen, in part, for its global presence and for its track record in building brands, as exemplified by its "brand stewardship" concept (see chapter 10). O&M's first efforts were new campaigns in the fall of 1994 to launch the Aptiva models (IBM's replacements for its four-year-old PS/1 home and small-office PCs) featuring MTV-like graphics and the TV actor, Paul Reiser. The ads ended with the tag line, "There is a difference—IBM." Additional ads promoted IBM's merged PS/2 and ValuePoint lines, called simply, IBM PC, and the new "Warp" version of their OS/2 operating system. Later ads used the tag line, "Solutions for a Small Planet" and showed people in different parts of the world discussing the benefits they had derived from their IBM computers in their native tongues with English subtitles added.

------

[a]David Kalish, "IBM's Brand Stand," *Marketing & Media* (May 1989): 71–76; Dennis Kneale, "IBM's Flawed Advertising Strategy to Get an Overhaul," *Wall Street Journal,* (October 22, 1993): B-1.

SERVICES

Although there have been strong service brands for years (e.g., American Express, British Airways, Hilton Hotels, Merrill Lynch, and, more recently, Federal Express), the pervasiveness and level of sophistication in branding services has accelerated in the past decade. Recent years have even seen corporate brand campaigns from professional service firms such as Coopers & Lybrand, KMPG Peat Marwick, and Anderson Consulting. As Interband's John Murphy notes, "In the last 30 years, some of the greatest branding successes have come in the area of services."

One of the challenges in marketing services is that, relative to products, they are more intangible and more likely to vary in quality depending on the particular person or people involved in providing the service. Consequently, branding can be particularly important to service firms to address potential intangibility and variability problems. Brand symbols may also be especially important as they help to make the abstract nature of services more concrete. Brands can help to identify and provide meaning to the different services provided by a firm. Branding has become especially important in financial services to help organize and label the myriad of new offerings in a manner that consumers can understand.

Branding a service can also be an effective way to signal to consumers that the firm has designed a particular service offering that is special and deserving of its own name. For example, British Airways not only branded its premium business class service as "Club Class," they also branded its regular coach service as "World Traveler," a clever way to communicate to their regular passengers that they are also special in some way and that their patronage is not taken for granted. Branding Brief 1–4 describes some of the epic branding battles that have emerged in the telecommunications industry.

RETAILERS AND DISTRIBUTORS

To the retailers or other channel members distributing products, brands provide a number of important functions. Brands can generate consumer interest, patronage, and loyalty in a store, and consumers learn to expect certain brands and products from a store. To the extent that "you are what you sell," brands help to create an image and establish a positioning for the store. Retailers can also create their own brand images by attaching unique associations to the quality of their service, their product assortment and merchandising, and pricing and credit policy. Finally, the appeal and attraction of brands can permit higher price margins, increased sales volumes, and greater profits. These brand name products may come from manufacturers or other external sources or from the store itself.

Long Distance Marketing Wars

Deregulation in the global telecommunication industry has created increased competition among brands in the 1990s. In the United States, for example, AT&T, MCI, and Sprint have waged a fierce battle for market share using traditional marketing tactics, including the introduction of various brands and subbrands. For example, all three firms created discount savings plans to reward loyal callers, gave them descriptive names, and heavily advertised and promoted them.

MCI's *Friends and Family* was the first such discount plan.[a] Launched in March 1991, the discount plan offered 20 percent discounts to groups of MCI customers who phoned one another and were willing to form a calling circle (a service feature that was initially difficult for AT&T to match because it lacked the advanced billing system needed to link accounts of customers from all over the country). In the process, MCI added to its corporate image as the "discount underdog" by adding the association of being "good guys." More recently, MCI has introduced *Friends and Family II,* which offered 40 percent savings, as well as *Personal Thanks*, a continuity program offering points toward airline tickets, merchandise, and free minutes.

AT&T's initial response, the "i plan," was confusing and ineffective. Their follow-up, AT&T *True USA Savings,* however, more directly challenged MCI's discount plan, promising that most customers would save more with its plan. AT&T also introduced a series of other services and features using the *True* prefix as a means of branding:

1. AT&T *True Rewards* was a continuity program where callers earned points for phone usage that could be redeemed for free phone calls, cash, or frequent flier miles with Delta, United, or USAir airlines.
2. AT&T *TrueVoice* was actually a service benefit. Based on innovative Bell Laboratories technology, AT&T claimed it brought the closest, truest long distance sound ever.
3. AT&T *TrueChoice* Calling Card allowed customers to choose their own personal calling card number.

Creating an umbrella of services around the *True* prefix was a clever way to build brand equity by reinforcing the heritage and authenticity of AT&T and the simplicity of its offerings.

The third entry in the market, Sprint, initially built its brand equity around the clarity of sound of fiber optic technology, represented literally (and symbolically) by a pin drop. Their discount plan, *The Most*, offered 20 percent discounts on a customer's most-called number and to all Sprint customers (and 36 percent if the most-called number was a Sprint customer). Their follow-up, *The Most II*, offered discounts of 20 percent if callers spent $30 to $74.99, 30 percent if callers spent $75 to $150, and 35 percent if callers spent over $150. They also introduced *Priority Rewards* continuity program, so that callers could earn points toward airline tickets, merchandise, and free talk time. More recently, they simpli-fied their message to concentrate on a "10 cents a minute" price message, cast-ing their popular spokesperson Candice Bergen as the "Dime Lady." In a cate-gory that consumers often find complex and confusing, the "Sprint Sense" message has resonated with consumers. Its success has led to similarly posi-tioned promotions such as "Fridays Free"—where small businesses can call all they want on Fridays for free.

Although the competitive ferocity in this market potentially tarnishes their brand images (AT&T spent $250 million, MCI spent $140 million, and Sprint spent $80 million in 1994 in often hard-hitting comparison advertising),[b] AT&T, MCI, and Sprint have all been able to build brand equity at both the corporate and individual service offering level through their branding strategies.

---

[a]Mark Lewyn, "MCI is Coming Through Loud and Clear," *Business Week* (January 25, 1993): 84–88.

[b]James Kim, "Discount War Can Be Confusing," *USA TODAY* (September 23, 1994): B1–2.

Retailers can introduce their own brands using their store names, by creating new names, or some combination of the two. Thus, many distributors, especially in Europe, have actually introduced their own brands, which they sell in addition to—or sometimes even instead of—manufacturers' brands. These products, referred to as "store brands" or "private label" brands, offer another way for retailers to increase customer loyalty and generate higher margins and profits. In Britain, five or six gro-cery chains account for roughly half of the country's food and package-goods sales, led by Sainsbury who owns approximately 15 percent of the market. Marks & Spencer sells only own-brand goods (under the label St. Michel) and, according to re-search, now owns one of the most powerful brand names in Britain. We consider store brands and private labels in greater detail in chapter 5. Branding Brief 1–5 de-scribes some of the branding challenges faced by long-time U.S. retail leader Sears, Roebuck & Co.

PEOPLE AND ORGANIZATIONS

Brands extend beyond products and services. People and organizations also can be viewed as brands. The naming aspect of the brand is generally straightforward in this case, and people and organizations also often have well-defined images understood and liked or disliked by others. This fact becomes particularly true when considering public figures such as politicians, entertainers, or professional athletes. All of these different public figures compete in some sense for public approval and acceptance and benefit from conveying a strong and desirable image.

For example, Cindy Crawford moved to the top of Video Story Board Tests' list of the most appealing TV endorsers in 1994, as measured by a survey of over 2000 consumers of the effectiveness and popularity of entertainers appearing in TV com-mercials, through skillfully managing her image. In essence, Cindy Crawford had be-

Brand Development at Sears

Sears, Roebuck & Co. became the nation's largest retailer by making household names of "hard goods" such as Craftsman tools, Kenmore appliances, Weatherbeater house paint, and DieHard auto batteries. Sales at Sears slumped through the 1980s as the retailer struggled to find the right brand image and marketing formula in the face of fierce competition from discounters such as Circuit City, Best Buy, and Home Depot, as well as a revived J. C. Penney. Sears attempted a number of different strategies during this time to turn things around, such as adopting an everyday low pricing strategy, closing its catalog business, organizing the store into seven "power formats" each with its own distinct selling place and style (i.e., women's apparel, appliances and electronics, home improvement, children's clothes, automotive, men's fashions, and furniture), and aggressively selling more national brand name products such as Panasonic and Whirlpool.

Sears executives were finally able to turn around the brand in perhaps a surprising and unlikely place. Although apparel was becoming an increasing large percentage of sales—70 percent of total nonfood sales were for apparel at shopping malls where more than two-thirds of Sears' 850 stores were located—women's clothing had never been a big seller at Sears. Although women at Sears covered a broad demographic spectrum—and, in fact, were making the majority of purchases in a number of departments—shoppers in their women's department tended to be a more narrowly defined market segment of "females over 40 with household incomes of less than $30,000." Sears was just not seen by middle-income working mothers, young adults, and others as the place to shop for fashionable clothes.

In the early 1990s, to better appeal to these groups, Sears revamped its women's apparel offerings to move toward trendier fashions (including some big-name brands such as Arrow shirts and Sperry Topsiders shoes), better-trained and higher quality service from salespeople, and slicker displays and presentations of clothes. Sears boosted ad spending 20 percent and launched a catchy new print and television ad campaign for its apparel with the tagline the "The Softer Side of Sears." Additionally, Sears closed poorly performing stores and embarked on a five-year, $4 billion store-refurbishing effort for others. As part of this facelift, the space-eating, but revenue-diminished, furniture section was moved into a new chain of shops called Homelife, freeing up more space for more profitable women's clothing. Driven by improved apparel sales, Sears' earnings rebounded and grew rapidly during the mid-1990s.[a]

---

[a]Kevin Kelly, "At Sears, the More Things Change . . . ," *Business Week* (November 12, 1990): 66–68; Kevin Kelly, "The Big Store May Be on a Roll," *Business Week* (August 30, 1993): 82–85; Susan Chandler, "Sears' Turnaround Is for Real—For Now," *Business Week* (August 15, 1994): 102–103.

come one of the leading "brands" in a newly formed "product category" of "super-model" and had attached a number of different products to her name, earning an estimated $6.5 million in 1994. At the time, she had her own exercise videos (which sold millions of copies), swimsuit calendars, and television show ("House of Style") on MTV, as well as a five-year, $7 million deal with Revlon and other endorsements with Pepsi and Kay Jewelers. Crawford's broad market appeal crosses geographical and age boundaries. Well aware of her image, she once commented that if she were to wear her hair up in a "high twist" on her TV show, viewers would invariably write in and complain that they wanted her hair to look "normal" and "wanted Cindy to look like Cindy."[22]

It is also true, however, that people do not have to be well-known or famous to be thought of as a brand. Anyone trying to build a career can be thought of as trying to create his or her own brand. Certainly, one key for a successful career is that certain people—co-workers, superiors, or even important people outside the company—know who you are and what kind of person you are in terms of your skills, talents, and attitude. By building up a name and reputation in a business context, a person is essentially creating his or her own brand. The right awareness and image can be invaluable in the manner by which people treat you and interpret your words, actions, and deeds.[23]

Similarly, organizations often take on meanings through their programs, activities, and products. Nonprofit organizations such as the Sierra Club, the American Red Cross, Amnesty International, and UNICEF have increasingly emphasized marketing. For example, National Geographic, founded in 1888 by thirty-three highly regarded scientists, is a nonprofit scientific and educational membership organization with a mission related to the increase and diffusion of geographic knowledge concerning the earth, sea, and sky.[24] Its products include National Geographic magazines, books, television shows, and gift items. Like the manufacturer of any consumer product, National Geographic conducts surveys that examine perceptions of its image and reactions to possible new products. Moreover, it has developed a marketing database that records transactions, permits market segmentation and targeting analysis, and calculates the lifetime values of its customers.

SPORTS, ART, AND ENTERTAINMENT

A special case of marketing people and organizations as brands is in the sports, art, and entertainment industries. Sports marketing has become highly sophisticated in recent years, employing traditional package-goods techniques. No longer content to allow win-loss records to dictate attendance levels and financial fortunes, many sports teams are being marketed through a creative combination of advertising, promotions, sponsorship, direct mail, and other forms of communication. By building awareness, image, and loyalty, these sports franchises are able to meet ticket sales targets regardless of what their team's actual performance might turn out to be. Brand symbols and logos in particular have become an important financial contributor to professional sports through licensing agreements.

Branding plays an especially valuable function in the arts and entertainment industries (e.g., with movies, television, music, and books). These offerings are good examples of experience goods—prospective buyers cannot judge quality by inspection and must use cues such as the particular people involved, the concept or rationale behind the project, word-of-mouth, and critical reviews. Thus, a movie can be seen as a product where the "ingredients" are the plots, actors, and director.[25] Certain movie titles such as "Star Wars," "Lethal Weapon," "Batman," "Die Hard," and "Star Trek" have established themselves as strong brands by combining all these ingredients into a formula that appeals to consumers and allows the studios to release sequels (essentially "brand extensions") that rely on the initial popularity of the title. For years, some of the most valuable movie franchises have involved recurring characters or ongoing stories, and many of the successful movies in recent years have been sequels. Their success comes from the fact that moviegoers know from the title and the people involved (actors, producers, directors, etc.) that they can expect certain things—a classic application of branding.

The existence of a strong brand name in the entertainment industry is valuable because of the strong feelings or even emotions that the names engender as a result of pleasurable past experiences. For example, in a review of the Fall 1994 TV season, one critic offered the following thoughts:[26]

> What if "Saturday Night Live" were called something else? Like "The Show Nobody Thinks Is Funny Show." Or "They Get Paid to Write This?" Maybe just "Bad Comedy—With Musical Guests." Would anyone watch? Doubtful. The "SNL" brand name sucks us in. . . .

A new album release from Walter Becker and Donald Fagen would probably not cause a ripple in the marketplace, but if hailed as coming from "Steely Dan" (their previous band), then strong sales would be virtually guaranteed. Observers believe that although Robert Plant and Jimmy Page's 1995 "Unledded" tour sold $33 million worth of tickets in North America and spawned album sales of about 1 million copies, these are a fraction of what they could have sold if they had reunited as "Led Zeppelin." Recognizing the power of his brand name, former Beatle Paul McCartney released an album in 1994, "Strawberry Oceans Ships Forest," that did *not* use his name but instead that of a hypothetical performer called "The Fireman." McCartney felt that he was liked for a certain kind of music and didn't want his fans to buy the album—which contained dance-oriented instrumentals in the spirit of reggae dub—and then be disappointed because it wasn't what they expected.[27] Branding Brief 1–6 describes some of the branding efforts in the fiercely competitive cable television industry.

GEOGRAPHICAL LOCATIONS

Geographical locations, like products and people, can also be branded. In this case, the brand name is relatively fixed by the actual name of the location. The power of branding is making people aware of the location and then linking desirable associations. Increased mobility of both people and businesses, growth in the tourism industry, and so on have all contributed to the rise of place marketing. Cities, states, regions, and countries are now actively promoted through advertising, direct mail, and other communication tools (see Branding Brief 1–7). The state of Alabama ran a clever campaign in the early 1990s that presented pictures and quotes of stereotypes

Branding Cable Television Networks

Many cable television networks have created extensive marketing programs to build an identity for their channels and create loyalty and regular viewership. The competition in the cable TV industry to achieve sufficient "mind share" with the consumers is critically important in a marketplace where viewers can switch between channels with the flick of a dial or the push of a button. Here, we highlight the branding efforts of two channels covering news, sports, and entertainment in very different ways.

MTV

Viacom's MTV music television is one network that has gone beyond playing music videos to capture (and sell) the lifestyle of a generation. With the slogan "MTV. You'll never look at music the same way again," it began 24-hour programming of music videos introduced by personable "VJs" with their launch in 1981. The cable channel's rebellious and irreverent manner was the perfect formula to attract the 12- to 34-year-olds of that generation. Quickly embraced by America's youth, MTV became a powerful tool for advertisers who saw it as a means to reach and influence teenagers and young adults. Ads employing cutting-edge animation and cinematic techniques and whose artistic sensibility seamlessly merged with the elaborately produced music videos were created with MTV in mind. Through their programming, personalities, and promotions, MTV created an extremely desirable brand image with associations of "young," "hip," and "daring." To capitalize on its popularity, regional versions of MTV have been exported to Europe, Asia, Latin America, and other parts of the world, and the MTV name has also been used to introduce new merchandising products and media. Unfortunately, although MTV is highly regarded by this younger market segment, most viewers were in the habit of only watching for short periods of time as they journeyed around the dial. To create the stable viewing patterns that advertisers desire, MTV has attempted to introduce shows that viewers would tune in to watch on a regular basis. Although some shows covered news and sports from a uniquely MTV point of view, the most successful ones were "Beavis and Butthead," "The Real World," and "MTV Unplugged." To compensate for the declining amount of programming time devoted to music, a new channel, "all music" M2, was launched in August 1996 and pitched to a slightly older audience.

CNN

Turner Broadcasting's Cable News Network (CNN) has also revolutionized television programming in many ways.[a] Introduced in 1980, it slowly built a following by combining detailed 24-hour-a-day news coverage, live broadcasts, and expert analysis and commentary. With its sister network, Headline News, it offers television viewers all over the world convenient, up-to-the minute, and in-depth newscasts. CNN lived up to its corporate slogan as "The World's News Leader" through unparalleled news coverage. CNN's ratings soared whenever a crisis or breaking news story occurred. During the early weeks of the Persian Gulf War in January 1991, CNN's daily 24-hour average rating reached almost a "7," or roughly 4 million viewers. Unfortunately, after the war ended, CNN's rating dropped back to their normal, pre-war ratings. As with MTV and many other cable channels, CNN's challenge has been to convert its valuable brand associations of professional, unbiased, and comprehensive news coverage to overcome its label as the "Crisis News Network" and attract the regular viewers that advertisers covet. To do so, CNN has moved beyond its regularly scheduled news shows (e.g., "Daybreak," "Newsday," and "PrimeNews") to establish more varied programming such as interview and talk shows (e.g., "Larry King Live" and "Crossfire") and specialized news shows (e.g., "Moneyline with Lou Dobbs," "CNN Sports Tonite," and "Showbiz Today"). These shows and the personalities hosting them are now actively advertised and promoted in print and TV media. Recognizing the value of its name, CNN is also selectively licensing its name to appropriate merchandise.

[a]Stephen Battaglio, "Calm After the Storm," *ADWEEK* (March 9, 1992): 13; Peter Waldman, "CNN Rechannels Efforts to Achieve Premier Status," *Wall Street Journal* (October 16, 1989): B–1; Wayne Walley, "The Mother of All Ratings Jumps," *Advertising Age* (April 8, 1991): 35–42.

of the state (e.g., women with bouffant hairdos), which were then refuted in the text of the ad—akin to a famous trade print ad campaign for Rolling Stone concerning the "perception" and "reality" of the image about their readers. The goals of these types of campaigns are to create awareness and a favorable image of a location that will entice temporary visits or permanent moves from individuals and businesses alike.

Examples of Strong Brands

It is clear from the examples above that virtually anything can be and has been branded. Which brands are the "strongest," that is, the most well-known or highly regarded? Certainly some of the best known brands can be found by simply walking down a supermarket aisle. It is also easy to identify a number of other brands with amazing staying power that have been market leaders in their respective categories for decades. For example, in ten major product categories, the number one U.S. brands from 1925 remain on top today: Kodak cameras and film, Goodyear tires, Nabisco crackers and cookies, Wrigley chewing gum, Del Monte canned fruit, Gillette razors and blades, Ivory soap, Coca-Cola soft drinks, Campbell's soup, and Lipton tea. Similarly, many brands that were number one in the United Kingdom in 1933 also remain on top today: Hovis bread, Stork margarine, Kellogg's corn flakes, Cadbury's chocolates, Gillette razors, Schweppes mixers, Brooke Bond tea, Colgate toothpaste, and Hoover vacuum cleaners. These brands have evolved over the years and have

---

Chasing the Tourist Dollar

The state of Florida has experienced a number of branding problems of late.[a] Although negative publicity about crime and attacks on foreign tourists have caused problems, perhaps the biggest challenge has come from the number and aggressiveness of rival destinations. A shift in consumer preferences for short vacations and a desire for new and different adventures have put the state at a disadvantage: Whereas the average American pleasure trip has decreased from 5.1 nights in 1989 to 4.3 nights in 1993, the average Florida visitor has been staying 12.3 nights, and Florida is viewed by many as an old destination. Moreover, Florida has been outspent by other states in communicating to consumers—the state's advertising budget of $6.7 million in 1994 was dwarfed by those of other areas (e.g., Las Vegas spent $33.5 million and even Mississippi, perhaps a seemingly unlikely tourist stop, spent $7.5 million).

Tourism-industry officials in Florida considered a number of solutions, including increased marketing expenditures. Perhaps the most important action was the enactment of a series of crime prevention measures. Special tourist-oriented police stepped up patrols of danger spots, license plates with special markings for rental cars were discontinued, and road signs were enlarged and increased in number to lead the way to popular tourist sites. To better attract European visitors, Florida marketing representatives launched an intensive effort throughout Europe to talk up the success of crime-control initiatives to tour operators abroad and the international press. Domestic efforts placed more emphasis on marketing the state as a whole rather than individual destinations.

The Florida Department of Commerce reported a record 41.3 million visitors to the Sunshine State in 1995, up 3.5 percent from its sluggish 1993 performance, and a robust 1996 was forecasted. Nevertheless, despite this rebound, tourism officials still long for the boom years of the 1980s and wonder how to best combat the "been there, done that" image that Florida evokes from many vacationers.

---

[a]Emory Thomas, "Crime Isn't All That's Hurting Florida Tourism," *Wall Street Journal* (November 3, 1994): B–1; Marta Brannigan, "Florida Basks in Warmth of More Tourists," *Wall Street Journal,* (February 20, 1996): A-2.

---

made a number of changes. In many cases, they barely resemble how they originally started. Branding Brief 1–8 describes the sometimes surprising and humble origins of a number of top brands.

What distinguishes leading brands? In later chapters, we will delve in into the success characteristics of brand leaders. A study by D'Arcy Masius Benton & Bowles (DMB&B) provides an interesting glimpse into the lives of "leadership brands."[28] Based on extensive consumer research, they conclude that leadership brands:

A Glimpse into the Past of Selected Brands[a]

Coca-Cola (aerated drink and manufacturer) As one of the best known and most 'international' of trade names, *Coca-Cola* was created in May 1886 by Frank M. Robinson, bookkeeper to the creator of the drink itself, Dr. John S. Pemberton, a druggist from Atlanta, Georgia, and was registered as a trademark on 31 January 1893. The name was based on two of the drink's constituents: extracts from *coca* leaves and from the *cola* nut. That coca leaves also yield cocaine is a connection that the manufacturers do not now prefer to emphasize, and it is certainly true that although the drink once contained a form of the drug, especially in the early days when it was advertised as an 'Esteemed Brain Tonic and Intellectual Beverage', it contains none now. The name itself is a remarkably successful one as a memorable and easily pronounceable trade name, having alliteration and three desirable 'k' sounds (compare *Kodak*). *Coca-Cola* gained popularity rapidly—it was first bottled in 1894—to such an extent that the manufacturers were obliged to register a second name for it used by the public as a 'pet' form: *Coke*. The second element of the name is not a registered trademark, so that 'cola' drinks exist on the market in a number of varieties. Among names of rival brands (imposters) were Coca, Cola, Fig Cola, Candy Cola, Cold Cola, Cay-Ola, and Koca-Nola. All these were outlawed by the courts in 1916.

Gillette (safety razors, blades, and toiletries by *Gillette* Industries) The name comes from the company's first president, King Camp Gillette, who traced his name back to the Gillet family of Somerset, England. Gillette patented the first disposable razorblades in 1902, having the previous year founded his company for the manufacture of razors and blades, initially as the American Safety Razor Co. In 1908 Wilkinson Sword tried unsuccessfully to trademark the name 'Gilledge' as a stropper to resharpen used blades. *Gillette* as a name has a favourable French appearance (although a bogus one) for products in the sophisticated toiletries market. Gillette's original blade had been perfected by William E. Nickerson, who designed equipment for the company. It was fortunate that he had not been the actual inventor, since 'Nickerson' would hardly make a suitable name for a company selling razors and blades.

Kodak (photographic products and cameras and manufacturer) A trade name that is as well known internationally as *Coca-Cola*. The two names, in fact, appeared within two years of each other: *Coca-Cola* in 1886 and *Kodak* in 1888. *Kodak* as a name has no meaning: it is not intended to suggest any word (as 'code' or 'compact'), nor does it derive from any word. It was invented by the American photographic pioneer, George Eastman, who patented it on 4 September 1888. Fortunately for posterity, Eastman has recorded the reasoning that prompted him to choose this particular name. He chose it, he says, "because I knew a trade name must be short, vigorous, incapable of being misspelled to an extent that would destroy its identity, and in order to satisfy trademark laws, it must mean nothing. The letter K has been a favourite with me—it seemed a strong, incisive sort of letter. Therefore, the word I wanted had to start with K. Then it became a question of trying out a great number of combinations of letters that made words starting and ending with K. The word Kodak is the result.' It has been pointed out that the name is additionally onomatopoeic—it suggests the clicking of a camera's shutter. It may also be relevant that 'K' was the first letter of Eastman's mother's family name. The name has sometimes been used generically in a number of languages for a camera. This prompted the *Verband Deutscher Amateurphotographen Vereine* ('Joint Society of German Amateur Photographic Associations') to issue the following warning (in German) in 1917: 'Whoever speaks of a *Kodak* meaning only a photographic camera in general is not mindful of the fact that he is damaging the German industry in favour of the Anglo-American by widespread use of this word.' George Eastman also invented the name of one of *Kodak*'s most popular cameras, the *Brownie.*

Shell (petroleum and manufacturer) The story of *Shell* began in the first half of the nineteenth century in the curio shop in East Smithfield, London, set up by a Jewish dealer, Marcus Samuel. Samuel's children had fastened seaside shells to their empty lunch boxes on returning from a holiday, and the dealer made up a number of such boxes and labelled them with the names of the resorts the shells had come from. For the more sophisticated demands of his lady customers he imported fancy polished shells from abroad. His shop soon became known as the Shell Shop, and business expanded rapidly so that by 1830 Marcus Samuel had built up an international trade in oriental curios and copra, as well as shells. When barrelled kerosene was added to his cargo list, the worldwide activities of the Shell Shop were consolidated as the *Shell* Transport and Trading Co. This was in 1897 when the firm had been taken over by Samuel's son, also called Marcus. (Marcus *père* died in 1870, aged 73.) The company adopted the scallop as its trademark in 1904.

Sony (electrical equipment and manufacturer) Many Japanese trade names turn out to be taken simply from the surname of a company founder or an inventor. *Sony* is rather different. When Japan's first transistor radio was produced by the Tokyo Tsushin Kogyo Kabushai Kaisha (company) in 1955 the directors understandably felt that they needed a much more 'streamlined' and international name for it than the full length company name. At first they considered 'TTK,' which was certainly better, but there already existed a TKK (Tokyo Kyuto KK, or Tokyo Express Co.) which would be confusing. Earlier, they had used 'Tape-corder' for their tape recorder and 'Soni' (from *'sonic'*) for this machine's tape. Considering, 'Soni,' the directors felt that this would probably be mispronounced in English, as 'so-nigh.' But the international (Latin) base *'son,'* meaning 'sound,' was good, and an alteration of the final 'i' to 'y' would suggest 'sonny,' and give the name a homely, affectionate touch. If, however, the actual name was spelled 'Sonny' the Japanese would pronounce this as 'son-ny,' and this might be associated with the Japanese word for 'loss,' *son.* This would not do, since the radio was clearly intended to produce a profit! Finally, the variant Sony was decided on for the transistor, and the name passed to the company as a whole in 1958.

---

[a]Reprinted from Adrian Room, *Dictionary of Trade Name Origins,* Routledge & Kegan Paul, 1982.

1. Have significant financial and perceptual benefits
2. Own a core benefit in the category with a balance of rational and emotional messages
3. Are consistent and focus on quality, not price
4. Use the full range of marketing tools to solidify performance

Another study also provides insight into consumer opinions of leading brands by ranking of brands according to consumers' perceptions of quality.[29] Specifically, about 2,000 randomly chosen U.S. respondents (ages 15 or older) are interviewed each year in the annual Equitrend survey by Total Research. They are asked to rate brands on a scale of 0 to 10, with 10 representing "outstanding/extraordinary quality," 5 representing "quite acceptable quality," and 0 representing "unacceptable/poor quality." No definitions of quality are provided, leaving it up to the consumer to decide how he or she judges quality in each case. The scores are averaged across consumers and converted to a 1–100 scale. Figure 1–3 shows the results of the 1996 survey.

At the same time, despite all of these successes, there are a number of brands who have lost their market leadership and, in some cases, even their very existence! Winston, after years of dominance in the cigarette category, lost its leadership position to Marlboro in 1975 and now trails that brand by a large margin. Volkswagen, once a top imported car in the United States, has seen sales drop precipitously and is currently attempting a comeback. Other seemingly invincible brands, such as IBM, American Express, and Sears, have run into difficulties and have seen their market preeminence challenged or even eliminated. Although in some cases these failures could be related to factors beyond the control of the firm, such as technological advances and/or shifting consumer preferences, in other cases the blame could probably be placed on the actions or inaction of the marketers behind these brands. Some of these marketers failed to account for changing market conditions and continued to operate with a "business as usual" attitude, or perhaps even worse, recognized that changes were necessary but were inadequate or inappropriate in their response.

How do you create a strong brand? How do you know whether you have a strong brand? How do you make sure that the strength of a brand does not become diminished over time? Before considering how the value or equity of a brand can be built, measured, and managed, we first examine the history of brands, explore how firms have managed brands over time, and consider what challenges are now faced by marketers interested in building strong brands.

Historical Origins of Branding[30]

As noted above, branding, in one form or another, has been around for centuries. The original motivation for branding was for craftsmen and others to identify the fruits of their labors so that customers could easily recognize them. Branding, or at least trademarks, can be traced back to ancient pottery and stonemason's marks, which were applied to handcrafted goods to identify their source. Pottery and clay lamps were sometimes sold far from the shops where they were made, and buyers looked for the stamps of reliable potters as a guide to quality. Marks have been found on early Chi-

1	Kodak Photographic Film	8.41
2	Disney World	8.40
3	National Geographic	8.39
4	The Discovery Channel	8.28
5	Mercedes-Benz Automobiles	8.22
6	Disneyland	8.20
7	Hallmark Greeting Cards	8.19
8	Waterford Crystal	8.18
9	Craftsman Power Tools	8.16
10	Fisher-Price Toys	8.16
11	Reynolds Wrap Aluminum Foil	8.09
12	Lexus Automobiles	8.09
13	Levi's Jeans	8.09
14	Makita Power Tools	8.03
15	Arm & Hammer Baking Soda	8.00
16	Hewlett-Packard Printers	7.97
17	Ziploc Bags	7.96
18	Chiquita Bananas	7.95
19	Duracell Batteries	7.94
20	M&M's Candy	7.92
21	The Learning Channel	7.89
22	Lego Toys	7.87
23	Hersey's Milk Chocolate Candy Bars	7.86
24	IBM Personal Computers	7.85
25	Universal Studios Florida	7.84
26	OshKosh B'Gosh Children's Clothing	7.83
27	Rubbermaid Household Products	7.82
28	BMW Automobiles	7.80
29	Maytag Major Appliances	7.80
30	The Disney Channel	7.79
31	Sony Televisions	7.79
32	Michelin Automobile Tires	7.78
33	The Summer Olympics	7.78
34	Glad-Lock Zipper Bags	7.77
35	Sea World	7.72
36	National Geographic Traveler	7.71
37	Tide Laundry Detergent	7.71
38	Lenox Crystal	7.71
39	Playskool Toys	7.71
40	Nike Athletic Shoes	7.71
41	Campbell's Soup	7.70
42	Black & Decker Power Tools	7.69
43	Tylenol Pain Reliever	7.68
44	Reeses Peanut Butter Cups	7.68
45	CNN (Cable News Network)	7.68
46	Visa Card	7.67
47	Energizer Batteries	7.66
48	Sony Compact Disc Players	7.64
49	Oreo Cookies	7.64
50	AT&T Long Distance Service	7.62
51	Dole Bananas	7.60
52	Hilton Hotels	7.60
53	Nike Activewear	7.58
54	Crest Toothpaste	7.58
55	Jeep Grand Cherokee Sport Utility Vehicle	7.58
56	Snickers Candy Bars	7.57
57	Tupperware Household Products	7.56
58	AAA (American Automobile Association)	7.55
59	PBS (Public Broadcasting)	7.55
60	Marriott Hotels	7.52
61	Stanley Non-Power Hand Tools	7.51
62	Goodyear Automobile Tires	7.50
63	GMC Suburban Sport Utility Vehicle	7.49
64	Busch Gardens	7.49
65	Orville Reddenbacher Popcorn	7.48
66	Little Tikes Toys	7.48
67	Cadillac Automobiles	7.48
68	Infinity Automobiles	7.47
69	ESPN	7.46
70	Compaq Personal Computers	7.46
71	Six Flags Theme Parks	7.46
72	Kenmore Major Appliances	7.43
73	Kitchenaid Major Appliances	7.43
74	Chevrolet Suburban Sport Utility Vehicle	7.43
75	Hyatt Hotels	7.42
76	Samsonite Luggage	7.42
77	G.E. Major Appliances	7.40
78	The Wall Street Journal	7.39
79	Coca-Cola	7.39
80	Reebok Athletic Shoes	7.39
81	Consumer Reports	7.39
82	Planters Peanuts	7.39
83	Whirlpool Major Appliances	7.38
84	Dewalt Power Tools	7.38
85	RCA Televisions	7.37
86	Smithsonian	7.37
87	The Home Depot	7.37
88	Advil Pain Reliever	7.36
89	Mattel Toys	7.34
90	Headline News	7.34
91	MasterCard	7.33
92	The Family Channel	7.33
93	AT&T Universal Card	7.33
94	Regional Bell Telephone Service	7.33
95	Nestlé Crunch Candy Bars	7.33
96	Wal-Mart Stores	7.32
97	Apple Macintosh Personal Computers	7.32
98	The Disney Store	7.32
99	Toyota Landcruiser Sport Utility Vehicle	7.31
100	Universal Studios Hollywood	7.31

FIGURE 1-3 Results of 1996 Equitrend Survey

nese porcelain, on pottery jars from ancient Greece and Rome, and on goods from India dating back to about 1300 B.C.

In medieval times, potters' marks were joined by printers' marks, watermarks on paper, bread marks, and the marks of various craft guilds. In some cases, these were used to attract buyers loyal to particular makers, but the marks were also used to police infringers of the guild monopolies and to single out the makers of inferior goods. An English law passed in 1266 required bakers to put their mark on every loaf of bread sold, "to the end that if any bread bu faultie in weight, it may bee then knowne in whom the fault is." Goldsmiths and silversmiths were also required to mark their goods, both with their signatures or personal symbols and with a sign of the quality of the metal. In 1597, two goldsmiths convicted of putting false marks on their wares were nailed to the pillory by their ears. Similarly harsh punishments were decreed for those who counterfeited other artisans' marks.

When Europeans began to settle in North America, they brought the convention and practice of branding with them. The makers of patent medicines and tobacco manufacturers were early U.S. branding pioneers. Medicine potions such as Swaim's Panacea, Fahnestock's Vermifuge, and Perry Davis' Vegetable Pain Killer became well-known to the public prior to the Civil War. Patent medicines were packaged in small bottles and, because they were not seen as a necessity, were vigorously promoted. To further influence consumer choices in stores, manufacturers of these medicines printed elaborate and distinctive labels, often with their own portrait featured in the center.

Tobacco manufacturers had been exporting their crop since the early 1600s. By the early 1800s, manufacturers had packed bales of tobacco under labels such as Smith's Plug and Brown and Black's Twist. During the 1850s, many tobacco manufacturers recognized that more creative names—such as Cantaloupe, Rock Candy, Wedding Cake, and Lone Jack—were helpful in selling their tobacco products. In the 1860s, tobacco manufacturers began to sell their wares in small bags directly to consumers. Attractive-looking packages were seen as important, and picture labels, decorations, and symbols were designed as a result.

The history of branding in the United States since 1860 can be divided into four main periods. We next consider some of the important developments in each.

EMERGENCE OF NATIONAL MANUFACTURER BRANDS: 1860–1914

In the United States after the Civil War, a number of forces combined to make widely distributed, manufacturer-branded products a profitable venture:

1. Improvements in transportation (e.g., railroad) and communication (e.g., telegraph and telephone) made regional and even national distribution increasingly easy.

2. Improvements in production processes made it possible to produce large quantities of high quality products inexpensively.

3. Improvements in packaging made individual (as opposed to bulk) packages that could be identified with the manufacturer's trademark increasingly viable.

4. Changes in U.S. trademark law in 1879, the 1880s, and 1906 made it easier to protect brand identities.

5. Advertising became perceived as a more credible option, and newspapers and magazines eagerly sought out advertising revenues.

6. Retail institutions such as department and variety stores and national mail order houses served as effective middlemen and encouraged consumer spending.

7. Population increased due to liberal immigration policies.

8. Increasing industrialization and urbanization raised the standard of living and aspirations of Americans, although many products on the market still were of uneven quality.

9. Literacy rose as the percentage of illiterate Americans dropped from 20 percent in 1870 to 10 percent in 1900.

All of these factors facilitated the development of consistent quality consumer products that could be efficiently sold to consumers through mass market advertising campaigns. In this fertile branding environment, mass-produced merchandise in packages largely replaced locally produced merchandise sold from bulk containers. This change brought about the widespread use of trademarks. For example, Procter & Gamble made candles in Cincinnati and shipped them to merchants in other cities along the Ohio and Mississippi rivers. In 1851, wharf hands began to brand crates of Procter & Gamble candles with a crude star. The firm soon noticed that buyers downriver relied on the star as a mark of quality, and merchants refused the candles if the crates arrived without the mark. As a result, the candles were marked with a more formal star label on all packages, were branded as "Star," and began to develop a loyal following.

The development and management of these brands was largely driven by the owners of the firm and their top-level management. For example, the first president of National Biscuit was involved heavily in the introduction in 1898 of Uneeda Biscuits, the first nationally branded biscuit. One of their first decisions was to create a pictorial symbol for the brand, the Uneeda biscuit slicker boy, who appeared in the supporting ad campaigns. H.J. Heinz built up the Heinz brand name through production innovations and spectacular promotions. Coca-Cola became a national powerhouse due to the efforts of Asa Chandler who actively oversaw the growth of its extensive distribution channel.

National manufacturers sometimes had to overcome resistance from consumers, retailers, wholesalers, and even employees from within their own company. To do so, these firms employed sustained "push" and "pull" efforts to keep both consumers and retailers happy and accepting of national brands. Consumers were attracted through the use of sampling, premiums, product education brochures, and heavy advertising. Retailers were lured by in-store sampling and promotional programs and shelf maintenance assistance.

As the use of brand names and trademarks spread, so did the practice of imitation and counterfeiting. Although the laws were somewhat unclear, more and more firms sought protection by sending their trademarks and labels to district courts for registration. Congress finally separated the registration of trademarks and labels in 1870 with the enactment of the country's first federal trademark law. Under the law, registrants were required to send a facsimile of their mark with a description of the type of goods on which it was used to the Patent Office in Washington along with a $25 fee. One of the first marks submitted to the Patent Office under the new law was the Underwood Devil, which was registered to William Underwood & Company of

Boston on November 29, 1870 for use on "Deviled Entrements." By 1890, most countries had trademark acts, establishing brand names, labels, and designs as legally protectable assets.

DOMINANCE OF MASS MARKETED BRANDS: 1915–1929

By 1915, manufacturer brands had become well-established in the United States on both a regional and national basis. The next fifteen years saw increasing acceptance and even admiration of manufacturer brands by consumers. The marketing of brands became more specialized under the guidance of functional experts in charge of production, promotion, personal selling, and other areas. This greater specialization led to more advanced marketing techniques. Design professionals were enlisted to assist in the process of trademark selection. Personal selling became more sophisticated as salesmen were carefully selected and trained to systematically handle accounts and seek out new businesses. Advertising combined more powerful creativity with more persuasive copy and slogans. Government and industry regulation came into place to reduce deceptive advertising. Marketing research became more important and influential in supporting marketing decisions.

Although functional management of brands had these virtues, it also presented problems. Because responsibility for any one brand was divided among two or more functional managers as well as advertising specialists, poor coordination was always a potential problem. For example, the introduction of Wheaties cereal by General Mills was nearly sabotaged by the company's salesmen who were reluctant to take on new duties to support the brand. As it turned out, three years after the introduction, when Wheaties was on the verge of being dropped, a manager from the advertising department at General Mills decided to become a product champion, and the brand went on to great success in the following decades.

CHALLENGES TO MANUFACTURER BRANDS: 1930–1945

The onset of the Great Depression in 1929 posed new challenges to manufacturer brands. Greater price sensitivity swung the pendulum of power in the favor of retailers who pushed their own brands and dropped non-performing manufacturer brands. Advertising came under fire as manipulative, deceptive, and tasteless and was increasingly being ignored by certain segments of the population. In 1938, the Wheeler Amendment gave power to the FTC to regulate advertising practices. In response to these trends, manufacturers' advertising went beyond slogans and jingles to give consumers specific reasons why they should buy advertised products.

There were few dramatic changes in marketing of brands during this time. As a notable exception, Procter & Gamble put the first brand management system into place where each of its brands had a manager assigned solely to that brand who was responsible for its financial success. Other firms were slow to follow, however, and relied more on their long-standing reputation for good quality—and a lack of competition—to sustain sales. During World War II, manufacturer brands became relatively scarce as resources were diverted to the war effort. Nevertheless, many brands continued to advertise and helped to bolster consumer demand during these tough times.

The Lanham Act of 1946 permitted federal registration of service marks—marks used to designate services rather than products—and collective marks such as union labels and club emblems.

ESTABLISHMENT OF BRAND MANAGEMENT STANDARDS: 1946–1985

After World War II, the pent-up demand for high quality brands led to an explosion of sales. Personal income grew as the economy took off, and market demand intensified as the rate of population growth exploded. Demand for national brands soared, fueled by a burst of new products and a receptive and growing middle class. Firm after firm during this time period adopted the brand management system.

In the brand management system, a brand manager took "ownership" of a brand. A brand manager was responsible for developing and implementing the annual marketing plan for his or her brand, as well as identifying new business opportunities. The brand manager might be assisted internally by representatives from manufacturing, the sales force, marketing research, financial planning, research and development, personnel, legal, and public relations and externally by representatives from advertising agencies, research suppliers, and public relations agencies.

Then as now a successful brand manager had to be a versatile "jack of all trades." For example, a marketing manager at Gillette once identified the following success factors to being a brand manager:[31]

1. A dedication to the brand, reflected in an effort to do what was best for the business
2. An ability to assess a situation and see alternative solutions
3. A talent for generating creative ideas and a willingness to be open to others' ideas
4. An ability to make decisions in a highly ambiguous environment
5. An ability to move projects through the organization
6. Good communication skills
7. A high energy level
8. A capacity for handling many tasks simultaneously

NEW BRANDING CHALLENGES AND OPPORTUNITIES: 1986–PRESENT

The sophisticated brand management systems implemented by so many firms were highly successful in creating powerful brand franchises in the 1950s, 1960s, and 1970s. This development did not go unnoticed by the financial community. The merger and acquisition frenzy of the 1980s resulted in Wall Street financiers seeking out undervalued companies from which investment or takeover profits could be made. One of the primary undervalued assets of these firms were their brands, given that they were off-balance-sheet items. Implicit in this Wall Street interest was a belief that strong brands resulted in better earnings and profit performance for firms, which, in turn, created greater value for shareholders.

For example, over the course of a short period of time in 1988, almost $50 billion changed hands in exchange for some well-known brands:[32]

1. American food, tobacco, and drink manufacturer RJR Nabisco was the center of a vicious tug-of-war between its own management and various outsiders desiring to buy the company. Eventually, the brand was sold to leveraged buyout specialists, Kohlberg, Kravis, and Roberts for $30 billion.

2. American food and tobacco manufacturer Philip Morris bought Kraft (home to Kraft cheese, Miracle Whip spread, Breyers ice cream, etc.) for $12.9 billion or more than four times its book value for tangible assets. An estimated $1100.6 million was for goodwill.[33] After the acquisition, Philip Morris substantially increased its intangible asset base and commenced systematically amortizing its assets.

3. Grand Metropolitan, a U.K. food and drinks company, acquired Pillsbury (home to Pillsbury baking products, Green Giant frozen and canned vegetables, Burger King, etc.) for $5.5 billion, a 50 percent premium on the American firm's pre-bid value and several times the value of its tangible assets.

4. Nestlé, a multinational powerhouse, acquired U.K.'s Rowntree (home to Kit Kat, After Eight, and Polo mints and other confectioneries) for $4.5 billion, more than five times its book value.

As these examples illustrate, the price premium paid for companies is often clearly justified on the basis of assumptions of the extra profits that could be extracted and sustained from their brands, as well as the tremendous difficulty and expense of creating similar brands from scratch.

Although there has been growing recognition of the value of brands, as reflected by these financial transactions, a number of developments have occurred in recent years that have significantly complicated marketing practices and pose challenges for brand managers (see Figure 1–4), as discussed next.[34]

Brand Proliferation

Perhaps the most important change is the proliferation of new brands and products, in part spurred by the rise in line and brand extensions. As a result, a brand name may now be identified with a number of different products of varying degrees of similarity. Coca-Cola now comes in diet, caffeine-free, and cherry-flavored forms. Procter & Gamble's Crest original toothpaste, introduced in 1955, has been joined by a number of line extensions: Crest Mint (1967), Advanced Formula Crest (1980), Crest Gel (1981), Crest Tartar Control (1985), Crest for Kids (1987), Crest Neat

---

Mature markets
More sophisticated and increasing competition
Difficulty in differentiating
Decreasing brand loyalty in many categories
Growth of private labels
Increasing trade power
Fragmentation of brand franchises
Fragmented media
Short-term performance orientation
Increasing promotional expenditures
Decreasing advertising expenditures

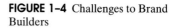

FIGURE 1-4 Challenges to Brand Builders

Squeeze (1991), Crest Baking Soda (1992), and Crest for Sensitive Teeth (1994). Procter & Gamble's Ivory soap has been extended to dishwashing detergent, laundry detergent, shampoo, and conditioner. With so many brands having introduced extensions, there are few single or "mono" product brands around.

Media Fragmentation

Another important change in the marketing environment is the erosion or fragmentation of traditional advertising media and the emergence of nontraditional media, promotion, and other communication alternatives. New ways to reach consumers and create brand value include sports and event sponsorship; in-store advertising; "mini-billboards" in transit vehicles, or parking meters, and in other locations; product placement in movies; and interactive, electronic media.

For a number of reasons, marketers have become disenchanted with traditional advertising media, especially network television. First, the cost of network TV has risen dramatically in many countries. Since the mid-1970s, the price of network TV advertising in the United States has far outpaced the rate of inflation but without accompanying increases in audience size. The cost-per-thousand (CPM) viewers, a standard measure of media efficiency, is now *five* times what it was in 1970. Second, commercial breaks on network TV have become more cluttered as advertisers increasingly decided to advertise with 15-second spots rather than the traditional 30- or 60-second spots. Third, the growth of independent stations and cable channels has resulted in a dramatic erosion of the network share of audience (from 91 percent in 1975 to under 50 percent by 1996). Fourth, the increase in remote controls and VCRs and the resulting "zipping," "zapping," "grazing," and "channel surfing," in the popular vernacular, has further reduced TV advertising effectiveness.[35] Finally, not only is it now difficult for marketers to reach consumers with advertising, it is also difficult to persuade them when they actually see or hear their communications. Charles Newman of Lever Bros. puts it this way:

> The dollars that were spent on advertising in the 1950s and 1960s are still paying off. The advertising done 30 years ago for the Marlboro Man is still paying off all around the world. It was so cheap to get a large share of voice in the 1950s—it would be impossible to duplicate that now. There was also more receptivity in the marketplace. Now there is a more world-weary, seen-it-all attitude. People are more likely not to believe what they see on TV, to tune things out. The more you turn up the volume, the more people resist, and it becomes harder and harder to implant in people's minds that things are desirable.[36]

For these and other reasons, the percentage of the communication budget devoted to advertising has shrunk over the years. Trade promotion, on the other hand, grew to half of all marketing communication spending by 1991 (from about a third in 1981). As chapter 6 describes, trade promotions often come in the form of financial incentives or discounts given to retailers, distributors, and other members of the trade to stock, display, and facilitate in other ways the sale of a product (e.g., through slotting allowances, point-of-purchase displays, contests and dealer incentives, training programs, trade shows, or cooperative advertising).

Many marketing critics, however, believe this rise in trade promotions has had deleterious effects. Besides inhibiting the use of franchise-building advertising, these diverted marketing funds led to some reductions in research and development budgets and staff. Retailers have come to expect and now demand trade discounts. Perhaps most importantly, the widespread discounting arising from trade promotions may have led to the increased importance of price as a factor in consumer decisions, breaking down traditional loyalty patterns.

Increased Competition and Costs

One reason marketers have been forced to use so many financial incentives or discounts is that the marketplace has become more competitive. Both demand and supply factors have contributed to the increase in competitive intensity. On the demand side, consumption for many products and services has flattened and hit the maturity stage, or even the decline stage, of the product life cycle. As a result, sales growth for brands can only be achieved at the expense of competing brands by taking away some of their market share. On the supply side, new competitors have emerged for a number of reasons. First, as noted above, many companies have taken their existing brands and launched products with the same name into new categories. Many of these brands provide formidable opposition. Second, deregulation of certain industries (e.g., telecommunications, financial services, health care, and transportation) has led to increased competition from outside traditionally defined product-market boundaries. Third, although firms have embraced globalization as a means to open new markets and potential sources of revenue, it has also resulted in an increase in the number of competitors in existing markets, threatening current sources of revenue. Finally, market penetration of generics, private labels, or low-priced "clones" imitating product leaders has increased. Private labels, or store brands, have grown on a worldwide basis. For example, in the analgesic market, private label share of sales rose from 19 percent in 1985 to 30 percent in 1991 in the United States, from 44 percent to 57 percent in the United Kingdom, and from 9 percent to 13 percent in Germany (West).[37] Retailers have gained power and often dictate what happens within the store. Their chief marketing weapon is price, and they have introduced and pushed their own brands and demanded greater compensation from trade promotions to stock and display national brands.

At the same time that competition is increasing, the cost of introducing a new product or supporting an existing product has increased rapidly, making it difficult to match the investment and level of support that brands were able to receive in previous years. A.C. Nielsen and NPD have been jointly maintaining a database of trial and repeat trends for the average consumer products. Product trial—defined as a household buying a particular consumer packaged goods product at least once during its introductory year—was around 15 percent in the latter half of the 1970s, had dropped to 13.4 percent in the first half of the 1980s, and further declined to 10.6 percent in the period from 1988 to 1991.[38]

Greater Accountability

Finally, in addition to all the foregoing reasons, marketers often find themselves responsible for meeting ambitious short-term profit targets because of financial market pressures and senior management imperatives. Stock analysts value strong and consistent earnings reports as an indication of the long-term financial health of a firm. As a result, marketing managers may find themselves in the dilemma of having to make decisions with short-term benefits but long-term costs (e.g., cutting advertising expenditures). Moreover, many of these same managers have experienced rapid job turnover and promotions and may not anticipate being in their current positions for very long. These different organizational pressures may encourage "quick-fix" solutions with perhaps adverse long-run consequences.

Purpose of the Book

As the above discussion points out, the complexity of both brand offerings and marketing communication options has significantly increased in recent years. A number of competitive challenges now exist for marketers. Many critics feel that the reaction by many marketers has been ineffective or, even worse, further aggravated the problem. Branding Brief 1–9 contains the remarks of one such critic. At the same time, a number of firms have introduced new marketing practices and systems. Perhaps one of the most compelling means to illustrate how much the marketing environment has changed is to consider some of the changes that have occurred at Procter & Gamble, the pioneer of the brand management system. Branding Brief 1–10 highlights some recent developments at that firm.

  Why is a special marketing text on brands needed? What does this book offer that is not covered in introductory or advanced marketing texts? Unfortunately, many of the important branding issues have been relatively neglected in these texts. Moreover, although many of the important and well-established principles of brand management are still basically valid (e.g., defining target markets, establishing differentiated product positions), as illustrated above, the context in which those principles must be applied to manage brands has dramatically changed. By putting more focus on the brand and accounting for these new developments, this book will provide students of marketing valuable knowledge, a broader perspective, and greater understanding of brand strategies and tactics. This book will consider a host of marketing issues from the point of view of branding. In doing so, issues that we may have otherwise overlooked will be examined and lessons that we may not have otherwise realized by practicing "marketing as usual" will be learned.

  In the remaining chapters, theories, models, and frameworks that accommodate and reflect these new developments will be presented to provide useful managerial guidelines and suggest promising new directions for future thought and research. In particular, a "common denominator" or unified conceptual framework based on the concept of brand equity will be introduced as a tool to interpret the potential effects of various brand strategies. Fundamentally, the brand equity concept stresses the importance of the role of the brand in marketing strategies. The concept of brand equity clearly builds on many previously identified principles about brand management. By adapting current theorizing and research advances to address the new challenges in brand management created by a changed marketing environment, however, the concept of brand equity can provide potentially useful new insights. Chapter 2 provides both an important overview on this topic and a blueprint for the rest of the book.

BRANDING BRIEF 1-9

Marketing's Crazy Eights

One thoughtful marketing critic, Alvin Achenbaum, maintains that, for whatever reason, marketing managers have often been guilty of one of the following eight sins:[a]

1. *Excessive product proliferation:* Line extensions where no real consumer need existed and category extensions where a new brand makes no sense or the brand image is inconsistent with the category.

2. *Widespread use of price competition:* Price discounting eroding brand loyalty.

3. *Retail bribery:* Retailers often demand and receive monetary inducements from manufacturers.

4. *Organizational inadequacy:* The brand management system often results in inexperienced and undersupported managers due to the rapid turnover.

5. *Short-term orientation:* Wall Street pressure for quarterly profit performance.

6. *Obsession with advertising creativity and a preoccupation with television:* Ads are often overresearched and, especially on television, expectations are too high for consumer response.

7. *Dubious planning processes:* Marketing plans too often are historical records of the past, not thoughtful forecasts of future events and what must be done about them.

8. *Market research double standard:* Although much research is being conducted and is serving as the basis for important marketing decisions, the research itself often lacks validity and may yield misleading findings.

Achenbaum continues by making eight recommendations to appropriately adapt to the new market conditions:[a]

1. Restore market growth.

2. Reevaluate product line policies.

3. Move the trade away from price promotion to revenue-building merchandising activities.

4. Readjust marketing communication programs to restore the former power of "pull" marketing.

5. Reorganize the brand management system.

6. Reevaluate allocation policies.

7. Rethink and revise marketing planning processes and create better strategic oversight.

8. Seek a basis for more effectively dealing with Wall Street's demands for short-term earnings.

---

[a]Alvin A. Achenbaum, "The Mismanagement of Brand Equity," ARF Fifth Annual Advertising and Promotion Workshop, February 1, 1992, © 1993 by the Advertising Research Foundation.

Procter & Gamble in the 1990s

In 1985, P&G posted its first annual earnings decline since 1952—a 29 percent decline to $635 million. Some of P&G's brand mainstays were being hammered by competition—both Crest toothpaste and Pampers diapers had seen their market share drop 20 percent over the previous eight-year period.[a] To get back on track, P&G made a number of internal and external changes in how it went about its business. P&G first changed its brand management system in October 1987, reorganizing along category lines.[b] Hailed by P&G as the biggest management change in thirty years, the reorganization created a new tier of marketing managers to oversee categories of products (e.g., laundry products, dishwashing products, and specialty products) and supervise individual brand managers. The strength of the original brand management system was that it created internal competition among brand managers. Although creating strong incentives, it also created conflicts and inefficiencies as brand managers fought over corporate resources. Given that the growth of the consumer market was slowing and becoming more fragmented, and that the increasingly powerful retail trade didn't think in terms of brands as much as categories, some type of overhaul was necessary. Category managers were supposed to take a broader view and seek out brand synergies and complementarity. In theory, the new organizational scheme was designed to make it easier to devise marketing strategies appropriate for brand portfolios within categories rather than coming up with competing brand strategies.

Bigger changes, however, were around the corner.[c] Beginning with the promotion of Ed Artzt to CEO in January 1990, the company introduced a number of changes that fundamentally changed the way it conducted its business. These changes primarily resulted from a shift in emphasis to a "value pricing" strategy. In 1991, P&G shifted to an everyday low pricing (EDLP) strategy, moving away from the conventional approach of maintaining high list prices interspersed with frequent and often substantial price discounts. There were a number of problems with the old pricing system. Many retailers didn't pass the discounts on to consumers. Some retailers engaged in forward buying and diverting tactics—stocking up on huge quantities and selling them after the discount expired or in regions that were not even "on deal." Consumers became conditioned to buying the brand only when it was discounted or on special or, even worse, looked to private label substitutes to obtain even lower prices. To stimulate sales, the frequency and depth of discounts kept increasing until at one point, 17 percent of all products sold by P&G, on average, were on deal. Escalating discounts and deals with the trade created cost whiplashes, and the company was making 55 daily prices on 80 or so brands, necessitating rework on every third order. Factories would alternate in a "bullwhip effect" between periods of intense overtime and underutilization. P&G plants ran at 55 percent to 60 percent of rated efficiency on average with huge variations in output.

P&G's solution to these problems was to implement its value pricing strategy, although they faced several challenges in making it successful. First, P&G

could not deliver everyday low prices without incurring everyday low costs. To reduce costs, P&G implemented a number of changes. To reduce overhead, P&G embarked on a "strengthening global effectiveness" (SGE) initiative that created eleven teams to collectively examine every part of the company to reduce overhead costs according to four simple guidelines: (1) Change the work, (2) do more with less, (3) eliminate rework, and (4) reduce costs that cannot be passed on to consumers. They simplified the distribution chain to make restocking more efficient for a number of products through a continuous product replenishment system. Improved ordering and EDLP increased factory efficiency to 80 percent. Greater production efficiency resulted in the closing of thirty factories and 13,000 jobs worldwide. By reducing management layers and streamlining work processes, P&G was able to further reduce the non-value-added costs of its products.

P&G also took a hard look at its product portfolios, deciding to simplify its brands and product lines. Recognizing that many of its brands offered line extensions of different sizes, flavors, and packages with virtually imperceptible differences that were expensive and slow-sellers, they decided to eliminate 25 percent of their stock-keeping units (SKUs). P&G also adopted a mega-branding approach. Where before they would introduce a new brand whenever a new technological change or segmentation opportunity presented itself, P&G instead began to introduce line and brand extensions off their biggest sellers, strengthening brand champions such as Charmin toilet paper, Crest toothpaste, Tide laundry detergent, and Pampers disposable diapers and revitalizing tired brands such as Ivory soap and Spic and Span floor cleaner. P&G also dropped or sold slow-selling brands altogether (e.g., Citrus Hill orange juice, Lava soap, and Bain de Soleil sun-care products) and combined weak brands with strong ones (e.g., White Cloud became Charmin Ultra toilet paper and Puritan was folded into Crisco Oil).

EDLP reduced list prices by 12 percent to 24 percent on nearly all of its U.S. brands and drastically reduced the use of coupons and trade promotions, cutting spending on the two by 40 percent. In their place, P&G put greater emphasis on brand-building advertising and marketing communications (totaling $3 billion in 1994). P&G also spent more than ever on research and development (over $1 billion in 1994) and cut the time to market for new products on a global basis by less than half. Moreover, only new products with a strong chance of making the top half or third of their category in unit sales were given the "green light." P&G also improved its relationship with retailers by simplifying price lists; implementing electronic ordering to reduce errors; coordinating delivery to reduce inventories; sharing sales data; and designing more effective store-specific promotions. As a result of these changes, P&G was rated by retailers in a national survey as the consumer-good company most helpful in making retailers more efficient.

As a result of all of these changes, P&G has come a long way from its previous high-price–high-cost strategy. Consumers still pay a premium to place P&G products on their shelves—a brand loyal family paid $725 more for a year's worth of P&G products than for private label or low-priced value brands in 1993. Yet, consumers have responded favorably—P&G's marketshares in two-thirds of the forty-plus product categories in which it competes were up in 1993 compared to the previous year. The aggressive program to lower prices, cut costs, and improve customer service by streamlining its once-cumbersome billing and delivery system has also paid off on the bottom line. In the fiscal year ending June 30, 1996, P&G reported record sales of $35.3 billion. P&G has subsequently rolled out its EDLP strategy into Europe.

---

[a]Alecia Swasy, "Slow and Steady: In a Fast-Paced World, Procter & Gamble Sets its Store in Old Values," *Wall Street Journal* (September 21, 1989): A–1.

[b]Zachary Schiller, "The Marketing Revolution at Procter & Gamble," *Business Week* (July 25, 1988): 72.

[c]Bill Saporito, "Behind the Tumult at P&G," *Fortune* (March 7, 1994): 74–82; Zachary Schiller, "Procter & Gamble Hits Back," *Business Week* (July 19, 1993): 20–22; Zachary Schiller, "Ed Artzt's Elbow Grease Has P&G Shining," *Business Week* (October 10, 1994): 84–86; Zachary Schiller, "Make It Simple," *Business Week* (September 9, 1996): 96–104.

Review

This chapter began by defining a brand as a name, term, sign, symbol, design, or some combination of these elements, intended to identify the goods and services of one seller or group of sellers and to differentiate them from those of competitors. The different components of a brand—that is, brand names, logos, symbols, package designs, and so on—are defined as brand elements. Brand elements come in many different forms. A brand is distinguished from a product, which is defined as anything that can be offered to a market for attention, acquisition, use, or consumption that might satisfy a need or want. A product may be a physical good, service, retail store, person, organization, place, or idea.

A brand is a product but one that adds other dimensions differentiating it in some way from other products designed to satisfy the same need. These differences may be rational and tangible—related to product performance of the brand—or more symbolic, emotional, or intangible—related to what the brand represents. Brands themselves are valuable intangible assets that need to be handled carefully. Brands offer a number of benefits to customers and the firms (see Figure 1–2). The key to branding is that consumers perceive differences among brands in a product category. A number of examples were provided to show how virtually any type of product can be branded by giving the product a name and attaching meaning to it in terms of what the product has to offer and how it differs from competitors. The chapter concluded by reviewing the historical origins of branding and outlining a number of branding challenges and opportunities faced by present-day marketing managers (see Figure 1–4).

Discussion Questions

1. What do brands mean to you? What are your favorite brands and why? Check to see how your perceptions of brands might differ from those of others.

2. Who do you think has the strongest brands? Why? What do you think of the Interbrand list of the strongest brands in Figure 1–3? Do you agree with the rankings? Why or why not?
3. Can you think of anything that cannot be branded? Pick an example that was not discussed in each of the categories provided (services, retailers and distributors, people and organizations, sports, art, and entertainment) and describe how it is a brand.
4. What do you think of the new branding challenges and opportunities that were listed? Can you think of any other issues?

Notes

1. Interbrand Group, *World's Greatest Brands: An International Review* (New York: John Wiley, 1992).
2. Adrian Room, *Dictionary of Trade Name Origins* (London: Routledge & Kegan Paul, 1982).
3. The second through fifth levels are based on a conceptualization in Theodore Levitt, "Marketing Success Through Differentiation—of Anything," *Harvard Business Review* (January–February 1980): 83–91.
4. Theodore Levitt, "Marketing Myopia," *Harvard Business Review* (July–August 1960): 45–56.
5. Alvin A. Achenbaum, "The Mismanagement of Brand Equity," ARF Fifth Annual Advertising and Promotion Workshop (February 1, 1993).
6. John Murphy, *Brand Strategy* (New York: Prentice-Hall, 1990): 4.
7. Jacob Jacoby, Jerry C. Olson, and Rafael Haddock, "Price, Brand Name, and Product Composition Characteristics as Determinants of Perceived Quality," *Journal of Consumer Research* 3(4) (1971): 209–216; Jacob Jacoby, George Syzbillo, and Jacqueline Busato-Sehach, "Information Acquisition Behavior in Brand Choice Situations," *Journal of Marketing Research* 11 (1977): 63–69.
8. Susan Fournier, "Understanding Consumer-Brand Relationships," working paper 96–018, Harvard Business School, Harvard University, Cambridge, MA, p. 3.
9. Philip Nelson, "Information and Consumer Behavior," *Journal of Political Economy* 78, (1970): 311–329; Michael R. Darby and Edi Karni, "Free Competition and the Optimal Amount of Fraud," *Journal of Law and Economics* 16 (April 1974): 67–88.
10. Allan D. Shocker and Richard Chay, "How Marketing Researchers Can Harness the Power of Brand Equity." Presentation to New Zealand Marketing Research Society, (August 1992).
11. Ted Roselius, "Consumer Ranking of Risk Reduction Methods," *Journal of Marketing*, by permission of the American Marketing Association.
12. Leslie de Chernatony and Gil McWilliam, "The Varying Nature of Brands as Assets," *International Journal of Advertising* 8 (1989, iss. 4): 339–349.
13. Constance E. Bagley, *Managers and the Legal Environment: Strategies for the 21st Century*, 2nd ed. (St. Paul, MN: West Publishing, 1995).
14. Tulin Erdem, "Brand Equity as a Signaling Phenomenon," working paper, Haas School of Business, University of California at Berkeley.
15. Betsy Morris, "The Brand's the Thing," *Fortune* (March 4, 1996): 72–86.
16. Charles Bymer, "Valuing Your Brands: Lessons from Wall Street and the Impact on Marketers," ARF Third Annual Advertising and Promotion Workshop (February 5–6, 1991).
17. Yumiko Ono, "Prescription-Drug Makers Heighten Hard-Sell Tactics," *Wall Street Journal* (August 29, 1994): B–1.

18. Pam Weisz, "Over-the-Counter Goes Under the Radar," *Brandweek* (June 3, 1996): 39–42.

19. Theodore Levitt, "Marketing Success Through Differentiation—of Anything," *Harvard Business Review* (January-February 1980): 83–91.

20. Tim Clark, "Package-Goods Execs Flood Into Software," *Advertising Age* (May 16, 1994): 4.

21. Chuck Pettis, *TechnoBrands* (New York: AMACOM, 1995).

22. Cathy Horyn, "Absolute Cindy," *Vanity Fair* (August 1994): 76.

23. University professors are certainly aware of the power of the name as a brand. In fact, one reason why many professors choose to have students identify themselves on exams by student numbers of some type is so that they will not be biased in grading by their knowledge of the student who prepared it. Otherwise, it may be too easy to give higher grades to those students that the professor likes or, for whatever reason, expects to have done well on the exam.

24. Robert P. Parker, "If You Got It Flaunt It," ARF Brand Equity Workshop, (February 15–16, 1994).

25. Joel Hochberg, "Package Goods Marketing vs. Hollywood," *Advertising Age* (January 20, 1992): 26.

26. Rick Marin, "Dear 'Saturday Night Live': It's Over. Please Die." *Newsweek* (October 17, 1994): 82.

27. Jeffrey A. Trachtenberg, "Now Available on Compact Disk! Featuring Songs by _____ ," *Wall Street Journal* (March 30, 1994): B–1.

28. Hank Berstein, "The Power of Leadership Brands," ARF Fourth Annual Advertising and Promotion Workshop (February 12–13, 1992).

29. Terry Lefton, "Measuring Quality Perception of America's Top Brands," *Brandweek* (April 4, 1991): 24–26.

30. Much of this section is adapted from an excellent article by George S. Low and Ronald A. Fullerton, "Brands, Brand Management, and the Brand Manager System: A Critical-Historical Evaluation," *Journal of Marketing Research* 31 (May 1994): 173–190 and an excellent book by Hal Morgan, *Symbols of America*, (New York: Viking, 1986).

31. Shirley Spence and Thomas Bonoma, "The Gillette Company: Dry Idea Advertising," Harvard Business School Case 9–586–042 (1986).

32. Interbrand Group, *World's Greatest Brands* (New York: John Wiley & Sons, 1992).

33. Peter Farquhar, Julia Y. Han, and Yuji Ijiri, "Recognizing and Measuring Brand Assets," MSI Report (Cambridge, MA: 1991).

34. Allan D. Shocker, Rajendra Srivastava, and Robert Ruekert, "Challenges and Opportunities Facing Brand Management: An Introduction to the Special Issue," *Journal of Marketing Research* 31 (May 1994): 149–158.

35. Alvin A. Achenbaum, "The Implication of Price Competition on Brands, Advertising and the Economy," ARF Fourth Annual Advertising and Promotion Workshop, (February 12–13, 1992). Zipping and zapping refer to the practice of fast-forwarding through ad breaks while watching taped TV programs and switching to other channels during commercial breaks while watching live TV programs. Channel grazing or surfing refers to watching snatches or a few minutes of one program, then another, and so on.

36. B.G. Yovovich, "What Is Your Brand Really Worth?," *Adweek's Marketing Week* (August 8, 1988). Reprinted by permission of ASM Communications.

35. Ian M. Lewis, "Brand Equity or Why the Board of Directors Needs Marketing Research," ARF Fifth Annual Advertising and Promotion Workshop (February 1, 1993).

36. Joel Rubinson, "Introduction to the Workshop," ARF Fourth Annual Advertising and Promotion Workshop (February 12–13, 1992).

CHAPTER 2   Brand Equity

Preview

Chapter 1 introduced some basic notions about brands and the role that they have played and are playing in marketing strategies. The chapter concluded by observing that marketers are now faced with an increasing number of tactical options that must be efficiently and effectively applied to an increasing number of product variations for the brand. The concept of brand equity was identified as having the potential to provide guidance to marketers to help them make those decisions.

In this chapter, we more formally introduce the brand equity concept, providing some perspective on its meaning and a detailed examination of one particular view of brand equity—the concept of customer-based brand equity—that will serve as the organizing framework for the rest of the book.[1] We consider the sources of customer-based brand equity and the outcomes or benefits that result from those sources. We then highlight some of the key issues in building, measuring, and managing customer-based brand equity. All through the chapter, we foreshadow material that will be dealt with in more detail in the remainder of the text.

Concept of Brand Equity

One of the most popular and potentially important marketing concepts to arise in the 1980s was the concept of brand equity. The emergence of brand equity, however, has meant both good news and bad news to marketers. The good news is that it has raised the importance of the brand in marketing strategy—which heretofore had been relatively neglected—and provided focus for managerial interest and research activity. The bad news is that the concept has been defined a number of different ways for a number of different purposes (see Figure 2–1), resulting in some confusion and even frustration with the term. To help illuminate the brand equity concept, some experts have even resorted to some fairly creative analogies to explain their points of view (see Branding Brief 2–1). Through it all, however, no common viewpoint has emerged as to how brand equity should be conceptualized and measured.

In a general sense, most marketing observers agree that brand equity is defined in terms of the marketing effects uniquely attributable to the brand. That is, brand equity relates to the fact that different outcomes result from the marketing of a product

The set of associations and behaviors on the part of the brand's customers, channel members, and parent corporation that permits the brand to earn greater volume or greater margins than it could without the brand name and that gives the brand a strong, sustainable, and differentiated advantage over competitors. (Marketing Science Institute)

The added value to the firm, the trade, or the consumer with which a given brand endows a product.[a] (Peter Farquhar, Claremont Graduate School)

A set of brand assets and liabilities linked to a brand, its name and symbol, that add to or subtract from the value provided by a product or service to a firm and/or to that firm's customers.[b] (David Aaker, University of California at Berkeley)

The sales and profit impact enjoyed as a result of prior years' marketing efforts versus a comparable new brand.[c] (John Brodsky, NPD Group)

Brand equity subsumes brand strength and brand value. Brand strength is the set of associations and behaviors on the part of a brand's customers, channel members, and parent corporation that permits the brand to enjoy sustainable and differentiated competitive advantages. Brand value is the financial outcome of management's ability to leverage brand strength via tactical and strategic actions in providing superior current and future profits and lowered risks.[d] (Raj Srivastava, University of Texas & Allan Shocker, University of Minnesota)

The measurable financial value in transactions that accrues to a product or service from successful programs and activities.[e] (J. Walker Smith, Yankelovich Clancy Schulman)

Brand equity is the willingness for someone to continue to purchase your brand or not. Thus, the measure of brand equity is strongly related to loyalty and measures segments on a continuum from entrenched users of the brand to convertible users. (Market Facts)

Brands with equity provide "an ownable, trustworthy, relevant, distinctive promise to consumers." (Brand Equity Board)

---

[a]Peter Farquhar, "Managing Brand Equity," *Marketing Research* (September 1989), pp. 1–11.
[b]David A. Aaker, *Managing Brand Equity*. New York: Free Press, 1991.
[c]John Brodsky, "Issues in Measuring and Monitoring," ARF Third Annual Advertising and Promotion Workshop, February 5–6, 1991.
[d]Rajendra Srivastava and Allan D. Schocker, "Brand Equity: A Perspective on Its Meaning and Measurement," Report No. 91-124. Cambridge, MA: Marketing Science Institute, October 1991.
[e]J. Walker Smith, "Thinking About Brand Equity and the Analysis of Customer Transactions," ARF Third Annual Advertising and Promotion Workshop, February 5–6, 1991.

FIGURE 2-1 Definitions of Brand Equity

BRANDING BRIEF 2-1

A Rose by Any Other Name

To help put the concept into perspective, people have compared brand equity to all types of things:

Josh McQueen of Leo Burnett makes an analogy with home equity[a]: "Home equity is the difference between the value of the home and the value of the remaining mortgage. Similarly, brand equity is the difference between the value of the brand to the consumer and the value of the product without that branding."

William Moran of Longman-Moran makes an analogy with love: "We all know there is such a thing, many of us have experienced it, but it is a slippery thing to define exactly, and it is even more difficult to agree on a definitive, quantitative expression of it. As a result, in any given instance there is no way to be sure whether it is being created or destroyed. Nonetheless, we know it is very valuable and worth a lot of effort to obtain, to nourish, and to sustain."[b]

Paul Zimmerman of Procter & Gamble compares brand equity to the "entropy" concept in thermodynamics. He relates how entropy is a property of the universe that reflects the lack of order in a system. Entropy has several components—energy and temperature—that can be varied in a system to keep it from being mixed up. "The analogy to brand equity is that equity, like entropy, can't be seen. Just like the components of entropy are measurable and useful to engineers and mathematicians, the components of brand equity are useful as the tools for business managers and market researchers."[c]

---

[a]Josh McQueen, "Leveraging the Power of Emotion in Building Brand Equity," ARF Third Annual Advertising and Promotion Workshop, February 5–6, 1991.

[b]William T. Moran, "The Search for the Golden Fleece: Actionable Brand Equity Measurement," ARF Third Annual Advertising and Promotion Workshop, February 5–6, 1991.

[c]Paul J. Zimmerman, "Second Day Introduction," ARF Fourth Annual Advertising and Promotion Workshop, February 12–13, 1992.

---

or service because of its brand name or some other brand element, as compared to outcomes if that same product or service did not have that brand identification. Although a number of different views of brand equity have been expressed, they all are generally consistent with the basic notion that brand equity represents the "added value" endowed to a product as a result of past investments in the marketing for the brand. Researchers studying brand equity at least implicitly agree on a number of other general points, too. They all acknowledge that there exist many different ways that value can be created for a brand; that brand equity provides a common denominator for interpreting marketing strategies and assessing the value of a brand; and that there exist many different ways that the value of a brand can be manifested or exploited to benefit the firm.

Despite this commonality, the specific approaches to motivating and defining brand equity can vary greatly depending on the perspective and purpose adopted. We next turn to one particular approach that will be used throughout the text.

Customer-Based Brand Equity

The framework of brand equity put forth by this text approaches brand equity from the perspective of the consumer.[2] Understanding the needs and wants of consumers and devising products and programs to satisfy them is at the heart of successful marketing. In particular, two fundamentally important questions faced by marketers are: What do different brands mean to consumers? and How does consumers' brand knowledge affect their response to marketing activity?

The customer-based brand equity framework incorporates recent theoretical advances and managerial practices in understanding and influencing consumer behavior. Specifically, *customer-based brand equity* is defined as the differential effect that brand knowledge has on consumer response to the marketing of that brand. A brand is said to have positive customer-based brand equity when customers react more favorably to a product and the way it is marketed when the brand is identified as compared to when it is not (e.g., when it is attributed to a fictitiously named or unnamed version of the product). Thus, a brand with *positive* customer-based brand equity might result in consumers being more accepting of a new brand extension, less sensitive to price increases and withdrawal of advertising support, or more willing to seek the brand in a new distribution channel. On the other hand, a brand is said to have *negative* customer-based brand equity if consumers react less favorably to marketing activity for the brand, as compared to an unnamed or fictitiously named version of the product.

There are three key ingredients to this definition: (1) "differential effect," (2) "brand knowledge," and (3) "consumer response to marketing." First, brand equity arises from differences in consumer response. If no differences occur, then the brand name product can essentially be classified as a commodity or generic version of the product. Second, these differences in response are a result of consumers' knowledge about the brand. Thus, although strongly influenced by the marketing activity of the firm, brand equity ultimately depends on what resides in the minds of consumers. Third, the differential response by consumers that makes up the brand equity is reflected in perceptions, preferences, and behavior related to all aspects of the marketing of a brand (e.g., choice of a brand, recall of copy points from an ad, actions in response to a sales promotion, or evaluations of a proposed brand extension).

The simplest way to illustrate what is meant by the concept of customer-based brand equity is to consider some of the typically observed results of product sampling or comparison tests. For example, with blind taste tests, one group of consumers samples a product without knowing which brand it is, whereas another group of consumers samples the product knowing which brand it is. Invariably, differences arise in the opinions of the two groups despite the fact that the two groups are literally consuming exactly the same product!

For example, Larry Percy reports the results of a beer tasting experiment that showed how discriminating consumers could be when given the names of the well-known brands of the beer they were drinking, but how few differences consumers could detect when they did not know the brand names of the beer they were drinking. Figure 2–2 displays the perceptual maps—visual tools to portray perceptual differences among brands expressed by consumers—that were derived from the two types of responses. As it turns out, even fairly knowledgeable consumers can have difficulty distinguishing different brands of beer (see Branding Brief 2–2). As another example, de Chernatony and Knox show how a sample of U.K. consumers were approximately equally split in those that had a preference for Diet Coke versus Diet Pepsi (44 percent to 51 percent, respectively) when tasting on a blind basis. When consumers tasted branded versions, however, Diet Coke was preferred by 65 percent of the sample and Diet Pepsi was preferred by only 23 percent (with the remainder seeing the brands as equal).[3]

When consumers report different opinions between branded and unbranded versions of identical products, it must be the case that knowledge about the brand, created by whatever means (e.g., past experiences, marketing activity for the brand), has somehow changed consumers' product perceptions. Examples of branded differences, such as those observed in the beer and diet cola experiments, can be found with virtually every type of product—conclusive evidence that consumers' perceptions of the performance of a product are highly dependent on their impressions of the brand that goes along with it. In other words, clothes may seem to fit better, a car may seem to drive more smoothly, the wait in a bank line may seem shorter and so on, depending on the particular brands involved.

BRAND KNOWLEDGE

From the perspective of the customer-based brand equity framework, brand knowledge is the key to creating brand equity. What marketers need, then, is an insightful way to represent how brand knowledge exists in consumer memory. An influential model of memory developed by psychologists is helpful in that regard.[4] The *associative network memory model* views memory as consisting of a network of nodes and connecting links where nodes represent stored information or concepts and links represent the strength of association between this information or concepts. Any type of information can be stored in the memory network, including information that is verbal, visual, abstract, or contextual in nature.

According to an associative network memory model, recall or retrieval of information occurs through a concept called *spreading activation*. At any point in time, an information node may be a source of activation because it is either presented external information (e.g., when a person reads or hears a word or phrase) or retrieved internal information currently being processed (e.g., when a person thinks about some concept). A particular node in memory is activated, and activation spreads from that node to other nodes connected to it in memory. When the activation of a particular node exceeds a threshold level, the contents of that node are recalled. The spread of activation depends on the number and strength of the links connected to the activated node: Concepts connected to the activated node whose linkages have the greatest strength will receive the most activation.

Consistent with the associative network memory model, brand knowledge is conceptualized here as consisting of a brand node in memory with a variety of associa-

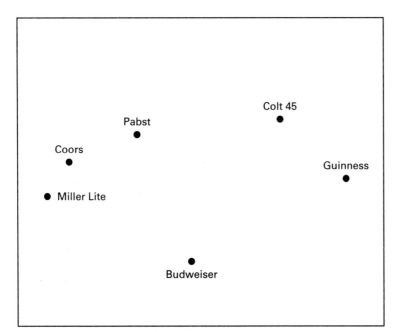

A. Taste Perceptions of Six Beer Brands When
the Drinker Knows What He Is Drinking

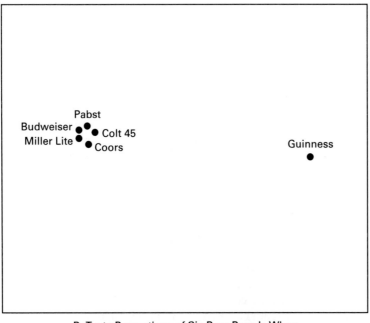

B. Taste Perceptions of Six Beer Brands When
the Drinker Does **Not** Know What He Is Drinking

FIGURE 2-2 Results of "Blind" Beer Taste Tests

BRANDING BRIEF 2-2

Australians Know Beer—Or Do They?

The reality is that in many product categories, brands are not that different in their actual product performance. Australians are well known for their beer-drinking loyalty and prowess. Australians have extremely strong and well-defined brand preferences, often based on regional differences. In Queensland, XXXX reigns supreme, where in the state of Victoria, beer drinkers ask for Victoria Bitter (VB). The only strong national brand is Foster's Lager, which has also been the recipient of a considerable financial investment to take advantage of its Australian heritage to develop markets worldwide.

Many Australian breweries make more than one beer, supporting them with different marketing programs and targeting different market segments. For example, the large Carlton and United Breweries (CUB) makes both Foster's Lager and Victoria Bitter. Recently, the *Sydney Morning Herald* reported that Castlemaine Perkins, a rival brewer to CUB, issued a press release claiming that examination and analysis of data on CUB's Foster's Lager and Victoria Bitter beers from four sources over a five-year period showed that the only consistent variation between the two beers was that VB had a higher *color* content!

Specifically, the press release reported that qualified chemists had examined six flavor profiles of the beers and concluded they showed similar analytical patterns. A spokesman for the analysts said the tests were standard industry ones using a technique called "wet chemistry" and included specific gravity (for the fullness in a beer), bitterness, pH, color, alcohol, head retention, carbonation, haze stability, aroma tests, and carbohydrate tests.

CUB's head brewer in Brisbane, Noel Jago, complained of an opposition smear campaign but admitted that most of CUB's full strength beers were similar and "reasonably close in many aspects." He maintained, however, that although the same hops, sugar, malt, and yeast were used in making the two beers, the difference was in the combination of basic ingredients. He also noted that the carbon dioxide, specific gravity, and other normal parameters were similar, but the fine tuning in fermentation and filtration made the difference.

"There is not a hell of a difference in taste but the difference is there," Jago said. He said anyone who doubted the difference in the beers was entitled to "come and see themselves."

---

tions linked to it. As a result of spreading activation, the strength and organization of these brand associations will be important determinants of the information that can be recalled about the brand to influence consumer response and brand-related decisions.

Extending this model, brand knowledge can be characterized in terms of two components: brand awareness and brand image. *Brand awareness* is related to the strength of the brand node or trace in memory, as reflected by consumers' ability to identify the brand under different conditions.[5] Brand awareness consists of *brand recognition*—reflecting the ability of consumers to confirm prior exposure to the brand—and *brand recall*—reflecting the ability of consumers to retrieve the brand when given the product category, the needs fulfilled by the category, or some other type of probe as a cue. *Brand image* is defined as consumer perceptions of a brand as reflected by the brand associations held in consumers' memory. Brand associations are the other informational nodes linked to the brand node in memory and contain the meaning of the brand for consumers. Associations come in all forms and may reflect characteristics of the product or aspects independent of the product itself.

For example, consider Apple computers. If someone asked you what came to mind when you thought of Apple computers, what might you say? You might reply with associations such as "user friendly," "creative," "for desktop publishing," or "used at many schools." Figure 2–3 displays some commonly mentioned associations about Apple computers. The associations that came to mind for you would make up your brand image for Apple. Through skillful marketing, Apple was able to achieve a rich brand image made up of a host of brand associations in the minds of consumers (although that image has perhaps become tarnished in recent years as the company has experienced marketplace setbacks). Different consumers might think of different associations for Apple, although many associations are likely to be shared by a majority of consumers. In that sense, we can refer to "the" brand image of Apple, but, at the same time, it must be recognized that this image may vary, perhaps even quite considerably, depending on the particular groups of consumers involved.

Other brands, of course, will be characterized by a different set of associations. For example, McDonald's marketing program attempts to create brand associations in consumers' minds to "quality," "service," "cleanliness," and "value." McDonald's rich brand image probably also includes strong associations to "Ronald McDonald," "Golden Arches," "for kids," and "convenient," as well as perhaps potentially negative associations such as "fast food." Coca-Cola's marketing program strives to link

User-friendly

Apple logo

Macintosh

PowerBook

Creative

Innovative

Fun

Friendly

Cool

Educational

Desktop publishing

Graphics

FIGURE 2-3 Examples of Possible Apple Computer Associations

brand associations in consumers' minds to "refreshment," "taste," "availability," "affordability," and "accessibility." Mercedes-Benz has achieved strong associations to "performance" and "status," whereas Volvo has created a strong association to "safety." Chapter 3 reviews in detail the different types of associations that can become linked to a brand.

Sources of Brand Equity

What causes brand equity to exist? How do marketers create it? Customer-based brand equity occurs when the consumer has a high level of awareness and familiarity with the brand and holds some strong, favorable, and unique brand associations in memory. The latter consideration is critical. For branding strategies to be successful and brand equity to be created, consumers must be convinced that there are meaningful differences among brands in the product or service category. The key to branding is that consumers must *not* think that all brands in the category are the same.

BRAND AWARENESS

In some cases, brand awareness alone is sufficient to result in more favorable consumer response, for example, in low involvement decision settings where consumers are willing to base their choices merely on familiar brands. In other cases, the strength, favorability, and uniqueness of the brand associations play a critical role in determining the differential response making up the brand equity. If the brand is perceived by consumers to be the same as a representative version of the product or service in the category, then consumer response to marketing for the brand would not be expected to vary from marketing attributed to a fictitiously named or unnamed product or service. If the brand has some salient, unique associations, then consumer response should differ.

Thus, establishing brand awareness and a positive brand image in consumer memory, in terms of strong, favorable, and unique brand associations, produces the knowledge structures that can affect consumer response and produce different types of customer-based brand equity. Brand awareness is created by increasing the familiarity of the brand through repeated exposure (for brand recognition) and strong associations with the appropriate product category or other relevant purchase or consumption cues (for brand recall).[6] Brand awareness can be characterized by depth and breadth: The depth of brand awareness relates to the likelihood that the brand can be recognized or recalled; the breadth of brand awareness relates to the variety of purchase and consumption situations in which the brand comes to mind.

Strategies to Increase Awareness
In the abstract, brand awareness is created by increasing the familiarity of the brand through repeated exposure, although this is generally more effective for brand recognition than for brand recall. Although brand repetition increases the strength of the brand node in memory and thus its recognizability, improving recall of the brand requires linkages in memory to appropriate product category, purchase situation, or consumption situation cues.

Two general guidelines are offered below for establishing brand awareness. First, it is important to visually and verbally reinforce the brand name with a full complement of reinforcing brand elements. In particular, to build awareness, it is often desirable to develop a slogan or jingle that creatively pairs the brand and the appropriate category, purchase, or consumption cues (and, ideally, the brand positioning as well, in terms of also building a positive brand image). Additional use can be made of the other brand elements—logos, symbols, characters, and packaging. The second important guideline for establishing brand awareness is to creatively pair the brand with its corresponding category or other appropriate cues through a wide range of communication options (advertising, promotion, sponsorship, and public relations). In other words, because anything that causes the consumer to experience the brand can potentially increase familiarity and awareness, a number of different communication options can be used.

BRAND IMAGE

A positive brand image is created by marketing programs that link strong, favorable, and unique associations to the brand in memory. The definition of customer-based brand equity does not distinguish between the source of brand associations and the manner in which they are formed; all that matters is the resulting favorability, strength, and uniqueness of brand associations. This realization has important implications for building brand equity. Besides marketer-controlled sources of information, brand associations can also be created in a variety of other ways: by direct experience; from information communicated by other commercial or non-partisan sources (e.g., *Consumer Reports* or other media vehicles) and word-of-mouth; and by inferences due to the identification of the brand with a company, country, channel of distribution, or some particular person, place, or event. Marketers should recognize the influence of these other sources of information by both managing them as well as possible and adequately accounting for them in designing communication strategies.

Strength of Brand Associations

Making sure that associations are linked sufficiently strongly to the brand will depend on how the marketing program and other factors affect consumers' brand experiences. Associations will vary in the strength of their connection to the brand node. Strength is a function of both the amount or quantity of processing that information receives and the nature or quality of that processing. The more deeply a person thinks about product information and relates it to existing brand knowledge, the stronger are the resulting brand associations. Two factors facilitating the strength of association to any piece of information are the personal relevance of the information and the consistency with which this information is presented over time. The particular associations that are recalled and salient will not only depend on the strength of association, but also depend on the context in which the brand is considered and the retrieval cues that are present to serve as reminders.

Think back to the earlier Apple computer example. Some associations that you listed were probably stronger than others and came to mind right away. These associations probably also varied in their uniqueness and favorability. If you were like others, one particularly strong association to Apple might have been "user friendly." The existence of this strong brand association has been a mixed blessing to Apple. On the plus side, many consumers value ease of use—especially those who buy personal computers for the home—and appreciate Apple in that regard. On the other hand, one drawback with a "user friendly" association is that many customers, especially those who buy personal computers for business applications, might infer that if a personal computer is easy to use, then it also must not be very powerful, a key choice consideration in that market. Recognizing this potential problem, Apple ran a clever ad campaign with the tag line, "The power to be your best," in an attempt to redefine what a powerful computer meant. The strategy behind the ads was that because Apple was easy to use, people in fact did just that—they used them!—a simple but important indication of "power."

Favorability of Brand Associations

Choosing which favorable and unique associations to link to the brand requires careful analysis of the consumer and competition to determine the optimal positioning for the brand. In the most basic sense, favorable brand associations are created by convincing consumers that the brand possesses relevant attributes and benefits that satisfy their needs and wants such that they form a positive overall brand attitude. Thus, favorable associations for a brand are those associations that are desirable to consumers and are successfully delivered by the product and conveyed by the supporting marketing program for the brand.

Favorable brand associations come in a variety of forms. Although they are primarily determined by intrinsic product-related factors, they may also be determined by more abstract non-product-related imagery related to typical or desirable users or usage situations for the brand. Not all brand associations will be deemed important and viewed favorably by consumers, nor will they be equally valued across different purchase or consumption situations.

For example, the associations that might come to mind when consumers think of Federal Express, a leading overnight delivery service, may be "fast," "dependable," and "convenient" with "purple and white packages and envelopes." Even though it is a strong brand association, the color of the packaging may matter little to most consumers when actually choosing an overnight delivery service, although it may perhaps play an important brand awareness function. On the other hand, fast, dependable, and convenient service may be more important in consumer choice, but even then only under certain situations. It may be that someone desires those benefits only when meeting an important deadline. If a consumer only needs a delivery "as soon as possible," then it may be that other less expensive options would be considered (e.g., the U.S. Postal Service's Priority Mail).

Uniqueness of Brand Associations

Finally, to create the differential response that leads to customer-based brand equity, it is important that some of the strongly held brand associations are not only favorable but also unique. Unique brand associations are distinct associations not shared with competing brands. Beliefs about unique attributes and benefits that consumers value more favorably than for competitive brands can lead to more favorable brand evaluations and a greater likelihood of choice. Thus, it is important to associate unique, meaningful "points of difference" to the brand to provide a competitive advantage and a reason why consumers should buy it.

For some brand associations, however, consumers only need to view them at least as favorably as competitors. That is, for some brand associations, it may be sufficient that they are seen as roughly equal in favorability with competing brand associations so that they function as "points of parity" in consumers' minds to negate potential points of difference for competitors. In other words, these associations are designed to provide "no reason why not" for consumers to choose the brand. Assuming that other brand associations are evident as points of difference, more favorable brand evaluations and a greater likelihood of choice should then result.

Benefits from Brand Equity

Customer-based brand equity occurs when consumer response to marketing activity differs when consumers know the brand from when they do not. The actual nature of how that response differs will depend on the level of brand awareness and how favorably and uniquely consumers evaluate brand associations, as well as the particular marketing activity under consideration. A number of benefits can result from a strong brand, in terms of both greater revenue and lower costs. For example, Ian Lewis from Time-Life categorizes the factors creating financial value for strong brands into two categories:[7] (1) factors related to *growth* (e.g., a brand's ability to attract new customers, resist competitive activity, introduce line extensions, and cross international borders), and (2) factors related to *profitability* (e.g., brand loyalty, premium pricing, lower price elasticity, lower advertising/sales ratios, and trade leverage). In this section, we consider in detail some of the benefits to the firm of having brands with a high level of awareness and a "positive" brand image. Figure 2–4 summarizes these benefits.

FIGURE 2–4 Brand Equity Benefits

Greater loyalty

Less vulnerability to competitive marketing actions

Less vulnerability to marketing crises

Larger margins

More inelastic consumer response to price increases

More elastic consumer response to price decreases

Greater trade cooperation and support

Increased marketing communication effectiveness

Possible licensing opportunities

Additional brand extension opportunities

GREATER LOYALTY AND LESS VULNERABILITY TO COMPETITIVE MARKETING ACTIONS AND CRISES

One characteristic of brands with a great deal of equity is that consumers feel much loyalty to the brand. For example, as noted above, many top brands have been market leaders for years despite the fact that there undoubtedly has been significant changes in both consumer attitudes and competitive activity over this period of time. Through it all, consumers have valued these brands—what they are and what they represent— sufficiently enough to stick with them and reject the overtures of competitors, creating a steady stream of revenues for the firm. Prior academic research in a variety of industry contexts also has found that brands with large market shares are more likely to have more loyal customers than brands with small market shares, a phenomenon dubbed "double jeopardy."[8]

Brand loyalty is closely related to brand equity but is a distinct concept. Brand loyalty is often measured in a behavioral sense through the number of repeat purchases. Yet, a consumer may continually purchase for reasons not related to a strong preference for the brand, as when the brand is prominently stocked or frequently promoted. Consumers may be in the habit of buying a particular brand without really thinking much about why. When confronted by a new or resurgent competitor providing compelling reasons to switch, consumers' ties to the brand may be tested for the first time.

The bottom line is that repeat buying is a necessary but not sufficient condition for being a brand loyal buyer in an attitudinal sense: Someone can repeat-buy but not be brand loyal in a literal sense. Brand loyalty is one of the many advantages of creating a positive brand image and manifestations of having brand equity. Thus, brand loyalty is related to, but distinct from, brand equity. Along these lines, some researchers make a further distinction with brand commitment. Brand commitment has been defined as the "clinch facet" of brand preference and the "attitudinal facet" of brand loyalty.[9] In other words, commitment is a stronger expression of brand preference and brand loyalty: Someone may favorably evaluate a brand and repeat-buy it but still not truly be committed to it.

Because brand loyalty is so closely related to brand equity, several additional points are worth noting. First, brand loyalty in a broad sense may not have declined as much in recent years as might appear to be the case according to the popular press.[10] For example, the DDB Needham Life Style study asks over 3000 consumers annually their agreement to questions such as, "I try to stick to well-known brand names." Although the proportion who agree to that statement declined from 77 percent in 1975 to 59 percent in 1993, most of that decline occurred prior to 1980. The intention to stick to well-known brand names has remained relatively stable over the last decade (see Figure 2–5). The study findings also reveal that the proportion of consumers who agree with the statement, "A store's own brand is usually a better buy than a nationally advertised brand," has declined only slowly over time, from 62 percent in 1975 to 55 percent in 1993, and the proportion of consumers who agree with the statement, "A nationally advertised brand is usually a better buy than a generic brand," has generally increased over time, from 23 percent in 1980 to 29 percent in 1991.

Thus, belief in the value of national brand names *in general* has remained strong over the last decade. On the other hand, consumer loyalty to *individual* brands is an-

FIGURE 2-5 Results of DDB Needham Life Style Study

	75	76	77	78	79	80	81	82	83	84	85	86	87	88	89	90	91	92	93	94	95	96	97
"I try to stick to well-known brand names."	77	78	75	74	70	60	62	60	59	60	62	65	61	63	61	62	61	58	59	54	58	56	57
"A store's own brand is usually a better buy than a nationally advertised brand."	62	60	60	58	59	61	63	57	57	59	58	56	52	52	55	51	54	55	55	58	58	58	56
"A nationally advertised brand is usually a better buy than a generic brand."	•	•	•	•	•	23	24	29	28	31	32	36	33	33	32	35	34	29	29	27	33	26	29

other matter. One study designed to answer that question examined 64 commonly used product categories (products with household penetration of at least 50 percent). In 52 of those categories, the proportion of users who were loyal to one brand declined from 1985 to 1991. Further evidence for the erosion of individual brand loyalty comes from research conducted by the Roper Organization. Roper asked women if they knew, before entering the store, which brand they would buy in selected categories such as mayonnaise, coffee, ice cream, and dry soup mixes. In all eight categories for which results were reported, brand loyalty fell from 1988 to 1991. In at least some of these cases, it could be said that loyalty declines had been as much a result of manufacturer's own strategies—inconsistent advertising, insufficient marketing support, ill-conceived product development or brand extensions—as compared to real changes in consumer behavior. In short, although consumers still seem to appreciate the value of manufacturers' brands in general, it should be recognized that actual loyalty will vary by product category and the marketing actions adopted for the brands within that category.

Returning to the benefits of brand equity, a brand with a positive brand image also is more likely to successfully weather a brand crisis or downturn in the brand's fortunes. Perhaps the most compelling example of this fact is Johnson & Johnson's Tylenol brand. Branding Brief 2–3 describes how J&J contended with a tragic product-tampering episode with their Tylenol pain reliever in the early 1980s. Despite having seen their market share drop from 37 percent to almost zero overnight and having been written off as a brand with no future, J&J was able to regain virtually all lost Tylenol market share through the skillful handling of a marketing crisis and a good deal of brand equity.

The important lesson from J&J's Tylenol crisis is that effective handling of a marketing crisis requires swift and sincere actions. There must be an immediate admission that something has gone wrong and that an effective remedy will be put in place. Moreover, the greater the brand equity, the more likely it is that these statements will have the necessary credibility with consumers so that they will be both understanding and patient as the firm sets out to resolve the crisis. Without some underlying brand equity, however, even the best laid plans for recovery may fall short to a suspicious or unknowing public. Many critics contend that the Exxon name will be tarnished for years from the Exxon Valdez accident and the resulting huge oil spill in Prince William Sound off the pristine Alaska coast, in part, because Exxon had not developed a favorable and strong enough brand image to inoculate itself from such unforeseen events.[11] Finally, it should also be recognized that even if not a crisis per se, a strong brand offers some protection in the case of a marketing downturn or when the brand's fortunes fall. Chapter 13 describes in more detail how to handle a marketing crisis.

LARGER MARGINS

Brands with positive customer-based brand equity should be able to command a price premium. Moreover, consumers should also have a more inelastic response to price increases and elastic responses to price decreases or discounts for the brand over time.[12] Consistent with this reasoning, research has shown that consumers loyal to a

Weathering a Brand Crisis: The Tylenol Experience[a]

Tylenol has been a true marketing success story. Originally introduced by Mc-Neil Laboratories as a liquid alternative to aspirin for children, it achieved non-prescription status when McNeil was bought by Johnson & Johnson (J&J) in 1959. J&J's initial marketing plan promoted a tablet form of the product for physicians to prescribe as a substitute for aspirin when allergic reactions occurred. Tylenol consisted of acetaminophen, a drug as effective as aspirin in the relief of pain and fever but without the stomach irritation that often accompanied aspirin. Backed by this selective physician "push," sales for the brand grew slowly but steadily over the course of the next fifteen years. By 1974, it reached $50 million in sales, or 10 percent of the analgesic market. In defending its turf from the competitive entry of Bristol-Myers' low-priced, but heavily promoted Datril competitor, J&J recognized the value of advertising Tylenol directly to consumers.

Thanks also to the successful introduction of a line extension, Extra-Strength Tylenol in tablet and capsule form, the brand's market share had risen to 37 percent of the pain reliever market by 1982. As the largest single brand in the history of health and beauty aids, Tylenol was used by 100 million Americans. The brand contributed 8 percent to J&J's sales but almost twice that percentage in terms of net profits to the company. Advertising support for the brand was heavy. A $40 million media campaign was scheduled for 1982 that used two different messages. The "hospital campaign" employed testimonials from people who had been given Tylenol in the hospital and reported that they had grown to trust it. The ad concluded with the tag line, "Trust Tylenol—hospitals do." The "hidden camera" campaign showed subjects who had been unobtrusively filmed while describing the symptoms of their headaches, trying Extra-Strength Tylenol as a solution, and vowing to use it again based on its effectiveness. This ad concluded with the tag line, "... the most potent pain reliever you can buy without a prescription."

All of this success came crashing to the ground with the news in the first week in October 1982 that seven people had died in the Chicago area after taking Extra-Strength Tylenol capsules that turned out to contain cyanide poison. Although it quickly became evident that the problem was restricted to that area of the country and had almost certainly been the work of some deranged person outside the company, consumer confidence was severely shaken. Most marketing experts believed that the damage to the reputation of the Tylenol brand was irreparable and that it would never fully recover. For example, well-known advertising guru Jerry Della Femina was quoted in the *New York Times* as saying "On one day, every single human being in the country thought that Tylenol might kill them. I don't think there are enough advertising dollars, enough marketing men, to change that ... You'll not see the name Tylenol in any form within a year." Tylenol's comeback from these seemingly insurmountable odds has become a classic example of how best to handle a marketing crisis.

Within the first week of the crisis, J&J issued a worldwide alert to the medical community, set up a 24-hour toll-free telephone number, recalled and analyzed sample batches of the product, briefed the Food & Drug Administration, and offered a $100,000 reward to apprehend the culprit of the tampering. During the week of October 5, J&J began a voluntary withdrawal of the brand by repurchasing 31 million bottles with a retail value of $100 million. They stopped advertising, and all communications with the public were in the form of press releases. To monitor consumer response to the crisis, J&J started to conduct weekly tracking surveys with 1000 consumer respondents. Ultimately, the company subsequently spent a total of $1.5 million for marketing research in the fourth quarter of 1982. The following week of October 12, they introduced a capsule exchange offer, promoted in half-page press announcements in 150 major markets across the country, inviting the public to mail in bottles of capsules to receive tablets in exchange. Although well-intentioned, this offer met with poor consumer response.

During the week of October 24, J&J made its return to TV advertising with the goals of convincing Tylenol users that they could continue to trust the safety of Tylenol products, as well as encouraging the use of the tablet form until tamper-resistant packaging was available. The spokesperson for the ad was Dr. Thomas N. Gates, the company's medical director, whose deep, reassuring voice exuded confidence and control. Looking calmly straight into the camera, he stated:

> You're all aware of the recent tragic events in which Extra-Strength Tylenol capsules were criminally tampered with in limited areas after they left our factories. This act damages all of us—you the American public because you have made Tylenol a trusted part of your healthcare and we who make Tylenol because we've worked hard to earn that trust. We will now work even harder to keep it. We have voluntarily withdrawn all Tylenol capsules from the shelf. We will reintroduce capsules in tamper-resistant containers as quickly as possible. Until then, we urge all Tylenol capsule users to use the tablet form and we have offered to replace your capsules with tablets. Tylenol has had the trust of the medical profession and 100 million Americans for over 20 years. We value that trust too much to let any individual tamper with it. We want you to continue to trust Tylenol.

The heavy media schedule for this ad ensured that 85 percent of the market viewed the ad at least four times during this week.

On November 11, 1982, six weeks after the poisonings and after intense behind-the-scenes activity, the Chairman of J&J announced during a live teleconference with 600 news reporters throughout the United States the return of Tylenol capsules to the market in a new, triple-seal package that was regarded as virtually tamper-proof. To get consumers to try the new packaging, the largest program of couponing in commercial history was undertaken. On November 28, 1982, sixty million coupons offering a free Tylenol product (valued up to $2.50) were distributed in Sunday newspapers nationwide. Twenty million more coupons were distributed the following Sunday. By the end of December, thirty percent of the coupons that had been issued had been redeemed. Accompanying these consumer marketing efforts, J&J also engaged in a number of activities to enlist the support of retailers in the form of trade promotions, sales calls, and others.

Convinced that market conditions were now stable enough to commence regular advertising, the agency developed three ad executions using the testimony of loyal Tylenol users with the goal of convincing consumers that they could continue to use Tylenol with confidence: The first ad execution contained excerpts of consumers' reactions to the tampering incident; the second ad brought back a Tylenol supporter from an ad campaign run before the tampering incident to reassert her trust in Tylenol; and the third ad used the testimony of a Tylenol user who reasoned that she could still trust the product given that hospitals still used it. The recall scores for two of the commercials were among the highest ever recorded by ASI, a well-known marketing research firm that conducted the ad testing for J&J. The return to advertising was also accompanied by additional coupon promotional offers to consumers.

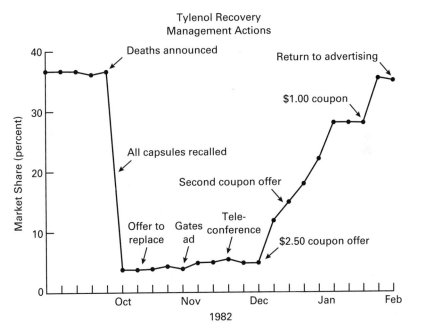

FIGURE 2-6 Tylenol Sales Growth

Incredibly, by February 1983, sales for Tylenol had almost *fully* returned to the lofty pretampering sales levels the brand had enjoyed six months earlier. Figure 2–6 displays the Tylenol sales growth with respect to management actions during this period. A decade later, the brand now is virtually a $1 billion brand—with extensions into cough and cold remedies. The next largest pain reliever competitor has only half the market share of Tylenol. Clearly, J&J's skillful handling of an extremely difficult situation was a major factor in the brand's comeback. Another important factor, however, was clearly the equity of the brand and its strong and valuable "trust" association built up over the years prior to the incident. The feelings of trust engendered by the brand helped to speed the brand recovery, a fact certainly evident to J&J (note the number of times the word "trust" appears in the initial Gates ad—5 times!!).

_____

[a]This brief is based on an excellent University of Chicago Graduate School of Business case written by John Deighton, "McNeil Consumer Products Company: Tylenol."

brand are less likely to switch in the face of price increases and more likely to increase the quantity of the brand purchased in the face of price decreases.[13] In an analysis of consumer goods manufacturers from the extensive PIMS database, Boulding, Lee, and Staelin found that, by providing unique and positive messages, a firm could insulate itself from future price competition, as witnessed by less negative future price elasticities. Conversely, they also found that nonunique messages could decrease future differentiation—price promotions for firms that priced above the industry average led to more negative future price elasticities.[14]

The results of a study by Intelliquest marketing research firm exploring the role of brand name and price in the decision purchase of business computer buyers is enlightening in that regard.[15] Survey respondents were asked: "What is the incremental dollar value you would be willing to pay over a no-name clone computer brand?" As Figure 2–7 shows, IBM commanded the greatest price premium, followed by Compaq and Hewlett-Packard. Some brands not listed evidently had negative brand equity as they actually received negative numbers! Clearly, according to this study, brands in the personal computer market have specific meaning that consumers value and will pay for.

At the same time, many firms have learned the hard way that consumers will not pay price premiums that exceed their perceptions of the value of a brand. Perhaps the most vivid illustration of this fact was the experience of Marlboro, Philip Morris' leading cigarette brand.[16] Branding Brief 2–4 describes how Philip Morris was forced to drop its prices on Marlboro so that it was more in line with discount and store brands who were gaining increased market share at Marlboro's expense. Although the Marlboro price discounts led to short-term profitability declines, they also led to regained market share that put the brand on stronger footing over the longer haul.

	Premium
IBM	$339
Compaq	$318
Hewlett Packard	$260
Dell	$230
Apple	$182
AST Computer	$ 17
Digital	$ 10

FIGURE 2–7 Price Sensitivity of Personal Computer Buyers

Marlboro's Price Drop

On April 2, 1993 or "Marlboro Friday," Philip Morris dropped a bombshell in the form of a three-page announcement: "Philip Morris USA … announced a major shift in business strategy designed to increase market share and grow long-term profitability in a highly price sensitive market environment." Quoting tobacco unit President-CEO William I. Campbell, the statement continued, "We have determined that in the current market environment caused by pro-longed economic softness and depressed consumer confidence, we should take those steps necessary to grow our market share rather than pursue rapid income growth rates that might erode our leading marketplace position." Specifically, Philip Morris announced four major steps:

1. An extensive retail promotional program.

2. Greatly expanded spending and attention to the Marlboro Adventure Team conti-nuity program begun in October 1992. Presented to consumers through direct mail and advertising, the program worked much like a catalog: Consumers who saved empty Marlboro packs could send them to Philip Morris in return for free mer-chandise.

3. An increased effort to take share in the discount cigarette market with a new push behind the company's low-priced Basic brand (although Philip Morris sold 48 per-cent of the premium cigarettes, they only held a 19 percent share of the discount market).

4. A major promotional cut in the price of Marlboro (roughly 40 to 50 cents a pack) that was expected to decrease earnings in Philip Morris' most profitable unit by 40 percent.

The fourth proposed action caught the eye of marketers and Wall Street alike. The action was justified by the results of a month-long test market in Portland, Oregon the previous December where a 40 cents decrease in pack price had in-creased market share by 4 points. The stock market reaction to the announce-ment was swift. By day's end, Philip Morris stock price had declined from $64.12 to $49.37, a 23 percent drop that represented a one-day loss of $13 billion in shareholder equity! There was a ripple effect in the stock market with signi-ficant stock price declines for other consumer goods companies with major brands (e.g., Sara Lee, Kellogg's, General Mills, and Procter & Gamble). The Dow Jones Industrial Average dropped 68.63 points, 30 points attributable to Philip Morris alone. One company that took one of the biggest hits was Coca-Cola, whose shareholders lost $5 billion in paper in the days following "Black Friday." Feeling that the stock market was overreacting, Coca-Cola manage-ment went to great pains to explain to the financial community that the market-ing situation faced by their brands differed from the Marlboro situation. Brand-ing Brief 2–5 contains some of the comparisons that they made in their presentation to analysts.

A number of factors probably provided the impetus for why Marlboro felt compelled to cut prices so dramatically. The economy certainly was still sluggish coming out of a recession. Private-label or store-brand cigarettes had been increasing in quality and were receiving more attention from customers and retailers. A prime consideration suggested by many was related to Philip Morris' hefty price increases. These price hikes had often occurred two to three times a year and had been above the rate of inflation (as much as 10 percent in a year). The 80 cents to a $1 difference between premium brands and discount brands that were prevailing at that time was thought to have resulted in steady sales increases for the discount brands. The growth in sales of those brands came at the expense of Marlboro market share, which had dropped to 22 percent and was further projected to decline to 18 percent if Philip Morris had made no changes.

By cutting the difference between discount cigarettes and Marlboro to roughly 40 cents, Philip Morris was able to woo back many customers. Within nine months after the price drop, their market share increased to almost 27 percent, eventually rising to almost 30 percent. Nevertheless, the lower prices had adverse profit implications, and by year-end, analysts had estimated that the strategy had cut Philip Morris' domestic tobacco unit's earnings by $2.3 billion to $2.84 billion.[a]

To maintain the long-term sales growth and profitability of the Marlboro brand, Philip Morris has since expanded its marketing programs by introducing a new continuity program called Marlboro Country Store (offering Western wear such as boots, cowboy hats, belt buckles, denim shirts, and leather jackets, discreetly stenciled with the Marlboro brand logo); test marketing a new, 15 millimeter shorter cigarette called Express for time-pressed and price-conscious consumers; and by slowly and carefully nudging up prices (a 4-cent increase in November 1992 seemed to be basically ignored by consumers). Subsequent marketing programs introduced a "Marlboro Unlimited" promotion where 2000 couples could win $1000 cash and a five-day outdoor vacation in the Western United States aboard a train brightly painted in the red and white colors of the cigarette pack.

---

[a]Laura Zinn, "The Smoke Clears at Marlboro," *Business Week* (January 31, 1994), pp. 76–77.

Two important lessons emerged from the Marlboro episode. First, strong brands *can* command price premiums. Once Marlboro's price difference entered a more acceptable range, consumers were then willing to pay the still-higher price to be able to buy Marlboro, and the sales of the brand started to increase. Second, strong brands cannot command an *excessive* price premium. The clear signal sent to marketers everywhere by Philip Morris' experience with Marlboro is that price hikes without corresponding investments in the value of the brand may increase the vulnerability of the brand to lower-priced competition. In these cases, consumers may be willing to "trade down" because they no longer can justify to themselves that the higher-priced brand is worth it.

Although much of the popular press attempted to exploit Marlboro's actions to proclaim that "brands were dead," nothing could have been further from the truth. In

---

BRANDING BRIEF 2-5

Soft Drinks Are Not Cigarettes

In the aftermath of the Marlboro price reduction announcement on April 2, 1993, Coca-Cola's stock took a beating, losing an astounding $5 billion in value! From a high of $45\,^3/_8$ the previous September, the stock had declined to 38, an almost 2-year low. Apparently, the stock market felt that the pressures that had forced Marlboro to cut prices and lower its profits were also being faced by Coca-Cola and others. On April 21, Coca-Cola scheduled a meeting with top financial analysts to dispel what they believed were misconceptions about its brand. Led by Roberto Goizueta, chairman and chief executive officer, the theme of the Coca-Cola presentation was "Soft Drinks Are Not Cigarettes." During the course of their talk, Coca-Cola management made the following points:[a]

1. Soft drink consumption had been steadily increasing in the United States. Cigarette consumption had been declining.

2. The retail price of a pack of Marlboros more than tripled between 1980 and 1992, leaving room for discounters to undercut the brand. On the other hand, the average retail price of Coca-Cola had remained virtually unchanged during this same period (around 2 cents per ounce).

3. Major cigarette makers, by selling both brand-name and private-label products, cannibalized their own sales and were their own worst enemy. Coca-Cola had no private label business in the United States.

4. The discount market for cigarettes increased from virtually nothing to 30 percent of United States sales in 1992. Private label soft drinks, on the other hand, accounted for only 8.7 percent of United States sales in 1992, a figure that was actually lower than twenty years ago.

5. More than 80 percent of Coca-Cola's earnings came from outside the United States, thus reducing its exposure to private label competitors in the United States.

Spreading the word concerning these differences seemed to help. Within a month, Coca-Cola's stock had increased to 42, just about where it had been at the time of the Marlboro announcement.

---

[a]Arthur M. Louis, "Coca-Cola's Stock Rescue Operation," *San Francisco Chronicle* (June 1, 1993), p. C1.

---

fact, a more accurate interpretation of the whole episode is that it showed that *new* brands were entering the scene, as evidenced by the ability of discount brands to create their own brand equity on the basis of strong consumer associations to "value." At the same time, existing brands, if properly managed can command loyalty, enjoy price premiums, and still be extremely profitable. For example, Frito-Lay dropped its prices 15 percent after losing two share points in the $13 billion salty snack market in the late

1980s. While also improving product quality and reducing costs, Frito-Lay regained 1.2 share points and enjoyed a 28 percent increase in profits.[17] Chapter 5 reviews pricing strategies and discount policies to build brand equity.

GREATER TRADE COOPERATION AND SUPPORT

Marketers often do not sell directly to consumers. In these cases, middlemen in the form of wholesalers, retailers, and other parties play an important role in the selling of the product. The activities of these channel of distribution members can thus facilitate or inhibit the success of the brand. If the brand has a positive brand image with consumers, then it is more likely that it will receive favorable treatment from the trade.

Specifically, a brand with a positive brand image is more likely to have retailers and other middlemen respond to the wishes of consumers and actively promote and sell the brand. Recognizing the likelihood of this consumer demand, channel members are also less likely to require any marketing "push" from the manufacturer and are more likely to be receptive to any marketing overtures that do arise from the manufacturer to stock, reorder, and display the brand.[18] Thus, they should be more likely to pass through trade promotions, demand smaller slotting allowances, give more favorable shelf space or position, and so on. Chapter 5 describes how marketers can work with retailers to maximize their brand equity.

INCREASED MARKETING COMMUNICATION EFFECTIVENESS

A host of advertising and communication benefits may result from creating awareness of and a positive image for a brand. These benefits can be seen by considering the manner by which a consumer responds to marketing communications and how the marketing communications program for a brand with a great deal of equity may be processed differently by consumers as a result. One well-established view of consumer response to marketing communications is *hierarchy of effects* models. These models assume that consumers move through a series of stages or mental states on the basis of marketing communications: exposure to, attention to, comprehension of, yielding to, retention of, and behaving on the basis of a marketing communication.

A brand with a great deal of equity already has created some knowledge structures in consumers' minds. The existence of these mental associations is extremely valuable as they increase the likelihood that consumers will pass through various stages of the hierarchy. For example, consider the effects of a positive brand image on the persuasive ability of advertising. As a result of having established brand awareness and strong, favorable, and unique brand associations, consumers may be more likely to notice an ad, may more easily learn about the brand and form favorable opinions, and may retain and act on these beliefs over time. Academic research has shown that familiar, well-liked brands are: (1) less susceptible to "interference" and confusion from competitive ads, (2) more responsive to creative strategies such as humor appeals, and (3) less vulnerable to negative reactions due to concentrated repetition schedules.

Because strong brand associations exist, lower levels of repetition may be necessary. For example, in a classic study of advertising weights, Anheuser-Busch ran a carefully conducted field experiment where the amount of Budweiser advertising shown to consumers in different matched test markets varied.[19] Seven different advertising expenditure levels were tested representing increases and decreases from the previous advertising expenditure levels: −100 percent (no advertising), −50 percent, 0 percent (same level), +50 percent, +100 percent (double the level of advertising), +150 percent, and +200 percent. These expenditure levels were run for one year and revealed that the "no advertising" level resulted in the same amount of sales as the current program. In fact, the 50 percent cut in advertising expenditures actually resulted in an *increase* in sales. The experimental results are consistent with the notion that strong brands such as Budweiser do not require the same advertising levels, at least over a certain period of time, as a less well-known or well-liked brand. These results should be interpreted carefully, however, as they do not suggest that large advertising expenditures did not play an important role in creating equity for the brand in the past, or that advertising expenditures could be cut way back without some adverse sales consequences at some point in the future.

Similarly, because brand knowledge structures exist, consumers may be more likely to notice a sales promotion, direct mail offering, or other sales-oriented marketing communications and respond favorably. For example, several studies have shown that promotion effectiveness is asymmetric in favor of a higher quality brand.[20] Chapter 6 outlines how to develop integrated marketing communication programs to build and capitalize on brand equity.

POSSIBLE LICENSING OPPORTUNITIES

A strong brand often has associations that may be desirable in other product categories. To capitalize on this value, a firm may choose to license its name, logo, or other trademark item to another company for use on their products and merchandise. Traditionally, licensing has been associated with characters such as Garfield the cat, Barney the dinosaur, and Disney's Mickey Mouse, or celebrities and designers such as Martha Stewart, Ralph Lauren, and Tommy Hilfiger. Recently, more conventional brands such as Harley Davidson, Caterpillar, and others have licensed their brands to others.

Licensing was a $80 billion industry in 1994. The rationale for licensing—the company obtaining the rights to use the trademark—is that consumers will pay more for the licensee's product because of the recognition and image lent by the trademark. For example, one marketing research study showed that consumers would pay $60 for cookware licensed under the Julia Child name as opposed to only $40 for the identical cookware bearing the Sears name.[21]

The rationale for the licensor—the company behind the trademark—relates to profits, promotion, and legal protection. In terms of profits, a firm can expect an average royalty of about 5 percent of the wholesale price of each product, ranging from 2 percent to 10 percent depending on the circumstances involved. Because there are no manufacturing or marketing costs, these revenues translate directly to profits. Licensing is also seen as a means to enhance the awareness and image of the brand. Linking the trademarks to other products may broaden its exposure and potentially increase the strength, favorability, and uniqueness of brand associations. Finally, licensing may provide legal protection for trademarks. Licensing the brand for use in certain product categories prevents other firms or potential competitors from legally using the brand name to enter those categories. For example, Coca-Cola entered licensing agreements in a number of product areas, including radios, glassware, toy trucks, and clothes, in part as legal protection. As it turns out, its licensing program has been so successful Coca-Cola has subsequently introduced a catalog sent directly to consumers offering a myriad of products bearing the Coca-Cola name (see Figure 2–8).

FIGURE 2–8 Excerpt from Coca-Cola Catalog

Despite the potential benefits from licensing related to profitability, image enhancement or legal protection, there are certainly risks. A trademark can become overexposed if marketers adopt a "saturation" policy. Consumers do not necessarily know the motivation or marketing arrangements behind a product and can become confused or even angry if the brand is licensed to a product that seemingly bears no relation. Moreover, if the product fails to live up to consumer expectations, the brand name could become tarnished. Chapter 7 discusses the pros and cons of licensing and its effect on brand equity in more detail.

ADDITIONAL BRAND EXTENSION OPPORTUNITIES

New product introductions are vital to the long-run success of a firm. When a firm introduces a new product, it has three main choices for its brand name:

1. It can develop a new brand name.
2. It can apply one of its existing names.
3. It can use a combination of a new brand name with an existing brand name.

When a firm uses an established brand name to enter a new market this is *brand extension* (approaches 2 and 3). Extensions can be classified into two general categories. A *line extension* is when a current brand name is used to enter a new market segment in the existing product class (e.g., with new varieties, new flavors, and new sizes). For example, Colgate has introduced a number of different varieties of toothpaste that come in different flavors, have different ingredients, or provide a specific benefit. A *category extension* is when the current brand name is used to enter a different product class. For example, Swiss Army Brands capitalized on the success of its knives to introduce watches and then sunglasses.

A brand with a positive brand image allows the firm to introduce appropriate new products as brand extensions. There are many advantages to introducing new products as extensions. An extension allows the firm to capitalize on consumer knowledge of the parent brand to raise the awareness of and suggest possible associations for the brand extension. Thus, extensions can potentially provide the following benefits to facilitate new product acceptance:

1. Reduce risk perceived by customers and distributors
2. Decrease cost of gaining distribution and trial
3. Increase efficiency of promotional expenditures
4. Avoid cost (and risk) of developing new names
5. Allow for packaging and labeling efficiencies
6. Permit consumer variety seeking

Besides facilitating new product acceptance, extensions can also provide feedback benefits to the parent brand and the company as a whole. Extensions may enhance the parent brand image by improving the strength, favorability, and uniqueness of brand associations and by improving perceptions of company credibility (in terms of perceived expertise, trustworthiness, or likability). Extensions may also help to convey the broader meaning of the brand to consumers, clarifying the core benefit proposition and business definition of the company. Finally, extensions may also bring new customers into the brand franchise and increase market coverage.

Along with these potential advantages, extensions certainly have some possible risks too. Certainly, they can fail. Moreover, extensions can potentially result in the following problems:

1. Cannibalizing sales of the parent brand
2. Hurting the image of the parent brand if the extension fails
3. Hurting the image of the parent brand even if the extension is successful
4. Forgoing the chance to develop a new brand name (opportunity cost).

Chapter 12 provides a conceptual model of how consumers evaluate brand extensions and presents a number of guidelines for marketers to maximize extension success and its effect on brand equity.

OTHER BENEFITS

Finally, brands with positive customer-based brand equity may provide other advantages to the firm not directly related to the products themselves, such as helping the firm to attract better employees, generating greater interest from investors, and garnering more support from shareholders.

Customer-Based Brand Equity Framework

In order to reap these potential benefits from brands, it is important that marketers know how to build, measure, and manage brand equity. The customer-based brand equity framework provides that guidance. In this section, we summarize the chief ingredients of the framework and indicate how they are treated in the rest of the text. Figures 2–9 to 2–11 schematically display some of the key components and guidelines for building, measuring, and managing customer-based brand equity that emerge from this framework.

BUILDING BRAND EQUITY

Building brand equity requires creating a brand that consumers are aware of and with which consumers have strong, favorable, and unique brand associations. In general, this knowledge-building will depend on three factors:

1. The initial choices for the brand elements or identities making up the brand
2. The supporting marketing program and the manner by which the brand is integrated into it
3. Other associations indirectly transferred to the brand by linking it to some other entity (e.g., the company, country of origin, channel of distribution, or another brand)

Figure 2–9 summarizes the key considerations in building brand equity discussed in this section. Each of the three factors is discussed in turn.

FIGURE 2-9 Building Customer-Based Brand Equity

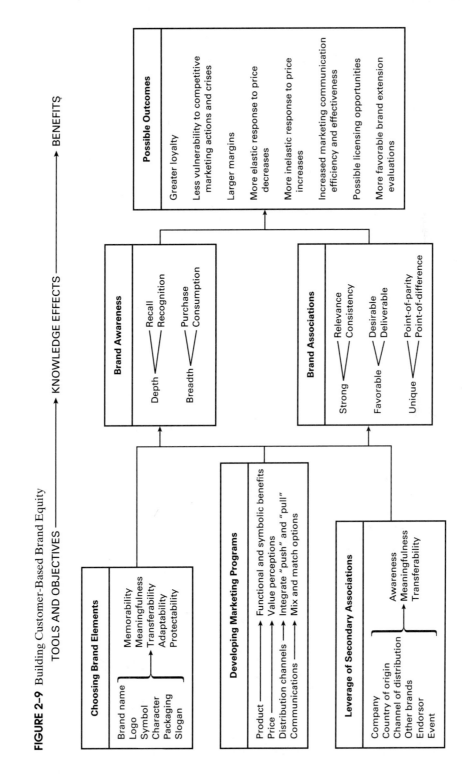

1. Brand Audit

   A. Brand inventory

   B. Brand exploratory

   C. Brand positioning

---

2. Brand Tracking

   A. Brand equity sources

   B. Brand equity outcomes

---

3. Brand Equity Management System

   A. Brand equity charter

   B. Brand equity report

   C. Brand equity director

FIGURE 2-10 Measuring Customer-Based Brand Equity

Choosing Brand Elements

A number of options exist and a number of criteria are relevant for choosing brand elements. A brand element is visual or verbal information that serves to identify and differentiate a product. The most common brand elements are brand names, logos, symbols, characters, packaging, and slogans. Brand elements can be chosen to enhance brand awareness or facilitate the formation of strong, favorable, and unique brand associations. The test of the brand-building contribution of brand elements is what consumers would think about the product *if* they only knew about its brand name, associated logo, or other elements.

In terms of choosing and designing brand elements to build brand equity, five general criteria can be used. Brand elements can be chosen according to their:

1. *Memorability*—easily recognized and recalled
2. *Meaningfulness*—credibility and suggestiveness, as well as fun, interesting, and rich in visual and verbal imagery
3. *Transferability*—mobile both within and across product categories, across geographical boundaries and cultures
4. *Adaptability*—flexible enough to be easily updated and made contemporary
5. *Protectability*—legally secure and competitively well-guarded

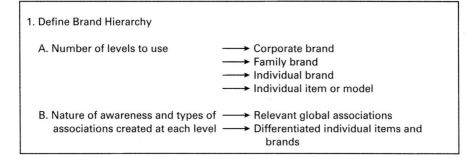

1. Define Brand Hierarchy

    A. Number of levels to use   ⟶ Corporate brand
                                        ⟶ Family brand
                                        ⟶ Individual brand
                                        ⟶ Individual item or model

    B. Nature of awareness and types of ⟶ Relevant global associations
        associations created at each level ⟶ Differentiated individual items and
                                                 brands

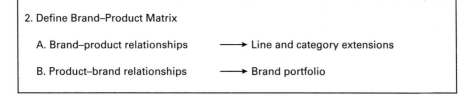

2. Define Brand–Product Matrix

    A. Brand–product relationships   ⟶ Line and category extensions

    B. Product–brand relationships   ⟶ Brand portfolio

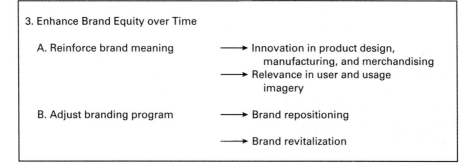

3. Enhance Brand Equity over Time

    A. Reinforce brand meaning   ⟶ Innovation in product design,
                                                 manufacturing, and merchandising
                                         ⟶ Relevance in user and usage
                                               imagery

    B. Adjust branding program   ⟶ Brand repositioning

                                         ⟶ Brand revitalization

4. Establish Brand Equity over Market Segments

    A. Identify differences   ⟶ How they purchase and use products
        in consumer behavior   ⟶ What they know and feel about
                                                 different brands

    B. Adjust branding program   ⟶ Choice of brand elements
                                         ⟶ Nature of supporting marketing program
                                         ⟶ Leverage of secondary associations

FIGURE 2-11 Managing Customer-Based Brand Equity

The first two criteria are more offensive considerations to create and build brand knowledge structures; the last three criteria are more defensive considerations to maximize and protect the value of those knowledge structures.

    Each of those criteria has its own set of more specific considerations. For example, the awareness or memorability of a brand name is improved the extent to which it is: (1) simple and easy to pronounce or spell; (2) familiar and meaningful; and (3) different, distinctive, and unusual. These first two criteria are more likely to improve brand name recall, whereas the third criterion is more likely to improve brand name recognition. Thus, many of the criteria may be conflicting and are somewhat contradictory depending on the choice of the brand element. For example, the more meaningful or suggestive a brand name, the more likely it is that it will not be legally protectable (it will already have been used by some other company or for some other product) or will not be transferable (it will not translate well into other languages). Moreover, some brand elements are more likely to satisfy certain criteria better than others. For example, one advantage to brand characters is that they afford creative potential as they are often fun, interesting, and likable. Slogans, on the other hand, may be more valuable in terms of memorability and other meaningfulness considerations.

Choosing the proper brand elements according to these criteria can help to contribute to brand equity by enhancing awareness and the formation of a positive brand image. Because different elements have different advantages, in most cases a subset or even all of the possible brand elements should be employed. Chapter 4 examines in detail the means by which the choice and design of brand elements can help to build brand equity.

Integrating the Brand into the Supporting Marketing Program

Although the judicious choice of brand elements can make some contribution to customer-based brand equity, the primary input comes from the marketing activities related to the brand. Strong, favorable, and unique brand associations can be created by marketing programs in a variety of well-established ways. In this text, we will only highlight some particularly important marketing mix considerations for building brand equity. Chapters 5 and 6 address these issues.

Product Strategy   The product is at the foundation of brand equity. In the design, manufacturing, and servicing of products, it is important that favorable brand associations are created by convincing consumers that the brand possesses relevant attributes and benefits that satisfy their needs and wants such that they form a positive overall brand attitude. As suggested above, these may be more functional in nature—related to actual product performance—or more symbolic in nature and not directly related to the product—such as with user or usage imagery. Perceived quality is a particularly important brand association that often drives consumer decisions. Because of the importance of consumers' actual product experiences in building brand equity, "after-marketing" activities have taken on increased importance.

Price Strategy   The pricing policy for the brand often creates strong associations in consumers' minds to the relevant price tier or level for the brand in the category, as well as to its corresponding price volatility or variance (e.g., in terms of the frequency, timing, and magnitude of discounts). Consumers will also often have associations to perceived value—the tradeoff between price and quality—that will be an important factor in their decisions. Consequently, in terms of the optimal pricing policy for the brand, it is important that marketers fully understand consumer perceptions of value for their own brand as well as for those of competitors.

Relatedly, value pricing is a strategy that attempts to properly blend product quality, product cost, and product price considerations to set prices in a way to fully satisfy the needs and wants of consumers and the profit objectives of the firm. Everyday low pricing is a complementary pricing approach to determine the nature of price discounts and promotions over time to maintain consistently low, value-based prices on major items on a day-to-day basis.

Channel Strategy   From a branding standpoint, there are three important channel considerations. First, consumers often have mental associations to retail stores or chains on the basis of product assortment, pricing and credit policy, quality of service, and so on. The associations making up the store image may be linked to its products (e.g., prestigious and exclusive brands versus bargain-driven and mass appeal). Manufacturers must determine to what extent they will benefit from, or even should try to explicitly capitalize on, these indirect associations in building their own brand equity.

Second, by their actions, retailers and other channel members can affect brand equity of the products they sell. Retailers can prominently display or mention the brand, increasing its awareness, or provide information in some manner that reinforces and strengthens the critical point-of-parity and point-of-difference brand associations. To realize these advantages, manufacturers must take an active role in helping retailers understand and appreciate how they can add value to brands. Effective branding programs will be those that successfully blend "push" and "pull" strategies. "Push" considerations include those marketing activities directed to channel members themselves to help them sell the product or "push" it on to the end consumer. "Pull" considerations include those marketing activities directed to the end consumer so that they will demand the product from the trade and thus "pull" it through the channel.

The third and final channel consideration concerns the actual nature of the channel design. To gain greater control and build stronger relationships with customers, manufacturers may need to introduce their own retail outlets or shops, as well as market directly to customers through various media.

Communication Strategies   The role of marketing communications is to contribute to brand equity by establishing the brand in memory and linking strong, favorable, and unique associations to it. A number of different marketing communication options exist to assist marketers. For example, alternative consumer communication options include media advertising (TV, radio, newspaper, and magazines), direct response advertising, outdoor advertising (billboards, posters, cinema, etc.), point-of-purchase advertising, trade promotions, consumer promotions, sponsorship or event marketing, and publicity or public relations.

From the perspective of customer-based brand equity—because all that matters is the resulting strength, favorability, and uniqueness of brand association—marketers should evaluate all possible communication options available to create knowledge structures according to effectiveness criteria as well as cost considerations. Along these lines, the growth of nontraditional media, promotions, and other marketing activity makes sense from the perspective of customer-based brand equity. Many of these alternatives can provide a cost-effective way to affect brand knowledge and thus, ultimately, sales.

Different communication options have different strengths, however, and can accomplish different objectives. For example, advertising is particularly well-suited for translating attributes to benefits and linking non-product, image attributes for the brand. Sponsorship and public relations are effective means of building brand awareness, especially brand recognition. Sales promotions and direct response offers can be relatively more effective at "closing the sale" for the brand and stimulating actual purchase.

Regardless of which options are chosen, the entire marketing program should be coordinated to create a consistent and cohesive brand image such that brand associations share content and meaning. The strength of brand associations from communication effects depends, in part, on how the brand elements are integrated in the various marketing communications (e.g., the position and prominence of the brand elements in a TV ad). Stronger brand associations to communication effects may be created by explicitly linking marketing communications to the brand. For example, identifiable visual scenes, characters, symbols, and verbal phrases or slogans can serve as cues or reminders to communication effects created by a TV ad and placed in or on product packages or places of business, coupons or other promotions, yellow pages ads, print ads, or other TV ads.

Thus, according to the customer-based brand equity framework, marketers must consider all available options to create brand knowledge structures—traditional as well as alternative or nontraditional marketing tactics—and must coordinate these options in their marketing programs to create congruent and strong brand associations. Mixing and matching communication options in this fashion should lead to a consistent and cohesive brand image.

Leveraging Secondary Associations

The third and final way to build brand equity is to leverage secondary associations. Brand associations may themselves be linked to other entities that have their own associations, creating "secondary" brand associations. In other words, a brand association may be created by linking the brand to another node or information in memory that conveys meaning to consumers. For example, the brand may be linked to certain source factors, such as the company (through branding strategies), countries or other geographical regions (through identification of product origin), and channels of distribution (through channel strategy), as well as to other brands (through ingredient or co-branding), characters (through licensing), spokespeople (through endorsements), sporting or cultural events (through sponsorship), or some other third-party sources (through awards or reviews). Because the brand becomes identified with another entity, even though this entity may not directly relate to the product or service performance, consumers may *infer* that the brand shares associations with that entity, thus producing indirect or secondary associations for the brand. In essence, the marketer is borrowing or "leveraging" some other associations for the brand to create some associations of its own and thus help to build its brand equity.

Secondary brand associations may be quite important if existing brand associations are deficient in some way. In other words, secondary associations can be leveraged to create strong, favorable, and unique brand associations that otherwise may be lacking. These secondary associations may lead to a transfer of global associations such as attitude or credibility (expertise, trustworthiness, and likability). These secondary associations may also lead to a transfer of more specific associations related to the product or service meaning and the attributes or benefits of the brand.

In general, the possibility of creating secondary associations must be judged by considering the awareness of the relevant entity and the nature and transferability of its associations. Has the target market heard of the company, person, place, or event that is to be linked to the brand? If so, what do people think of it? Successful transfer of associations will only occur when the other entity in question has sufficient awareness and the desired meaning. Additionally, how likely is that some of their associations would actually transfer and become linked to the brand? If the associations for the other entity are too strong or restrictive or are not seen as relevant to the brand, consumers may fail to create the desired secondary association. For example, if consumers feel that a certain celebrity is insincerely endorsing a product only for the money, then whatever goodwill or relevant associations that the company might be hoping to transfer to the brand would be unlikely to materialize.

MEASURING BRAND EQUITY

The initial choices for brand elements, the nature of the supporting marketing program, and the leverage of secondary associations are all ways to build consumer knowledge structures and create sources of brand equity. Because the value of the brand equity concept lies in its ability to guide strategic decisions, it is important that marketers are able to accurately measure both these sources of brand equity as well as the outcomes or brand equity benefits that then result. Conceptually, there are two basic complementary approaches to measuring customer-based brand equity.

Measuring Sources of Brand Equity

The *indirect approach* attempts to assess potential sources for customer-based brand equity by measuring brand knowledge structures, that is, consumers' brand awareness and brand image. The indirect approach is useful for identifying what aspects of the brand knowledge may potentially cause the differential response that creates customer-based brand equity. Because any one measure typically only captures one particular aspect of brand knowledge, multiple measures should be employed to account for the multidimensional nature of brand knowledge. Brand awareness can be assessed through a variety of aided and unaided memory measures that can be applied to test brand recall and recognition. The strength, favorability, and uniqueness of brand associations can be assessed through a variety of qualitative and quantitative techniques. Chapter 8 reviews the logic and techniques to measure sources of brand equity.

Measuring Outcomes of Brand Equity

The *direct approach* to measuring customer-based brand equity, on the other hand, attempts to more directly assess the impact of brand knowledge on consumer response to different elements of the marketing program for the firm. The direct approach is useful in approximating the possible outcomes and benefits that arise from the differential response that creates customer-based brand equity. The two main ways to measure the outcomes and benefits of brand equity are comparative methods (means to better assess the effects of consumer perceptions and preferences on aspects of the marketing program) and holistic methods (attempts to come up with estimates of the overall value of the brand).

Comparative methods involve experiments that examine consumer attitudes and behaviors towards a brand and its marketing activity that arise from having a high level of awareness and strong, favorable, and unique associations. *Brand-based comparative approaches* typically involve experiments where one group of consumers responds to an element of the marketing program or some marketing activity when it is attributed to the brand and another group of identically matched consumers responds to that same element when it is attributed to a competitive or fictitiously named version of the product or service. Comparing responses of the two groups thus provides an estimate of the effects due to specific knowledge about the brand that goes beyond more general knowledge of the product or service category. *Marketing-based comparative approaches*, on the other hand, use experiments where consumers respond to changes in elements of the marketing program or marketing activity for the target brand or competitive brand.

Holistic methods attempt to place an overall value for the brand in either abstract utility terms or concrete financial terms. Thus, holistic methods attempt to "net out" various considerations to determine the unique contribution of the brand. The *residual approach* attempts to examine the value of the brand by subtracting out consumers' preferences for the brand based on physical product attributes alone from their overall brand preferences. The *valuation approach* attempts to place a financial value on the brand for accounting purposes, mergers and acquisitions, or other such reasons. Chapter 9 outlines all of the various ways to measure outcomes of brand equity in detail.

Brand Equity Measurement System

To apply these two different types of measures in a managerial setting, it is necessary to design and put into place a brand equity measurement system. A *brand equity measurement system* is a set of research procedures designed to provide timely, accurate, and actionable information for marketers so that they can make the best possible tactical decisions in the short run and strategic decisions in the long run. As described in chapter 10, implementing such a system involves three steps (see Figure 2–10):

Conducting the Brand Audit A *brand audit* is a comprehensive examination of a brand involving activities to assess the health of the brand, uncover its sources of equity, and suggest ways to improve and leverage that equity. A brand audit requires understanding sources of brand equity from the perspective of both the firm and the consumer. Specifically, the brand audit consists of three activities:

1. *Brand inventory.* The purpose of the brand inventory is to provide a complete, up-to-date profile of how all the products and services sold by a company are marketed and branded. For each product, the relevant brand elements must be identified, as well as the supporting marketing program. This information should be summarized visually and verbally. Although primarily a descriptive exercise, some useful analysis can be conducted as to the consistency of branding and marketing efforts.

2. *Brand exploratory.* The brand exploratory is research activity designed to identify potential sources of brand equity. The brand exploratory provides detailed information as to

what consumers think of and feel about the brand. Although reviewing past studies and interviewing relevant personnel inside or outside the company involved in marketing the brand provides some insights, additional research is often required. To allow a broader range of issues to be covered and also to permit those issues to be pursued in depth, the brand exploratory often employs qualitative research techniques. To provide a more specific assessment of the sources of brand equity, a followup quantitative phase is often necessary.

3. *Brand positioning*. The brand exploratory provides information on potential sources of brand equity. Brand positioning analysis reviews information to determine the desired brand awareness and brand image. Arriving at a positioning for the brand requires decisions in four areas: target market, nature of competition, point-of-parity associations, and point-of-difference associations. The first two considerations help to define the frame of reference for the brand. The latter two considerations help to create the exact location of the brand in consumer minds.

The essence of brand positioning is that the brand has some sustainable competitive advantage or "unique selling proposition" that gives consumers a compelling reason why they should buy that particular brand. Thus, one critical success factor for a brand is that it has some strongly held, favorably evaluated associations that function as *points of difference* and are unique to the brand and imply superiority over other competing brands. These potential differences should be judged on the basis of desirability (from a consumer perspective) and deliverability (from a firm perspective).

At the same time, it is also the case that some strongly held, favorably evaluated associations only need to function as *points of parity* and be seen as about the same as with competing brands. Shared associations can help to establish category membership and define the nature of competition with other products and services. Most importantly, shared associations can also prevent other brands from establishing competitive advantages and points of difference.

Point-of-difference and point-of-parity associations will depend on the particular frame of reference that is chosen. In other words, the uniqueness and shared nature of associations can only be assessed by considering the perceptions toward the brand by a certain group of consumers with respect to a defined set of competitors.

Developing Brand Tracking Procedures   Once the brand positioning is chosen as part of the brand audit or in some other way, a marketing program can be put into place to build the desired brand knowledge structures and maximize the potential benefits that may result. To check the success of the marketing program, tracking studies are often conducted. Whereas the brand audit is done on a non-recurring basis to help sharpen or change the brand positioning, tracking studies involve information collected from consumers on a routine basis over time. The purpose of tracking studies is to monitor the strength, favorability, and uniqueness of those brand associations that represent key sources of brand equity. Additionally, tracking studies also measure relevant outcomes of brand equity such as overall attitudes or preference for the brand, reported past usage and intended future usage, price sensitivity, and so on. Tracking studies can also analyze the marketing program with respect to its effects on the current brand image and how it can help to achieve the desired brand image.

Creating a Brand Equity Management System   To fully benefit from the research findings that emerge from the brand audit and brand tracking studies, a brand equity management system needs to be implemented within the firm. Such a system would include, minimally, the following three ingredients:

1. *Brand equity charter*. The company view of brand equity should be formalized into a document, the *brand equity charter*, that provides relevant guidelines to marketing managers. This document should minimally define the brand equity concept and explain its importance, specify what the assumed equity is for all relevant brands (e.g., in terms of key associations), explain how brand equity is measured by the firm in terms of the content and structure of tracking studies and the resulting Brand Equity Reports, and suggest general principles for managing brand equity.

2. *Brand equity report*. The results of the tracking survey and other relevant outcome measures should be assembled into *brand equity reports* that are distributed to management on a regular basis (monthly, quarterly, or annually). The report ideally would combine relevant tracking information with other internal information and effectively integrate all these different measures into an interpretable and actionable form.[22] In this way, the brand equity report would provide descriptive information as to *what* is happening within a brand as well as diagnostic information as to *why* it is happening

3. *Brand overseers*. Finally, a director(s) or vice-president(s) of brand or equity management should be appointed within the organization. The person or persons in that position would be responsible for overseeing the implementation of the brand equity charter and brand equity reports. Their task would be to make sure that, as much as possible, product and marketing actions across divisions and geographical boundaries are performed in a way that reflected the spirit of the brand equity charter and the substance of the brand equity report to maximize the long-term equity of brands.

MANAGING BRAND EQUITY

Brand equity management concerns those activities that take a broader and more diverse perspective of the brand's equity—understanding how branding strategies should reflect corporate concerns and be adjusted, if at all, over time, geographical boundaries, or market segments. Effectively managing brand equity includes defining the branding strategy by defining the brand hierarchy and brand-product matrix and devising policy for brand fortification and leverage over time and geographical boundaries (see Figure 2–11).

Defining the Branding Strategy

The branding strategy of the firm provides the general guidelines as to which brand elements a firm chooses to apply across the products it offers for sale. The two main tools in defining the corporate branding strategy are the brand-product matrix and the brand hierarchy.

Brand-Product Matrix The brand-product matrix is a graphical representation of all the brands and products sold by the firm. The matrix or grid has the brands as rows and the corresponding products as columns. The rows of the matrix represent brand-product relationships and capture the brand extension strategy of the firm with respect to a brand. The columns represent product-brand relationships and reflect the brand portfolio strategy for the firm.

Brand-product relationships capture the brand extension strategy of the firm. Potential extensions must be judged by how effectively they leverage the existing brand equity to the new product, as well as how well they, in turn, contribute to the equity of the existing brand. In other words, what is the level of awareness likely to be and what is the expected strength, favorability, and uniqueness of brand associations of the particular extension product? At the same time, how does the introduction of the extension affect the prevailing levels of awareness and strength, favorability, and uniqueness of brand associations of the existing products associated with the brands. A number of guidelines exist for optimal brand extension strategies.

Product-brand relationships capture the brand portfolio strategy in terms of the number and nature of brands to be marketed in each category. Different brands may be necessary to appeal to different market segments. Brands can also take on very specialized roles in the portfolio—as flanker brands to protect more valuable brands, as low-end entry level brands to expand the customer franchise, as high-end prestige brands to enhance the worth of the entire brand line, or as cash cows to milk all potentially realizable profits. As part of the long-term perspective in managing a brand portfolio, it is necessary that the role of different brands and the relationships among different brands in the portfolio be carefully considered over time. In particular, a brand migration strategy needs to be designed and implemented so that consumers understand how various brands in the portfolio can satisfy their needs as they potentially change over time or as the products and brands themselves change over time.

A branding strategy can be characterized according to its breadth (in terms of brand-product relationships and brand extension strategy) and its depth (in terms of product-brand relationships and the brand portfolio or mix). The breadth of the branding strategy concerns the product mix and which products the firm should manufacture and/or sell. Decisions must be made as to how many different product lines the company should carry (the breadth of the product mix), as well as how many variants should be offered in each product line (the depth of the product mix). The depth of the product mix concerns the brand portfolio and the set of all brands and brand lines that a particular seller offers for sale to buyers.

Brand Hierarchy   The *brand hierarchy* reveals an explicit ordering of brands by displaying the number and nature of common and distinctive brand components across the firm's products. By capturing the potential branding relationships among the different products sold by the firm, a brand hierarchy is a useful means to graphically portray a firm's branding strategy. One simple representation of possible brand components and levels of a brand hierarchy, from top to bottom, is composed of: (1) corporate or company brand, (2) family brand, (3) individual brand, and (4) modifier (individual item or model).

Brand names of products are typically not restricted to one name but often consist of a combination of multiple brand name components. For example, a brand such as the Toyota Camry V6 XLE automobile is a combination of brand names from three different levels (the company name, individual brand name, and individual model name). Implementing a brand hierarchy and arriving at a branding strategy necessitates designing the proper brand hierarchy in terms of the number and nature of brand elements and designing the optimal supporting marketing program in terms of creating the desired amount of brand awareness and type of brand associations at each level.

In designing the proper brand hierarchy, decisions must be made as to the number of levels of the hierarchy to use, how brands from different levels of the hierarchy are combined, if at all, for any one product, and how any one brand is linked, if at all, to multiple products. Sub-brand strategies combine brands from different levels. For example, one particularly useful sub-branding strategy is where existing brand names (either the company or family brand name) is combined with a new brand name. Such a strategy offers two potential benefits in that it can both allow for leverage of secondary associations by facilitating access to perceptions and preferences toward the existing brands and allow for the creation of product-specific brand beliefs.

In general, it is advisable with sub-brand strategies to create global brand associations at higher levels that are relevant to as many brands as possible at the next lower level (e.g., from the company name or family brand name to individual brands, items, or models) and clearly differentiate brands at the same levels. It is also necessary to define the relative emphasis or prominence that brands at different levels should receive when combined to brand any one product.

Chapter 11 reviews issues with respect to branding strategies and the concepts of the brand-product matrix and brand hierarchy. Chapter 12 concentrates on the topic of brand extensions.

Managing Brand Equity over Time

Effective brand management requires taking a long-term view of marketing decisions. Because consumers' responses to marketing activity depend on what they know and remember about a brand, short-term marketing actions, by changing brand knowledge, *necessarily* increase or decrease the success of future marketing actions. Thus, one of the difficulties in taking a long-term view of marketing activity is the ability to predict how a proposed marketing action changes consumer knowledge and how this changed knowledge structure influences consumer response to future marketing actions. A long-term perspective of brand management recognizes that any changes in the supporting marketing program for a brand may, by changing consumer knowledge, affect the success of future marketing programs. Additionally, a long-term view results in proactive strategies designed to maintain and enhance customer-based brand equity over time in the face of external changes in the marketing environment and internal changes in a firm's marketing goals and programs. Chapter 13 outlines issues related to managing brand equity over time.

Managing brand equity involves reinforcing brands or, if necessary, revitalizing brands. Brand equity is reinforced by marketing actions that consistently convey the meaning of the brand to consumers in terms of what products the brand represents, what core benefits it supplies, what needs it satisfies, and how the brand makes those products superior and which strong, favorable, and unique brand associations exist in the minds of consumers. The most important consideration in reinforcing brands is the consistency of the marketing support that the brand receives both in terms of the amount and nature of that support. Consistency does not mean that marketers should avoid making any changes in the marketing program: Many tactical changes may be necessary to maintain the strategic thrust and direction of the brand. Unless there is some change in the marketing environment, however, there is little need to deviate from a successful positioning. In such cases, the critical points of parity and points of difference that represent sources of brand equity should be vigorously preserved and defended.

Reinforcing the brand meaning depends on the nature of the brand association involved. For brands whose core associations are primarily product-related attributes and/or functional benefits, innovation in product design, manufacturing, and merchandising is especially critical to maintaining or enhancing brand equity. For brands whose core associations are primarily non-product-related attributes and symbolic or experiential benefits, relevance in user and usage imagery is especially critical to maintaining or enhancing brand equity. In managing brand equity, it is important to recognize the trade-offs that exist between those marketing activities that fortify the brand and reinforce its meaning and those that attempt to leverage or borrow from its existing brand equity to reap some financial benefit. At some point, failure to fortify the brand will diminish brand awareness and weaken brand image. Without these sources of brand equity, the brand itself may not continue to yield as valuable benefits.

Revitalizing a brand requires either that lost sources of brand equity are recaptured or that new sources of brand equity are identified and established. According to the customer-based brand equity framework, two general approaches are possible: (1) expanding the depth and/or breadth of brand awareness by improving brand recall and recognition of consumers during purchase or consumption settings, and (2) improving the strength, favorability, and uniqueness of brand associations making up the brand image. This latter approach may involve programs directed at existing or new brand associations.

With a fading brand, the depth of brand awareness is often not as much of a problem as the breadth—consumers tend to think of the brand in very narrow ways. Strategies to increase usage of and find uses for the brand may be necessary. Although changes in brand awareness are probably the easiest means of creating new sources of brand equity, a new marketing program may need to be implemented to improve the strength, favorability, and uniqueness of brand associations. As part of this repositioning, new markets may have to be tapped. The challenge in all of these efforts to modify the brand image is to not destroy the equity that already exists with current customers.

A number of different possible strategies designed to both acquire new customers and retain existing ones are possible. Different possible strategies are also available to retire those brands whose sources of brand equity had essentially dried up or that had acquired damaging and difficult-to-change associations. Enhancing brand equity over time also requires that the branding strategy itself may have to change somewhat. Adjustments in the branding program may involve brand consolidations (where two brands are merged), brand deletion (where brands are dropped), and brand name changes.

Establishing Brand Equity over Geographic Boundaries, Cultures, and Market Segments

An important consideration in managing brand equity is recognizing and accounting for different types of consumers in developing branding and marketing programs. International issues and global branding strategies are particularly important in these decisions. To develop a global marketing program, it is necessary for marketers to first identify differences in consumer behavior in the relevant regions. How does the manner by which new consumers purchase and use products and think and feel about brands differ from customers in existing markets? Once these differences are thoroughly understood, it is then possible to adjust the branding program to max-imize brand equity in a global context. These changes may involve the choices of brand elements, the nature of the supporting marketing program, and the leverage of secondary associations. A number of issues exist concerning the extent to which a global marketing program should be standardized versus customized and how mar-keting programs can be adapted to different geographic, cultural, or demographic segments. Chapter 14 examines issues related to broadening of brand equity across market segments.

Review

In this chapter, we first defined the important concept of brand equity in terms of the marketing effects uniquely attributable to a brand. The concept of customer-based brand equity was then introduced. Customer-based brand equity was defined as the differential effect that brand knowledge has on consumer response to the marketing of that brand. A brand is said to have positive customer-based brand equity when cus-tomers react more favorably to a product and the way it is marketed when the brand is identified as compared to when it is not (e.g., when it is attributed to a fictitiously named or unnamed version of the product).

Brand knowledge was defined in terms of an associative network memory model as a network of nodes and links where the brand node in memory has a variety of as-sociations linked to it. Brand knowledge can be characterized in terms of two compo-nents: brand awareness and brand image. Brand awareness is related to the strength of the brand node or trace in memory, as reflected by consumers' ability to recall or recognize the brand under different conditions. Brand awareness can be characterized by depth and breadth. The depth of brand awareness relates to the likelihood that the brand can be recognized or recalled. The breadth of brand awareness relates to the variety of purchase and consumption situations in which the brand comes to mind. Brand image is defined as consumer perceptions of a brand as reflected by the brand associations held in consumers' memory.

Customer-based brand equity occurs when the consumer has a high level of awareness and familiarity with the brand and holds some strong, favorable, and unique brand associations in memory. In some cases, brand awareness alone is suffi-cient to result in more favorable consumer response, such as in low involvement deci-sion settings where consumers are willing to base their choices merely on familiar brands. In other cases, the strength, favorability, and uniqueness of the brand associa-tions play a critical role in determining the differential response making up the brand equity.

Associations will vary in the strength of their connection to the brand node. Strength is a function of both the amount or quantity of processing the information receives and the nature or quality of that processing. The more deeply a person thinks about product information and relates it to existing brand knowledge, the stronger the resulting brand associations. Two factors facilitating the strength of association to any piece of information is the personal relevance of the information and the consistency with which this information is presented over time.

Favorable associations for a brand are those associations that are desirable to consumers and are successfully delivered by the product and conveyed by the supporting marketing program for the brand. Not all brand associations will be deemed important and viewed favorably by consumers, nor will they be equally valued across different purchase or consumption situations.

To create the differential response that leads to customer-based brand equity, it is important to associate unique, meaningful points of difference to the brand to provide a competitive advantage and a reason why consumers should buy it. For some brand associations, however, it may be sufficient that they are seen as roughly equally favorable with competing brand associations so that they function as points of parity in consumers' minds to negate potential points of difference for competitors. In other words, these associations are designed to provide no reason why not for consumers to choose the brand.

Assuming a positive brand image is created by marketing programs that link strong, favorable, and unique associations to the brand in memory, a number of benefits can result (see Figure 2–4). The chapter concluded by summarizing the chief ingredients to the customer-based brand equity framework that provides guidance as to how to build, measure, and manage brand equity (see Figures 2–9 to 2–11). Building brand equity will depend on three factors: (1) the initial choices for the brand elements or identities making up the brand, (2) the way the brand is integrated into the supporting marketing program, and (3) the associations indirectly transferred to the brand by linking the brand to some other entity (e.g., the company, country of origin, channel of distribution, or another brand). Measuring brand equity requires measuring sources and outcomes of brand equity and implementing a brand equity measurement system. Managing brand equity concerns those activities that take a broader and more diverse perspective of the brand's equity—understanding how branding strategies should reflect corporate concerns and be adjusted, if at all, over time or over geographical boundaries. Effectively managing brand equity includes defining the branding strategy for the firm by defining the brand hierarchy and brand-product matrix and devising policy for brand fortification and leverage over time and over geographical boundaries.

Organization of the Book

These first two chapters have discussed the importance of and challenge in handling brands, as well as briefly highlighted some of the decisions that have to be made in building, measuring, and managing brand equity and the tools that can be used to help make those decisions. The remainder of the book addresses in much greater depth how to build brand equity (chapters 3–7 in Part II), measure brand equity (chapters 8–10 in Part III), and manage brand equity (chapters 11–14 in Part IV). The concluding chapter (15) and appendices provides some additional applications.

Discussion Questions

1. Pick a brand. Attempt to identify its sources of brand equity. Assess its level of brand awareness and the strength, favorability, and uniqueness of its associations.
2. Pick a brand. Assess the extent to which the brand is achieving the various benefits of brand equity.

Notes

1. Kevin Lane Keller, "Conceptualizing, Measuring, and Managing Customer-Based Brand Equity," *Journal of Marketing* (January 1993), pp. 1–29.
2. As with product, we use the term "consumer" broadly to encompass all types of customers, including individuals as well as organizations.
3. Leslie de Chernatony and Simon Knox, "How an Appreciation of Consumer Behaviour Can Help in Product Testing," *Journal of Market Research Society*, 32 (3) (July 1990), p. 333.
4. John R. Anderson, *The Architecture of Cognition*, Cambridge, MA: Harvard University Press, 1983; Robert S. Wyer, Jr. and Thomas K. Srull, "Person Memory and Judgment," *Psychological Review,* 96(1) (1989), 58–83.
5. John R. Rossiter and Larry Percy, *Advertising and Promotion Management*, New York: McGraw-Hill, 1987.
6. Joseph W. Alba and J. Wesley Hutchinson, "Dimensions of Consumer Expertise," *Journal of Consumer Research*, 13 (March, 1987), pp. 411–453.
7. Ian M. Lewis, "Brand Equity or Why the Board of Directors Needs Marketing Research," ARF Fifth Annual Advertising and Promotion Workshop, February 1, 1993.
8. Andrew S.C. Ehrenberg, Gerard J. Goodhardt, and T. Patrick Barwise, "Double Jeopardy Revisited," *Journal of Marketing*, 54 (July, 1990), pp. 82–91.
9. Jacob Jacoby and Robert Chestnut, *Brand Loyalty: Measurement and Management*, New York: Ronald Press, 1978.
10. Tod Johnson, "The Inherent Value of Brands: Results From Over Fifteen Years of Brand Loyalty Data," Third Annual ARF Advertising and Promotion Workshop; James C. Crimmins, "Better Measurement and Management of Brand Equity," Fourth Annual ARF Advertising and Promotion Workshop, February 12–13, 1992.
11. Susan Caminit, "The Payoff from a Good Corporate Reputation," *Fortune* (February 10, 1992), pp. 74–77.
12. Hermann Simon, "Dynamics of Price Elasticity and Brand Life Cycles: An Empirical Study," *Journal of Marketing Research*, 16 (November 1979), pp. 439–452.
13. Lakshman Krishnamurthi and S.P. Raj, "An Empirical Analysis of the Relationship Between Brand Loyalty and Consumer Price Elasticity," *Marketing Science* (Spring 1991), 10(2), 172–183.
14. William Boulding, Eunkyu Lee, and Richard Staelin, "Mastering the Mix: Do Advertising, Promotion, and Sales Force Activities Lead to Differentiation?", *Journal of Marketing Research*, 31 (May, 1994), pp. 159–172.
15. Kyle Pope, "Computers: They're No Commodity," *Wall Street Journal* (October 15, 1993), p. B1.
16. Ira Teinowitz, "Marlboro Friday: Still Smoking," *Advertising Age* (March 28, 1994), p. 24.
17. Lois Therrien, "Brands on the Run," *Business Week* (April 9, 1993), pp. 26–29.

18. David B. Montgomery, "New Product Distribution: An Analysis of Supermarket Buyer Decisions," *Journal of Marketing Research*, 12(3), (1978), 255–264.

19. Russell L. Ackoff and James R. Emshoff, "Advertising Research at Anheuser-Busch, Inc. (1963–1968), *Sloan Management Review* (Winter 1975), pp. 1–15.

20. See Robert C. Blattberg, Richard Briesch, and Edward J. Fox, "How Promotions Work," *Marketing Science*, 14, G122–G132. See also Bart J. Bronnenberg and Luc Wathieu, "Asymmetric Promotion Effects and Brand Positioning," working paper, University of Texas, showing how the relative promotion effectiveness of high and low quality brands depends on their positioning along both price and quality dimensions.

21. Frank E. James, "I'll Wear the Coke Pants Tonight; They Go Well With My Harley-Davidson Ring," *Wall Street Journal* (June 6, 1985), Sect. 2, p. 31.

22. Joel Rubinson, "Brand Strength Means More Than Market Share," ARF Fourth Annual Advertising and Promotion Workshop, February 12–13, 1992.

CHAPTER # Brand Knowledge Structures

Preview

The first two chapters have provided some perspective on branding, defined and described the concept of customer-based brand equity, and highlighted some basic considerations as to how brand equity can be built, measured, and managed. Customer-based brand equity was defined as the differential effect that brand knowledge has on customer response to the marketing of that brand. According to the customer-based brand equity framework, brand knowledge in consumers' minds is central to the creation and management of brand equity. Brand knowledge can be conceptualized in terms of a brand node in memory with brand associations, varying in strength, connected to it. Brand equity is then a function of the level, or depth and breadth, of brand awareness and the strength, favorability, and uniqueness of brand associations.

In the next five chapters, we consider in greater detail how brand knowledge structures can be created to build sources of brand equity. In this chapter, we first review the different types of brand awareness and the resulting consequences of having a high level of awareness. Next, we classify the different types of associations that can be linked to the brand as part of its brand image. We then present general factors affecting the strength, favorability, and uniqueness of brand associations. The chapter concludes by considering how to define desired or ideal brand knowledge structures and how to position a brand. Chapters 4 through 7 then describe specific strategies and tactics that the firm can take to build brand equity.

Brand Awareness

As described in chapter 1, the process of branding requires "labeling" a product through one or more brand elements (e.g., a brand name, logo, or symbol) and creating "meaning" for the brand as to what it is and how it is different from other brands through product design and the manner by which it is marketed. In terms of the former consideration, *brand awareness* is related to the strength of the resulting brand node or trace in memory, as reflected by consumers' ability to identify the brand under different conditions. In other words, how well do the brand elements serve the function of identifying the product?

Creating brand awareness involves giving the product an identity by linking brand elements to a product category and associated purchase and consumption or usage situations. From a strategic standpoint, it is important to have high levels of brand awareness under a variety of conditions and circumstances. In this section, we consider the two main types of brand awareness—brand recognition and brand recall—and examine the various advantages of having a high level of brand awareness. We also explore issues related to how brand knowledge is organized in memory by considering category structure.

TYPES OF BRAND AWARENESS

Brand awareness consists of brand recognition and brand recall performance. *Brand recognition* relates to consumers' ability to confirm prior exposure to the brand when given the brand as a cue. In other words, brand recognition requires that consumers can correctly discriminate the brand as having been previously seen or heard. For example, when consumers go to the store, will they be able to recognize the brand as one to which they had already been exposed? *Brand recall* relates to consumers' ability to retrieve the brand from memory when given the product category, the needs fulfilled by the category, or a purchase or usage situation as a cue. In other words, brand recall requires that consumers correctly generate the brand from memory when given a relevant probe. For example, recall of Kellogg's Corn Flakes will depend on consumers' ability to retrieve the brand when they think of the cereal category or what they should eat for breakfast or a snack, either at the store (when making a purchase) or at home (when making a consumption choice).

As is the case with most information in memory, it is generally easier to recognize a brand than it is to recall it from memory. The relative importance of brand recall and recognition will depend on the extent to which consumers make product-related decisions with the brand present or not.[1] For example, if product decisions are made in the store, brand recognition may be more important because the brand will actually be physically present. Outside the store or in any situation where the brand is not present, on the other hand, it is probably more important that the consumer be able to actually recall the brand from memory.

Brand awareness can be characterized according to depth and breadth. The *depth* of brand awareness concerns the likelihood that a brand element will come to mind and the ease with which it does so. For example, a brand that can be easily recalled has a deeper level of brand awareness than one that only can be recognized. The *breadth* of brand awareness concerns the range of purchase and usage situations where the brand element comes to mind. The breadth of brand awareness depends to a large extent on the organization of brand and product knowledge in memory.

To illustrate some of the issues involved, consider the breadth and depth of brand awareness for Tropicana orange juice. At the most basic level, it is necessary that consumers recognize the brand when it is presented or exposed to them. Beyond that, consumers should think of Tropicana whenever they think of orange juice, particularly when they are considering a purchase in that category. Additionally, consumers ideally would think of Tropicana whenever they were deciding which type of beverage to drink, especially when seeking a "tasty but healthy" beverage—some of the needs presumably satisfied by orange juice. Thus, consumers must think of Tropicana in terms of satisfying a certain set of needs whenever those needs arise. One of the challenges for any provider of orange juice in that regard is to link the product to usage situations outside of the traditional breakfast usage situation—hence the industry campaign to boost consumption of Florida orange juice that used the slogan, "It's not just for breakfast anymore."

As suggested by the Tropicana example, to fully understand brand recall, it is important to appreciate *product category structure* or how product categories are organized in memory. Typically, marketers assume that products are often grouped at varying levels of specificity and can be organized in a hierarchical fashion. For example, according to Mita Sujan, a pioneer in the study of consumer categorization processes:[2] "One could group a set of products into broad, superordinate product classes such as 'cars' or 'cameras'; into less inclusive product categories such as '35mm cameras' or '110 cameras'; into more specific product types such as '35mm cameras with advanced features' or into many specific brand-level categories such as 'Canon AE-1 cameras' or 'Minolta XD 11 cameras.' " Thus, in consumers' minds, a product hierarchy often exists with product class information at the highest level, product category information at the second highest level, product type information at the next level, and brand information at the lowest level.

The beverage market provides a good setting to examine issues in category structure and the effects of brand awareness on brand equity. Figure 3–1 contains a schematic depiction of one possible hierarchy that might exist in consumers' minds. According to this representation, consumers first distinguish between flavored or non-flavored beverages (water). Next, they distinguish between non-alcoholic and alcoholic flavored beverages. Non-alcoholic beverages are further distinguished in consumers' minds by whether they are hot (coffee or tea) or cold (milk, juices or soft drinks); alcoholic beverages are further distinguished by whether they are wine, beer, or distilled spirits. Even further distinctions are possible. For example, the beer category could be further divided into no-alcohol, low-alcohol (or "light"), and full-strength beers. Full-strength beers can be further distinguished along a number of different dimensions—by variety (e.g., ale or lager), by brewing method (e.g.,

FIGURE 3–1 Beverage Category Hierarchy

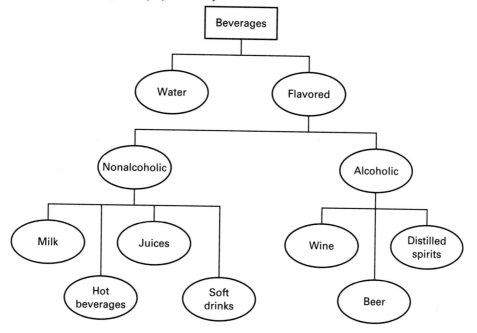

draft, ice, or dry), by price and quality (discount, premium, or super-premium), and so on.

The organization of the product category hierarchy that generally prevails in memory will play an important role in consumer decision making. For example, consumers often make decisions in what could be considered a "top-down" fashion. Based on this simple representation, a consumer would first decide whether to have water or some type of flavored beverage. If the consumer chose a flavored drink, then the next decision would be whether to have an alcoholic or non-alcoholic drink, and so on. Finally, consumers might then choose the particular brand within the particular product category or product type with which they are interested. The depth of brand awareness would then relate to the likelihood that the brand came to mind, whereas the breadth of brand awareness would relate to the different types of situations in which the brand might come to mind. In general, soft drinks have much breadth in awareness in that they come to mind in a variety of different consumption situations. A consumer may consider drinking one of the different cola varieties of Coke virtually anytime, anywhere. Other beverages have much more limited perceived consumption situations, for example, alcoholic beverages, milk, and juices.

Strategically, understanding the product hierarchy has important implications for how to improve brand awareness, as well as how to properly position the brand (as will be addressed later in this chapter). In terms of building awareness, in many cases, it is not only the depth of awareness that matters but also the breadth and properly linking the brand to various categories and cues in consumers' minds. In other words, it is important that the brand not only be "top-of-mind" and have sufficient "mind share" but it must also do so at the right times and places. Breadth is an often neglected consideration, even for brands that are category leaders. For many brands, the key question is not whether consumers can recall the brand, but instead, where do they think of the brand, when they do think of the brand, and how easily and often do they think of the brand?

The importance of categorization and the product category hierarchy concept can be seen by considering various scenarios, again in the beverage industry. Take Snapple for instance. From its start as an iced tea, Snapple essentially pioneered a new category of "new age" beverages. In creating this category, Snapple strategically positioned itself as having more flavor than bottled waters but being more healthful than soft drinks and lighter than fruit juices. From an awareness standpoint, it is therefore important that consumers consider drinking Snapple in exactly the same type of situations as those other beverages. Although Snapple achieved much early success, such a categorization can be tricky given the pervasiveness and intensity of marketing activity in the beverage market. For example, Seven-Up has struggled for years to create the proper categorization for its brand in the beverage market. The historical positioning of 7UP as an "Uncola" has been one way that Seven-Up marketing managers have tried to transcend the brand's early origins as a mixer to expand its sales opportunities. The hope has been that consumers would categorize 7UP as a "cola alternative" in the soft drink category and thus think of it whenever they might think of drinking a Coke or Pepsi. The strategy has met with mixed success, and despite new packaging and a new jingle ("It's an Up Thing"), 7UP has fallen considerably behind its chief competitor, Coca-Cola's Sprite brand.

CONSEQUENCES OF BRAND AWARENESS

What are the advantages of creating a high level of brand awareness? Brand awareness plays an important role in consumer decision making for three main reasons.

First, as suggested above, it is important that consumers think of and consider the brand whenever they are making a purchase for which the brand could potentially be acceptable, or whenever they are consuming a product whose needs the brand could potentially satisfy. In particular, raising brand awareness increases the likelihood that the brand will be a member of the *consideration set*, the handful of brands that receives serious consideration for purchase.[3] Much research has shown that consumers are rarely loyal to only one brand but instead have a set of brands that they would consider buying and another—possibly smaller—set of brands that they actually buy on a regular basis. Because consumers typically only consider a few brands for purchase, making sure that the brand is in the consideration set also means that *other* brands may be less likely to be considered or recalled. Research in psychology on "part-list cuing effects" has shown that recall of some information can inhibit recall of other information.[4] In a marketing context, that means that if a consumer thinks of going to Burger King for a quick lunch, he or she may be less likely to think of going to other types of fast food restaurants such as Kentucky Fried Chicken or Taco Bell.[5]

The second advantage of creating a high level of brand awareness is that brand awareness can affect choices among brands in the consideration set, even if there are essentially no other associations to those brands. For example, consumers have been shown to adopt a decision rule in some cases to buy only more familiar, well-established brands.[6] Thus, in low-involvement decision settings, a minimum level of brand awareness may be sufficient enough for product choice, even in the absence of a well-formed attitude.[7] One influential model of attitude change and persuasion, the elaboration-likelihood model, is consistent with the notion that consumers may make choices based on brand awareness considerations when they have low involvement. Low involvement results when consumers lack either purchase motivation (e.g., when consumers don't care about the product or service) or purchase ability (e.g., when consumers do not know anything else about the brands in a category).[8]

In terms of consumer purchase motivation, although products and brands may be critically important to marketers, to many consumers in many categories, choosing a brand is not a "life or death" decision. For example, despite spending millions of dollars in TV advertising over the years to persuade consumers of product differences, one recent survey showed that 40 percent of consumers believed all brands of gasoline were about the same or did not know which brand of gasoline was best. A lack of perceived differences among brands in a category is likely to lead to unmotivated consumers in the brand choice process.

In terms of consumer purchase ability, consumers in some product categories just do not have the necessary knowledge or experience to be able to judge product quality even if they so desired. The obvious examples are products with a high degree of technical sophistication. Yet, at the same time, there are other instances with seemingly less complicated product specifications where consumers still may lack the necessary ability to judge quality. Consider the college student who has not really had to cook or clean before on his or her own roaming the supermarket aisles for the first time. The reality is that product quality is often highly ambiguous and difficult to judge without a great deal of prior experience and expertise. In such cases, consumers will use whatever short-cut or heuristic that they can come up with to make their decisions in the best manner possible. At times, they may end up just choosing the brand with which they are most aware and familiar. We discuss the role of perceived quality in consumer decisions in greater detail below.

Finally, the third way that brand awareness affects consumer decision making is by influencing the formation and strength of brand associations that make up the brand image. A necessary condition for the creation of a brand image is that a brand node has been established in memory, and the nature of that brand node should affect how easily different kinds of information can become attached to the brand in memory as brand associations. As will be described in chapter 4, the first step in building brand equity is to register the brand into the minds of consumers, and the choice of the brand elements may make that task easier or more difficult.

ESTABLISHING BRAND AWARENESS

How do you create brand awareness? In general, the more a consumer "experiences" the brand by seeing it, hearing it, or thinking about it, the more likely it is that the brand becomes strongly registered in memory. Thus, anything that causes consumers to experience a brand name, symbol, logo, character, packaging, or slogan can potentially increase familiarity and awareness of that brand element—through advertising and promotion, sponsorship and event marketing, publicity and public relations, and outdoor advertising. Although brand repetition increases brand recognition, improving brand recall requires links in memory to the appropriate product category or other situational purchase or consumption cues. That is, although brand repetition increases the strength of a brand in memory and thus its recognizability, improving recall of a brand requires linkages in memory to the appropriate cues such as the product or service category. Pairing a brand with its corresponding product or service category through sponsorship, advertising, promotion, and the like can help to establish these links and facilitate brand recall.

It should be noted that the manner by which the brand and its corresponding category are paired (e.g., as with an advertising slogan) will also be influential in determining the strength of product category links. For brands with strong category associations (e.g., Ford), the distinction between brand recognition and recall may not matter much. For brands that may not have the same level of initial category awareness, such as in competitive markets or when the brand is new to the category, then it is more important to emphasize category links in the marketing program. Moreover, as will be discussed in chapter 11, strongly linking the brand to the proper category or other relevant cues may become especially important over time if the product meaning of the brand changes (e.g., through brand extensions or mergers or acquisitions).

Brand Image

Brand awareness is a necessary, but not always sufficient, step in building brand equity. Other considerations, such as the image of the brand, often come into play. Brand image long has been recognized as an important concept in marketing.[9] Although there has not always been agreement on how to measure brand image,[10] one generally accepted view is that, consistent with an associative network memory model, *brand image* can be defined as perceptions about a brand as reflected by the brand associations held in consumer memory.[11] Brand associations are the other informational nodes linked to the brand node in memory and contain the meaning of the brand for consumers. The strength, favorability, and uniqueness of brand associations play an important role in determining the differential response that makes up brand equity, especially in high involvement decision settings where consumer motivation and ability are sufficiently present. Before considering these three dimensions in more detail, it is useful to first describe the different types of brand associations that may exist in consumer memory.

TYPES OF BRAND ASSOCIATIONS

As the Apple computer example in chapter 2 showed, brand associations come in many different forms. One way to distinguish among brand associations is by their level of abstraction, that is, by how much information is summarized or subsumed in the association.[12] Along these lines, brand associations can be classified into three major categories of increasing scope: attributes, benefits, and attitudes. Several additional distinctions can also be made within these categories according to the qualitative nature of the association. Figure 3–2 schematically summarizes the different types of brand associations and dimensions of brand knowledge which we now discuss in detail.

Attributes

Attributes are those descriptive features that characterize a product or service, such as what a consumer thinks the product or service is or has and what is involved with its purchase or consumption. Attributes can be categorized in a variety of ways.[13] Here, we distinguish attributes according to how directly they relate to product or service performance: *Product-related attributes* are defined as the ingredients necessary for performing the product or service function sought by consumers, and *non-product-related attributes* are defined as external aspects of the product or service that often relate to its purchase or consumption in some way. Issues surrounding each are discussed in turn.

Product-Related Attributes   Product-related attributes refer to a product's physical composition or a service's requirements and are what determine the nature and level of product performance. Product-related attributes can be further distinguished according to essential ingredients and optional features, either necessary for a product to work, or allowing for customization and more versatile, personalized usage. Product-related attributes vary by product or service category:[14]

1. Some categories have few ingredients or features. For bread, essential ingredients might include the grain and yeast flavors, texture, nutrition content (in terms of complex carbohydrates, fiber, protein, iron, and vitamins and minerals), with few other distinguishing features.

2. Other products have many essential ingredients but few features. For a toaster oven, essential ingredients might include a housing of plastic and metal, an oven pan, hinged

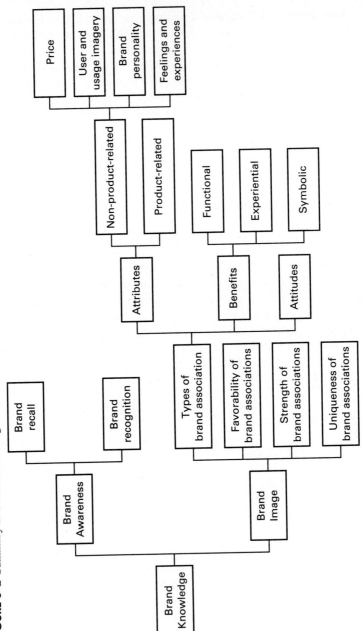

FIGURE 3–2 Summary of Brand Knowledge

crumb tray, and broiling grid, a clear glass door, 1200- to 1600-watt draw, and 2- to 3-foot power cord. Optional features might include safety features (such as automatic shut-off when door is opened), a toast-ready bell, and certain settings.

3. Finally, some products have numerous ingredients and features. For a portable tape player or "boom box," essential ingredients might include an AM/FM stereo radio, programmable CD player, and at least one cassette deck, at least two speaker drives, an ability to record from radio or CD player, an AC power cord, an ability to operate on batteries (generally eight D cells), and a telescoping antenna that pivots. Features might include a clock, extra bass, graphic equalizer, inputs/outputs, lights, and surround sound with extra features for the CD player and cassette deck.

Non-Product-Related Attributes   Non-product-related attributes may affect the purchase or consumption process but do not directly affect the product performance. Non-product-related attributes arise from the marketing mix and how the product is marketed. All kinds of associations can become linked to the brand that do not directly relate to product performance, for example, the color of the product or look of its package, the company or person that makes the product and the country in which it is made, the type of store in which it is sold, the events for which the brand is a sponsor and the people who endorse the brand, and so on. These types of associations are discussed in detail in chapters 4 and 7. In this section, we highlight five other types of non-product-related attributes:

1. Price
2. User imagery (i.e., what type of person uses the product or service)
3. Usage imagery (i.e., where and under what types of situations the product or service is used)
4. Feelings and experiences
5. Brand personality

Price.   The price of the product or service is considered a non-product-related attribute since it represents a necessary step in the purchase process but typically does not directly relate to the product performance or service function. Price is a particularly important attribute association because consumers often have strong beliefs about the price and value of a brand and may organize their product category knowledge in terms of the price tiers of different brands.[15] Chapter 5 describes issues with price associations in greater detail.

User and usage imagery.   User and usage imagery attributes can be formed directly from a consumer's own experiences and contact with brand users or indirectly through the depiction of the target market and usage situation as communicated in brand advertising or by some other source of information (e.g., word-of-mouth).

Associations of a typical brand user may be based on descriptive demographic factors or more abstract psychographic factors. For example, demographic factors might include:

1. *Gender:* Virginia Slims cigarettes and Secret deodorant have "feminine" associations whereas Marlboro cigarettes and Right Guard deodorant have more "masculine" associations.

2. *Age:* Pepsi cola, Powerade energy sports drink, and Fuji film position themselves as younger than Coke, Gatorade, and Kodak, respectively.

3. *Race:* Goya foods have a strong identification with the Hispanic market.

4. *Income:* During the 1980s BMW automobiles became associated with "yuppie" owners, young, affluent, urban professionals.

The types of psychographic factors making up user imagery might include attitudes toward career, possessions, social issues, or political institutions.

As an example of user imagery, a recent study determined how one market segment of American beer drinkers—men aged 21 to 49 who drink at least six beers weekly—envisioned the typical user of three major brands of beer.[16] Specifically, 100 of these consumers were each given the same 98 photographs of different people and were asked to match each picture with the brand of beer that the person in the photograph probably drank. The following portraits emerged:

- Budweiser drinker: Tough, grizzled, blue collar
- Miller drinker: Light-blue collar, civilized, and friendly
- Coors drinker: Somewhat more feminine image

Consumers were also asked whether they identified with the photo subjects they assigned to each brand. The highest scores went to Miller (66 percent), with Coors and Budweiser trailing (43 percent and 42 percent, respectively).

Associations of a typical usage situation may be based on the time of day, week, or year, the location (inside or outside the home), or the type of activity (formal or informal). For example, advertising for Snickers emphasizes how the candy bar is "packed with peanuts" and therefore "satisfies" as a healthy, filling snack. Miller High Life has been advertised in terms of "Miller Time"—a relaxing, rewarding part of the day. Norwegian Cruise Lines advertises that "it's different out there" in sexy, youthful ads. Excedrin has been advertised according to usage application as the "headache medicine" to contrast it from Tylenol's perceived usage advantage as the best pain reliever to alleviate aches and pains. For a long-time, pizza chain restaurants had strong associations to their channels of distribution and the manner by which customers would purchase and eat the pizza—Domino's was known for delivery, Little Caesar for carry-out, and Pizza Hut for dine-in service—although in recent years each of these major competitors has made inroads in the traditional markets of the others.

Feelings and experiences.   Josh McQueen from Leo Burnett ad agency notes that for the 200 or so brands that are handled by the agency, emotional rewards are often at the heart of the motivation that builds the value of brand equity. According to McQueen, emotions help give products meaning and increase product use satisfaction while also potentially enhancing product perceptions. The feelings associated with a brand and the emotions they evoke can become so strongly associated that they are accessible during product consumption or use. Researchers have defined transformational advertising as advertising designed to change consumer's perceptions of the actual usage experience with the product.[17] For example, Coast soap advertises its brand as the "eye-opener" in an attempt to change consumers' perceptions about what it feels like to use the product (i.e., "invigorating").

Julie Edell and Marian Moore from Duke University have studied feelings in an advertising context and have identified four different types of feelings consumers can experience while viewing a television ad:[18]

1. *Upbeat feelings:* Amused, carefree, cheerful, happy, playful, and silly
2. *Warm feelings:* Affectionate, hopeful, kind, peaceful, and warm
3. *Disinterested feelings*: Critical, disinterested, offended, skeptical, and suspicious
4. *Uneasy feelings:* Sad, uneasy, lonely, anxious, regretful, and concerned

Through repeated advertising exposure or some other means, it would seem that at least some of these feelings may also become associated to the brand. For example, Pacific Bell ran a highly successful campaign in California in the mid-1980s that focused on the emotional rewards of calling someone on the telephone as opposed to more practical or functional reasons.

Brand personality.   Brands may also take on personality traits similar to people.[19] A brand, like a person, can be characterized as being "modern," "old fashioned," "lively," or "exotic." Brand personality reflects how people feel about a brand rather than what they think the brand is or does.[20] A brand with the right personality can result in a consumer feeling that the brand is relevant and "my kind of product." A consumer may be more willing to invest in a relationship or even develop a "friendship" with the brand as a result. Advertising in particular often needs to reflect the appropriate brand personality. The first question members of the creative department in an ad agency often ask a new client is, "What is the personality of the brand?" The answer that is given often takes on great importance as they develop the ad campaign.

A market research study on coffee conducted a few years ago reveals how the personality of a brand can impact its performance.[21] Initial research showed that Maxwell House was seen by consumers as a reliable, honest brand of coffee, whereas Folgers, as the result of a long-standing ad campaign, was seen by consumers as the "mountain-grown" coffee. Despite seemingly favorable perceptions for both brands, Maxwell House was losing market share. One possible reason why was uncovered in a followup research study that asked consumers to describe what sort of person each brand might represent. Although consumers described Folgers as "exciting" and "smart-looking," Maxwell House was described as somewhat "likable" but "boring." Consumers felt the Maxwell House brand didn't care about them and took their business for granted. These research insights suggested that the brand personality of Maxwell House needed to be changed for the brand to regain its footing in the marketplace.

How does brand personality get formed? Branding Brief 3–1 describes some of the trials and tribulations in creating a brand personality for Dr. Pepper soft drink. Although any aspect of the marketing program may affect brand personality, advertising may be especially influential because of the inferences consumers make about the underlying user or usage situation depicted in an ad. Advertisers may imbue a brand with personality traits through anthropomorphization and product animation techniques (e.g., California Raisins), personification through the use of brand characters (e.g., Jolly Green Giant), or the creation of user imagery (e.g., Charlie girl).[22] More generally, advertising may affect brand personality by the manner in which it depicts the brand, for example, by the actors in an ad, the tone or style of the creative strategy, and the emotions or feelings evoked by the brand.

BRANDING BRIEF 3-1

To Be a Pepper or Not to Be a Pepper . . .

Defining the target market can have profound implications on the resulting positioning. The extent to which users and non-users agree can provide strategic direction. Dr. Pepper is an unusual tasting soft drink with an unusual name. Its first major ad campaign stressed that it was "America's Most Misunderstood Soft Drink," establishing the brand as a feisty, irreverent underdog that stood out from the crowd. Later ads repositioned the brand, however, in different directions.

For example, to capitalize on its growing popularity, the "Be a Pepper" campaign was launched. This mainstream shift created problems because although some loyal Dr. Pepper drinkers still saw the brand as original, fun, and offbeat, in spite of the advertising, others rejected the new mainstream appeal. Recognizing this shift, Dr. Pepper returned to a campaign stressing the brand's individuality by urging consumers to "Hold Out for the Out of the Ordinary." The shift brought new and old users into the fold and led to sales growth in the 1980s. More recently, however, Dr. Pepper has reverted back to a more mass appeal, invoking heart-tugging images of small-town America.[a] This shift created an opportunity for the brand to recapture its heritage with these underdog supporters. New ads proclaim that the brand is "Just What the Dr. Ordered."

In the soft drink category, for years there was a high degree of agreement in brand personality for the two giants—Coke and Pepsi. Pepsi had always differentiated itself on the basis of a younger and more energetic image. Coke, on the other hand, had been seen as more mainstream and predictable. To better counteract Pepsi's appeal, Coke developed the youthful, unorthodox "Always" ad campaign. As compared to these brand leaders, however, Dr. Pepper has had a hard time finding the right brand personality to retain current customers and attract new ones.

---

[a]Ronald Alsop, "Dr. Pepper Is Bubbling Again After Its 'Be a Pepper' Setback," *Wall Street Journal* (September 26, 1985), p. 33. Betsy Sharkey, "David Naughton: Wouldn't He Like to Be a Pepper II?" *ADWEEK* (May 16, 1988), p. 10. Kevin Goldman, "Dr. Pepper Wraps Ads in Stars and Stripes," *Wall Street Journal*, Oct. 4, 1993, p. 133.

Although user imagery, especially as depicted by advertising, is a prime source of brand personality, user imagery and brand personality may not always be in agreement. In product categories where product-related attributes are more central in consumer decisions (e.g., food products), brand personality and user imagery may be much less related, but differences may arise in other instances. For example, at one point in time, Perrier's brand personality was "sophisticated" and "stylish" where its actual user imagery was not as flattering or subdued but seen more as "flashy" and "trendy."

As another example of the relationship between brand personality and user imagery, consider the history of *USA Today*. When the newspaper was first introduced, a research study exploring consumer opinions of the newspaper indicated that the benefits of *USA Today* perceived by readers and non-readers were highly consistent. Similarly, perceptions of the *USA Today* brand personality—as colorful, friendly, and simple—were also highly related. User imagery, however, differed dramatically: Non-readers viewed a typical *USA Today* reader as a shallow "air head"; readers, on the other hand, saw a typical *USA Today* reader as a well-rounded person interested in a variety of issues. Based on these findings, an advertising campaign was introduced to appeal to non-readers that showed how prominent people endorsed the newspaper.[23]

In those categories where user and usage imagery are important to consumer decisions, however, brand personality and user imagery are more likely to be related, such as with cars, beer, liquor, cigarettes, and cosmetics. Thus, consumers often choose and use brands that have a brand personality that is consistent with their own self-concept, although in some cases the match may be based on consumer's desired self-image rather than their actual self-image.[24]

Benefits

The second main type of associations is benefits. Benefits are the personal value and meaning that consumers attach to the product or service attributes—what consumers think the product or service can do for them and what it represents more broadly. For example, the benefits of an air conditioner might include comfort, how quietly it performs, and how it performs under adverse weather conditions. Benefits can be further distinguished into three categories according to the underlying motivations to which they relate: functional benefits, symbolic benefits, and experiential benefits.[25]

Functional benefits are the more intrinsic advantages of product or service consumption and usually correspond to product-related attributes. These benefits are often linked to fairly basic motivations such as physiological and safety needs and involve a desire to satisfy problem removal or avoidance.[26] For example, functional benefits of a shampoo might be that it eliminates dandruff, removes greasiness, makes hair and scalp healthy, and gives hair moisture and body. Representative brands with strong functional benefit associations might include Arm & Hammer, Ivory, Vaseline, Steelcase, Timex, and Volkswagen.

Symbolic benefits are the more extrinsic advantages of product or service consumption and usually correspond to non-product-related attributes, especially user imagery. Symbolic benefits relate to underlying needs for social approval or personal expression and outer-directed self-esteem. Thus, consumers may value the prestige, exclusivity, or fashionability of a brand because of how it relates to their self-concepts.[27] For example, symbolic benefits of a shampoo might be that it assures users that they are using a product only used by "beautiful people" who appreciate the "good things in life."

Symbolic benefits should be especially relevant for socially visible, "badge" products. A badge product is one where consumers believe that brand usage signals or conveys some information about the person to others. Figure 3–3 contains the results of a recent survey conducted in Australia to determine the extent to which consumers felt that brand choices and usage in various product categories indicated the personality or suggested something about the brand user. Representative brands with strong symbolic benefits might include Brooks Bros., Calvin Klein, Lenox, Rolex, Gucci, Jaguar, and Tiffany.

Product Personalities Agree Ratings	
Q. Do you agree or disagree that you can tell something about a person by the brand of _____ he/she buys?	
Product categories:	%
Perfume (women only)	78
Department store	69
Wine	68
Aftershave (men only)	62
Boxed chocolates	49
Instant coffee	47
Beer	46
Cigarettes	40
Pet food	32
Toilet paper	30
Toothpaste	27
Facial tissues	27
Potato chips	20

Sample: 1300. *Source:* Frank Small & Associates

FIGURE 3-3 Perceptions of Category Users

Experiential benefits relate to what it feels like to use the product or service and can correspond to both product-related attributes as well as non-product-related attributes such as usage imagery. These benefits satisfy experiential needs such as sensory pleasure (sight, taste, sound, smell, or feel), variety, and cognitive stimulation. For example, experiential benefits of a shampoo might involve its scent and lather and the feelings of beauty and cleanliness when applying or using the product. Representative brands with strong experiential benefit associations might include Disney, Kodak, Mountain Dew, Nike, and Carnival cruise lines.

Attitudes

The most abstract and highest-level type of brand associations are attitudes. *Brand attitudes* are defined in terms of consumers' overall evaluations of a brand.[28] Brand attitudes are important because they often form the basis for actions and behavior that consumers take with the brand (e.g., brand choice). Consumers' brand attitudes generally depend on specific considerations concerning the attributes and benefits of the brand. For example, the multi-attribute attitude model in psychology suggests that overall brand attitudes depend on the strength of association between the brand and salient attributes or benefits and the favorability of those attribute or benefit beliefs.

Consider Sheraton hotels. A consumer's attitude toward Sheraton depends on how much he or she believes that the brand is characterized by certain associations that matter to the consumer for a hotel chain (e.g., locational convenience; room comfort, design, and appearance; service quality of staff; recreational facilities; food service; security; prices). Branding Brief 3–2 describes in more detail how social psychol-

---

Understanding Brand Attitudes

There are several different ways to conceptualize or model attitudes. Here we highlight two such ways with clear branding implications. One view takes the position that consumers form attitudes because they provide a function of some kind for a person. One social psychologist, Daniel Katz, developed a functional theory of attitudes to account for the different types of roles that attitudes can play. He identified four main functions:

1. The *utilitarian function* deals with attitudes formed on the basis of rewards and punishments.
2. The *value-expressive function* deals with attitudes formed to express an individual's central value or self-concept.
3. The *ego-defensive function* deals with attitudes formed to protect an individual from either external threats or internal feelings of insecurity.
4. The *knowledge function* deals with attitudes formed to satisfy an individual's need for order, structure, and meaning.

Consumers thus form attitudes toward brands to provide the function they are seeking. Thus, they might like and use certain brands because they satisfy their needs (utilitarian function), allow themselves to express their personality (value-expressive function), bolster a perceived weakness they have (ego-defensive function), or simplify decision making (knowledge function).

Perhaps the most widely accepted approach to actually modeling attitudes is based on a multi-attribute formulation, in which brand attitudes are seen as a function of the associated attributes and benefits that are salient for the brand. Fishbein and Ajzen[a] have proposed what has been probably the most influential multi-attribute model of models. As applied to marketing, this *expectancy-value* model views brand attitudes as a multiplicative function of the salient beliefs that a consumer has about the brand (i.e., the extent to which consumers think that the brand possesses certain attributes or benefits) and the evaluative judgment of those beliefs (i.e., how good or bad it is that the brand possesses those attributes or benefits).

Thus, overall brand attitudes depend on the strength of association between the brand and salient attributes or benefits and the favorability of those beliefs. According to the multi-attribute model, belief strength can be measured by having consumers rate the probability that the brand possesses each of the salient attributes or benefits, as follows.

How likely is it that Colgate toothpaste fights tooth decay?

Extremely   Extremely
Unlikely   1 2 3 4 5 6 7   Likely

Similarly, belief evaluations can be measured by having consumers rate the favorability of the salient attributes or benefits.

How good or bad is it that Colgate toothpaste fights tooth decay?

Very								Very
Bad	-3	-2	-1	0	1	2	3	Good

Overall brand attitudes are then the sum of each attribute belief strength multiplied by its favorability. Fishbein and Ajzen also developed the theory of reasoned action to extend the multi-attribute model to include interpersonal, social effects. According to the theory, attitudes toward brands can also depend on consumers' beliefs about other people's opinions as well as consumers' motivation to comply with these other people's wishes.

---

[a]Martin Fishbein and Icek Ajzen, *Belief, Attitude, Intention, and Behavior: An Introduction to Theory and Research.* Reading, MA: Addison-Wesley, 1975. Icek Ajzen and Martin Fishbein, *Understanding Attitudes and Predicting Social Behavior.* Upper Saddle River, NJ: Prentice Hall, 1980.

ogists have conceptualized and operationalized the multi-attribute model and how it has been applied in marketing. It is important to note that brand attitudes can be formed on the basis of: 1) beliefs about product-related attributes and functional benefits and/or 2) beliefs about non-product-related attributes and symbolic and experiential benefits.

One important reason why brand attitudes are considered to be a brand association is that they can vary in strength. Attitude strength has been measured in psychology by the reaction time to evaluative queries about the attitude object: Individuals who can evaluate an attitude object quickly are assumed to have a highly accessible attitude.[29] Research has shown that attitudes formed from direct behavior or experience are more accessible than attitudes based on information or other indirect forms of behavior.[30] Highly accessible brand attitudes are more likely to be activated spontaneously upon exposure to the brand and guide subsequent brand choices.[31] Because of the embedded meaning that they contain, abstract associations such as attitudes, or even benefits to some extent, tend to be inherently more evaluative than attributes. Because of this evaluative nature, more abstract associations can be more durable and accessible in memory than the underlying attribute information.[32] Moreover, brand attitudes may be stored and retrieved in memory separately from the underlying attribute information.[33] In fact, Claremont's Peter Farquhar believes that one key element of brand equity is attitude accessibility.[34]

In summary, a number of different types of associations may become linked to the brand. To create brand equity, it is important that the brand have some strong, favorable, and unique brand associations *in that order*. In other words, it doesn't matter how unique a brand association is unless consumers evaluate the association favorably, and it doesn't matter how desirable a brand association is unless it is sufficiently strong enough so that consumers actually recall it. At the same time, it should be recognized that not all strong associations are favorable and not all favorable associations are unique. Creating strong, favorable, and unique associations are a real challenge to marketers. We next consider some of the basic issues with respect to each of these three vital dimensions of brand equity.

STRENGTH OF BRAND ASSOCIATIONS

Associations can be characterized by the strength of connection to the brand node. The strength of brand associations are critical determinants of what information will be recalled by consumers and can therefore affect their brand decisions. In this section, we will consider the factors that, in general, affect the strength and recallability of a brand association. Chapters 4 through 7 provide more concrete guidelines.

Consumer beliefs about brand attributes and benefits can be formed in three main ways: (1) on the basis of direct experience with the brand; (2) on the basis of some form of communication about the brand (either from the firm or from some other non-partisan third-party sources); or (3) on the basis of some assumptions or inferences made from some other brand-related information. In general, the source of information creating the strongest brand associations is direct experience. This type of information can be particularly influential in consumers' product decisions, as long as consumers know how to interpret their experiences. As Figure 3–4 shows, according to at least one consumer survey, knowing what to expect from a product because of past experience was the most common reason for buying a particular brand. The next strongest associations are likely to be formed on the basis of word-of-mouth (friends, family, etc.) or other noncommercial sources of information (consumer unions, the popular press, etc.). Word-of-mouth is likely to be particularly important for restaurants, entertainment, banking, and personal services. Company-influenced sources of information such as advertising are often likely to create the weakest associations and thus may be the most easily changed.

FIGURE 3–4 Consumer Reasons for Brand Choice

(percent of adults who said that specified reasons were most important in deciding to buy a brand, 1992)

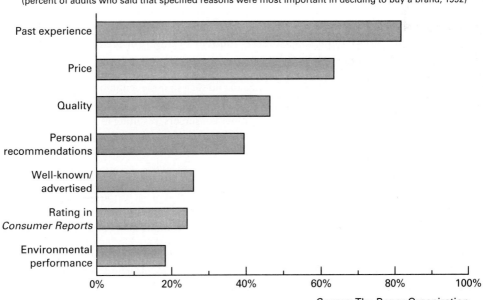

Source: The Roper Organization

Research in psychology provides some useful insights into some factors affecting association strength. In general, the strength of an association depends on how information is initially processed as it enters consumers' memory and where it is actually located as a result. Psychologists refer to these two processes as memory *encoding* and *storage*. Encoding processes can be characterized according to the amount or *quantity* of processing that information receives at encoding (i.e., how much a person thinks about the information) and the nature or *quality* of the processing that information receives at encoding (i.e., the manner in which a person thinks about the information). The quantity and quality of processing will be an important determinant of the strength of an association. Prior research has shown that a number of factors affect the quantity and quality of encoding processes and the accessibility of information from memory and the ability of consumers to recall or retrieve brand associations.[35] Here, we briefly highlight some of those factors.[36]

Quality and Quantity of Processing

In terms of qualitative considerations, in general, the more attention that is placed on the meaning of information during encoding, the stronger the resulting associations in memory will be.[37] Thus, when a consumer actively thinks about and "elaborates" on the significance of product or service information, stronger associations are created in memory. Another key determinant of the strength of a newly formed association will be the content, organization, and strength of existing brand associations in memory. All else equal, it will be easier for consumers to create an association to new information when extensive, relevant knowledge structures already exist in memory. One reason why personal experiences create such strong brand associations is that information about the product is likely to be related to existing knowledge due to its self-relevance.

To illustrate the issues involved, consider the brand associations that might be created by a new TV ad campaign employing a popular celebrity endorser designed to create a new benefit association for a well-known brand. For example, assume Bruce Springsteen and the song "Born to Run" were used to promote the "thrill" and "timeless appeal" of driving a Chevrolet. A number of different scenarios characterize how consumers might process such an ad:

1. Some consumers may barely notice the ad such that the amount of processing devoted to the ad is extremely low, resulting in weak to nonexistent brand associations.

2. The ad may catch the attention of other consumers, resulting in sufficient processing, but these consumers may devote most of the ad thinking about the song and wondering why Springsteen decided to endorse a Chevy (and whether he actually drove one), resulting in strong associations to Springsteen but not to Chevrolet.

3. Finally, another group of consumers may not only notice the ad but may think of how they had a wrong impression of Chevy and that it is "different" from the way they thought and that it looked fun to drive. The endorsement by Springsteen in this case helped to transfer and create some positive associations to the brand.

In addition to congruency or consistency with existing knowledge, the ease with which new information can be integrated into established knowledge structures clearly depends on the nature of that information, in terms of characteristics such as its inherent simplicity, vividness, and concreteness.

In terms of quantitative considerations, repeated exposures to information provide greater opportunity for processing and thus the potential for stronger associations. Recent advertising research in a field setting, however, suggests that qualitative considerations and the manner or style of consumer processing engendered by an ad are generally more important than the cumulative total of ad exposures per se.[38] In other words, high levels of repetition for an uninvolving, unpersuasive ad is unlikely to have as much sales impact as lower levels of repetition for an involving, persuasive ad.

In short, a number of factors will affect the strength of brand associations. Perhaps the two most important factors are the relevance of the brand information and the consistency with which that brand information is presented to consumers at any one point in time, as well as over time.

Recall of Brand Associations

According to the associative network memory model described in chapter 2, the strength of a brand association increases both the likelihood that that information will be accessible and the ease with which it can be recalled by "spreading activation." Accessible, recalled information is important as it can create the differential response that makes up customer-based brand equity. Successful recall of brand information by consumers does not depend only on the initial associative strength of that information in memory, however, but also on other considerations. Three such factors are particularly important.

First, the presence of *other* product information in memory can produce interference effects and reduce the accessibility of similar brand information in memory. Specially, the presence of other information in memory may cause the target information to be either overlooked or confused with this other information. Second, the time since exposure to information at encoding affects the strength of a new association—the longer the time delay, the weaker the association. The time elapsed since the last exposure opportunity, however, has been shown generally to only produce gradual decay. That is, cognitive psychologists believe that memory is extremely durable so that once information becomes stored in memory, its strength of association decays very slowly.[39] Third, the number and type of external retrieval cues that are available will be key factors affecting memory accessibility. That is, information may be "available" in memory (i.e., potentially recallable) but may not be "accessible" from memory (i.e., unable to be recalled) without the proper retrieval cues or reminders. Thus, the particular associations for a brand that are salient and "come to mind" depend on the context in which the brand is considered. The more cues linked to a piece of information, however, the greater the likelihood that the information can be recalled.

The entire marketing program and all activities related to the brand will affect the strength of brand associations. For example, the Body Shop created a global brand image without even using conventional advertising! Their strong associations to personal care and environmental concern occurred through their products (natural ingredients only, never tested on animals, etc.), packaging (simple, refillable, recyclable), merchandising (detailed point-of-sale posters, brochures, and displays), staff (encouraged to be enthusiastic and informative concerning environmental issues), sourcing policies (using small local producers from around the world), social action program (requiring each franchisee to run a local community program), and public relations programs and activities (taking visible and sometimes outspoken stands on various issues). (See Branding Brief 7–1.) Starbucks coffee is another more recent example of creating an amazingly rich brand image without the benefit of any advertising to speak of.

In many cases, marketing communication programs make the primary contribution to the creation of strong brand associations and recalled communication effects through a variety of means, such as: (1) by using creative communications that cause consumers to elaborate on brand-related information and relate it appropriately to existing knowledge; (2) by exposing consumers to communications repeatedly over time; and (3) by ensuring that many retrieval cues are present as reminders. Chapter 6 reviews in detail how integrated marketing communication programs can contribute to brand equity.

FAVORABILITY OF BRAND ASSOCIATIONS

Associations differ according to how favorably they are evaluated. The success of a marketing program is reflected in the creation of favorable brand associations, such as when consumers believe that the brand possesses attributes and benefits that satisfy their needs and wants such that a positive overall brand attitude is formed. Favorability, in turn, will be a function of the desirability and deliverability of the brand association.

Desirability

In terms of desirability, how important or valued is the image association to the brand attitudes and decisions made by consumers? It is often useful to explore underlying consumer motivations in a product category to uncover the relevant associations. For example, Maslow's hierarchy maintains that consumers have different priorities and levels of needs.[40] From lowest to highest priority, they are:

1. Physiological needs (food, water, air, shelter, sex)
2. Safety and security needs (protection, order, and stability)
3. Social needs (affection, friendship, belonging)
4. Ego needs (prestige, status, self-respect)
5. Self-actualization (self-fulfillment).

According to Maslow, higher-level needs become relevant once lower-level needs are satisfied. Marketers have also recognized the importance of higher-level needs. For example, "means-end chains" have been devised as a way of understanding higher level meanings of brand characteristics.[41] A means-end chain takes the following structure: Attributes lead to benefits that, in turn, lead to values. In other words, a consumer chooses a product that delivers attributes (A) that provide benefits or has certain consequences (B/C) that satisfies values (V). For example, in a study of salty snacks, one respondent noted that a flavored chip (A) with a strong taste (A) would mean that she would eat less (B/C), not get fat (B/C), and have a better figure (B/C), all of which would enhance her self esteem (V).

Consumers may have many different values that matter to themselves, although one useful scale is based on eight different categories of values:[42]

Self-respect	Self-fulfillment
Security	Being well-respected
Warm relationships	Sense of belonging
Sense of accomplishment	Fun-enjoyment-excitement

Deliverability

Creating a favorable association also requires that the firm be able to deliver on the desired association. In terms of deliverability, the main question is, What would be the cost or investment necessary and length of time involved to create or change the desired association(s)? Deliverability is more complex than that, however, and depends on three main factors—the actual or potential ability of the product to perform, the current or future prospects of communicating that performance, and the sustainability of the actual and communicated performance over time.

The first factor affecting deliverability relates to the actual or potential ability of the product to perform at the level stated. The product design and marketing offering must be able to support the desired association. Does communicating the desired association involve real changes to the product itself or just perceptual ones as to how the consumer thinks of the product or brand? It is obviously easier to convince consumers of some fact about the brand that they were unaware of and may have overlooked than to make changes in the product *and* convince consumers of these changes.

The second factor affecting deliverability is the current or future prospects of communicating information to create or strengthen the desired associations. The key issue here is consumers' perceptions of the brand and the resulting brand associations. It is very difficult to try to create an association that is not consistent with existing consumer knowledge or that consumers, for whatever reason, have trouble believing in. For example, when Gillette introduced the "blue blade" in the 1930s, although the razor offered superior performance, its real innovation was its color. It deliberately was given a blue lacquer color so as to distinguish it from other steel blades and better communicate its uniqueness.[43] More recently, marketers at Chesebrough-Pond's attribute the success of their Mentadent toothpaste in part to the fact that consumer interest was piqued because the product looked and felt different from any other toothpaste on the market and thus vividly demonstrated its innovative nature.

The communicability of a brand association can depend on many things but perhaps the most important one is whether consumers can be given a compelling reason and understandable rationale as to why the brand will deliver the desired benefit. In other words, what factual, verifiable evidence or proof can be given as support such that consumers will actually believe in the brand and its desired associations?

Finally, the third factor affecting the deliverability of a brand association is the sustainability of the actual and communicated performance over time. Is it the case that the favorability of a brand association can be reinforced and strengthened over time? Sustainability will depend on internal commitment and use of resources as well as external market forces.

It should be recognized that not all associations for a brand will be relevant and valued in a purchase or consumption decision. This may be particularly true for certain non-product-related associations. For example, consumers often have an association in memory to the color of the product or package for brands. Although this association may facilitate brand recognition or awareness or lead to inferences about product quality in some cases, it may not always be considered a meaningful factor in a purchase decision. Moreover, the evaluations of brand associations may be situationally or context-dependent and vary according to the particular goals that consumers have in their purchase or consumption decision.[44] An association may be valued in one situation but not another.[45] For example, speed and efficiency of service may be more important when a consumer is under time pressure but may have little impact when a consumer is less hurried.

UNIQUENESS OF BRAND ASSOCIATIONS

Brand associations may or may not be shared with other competing brands. The essence of brand positioning is that the brand has a sustainable competitive advantage or "unique selling proposition" that gives consumers a compelling reason why they should buy that particular brand.[46] These differences may be communicated explicitly by making direct comparisons with competitors or may be highlighted implicitly without stating a competitive point of reference. Furthermore, they may be based on product-related or non-product-related attributes or functional, experiential, or image benefits. In fact, in many categories, non-product-related attributes, such as user type or usage situation, may more easily create unique associations.

The existence of strongly held, favorably evaluated associations that are unique to the brand and imply superiority over other brands is critical to a brand's success. Yet, unless the brand faces no competition, it will most likely share some associations with other brands. Shared associations can help to establish category membership and define the scope of competition with other products and services.[47]

Research on noncomparable alternatives suggests that even if a brand does not face direct competition in its product category, and thus does not share product-related attributes with other brands, it can still share more abstract associations and face indirect competition in a more broadly defined product category.[48] Thus, although a railroad may not compete directly with another railroad, it still competes indirectly with other forms of transportation, such as airlines, cars, and buses. A maker of educational CD-ROM products may be implicitly competing with all kinds of other forms of education and entertainment, such as books, videos, television, and magazines.

A product or service category can also be characterized by a set of associations that include specific beliefs about any member in the category, as well as overall attitudes toward all members in the category. These beliefs might include many of the relevant product-related attributes for brands in the category, as well as more descriptive attributes that do not necessarily relate to product or service performance (e.g., the color of a product, such as red for ketchup). Certain attributes or benefits may be considered "prototypical" and essential to all brands in the category, and a specific brand may exist that is considered to be an "exemplar" and most representative of the product or service category.[49] For example, consumers might expect a running shoe to provide support and comfort, be built well enough to withstand repeated wearings, and provide other features, and they may believe that Asics or some other leading brand best represents a running shoe. Similarly, consumers might expect a bank to offer a variety of checking and savings accounts and provide branch and electronic delivery services, and they may consider Citibank or some other market leader to be the best example of a bank.

Because the brand is linked to the product category, some category associations may also become linked to the brand, either in terms of specific beliefs or overall attitudes. Product category attitudes can be a particularly important determinant of consumer response. For example, if a consumer thinks that all brokerage houses are basically "greedy" and that brokers are "in it for themselves," then he or she probably will have similarly unfavorable beliefs about and negative attitudes toward any particular brokerage house simply by virtue of its membership in the category. Thus, in almost all cases, some product category associations that are linked to the brand will also be shared with other brands in the category. Note that the strength of the brand associations to the product category will be an important determinant of brand awareness.[50] We consider additional aspects of uniqueness of brand associations in terms of brand positioning and points of parity and points of difference in the next section.

Determining the Desired Brand Knowledge Structures

The previous discussion described how to profile *existing* brand knowledge structures. In this section, we consider how marketers might determine *desired* brand knowledge structures, that is, what they would like consumers to know about the brand as opposed to what they might already currently know. Determining the desired brand knowledge structures involves positioning a brand. Brand positioning has been defined as the "act of designing the company's offer and image so that it occupies a distinct and valued place in the target customer's minds."[51] Thus, positioning, as the name implies, involves finding the proper location in the minds of a certain market segment so that they think about the product in the "right" or desired way. According to the customer-based brand equity model, deciding on a positioning requires determining a frame of reference—by identifying the target market and the nature of competition—and the ideal point-of-parity and point-of-difference brand associations. In other words, it is necessary to decide: (1) who the target consumer is, (2) who the main competitors are, (3) how the brand is similar to these competitors, and (4) how the brand is different from these competitors. These ingredients are each discussed in turn. Branding Brief 3–3 presents an interesting analysis of the positioning of some top brands.

TARGET MARKET

Identifying the consumer target is important because different consumers may have different brand knowledge structures and thus perceptions and preferences for the brand. Without this understanding, it may be difficult to be able to state which brand associations are strongly held, favorable, and unique. There are a number of important considerations in defining and segmenting a market and choosing target market segments. Here, we highlight a few.

What Makes a Brand Different?

A recently reported study examined the factors that discriminate a number of top brands.[a] Specifically, category users were surveyed concerning their brand perceptions in the following product categories:

1. Airlines (American, Continental, and United)
2. Beer (Budweiser, Coors, and Miller)
3. Coffee (Folgers, Maxwell House, and Nestle)
4. Fast Food (Burger King, McDonald's, and Wendy's)
5. Hotels (Hilton, Holiday Inn, and Marriott)
6. Long Distance Telephone (AT&T, MCI, and Sprint)
7. Soup (Campbell's, Lipton, and Progresso)

Study respondents rated the brands on a number of functional, economic, psychological, social, and cultural factors. The results were analyzed with some advanced multivariate techniques to yield the perceptual space shown below. Several observations are relevant. First, brand type can be more important than category to the positioning of a brand. Thus, Campbell's soup may have as much as common in many ways with Maxwell House coffee than with Lipton or Progresso soup. Second, within a category, there was a brand hierarchy in terms of the five factors that subjects rated. The functional and economic dimensions were the ones found to be most desirable, however, the dimensions most closely associated with brand choice dealt with the cultural, social, and psychological factors.

The researchers who conducted the study interpreted these findings as indication that an "equity hierarchy" existed with the stated economic and func-

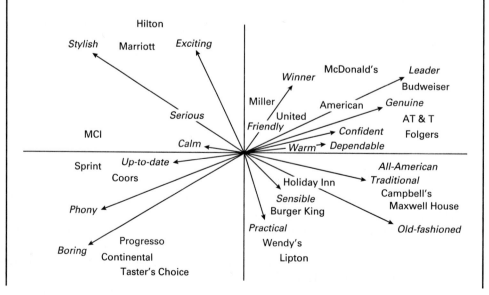

tional dimensions as a "cost of entry" base and the derived cultural, social, and psychological dimensions as the key brand choice differentiators. In other words, the study findings could be interpreted in terms of the positioning concepts presented here as stating that economic and functional characteristics are often points-of-parity associations and cultural, social, and psychological factors are often points-of-difference associations, at least with these generally mature, well-known brands.

---

[a]James F. Donius, "Brand Equity: A Holistic Perspective," ARF Brand Equity Conference, February 15–16.

A *market* is the set of all actual and potential buyers who have sufficient interest in, income for, and access to a product. In other words, a market consists of all consumers with sufficient motivation, ability, and opportunity to buy a product. *Market segmentation* involves dividing the market into distinct groups of homogeneous consumers who have similar needs and consumer behavior and thus require similar marketing mixes. Defining a market segmentation plan involves tradeoffs between costs and benefits. The more finely segmented the market, the greater the likelihood that the firm will be able to implement marketing programs that better meet the needs of consumers in any one segment. The advantage of a more positive consumer response from a customized marketing program, however, can be offset by the greater costs from a lack of standardization.

Figures 3–5 and 3–6 display some possible segmentation bases for consumer and industrial markets, respectively. In general, these bases can be classified as *descriptive* or customer-oriented (related to the kind of person or organization) versus *behavioral* or product-oriented (related to how the customer thinks of or uses the brand or product). Behavioral segmentation bases are often most valuable in understanding branding issues because they have clearer strategic implications. For example, defining a benefit segment makes it clear what should be the ideal point of difference or desired benefit with which to establish the positioning. Take the toothpaste market. One research study uncovered four main segments:[52]

1. *The Sensory Segment:* Seeking flavor and product appearance
2. *The Sociables:* Seeking brightness of teeth
3. *The Worriers:* Seeking decay prevention
4. *The Independent Segment:* Seeking low price

Given this market segmentation scheme, marketing programs could be put into place to attract one or more segments. For example, Close-Up has targeted the first two segments, whereas Crest has primarily concentrated on the third segment (although introducing flavor extensions such as Winterfresh Gel to address the Sensory Segment). Leaving no stone unturned, Beecham's Aquafresh has gone after all three of these segments, designing the toothpaste to have three stripes to dramatize each of the three different product benefits. Branding Brief 3–4 describes a benefit segmentation plan of gasoline buyers devised by Mobil.

BEHAVIORAL

- User status
- Usage rate
- Usage occasion
- Brand loyalty
- Benefits sought

DEMOGRAPHIC

- Income
- Age
- Sex
- Race
- Family

PSYCHOGRAPHIC

- Values, opinions, and attitudes
- Activities and lifestyle

GEOGRAPHIC

- International
- Regional

FIGURE 3–5 Possible Consumer Segmentation Bases

NATURE OF GOOD

- Kind
- Where used
- Type of buy

BUYING CONDITION

- Purchase location
- Who buys
- Type of buy

DEMOGRAPHIC

- SIC code
- Number of employees
- Number of production workers
- Annual sales volume
- Number of establishments

BUYING CONDITION

- Purchase location
- Who buys
- Type of buy

FIGURE 3–6 Possible Business-to-Business Segmentation Bases

Dividing Up Gasoline Buyers[a]

In the 1950s, oil companies offered trading stamps, glasses, windshield washing services, and other incentives to differentiate their brands. In recent years, however, gasoline marketing has been based more on attracting customers with low prices. In an attempt to break out of the sometimes vicious and unprofitable price wars that would result, Mobil interviewed 2000 consumers to gain new insights into what gas customers wanted. According to their study, only 20 percent of Mobil's customers bought gasoline based solely on price. The surveys led them to conclude that many motorists would forsake gasoline discounters in favor of a "quality buying experience."

Specifically, Mobil's research turned up five primary purchasing groups, labelled the Road Warriors, True Blues, Generation F3 Drivers (for fuel, food, and fast), Homebodies, and Price Driven. Different groups exhibited different needs and spending habits: The Price Driven group spent no more than $700 annually whereas the biggest spenders, the Road Warriors and True Blues, averaged at least $1200 a year (see Figure 3–7). Mobil decided to target these big spenders, as well as Generation F3 Drivers (because Mobil felt many of them were destined to become Road Warriors).

Taxonomy at the Pump: Mobil's Five Types of Gasoline Buyers

Road Warriors:	True Blues:	Generation F3:	Homebodies:	Price Driven:
Generally higher-income middle-aged men who drive 25,000 to 50,000 miles a year . . . buy premium with a credit card . . . purchase sandwiches and drinks from the convenience store . . . will sometimes wash their cars at the carwash.	Usually men and women with moderate to high incomes who are loyal to a brand and sometimes to a particular station . . . frequently buy premium gasoline and pay in cash.	(for fuel, food and fast): Upwardly mobile men and women—half under 25 years of age—who are constantly on the go . . . drive a lot and snack heavily from the convenience store.	Usually housewives who shuttle their children around during the day and use whatever gasoline station is based in town or along their route of travel.	Generally aren't loyal to either a brand or a particular station, and rarely buy the premium line . . . frequently on tight budgets . . . efforts to woo them have been the basis of marketing strategies for years.
16% of buyers	**16 % of buyers**	**27% of buyers**	**21% of buyers**	**20% of buyers**

FIGURE 3–7 Mobil Gasoline Buyer Segmentation Plan

To better appeal to the non-price-driven segments, Mobil devised a new strategy it dubbed "Friendly Serve" to improve the quality of service at its stations. Cleaning up its facilities, increasing the lighting, spiffing up the restrooms, adding helpful attendants in test markets allowed Mobil to increase prices and improve its profitability in selected stations.

---

[a]Reprinted by permission of *Wall Street Journal,* © 1995 Dow Jones and Company, Inc. All rights reserved worldwide.

Often the underlying rationale for demographic segmentation bases basically involves more behavioral considerations. For example, marketers may choose to segment a market on the basis of age and target a certain age group. However, the underlying reason why that age group may be an attractive market segment may be because they are particularly heavy users of the product, are unusually brand loyal, or are most likely to seek the benefit that the product is best able to deliver. In some cases, however, broad demographic descriptors may mask important underlying differences.[53] A target market of "women aged 25 to 54" may contain a number of very different segments who may require totally different marketing mixes. The main advantage of demographic segmentation bases is that the demographics of traditional media vehicles are generally well-known from consumer research and, as a result, it has been easier to buy media on that basis. With the importance of nontraditional media and other forms of communication, as well as the capability to build databases to profile customers on a behavioral and media usage basis, however, this advantage has become less important.

A number of criteria have been offered to guide segmentation and target market decisions, such as the following:[54]

1. *Identifiability:* Can segment identification be easily calculated?
2. *Size:* Is there adequate sales potential in the segment?
3. *Accessibility:* Are specialized distribution outlets and communication media available to reach the segment?
4. *Responsiveness to marketing programs:* How favorably will the segment respond to a tailored marketing program?

The obvious overriding consideration in defining market segments is profitability. In many cases, profitability can be related to behavioral considerations. For example, Baldinger analyzes the implications of a brand loyalty segmentation scheme with four segments dubbed "Loyals," "Rotators," "Deal Selectives," and "Price Drivens." Along these lines, Market Facts research supplier has developed a Conversion Model to measure the strength of the psychological commitment between brands and consumers and their openness to change.[55] To determine the ease with which a consumer can be converted to another choice, the model assesses commitment based on factors such as consumer attitudes towards and satisfaction with current brand choices in a category and the importance of the decision to select a brand in the category. The model segments *users* of a brand into four groups based on strength of commitment, from low to high, as follows: Convertible, Shallow, Average, and Entrenched. The model also classifies *non-users* of a brand into four other groups based on their openness to trying the brand, from low to high, as follows: Strongly Unavailable, Weakly Unavailable, Ambivalent, and Available.

Figure 3–8 displays an application of the Conversion Model to the carbonated soft drink market in the summer of 1991. Market Facts defines the near-term potential of a brand and its future health as the difference between the Available Non-User and Convertible User segments. On that basis, Market Facts believed that growth potential was found for several non-cola soft drinks and later reported some confirmatory market evidence.

FIGURE 3–8 Market Facts Conversion Model: Application to Carbonated Soft Drinks

Preaching to Convertibles

At the core of Market Facts' Conversion Model is a religion-based theory of how human commitment is formed. The model segments consumers according to the strength of their attachment to a particular brand. The direction of the difference between the sizes of the Convertible and Available segments is a strong indicator of future brand health.

	Coca-Cola	Pepsi-Cola	Diet Coke	Diet Pepsi	Dr Pepper	7-Up	Sprite	Minute Maid	Orange Crush	Mountain Dew
Users	*40%*	*34%*	*20%*	*16%*	*21%*	*15%*	*14%*	*6%*	*6%*	*7%*
Entrenched	4	4	1	1	3	1	1	0	•	•
Average	21	19	10	9	13	8	6	2	3	4
Shallow	12	9	7	4	4	5	6	3	2	2
Convertible	3	2	2	2	1	1	2	1	1	1
Near-Term Potential	*−1*	*+2*	*−1*	*+1*	*+3*	*+5*	*+4*	*+3*	*+5*	*+2*
Available	2	4	1	3	4	6	6	4	6	3
Ambivalent	9	12	6	7	12	17	15	10	13	10
Weakly Unavailable	11	13	9	11	15	22	20	18	19	16
Strongly Unavailable	38	37	64	63	48	40	45	61	56	64
Nonusers	*60%*	*66%*	*80%*	*84%*	*79%*	*85%*	*86%*	*94%*	*94%*	*93%*

NATURE OF COMPETITION

It is difficult to disentangle target market decisions from decisions concerning the nature of competition for the brand because they are often so closely related. In other words, deciding to target a certain type of consumer often, at least implicitly, defines the nature of competition because certain firms have decided to also target that segment in the past (or plan to do so in the future) or consumers in that segment already may look to certain brands in their purchase decisions. Other issues can be raised in defining the nature of competition and deciding which products and brands are most likely to be seen as close substitutes. For example, the nature of competition may depend on the channels of distribution chosen. Competitive analysis will consider a host of factors—including the resources, capabilities, and likely intentions of various other firms—to choose markets where consumers can be profitably serviced (see also Chapter 11).[56]

One lesson stressed by many marketing strategists is not to be too narrow in defining competition. Often, competition may occur at the benefit level rather than the attribute level. Thus, a luxury good with a strong hedonic benefit (e.g., stereo equipment) may compete as much with a vacation as with other durable goods (e.g., furniture). As noted above, products are often organized in consumers' minds in a hierarchical fashion such that competition can be defined at a number of different levels. Take Dr. Pepper as an example: At the product type level, it competes with non-cola, flavored soft drinks; at the product category level, it competes with all soft drinks; and at the product class level, it competes with all beverages. The target and competitive frame of reference chosen will dictate the breadth of brand awareness and the situations and types of cues that should become closely related to the brand. Recognizing the nature of different levels of competition also has important implications for the desired brand associations, as described next.

POINTS OF PARITY AND POINTS OF DIFFERENCE

Once the appropriate frame of reference for positioning has been fixed by defining the customer target market and nature of competition, the basis of the positioning itself can be defined. Arriving at the proper positioning requires establishing the correct point-of-difference and point-of-parity associations.[57]

Points-of-Difference Associations

Points of difference are those associations that are unique to the brand that are also strongly held and favorably evaluated by consumers. These points of difference may be based on any type of association—attribute, benefit, or attitude—although the more abstract and the higher the level of the association, the more likely it is to be a sustained source of brand equity.

The concept of points of difference has much in common with several other well-known marketing concepts. For example, it is similar to the notion of "unique selling proposition" (USP), a concept pioneered by Rosser Reeves and the Ted Bates advertising agency in the 1950s. The original idea behind USP was that advertising should give consumers a compelling reason to buy a product that competitors could not match. With this approach, the emphasis in designing ads was placed on communicating a distinctive, unique product benefit (i.e., the ad message or claims) and not on the creative (i.e., the ad creative or execution). In other words, USP emphasized *what* was said in an ad as opposed to *how* it was said. As a result, ads single-mindedly, and sometimes literally, hammered home the key consumer benefit.

For example, one notable albeit widely disliked example was an ad for Anacin aspirin. The ad schematically showed three boxes in the skull of a headache sufferer. In turn, a pounding hammer, a coiling spring, and a crackling lightening bolt were relieved by little bubbles of Anacin making their way up from the user's stomach, as the announcer stated: "Are you looking for fast, fast, fast relief? Then take Anacin. Anacin stops headaches pain fast, relieves tension fast, and calms jittery nerves fast. Anacin—for fast, fast, *fast* relief." In 1954, American Home Products backed these Anacin ads with a lavish media budget. Although disliked, the message got through, and the brand gained considerable market share.

Another related concept is "sustainable competitive advantage." Sustainable competitive advantage (SCA) relates, in part, to a firm's ability to achieve an advantage in delivering superior value in the marketplace for a prolonged period of time.[58] Although the SCA concept is somewhat broader—SCAs could be based on business practices such as human resource policies—it also emphasizes the importance of differentiating products in some fashion. Thus, the concept of point of difference is closely related to unique selling proposition and sustainable competitive advantage and maintains that a brand must have some strong, favorable, and unique associations to differentiate itself from other brands.

Consumers' actual brand choices often will depend on the perceived uniqueness of brand associations. These points of difference may involve product-related attributes (e.g., the fact that Kraft Singles cheese has 5 oz. of milk), benefits (e.g., the fact that Magnavox products have "consumer friendly" technological features such as television sets with a button to help locate misplaced remotes and "Smart Sound" to automatically level out spikes in television volume), or even attitudes (e.g., the fact that British Airways is advertised as the "world's favourite airline"). In other cases, points-of-difference associations involve non-product-related attributes (e.g., the western imagery of Marlboro cigarettes). Many top brands attempt to create a point of difference on "overall superior quality," whereas a positioning strategy adopted by a number of other firms is to create a point of difference for their brands as the "low-cost provider" of a product or service. Thus, a host of different types of points of difference are possible.

Points-of-Parity Associations

Points of parity, on the other hand, are those associations that are not necessarily unique to the brand but may in fact be shared with other brands. These types of associations come in two basic forms. First, *category point-of-parity associations* are those associations that consumers view as being necessary to be a legitimate and credible product offering within a certain category. In other words, they represent necessary, but not sufficient conditions for brand choice. In terms of the discussion of product levels from chapter 1, these attribute associations are minimally at the generic product level and most likely at the expected product level. Thus, consumers would not consider a bank truly a bank unless it offered a range of checking and savings plans; provided safety deposit boxes, travelers cheques, and other such services; had convenient hours and automated teller machines; and other features.

Second, *competitive point-of-parity associations* are those associations designed to negate competitors' points of difference. In other words, if in the eyes of consumers, the brand association designed to be the competitor's point of difference (e.g., a product benefit of some type) is as strongly held for the target brand as for competitor's brands *and* the target brand is able to establish another association as strong, favorable, and unique as part of its point of difference, then the target brand should be in a superior competitive position. In other words, if a brand can "break even" in those areas where its competitors are trying to find an advantage *and* can achieve advantages in some other areas, the brand should be in a strong—and perhaps unbeatable—competitive position.

Often, the key to positioning is not so much in achieving a point of difference as in achieving necessary or competitive points of parity! For example, consider the introduction of Miller Lite beer.[59] When Philip Morris bought Miller Brewing, its flagship High Life brand was not competing particularly well, leading the company to decide to introduce a light beer. The initial advertising strategy for Miller Lite was to assure parity with a necessary and important consideration in the category by stating that it "tastes great" while at the same time creating a point of difference with the fact that it contained one-third less calories (96 calories vs. 150 calories for conventional 12-ounce full-strength beer) and was thus "less filling." As is often the case, the point of parity and point of difference were somewhat conflicting, as consumers tend to equate taste with calories. To overcome potential consumer resistance to this notion, Miller employed credible spokespeople, primarily popular former professional athletes who would presumably not drink a beer unless it tasted good. These ex-jocks were placed in amusing situations in ads where they debated the merits of Miller Lite as to which of the two product benefits—"tastes great" or "less filling"—was more descriptive of the beer. The ads ended with the clever tagline, "Everything you've always wanted in a beer . . . and less."[60]

Other examples of the importance of creating points of parity abound. Hyundai initially established a strong point of difference on low cost and economy for its cars but later attempted to create more favorable user imagery to establish a point of parity with better admired and more glamorous competitors. As another example, consider the marketing dilemma faced by Cable News Network (recall Branding Brief 1–6). Despite moments of ratings success, CNN has been plagued by low regular viewership and has been dubbed "talk radio" with pictures. It could be argued that although they have strong points of difference on the basis of "in depth" and "up-to-the-minute," they may lack necessary points of parity. For example, versus networks they may need to establish a competitive evening news program with all the necessary ingredients (e.g., a well-identified time slot, anchor personalities, portfolio of news stories) to create both necessary and competitive points of parity.

Competitive Frame of Reference

The competitive frame of reference will dictate the points of parity and points of difference. Choosing to compete in different categories often results in different competitive frames of reference and thus different points of parity and points of difference. For example, consider the possible positioning options for Federal Express, the U.S. market share leader in the overnight delivery service (ONDS) category. Within the ONDS category, Federal Express created strong, favorable, and unique associations to consumer benefits that they were the fastest and most dependable delivery service around (as reinforced by their introductory advertising tag line, "When it absolutely, positively has to be there overnight"). This association provided a key point of difference to traditional mail deliveries by the U.S. Postal Service (which would typically take two or more days depending on the destination involved), as well as other ONDS who found it difficult, at least initially, to match Federal Express' high level of service quality.

If Federal Express were to define its competition as other brands in the ONDS category then it might continue to design marketing programs to enhance its associations for speed, reliability, and confidence. On the other hand, what other forms of competition does Federal Express face? As a market leader, it could be argued that its competition comes to a large extent from other types of products that can satisfy needs similar to those satisfied by Federal Express. For example, take fax machines as a case in point. It certainly would be true that many documents that would have been sent a few years ago by overnight delivery, and most likely by Federal Express, can now be sent more quickly and easily via a fax machine. In that sense, some of Federal Express' stiffest competition may come from other forms of document transmission and delivery. In the case of fax machines, Federal Express' key point of difference of "speedy delivery" is rendered meaningless by the instantaneous capabilities of fax machines, suggesting that other points of difference are necessary. On the other hand, the confidence and risk reduction of sending a document by Federal Express may still be relevant when competing with fax delivery. Although a fax may not find its way to the intended person in a timely manner, Federal Express may be more likely to "hit the right mark." Thus, Federal Express may decide to emphasize security and confidentiality as compared to fax machines. Along those lines, note that its new tracking capabilities may actually help Federal Express to compete with both types of its main competitors—other ONDS carriers as well as alternative delivery forms such as fax machines.

As another example, Enterprise Rent-A-Car has challenged Hertz's supremacy in the rental car market by tailoring its marketing program to a relatively neglected target market.[61] While Hertz, Avis, Alamo, and others specialize in airport rental cars for business and leisure travelers, Enterprise has attacked the low-budget, insurance-replacement market by primarily renting to customers whose cars have been wrecked or stolen. Enterprise charges low rental rates by avoiding expensive airport and downtown locations, by only opening for daylight hours, and by holding onto its fleet of cars for a longer period of time before replacing them. Enterprise also distinguishes itself, in part, by offering to pick customers up so that they are able to rent its cars. Enterprise has a limited advertising budget, relying more on a grassroots marketing push based on referrals from insurance agents and adjusters, car dealers, body shops, and garages. By creating points of difference of low cost and convenience in an overlooked market, Enterprise has posted a monthly profit for the last twenty years.

Desirability and Deliverability

As with any association, for points of difference to be favorable, they must be desirable and deliverable. In 1992, a number of brands in different product categories (colas, dish washing soaps, beer, deodorant, gasoline, etc.) introduced clear versions of their products to better differentiate themselves.[62] Although "clear" perhaps signaled natural, pure, and lightness to consumers initially, a proliferation of clear versions of products that did not reinforce these other associations blurred its meaning. The "clear" association does not seem to be of enduring value or sustainable as a point of difference. In many cases, these brands have seen declining market share or have disappeared all together. Similarly, many marketing experts criticized PepsiCo's decision to market Diet Pepsi as a "fresh" beverage by placing freshness dating on the package as positioning on the basis of an attribute and benefit that was not really relevant to consumers.[63] Anheuser-Busch has recently followed suit with its Budweiser beer, although in this case it is easier to see how freshness could be seen as more likely to be important to consumers in this market (e.g., the perceived freshness of bottled and canned beer vs. draft beer).

On the other hand, General Motors' Saturn has created a unique position in the U.S car market by establishing associations that are highly relevant to a certain consumer segment. According to GM Chairman John Smale, Saturn's brand promise (and point of difference) is that it is the car to buy for consumers who "want a car built, sold, and serviced by people who really care—people whose No. 1 priority is to satisfy you and build and preserve a relationship with you, no matter what it takes." The entire marketing program creates associations to Saturn as coming from a "dedicated and caring" car company[64] (see Figure 3–9 for an example of a Saturn ad).

The concepts of points of difference and points of parity are powerful tools to guide positioning. Branding Brief 3–5 describes how they relate to political campaigns. A number of considerations come into play in conducting positioning analysis and deciding on the desired brand image (see chapter 10).[65] Determining the proper competitive frame of reference depends on understanding consumer behavior and the consideration sets consumers adopt in making brand choices. Determining points-of-difference associations that are strong, favorable, and unique are based on desirability and deliverability considerations, which are combined to determine the resulting anticipated levels of sales and costs that might be expected with the positioning. In general, it is difficult to create more than one or perhaps two major points of difference, at least at the benefit level.

Once the brand positioning strategy has been determined, the actual marketing program to create, strengthen, or maintain brand associations can be put into place. In this chapter, we considered some general principles in building brand knowledge structures. Chapters 4 through 7 describe some of the important marketing mix issues in designing supporting marketing programs and other marketing activity to build brand equity.

Review

Consumers' brand knowledge structures provide the key to brand equity. Brand knowledge consists of brand awareness and brand image. *Brand awareness* is related to the strength of the resulting brand node or trace in memory, as reflected by consumers' ability to identify the brand under different conditions. Brand awareness consists of brand recognition and brand recall performance. *Brand recognition* relates to consumers' ability to confirm prior exposure to the brand when given the brand as a cue. *Brand recall* relates to the consumers' ability to retrieve the brand from memory

It seems that besides coupes, wagons and sedans, we also make one heck of a final exam.

We've heard of many instances where Saturns have been given as graduation gifts. (Most of us here remember getting pen and pencil sets.) In that case, we suspect this year's graduating class will be quite impressed with the newly redesigned Saturn coupe.

Apparently, a Saturn showroom isn't the only place you can go to learn more about Saturn. All across the country, some pretty prestigious universities are offering us up as a case study in everything from organizational theory to marketing to global logistics. Not only that, we're on the recommended reading list of a few sociology departments, as well. This is pretty heady stuff, especially when you consider we didn't even exist as a company until a few years ago. And now to be held up as a role model for future MBAs to study, why, it's quite an honor. It's also a very good example of what happens when you do your homework.

The 1997 Saturn SC1

 It doesn't take a genius to see that part of the Saturn difference lies in the relationship between labor and management. Gone are things like time clocks and foremen. Instead, everyone rolls up their sleeves and makes decisions together. Funny what happens when you treat everyone the same; things actually get done.

A DIFFERENT KIND *of* COMPANY. A DIFFERENT KIND *of* CAR.

This 1997 Saturn SL2 and this SC1 both have an M.S.R.P. of $12,895, including retailer prep and transportation. Of course, the total cost will vary seeing how options are extra, as are things like tax and license. We'd be happy to provide more detail at 1-800-522-5000 or look for us on the Internet at http://www.saturncars.com ©1996 Saturn Corporation.

FIGURE 3-9 Example of Saturn Ad

Positioning Politicians

The importance of marketing has not been lost on politicians and, although there are a number of different ways to interpret their words and actions, one way to interpret campaign strategies is from a brand equity perspective. For example, consultants to political candidates stress the importance of having "high name ID" or, in other words, a high level of brand awareness. In major races, at least 90 percent is desired. They also emphasize "positives-negatives"—voter responses when asked if they think positively or negatively of a candidate.[a] A 3:1 ratio is desired (and 4:1 is seen as even better). This measure corresponds to a brand attitude in marketing terms.

The importance of positioning a political candidate can be seen by examining George Bush's textbook presidential campaign of 1988. Bush had been Vice President for 8 years under Ronald Reagan and was perceived by many as a moderate Republican. His Democratic opponent, on the other hand, the governor of Massachusetts, Michael Dukakis, was seen by many as being a traditional Democrat. Bush's campaign team included campaign chairman James Baker, pollster Robert Teeter, director of communications Roger Ailes, and the Frankenberry, Laughlin, and Constable ad agency. Their goal in the campaign was to convince voters that the country was in good shape and that Bush was therefore the best choice to succeed Ronald Reagan. Because of existing perceptions of the two men, they also needed to change the public's image of both Bush and Dukakis. Early in the campaign, Bush's ratio of positives to negatives was 40 percent to 43 percent—and no presidential candidate had ever had negatives above 40 percent and gone on to win the election!

The objective of the Republican campaign was to move Bush to the "center" of the political spectrum and make him a "safe" choice, a person who combined compassion with toughness and who was experienced and presidential in stature. The Republican campaign objective with Dukakis, on the other hand, was to make him seem liberal and move him to the left, emphasizing the risk of change. In terms of actual policies, the Republican strategy could be viewed as a classic application of positioning principles. Its goal was to create a point of difference on traditional Republican issues such as defense, the economy (and taxes), and crime and create a point of parity—thus negating their opponent's point of difference—on traditional Democratic issues such as the environment, education, and abortion rights.

The actual campaign was a fully integrated modern communications program, skillfully blending public relations and media news coverage with paid advertising. Campaign messages were researched carefully by focus groups and other means. Bush's convention speech and the line, "a thousand points of light" became the centerpiece for several ads. Many ads were soft, positive spots, designed to combat Bush's "nerd" or "wimp" image or to portray Bush's career as a number of successful missions, leading up to the penultimate job of president. Other ads were hard-hitting negative spots, designed to attack

Dukakis' image on the environment (in the famous Boston harbor spot), crime (in the equally famous prison furloughs ad that became associated with convict Willie Horton), the economy (in ads blasting the success of the "Massachusetts Miracle"), and defense (in the famous tank ride ad, taken off the air from a news sound bite, showing Dukakis riding a tank with a helmet on and gesturing thumbs up, perhaps looking a bit too much like *Mad* magazine's Alfred E. Neuman).

As a result of this well-designed and well-executed campaign, by the time of the election, Bush's ratio of positives to negatives had dramatically shifted to 60 percent to 20 percent. Equally important, on those key Democratic issues that were to be their points of difference, the Republicans were able to "break even." For example, when voters were asked in exit polls which presidential candidate would be better for the environment, they were almost exactly equally split between the two candidates. Having successfully achieved these points of parity and points of difference in the minds of the voters, Bush won in a landslide.

Although the Republicans ran a near flawless campaign in 1988, that was not the case in 1992. The new Democratic candidate, Bill Clinton, was a fierce campaigner who ran a very focused campaign designed to create a key point of difference on one main issue—the economy. Rather than attempting to achieve a point of parity on this issue, Bush, who was running for re-election, campaigned on other issues such as family values. By conceding a key point of difference to the Democrats and failing to create a compelling one of his own, Bush and the Republicans were defeated handily. Failing to learn from their mistakes, the Republicans ran a meandering campaign in 1996 that failed to achieve points of parity or points of difference. Not surprisingly, their presidential candidate, Bob Dole, lost decisively to the incumbent Bill Clinton.

---

[a]Typically, the pollsters employ five point scales to the question, "Do you think positively or negatively of the candidate?" The bottom two points and top two points are collapsed together to reflect negative and positive opinions, respectively.

when given the product category, the needs fulfilled by the category, or a purchase or usage situation as a cue. Brand awareness also can be characterized according to depth and breadth. The *depth* of brand awareness concerns the likelihood that the brand will come to mind and the ease with which it does so. The *breadth* of brand awareness concerns the number of purchase and usage situations or cues where the brand comes to mind.

Brand awareness can play an important role in consumer decision making in three main ways: (1) by affecting inclusion in consideration set, (2) by affecting likelihood of choice in low involvement settings (due to lack of consumer motivation or ability), and (3) by affecting creation of brand associations and brand image. In general, brand awareness is created by increasing the familiarity of the brand through repeated exposure, although brand recall requires links in memory to the appropriate product category or other cues.

Brand image is comprised of the perceptions about a brand held in memory by consumers, as reflected by the brand associations. Brand associations come in many different forms: product-related and non-product-related attributes; functional, symbolic, and experiential benefits; and attitudes. For brand equity to occur, some of these associations must be strong, favorable, and unique. Strong associations occur with sufficient quantity and quality of processing. In particular, strong associations are more likely to result with information deemed relevant and presented consistently over time. Favorable brand associations occur when consumers believe that the brand possesses attributes and benefits that satisfy their needs and wants such that a positive overall brand attitude is formed. Favorability, in turn, will be a function of the desirability and deliverability of the brand association. Finally, in terms of uniqueness, brand associations may or may not be shared with other competing brands. Points of difference are those associations that are unique to the brand that are also strongly held and favorably evaluated by consumers. Points of parity, on the other hand, are those associations that are not necessarily unique to the brand but may in fact be shared with other brands. Category point-of-parity associations are those associations that consumers view as being necessary to be a legitimate and credible product offering within a certain category. Competitive point-of-parity associations are those associations designed to negate competitor's points of difference.

Determining the desired brand knowledge structures involves positioning a brand in the minds of consumers. According to the customer-based brand equity model, deciding on a positioning requires determining a frame of reference—by identifying the target market and the nature of competition—and the ideal point-of-parity and point-of-difference brand associations. Deciding on these four ingredients will then determine the brand positioning and dictate the desired brand knowledge structures.

Discussion Questions

1. Apply the categorization model to a product category other than beverages. How do consumers make decisions whether to buy the product and how do they arrive at their final brand decision? What are the implications for brand equity management for the brands in the category?
2. Pick a brand. Describe its breadth and depth of awareness.
3. Pick a category basically dominated by two main brands. Evaluate the positioning of each brand. Who are their target markets? What are their main points of parity and points of difference? Have they defined their positioning correctly? How might it be improved?

Notes

1. James R. Bettman, *An Information Processing Theory of Consumer Choice.* Reading, MA: Addison-Wesley, 1979; John R. Rossiter and Larry Percy, *Advertising and Promotion Management.* New York: McGraw-Hill, 1987.
2. Mita Sujan and Christine Dekleva, "Product Categorization and Inference Making: Some Implications for Comparative Advertising," *Journal of Consumer Research,* 14 (December 1987), pp. 372–378.

3. William Baker, J. Wesley Hutchinson, Danny Moore, and Prakash Nedungadi, "Brand Familiarity and Advertising: Effects on the Evoked Set and Brand Preference," in Richard J. Lutz (ed.), *Advances in Consumer Research,* Vol. 13. Provo, UT: Association for Consumer Research, 1986, pp. 637–642; Prakash Nedungadi, "Recall and Consumer Consideration Sets: Influencing Choice without Altering Brand Evaluations," *Journal of Consumer Research,* 17(December 1990), pp. 263–276.

4. For example, see Henry L. Roediger, "Inhibition in Recall from Cuing with Recall Targets," *Journal of Verbal Learning and Verbal Behavior,* 12 (1973), 644–657 and Raymond S. Nickerson, "Retrieval Inhibition from Part-Set Cuing: A Persisting Enigma in Memory Research," *Memory and Cognition,* 12 (November 1984), pp. 531–552.

5. In an interesting twist, it is also the case, however, that consumers would be more likely to recall closely related brands in the category, e.g., Wendy's. See Prakash Nedungadi, "Recall and Consumer Consideration Sets: Influencing Choice Without Altering Brand Evaluations," *Journal of Consumer Research,* 17 (December 1990), pp. 263–276.

6. Jacob Jacoby, George J. Syzabillo, and Jacqeline Busato-Schach, "Information Acquisition Behavior in Brand Choice Situations," *Journal of Consumer Research,* Vol. 3 (1977), pp. 209–216; Ted Roselius, "Consumer Ranking of Risk Reduction Methods," *Journal of Marketing,* 35 (January 1977), pp. 56–61.

7. James R. Bettman and C. Whan Park, "Effects of Prior Knowledge and Experience and Phase of the Choice Process on Consumer Decision Processes: A Protocol Analysis," *Journal of Consumer Research,* 7 (December 1980), pp. 234–48; Wayne D. Hoyer and Steven P. Brown, "Effects of Brand Awareness on Choice for a Common, Repeat-Purchase Product," *Journal of Consumer Research,* 17 (September 1990), pp. 141–48; C. W. Park and V. Parker Lessig, "Familiarity and Its Impact on Consumer Biases and Heuristics," *Journal of Consumer Research,* 8 (September 1981), pp. 223–30.

8. Richard E. Petty and John T. Cacioppo, *Communication and Persuasion.* New York: Springer-Verlag, 1986.

9. Burleigh B. Gardner and Sidney J. Levy, "The Product and the Brand," *Harvard Business Review* (March–April 1955), pp. 33–39.

10. Dawn Dobni and George M. Zinkhan, "In Search of Brand Image: A Foundation Analysis," in *Advances in Consumer Research,* Vol. 17, Marvin E. Goldberg, Gerald Gorn, and Richard W. Pollay, eds. Provo UT: Association for Consumer Research, 1990, pp. 110–119.

11. H. Herzog, "Behavioral Science Concepts for Analyzing the Consumer," in *Marketing and the Behavioral Sciences,* Perry Bliss, ed. Boston, MA: Allyn and Bacon, 1963, pp. 76–86 and Joseph W. Newman, "New Insight, New Progress for Marketing," *Harvard Business Review* (November–December 1957), pp. 95–102.

12. Joseph W. Alba and J. Wesley Hutchinson, "Dimensions of Consumer Expertise," *Journal of Consumer Research,* 13 (March 1987), pp. 411–53; Amitava Chattopadhyay and Joseph W. Alba, "The Situational Importance of Recall and Inference in Consumer Decision Making," *Journal of Consumer Research,* 15 (June 1988), pp. 1–12; Michael D. Johnson, "Consumer Choice Strategies for Comparing Noncomparable Alternatives," *Journal of Consumer Research,* 11 (December 1984), pp. 741–53; Edward J. Russo and Eric J. Johnson, "What Do Consumers Know About Familiar Products," in *Advances in Consumer Research,* Vol. 7, Jerry C. Olson, ed. Ann Arbor, MI: Association for Consumer Research, 1980, pp. 417–423.

13. James H. Myers and Allan D. Shocker, "The Nature of Product-Related Attributes," in *Research in Marketing,* Vol. 5, 1981, Jagdish Sheth, ed. Greenwich, CT: JAI Press.

14. These attributes are found in *Consumer Reports* reviews in 1994.

15. Robert C. Blattberg and Kenneth J. Wisniewski, "Price-Induced Patterns of Competition," *Marketing Science,* 8 (Fall 1989), pp. 291–309.

16. Patricia Sellers, "A Whole New Ball Game in Beer," *Business Week* (September 19, 1994), pp. 79–86.

17. William D. Wells, "How Advertising Works," unpublished paper, 1980. Christopher P. Puto and William D. Wells, "Informational and Transformational Advertising: The Differential Effects of Time," in Thomas C. Kinnear (ed.), *Advances in Consumer Research,* Vol. 11. Ann Arbor, MI: Association for Consumer Research, 1983, pp. 638–643. Stephen J. Hoch and John Deighton, "Managing What Consumers Learn From Experience," *Journal of Marketing,* 53 (April 1989), pp. 1–20.

18. Julie A. Edell and Marian C. Burke, "The Power of Feelings," *Journal of Consumer Research,* 14 (1987), pp. 421–433.

19. Joseph T. Plummer, "How Personality Makes a Difference," *Journal of Advertising Research,* Vol. 24 (December 1984/January 1985), pp. 27-31.

20. Bill Abrams, "Admen Say 'Brand Personality' Is as Crucial as the Product, " *Wall Street Journal,* (August 13, 1981) p. B3.

21. Jamie Beckett, "Why Companies Want You to Talk to Your Coffee," *San Francisco Chronicle,* (July 6, 1992), p. B3.

22. Jennifer Aaker, "Conceptualizing and Measuring Brand Personality," *Journal of Marketing Research,* in press and Susan Fournier, "Understanding Consumer-Brand Relationships," Working Paper 96–018, October 1995, Harvard Business School.

23. Jay Dean, "A Practitioner's Perspective on Brand Equity," in *Proceedings of the Society for Consumer Psychology,* 1994, eds. Wes Hutchinson and Kevin Lane Keller. Clemson, SC: CtC Press, pp. 56–62.

24. M. Joseph Sirgy, "Self Concept in Consumer Behavior: A Critical Review," *Journal of Consumer Research,* 9 (December 1982), pp. 287–300.

25. C. Whan Park, Bernard J. Jaworski, and Deborah J. MacInnis, "Strategic Brand Concept-Image Management," *Journal of Marketing,* 50 (October 1986), pp. 621–35.

26. Abraham H. Maslow, *Motivation and Personality,* 2nd ed. New York: Harper & Row, 1970. Geraldine Fennell, "Consumer's Perceptions of the Product-Use Situations," *Journal of Marketing,* 42 (April 1978), pp. 38–47. John R. Rossiter and Larry Percy, *Advertising and Promotion Management.* New York: McGraw-Hill, 1987.

27. Michael R. Solomon, "The Role of Products as Social Stimuli: A Symbolic Interactionsim Perspective," *Journal of Consumer Research,* 10 (December 1983), pp. 319–29.

28. William L. Wilkie, *Consumer Behavior,* 2nd ed. New York: John Wiley & Sons, 1990.

29. Russell H. Fazio, David M. Sanbonmatsu, Martha C. Powell, and Frank R. Kardes, "On the Automatic Activation of Attitudes," *Journal of Personality and Social Psychology,* 50 (February 1986), pp. 229–238.

30. Russell H. Fazio and Mark Zanna, "Direct Experiences and Attitude Behavior Consistency," in *Advances in Experimental Social Psychology,* Vol. 14. Leonard Berkowitz, ed. New York: Academic Press, 1981, pp. 161–202.

31. Ida E. Berger and Andrew A. Mitchell, "The Effect of Advertising on Attitude Accessibility," *Journal of Consumer Research,* 16 (December 1989), pp. 280–8. Russell H. Fazio, Martha C. Powell, and Carol J. Williams, "The Role of Attitude Accessibility in the Attitude and Behavior Process," *Journal of Consumer Research,* 16 (December 1989), 288–16.

32. Amitava Chattopadhyay and Joseph W. Alba, "The Situational Importance of Recall and Inference in Consumer Decision Making," *Journal of Consumer Research,* 15 (June 1988), pp. 1–12.

33. Lynch, John G. Jr., Howard Mamorstein, and Michael Weigold, "Choices From Sets Including Remembered Brands: Use of Recalled Attributes and Prior Overall Evaluations," *Journal of Consumer Research,* 15 (September 1988), pp. 169–184.

34. Peter H. Farquhar, "Managing Brand Equity," *Marketing Research,* 1 (September 1989), pp. 24–33.

35. John R. Anderson, *The Architecture of Cognition.* Cambridge, MA: Harvard University Press, 1983.

36. For additional discussion, see John G. Lynch Jr. and Thomas K. Srull, "Memory and Attentional Factors in Consumer Choice: Concepts and Research Methods," *Journal of Consumer Research,* 9 (June 1982), pp. 18–36 and Joseph W. Alba, J. Wesley Hutchinson, and John G. Lynch, Jr., "Memory and Decision Making," in *Handbook of Consumer Theory and Research,* Harold H. Kassarjian and Thomas S. Robertson (eds.). Upper Saddle River, NJ: Prentice Hall, 1992, pp. 1–49.

37. Fergus I. M. Craik and Robert S. Lockhart, "Levels of Processing: A Framework for Memory Research," *Journal of Verbal Learning and Verbal Behavior,* 11 (1972), pp. 671–684; Fergus I. M. Craik and Endel Tulving, "Depth of Processing and the Retention of Words in Episodic Memory," *Journal of Experimental Psychology,* 104 (3) (1975), pp. 268–294; Robert S. Lockhart, Fergus I. M. Craik, and Larry Jacoby, "Depth of Processing, Recognition, and Recall," in *Recall and Recognition,* John Brown, ed. New York: John Wiley & Sons, 1976.

38. Magid Abraham and Leonard Lodish, *Advertising Works: A Study of Advertising Effectiveness and the Resulting Strategies and Tactical Implications.* Chicago, IL: Information Resources, 1989.

39. Elizabeth F. Loftus and Gregory R. Loftus, "On the Permanence of Stored Information in the Human Brain," *American Psychologist,* 35 (May 1980), pp. 409–420.

40. Abraham Maslow, *Motivation and Personality,* 2nd ed. New York: Harper & Row, 1970.

41. Thomas J. Reynolds and Jonathan Gutman, "Laddering Theory: Method, Analysis, and Interpretation," *Journal of Advertising Research* (February/March 1988), pp. 11–31.

42. Lynn R. Kahle, Basil Poulos, and Ajay Sukhdial, "Changes in Social Values in the United States During the Past Decade," *Journal of Advertising Research* (February/March 1988), pp. 35–41.

43. Gerard Lambert, *All Out of Step.* Garden City, NY: Doubleday & Co., 1956, p. 188 summarized in William Weilbacher, *Brand Marketing*, Chicago, IL: NTC Business Books, 1993, pp. 30–31.

44. George S. Day, Allan D. Shocker, and Rajendra K. Srivastava, "Customer-Oriented Approaches to Identifying Products-Markets," *Journal of Marketing*, 43 (Fall 1979), pp. 8–19.

45. K. E. Miller and J. L. Ginter, "An Investigation of Situational Variation in Brand Choice Behavior and Attitude," *Journal of Marketing Research,* 16 (February 1979), pp. 111–123.

46. David A. Aaker, "Positioning Your Brand," *Business Horizons,* 25 (May/June 1982), pp. 56–62; Al Ries and Jack Trout, *Positioning: The Battle for Your Mind.* New York: McGraw-Hill, 1979; Yoram Wind, *Product Policy: Concepts, Methods, and Strategy.* Reading, MA: Addison-Wesley, 1982.

47. Deborah J. MacInnis and Kent Nakomoto, "Factors That Influence Consumers' Evaluations of Brand Extensions," working paper, Karl Eller School of Management, University of Arizona, 1991; Mita Sujan and James R. Bettman, "The Effects of Brand Positioning Strategies on Consumers' Brand and Category Perceptions: Some Insights from Schema Research," *Journal of Marketing Research,* 26 (November 1989), pp. 454–467.

48. James R. Bettman and Mita Sujan, "Effects of Framing on Evaluation of Comparable and Noncomparable Alternatives by Expert and Novice Consumers," *Journal of Consumer Research,* 14 (September 1987), pp. 141–154; Michael D. Johnson, "Consumer Choice Strategies for Comparing Noncomparable Alternatives," *Journal of Consumer Research,* 11 (December 1984), pp. 741–753; C. Whan Park and Daniel C. Smith, "Product Level Choice: A Top-Down or Bottom-Up Process?" *Journal of Consumer Research,* 16 (December 1989), pp. 289–299.

49. Joel B. Cohen and Kanul Basu, "Alternative Models of Categorization: Towards a Contingent Processing Framework," *Journal of Consumer Research,* 13 (March 1987), pp. 455–472; Prakash Nedungadi and J. Wesley Hutchinson, "The Prototypicality of Brands: Relationships With Brand Awareness, Preference, and Usage," in Elizabeth C. Hirschman and Morris B. Holbrook, eds., *Advances in Consumer Research,* Vol. 12. Provo, UT: Association for Consumer Research, 1985, pp. 489–503; Eleanor Rosch and Carolyn B. Mervis, "Family Resemblance: Studies in the Internal Structure of Categories," *Cognitive Psychology,* 7 (October 1975), pp. 573–605; James Ward and Barbara Loken, "The Quintessential Snack Food: Measurement of Prototypes," in Richard J. Lutz (ed.), *Advances in Consumer Research,* Vol. 13. Provo, UT: Association for Consumer Research, 1986, pp. 126–131.

50. Prakash Nedungadi and J. Wesley Hutchinson, "The Prototypicality of Brands: Relationships With Brand Awareness, Preference, and Usage," in Elizabeth C. Hirschman and Morris B. Holbrook, eds., *Advances in Consumer Research,* Vol. 12. Provo, UT: Association for Consumer Research, 1985, pp. 489–503; James Ward and Barbara Loken, "The Quintessential Snack Food: Measurement of Prototypes," in Richard J. Lutz (ed.), *Advances in Consumer Research,* Vol. 13. Provo, UT: Association for Consumer Research, 1986, pp. 126–131.

51. Philip Kotler, *Marketing Management,* 8th ed. Upper Saddle River, NJ: Prentice Hall, 1994.

52. Russell I. Haley, "Benefit Segmentation: A Decision-Oriented Research Tool," *Journal of Marketing,* 32 (July 1968), pp. 30–35.

53. Also, it may be the case that the actual demographic specifications given do not fully reflect consumers' underlying perceptions. For example, when the Ford Mustang was introduced, the intended market segment was much younger than the ages of the actual customers who bought the car. Evidently, these consumers felt or wanted to feel younger psychologically than they really were.

54. Ronald Frank, William Massey, and Yoram Wind, *Market Segmentation.* Upper Saddle River, NJ: Prentice Hall, 1972.

55. Chip Walker, "How Strong Is Your Brand," *Marketing Tools* (January/February 1995), pp. 46–53.

56. A complete treatment of this material is beyond the scope of this chapter. Useful reviews can be found in any good marketing strategy text. For example, see Chapter 3 of Donald R. Lehmann and Russell S. Winer, *Product Management.* Upper Saddle River, NJ: Prentice Hall, 1994.

57. The concept of "points of parity" and "points of difference" and many of the other ideas in this section were first developed by Northwestern University's Brian Sternthal.

58. John Czepiel, *Competitive Marketing Strategy.* Upper Saddle River, NJ: Prentice Hall, 1992.

59. Brian Sternthal, "Miller Lite Case," Kellogg Graduate School of Management, Northwestern University.

60. Interestingly, when Miller Lite was first introduced, the assumption was that the relevant motivation underlying the benefit of "less filling" for consumers was that they could drink more beer. Consequently, Miller targeted heavy users of beer with a sizable introductory ad campaign concentrated on mass market sports programs. As it turned out, the initial research showed that the market segment they attracted was more the moderate user—older

and upscale. Why? The brand promise of "less filling" is actually fairly ambiguous. To this group of consumers, less filling meant that they could drink beer and stay mentally and physically agile (sin with no penalty!). From Miller's standpoint, attracting this target market was an unexpected but happy outcome as it meant that there would be less cannibalization with its more mass-market High Life brand. To better match the motivations of this group, there were some changes in the types of athletes in the ads, e.g., ex-bull fighters to better represent mental and physical agility.

61. Greg Burns, "It Only Hertz When Enterprise Laughs," *Business Week* (December 12, 1994), p. 44.

62. Kathleen Deveny, "Anatomy of a Fad: How Clear Products Were Hot and Then Suddenly Were Not," *Wall Street Journal* (March 15, 1994), p. B1.

63. Michael J. McCarthy, "Pepsi Dates Diet Drink for Freshness in Risky Test to Gain Marketing Edge," *Wall Street Journal* (September 7, 1993), p. B4. Brad Morgan, "Spreading a Freshness Lesson Gleaned from Campaign History," *Brandweek* (April 25, 1994), p. 18.

64. John Smale, "Smale on Saturn—Don't Change What's Working," *Advertising Age* (March 28, 1994), p. S24.

65. Philip Kotler, *Marketing Management,* 8th ed. Upper Saddle River, NJ: Prentice Hall, 1994.

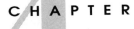

CHAPTER

Choosing Brand Elements to Build Brand Equity

Preview

Brand elements, sometimes called brand identities, are those trademarkable devices that serve to identify and differentiate the brand. The main brand elements are brand names, logos, symbols, characters, slogans, jingles, and packages. Independent of the decisions made about the product and how it is marketed, brand elements can be chosen in a manner to build as much brand equity as possible. That is, brand elements can be chosen to both enhance brand awareness and facilitate the formation of strong, favorable, and unique brand associations. The test of the brand-building ability of brand elements is what consumers would think about the product *if* they only knew about its brand name, associated logo, and other characteristics.

In this chapter, we consider how different brand elements can be chosen to build brand equity. After describing the general criteria to choose brand elements, we consider specific tactical issues for each of the different types of brand elements. The chapter concludes by addressing how a marketer should optimally choose a set of brand elements to build brand equity.

Brand Element Choice Criteria

In general, there are five choice criteria in choosing brand elements (as well as more specific choice considerations in each case as shown in Figure 4–1):

1. Memorability
2. Meaningfulness
3. Transferability
4. Adaptability
5. Protectability

The first two criteria—memorability and meaningfulness—can be characterized as "brand building" in terms of how brand equity can be built through the judicious choice of a brand element. The latter three, however, are more "defensive" in nature and are concerned with how the brand equity contained in a brand element can be leveraged and preserved in the face of different opportunities and constraints. We next briefly consider each of these general criteria.

MEMORABILITY

A necessary condition for building brand equity is achieving a high level of brand awareness. Towards that goal, brand elements can be chosen that are inherently memorable and therefore facilitate recall and/or recognition in purchase and/or consump-

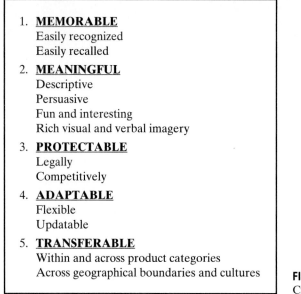

1. **<u>MEMORABLE</u>**
   Easily recognized
   Easily recalled
2. **<u>MEANINGFUL</u>**
   Descriptive
   Persuasive
   Fun and interesting
   Rich visual and verbal imagery
3. **<u>PROTECTABLE</u>**
   Legally
   Competitively
4. **<u>ADAPTABLE</u>**
   Flexible
   Updatable
5. **<u>TRANSFERABLE</u>**
   Within and across product categories
   Across geographical boundaries and cultures

FIGURE 4-1 Brand Elements Choice Criteria

tion settings. In other words, the intrinsic nature of certain names, symbols, logos, and the like—their semantic content, visual look, and so on—may make them more memorable and therefore contribute to brand equity. For example, naming a brand of propane gas cylinders, "Blue Rhino," and reinforcing it with a powder blue mascot with a distinctive yellow flame, as was the case with one firm, is likely to stick in the minds of consumers. Blue Rhino seeks the lion's share of replacement sales for the propane tanks of backyard gas grills by promising consumers convenience, safety, and reliability.

MEANINGFULNESS

Besides choosing brand elements to build awareness, brand elements can also be chosen whose inherent meaning enhances the formation of brand associations. Brand elements may take on all kinds of meaning, varying in descriptive, as well as persuasive, content. For example, chapter 1 described how brand names could be based on people, places, animals, birds, or other things or objects. Two particularly important dimensions or aspects of the meaning of a brand element are the extent to which it conveys general information about the nature of the product category and/or specific information about particular attributes and benefits of the brand.

First, in terms of descriptive meaning, to what extent does the brand element suggest something about the product category? How likely would it be that a consumer could correctly identify the corresponding product category or categories for the brand based on any one particular brand element? Relatedly, does the brand element seem credible in the product category? In other words, is the content of a brand element consistent with what consumers would expect to see from a brand in that product category? Second, in terms of persuasive meaning, to what extent does the

brand element suggest something about the particular kind of product that the brand would likely be, for example, in terms of key attributes or benefits? Does it suggest something about a product ingredient or the type of person who might use the brand? The associations suggested by a brand element may not always be related to the product: Brand elements can be chosen that are rich in visual and verbal imagery and inherently fun and interesting.

A memorable and meaningful set of brand elements offers many advantages. Because consumers often do not examine much information in making product decisions, it is often desirable that brand elements be easily recognized and recalled and inherently descriptive and persuasive. Moreover, memorable or meaningful brand names, logos, symbols, and so on reduce the burden on marketing communications to build awareness and link brand associations. The different associations that arise from the likability and appeal of the brand elements also may play a critical role in the equity of a brand, especially when few other product-related associations exist. Often, the less concrete the possible product benefits, the more important is the creative potential of the brand name and other brand elements to capture intangible characteristics of a brand.

TRANSFERABILITY

The third general criterion concerns the transferability of the brand element, both in a product category and geographic sense. First, to what extent can the brand element add to brand equity of new products sharing that element introduced either within the product class or across product classes? In other words, how useful is the brand element for line or category extensions, such as when the brand is used to introduce new products in the same or different categories? Second, to what extent does the brand element add to brand equity across geographical boundaries and market segments? To a large extent this depends on the cultural content and linguistic qualities of the brand element. For example, one of the main advantages of non-meaningful names (e.g., Exxon) is that they translate well into other languages since they have no inherent meaning. The mistakes that even top companies have made in translating their brand names, slogans, and packages into other languages and cultures over the years have become legendary. Figure 4–2 lists some well-known global branding mishaps.

ADAPTABILITY

The fourth consideration concerns the adaptability of the brand element over time. Because of changes in consumer values and opinions, or just because of a need to remain up-to-date or contemporary, brand elements often must be updated over time. The more adaptable and flexible the brand element, the easier it is to update it. For example, logos and characters can be given a new look or a new design to make them appear more modern and relevant.

PROTECTABILITY

The fifth and final general consideration concerns the extent to which the brand element is protectable—both in a legal and competitive sense.

1. When Braniff translated a slogan touting its upholstery, "Fly in leather," it came out in Spanish as "Fly naked."

2. Coors put its slogan, "Turn it loose," into Spanish, where it was read as "Suffer from diarrhea."

3. Chicken magnate Frank Perdue's line, "It takes a tough man to make a tender chicken," sounds much more interesting in Spanish: "It takes a sexually stimulated man to make a chicken affectionate."

4. Why Chevy Nova never sold well in Spanish speaking countries: "No va" means "it doesn't go" in Spanish.

5. When Pepsi started marketing its products in China a few years back, its slogan, "Pepsi Brings You Back to Life," was translated pretty literally. The slogan in Chinese really meant, "Pepsi Brings Your Ancestors Back from the Grave."

6. When Coca-Cola first shipped to China, it named the product something that when pronounced sounded like "Coca-Cola." The only problem was that the characters used meant "Bite the wax tadpole." They later changed to a set of characters that meant "Happiness in the mouth."

7. A hair products company, Clairol, introduced the "Mist Stick," a curling iron, into Germany, only to find out that "mist" is slang for manure.

8. When Gerber first started selling baby food in Africa, it used the same packaging as in the United States with the cute baby on the label. Later, they found out that in Africa companies routinely put pictures on the label of what's inside, since most people can't read.

FIGURE 4-2 Global Branding Mistakes

In terms of legal considerations, it is important to: (1) Choose brand elements that can be legally protectable on an international basis, (2) formally register them with the appropriate legal bodies, and (3) vigorously defend trademarks from unauthorized competitive infringement. The necessity of legally protecting the brand is dramatized by seeing the billions of dollars in losses in the United States alone from unauthorized use of patents, trademarks, and copyrights.

A closely related consideration is the extent to which the brand element is competitively protectable. Even if a brand element can be protected legally, it still may be the case that competitive actions can take away much of the brand equity provided by the brand elements themselves. If a name or package, for example, is too easily copied, much of the uniqueness of the brand may go away. For example, consider the ice beer category. Although Molson Ice was one of the early entries in the category, its pioneering advantage from a branding standpoint was quickly lost when Miller Ice and what later became Bud Ice were introduced. Thus, it is important to reduce the likelihood that competitors can imitate the brand by creating a derivative based on salient prefixes or suffixes of the name or emulating the package look.

Brand Element Options and Tactics

The value of choosing brand elements strategically to build brand equity can be seen by considering the advantages of having chosen "Apple" as the name for a personal computer. Apple was a simple but well-known word that was distinctive in the product category—factors facilitating the development of brand awareness. The meaning of the name also gave the company a "friendly shine" and warm brand personality. Moreover, the name could also be reinforced visually with a logo that could easily transfer across geographical and cultural boundaries. Finally, the name could serve as a platform for sub-brands (e.g., as with the Macintosh), aiding the introduction of brand extensions. Thus, as the Apple example illustrates, the judicious choice of a brand name can make a useful contribution to the creation of brand equity.

What would an ideal brand element be like? Consider brand names, perhaps the most central of all brand elements. Ideally, a brand name would be easily remembered, highly suggestive of both the product class and the particular benefits that served as the basis of its positioning, inherently fun and interesting, rich with creative potential, transferable to a wide variety of product and geographic settings, enduring in meaning and relevant over time, and strongly protectable both legally and competitively.

Unfortunately, it is difficult to choose a brand name—or any brand element for that matter—that would satisfy all of these different criteria. For example, as noted above, the more meaningful the brand name, the more likely it is that the brand name will not be very transferable to other cultures due to translation problems. Moreover, brand names are generally less adaptable over time. Because of the fact that it is virtually impossible to find one brand element that will satisfy all the choice criteria, multiple brand elements are typically employed. The following sections outline in detail the major considerations with each type of brand element. The chapter concludes by discussing how to "put all of this together" to design a set of brand elements to build brand equity.

BRAND NAMES

The brand name is a fundamentally important choice as it often captures the central theme or key associations of a product in a very compact and economical fashion. Brand names can be an extremely effective "shorthand" means of communication. Whereas the time it takes consumers to comprehend marketing communications can range from a half a minute (for an advertisement) to potentially hours (for a sales call), the brand name can be noticed and its meaning registered or activated in memory within just a few seconds. Because the brand name becomes so closely tied to the product in the minds of consumers, however, it is also the most difficult brand element for marketers to subsequently change. Consequently, brand names are often systematically researched before being chosen. The days when Henry Ford II could name his new automobile the "Edsel" after the names of family members seem to be long gone. As an example of the significant expense that can be incurred in branding research, Procter & Gamble reportedly spent $1 million developing the name, packaging, and image for Coast soap before its introduction.

Is it difficult to come up with a brand name? Ira Bachrach, a well-known branding consultant, notes that although there are 140,000 words in the English vocabulary, the average American only recognizes 20,000 words and his consulting company, NameLab, sticks to the 7000 words that make up the vocabulary of most TV programs and commercials. Although that may sound like a lot of choices, each year tens of thousands of new brands are registered as legal trademarks. In fact, arriving at a satisfactory brand name for a new product can be a painfully difficult and prolonged process. After realizing that most of the desirable brand names are already legally registered, many a frustrated executive has lamented that "all of the good ones are taken."

In some ways, this difficulty should not be surprising. Any parent can probably sympathize with how hard it can be to choose a name for a child—as evidenced by the thousand of babies born each year without names because their parents have not decided on, or perhaps not agreed upon, a name yet! It is rare that naming a product can be as easy as it was for Ford when it introduced the Taurus automobile. As it turns out, "Taurus" was the code name given to the car during its design stage as a result of the fact that the chief engineer and product manager's wives were both born under that astrological sign. As luck would have it, upon closer examination, the name turned out to have a number of desirable characteristics. Consequently, it was chosen as the actual name for the car, saving thousands of dollars in additional research and consulting expenses and much mental wear and tear.

Naming Guidelines

Selecting a brand name for a new product is certainly an art and a science. In this section we provide some general guidelines for choosing a name. We only focus on coming up with a completely new brand name for the product. Chapter 11 considers how a company can use existing brand or company names in various ways to name new products. As with any brand element, brand names must be chosen with the five general criteria in mind. After outlining some more specific naming criteria, we will describe the process by which a name should be chosen.

Brand Awareness   In general, it is believed that brand awareness is improved the extent to which brand names are chosen that are simple and easy to pronounce or spell; familiar and meaningful; and different, distinctive, and unusual.[1]

Simple and easy to pronounce or spell.   First, to enhance brand recall, it is desirable that the brand name is simple and easy to pronounce or spell. Simplicity reduces the cognitive effort by consumers to comprehend and process the brand name. Short names often facilitate recall because they are easy to encode and store in memory (e.g., Aim toothpaste, Raid pest spray, Bold laundry detergent, Suave shampoo, Off insect repellent, Jiff peanut butter, Ban deodorant, and Bic pens). Even longer names can be shortened to ease recallability. For example, over the years Chevrolet cars have also become known as "Chevy," Budweiser beer has also become known as "Bud," and Coca-Cola has also become known as "Coke."

Pronounceability is critical to obtain valuable repeated word-of-mouth exposure that helps to build strong memory links. Pronounceability also affects entry into consideration sets and the willingness of consumers to order or request the brand orally. Rather than risk the embarrassment of mispronouncing a difficult name (e.g., as might be the case with such potentially difficult-to-pronounce names as Hyundai automobiles, Fruzen Gladje ice cream, or Faconnable clothing), consumers may just avoid pronouncing it altogether. Clearly, it is a challenge to build brand equity for a brand with a difficult-to-pronounce name because so much of the initial marketing efforts have to be devoted to educating consumers as to just the proper way to pronounce the name. In the case of Wyborowa imported Polish vodka (pronounced Vee-ba-rova), management actually resorted to running a print ad to help consumers pronounce the brand name—a key consumer behavior success factor in the distilled spirits category.

Ideally, the brand name would have a clear, understandable, and unambiguous pronunciation and meaning. The way the brand is pronounced may affect its meaning. One research study showed that certain hypothetical products that had brand names that were acceptable in both English and French languages (e.g., Vaner, Randal, and Massin) were perceived as more "hedonic" (i.e., providing much pleasure) and better liked when pronounced in French than in English.[2]

Consumers may take away different perceptions of the brand if ambiguous pronunciation of its name results in different meanings. For example, research showed that the interpretation of the Honda Precis varied depending on how consumers thought the name was pronounced.[3] Although the name was meant to imply that the car was "precise and accurate," if consumers thought it was pronounced PREE-sus, they were more likely to think of it as an economy car (the intended positioning); on the other hand, if they thought it was pronounced PRAY-see, they were more likely to think of it as a luxury or sports car; and if they thought it was pronounced PRAY-sus, they were more likely to think of it as a family car.

Pronounceability problems may arise from not conforming to linguistic rules. Although Honda chose the name "Acura" because it was associated with words connoting precision in several languages, they initially had some trouble with consumer pronunciation of Acura (pronounced AK-yur-a) in the American market, perhaps in part because they chose not to use the more phonetically simpler English spelling of the name as Accura (with a double "C").

To improve pronounceability and recallability, many marketers seek a desirable cadence and pleasant sound in their brand names. For example, brand names may use alliteration (repetition of consonants; e.g., Coleco), assonance (repetition of vowel sounds; e.g., Ramada Inn), consonance (repetition of consonants with intervening vowel change; e.g., Hamburger Helper), or rhythm (repetition of pattern of syllable stress; e.g., Better Business Bureau). Some words employ onomatopoeia—words composed of syllables when pronounced that generate a sound strongly suggestive of the word meaning (e.g., Sizzler steak house, Cap'n Crunch cereal, Ping golf clubs, or Schweppes carbonated beverages).

Familiar and meaningful.   A second consideration to enhance brand recall is that the brand name is familiar and meaningful so that it is able to tap into existing knowledge structures. Brand names may be more concrete or abstract in their meaning. As pointed out in chapter 1, all types of categories of objects can be used to form a name (e.g., people, places, animals, birds, or different kinds of inanimate objects). Because these objects already exist in memory in verbal and visual form, less learning has to occur. Links can be more easily formed to the object name and product, increasing memorability.[4] One research study of hypothetical brand names showed that "high imagery" brand names, (e.g., Ocean, Frog, Plant, and Paper) were significantly more memorable across a variety of recall and recognition measures than "low imagery" words (e.g., History, Truth, Moment, and Memory).[5] Thus, when a consumer sees an ad for the first time for a car called "Neon," the fact that consumers already have the word stored in memory should make it easier to encode the product name and thus improve its recallability.

To help create strong brand-category links and aid brand recall, the brand name may also be chosen to suggest the product or service category (e.g., JuicyJuice 100 percent fruit juices, Ticketron ticket selling service, and *Newsweek* weekly news magazine). Brand elements that are highly descriptive of the product category or its attribute and benefits, however, may be potentially quite restrictive.[6] For example, it may be difficult to introduce a soft drink extension for a brand called JuicyJuice!

Different, distinctive, and unusual. Although choosing a simple, easy-to-pronounce, familiar, and/or meaningful brand name can improve its recallability, to improve brand recognition, it is important that brand names be different, distinctive, and unusual. As Chapter 3 noted, recognition depends more on discriminability, and more complex brand names are more easily distinguished. The distinctiveness of a brand name is a function of its inherent uniqueness as well as its uniqueness in the context of other competing brands in the product category. Distinctive words may be seldom used or atypical words for the product category (e.g., Apple computers), unusual combinations of real words (e.g., Toys-R-Us), or completely made-up words (e.g., Xerox or Exxon). Even made-up brand names, however, have to satisfy prevailing linguistic rules and convention (e.g., try to pronounce names without vowels such as Blfft, Xgpr, or Msdy!).

As with all brand choice criteria, tradeoffs must be recognized. Even if a distinctive brand name is advantageous for brand recognition, it also has to be seen as credible and desirable in the product category. A notable exception, Smuckers jelly has tried to turn the handicap of its distinctive, but potentially dislikable, name into a positive through its slogan, "With a Name Like Smuckers, It Has to Be Good!"

Brand Associations   Although choosing a memorable name is valuable, it is often necessary for the brand to have broader meaning to consumers than just its product category. Because the brand name is a compact form of communication, the explicit and implicit meanings that consumers extract from the name can be critical. In particular, the brand name may be chosen to reinforce an important attribute or benefit association that makes up its product positioning (e.g., as with ColorStay lipsticks, SnackWell reduced fat snacks, Die-Hard auto batteries, Mop'n Glow floor wax, Lean Cuisine low calorie frozen entrees, Shake'n'Bake chicken seasoning, and Cling-Free static buildup remover). Besides performance-related considerations, brand names also can be chosen to communicate more abstract considerations. For example, brand names may be more intangible or emotion-laden to arouse certain feelings (e.g., Joy dishwashing liquid, Caress soap, and Obsession perfumes).

A descriptive brand name should make it easier to link the reinforced attribute or benefit.[7] That is, it should be easier to communicate to consumers that a laundry detergent "adds fresh scent" to clothes if it were given a name such as "Blossom" than if it were given a neutral, nonsuggestive name such as "Circle."[8] Although brand names chosen to reinforce the initial positioning of a brand may facilitate the linkage of that brand association, they may also make it harder to link new associations to the brand if it later has to be repositioned.[9] For example, if a brand of laundry detergent were to be initially named Blossom and positioned as "adding fresh scent," it may be more difficult to attempt to later reposition the product, if necessary, and add a new brand association, for example, that the product "fights tough stains." Consumers may find it more difficult to accept or just too easy to forget the new positioning when the brand name continues to remind them of other product considerations.

With sufficient time and the proper marketing programs, however, the restrictive nature of suggestive names sometimes can be overcome. For example, consider Compaq computers. When two former Texas Instruments engineers were considering the name for their new line of portable personal computers, they chose the name "Compaq" because the name appropriately suggested a small computer. Through subsequent introductions of "bigger" personal computers, advertising campaigns, and other marketing activity, Compaq has been able to transcend the initial positioning suggested by its name. Similarly, Johnson & Johnson Baby Shampoo was also able to transport its "gentleness" association to a more adult audience when it was forced to reposition in the 1970s when the birth rate declined. Nevertheless, it must be recognized that such marketing maneuvers can be a long and expensive process. Imagine the difficulty of repositioning brands such as "I Can't Believe It's Not Butter" or "Gee, Your Hair Smells Terrific!" Thus, it is important in choosing a meaningful name to consider the possible contingencies in later repositioning and the necessity of having to link other associations at some point that become relevant or desirable with consumers.

Fictitious names.   Meaningful names are not restricted to only real words. Consumers can extract meaning, if they so desire, even out of made-up or "fanciful" brand names. For example, one study of computer-generated brand names containing random combinations of syllables found that "whumies" and "quax" were found to be remindful of a breakfast cereal and "dehax" was remindful of a laundry detergent.[10] Thus, consumers were able to extract at least some product meaning out of these essentially arbitrary names when instructed to do so. Nevertheless, the likelihood of consumers extracting meaning out of highly abstract names will depend on their motivation to do so. In many cases, consumers may not be so inclined.

Made-up brand names, however, are generally devised more systematically. Fictitious words are typically based on combinations of morphemes. A morpheme is the smallest linguistic unit having meaning. There are 6000 morphemes in the English language, including real words (e.g., "man") as well as prefixes, suffixes, or roots. For example, Compaq computer's name comes from a combination of two morphemes indicating "computers and communication" and a "small, integral object." The use of the less common morpheme "paq" as an ending—instead of pak, pac, or pach—was an attempt to suggest something scientific and unusual. Similarly, Nissan's Sentra automobile is a combination of two morphemes suggesting "central" and "sentry."[11] By combining carefully chosen morphemes, it is possible to construct brand names that actually have some relatively easily inferred or implicit meaning.

Even individual letters can contain meaning that may be useful in developing a new brand name. For example, some words begin with phonemic elements called "plosives" (i.e., the letters b, c, d, g, k, p, and t) whereas others use "sibilants" (i.e., sounds like s and soft c). Plosives escape from the mouth more quickly than sibilants and are harsher and more direct. Consequently, they are thought to make names more specific and less abstract and be more easily recognized and recalled.[12] One survey of the top 200 brands in the *Marketing and Media Decision*'s lists for the years 1971 to 1985 found a preponderance of brand names using plosives.[13] On the other hand, because sibilants have a softer sound, they tend to conjure up romantic, serene images and are often found with products such as perfumes (e.g., Cie, Chanel, and Cerissa).[14] One study found a relationship between certain characteristics of the letters of brand names and product features: As consonant hardness and vowel pitch increased in hypothetical brand names for toilet paper and household cleansers, consumer perception of the harshness of the product also increased.[15]

Brand names are not restricted to letters alone. Alphanumeric brand names contain one or more numbers in either digit form (e.g., 5) or in written form (e.g., "five").[16] Alphanumeric brand names may include a mixture of letters and digits (e.g., WD-40), a mixture of words and digits (e.g., Formula 409), or mixtures of letters or words and numbers in written form (e.g., Saks Fifth Avenue). Alphanumeric brand names may also be used to designate generations or relationships in a product line in terms of particular product models (e.g., BMW's 3, 5, and 7 series). Paiva and Costa conducted exploratory research of consumer perceptions of alphanumeric names. Not surprisingly, alphanumeric brand names often were associated with technology, although the particular perceptions depended on a number of factors, including the visual or aural aspects of the name, the actual numbers that were used in the name, and the words or letters that, along with the number(s), comprised the brand name.

A number of linguistic issues could be raised with brand names. Figure 4–3 contains an overview of different categories of linguistic characteristics with definitions and examples.

Naming Procedures

A number of different procedures or systems have been suggested for naming new products (see Figure 4–4 for the approach recommended by John Murphy of top naming firm Interbrand). Although some differences exist, most systems developing brand names can be seen as basically adopting a procedure something along the following lines:

1. In general, the first step in selecting a brand name for a new product is to define the branding objectives in terms of the five general criteria noted above. It is particularly important to define the ideal meaning that the brand should take. It is also necessary to recognize the role of the brand within the corporate branding hierarchy and how the brand should relate to other brands and products (as will be discussed in chapter 11). In many cases, existing brand names, at least in part, may be used.

2. With the strategic branding direction in place, the second step involves generating as many names and concepts as possible. Any potential source of names can be used: Company management and employees; existing or potential customers (including retailers or suppliers if relevant); ad agencies, professional name consultants, or specialized computer-based naming companies; and so on. Tens, hundreds, or even thousands of names may result from this step.

Characteristics	Definitions and/or Examples
Phonetic devices	
(1) Alliteration	Consonant repetition (Coca-Cola)
(2) Assonance	Vowel repetition (Kal Kan)
(3) Consonance	Consonant repetition with intervening vowel changes (Weight Watchers)
(4) Masculine rhyme	Rhyme with end of syllable stress (Max Pax)
(5) Feminine rhyme	Unaccented syllable followed by accented syllable (American Airlines)
(6) Weak/imperfect/slant rhyme	Vowels differ or consonants similar, not identical (Black & Decker)
(7) Onomatopoeia	Use of syllable phonetics to resemble the object itself (Wisk)
(8) Clipping	Product names attenuated (Chevy)
(9) Blending	Morphemic combination, usually with elision (Aspergum, Duracell)
(10) Initial plosives	*/b/, /c-hard/, /d/, /g-hard/, /k/, /p/, /q/, /t/* (Bic)
Orthographic devices	
(1) Unusual or incorrect spellings	Kool-Aid
(2) Abbreviations	7-Up for Seven-Up
(3) Acronyms	Amoco
Morphological devices	
(1) Affixation	Jell-O
(2) Compounding	Janitor-in-a-Drum
Semantic devices	
(1) Metaphor	Representing something as if it were something else (Arrid). Simile was included with metaphor when a name described a likeness and not an equality (AquaFresh).
(2) Metonymy	Application of one object or quality for another (Midas).
(3) Synecdoche	Substitution of a part for the whole (Red Lobster).
(4) Personification/pathetic fallacy	Humanizing the nonhuman or ascription of human emotions to the inanimate (Betty Crocker).
(5) Oxymoron	Conjunction of opposite (Easy-Off).
(6) Paranomasia	Pun and word plays (Hawaiian Punch).
(7) Semantic appositeness	Fit of name with object (Bufferin).

FIGURE 4-3 Brand Name Linguistic Characteristics

3. Next, the names must be screened based on the branding objectives and marketing considerations identified in step 1, as well as just common sense, to produce a more manageable list. For example, General Mills starts by eliminating:
   - Names that have unintentional double meaning
   - Names that are patently unpronounceable, already in use, or too close to an existing name
   - Names that have obvious legal complications
   - Names that represent an obvious contradiction of the positioning

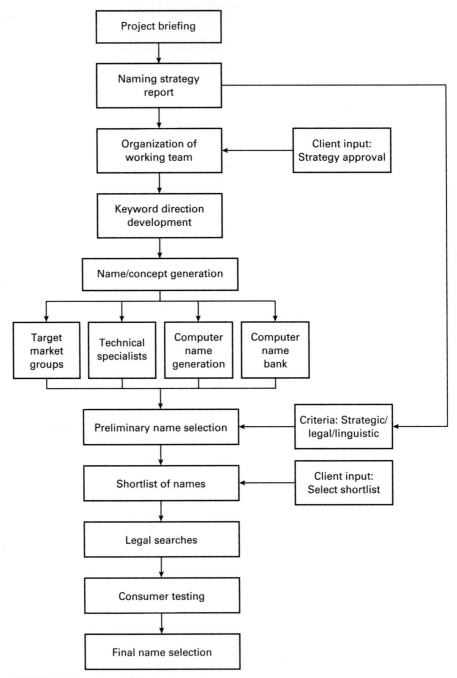

FIGURE 4-4 Interbrand Naming Procedure

They next have in-depth evaluation sessions with management personnel and marketing partners to narrow the list down to a handful of names or so. Often, a "quick-and-dirty" legal search may be conducted to help screen out legal "problem-children." Branding Brief 4–1 describes how General Mills developed the Triples brand of cereal.

4. The fourth step involves collecting more extensive information on each of the final five to ten or so names. Before spending large amounts of money with consumer research, it is usually advisable to do an extensive international legal search. Because of the costs involved, searches are sometimes done on a sequential basis, only testing those names in a new country that survived the legal screen from the previous country.

5. Next, consumer research is often conducted to confirm management expectations as to the memorability and meaningfulness of the names. Consumer testing can take on all forms. Many firms attempt to stimulate the actual marketing program for the brand and consumer's likely purchase experiences as much as possible.[17] Thus, consumers may be shown the product and its packaging, price, or promotion so that they understand the rationale for the brand name and how it will be used. Realistic three-dimensional packages as well as concept boards or animatic advertising may also be shown. Multiple samples of consumers may have to be surveyed depending on the target markets involved (e.g., to capture differences in regional or ethnic appeal). The effects of the brand name with repeated exposure and when spoken versus when written can also be factored in.

6. Finally, based on all of the information collected from the previous step, management can choose the name that maximizes the firm's branding and marketing objectives and then formally register the name.

LOGOS AND SYMBOLS

Although the brand name typically is the central element of the brand, visual brand elements often play a critical role in building brand equity, especially in terms of brand awareness. Logos have a long history as a means to indicate origin, ownership, or association. For example, families and countries have used logos for centuries to visually represent their names (e.g., the Hapsburg Eagle of the Austro-Hungarian Empire).

There are many types of logos, ranging from corporate names or trademarks (i.e., word marks) written in a distinctive form, on one hand, to entirely abstract logos that may be completely unrelated to the word mark, corporate name, or corporate activities, on the other hand.[18] Examples of brands with strong word marks (and no accompanying logo separate from the name) include Coca-Cola, Dunhill, and Kit-Kat. Examples of abstract logos include the Mercedes star, Rolex crown, CBS eye, Nike swoosh, and the Olympic rings. These non-word mark logos are also often called symbols.

Many logos are between these two extremes. Often logos are devised as symbols to reinforce or embellish the brand meaning in some way. Some logos are literal representations of the brand name, enhancing brand awareness (e.g., the Arm and Hammer, American Red Cross, and Apple logos). Logos can be quite concrete or pictorial in nature (e.g., the American Express centurion, Land o' Lakes butter Native American, the Morton salt girl with umbrella, and Ralph Lauren's polo player). Certain elements of the product or company can become a symbol (e.g., the Goodyear blimp, McDonald's golden arches, and Playboy bunny).

The importance of logos and symbols can be seen by the results of a study that asked 150 consumers their impressions of companies based on their names alone and also when their logos were present. The results could differ fairly dramatically de-

==

Branding a New Cereal[a]

In 1991, General Mills set out to introduce a new brand of cereal. Cereal is the third largest grocery store category behind cookies/crackers and bakery products, with extremely broad consumer appeal, as reflected by the category's 97 percent household penetration and the average of seven to nine brands in inventory per household. The cereal category had grown rapidly over the last decade, tripling in volume, resulting in some fierce competition from new entrants as over 200 brands fought for shelf space. Although Kellogg was the market share leader with 37.2 percent share in 1991, General Mills had been making significant inroads, increasing market share from 20.4 percent in 1985 to 24.6 percent in 1991.

General Mills's "Big G" power brands of cereals—defined as those cereal brands with dollar shares above 1 percent—included Cheerios, Honey Nut Cheerios, Apple Cinnamon Cheerios, Wheaties, Raisin Nut Bran, Oatmeal Raisin Crisp for adults and Lucky Charms, Trix, Cinnamon Toast Crunch, Kix, and Golden Grahams for kids. New product introductions are critical in the cereal market. Although General Mills had experienced some failures (e.g., Powdered Donutz and Protein Plus cereals), it had the best new product success rate in the industry, achieving at least 1/2 percent category share after the first year for eight of the fourteen last new brands it had introduced.

Cereals have three main attributes that determine their look and taste:

1. *Texture:* puff, flake, shredded, and/or chex
2. *Grain Type:* oats, bran, wheat, rice, and/or corn
3. *Nutrition:* fortified, multigrain, fiber, fruit, and/or pre-sweetened

Most cereals use a combination of these three attributes to differentiate themselves from other brands in the market. In looking for a new opportunity, General Mills considered which of the leading power cereal brands were most vulnerable. It determined that although Kellogg's Rice Krispies (KRK) controlled about 3 percent of the market, there was virtually no competition for the puffed rice business. General Mills decided to position their new product against KRK. After extensive concept and product testing, they decided that the best product options were a three-color, lightly sugar-coated, multigrain product that came in two package sizes (13 and 19 oz.). Blind taste tests revealed that this new product formulation was preferred over KRK by 51 percent to 37 percent.

In terms of product positioning, the primary selling proposition was defined as "a light and crispy cereal like KRK but with the hearty taste of three grains." Executionally, marketing communications were to have an upbeat, fun, and friendly tone that made the product look and sound appetizing. It was decided that the product name should communicate "three grains," "crispiness," and "all family." General Mills applied an extensive set of evaluation criteria in choosing the name, including the following: positioning, memorability, exclusivity, intrinsic merit, imagery, spellability, execution potential, credibility, consumer orientation, and legal considerations.

Based on these criteria, four alternatives were developed and screened: (1) Triple Crisp, (2) Triples, (3) Multigrain Crispers, and (4) Trios. The name "Triples" was selected because it was seen as upbeat, simple, exclusive, clever, and memorable, with no legal issues. Packaging was also seen as playing as important a role as other parts of the marketing mix and specific objectives were defined. A teal colored box was chosen based on consumer feedback because it was differentiated from KRK, had stronger shelf impact, was unique to the category, communicated "crispier" more effectively, and was thought to appeal in a fun way to the whole family.

The product was priced to be competitive with KRK ($2.49). In developing the introductory ad campaign, three different campaigns were tested: "Love, Love, Love," "Triple Take," and "Open Your Eyes." Based on ASI consumer testing, the first option was chosen because it received the highest measures in both brand name recall and attention measures. Heavy spending levels for advertising were chosen for the first year—a record-breaking $34 million. Given the importance of early trial, an aggressive promotion plan was also implemented using direct mail sampling; frequent, high value couponing with broad reach and targeted vehicles to consumers; and introductory allowances, display incentives, and shelf management guidelines to the trade.

General Mills started selling Triples in November 1990, shipping the product in January 1991, and advertising and couponing in February 1991. Year 1 retail sales were $60 million as 2.1 million twelve-pack cases were sold. By August 1991, Triples had reached its goal of 1 percent share of the cereal market, achieving power brand status. This early success elicited a strong competitive response by KRK, however, and Triples faced a formidable challenge to retain its market share over the long-term.

---

[a]Material presented at Stanford University by General Mills marketing executives.

pending on the company involved. Clearly, logos have meaning and associations that change consumer perceptions of the company. Like brand names, logos can acquire associations through their inherent meaning as well as through the supporting marketing program. In terms of inherent meaning, even fairly abstract logos can have different evaluations depending on the shapes involved. As with names, more abstract logos can be quite distinctive and thus recognizable. Nevertheless, because abstract logos may lack the inherent meaning present with a more concrete logo, one of the dangers of an abstract logo is that consumers may not understand what the logo is intended to represent without a significant marketing initiative to explain its meaning.

Benefits
Because of their visual nature, logos and symbols are often easily recognized and a valuable way to identify products, although a key concern is how well they become linked in memory to the corresponding brand name and product to boost brand recall. That is, consumers may recognize certain symbols but be unable to link them to any specific product or brand.

Another branding advantage of logos is their versatility: Because logos are often nonverbal, they can be updated as needed over time and generally transfer well across cultures. Because logos are often abstract without much product meaning, they also can be relevant and appropriate in a range of product categories. For example, corporate brands often develop logos because their identity may be needed on a wide range of products, although perhaps in more of a subordinate way as a means to endorse different sub-brands. Logos can allow the corporate brand to play a more explicit secondary role for these various products.

Finally, abstract logos are often useful when the use of the full brand name is restricted in some way. National Westminster Bank in the United Kingdom, for example, created a triangular device as a logo in part because the name itself was long and cumbersome and the logo could more easily appear as an identification device on checkbooks, literature, signage, and promotional material.[19]

Logos and symbols can be particularly important in services because of their intangible, abstract nature. For example, many insurance firms use symbols of either strength (e.g., the Rock of Gibraltar for Prudential and the stag for Hartford), security (e.g., the Traveller's umbrella, the "good hands" of Allstate, and the hard hat of Fireman's Fund), or some combination of the two (e.g., the castle for Fortis).

In the telecommunication industry, Sprint capitalized on an early ad campaign to create a powerful symbol. In introductory TV ads, Sprint demonstrated its fiber optic system by the fact that someone could literally hear a pin drop over the phone. Now, Sprint ads use the concept of a "pin drop" as a metaphor both visually and verbally to: (1) reinforce its early heritage, (2) communicate a still important product benefit (sound quality), and (3) signal an important corporate image dimension (innovation). Similarly, Memorex has used a shattered glass—introduced in earlier TV ads featuring Ella Fitzgerald and others—as a symbol to reinforce the audio reproduction qualities of its audiotape and communicate and signal other qualities of the brand.

Unlike brand names, logos can also be easily changed over time to achieve a more contemporary look. In doing so, however, it is important to make gradual changes that do not lose sight of the inherent advantages of the logo. In the 1980s, the trend for many firms was to create more abstract, stylized versions of their logos. In the process, some of the meaning, and thus equity, residing in these logos was lost. Recognizing their potential contribution to brand equity, some firms eventually reverted back to a more traditional look to their symbols or even brought back old symbols that had been tossed aside altogether (e.g., Lincoln-Mercury's cougar). For example, although Prudential had been through fourteen different versions of its Rock of Gibraltar logo, when it adopted a new version in 1983 that simply consisted of black and white slanting lines, some consumers just could not make a connection from the new logo to the traditional logo and what it had represented. As a result, Prudential subsequently introduced a sixteenth version that was still modern but clearly recognizable as the Rock of Gibraltar.

CHARACTERS

Characters represent a special type of brand symbol—one that takes on human or real-life characteristics. Brand characters typically are introduced through advertising and can play a central role in these and subsequent ad campaigns and package designs. Like other brand elements, brand characters come in many different forms. Some brand characters are animated (e.g., Pillsbury's Poppin' Fresh Doughboy, the Keebler Elves, and numerous cereal characters such as Tony the Tiger, Toucan Sam, and Cap'n Crunch) whereas others are live action figures (e.g., Marlboro cowboy, Mr. Whipple, or Ronald McDonald). In general, animated characters are more likely than live action characters to actually have a visible presence on packages. Figure 4–5 contains a more complete list of some popular brand characters.

One of the most powerful brand characters ever introduced is Pillsbury's Jolly Green Giant.[20] His origin can be traced back to the 1920s when the Minnesota Valley Canning Co. placed a green giant on the label of a new variety of sweet, large English peas as a means to circumvent trademark laws that prevented them from naming the product "Green Giant." Minnesota Valley Canning became Leo Burnett's first client after forming his agency in 1935, and after adding the word "jolly," the agency used the Jolly Green Giant character in print ads beginning in 1930 and in TV ads beginning in the early 1960s. At first, TV ads featured an actor wearing green body makeup and a suit of leaves. Later, the ads moved to full animation. Creatively, the ads have been very consistent. The Green Giant is always in the background, with his features obscure, and he only says "Ho-Ho-Ho." He moves very little, doesn't walk, and never leaves the "valley." The Green Giant has been introduced into international markets, following basically the same set of "rules."

The Little Sprout character was introduced in 1973 to bring a new look to the brand and allow for more flexibility. Unlike the Green Giant, the Little Sprout is a chatterbox, often imparting valuable product information. The characters and setting are always the same in Green Giant ads, although the story itself may differ depending on the product circumstances. Through it all, however, the Green Giant retains the same personality and continues to represent the key brand associations of "freshness," "quality," and "consistency." The Green Giant brand has enormous equity to Pillsbury, and it has found that using the name and character on a new product has been an effective signal to consumers that the product is "wholesome" and "healthy."

Benefits

Brand characters can provide a number of brand equity benefits. Because they are often colorful and rich in imagery, they tend to be attention-getting. Consequently, brand characters can be quite useful for creating brand awareness. Brand characters can also help to communicate a key product benefit. For example, Maytag's Lonely Repairman has helped to reinforce the key "reliability" product association (see Figure 4–6). Perhaps a more common image enhancement is related to brand personality and just the sheer likability of the brand. The human element of brand characters can help to create perceptions of the brand as being fun, interesting, or other favorable impressions. For example, recall from chapter 1 how the California Raisins helped to improve the product image of raisins as being more "hip" and "modern." As a result of the meaning and various feelings that can become attached, popular characters often are valuable licensing properties, providing direct revenue and additional brand exposure (see chapter 7). Finally, because brand characters do not typically have direct product meaning, they may also be transferred relatively easily across product categories. For example, Aaker notes that, "the Keebler's elf identity (which combines a sense of homestyle baking with a touch of magic and fun) gives

Brand	Character	Category
Aunt Jemima	Aunt Jemima	prepared foods
Bartles & Jaymes	Frank Bartle, Ed Jayme	alcoholic beverages
Borden	Elsie the Cow	dairy products
Bounty	Rosie the Waitress	paper towels
Budweiser	Spuds McKenzie	alcoholic beverages
Butterworth	Mrs. Butterworth	pancake syrup
California Raisins	Dancin' Raisins	produce
Cap'n Crunch	Cap'n Crunch	RTE cereals
Cheetos	Chester Cheeta	cheese snacks
Chicken of the Sea	Mermaid	canned fish
Colombian	Juan Valdez	coffee
Denny's	The Corlick Sister	food service
Domino's Pizza	The Noid	food service
Dunkin' Donuts	Donut Man	food service
Embassy Suites	Garfield	hotel
Energizer	Bunny	batteries
Fancy Feast	Fancy Feast Cat	pet food
Froot Loops	Toucan Sam	RTE cereals
Fruit of the Loom	Fruit Guys	underwear
Frosted Flakes	Tony the Tiger	RTE cereals
Green Giant	Green Giant/Little Sprout	vegetables
Hamburger Helper	Helping Hand	prepared foods
Hathaway Shirts	Man with eye-patch	apparel
Hawaiian Punch	Punchy	soft drinks
Hush Puppies	Hush Puppies puppy	apparel
Isuzu	Joe Isuzu ("The Liar")	automobiles
Keebler	Keebler Elves	cookies & crackers
Kool-Aid	Kool-Aid Kid	soft drinks
Kraft Macaroni 'n' Cheese	"Elizabeth"	prepared foods
Lucky Charms	Leprechaun	RTE cereals
Marlboro	Marlboro Cowboy	cigarettes
Maytag	Maytag Repairman	household appliances
McDonald's	Ronald McDonald	food service
McDonald's	Mac Tonight	food service
Merrill Lynch	Merrill Lynch Bull	financial services
Metropolitan	Peanuts	insurance
Michelin	Michelin Man	tires
Mr. Clean	Mr. Clean	floor cleaner
Mrs. Butterworth	Mrs. Butterworth	prepared foods
New Yorker Magazine	Eustace Tilley	publications
Nine-Lives	Morris the Cat	pet food
NTHSA	Vince & Larry	highway safety
Owens-Corning	Pink Panther	insulation
Palmolive	Madge the Manicurist	dishwashing liquid

FIGURE 4-5 Some Notable Past and Present Brand Characters[a]

Brand	Character	Category
Pepperidge Farm	Clarence	cookies & crackers
Peter Pan	Peter Pan	peanut butter
Planters	Mr. Peanut	nuts
Pillsbury	Poppin' Fresh (doughboy)	refrigerated dough
Qantas	Qantas Koala	airline
RCA	Nipper	audio-video equipment
Rice Krispies	Snap, Crackle, & Pop	RTE cereals
Schweppes	Commander Whitehead	beverages
Seven-Up	Seven-Up Spots	soft drinks
Snuggle	Snuggle Bear	fabric softener
Star-Kist	Charlie the Tuna	canned fish
Sugar Pops	Dig'um the Frog	RTE cereals
Tanqueray	Mr. Jenkins	gin
Trix	Trix Rabbit	RTE cereals
Union 76	Murph	gasoline
Vlasic	Stork	pickles

[a]Many thanks to Christie Brown for helping to put together this list.

FIGURE 4–5 Some Notable Past and Present Brand Characters[a] (*continued*)

the brand latitude to extend into other baked goods—and perhaps even into other types of food where homemade magic and fun might be perceived as a benefit."[21]

Cautions

There are some cautions and drawbacks to using brand characters. Brand characters can be so attention-getting and well-liked that they dominate other brand elements and actually dampen brand awareness. For example, when Ralston Purina introduced its drumming pink bunny that "kept going . . . and going . . . and going" in ads for its Eveready Energizer battery, many consumers were so captivated by the character that they paid little attention to the name of the advertised brand. As a result, they often mistakenly believed that the ad was for Eveready's chief competitor, Duracell. Consequently, Eveready found it necessary to add the pink bunny as a reminder to its packages, promotions, and other marketing communications to create stronger brand links.

Characters often must be updated over time so that their images and personalities are still relevant to the target market. The Campbell Soup kids have become more "buff" over time—taller, trimmer, and more athletic. Aunt Jemima has also lost some weight over the years and has a much different and contemporary look—she no longer wears a bandanna but sports a perky perm and pearl earrings instead.[22] Over a fifty-year period, there have been over 200 different "Breck Girls" who have appeared in ads for the shampoo—including Cybill Shepherd, Jaclyn Smith, Kim Basinger, and Brooke Shields.[23] In general, the more realistic the brand character, the more important it is to keep it up-to-date. One advantage of fictitious animated char-

FIGURE 4-6 Sample Maytag Ad

acters is that their appeal can be more enduring and timeless. Branding Brief 4–2 describes the efforts by General Mills to evolve the Betty Crocker character over time.

Current Developments

Brand characters continue to be introduced to help brands break through the marketplace clutter and create a point of difference. The 1980s saw the introduction of such notable characters as Joe Camel for Camel cigarettes, Joe Isuzu for Isuzu automobiles, and Domino's Pizza Noid. More recently, the most expensive liquor advertising campaign ever ($27 million) launched the character Mr. Jenkins for Tanqueray gin.[24] The liquor industry, in general, has struggled with attracting new consumers as they have watched their sales and shares slip in the beverage market as a whole. For years, Tanqueray's product image mirrored its user imagery—older, conservative, and stuffy. Tanqueray's ad agency, Deutsch, decided to try to turn these potential negatives into a positive by "taking older and turning it into more sophisticated; taking stuffiness and turning it into urbanity and wit; and taking conservative and turning it into restraint and a highly evolved sense of humor."

Deutsch decided to create a character who would seem sophisticated and elegant but also with a devilish side; someone who came across as honest and who could talk about life in real terms but could also find fun in traditionally unfunny situations. They chose the name Mr. Jenkins because it was "plain vanilla"—neither too snooty nor too ethnic. To find the right look for the character, they searched everywhere. Finally, in an article in *Town and Country* magazine about the social scene in West Palm Beach, Florida, they found the photo of Ridgely Harrison III, a 68-year-old retired executive who, in the words of the agency, "looked cool for an old guy." The agency crafted the image of the character to communicate the desired image of the brand: "the dualities of a clear liquor that yet had taste and complexity, who could relate to the older franchise but still have a lot of relevance for the younger audience." The ads placed Mr. Jenkins in settings "where his droll insights exposed pretense and skewered pomposity." One ad's headline read: "The applause was deafening when Mr. Jenkins told Stewart, the pianist, that if he didn't finish his 'Feelings' medley, he'd find himself wearing Mr. Jenkins' Tanqueray martini." Although some critics found fault and even parodied ads with the acerbic Mr. Jenkins, sales in the first year of the campaign increased 15 percent.

SLOGANS

Slogans are short phrases that communicate descriptive or persuasive information about the brand. Slogans typically appear in advertising but can play an important role on packaging and in other aspects of the marketing program. Slogans are powerful branding devices because, like brand names, they are a extremely efficient, shorthand means to build brand equity. Slogans can function as useful "hooks" or "handles" to help consumers grasp the meaning of a brand in terms of what the brand is and what makes it special.

Benefits

Slogans can be devised in a number of different ways to help build brand equity. Some slogans help to build brand awareness by playing off the brand name in some way (e.g., "My Doctor Said Mylanta," "Step up to the Mic" for Micatin, or "Aetna,

Bringing Betty Crocker into the 1990s

In 1921, Washburn Crosby Co., makers of Gold Medal flour, launched a picture puzzle contest. The contest was a huge success—the company received 30,000 entries—and several hundred contestants sent along requests for recipes and advice about baking. To handle these requests, the company decided they needed to create a spokesperson. They chose the name Betty Crocker because "Betty" was a popular, friendly sounding first name and "Crocker" was a reference to William G. Crocker, a well-liked, recently retired executive. The company merged with General Mills in 1928, and the newly merged company introduced the Betty Crocker Cooking School of the Air as a national radio program. During this time, Betty was given a voice and her signature began to appear on nearly every product that the company produced.

In 1936, the face was drawn by artist Neysa McMein as a composite of some of the home economists at the company. Prim and proper, Betty was shown with pursed lips, a hard stare, and graying hair. The appearance of Betty Crocker has been updated a number of times over the years (see Figure 4–7), making her appear more friendly (although she never lost her reserved look). Before her makeover in 1986, Betty Crocker was seen as honest and dependable, friendly and concerned about customers, and a specialist in baked goods, but also out-of-date, old and traditional, a manufacturer of "old standby products," and not particularly contemporary or innovative. The challenge was to

FIGURE 4-7 Betty Crocker Through The Years

give Betty a look that would attract younger consumers but not alienate older ones who remembered her as the stern homemaker of the past. There needed to be a certain fashionableness about her, not too dowdy, not too trendy, since the new look would need to be around for five to ten years. Her look also needed to be relevant to working women, too. Finally, for the first time, Betty Crocker's look was to also appeal to men, given the results of a General Mills study that showed that 30 percent of American men sometimes cooked for themselves.

Betty was given a more casual wash-and-wear look to her hair (as compared to the beauty parlor permanents of her predecessors), and her traditional red-and-white outfit was made a stylish suit and blouse complimented with a big bow and hoop earrings. The makeover seems to have taken—although Betty Crocker was close to 75, she didn't look a day over 35! Although the Betty Crocker name is on 200 or so products (for Betty Crocker Desserts, Helper Dinner Mixes, Fruit Snacks, and Pop Secret Microwave Popcorn), her visual image has since been largely replaced by the red spoon symbol on package fronts and basically only appears on cookbooks and in advertising.

I'm Glad I Met Ya"). Some slogans build brand awareness even more explicitly by making strong links between the brand and corresponding product category by combining both entities in the slogan (e.g., "If You're Not Wearing Dockers, You're Just Wearing Pants"). Most importantly, slogans can help to reinforce the brand positioning and desired point of difference (e.g., "Sometimes You Need a Little Finesse, Sometimes You Need a Lot," "It's Hard to Stop a Trane," and "Help Is Just Around the Corner. True Value Hardware"). For market leaders, slogans often employ "puffery" where the brand is praised with subjective opinions, superlatives, and exaggerations (e.g., Keebler's "Uncomparably Good"; Anheuser-Busch's "When You've Said Budweiser, You've Said It All"; and Bayer's "Bayer Works Wonders").

Slogans often become closely tied to advertising campaigns and are used as taglines to summarize the descriptive or persuasive information conveyed in the ads. In categories where advertising plays a key role in building brand equity, slogans may be an important means of differentiation. For example, in the soft drinks category, millions of dollars in advertising are spent to craft an image for a brand. Consequently, slogans have become a valuable branding tool in terms of crafting a brand image, as illustrated by the recent histories of the two competing cola giants:

1. Coca-Cola, as the market leader in soft drinks, is especially concerned with creating catchy, well-liked slogans.[25] Perhaps their most successful slogan, "It's the Real Thing," dates back to 1969. Since that time, they have introduced several variations of this puffery-based slogan, such as, "Coke Is It," "Catch the Wave," "Can't Beat the Feeling," and "Can't Beat the Real Thing." Most recently, they have adopted the slogan, "Always Coca-Cola." For their Diet Coke brand extension, Coca-Cola used the slogan, "Just for the Taste of It," for eleven years after its introduction in 1982. The first followup slogan, "Taste It All," and its corollary, "One Awesome Calorie," were not well-received, however, and lasted only seven months, leading to the firing of the ad agency that held the account. The new slogan became, "This is Refreshment."

2. Pepsi-Cola has also chosen its slogans carefully from its original "Pepsi Generation," which evolved over time to "The Choice of a New Generation," before being replaced by the questionably received and never fully realized, "Gotta Have It." They subsequently adopted a more traditionally respectful, "Be Young. Have Fun. Drink Pepsi." Next, they went with the broader appealing slogan, "Nothing Else Is a Pepsi." More recently, however, they returned to the youthful appealing, "Generation Next." For Diet Pepsi, after years of changing slogans, the company struck gold in 1990 with popular television ads featuring Ray Charles (and the Raylettes) with the tagline, "You've Got the Right One, Baby," and the clever catch phrase, "Uh-huh!"

Designing Slogans

Some of the most powerful slogans are those that contribute to brand equity in multiple ways. Slogans can play off the brand name in a way to build both awareness *and* image (e.g., "Get Certain. Get Certs," "Maybe She's Born With It, Maybe It's Maybelline," or "The Big Q Stands for Quality" for Quaker State). Slogans also can contain meaning that is relevant in both a product-related *and* non-product-related sense. For example, consider the Champion sportswear slogan, "It Takes a Little More to Make a Champion." The slogan could be interpreted in terms of product performance, as meaning that Champion sportswear is made with a little extra care or with extra special materials, but also could be interpreted in terms of user imagery as meaning that Champion sportswear is associated with top athletes. This combination of superior product performance and aspirational user imagery is a powerful platform from which to build brand image and equity. Benetton has an equally strong slogan from which to build brand equity ("United Colors of Benetton") but, as Branding Brief 4–3 describes, it has not always been used to full advantage.

Updating Slogans

Some slogans become so strongly linked to the brand that it becomes difficult to subsequently introduce new ones (take the slogan quiz in Figure 4–8 and check at the bottom of the page to see how many slogans you can correctly identify). For example, Miller Lite beer has struggled to find a successor to its memorable "Tastes Great . . . Less Filling" slogan, most recently adopting the hopeful refrain, "Life Is Good" before moving to the controversial "Made by Dick" ads with its sometimes bizarre Miller Time refrain. Timex watches finally gave up trying to replace its classic, "Takes a Licking and Keeps on Ticking," and has returned to the tagline in its advertising. Seven-Up tried four different successors to their popular "Uncola" slogan—"Freedom of Choice," "Crisp and Clean and No Caffeine," "Don't You Feel Good About Seven-Up," and "Feels So Good Coming Down"—but none seemed to surpass the original.

Thus, a slogan that becomes so strongly identified with the brand can potentially "box it in." Successful slogans can take on lives of their own and become public catch phrases (as with Wendy's "Where's the Beef" in the 1980s and Bud Light's "Yes I Am" and "I Love You, Man" in the 1990s), but there can also be a down side to this success—slogans can quickly become overexposed and lose specific brand or product meaning.

Once a slogan achieves such a high level of recognition and acceptance, it may still contribute to brand equity, but probably as more of a reminder of the brand. Consumers may be unlikely to consider what the slogan means in a thoughtful way after

Benetton's Brand Equity Management

One of the world's top clothing manufacturers (with global sales at $2 billion), Benetton has experienced some ups and downs in managing its brand equity. Benetton built a powerful brand by creating a broad range of basic and colorful clothes that appealed to a wide range of consumers. Their corporate slogan, "United Colors of Benetton" would seem to almost perfectly capture their desired image and positioning. It embraces both product considerations (the colorful character of the clothes) and user considerations (the diversity of the people who wore the clothes), providing a strong platform for the brand. Benetton's ad campaigns reinforced this positioning by showing people from a variety of different racial backgrounds wearing a range of different colored clothes and products.

Benetton's ad campaigns switched directions, however, in the 1980s, addressing controversial social issues. Created in-house, they were shot by famed photographer, Oliverio Toscani. In the ensuing years, Benetton print ads and posters featured such unusual and sometimes disturbing images as a white child wearing angel's wings alongside a black child sporting devil's horns; a priest kissing a nun; an AIDS patient and his family in the hospital moments before his death; and, in an ad only run once in a French daily, *Liberation*, 56 close-up photos of male and female genitalia. In 1994, Benetton launched a $15 million ad campaign in newspapers and billboards in 110 countries featuring the torn and bloodied uniform of a dead Bosnian soldier. Critics have labeled these various campaigns as gimmicky, "shock" advertising and accused Benetton of exploiting sensitive social issues to sell sweaters. One fact is evident. Although these new ad campaigns may be appreciated by and effective with a certain market segment, they are certainly more "exclusive" in nature—distancing the brand from many other consumers—than the early Benetton ad campaigns that were so strikingly inviting to consumers and "inclusive" in nature.

Benetton's new ad campaigns have not been well received by its retailers and franchise owners. The ad displaying the dead Bosnian soldier received an especially hostile reaction all over Europe. In the United States, some of Benetton's more controversial ads have been rejected by the media, and Benetton's U.S. retailers commissioned their own campaign from Chiat-Day ad agency in an attempt to create their own, more sophisticated image for the brand. One group of retailers in Germany—Benetton's second largest market—objected so strongly to 1994's $80 million global campaign that they refused to pay certain merchandising and franchise fees, claiming that their sales had plunged almost 30 percent to 50 percent since Benetton began running its most controversial ads in 1992. As one spokesperson to the group said, "Benetton's ad strategy is morally condemnable, legally untenable, and economically extremely damaging.... They have ruined their own brand with tasteless ads." Benetton responds that it is only "highlighting social problems."

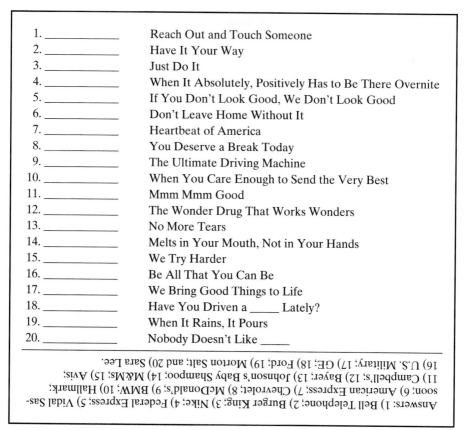

1. _____   Reach Out and Touch Someone
2. _____   Have It Your Way
3. _____   Just Do It
4. _____   When It Absolutely, Positively Has to Be There Overnite
5. _____   If You Don't Look Good, We Don't Look Good
6. _____   Don't Leave Home Without It
7. _____   Heartbeat of America
8. _____   You Deserve a Break Today
9. _____   The Ultimate Driving Machine
10. _____   When You Care Enough to Send the Very Best
11. _____   Mmm Mmm Good
12. _____   The Wonder Drug That Works Wonders
13. _____   No More Tears
14. _____   Melts in Your Mouth, Not in Your Hands
15. _____   We Try Harder
16. _____   Be All That You Can Be
17. _____   We Bring Good Things to Life
18. _____   Have You Driven a _____ Lately?
19. _____   When It Rains, It Pours
20. _____   Nobody Doesn't Like _____

Answers: 1) Bell Telephone; 2) Burger King; 3) Nike; 4) Federal Express; 5) Vidal Sassoon; 6) American Express; 7) Chevrolet; 8) McDonald's; 9) BMW; 10) Hallmark; 11) Campbell's; 12) Bayer; 13) Johnson's Baby Shampoo; 14) M&Ms; 15) Avis; 16) U.S. Military; 17) GE; 18) Ford; 19) Morton Salt; and 20) Sara Lee.

FIGURE 4-8 Famous Slogans Quiz

seeing or hearing it so many times. At the same time, a potential difficulty arises if the slogan continues to convey some product meaning that the brand no longer needs to reinforce. In this case, by not facilitating the linkage of new, desired brand associations, the slogan can become restrictive and fail to allow the brand to be updated as much as desired or necessary.

Because slogans are perhaps the easiest brand element to change over time, there is more flexibility in managing them. In changing slogans, however, as with changing other brand elements, it is important to:

1. Recognize how the slogan is contributing to brand equity, if at all, through enhanced awareness or image
2. Decide how much of this equity enhancement, if any, is still needed
3. Retain as much as possible the needed or desired equities still residing in the slogan while providing whatever new twists of meaning are needed to contribute to equity in other ways

In many cases, moderate modifications of an existing slogan (as was done with Coke) may prove more fruitful than introducing a new slogan with a completely new set of meanings.

JINGLES

Jingles are musical messages written around the brand. Typically composed by professional songwriters, they often have enough catchy hooks and choruses to become almost permanently registered in the minds of listeners—sometimes whether they want them to or not! During the first half of the twentieth century, when broadcast advertising was confined primarily to radio, jingles became important branding devices. Figure 4–9 contains a few famous brand jingles—sing along if you want (and can remember)!

Jingles can be thought of as extended musical slogans and in that sense can be classified as a brand element. Because of their musical nature, however, jingles are not nearly as transferable as other brand elements. Jingles can communicate brand benefits but, because of their musical foundation, jingles typically convey product meaning in a non-direct and fairly abstract fashion. The potential associations that might occur for the brand from jingles are probably more likely to relate to feelings and personality and other such intangibles. Jingles are perhaps most valuable in terms of enhancing brand awareness. Often, the jingle will repeat the brand name in clever and amusing ways that allow consumers multiple encoding opportunities. Because of their catchy nature, consumers are also likely to mentally rehearse or repeat the jingle even after seeing or hearing the ad, providing even additional encoding opportunities.

PACKAGING

Packaging involves the activities of designing and producing containers or wrappers for a product. Like other brand elements, packages have a long history. Early humans used leaves and animal skin to cover and carry food and water. Glass containers first appeared in Egypt as early as 2000 B.C. Later, the French emperor Napoleon awarded 12,000 francs to the winner of a contest to find a better way to preserve food, leading to the first crude method of vacuum-packing.[26]

From the perspective of both the firm and consumers, packaging must achieve a number of objectives:[27]

1. Identify the brand
2. Convey descriptive and persuasive information
3. Facilitate product transportation and protection
4. Assist at-home storage
5. Aid product consumption

To achieve the marketing objectives for the brand and satisfy the desires of consumers, the aesthetic and functional components of packaging must be chosen correctly. Aesthetic considerations relate to a package's size and shape, material, color, text, and graphics. Innovations in printing processes now permit eye-catching and appealing graphics that convey elaborate and colorful messages on the package at the "moment of truth" at the point-of-purchase.[28] Functionally, structural design is crucial. For example, packaging innovations with food products over the years have resulted in packages being resealable, tamperproof, and more convenient to use (e.g., easy-to-hold, easy-to-open, or squeezable). Changes in canning have made vegetables crunchier, and special wraps have extended the life of refrigerated food.[29]

I'D LIKE TO BUY THE WORLD A COKE
(COCA COLA)

I'd like to buy the world a home
And furnish it with love
Grow apple trees and honey bees
And snow-white turtle doves
I'd like to teach the world to sing
In perfect harmony
I'd like to buy the world a Coke
And keep it company
That's the real thing

I'd like to teach the world to sing
In perfect harmony
And I'd like to buy the world a Coke
And keep it company
It's the real thing
Coke is
(Repeat)

THE DOGS KIDS LOVE TO BITE
(ARMOUR HOT DOGS)

Hot dogs, Armour hot dogs
What kinds of kids eat Armour hot
dogs
Fat kids, skinny kids, kids who climb
on rocks
Tough kids, sissy kids
Even kids with chicken pox
Love hot dogs, Armour hot dogs
The dogs kids love to bite!

Pickin' it up on the old banjo
Put on the mustard, and away we go
When men bite dogs, it's news they say
But when kids bite dogs they yell
hooray!
For hot dogs,
Armour hot dogs
The dogs kids love to bite!

BE A PEPPER
(DR. PEPPER)

I drink Dr. Pepper, and I'm proud
I used to be alone in a crowd
But now you look around these days
There seems to be a Dr. Pepper crowd

Oh, You're a Pepper
I'm a Pepper, he's a Pepper, she's a
Pepper, we're a Pepper
Wouldn't you like to be a Pepper, too
I'm a Pepper, he's a Pepper, she's a
Pepper
If you drink Dr. Pepper, you're a Pep-
per, too

Us Peppers are an interesting breed
An original taste is what we need
Ask any Pepper and he'll say
Only Dr. Pepper tastes that way

I'm a Pepper, he's a Pepper, she's a
Pepper, we're a Pepper
Wouldn't you like to be a Pepper, too
Be a Pepper, drink Dr. Pepper . . .
(Repeat)

IF YOU'VE GOT THE TIME
(MILLER HIGH LIFE)

If you've got the time
We've got the beer
Miller beer
Miller tastes too good to hurry through

But when it's time to relax
Miller stands clear
Beer after beer
If you've got the time, you've got the
time
We've got the beer
Miller beer

FIGURE 4-9 Popular Jingles

Despite these advances, research has shown that consumers are still not satisfied and, for example, seek food packages that[30] (1) are tamperproof, easy to both open and close, and designed to keep products fresh; (2) come in single-serving portions or bulk assortments that can feed a small or large family but can be safely stored for long periods of time; and (3) are convenient (e.g., so that the package can be popped directly into the microwave—which roughly 80 percent of American families have—or the conventional oven). Of course, consumers want all of this done with as little adverse effect on the environment as possible (meaning that the package is recyclable, biodegradable, etc.). Despite all of the recent attention in food packaging, opportunities remain as consumers still report many problems with in-home use or storage. In a recent survey, consumers complained about food packages that stick, rip, or don't protect their contents. According to the study, the worst offenders were cookie, cracker, and chip bags; carbonated beverage cans; plastic lunch meat wrappers; sugar and flour bags; and cereal boxes. Out of frustration, some consumers were actually even doing their own repackaging at home![31]

Structural design improvements in packaging reflect research and development advances that do not always come easy. For example, the move to microwavable food products was complicated by the fact that, unlike the precision of temperatures on a conventional oven, microwaves vary to a greater deal in terms of their temperature settings. Nevertheless, functional packaging innovations can have a powerful impact on sales. For example, Minnetonka's Close-Up toothpaste was able to make a splash in the U.S. toothpaste market by introducing a pump dispenser.

Benefits

Packaging can have important brand equity benefits for a company. Often, one of the strongest associations that consumers have with a brand relates to the look of its packaging. For example, if you ask the average consumer what comes to mind when they think of Heineken beer, a common response is "green bottle." The package appearance can become an important means of brand recognition. Moreover, the information conveyed or inferred from the package can build or reinforce valuable brand associations. For example, certain colors suggest the image of a product. Although often avoided as being too funereal, black has become more popular as a means of communicating quality and elegance (e.g., Breyers ice cream adopted a round container and black background to cultivate a more upscale image). With a need to upgrade the perceived quality of their store brands, and in recognition of the power of bold graphics, supermarket retailers have been careful to design attractive, upscale packages on their own premium branded products.

Structural packaging innovations can create a point of difference that permits a higher margin. New packages can also expand a market and capture new market segments. For example, although V-8 had been a big seller for Campbell, consumer research found that soft sales among a younger target market was partly a result of the fact that these consumers simply did not shop the canned-good aisles where the brand was being stocked. Consequently, Campbell experimented by putting V-8 juice in cartons and six-packs so that they could be stocked in the more accessible refrigerator and beverage sections. Sales jumped 15 percent as a result.[32]

One of the major packaging trends of recent years is to make both bigger and smaller packaged versions of products (as well as portions!) to appeal to new market segments.[33] Jumbo products have been successfully introduced with hot dogs, pizzas, English muffins, frozen dinners, and beer. For example, Pillsbury's introduction of its Grand biscuits—40 percent larger than its existing offerings—was the most successful new product in the company's 126-year history.

Package design also has become more important in recent years as brand proliferation continues and advertising is seen as becoming less cost-effective. Packaging can be a means to have strong appeal on the shelf and stand out from the clutter. The importance of packaging at the point-of-purchase can be seen by recognizing that the average supermarket shopper is exposed to 15,000 to 20,000 products in a shopping visit that lasts less than 30 minutes and where many purchases may be unplanned. However, packaging is not important in only supermarket settings. For example, Microsoft changed its packages away from forest green—which was seen as not eye catching enough and more appropriate for chewing gum or frozen vegetables—to red and royal blue. Microsoft believes that the new packaging made a valuable contribution to its marketing success.[34]

For many consumers, the first encounter with a new brand may be on the supermarket shelf or in the store. Because few product differences exist in some categories, packaging innovations can provide at least a temporary edge on competition. For these reasons, packaging has been seen as a particularly cost-effective way to build brand equity.[35] Along these lines, packaging is sometimes called the "last five seconds of marketing" as well as "permanent media."

In mature markets especially, package innovations can provide a short-term sales boost. For example, packaging innovations such as the 2-liter jug bottle and the 12-pack carton helped soft drink makers experience steady 5 percent to 7 percent growth in the 1980s. With the rate of growth of the soft drink industry slowing down to 2 percent to 3 percent in the 1990s, soft drink makers have sought new packaging innovations to fuel additional growth. As a result, Pepsi-Cola introduced the 24-pack Cube, 12-ounce resealable bottles, 8-ounce Pepsi Mini cans, and the wide-mouth, 1-liter Big Slam bottle. Even the traditional look of Pepsi's packaging, which had not been changed since 1973, has been updated, giving it a streamlined, more contemporary version of the red and blue swirl first introduced in 1943. Starting in overseas markets, Pepsi has been testing even more dramatic packaging and logo changes, moving to a space-age blue look. Not to be outdone, Coca-Cola recently returned to some of its brand heritage to feature its patented contour bottle, originally introduced in 1915. Aided by a supporting ad campaign, Coke sales due to the contour bottle have shot up.[36]

Packaging innovations such as Snapple's widemouth glass bottle have also contributed to strong market performance for other beverages. Arizona's iced teas and fruit drinks in oversize (24-ounce), pastel-colored cans with a Southwestern motif became a $300 million brand in a few years with no marketing support beyond point-of-purchase and rudimentary outdoor ads, designed in-house![37]

Also picking up on the packaging trend—and in the face of slumping sales— wine makers have gone beyond pretty labels to consider selling the fruits of their labor in bottles of different shapes and sizes.[38] As one packaging expert noted, "Wine makers are finding out that packaging can be a real important part of a product's appeal. Not just a prettier label but a functionally different package." To illustrate some of the changes, note the following observation by one marketing commentator:

If you're taking a lunch break on the ski slopes, you can open up a 187 milliliter screw-cap bottle, the size that used to be found only on planes but now can be bought in supermarkets and at mountaintop ski cafes. If you're expecting lots of relatives for the holidays, you can try a five-liter bag-in-a-box. If you're having an intimate dinner with a temperate date, uncork a 500 milliliter bottle, which holds four glasses instead of the six in the standard 750 milliliter bottle.

Although still relatively small in absolute terms, these new packages have seen the fastest relative growth in sales in the category. New packages are even being used for varietal wines (i.e., wines identified with a particular grape such as with chardonnays), as well as with the blended jug or generic wines. Wine makers are hoping that at least some consumers will trade image and status for convenience (with smaller bottles) and value (with bigger bottles).

Finally, it should also be recognized that consumer exposure to packaging is not restricted to only the point-of-purchase and moments of consumption, as brand packages often play a starring role in advertising. One survey of 200 TV commercials in ten mass-market product categories indicated that the package was featured, on average, roughly 12 seconds out of a 30-second spot.[39] Newer products, or variations or updates of older ones, tended to feature the package longer, a sensible advertising strategy for brands with marketing objectives to build brand recognition. Print ads also often prominently display the package.

Package Design

For all these reasons, package design has been elevated in its importance and has now become an integral part of product development and launch. In fact, the cost of packaging across all U.S. firms has been estimated by some to be as much as $50 billion annually, an amount that would even exceed total ad expenditures. Branding Brief 4–4 describes the activities of Landor Associates, one of the leading package design and image management firms in the world.

As with the choice of a brand name, package design has become a much more sophisticated process. In the past, package design was often an afterthought, as colors and materials were often chosen fairly arbitrarily. For example, legend has it that the color of the famous Campbell soup can was a result of the fact that one executive at the company liked the look of the red and white uniforms of Cornell University's football team! These days, specialized package designers bring artistic techniques and scientific skills to package design in an attempt to meet the marketing objectives for a brand. These consultants conduct detailed analyses to break down the package into a number of different "elements." They decide on the optimal look and content of each element and the proper packaging "hierarchy" in terms of which elements should be dominant in any one package (e.g., the brand name, illustration, or some other graphical element) and how the elements should relate. When brand extensions are introduced, these designers can also decide which elements should be shared across packages and which elements should differ (and how).

Designers often refer to the "shelf impact" of a package—the visual effect that the package has at the point of the purchase when seen in the context of other packages in the category. For example, "bigger and brighter" packages are not always better when competitors' packages are also factored in. Although some information is legally required on packages (e.g., nutrition information for food packages), a number

---

Corporate Make-Over Experts Landor Associates

One of the premier image consultants and strategic designers in the world, Landor Associates, called the Ferryboat Kalmath, anchored at Pier 5 in San Francisco, home for years. Although it has since moved into more spacious headquarters, Landor has retained the ferryboat as a symbol of the creativity and innovation that it feels it brings to its marketing assignments. Landor has provided a wide range of services to a varied list of clients. Some of the professional services Landor provides include corporate image management; naming systems; corporate, brand, and retail identity systems design, identity systems documentation, consumer research, retail space planning, brand value analysis, product positioning, communication strategies, corporate positioning, signage systems development, and corporate culture integration.

Landor has provided the name and graphic identity for Touchstone Pictures, Saturn automobiles, Dollar Rent-A-Car; devised packaging for Miller Genuine Draft; created the Cotton Mark—the first of any commodity product to add value through strategic branding; has redone packages for brands such as Coca-Cola, Maxwell House, V-8, Hawaiian Punch, Jergens soaps and lotions, and Oral-B; has created a branding and packaging system for 3M, General Electric, Birds Eye, Lean Cuisine, and Black & Decker; and has defined corporate identity for numerous airlines, including British Airways.

A case study can help to illustrate the kinds of services provided by an image consultant such as Landor. In 1984, Castle and Cooke, with corporate sales of $1.5 billion, decided on an aggressive new strategic direction for its Dole brand, which it had marketed since the 1930s. Castle and Cooke's objectives were to correct declining volume in the base canned pineapple business and to leverage the brand into other categories beyond pineapple. To capitalize on consumer trends towards healthier, more active lifestyles and demand for lighter, more nutritious diets, Castle and Cooke set the strategic objective of "becoming a leading worldwide supplier and marketer of premium quality, value-added fresh fruit, vegetables, and packaged goods."

While predesign research indicated that Dole was one of the most trusted and respected brand names in the food business, the Dole imagery and brand values were underutilized. Although the brand conveyed an image of premium quality, value, and natural healthfulness, consumers were still somewhat confused about the brand because of the fragmented projection of multiple visual images through Dole's various categories and product lines. Consumers did not connect the name Dole with any distinct visual image. Clearly, a single consistent visual identity was needed that would enhance Dole's brand presence throughout food markets worldwide and be relevant across a wide range of fresh and processed products.

Capitalizing on the strengths of positive Dole brand associations and the elasticity of the Dole name itself, Landor created a bold new global brand identity which was intended to bring consistency, meaning, and personality to the Dole brand. While retaining the basic colors and the rich heritage from the

long-time association with pineapple and the sunny fields of Hawaii, the new identity also attempted to capture the company's expanded business and marketing directions. The Dole symbol was integrated into the name itself, creating a singular Dole identity focal point. Rays of sunshine bursting through the "O" were to literally represent Dole's "sunshine foods" products and to provide a flexible umbrella identity for healthy and natural food items the company would market in the future. The dramatic new identity was applied to all existing and new products—canned, fresh, refrigerated and frozen—in the U.S. and abroad, to give Dole a motivating consistent identity and create synergy throughout Dole's expanding presence within the supermarket.

The new Dole brand identity and packaging system were evaluated by consumer research in the United States, Japan, and West Germany with consumers preferring the new identity over the old one by an overwhelming margin of more than 70 percent. In consumer testing, the new system was viewed as having improved brand registration and shelf impact and exceeded the previous identity across all imagery attributes, including the critical image clusters of "good quality," "natural," and "appetite appeal."

of decisions can be made about design elements to improve brand awareness and facilitate the formation of brand associations.

Perhaps one of the most important visual design elements for a package is its color. Some package designers believe that consumers have a "color vocabulary" when it comes to products and expect certain types of products to have a particular look. For example, it is believed that it would be difficult to sell milk in anything but a white carton or club soda in anything but a blue package. At the same time, certain brands are also thought to have "color ownership" such that it would be difficult for other brands to use a similar look. One leading design executive outlined the following brand color palette:[40]

Red:	Ritz crackers, Folgers coffee, Colgate toothpaste, and Coca-Cola soft drinks.
Orange:	Tide laundry detergent, Wheaties cereal, and Stouffers frozen dinners.
Yellow:	Kodak film, Juicy Fruit chewing gum, Cheerios cereal, and Bisquick biscuit mix.
Green:	Del Monte canned vegetables, Green Giant frozen vegetables, and 7UP soft drink.
Blue:	IBM computers, Windex cleaner, and Downy fabric softener.

Packaging color can affect consumers' perceptions of the product itself.[41] For example, consumers ascribe sweeter taste to orange drinks the darker the orange shade of the can or bottle. Researchers at Derni Corp. found that when they changed the color of the packaging of their Barrelhead Sugar-Free Root Beer from beige to blue, people were more likely to agree that it "tasted like old-fashioned root beer served in frosty mugs." Similarly, marketers of Miller High Life beer struggled for years with the fact that a clear bottle made their beer seem less hearty than the market leader,

Budweiser, which was sold in a dark bottle. They finally resorted to an ad campaign to try to correct the misperception.

In addition to the specific product inferences signaled by the color and other packaging design elements, it is also important that any other associations conveyed by the packaging be consistent with information conveyed by other aspects of the marketing program. In particular, as will be pointed out in chapter 6, packaging should be designed in some cases to directly reinforce advertising in certain ways.

Packaging Changes

Packages are changed for a number of reasons.[42] Packaging may be upgraded to signal a higher price, to more effectively sell products sold through new or shifting distribution channels (e.g., when Kendall Oil found more of its sales coming from supermarkets and hardware stores rather than service stations, it redid its packages to make them more appealing to do-it-yourselfers), or when there is a significant product line expansion that would benefit from a common look (e.g., as with Planter's nuts, Weight Watchers foods, or Stouffers frozen foods). Package redesign may also accompany a new product innovation to signal changes to consumers. For example, when Procter & Gamble introduced Liquid Tide laundry detergent, the company felt that the 10 percent market share that the brand achieved was helped by the addition of a well-received drip-proof spout and bottle cap package design.[43]

Perhaps the most common reason for package redesign is that the old package just looks outdated. Under these circumstances, it is important when the packaging is changed that the key package equities that have been built up are not lost as a result. Packaging often has some unique graphic features that have achieved a high level of awareness and preference. The need to create a more contemporary look must be reconciled with the need to preserve existing packaging equities.

For example, marketing managers at Bayer maintain that its aspirin packaging has two key graphic features—the yellow box and the Bayer Shield. Although their packaging may be updated, Bayer management has said that these two features will always be prominent.[44] Similarly, when marketers at Ralston-Purina made the first-ever packaging change in an attempt to rejuvenate sales of their fading market leader, Purina Dog Chow dog food, they made sure to balance old elements with new elements.[45] The nine drawings of dog breeds that were seen as old-fashioned and too rural by consumers were replaced by a photo of a single dog and a boy. Retained, however, were key packaging features such as a dark green background, yellow lettering, and the slogan, "All you add is love."

In some cases, package designs have to be changed frequently to keep the product contemporary and relevant to a younger audience. For example, Procter & Gamble's Clearasil acne medication gets a package change every few years because the company believes that teens in that market tend to buy the newest looking product in that market.[46]

To identify or confirm key package equities, it is often necessary to conduct consumer research. For example, when Nabisco set out to redesign the package for its 86-year-old Milk-Bone brand of dog biscuits, as part of a research study, they asked some of their loyal customers to draw the package from memory. Most people drew the dog bone shape that was the brand's logo correctly but had some difficulty drawing the head of the dog that appeared on the front of the package despite its prominent placement there. These people also tended to ignore other packaging elements that informed them of the biscuits' nutritional and teeth-cleaning advantages altogether. The researchers interpreted the findings to mean that the Milk-Bone brand did not necessarily signify "clean teeth" to consumers as much as "love and affection." They also concluded that the brand's key packaging equity was wrapped up in the dog, the biscuit, and the bone shape. As a result, the package was redesigned by removing much of the informational clutter, placing the dog bone logo higher and more prominent on the box; and making the dog, which previously was shown staring off blankly into space, appear more engaging by having it look straight ahead, as if at the consumer. The package redesign was thought to have contributed to a halt in the sales erosion that the brand had been experiencing.[47]

Although packaging changes may seem expensive, they can be cost-effective as compared to other marketing communication costs. Reshaping a bottle may cost as much as $300,000 because of changes in production equipment, but this expense is only roughly the cost of producing one 30-second commercial or the cost of airing a 30-second commercial once on a popular American prime-time TV series. New graphics and photographs—the simplest and most common redesign—may cost just a few thousand dollars. A new package design may take three to four months and cost around $50,000. Most importantly, these packaging changes can have immediate impact on sales. For example, sales of the Heath candy bar increased 25 percent after its wrapper was redone. Similarly, Rice-A-Roni's sales increased 20 percent in the first year after a packaging revitalization.

In making a packaging change, it is important to recognize its effect on the original or current customer franchise for the brand. For example, to capitalize on the draft beer sales momentum started by Miller Genuine Draft, Adolph Coors changed the labels of its cans and bottles for its flagship Coors brand to read "Original Draft" instead of "Banquet Beer." Although Coors picked up some of the younger customers that it was hoping to attract, it also, unfortunately, lost some of its older, existing customers, especially in its strongholds in California and Texas where Coors had been sold for years. These customers believed that the beer itself had actually changed, and nothing Coors did or said convinced these long-time customers otherwise. Thus, despite the fact that Coors had actually sold draft (i.e., unpasteurized) beer since 1959, it reverted back to the old name and look for the beer six months later.[48]

Summary

The importance of packaging is reflected in the fact that some marketing observers refer to it as the "fifth 'P'" of the marketing mix. Packaging can play an important role in building brand equity directly through points of difference created by functional or aesthetic elements of the packaging or indirectly through the reinforcement of brand awareness and image.

Putting It All Together

The above discussion highlighted some key considerations for brand names, logos, symbols, characters, slogans, jingles, and packages. Each of these different brand elements can play a different role in building brand equity. Conceptually, it is necessary to "mix and match" these different brand elements to maximize brand equity. That is, as noted above and summarized in Figure 4–10, each brand element has certain strengths and weaknesses. Thus, marketers must "mix" brand elements by choosing different brand elements to achieve different objectives. At the same time, marketers must "match" brand elements by making sure that certain brand elements are chosen to reinforce each other by shared meaning. For example, research has shown that meaningful brand names that are visually represented through logos are easier to remember than without such reinforcement.[49]

The entire set of brand elements can be thought of as making up the *brand identity*. Brand identity reflects the contribution of all brand elements to awareness and image. The cohesiveness of the brand identity depends on the extent to which the brand elements are consistent. Ideally, brand elements would be chosen to support other brand elements that could easily be incorporated into other aspects of the brand and marketing program. Some strong brands have a number of valuable brand elements that directly reinforce each other. For example, consider Charmin toilet tissue. Phonetically, the name itself probably conveys softness. The brand character, Mr.

Brand Element	*Criterion*	
	Memorability	*Meaningfulness*
Brand name	Can be chosen to enhance brand recall and recognition	Can reinforce almost any type of association although sometimes only indirectly
Logo and symbol	Generally more useful for brand recognition	Can reinforce almost any type of association although sometimes only indirectly
Characters	Generally more useful for brand recognition	Generally more useful for non-product-related imagery and brand personality
Slogans	Can be chosen to enhance brand recall and recognition	Can convey almost any type of association explicitly
Packaging	Generally more useful for brand recognition	Can convey almost any type of association explicitly
	Protectability	*Transferability*
Brand name	Generally good but with limits	Can be somewhat limited
Logo and symbol	Excellent	Excellent
Characters	Excellent	Can be somewhat limited
Slogans	Excellent	Can be somewhat limited
Packaging	Can be closely copied	Good
	Adaptability	
Brand name	Difficult	
Logo and symbol	Can typically be redesigned	
Characters	Can sometimes be redesigned	
Slogans	Can be modified	
Packaging	Can typically be redesigned	

FIGURE 4–10 Critique of Brand Element Options

Whipple, and the brand slogan, "Please Don't Squeeze the Charmin," also help to reinforce the key point of difference for the brand of "softness."

Brand names characterized by rich, concrete visual imagery often can yield powerful logos or symbols. For example, Cutty Sark has used its schooner sailing ship as a logo on all types of merchandise. L'eggs pantyhose is sold in an egg-shaped package that directly reinforces the name. Wells Fargo, a large California-based bank, has a brand name rich in western heritage that can be exploited all through its marketing program. Wells Fargo has adopted a stagecoach symbol and has named individual services to be thematically consistent, for example, creating investment funds under the Stagecoach Funds brand umbrella.

Review

Brand elements are those trademarkable devices that serve to identify and differentiate the brand. The main brand elements are brand names, logos, symbols, characters, slogans, jingles, and packages. Brand elements can be chosen to both enhance brand awareness and facilitate the formation of strong, favorable, and unique brand associations.

In choosing and designing brand elements, five criteria are particularly important. First, brand elements can be chosen to be inherently memorable, both in terms of brand recall and recognition. Second, brand elements can be chosen to be inherently meaningful such that they convey information about the nature of the product category and/or particular attributes and benefits of a brand. The information conveyed by brand elements does not necessarily have to relate to the product alone and may reflect brand personality, user or usage imagery, or feelings. Third, brand elements can be chosen to be transferable within and across product categories (i.e., to support line and brand extensions) and across geographical and cultural boundaries and market segments. Fourth, brand elements can be chosen to be adaptable and flexible over time. Finally, brand elements must be chosen that are legally protectable and, as much as possible, competitively defensible. Branding Brief 4–5 outlines some of the key legal considerations in protecting the brand.

A number of considerations were reviewed for each different type of brand element. Because different brand elements have different strengths and weaknesses, it is important to "mix and match" brand elements to maximize their collective contribution to brand equity. Brand elements are "mixed" by choosing different brand elements to achieve different objectives. Brand elements are "matched" by designing some brand elements to be mutually reinforcing and sharing some meaning.

Discussion Questions

1. Pick a brand. Identify all of its brand elements and assess their ability to contribute to brand equity according to the choice criteria identified in the chapter.
2. What are some other examples of slogans not listed in the chapter that make strong contribution to brand equity? Why? Can you think of any "bad" slogans? Why do you consider them to be so?
3. Choose a package for any supermarket product. Assess its contribution to brand equity. Justify your decisions.

Legal Branding Considerations[a]

BACKGROUND

According to Cohen, under common law, "a 'technical' trademark is defined as any fanciful, arbitrary, distinctive, and non-descriptive mark, word, letter, number, design, or picture that denominates and is affixed to goods; it is an inherently distinctive trade symbol that identifies a product."[b] She maintains that *trademark strategy* involves proper trademark planning, implementation, and control, as follows.

1. *Trademark planning* requires selecting a valid trademark, adopting and using the trademark, and engaging in search and clearance processes.

2. *Trademark implementation* requires effectively using the trademark in enacting marketing decisions, especially with respect to promotional and distributional strategies.

3. *Trademark control* requires a program of aggressive policing of a trademark to ensure its efficient usage in marketing activities, including efforts to reduce trademark counterfeiting and to prevent the trademark from becoming generic, as well as instituting suits for infringement of the trademark.

In this brief, we highlight a few key legal branding considerations. For more comprehensive treatments, it is necessary to consider other sources.[c]

COUNTERFEIT AND IMITATOR BRANDS

Why is trademark protection of brand elements such as brand names, logos, and symbols such an important brand management priority? Counterfeiting alone costs U.S. companies an astounding $200 billion a year, and an estimated 5 percent of products sold worldwide are phony. Virtually any product is fair game for illegal counterfeiting or questionable "copycat" mimicking—from Nike apparel to Windows 95 software and from Similac baby formula to ACDelco auto parts.[d] Pirated products from China, Vietnam, and Russia, in particular, have flooded global markets.

In addition, some products attempt to gain market share by imitating successful brands. These copycat brands may mimic any one of the possible brand elements: close brand name replicates or duplicative or similar trade dress. For example, Calvin Klein's popular Obsession perfume and cologne has had to withstand imitators such as Compulsion, Enamoured, and Confess whose package slogan proclaimed, "If you like Obsession, you'll love Confess." Many copycat brands are put forth by retailers as store brands, putting national brands in the dilemma of protecting their trade dress by cracking down on some of their best customers. Complicating matters is that if challenged, many private labels contend, with some justification, that they should be permitted to continue labeling and packaging practices that have come to identify entire categories of products rather than a single national brand.[e] In other words, certain packaging looks may become a necessary point of parity in a product category.

A common victim of brand cloning, Contac cold medication underwent its first packaging overhaul in 33 years to better prevent knockoffs as well as update its image. Many national brand manufacturers are also responding through legal action. For national brands, the key is proving that brand clones are misleading consumers who may think that they are buying national brands. The burden of proof is to establish that an appreciable number of reasonably acting consumers are confused and mistaken in their purchases.[f] In such cases, several factors might be considered by courts in determining likelihood of confusion, such as: (1) strength of the national brand's mark, (2) relatedness of the national brand and brand clone products, (3) similarity of the marks, (4) evidence of actual confusion, (5) similarity of marketing channels used, (6) likely degree of buyer care, (7) the brand clone's intent in selecting the mark, and (8) likelihood of expansion of the product lines.

Stanford University's Itamar Simonson provides an in-depth discussion of these issues and methods to assess the likelihood of confusion and "genericness" of a trademark. He stresses the importance of recognizing that consumers may vary in their level or degree of confusion and that it is difficult as a result to identify a precise threshold level above which confusion "occurs." He also notes how survey research methods must accurately reflect the consumers' state of mind when engaged in marketplace activities.[g]

HISTORICAL AND LEGAL PRECEDENCE

Legally, a brand name is a "conditional-type property"—protected only after it has been used in commerce to identify products (goods or services) and only in relation to those products or to closely related offerings. To preserve a brand name's role in identifying products, federal law protects brands from actions of others that may tend to cause confusion concerning proper source identification.

By contrast with the case of confusion, *trademark appropriation* is a developing area of state law that can severely curtail even those brand strategies that do not "confuse" consumers. Appropriation refers to enhancing the image of a new offering via the use of some property aspect of an existing brand. Thus, appropriation resembles theft of an intangible property right. The typical argument to prevent imitations is that, even in the absence of confusion, a weaker brand will tend to benefit by imitating an existing brand name.

Protection from "dilution" arose in 1927 when a legal ruling declared that "once a mark has come to indicate to the public a constant and uniform source of satisfaction, its owner should be allowed the broadest scope possible for the 'natural expansion of his trade' to other lines or fields of enterprise." From this, two brand-related rights followed: (1) the right to preempt and preserve areas for brand extensions and (2) the right to stop the introduction of similar or identical brand names even in the absence of consumer confusion so as to protect a brand's image and distinctiveness from being diluted.

New American laws register trademarks for only ten years (instead of twenty) and to renew trademarks, firms must prove they are using the name and not just holding it in reserve. To determine legal status, marketers must search trademark registrations, brand name directories, phone books, trade journals and advertisements, and so on. In 1991, 120,000 trademark applications were filed with the U.S. Patent and Trademark Office, including a large number filed by foreign companies from Canada, Germany, Britain, and Japan.

Figure 4–11 describes some broad guidelines concerning trademark protection. The remainder of this brief describes some of the particular issues involved with two important brand elements—brand names and packaging.

A number of experts have put forth advice and checklists concerning trademark protection.[a] Among the guidelines that have been suggested include the following:

1. Register the trademark formally, also any symbol or stylized use of it and color.
2. Whenever the trademark appears in print make sure that it stands out from the surrounding text. To do this, always capitalize the first letter of your trademark and perhaps use italics or bold print.
3. Always follow the trademark with a generic or dictionary name.
4. Always use the trademark as an adjective, never as a noun; never pluralize the trademark; never use it in the possessive; never use it as a verb.
5. Never "fool around" with the spelling of the trademark.
6. Maintain a consistent visual identity for the trademark; do not allow a proliferation of different graphic treatments.
7. Use appropriate registration marks.
8. Educate all personnel on proper trademark use, especially secretaries, distributors, dealers, and others who might promote it or otherwise frequently use it.
9. Challenge each misuse of the trademark, particularly by others in the marketplace.
10. Maintain thorough records of "due diligence" in correctly using and protecting the trademark.

[a]These guidelines are based on material found in Jack Alexander, "What's In a Name? Too Much, Said the FCC," *Sales & Marketing Management* (January 1989), pp. 75–78 and John M. Murphy, *Brand Strategy*, Chapter 14. London: Prentice Hall, 1990.

FIGURE 4–11 Protecting Trademarks

TRADEMARK ISSUES WITH NAMES

Without adequate trademark protection, brand names can become legally declared generic, as was the case with vaseline, victrola, cellophane, escalator, and thermos. For example, when Bayer set out to trademark the "wonder drug" acetylsalicyclic acid, they failed to provide a "generic" term or common descriptor for the product and provided only a trademark, aspirin. Without any other option available in the language, the trademark became the common name for the product. In 1921, a U.S. District Court ruled that Bayer had lost all its rights in the trademark. Other brand names have struggled to retain their legal trademark status, e.g., Band Aids, Kleenex, Scotch Tape, Q-Tips, and Jello. Xerox spends $100,000 a year explaining that you don't "Xerox" a document, you photocopy it.[h]

Legally, the courts have created a hierarchy for determining eligibility for registration. In descending order of protection, these categories are:

1. Fanciful (Kodak)
2. Arbitrary (Camel)
3. Suggestive (Eveready)
4. Descriptive (Ivory)
5. Generic (Aspirin)

Thus, fanciful names are the most easily protected but at the same time, are less suggestive or descriptive of the product itself, suggesting the type of tradeoffs involved in choosing brand elements. Generic terms are never protectable. Marks that are difficult to protect include those that are surnames, descriptive terms or geographical names, or those that relate to a functional product feature. Marks that are not inherently distinctive and thus are not immediately protectable may attain trademark protection if they acquire secondary meaning.

Secondary meaning refers to the fact that the mark has a new meaning rather than the older (primary) meaning. The secondary meaning must be the meaning the public usually attaches to the mark and indicates the association between the mark and goods from a single source. Secondary meaning is usually proven through extensive advertising, distribution, availability, sales volume, length, and manner of use, and market share.[i] Secondary meaning is necessary to establish trademark protection for descriptive marks, geographic terms, and personal names.

TRADEMARK ISSUES WITH PACKAGING

In general, names and graphic designs are more legally defensible than shapes and colors. The issue of legal protection of the color of packaging for a brand is a complicated one. One federal appeals court in San Francisco recently ruled that companies cannot get trademark protection for a product's color alone.[j] The court ruled against a small Chicago manufacturer who makes green-gold padding used by dry cleaners and garment makers on machines that press clothes who filed suit against a competitor who had started selling padding of the same hue. In rejecting protection for the color alone, the court said manufacturers with distinctively colored products can rely on existing law that protects "trade dress" related to the overall appearance of the product: "Adequate protection is available when color is combined in distinctive patterns or designs or combined in distinctive logos."

Color is one factor, but not a determinative one, under a trade dress analysis. This ruling differed from a landmark ruling in 1985 arising from a suit by Owens-Corning Fiberglass Corp. who sought to protect the pink color of its insulation. A Washington court ruled in Owens-Corning's favor. Other courts have made similar rulings, but at least two other appeals courts in other regions of the country have subsequently ruled that colors cannot be trademarked. Note that these trademark rulings apply only when color is not an integral part of the product.

---

[a]Much of this brief is based on several excellent sources: Dorothy Cohen, "Trademark Strategy," *Journal of Marketing*, 50 (January 1986), pp. 61–74; Dorothy Cohen, "Trademark Strategy Revisited," *Journal of Marketing*, 55 (July 1991), pp. 46–59.

[b]Dorothy Cohen, "Trademark Strategy," *Journal of Marketing*, 50 (January 1986), pp. 61–74.

[c]For example, see Judy Zaichowsky, *Defending Your Brand Against Imitation*. Westpoint, CO: Quorom Books, 1995.

[d]David Stipp, "Farewell, My Logo," *Fortune* (May 27, 1996), pp. 128–140.

[e]Paul F. Kilmer, "Tips for Protecting Brand from Private Label Lawyer," *Advertising Age* (December 5, 1994), p. 29.

[f]Greg Erickson, "Seeing Double," *Brandweek* (October 17, 1994), pp. 31–35.

[g]Itamar Simonson, "Trademark Infringement from the Buyer Perspective: Conceptual Analysis and Measurement Implications," *Journal of Public Policy & Marketing*, 13 (2) (Fall 1994), pp. 181–199.

[h]Constance E. Bagley, *Managers and the Legal Environment: Strategies for the 21st Century*, 2nd ed., Minneapolis, MN: West Publishing, 1995.

[i]Garry Schuman, "Trademark Protection of Container and Package Configurations—A Primer," *Chicago Kent Law Review*, 59 (1982), pp. 779–815.

[j]Junda Woo, "Product's Color Alone Can't Get Trademark Protection," *Wall Street Journal* (January 5, 1994), p. B-8.

Notes

1. An excellent overview of the topic, some of which this section draws on, can be found in Kim R. Robertson, "Strategically Desirable Brand Name Characteristics," *Journal of Consumer Marketing*, 6 (4), 1989, pp. 61–71.

2. Frances Leclerc, Bernd H. Schmitt, and Laurette Dube, "Foreign Branding and Its Effects on Product Perceptions and Attitudes," *Journal of Marketing Research*, 31 (May 1994), pp. 263–270.

3. Ronald Alsop, "Firms Create Unique Names, But Are They Pronounceable," *Wall Street Journal* (April 2, 1987), B1.

4. Robert N. Kanungo, "Effects of Fittingness, Meaningfulness, and Product Utility," *Journal of Applied Psychology*, 52 (1968), pp. 290–295.

5. Kim R. Robertson, "Recall and Recognition Effects of Brand Name Imagery," *Psychology and Marketing*, Vol. 4 (1987), pp. 3–15.

6. Kevin Lane Keller, Susan Heckler, and Michael J. Houston, "The Effects of Brand Name Suggestiveness on Advertising Recall," *Journal of Marketing*, January 1998, in press.

7. William L. Moore and Donald R. Lehmann, "Effects of Usage and Name on Perceptions of New Products," *Marketing Science*, 1(4) (1982), pp. 351–370.

8. Kevin Lane Keller, Susan Heckler, and Michael J. Houston, "The Effects of Brand Name Suggestiveness on Recall of Advertising Effects," *Journal of Marketing*, January 1998, in press.

9. Kevin Lane Keller, Susan Heckler, and Michael J. Houston, "The Effects of Brand Name Suggestiveness on Recall of Advertising Effects," *Journal of Marketing*, January 1998, in press.

10. Robert A. Peterson and Ivan Ross, "How to Name New Brands," *Journal of Advertising Research*, 12 (6) (December 1972), pp. 29–34.

11. Robert A. Mamis, "Name Calling," *Inc.* (July 1984).

12. Bruce G. Vanden Bergh, Janay Collins, Myrna Schultz, and Keith Adler, "Sound Advice on Brand Names," *Journalism Quarterly*, 61 (4) (1984), pp. 835–840.

13. Bruce G. Vanden Bergh, Keith Adler, and Lauren Oliver, "Linguistic Distinction Among Top Brand Names," *Journal of Advertising Research* (August/September 1987), pp. 39–44.

14. Daniel L. Doeden, "How to Select a Brand Name," *Marketing Communications* (November 1981), pp. 58–61.

15. Timothy B. Heath, Subimal Chatterjee, and Karen Russo, "Using the Phonemes of Brand Names to Symbolize Brand Attributes," in *The AMA Educator's Proceedings: Enhancing Knowledge Development in Marketing*. William Bearden and A. Parasuraman, eds. Chicago: American Marketing Association.

16. Much of this passage is based on Teresa M. Paiva and Janeen Arnold Costa, "The Winning Number: Consumer Perceptions of Alpha-Numeric Brand Names," *Journal of Marketing*, 57 (July 1993), 85–98.

17. John Murphy, *Brand Strategy*, Prentice-Hall, 1990, p. 79.

18. John Murphy, *Brand Strategy*, Prentice-Hall, 1990.

19. John Murphy, *Brand Strategy*, Prentice-Hall, 1990.

20. Cyndee Miller, "The Green Giant: An Enduring Figure Lives Happily Ever After," *Marketing News* (April 15, 1991), p. 2.

21. David A. Aaker, *Building Strong Brands*. New York: Free Press, 1996, p. 203.

22. Yukimo Ono, "Aunt Jemima Brand Hires Gladys Knight," *Wall Street Journal* (September 16, 1994), p. B-3.

23. Charles Goodrum and Helen Dalyrmple, *Advertising in America*. New York: Harry N. Abrams, Inc., 1990.

24. Jerry Carroll, "Mr. Jenkins Has His Eye On You," *San Francisco Chronicle* (December 11, 1994), p. S1.

25. Joanne Lipman, "Coca-Cola Is Close to Picking New Slogan," *Wall Street Journal* (September 28, 1992), p. B-10. Kevin Goldman, "Diet Coke Loses Its Taste for Latest Slogan," *Wall Street Journal* (July 13, 1993), p. B-5. Kevin Goldman, "Lintas's Campaign for Diet Coke Fizzles," *Wall Street Journal* (May 28, 1993), p. B-3. Kevin Goldman, "Interpublic's Lintas Loses Diet Coke Job," *Wall Street Journal* (October 6, 1993), p. B-10. Kevin Goldman, "Refreshment Bears Weight for Diet Coke," *Wall Street Journal* (January 13, 1994), p. B-6.

26. Nancy Croft, "Wrapping Up Sales," *Nation's Business* (October 1985), pp. 41–42.

27. Susan B. Bassin, "Value-Added Packaging Cuts Through Store Clutter," *Marketing News* (September 26, 1988), p. 21.

28. Raymond Serafin, "Packaging Becomes an Art," *Advertising Age* (August 12, 1985), p. 66.

29. Trish Hall, "New Packaging May Soon Lead to Food That Tastes Better and Is More Convenient," *Wall Street Journal* (April 21, 1986), p. 25.

30. M. McDevitt Rubin, "Practical Packaging," *Pittsburgh Press* (December 15, 1992), p. 29.

31. Stephen MacDonald, "Food Packages Rile Consumers," Form + Function, *Wall Street Journal* (November 11, 1987), p. 29.

32. Susan Spillman, "Right Package is Vital to Wrap Up More Sales," *USA Today* (February 13, 1993); p. B-1.

33. Eben Shapiro, "Portions and Packages Grow Bigger and BIGGER," *Wall Street Journal* (October 12, 1993), p. B-1.

34. Ronald Alsop, "Color Grows More Important in Catching Consumers' Eyes," *Wall Street Journal* (November 29, 1984), p. 37.

35. Alecia Swasy, "Sales Lost Their Vim? Try Repackaging," *Wall Street Journal* (October 11, 1989), p. B-1.

36. Eleena de Lisser, "Pepsi Puts Spotlight on New Packaging," *Wall Street Journal* (August 11, 1993), p. B-1.

37. Gerry Khermouch, "John Ferolito, Don Vultaggio," *Brandweek* (November 14, 1995), p. 57.

38. Lourdes Lee Valeriano, "Wine Is Bottled in More Shapes and Sizes," *Wall Street Journal* (December 9, 1993), p. B-1.

39. "Packaging Plays Starring Role in TV Commercials," *Marketing News* (January 30, 1987), p. 6.

40. Michael Purvis, President of Sidjakov, Berman, and Gomez, as quoted in Carla Marinucci, "Advertising on the Store Shelves," *San Francisco Examiner* (October 20, 1986), pp. C1–C2.

41. Ronald Alsop, "Color Grows More Important in Catching Consumers' Eyes," *Wall Street Journal* (November 29, 1984), p. 37.

42. Bill Abrams and David P. Garino, "Package Design Gains Stature as Visual Competition Grows," *Wall Street Journal* (March 14, 1979), p. 48.

43. Amy Dunkin, "Want to Wake Up a Tired Old Package? Repackage It," *Business Week* (July 15, 1985), pp. 130–134.

44. J. David Mahder, "Unleashing the Power of Bayer Equity," ARF Fifth Annual Advertising and Promotion Workshop, February 1, 1993.

45. Bill Abrams and David P. Garino, "Package Design Gains Stature as Visual Competition Grows," *Wall Street Journal* (March 14, 1979), p. 48.

46. Alecia Swasy, "Sales Lost Their Vim? Try Repackaging," *Wall Street Journal* (October 11, 1989), p. B-1.

47. Pam Weisz, "Repackaging," *Brandweek* (February 27, 1995), pp. 25–27.

48. Marj Charlier, "Beer Drinkers in Texas, California Don't Swallow Change in Coors Label," *Wall Street Journal* (December 29, 1988), p. B-4; "And So It's Back to Drawing Board for Original Draft," *Wall Street Journal* (January 20, 1989), p. B4.

49. Terry L. Childers and Michael J. Houston, "Conditions for a Picture Superiority Effect on Consumer Memory," *Journal of Consumer Research*, 11 (September 1984), pp. 551–563; Kathy A. Lutz and Richard J. Lutz, "Effects of Interactive Imagery on Learning: Application to Advertising," *Journal of Applied Psychology*, 62(4) (1977), pp. 493–498.

 CHAPTER

Designing Marketing Programs to Build Brand Equity

Preview

Although the judicious selection of brand elements and the resulting brand identity can make an important contribution to customer-based brand equity, the primary input comes from marketing activities related to the brand and the resulting marketing program. In this chapter, we will consider product, pricing, and distribution strategies to build brand equity. Chapter 6 considers how marketers can create integrated marketing communication programs to build brand equity. In both of these chapters, our intent is to focus on marketing mix issues primarily from a branding perspective. Our interest is in how marketing programs should be optimally designed to build brand equity. We also consider how the brand itself can be effectively integrated into the marketing program to maximize the creation of brand equity. To obtain a broader perspective on marketing mix issues, however, it is necessary to consult a basic marketing management text, as well as the specific references noted below.[1] After reviewing product, pricing, and channels strategies, the chapter concludes by considering the important topic of private labels.

Product Strategy

The product itself is at the heart of brand equity, as it is the primary influence of what consumers experience with a brand, what they hear about a brand from others, and what the firm can tell customers about the brand in its communications. Designing and delivering a product that fully satisfies consumer needs and wants is a prerequisite for successful marketing, regardless of whether the product is a tangible good, service, or organization. To create brand loyalty, consumers' experiences with the product must at least meet, if not actually surpass their expectations. Numerous studies have shown that high-quality brands tend to perform better financially, for example, yielding higher returns on investment.[2]

In this section, we will consider how consumers form their opinions of the quality of a product and their attitudes toward brands as well as the resulting implications for product strategy. We begin by examining perceived quality.

PERCEIVED QUALITY

Perceived quality has been defined as customers' perception of the overall quality or superiority of a product or service relative to relevant alternatives and with respect to its intended purpose. Thus, perceived quality is a global assessment based on customer perceptions of what they think constitutes a quality product and how well the brand rates on those dimensions. Achieving a satisfactory level of perceived quality has become more difficult as continual product improvements over the years have led to heightened consumer expectations of product quality.[3]

Much research attention has been devoted to understanding how consumers form their opinions about perceived quality. The specific attributes or benefits that become associated with favorable evaluations and perceptions of product quality can vary from category to category. Figure 5–1 displays some product attributes and benefits that were selected as part of a research study to be meaningful across seven different product classes. Nevertheless, prior research has identified the following general dimensions of product quality.[4]

1. *Performance:* Levels at which the primary characteristics of the product operate (e.g., low, medium, high, or very high)
2. *Features:* Secondary elements of a product that complement the primary characteristics
3. *Conformance quality:* Degree to which the product meets specifications and is absent of defects
4. *Reliability:* Consistency of performance over time and from purchase to purchase
5. *Durability:* Expected economic life of the product
6. *Serviceability:* Ease of servicing the product
7. *Style and Design:* Appearance or feel of quality

Consumer beliefs along these dimensions often underlie perceptions of the quality of the product, which, in turn, can influence attitudes and behavior towards a brand.

Reflecting the importance of product quality, a number of firms have embraced concepts such as "quality function deployment" (QFD) and "total quality management" (TQM) to direct their efforts to maximize the quality of their products. Proponents of TQM adhere to a number of general tenets, such as the following:[5]

FIGURE 5–1 Representative Set of Specific Attributes and Benefits for Seven Product Categories[a]

Flavor/taste	Weight	Construction material
Caffeine content	Warranty	Availability
Price	Durability	Serviceability
Packaging	Convenience	Compatibility
Size	Color	Energy-efficiency
Calories	Style	Instructions
Brand name	Comfort	Automation
Sweetness	Freshness	Ease of use

Note: The product categories studied were cola-based sodas, personal stereos, orange juice, sneakers, refrigerators, 35mm SLR cameras, and point & shoot cameras.

[a]Rajeev Batra, Donald R. Lehmann, and Dipinder Singh, "The Brand Personality Component of Brand Goodwill: Some Antecedents and Consequences," in David A. Aaker and Alexander L. Biel, *Brand Equity and Advertising,* Lawrence Erlbaum Associates, 1993, Hillsdale, NJ, pp. 83–96.

- Quality must be perceived by customers.
- Quality must be reflected in every company activity, not just in company products.
- Quality requires total employee commitment.
- Quality requires high quality partners.
- Quality can always be improved.
- Quality improvement sometimes requires quantum leaps.
- Quality does not always cost more.
- Quality is necessary but may not be sufficient.
- A quality drive cannot save a poor product.

TQM principles have provided some useful structure and guidance to marketing managers interested in improving product quality. In practicing TQM, however, some firms have run into implementation problems as they became overly focused—perhaps even obsessed—with processes and *how* they were doing business, losing sight of the needs and wants of customers and *why* they were doing business. In some cases, companies were able to successfully achieve benchmarks against top quality standards—but only by incurring prohibitive increases in costs at the same time. For example, scientific equipment maker Varian totally embraced TQM principles but found itself losing money as it became inwardly focused, rushing to meet production schedules and deadlines that it now feels may not have been that important to its customers to begin with.

In a reaction to this somewhat myopic behavior, some companies now concentrate their efforts on "return on quality." ROQ adherents advocate only improving quality on those dimensions that produce tangible customer benefits, lower costs, or increased sales. This bottom-line orientation forces companies to make sure that the quality of the product offerings is in fact the quality consumers actually want, leading to recommendations such as those found in Figure 5–2.[6]

PERCEIVED VALUE

Consumers often combine quality perceptions with cost perceptions to arrive at an assessment of the value of a product. In considering consumer value perceptions, it is important to realize that costs are not just restricted to the actual monetary price but may reflect opportunity costs of time, energy, and any psychological involvement in the decision that consumers might have.[7]

From a firm's perspective, it is necessary to take a broad view of value creation. Harvard's Michael Porter has proposed the *value chain* as a strategic tool for identifying ways to create more customer value.[8] He views firms as a collection of activities that are performed to design, produce, market, deliver, and support products. The value chain identifies five primary value-creating activities (inbound logistics, operations, outbound logistics, marketing and sales, and service) and four support activities that occur all through these primary activities (firm infrastructure, human resources management, technology development, and procurement). According to Porter, firms can achieve competitive advantages by improving performance and reducing costs in any or all of these value-creating activities. He also emphasizes the importance of effectively managing core business processes and cross-functional integration and cooperation.

Porter also notes how firms can create competitive advantages by partnering with other members of the value chain to improve the performance of the customer value-delivery system (e.g., suppliers into, as well as distributors out of, the firm's value chain). For example, Procter & Gamble works closely with retailers such as Wal-Mart to ensure that P&G brands can be quickly and efficiently distributed to stores. Some of P&G's employees even have assignments in Bentonville, Arkansas—site of Wal-Mart's headquarters—to better coordinate these efforts! From a branding perspective, all of these various activities are potentially a means of creating strong, favorable, and unique brand associations that can serve as sources of brand equity.

Thus, product quality depends on more than product performance—on broader product-related concerns as well. For example, product quality may also be impacted by factors such as the speed, accuracy, and care of product delivery and installation; the promptness, courtesy, and helpfulness of customer service and training; the quality of repair service; and so on. Moreover, as pointed out in chapter 2, brand attitudes may not necessarily be based only on functional benefits and product-related concerns but may also depend on more abstract non-product factors in terms of the symbolism or personality reflected in the brand. These "augmented" aspects of a product are often crucial to its equity—the imagery, personality, prestige or status of a brand that reflects user and usage experiences. Finally, as noted in chapter 3, in numerous instances, consumer evaluations may not correspond to the perceived quality of the product and may be formed by less thoughtful decision making, such as on the basis of

FIGURE 5-2 Guidelines for "Return on Quality" Strategies[a]

1. *Start with an effective quality program.* Companies that don't have the basics, such as process and inventory controls and other building blocks, will find a healthy return on quality elusive.

2. *Calculate the cost of current quality initiatives.* Cost of warranties, problem prevention, and monitoring activities all count.

3. *Determine what key factors retain customers—and what drives them away.* Conduct detailed surveys. Forecast market changes, especially quality and new product initiatives of competitors.

4. *Focus on quality efforts most likely to improve customer satisfaction at a reasonable cost.* Figure the link between each dollar spent on quality and its effect on customer retention and market share.

5. *Roll out successful programs after pilot-testing the most promising efforts and cutting the ones that don't have a big impact.* Closely monitor results. Build word of mouth by publicizing success stories.

6. *Improve programs continually.* Measure results against anticipated gains. Beware of the competition's initiative and don't hesitate to revamp programs accordingly. Quality never rests.

[a]David Greising, "Quality: How to Make It Pay," *Business Week* (August 8, 1994), pp. 54–59.

simple heuristics and decision rules (e.g., brand reputation or product characteristics such as color or scent).

ENHANCING CONSUMPTION EXPERIENCES

As with brand awareness, both purchase *and* consumption issues should be reflected in product strategies to achieve the desired brand image. Much marketing activity is devoted to finding ways to encourage trial and/or repeat purchases by consumers. Perhaps the strongest and potentially most favorable associations, however, result from actual product experience. Unfortunately, not nearly enough marketing attention seems to be devoted to finding new ways for consumers to truly appreciate the advantages and potential capabilities of products. Perhaps in response to that oversight, one notable trend in marketing is the growing importance of aftermarketing, that is, those marketing activities that occur *after* customer purchase. Innovatively designed, thoroughly tested, carefully produced, and effectively communicated products are without question the most important considerations in enhancing consumption experiences and building brand equity. Nevertheless, a number of other means exist to enhance consumption experiences. In this section, we address some other relatively neglected issues concerning aftermarketing and how marketers can enhance consumption experiences to build brand equity.

For example, instruction manuals for many products are too often an afterthought, put together by engineers who use overly technical terms and convoluted language.[9] As a result, consumers' initial product experiences may be frustrating or, even worse, unsuccessful. Furthermore, in many cases, even if consumers are able to figure out how to make the product perform its basic functions, many more advanced features—highly desirable and potentially unique to the brand—may not be fully appreciated by consumers. In other words, if a consumer cannot set the clock on his or her VCR, what difference does it make if it has 14-day multiple programmability? To enhance consumers' consumption experiences, it is important to develop user manuals that clearly and comprehensively describe both what the product potentially can do for consumers and how consumers can realize these product benefits. To achieve these goals, user manuals increasingly may need to utilize multimedia formats—video, CD-ROM, or computer diskettes—to graphically, succinctly, and persuasively portray product functions and benefits.

Aftermarketing, however, involves more than the design and communication of product instructions. As one expert in the area notes, "The term 'aftermarketing' describes a necessary new mindset that reminds businesses of the importance of building a lasting relationship with customers to extend their lifetimes. It also points to the crucial need to better balance the allocation of marketing funds between conquest activities (like advertising) and retention activities (like customer communication programs)." He offers examples of seven specific activities to nurture loyalty and build relationships with customers:[10]

1. Establishing and maintaining a customer information file
2. "Blueprinting" customer contacts
3. Analyzing customer feedback

4. Conducting customer satisfaction surveys
5. Formulating and managing communication programs
6. Hosting special customer events or programs
7. Identifying and reclaiming lost customers

Creating stronger ties with consumers can be as simple as creating a well-designed customer service department, easily accessible with a toll-free 800 phone number or a web site accessed through the internet. Loyalty or frequency programs have become one popular means by which marketers can create stronger ties to customers. The purpose of frequency marketing has been defined as "identifying, maintaining, and increasing the yield from a firm's 'best' customers through long-term, interactive, value-added relationships." Firms in all different kinds of industries—most notably in the airlines industry—have established loyalty programs through different mixtures of specialized services, newsletters, premiums, and incentives. Often these loyalty programs involve extensive co-branding arrangements or brand alliances. Figure 5–3 shows the breadth of the American Airlines AAdvantage program.

Those marketers who will be most successful at building customer-based brand equity will take all the necessary steps to make sure they fully understand their customers and how they can deliver superior value *after* purchase. For example, Intuit, makers of the Quicken personal financial management software package, routinely sends its researchers home with first-time buyers to check that their software is easy to install and to identify any sources of problems that might arise.

SUMMARY

The product is at the heart of brand equity. Products must be designed, manufactured, marketed, sold, delivered, and serviced in a way to create a positive brand image through strong, favorable, and unique brand associations. Product strategy entails choosing both tangible and intangible benefits to be embodied by the product and surrounding marketing activities that are desired by consumers as well as deliverable by the marketing program. A range of possible associations can become linked to the brand, some more functional and product-related and some more symbolic and non-product-related. Perceived quality is a particularly important brand association that often drives consumer decisions. Because of the importance of consumers' actual product experiences in building brand equity, "aftermarketing" activities have taken on increased importance.

Pricing Strategy

Price is the one revenue-generating element of the marketing mix, and price premiums are one of the most important benefits of creating brand awareness and strong, favorable, and unique brand associations. In this section, we will consider the different kinds of price perceptions that consumers might form and different pricing strategies that the firm might adopt to build brand equity.

A'Advantage®
AmericanAirlines

Airlines ◄

American Eagle®
Canadian Airlines International
Cathay Pacific Airways
Hawaiian Airlines
Japan Airlines*
Qantas Airways
Reno Air
Singapore Airlines
South African Airways*

Car Rental ◄

Alamo Rent A Car
Avis Rent A Car
Hertz

Hotels ◄

Fairmont Hotels*
Forte Hotels
Hilton and Conrad Hotels
Hilton International
Holiday Inn®
Inter•Continental Hotels
ITT Sheraton
Loews Hotels*
Marriott Hotels • Resorts • Suites
Red Lion Hotels & Inns
Sandals Resorts
Vista Hotels
Wyndham Hotels & Resort

Financial Services ◄

AMR Investment Services
Citibank A'Advantage Card

Long Distance Service ◄

MCI

Special Services ◄

A'Advantage® Dining*
The American Traveler® Catalog
FTD Direct

* Indicates new participants.

A Day in the Life of an A'Advantage Member

Flying is a great way to earn A'Advantage miles, but now it's easier than ever to earn a bundle of miles!

In addition to flying on American Airlines and our AAdvantage airline participants, you can earn miles from all the companies listed in the column to the left. Below is an example of how miles might potentially add up in a typical day. As you read through, note how many more miles you can earn whenever you charge goods or services on your Citibank AAdvantage card – one mile for every dollar you spend!*

Time	Activity	Miles
7:00 a.m.	Pick up dry cleaning: (30 Citibank AAdvantage miles)	
7:45 a.m.	Renew gym membership: (420 Citibank AAdvantage miles)	
10:55 a.m.	Fly from Dallas/Fort Worth to Miami: (1,048 Citibank AAdvantage miles)	1,121 miles
3:15 p.m.	Drive away in an AAdvantage participant rental car: (60 Citibank AAdvantage miles)	500 miles
4:00 p.m.	Check into AAdvantage participant hotel room: (75 Citibank AAdvantage miles)	500 miles
7:00 p.m.	Dinner with clients (AAdvantage Dining): (90 Citibank AAdvantage miles)	270 miles
8:45 p.m.	Call home using MCI® AAdvantage Calling Card and help daughter with algebra homework: (10 Citibank AAdvantage miles)	50 miles
10:15 p.m.	Call FTD Direct and order a floral arrangement for wife to celebrate upcoming wedding anniversary: (45 Citibank AAdvantage miles)	400 miles
	AAdvantage miles	2,841 miles
	Citibank AAdvantage miles	1,768 miles
	Total miles	**4,609 miles!**

Each time a new participant joins the program, you'll see an announcement in your AAdvantage Newsletter. Keep watching to find out even more ways you can earn miles, day by day. Before you know it, you'll have enough to claim a travel award for the vacation of your dreams.

* The maximum number of AAdvantage miles you can earn with the Citibank AAdvantage card is 60,000 per calendar year. American Airlines A'Advantage Platinum® and A'Advantage Gold® members are excluded from this limit.

FIGURE 5-3 AAdvantage Program Partnerships

CONSUMER PRICE PERCEPTIONS

The pricing policy for the brand can create associations in consumers' minds to the relevant price tier or level for the brand in the category, as well as to its corresponding price volatility or variance (in terms of the frequency or magnitude of discounts, etc.). In other words, the pricing strategy can dictate how consumers categorize the price of the brand (e.g., as low-, medium-, or high-priced) and how firm or flexible consumers see that price (e.g., as frequently or infrequently discounted).

Consumers often rank brands according to price tiers in a category.[11] For example, Figure 5–4 shows the price tiers that resulted from a study of the ice cream market.[12] In that market, as the figure shows, there is also a relationship between price and quality. Within any price tier, as the figure also shows, there is a range of acceptable prices, called "price bands." The price bands provide managers with some indication of the flexibility and breadth they can adopt in pricing their brands within a particular price tier.

Besides these descriptive "mean and variance" price perceptions, consumers may have price perceptions of brands that have more inherent product meaning. In particular, in many categories, consumers may infer the quality of a product on the basis of its price. Relatedly, as noted above, consumers may also combine their perceptions of the quality of the product with their perceptions of the price of the product to arrive at an assessment of its perceived value. Consumer associations of per-

FIGURE 5–4 Price Tiers in the Ice Cream Market

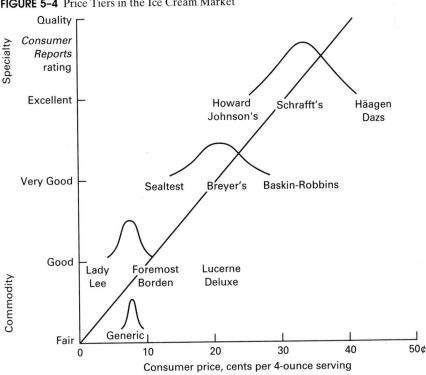

ceived value are often an important factor in their decisions. Accordingly, many marketers have adopted *value-based pricing strategies*—attempting to sell the right product at the right price—to better meet consumer wishes, as described below.

Consumers' perceptions of value should obviously exceed the cost to the company of making and selling the product. As chapter 2 pointed out, consumers are willing to pay a premium for certain brands because of what those brands represent to them. Based on tangible or intangible considerations, consumers place a value on the unique aspects of a brand that justifies a higher price in their minds. For example, at one time, Hitachi and GE jointly owned a factory in England that made identical televisions for the two companies. The only difference was the brand name on the television. Nevertheless, the Hitachi televisions sold for a $75 premium over the GE televisions. Moreover, Hitachi sold twice as many sets as GE, despite the higher price![13] Similarly, industry analysts believe that Mondavi wines command higher prices than wines of similar quality from other producers because of their name and what it means to consumers.[14]

In short, price has complex meaning and can play multiple roles to consumers. From a branding perspective, it is important to understand all price perceptions that consumers have for a brand. As part of this understanding, it is necessary to uncover quality and value inferences and any price premiums that exist.

SETTING PRICES TO BUILD BRAND EQUITY

Choosing a pricing strategy to build brand equity involves determining:

- A method or approach for how current prices will be set
- A policy or set of guidelines for the depth and duration of promotions and discounts over time

There are many different approaches to setting prices that depend on a number of considerations. Here, we highlight a few of the most important issues as they relate to brand equity.[15]

Factors related to the costs of making and selling products and the relative prices of competitive products are important determinants of the optimal pricing strategy. For example, two very different pricing strategies often employed in introducing a new product are penetration pricing and skimming pricing. With *penetration pricing*, margins are minimized (and sometimes even negative) in an attempt to capture and defend market share. This strategy is often adopted when strong experience curve effects are believed to exist such that the cost of making and marketing a product are expected to decline sharply with increases in cumulative production over time. The idea is that low prices lead to increased sales volume and market share that, in turn, leads to lower costs and greater profits over time. With *skimming pricing*, on the other hand, margins are maximized in an attempt to extract as much profit as possible. Such a strategy is seen as appropriate if it can be assumed that consumers see price as a signal of quality and if there is lack of strong competitors.

Increasingly, firms are placing greater importance on consumer perceptions and preferences in developing their pricing strategy. Many firms now are employing a "value pricing" approach to set prices and an "everyday low pricing" approach to determine their discount pricing policies over time. We describe both approaches in turn.

Value Pricing

Penetration and skimming pricing represent two extreme pricing strategies. A pricing strategy that typically results in prices in between these two is *value pricing*. The objective with value pricing is to uncover the right blend of product quality, product costs, and product prices that fully satisfy the needs and wants of consumers and the profit targets of the firm. As a concept, marketers have employed value pricing in various ways for years. Its increased adoption as a pricing strategy in recent years, however, is a result of several factors.

First, the last decade or so has seen slower growth in disposable income. Consequently, as baby boomers—born between 1946 and 1964—move into later stages of the family life cycle, they have struggled with meeting new and difficult financial demands such as paying for children's college tuition, saving for retirement, and so on. With a more debt-burdened and cost-conscious consumer base, many firms have found it more difficult to raise prices than in previous years.[16] Chapter 2 described consumer defections from Marlboro to lower-priced private label cigarettes as a result of sustained price hikes. Other brands have also met with resistance to higher prices from consumers—often for the first time in their history. A *Wall Street Journal* study of retail supermarkets in 1993 found that many products that had experienced significantly higher prices had also experienced lower unit sales. For example, although the baby formula market had been characterized by a great deal of loyalty over the years—despite fairly steady price increases—Enfamil found that its sales declined over 20 percent when their prices rose an average of 18 percent.

In this new consumer climate, several firms have been successful by adopting a value-pricing strategy. For example, Wal-Mart's slogan of "We Sell For Less" describes the pricing strategy that has allowed them to become the world's largest retailer; Southwest Airlines combined low fares with no-frills—but friendly—service to become a powerful force in the airline industry; and Taco Bell reduced operating costs enough to lower prices of many of the items on its menu to under $1, sparking an industry-wide trend in fast foods. The success of these and other firms have dramatized the potential benefits of implementing a value pricing strategy.

As might be expected, there are a number of opinions as to the keys for success in adopting a value-based pricing approach (see Figure 5–5 for one such set of views). In general, an effective value pricing strategy should strike the proper balance among:

1. Product design and delivery
2. Product costs
3. Product prices

In other words, the right kind of product has to be made the right way and sold at the right price. We next consider issues related to each of these three areas.

Product Design and Delivery   The first key is the proper design and delivery of the product. There are a number of means of enhancing product value through well-conceived and executed marketing programs that are covered in this and other chapters of the book. Some of the more popular means include product quality improvements, better service offerings or a longer warranty period, impactful, breakthrough advertising to enhance the product's image, value-added services in the distribution

In examining the current marketing climate, one marketing commentary offered the following value pricing recommendations:[a]

TARGET PRICING. Forget traditional cost-plus pricing. Instead, reverse the equation for price-driven costing. Meeting price targets means reengineering the corporation to speed up new-product development, simplify design, and reorganize the work flow.

VALUE PRICING. Coupons, discounts, and rebates have gotten out of hand. Cut back on expensive promotions and instead offer stable, low, everyday prices.

STRIPPING DOWN. Offer cost-conscious customers quality products with fewer bells and whistles at a cheaper price.

ADDING VALUE. Introduce innovative products sold at a modest premium. Back them with strong merchandising and advertising campaigns.

GETTING CLOSE TO CUSTOMERS. Find out what customers really want and give that to them. Use the new information technologies to closely track their needs and your costs.

GOING GLOBAL. The future is now. It's a way to increase unit volume, and less mature markets offer more pricing flexibility.

[a]Christopher Farrell, "Stuck! How Companies Cope When They Can't Raise Prices," *Business Week* (November 15, 1993), pp. 146–150.

FIGURE 5-5 Strategies for Thriving in Disinflationary Times

channels from technical support or financing, and improved sales force training on the basis of product value.[17]

Proponents of value pricing point out that the concept does *not* mean just selling "stripped-down" versions of products at lower prices. For example, by combining high performance at lower prices, Japanese luxury cars such as Lexus and Infiniti have been able to create strong value perceptions and sales in the United States versus their American and European competitors. Auto critics cheered when the 1997 Camry was introduced and reviewed as roomier, smoother, faster, and quieter—and cheaper! Some companies actually have been able to *increase* prices in some cases by introducing new or improved "value-added" products. In certain product categories, marketers have been able to couple product innovations and improvements—from new flavors and bottle designs for iced teas to newly designed toothbrushes with special features such as rippled bristles and handles with tiny shock absorbers—with higher prices that strike an acceptable balance to at least some market segments. For example, when Clorox and S.C. Johnson launched new drain cleaners that included micro-organisms to eat away at the buildup in drains, although prices in the category rose almost 15 percent, sales still increased 20 percent.[18]

Product Costs   The second key to a successful value pricing strategy is to lower costs as much as possible. Meeting cost targets invariably requires additional cost savings through productivity gains, outsourcing, material substitution (less expensive or less wasteful materials), product reformulations, process changes (automation or other factory improvements), and so on.[19] As one marketing executive put it:

> The customer is only going to pay you for what he perceives as real value-added. When you look at your overhead, you've got to ask yourself if the customer is really willing to pay for that. If the answer is no, you've got to figure out how to get rid of it or you're not going to make money.[20]

For example, by investing in efficient manufacturing technology, Sara Lee has been able to maintain adequate margins for years on its L'eggs women's hosiery with minimal price increases. The combination of low prices and the strong L'eggs brand image has resulted in an almost 50 percent market share.[21] At the same time, cost reductions cannot sacrifice quality. Delta Airline's $1.6 billion cost-cutting efforts in 1995 resulted in the airline dropping to last place among the ten largest carriers in on-time performance and struggling with customer complaints about ticketing delays, dirty planes, and mishandled bags. Morale among Delta employees slipped, too. Admitting that it "cut too deeply," Delta took steps to restore its quality of service.[22]

Product Prices   The final key to a successful value pricing strategy is to understand exactly how much value consumers perceive in the brand and thus to what extent they will pay a premium over product costs. A number of techniques are available to estimate these consumer value perceptions (see chapter 9 for a review). Perhaps the most straightforward approach involves just asking consumers directly their perceptions of price and value in different ways.

The price suggested by estimating perceived value can often be used as a starting point in determining actual market place prices, adjusting by cost and competitive considerations as necessary. For example, General Motors Corp.'s Cadillac Division has used "target pricing" to arrive at the prices of its luxury cars. GM marketers determined the optimal price based on assumptions about the consumer and then figured out how to make the car at the right cost to ensure the necessary profit.[23] Similarly, to halt a precipitous slide in market share for its flagship 9-Lives brand, the Pet Products Division of H. J. Heinz took a new tack in their pricing strategy. They found from research that, despite the fact that their cat food cost between 29 and 35 cents per can, consumers wanted to be able to buy cat food at the price of "four cans for a dollar." As a result, Heinz reshaped its product packaging and redesigned its manufacturing processes to be able to hit the necessary cost, price, and margin targets. Despite lower prices, profits for the brand doubled.

From a brand equity perspective, it is important that consumers find the price of the brand appropriate and reasonable *given* the benefits that they feel they accrue. To achieve the proper balance of perceived value, there is always tension between lowering prices on one hand, and increasing consumer perceptions of product quality on the other hand. Academic researchers Lehmann and Winer believe that although price reductions are more commonly employed to improve perceived value, in reality they are often more expensive than adding value through various brand-building marketing activities.[24] Their argument is that the lost revenue from a lower margin on each item sold is often much greater than the added cost of value-added activities, primarily because many of these costs are fixed and spread over *all* the units sold, as opposed to the *per unit* reductions that result from lower prices.

In short, a successful value pricing strategy requires skillful decisions in a number of areas. As one commentary noted:

> The delivery of value to the customer is the nexus at which all aspects of commerce converge. It calls for a clear understanding of customer needs, superior product design, intelligent application of technology, relentless focus on quality, cost control, and productivity—and a pugnacious insistence on one-upping the competition. This is the most basic test of business effectiveness. Those who don't pass it may not be with us when the value decade is done.[25]

EDLP

Value pricing is an approach for setting prices. A closely related pricing policy— everyday low pricing (or "EDLP")—has received increased attention as a means of determining the nature of price discounts and promotions over time. EDLP eschews the sawtooth, whiplash pattern of alternating price increases and decreases or discounts to establish a more consistent set of "everyday" base prices on products. In many cases, these EDLP prices are based on the value pricing considerations noted above.

As noted in chapter 1, Procter & Gamble made a well-publicized conversion to EDLP. By reducing list prices on half of its brands and eliminating many temporary discounts, P&G reported that they saved $175 million in 1991, or 10 percent of their previous year's profits. Advocates of EDLP argue that maintaining consistently low prices on major items every day will help build brand loyalty, fend off private-label inroads, and reduce manufacturing and inventory costs.[26] Branding Brief 5–1 describes some of the efforts by marketers to cut prices in the cereal market.

Even strict adherents to EDLP, however, see the need for some types of price discounts over time. Well-conceived, timely sales promotions can provide important financial incentives to consumers and induce sales. If that is the case, why do firms seek greater price stability? Manufacturers can be hurt by an overreliance on trade and consumer promotions and the resulting fluctuations in prices for several reasons.

As has been well documented, trade discounts have risen considerably in recent years in both breadth (e.g., the percentage of the total marketing communications expenditures devoted to trade promotions increased dramatically in the last several decades—from a third to almost a half of the budget total) and depth (e.g., the extent of the average price discount, which previously was only 4 percent, more commonly became around 10 percent to 15 percent). Unfortunately, many of these trade promotion dollars are not always passed along as savings to consumers.[27] For example, although trade promotions are only supposed to result in discounts on products for a certain length of time and in a certain geographical region, that is not always the case. With *forward buying,* retailers order more product than they plan to sell during the promotional period so that they can later obtain a bigger margin by selling the remaining goods at the regular price after the promotional period has expired. With *diverting,* retailers pass along or sell the discounted products to retailers outside the designated selling area.

------------------------------- BRANDING BRIEF 5-1 -------------------------------

Pricing Showdown in the Cereal Market[a]

The cereal category has experienced interesting price competition in recent years. In the late 1980s and early 1990s, the cereal industry as a whole aggressively raised list prices on items as much as 5 percent to 6 percent every eight months. In order to disguise the higher prices, cereal makers attempted to offset them with a host of coupons, trade promotions, and other deals (such as two-for-the-price-of-one and buy-one-get-one or "bogo" offers)—a strategy dubbed "price-up, deal back."

On April 4, 1994 ("Cheerios Monday"), General Mills, the number two player in the $8.7 billion cereal market with a 29 percent share, announced that it would lower prices between 30 cents and 70 cents a box (or 11 percent on average) on its eight most popular ready-to-eat cereals (Cheerios, Honey Nut Cheerios, Multi Grain Cheerios, Wheaties, Whole Grain Total, Golden Grahams, Lucky Charms, and Trix). General Mills also announced that it was cutting coupon and other promotional expenditures by $175 million.

General Mills was motivated by a number of reasons. With prices as much as 25 percent lower, private label cereals had begun to make some significant inroads on sales, increasing their share of the market to 5.2 percent. Because of pervasive sales promotions, more than 60 percent of all cereal purchases were being made with some kind of coupon or discount. As Steve Sanger, president of General Mills, stated:

> The practice of pricing up and discounting back has become more and more inefficient for manufacturers and retailers and burdensome for consumers. There's tremendous cost associated with printing, distributing, handling, and redeeming coupons. Because of this inefficiency, the 50 cents that the consumer saves by clipping a coupon can cost manufacturers as much as 75 cents. It just doesn't make sense.

These actions were all part of a broader General Mills program to both reduce unnecessary costs (e.g., through improved manufacturing productivity) and increase consumer value (e.g., through enhanced ingredients such as an additional 25 percent fruit and nut pieces in select cereals in 1993 and reformulated Wheaties and Cheerios in 1994). General Mills' avowed marketing strategy was to improve one-third of its product line every year and introduce and maintain superior products with a meaningful point of difference backed by strong advertising.

Kellogg, the market leader with a 36 percent share, followed quickly with an announcement that it would stop offering the buy-one-get-one-free offers and attempted to hold firm on price increases by cutting costs. Recognizing a competitive opportunity, marketers of the number three and four cereal suppliers, Post and Quaker Oats, initially decided to continue to offer $1-plus coupons. Eventually, however, Post enacted a 20 percent across-the-board price cut and began to issue a new, all-purpose coupon that would apply to all sizes of all of its cereals. Kellogg soon thereafter reduced prices an average 19 percent on nearly two-thirds of its line.

The dust is settling on these various pricing maneuvers. One worry for General Mills was that the retail grocers would see their reduced wholesale prices as a means of increasing their profit margins by not reducing shelf prices. Research showed, however, that many retailers actually did reduce shelf prices for the eight Big G brands targeted for cuts (75 percent of all stores had instituted some price cuts, with those retailers passing along 75 percent of General Mills funding onto consumers). Although their quarterly earnings declined 10 cents a share because of the price actions, General Mills believed that their strategy was the right one for the cereal industry in the long run.

---

[a]Richard Gibson, "General Mills to Slash Prices of Some Cereals," *Wall Street Journal* (April 5, 1994), p. A-4; John McManus, "Sanity's at Stake in Steve Sanger's Cereal Showdown," *Brandweek* (April 25, 1994), p. 16; Betsy Spethman, "Kellogg Counters Big G Price Cuts: 'Bogo' a No Go June 1," *Brandweek* (April 25, 1994), p. 3, Julie Liesse and Kate Fitzgerald, "General Mills Price Cuts Fail to Stem Couponing," *Advertising Age* (August 1, 1994), p. 26.

Although these practices may seem to provide some financial benefits to the retailer, critics argue that they can produce a false economy. Often overlooked is the extra expenses involved due to additional warehouse facilities, shipping costs, overhead costs, and so on. In justifying its switch to EDLP, Procter & Gamble argued that only 30 percent of its trade promotion dollars actually reached consumers in the form of lower prices—35 percent was thought to be lost in the form of higher retailer costs while another 35 percent was thought to be taken as direct profits by the retailers. By reducing both the number of trade discounts, as well as its wholesale list prices, P&G attempted to leave retailers in close to the same "net" profitability position but restore the price integrity of their brands in the process. From the manufacturer's perspective, these retailer practices created production complications: Factories had to run overtime because of excess demand during the promotion period but had slack capacity when the promotion period ended, costing manufacturers millions. On top of it all, on the demand side, many marketers felt that the "see-saw" of high and low prices on products actually trained consumers that they should wait to buy the brand only when it was discounted or on special, thus eroding its perceived value.

In summary, to build brand equity, marketers must determine strategies for setting prices and adjusting them, if at all, over the short and long run. Increasingly, these decisions will reflect consumer perceptions of value. The benefits delivered by the product and its relative advantages with respect to competitive offerings, among other factors, will determine what consumers see as a "fair price." Value pricing then strikes the balance among product design, product costs, and product prices. Everyday low pricing is a complementary pricing approach to determine the nature of price discounts and promotions over time that maintains consistently low, value-based prices on major items on a day-to-day basis.

Channel Strategy

The manner by which a product is sold or distributed can have a profound impact on the resulting equity and ultimate sales success of a brand. *Marketing channels* are defined as "sets of interdependent organizations involved in the process of making a product or service available for use or consumption."[28] Channel strategy involves the design and management of intermediaries such as wholesalers, distributors, brokers, and retailers. In this section we consider how channel strategy can contribute to brand equity.[29]

CHANNEL DESIGN

A number of possible channel types and arrangements can be selected. Broadly, they can be classified into direct and indirect channels. *Direct channels* involve selling through personal contacts from the company to prospective customers by mail, phone, electronic means, in-person visits, and so on. *Indirect channels* involve selling through third-party intermediaries such as agents or broker representatives, wholesalers or distributors, and retailers or dealers.

Much research has considered the pros and cons of selling through various channels. Although the decision ultimately depends on the relative profitability of the different options, some more specific guidelines have been proposed. For example, one study for industrial products suggests that direct channels may be preferable when:[30]

- Product information needs are high
- Product customization is high
- Product quality assurance is important
- Purchase lot size is important
- Logistics are important

On the other hand, this study suggests that indirect channels may be preferable when:

- A broad assortment is essential
- Availability is critical
- After-sales service is important

Exceptions to these generalities exist, however, especially depending on the market segments involved.

It is rare that a manufacturer will use only a single type of channel. More likely, it will be the case that a hybrid channel design with multiple channel types will be employed.[31] In designing a hybrid channel system, the tradeoff is with having too many channels (leading to conflict among channel members and/or a lack of support) or too few channels (resulting in market opportunities being overlooked). As both direct and indirect channels are often used, it is worthwhile to consider the brand equity implications of the two major channel design types, as follows.

INDIRECT CHANNELS

Although indirect channels can consist of a number of different types of intermediaries, we will concentrate our discussion on retailers. Retailers tend to have the most visible and direct contact with customers and therefore have the greatest opportunity to impact brand equity. Retailers come in many forms. Consumers may have associations to any one retailer on the basis of a number of factors, such as the retailer's product assortment, pricing and credit policy, quality of service, and so on. Through the products and brands they stock, the means by which they sell and so on, retailers strive to create their own brand equity by establishing awareness and strong, favorable, and unique associations.

At the same time, retailers can have a profound influence on the equity of the brands they sell. The interplay between the store image and the brand images of the products they sell is an important one. In chapter 7, we examine how the brand image of a retailer can be "transferred" to the products it sells. That is, because of the knowledge and associations that consumers have with retailers, consumers infer or make certain assumptions about the products they sell—for example, "this store only sells good quality, high value merchandise, so this particular product must also be good quality and high value." In chapter 15, we describe how retailers can build their own brand images and equity. In this section, we consider how the marketing activity of retailers can directly affect the brand equity of the products they sell.

Push and Pull Strategies

Beside indirect means of image transfer, retailers can more directly affect the equity of the brands they sell. By the actions they take in stocking and selling products, retailers can enhance or detract from brand equity, suggesting that manufacturers must take an active role in helping retailers add value to their brands.

Yet, at the same time, a battle has emerged in recent years between manufacturers and retailers making up their channels of distribution. Because of greater competition for shelf space between what many retailers feel are increasingly undifferentiated brands, among other factors, retailers have gained in power and are now in a better position to set the "terms of trade" with manufacturers. Increased power means that retailers can command more frequent and lucrative trade promotions. Figure 5–6 shows the dependence that various major manufacturers have on certain retailers that they supply. Increasingly, supermarket retailers are demanding compensation to even stock a new brand in the form of cash payments for the shelf space itself (e.g., slotting

FIGURE 5–6 Dependence of Major Manufacturers on Certain Retailers

Company	Share of selected suppliers' sales generated by key retail accounts
Gibson Greetings	35% from 5 retailers. 13% from Phar-Mor.
Gitano	56% from 10 retailers. 26% from Wal-Mart.
Haggar	22.6% from J.C. Penney. 10% from Wal-Mart.
Hasbro	75% from 10 retailers. 17% from Toys 'R' Us.
Huffy	23% from Kmart & Toys 'R' Us.
Mattel	13% from Toys 'R' Us.
Mr. Coffee	21% from Wal-Mart. 10% from Kmart.
Procter & Gamble	11% from Wal-Mart.
Rubbermaid	11% from Wal-Mart.
Royal Appliance	53% from 5 retailers. 27% from Wal-Mart.
The Scotts Co.	26% from Wal-Mart, Kmart, & Home Depot.

allowances), introductory deals (e.g., one free with three), postponed billing or extended credit (e.g., dating), payment for retailer advertising or promotion in support of the new brand, and so on.[32] Even after stocking brands, retailers can still later require generous trade promotions to keep them on the shelf.

Thus, retailers have increased their power over manufacturers. One way for manufacturers to regain some of their lost power over retailers is by creating strong brands through some of the brand-building tactics described in this book, for example, by selling innovative and unique products—properly priced and advertised—that consumers demand. In this way, consumers may ask or even pressure retailers to stock and promote manufacturers' products. By devoting marketing efforts at the end consumer, a manufacturer is said to employ a *pull strategy*, as the idea is that consumers are using their buying power and influence on retailers to "pull" the product through the channel. Alternatively, marketers can devote their selling efforts towards the channel members themselves, providing direct incentives for them to stock and sell products to the end consumer. This approach is called a *push strategy* as the manufacturer is attempting to reach the consumer by "pushing" the product through each step of the distribution chain.

Although certain brands seem to emphasize one strategy more than another—"push" strategies are usually associated with more selective distribution and "pull" strategies with broader, more intensive distribution—in general, the most successful branding programs often skillfully blend "push" and "pull" strategies. For example, when Goodyear Tire & Rubber introduced its Aquatred tire, an all-season radial designed to provide better traction on wet roads, it was priced 10 percent higher than Goodyear's previous top-of-the line mass market tire. Nevertheless, Goodyear was able to sell 2 million Aquatreds in the first two years of its introduction by combining strong merchandising support to tire dealers and a persuasive advertising campaign directed to consumers (see Figure 5–7).[33]

Channel Support

There are a number of different services potentially provided by channel members that can enhance the value to consumers of purchasing and consuming a brand-name product (see Figure 5–8). Although firms are increasingly attempting to provide some of the services themselves—e.g., such as the advent of toll-free 800 phone numbers and internet-accessible web sites, have made it easier for firms to provide customer assistance—establishing a "marketing partnership" with retailers may nevertheless be critical to ensure proper channel support and the execution of all of these various services. Two aspects of such a partnership involve retail segmentation activities and co-operative advertising programs, as follows.

Retail Segmentation   A manufacturer can initiate a number of marketing and merchandising programs to assist retailers' selling efforts. One important realization in developing these programs is that retailers have to be treated as if they were "customers" too. Because of their different marketing capabilities and needs, retailers may need to be divided into segments or even treated individually in designing the optimal marketing program so that they will provide the necessary brand support. In other words, different retailers may need to be given different product mixes, special delivery systems, customized promotions, or even their own branded version of the products.

RAIN GEAR.

Water, water everywhere. The slippery kind. That's when you'll sure be glad you've got Goodyear's all-season Aquatred.® Because Aquatred has an advanced

60000

A 60,000-mile limited treadlife warranty. Ask for details.

deep-groove AquaChannel™ that sweeps water away at more than a gallon a second. Leaving you

feeling secure and in control of the situation.

So gear up for inclement weather. With Aquatred. Only from Goodyear.

☐ *AquaChannel sweeps water away at more than a gallon a second.*
☐ *Unique Goodyear compound adds to the Aquatred's superb road grabbing wet traction.*
☐ *The AquaChannel design is now used in Goodyear's Formula One racing rain tire.*

THE BEST TIRES IN THE WORLD HAVE
GOODYEAR WRITTEN ALL OVER THEM.

FIGURE 5–7 Sample Goodyear Ad

For example, Shugan refers to *branded variants* as branded items that are not directly comparable to other items carrying the same brand name.[34] Branded variants can be found in a diverse set of durable and semi-durable good categories, such as alarm clocks, answering machines, appliances, baby items, binoculars, dishwashers, luggage, mattresses, microwaves, sports equipment, stereos, televisions, tools, and watches. Manufacturers create branded variants in many ways, including changes in color, design, flavor, options, style, stain, motif, features, and layout. Branded variants are a means to reduce retail price competition because they make direct price comparisons by consumers difficult. Thus, different retailers may be given different items or models of the same brand to sell. Shugan and his colleagues show that as the manufacturer of a product offers more branded variants, a greater number of retail stores carry the product, and these stores offer higher levels of retail service for these products.[35]

Cooperative Advertising   One relatively neglected means of increasing channel support is through better designed and implemented cooperative advertising programs. Traditionally, with co-op advertising, a manufacturer pays for a portion of the advertising that a retailer runs to promote the manufacturer's product and its availability in the retailer's place of business. Manufacturers generally share the cost of advertising run by the retailer on a percentage business—usually 50-50—up to a certain limit. To be eligible to receive co-op funds, manufacturers usually have some stipulations as to the nature of brand exposure in the ad. The total amount of cooperative advertising funds the manufacturer provides to the retailer is usually based on a percentage of dollar purchases made by the retailer from the manufacturer.[36] Estimates of the total amount spent by companies on cooperative advertising is huge, ranging from $5 billion to $6 billion.

FIGURE 5-8 Services Provided by Channel Members[a]

Marketing research	Gathering information necessary for planning and facilitating interactions with customers.
Communications	Developing and executing communications about the product and service.
Contact	Seeking out and interacting with prospective customers.
Matching	Shaping and fitting the product/service to the customer's requirements.
Negotiations	Reaching final agreement on price and other terms of trade.
Physical distribution	Transporting and storing goods (inventory).
Financing	Providing credit or funds to facilitate the transaction.
Risk-taking	Assuming risks associated with getting the product or service from firm to customer.
Service	Developing and executing ongoing relationships with customers, including maintenance and repair.

[a]Donald Lehmann and Russell Winer, *Product Management*. Burr Ridge, IL: Irwin, 1994.

The rationale behind cooperative advertising for manufacturers is that it is a means of concentrating some of the communication efforts at a more local level where they may potentially have more relevance and selling impact with consumers. Unfortunately, the image about the brand communicated through co-op ads is not so tightly controlled, and there is a danger that the emphasis in a co-op ad may be too much on the store or on a particular sale it is running. Perhaps even worse, there is also a danger that a co-op ad may communicate a message about the brand that even runs counter to its desired image.

Some manufacturers are attempting to gain better control over their cooperative advertising by providing greater assistance to retailers. For example, Goodrich created an image ad for their tires that could also be recut to plug various local dealerships at the same time. Rubbermaid has collaborated with big retailers such as Wal-Mart and Home Depot to find ad approaches that achieve the "best of both worlds," allowing Rubbermaid to create more awareness and loyalty for its brand while creating sales momentum for the retailer in the same ad.[37]

Increasingly, it would seem desirable to achieve synergy between the manufacturer's own ad campaigns for a brand and its corresponding co-op ad campaigns with retailers. The challenge in designing effective co-op ads will continue to be how to strike a balance between pushing the brand while selling the store at the same time. In that sense, cooperative advertising will have to "live up to its name," and manufacturers will have to get involved in the design and execution of retailers' campaigns rather than just handing over money or supplying generic, uninspired ads.

In summary, in eliciting channel support, manufacturers must be creative in how they develop marketing and merchandising programs aimed at the trade or any other channel members. In doing so, it is important to consider how channel activity can encourage trial and communicate or demonstrate product information to build brand awareness and strong, favorable, and unique brand associations. Branding Brief 5–2 describes how DuPont skillfully combined push and pull strategies to build brand equity for its Stainmaster carpets.

DIRECT CHANNELS

For some of the reasons noted above, manufacturers may choose to sell directly to consumers. Chapter 6 describes some general issues surrounding direct marketing in terms of how it fits into the marketing communications mix. Here, we consider some of the brand equity considerations with selling through direct channels.

Company-Owned Stores

To gain control over the selling process and build stronger relationships with customers, some manufacturers are introducing their own retail outlets, as well as selling their product directly to customers through various means. These channels can take many forms. The most extensive form involves company-owned stores. Hallmark, Goodyear, and others have sold their own products in their own stores for years. Recently, a number of firms—including some of the biggest marketers around—have set up their own stores:

Blending Push and Pull at DuPont[a]

DuPont blends push strategies aimed at retailers and pull strategies targeting consumers to build strong brand equity. Their basic marketing formula includes the following ingredients:

1. Superior products addressing relevant consumer need
2. Distinctive advertising executions backed up by heavy advertising expenditures
3. Powerful trade promotions with much impact at the point of sale
4. Long-term consumer warranties followed up with a toll-free number
5. Fostering the general reputation of DuPont as a supplier of innovative quality products (e.g., Nylon, Dacron, Orlon, and Teflon)

The 1986 introduction of DuPont Stainmaster carpet represents perhaps a textbook example of how to efficiently build a brand by blending push and pull strategies. Stainmaster addressed one of the most important benefits that consumers sought in carpets—soil and stain resistance. Armand Zinnato, one of DuPont's research chemists, discovered that certain dye-resistant agents previously used to improve wash-fastness would also impart previously unobtainable stain-resistance. Recognizing the difficulty in obtaining broad patent protection, DuPont embarked on an aggressive consumer-marketing program.

TRADE PROGRAM

At the launch, DuPont limited Stainmaster to two major distributors and 1,500 retailers. A training program for the sales forces included audiovisual presentations and personal presentations by DuPont employees. Fifty field representatives were sent out to cover major markets. Support at the retail level was intensive, with DuPont supplying posters, banners, labels, and tags. "We had more merchandising tools than dealers dreamed possible," said Gary Johnston, marketing communications supervisor in the Flooring Systems Division. A key feature was a demonstration unit that allowed customers to dip a toothbrush-like "swizzle stick," with one treated and one untreated group of tufts, into various stains and go through the simple stain-removal process to see for themselves how Stainmaster worked.

Dealers received a 12-page catalog describing what DuPont had to offer in merchandising DuPont Certified Stainmaster carpet, as well as the company's Antron nylon and Dacron polyester products. Other literature available to the dealers included cards, brochures, cleaning instructions, and DuPont's *Complete Book of Carpeting*. Store and product identification for dealers comprised of hanging mobiles with Stainmaster logos, large canvas banners that could be hung outside showrooms, in-store wall and window posters, carpet-identification medallions, sales tags, and photo boards depicting the Stainmaster TV commercials. Promotional activities to encourage dealers to hold special events or sales to promote Stainmaster included a "Pet Parade" in Los Angeles that featured hundreds of animals from cats to monkeys strutting along a length of red carpet made with Stainmaster.

Among the cooperative advertising available to retailers were Stainmaster newspaper ad slicks with room to add the showroom name; Stainmaster TV tapes, which became 30-second TV spots when dealers added their names to the 8-second tag; 30-second radio commercials with time included for the dealer's tag. Any retail carpet dealer purchasing a total of more than 5,000 square yards of Stainmaster carpet in a six-month period accrued co-op advertising dollars for DuPont Stainmaster carpet. This program used mill and distributor data to calculate the square yardage sold by retailers.

ADVERTISING

The Stainmaster consumer advertising campaign focused on quality, style, fashion, and performance. The TV campaign opened with ad spots on 8 of the top 10 prime-time programs and consisted of some 1.7 billion gross impressions by the end of 1987. The newspaper coverage extended to the top 70 markets, 30 more than DuPont had ever covered before. One of DuPont's ads for Stainmaster was in the top 10 best-noted TV commercials for the first half of 1987, and the clever introductory spot, "Landing," won a Clio award that year for advertising creativity.

WARRANTY

DuPont's "repair or replace" warranty for Stainmaster consisted of a full five-year stain-resistance warranty (covering most common household food and beverages), a five-year wear-resistance warranty (no more than 10 percent wear in any area, except stairs), and a lifetime anti-static warranty. The duration of the warranty came out of product testing.

TOLL-FREE NUMBER

For Stainmaster carpet dealers and buyers, DuPont introduced a toll-free 800 number tended by operators trained in carpet-stain treatments and backed up by a sophisticated computer system for dealer ordering of sales material and recording of warranties. Initially, the vast majority of the calls were from dealers requesting sales aids, point-of-purchase materials, extra warranty cards, swizzle sticks for in-store displays, and product information. Mills called for extra swizzle sticks, training tapes, or information literature. Later, more calls were placed by consumers.

Calls from consumers basically fit three categories: those wanting product information, those asking where to buy carpets of Stainmaster, and consumers with questions on performance and cleanability. After verifying the latter's purchase and warranty coverage, operators would talk the caller through the cleaning process. The method of stain removal varied as to length and number of steps by the type of stain and length of time it had lain untended. Operator training required them to have tested Stainmaster carpets personally. If an operator could not correct the problem, he or she would take the customer's num-

ber and have one of the DuPont scientists call back the next day. If all these approaches failed, DuPont would send a local professional cleaner to the resident.
As a last resort, DuPont replaced the carpet.

RESULTS

The marketing program for Stainmaster exceeded DuPont's expectations. Consumer research indicated that recall of Stainmaster advertising far surpassed
that of competitors. More importantly, 60 percent of carpet sold at retail in 1988
had enhanced stain resistance and roughly three-fourths of those sales went to
Stainmaster, often at a price premium.

———

[a]Bette Collins and Paul Farris, "Stainmaster," UVA-M-357, Darden Graduate School of Business,
University of Virginia, Charlottesville, VA and Paul Farris, "Stainmaster Teaching Note," UVA-
M-357TN, Darden Graduate School of Business, University of Virginia, Charlottesville, VA.

1. In December 1994, after the Federal Trade Commission amended a 16-year ban against
   the jeans-maker from selling its own wares, Levi-Strauss announced that it was planning
   to open 200 stores and outlets over the next five years.[38] The planned stores included
   Original Levi's Stores, Dockers Shops, and Dockers Outlet Stores, initially located
   mostly in downtown areas and upscale suburban malls.

2. Nike has introduced its Nike Town stores, which stock essentially all of the products Nike
   sells. Each store consists of a number of individual shops or pavilions that feature shoes,
   clothes, and equipment for a different sport (e.g., tennis, jogging, biking, or watersports)
   or different lines within a sport (e.g., there are three basketball shops and two tennis
   shops). Each shop develops its own concepts based with lights, music, temperature, and
   unique multimedia displays.

3. The Disney Store, started in 1987, sells exclusive Disney branded merchandise, ranging
   from toys and videos to collectibles and clothing, priced from $3 to $3000. Disney views
   the stores as an extension of the "Disney experience," referring to customers as guests
   and employees as cast members. By 1995, there were roughly 500 specialty shops worldwide as part of an aggressive expansion program. Disney also recently opened its first
   Walt Disney Gallery to sell only high-end merchandise and plans to hook those bou-
   tiques onto some of their existing specialty stores.

A number of other brands have created their own stores, for example, Bang
& Olufsen audio equipment, OshKosh B'Gosh children's wear, Warner Bros. entertainment, and Speedo Authentic Fitness swimwear. Even Dr. Martens—a somewhat
obscure brand best known for its thick-soled lace-up boots—opened a five-story
13,957-square-foot store in London, trying to transform the brand into more of a
lifestyle brand.

These "company stores" provide many benefits.[39] Primarily, they are a means to
showcase the brand and all of its different product varieties in a manner not easily
achieved through normal retail channels. For example, Nike might find its products
spread all through department stores and athletic specialty stores. These products
may not be displayed in a logical, coordinated fashion, and certain product lines may
not even be stocked at all. By opening its own stores, Nike can effectively put its "best

foot forward" by showing the depth, breadth, and variety of Nike branded products. These types of stores also can provide the added benefit of functioning as a test market to gauge consumer response to alternative product designs, presentations, and prices, allowing firms to "keep their fingers on the pulse" of consumers' shopping habits.

One issue with company stores, of course, is potential conflict with existing retail channels and distributors. In many cases, however, these stores can be seen as a means of bolstering brand image and building brand equity rather as a direct sales device per se. For example, Nike views its stores as essentially an advertisement and tourist attraction as much as a retail store. Nike reports that research studies have confirmed that Nike Town stores enhanced the Nike brand image by presenting the full scope of Nike's sports and fitness lines to customers and "educating them" on the value, quality, and benefits of Nike products. Their research also revealed that although only about 25 percent of visitors actually made a purchase at a Nike Town store, 40 percent of those who did not buy during their visit eventually purchased Nike products from some other retailers.

These manufacturer-owned stores can also be seen as a means of hedging bets with retailers who continue to push their own labels. With one of their main suppliers, J.C. Penney, pushing its own Arizona brand of jeans, Levi's can protect its brand franchise to some extent by establishing its own distribution channel. Nevertheless, many retailers and manufacturers are dancing around the "turf issue," avoiding head-on clashes in establishing competitive distribution channels. Manufacturers in particular have been careful to stress that their stores are not a competitive threat to their retailers but rather "showcases" that can help sell merchandise for any retailer carrying their brand.[40]

Other Means

Besides going to their own stores, some marketers—such as Nike, Polo, Levi's (with Dockers)—are attempting to create their own shops within major department stores. This approach offers the desirable dual benefits of appeasing retailers—and perhaps even benefiting from the retailer's brand image—while at the same time allowing the firm to retain control over the design and implementation of the product presentation at the point of purchase.

Finally, another channel option is to sell directly to consumers via phone, mail, or electronic means. Retailers have sold their goods through catalogs for years. Although a long-time successful strategy for brands such as Mary Kay and Avon, many mass marketers are increasing their direct selling efforts, especially those who also sell through their own retail stores (e.g., Levi-Strauss, Nike, and Disney). Sony introduced *Sony Style* magazine as means of providing customers detailed information on a full range of their products. Again, these vehicles not only help to sell products but also can contribute to brand equity by increasing consumer awareness of the range of products associated with a brand and their understanding as to the key benefits of those products. As chapter 6 describes, although direct marketing efforts can be executed in many ways—catalogs, videos, or physical sites—they all represent an opportunity to engage in a dialogue and establish a relationship with consumers. Branding Brief 5–3 describes some of the "trendsetting" best direct response campaigns as judged by the Direct Marketing Association with their 1996 Echo Awards.[41]

Direct Marketing Association 1996 Echo Award Winners

SAUCONY

Saucony designs and manufactures a line of high performance athletic footwear for running, walking, court use, and cross-training. Saucony products are regarded by serious athletes as superior, high technology designed products, ranging in price from $60 to $120 per pair. Saucony's audience is best defined as consumers who are runners, walkers, court enthusiasts, or court trainers. Each of these audience segments shares the following interests in footwear: comfort, proper fit, superior technology, high performance, and value.

Saucony wanted to explore the potential of the World Wide Web. A sampling of its audience indicated that enough customers and prospects were online to warrant the development of a web site. Saucony hoped the interactive nature of the web would provide the following:

- Customized information ("electronic literature fulfillment") to respondents
- More information than is generally otherwise available in traditional media
- A compressed time line from point of initial inquiry to point of initial purchase
- A database of prospects and new customers
- Measured inquiries, coupon requests, coupon redemptions, and sales
- Reduced cost per inquiry and cost per sale

Saucony's strategy focused on providing information, education, direction, and incentive in a self-paced, entertaining, online experience. They conceived and created a web site with the following elements and characteristics:

1. The site is hosted by a Saucony employee, George, who is an accomplished runner. The content is therefore perceived as credible because it is hosted and created *by* a serious athlete *for* serious athletes.
2. George invites the viewer to "look around" Saucony headquarters and further invites the viewer into the Saucony locker room.
3. Once in the locker room, George invites the viewer to find out more about Saucony products and technology.
4. He offers to help the viewer pick a pair of shoes. This is accomplished by answering a few questions in the "Shoe-zer" such as height, weight, frame, type of sport, frequency of workouts, and within seconds the appropriate shoe or shoes are displayed on the screen. Technical specs are displayed on the screen as well.
5. Next George offers to tell the viewer where these shoes can be purchased. He invites the viewer to tell him where he lives and quickly shows a listing of the "Extra Mile Club" dealers in the neighborhood.
6. Then George encourages the viewer to sign up for the "Extra Mile Club," a frequency/loyalty program, with a special "web offer." If the viewer signs up immediately, George lets him print out a discount coupon to be redeemed at the aforementioned retailers.

7. New and existing customers are encouraged to register all purchases to accrue points in the "Extra Mile Club." Points can be redeemed for gym bags, running jackets, and ultimately a free pair of shoes.

8. Saucony plans to mail and email special promotions to this fertile new database.

The entire project was conceived, created, tested, and launched in less than five weeks. The content of the site was also used in a multimedia presentation at the Saucony worldwide sales conference in July. In early August, the site went "live" on the World Wide Web. The total budget including strategy, creative development, html, cgi, and installation onto server was $30,000. Cost per response as of entry submission was six cents per visit and dropping. The number of visits to site averages 5,000 per day. Total visits from August, 1995 to March 31, 1996 equals 650,000. The Saucony URL is http://www.saucony.com.

HJ HEINZ & COMPANY AUSTRALIA LIMITED

The Heinz Baby Program commenced in April 1995 and is ongoing. It was developed by Heinz, Australia's trusted leader in baby food, to provide baby feeding information and services for new parents. A series of five information-packed handbooks are delivered at the right time for each stage of baby's feeding and nutritional needs. In addition, free gifts, samples, special offers, mail order catalogs and an 800 number Baby Feeding Helpline were also established. The consumer target audience consists of new mothers, both first time and those who have been through the experience before. Many of these consumers have an overall perception that it is better to feed their babies home prepared food than give their babies canned food. The program is introduced to mothers while in the hospital through a "Bounty Bag." Response ads were also placed in key women's and parents' publications (in this case, *Australian Parents, Mother and Baby, Australian Women's Weekly, Family Circle,* and *Baby Care* book).

Heinz has a 90+ market share and is a clear leader in the prepared food category in Australia. For fifty years Heinz has been making and selling baby food in Australia and the company has built up a wealth of information and expertise in the area of infant feeding and nutrition. The objectives of the program were to create a stronger relationship with new parent households that results in better understanding of baby feeding needs, recognition of Heinz's in-depth expertise in all aspects of feeding and nutrition (not just prepared food), increased trust in the quality and suitability of Heinz products, and growth in prepared baby food usage. Some of the obstacles to achieving these objectives include:

- Leveling of birth rate
- Decreasing per capita consumption of prepared food
- Combatting the misconception about prepared baby food and food in general
- Competing versus a new company in the market—Gerber

The strategy was to concentrate marketing dollars on the one in seven households in Australia with babies by using gifts and services to build a relationship with mothers; provide samples and incentives to stimulate trial and ongoing purchase; initiate cooperative offers to provide appreciated values to members (and help to defray costs). With over 75, 000 members enrolled in the first year, the Heinz Baby Program is already reaching one in four to five babies in Australia. Member response to the various offers range from 6.5 to 11 percent generating hundreds of calls each week to the Baby Feeding Helpline. Member feedback has been extremely positive and longer term impact on brand position, attitude, and usage is under evaluation.

HARLEY-DAVIDSON MOTOR COMPANY

Harley-Davidson Motor Company, the only major American-based motorcycle manufacturer, produces heavyweight motorcycles and a complete line of related parts, accessories, clothing, and collectibles. The primary target audience for the campaign was Harley-Davidson motorcycle owners. The secondary audience was non-owners with an interest in the Harley-Davidson brand. The campaign included newspaper, television, and radio, to be placed locally by the dealer network. Direct mail was also included using a rented file of motorcycle owners. The overall worldwide motorcycle market is growing and the demand for Harley-Davidson motorcycles exceeds the supply.

The objective of the program was to achieve a measurable increase in dealership traffic and sales from the previous fourth quarter by building the image and identity of the Harley-Davidson dealer. Due to the shortage of motorcycles, the campaign focused on Harley-Davidson parts, accessories, clothing, and collectibles. One of the major obstacles to achieving the objective is that the Harley-Davidson dealer is the true contact point for the brand, but the existence of "chop shops," Easyriders, and other aftermarket stores have blurred the understanding of what is and isn't a "Harley store."

A campaign was designed to build the Harley-Davidson brand image, dealership loyalty, and dealership traffic by establishing the Harley "Genuine Dealer" as a key contact point for the brand. To kick off the campaign the dealers received a Genuine Dealer promotion kit that included:

- Genuine Dealer Self-Promotion Materials: The self-promotion materials included a :25/:05 television spot, three black-and-white small space ads, one :25/:05 radio spot, and a store hours sign.
- Genuine Dealer Holiday Materials: The purpose of this portion of the campaign was to provide the dealers with materials to sell MotorClothes and collectibles during the 1995 holiday season. The materials included three black-and-white small space ads, one :25/:05 radio spot, an FSI, and a direct mail piece.
- Genuine Dealer/Genuine Motor Accessories Materials: The dealers also had the opportunity to participate in a direct mail program involving a free pin offer to stimulate sales of parts and accessories.

The Genuine Dealer Program budget totaled $636,000 including creative development, preproduction, production, list rental, and postage. Media is not included because it was placed locally by the dealer network.

As a result of this integrated promotional campaign, Harley-Davidson reported record sales and earnings for its fourth quarter and year ended December 31, 1995. The fourth quarter 1995 Parts and Accessories/MotorClothes sales at Harley-Davidson dealers increased 18.5 percent from the previous year. Much of this increase has been directly attributed to the Genuine Dealer Promotion. At a cost of $636,000, the Genuine Dealer Program generated an additional $91,000,000 of revenue in the fourth quarter of 1995.

LAND ROVER

We have a saying in the United States, "If it ain't broke, don't fix it." The London agency Craik Jones Watson Mitchell Voelkel must have had this concept in mind for its 1995 campaign on behalf of the new Range Rover 4×4. Last year, the agency won a Gold Echo/Gold Mailbox Award for a campaign that introduced owners of the classic Range Rover to the new model through a series of exquisite mailers and lavish preview events. This year, Craik Jones takes home a Gold Echo for enticing some 3,200 Range Rover owners to attend an even fancier affair celebrating the good life: stately homes, popular British sports, fine food, and of course, the Range Rover.

With its impressive height, wood-and-leather interior, and high performance on- and off-road, Range Rover is known for providing a unique driving experience. Priced at £35,000 ($52,000), its owners tend to be successful family men and women, aged 30 to 50. The difficulty is to get this audience—mostly self-employed or senior company executives—to take a day out of their demanding schedules to look at new cars in showrooms. A hook was needed. Research indicated that Range Rover drivers had a burning desire to drive off-road in the most challenging conditions (but not necessarily in their own cars). They also wanted a taste of being part of the British landed gentry—the class of people known for their mansions and castles in the rolling countryside.

So Land Rover organized a series of events, "A Country Affair," which combined off-road driving at stately homes throughout England. Here, Range Rover owners could put the new model through its paces and enjoy a first-class catered affair. They could also get tips from top pros and coaches in a variety of sports. Land Rover dealers hand picked 4,000 names from their files to receive invitations to the nearest event. The word "invitations," however, doesn't quite do justice to the mailing piece that was used. What recipients found in their mailboxes were 12-page hardcover books, inviting them to take part in a day of test driving, archery, skeet shooting, fly casting, croquet, and golf clinics, all with professional coaching and supervision. Printed on heavy, textured paper, the books looked as if they had been handwritten in pencil and were fully illustrated with watercolor paintings of the vehicle and the events on the itinerary. Tucked inside the front cover was an R.S.V.P. card, with map and directions, and postage-paid return envelope.

The goal of the campaign, which ran July through September 1995, was threefold: To enhance the customers' perception of the brand; to build loyalty by catering to customers' interests; and ultimately, to encourage customers to purchase the new Range Rover. An astonishing 82 percent of the recipients attended "A Country Affair." With the total communication budget (creative, preproduction, production and postage) at £150,000 ($225,000), cost per response was £45.7 ($68.60). Of those, 24 percent eventually purchased new Range Rovers. And since customers were encouraged to bring a colleague, the manufacturer added valuable names of many more like-minded consumers to its prospecting database. The resulting sales were so strong that dealers asked the agency to cancel a followup mailing that included a purchase offer. Dealers are already clamoring for the event to be repeated annually.

In summary, channels are the means by which firms distribute their products to consumers. Channel strategy to build brand equity involves designing and managing direct and indirect channels to build brand awareness and improve the strength, favorability, and uniqueness of brand associations. Direct channels can enhance brand equity by allowing consumers to better understand the depth, breadth, and variety of the products associated with the brand as well as any distinguishing characteristics. Indirect channels can influence brand equity through the actions taken and support given to the brand by intermediaries such as retailers and the transfer of any associations that these intermediaries might have to the brand.

In concluding this chapter, we turn to the issue of private labels or store brands. After portraying private label branding strategies, we describe how major manufacturers' brands have responded to their threat.

Private Labels

Although different terms and definitions are possible, we refer to *private labels* as products marketed by retailers and other members of the distribution chain. Private labels can be called *store brands* when they actually adopt the name of the store itself in some way (e.g., Safeway Select). Private labels should not be confused with *generics* whose simple black and white packaging typically provides no information as to who made the product. Private label brands typically cost less to make and sell than the national or manufacturer brands with which they compete. Thus, the appeal to consumers of buying private labels and store brands often is the cost savings involved; the appeal to retailers of selling private labels and store brands is that their gross margin is often 25 percent to 30 percent—nearly twice than that for national brands.

The history of private labels is one of many ups and downs. The first private-label grocery products in the United States were sold by the Great Atlantic and Pacific Tea Company (later known as A&P), which was founded in 1863. During the first half of the twentieth century, a number of store brands were successfully introduced. Under competitive pressure from the sophisticated mass-marketing practices adopted by large packaged goods companies in the 1950s, private labels fell out of favor with consumers. The recession of the 1970s, however, saw the successful introduction of low-cost, basic quality, and minimally packaged generic products that appealed to bargain-seeking consumers. During the subsequent economic upswing, though, the lack of perceived quality eventually hampered generic sales, and many consumers returned back yet again to national or manufacturers' brands.

Because the appeal of private labels to consumers has traditionally been their lower cost, the sales of private labels generally have been highly correlated with personal disposable income (see Figure 5–9). To better compete in today's marketplace, private label makers have begun improving quality and expanding the variety of their private-label offerings to include even premium products. Because of these and other actions, private label sales have recently made some major inroads in new markets. In this section, we will examine how private labels have achieved this growth and study some particularly successful examples.

PRIVATE LABEL STATUS

In the United States, private label goods in 1993 accounted for 19.7 percent of all units sold in grocery stores and nearly 15 percent of total supermarket dollar volume. In other countries, these percentages are often quite higher. For example, private labels in the United Kingdom make up over a third of sales at grocery stores, in part because the grocery industry is more concentrated there. The five largest grocery chains make up 62 percent in sales in the United Kingdom (but only 21 percent in the United States). Two of the large U.K. grocery chains are Tesco and Sainsbury. Tesco has two major labels: Tesco Own and the 50 percent lower-priced Tesco Value. Sainsbury's slogan and the basis for its positioning in the United Kingdom is "Good Food Costs Less," which they have capitalized on to introduce a wide range of supermarket food products.

Private label appeal is widespread. In supermarkets, private label sales have always been strong in product categories such as dairy goods, vegetables, and beverages. More recently, private labels have been successful in previously "untouchable"

FIGURE 5-9 Relationship of Income and Sales of Private Labels

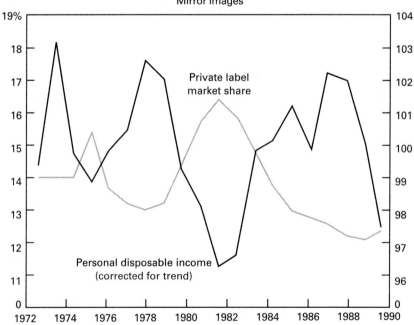

categories such as cigarettes, disposable diapers, and cold remedies. One study indicated that although the 17 percent of households who shop primarily on the basis of price and are classified as "heavy" private label buyers account for 42 percent of total private labels sales, nearly one-third of *all* consumers now regularly buy some private label goods. In fact, users of private labels in bottled water and diapers are even more upscale—with average incomes of $25,000 to $55,000—and older—with average ages in the 30s—than buyers of national brands in the category.

Nevertheless, some categories have not seen a strong private label presence. Many shoppers, for example, still seem unwilling to trust their hair, complexion, dental care, and so on to store brands. Private labels also have been relatively unsuccessful in other categories such as tuna fish, baby food, and beer. One implication that can be drawn from this pattern of product purchases is that consumers are being more selective in what they buy, no longer choosing to only buy national brands. For less-important products in particular, consumers seem to feel "that top-of-the-line is unnecessary and good is good enough."[42] Categories that are particularly vulnerable to private label advances would be those where there is little perceived quality differences among brands in the eyes of a sizable group of consumers, for example, OTC pain relievers, bottled water, plastic bags, paper towels, dairy products, and soft drinks.

PRIVATE LABEL BRANDING STRATEGY

Although the growth of private labels has been interpreted by some as a sign of the "decline of brands," it could easily be argued that the *opposite* conclusion may in fact be more valid, as private label growth could be seen in some ways as a consequence of cleverly designed branding strategies. In terms of building brand equity, the key point of difference to consumers for private labels has always been "good value," a desirable and transferable association across many product categories. As a result, private labels can be extremely "broad," and their names can be applied across many different products.

As with national brands, implementing a value pricing strategy for private labels requires determining the right price and product offering. For example, one reported guideline is that the typical "no-name" product has to sell for at least 15 percent below a national brand, on average, to be successful. The challenge for private labels, however, has been to determine the appropriate product offering. Specifically, to achieve the necessary points of parity, or even to create their own points of difference, private labels have been improving quality, and as a result are now even aggressively positioning against national brands. Many supermarket chains have even introduced their own premium store brands such as Safeway (Select), Von's (Royal Request), and Ralph's (Private Selection).

For example, A&P positioned its premium Master's Choice brand to fill the void between the mass-market national brands and the more upscale specialty brands that they sell. They have used the brand across a wide range of products such as teas, pastas, sauces, and salad dressings. Sellers of private labels are also adopting much more extensive marketing communication programs to spread the word about their brands. For example, A&P includes a glossy Master's Choice insert and also uses Act Media shopping carts, freezer vision, instant coupon machines, and a television advertising campaign in selling the America's Choice brand. Branding Brief 5–4 describes how Loblaws has been successful at creating its own brands.

BRANDING BRIEF 5-4

Building Brands at Loblaw[a]

Loblaw is Canada's largest food distributor. Loblaw's business success is attributable to a number of strategic considerations:

1. *Real estate strategy.* In 1985, Loblaw embarked on a five-year, $1.26 billion capital expenditure program designed to upgrade existing units and to add new units. This money was spent to build new combination stores, build and refurbish supermarkets, acquire franchise businesses, and build wholesaling and servicing elements. Unlike the majority of firms in the supermarket industry, Loblaw believed in owning the real estate and leasing the fixtures for its retail operations (to provide cost-effective exit strategies). Loblaw also sought out and willingly paid for prime store locations.

2. *Store design strategy.* To more profitably manage their stores, Loblaw divided its 1200 stores into four formats: (1) No frills (under 20,000 square feet), (2) Conventional supermarkets (between 18,000 and 35,000 square feet), (3) Superstores (between 60,000 and 80,000 square feet), and (4) Combination stores or "Super-Centres" (between 100,000 and 140,000 square feet). Each format was designed and run differently to better meet the needs of their target market segment.

3. *Procurement strategy.* Loblaw organized procurement through a company they formed called Intersave, which consolidated retail and wholesale; centralized finance, real estate, and procurement activities; installed state-of-the-art computer systems to gather product movement, profitability, and merchandise information. Because procurement is 80 percent of the cost of goods sold, reductions in costs here had big impact.

4. *Branding strategy.* Loblaw decided that a successful house brand was one way to ensure customer loyalty to the chain itself. Loblaws followed many basic branding principles in getting their branding program off the ground, as follows.

Loblaw was the first store in Canada to introduce generics in 1978, reflecting a carefully crafted strategy to build an image of quality and high value in six areas:

- Product selection (fancy grade products)
- Quality testing
- Packaging (bright, upbeat colors)
- Advertising (print, billboard, and TV media)
- Displays (color-coordinated)
- Guarantees

By 1983, they carried over 500 generic products that accounted for 10 percent of Loblaw's sales. This success was due to innovative marketing, low costs, and a large network of suppliers. Generics were restricted to major product categories to provide volume necessary for the program to be successful. Other categories presented different opportunities, and in 1984 Loblaw chose to introduce another brand, President's Choice, that was designed to offer unique value through exceptional quality and moderate prices. These categories ranged from basic supermarket categories such as chocolate chip cookies, colas, and cereals to more exotic categories such as Devonshire custard from England and gourmet Russian mustard. The chocolate chip cookie had a higher percentage of chips (40 percent) than other brands and used real butter. Its high quality was evidenced by the fact that it was rated as the best in the category by Consumer Reports. These products also used distinctive and attractive packaging with modern lettering and colorful labels and names ("decadent" cookies, "ultimate" frozen pizza, and "too good to be true" peanut butter).

FIGURE 5-10 Sample Insider's Report

In terms of marketing communications, Loblaw consolidated its budget. Even though its advertising/sales ratio (2 percent) was less than half that of major brands, they were able to put into place a strong promotional program with much in-store merchandising. Loblaw also introduced its *Insider's Report*, a quarterly publication featuring its own store brands and offering consumers shopping tips (see Figure 5–10). The president of the corporate label group at the time, Dave Nichols, became a spokesperson both inside and outside the company.

By 1989, approximately 2200 No Name brands and 700 President's Choice brands made up 30 percent of Loblaw's total sales while earning an average of 15 percent higher margin than the major brands. Approximately 200 new store brands were being introduced annually with three-quarters of them being successful (as compared to a 10% or so success rate for major brands).

[a]Mary L. Shelman and Ray A. Goldberg, "Loblaw Companies Limited," HBS# 9-588-039. Gordon H. G. McDougall and Douglas Snetsinger, "Loblaw," in Lovelock and Weinberg, *Marketing Challenges*, 3rd ed. New York: McGraw-Hill, 1993, pp. 169–185.

Three companies that have successfully established their own private labels to compete with national packaged goods giants are Paragon, Cott, and Perrigo. Paragon, recently spun off from Weyerhaeuser, is a half-billion dollar player in the diaper business. It has made significant inroads in Procter & Gamble's sales by combining a high-quality product with competitive prices. Toronto-based Cott has been around for 40-plus years, selling its own cola with the slogan, "It's Cott to be Good." In 1991, it became a private label supplier of cola for Safeway Select, President's Choice, and Master's Choice. Cott quickly gained 1 percent of this huge $30 billion market. Cott uses syrup supplied by RC Cola in its cola product and employs a top design firm in its packaging.[43] Finally, Perrigo, another private label supplier and producer, has grown to be become a major player in the $3 billion private-label health and beauty aids business. Perrigo's approach is to sell look-alike products or "knockoffs" at lower prices by not advertising and doing little original research. Instead, Perrigo's chemists simply take apart major brands and then put them back together again with a slight twist in ingredients, when necessary, to avoid patent infringement.[44]

MAJOR BRAND RESPONSE TO PRIVATE LABELS

Chapter 1 described Procter & Gamble's value-pricing program and strategies to combat competitive inroads from private labels and other brands. Other major national brands also have been successful at fending off private labels. For example, H.J. Heinz retained more than 50 percent market share in the ketchup category for years. Heinz's ingredients for success included a distinctive, slightly sweet tasting product; a carefully monitored price gap with competitors; and aggressive packaging, product development, and promotional efforts (e.g., as evidenced by their introduction in years past of a squeezable bottle, flavored ketchup, and a rejuvenated "Anticipation" advertising campaign). Branding Brief 5–5 describes some of the marketing activity at

---

BRANDING BRIEF 5-5

Razor-Sharp Branding at Gillette

One of the strongest brands in the world is Gillette. The company owns roughly two-thirds of the U.S. blade and razor market and even more in Europe and Latin America. In fact, more than 70 percent of sales and profits come from overseas operations in 200 countries. Moreover, their 10 percent profit margin is substantially higher than at most packaged goods companies. How has Gillette been so successful? Its marketing and branding practices provide a number of useful lessons to marketers.[a]

Fundamentally, Gillette continually innovates to produce a demonstrably superior product. More than 40 percent of Gillette's sales in the first half of the 1990s came from new products. Gillette's credo is to "increase spending in 'growth drivers'—R&D, plant and equipment, and advertising—at least as fast as revenues go up." As Gillette's CEO proclaims, "Good products come out of market research. Great products come from R&D." To clearly differentiate its brands, Gillette refuses to manufacture private-label products.

Gillette's marketing philosophy is not to sell products but to capture customers by selling razors and, more importantly, all of the blade refills. The operating margins of blades is 40 percent of revenues. All told, the blade and razor business generates one-third of corporate revenues but two-thirds of profits. Additional products sold by Gillette—Braun small appliances, Oral-B toothbrushes, and Papermate, Parker, and Waterman pens—also command premium prices and margins through proprietary design. In 1996, Gillette struck a deal to buy battery manufacturer Duracell. All these consumer product businesses share common traits: They are No. 1 worldwide in their markets, profitable, fast-growing, and anchored by a strong technological base.

Gillette's experience with Sensor is instructive. Sales of Sensor worldwide in 1993 exceeded $500 million. The men's and women's versions of Sensor together account for 61.2 percent of the $61.3 million non-disposable razor category in the United States. Sensor, a twin-bladed razor mounted on tiny springs, is priced at $3.49. Because Gillette designs and builds all of its own—often complicated—manufacturing equipment, it is difficult for competitors to clone Gillette products. For example, although Schick won the rights to the Sensor patent, the company lacked the laser-welding machines needed to produce a Sensor clone. Gillette's pricing also helps to stem private label competition. The typical American man buys thirty blades in a year. If he buys Sensor, however, which costs 70 cents per blade, that adds up to $21 per year. Although a cost-conscious shopper could buy thirty generic blades for $9, Gillette believes most consumers would not trade down to a potentially less pleasurable daily shaving experience to save $12.

Gillette always backs its products with strong advertising and promotional support. Gillette's newest innovation in shaving technology, the Sensor Excel, adds five rubbery strips or "microfins" in front of the razor blade (to stretch the skin) and a larger lubricating strip to make shaving smoother and more comfortable—at a price 15 percent to 20 percent higher than that of the original

Sensor. Sensor Excel was introduced with a $40 million ad campaign (created by Gillette's long-time agency, BBDO), free-standing inserts and other promotions, and sampling activities. The TV ads use a montage of slow-motion scenes of men shown in different roles with upbeat background music and the now-familiar tag line "The Best a Man Can Get."

---

[a]Patricia Sellers, "Brands, It's Thrive or Die," *Fortune* (August 23, 1993), pp. 52–56. Linda Grant, "Gillette Knows Shaving—and How to Turn Out Hot New Products," *Fortune* (October 14, 1996), pp. 207–210.

Gillette, perhaps one of the most successful builders of global brands (and defender against private labels). More generally, to compete with private labels, a number of different tactics have been adopted by marketers of major national or manufacturer brands, as follows (see Figure 5–11).

First, marketers of major brands have attempted to decrease costs and reduce prices to negate the primary point of difference of private labels and achieve a critical point of parity. In many categories, prices of major brands had crept up to where price premiums over private labels were 30 percent to 50 percent, or even 100 percent! In those categories where consumers make frequent purchases, the cost savings of "trading down" to a private label brand was quite substantial as a result. For example, before Marlboro dropped its prices, a smoker who purchased, on average, ten packs of cigarettes a week could have saved over $500 a year by switching from a premium brand such as Marlboro that cost $2 a pack to a private label brand that only cost $1 a pack!

In instances where major brands and private labels are on more equal footing with regard to price, major brands often compete well because of other favorable brand perceptions that consumers might have. For example, when Star Kist cut prices

1. Decrease costs.
2. Cut prices.
3. Increase R & D expenditures to improve products and identify new product innovations.
4. Increase advertising and promotion budgets.
5. Eliminate stagnant brands and extensions and concentrate efforts on smaller number of brands.
6. Introduce discount "fighter" brands.
7. Supply private label makers.
8. Track store brands growth and compete market by market.

FIGURE 5-11 Major Brand Response to Private Labels

on its tuna to only five cents higher than private labels—given the positive image their brand had with consumers—they were able to slice the private label share in the category in half (from 20 percent to 10 percent). Marketers of major brands have cut prices on older brands to make them more appealing. Procter & Gamble cut prices on a number of old standbys (e.g., Joy dishwashing detergent, Era laundry detergent, Luvs disposable diapers, and Camay beauty soap) by 12 percent to 33 percent, shifting them into the mid-tier level of pricing. Miller Brewing Co. dropped prices on its Miller High Life brand 20 percent, while also reviving the old "Miller Time" advertising theme, increasing sales 20 percent as a result.

It should be noted that one problem faced by marketers of major brands is that it can be difficult to actually lower prices even if they so desire. Supermarkets may not pass along the wholesale price cuts they are given. Moreover, marketers of major brands may not want to alienate retailers by attacking their store brands too forcefully, especially in "zero-sum" categories where their brands could be easily replaced. For example, for its Luvs brand of diapers, P&G eliminated jumbo packs, streamlined package designs, simplified printing, and trimmed promotions, increasing retail margins from 3.3 percent to 8.6 percent as a result. Nevertheless, faced with margins on store brand diapers of 8 percent to 12 percent, the Safeway supermarket chain still chose to drop the brand altogether anyway.

Besides these various pricing moves to achieve points of parity, marketers of major brands have also used other tactics to achieve additional points of difference to combat the threat of private labels. They have increased R&D expenditures to improve products and identify new product innovations. They have increased advertising and promotion budgets. They have also tracked store brand growth more closely and are competing on a more market-by-market basis. Marketers of major brands have also adjusted their brand portfolios. They have eliminated stagnant brands and extensions and concentrated their efforts on smaller number of brands. They have introduced discount "fighter" brands especially designed and promoted to compete with private labels.

One controversial move by some marketers of major brands is to actually supply private label makers. For example, Ralston-Purina, Borden, ConAgra, and Heinz have all admitted to supplying products—sometimes lower in quality—to be used for private labels. Other marketers, however, criticize this "if you can't beat them, join them" strategy, maintaining that these actions, if revealed, may create confusion or even reinforce a perception by consumers that all brands in a category are essentially the same.

FUTURE DEVELOPMENTS

Many marketers feel that the brands most endangered by the rise of private labels are second-tier brands that have not been as successful at establishing as clear an identity as market leaders. For example, in the laundry detergent category, the success of a private label brand such as Wal-Mart's Ultra Clean is more likely to come at the expense of brands such as Oxydol, All, or Fab rather then market leader Tide. Highly priced, poorly differentiated and undersupported brands thus are especially vulnerable to private label competition.

At the same time, retailers will also need the quality and image that go along with well-researched, efficiently manufactured, and professionally marketed major brands if nothing else because of the wishes of consumers. When A&P let store brands soar to 35 percent of its dry grocery sales mix in the 1960s, many shoppers defected. The private label share of A&P's product mix now is 18 percent.

Review

In this chapter, we considered product, pricing, and distribution strategies to build brand equity. A number of issues were reviewed and guidelines proposed in each area. In closing, it is useful to highlight a few key principles for each of these three elements of the marketing mix. First, in terms of product design, both tangible and intangible considerations are important. Successful brands often create strong and favorable associations to both functional and symbolic benefits. Although perceived quality is often at the heart of brand equity, it is important to recognize the range of possible associations that may become linked to the brand. Second, in terms of pricing strategies, it is important for marketers to fully understand consumer perceptions of value for the brand. Increasingly, firms are adopting value-based pricing strategies to set prices and everyday low pricing strategies to guide their discount pricing policy over time. Value-based pricing strategies attempt to properly balance product design and delivery, product costs, and product prices. Everyday low pricing strategies attempt to establish a stable set of "everyday" prices and only introduces price discounts very selectively. Third, in terms of channel strategies, it is important to: (1) appropriately match brand and store images to maximize leverage of secondary associations; (2) integrate "push" strategies for retailers with "pull" strategies for consumers; and (3) consider a range of direct and indirect distribution options.

The chapter concluded by describing private label branding strategies and how major manufacturers have responded. In the following chapter, we consider how to develop integrated marketing communication programs to build brand equity.

Discussion Questions

1. Think about the products you own. Assess their product design. Critique their "after-marketing" efforts. Are you aware of all of the products' capabilities? Identify a product where you feel you are not fully capitalizing on all of its benefits. How might you suggest improvements?

2. Choose a product category. Profile all the brands in the category in terms of pricing strategies and perceived value. If possible, review the brands' pricing histories. Have these brands set and adjusted prices properly? What would you do differently?

3. Take a trip to a department store. Evaluate the in-store marketing effort. Which categories or brands seem to be receiving the biggest in-store "push"? What unique in-store merchandising efforts do you see?

4. Take a trip to a supermarket. Observe the extent of private-label brands. In which categories do you think private labels might be successful? Why?

Notes

1. Philip Kotler, *Marketing Management*, 8th ed. Upper Saddle River, NJ: Prentice Hall, 1994.

2. David A. Aaker and Robert Jacobson, "The Strategic Role of Product Quality," *Journal of Marketing* (October 1987), pp. 31–44.

3. Stratford Sherman, "How to Prosper in the Value Decade," *Fortune* (November 30, 1992), p. 91.

4. David Garvin, "Product Quality: An Important Strategic Weapon," *Business Horizons*, 27 (May–June 1985), pp. 40–43. Philip Kotler, *Marketing Management*, 8th ed. Upper Saddle River, NJ: Prentice Hall, 1994.

5. Philip Kotler, *Marketing Management*, 8th ed. Upper Saddle River, NJ: Prentice Hall, 1994.

6. David Greising, "Quality: How to Make It Pay," *Business Week* (August 8, 1994), pp. 54–59. Roland T. Rust, Anthony J. Zahorik, and Timothy L. Keiningham, "Return on Quality (ROQ): Making Service Quality Financially Accountable," Marketing Science Institute Report Number 94-106, April 1994.

7. Philip Kotler, *Marketing Management*, 8th ed. Upper Saddle River, NJ: Prentice Hall, 1994.

8. Michael E. Porter, *Competitive Advantage.* New York: Free Press, 1985.

9. Lourdes Lee Valeriano, "Loved the Present! Hated the Manual!," *Wall Street Journal* (December 15, 1994), p. B-1.

10. Terry Vavra, *Aftermarketing: How to Keep Customers for Life Through Relationship Marketing.* Homewood, IL: Irwin Professional Publishers, Business One Irwin: 1992.

11. Robert C. Blattberg and Kenneth Wisniewski, "Price-Induced Patterns of Competition," *Marketing Science*, 8 (Fall 1989), pp. 291–309.

12. Elliot B. Ross, "Making Money with Proactive Pricing," *Harvard Business Review* (November-December 1984), pp. 145–155.

13. Norman Berry, "Revitalizing Brands," *The Journal of Consumer Marketing*, 5 (3) (1988), pp. 15–20.

14. Sally Lieberman, "Mondavi Uncorks New Wine, Stock," *San Francisco Examiner* (May 2, 1993), p. E-1.

15. For a more detailed and comprehensive treatment of pricing strategy, see Thomas T. Nagle, *The Strategy of Tactics of Pricing.* Upper Saddle River, NJ: Prentice Hall, 1987. Kent B. Monroe, *Pricing: Making Profitable Decisions*, 2nd. ed. New York: McGraw-Hill, 1990.

16. Yumiko Ono, "Companies Find That Consumers Continue to Resist Price Boosts," *Wall Street Journal* (March 8, 1994), p. B-8.

17. Donald Lehmann and Russell Winer, *Product Management.* Burr Ridge, IL: Irwin, 1994.

18. Kathleen Deveny, "Some Firms Buck Price-Trimming Trend," *Wall Street Journal* (August 19, 1993), p. B-1.

19. Allan J. Magrath, "8 Timeless Truths About Pricing," *Sales & Marketing Management* (October 1989), pp. 78–84.

20. Thomas J. Malott, CEO of Siemens that makes heavy electrical equipment and motors, quoted in Stratford Sherman, "How to Prosper in the Value Decade," *Fortune* (November 30, 1992), pp. 90–103.

21. Christopher Power, "Value Marketing," *Business Week* (November 11, 1991), pp. 132–140.

22. Martha Brannigan and Eleena de Lisser, "Cost Cutting at Delta Raises the Stock Price but Lowers the Service," *Wall Street Journal* (June 20, 1996), pp. A1, A8.

23. Christopher Farrell, "Stuck! How Companies Cope When They Can't Raise Prices," *Business Week* (November 15, 1993), pp. 146–150.

24. Donald Lehmann and Russell Winer, *Product Management*. Burr Ridge, IL: Irwin, 1994.

25. Stratford Sherman, "How to Prosper in the Value Decade," *Fortune* (November 30, 1992), pp. 90–103

26. Richard Gibson, "Retailing: Broad Grocery Price Cuts May Not Pay," *Wall Street Journal* (May 7, 1993), p. B1.

27. Zachary Schiller, "Not Everyone Loves a Supermarket Special," *Business Week* (February 17, 1992), pp. 64–66.

28. Philip Kotler, *Marketing Management*, 8th ed. Upper Saddle River, NJ: Prentice Hall, 1994.

29. For a more detailed and comprehensive treatment of channel strategy, see Louis W. Stern and Adel I. El-Ansary, *Marketing Channels*, 5th ed. Upper Saddle River, NJ: Prentice Hall, 1996.

30. V. Kasturi Rangan, Melvyn A. J. Menezes, and E.P. Maier, "Channel Selection for New Industrial Products: A Framework, Method, and Applications," *Journal of Marketing*, 56 (July 1992), pp. 69–82.

31. Rowland T. Moriarty and Ursula Moran, "Managing Hybrid Marketing Systems," *Harvard Business Review,* 68 (1990), pp. 146–155.

32. William M. Weilbacher, *Brand Marketing*. Lincolnwood, IL: NTC Business Books. 1993, p. 53.

33. Christopher Farrell, "Stuck! How Companies Cope When They Can't Raise Prices," *Business Week* (November 15, 1993), pp. 146–150.

34. Steven M. Shugan, "Branded Variants," *Research in Marketing*, AMA Educators' Proceedings, Series #55. Chicago, IL: AMA, 1989, pp. 33–38.

35. Mark Bergen, Shantanu Dutta, and Steven M. Shugan, "Branded Variants: A Retail Perspective," *Journal of Marketing Research* (February 1995), p. 9.

36. George E. Belch and Michael A. Belch, *Introduction to Advertising and Promotion*. Burr Ridge, IL: Irwin, 1995.

37. Raju Narisetti, "Joint Marketing with Retailers Spreads," *Wall Street Journal* (October 24, 1996), p. B6.

38. Bill Richards, "Levi-Strauss Plans to Open 200 Stores in 5 Years, With Ending of FTC Ban," *Wall Street Journal* (December 22, 1994), p. A-2.

39. Mary Kuntz, "These Ads Have Windows and Walls," *Business Week* (February 27, 1995), p. 74.

40. Elaine Underwood, "Store Brands," *Brandweek* (January 9, 1995), pp. 22–27.

41. DM Editorial Staff, "1996 Echo Awards—Spotting the Trendsetters," *Direct Marketing*, 59 (7) (November 1996), pp. 10–17.

42. Chip Walker, "What's In a Name," *American Demographics* (February 1991), p. 54.

43. Patricia Sellers, "Brands, It's Thrive or Die," *Fortune* (August 23, 1993), pp. 52–56.

44. Gabriella Stern, "Cheap Imitation: Perrigo's Knockoffs of Name-Brand Drugs Turn Into Big Sellers," *Wall Street Journal* (July 15, 1993), pp. A1, A9.

 **CHAPTER**

Integrating Marketing Communications to Build Brand Equity

Preview

The previous chapter described how product, price, and distribution strategies can contribute to brand equity. In this chapter, we consider the final and perhaps most flexible element of the marketing mix. *Marketing communications* are the means by which firms attempt to inform, persuade, and remind consumers, directly or indirectly, about the brands that they sell. In a sense, marketing communications represent the "voice" of the brand and are a means by which it can establish a dialogue and build relationships with consumers. Although advertising is often a central element of a marketing communications program, it is usually not the only one—or even the most important one—in terms of building brand equity. Figure 6–1 displays some of the commonly used marketing communication options for the consumer market.

FIGURE 6–1 Alternative Marketing Communication Options

1. Media Advertising
   - TV
   - Radio
   - Newspaper
   - Magazines

2. Direct Response Advertising
   - Mail
   - Telephone
   - Broadcast media
   - Print media
   - Computer-related
   - Media-related

3. Place Advertising
   - Bulletins
   - Billboards
   - Posters
   - Cinema
   - Transit

4. Point-of-Purchase Advertising
   - Shelf talkers
   - Aisle markers
   - Shopping cart ads
   - In-store radio or TV

5. Trade Promotions
   - Trade deals & buying allowances
   - Point-of-purchase display allowances
   - Push money
   - Contests and dealer incentives
   - Training programs
   - Trade shows
   - Cooperative advertising

6. Consumer Promotions
   - Samples
   - Coupons
   - Premiums
   - Refunds/rebates
   - Contests/sweepstakes
   - Bonus packs
   - Price-offs

7. Event Marketing and Sponsorship
   - Sports
   - Arts
   - Entertainment
   - Fairs and festivals
   - Cause-related

8. Publicity and Public Relations

9. Personal Selling

Although advertising and other communication options can play different roles in the marketing program, one important purpose of all marketing communications is to contribute to brand equity. According to the customer-based brand equity model, marketing communications can contribute to brand equity by creating awareness of the brand and/or linking strong, favorable, and unique associations to the brand in consumers' memory. In addition to forming the desired brand knowledge structures, marketing communication programs also can provide incentives that elicit the differential responses that make up customer-based brand equity. Thus, perhaps the simplest but most useful way to judge advertising and or any other communication options is in its ability to achieve the desired brand knowledge structures and elicit the differential response that makes up brand equity. For example, how well does a proposed ad campaign contribute to awareness or creating, maintaining, or strengthening certain brand associations? To what extent does a promotion encourage consumers to buy more of a product? At what price premium?

The flexibility of marketing communications lies in part with the number of different ways that they can contribute to brand equity. At the same time, brand equity provides the focus as to how all of the different marketing communication options should best be designed and implemented. In this chapter, we consider how to optimally develop marketing communication programs to build brand equity. Our assumption is that the other elements of the marketing program have been properly put into place. Thus, the optimal brand positioning has been defined—especially in terms of the desired target market—and product, pricing, and distribution decisions have been made.

To motivate the complexity in designing marketing communication programs, we begin by reviewing a simple information-processing model of communications. To provide necessary background, we next evaluate the major communication options in terms of their roles in contributing to brand equity and some of their main costs and benefits. The chapter concludes by considering how to "mix and match" communication options—that is, how to employ a range of communication options in a coordinated or integrated fashion—to build brand equity. For brevity, we will not consider a number of specific but important marketing communication issues such as media scheduling, budget estimation techniques, and research approaches.[1]

Information Processing Model of Communications

A number of different models have been put forth over the years to explain the communication process and the steps involved in the persuasion process—recall the hierarchy of effects discussion from chapter 2. For example, William McGuire, an influential social psychologist from Yale, maintains that for a person to be persuaded by any form of communication—a TV advertisement, newspaper editorial, classroom lecture—the following six steps must occur:

1. *Exposure:* The person must see or hear the communication.
2. *Attention:* The person must notice the communication.
3. *Comprehension:* The person must understand the intended message or arguments of the communication.

4. *Yielding:* The person must respond favorably to the intended message or arguments of the communication.

5. *Intentions:* The person must plan to act in the desired manner of the communication.

6. *Behavior:* The person must actually act in the desired manner of the communication.

The difficulty in creating a successful marketing communication program can be seen by recognizing that each one of the six steps must occur for a consumer to be persuaded. If there is a breakdown or failure in any step along the way, then successful communication will not result. For example, consider the potential pitfalls in launching a new advertising campaign:

1. A consumer may not be exposed to an ad because the media plan missed the mark.

2. A consumer may not notice an ad because of a boring and uninspired creative strategy.

3. A consumer may not understand an ad because of a lack of product category knowledge or technical sophistication or because of a lack of awareness and familiarity about the brand itself.

4. A consumer may fail to respond favorably and form a positive attitude because of irrelevant or unconvincing product claims.

5. A consumer may fail to form a purchase intention because of a lack of an immediate perceived need.

6. A consumer may fail to actually buy the product because of a failure to remember anything from the ad when confronted with the available brands in the store.

To show how fragile the whole communication process is, assume that the probability of *each* of the six steps being successfully accomplished is 50 percent—most likely an extremely generous assumption. The laws of probability suggest that the probability of *all* six steps successfully occurring, assuming they are independent events, would be $.5 \times .5 \times .5 \times .5 \times .5 \times .5$, which equals 1.5625 percent. If the probability of each step occurring, on average, was a perhaps more reasonable 10 percent, then the joint probability of all six events occurring would be .0001. In other words, only 1 in 10,000! No wonder advertisers sometimes lament the limited power of advertising!

One implication of the information processing model is that to increase the odds for a successful marketing communications campaign, marketers must attempt to increase the likelihood that *each* step occurs. For example, from an advertising standpoint, the ideal ad campaign would ensure that:

1. The right consumer is exposed to the right message at the right place and at the right time.

2. The creative strategy for the advertising causes the consumer to notice and attend to the ad but does not distract from the intended message.

3. The ad properly reflects the consumer's level of understanding about the product and the brand.

4. The ad correctly positions the brand in terms of desirable and deliverable points-of-difference and points-of-parity.

5. The ad motivates consumers to consider purchase of the brand.

6. The ad creates strong brand associations to all of these stored communication effects so that they can have an effect when consumers are considering making a purchase.

Clearly, marketing communication programs must be designed and executed carefully if they are to have the desired effects on consumers. In the following section, we will survey and critique the major marketing communication options: broadcast, print, direct response, and place advertising media; consumer and trade promotions; event marketing and sponsorship; publicity and public relations; and personal selling.

Overview of Marketing Communication Options

ADVERTISING

Advertising can be defined as any paid form of nonpersonal presentation and promotion of ideas, goods, or services by an identified sponsor. Advertising plays an important and often controversial role in contributing to brand equity. Although advertising is recognized as a powerful means of creating strong, favorable, and unique brand associations, it is controversial because the specific effects of advertising are often difficult to quantify and predict. Nevertheless, a number of studies using very different approaches have shown the power of advertising to affect brand sales.

For example, the American Association of Advertising Agencies has compiled a list of some of the studies demonstrating the productivity of advertising expenditures. They report analyses of advertising effects using the PIMS ("Profit Impact of Marketing Strategy") database, which contains both marketing and financial information on 750 consumer businesses in a variety of industries. One such PIMS study by the Center for Research and Development showed that firms that increased advertising during a recessionary period gained a half to a full market share point coming out of the recession, whereas those firms who cut their advertising budget only gained two-tenths of a share point.[2]

Other comprehensive studies also document the power of advertising. For example, an analysis of the effects of advertising on sales using Nielsen's single-source data base of 142 packaged goods brands from 1991–1992 revealed that approximately half the time, advertising "worked." Specifically, 70 percent of the ad campaigns in the sample boosted sales immediately, although the effect was only strong in 30 percent of the cases. Forty-six percent of campaigns appeared to yield a long-term sales boost. Additional analyses revealed other interesting study findings, indicating that:

1. Increased sales could come from a single advertisement.
2. "Blitz campaigns" with concentrated exposure schedules could suffer from diminished returns such that ads shown less frequently over a longer period of time were more effective.
3. Advertising was more likely to increase both sales and profits than "money-off" sales promotions, which almost always lost money.[3]

Similarly, another comprehensive study of advertising effectiveness conducted by a major research supplier, Information Resources Inc., with a different data base reinforces these findings and provides several additional observations as to how advertising, as well as promotion, works (see Branding Brief 6–1).[4]

Besides these broad-based studies, numerous anecdotal case studies point to the power of advertising. To highlight just one, sales of Frito-Lay's Baked Lay's line of low-fat chips in its first year reached $200 million, far exceeding sales plans for the

Advertising Works!: IRI's Study of Advertising Effectiveness

Information Resources Institute (IRI) recently provided a unique, in-depth examination into how advertising works. IRI uses a "single-source" testing service called BehaviorScan. Single-source research suppliers track behavior of individual households from TV sets to checkout counters in supermarkets in test markets across the United States. Consumers in test markets who sign up to be a member of IRI's "Shoppers Hotline" panel agree to have microcomputers record when the TV set is on and to which station it is tuned, and electronic scanners record UPC codes of their household purchases at supermarkets. IRI has the capability to send different commercials to different preselected homes to test the effects of advertising copy and weights. BehaviorScan can also test the effects of store feature, displays, coupons, and so on.

In 1989, IRI reviewed the results of 389 research studies conducted over the previous seven years and offered the following generalizable principles concerning advertising and promotion effectiveness:

1. *TV advertising weight alone is not enough.* Only roughly half of TV advertising heavy-up plans have a measurable effect on sales, although when they do have an effect it is often large. The success rate is higher on new products or line extensions than on established brands.

2. *TV advertising is more likely to work when there are changes in copy or media strategy* (e.g., a new copy strategy or an expanded target market).

3. *When advertising is successful in increasing sales, its impact lasts beyond the period of peak spending.* Recent evidence shows the long-term positive effects of advertising lasting up to two years after peak spending. Moreover, the long-term incremental sales generated are approximately double the incremental sales observed in the first year of an advertising spending increase.

4. *About 20 percent of advertising plans pay out in the short-term.* However, when the long-term effect of advertising is considered, it is likely that most advertising plans that show a significant effect in a split cable experiment would pay out.

5. *Promotions almost always have a measurable impact on sales. However, the effect is usually purely short term.*

6. *Payout statistics on promotions are dismal.* Roughly 16 percent of trade promotions are profitable. Furthermore, promotions' effects are often purely short term, except for new products.

7. *The above statistics on advertising and promotion payouts show that many brands are overspending on marketing support.* Many classes of spending can be reduced at an increase in profits.

8. *Allocating marketing funds involves a continuous search for marketing programs that offer the highest return on the marketing dollar.* Trade-offs between advertising, trade, and consumer promotions can be highly profitable when based on reliable evaluation systems measuring this productivity at any point in time.

9. *The current trend towards promotion spending is not sound from a marketing productivity standpoint.* When the strategic disadvantages of promotions are included, that is, losing control to the trade and training consumers to buy only on deal, then the case is compelling for a re-evaluation of current practices and the incentive systems responsible for this trend.

brand. During that first year, Frito-Lay had spent about $15 to $20 million to advertise Baked Lay's with ads featuring Miss Piggy and supermodels such as Vendala, Kathy Ireland, and Naomi Campbell. Critics note that the combination of entertainment and product benefits in the well-received ads were indispensable in fueling sales of the otherwise slow-starting product.[5]

Given the complexity of designing advertising—the number of strategic roles it might play, the sheer number of specific decisions involved, and its complicated effect on consumers—a comprehensive set of detailed managerial guidelines are difficult to provide. Different advertising media clearly have different strengths, however, and therefore are best suited to play certain roles in a communication program. Figure 6–2 provides a breakdown of national advertising spending by major advertising media, and Figure 6–3 summarizes advantages and disadvantages of the main advertising media. In this section, some key issues about each media type are highlighted in turn.

Television

Television is generally acknowledged as the most powerful advertising medium as it allows for sight, sound, and motion and reaches a broad spectrum of consumers. Virtually all American households have televisions and the amount of time that television sets are on each day, on average, is a staggering seven hours! The wide reach of TV advertising translates to low cost per exposure. From a brand equity perspective, TV advertising has two particularly important strengths. First, TV advertising can be an effective means of vividly demonstrating product attributes and persuasively explaining their corresponding consumer benefits. Second, TV advertising can be a compelling means for dramatically portraying non-product-related user and usage imagery, brand personality, and so on.

On the other hand, television advertising has its drawbacks. Because of the fleeting nature of the message and the potentially distracting creative elements often found in a TV ad, product-related messages and the brand itself often can be overlooked by consumers while viewing a TV ad. Moreover, the large number of ads and non-programming material on television creates much clutter that makes it easy for consumers to ignore or forget ads. Another important disadvantage of TV ads is the high cost of production and placement. Even though the price of TV advertising has skyrocketed, the share of the prime time audience for the major networks has steadily declined, from around 90 percent in the mid-1970s to under 60 percent by the mid-1990s. By a number of measures, the effectiveness of any one ad,

	$MM	% of total
TV	29,400	22.7%
Radio	8,654	6.7%
Newspaper	30,737	23.8%
Magazines	7,000	5.4%
Direct response	23,391	23.4%
Outdoor	1,031	0.8%
Other	29,086	22.5%
TOTAL	129,299	

FIGURE 6-2 Marketing Communication Expenditures (United States, 1993)

Media	Advantages	Disadvantages
Television	Mass coverage High reach Impact of sight, sound, and motion High prestige Low cost per exposure Attention getting Favorable image	Low selectivity Short message life High absolute cost High production costs Clutter
Radio	Local coverage Low cost High frequency Flexible Low production costs Well-segmented audiences	Audio only Clutter Low attention getting Fleeting message
Magazines	Segmentation potential Quality reproduction High information content Longevity Multiple readers	Long lead time for ad placement Visual only Lack of flexibility
Newspapers	High coverage Low cost Short lead time for placing ads Ads can be placed in interest sections Timely (current ads) Reader controls exposure Can be used for coupons	Short life Clutter Low attention-getting capabilities Poor reproduction quality Selective reader exposure
Outdoor	Location specific High repetition Easily noticed	Short exposure time requires short ad Poor image Local restrictions
Direct mail	High selectivity Reader controls exposure High information content Opportunities for repeat exposures	High cost/contact Poor image (junk mail) Clutter

FIGURE 6-3 Advertising Media Characteristics

on average, has diminished. For example, Video Storyboards reported that the number of viewers who reported that they paid attention to TV ads dropped significantly in the last decade.

Nevertheless, properly designed and executed TV ads can affects sales and profits. For example, over the years, one of the most consistently successful TV advertisers has been Apple. Their "1984" ad for the introduction of its Macintosh personal computer—portraying a stark Orwellian future with a feature film look—only ran once on TV but is one of the best known ads ever. In the decade that followed, Apple advertising successfully created awareness and image for a series of products. Each year, the American Marketing Association awards "Effies" to those brands whose ad-

AMA's Effie Awards for Best Advertising

TIMEX INDIGLO

Emerson not withstanding, Timex knew that just because it had a great product innovation, the world would not beat a path to its door unless it had a good campaign. Fallon McElligott got the assignment. A major innovation in illuminating watch dials, the Indiglo is a paper-thin light in the dial of the watch. Previously, watch night lights were small bulbs that were attached at one end of the dial. They were both less attractive and less effective. Not one to hide its light under a basket, Timex and Fallon McElligott developed a series of playful ads that brought the innovation to the attention of consumers. In one television spot, a firefly falls in love with an Indiglo Timex. In another, Manhattan goes completely dark in a raging thunderstorm. Luckily for the city, the Statue of Liberty comes to life and turns on her Indiglo, which illuminates New York harbor. The ad campaign improved the watchmaker's bottom line: Timex's share of the watch market has improved to 33 percent, up from 25 percent, Watson said. Meanwhile, Indiglos now account for more than 40 percent of overall Timex sales.

MCDONALD'S

If you want to know about the psychology of tweens, just go to McDonald's and Leo Burnett. The pair was able to reverse a five-year decline in McDonald's share of the tween market by capitalizing on that segment's desire for freedom. The campaign began after McDonald's realized that tweens were no longer motivated by Happy Meals and other promotions aimed at kids younger than them. One spot focused on what it would be like if tweens ran the world, which for the 8- to 13-year-old age group consists largely of school. It illustrated the mix of tween concerns and desires. For instance, the water fountains would dispense McDonald's milk shakes, while Michael Jordan would be their gym teacher. They could have class underwater to learn about whales and take field trips to McDonald's. And the kid who picked on them in social studies would have permanent detention. "They are not in a hurry to grow up," said Laurie Stearn, a Burnett account supervisor. "They wanted the privileges of being an adult but not the responsibilities." The campaign struck a chord with tweens. McDonald's share increased for the first time in five years while the shares of competitors declined.

EXCEDRIN

Excedrin's "The Headache Medicine" campaign is a case study in market segmentation. Where once there stood the pain reliever market, Bristol-Myers Squibb and Bozell Worldwide created the subsegment of headache relievers and then positioned Excedrin as its sole occupant. After being plagued by market-share declines over several years, the campaign damned Excedrin's toughest competitor with strong praise. The campaign involved a series of television spots that had Tylenol users praising its pain-relieving powers. The crucial moment of the spots comes when the spokesperson says: "But for headaches, I use Excedrin." "We developed a campaign that breaks all the rules," said Jim Harrington, a partner at Bozell. The praise of Tylenol makes the campaign believable. Harrington added that there is clinical proof that Excedrin is a superior headache medicine. "The campaign has been on air for 23 months and we have had 23 straight months of sales increases after 8 or 9 years of sales declines," Harrington said. "It has helped generate all sorts of new trials."

KOOL-AID

Faced with double-digit declines in the Hispanic consumer franchise, Kraft General Food's Kool-Aid business needed a new product to revive sales in that segment. Working with Mendoza, Dillon & Asociados, it launched the Pina Pineapple flavor in what was the brand's first bilingual package. The launch was undertaken after market research that determined that the flavor would be able to appeal across the whole segment. "The research showed that this one flavor was universal to everyone [in the segment]," said Jackie Hernandez-Brown, account supervisor. Mendoza, Dillon put together an integrated campaign that included 15-second television spots, coupons, samples, and a sweepstakes. The television spots showed a lush pineapple that was followed by the Kool-Aid symbol and a family enjoying the new flavor. Hispanic sales showed increases for the first time in years, and Pina Pineapple sales were 175 percent of goal. The campaign also created a halo effect that boosted sales of other flavors that were purchased by consumers in addition to Pina Pineapple, Brown said.

THE BALTIMORE OPERA

For a generation raised on the Rolling Stones and the Grateful Dead, opera is not high on the list of entertainment alternatives. But an ad campaign developed by the Baltimore Opera and Gray Kirk/VanSant Advertising repositioned the opera company to make its performances more appealing to people older than 35 with household incomes greater than $50,000. "We wanted to change attitudes," said Jeff Millman, svp at Gray Kirk/VanSant. To carry out that message, Gray Kirk/VanSant put together a humorous 30-second television spot about a man attending a live performance of an Italian opera. After every few sentences, a man in a tuxedo would appear and whisper a translation into the opera-goer's ear. The translated lyrics included: "The fire is burning in my heart and my loins." "I yearn for the taste of your ruby red lips," and "I cannot hide my feelings for you any longer." The commercial concludes that English translations are available at all performances. After falling for a number of years, subscriptions are now at their highest level ever. Demand for the opera is so great that the company has been adding performances.

vertising campaigns have had a demonstrable impact on sales and profits. Branding Brief 6–2 contains several of the 1994 winners.

Guidelines   In designing and evaluating an ad campaign, it is important to distinguish the *message strategy* or positioning of an ad (i.e., what the ad attempts to convey about the brand) from its *creative strategy* (i.e., how the ad expresses the brand claims). Designing effective advertising campaigns is both an "art" and a "science": The "artistic" aspects relate more to the creative strategy of the ad and its executional information; the "scientific" aspects relate more to the message strategy of the ad and the brand claim information it contains. Thus, as Figure 6–4 describes, the two main concerns in devising an advertising strategy are:

FIGURE 6–4 Factors in Designing Effective Advertising Campaigns[a]

1. **Define Positioning to Establish Brand Equity**

   Competitive Frame of Reference
   - Nature of competition
   - Target market

   Point of Parity Attributes or Benefits
   - Product-related
   - Non-product-related

   Point of Difference Attributes or Benefits
   - Product-related
   - Non-product-related

2. **Identify Creative Strategy to Communicate Positioning Concept**

   Informational (Benefit Elaboration)
   - Problem-solution
   - Demonstration
   - Product comparison
   - Testimonial (unknown consumer or celebrity)

   Transformational (Imagery Portrayal)
   - Typical or aspirational usage situation
   - Typical or aspirational user of product
   - Brand personality

   Motivational ("Borrowed Interest" Techniques)
   - Humor
   - Warmth
   - Sex appeal
   - Music
   - Fear
   - Special effects

   ---
   [a]Based on an insightful framework put forth in John R. Rossiter and Larry Percy, *Advertising and Promotion Management*, New York: McGraw-Hill, 1987.

1. Defining the proper positioning to maximize brand equity
2. Identifying the best creative strategy to communicate or convey the desired positioning

Chapter 3 described a number of issues with respect to properly positioning a brand to maximize brand equity. In terms of arriving at the best creative strategy, creative strategies can be broadly classified as either "informational" (i.e., elaborating on a specific product-related attribute or benefit) or "transformational" (i.e., portraying a specific non-product-related benefit or image).[6] These two general categories of approaches each encompass several different specific creative approaches. Regardless of which general creative approach is taken, however, certain motivational or "borrowed interest" devices—such as the presence of cute babies, frisky puppies, popular music, well-liked celebrities, amusing situations, provocative sex appeals, or fear-inducing threats—are often employed to attract consumer attention and raise their involvement with an ad. Such techniques are thought to be necessary in the tough new media environment characterized by low involvement consumer processing and much competing ad and programming clutter. Unfortunately, these attention-getting tactics are often *too* effective and distract from brand or product claims. Thus, the challenge in arriving at the best creative strategy is figuring out how to "break through the clutter" to attract the attention of consumers, but still be able to deliver the intended message at the same time.

What makes an effective TV ad? Fundamentally, a TV ad should contribute to brand equity in some demonstrable way, such as by strengthing a key association or adding another one. To successfully communicate with consumers and build brand equity, some other commonly cited criteria suggest that a TV ad should:[7]

1. Focus on the appropriate target market
2. Properly and uniquely position the brand
3. Cut through the clutter and attract attention
4. Correctly account for consumer brand and product knowledge
5. Be simple and clear
6. Be memorable and strongly associated with the brand
7. Have sustaining power and durability over time
8. Impact sales

Although managerial judgment using criteria such as these can and should be employed in evaluating advertising, research also can play an important role. Advertising strategy research is often invaluable in clarifying communication objectives, target markets, and positioning alternatives. In terms of evaluating the effectiveness of message and creative strategies, "copy testing" is often conducted where a sample of consumers is exposed to candidate ads and their reactions gauged in some manner. There are many different ways to copy test an ad, depending on decisions in areas such as the following:[8]

- Type of advertisement used (e.g., mock-up or finished ad)
- Frequency of exposure (e.g., single or multiple)
- How the ad is shown (e.g., isolated; in ad clutter; or in a program or magazine)
- Where the exposure occurs (e.g., in a shopping center facility; at home on TV or through mail; or in a theater)

- How sample respondents are obtained (e.g., pre-recruited or not)
- Geographic scope (e.g., one city or many)

Moreover, besides these methodological or data collection issues, perhaps the most important decision is what type(s) of measures to use to judge the ad (e.g., based on recall, recognition, persuasion, and/or behavior).

Unfortunately, copy test results may vary considerably depending on what decisions are made in these different areas. Consequently, the results of an ad copy test must be interpreted as one possible data point that should be combined with managerial judgment and other information in evaluating the merits of an ad. Copy testing is perhaps most useful when managerial judgment reveals some fairly clear positive *and* negative aspects to an ad and is therefore somewhat inconclusive. In this case, copy testing research may shed some light as to how these various conflicting aspects "net out" and collectively affect consumer processing. Regardless, copy testing results should not be seen as a means of making a "go" or "no-go" decision and ideally should play a diagnostic role in helping to understand *how* an ad works.

Future Prospects   In the new computer era, the future of television and traditional mass-marketing advertising is uncertain. In a well-publicized speech, Edwin L. Artz, then chairman and CEO of Procter & Gamble, sent an ominous message to Madison Avenue at the 1994 American Association of Advertising Agencies convention. Artz sternly advised agencies to embrace new technologies or risk becoming irrelevant. "From where we stand today, we can't be sure that ad-supported TV programming will have a future in the world being created—a world of video-on-demand, pay-per-view, and subscription television. . . . We've got to get together as an industry to better define the video market of the future and to understand how consumer viewing habits will change as a result of these new technologies." Other advertisers warn of eventually bypassing ad agencies via interactive shopping channels, CD-ROM catalogs, multimedia kiosks, and on-line services.[9]

Nevertheless, at least for some, the power of TV ads remains. As one advertising executive put it, "Nothing competes with primetime television when it comes to communicating with a mass audience. Other mediums can't entertain and inform in the same captivating way."

Radio

Radio is a pervasive medium as 96 percent of all Americans 12 years and older listen to the radio daily and, on average, over twenty hours a week. Perhaps the main advantage to radio is flexibility—stations are very targeted, ads are relatively inexpensive to produce and place, and short closings allow for quick responses. Radio is a particularly effective medium in the morning and can effectively complement or reinforce TV ads. Obvious disadvantages of radio, however, are the lack of visual image and relatively passive nature of consumer processing that results.

Several brands have effectively built brand equity with radio ads. One notable example is Motel 6, the nation's largest budget motel chain, founded in 1962—when the "6" stood for $6 a night. After finding its business fortunes hitting bottom in 1986 with an occupancy rate of only 67 percent, Motel 6 made a number of marketing changes, including the launch of a radio campaign of humorous 60-second ads featuring folksy contractor-turned-writer Tom Bodett. Containing the clever tagline, "We'll leave the light on for you," and backed by a $5 million media buy, the radio campaign led to a rise in occupancy to 73 percent in 1987, with earnings returning to the black the following year.

What makes an effective radio ad?[10] Radio has been less studied than other media. Because of its low involvement nature and limited sensory options, radio advertising often must be fairly focused. For example, advertising pioneer David Ogilvy believes four factors are critical:[11]

1. Identify your brand early in the commercial.
2. Identify it often.
3. Promise the listener a benefit early in the commercial.
4. Repeat it often.

Nevertheless, radio ads can be extremely creative. The lack of visual images is seen by some as a plus because they feel that the clever use of music and other sounds and humor and other creative devices can tap into the listener's imagination in a way to create powerfully relevant and liked images.

Print

Print media offers a stark contrast to broadcast media. Most importantly, because of its self-paced nature, magazines and newspapers can provide much detailed product information. At the same time, the static nature of the visual images in print media makes it difficult to provide dynamic presentations or demonstrations. Another disadvantage of print advertising is that it can be a fairly passive medium.

In general, the two main print media—magazines and newspapers—have many of the same advantages and disadvantages. Newspapers, however, are more timely and pervasive. Daily newspapers are read by roughly three-fourths of the population and tend to be used a lot for local, especially retailer, advertising. On the other hand, although advertisers have some flexibility in designing and placing newspaper ads, poor reproduction quality and short shelf lives can diminish some of the possible impact of newspaper advertising as compared to magazine advertising.

Although print advertising is particularly well-suited to communicating product information, it can also effectively communicate user and usage imagery. For example, one famous print ad campaign is the "Portraits" series by American Express that featured brilliant shots by famed photographer Annie Leibovitz of celebrity cardholders such as Tom Seaver, Ray Charles, and couples such as Jessica Tandy and Hume Cronyn in unique, attention-getting poses. Launched in 1987, the strategy behind the "Membership has its privileges" campaign, created by ad agency Ogilvy & Mather, was to attempt image-building in print and dramatize the product benefits in TV—the reverse of the typical use of these media by most advertisers.[12] Other brands such as Calvin Klein and Guess have also created strong non-product associations through print advertising. Some brands attempt to communicate both product benefits and user or usage imagery in their print advertising—car makers such as Ford, Lexus, and Volvo or cosmetic makers such as Maybelline and Revlon.

Figure 6–5 displays the most successful print campaigns of 1994 according to the consumer research by Video Storyboards Inc. One brand appearing on the list is Absolut vodka, which has had one of the longest running and perhaps most successful print ad campaigns ever. In 1980, Absolut was a tiny brand, selling 12,000 cases a year.

Video Storyboard Tests surveys 20,000 consumers annually whose responses serve as the basis for their ranking of the "most outstanding" print ads. The winners (with agencies in parentheses):

1. Ford (J. Walter Thompson/Wells Rich and Green)
2. Guess (in-house)
3. Calvin Klein (in-house)
4. Revlon (Tarlow)
5. Reebok (Leo Burnett)
6. Marlboro (Leo Burnett)
7. Sears (Young and Rubicam, Ogilvy & Mather)
8. Absolut (TBWA)
9. Camel (Mezzina/Brown)
10. Lexus (Saatchi & Saatchi's Team One)

FIGURE 6–5 Top Print Ad Campaigns of 1994

Research conducted at that time had pointed out a number of liabilities for the brand: The name was seen as too gimmicky, the bottle shape was ugly, and bartenders found it hard to pour; shelf prominence was limited; and there was no credibility for a vodka brand made in Sweden. Michel Roux, President of Carillon (Absolut's importer) and TBWA (Absolut's New York ad agency) decided to use the oddities of the brand—its quirky name and bottle shape—to create brand personality and communicate quality and style in a series of creative print ads. Each ad in the campaign visually depicts the product in an unusual fashion and verbally reinforces the image with a simple two-word headline using the brand name and some other word in a clever play on words. For example, the first ad showed the bottle prominently displayed, crowned by an angel's halo, with the headline "Absolut Perfection" appearing at the bottom of the page (see Figure 6–6). Followup ads explored various themes (e.g., seasonal, geographical, celebrity artists) but always attempted to put forth a fashionable, sophisticated, and contemporary image. By 1991, Absolut had become the market leader of the imported vodka sector, with sales of 2.7 million cases and a 62 percent market share.

Guidelines   What makes an effective print ad? Although the evaluation criteria noted above for television advertising basically apply, print advertising has some special requirements and rules. For example, research on print ads in magazines reveals that it is not uncommon for two-thirds of a magazine audience to not even notice any one particular print ad, and only 10 percent or so of the audience to read much of the copy of any one ad. Many readers only glance at the most visible elements of a print ad, making it critical that an ad communicate clearly, directly, and consistently in the ad illustration and headline. Figure 6–7 contains some important print ad creative criteria.[13]

Direct Response
In contrast to advertising in traditional broadcast and print media, which typically communicates to consumers in a non-specific and non-directive manner, *direct*

FIGURE 6-6 Absolut Perfection Ad

In judging the effectiveness of a print ad, in addition to considering the communication strategy (e.g., target market, communication objectives, and message strategy), the following questions should be answered affirmatively concerning the executional elements:[a]

1. Is the message clear at a glance? Can you quickly tell what the advertisement is all about?
2. Is the benefit in the headline?
3. Does the illustration support the headline?
4. Does the first line of the copy support or explain the headline and illustration?
5. Is the ad easy to read and follow?
6. Is the product easily identified?
7. Is the brand or sponsor clearly identified?

---

[a]Philip Ward Burton and Scott C. Purvis, *Which Ad Pulled Best*, 5th ed., Lincolnwood, IL: NTC Business Books, 1987.

FIGURE 6–7 Print Ad Evaluation Criteria

response refers to the use of mail, telephone, and other nonpersonal contact tools to communicate with or solicit a response from specific customers and prospects. Direct response can take many forms and is not restricted to just solicitations by mail, telephone, or even within traditional broadcast and print media. For example, General Motor's Buick Division, Chase Manhattan Bank, and others have sent computer disks to targeted consumers to introduce some new products and services. Videocassettes have become an increasingly affordable means to market directly, costing only $2 a tape to make (although production costs can add another $50,000 or so).[14] Soloflex has been selling its home-gym products via video since 1983 and reports that sales are twice that of conventional brochures.[15]

One increasingly popular means of direct marketing is *infomercials*.[16] In a marketing sense, an infomercial attempts to combine the sell of commercials with the draw of educational information and entertainment. As such, infomercials can be thought of as a cross between a sales call and a television ad. Infomercials can vary in length but are often 30-minute video programs that are made at the cost of $250,000 to $500,000. A number of individuals have become famous with late-night channel switchers from pitching their wares (e.g., Tony Robbins, Victoria Principal, Susan Powter, Barbara DeAngeles, Kathy Smith, Dionne Warwick, Vanna White, and others). More recently, mainstream marketers such as Texaco, Volvo, Norelco, Club Med, and Fidelity Investments have begun airing infomercials. Even Procter & Gamble introduced an infomercial in the summer of 1994 for Fixodent, its top-selling denture adhesive.

Perhaps the most widely anticipated new direct marketing technique involves the electronic possibilities offered by computers and the "information super highway." Branding Brief 6–3 describes some of the marketing and branding developments on the Internet and World Wide Web.

Riding the Interactive Marketing Wave[a]

As access to the internet becomes easier with the growth of online services, the penetration of Netscape and other software, marketers are increasingly attempting to build a presence in cyberspace on the World Wide Web. The approaches vary widely as does the nature of the advertisers themselves. In general, consumer sites tend to offer entertainment, information, and various services, avoiding overt hard-sell advertising. Some of the appeals offered by the early pioneers of "virtual marketing" include:

1. *Ragu:* Ragu attempted to provide useful information updated regularly to bring browsers back. Their "Mama's Cucina" site offered Italian phrases and lessons, recipes, coupons, and sweepstakes.

2. *Miller Genuine Draft:* Miller's virtual Tap Room, one of the earliest consumer products sites, included a question-and-answer page called, "Ask the Brew Master," offbeat regional news stories, and items on sports Miller sponsored such as race-car driving.

3. *Reebok:* Reebok's site offered colorful graphics, athlete interviews, sports tips and human rights news.

4. *Zima:* Zima adopted a hip and entertaining tone and ran an ongoing soap opera featuring Zima-loving characters, as well as product news and games.

5. *MCI Business Markets:* Modeled like a computer game, MCI's Gramercy Press site included pages that lead to a myriad of other pages, all featuring the fictional characters who made up MCI's TV campaign at the time.

More recently, the 1996 CASIE awards for "outstanding, effective" online marketing went to web sites for the AT&T Olympic Games Connection, Caverjet (Upjohn Pharmacia), Cover Girl Cosmetics (Procter & Gamble), Kasparov vs. Deep Blue (IBM), L.L. Bean, MCI, Pepsi World, Sotheby's, U.S. Robotics, and Zima.com (Coors Brewing Co.). Six companies were honored for interactive advertising campaigns: Altoids, AT&T's Intermecial campaign, Compaq, Maxwell House Coffee, McDonald's, and Portland General Electric.

Many web marketers collect names and addresses for databases and conduct e-mail surveys and online focus groups. A decent web site that can sustain viewer interest can be built for less than $150,000 but can also cost more, too. Designing web sites requires creating eye-catching pages that can sustain browsers' interest, employing the latest technology, and effectively communicating the corporate message. One top designer notes that it is important that users feel as if they have just entered a new, cohesive world, requiring that different pages and content areas within a site have consistent design elements, colors, and placement. To spread the word about their web sites, advertisers adopt a number of approaches. For example, Zima prints its web address on bottles and buys electronic billboards at other popular web sites.

The main advantages to marketing on the web are the low cost and the level of detail and degree of customization it offers. All kinds of information can be stored in a web site—company or product information, news, updates or

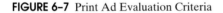

press releases, advertising or promotional material, and so on. By capitalizing on its interactive nature, marketers can construct web sites that allow for any consumer to choose that brand information that is relevant to his or her needs or desires. The interactive nature of web sites also may be more involving and engaging for consumers, allowing for solid relationship building. Interactive marketing offers other possible advantages. A small company may seem bigger and an old brand can seem more contemporary with a well-designed web site. The target market for a brand can be more geographically dispersed with a web site that offers ordering capabilities. A web site can be linked to other brands or companies to easily exploit partnership relationships.

There are also some drawbacks and cautionary notes that can be raised about interactive marketing. Research evidence about consumer behavior and best management practices for interactive marketing is still emerging. A brand's target market—especially if older—may not have adopted interactive technology. More generally, the internet still relies on a "pull" approach as consumers have to decide to visit a site. Given the large number of choices and clutter on the internet, interactive marketing may not be intrusive enough. If consumers are dissatisfied when they visit a web site, it may be difficult to convince them to return.

In creating these online information sources for consumers for brand or company web sites, it is important to deliver timely and reliable information. In August 1996, the *Wall Street Journal* sent a flurry of e-mails to twenty-four top consumer marketing companies (e.g., asking 3M if Post-It Notes get less sticky from just sitting around; asking Budweiser how it came up with 110 days as the freshness standard for its new labeling; asking Reebok if it is dangerous to wear running shoes to play basketball; and so on). Only three companies adequately answered within a day—others took longer or failed to reply back altogether.

Marketing on the web will clearly change dramatically as its technology changes. For example, when software ensuring secure transactions becomes standard and well-accepted, an online marketplace can emerge where brands can be sold to consumers directly and inexpensively. Traditional print and broadcast ads, however, may not translate well to a high-tech media form, and information may need to be conveyed differently. The challenge will be to entertain people but still communicate desired information.

---

[a]Robin Frost, "Web Design: More Than Just a Pretty Picture," *Wall Street Journal* (October 31, 1996), pp. B6, B8.

Guidelines   Direct marketing has consistently outgrown every media spending category since 1986. This steady growth is a function of technological advances (e.g., the ease of setting up toll-free 800 numbers), changes in consumer behavior (e.g., increased need for convenience), and the needs of marketers (e.g., the desire to avoid wasteful communications to non-target customers or customer groups). The advantages of direct response is that it facilitates the establishment of relationships with consumers by marketers. In fact, direct marketing is often seen as a key component of "relationship marketing"—an important trend in marketing. With relationship marketing, marketers attempt to transcend the simple purchase exchange process with consumers to make more meaningful and richer contacts.

Direct communications through newsletters, catalogs, and electronic home pages allow marketers to explain to consumers new developments with their brands on an ongoing basis, as well as allow consumers to provide feedback to marketers as to their likes and dislikes and specific needs and wants. By learning more about customers, marketers can fine-tune marketing programs to offer the right products to the right customers at the right time.

As the name suggests, the goal of direct response is to elicit some type of behavior from consumers. It is easier to measure the effects of direct marketing efforts—people either respond or not. The disadvantages to direct response, however, are the intrusiveness and clutter involved. For example, 62 billion pieces of third-class mail were sent to American homes in 1993!

To implement an effective direct-marketing program, three critical ingredients are developing an up-to-date and informative list of current and potential future customers, putting forth the right offer in the right manner, and tracking the effectiveness of the marketing program. To better implement direct marketing programs, many marketers are embracing database marketing. Regardless of the particular means of direct marketing, marketers can potentially benefit from database marketing to create targeted communications and marketing programs tailored to the needs and wants of specific consumers. Database marketers collect names and information from consumers on their attitudes and behavior into a comprehensive database. Besides ordering products, names and information can be collected from consumers in a variety of ways, such as by sending in a coupon, filling out a warranty card, or entering a sweepstakes.

Database marketing is generally thought to be more effective at helping firms to retain existing customers than to attract new ones. As a guideline, many marketers believe that database marketing makes more sense the higher the price of the product and the more often it is bought. Database marketing pioneers include a number of financial-services firms and airlines. Even packaged goods companies, however, are exploring the possible benefits of database marketing. For example, Procter & Gamble created a database to market its Pampers disposable diaper, allowing P&G to send out "individualized" birthday cards for babies and reminder letters to parents to move their child up to the next size.[17] Database management tools will become a priority to marketers as they attempt to track the lifetime value of customers.

Place

The last category of advertising is also often called "non-traditional," "alternative," or "support" advertising media because it has arisen in recent years as a means to complement more traditional advertising media. *Place advertising*, also called out-of-home advertising, is a broadly defined category that captures advertising outside traditional media. Increasingly, ads and commercials are showing up in unusual spots. The rationale often given is that because traditional advertising media—especially television advertising—is seen as becoming less effective, marketers are better off reaching people in other environments, such as where they work, play, and, of course, shop. Some of the options available include the following.

Billboards   In 1925, Burma-Shave placed a set of four billboards in sequence along roads nationwide with the jingle:

> *Shave the modern way.*
> *Fine for the skin.*
> *Druggists have it.*
> *Burma-Shave.*

The success of Burma-Shave billboards convinced marketers that consumers would notice and remember simple messages conveyed in "unexpected" places. Billboards have been transformed over the years and now employ colorful graphics and unusual, even three-dimensional, images to attract attention. Billboards do not even necessarily have to stay in one place. Marketers can buy ad space on billboard-laden trucks that are driven continuously all day in marketer-selected areas. For example, Oscar-Mayer sends six "Wienermobiles" traveling across the United States each year to increase brand exposure and goodwill.

Moreover, billboard-type ads are now showing up everywhere. Transit ads on buses, subways, and commuter trains—around for years—have now become a valuable means to reach working women. Goodyear, whose brand-emblazoned blimp enjoyed clear skies for over fifty years, has been subsequently joined by Fuji, Metropolitan Life, Blockbuster Video, and others in sponsoring blimps. Advertisers now can buy space in stadiums and arenas and on garbage cans, bicycle racks, parking meters, airport luggage carousals, the bottom of golf cups, and on gasoline pumps. Advertisers can even buy space in toilet stalls and above urinals where, according to research studies, office workers visit an average of three to four times a day for roughly four minutes per visit.[18]

Videocassettes, Movies, Airlines, Lounges   Increasingly, advertisers are placing traditional TV and print ads in unconventional places.[19] Companies like Whittle Communication and Turner Broadcasting have tried placing TV and commercial programming into waiting rooms at doctors' offices, classrooms, airport lounges, and other public places. Airlines now offer media-sponsored audio and video programming that accept advertising (e.g., USA Today Sky Radio and National Geographic Explorer) and include catalogs in seat pockets for leading mail order companies (e.g., High Street Emporium). Movie theater chains such as the 271-theater Cineplex Odeon now run 30-, 60-, or 90-second ads. After a Diet Pepsi ad appeared on the videocassette of the blockbuster hit "Top Gun" in 1986, advertisers began to place ads on videocassettes. In 1985, Bloomingdale's included five pages of print ads for brands such as Calvin Klein sportswear and Lincoln-Mercury automobiles in its catalog. Other catalog providers have followed suit, entertaining ads from a variety of upscale marketers.

Although literally the same ads that also appear on TV or in magazines often appear in these unconventional places, many advertisers believe it is important to create specially designed ads for these out-of-home exposures. For example, Schweppes created a special ad featuring the popular comedic actor John Cleese that ran at the beginning of the videocassette for "A Fish Called Wanda," a movie in which he also starred.

Product Placement   Many major marketers pay fees of $50,000 to $100,000 and even higher so that their products can make cameo appearances in movies and on television—the exact amount depending on the amount and nature of the brand exposure. This practice got a boost in 1982 when, after Mars declined an offer for its M&M's brand, the sales of Reese's Pieces increased 65 percent after prominently appearing in the blockbuster movie "E.T.: The Extra Terrestrial."[20]

Product placements can be combined with special promotions to publicize the brand's entertainment tie-ins. Some firms benefit from product placement at no cost by supplying their product to movie companies (e.g., Nike does not pay to be in movies but often supplies shoes, jackets, bags, and other products) or just because of the creative demands of the storyline (e.g., Red Stripe beer received a prominent plug in the movie "The Firm" for a token $5000 because the director felt that the beer was consistent with the Caribbean island mood of a particular scene).[21] To test the effects of product placement, marketing research companies such as CinemaScore conducts viewer exit surveys to determine which brands actually were noticed during the movie showing.

Point-of-Purchase   A myriad of possibilities have emerged in recent years as ways to communicate with consumers at the point of purchase (P-O-P). In-store advertising includes ads on shopping carts, cart straps, aisles, or shelves, as well as promotion options such as in-store demonstrations, live sampling, and instant coupon machines. P-O-P radio provides FM-style programming and commercial messages to 6500 food stores and 7900 drugstores nationwide. Programming includes a store-selected music format, consumer tips, and commercials.

The appeal of point-of-purchase advertising lies in the fact that numerous studies have shown that consumers in many product categories make the bulk of their final brand decisions in the store. For example, according to a study by Actmedia—who places ads in 7,000 supermarkets nationwide—70 percent of all buying decisions are made in the store. In-store media is used to increase the number and nature of spontaneous and planned buying decisions.

In summary, nontraditional media present some interesting options for marketers to reach consumers in new ways. Ads now can appear virtually anywhere where it might be the case that consumers have a few spare minutes or even seconds and thus enough time to notice them. The main advantage of nontraditional media is that a very precise and—because of the nature of the setting involved—captive audience often can be reached in a cost-effective manner. For example, one fast-growing, nontraditional media buy is ski resort-based advertising. By placing ads in and around ski lifts and lodges, advertisers can reach an active, well-off and young audience not easily reached by traditional media.[22] Because out-of-home ads must be quickly processed, however, the message must be simple and direct. In fact, outdoor advertising is often called the "15-second sell." Thus, strategically, out-of-home advertising is often more effective at enhancing awareness or reinforcing existing brand associations rather than creating new ones.

The challenge with nontraditional media is demonstrating its reach and effectiveness through credible, independent research. The early 1990s recession found many advertisers returning to more traditional, measurably efficient forms of advertising. Afraid to take chances on unproven options, many advertisers decided a better approach was more creative uses of traditional media.[23] Another worry with nontraditional media is consumer backlash for over-commercialization. Perhaps because of the sheer pervasiveness of advertising, however, consumers seem to be less bothered by nontraditional media now than in the past. For example, unlike Europeans, Americans resisted the notion of on-screen advertising in movie theaters and videos.[24] Yet, almost half of all theaters now run ads, albeit often bigger and more cinematic than their small-screen companions.

Consumers must be favorably impacted in some way to justify the marketing expenditures for nontraditional media, and some firms offering ad placement in supermarket checkout lines, fast food restaurants, physicians' waiting rooms, health clubs, and truck stops have suspended business at least in part because of a lack of consumer interest. The bottom line, however, is that there will always be room for creative means of placing the brand in front of consumers. The possibilities are endless. For example, who could have guessed that RJR Nabisco would distribute sandals with the word "Camel" carved onto the bottom of their soles so that beachgoers could leave "Camel tracks" in the sand to help promote its cigarette![25]

PROMOTIONS

Sales promotions can be defined as short-term incentives to encourage trial or usage of a product or service.[26] Sales promotions can be targeted at either the trade or at end-consumers and, like advertising, sales promotions come in all forms (see Figure 6–1). Where advertising provides consumers a *reason* to buy, sales promotions offer consumers an *incentive* to buy. Thus, sales promotions are designed to:

- Change the behavior of the trade so that they carry the brand and actively support it
- Change the behavior of consumers so that they buy a brand for the first time, buy more of the brand, or buy the brand earlier and/or more often

Critics maintain that the use of sales promotions grew in the 1980s for a number of reasons, as follows (see Figure 6–8). Brand management systems with quarterly evaluations were thought to encourage short-term solutions, and an increased need for accountability seemed to favor communication tools like promotions whose behavioral effects are more quickly and easily observed than the often "softer" perceptual effects of advertising. Economic forces worked against advertising effectiveness as ad rates rose steadily despite what was perceived as an increasingly cluttered media environment and fragmented audience. Consumers were thought to be making more in-store decisions and be less brand loyal and immune to advertising than in the past.

1. Short-term solutions
2. Need for accountability
3. Economic factors
4. Consumer behavior
5. Product life cycle
6. Pricing trends
7. Power of retailer

FIGURE 6–8 Reasons for the Growth of Sales Promotions

Many mature brands were seen as less easily differentiated. On top of it all, retailers were seen as becoming more powerful.

For all these reasons, consumer and trade promotions were viewed by some marketers as a more effective means than advertising to influence the sales of a brand. Trade promotions were especially favored because of the necessity of securing distribution so that consumers could even have the opportunity to buy the brand if they so chose. Thus, Donnelly Marketing's Annual Survey of Promotional Practices in 1993 indicated that trade promotion accounted for 47 percent, consumer promotion 28 percent, and media ad budgets 25 percent of total marketing budgets.[27]

There clearly are advantages to sales promotions. Consumer sales promotions permit manufacturers to price discriminate by effectively charging different prices to groups of consumers who vary in their price sensitivity. Besides conveying a sense of urgency to consumers, carefully designed promotions can build brand equity through information conveyed or actual product experience that helps to create strong, favorable, and unique associations. Sales promotions can encourage the trade to maintain full stocks and actively support the manufacturer's merchandising efforts.

On the other hand, from a consumer behavior perspective, there are a number of disadvantages of sales promotions, such as decreased brand loyalty and increased brand switching, as well as decreased quality perceptions and increased price sensitivity. One survey of top U.S. marketing executives indicated that many believed that the heavy use of coupons and discounting negatively affected a brand's long-term image and positioning. Another disadvantage of sales promotions is that in some cases it may merely subsidize buyers who would have bought the brand anyway. Moreover, new consumers attracted to the brand may attribute their purchase to the promotion and not to the merits of the brand per se and, as a result, may not repeat buy when the promotional offer is withdrawn. Finally, the trade may not actually provide the agreed upon merchandising and engage in nonproductive activities such as forward buying and diversion (see chapter 5). Because of these perceived drawbacks with sales promotions, recent years have seen some shift back to traditional forms of advertising.

There are a number of specific possible objectives to promotions (see Figure 6–9). In designing a sales promotion, Harvard's John Quelch argues that six issues must be addressed:

1. What type of promotion should be used?
2. To what pack sizes or models should the promotion apply?
3. In which geographical markets should the promotion be offered?
4. When should the promotion be offered and for how long?
5. What explicit or implicit discount should the promotion include?
6. What terms of sale should be attached to the promotion?

Figure 6–10 lists some of the additional considerations he identifies for each of these six issues. He argues that the actual choices made in each of these areas will depend on a number of factors, such as the level of consumer involvement, inventory risk, and franchise strength of the brand. Next, we consider some specific issues related to consumer and trade promotions.

I. CONSUMER TARGET
  - To persuade *new category users* to try the category and Brand X in particular and thereby increase primary as well as selective demand.
  - To persuade *existing category users* to include Brand X in their evoked sets and to try and/or switch to Brand X.
  - To persuade *existing Brand X* users to
    - continue to purchase Brand X and not to switch.
    - increase their purchase frequency of Brand X.
    - purchase now rather than later by overcoming reasons for postponement.
    - adopt new uses for Brand X and so use more product, resulting in higher purchase quantities and purchases of larger sizes.
    - purchase multiple units of Brand X to take them out of the marketplace for an extended time period.

II. TRADE TARGET
  A. *Distribution*
    - To maintain or increase existing distribution, shelf facings, and shelf locations for Brand X.
    - To persuade existing outlets to stock additional open stock models and/or temporary promotional models of Brand X.
    - To persuade the trade to stock a complete line of a producer's products.
  B. *Support*
    - To persuade existing outlets to provide temporary price cuts, special displays, and advertising features for Brand X.
    - To provide retailers with an opportunity to increase in-store excitement and, thereby, to persuade them to promote Brand X aggressively in their stores.
    - To achieve secondary placements of Brand X near related items in stores where it already has distribution.
  C. *Inventories*
    - To increase the average trade account order size for Brand X.
    - To increase Brand X's share of trade inventories to preempt competition and motivate special merchandising support to sell them through.
    - To flush trade inventories of Brand X if they are excessive or if Brand X is being discontinued in favor of another item requiring shelf space.
  D. *Good Will*
    - To insulate the trade from consumer-price negotiation at the point-of-purchase (when Brand X is a durable good).
    - To insulate the trade from a temporary sales reduction that might be caused by an increase in the price of Brand X.

---

[a]Reprinted from John A. Quelch, "Note on Sales Promotion Design," Harvard Business School N-589–021.

FIGURE 6-9 Possible Promotion Objectives for Brand X[a]

1. Type
   - Immediate vs. delayed value
   - Price cut vs. added value
2. Product Scope
   - Multiple or selective
   - More or less popular
   - In-line or out-of-line
3. Market Scope
   - National or regional
4. Timing
   - When to promote (in- or off-season)
   - When to announce (early or later)
   - Duration (long or short)
   - Frequency (high or low)
5. Discount Rate
   - Deep or shallow
6. Terms
   - Tight or loose

[a]Adapted from John A. Quelch, "Note on Sales Promotion Design," Harvard Business School N-589–021.

FIGURE 6-10 Issues in Designing Sales Promotions[a]

Consumer Promotions

Consumer promotions are designed to change the choices, quantity, and/or timing of consumers' product purchases. Although consumer sales promotions come in all forms, a distinction has also been made between customer franchise building promotions (e.g., samples, demonstrations, and educational material) and non-customer franchise building promotions (e.g., price-off packs, premiums, sweepstakes, and refund offers).[28] Customer franchise building promotions are promotions that are seen as enhancing the attitudes and loyalty of consumers towards a brand—in other words, those promotions that impact brand equity.

Thus, sales promotions increasingly are being judged by their ability to contribute to brand equity as well as generate sales. Branding Brief 6–4 describes several winners of the Promotion Marketing Association's Reggie Awards for the best promotions of 1994. As reflected by these examples, creativity is as critical to promotions as to advertising or any other form of marketing communications. Gillette's promotion where one fan was picked to shoot a three-pointer for $1 million at the NCAA basketball championship resulted in 2 million fans—who had to buy a Gillette product to enter—signing up.[29] Gillette has devised similar promotions in other sports such as baseball and golf.

Promotion strategy must reflect the attitudes and behavior of consumers. The last decade or so has seen a steady decrease in the percentage of coupons redeemed by consumers: The redemption rate was 3.5 percent in 1983, but dropped to only 2.3

──────────── BRANDING BRIEF 6-4 ────────────

PMA's Reggie Awards for Best Promotions

BFGOODRICH TIRES

BFGoodrich Tires faced a problem many companies are experiencing today—how to focus attention on value in a market where rampant price slashing is eroding brand equity. And, they came up with a promotional concept that ingeniously tied together two distant market segments.

The award-winning promotion capitalized on the lifestyle trend of enjoying the great outdoors with the philosophy that if consumers were communing with nature on foot or in their vehicle, they should have the best all-terrain treads on their feet *and* off-road vehicle. In a departure from typical price promotion, BFGoodrich Tires offered consumers a high-perceived-value product—Timberland Eurohiker boots for free with the purchase of a set of any BF-Goodrich Light Truck Tires.

Program objectives for consumers included building the brand and reinforcing the "fun, innovative, and sporty" position. The promotion also aimed to generate consumer purchases via an added-value promotion, rather than through a price promotion, thereby sustaining market share. For trade, the objectives were to encourage greater key account participation and merchandising support and offer promotion options on a local, account-specific basis for maximum effectiveness.

An integrated marketing campaign supported the promotion. A national print ad campaign in outdoor and car enthusiast magazines reached more than 1.1 million readers, and local newspaper and radio ads also supported the promotion. Five-foot-tall in-store displays showed huge logs with Timberland boots perched atop them, and brochures with off-road hiking and driving safety tips were offered. Three local promotion options were offered to the retailer to run in tandem with the national program: the "Back Country Adventure," a local sweepstakes; "Capture the Great Outdoors," a photo contest of the best outdoor shot incorporating Timberland and BFGoodrich products; and "Get Serious Scavenger Hunt," an off-road scavenger hunt/road rally for fun and prizes.

BFGoodrich Tires built the brand by motivating consumers to buy its tires for value and quality not price. The brand's strategic partnership with Timberland reinforced the brand image of quality, value, performance, durability, and authenticity. Sales reflected this: BFGoodrich sold more than 70,000 tires during the two-month period, as reflected by the 17,500 orders for Timberland free boots. By contributing to "Tread Lightly!", a not-for-profit organization dedicated to nature preservation, the company established goodwill and demonstrated a commitment to responsible off-road driving. The unique nature of the promotion, compounded by value-added incentives for the trade, increased merchandising by 80 percent. Most important, the promotion was fun, inspiring non-promoting accounts to become active with BFGoodrich Tires.

PEPPERIDGE FARM

Within an intensely competitive snack crackers market, the small size and unique shape of Pepperidge Farm's Goldfish Tiny Crackers have made the brand a favorite, especially among families with young children. In recent years, however, Goldfish brand loyalty has been eroded by competitor price slashing, private label entries, and the popularity of reduced-fat products. Faced with these challenges, Pepperidge Farm teamed up with McCracken Brooks Communications to develop a major consumer and trade event in the critical summer snack season.

McCracken Brooks Communications helped Pepperidge Farm Goldfish Tiny Crackers "reel in" profits during the summer of 1994 by elevating the product's brand equity and infusing the Goldfish cracker shape with personality. The "Goldfish Character" was the focus of all marketing communications and the basis for an original line of Goldfish Gear merchandise.

Key components of the promotion included integrating the Goldfish character into every element of the sell-in. Sales brochures sent to retailers reinforced the message of increased sales through multiple product purchases and depicted an ideal display configuration. Beach umbrellas featuring the Goldfish character were used to anchor in-store displays, and a line of exclusive custom-made Goldfish Gear merchandise was made available to consumers through proofs-of-purchase. Merchandise included Goldfish Gear t-shirts, baseball caps, beach/golf umbrellas, children's backpacks, and portable snack keepers.

The Pepperidge Farm Goldfish Tiny Crackers Goldfish Gear Promotion was the most successful promotion in the brand's history, not only increasing short-term volume 600 percent over earlier promotions, but delivering a sustained volume lift of 13 percent over a prolonged period into the fall. In addition, the success of the promotion demonstrated the brand's potential and the value of the "Goldfish" brand equity to distributors, the trade, and within Pepperidge Farm itself.

SATURN CORPORATION

Saturn Corporation, a division of General Motors, competes in a market segment where consumers are well-educated, savvy, and predisposed to buying import cars. To win market share from such popular cars as the Honda Civic and Toyota Corolla, Saturn created "the Saturn Difference," a comprehensive, customer-focused culture aimed at satisfying consumers committed to buying imports.

The Saturn Homecoming was a unique promotional event designed to build customer loyalty and enthusiasm by reinforcing the company's relationship with its owners, and to build the Saturn brand by further strengthening "The Saturn Difference" positioning. Owners came from as far away as Alaska and Taipei to visit the birthplace of their vehicle. A couple attending the event even got married by a United Auto Workers chaplain with the Saturn President giving the bride away. The Saturn Corporation entertained more than 40,000 people for the weekend; close to 100,000 owners attended Saturn retail-sponsored events nationwide.

The June 24–25 event held at the company plant in Spring Hill, Tennessee, was hosted by Olympic gold medalist Dan Jansen and featured performances by country music star Wynonna and rhythm & blues stars BeBe and CeCe Winans. Proceeds from the event benefited the Make-A-Wish Foundation—enabling Saturn owners and the corporation to continue building the brand while helping others.

The promotion consisted of three phases. The research phase started in 1992 when a survey revealed that an astonishing 21,000 owners (not including guests) would attend. In phase two, Saturn invited more than 600,000 owners to visit Spring Hill in June. Phase three involved launching a national advertising campaign, transforming a 70-acre unused soy field to a summer fair location and recruitment of the Saturn "Home Team"—a team of employees wearing baseball shirts with the number "2," because the customer is number "1." The homecoming event included a plant tour, Camp Saturn for children, who were entertained by some very special Disney characters, and an antique and custom vehicle show.

Although most of the auto industry was experiencing sales increases, Saturn remained ahead of the pace with a 25 percent increase in sales in 1994 compared to January–November 1993. The promotion built the brand by involving Saturn owners in a piece of Saturn History.

---

percent in 1993.[30] Although there are a number of possible explanations, certainly one contributing factor is the large amount of coupon clutter. Marketers distributed 300 billion coupons valued at $175 billion, about 85 percent of which were in Sunday newspapers. As a result, one area of promotional growth is in-store coupons, which marketers have increasingly turned to as redemption rates of traditional out-of-store coupons slip.

Trade Promotions

Trade promotions are typically designed to either secure shelf space and distribution for a new brand or to achieve more prominence on the shelf and in the store. Shelf and aisle positions in the store are important because they affect the ability of the brand to catch the eye of the consumer—placing a brand on a shelf at eye level may double sales as compared to placing it on the bottom shelf.[31]

Because of the large amount of money spent on trade promotions, there is increasing pressure to make trade promotion programs more effective, as suggested by the following commentary:

> Increasingly the answer that glues the two into a workable partnership is account-specific promotions, tailored to each retailer, with budgets carved up to suit each market's demands. Manufacturers are decentralizing promotions, giving more responsibility for trade budgets to field salesmen. Big companies are setting up internal departments to implement and track these myriad local promotions; mid-size and smaller companies who can't afford the infrastructure are turning to outside services.[32]

Additionally, as noted in chapter 5, some firms are attempting to substitute consumer-oriented promotions and advertising that can build the brand in a way to satisfy retailers and manufacturers. For example, since 1992, Procter & Gamble has run brand-specific TV and direct mail advertising customized for Wal-Mart, Kmart, Target, and other retailers.

EVENT MARKETING AND SPONSORSHIP

Event marketing refers to public sponsorship of events or activities related to sports, art, entertainment, or social causes. Although the origin of event marketing can be traced back to philanthropic activities from over a century ago, many observers identify mega-events in the mid-1980s such as the 1984 Summer Olympics, Statue of Liberty Centennial, and Live Aid concert as arousing marketers' interest in sponsorship in the United States.[33] According to the International Events Group, event sponsorship has grown rapidly in recent years, from $2.5 billion in 1990 to $3.7 billion in 1993. Many companies now have event-marketing departments with separate budgets. As Figure 6–11 shows, the vast majority of event expenditures go towards sports. Once employed mostly by only cigarette, beer, and auto companies, sports marketing is now being embraced by virtually every type of company, including consumer packaged goods and high-technology companies. Moreover, virtually every sport—from sled-dog racing to croquet and from tractor pulls to professional beach volleyball—now receives corporate backing of some kind.[34]

Perhaps the most popular sport sponsorship in the United States is auto racing. In 1994, the National Association for Stock Car Racing (NASCAR) attracted 3.4 million fans and over 200 million television viewers to its Winston Cup Series.[35] R.J. Reynolds paid almost $5 million for the rights to link the 29 races to its Winston brand, but over 100 other corporations are also involved in NASCAR racing. Sponsoring companies include Canon, Eastman Kodak, Gillette, McDonald's, and others; and sponsoring brands include Tide, Country Time, Purex, Kellogg's Corn Flakes, and others. Perhaps the main appeal to NASCAR sponsors is the large amount of exposure time for their brands, because the cars, visible for much of the event, are typically emblazoned with the brand logo. Moreover, NASCAR fans are an attractive audience to corporate sponsors as they tend to support NASCAR sponsors, more so than is the case for fans of other sports.

	1993 Expenditures	Percentage
Sports	$2.4 bil	66%
Pop Music/ Entertainment Tours	$361 mil	10%
Festivals, Fairs, Annual Events	$333 mil	9%
Causes	$314 mil	8%
Arts	$245 mil	7%

FIGURE 6-11 Sponsorship Expenditures

Rationale

Event sponsorship provides a different kind of communication option to marketers. By becoming part of a special and more personally relevant moment in consumer lives, involvement with events can broaden and deepen the relationship of the sponsor with their target markets. Marketers report a number of reasons why they sponsor events:

1. *Identify with a particular target market or lifestyle.* Marketers can link their brands to events popular with either a select or broad group of consumers. Customers can be targeted geographically, demographically, psychographically, or behaviorally according to events. In particular, events can be chosen based on attendees' attitudes and usage toward certain products or brands. For example, one survey found that golf fans are 50 percent more likely to own IRAs and 100 percent more likely to own stock than the average affluent male. Volvo sponsored tennis tournaments because of a belief that tennis players were prime customers for its product. Similarly, Subaru believed there was a similar match between skiing events and potential buyers of its 4-wheel drive vehicles.

2. *Increase awareness of company or product name.* Sponsorship often offers sustained exposure to a brand, a necessary condition to build brand recognition. By skillfully choosing sponsorship events or activities, identification with a product and thus brand recall can also be enhanced. For example, Dutch Boy sponsors an "In the Paint" graphic in televised NBA coverage to update key game statistics (as hoop fans know, the area within the foul lines on a basketball court is referred to as "the paint"), and AT&T sponsors a long-distance shootout during NBA All Star Weekend as a contest to identify the best professional three-point shooter.

3. *Create or reinforce consumer perceptions of key associations.* Events themselves have associations that help to create or reinforce brand associations. For example, Anheuser-Busch chose to have Bud Light become a sponsor of the Ironman and other triathlons because it wanted a "healthy" image for the beer and did not want it to be seen as a beer for "wimps" (see chapter 7). In some cases, the product itself may be used at an event, providing demonstration of its abilities. For example, Seiko has been the official timer of the Olympics for years. As part of Motorola's 1996 Olympic sponsorship in Atlanta, they donated 10,000 two-way radios, 6,000 pagers, 1,500 computer modems, and 1,200 cellular phones.

4. *Enhance corporate image dimensions.* Sponsorship is seen as much more of a "soft sell" and a means to improve perceptions that the company is likable, prestigious, and so on. In doing so, it is often hoped that consumers will credit the company and favor it in later product choices.

5. *Express commitment to the community or on social issues.* Often called cause-related marketing, these sponsorships often involve corporate tie-ins with nonprofit organizations and charities (see chapter 11). An early pioneer in this area, American Express supported more than 70 causes in 18 countries with $8.6 million in donations from 1981 to 1986. As another example, Colgate-Palmolive has sponsored the Starlight Foundation—which grants wishes to young people who are critically ill—for years.

6. *Entertain key clients or reward key employees.* Many events have lavish hospitality tents and other special services or activities that are only available for sponsors and their guests. Involving clients with the event in these and other ways can engender goodwill and establish valuable business contacts. From an employee perspective, events can build participation and morale or be used as an incentive. For example, when John Hancock, as

part of its Winter Olympic sponsorship in 1994, offered trips to Lillehammer, Norway as a reward to agents who generated $100,000 in commissions, twice the number of agents qualified than in years past.

7. *Permit merchandising or promotional opportunities.* Many marketers tie in contests or sweepstakes, in-store merchandising, direct response, or other marketing activities with their event. When Sprint sponsored the World Cup in 1994, its related activities included long-distance calling cards picturing soccer stars, a geography program for Latin America schools tied to game results, and discounts on long-distance calls for soccer-related businesses and local soccer groups.[36]

Despite these potential advantages, there are a number of potential disadvantages to sponsorship. The success of an event can be unpredictable and out of the control of the sponsor. For example, the hopes of Kodak as sponsor of the Great American Balloonfest were blown away when bad weather hampered the planned set of events. There can be much clutter in sponsorship. Recognizing this problem, the Olympic Organizing Committee in 1988 began to offer worldwide exclusivity contracts to display the Olympics rings logo in various product categories. Finally, although many consumers will credit sponsors for providing necessary financial assistance to make an event possible, some consumers may still resent the commercialization of events through sponsorship.

Guidelines

Developing successful event sponsorship involves choosing the appropriate events, designing the optimal sponsorship program, and measuring the effects of sponsorship on brand equity.[37]

Choosing Sponsorship Opportunities   Because of the huge money involved and number of event opportunities that exist, many marketers are becoming much more strategic about the events with which they will get involved and the manner by which they will do so. As it is, the sophistication in marketing events in the United States lags behind many countries in Europe and elsewhere where restricted media options have spawned greater sponsorship activity over the years.

There are a number of potential guidelines in choosing events (see chapter 7). Fundamentally, the marketing objectives and communication strategy that have been defined for the brand must be met by the event. Thus, the audience delivered by the event must match the target market of the brand. Moreover, the event must have sufficient awareness, possess the desired image, and be capable of creating the desired effects with that target market. Of particular concern is whether consumers make favorable attributions to the sponsor for its event involvement. An "ideal event" might be one

1. Whose audience closely matches the ideal target market
2. That generates much favorable attention
3. That is unique but not encumbered with many sponsors
4. That lends itself to ancillary marketing activities
5. That reflects or even enhances the brand or corporate image of the sponsor

Philips Electronics, the $30 billion Dutch industrial giant, has been an active sponsor of sports, including a $20 million sponsorship of the 1994 World Cup soccer tournament. Philips offers the following ten commandments of sponsorship:[38]

1. There shall be a natural relationship to products.
2. The event shall fit the marketing game plan.
3. There shall be a mass audience.
4. There shall be direct exposure.
5. The project shall not be risky.
6. Results shall not depend on an athlete or team.
7. There shall be a major role for the company.
8. There shall be no legal, environmental, or other hazards.
9. The event shall be well-organized.
10. There shall be continuity with past sponsorships.

Of course, rather than linking itself to an event, some sponsors create their own. The cable sports network ESPN created the Extreme Games—later called the X Games—to capture youth-oriented activities (e.g., road-luge racing, in-line skating, skateboarding, bungee jumping, and sky surfing) that appealed to a market segment not as easily attracted to traditional sports.

Designing Sponsorship Programs   Many marketers believe that it is the marketing program accompanying a sponsorship that ultimately determines its success. A sponsor can strategically identify itself at an event in a number of ways, including banners, signs, and programs. For more significant and broader impact, however, sponsors typically supplement such activities with samples, prizes, advertising, retail promotions, and publicity. Marketers often note that from at least two to three times the amount of the sponsorship expenditure should be spent on related marketing activities. For example, Visa leveraged its exclusive Olympic sponsorship in 1992 with an aggressive ad campaign reinforcing its worldwide acceptance ("We're everywhere you want to be").

David D'Allesandro, long-time sports marketing director at John Hancock, believes the key to successful sponsorship is leveraging the event so that it goes beyond simple calculations like cost-per-thousand TV advertising exposures. John Hancock uses sponsorships to entertain big clients, attract new customers, inspire current salespeople, recruit new salespeople, and raise employee morale. For Hancock, D'Allesandro believes the best events are either very big in scope, like the Olympics, or very localized, like a youth hockey clinic with an Olympian.

Branding Brief 6–5 identifies winners of Brandweek's 8th Annual Event Marketing Awards. Events were judged on the following criteria: (1) competitiveness of the theme, (2) appeal to target audience, (3) appropriateness to the objective, (4) execution of the event, (5) merchandising techniques and tie-ins, and (6) effectiveness.

Measuring Sponsorship Activities   There are two basic approaches to measuring the effects of sponsorship activities: the *supply-side* method focuses on potential expo-

---

Winners of Brandweek's 8th Annual Event Marketing Awards[a]

MASTERCARD WORLD CUP PROMOTION

It was easily MasterCard's biggest sponsorship, at $25 million. It spawned 35 separate programs, beginning in 1992, that combined with promotions, advertising, and event signage to produce a de facto ownership of World Cup. In the opinion of the judges, MasterCard superseded the other top-level World Cup sponsors, like Fuji, GMC Trucks, and Coke and earned the credit-card association top honors for best overall use of sponsorship.

Tying in its three major constituencies of issuing banks, merchants, and cardholders with a plethora of well-orchestrated programs and designing an effectively ambush-proof "host of the World Cup" positioning, MasterCard galvanized support in the nine U.S. cities where World Cup games were held. There were merchant seminars, mall promotions, and welcome centers. MasterValues, the brand's largest annual promotion, was combined with local World Cup versions in host cities. Additional promotions included allowing member banks to sell World Cup merchandise to cardholders and using logos in banks' and merchants' marketing materials.

Advertising and PR efforts produced what MasterCard estimated as a worldwide total of four billion impressions. Even without the wide selection of World Cup marketing activities, it might have been worth $25 million just to have the MasterCard logo behind the goal where an estimated two billion fans watched as Brazil won the championship, beating Italy in a penalty-kick shootout.

Few numbers are available yet, but the most telling evidence about the relative success of the sponsorship is the expectation by member banks that MasterCard's sponsorship of World Cup '98 is a lock. While nothing has been finalized, MasterCard president/CEO Gene Lockhart has twice referred to MasterCard's involvement in the next World Cup at member gatherings. "Even without a lot of hard numbers, we know members think it was a success, because they all assume we'll do it again," said Mava Heffler, VP, promotions.

YUKON JACK WORLD ARM WRESTLING CHAMPIONSHIPS

Probably the most daunting problem facing any marketer contemplating a sports sponsorship is avoiding getting lost in the clutter. With the high price tags that accompany sports sponsorships many opt to create their own events with varying degrees of success. Heublein's Yukon Jack World Arm Wrestling Championships were impressive in reaching the target of legal drinking age to 24-year-old males coveted by the brand, helping to win new trade accounts, and enhancing sales and the brand's image by creating a proprietary association between the liqueur and the arm wrestling.

Support in the fifteen markets where the event was held was limited to public relations and point-of-purchase materials, with advance signage also posted in health clubs and gyms, sports bars, and corner taverns. Drink specials were also arranged for at participating bars to encourage sampling. Premiums including caps, shirts, and shot glasses were given to participants and spectators on the days of the actual event. In markets where an official event was not held, POP was also used at select accounts. The total trade budget for the event was $450,000.

In the event's seventh year, results were laudable. Account depletions increased by 50 percent compared to the same period the previous year without the event. On-premise drink specials generated 75 percent more sales than the average night and seven accounts that held an event now carry the brand because of sales generated by the arm-wrestling program. For 1993–1994, sales were up 12 percent. The event is growing as well. The number of competitors grew by 1,500, or 25 percent, and the number of spectators grew 20 percent to 13,000. More markets are planned for the next round and a special based on the competition will air on the Nashville Network.

CBS COLLEGE TOUR

In an increasingly crowded broadcast marketplace, CBS wanted to generate interest in its programming and provide promotional opportunities for its sponsors. The solution, the network decided, was to go back to school. The CBS College Tour, put together by the Contemporary Group, brought nine sponsors to 44 college campuses with interactive exhibits themed to CBS shows.

At L'Oreal's "Studio CBS" exhibit, for example, students performed scenes from CBS's daytime soaps and received a video of their performances. At the Nestle exhibit, students competed for prizes in a version of the game show *The Price is Right.* More than 250,000 students attended the event, which was promoted on CBS stations and in print ads and flyers posted on campuses.

"The College Tour really defines event marketing at its best," said George Schweitzer, exec vp for marketing and communications at CBS. "For the consumer, there's lots of fun there. For the sponsors, it provided them with a tremendous way to reach a very hard-to-target audience segment, college students, and do it with the borrowed equity of CBS." The network also gained exposure for its shows among a population where the average person watches more than thirteen hours a week of television.

Schweitzer said the tour is somewhat of a logistical nightmare, with two 18-wheelers trucking the exhibits from campus to campus. But sponsors seem to think it's worth the trouble. Six are returning for the 1994–1995 tour, which began in August; AT&T, Ford, L'Oreal, MasterCard, Nestle, and Warner-Lambert. They will be joined by three new sponsors: Disney, Subway, and American Home Products. "The greatest sign of success is we have advertisers who keep wanting to come back to be in it again and we have colleges who keep wanting us to come back," said Schweitzer. "You can't do better than that."

---

[a]*Brandweek* (December 19, 1994), pp. 31–43.

sure to the brand by assessing the extent of media coverage, and the *demand-side* method focuses on reported exposure from consumers. We examine each in turn.

Supply-side measures of sponsorship effects.   Supply-side methods attempt to approximate the amount of time or space devoted in media coverage of an event. For example, the number of seconds that the brand is clearly visible on a television screen or column inches of press clippings covering an event that mention the brand can be estimated. This measure of potential "impressions" delivered by an event sponsorship is then translated into an equivalent "value" in advertising dollars according to the fees associated in actually advertising in the particular media vehicle.

For example, John Hancock in 1991 calculated that the value of press coverage of the college football bowl that they sponsored—which included 7829 stories and some TV reports—was worth $1.1 million. Broadcast of the game by the CBS network included approximately 60 minutes of exposure to the brand in the four-hour telecast, which, when combined with its pre-game promotions, added another $4 million in value. All told, Hancock believed the financial benefit of the sponsorship, based on the amount of coverage and what Hancock would have to pay for the same amount of ad space in print or commercial time on TV, was $5.1 million. Given the total cost of the sponsorship was $1.6 million (which included $1 million in sponsorship fees, $500,000 in TV rights fees, 10.5 minutes of paid commercial time during the TV broadcast, and $100,000 for various charities scholarships, and a game banquet in the host city of El Paso), John Hancock believed the sponsorship was effective.[39]

Although supply-side exposure methods provide quantifiable measures, their validity can be questioned. The difficulty lies in the fact that equating media coverage with advertising exposure ignores the content of the respective communications that consumers receive. The advertiser uses media space and time to communicate a strategically designed message. Media coverage and telecasts only expose the brand and don't necessarily embellish its meaning in any direct way. Although some public relations professionals maintain that positive editorial coverage can be worth five to ten times the advertising equivalency value, it is rare that sponsorship affords the brand such favorable treatment. As one set of critics noted:[40]

> Equating incidental visual and audio exposures with paid advertising time is, we feel, questionable at best. A commercial is a carefully crafted persuasive declaration of a product's virtues. It doesn't compete for attention with the actual on-camera action of a game or race. A 30-second exposure of a billboard in the background can't match the value of 30 seconds in which the product is the only star.

Demand-side measures of sponsorship effects.   An alternative measurement approach is the "demand side" method that attempts to identify the effects that sponsorship has on consumers' brand knowledge structures. Thus, tracking or custom surveys can explore the ability of the event sponsorship to impact awareness, attitudes, or even sales.

Event spectators can be identified and surveyed after the event to measure sponsor recall of the event as well as attitudes and intentions toward the sponsor as a result. For example, a survey by DDB Needham in 1992 indicated that 22 of 37 Olympic sponsors created no connection in consumer minds with the event.[41] A random survey of viewers who watched ten or so hours of television coverage of the 1993 U.S. Open tennis tournament found that only 7 percent knew who sponsored the men's singles title (Nissan Motor Corp.'s Infiniti brand) and only 14 percent knew who sponsored the women's singles title (Bristol-Meyer's Clairol brand).

PUBLIC RELATIONS AND PUBLICITY

Public relations and publicity relates to a variety of programs and is designed to promote and/or protect a company's image or its individual products. Publicity refers to nonpersonal communications that involve press releases, media interviews, press conferences, feature articles, newsletters, photographs, films, tapes, and so on. Public relations also may involve annual reports, fund-raising and membership drives, lobbying, special event management, and public affairs.

The marketing value of public relations got a big boost in 1983 when public relations firm Burson-Masteller's skillful handling of Johnson & Johnson's Tylenol product-tampering incident was credited with helping to save the brand (see chapter 2). Around that time, politicians also discovered the power of campaign "sound bites" that were picked up by the press as a means for broad, cost-efficient candidate exposure.

Marketers now recognize that although public relations is invaluable during a marketing crisis, it is also needs to be a routine part of any marketing communications program. Even companies who primarily use advertising and promotions can benefit from well-conceived and well-executed publicity. For example, McDonald's spends roughly $1 million on advertising each day and runs a number of different promotions featuring price discounts, movie tie-ins, product giveaways, and sweepstakes. To celebrate the twenty-fifth anniversary of the Big Mac, besides its basic advertising and promotion efforts, McDonald's created a media blitz over a concentrated period of time through a comprehensive "Big Mac Media Attack" consisting of:

1. A press kit distributed to local and national media contacts worldwide containing press releases explaining the origin and evolution of the Big Mac over time.
2. An anniversary party event held in Pittsburgh, the home of the Big Mac, followed up newswire photos.
3. Audio and video packages distributed to U.S. radio and television stations with footage of the Pittsburgh event, interviews with McDonald's representatives, historic and current Big Mac commercials, and other elements.

McDonald's research indicated that the media program resulted in nearly 300 million publicity impressions (60 percent in newspapers; 30 percent in television; and 10 percent in radio), a 119 percent increase in consumer awareness of the anniversary, and a 13 percent increase in sales of Big Macs for a comparable period the year before.

PERSONAL SELLING

Personal selling involves face-to-face interaction with one or more prospective purchasers for the purpose of making sales. Personal selling represents a communication option with pros and cons almost exactly the opposite of advertising. Specifically, the main advantage to personal selling is that a detailed, customized message can be sent to customers where feedback can be gathered to help close the sale. Prospective customers can be identified and qualified and tailored solutions can be offered. Products often can be demonstrated with customer involvement as part of the sales pitch for the brand. Personal selling can also be beneficial after the sale to handle customer problems and ensure customer satisfaction. The main disadvantage to personal selling is the high cost involved and its lack of breadth. For many mass market products, personal selling would be cost prohibitive.[42]

Personal selling practices have changed in recent years as recognition of the importance of competing with sales and customer service.[43] According to a *Business Week* cover story, "smart selling" means focusing the entire company on its customers, including changing how salespeople are hired, trained, and paid. These commentators believe that the keys to better selling are to:

1. *Rethink training*. Forget high pressure, slam-dunk selling. Sales reps need new skills: They must learn to become customer advocates whose detailed knowledge of their customers' businesses helps them spot sales opportunities and service problems.

2. *Get everyone involved*. Salespeople should no longer act solo. Everyone in a company from product designers to plant managers and financial officers must be a part of selling to and serving customers.

3. *Inspire from the top*. Chief executives and top managers must frequently, visibly lead the smart-selling charge in their companies. Having the boss call regularly on customers and lead sales training sessions is a must.

4. *Change the motivation*. Salespeople need constant recognition—but not in the form of the old-fashioned commission. That can be an incentive to scoring a quick sales hit. Instead, include measures of long-term customer satisfaction in calculating compensation.

5. *Forge electronic links*. Use computerized marketing and distribution technology to track relationships with customers, make sure the right products get to the right stores at the right times, and make order-taking easy. It all adds up to high-tech intimacy.

6. *Talk to your customers*. Make frequent phone calls, assign a company employee to a customer's plant or drop notes to frequent shoppers. Customers like the attention, and the added communication makes for better intelligence gathering.

Developing Integrated Marketing Communication Programs

The strategy behind marketing communication programs has changed dramatically over the years. In Figure 6–12, Leo Burnett USA, an ad agency famous for its media planning and buying skills, offers a simple contrast in how marketing communication planning has changed over the years. The previous section examined the various communication options available to marketers in depth. This section considers how to develop an integrated marketing communication program in terms of the optimal range of options that should be chosen and the relationships among those options. To foreshadow the main theme that is developed in this discussion, it is recommended that marketers "mix and match" communication options to build brand equity, that is, choose a variety of different communication options that share common meaning and content.

THEN	NOW
One target, defined by demographics	Multiple targets, defined by behavior and ranked by profit to brand
Consumer "mass media"	Consumer mass media Direct media Sales promotion Event marketing Marketing PR
Marketing and creative strategies developed, then media bought	Creative strategy includes media planning

FIGURE 6–12 Leo Burnett's Changes in Media Strategies

"MIXING" COMMUNICATION OPTIONS

Establishing brand awareness and a positive brand image in consumers' minds produces the knowledge structures that can affect consumer response and generate customer-based brand equity. One implication of the conceptualization of customer-based brand equity is that the *manner* in which brand associations are formed does not matter—only the resulting favorability, strength, and uniqueness of brand associations matter. In other words, if a consumer has an equally strong and favorable brand association from Rolaids antacids to the concept "relief" because of exposure to a "problem-solution" television ad that concludes with a tag line "Rolaids spells relief" *or* because of knowledge of the fact that Rolaids sponsors the "Relief Pitcher of the Year" award for major league baseball, the impact in terms of customer-based brand equity should be identical *unless* additional associations are created (e.g., "advertised on television") or existing associations are affected in some way (e.g., "speed or potency of effects").

Thus, from the perspective of customer-based brand equity, marketers should evaluate *all* possible communication options available to create knowledge structures according to effectiveness criteria as well as cost considerations. This broad view of brand building activities is especially relevant when considering marketing communication strategies to improve brand awareness. As noted in chapter 3, brand awareness is closely related to brand familiarity and can be viewed as a function of the number of brand-related exposures and experiences that have been accumulated by the consumer.[44] Thus, *anything* that causes the consumer to notice and pay attention to the brand can increase brand awareness, at least in terms of brand recognition. Obviously, the visibility of the brand in many sponsorship activities suggests that these activities may be especially valuable for enhancing brand recognition.

To enhance brand recall, however, more intense and elaborate processing of the brand may be necessary so that stronger brand links to the product category are established to improve memory performance. Similarly, because brand associations can be created in the abstract in many different ways, *all* of the possible marketing communication options reviewed above should be considered to create the desired brand image and knowledge structures.

Consistent with this view, Schultz, Tannenbaum, and Lauterborn conceptualize integrated marketing communications in terms of "contacts."[45] They define a *contact* as any information-bearing experience that a customer or prospect has with the brand, the product category, or the market that relates to the marketer's product or service. According to these authors, there are numerous ways in which a person can come in contact with a brand:

> For example, a contact can include friends' and neighbors' comments, packaging, newspaper, magazine, and television information, ways the customer or prospect is treated in the retail store, where the product is shelved in the store, and the type of signage that appears in retail establishments. And the contacts do not stop with the purchase. Contacts also consist of what friends, relatives, and bosses say about a person who is using the product. Contacts include the type of customer service given with returns or inquiries, or even the types of letters the company writes to resolve problems or to solicit additional business. All of these are customer contacts with the brand. These bits and pieces of information, experiences, and relationships, created over time, influence the potential relationship among the customer, the brand, and the marketer.

Determining Optimal Mix

In making the final decision as to how much and what kinds of marketing communications are necessary, economic theory would suggest placing dollars into a marketing communication budget and across communication options according to marginal revenue and cost. For example, the communication mix would be optimally distributed when the last dollar spent on each communication option generated the same return. Because such information may be difficult to obtain, other models of budget allocation emphasize more observable factors such as stage of brand life cycle, objectives and budget of the firm, product characteristics, size of budget, and media strategy of competitors. These factors are typically contrasted with the different characteristics of the media.

For example, marketing communication budgets tend to be higher when there is low channel support, much change in the marketing program over time, many hard-to-reach customers, more complex customer decision making, differentiated products and non-homogeneous customer needs, and frequent product purchases in small quantities.[46] Personal selling tends to become a more dominant element in the communication mix when the brand has a high unit value, is technical in nature, requires demonstration, must be tailored to the specific needs of customers, is purchased infrequently or involves a trade-in; when the firm has a limited communications budget; and when customers are easily identified.[47]

Besides these efficiency considerations, different communication options also may be chosen to target different market segments. For example, advertising may attempt to bring new customers into the market or attract competitor's customers to the brand, whereas promotions may attempt to reward loyal users of the brand, or vice versa.

"MATCHING" COMMUNICATION OPTIONS

There are a number of means of creating integrated marketing communications (IMC) programs. In general, any IMC program can be evaluated along two dimensions—consistency and complementarity. *Consistency* considerations relate to the extent to which information conveyed in different communication options is consistent and thus mutually reinforcing. *Complementarity* considerations relate to the extent to which different communication options are designed in a way such that the strengths in one option help to negate the disadvantages of another option. In other words, the ideal communications program would have a large number of communication options sharing some core meaning but differing in a way to capitalize on the advantages but compensate for the disadvantages of each option. We review both considerations in turn.

Consistency Considerations

Regardless of which communication options are chosen, the entire marketing communication program should be coordinated to create a consistent and cohesive brand image, that is, where brand associations share content and meaning. The consistency and cohesiveness of the brand image is important because it determines how easily existing associations can be recalled and how easily additional associations can become linked to the brand in memory.

In general, information that is consistent in meaning is more easily learned and recalled than unrelated information—though the unexpectedness of information inconsistent in meaning with the brand sometimes can lead to more elaborate processing and stronger associations than even consistent information.[48] Nevertheless, with inconsistent associations and a diffuse brand image, consumers may overlook some associations or, because they are confused about the meaning of the brand, form less strong and favorable new associations.

Therefore, in the long run, different communication elements should be designed and combined so that they work effectively together to create a consistent and cohesive brand image. As branding expert Larry Light states: "The total brand experience must be a result of an integrated, focused, strategically sound, differentiated, consistent, branded marketing program. Inconsistency, instead of integration, leads to uncertainty. Yet, uncertainty and inconsistency do seem to be the result of a lot of today's marketing practices."[49]

Note also that there may actually be memory advantages to using multiple communication options to create positive brand images. The *encoding variability principle* in psychology argues that presenting information in varied contexts causes information to be encoded in slightly different ways. As a result, multiple retrieval routes are formed in memory—each converging on the to-be-remembered information—thereby enhancing recall.[50] In other words, multiple ways to learn information provide multiple cues to recall information, thereby improving memory performance. Thus, the encoding variability principle suggests that an integrated marketing communications program, by employing multiple communication elements, may be an effective way to create, maintain, or strengthen brand associations in memory.

Complementarity Approaches

Communication options are often more effective when used in tandem. For example, research has shown that promotions can be more effective when combined with advertising.[51] Similarly, a famous McGraw-Hill ad campaign shows the benefits of prior trade advertising to facilitate selling efforts (see Figure 6–13). In both cases, the awareness and attitudes created by advertising campaigns can improve the success of more direct sales pitches. Thus, the ideal marketing communication program would ensure that the communication options chosen would be mutually compensatory and reinforcing to create desired consumer knowledge structures.

In particular, marketing communications must sometimes be explicitly tied together to create or enhance brand equity. For example, TV ads often do not "brand" well—that is, weak links may exist from the communication effects created by a TV ad to knowledge about the brand in memory—for the following three main reasons.

1. *Competitive clutter.* Competing ads in the product category can create "interference" and consumer confusion as to which ad goes with which brand.[52] Numerous instances can be found where consumers mix up competing ads and brands. For example, Eveready introduced a clever ad campaign in 1989 for their Energizer batteries that featured a pink toy bunny that kept on "going . . . and going . . . and going." Unfortunately, consumer research by Video Storyboard uncovered that of the people in their annual survey who named the popular commercial as their favorite of the year, 40 percent mistakenly attributed it to Eveready's main competitor, Duracell—only 60 percent correctly identified it as an Energizer ad! To exacerbate this interference problem, it is often the case that competing ads appear in the same media vehicle because they typically target the same consumers. For example, an analysis of one recent week of prime time television advertising found that of the fifty-seven commercials that ran in an average hour, twenty-four, or 42 percent, faced at least one competitor running an ad during that same time period.[53]

2. *Ad content and structure.* Factors related to the content and structure of the ad itself can result in weak links from the brand to communication effects created by ad exposure. For example, as noted above, advertisers have a vast range of creative strategies and techniques at their disposal to improve consumer motivation and lead to greater involvement and enhanced ad processing on their part. Although these "borrowed interest" tactics may effectively grab consumers' attention for an ad, the resulting focus of attention and processing may be directed in a manner that does *not* create strong brand associations. For example, when the popular actor James Garner was advertising for Polaroid, marketing research surveys routinely noted that many interview respondents mistakenly attributed his promotion to Kodak, their chief competitor. Moreover, when these attention-getting creative tactics are employed, the position and prominence of the brand in the ad is often downplayed. Delaying brand identification or providing few brand mentions in an ad may also raise processing intensity but result in attention directed away from thinking about the brand. Furthermore, limited brand exposure time in the ad allows little opportunity for elaboration of existing brand knowledge, also contributing to weak brand links.[54]

3. *Consumer involvement.* Finally, in certain circumstances, consumers may not have any inherent interest in the product or service category or may lack knowledge of the specific brand (e.g., in the case of a low share brand, a new market entry). The resulting decrease in consumer motivation and ability to process also translates to weaker brand links. Similarly, a change in advertising strategy to target a new market segment or add a new attribute, benefit, or usage association to the brand image may also fail to produce strong brand links because consumers lack the ability to easily relate this new advertising information to existing brand knowledge.[55]

Thus, for a variety of reasons, consumers may fail to correctly identify advertising with the advertised brand or, even worse, incorrectly attribute advertising to a

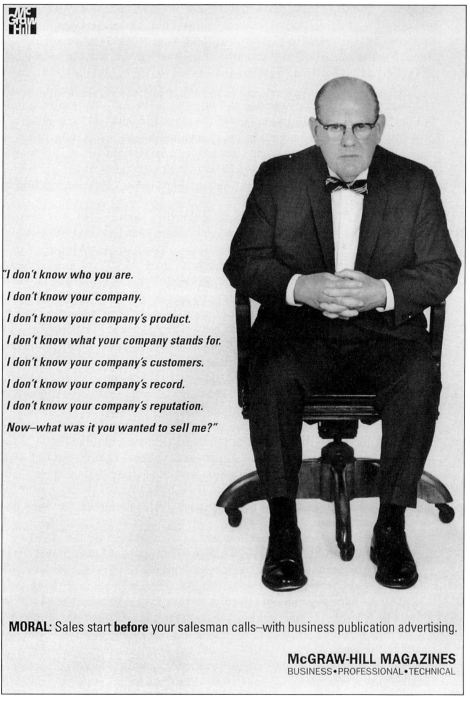

FIGURE 6-13 McGraw-Hill Trade Ad

competing brand. In these cases, advertising "worked" in the sense that communication effects—ad claims and executional information, as well as cognitive and affective responses by consumers to that information—were stored in memory. Yet advertising "failed" in the sense that these communication effects were *not* accessible when critical brand-related decisions were made.

To address this problem, one common tactic marketers employ to achieve ad and point-of-purchase congruence and improve ad recall is to make the brand name and package information prominent in the ad. Unfortunately, this increase in brand emphasis means that communication effects and brand associations that can potentially affect brand evaluations are less likely to be able to be created by the ad and stored in consumer memory. In other words, although consumers are better able to recall the advertised brand with this tactic, there is *less* other information about the brand to actually recall.

A potentially more effective tactic to improve consumer's motivation and ability to retrieve communication effects when making a brand-related decision is advertising retrieval cues. An *advertising retrieval cue* is visual or verbal information uniquely identified with an ad evident when consumers are making a product or service decision. Their purpose is to maximize the probability that consumers who have seen or heard the cued ad retrieve from long-term memory the communication effects that were stored from earlier processing of that ad. Ad retrieval cues may consist of a key visual, a catchy slogan, or any unique advertising element that serves as an effective reminder to consumers. For example, in an attempt to remedy the problem they had with mistaken attributions, Quaker Oats placed a photograph of the "Mikey" character from the popular Life cereal ad on the front of the package. More recently, Eveready featured a picture of its pink bunny character on the packages for its Energizer batteries to reduce consumer confusion with Duracell.

Ad retrieval cues can be placed in the store (e.g., on the package or as part of a shelf-talker or some other point-of-purchase device), combined with a promotion (e.g., with a FSI coupon), included as part of a Yellow Pages directory listing, or embedded in any marketing communication option where recall of communication effects can be advantageous to marketers. By using ad retrieval cues, greater emphasis can be placed in the ad on supplying persuasive information and creating positive associations so consumers have a reason *why* they should purchase the brand. Ad retrieval cues allow for creative freedom in ad execution because the brand and package need not be the centerpiece of the ad. The effectiveness of ad retrieval cues depends on how many communication effects are potentially retrievable and how likely these communication effects are to be retrieved from memory with only the brand as a cue, as compared to the executional information making up the ad retrieval cue. An ad retrieval cue is most effective when many communication effects are stored in memory but are only weakly associated to the brand because of one or more of the various factors noted above.

Other strategies besides ad retrieval cues may be employed to maximize the brand equity arising from TV advertising. Print and radio reinforcement of TV ads—where the video and audio components of a TV ad serve as the basis for the respective type of ads—can be an effective means to leverage existing communication effects from TV ad exposure and more strongly link them to the brand. Cueing a TV ad with an explicitly linked radio or print ad can create similar or even enhanced processing outcomes that can substitute for additional TV ad exposures. Moreover, a potentially useful although rarely employed media strategy is to run explicitly linked print or radio ads *prior* to the accompanying TV ad. The print and radio ads in this case function as a "teaser" and increase consumer motivation to process the more "complete" TV ad, consisting of both audio and video components.

As another strategy, different combinations of TV ad excerpts within a campaign (e.g., 15-second spots consisting of highlights from longer 30- or 60-second spots for those campaigns characterized by only one dominant ad execution or umbrella ads consisting of highlights from a pool of ads for those campaigns consisting of multiple ad executions) and across campaigns over time (e.g., including key elements from past ad campaigns that are strongly identified with the brand as part of the current ad campaign) may be particularly helpful for strengthening dormant associations and facilitating the formation of consumer evaluations of and reactions to the ads and their linkage to the brand.

The basic rationale for these different strategies is that TV ads should not be considered as discrete units that are created for a particular ad campaign and therefore run for a certain length of time before being replaced by a new ad campaign. Rather, TV ads should be thought of more broadly as consisting of different ingredients or pieces of information that advertisers might choose to combine in different ways over time to improve their brand-building abilities. The most important ingredients are those identifiable visual scenes, characters, symbols, and verbal phrases or slogans that can serve as cues or reminders to communication effects created by a single TV ad, an ad campaign with multiple TV ads, or a previous ad campaign.

Combining these ingredients to leverage communication effects over time offers several potential benefits. First, it can help to maintain the strength of unique and favorable brand associations. In particular, without such reminders, the heritage of a brand and its original associations may become weakened because the ad campaign was not being currently aired or a new ad campaign was using different appeals or creative strategies to reposition or modernize the brand. Second, it can facilitate the formation of favorable attitudes by consumers towards the advertising and brand. In other words, consumers may be likely to say, "I like the ads for that brand." As noted above, these attitudes toward the ad can favorably impact brand evaluations, especially for low-involvement consumer decisions.

Note that an implicit issue in this discussion is the optimal continuity to have with advertising and communication campaigns over time. Congruity theory would suggest that a moderate amount of change is appropriate.[56] Too little change may not be noticed by consumers and thus have no effect. On the other hand, more dramatic changes may confuse consumers and result in their still continuing to think of the brand in the "old way." Because of strong associations already in memory, consumers may either fail to incorporate new ad information into their brand knowledge structures or fail to retrieve new ad information when making later product or service decisions. In many cases, a moderate change, such as retaining the current positioning but communicating it with a new creative, may be the most effective way to maintain or enhance the strength of brand associations. If the favorability or uniqueness of brand associations is deficient in some way, however, then a more severe change in positioning emphasizing different points of parity or points of difference may be necessary.

Review

The purpose of this chapter was to provide conceptual frameworks and managerial guidelines as to how marketing communications can be integrated to enhance brand equity. The chapter addressed this issue from the perspective of customer-based brand equity, which maintains that brand equity is fundamentally determined by the brand knowledge created in consumers' minds by the supporting marketing program.

Two key implications emerged from this discussion. First, from the perspective of customer-based brand equity, all possible communication options should be evaluated in terms of their ability to affect brand equity. In particular, the customer-based brand equity concept provides a common denominator by which the effects of different communication options can be evaluated: Each communication option can be judged in terms of the effectiveness and efficiency by which it affects brand awareness and by which it creates, maintains, or strengthens favorable and unique brand associations. Different communication options have different strengths and can accomplish different objectives. Thus, it is important to employ a "mix" of different communication options, each playing a specific role in building or maintaining brand equity.

The second important insight that emerges from the conceptual framework is that the marketing communication program should be put together in a way such that the whole is greater than the sum of the parts. In other words, as much as possible, there should be a "match" among certain communication options so that the effects of any one communication option are enhanced by the presence of others. In particular, marketing communications often must be explicitly linked (i.e., cued) to allow for the necessary interactions to create a positive brand image. Specifically, marketers often should integrate marketing communications by literally taking visual or verbal information from one communication element and using it in different ways in another communication element. The rationale is that this information can cue or serve as a

FIGURE 6-14 General Marketing Communication Guidelines

1. *Be analytical:* Use frameworks of consumer behavior and managerial decision making to develop well-reasoned communication programs.
2. *Be curious:* Better understand customers by using all forms of research and always be thinking of how you can create added value for consumers.
3. *Be single-minded:* Focus message on well-defined target markets (less can be more).
4. *Be integrative:* Reinforce your message through consistency and cuing across all communication options and media.
5. *Be creative:* State your message in a unique fashion; use alternative promotions and media to create favorable, strong, and unique brand associations.
6. *Be observant:* Keep track of competition, customers, channel members, and employees through monitoring and tracking studies.
7. *Be patient:* Take a long-term view of communication effectiveness to build and manage brand equity.
8. *Be realistic:* Understand the complexities involved in marketing communications.

reminder to related information. By enhancing consumer motivation, ability, and opportunity to process and retrieve brand-related information, these cues can facilitate the formation of strong, favorable, and unique brand associations. Explicitly integrating media in this manner also increases the likelihood that brand knowledge is used in consumer product and service decisions. In these ways, explicitly integrated media can contribute to brand equity.

In closing, the basic message of this chapter is simple: Advertisers need to evaluate marketing communication options strategically to determine how they can contribute to brand equity. To do so, advertisers need some theoretical and managerial guidelines by which they can determine the effectiveness and efficiency of various communication options both singularly and in combination with *other* communication options. Figure 6–14 provides the author's philosophy concerning the design, implementation, and interpretation of marketing communication strategies.

Discussion Questions

1. Pick a brand and gather all its marketing communication materials. How effectively has it mixed and matched marketing communications? Has it capitalized on the strengths of different media and compensated for its weaknesses at the same time? How explicitly has it integrated its communication program?
2. What do you see as the role of the internet for building brands? How would you build a web site for a major brand, e.g., Nike, Disney, or Levi-Strauss?
3. From a current issue of *Newsweek* or *Time* magazine, decide which print ad you feel is the best and which ad you feel is the worst based on the criteria described in the chapter.

Notes

1. To obtain a broader perspective, it is necessary to consult good advertising texts such as George E. Belch and Michael A. Belch, *Introduction to Advertising and Promotion*, 3rd ed. Homewood, IL: Irwin, 1995; Rajeev Batra, John G. Meyers, and David A. Aaker, *Advertising Management*, 5th ed., Upper Saddle River, NJ: Prentice Hall, 1996; or John R. Rossiter and Larry Percy, *Advertising and Promotion Management*, New York: McGraw-Hill, 1987.
2. Alexander L. Biel, "Converting Image Into Equity," in David A. Aaker and Alexander L. Biel (eds.), *Brand Equity & Advertising*. Hillsdale, NJ: Lawrence Erlbaum Associates, 1993, pp. 67–82.
3. "How to Turn Junk Mail into a Goldmine—Or Perhaps Not," *The Economist* (April 1, 1995), pp. 51–52.
4. Leonard M. Lodish, Magid Abraham, Stuart Kalmenson, Jeanne Livelsberger, Beth Lubetkin, Bruce Richardson, and Mary Ellen Stevens, "How T.V. Advertising Works: A Meta Analysis of 389 Real World Split Cable T.V. Advertising Experiments," *Journal of Marketing Research*, 32 (May 1995), pp. 125–139; Magid Abraham and Leonard Lodish, *Advertising Works: A Study of Advertising Effectiveness and the Resulting Strategies and Tactical Implications*, Chicago, IL: Information Resources, Inc., 1989.
5. Dottie Enrico, "Consumers Pig Out on Baked Lay's Campaign," *USA Today* (October 7, 1996), p. B8.

6. John Rossiter and Larry Percy, *Advertising and Promotion Management*. New York: McGraw-Hill, 1987.

7. Michael Ray, *Advertising and Communications Management*. Upper Saddle River, NJ: Prentice Hall, 1982.

8. Rajeev Batra, John G. Meyers, and David A. Aaker, *Advertising Management*, 5th ed., Upper Saddle River, NJ: Prentice Hall, 1996.

9. John Flinn, "Advertising's New Age," *San Francisco Chronicle* (October 23, 1994), p. B14.

10. For a comprehensive overview, see Bob Schulberg, *Radio Advertising: The Authoritative Handbook*. Lincolnwood, IL: NTC Books, 1990.

11. David Ogilvy, *Ogilvy on Advertising*. New York: Vintage Books, 1983.

12. Judith Graham, "AmEx 'Portraits' Stresses Values," *Advertising Age* (January 1, 1990), p. 12.

13. For more discussion on these guidelines, see Burton and Purvis, *Which Ad Pulled Best*, 5th ed. Lincolnwood IL: NTC Business Books, 1987.

14. Yumiko Ono, "Direct Marketers Press Fast-Forward on Using Videotapes as Costs Decline," *Wall Street Journal* (October 31, 1994), p. A-8.

15. Julia Reed, "Ads Where You Least Expect Them," *U.S. News and World Report* (March 9, 1987), p. 46.

16. Kevin Goldman, "P&G Experiments With an Infomercial," *Wall Street Journal* (July 8, 1994), p. B-9.

17. "How to Turn Junk Mail into a Goldmine—Or Perhaps Not," *The Economist* (April 1, 1995), pp. 51–52. Gary Levin, "Going Direct Route," *Advertising Age* (November 11, 1991), p. 37.

18. Jeff Pelline, "New Commercial Twist in Corporate Restrooms," *San Francisco Chronicle* (October 6, 1986), p. 27.

19. Chuck Stogel, "Quest for the Captive Audience," *Superbrands 1992*, pp. 106–107.

20. David T. Friendly, "Selling It at the Movies," *Newsweek* (July 4, 1983), p. 46.

21. Joanne Lipman, "In Film Product Placement, Needs of Story Can Bring Free Display," *Wall Street Journal* (November 25, 1991), p. B6. Laura Bird, "A Star Is Brewed as Obscure Beer Scores with Role in Hit Movie," *Wall Street Journal* (July 8, 1993), p. B-6.

22. Junu Bryan Kim, "Research Makes Ski Run Easier," *Advertising Age* (August 19, 1991), p. 30.

23. Scott Hume, "Steady Diet of Basics Leaves Little Room for Offbeat," *Advertising Age* (August 19, 1991), p. 27.

24. Scott Hume and Marcy Magiera, "What do Moviegoers Think of Ads?," *Advertising Age* (April 23, 1990), p. 4.

25. *Consumer Reports* (December 1982), pp. 752–755.

26. For an excellent summary of issues related to the type, scope, and tactics of sales promotions design, see John A. Quelch, "Note on Sales Promotion Design," Harvard Business School 589–021 (August 24, 1988).

27. Eric Hollresier, Trading Up from Tactics to Strategy in the Trade Game," *Brandweek* (October 3, 1994), Boston, MA. pp. 26–33.

28. Michael L. Ray, *Advertising and Communication Management*. Upper Saddle River, NJ: Prentice Hall, 1982.

29. Chris Roush, "A Sports Marketer with a Mean Curve," *Business Week* (September 12, 1994), p. 96.

30. Kathleen Deveny and Richard Gibson, "Awash in Coupons? Some Firms Try to Stem the Tide," *Wall Street Journal* (May 10, 1994), p. B1.

31. John R. Rossiter and Larry Percy, *Advertising and Promotion Management*. New York: McGraw-Hill, 1987.

32. Eric Hollreiser, "Trading Up from Tactics to Strategy in the Trade Game," *Brandweek* (October 3, 1994), pp. 26–33.

33. See Peggy Cunningham, Shirley Taylor, and Carolyn Reeder, "Event Marketing: The Evolution of Sponsorship from Philanthropy to Strategic Promotion," pp. 407–425.

34. Michael Oneal and Peter Finch, "Nothing Sells Like Sports," *Business Week* (August 31, 1987), pp. 48–53.

35. Nancy Ten Kate, "Make It An Event," *American Demographics* (November 1992), pp. 40–44.

36. Chris Roush, "A Sports Marketer With a Mean Curve," *Business Week* (September 12, 1994), p. 96.

37. The Association of National Advertisers has a useful source, *Event Marketing: A Management Guide*, which is available by contacting them at 155 East 44th Street, New York, NY 10017.

38. Patrick Oster, "Philips: Playing by Its Own Rules at the World Cup," *Business Week* (June 20, 1994), p. 80.

39. Michael J. McCarthy, "Keeping Careful Score on Sports Tie-Ins," *Wall Street Journal* (April 24, 1991), p. B1.

40. William L. Shankin and John Kuzma, "Buying That Sporting Image," *Marketing Management* (Spring 1992), p. 65.

41. Jim Crimmins, "Most Sponsorships Waste Money," *Advertising Age* (June 21, 1993), p. S-2.

42. John Quelch, "Communications Policy," Teaching Note 5–585–021. Boston, MA. HBS Case Services, 1984.

43. Christopher Power, "Smart Selling," *Business Week* (August 3, 1992), pp. 46–52.

44. Joseph W. Alba and J. Wesley Hutchinson, "Dimensions of Consumer Expertise," *Journal of Consumer Research*, 13 (March 1987), pp. 411–453.

45. Don E. Schultz, Stanley I. Tannenbaum, and Robert F. Lauterborn, *Integrated Marketing Communications*. Lincolnwood, IL: NTC Business Books, 1993.

46. Thomas C. Kinnear and Kenneth L. Bernhardt, *Principles of Marketing*, 2nd ed. Glenview, IL: Scott Foresman and Co., 1986.

47. Philip L. Kotler, *Marketing Management*, 9th ed. Upper Saddle River, NJ: Prentice Hall, 1997.

48. Susan E. Heckler and Terry L. Childers, "The Role of Expectancy and Relevancy in Memory for Verbal and Visual Information: What is Incongruency?" *Journal of Consumer Research*, 18 (March 1992), pp. 475–492; Michael J. Houston, Terry L. Childers, and Susan E. Heckler, "Picture-Word Consistency and the Elaborative Processing of Advertisements," *Journal of Marketing Research*, 24 (November 1987), pp. 359–369; Thomas K. Srull and Robert S. Wyer, "Person Memory and Judgment," *Psychological Review*, 96(1) (1989), pp. 58–83.

49. Larry Light, "Bringing Research to the Brand Equity Process," ARF Brand Equity Workshop, February 15–16, 1994.

50. For example, see Daniel R. Young and Francis S. Belleza, "Encoding Variability, Memory Organization, and the Repetition Effect," *Journal of Experimental Psychology: Learning, Memory, and Cognition*, 8(6) (1982), pp. 545–559.

51. William T. Moran, "Insights from Pricing Research," in E.B. Bailey (ed.), *Pricing Practices and Strategies*. New York: The Conference Board, 1978, pp. 7–13.

52. Raymond R. Burke and Thomas K. Srull, "Competitive Interference and Consumer Memory for Advertising," *Journal of Consumer Research*, 15 (June 1988), pp. 55–68; Kevin Lane Keller, "Memory Factors in Advertising: The Effect of Advertising Retrieval Cues on Brand Evaluations," *Journal of Consumer Research*, 14 (December 1987), pp. 316–333; Kevin Lane Keller, "Memory and Evaluations in Competitive Advertising Environments," *Journal of Consumer Research*, 17 (March 1991), pp. 463–476. Robert J. Kent and Chris T. Allen, "Competitive Interference Effects in Consumer Memory for Advertising: The Role of Brand Familiarity," *Journal of Marketing*, 58 (July 1994), pp. 97–105.

53. *Advertising Age* (October 14–20), 1991.

54. David Walker and Michael J. von Gonten, "Explaining Related Recall Outcomes: New Answers From A Better Model," *Journal of Advertising Research* 29 (1989), 11–21.

55. Susan E. Heckler, Kevin Lane Keller, and Michael J. Houston, "The Effects of Brand Name Suggestiveness on Advertising Recall," *Journal of Marketing,* January 1988, in press.

56. Joan Meyers-Levy and Alice M. Tybout, "Schema Congruity as a Basis for Product Evaluation," *Journal of Consumer Research*, 16 (June 1989), pp. 39–54.

CHAPTER 7

Leveraging Secondary Brand Associations to Build Brand Equity

Preview

The previous chapters described how brand equity could be built through the choice of brand elements (chapter 4) or through the supporting marketing program and product, price, distribution, and marketing communication strategies (chapters 5 and 6). In this chapter, we consider the third means by which brand equity can be built—through the leverage of secondary brand associations. That is, brands may themselves be linked to other entities with their own associations. By becoming identified with these other entities in some manner, consumers may assume or infer that some of the associations that characterize the other entities may also be true for the brand. Thus, in effect, some associations become "transferred" from other entities to the brand. In other words, the brand essentially "borrows" some associations and, depending on the nature of those associations, perhaps some brand equity from other entities.

We refer to this indirect approach to building brand equity as "leveraging" secondary associations for the brand. Secondary brand associations may be quite important if existing brand associations are deficient in some way. In other words, secondary associations can be leveraged to create strong, favorable, and unique associations that may otherwise not be present. In this chapter, we will consider the following eight different means by which secondary associations can be created by linking the brand to:

1. Companies (e.g., through branding strategies)
2. Countries or other geographical areas (e.g., through identification of product origin)
3. Channels of distribution (e.g., through channels strategy)
4. Other brands (e.g., through co-branding)
5. Characters (e.g., through licensing)
6. Spokespeople (e.g., through endorsements)
7. Events (e.g., through sponsorship)
8. Other third-party sources (e.g., through awards or reviews)

The first three entities all reflect source factors—who makes the product, where the product is made, and where it is purchased. The remaining entities deal with related people, places, or things.

As an example of some of the issues involved, assume Salomon—makers of alpine and cross country ski bindings, ski boots, and skis—decided to introduce a new tennis racquet called the "Avenger." Although Salomon has been selling safety bindings for skis since 1947, much of Salomon's recent growth has been fueled by its diversification into ski boots and the introduction of a revolutionary new type of ski called the monocoque. Salomon's innovative, stylish, and top quality products have led to strong leadership positions. In creating the marketing program to support the new Avenger tennis racquet, Salomon could attempt to leverage secondary brand associations in a number of different ways, as follows.

First, Salomon could leverage associations to the corporate brand by "sub-branding" the product, that is, by calling it Avenger by Salomon. Consumers' evaluations of the new product extension would be influenced by the extent to which consumers held favorable associations about Salomon as a company or brand because of their skiing products *and* felt that such knowledge was predictive of a tennis racquet that the company made. Second, Salomon could try to rely on its European origins—its headquarters are near Lake Annecy at the foot of the Alps mountains—although such a location would not seem to have much relevance to tennis. Third, Salomon could also try to sell through upscale, professional tennis shops and clubs in a hope that their credibility would "rub off" on the Avenger brand. Fourth, Salomon could attempt to co-brand by identifying a strong ingredient brand for its grip, frame, or strings (e.g., as Wilson did by incorporating Goodyear tire rubber on the soles of its ProStaff Classic tennis shoes). Fifth, although it is doubtful that a licensed character could be effectively leveraged, Salomon obviously could attempt to find one or more top professional players to endorse the racquet or choose to become a sponsor of tennis tournaments or even the entire professional ATP men's or WTA women's tennis tour. Finally, Salomon could attempt to secure and publicize favorable ratings from third party sources (e.g., *Tennis* magazine).

Thus, independent of the associations created by the racquet itself, its brand name, or any other aspects of the marketing program, Salomon may be able to build equity by linking the brand to these other entities. In this chapter, we first consider the nature of associations that can be leveraged or transferred from other entities and the process by which they do so. We then consider in detail each of the eight different means of leveraging secondary brand associations.

Conceptualizing the Leveraging Process

In simple terms, the basic mechanism involved with leveraging secondary brand associations is as follows. Consumers have some knowledge of an entity—certain beliefs and attitudes—that they have learned over time. When a brand is identified as being linked to that entity, consumers may infer that some of the associations that characterize the entity may also characterize the brand. A number of different theoretical mechanisms from psychology would predict such an inferencing effect. For example, such reasoning by consumers could merely be a result of "cognitive consistency" considerations: In the minds of consumers, if it is true for the entity, then it must be true for the brand.

In terms of conceptualizing the inferencing process more formally, two factors are particularly important in predicting the extent of leverage that might result from linking the brand to another entity in some manner:

1. *Awareness and knowledge of the entity:* If consumers have no familiarity with or knowledge of the entity, then obviously there is nothing that can be transferred. Ideally, consumers would be aware of the entity and hold some strong, favorable, and perhaps even unique associations.

2. *Meaningfulness of the entity's associations:* Given that the entity has some potentially positive associations, to what extent are those associations relevant and meaningful for the brand? The meaningfulness of these other associations may vary depending on the brand and product context. Some associations may seem relevant to and valuable for the brand whereas others may seem to consumers to have little connection.

3. *Transferability of the entity's associations:* Assuming that some potentially useful and meaningful associations exist for the entity and could possibly be transferred to the brand, to what extent will those associations actually become linked to the brand? Thus, a key issue is the extent to which these other associations will in fact become strong, favorable, and unique in the context of the brand.

In other words, the basic questions with transferring secondary associations from another entity are: What do consumers know about the other entity? and Does any of this knowledge affect what they think about the brand when it becomes linked or associated in some fashion with this other entity?

Theoretically, any association may be inferred from other entities to the brand. It is useful to make a distinction, as was done in chapter 3, between global associations (overall attitudes toward the entity) and more specific brand associations (attributes or benefits that directly relate to product meaning). In general, it may be more likely for global associations to transfer from the entity than more specific associations. Many specific associations are likely to be seen as irrelevant or too strongly linked to the original entity to transfer to the brand.

The process by which associations from another entity can be transferred to a brand will be discussed in detail in discussing brand extensions in chapter 12, but several points deserve comment here. The inferencing process will depend largely on the strength of the linkage or connection in consumers' minds between the brand and other entity. The more consumers see fit or similarity of the entity to the brand, the more likely it is that consumers will infer similar associations to the brand.

In general, secondary associations are most likely to affect evaluations of a new product when consumers lack either the motivation or ability to judge more product-related concerns. In other words, when consumers either don't care much about choosing a particular brand or don't feel that they possess the knowledge to choose the appropriate brand, they may be more likely to make brand decisions on the basis of such secondary considerations as the country from which the product came, the store in which the product is sold, and so on.

Thus, a number of different theoretical mechanisms are possible by which another entity, such as country of origin, may influence product evaluations: (1) as a product attribute whose favorability combines with the favorability of other attributes and benefits to influence overall brand evaluations, (2) as a signal to infer more other specific product characteristics, (3) as a heuristic cue to simplify an evaluation, or (4) as a standard relative to which the product is compared.[1]

GUIDELINES

Choosing to emphasize the company or a particular person, place, or event should be based on consumers' awareness of that entity, as well as how the beliefs and attitudes of the entity might possibly become linked to the brand. A leveraging strategy makes sense when consumers have associations in memory to another entity that are congruent with desired brand associations. For example, consider a country such as New Zealand, which is known for having more sheep than people. A New Zealand sweater manufacturer that positioned its product on the basis of its "New Zealand wool" presumably could more easily establish strong and favorable brand associations because New Zealand may already mean "wool" to many people.

At the same time, secondary brand associations may be risky because some control of the brand image is given up. The company, person, place, event, or thing that makes up the primary brand association will undoubtedly have a host of associations of which only some smaller set will be of interest to the marketer. Managing the transfer process so that only the relevant secondary associations become linked to the brand may be difficult. Moreover, these images may change over time as consumers learn more about the entity, and new associations may or may not be advantageous for the brand.

Next, we consider some of the main ways by which secondary brand associations can become linked to the brand.

Company

The branding strategies adopted by the company that makes a product will be an important determinant of the strength of association from the brand to the company and any other existing brands. Three main branding options exist for a new product:

1. Create a new brand
2. Adopt or modify an existing brand
3. Combine an existing and new brand

Existing brands may be related to a company (e.g., Procter & Gamble) or family brand (e.g., Ivory) and may involve names, logos, symbols, and so on. To the extent that the brand is linked to another existing brand, as with options 2 and 3, then associations to the other brand may also become linked to the brand. In particular, a corporate or family brand can be a source of much brand equity. For example, a corporate brand may evoke associations of common product attributes, benefits, or attitudes; people and relationships; programs and values; and corporate credibility. Branding Brief 7–1 describes how the Body Shop was able to create a strong corporate image that impacts all the products it sells.

Leveraging a corporate brand may not always be useful, however, depending on the awareness and image involved. For example, Beatrice once attempted to create a corporate brand umbrella around some of the diverse products it sold at the time, such as Hunt Wesson foods, Stiffel lamps, and Orville Redenbacher popcorn. An expensive ad campaign uniting the products around the theme, "You've Known Us All Along," failed to connect with consumers. In fact, in some cases, large companies are deliberately introducing new brands in an attempt to convey a "smaller" image.[2] For example, Gallo created the two folksy farmers, Ed Bartles and Frank James, to sell their wine cooler product. Philip Morris' Miller unit has used its Plank Road Brewery brand to introduce Icehouse and Red Dog beers. Philip Morris also invented a whole new tobacco company to market a new discount cigarette, Dave's. Promotional material read:

> Down in Concord, North Carolina, there's a guy named Dave. Dave is an entrepreneur who believes in the value of homemade products and the concept of offering folks quality cigarettes at the right price . . . Dave guarantees, "If you don't like 'em, I'll eat 'em."

Image Management The Body Shop Way[a]

BACKGROUND

In 1976, Anita Roddick opened the first Body Shop in Brighton, a little village on the south coast of England. Anita was inspired by her observations of different cultures' methods of skin and hair care and driven by the need to feed her two daughters while her husband, Gordon, fulfilled a boyhood dream to ride a horse from Buenos Aires to New York. In her first store, Anita offered some 25 natural body products.

In 1993, The Body Shop opened its one-thousandth store in Mexico City, Mexico and now operates in 45 countries. Of these 1000 stores, less than 10 percent were company owned—the rest were franchised. At that time, over 7,000 people worked for The Body Shop and its franchises around the world. The company offered approximately 420 products and 560 sundry items as well as customized customer care.

The Body Shop has not only been a successful natural body products company, but has also been an organization that under the Roddicks' guidance has attempted to make a difference in the lives of humans and animals and the protection of the environment. To this end, The Body Shop is against animal testing, actively attempts to minimize its impact on the environment, engages in fair trading relationships, and encourages education, awareness, and community involvement among its staff.

BUILDING BRAND EQUITY AT THE BODY SHOP

The Body Shop has sought to build brand equity through its product, packaging, distribution, promotion, price, and its philosophy of "profits with principles," as follows.

Product

The Body Shop offers customers over 400 naturally based body care products, over 550 sundry items, and customized care. The product line ranges from traditional lotions and creams, shampoos and conditioners to perfumes, shower gels, soaps, foot scrubs, face scrubs and masks, eye gels, massage oils, suntan products, baby care products, men's after-shave, shaving cream and cologne, and women's cosmetics. Products are based on natural ingredients, particularly fruits, vegetables, flowers, and herbs. The products are colorful, fragrant, and high quality. The Body Shop also carries a diverse selection of sundry items, some of them body-related such as face and back mitts, combs and brushes, nail scrubbers and clippers, pumice foot scrubbers, back massagers, cosmetic cases, and soap dishes and some other non-related items such as writing paper, candles, and bracelets. Every store has a perfume bar that can be used for scenting oils and lotions at no extra charge; a gift basket making service, fully trained staff, and regular in-store activities such as free makeovers and foot and hand massages.

Packaging

Since its early days, The Body Shop has tried to avoid packaging excesses for its products. In the beginning, Anita asked customers to bring bottles back for refilling because the company didn't have a large bottle inventory. Today, The Body Shop has made refilling and recycling of bottles an integral part of the company's overall environmental stewardship program. The bottles that were originally chosen for their simplicity and low cost are still the primary packaging form today. The simple green label with the Body Shop logo with the product name still identifies at least half the products. All products in the traditional bottles are offered in five sizes from very small testers (2 ounces) to large economy sizes (24 ounces).

In recent years, however, as products have proliferated and become more sophisticated, new packaging forms and new labels have been introduced. Mango Body Butter is an example of a product that sports entirely new packaging and labeling. It is contained in a yellow flat jar with a large yellow lid with the words mango body butter in large type. The Body Shop name and logo still appear but they are smaller and less significant part of the label.

In addition, The Body Shop has eight sub-brands, almost all of which are identified with new labeling and some very new package forms as well. While the packaging is more sophisticated and helps to identify the new products and the sub-brand product from the older, more original products, these labeling and packaging changes add new dimensions and complexities to the brand recognizability.

The eight sub-brands include:

1. *Trade Not Aid:* A variety of products including Brazil Nut Conditioner and Blue Corn Line of products that are sourced through direct trade initiatives.
2. *Mostly Men:* Shaving cream, an aftercare, an aftershave gel, a skin protector, a deep cleansing and an everyday bath and shower gel, a soap, a face scrub, and a face wash.
3. *Mama Toto:* A line for pregnant mothers and infants with a book, *The Rituals of Child Birth and Rearing,* baby lotion, baby shampoo, baby powder, nipple cream, and cooling leg gel.
4. *Endangered Species:* Glycerin soaps, sponges, and scrub brushes in the shape of endangered species animals.
5. *Aromatherapy:* Essential oils, a bath oil, a scalp oil, and a warming cream.
6. *Watermelon Sun:* Sun spray, sun lotion, sun block, aftersun, and self-tan.
7. *Colourings Cosmetics:* Blushes, powders, cover-ups, foundations, lipsticks, eye shadows, mascaras, and eye pencils.

Another important aspect of The Body Shop packaging is that one bottle of every product is designated by a large yellow sticker as a tester so that customers have a chance to compare the various lotions or smell the fragrant shampoos before buying.

Distribution

The Body Shop's main outlet for product distribution is its own retail stores. The Body Shop products are not sold through other channels. All over the world The Body Shop stores "look and feel" the same. The typical outside "look" is a dark green wooden facade with large floor-to-ceiling display windows accented with bright, colorful, catchy campaign or promotional posters. A recent poster campaign for Mother's Day included a large poster that read "Since God couldn't be everywhere, she made mothers." Above the entrance to every store "The Body Shop" is written in yellow letters. From every doorway also hangs a green sign with The Body Shop name and logo.

The look inside is also consistent across all stores: mainly dark green with green and chrome shelves, mirrors beside and behind the shelves, marble floors, more bright posters, more colorful promotional materials and, of course, products. Bottles, jars, pots, and tubes line the walls of the stores arranged by product categories. The products are essentially uniform throughout all the stores worldwide (some countries have slightly different lines depending on customer preferences), and they are an important aspect of the store's appearance. The stores always have a strong fragrant smell—it is hard to walk by a Body Shop without smelling it.

The Body Shop has also recently begun to distribute its product in the United States through a mail order catalog. Like the stores, the catalog is laid out according to product categories. Product photos in the catalog are bright and colorful like the products in the stores. Many of the products are shown to scale, so that customers can assess the relative size of the products they are buying. Many of the products are actually shown with lids off so that unfamiliar shoppers can actually see the product. This "show the product" feature tries to emulate the ever-present "tester" bottle in the stores. Through the catalog, customers can buy almost all the same products, including gift packs, that they could buy in the retail stores. Although the prices are the same in the catalog as in the stores, shipping and handling costs make buying from the catalog more expensive. However, the catalog provides customers with a service for sending friends and family members Body Shop products wherever they are. Catalogs can be purchased in the stores for $1.00 and they are periodically mailed directly to residences.

Promotion

Since the early days, The Body Shop attempted to avoid the "narrow images" of "flawless beauty" portrayed in traditional cosmetic advertising. The company philosophy is strongly against making unfulfillable promises about the results that Body Shop products will provide. Instead, The Body Shop is committed to promoting a wider vision of beauty that focuses on traditional methods of caring for the skin, hair, face, and body. Since 1973, The Body Shop has followed a strategy of avoiding direct advertising and relying heavily on in-store promotion, word-of-mouth, and public relations/third party reporting.

The in-store promotion is abundant. Bright, colorful posters announcing holidays, supporting AIDS protection, or promoting particular product lines are in all the display windows. On the counters and shelves are colorful brochures describing the No Animal Testing Policy, Trade Not Aid Policy, AIDS Protect and Respect Campaign, and the Endangered Species Campaign. Also displayed on counters are informational newspapers called broad sheets, which also are occasionally mailed directly to residences. Descriptive green tags sit on all the shelves below the products. These tags identify each product, its active ingredients and its uses or benefits.

Price

The Body Shop has tried to set a price for all its products that signals high quality without being exorbitant. The prices fall somewhat below comparable body products and cosmetics found at the counters in departments stores. The Body Shop offers five sizes for most products, which also helps to promote price points for various buyers.

The prices are approximately 10 percent less than the moderately priced cosmetic products such as Clinique and approximately 15 percent less than higher priced products such as Estee Lauder and Chanel. The Body Shop products comparably priced to a direct competitor like H20 and about 5 percent less than Estee Lauder's Origins. The Body Shop is significantly higher priced than department store copies like Nordstrom's Own Label natural products.

Profits with Principles

In addition to the traditional "4 P's" marketing mix, The Body Shop has a "Fifth P" in its marketing mix to build brand equity—its corporate philosophy of "Profits with Principles," also known as "Doing Good by Doing Well." The Body Shop carries out its philosophy in three main areas—environmental stewardship, fair trade, and community development and activism—as follows.

Environmental Stewardship

In 1987, The Body Shop established the Environmental Department and has introduced environmental management into every level of its operation. In 1993, The Body Shop released Green Book 2, the second comprehensive and independently verified internal Environmental Audit, which showed encouraging results. Moreover, the company is trying to become energy self-sufficient by building a wind-farm in Radnoshire, Wales to put back into the national grid what the Watersmead facility consumes.

Fair Trade

The Body Shop believes that all of its trading should incorporate the ethics of the company. Specifically, trading should help create livelihoods for economically stressed communities. Although direct sourcing from such communities is currently just a small percentage of the trade, The Body Shop intends to increase this practice wherever possible.

The Body Shop's drive toward direct trade is currently called "Trade Not Aid." Trade Not Aid creates mutually beneficial trading links between The Body Shop and indigenous people and other communities in need, such as the Kayapo Indians in Brazil or the Santa Ana Indians in New Mexico.

Community Development and Activism

In addition to fair trading relationships, The Body Shop also supports over 600 community development and social change activities throughout the world. Some of these include an Eastern European Relief Drive to create an orphanage for children in Albania and Romania, an aromatherapy massage project to comfort people with AIDS in the United States, a drive to provide support, housing, and jobs for the homeless in Canada. The Body Shop has run a national HIV/AIDS awareness campaign in the U.S. stores and held a voter registration drive for the presidential election in 1992. In November 1992, The Body Shop opened a store in Harlem, New York. After the initial start-up costs are recouped, 50 percent of the shop's profits will be donated to community organizations in Harlem. The remaining 50 percent will benefit a fund to establish similar stores around the country.

FUTURE CHALLENGES

The Body Shop has built brand equity despite the fact that the company for years did no traditional consumer advertising. The Body Shop has limited its communication efforts to its in-store presentation and promotion, public relations and publicity, and word of mouth. The decision not to advertise, however, has given The Body Shop fewer options for communicating its image and less control over the image that is communicated to the public than other companies. This has resulted in an equity that varies greatly depending on the nationality and experiences of the consumer.

Further complicating their brand equity challenge is the fact that The Body Shop is trying to communicate many complicated and information-based messages. Through the first fifteen years of the company's growth, The Body Shop, mostly through the press, effectively reached consumers because its messages were unique. They were the only naturally based, cruelty-free, personal care product company, and one of the only companies in any industry to emphasize environmental friendliness and social responsibility as a core part of doing business. With the current onslaught of new competitors, especially in the U.S. market, however, these communication vehicles are becoming less effective. The story is no longer "new" or "unique." The Body Shop must determine how best to remain relevant and competitive with consumers.

---

[a]This brief is based on published sources and a brand audit conducted as part of a Stanford business school class project by Janet Kraus, Kathy Apruzzese, Maria Nunez, and Karen Reaudin.

Chapter 11 considers the pros and cons of various branding strategies, including corporate and family branding strategies, and examines how different types of brand associations may potentially be linked to a new product by using an existing brand in some way to brand the new product.

Finally, it should be recognized that brands and companies are often unavoidably linked to the category and industry in which they compete, sometimes with adverse consequences. Some industries are characterized by fairly divided opinions, but consider the challenges faced by a brand in the oil and gas industry, which is generally viewed in a negative light. By virtue of membership in the category in which they compete, an oil company may expect to face a potentially suspicious or skeptical public *regardless* of what they do otherwise.

Country-of-Origin and Other Geographical Areas

Besides the company that makes the product, the country or geographical location from which it is seen as coming from may also become linked to the brand and generate secondary associations. Many countries have become known for expertise in certain product categories or for conveying a particular type of image. As noted by many, the world is becoming a "cultural bazaar" where consumers can pick and choose brands originating in different countries based on their beliefs about the quality of certain types of products from certain countries or the image that these brands or products communicate. Thus, a consumer may, from anywhere in the world, choose to wear Italian suits, exercise in American athletic shoes, listen to a Japanese compact disc player, drive a German car, or drink English beer. Choosing brands with strong national ties may reflect a deliberate decision to maximize product utility and communicate self-image based on what consumers believe about products from those countries.

Thus, a number of brands are able to create a strong point of difference in part because of consumers' identification of and beliefs about the country of origin. For example, consider the following strongly-linked brands and countries:

Levi's jeans—United States	Dewar's whiskey—Scotland
Nike athletic shoes—United States	Kikorian soy sauce—Japan
Coke soft drink—United States	Bertolli olive oil—Italy
Marlboro cigarettes—United States	Gucci shoes & purses—Italy
Chanel perfume—France	Mont Blanc pens—Switzerland
Foster's beer—Australia	BMW—Germany

Branding Brief 7–2 describes some of the difficulties Britain has had with its image and the implications for the products it sells.

Other geographical associations besides country-of-origin are possible, such as states, regions, and cities. Establishing a geographical or country-of-origin association can be done in different ways. The location can actually be embedded in the brand name (e.g., Idaho potatoes, Maine blueberries, California peaches, Irish Spring soap, or South African Airways) or combined with a brand name in some way (e.g., Bailey's Irish Cream). Alternatively, the location may become the dominant theme in brand

---

Keep a Stiff Upper Lip?: Britain's Imperially Flawed Image[a]

If Britain were a brand, how would it sell? A report by advertising agency BMP DDB Needham in London recently addressed that question in a study that ended up being a harsh indictment of Britain's image abroad. The author of the agency's report, Anneke Elwes, compared Britain's image to that of a gentlemen's club—"aging, elitist and a bastion of conservative and traditional values . . . Its values are stuffy and male . . . It is no longer aspirational or even relevant to a new generation whose interests and concerns are of today, not yesterday." Ms. Elwes acknowledged that the theme of British-style tradition had been exploited by many advertisers, but that by exclusively marketing its past, Britain was failing to associate itself with progress.

In compiling the report, the agency carried out extensive group discussions with British men and women, teenagers, and foreign nationals living in Britain, as well as conducting surveys through its international offices in Western and Eastern Europe, the United States, India, Asia, Australia, and New Zealand. Although the impressions varied by region, collectively they suggested that Britain has an image problem. Some of the specific regional impressions were as follows.

AUSTRALASIA

Among Asian respondents, Britain was characterized by masculine reserve and arrogance and was seen as a "has-been, irrelevant" nation. One Asian respondent wasn't impressed with the famed British civility. "Their politeness merely hides contempt," he remarked. It was viewed as coming up short on new ideas, entrepreneurial zeal, innovation, and business in general.

Consumers in Australia and New Zealand admired British institutions but saw the country as aggressive and war-mongering and unwilling to move with the times. For many, the country triggered images of the quaint picture of British country life, but that was quickly supplanted by more urban images of darkness, dirt, and overcrowding.

EUROPE

Western Europeans painted a kinder picture. Respondents acknowledged London as a great bustling city with a richer variety than anywhere else in the world. They had positive images of the English countryside and the respect for culture and tradition. And Britons, Western Europeans said, are good at comedy, literature, music, stylish sports cars, and caring for their homes and gardens. But it went downhill from there. One panelist remarked that Britons are "ugly people with bad taste." And that they're bad at food, dressing, industry, and "being European."

Among East Europeans in the survey, there seemed to be a respect for Britain's status as an island nation; the country was seen as strongly independent and self-confident. For them, Britain conjured up images of Rolls-Royce cars, the BBC, the British press, and universities.

AMERICANS

The report found that Americans had the most limited views of Britain. Croquet, tea time, Robin Hood, and James Bond were some of the more popular images. Most knowledge about Britain in America came from films such as "Howard's End," but the country was viewed as dull, conventional, and stuffy. Among panelists the adjectives that best described Britain were "proud, civilized, cultured, arrogant, and cold." Britons weren't "emotional, temperamental, aggressive, adventurous, or fun-loving" the panel concluded.

So what does all this mean for British advertisers? Ms. Elwes concluded that Britain needed to expand its "brand equity" beyond the values of tradition and stability.

> Britishness is a dated concept. Advertisers should play on more positive concepts such as the British love of individualism. For some, that image is conveyed through pink-haired punk rockers; for an Italian respondent, it is the fact that in Britain, your socks don't have to match your shirt. For a respondent from Thailand, it was that even the wealthy ride the bus and "no one minds." The paradox is that despite the reserve and inhibition of the British, there is still freedom to do your own thing *and* defy convention.

---

[a]Tara Parker-Pope, "Britain Suffers From Stuffy Image Abroad An Ad Agency Finds," *Wall Street Journal* (January 4, 1995), p. A8.

---

advertising (e.g., Foster's or Coors beer). Some countries have even created advertising campaigns to promote their own products. For example, Puerto Rico advertises the quality of their rums. Other countries have actually developed and advertised labels or seals for their products. Taiwan has developed its "Symbol of Excellence," which they award to certain qualifying manufacturers, that allows them to display a red label stating, "It's Very Well Made in Taiwan," on their products. They also give an award of even higher distinction—"The Gold Award of Excellence"—that is awarded based on a competition with an international panel of judges. Figure 7–1 displays the 1994 winners. Branding Brief 7–3 describes New Zealand's attempt to create a brand, "The New Zealand Way."

By virtue of the fact that it is typically a legal necessity that the country of origin appear visibly somewhere on the product or package, associations to the country of origin almost always have the potential to be created at the point of purchase and impact brand decisions there. The question really becomes one of relative emphasis and the role of country of origin or other geographical regions throughout the marketing program. Becoming strongly linked to a country of origin or specific geographical region is not without potential disadvantages. Events or actions associated with the country may color people's perceptions.

In an ad headlined, "Excellence, Made in Taiwan," the 1994 Gold Award of Excellence winners were described as follows.

1. *Kunnan* The world's first one-piece, metal composite driver offers unprecedented power and accuracy.
2. *Merida* Created the world's first bike with traditional styling and innovative mountain bike technology.
3. *Proton* Proton's newest TV/monitor handles every conventional signal out there now, and even those predicted for the future.
4. *Feeler* Innovative design enables the vertical machining center to dramatically improve the accuracy in parts for heavy industry.
5. *Philips* The Brilliance 1720 color monitor won the prestigious Deming award in Japan.
6. *Startek* The fingerprint verifier is the world's most advanced security system for both home and business.
7. *UMC* United Microelectronics Corp. introduced the world's first dual frequency chipset design.
8. *Giant* The Monex is the ultimate lightweight mountain bike, weighing only 9.8 Kg.

FIGURE 7-1 Taiwan's 1994 Gold Awards of Excellence

For example, strong connections to a country may pose problems if the firm desires to move production elsewhere. Consider the situation faced with Waterford Wedgwood PLC's famous, ornate crystal, which has been promoted as the ultimate in Irish handmade luxury for decades. Ads have called Waterford "the ambassador of a nation" and attributed its brilliance to "deep, prismatic cutting that must be done entirely by skilled hands rather than machines." Because of cost considerations, Waterford has had to confront the issue of shifting production out of Ireland and using machines to make some lines. As it turns out, Waterford has been encouraged to make such a move by the fact that consumer research in the United States—home to more than 70 percent of Waterford's crystal sales—indicates that what appears to matter to its customers there is the Waterford label and not where the crystal is made per se. Nevertheless, many retailers worried that such a move could destroy the very precious brand image that Waterford had built.

Finally, the favorability of a country-of-origin association must be considered both in a domestic and foreign perspective. In the domestic market, country-of-origin perceptions may stir consumers' patriotic notions or remind them of their past. As international trade grows, consumers may view certain brands as symbolically important of their own cultural heritage and identity. Patriotic appeals have been the basis of marketing strategies all over the world. Patriotic appeals, however, can lack uniqueness and even be overused. For example, during the Reagan administration in the mid-1980s, a number of different U.S. brands in a diverse range of product cate-

Selling Brands the New Zealand Way

In 1991, New Zealand set out to create "The New Zealand Way" (NZW) brand. The key objective of the New Zealand Brand Campaign was to build a strong national umbrella brand that added value to the marketing of New Zealand origin products and services by: (1) differentiating New Zealand branded products and services in international markets, (2) raising the awareness of New Zealand's unique values and personality, and (3) utilizing the promotional activities of the New Zealand Tourism Board, Tradenz (a government trade development board) and manufacturers to heighten the profile of branded New Zealand products and services. The NZW brand was to position a broad range of the country's tourism and trade products and services at the forefront of world markets.

The focal point for communicating the personality and meaning of the NZW brand was to be the brand design and the campaign that was to be built around it. The three components of the NZW brand design were: (1) the brand logo, (2) a descriptor word or short phrase (e.g., quality), and (3) the slogan, "The New Zealand Way." The descriptor words were to allow users of the NZW brand to customize it to suit their marketing program. Any words or short phrases could be licensed as descriptors as long as they were seen as compatible with the overall personality of the NZW brand, described below. The campaign to launch and support the NZW brand included a range of promotional techniques such as public relations, direct marketing, and events in key geographical markets.

The desired associations for the NZW brand to be created by the campaign were:

1. *Quality excellence* epitomized by the consistent delivery of products and services that meet and exceed the expectations of the customer.

2. *Environmental responsibility* reinforced by New Zealand's leadership in the efficient and sustainable use of environmental resources and delivery of fresh and natural products.

3. *Innovation* characterized by the unique personality of New Zealanders who seek out new solutions and that disregards the ingrained and inhibiting conventions of its trading partners.

4. *Contemporary values* reflected in the positioning of its products and services at the forefront of contemporary market trends and requirements.

5. *Honesty, integrity, and openness* personified in the business practices, lifestyles, and character of New Zealanders.

6. *Achievement* reflected in the endeavors and outstanding accomplishments of New Zealanders in business, sports, and the arts.

gories (e.g., cars, beer, clothing) used pro-American themes in their advertising, perhaps diluting the efforts of all as a result.

Channels of Distribution

Chapter 5 described how members of the channels of distribution can directly affect the equity of the brands they sell by the supporting actions that they take. It also was noted that retail stores can indirectly affect the brand equity of the products they sell by influencing the nature of associations that are inferred about these products on the basis of the associations linked to retail stores in the minds of consumers. In this section, we consider how retail stores can indirectly affect brand equity through this "image transfer" process.

Because of associations to product assortment, pricing and credit policy, quality of service, and so on, retailers have their own brand images in consumers' minds. Retailers create these associations through the products and brands they stock, the means by which they sell them, and so on. To more directly shape their image, many retailers aggressively advertise and promote directly to customers. Given that a store has some associations in the minds of consumers, these associations may be linked to the products they sell or affect existing brand associations for these products in some way. For example, a consumer may infer certain characteristics about a product on the basis of where it is sold, for example, "If it is sold by Nordstrom, it must be good quality." The same brand may be perceived differently depending on whether it is sold in a store seen as prestigious and exclusive or a store seen as for bargain shoppers and having more mass appeal.

The transfer of store image associations can be either positive or negative for a brand. For many high-end brands, a natural growth strategy is to expand their customer base by tapping new channels of distribution. Such strategies can be dangerous, however, depending on how existing customers and retailers react. When Levi-Strauss & Co. decided to expand the distribution channels for their Levi's jeans in the early 1980s beyond department and specialty shops to include mass market chains Sears and J. C. Penney's, R.H. Macy's decided to drop the brand because they felt its image had been cheapened.

OshKosh B'Gosh faced a similar dilemma in 1991 as it sought to increase sales of its trendy children's overalls, cotton separates, and dress clothes. Part of its strategy involved expanding its distribution from existing upscale department and specialty stores to also include Sears and J. C. Penney's stores.[3] As was the case with Levi's, some department stores reacted negatively. The main objection from these existing channels was that, because of competitive pressure from lower-priced chain stores, they were forced to reduce their prices on OshKosh items to remain competitive, cutting into their margins. To keep these customers happy, OshKosh decided to offer department stores some exclusive, higher-margin items. Although there was some decrease in volume from disgruntled department store buyers, OshKosh felt that this loss was more than made up by volume from the new mass market outlets. Because of its strong relationship with consumers and perceived commitment to quality, however, OshKosh believes that its brand image was not tarnished in the process.

Co-Branding

As noted above, a new product can become linked to an existing corporate or family brand that has its own set of associations through a brand extension strategy. An already introduced brand can also leverage associations by linking itself to other existing brands from the same or different company. *Co-branding*—also called brand bundling or brand alliances—occurs when two or more existing brands are combined into a joint product and/or marketed together in some fashion.[4] A special case of this strategy is ingredient branding, which will be discussed in the next section.[5]

Co-branding has been around for years, for example, Betty Crocker paired with Sunkist Growers in 1961 to successfully market a lemon chiffon cake mix.[6] As a means of building brand equity, interest in co-branding has increased in recent years. For example, Leaf Specialty's Heath toffee candy bar has not only been extended into several new products—for example, Heath Sensations (tiny bite-sized candies) and Heath Bits and Bits of Brickle (chocolate covered and plain toffee baking products)—but also has been licensed to a variety of vendors, such as Dairy Queen (with its Blizzard drink), Ben and Jerry's (with its ice cream products), Nestlé (with its ice cream bar), and Pillsbury (with its cake frosting).[7] Figure 7–2 displays some supermarket examples of co-branding. One of the more active co-branding areas has been with consumer charge and credit cards. Branding Brief 7–4 describes some of the history and new developments there.

The main advantage to co-branding is that a product may be more uniquely and convincingly positioned by virtue of the multiple brands involved. Co-branding can create more compelling points of difference and/or points of parity for the brand than might have been otherwise feasible. As a result, co-branding can generate greater sales from the existing target market as well as open additional opportunities with new consumers and channels. Co-branding can reduce the cost of product introduction because two well-known images are combined, accelerating potential adoption.

In poorly differentiated categories especially, co-branding may be an important means of creating a distinctive product. For example, when Kellogg's partnered with

---

Aunt Jemima oatmeal waffles with Quaker oatmeal
Beech-Nut baby foods with Chiquita bananas
Ben and Jerry's Heath Bar Crunch ice cream
Betty Crocker Supreme Bar Mix with Sunkist lemon
Betty Crocker brownie mix with Hershey chocolate syrup
Fat Free Cranberry Newtons with Ocean Spray cranberries
Kellogg's Pop-Tarts with Smuckers fruit filling
Pillsbury's Oreo Bars baking mix and frosting
Reese's Peanut Butter Puffs cereal
Nestlé's Cheerios cookie bars
M&M Cookie Bars baking mix

FIGURE 7–2 Co-Branding Examples

Co-Branding Bank Cards

For years, the credit card business was dominated by bank-issued Visa and MasterCard cards. More recently, banks have been combining their name with other brand names to offer "co-branded" cards. To issue a co-branded credit card, a card issuer joins up with a provider of goods or services to sponsor a card that provides users with some type of incentive to charge purchases on the card. From a company standpoint, it is a means to boost loyalty among its customer franchise. Different cards offer different value propositions. Hundreds of co-branded cards have now been introduced. Figure 7–3 displays some the largest issuers of Visa/MasterCard co-branded cards.

Issuer	Number Co-branded (millions)	Co-branded Partners
Citibank	12	Ford Motor, American Airlines, MCI, Apple Computer, Sharper Image
Household Bank	10	General Motors, Ameritech, Charles Schwab
Associates National	2	GTE, Unocal, Amoco, Diamond Shamrock, Western Union, Casual Corner
Chemical Bank	2	Shell Oil
Banc One	2	AAA, Dean Witter, Paine Webber, Compucard

FIGURE 7–3 Largest Issuers of Visa & MasterCard Co-branded Cards

Launching a new co-branded credit card in such a fiercely competitive market is difficult and requires careful product design and implementation. To illustrate, consider the 1993 launch of the Shell MasterCard from Chemical Bank—the first national co-branded bank card between the banking and oil industries. The card program was designed so that the average driver could, by using the Shell MasterCard, achieve a 10 percent reduction in annual gasoline costs. Specifically, the following plan was offered to consumers: The first $70 in rebates were awarded on the basis of a 2 percent rebate on general purchases and a 3 percent total rebate on Shell gasoline purchases; after earning $70 in rebates, cardholders continued to earn a 1 percent rebate on Shell gasoline purchases for the remainder of that anniversary year; no annual fee was charged for the first year, and charter members would not be charged an annual fee as long as they used their card for at least six purchases a year.

A fully integrated marketing communications program supported the launch of the Shell MasterCard. The initial offering included press releases, an extensive national television and print advertising, and 9 million direct mail solicitations, including 4 million current Shell Credit Card holders. Take-one applications, supported with point-of-sale merchandising, also were displayed at Shell's 8700 U.S. service stations. After only two months, the Shell Chemical

Bank MasterCard had surpassed the 1 million account mark, the second most successful card launch in history (the Household Bank–General Motors card was the fastest grower ever, achieving the 1 million account mark after only 28 days). Having observed Shell's success, other major oil companies such as Texaco, Amoco, and Mobil introduced their own co-branded credit cards.

ConAgra to introduce a new line of cereal under ConAgra's popular Healthy Choice brand name, Kellogg's conducted research to see how a co-branded line would fit its business. Kellogg's found that the Healthy Choice name would "cut through the clutter" in the cereal market, quickly establish a level of credibility in nutrition, and overcome a lot of the initial hurdles associated with a new cereal.[8]

The potential disadvantage of co-branding are the risks and lack of control from becoming aligned with another brand in the minds of consumers. Consumers' expectations about the level of involvement and commitment with co-brands is likely to be high. Unsatisfactory performance, thus, could have negative repercussions for the brands involved. If the other brand is one that has entered into a number of co-branding arrangements, there also may be a risk of overexposure that would dilute the transfer of any association.

GUIDELINES

To create a strong co-brand, it is important that both brands entering the agreement have adequate brand awareness and strong, favorable, and unique associations. Thus, a necessary but not sufficient condition for co-branding success is that the two brands separately have some brand equity. The most important requirement is that there is a logical fit between the two brands such that the combined brand or marketing activity maximizes the advantages of the individual brands while minimizing the disadvantages. For example, Fisher-Price and Compaq teamed up to introduce a set of jointly branded Wonder Tools software and computer accessories. Reflecting the complementarity of the strategy, ads stressed, "Nobody Knows Fun Like Fisher-Price, Nobody Knows Computers Like Compaq."

On the other hand, some eyebrows were raised when Daimler-Benz AG's Mercedes Benz unit agreed to manufacture a "Swatchmobile," named after SMH's colorful and fashionable lines of Swatch watches.[9] Personally championed by SMH's charismatic chairman, Nicolas Hayek, the car is to be designed to be small (less than 10 feet long) and low cost (under $10,000). The car is also supposed to combine the three most important features of Swatch watches—affordability, durability, and stylishness—with an important feature of a Mercedes Benz automobile—safety and security in a crash. A number of critics believe the Mercedes Benz image could suffer if the car is unsuccessful, a very possible outcome given the fact that many products bearing the Swatch name—for example, Swatch branded clothes, bags, telephones, pagers, and sunglasses—have already seen disappointing sales or been dropped altogether.

The need for complementary brand equity is reinforced by some academic research by Park, Jun, and Shocker. They compare co-brands to the notion of "conceptual combinations" in psychology. A conceptual combination (e.g., "apartment dog") consists of a modifying concept or "modifier" (e.g., apartment) and a modified concept or "header" (e.g., dog). In general, research in psychology has shown that the modified concept plays a more important role in a person's impression of the composite. Experimentally, Park and his colleagues explored the different ways that Godiva (associated with expensive, high-calorie boxed chocolates) and Slim-Fast (associated with inexpensive, low-calorie diet food) could introduce a chocolate cake mix separately or together through a co-brand. They found that the co-branded version of the product was better accepted than if either brand attempted to extend individually into the cake mix category. They also found that consumers' impressions of the co-branded concept were driven more by the header brand (e.g., Slim-Fast chocolate cake mix by Godiva was seen as lower-calorie than if the product was called Godiva chocolate cake mix by Slim-Fast; the reverse was true for associations of richness and luxury).[10] Relatedly, they also found that consumers' impressions of Slim-Fast after exposure to the co-branded concept were more likely to change when it was the header brand than when it was the modifier brand. Their findings show how carefully selected brands can be combined to overcome potential problems of negatively correlated attributes (e.g., rich taste and low calories).

Besides these strategic considerations, co-branding ventures must be entered into and executed carefully. There must be detailed plans to legalize contracts, make financial arrangements, and coordinate marketing programs. As one executive at Nabisco put it, "Giving away your brand is a lot like giving away your child—you want to make sure everything is perfect." The financial arrangement between brands may vary, although one common approach involves a licensing fee and royalty from the brand more involved in the production process.

Ingredient Branding

A special case of co-branding is *ingredient branding*, which involves creating brand equity for materials, components, and parts that are necessarily contained within other branded products. Some well-known ingredient brands include Dolby noise reduction, Goretex water-resistant fibers, Teflon nonstick coatings, Stainmaster stain-resistant fibers, and Scotchgard fabrics. Ingredient brands attempt to create sufficient awareness and preference for their product such that consumers will not buy a "host" product that does not contain the ingredient.

From a consumer behavior perspective, branded ingredients are often seen as a signal of quality. In a fascinating study, Carpenter, Glazier, and Nakamoto found that the inclusion of a branded attribute (e.g., "Alpine Class" fill for a down jacket) significantly impacted consumer choices *even when consumers were explicitly told that the attribute was not relevant to their choice.* Clearly, consumers inferred certain quality characteristics as a result of the branded ingredient.[11] The uniformity and predictability of ingredient brands can reduce risk and reassure consumers. As a result, ingredient brands can become industry standards to consumers such that they would not buy a product that did not contain the ingredient. Consumers do not necessarily have to know exactly how the ingredient works—just that it adds value.

Ingredient branding has become more prevalent as mature brands seek cost-effective means to differentiate themselves on one hand, and potential ingredient products seek means to expand their sales opportunities on the other hand. The pervasiveness of ingredient branding is compellingly demonstrated by Claremont's Peter Farquhar, who cites a catalog description for L.L. Bean's winter sports gloves that boast of a:

> . . . breathable Gore-Tex waterproof liner. Fully insulated with Hollofil II. Back of glove is layered with Thinsulate for added warmth . . . Outer shell is Antron nylon with adjustable Velcro closures . . . $45.00

Thus, as in this example, one product may contain a number of different branded ingredients.

The advantages and disadvantages of ingredient branding are similar to those of co-branding.[12] From the perspective of the firm making and supplying the ingredient, the benefit of branding its products as ingredients is that by creating consumer "pull," greater sales can be generated at a higher margin than would have otherwise occurred. Additionally, there may be more stable and broader customer demand and better longer-term supplier–buyer relationships. Enhanced revenues may accrue from having two revenue streams—the direct revenue from the cost of the supplied ingredients, as well as the possible extra revenue from the royalty rights paid to display the ingredient brand.

The manufacturer of the host product, for its part, can leverage the equity from the ingredient brand to enhance its own brand equity. For example, Delicious Cookie Co. has leveraged some better known and liked brands such as Land o' Lakes butter, Skippy peanut butter, Chiquita bananas, Musselman's applesauce, and Heath toffee candy bars to establish brand equity for its own cookies. On the demand side, the host product brands may achieve access to new product categories, different market segments, and more distribution channels than they otherwise could have expected. On the supply side, the host product brands may be able to share some production and development costs with the ingredient supplier.

Ingredient branding is not without its risks and costs. The costs of a supporting marketing communication program can be high—advertising to sales ratios for consumer products often surpass 5 percent—and many suppliers are relatively inexperienced in designing mass media communications that may have to contend with inattentive consumers and non-cooperative middlemen. As with co-branding, there is a loss of control as marketing programs for the supplier and manufacturer may have different objectives and thus may send different signals to consumers. Some manufacturers may be reluctant to become supplier dependent or may not believe that the branded ingredient adds value, resulting in a loss of possible accounts. Manufacturers may resent any consumer confusion as to what is the "real brand" if the branded ingredient gains too much equity. Finally, the sustainability of the competitive advantage may be somewhat uncertain as brands who follow may benefit from the increased understanding of the role of the ingredient by consumers. As a result, follower brands may not have to communicate the importance of the ingredient as much as why their ingredient is better than the pioneer or other brands.

GUIDELINES

Ingredient branding programs build brand equity in some of the same ways that conventional branding programs do. For example, Monsanto launched an intensive marketing program to create awareness of and an image for its patented aspartame artificial sweetener, NutraSweet, as a sugar substitute for foods and beverages. The NutraSweet brand consists of a name to communicate two key associations to consumers—"nutritious" and "sweet"—as well as a symbol of a red swirl. An extensive advertising campaign was launched to communicate the natural benefits of NutraSweet and establish a key point of parity (see Figure 7–4 for an example of a print ad). Another important aspect of the branding program was the stipulation that all products containing NutraSweet were required to bear the brand name and symbol. Although NutraSweet's patent expired in December 1992, much equity had been created with consumers before that time. The success of the branding program is evident in research by a potential competitor, Alberto-Culver, that revealed that about 95 percent of sweetener users knew what NutraSweet was, whereas only 10 percent were familiar with the generic term "aspartame."

What are the success requirements for ingredient branding? Branding Brief 7–5 describes ingredient branding efforts at DuPont, who has successfully introduced a number of such brands. In general, consumers must first perceive that the ingredient matters to the performance and success of the end product. Ideally, this intrinsic value would be easily visible or experienced. Second, the ingredient must have an innovation or some other substantial advantage over existing alternatives. Third, a coordinated "push" and "pull" program must be put into place such that consumers understand the importance and advantages of the branded ingredient. Often this will involve consumer advertising and promotions and—sometimes in collaboration with manufacturers—retail merchandising and promotion programs (recall DuPont's Stainmaster experiences from Branding Brief 5–2). As part of the "push" strategy, some communication efforts may also need to be devoted to gaining cooperation and support of manufacturers or other channel members. Fourth, a distinctive symbol or logo must be designed to clearly signal to consumers that the host product contains the ingredient. Ideally, the symbol or logo would function essentially as a "seal" and would be simple and versatile—such that it could appear virtually everywhere and credibly communicate quality and confidence to consumers.

Licensing

Licensing involves contractual arrangements whereby firms can use the names, logos, characters, and other facets of other brands to market their own brands for some fixed fee. Essentially, a firm is "renting" another brand to contribute to the brand equity of their own product. Because it can be a short-cut means of building brand equity, licensing has gained in popularity—retail sales of licensed products jumped from $4 billion in 1977 to $70 billion in 1994.[13]

Entertainment licensing has also become big business in recent years. Successful licensers include movie titles and logos (e.g., "Star Wars," "Jurassic Park," and "The Lion King"), comic strip characters (e.g., Garfield and Peanuts characters), television

Your body doesn't know NutraSweet from beans.

Or peas. Or grapes. Or milk. Or chicken, for that matter.

Because NutraSweet brand sweetener is made of two building blocks of protein, like those that make up things we eat every day.

And that means your body digests NutraSweet the same way it does fruits, vegetables, dairy products, and meats. So even though NutraSweet doesn't come from nature, as far as your body's concerned, it might as well have.

No wonder people go out of their way to find NutraSweet in their favorite products.

After all, with a sweetening ingredient that tastes just like sugar—and your body treats like a bean—who could possibly resist?

© 1988 The NutraSweet Co.

FIGURE 7–4 Sample NutraSweet Ad

Ingredient Branding the DuPont Way

Perhaps one of the most successful ingredient brand marketers is DuPont, which has successfully branded ingredients such as Teflon, Dacron, Kevlar, Lycra, Comforel, and Stainmaster. Early on, DuPont learned an important branding lesson the hard way. By not protecting the name of their first organic chemical fiber, nylon, it was not trademarkable and became generic. In total, DuPont now sells over 30,000 products across 1500 different product lines. DuPont has roughly 2000 different brands and 15,000 brand registrations to support those products. A key question that DuPont constantly confronts is whether to brand a product as an "ingredient brand." To address this question, DuPont typically applies several criteria, both quantitative and qualitative in nature.

For example, on the quantitative side, DuPont has a model which estimates the return on investment of promoting a product as an ingredient brand. Inputs to the model include brand resource allocations such as advertising, trade support, etc. while outputs relate to favorability ratings and potential sales. The goal of the model is to determine whether branding an ingredient can be financially justified, especially in industrial markets. On the qualitative side, DuPont assesses how an ingredient brand can help a product's positioning. If competitive and consumer analyses reveal that conveying certain associations would boost sales, DuPont is more likely to brand the ingredient. For example, one reason that DuPont launched their stain-resistant carpet under the ingredient brand Stainmaster was that it sought to better communicate a "tough" association which they believed would be highly valued in this market.

DuPont maintains that an appropriate, effective ingredient branding strategy leads to a number of competitive advantages, such as higher price premiums (which DuPont finds often averages 20 percent), enhanced brand loyalty, and increased bargaining power with other members of the value chain. As described in Branding Brief 5–2, DuPont employs both push and pull strategies to create their ingredient brands. Consumer advertising creates consumer "pull" by generating interest in the brand and a willingness to specifically request it. Extensive trade support in the form of co-op advertising, training, and trade promotions creates "push" by fostering a strong sense of loyalty to DuPont from other members of the value chain. This loyalty helps DuPont negotiate favorable terms from distributors and leads to increased cooperation when new products are introduced.

Because many of these ingredient brands are sub-branded under their corporate brand name, DuPont also supports their corporate brand through advertising and other means (see chapter 6). Their most recent corporate brand commercial—the "Originators" campaign—promoted new and existing products by focusing on the reflections of the actual DuPont scientists who invented them. The ads mixed black-and-white portraiture of the originators with colorful, cartoon-like "thoughts." For example, one ad described the creation of Kevlar and how it is used in a variety of ways, from skis and tennis rackets to bullet resistant vests. The ads end with DuPont's long-time slogan, "Better Things for Better Living."

One of DuPont's greatest success stories is probably Lycra, the super-elastic polymer invented in DuPont labs in 1959.[a] Generically known as "spandex," Lycra got its start as an ingredient for girdles. Lycra's use has expanded steadily since, from bathing suits in the 1970s to bicyclists' pants and aerobic outfits in the 1980s. More recently, nylon-Lycra bike shorts and exercise wear have become fashionable as every-day wear, especially with young adults.

In building the brand, DuPont has applied its well-known formula for success—one part product development and one part consumer marketing. Over the years, DuPont scientists have invented new versions of Lycra that have expanded the uses for this versatile fiber. Originally too bulky for lightweight items, finer versions of Lycra have since been developed that can be knitted or woven into delicate fabrics and lightweight items such as panty hose and dresses. Mastering new and often difficult-to-make versions have made Lycra synonymous with the freedom of movement that comes from spandex. As one sportswear maker puts it, "I wouldn't buy any spandex that wasn't from DuPont." To reach consumers, DuPont actively advertises the benefits of Lycra—proclaiming "Clothes that Move the Way You Do" in a print and TV advertising campaign that also includes the tag line, "Nothing Moves like Lycra." This global campaign targets both consumers and the trade. DuPont actively works with other fiber producers to educate consumers on the differences a little Lycra makes. It has also teamed up with industry trade group, Cotton Inc., to develop a "Made with Cotton and Lycra" logo for clothes handtags.

The success of these efforts can be seen by the results of a recent DuPont study where consumers said they would pay 20 percent more for a skirt made of wool plus Lycra than for an all-wool version. Despite losing its original patent years ago, DuPont has earned a worldwide leadership position in the spandex market with the Lycra brand.

---

[a]Monica Roman, "How DuPont Keeps 'Em Coming Back For More," *Business Week* (August 20, 1990), p. 68.

---

characters (e.g., Sesame Street, Mighty Morphin' Power Rangers, and the Simpsons), and cartoon characters (e.g., Warner Bros. Looney Tunes characters and the Flintstones). Some classic character properties include Cabbage Patch, Care Bears, and Strawberry Shortcake. Perhaps the champion of licensing is Walt Disney Co. Branding Brief 7–6 describes some of its licensing practices and strategies.

Licensing can be quite lucrative for the licensor. Licensing has long been an important business strategy with designer apparel and accessories. Designers such as Donna Karan, Calvin Klein, Pierre Cardin, and others command large royalties for the rights to use their names on a variety of merchandise such as clothing, belts, ties, luggage, and so on. Teenage Mutant Ninja Turtles products, first introduced in 1988, were licensed for better or worse to more than a hundred businesses and generated an

Licensing the Disney Way

The Walt Disney Company is routinely recognized as having one of the strongest brands in the world. Much of its success lies in its flourishing television, movie, theme park, and other entertainment ventures. These different vehicles have created a host of well-loved characters and a reputation for quality entertainment. Disney Consumer Products is designed to keep the Disney name and characters fresh in the consumers' minds through seven business areas in the following ways:

1. *Merchandise licensing:* Selectively authorizing the use of Disney characters on high quality merchandise
2. *Publishing:* Telling the Disney story in books, magazines, comics, and art
3. *Music and audio:* Playing favorite Disney songs and stories on tape and compact disc
4. *Computer software:* Programming Disney "fun" into home computers and computer game systems
5. *Educational production:* Casting the characters in award-winning films for schools and libraries
6. *The Disney Store:* Bringing the Disney magic to premium shopping centers in the United States and overseas
7. *Catalog marketing:* Offering Disney and Disney-quality products via top catalogs, managed by Disney's subsidiary, Childcraft Inc.

The pervasiveness of these product offerings is staggering—all in all, there are over 3 billion entertainment-based impressions of Mickey Mouse received by children in total every year, equivalent to 10 million impressions a day.

Disney believes that the fact that its characters have appeared on quality merchandise for years has added greatly to its popularity. The philosophy of Walt Disney, the founder of the company, was to present his characters in toys with real play value or in high quality merchandise that would then extend the fun of the filmed entertainment and enhance the company's reputation for excellence. The first handmade Mickey Mouse appeared in 1930. Disney Licensing is now responsible for some 3000 contracts for 16,000 products with top manufacturers worldwide, licensing their standard characters (i.e., Mickey, Minnie, Donald, Goofy, and Pluto) and filmed entertainment (i.e., theatrical releases such as "Aladdin," "Lion King," and "Pocohantas," and TV properties such as "Home Improvement").

To capitalize on the popularity of these characters, Disney has developed a family of brands for Disney-licensed products, each one featuring Mickey Mouse, Minnie Mouse, or some other classic Disney characters. Each brand was created for a special age group and distribution channel. Baby Mickey & Co., targeting infants, and Mickey & Co., targeting kids and adults, are sold at department and specialty gift stores. Disney Babies, targeting infants, Mickey's Stuff for Kids, targeting boys and girls, and Mickey Unlimited, targeting teens

and adults, are sold through mass market channels. The brand combined the names and characters into a specially designed logo. Each could be used in a wide range of product categories, including apparel and accessories, toys, home furnishings, social expressions/novelties, sporting goods, and gifts.

Artists in Licensing's Creative Resources department work closely with manufacturers on all aspects of product marketing, including design, prototyping, manufacturing, packaging, and advertising. At each step, care is taken to ensure that the products are faithful to the look and personality of the characters. To protect and enhance the value of its brands, Disney issues a thick notebook of standards of brand identities for Disney licensing that specifies color treatment of the logo; proper use of secondary graphic elements or "trade dress" (distinctive color schemes, shapes, images, background patterns or typography) in packaging, retail signage, or other communications; minimum unobstructed surrounding area; artwork reproduction procedures; use of the brand name outside the logo; and the Disney copyright notice. Disney maintains a team of employees who strictly interpret these guidelines, fiercely guarding the image of the characters.

---

estimated $1 billion in sales in 1991 for products bearing the turtle name, ranging from conventional souvenirs and T-shirts to more exotic alternatives such as vanilla-flavored pizza candy and even pork rinds! Everyone seems to get into the act with licensing. Sports licensing of clothing apparel and other products has grown considerably to a $11.1 billion business by 1992. Even the Rolling Stones released a line of 80 licensed goods (including T-shirts, ties, and even a credit card) sold at concerts during their Voodoo Lounge tour, via home shopping shows, on computer networks, and through a 16-page catalog.

GUIDELINES

One danger in licensing is that manufacturers can get caught up in licensing a brand that might be popular at the moment but is really only a "fad" and just produces short-lived sales. Because of multiple licensing arrangements, licensing entities easily can become overexposed and wear out quickly as a result. For example, after their high water mark in 1991, sales of licensed Teenage Mutant Ninja Turtles merchandise dropped to $100 million in 1993. Licensed merchandise sales of Barney products hit a $500 million jackpot in 1993 but faded significantly the following year before making a comeback in 1996. Sales of Izod Lacoste—with its familiar alligator crest—peaked at $450 million in 1982 but dwindled to an estimated $150 million in shirt sales in 1990 after the brand became overexposed and discount priced.[14]

Firms are taking a number of steps to protect themselves in their licensing agreements, especially those firms that have little brand equity of their own and rely on the image of their licensors.[15] For example, firms are obtaining licensing rights to a broad range of licensed entities—some of which are relatively more enduring in nature—to diversify their risk. Licensees are developing unique new products and sales and marketing approaches so that their sales are not just merely a function of the popularity of other brands. Some firms conduct marketing research to ensure the proper match of product and licensed entity or to provide more precise sales forecasts for effective inventory management.

Corporate trademark licensing—one of the fastest-growing segments of the licensing industry—is when company names, logos, or brands are licensed on various, often unrelated products.[16] For example, Harley-Davidson chose to license its name—synonymous with motorcycles and a certain lifestyle—to a polo shirt, gold ring, and even a wine cooler! Other seemingly narrowly focused brands such as Jeep, Caterpillar, Deere, and Louisville Slugger have also entered a broad portfolio of licensing arrangements. In licensing their corporate trademark, firms may have different motivations, including generating extra revenues and profits, protecting their trademarks, increasing their brand exposure, or enhancing their brand images. The profit appeal can be enticing as there are no inventory, no accounts receivables, no manufacturing expenses, and so on. In an average deal, a licensee pays a corporation a royalty of about 5 percent of the wholesale price of each product, although the actual percentage can vary from 2 percent to 10 percent. As noted in chapter 5, some firms now sell licensed merchandise through their own catalogs (see the Coca-Cola catalog in Figure 7–5). The risk, however, is that the product does not live up to the reputation established by the brand.

Celebrity Endorser

Using well-known and admired people to promote products has a long marketing history. Even former U.S. president Ronald Reagan has been a celebrity endorser in the past, pitching several different products—including cigarettes—during his acting days. The rationale is that a famous person can draw attention to a brand, as well as shape the perceptions of the brand by virtue of the inferences that consumers make based on the knowledge that they have about the famous person. Consequently, in choosing a celebrity endorser, it is important that the celebrity is well-known enough so that both awareness of and image for the brand may be improved. In particular, a celebrity endorser should have a high level of visibility and a rich set of potentially useful associations.[17] Ideally, a celebrity endorser would be seen as credible in terms of expertise, trustworthiness, and/or likability or attractiveness as well as having specific associations with potential product relevance of some kind. Each year, research company Video Storyboard Test rates the effectiveness and popularity of entertainers who appear in commercials based on a consumer survey. The results for 1996 appear in Figure 7–6.

A number of different brands have created strong associations to celebrities that have served as sources of brand equity. For example, actress Candice Bergen has appeared in almost 100 commercials for Sprint since 1990 and has helped to give the brand more of a smart, feisty, and irreverent image. Prior to that, actor Cliff Robertson was a credible and believable spokesperson for AT&T for years. Founder and Chairman Dave Thomas has been an effective pitchman for his Wendy's restaurant chain because of his down-home, unpretentious style and strong product focus. Similarly, Lee Iacocca was seen as a feisty, patriotic symbol for Chrysler automobiles while he was chairman there. Finally, perhaps the brand that benefited the most from asso-

FIGURE 7–5 Excerpt from Coca-Cola Catalog

NEW!

Stars, stripes and "Coca-Cola" forever.
F. Celebrate America's birthday with "Coca-Cola" Fourth of July pins. The three pins are semicloisonné with gold plating and military clutch backings. Only 1,000 of each have been produced. They measure from 1¼" to 1½" high.
#4033 Set of 3
Fourth of July Pins $15

New pins for a new year.
G. Set of three 1997 holiday pins pay tribute to Valentine's Day, Mother's Day and St. Patrick's Day. All are semicloisonné with gold plating and military clutch backings. Only 1,000 of each have been produced. Measure approximately 1¼" across.
#1794 Set of 3
1997 Holiday Pins $15

"Ice-cold" fun.
E. This heirloom-quality collectible depicts the frisky "Coca-Cola" Polar Bear cubs enjoying a winter's day. The delightful scene is captured beneath a sparkling clear dome resting on a "Coca-Cola" bottle crown. Production has been limited to 95 casting days and each piece is hand-numbered. Measures 5½"H.
#1788 Polar Bear Bell Jar $45

Discover the rich history of The Coca-Cola Company.
K. This deluxe book with text by Ann Hoy celebrates the Company's first hundred years in lush full-color detail. Interesting facts and photographs tell the story of the "birth" of "Coke," show the many nostalgic advertising campaigns and more. 11" x 14", hardbound; 159 pages.
#1450 Coca-Cola: The First Hundred Years Book $59

Remember 1996.
H. Commemorate the 1996 holiday season with this set of three colorful semicloisonné pins. Each pin measures 1¼" and has beautiful gold detailing.
#7284 Holiday Pins - Set of 3 $12

Soon to be history!
J. Wool cap in green and red is from a limited edition of 2,500. Individually numbered on the side in embroidery.
#4159 Holiday Limited Edition Cap $34

FIGURE 7–5 Excerpt from Coca-Cola Catalog (*continued*)

Top Entertainment Endorsers			
Ranking			
'96	*'95*	*Name*	*Endorsements*
1	1	Candice Bergen	Sprint
2	*	Whoopi Goldberg	MCI
3	2	Bill Cosby	Jell-O
4	7	Jerry Seinfeld	American Express
5	5	Cindy Crawford	Revlon, Pepsi
6	3	Elizabeth Taylor	Black Pearls perfume
7	10	Kate Jackson	Lincoln-Mercury
8	*	Rosie O'Donnell	Kmart
9	*	Jonathan Pryce	Infiniti
10	9	Cybill Shepherd	L'Oreal

*Not ranked

FIGURE 7-6 Top TV Endorsers Ranked by Consumer Appeal

ciations with celebrities is Miller Lite, which used famous retired athletes in amusing ads to communicate product credibility ("good taste") and likability. Branding Brief 7–7 describes some sponsorship issues on the PGA golf tour.

POTENTIAL PROBLEMS

There are a number of potential problems with linking a celebrity endorser to a brand. First, celebrity endorsers can be overused by endorsing too many products such that they lack any specific product meaning or are just seen as overly opportunistic or insincere. Over the years, comedian Bill Cosby has pitched for Jell-O, E.F. Hutton, Ford Motor Co., Coca-Cola, Texas Instruments, and Kodak, among others. It could be argued that Michael Jordan, as talented a basketball player and as likable a person as he might be, may lose effectiveness as an endorser when he is associated with so many brands and products. In 1996, he earned an estimated $40 million in endorsements while starring in ads for Gatorade sports drink, Hanes underwear, McDonald's restaurants, Nike athletic shoes, Rayovac batteries, Wheaties cereal, and WorldCom long distance telecommunications. He even supported his own brand in the form of the introduction of Michael Jordan men's cologne.

Second, there must be a reasonable match between the celebrity and the product. Many past endorsements would seem to fail this test. A classic mismatch occurred when the CEO of Bristol-Meyers insisted on using his favorite Western actor, rugged John Wayne, as the spokesperson for Datril pain reliever! Tennis star John McEnroe was the spokesperson for Bic disposable razors despite his ubiquitous two-day stubble on the tennis court. George C. Scott, an Oscar winner for his patriotic movie portrayal of Patton, would have seemed to have been a curious choice to endorse the French Renault car. Some potentially better matches in recent years might include singer Tina Turner for Hanes Resilience panty hose, actor Paul Hogan of "Crocodile

Hitting the Sponsorship Sweet Spot on the PGA Tour[a]

One good example of leveraging secondary associations is with sports marketing. Marketers selling sports-related products often line up professional athletes, coaches, or teams as endorsers to lend credibility to their products. Perhaps the best example of the power of these secondary associations is with golf equipment and clothing. Believers in the pyramid of influence, many golf manufacturers believe that the clothing, shoes, equipment, and other merchandise adopted by top professional golfers "trickle down" and are important considerations in the choices made by recreational golfers. In other words, the hope is that endorsements by top professionals increase the likelihood that recreational golfers will believe "if you use this equipment, you can play like the pros."

Player endorsements of golf clubs and balls have long been a part of golf. The very first pro endorsement came about when Harry Vardon, after winning his second British Open victory, signed with Spalding in 1898 to play a guttapercha ball. In the 1920s, Wilson established an advisory staff of top pros, including Gene Sarazan, Sam Snead, and Patty Berg. Not to be outdone, MacGregor, formerly a dominant force in the market, signed Byron Nelson and Ben Hogan in 1939 and Jack Nicklaus in 1961 to expensive contracts. Amana became the first non-golf company to achieve a major tour presence when it began to pay players a small fee for wearing its hats and visors with Munsingwear apparel quickly following. Starting in the mid-1980s, players' hats became used to display logos for all types of brand—banks, investment firms, watches, and so on.

In the 1990s, millions of dollars are spent ensuring that top players use and publicize various golf brands. These endorsements are often backed by expensive ad campaigns spotlighting the players and their endorsements. Although players endorse all types of products, including clothing, shoes, cars, sunglasses, airlines, electronics, training aids, and so on, perhaps the golf clubs themselves are the most lucrative and involving endorsements. Compensation can even include royalties from clubs sold, stock options (e.g., Chi Chi Rodriguez reportedly made $10 million on stock options with Callaway Golf) and even company ownership (e.g., Greg Norman is said to have made almost $40 million on an investment in Cobra Golf). Male golfers on the PGA TOUR, on average, expect to double their tournament earnings from off-the-course activities and endorsements. Golf club contracts range from $100,000 a year at entry level to $250,000 a year for the average player to $1 million or more for the very top players, although these numbers have been changing.

Increasingly, golf club makers require that their professional endorsers use the exact same type of clubs that can be bought by the recreational player (e.g., perimeter-weighted, cast, stainless steel irons), although often with adverse consequences for the players. Used to the classic forged-steel "player's blade," some top pros such as Payne Stewart and Lee Janzen found their games suffered when they switched clubs to satisfy endorsement contracts. The golf

club makers, who spend 5 to 10 percent of their marketing budget on tour players and promotion products, justify such stipulations by the effects that they believe that player endorsements have on consumers. As the head of one golf
equipment company maintains, "We know it works; we don't need marketing
research to tell us that."

---

[a]Peter McCleery, "The Endorsement Game," *Golf Digest* (December 1994), pp. 80–85, 148–149.

Dundee" fame for Subaru's line of Outback sports utility vehicles, and long-time tennis star Jimmy Connors for Nuprin pain reliever.

Third, celebrity endorsers can get in trouble or lose popularity, diminishing their
marketing value to the brand. The Beef Council's advertising strategy of employing
celebrity actors and actresses as spokespeople in the mid-1980s back-fired when actress Cybill Shepard admitted in a magazine article that she did not actually eat much
red beef and the other spokesperson, actor James Garner, underwent quintuple-
bypass heart surgery. Thus, linking the brand to a celebrity results in a certain lack of
control as a number of spokespeople over the years have run into legal difficulties,
personal problems, or controversy of some form that diminished their marketing
value (e.g., as was the case with boxer Mike Tyson, entertainers Michael Jackson and
Madonna, and others).

Fourth, many consumers feel that celebrities are only doing the endorsement for
the money and do not necessarily believe in or even use the endorsed brand. Even
worse, some consumers feel that the salaries for celebrities to appear in commercials
add a significant and unnecessary cost to the brand. In reality, celebrities often do not
come cheap and can demand literally millions of dollars to endorse a brand. Celebrities also can be difficult with which to work and may not willingly follow the marketing direction of the brand. Tennis player Andre Agassi tried Nike's patience when—
at the same time he was advertising for Nike—he appeared in commercials for the
Canon Rebel camera. In these ads, he looked into the camera and proclaimed,
"Image is Everything"—perhaps the antithesis of the "authentic athletic performance" positioning that is the foundation of the Nike brand equity!

Finally, as noted in chapter 6, celebrities may distract attention from the brand
in ads such that consumers notice the stars but have trouble remembering the advertised brand. For example, Susan Lucci appeared on Video Storyboards top 10 endorser list in 1993. Unfortunately only 15 percent of those surveyed knew she was promoting Fords—75 percent had no idea and, even worse, 10 percent thought she was
representing rivals Chevrolet or Plymouth. Similar confusion has prevailed in the soft
drink category where at one time, so many brands were using celebrities, consumers
virtually needed a scorecard to keep track!

GUIDELINES

To overcome these problems, celebrity spokespeople must be evaluated, selected, and
used strategically. First, it is important to choose a well-known and well-defined
celebrity whose associations are relevant to the brand and likely to be transferable. In

discussing Andre Agassi's role as a Nike endorser, Nike CEO Phil Knight made the following observation.[18]

> What's interesting about tennis is not hitting the ball back and forth across the net but the personalities. We've been pleased that we've always had interesting personalities endorsing our products. Andre certainly has a lot of flair and has created a lot of interest. It's surprising even to me how he's transcended the sport.

Thus, there must be a logical fit between the brand and person.[19] To reduce confusion or dilution, the celebrity ideally would not be linked to a number of other brands or overexposed. After winning Olympic gold in 1984, Mary Lou Retton appeared in commercials for so many brands (e.g., McDonald's restaurants, Vidal Sassoon shampoo, Wheaties cereal, Pony Sports shoes, Super Juice frozen juice bars, and Energizer batteries) that one marketing critic wearily complained, "I've seen more of her in the past year than I have of my mother—and I love my mother more!"[20] To broaden the appeal and reduce the risks of linking to one celebrity, some marketers have employed several celebrities. Second, the celebrity must be used in the advertising and communication program in a creative fashion that highlights the relevant associations and encourages their transfer. For example, comedian Jerry Seinfeld's popular commercials for American Express have used the same unflappable charm and knack for finding himself in unusual situations that he displays on his TV show. Finally, marketing research must be undertaken to help identify potential endorser candidates and facilitate the development of the proper marketing program, as well as track their effectiveness.

Sporting, Cultural, or Other Events

Chapter 6 described in detail the rationale for event marketing and sponsorship and provided guidelines as to how to choose the appropriate event, design the optimal sponsorship program, and measure the effects of sponsorship on brand equity. One benefit of event marketing noted there was that it was a means of creating or reinforcing consumer perceptions of key associations. Events have their own set of associations and may become linked to a sponsoring brand under certain conditions.

The main means by which an event can transfer any associations is probably on the basis of various dimensions of credibility. A brand may seem as more likable or perhaps even trustworthy or expert on the basis of becoming linked to an event. For example, event sponsorship has played an important role in building brand equity for Visa credit cards.[21] Back in 1985, Visa and MasterCard were seen as essentially identical products that faced stiff competition from other brands, particularly American Express, which had a strong and desirable image with consumers. Visa set out to create a differentiating and enduring perception of its brand as the best payment system for all types of purchases. Visa was positioned as the brand with superior acceptance by virtue of hard-hitting comparative ads with American Express. The "It's Everywhere You Want to Be" campaign featured interesting, unique, and prestigious locations where consumers might expect American Express to be accepted but where consumers were told to, "Bring Your Visa Card, Because They Don't Take American Express." In terms of event marketing, Visa aligned itself with high profile events—sporting events, concert tours, and so on—that similarly did not take American Express and backed up its sponsorships with additional comparative advertising campaigns.

Starting in 1988, the Olympics became Visa's biggest event association. Visa's Olympic involvement has helped to reinforce its desired positioning as a high quality, globally accepted product. Visa's Olympic support and sponsorship were reinforced in many ways. Ads for the 1992 Olympic games focused on how tough the competition would be at the games, ". . . but not as tough as the sellers at the ticket window if you don't have your Visa card." To support Olympic fundraising, cardholder transactions were tied to Visa donations to certain Olympic teams in several countries. Visa also provided direct financial support to certain Olympic teams. Visa's "Olympics of the Imagination" brought school children from all over the world to the Olympics as part of an art competition tied into the Olympics. Visa adopted similar activities for the 1996 Olympic Games in Atlanta.

The effects of these sponsorship and other communication efforts have been dramatic. Research has shown that Visa is now perceived as more widely accepted and, as a result, the card of choice for personal and family shopping, personal travel and entertainment, and even international travel, a former American Express stronghold.

In summary, sponsored events can contribute to brand equity by becoming associated with the brand and improving brand awareness, adding new associations, or improving the strength, favorability, and uniqueness of existing associations. The extent to which this transfer takes place will depend on which events are selected and how the sponsorship program is designed and integrated into the entire marketing program to build brand equity. Branding Brief 7–8 describes sponsorship strategies for the Olympics in broader terms.

Third-Party Sources

Finally, it should be noted that secondary associations can be created in a number of different ways by linking the brand to various third-party sources. For example, the Good Houskeeping seal has been seen as a mark of quality for decades. Endorsements from leading magazines (e.g., P.C. magazine), organizations (e.g., American Dental Association), and experts (e.g., film critics Gene Siskel and Roger Ebert) can obviously improve perceptions of and attitudes toward brands. J.D. Powers and Associates' well-publicized Customer Satisfaction Index helped to cultivate an image of quality for Japanese auto makers in the 1980s, with a corresponding adverse impact on the quality image of their U.S rivals. In the 1990s, they began to rank quality in other industries, such as airlines, credit cards, rental cars, and phone service, and top-rated brands in these categories began to feature their awards in ad campaigns.

Third-party sources may be seen as especially credible sources. As a result, they are often featured in advertising campaigns and selling efforts. For example, MCI chose to showcase the results of one such independent survey.

BRANDING BRIEF 7-8

Going for Corporate Gold at the Olympics[a]

Competition at the Olympics is not restricted to just the athletes. A number of corporate sponsors also vie to make their sponsorship dollars earn the highest return possible. For the 1996 Summer Olympic Games in Atlanta, 45 corporations paid a record $627.7 million dollars for the rights of sponsorship, totaling 40 percent of the anticipated revenue.

Corporate sponsorship of the Olympics exploded with the commercial success of the 1984 Summer Games in Los Angeles. Many international sponsors realized positive image-building and increased market share (e.g., Fuji). In Atlanta, top-tier worldwide corporate sponsors spent $40 million for the rights to display all Olympic logos and exclusive rights to the five-ring logo in their ads and on their packaging and to secure prime access to tickets, hotel rooms, athletes, cultural events, and the hospitality village (see Figure 7–7 for sponsoring brands). Centennial Olympic Games Partners had the same access as Worldwide Sponsors but could only use Atlanta Games and U.S. Team logos. Centennial Olympic Game Sponsors provided services to the Games and could negotiate event tickets and access to athletes.

WORLDWIDE SPONSORS

Bausch & Lomb	Time, Inc./Sports Illustrated
Coca-Cola	UPS
IBM	Visa
John Hancock	Xerox
Eastman Kodak	
Matshuita/Panasonic	

CENTENNIAL OLYMPIC GAMES PARTNERS

Anheuser-Busch	McDonald's
AT&T	Motorola
Delta Airlines	NationsBank
Home Depot	Sara Lee/Champion
IBM	SMH/Swatch

CENTENNIAL OLYMPIC GAMES SPONSORS

Avon	King World
BellSouth	Nissan
Blue Cross and Blue Shield	Randstad Staffing Services
BMW	Scientific-Atlanta
Borg-Warner Security	Sensormatic Electronics
General Motors	World Travel Partners
Holiday Inn	York International

FIGURE 7-7 1996 Olympic Summer Games Sponsorship Levels

In addition to the 40 "sponsors," there were an additional 75 "suppliers" and another 125 or so "licensees." Besides direct expenditures, firms spent hundreds of millions more on related marketing efforts. Coca-Cola's total Olympic-related expenditure reportedly topped $500 million and included funding for the Torch Relay and a mega-retail promotion, Coke's Red Hot Olympic Summer. AT&T was the official "presenter" of the 21–acre tent-filled commercial showcase, Centennial Olympic Park (which included Bud World and the Swatch Pavilion), and erected a giant communications center in the Olympic Village.

Olympic sponsorship is controversial in terms of its marketing impact. For example, despite the fact that Hilton was the official hotel of the 1992 Summer Games, only 8 percent of consumers were aware of the sponsorship just weeks after the Olympics ended. Even worse, 9 percent thought the sponsor was Holiday Inn. Similarly, Kellogg also was a 1992 sponsor but only 20 percent of consumers named Kellogg's Corn Flakes as a brand sponsor while 35 percent named Wheaties. In 1996, licensees fell short of their goal of a $1 billion in total sales.

In some cases, sponsorship confusion may be due to "ambush marketing." With ambush marketing, advertisers attempt to falsely give consumers the impression that they are Olympic sponsors by means such as: (1) running Olympic-themed ads that publicize other forms of sponsorship (sponsor of a national team, network telecast, etc.); (2) identifying the brand as an official supplier; or (3) using current or former Olympians as endorsers. For example, to retaliate against Visa's ads stressing its exclusive Olympic acceptability, American Express ran ads that focused on its card's presence in Olympic host cities. To improve the marketing effectiveness of sponsorship, the Olympic committee has vowed to fight ambush marketing as well as attempted to reduce the number of sponsors to avoid clutter. Spending $10 million on the Atlanta games, they forced Fuji to cover up 18 Atlanta area billboards featuring the USA Track & Field Federation seal and decathlete Dan O'Brien after the USOC ruled that the ads would undercut Fuji rival Eastman Kodak, which was an official sponsor.

Nevertheless, Olympic sponsorship remains highly controversial. Many corporate sponsors continue to believe that their Olympic sponsorship yields many significant benefits, creating an image of good will for their brands; serving as a platform to enhance awareness and communicate messages; and affording numerous opportunities to reward employees, entertain clients, and so on. Other criticize the event as horribly overcommercialized, citing the Atlanta summer games as an example. In any case, as suggested in chapter 6, it is clear that the success of Olympic sponsorship—like any sports sponsorship—depends in large part with how well the sponsorship is executed and incorporated into the entire marketing plan. And as might be expected, firms are already lining up to pay the $45 million top ticket for sponsorship of the 2000 Summer Olympic Games in Sydney.

---

[a]Bruce Horovitz, "Sponsors Warm Up a Year Before Games," *USA Today* (July 19, 1995), pp. 1B, 2B. Olympic Partnership, Special Advertising Section, *Sports Illustrated,* July 1996.

Review

This chapter considered the process by which other entities—the company that makes a product, where the product is made, where it is purchased, as well as related people, places, or things—can be leveraged to create secondary associations. The main premise is that by linking the brand to other entities with their own set of associations, consumers may expect that some of these same associations may also characterize the brand. Thus, independent of how a product is branded, the nature of the product itself and its supporting marketing program, brand equity can be created by "borrowing" it from other sources. Creating secondary associations in this fashion may be quite important if the corresponding brand associations are deficient in some way. Secondary associations may be especially valuable as a means to link favorable brand associations that can serve as points of parity or to create unique brand associations that can serve as points of difference in positioning a brand.

The chapter reviewed eight different ways to leverage secondary associations to build brand equity by linking the brand to: (1) the company making the product, (2) the country or some other geographical location in which the product originates, (3) retailers or other channel members who sell the product, (4) other brands, including ingredient brands, (5) licensed characters, (6) famous spokespeople or endorsers, (7) events, and (8) other third-party sources. In general, the extent to which any of these entities can be leveraged as a source of equity will depend on consumer awareness and knowledge of the entity and how easily the appropriate associations of the entity transfer to the brand. In general, global credibility or attitudinal dimensions may be more likely to transfer than specific attribute and benefit associations, although the latter can be transferred, too. Linking the brand to other entities, however, is not without risk. Some control is given up, and managing the transfer process so that only the relevant secondary associations become linked to the brand may be difficult.

Discussion Questions

1. The Boeing Company makes a number of different types of aircraft for the commercial airline industry, the 727, 747, 757, and most recently, 777 jet models. Boeing has roughly a two-thirds market share worldwide in its classes and competes with McDonnell Douglas, Airbus, and Fokker. Is there any way for Boeing to adopt an ingredient branding strategy with its jets? How? What would be the pros and cons?

2. After winning the Super Bowl, the star wide receiver of the San Francicso 49ers, Jerry Rice, complained bitterly about his lack of endorsement offers. Similarly, after every Olympics, a number of medal-winning athletes lament their lack of commercial recognition. From a branding perspective, how would you respond to the complaints of these athletes?

3. Pick a brand. Evaluate how it leverages secondary associations. Can you think of any ways that the brand could more effectively leverage secondary brand associations?

Notes

1. Wai-Kwan Li and Robert S. Wyer, Jr., "The Role of Country of Origin in Product Evaluations: Informational and Standard-of-Comparison Effects," *Journal of Consumer Psychology*, 3(2) (1994), pp. 187–212.

2. Suen L. Hwang, "Philip Morris Makes Dave's—but Sh! Don't Tell," *Wall Street Journal* (March 2, 1995), p. B-1.

3. Julia Flynn Siler, "OshKosh B'gosh May Be Risking Its Upscale Image," *Business Week* (July 15, 1991), p. 140.

4. Akshay R. Rao and Robert W. Ruekert, "Brand Alliances as Signals of Product Quality," *Sloan Management Review* (Fall 1994), pp. 87–97. Akshay R. Rao, Lu Qu, and Robert W. Ruekert, "Brand Alliances as Information about Unobservable Product Quality," working paper, University of Minnesota.

5. Robin L. Danziger, "Cross Branding with Branded Ingredients: the New Frontier," ARF Fourth Annual Advertising and Promotion Workshop, February 12–13.

6. Kim Cleland, "Multimarketer Melange an Increasingly Tasty Option on the Store Shelf," *Advertising Age* (May 2, 1994), p. S-10.

7. Teresa Gubbins, "Spinoffs Take Products All Over the Store," *Dallas Morning News* (June 15, 1994), p. 2F.

8. Betsy Spethmann and Karen Benezra, "Co-brand or Be Damned," *Brandweek* (November 21, 1994), pp. 21–24.

9. Kevin Helliker, "Can Wristwatch Whiz Switch Swatch Cachet to an Automobile," *Wall Street Journal* (March 4, 1994), p. A1; Audrey Choi and Margaret Studer, "Daimler-Benz's Mercedes Unit to Build A Car with Maker of Swatch Watches," *Wall Street Journal* (February 23, 1994), p. A-14.

10. C. Whan Park, Sung Youl Jun, and Allan D. Shocker, "Composite Branding Alliances: An Investigation of Extension and Feedback Effects," *Journal of Marketing Research* (November 1996), p. 453–467.

11. Gregory S. Carpenter, Rashi Glazer, and Kent Nakamoto, "Meaningful Brands from Meaningless Differentiation: The Dependence on Irrelevant Attributes," *Journal of Marketing Research* (August 1994), pp. 339–350.

12. Donald G. Norris, "Ingredient Branding: A Strategy Option with Multiple Beneficiaries," *Journal of Consumer Marketing*, 9 (3) (1992), pp. 19–31.

13. Philip Kotler, *Marketing Management: Analysis, Planning, Implementation, and Control*, 8th ed., Upper Saddle River, NJ: Prentice Hall, 1994.

14. Teri Agins, "Izod Lacoste Gets Restyled and Repriced," *Wall Street Journal* (July 22, 1991), p. B-1.

15. Udayan Gupta, "Licensees Learn What's In a Pop-Culture Name: Risk," *Wall Street Journal* (August 8, 1991), p. B-2.

16. Frank E. James, "I'll Wear the Coke Pants Tonight; They Go Well With My Harley-Davidson Ring," *Wall Street Journal* (June 6, 1985), p. 31.

17. Grant McCracken, "Who is the Celebrity Endorser? Cultural Foundations of the Endorsement Process," *Journal of Consumer Research*, 16 (December 1989), pp. 310–321.

18. Doug Smith, "Always the Showman; Now a Winner," *USA Today* (January 11, 1985), pp. 1C, 2C.

19. Shekra Misra and Sharon E. Beatty, "Celebrity Spokesperson and Brand Congruence," *Journal of Business Research*, 21 (1990), pp. 159–173.

20. Roderick Townley, "Is That Winning Smile Losing Its Charm?" *TV Guide* (June 28, 1986), pp. 41–42.

21. Janet Soderstrom, "Brand Equity. It's Everywhere You Want to Be," talk given at Branding Conference, San Francisco, California, October 26, 1995.

CHAPTER 8

Measuring Sources of Brand Equity

Preview

The previous five chapters of Part II described various strategies and approaches to build brand equity. In the next three chapters, which make up Part III, we take a detailed look at what consumers know about brands, what marketers want them to know, and how marketers can develop measurement procedures to assess how well they are doing. Understanding the current and desired brand knowledge structures of consumers is vital to effectively building and managing brand equity. As Gardner and Levy note in a classic marketing article:[1]

> The image of a product associated with the brand may be clear-cut or relatively vague; it may be varied or simple; it may be intense or innocuous. Sometimes the notions people have about a brand do not seem very sensible or relevant to those who know what the product is "really" like. But they all contribute to the customer's deciding whether or not the brand is "for me." These sets of ideas, feelings, and attitudes that consumers have about brands are crucial to them in picking and sticking to ones that seem most appropriate.

Ideally, marketers would be able to construct detailed "mental maps" of consumers to understand exactly what exists in their minds concerning brands—all their opinions, feelings, beliefs, and attitudes towards different brands. These mental blueprints would then provide managers strategic and tactical guidance to help them make brand decisions. Unfortunately, these brand knowledge structures—because they only reside in consumers' minds—are not so easily measured.

Nevertheless, effective brand management requires a thorough understanding of the consumer. Often a simple insight as to how consumers think of or use products and the particular brands in a category can result in profitable changes in the marketing program. As a result, many large companies conduct exhaustive research studies to learn as much as possible about consumers, and a number of detailed, sophisticated research techniques and methods have been developed to help marketers better understand consumer knowledge structures. Branding Brief 8–1 describes the lengths to which marketers have gone in the past to learn about consumers. Much has been written on these consumer behavior topics. In this chapter, only some of the important considerations that are critical to the measurement of brand equity are highlighted.[2] Figure 8–1 outlines some general considerations in understanding consumer behavior.

The customer-based brand equity model provides guidance as to how brand equity can be measured. Given that customer-based brand equity is defined as the differential effect that knowledge about the brand—in terms of brand awareness and strong, favorable, and unique brand associations—has on customer response to the marketing of that brand, there would seem to be two basic approaches to measuring brand equity. An indirect approach could assess potential sources of customer-based brand equity by identifying and tracking consumers' brand knowledge structures. A direct approach, on the other hand, could measure customer-based brand equity more directly by assessing the actual impact of brand knowledge on consumer response to different elements of the marketing program.

The two general approaches are complementary and both should be employed by marketers. In other words, for brand equity to provide a useful strategic function and guide marketing decisions, it is important for marketers to fully understand the sources of brand equity, how they affect outcomes of interest (e.g., sales), and how all of this information changes, if at all, over time. Chapter 3 provided a framework to conceptualize consumers' brand knowledge structures. This chapter uses this information to consider approaches to measure brand knowledge and the sources of brand equity. Chapter 9 reviews approaches to measure the outcomes of brand equity, and chapter 10 puts all of these ideas together to develop a brand equity measurement system.

Digging Beneath the Surface to Understand
Consumer Behavior

Most consumer research relies on surveys to obtain consumers' reported beliefs, attitudes, and behavior. Rather than talking to consumers, however, useful marketing insights sometimes emerge from unobtrusively observing consumer behavior. In many instances, consumer behavior that is observed differs from the behavior that consumers report in surveys.[a] For example, Hoover Co. become suspicious when people claimed in surveys that they vacuumed their houses for an hour a week. To check, they installed timers to certain models and exchanged them for the same models in consumers' homes. The timers showed that people actually spent only a little over *half* an hour vacuuming each week. People were exaggerating the amount that they did.

One University of Arizona professor, William Rathje, goes to the extreme of analyzing household trash to determine the types of foods and quantities of food that people consume. He found that people really don't have a very good idea of how much and what types of food they really eat and tend to overestimate. Similarly, much research has shown that people report that they eat healthier food than would appear to be the case if you opened their cabinets!

Toothpaste makers know a whole host of facts from observing consumers. For example, the favorite color for a toothbrush is blue; 37 percent of the U.S. population use a toothbrush over six months old; and 47 percent put water on the brush before applying the toothpaste; 15 percent put water on afterwards; and 24 percent do both; and 14 percent don't put water on at all. They have also learned a lot about consumer complaints concerning toothpaste: 21 percent of the U.S. population have some difficulty handling one of the tubes; 16 percent have trouble squeezing the last toothpaste out of the tube; 5 percent can't unscrew the toothpaste cap or lose it; and 7 percent have trouble with the tube breaking. As a consequence of this research, the "pump" packaging was introduced to facilitate product usage.

As another example, Kodak studied over 10,000 photos to see what kinds of mistakes amateur photographers make, leading to the successful introduction of the disk camera in 1982 to reduce the number of out-of-focus and underexposed shots. Finally, after conducting traditional focus groups for their Breyers ice cream account, researchers at Young and Rubicam ad agency decided to go the extra step and visit six consumers at home to observe their ice cream eating first hand.[b] They found that people's emotional response to ice cream was a very sensual, inner-directed experience.

This type of research has its roots in ethnography, an anthropological term for the study of cultures in their natural surroundings (although traditional ethnographic studies involve living with people for extended periods of time and not the relatively short period of time usually involved in marketing studies). The intent behind these in-depth, observational studies is for consumers to "drop their guard" and provide a more realistic portrayal of who they are rather than who they would like to be. On the basis of ethnographic research to uncover consumers' true feelings, ad campaigns have been created for a Swiss chocolate maker with the theme "The True Confessions of a Chocaholic" (because chocolate lovers often hid stashes all through the house); for Tampax Tampons with the theme "More Women Trust Their Bodies to Tampax" (because teen users wanted the freedom to wear body conscious clothes); and for Crisco shortening with the theme "Recipe for Success" (because people often baked pies and cookies in a celebratory fashion).

---

[a]John Koten, "You Aren't Paranoid If You Feel Someone Eyes You Constantly," *Wall Street Journal* (March 29, 1985), p. 1.

[b]Ronald Alsop, "People Watchers' Seek Clues to Consumers' True Behaviors," *Wall Street Journal* (September 4, 1986), p. B1.

In general, measuring sources of brand equity requires that the brand manager fully understand how customers shop for and use products and services and, most importantly what customers think of various brands. In particular, measuring sources of customer-based brand equity requires measuring various aspects of brand awareness and brand image that potentially can lead to the differential customer response that creates brand equity. To some extent, consumer reactions to a brand may be based on their "gestalt" knowledge. In other words, consumers may have a more holistic view of brands that is difficult to decompose into component parts. Yet, in many cases, consumers' perceptions of a brand can be isolated and assessed in greater detail. The remainder of this chapter describes both qualitative and quantitative approaches to identify potential sources of brand equity.

FIGURE 8-1 Understanding Consumer Behavior[a]

Who buys our product or service?
Who makes the decision to buy the product?
Who influences the decision to buy the product?
How is the purchase decision made? Who assumes what role?
What does the customer buy? What needs must be satisfied?
Why do customers buy a particular brand?
Where do they go or look to buy the product or service?
When do they buy? Any seasonality factors?
What are customers' attitudes toward our product?
What social factors might influence the purchase decision?
Do the customers' lifestyles influence their decisions?
How is our product perceived by customers?
How do demographic factors influence the purchase decision?

---

[a]Based on list from George Belch and Michael Belch, *Advertising and Communication Management*, 3rd ed. Homewood, IL: Irwin, 1995.

Qualitative Research Techniques

As chapter 3 noted, there are a number of different types of associations that can become linked to the brand. For example, consider the possible attribute and benefit beliefs that might exist for Levi's 501 brand of jeans:

Product-related attributes:	Blue denim, shrink-to-fit cotton fabric, button-fly, two horse patch, and small red pocket tag
User imagery:	Western, American, blue collar, hard working, traditional, strong, rugged, and masculine
Usage imagery:	Appropriate for outdoor work and casual social situations
Brand personality:	Honest, classic, contemporary, approachable, independent, and universal
Functional benefits:	High quality, long-lasting, and durable
Experiential benefits:	Comfortable fitting and relaxing to wear
Symbolic benefits:	Feelings of self-confidence and self-assurance

There are also many different ways to uncover the types of associations linked to the brand and their corresponding strength, favorability, and uniqueness. Qualitative research techniques are often employed to identify possible brand associations and sources of brand equity. *Qualitative research techniques* are relatively unstructured measurement approaches whereby a range of possible consumer responses are permitted. Because of the freedom afforded both researchers in their probes and consumers in their responses, qualitative research can often be a useful "first step" in exploring consumer brand and product perceptions.

Qualitative research has a long history in marketing. Ernest Dichter, one of the early pioneers in consumer psychoanalytic research, first applied these research principles in a study for Plymouth automobiles in the 1930s.[3] His research revealed the important—but previously overlooked—role that women played in the automobile purchase decision. Based on his consumer analysis, a new print ad strategy was employed for Plymouth that highlighted a young couple gazing admiringly at a Plymouth automobile under the headline, "Imagine Us In A Car Like That." His subsequent work had an important impact on a number of different ad campaigns.[4] Some of Dichter's assertions were fairly controversial. Based on his research, Dichter argued that women used Ivory soap to wash away their sins before a date. He also equated convertibles with mistresses and suggested "Putting the Tiger in the Tank" for Exxon.

We next review a number of qualitative research techniques that can be employed to identify sources of brand equity.

FREE ASSOCIATION

The simplest and often most powerful way to profile brand associations involves free association tasks whereby consumers are asked what comes to mind when they think of the brand without any more specific probe or cue than perhaps the associated product category (e.g., "What does the Rolex name mean to you?" or "Tell me what comes to mind when you think of Rolex watches."). The primary purpose of free association tasks is to identify the range of possible brand associations in consumers' minds, but they may also provide some rough indication of the relative strength, favorability, and uniqueness of brand associations, too, as follows.[5]

Coding free association responses in terms of the order of elicitation—early or late in the sequence—can yield at least a rough measure of strength.[6] For example, if many consumers mention "fast and convenient" as one of their first associations when given "McDonald's restaurants" as a probe, then it is likely that the association is a relatively strong one and likely to impact consumer decisions. Associations later in the list, on the other hand, may be weaker and thus more likely to be overlooked during consumer decision making. Comparing associations to those elicited for competitive brands also can provide some indication of their relative uniqueness. Finally, even favorability, to some extent, may be discerned on the basis of how associations are stated and phrased.

Answers to these questions help marketers to clarify the range of possible associations and assemble a brand profile.[7] To better understand the favorability of associations, consumers can be asked followup questions as to the favorability of associations they listed or, more generally, what they like best about the brand. Similarly, consumers can also be asked direct followup questions as to the uniqueness of associations they listed or, more generally, what they find unique about the brand. Thus, additionally useful questions include:

- What do you like best about the brand? What are its positive aspects? What do you dislike? What are its disadvantages?
- What do you find unique about the brand? How is it different from other brands? In what ways is it the same?

These simple, direct measures can be extremely valuable at determining core aspects of a brand image. To provide more structure and guidance, consumers can be asked further followup questions to describe what the brand means to them in terms of "who, what, when, where, why, and how" type of questions such as:

- Who uses the brand? What kind of person?
- When and where do they use the brand? What types of situations?
- Why do people use the brand? What do they get out of using it?
- How do they use the brand? What do they use it for?

Guidelines

The two main issues to consider in conducting free association tasks are how to set up the questions in terms of the types of probes to give to subjects, and how to code and interpret the resulting data. First, with regards to question structure, in order not to bias results, it is best to move from more general considerations to more specific considerations, as illustrated above. Thus, consumers can be asked first what they think of the brand as a whole without reference to any one particular category, followed by specific questions as to particular products and aspects of the brand image. As with many qualitative research techniques, consumers' responses with open-ended probes can be made either orally or written. The advantage of oral responses is that subjects may be less deliberate and more spontaneous in their reporting.

Second, in terms of coding the data, the protocols provided by each consumer can be divided up into phrases and aggregated across consumers in categories. Figure 8–2 provides some examples of possible free associations for some popular brands.

Because of their more focused nature, responses to specific probes and followup questions are naturally easier to code.

PROJECTIVE TECHNIQUES

Uncovering the sources of brand equity requires that consumers' brand knowledge structures be profiled as accurately and completely as possible. Unfortunately, under certain situations, consumers may feel that it would be socially unacceptable or undesirable to express their true feelings—especially to an interviewer that they don't even know! As a result, they may find it easier to fall back on stereotypical, "pat" answers

FIGURE 8-2 Sample Free Associations[a]

AT&T

Long Distance Calls
Old/Conservative/Long-time/Traditional
True Voice & World Savings
High Quality
Baby Bells
Stable/Dependable/Trustworthy
Helpful/Friendly/Caring
Big/Global/Powerful
Technically Advanced/Hi-Tech

BMW

German Auto
High Quality
High Performance
Expensive
Upscale/High Class/Classy/Prestigious
Yuppie
Ultimate Driving Machine
Sporty/Fast

BUDWEISER

Beer
King of Beers
Clydesdale Horses
Blue Collar
Inexpensive
Watery
American

BURGER KING

Fast Food
Whopper
Flame Broiled
Have It Your Way
Fatty/Greasy/Sloppy Burgers

CAMPBELL'S

Canned Soup
Nutritious/Healthy/"Good Food"
Red & White Can
Rainy & Cold Weather
Salty
Childhood/Kids
Feel Good

---

[a]These free associations are based on responses by students in brand management classes at Stanford University and the University of North Carolina at Chapel Hill.

that they believe would be acceptable or perhaps even expected by the interviewer. This unwillingness or inability to reveal true feelings may be particularly evident when consumers are asked about brands characterized by non-product-related image associations. For example, it may be difficult for consumers to admit that a certain brand name product has prestige and enhances their self-image. As a result, consumers may instead refer to some particular product feature as the reason why they like or dislike the brand. Alternatively, it may just be that consumers find it difficult to identify and express their true feelings when asked directly *even if they attempt to do so*. For either of these reasons, an accurate portrayal of brand knowledge structures may be impossible without some rather unconventional research methods.

Projective techniques are diagnostic tools to uncover the true opinions and feelings of consumers when they are unwilling or otherwise unable to express themselves on these matters. The idea behind projective techniques is that consumers are presented with an incomplete stimulus and asked to complete it or given an ambiguous stimulus that may not make sense in and of itself and are asked to make sense of it. In doing so, the argument is that consumers will reveal some of their true beliefs and feelings. Thus, projective techniques can be especially useful when deeply rooted personal motivations or personally or socially sensitive subject matters may be operating.

In psychology, the most famous example of a projective technique is the *Rorschach test,* where ink blots are presented to experimental subjects who are then asked what the ink blots remind them of. In responding, it is believed that subjects reveal certain facets of their own, perhaps subconscious, personality. Projective techniques have a long history in marketing, beginning with the motivation research of the late 1940s and 1950s.[8] A classic marketing example of projective techniques comes from an experiment exploring hidden feelings towards instant coffee conducted by Mason Haire in the late 1940s, summarized in Branding Brief 8–2.[9] Although projective techniques do not always yield as powerful results as in that example, they often provide useful insights that help to assemble a more complete picture of consumers and their relationships with brands. All kinds of projective techniques are possible. Here we highlight a few.[10]

Completion and Interpretation Tasks

As mentioned above, classic projective techniques use incomplete or ambiguous stimuli to elicit consumer thoughts and feelings. One such approach is with "bubble exercises" based on cartoons or photos where different people are depicted buying or using certain products or services. Empty bubbles, as found in cartoons, are placed in the scenes to represent the thoughts, words, or actions of one or more of the participants in the scene. Consumers are then asked to figuratively "fill in the bubble" by indicating what they believed was happening or being said in the scene. The stories and conversations told through bubble exercises and picture interpretations can be especially useful to assess user and usage imagery for a brand.

McCann-Erickson ad agency has used a variation of this approach involving figure drawings by consumers to discover hidden thoughts and feelings for different brands.[11] For example, in working on their American Express account, researchers at the agency found in focus groups that consumers did not distinguish their perceptions of gold-card and green-card holders. Follow-up research instructing consumers to produce figure drawings, however, was more insightful. For example, one consumer por-

---

BRANDING BRIEF 8-2

Once Upon a Time . . . You Were What You Cooked

One of the most famous applications of psychographic techniques was by Mason Haire in the 1940s. The purpose of Mason Haire's experiment was to uncover consumers' true beliefs and feelings toward Nescafe instant coffee. The impetus to the experiment was the results of a survey conducted to determine why the initial sales of Nescafe instant coffee were so disappointing. The survey asked subjects if they used instant coffee and, if not, what they disliked about it. The majority of the people who reported that they didn't like the product stated that it was because they didn't like the flavor. On the basis of consumer taste tests, however, Nescafe's management knew that consumers found that the taste of instant coffee was acceptable when they didn't know what type of coffee they were drinking. Suspecting that consumers were not expressing their true feelings, Haire designed a clever experiment to discover what was really going on.

Haire set up two shopping lists containing the same six items. Shopping List 1 specified Maxwell House Drip Ground Coffee whereas Shopping List 2 included Nescafe Instant Coffee, as follows:

Shopping List 1	*Shopping List 2*
Pound and a half of hamburger	Pound and a half of hamburger
2 loaves Wonder bread	2 Loaves Wonder bread
Bunch of carrots	Bunch of carrots
1 can Rumford's Baking Powder	1 can Rumford's Baking Powder
Maxwell House Coffee (drip ground)	Nescafe instant coffee
2 cans Del Monte peaches	2 cans Del Monte peaches
5 lbs. potatoes	5 lbs. potatoes

Two groups of identically matched subjects were each given one of the lists and asked to: "Read the shopping list below. Try to project yourself into the situation as far as possible until you can more or less characterize the woman who bought the groceries." Subjects then wrote a brief description of the personality and character of that person. After coding the responses into frequently mentioned categories, two starkly different profiles emerged:

	List 1 *(Maxwell House)*	*List 2* *(Nescafe)*
Lazy	4%	48%
Fails to plan household purchases and schedules well	12%	48%
Thrifty	16%	4%
Not a good wife	0%	16%

Haire interpreted these results as indicating that instant coffee represented a departure from homemade coffee and traditions with respect to caring for one's family. In other words, at that time, the "labor-saving" aspect of instant coffee, rather than being an asset, was a *liability* in that it violated consumer traditions. Consumers were evidently reluctant to admit this fact when asked directly but were better able to express their true feelings when asked to project to another person. The strategic implications of this new research finding were clear. Based on the original survey results, the obvious positioning for instant coffee with respect to regular coffee would have been to establish a point of difference on "convenience" and a point of parity on the basis of "taste." Based on the projective test findings, however, it was clear that there also needed to be a point of parity on the basis of user imagery. As a result, a successful ad campaign was launched that promoted Nescafe coffee as a way for housewives to free up time so they could devote additional time for more important household activities.

trayed a gold-card user as a broad-shouldered man standing in an active position. The green-card user, on the other hand, was drawn as a "couch potato" in front of a TV set. Based on this drawing and those of others, the agency decided to market the gold card as a "symbol of responsibility for people who have control over their lives and finances."

Comparison Tasks

Another technique that may be useful when consumers are not able to directly express their perceptions of brands is comparison tasks where consumers are asked to convey their impressions by comparing brands to people, countries, animals, activities, fabrics, occupations, cars, magazines, vegetables, nationalities, or even other brands.[12] For example, consumers might be asked: "If Wheaties cereal were a car, which one would it be? If it were an animal, which one might it be? Looking at the people depicted in these pictures, which ones do you think would be most likely to eat Wheaties?" In each case, consumers could be asked a followup question as to why they made the comparison they did. The objects chosen to represent the brand and the reasons why they were chosen can provide a glimpse into the psyche of the consumer with respect to a brand. In particular, uncovering the types of associations or inferences that reflect these choices can be useful once again in understanding user or usage imagery for the brand and other types of non-product-related associations.

For example, a Young & Rubicam study found that consumers had the following brand associations when asked to make comparisons based on probes to personality traits, animals, activities, fabric, occupations, and magazines for four major brands:[13]

Kentucky Fried Chicken	Holiday Inn	Bird's Eye	Oil of Olay
Ordinary	Friendly	Reliable	Youthful
Zebra	Mink	Bat	Mink
Camping	Travel	Cooking	Swimming
Denim	Polyester	Cotton	Silk
Housewife	Trucker	Housewife	Secretary
TV Guide	Business Week	Woman's Daily	Vogue

In an interesting study, Northwestern University's Sid Levy and Bobby Calder studied the image of the Army by asking pre-recruits, current recruits in training, and recruits who either failed to make the Army or who were rejected by the Army which animals out of a list of twelve were most like and least like the Army. In analyzing the responses, the researchers were able to develop a "vitality index" based on the predatory or domestic nature of the animals (e.g., lion and tigers versus cats and dogs) that were used to profile the different groups. As it turned out, pre-recruits had the "wildest" image of Army. Recruits actually in the army had more domesticated views, perhaps because they were being ordered around a lot. Those rejected by the army had the lowest vitality index.

ZALTMAN METAPHOR ELICITATION TECHNIQUE (ZMET)

One interesting new approach to better understanding how consumers view brands is the Zaltman Metaphor Elicitation Technique (ZMET).[14] ZMET was developed by Harvard's Gerald Zaltman and the University of Connecticut's Robin Higie Coulter as a result of a belief that important opportunities to learn from consumers were being overlooked as a result of ignoring nonverbal channels of communication as part of the research process. They designed ZMET as a research tool to surface the mental models that drive consumer thinking and behavior and characterize these models in actionable ways using consumers' metaphors. In a broad sense, a metaphor involves the understanding and experiencing of one thing in terms of another. Specifically, ZMET is based on seven basic premises:

1. Most human communication is nonverbal.
2. Thoughts typically occur as nonverbal images even though they are often expressed verbally.
3. Metaphors are essential units of thought and are the key windows/mechanism for viewing consumer thought and feelings and for understanding behavior.
4. Sensory images provide important metaphors.
5. Consumers have mental models—interrelated ideas (concepts or constructs) about a market experience—that represent their knowledge and behavior.
6. Hidden or deep structures of thought can be accessed.
7. Emotion and reason are forces that commingle in the minds of consumers.

ZMET employs qualitative methods to tap into consumers' visual and other sensory images and elicit the metaphors, constructs, and mental models that drive consumers' thinking and behavior. Methodologically, a small group of twenty or so individuals are recruited to participate in a research study that requires them to take photographs and/or collect pictures (from magazines, books, newspapers or other sources) that indicate what the brand means to them or some other task. Study participants come in a week or ten days after initial recruitment for a two-hour personal, one-on-one interview conducted as a "guided conversation." The guided conversation includes a series of steps that includes some or all of the following:

1. *Storytelling.* Participants describe the content of each picture.
2. *Missed images.* Participants describe the picture(s) that he or she was unable to obtain and explain their relevance.

3. *Sorting task.* Participants sort pictures into meaningful groups and provide a label or description for each group.

4. *Construct elicitation.* Participants reveal basic constructs and their interconnections using images as stimuli through the Kelly Repertory grid (described below) and laddering techniques (described in chapter 3).

5. *The most representative picture.* Participants indicate which picture is most representative.

6. *Opposite images.* Participants indicate pictures that describe the opposite of the brand or the task that they were given.

7. *Sensory images.* Participants indicate what does and does not describe the concept in terms of color, emotion, sound, smell, taste, and touch.

8. *Mental map.* After reviewing all of the constructs discussed and asking participants if the constructs are accurate representations of what was meant and if any important ideas are missing, participants create a map or causal model connecting the constructs that have been elicited.

9. *Summary image.* Participants create a summary image or montage using their own images (sometimes augmented by images from an image bank) to express important issues. Digital imaging techniques may be employed to facilitate the creation of the image.

10. *Vignette.* Participants put together a vignette or short video to help communicate important issues.

Once the participants' interviews are completed, researchers identify key themes or constructs, code the data, and assemble a consensus map involving the most important constructs. Quantitative analyses of the data can provide information for advertising, promotions, and other marketing-mix decisions. Accordingly, ZMET has been applied in a variety of different ways, including as a means to help understand consumers' images of brands, products, and companies. Figure 8–3 displays a consensus map that emerged from a study of intimate apparel.

Relatedly, Duke's Gerri Henderson and her colleagues show how network analysis can be used to represent consumer brand associations and uncover the knowledge structures of consumers.[15] Their approach employs a variety of methods to elicit brand associations, such as free elicitation or response and a modified Kelly repertory grid. As applied to branding, use of the Kelly repertory grid involves presenting consumers with a series of brand triads. With each triad, consumers are asked to identify which two brands are most alike, and thus different from the third brand, and then probed for their reasoning. Consumer responses to these various methods formed the dimensions upon which all brands were evaluated. Based on this information, matrices were created with brands and dimensions as both rows and columns. Entries in the matrix thus represented the relationship among and between brands and dimensions. Dimensions could reflect any type of brand association—for example, physical product attributes as well as people, places, and occasions. Network analysis can then be used to reveal a network of associations between all brands and all dimensions. The researchers applied this technique to sports cars—Figure 8–4 displays the graphical output from their analysis of one experimental subject.

FIGURE 8–3 ZMET Application to Intimate Apparel Market

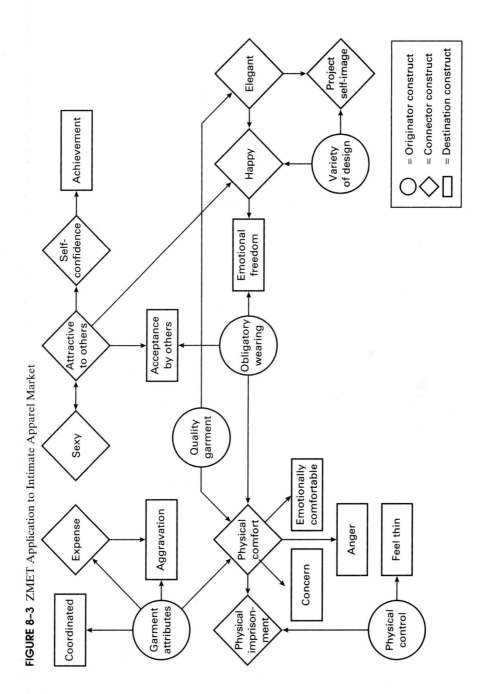

= Originator construct
= Connector construct
= Destination construct

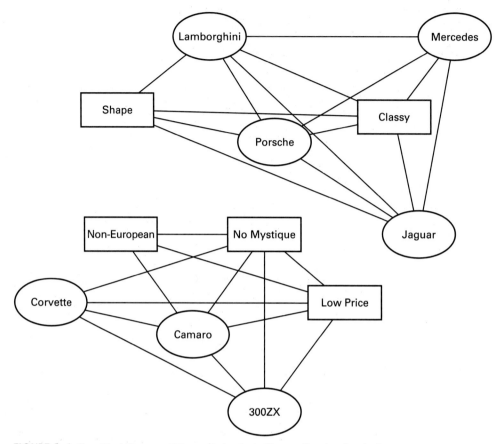

FIGURE 8–4 Graphical Output of Network Analysis (Sports Car Application)

BRAND PERSONALITY AND VALUES

As defined in chapter 3, brand personality is the human characteristics or traits that can be attributed to a brand. Brand personality can be measured in different ways. Perhaps the simplest and most direct way is to solicit open-ended responses to a probe such as:

> If the brand were to come alive as a person, what would it be like, what would it do, where would it live, what would it wear, who would it talk to if it went to a party (and what would it talk about)?

If consumers have difficulty getting started in their descriptions, they can be given an easily understood example or prompt as a guide. For example, consumers could be told that if Campbell's soup were to be described as a person, one possible response might be:[16]

> Mrs. Campbell is a rosy-cheeked and plump grandmother who lives in a warm, cozy house and wears an apron as she cooks wonderful things for her grandchildren.

Other means are possible to capture consumers' point of view. For example, consumers could be given a variety of pictures or a stack of magazines and asked to assemble a profile of the brand. These pictures could be of celebrities or anything else. Along these lines, ad agencies often conduct "picture sorting" studies to clarify who are typical users of a brand.

Brand personality can be assessed more definitively through adjective checklists or ratings. U.C.L.A.'s Jennifer Aaker conducted a research project looking at brand personalities that provides an interesting glimpse into the personality of a number of well-known brands, as well as a methodological means to examine the personality of any one brand.[17] Based on an extensive data collection involving ratings of 114 personality traits on 37 brands in various product categories by over 600 individuals representative of the U.S. population, she created a reliable, valid, and generalizable scale of brand personality that reflected the following five factors (with underlying facets) of brand personality:

1. Sincerity (down-to-earth, honest, wholesome, and cheerful)
2. Excitement (daring, spirited, imaginative, and up-to-date)
3. Competence (reliable, intelligent, and successful)
4. Sophistication (upper class and charming)
5. Ruggedness (outdoorsy and tough)

Figure 8–5 includes the specific trait items that make up the Aaker brand personality scale. Respondents in her study rated how descriptive each personality trait was for each brand according to a seven-point scale ("1" = not at all descriptive; "7" = extremely descriptive), which were then averaged to provide summary measures. Figure 8–6 contains the actual ratings of the 37 brands from the study on the five factors. Note that certain brands tended to be strong on one particular factor (e.g., Campbell's with "Sincerity"; MTV with "Excitement"; CNN with "Competence"; Revlon with "Sophistication"; and Levi's with "Ruggedness"). Other brands (e.g., Hallmark) were high on more than one factor. Some brands (e.g., MCI) scored poorly on all factors!

Taking the brand personality concept the next step, Harvard's Susan Fournier has conducted a number of interesting studies exploring consumer-brand relationships. Branding Brief 8–3 (p. 324–25) describes the results of some of her work.

In summary, qualitative research techniques are a creative means of ascertaining consumer perceptions that may otherwise be difficult to uncover. The range of possible qualitative research techniques is only limited by the creativity of the marketing researcher. Branding Brief 8–4 (p. 326) describes the findings of a research study that employed multiple qualitative research techniques to discover consumers' true feelings and beliefs about two brands of imported vodka, Absolut and Stolichnaya.

There are also drawbacks to qualitative research. The in-depth insights that emerge have to be tempered by the fact that the samples involved are often very small and may not necessarily generalize to broader populations. Moreover, given the qualitative nature of the data, there may also be questions of interpretation. Different researchers examining the same results from a qualitative research study may draw very different conclusions. Several practical issues in conducting qualitative research are

FIGURE 8-5 Brand Personality Scale Measures

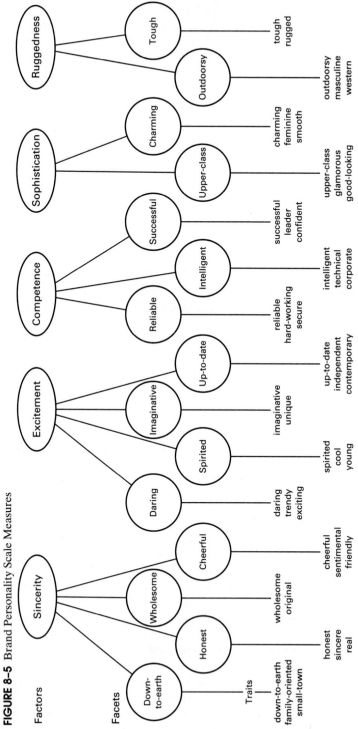

Factors

Facets

Traits

Sincerity			
Down-to-earth	Honest	Wholesome	Cheerful
down-to-earth family-oriented small-town	honest sincere real	wholesome original	cheerful sentimental friendly

Excitement			
Daring	Spirited	Imaginative	Up-to-date
daring trendy exciting	spirited cool young	imaginative unique	up-to-date independent contemporary

Competence		
Reliable	Intelligent	Successful
reliable hard-working secure	intelligent technical corporate	successful leader confident

Sophistication	
Upper-class	Charming
upper-class glamorous good-looking	charming feminine smooth

Ruggedness	
Outdoorsy	Tough
outdoorsy masculine western	tough rugged

| Indexed Profiles of 37 Brand Personalities: Based on the Five Factors | | | | | | | |

FACTOR (1–5)

	AT&T	Advil	AMEX	Apple	Avon	Campbell's	Charlie	Cheerios
Sincerity	1.06	.92	.83	.92	1.08	1.25	.83	1.14
Excitement	.91	.72	.83	.95	1.03	.87	.96	.77
Competence	1.15	.95	.99	1.07	1.01	1.01	.77	.88
Sophistication	.85	.75	.87	.86	1.22	.89	1.13	.76
Ruggedness	.94	.90	.83	.92	.92	.93	.77	.84
	CNN	Crest	Diet Coke	ESPN	Guess?	Hallmark	Hershey's	IBM
Sincerity	.99	1.09	.94	.99	.88	1.27	1.11	.89
Excitement	1.02	.84	.93	1.10	1.15	1.21	.88	.91
Competence	1.18	.99	.85	1.04	.90	1.12	.89	1.10
Sophistication	.93	.87	.90	.89	1.24	1.31	.96	.84
Ruggedness	1.01	.94	.89	1.23	1.03	.96	.85	.91
	K-Mart	Kodak	LEGO	Lee	Levi's	Lexus	Mattel	McDonald's
Sincerity	1.07	1.10	1.11	1.14	1.20	.87	1.13	1.12
Excitement	.85	.99	1.10	1.00	1.11	1.12	1.10	.97
Competence	.97	1.08	1.01	.99	1.05	1.07	1.04	1.02
Sophistication	.78	.96	.87	1.09	1.13	1.27	.90	1.02
Ruggedness	.91	1.02	1.10	1.34	1.43	1.03	1.13	.90
	MCI	Mercedes	Michelin	MTV	Nike	Oil of Olay	Pepsi	Porsche
Sincerity	.81	.84	.96	.70	.98	1.00	1.02	.71
Excitement	.82	1.07	.86	1.27	1.17	.85	1.04	1.26
Competence	.90	1.06	1.03	.82	1.03	.94	.89	.95
Sophistication	.73	1.31	.82	1.02	1.05	1.17	.95	1.37
Ruggedness	.75	.99	1.20	.93	1.36	.76	.99	1.07
	Reebok	Revlon	Saturn	Sony	Visa			
Sincerity	.94	.96	.96	.87	.90			
Excitement	1.12	1.06	1.05	.94	.87			
Competence	.97	.98	.99	1.02	1.02			
Sophistication	1.00	1.31	1.08	.89	.87			
Ruggedness	1.30	.85	1.00	.90	.87			

FIGURE 8–6 Personality Ratings of Selected Brands

discussed in Branding Brief 8–5. Chapter 10 also discusses in greater detail the role of qualitative research in a brand equity measurement system.

Quantitative Research Techniques

Although qualitative measures are useful to identify the range of possible associations to a brand and their characteristics in terms of strength, favorability, and uniqueness, a more definitive portrait of the brand often is desirable to permit more confident and defensible strategic and tactical recommendations. Whereas qualitative research typically elicits some type of verbal responses from consumers, quantitative research typi-

---

BRANDING BRIEF 8–3

Brands as Relationship Partners

Harvard's Susan Fournier has proposed a number of interesting ideas concerning brand equity by developing a framework for conceptualizing and understanding the relationships consumers form with brands. She created her framework by systematically applying and extending the metaphor of interpersonal relationships into the brand domain. She argues that: (1) brands can and do serve as viable relationship partners, (2) consumer-brand relationships are valid at the level of lived experience, and (3) consumer-brand relationships are actionable in terms of setting marketing strategy. She maintains that the everyday execution of marketing mix decisions constitutes a set of behaviors enacted on the part of the brand. For example, she notes how the following actions by a brand result in certain inferences about traits of the brand by consumers.

Brand Action	*Trait Inference*
Brand is repositioned and changing its marketing program constantly	Flighty, schizophrenic
Brand sells in selective outlets at a high price	Snobbish, sophisticated
Brand is often discounted or on deal	Cheap, uncultured
Brand is highly visible and advertises frequently	Friendly, popular
Brand supports environmental, educational, or social causes	Helpful, supportive
Brand offers length warranty and customer hot-line	Reliable, dependable

---

1. *Committed partnerships:* Loyal, exclusive relationship with Zest soap, "because it is simply the best soap you can buy and no other will suffice."

2. *Flings:* A one-shot, frivolous engagement with Crest Sparkles toothpaste, "just for the sheer fun of it."

3. *Secret affairs:* Occasional enjoyment of a Marlboro Light cigarette by a reformed smoker.

4. *Rebound relationships* (and associated enemyships): Purchase of a Honda lawnmower (out of anger at the failure of a Lawnboy servicing department).

5. *Arranged marriages:* Switch to Hellman's mayonnaise from long-standing Miracle Whip usage because the new husband insisted.

6. *Marriages of convenience:* A loyalty with DeMoulas Salad Dressing is initiated by the fact that someone left it behind at a picnic.

7. *Social sanctions:* Purchase of Murphy's Oil Soap for hardwood floor cleaning because it is the only brand recommended by the floor installer.

8. *Childhood buddies:* Warmly reminiscent memories of childhood sparked by consumption of Oreo cookies, Jell-O cooked pudding, and Hershey's Kisses.

9. *Fairweather friends:* Use of Tide . . . "Whenever it is on sale, and only when it is on sale."

10. *Enslavements/dependencies:* Trapped and constrained in software choices by Microsoft Windows operating system preinstalled on machine.

11. *Compartmentalized friendships:* Situationally restricted relationship with Avia tennis shoes worn only on the court.

FIGURE 8-7 Consumer Brand-Relationship Forms

To apply these ideas, Fournier conducts lengthy in-depth interviews. The interviews are designed to yield two complementary types of information: a first-person description of the informant's brand usage history and the context of the informant's life story and current life situation. Based on her research, Fournier has defined eleven possible consumer-brand relationship forms (see Figure 8–7).

cally employs various types of scale questions so that numerical representations and summaries can be made. Quantitative measures of brand knowledge can be employed to better assess the depth and breadth of brand awareness and the strength, favorability, and uniqueness of the brand associations. Quantitative measures are often the primary ingredient in tracking studies that monitor brand knowledge structures of consumers over time, as discussed in chapter 10.

AWARENESS

Recall that brand awareness is related to the strength of the brand in memory, as reflected by consumers' ability to identify various brand elements (i.e., the brand name, logo, symbol, character, packaging, and slogan) under different conditions. Brand awareness relates to the likelihood that a brand will come to mind and the ease with which it does so given different type of cues.

Several measures of awareness of brand elements can be employed.[18] Choosing the appropriate measure depends on the relative importance of brand awareness for consumer behavior in the category and the resulting role it plays to the success of the marketing program for the brand, as discussed in chapter 3. For example, if research reveals that many consumer decisions are made at the point of purchase where the brand name, logo, packaging, and so on will be physically present and visible, then brand recognition will be important. If research reveals that consumer decisions are mostly made in other settings away from the point of purchase where the brand elements are not physically present, on the other hand, then brand recall will be more important. As a cautionary note, even though brand recall per se may be viewed as less important when consumer decisions are made at the point of purchase, consumers' brand evaluations and choices will still often depend on what *else* they recall about the brand given that they are able to recognize it there.

Chasing the Spirit of Imported Vodka

Young & Rubicam ad agency conducted an in-depth eight-step examination of two popular imported vodkas, Absolut and Stolichnaya ("Stoli"). The research involved the following eight steps:

1. A list of approximately forty traits were written on pieces of cardboard. Consumers were asked to put each trait in one of four piles according to which brand they associated with the given trait: Stoli, Absolut, neither, or both.

2. Consumers were given a stack of pictures of people culled from various magazines. Consumers then placed them into one of three piles depending on how well they associated the person with the brand—Stoli, Absolut, or neither.

3. Consumers completed a bubble exercise where they were given pictures of people with bubbles indicating their words and asked, "Imagine one of the people from the Absolut pile ran into the person in the Stoli pile. Write down in the bubbles what they would say to each other."

4. Consumers were asked the best and worst thing about each brand.

5. Consumers described the bottles of each brand in an open-ended fashion and then were asked several specific followup questions: "If you had to make a judgment about the bottle—without knowing anything about its contents—what would you think?" and "What do you think about the label?"

6. Consumers were asked, "Imagine the Absolut and Stoli bottles were talking to each other. What would they say?"

7. Consumers were asked what they associated with the countries of origin for the brands—Sweden and Russia.

8. Consumers were asked, "If the bottles became a person, how would you see them? What kind of cars would they drive, clothes would they wear, how old would they be, what gender, etc?"

The study findings indicated that the Absolut brand personality was seen as "cool" and "stylish." To a large extent these associations came from the user imagery of Absolut drinkers as young, hip people, but lots of imagery came from the stylish, contemporary look of the bottle and advertising itself. Stoli was seen as "older" and more "traditional."

Recognition

In the abstract, recognition processes require that consumers be able to discriminate a stimulus—a word, object, image—as something they have previously seen. Brand recognition relates to consumers' ability to identify the brand under a variety of circumstances and can involve identification of any of the brand elements. The most basic type of recognition procedures gives consumers a set of single items visually or orally and asks them if they thought that they had previously seen or heard these items. To provide a more sensitive test, it is often useful to include decoys or lures—items that consumers could not have possibly seen. In addition to "yes" or

---

┌───┐

Focus Group Guidelines

With qualitative research, consumer responses may be collected in small groups called "focus groups" or individually, depending on the depth and nature of the task involved with the qualitative technique. Focus groups are a data collection tool that gathers the opinions of six to ten people who are carefully selected based on certain demographic, psychographic, or other considerations and brought together to freely discuss various topics of interest at length. A professional research moderator provides questions and probes based on a discussion guide or agenda prepared by the responsible marketing managers to ensure that the right material gets covered. However, moderators often follow and lead the discussion at times to track down some potentially useful insight as they attempt to discern the real motivations of consumers and why they are saying and doing certain things. The sessions are typically taped in some fashion and marketing managers often remain behind two-way mirrors in the room.

Focus groups, like any research technique, can be abused if not conducted carefully.[a] The key for marketers to successfully use any of these qualitative approaches in a focus group setting is to *listen*. Consumer responses must be interpreted, so it is critical that biases are eliminated as much as possible. On the positive side, many useful insights can emerge from thoughtfully run focus groups. On the negative side, it may be expensive to recruit qualified subjects ($3000 to $5000 per group). Even when multiple groups are involved, it may be difficult to generalize the results to a broader population. For example, within the United States, focus group findings often vary from region to region. One New York firm specializing in focus group research claimed that the best city to conduct focus groups was Minneapolis because they could get a fairly well-educated sample of people who were honest and forthcoming about their opinions. They maintained that other cities could be more useful, however, for special purposes, for example, focus group participants in Houston provided valuable information on underarm deodorants because they were used to having to contend with the relentless heat and humidity of that city. Many marketers interpret focus groups carefully in New York and other Northeastern cities because the people in these areas tend to be highly critical and generally do not report that they like much.

---

[a]Sarah Stiansen, "How Focus Groups Can Go Astray," *AdWeek* (December 5, 1988), pp. FK 4–6.

└───┘

"no" responses, consumers also can be asked to rate how confident they are in their recognition of an item.

There are a number of additional, somewhat more subtle recognition measures that involve "perceptually degraded" versions of the brand. In some cases, the brand element may be visually masked or distorted in some way or shown for extremely brief duration. For example, brand name recognition could be tested with missing letters. Figure 8–8 tests your ability to recognize brand names under less than full information. These more subtle measures may be particularly important for brands which have a high level of recognition.

In terms of packaging, brand recognition is especially important, and some marketing researchers have used creative means to assess the visibility of package design. As a starting point, they consider the benchmark or "best case" of the visibility of a package when a consumer:

1. With 20-20 vision
2. Is face-to-face with a package
3. At a distance of less than five feet
4. Under ideal lighting conditions.

A key question then is whether the package design is robust enough so that it is still recognizable if one or more of these four conditions are not present. Because shopping is often not conducted under "ideal" conditions, such insights are important. For example, one research study indicated that one out of six members of the population

FIGURE 8–8 Don't Tell Me, It's on the Tip of My Tongue . . .

A brand name with a high level of awareness will be recognized under less than ideal conditions. Consider the following list of incomplete names (i.e., word-fragments). Which ones do you recognize? Compare your answers to the answer key in the footnote to see how well you did.[a]

1. D _ _ N E _
2. K O _ _ K
3. D U _ A C _ _ _
4. H Y _ T _
5. A D _ _ L
6. M _ T _ E L
7. D _ L T _
8. N _ Q U _ L
9. G _ L L _ T _ _
10. H _ _ S H _ Y
11. H _ L L _ _ R K
12. M _ C H _ _ I N
13. T _ P P _ R W _ _ E
14. L _ G _
15. N _ K _

_____

[a]1. Disney 2. Kodak 3. Duracell 4. Hyatt 5. Advil 6. Mattel 7. Delta 8. NyQuil 9. Gillette 10. Hershey 11. Hallmark 12. Michelin 13. Tupperware 14. Lego 15. Nike

who wear eye glasses do not wear them when shopping in a supermarket![19] A key question then is whether a package is still able to effectively communicate to consumers under such conditions.

Research methods using tachistoscopes (T-scopes) and eye tracking techniques exist to test the effectiveness of alternative package designs according to a number of specific criteria:

1. Degree of shelf impact
2. Impact and recall of specific design elements
3. Distance at which the package can first be identified
4. Angle at which the package can first be identified
5. Speed with which the package can be identified
6. Perceived package size
7. Copy visibility and legibility

These additional measures can provide more sensitive measures of recognition than simple "yes" or "no" tasks. By applying these direct and indirect measures of brand recognition, marketers can determine which brand elements exist in memory and, to some extent, the strength of their association. One advantage to brand recognition measures versus recall measures is that they can be used in any modality. For example, because brand recognition is often visual in nature, visual recognition measures can be used. It may be difficult for consumers to describe a logo or symbol in a recall task either verbally or pictorially but much easier for them to assess the same elements visually in a recognition task.

Nevertheless, brand recognition measures only really provide an approximation as to *potential* recallability. To determine whether the brand elements will actually be recalled under various circumstances, measures of brand recall are necessary.

Recall

Brand recall relates to consumers' ability to identify the brand under a variety of circumstances. With brand recall, consumers must retrieve the actual brand element from memory when given some related probe or cue. Thus, brand recall is a more demanding memory task than brand recognition because consumers are not just given a brand element and asked to identify or discriminate it as one they had or had not already seen.

Different measures of brand recall are possible depending on the type of cues provided to consumers. *Unaided recall* on the basis of "all brands" provided as a cue is likely to identify only the very strongest brands. *Aided recall* uses various types of cues to help consumer recall. One possible sequence of aided recall might use progressively narrowly defined cues—such as product class, product category, and product type labels—to provide insight into the organization of consumers' brand knowledge structures. For example, if recall of the Porsche 944, a high performance German sports car, in non-German markets was of interest, the recall probes could begin with "all cars" and move to more and more narrowly defined categories such as "sports cars," "foreign sports cars," or even "high performance German sports cars." For example, consumers could be asked: "When you think of foreign sports cars, which brands come to mind?"

Other types of cues may be employed to measure brand recall. For example, consumers could be probed on the basis of product attributes ("When you think of chocolate, which brands come to mind?") or usage goals ("If you were thinking of having a healthy snack, which brands come to mind?"). Often, to capture the breadth of brand recall, it may be important to examine the context of the purchase decision or consumption usage situation. For example, consumers could be probed according to different purchase motivations as well as different times and places when the product could be used to see which brands came to mind (e.g., different times of the day, days of the week, or times of the year; at home, at work, or on vacation). The more that brands have strong associations to these non-product considerations, the more likely it is that they will be recalled when they are given those situational cues. Combined measures of recall based on product attribute or category cues as well as situational or usage cues give an indication of breadth of recall.

Brand recall also can provide some insight into category structure and brand positioning in consumers' minds. Past research has shown that brands tend to be recalled in categorical clusters when consumers are given a general probe. Certain brands are grouped together because they share certain associations and are thus likely to cue and remind consumers of each other if one is recalled.[20] For example, academic researchers Joe Alba and Wes Hutchinson provide an analysis of a brand recall protocol produced by a consumer in response to instructions to list the brand names of any products that could be used to treat the symptoms of the common cold (see Figure 8–9). They draw the following conclusions:

> Brand name clustering is clearly related to benefit categories (based on product class tables given in the Handbook of Nonprescription Drugs 1979). For instance, Alka-Seltzer Plus, Congesprin, NyQuil, and Comtrex are all multi-ingredient drugs that contain a decongestant and an analgesic, and can be used to treat head colds. NyQuil and Comtrex also contain a cough suppressant and, in principle, could have been clustered with cough remedies such as Robitussin or Vicks Formula 44. It is of interest to note that Vicks Formula 44-D was clustered with cough remedies even though it contains a decongestant and is functionally similar to NyQuil and Comtrex. This is probably the result of successful positioning on the part of Vicks, in as much as they also make NyQuil and need to avoid cannibalization.

Besides being judged as correctly recalled, brand recall can be further distinguished according to order, as well as latency or speed of recall. In many cases, people will recognize a brand when it is shown to them and will recall it if they are given a sufficient number of cues. Thus, potential recallability is high. The bigger issue is the salience of the brand—do consumers think of the brand under the right circumstances, for example, when they could be either buying or using the product? How quickly do they think of the brand? Is it automatically or easily recalled? Is it the first brand recalled?

Corrections for Guessing   With any research measure, there is always an issue of consumers making up responses or guessing. That problem may be especially true with certain types of aided awareness or recognition measures for the brand. *Spurious awareness* occurs when consumers erroneously claim that they recall something that

FIGURE 8-9 Example of Brand Name Clustering

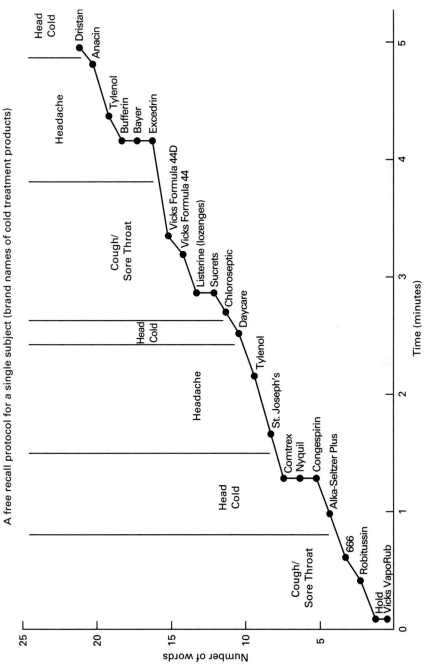

A free recall protocol for a single subject (brand names of cold treatment products)

331

they really don't remember and that maybe doesn't even exist! For example, one market research firm, Oxtoby-Smith, conducted a benchmark study of awareness of health and beauty products.[21] In the study, they asked consumers questions like:

> The following is a list of denture adhesive brand names. Please answer yes if you've heard the name before and no if you haven't. Okay? Orafix? Fasteeth? Dentu-Tight? Fixodent?

Although 16 percent of the sample reported that they had heard of Dentu-Tight, there was only one problem—it didn't really exist! Similarly high levels of reported recall were reported for plausible sounding but fictitious brands such as Four O'Clock Tea (8 percent), Leone Pasta (16 percent), and Mrs. Smith's Cake Mix (31 percent). On the basis of their study, Oxtoby-Smith found that spurious awareness of new health and beauty products was around 8 percent and was even higher in some product categories. In one case, a proposed line extension was mistakenly thought to already exist by about 50 percent of the sample (a finding that no doubt sent a message to the company that they should go ahead and introduce the product!).

From a marketing perspective, the problem with spurious awareness is that it may send misleading signals as to the proper strategic direction for a brand. For example, Oxtoby-Smith reported that one of its clients was struggling with a 5 percent market share despite the fact that 50 percent of survey respondents reported that they were aware of the brand. On the surface, it would seem that the recommended strategy would be to improve the image of the brand and attitudes toward it in some way. Upon further examination, it was determined that spurious awareness accounted for *almost half* of the survey respondents who reported brand awareness, suggesting that a more appropriate solution to the true problem would be to first build awareness to a greater degree. Marketers should be sensitive to the possibilities of misleading signals because of spurious brand awareness, especially with new brands or ones with plausible sounding names.

Strategic Implications   The advantage to aided recall measures is that they yield insight into how brand knowledge is organized in memory and what kind of cues or reminders may be necessary for consumers to be able to retrieve the brand from memory. Understanding recall when different levels of product category specificity are used as cues is important because it has implications for how consideration sets are formed and product decisions are made by consumers.

For example, again take the case of the Porsche 944. Assume that consumer recall of this particular car model was fairly low when all cars were considered but very high when foreign sports cars were considered. In other words, consumers strongly categorized the Porsche 944 as a prototypical sports car but only tended to think of it in that way. If that were the case, for more consumers to entertain the possibility of buying a Porsche 944, it may be necessary to broaden the meaning of Porsche so that it had a stronger association to cars in general. Of course, such a strategy would run the risk of alienating existing customers who had been initially attracted by the "purity" and strong identification of the Porsche 944 as a sports car. Deciding on the appropriate strategy would depend on the relative costs and benefits of targeting the two different segments.

Understanding when the product is recalled on the basis of situational cues also often yields important strategic guidance. For example, in many cases, the best route for improving sales for a brand is not by increasing consumer attitudes toward the brand but, instead, by increasing the situations when consumers would consider using the brand. As an example, consider the marketing challenges for Campbell's soup. Their advertising strategy in recent years has emphasized either taste (with their long-time advertising slogan, "Mmm, Mmm, Good") or nutrition (with the advertising slogan, "Never Underestimate the Power of Soup"). Part of their difficulty in increasing sales may not lie so much with the attitudinal considerations addressed by those ad campaigns as with memory considerations and the fact that people do not think of eating soup as often as they should in certain meal occasions. For example, although soup is often eaten as a side dish or appetizer when people eat out at restaurants, it is probably often overlooked with more common dinner occasions at home. Creating a communication program that provides reminders to those consumers who already have a favorable attitude towards soup to help them to remember it in more varied consumption settings may be the most profitable way to grow the Campbell's soup franchise. In other words, it may be harder to try to *change* existing brand attitudes than to *remind* people of their existing attitudes toward a brand where appropriate.

The important point to note is that the category structure that exists in consumers' minds, as reflected by brand recall performance, can have profound implications for consumer choice and marketing strategy. An experiment by Prakash Nedungadi provides a compelling demonstration of this fact.[22] As a preliminary step, Nedungadi first examined the category structure for "fast food" restaurants that existed in consumers' minds. He found that a major subcategory was "hamburger chains" and a minor subcategory was "sandwich shops." He also found, on the basis of usage and linking surveys, that within the subcategory of national hamburger chains, a major brand was McDonald's and a minor brand was Wendy's, and within the subcategory of local sandwich shops, a major brand was Joe's Deli (in his testing area) and a minor brand was Subway. Consistent with this reasoning, in an unaided recall and choice task, consumers were more likely to remember and select a brand from a major subcategory than from a minor subcategory and, within a subcategory, a major brand versus a minor brand.

Next, Nedungadi looked at the effects of different brand "primes" on subsequent choices among the four fast food restaurants. Brands were primed by having subjects in the experiment first answer a series of seemingly unrelated questions—including some questions about the brand to be primed—before making their brand selections. Because of this initial exposure to the brand, a target brand was "primed" in memory and therefore potentially more accessible during the choice task. Two key findings emerged. First, a major brand that was primed was more likely to be selected in the later choice task even though the attitudes toward the brand were no different from those of a control group. In other words, merely making the brand more accessible in memory increased the likelihood that it would be chosen *independent of any differences in brand attitude*. Second, priming a minor brand in a minor subcategory actually benefited the *major* brand in that subcategory more. In other words, by drawing attention to the minor subcategory of sandwich shops—which could easily be overlooked—the minor brand, Subway, indirectly primed the major brand, Joe's Deli, in the subcategory.

The Nedungadi study findings clearly demonstrate the importance of understanding the category structure that exists in consumer memory, as well as the value in strategies to increase the recall or accessibility of brands during choice situations. More generally, the insights gleaned from measuring brand recall are valuable for developing brand identity and integrated marketing communication programs, as Chapters 4 and 6 showed. For example, brand recall can be examined for each brand element to explore the extent to which any one brand element—the name, symbol, logo, and so on—suggests another brand element. In other words, is it the case that consumers are aware of all the different brand elements and understand how they relate?

IMAGE

One vitally important aspect of the brand is its image, as reflected by the associations that consumers hold toward the brand. Strong, favorable, and unique associations provide the foundation for customer-based brand equity. As noted above, brand associations come in many different forms and can be classified along many different dimensions. It is useful to make a distinction between more "lower-level" considerations related to consumer perceptions of specific attributes and benefits versus more "higher-level" considerations related to general preferences and various attitudes and behaviors. As noted in chapter 3, there is an obvious relationship between the two levels as consumers' overall brand attitudes and behavior typically depend on perceptions of specific attributes and benefits about the brand. We next consider both types of associations.

Specific, Lower-Level Brand Associations

Beliefs are descriptive thoughts that a person holds about something.[23] Brand association beliefs are those specific attributes and benefits linked to the brand and its competitors. For example, consumers may have brand association beliefs for Sega home video games such as "fun and exciting," "cool and hip," "colorful," "good graphic quality," "advanced technology," "variety of software titles," and "sometimes violent." They may also have associations to the "Sonic the Hedgehog" character and the slogan, "Welcome to the Next Level." Sega user imagery may be "used by a teenager or 20-something male who is serious about playing video games, especially sports games."

The qualitative research approaches described above are useful in uncovering these different type of salient brand associations making up the brand image. To better understand their potential contribution to brand equity, the belief associations that are identified need to be assessed on the basis of one or more of the three key dimensions—strength, favorability, and uniqueness—making up the sources of brand equity. As a first cut, open-ended measures could be employed, as noted above, that tap into the strength, favorability, and uniqueness of brand associations, as follows:

1. What are the strongest associations you have to the brand? What comes to mind when you think of the brand? (Strength)

2. What is good about the brand? What do you like about the brand? What is bad about the brand? What do you dislike about the brand? (Favorability)

3. What is unique about the brand? What characteristics or features does the brand share with other brands? (Uniqueness)

To provide more specific insights, these belief associations could be rated on scales according to strength, favorability, and uniqueness along the following lines, as illustrated with Lipton iced tea:

1. To what extent do you feel the following product characteristics are descriptive of Lipton iced tea (where 1 = strongly disagree and 7 = strongly agree)?

   _____ convenient

   _____ refreshing and thirst quenching

   _____ real and natural

   _____ good-tasting

   _____ contemporary and relevant

   _____ used by young professionals

2. How good or bad is it for iced tea to have the following product characteristics (where 1 = very bad, and 7 = very good)?

   _____ convenient

   _____ refreshing and thirst quenching

   _____ real and natural

   _____ good-tasting

   _____ contemporary and relevant

   _____ used by young professionals

3. How unique is Lipton iced tea in terms of the following product characteristics (where 1 = not at all unique and 7 = highly unique)?

   _____ convenient

   _____ refreshing and thirst quenching

   _____ real and natural

   _____ good-tasting

   _____ contemporary and relevant

   _____ used by young professionals

Any potentially relevant association can and should be measured, including those product-related attributes and benefits related to dimensions of product quality—such as (where appropriate) performance, features, conformance quality, reliability, durability, serviceability, and style and design—as well as non-product-related attributes and benefits related to user and usage imagery and brand personality.

There are many possible ways to ask these questions and actually scale these brand beliefs and perceptions. Generally, they take the form of semantic differential (bipolar adjectives) or Likert-type scales (as above), but all types of scales are possible. Moreover, different scales can be constructed depending on the decisions taken with respect to a number of considerations, such as the following:

1. Absolute or comparative scales
2. Verbal, numerical, or spatial scales
3. The number of points on the scale (e.g., whether they should be odd or even)

4. Balanced or unbalanced scales

5. The treatment of "no opinion" or "don't know" responses in the scale

Much research has considered the implications of these and other methodological choices. For example, Barnard and Ehrenberg experimentally examined three different measures of consumer beliefs about different attributes:[24]

1. *Free choice:* On an attribute by attribute basis, subjects indicated for a list of brands which one(s) possessed the attribute.

2. *Scaling:* Subjects indicated the association of a brand with an attribute by ticking a box on a 5-step scale from "agree a lot" to "disagree a lot" with a "no opinion" box provided.

3. *Ranking:* Subjects rank-ordered the different brands according to how closely associated they were with an attribute.

They found that the three measurement approaches placed the brands in roughly the same relative positions on each attribute dimension, suggesting that the choice between absolute and comparative scales, at least in their context, may not have been that critical in measuring brand beliefs. For detailed discussion of these more specific scaling or survey issues, however, it is necessary to consult a good marketing research text.[25]

General, Higher-Order Brand Associations

The purpose of measuring higher-order brand associations is to find out how consumers combine all of the specific considerations about the brand in their minds to form different types of brand evaluations, as reflected by their attitudes, intentions, and behavior.

Brand Attitudes   There are a number of possible measures that capture consumer brand attitudes. For example, consider the following different indicators of consumers' brand attitudes towards Levi's 501 jeans:

Overall brand attitudes

- How favorable is your overall attitude toward Levi's 501 jeans?
- How much do you like Levi's 501 jeans?
- How well do Levi's 501 jeans satisfy your needs?
- Is Levi's 501 the best brand of jeans for you?
- How likely would you be to recommend Levi's 501 jeans to others?

Attitudes toward product-related attributes and benefits

- Considering the product alone, how good are Levi's 501 jeans?
- How well made are Levi's 501 jeans?
- How would you rate the overall quality of Levi's 501 jeans?

Attitudes toward non-product-related attributes and benefits

- How well does the image of Levi's 501 jeans fit your personality?
- How positive are your feelings toward Levi's 501 jeans?
- How much do you like people who wear Levi's 501 jeans?

Attitudes toward price and value

- Are Levi's 501 jeans worth a premium price?
- How good a value are Levi's 501 jeans?
- Are Levi's 501 jeans a fair value?

- Do you get what you pay for with Levi's 501 jeans?
- Considering the price you pay relative to quality, how would you rate the overall value of Levi's 501 jeans?

Attitudes toward the company

- How good is the overall reputation of Levi-Strauss?
- How trustworthy is Levi-Strauss?
- How likable is Levi-Strauss?
- To what extent is Levi-Strauss a market leader in jeans?
- How strong is the tradition of Levi-Strauss in jeans?

These different measures of brand preference and overall attitudes are useful in capturing the favorability of these key brand associations. As chapter 3 noted, overall brand attitudes can also vary in their strength. Attitude accessibility can be measured on a microcomputer by seeing how long it takes a consumer to indicate his or her brand evaluation ratings. Although these differences may be in microseconds, they may still be significant managerially. Finally, brand attitudes can also be measured in a comparative manner to assess their uniqueness by eliciting relative preference, for example, by adding a phrase such as, "as compared to Lee's jeans" or some other relevant competitor in the Levi's example above.

A more complicated and quantitative technique to assess overall brand uniqueness is multidimensional scaling or perceptual maps. Multidimensional scaling (MDS) is a procedure to determine the perceived relative image of a set of objects, such as products or brands. MDS transforms consumer judgments of similarity or preference into distances represented in perceptual space. For example, if brands A and B are judged by respondents to be the most similar of a set of brands, the MDS algorithm will position brands A and B so that the distance between them in multidimensional space is smaller than the distance between any other two pairs of brands. Respondents may base their similarity between brands on any basis—tangible or intangible.[26] (Recall the results of the beer testing experiment in Figure 2–2 of chapter 2.)

Relatedly, European academic branding experts Kapferer and Laurent have proposed a scale to measure the brand sensitivity of a product class as a whole.[27] They characterize brand sensitivity in terms of the relationship among brands for a given consumer in a given product class, particularly with respect to comparisons between national brands versus unbranded products or private labels in that product class. The types of items in their scale are displayed in Figure 8–10. According to their approach, the strength of a brand would be reflected by the number of its customers who are brand sensitive. Brand sensitivity can be seen as a potential proxy for or measure of brand uniqueness. In other words, if consumers are not brand sensitive in a category as a whole, it is unlikely that any one specific brand will be unique.

Brand Intentions   Another set of possible measures are related to brand intentions. Intention measures could focus on the likelihood of buying the brand or the likelihood of switching from the brand to another brand. Research in psychology suggests that purchase intentions are most likely to be predictive of actual purchase when there is correspondence between the two in:

- Action (e.g., buying for own use or to give as a gift)
- Target (e.g., specific type of product and brand)

DIRECT QUESTIONS

Forced choice between two items

1. For PRODUCT . . .
   "I prefer to buy a well known brand" or
   "I don't mind buying the store brand"

Four Likert items

2. "When I buy a PRODUCT, I look at the brand."
3. "I do not choose a PRODUCT according to the brand."
4. "For a PRODUCT, the brand name is not that important."
5. "When I buy a PRODUCT, I take account of the brand."

INDIRECT MEASURES

6. A dollarmetric measure involving three well-known brands: the last brand purchased by consumer in the product category and the first other two brands mentioned in a spontaneous brand awareness question. Would the consumer maintain his/her choice if the price differential increased by 10 percent, 25 percent, 50 percent between the chosen brand and the other two competitors?
7. A dollarmetric measure between the last brand bought by consumer and a private label or store brand in the product category.
8. A mini-information display board choice task. Five brands and five product attributes (including brand name and price) were included in a grid and consumers were asked to choose a brand. Brand sensitivity was indicated by usage of the brand name attribute in making the choice.

FIGURE 8-10 Kapferer and Laurent's Brand Sensitivity Measure

- Context (e.g., in what type of store based on what prices and other conditions)
- Time (e.g., within a week, month, or year)[28]

In other words, when asking a consumer to forecast his or her likely purchase of a product or a brand, it is important to specify *exactly* the circumstances involved—the purpose of the purchase, the location of the purchase, the time of the purchase, and so on. For example, consumers could be asked,

> Assume your refrigerator broke down over the next weekend and could not be inexpensively repaired. If you went to your favorite appliance store and found all the different brands competitively priced, how likely would you be to buy a General Electric refrigerator?

Consumers could indicate their purchase intention on an 11-point probability scale such as: 0 = definitely would not buy, . . . , 10 = definitely would buy.

Brand Behaviors   Finally, perceptions of brand purchase, usage, or loyalty could be probed. Consumers could be asked to what extent buying or using the brand would generally be:

- Beneficial versus Harmful
- Pleasant versus Unpleasant
- Awful versus Nice
- Wise versus Foolish

Other measures could capture reported brand usage and loyalty. Consumers could be asked these issues directly. Alternatively, consumers could be asked the percentage of their last purchases in the category that went to the brand (past purchase history) and the percentage of the planned next purchases that would go the brand (intended future purchases). For example, the marketers or brand managers of Fuji film might ask the following questions:

1. Which brand of film do you usually buy?
2. Which brand of film did you buy last time?
3. Do you have any film on hand? Which brand?
4. Which brands of film did you consider buying?
5. Which brand of film will you buy next time?
6. Do you expect to take pictures in the next two weeks?
7. Have you taken any pictures in the last two weeks?

These types of questions can provide information on brand attitudes and usage for Fuji, potential gaps with competitors, and who might be in the consideration set at the time of purchase. These measures could be open-ended, dichotomous (forcing consumers to choose a brand), or involve multiple choice or rating scales. The answers to these types of question also could be compared to actual measures of consumer behavior to assess whether consumers are accurate in their predictions. For example, if 30 percent of consumers reported, on average, that they thought that they would take pictures in the next two weeks but only 15 percent of consumers reported two weeks later that they actually had taken pictures in the last two weeks, then Fuji brand managers might need to devise strategies to better convert intentions to actual behavior.

Relatedly, industry consultants Longman and Moran have developed a measure of *substitutability* related to brand behaviors that they see as a key source of brand equity. Their measure is based on a scale produced by the answers to two questions:

- Which brand did you buy last time?
- If the brand had not been available, what would you have done (i.e., waited, gone to another store, or bought another brand—and if another brand, which one)?

Based on their responses, consumers are placed into one of six segments that are assumed to be of decreasing value for the brand:

1. People who bought your brand last time and who would have waited or gone to another store to buy your brand.
2. People who bought your brand last time but would have accepted any other brand as a substitute.

3. People who bought your brand last time but specified a particular other brand as a substitute.

4. People who bought another brand last time but named your brand as a possible substitute.

5. People who bought another brand last time and did not name your brand as a substitute.

6. People who bought another brand last time and would have waited or gone to another store to buy that brand.

They view repeat rate—how many of the people who bought your brand last time and would buy it again this time—as a key indicator of brand equity: The higher the repeat rate, the greater the brand equity and the greater the marketing profitability; the less that people are willing to accept substitute brands, the more that they are likely to repeat buy.

Review

This chapter has described different ways to measure consumers' brand knowledge structures. Qualitative research techniques were reviewed as a means to identify possible brand associations. Quantitative research techniques were reviewed as a means to better approximate the breadth and depth of brand awareness and the strength, favorability, and uniqueness of brand associations. In contrasting the two approaches, because of their unstructured nature, qualitative measures are especially well-suited

FIGURE 8-11 Summary of Qualitative and Quantitative Measures

I. Qualitative Research Techniques
   Free Association
   Adjective Ratings and Checklists
   Projective Techniques
   Photo Sorts
   Bubble Drawings
   Story-Telling
   Personification Exercises
   Role-playing

II. Quantitative Research Techniques
   A. Brand Awareness
      Direct and indirect measures of brand recognition
      Aided and unaided measures of brand recall
   B. Brand Image
      Open-ended and scale measures of specific attributes and benefits
         Strength
         Favorability
         Uniqueness
      Overall attitudes, intentions, and behavior

to provide an in-depth glimpse of what brands and products means to consumers. To obtain more precise and generalizable information, however, quantitative scale measures are typically employed.

Figure 8–11 summarizes some of the different types of measures that were discussed in the chapter.

Discussion Questions

1. Pick a brand. Employ projective techniques to attempt to identify sources of its brand equity. Which measures work best? Why?
2. Pick a brand. How would you best profile consumers' brand knowledge structures? How would you use quantitative measures?

Notes

1. Burleigh B. Gardner and Sidney J. Levy, "The Product and the Brand," *Harvard Business Review* (March-April 1955), p. 35.
2. One of the leading textbooks in this area is J. Paul Peter and Jerry C. Olson, *Consumer Behavior and Marketing Strategy*, 3rd ed., Homewood, IL: Irwin, 1993.
3. John Motavalli, "Probing Consumer Minds," *AdWeek* (December 7, 1987), pp. F.K.4-8.
4. Ernest Dichter, *Handbook of Consumer Motivations*. New York: McGraw-Hill, 1964.
5. H. Shanker Krishnan, "Characteristics of Memory Associations: A Consumer-Based Brand Equity Perspective," *International Journal of Research in Marketing* (October, 1996), p. 389–405.
6. J. Wesley Hutchinson, "Expertise and the Structure of Free Recall," in Richard P. Bagozzi and Alice M. Tybout, eds., *Advances in Consumer Research,* Vol. 10, Ann Arbor, MI: Association of Consumer Research (1983), pp. 585–589.
7. Yvan Boivin, "A Free Response Approach to the Measurement of Brand Perceptions," *International Journal of Research in Marketing*, 3 (1986), 11–17.
8. Sydney J. Levy, "Dreams, Fairy Tales, Animals, and Cars," *Psychology and Marketing*, 2 (2) (1985), pp. 67–81.
9. Mason Haire, "Projective Techniques in Marketing Research," *Journal of Marketing*, (April 1950), pp. 649–656. Interestingly, a followup study conducted several decades later suggested that instant coffee users were no longer perceived as psychologically different from drip grind users (See Frederick E. Webster, Jr. and Frederick Von Pechmann, "A Replication of the 'Shopping List' Study," *Journal of Marketing*, 34 (April 1970), pp. 61–63).
10. Sydney J. Levy, "Dreams, Fairy Tales, Animals, and Cars," *Psychology and Marketing*, 2 (2) (1985), pp. 67–81.
11. Ronald Alsop, "Advertisers Put Consumers on the Couch," *The Wall Street Journal* (May 13, 1988), p. 21.
12. Jeffrey Durgee and Robert Stuart, "Advertising Symbols and Brand Names that Best Represent Key Product Meanings," *Journal of Consumer Marketing*, 4 (3) (1987), pp. 15–24.
13. Jay Dean, "A Practitioner's Perspective or 15 Things I've Learned about Brand Personality," paper presented at Society of Consumer Psychology annual meeting, February 1994.
14. Gerald Zaltman and Robin Higie, "Seeing the Voice of the Customer: The Zaltman Metaphor Elicitation Technique," Marketing Science Institute Report Number 93–114.

Gerald Zaltman and Robin Higie, "Seeing the Voice of the Customer: Metaphor-Based Advertising Research," *Journal of Advertising Research* (July/August 1995), pp. 35–51.

15. Geraldine R. Henderson, Dawn Iacobucci, and Bobby J. Calder, "Brand Diagnostics: The Use of Consumer Associative Networks for the Brand Manager," working paper, Fuqua School of Business, Duke University.

16. Jennifer Aaker, "Dimensions of Measuring Brand Personality," *Journal of Marketing Research*, 34 (August 1997), pp. 347–356.

17. Jennifer Aaker, "Dimensions of Measuring Brand Personality," *Journal of Marketing Research*, 34 (August 1997), pp. 347–356.

18. Thomas K. Srull, "Methodological Techniques for the Study of Person Memory and Social Cognition," in Robert S. Wyer and Thomas K. Srull, eds., *Handbook of Social Cognition*, Vol. 2. Hillsdale NJ: Lawrence Erlbaum, 1984, pp. 1–72.

19. Bill Abrams and David P. Garino, "Package Design Gains Stature as Visual Competition Grows," *Wall Street Journal* (August 6, 1981), p. 25.

20. Joseph W. Alba and J. Wesley Hutchinson, "Dimensions of Consumer Expertise," *Journal of Consumer Research*, 13 (March 1987), pp. 411–454.

21. Raymond Gordon, "Phantom Products," *Forbes* (May 21, 1984), pp. 202–4.

22. Prakash Nedungadi, "Recall and Consumer Consideration Sets: Influencing Choice without Altering Brand Evaluations," *Journal of Consumer Research*, 17 (December 1990), pp. 263–276.

23. Philip Kotler, *Marketing Management: Analysis, Planning, Implementation, and Control*, Prentice Hall. Upper Saddle River, NJ, 1994. 8th ed. (1991-7th ed.)

24. Neil R. Barnard and Andrew S. C. Ehrenberg, "Robust Measures of Consumer Brand Beliefs," *Journal of Marketing Research*, 26 (November 1990), pp. 477–484.

25. For example, see Gilbert A. Churchill, Jr., *Marketing Research*, 5th ed. Chicago: Dryden, 1991; or David A. Aaker, *Marketing Research*, 5th ed. New York: John Wiley & Son, 1995.

26. Joseph F. Hair, Jr., Rolph E. Anderson, Ronald Tatham, and William C. Black, *Multivariate Data Analysis*, 4th ed., Upper Saddle River, NJ: Prentice Hall, 1995.

27. Jean-Noel Kapferer and Gilles Laurent, "Consumers' Brand Sensitivity: A New Concept for Brand Management," working paper, Centre HEC-ISA. Jean-Noel Kapferer and Gilles Laurent, "Consumer Brand Sensitivity: A Key to Measuring and Managing Brand Equity," presentation at Marketing Science Institute Conference, "Defining, Measuring, and Managing Brand Equity," March 1–3, 1988, Austin, TX.

28. Icek Ajzen and Martin Fishbein, *Understanding Attitudes and Predicting Social Behavior*. Upper Saddle River, NJ: Prentice Hall, 1980.

CHAPTER 9

Measuring Outcomes of Brand Equity

Preview

The previous chapter described different approaches to measure consumers' brand knowledge structures to be able to identify and quantify potential sources of brand equity. By applying these measurement techniques, marketers should be able to gain a good understanding of the depth and breadth of awareness and the strength, favorability, and uniqueness of associations for their brands. The customer-based brand equity model states that as a consequence of creating such knowledge structures, consumers respond more favorably to the marketing activity for a brand than if the brand had not been identified to consumers. As described in chapter 2, a product with positive brand equity can potentially enjoy the following seven important customer-related benefits:

1. Be perceived differently and produce different interpretations of product performance.
2. Enjoy greater loyalty and be less vulnerable to competitive marketing actions.
3. Command larger margins and have more inelastic responses to price increases and elastic responses to price decreases.
4. Receive greater trade cooperation and support.
5. Increase marketing communication effectiveness.
6. Yield licensing opportunities.
7. Support brand extensions.

The customer-based brand equity model maintains that these benefits, and thus the ultimate value of a brand, depends on the underlying components of brand knowledge and sources of brand equity. As chapter 8 described, these individual components can be measured, but their resulting value still must be estimated in some way. In this chapter, we examine measurement procedures to assess the effects of brand knowledge structures on these and other outcomes of interest to marketers. In doing so, we are able to get a much clearer picture of the value of a brand.

First, we review comparative methods—a means to better assess the effects of consumer perceptions and preferences on consumer response to various aspects of the marketing program and the specific benefits of brand equity. Next, we consider holistic methods—an attempt to come up with an estimate of the overall or summary value of a brand.[1]

Comparative Methods

Comparative methods involve experiments that examine consumer attitudes and behavior toward a brand to more directly estimate the benefits arising from having a high level of awareness and strong, favorable, and unique brand associations. There are two types of comparative methods. *Brand-based comparative approaches* use experiments in which one group of consumers responds to an element of the marketing program or some marketing activity when it is attributed to the target brand and another group responds to that same element or activity when it is attributed to a competitive or fictitiously named brand. *Marketing-based comparative approaches* use experiments where consumers respond to changes in elements of the marketing program or marketing activity for the target brand or competitive brands.

In other words, the brand-based comparative approach holds the marketing program fixed and examines consumer response based on changes in brand identification, whereas the marketing-based comparative approach holds the brand fixed and examines consumer response based on changes in the marketing program. We describe these two approaches in turn. *Conjoint analysis* is then described as a technique that, in effect, combines the two approaches.

BRAND-BASED COMPARATIVE APPROACHES

As a means of measuring the outcomes of brand equity, brand-based comparative approaches hold the marketing element or activity under consideration fixed and examine consumer response based on changes in brand identification. These measurement approaches typically employ experiments where one group of consumers respond to questions about the product or some aspect of its marketing program when it is attributed to the brand and one (or more) groups of consumers respond to the same product or aspect of the marketing program when it is attributed to some other brand or brands, typically a fictitiously named or unnamed version of the product or service or one or more competitive brands. Comparing the responses of the two groups provides some useful insights into the equity of the brand. Consumer responses may be on the basis of beliefs, attitudes, intentions, or actual behavior.

Competitive brands can be a useful benchmark with brand-based comparative approaches. Although consumers may interpret marketing activity for a fictitiously named or unnamed version of the product or service in terms of their general product category knowledge (e.g., by assuming prototypical product or service specifications and price, promotion, and distribution strategies for the anonymous entry in the category), they may also have a particular brand or "exemplar" in mind. This exemplar may be the category leader or some other brand that consumers feel is representative of the category (e.g., their most preferred brand). Inferences for any missing information may be made based on their knowledge of this particular brand in memory. Thus, it may be instructive to examine how consumers evaluate a proposed new ad campaign, new promotion offering, new product, etc. when it is also attributed to one or more major competitors.

Applications

The classic example of the brand-based comparative approach is "blind testing" research studies where consumers examine or use a product with or without brand identification. For example, recall the beer taste test results from chapter 2 that showed how dramatically consumer perceptions differed depending on the presence or absence of brand identification. Thus, one natural application of the brand-based comparative approach is with product purchase or consumption—as long as the brand identification can be hidden in some way for the "unbranded" control group. Products could be existing ones or proposed new extensions.

Brand-based comparative approaches are also useful to determine brand equity benefits related to price margins and premiums. For example, when American Motors first tested (what was then called) the Renault Premier automobile, they conducted an experiment to come up with a financial value for the brand name.[2] One group of consumers were shown an "unbranded" model of the car. After visually inspecting the car, consumers in this group were asked what they would pay for it. For the un-branded version, consumers reported on average that they would pay about $10,000. Other groups of consumers went through the same inspection and measurement procedure when the car was identified as one of various other brand names. When the car was identified as the Renault Premier, consumers priced the car at around $13,000, and when it was identified as a Chrysler, the average reservation price was even slightly higher. After Chrysler subsequently bought American Motors, the car was later introduced as the Chrysler Eagle Premier, and the two models sold for $12,400 and $14,100.

Assessing customer-based brand equity with marketing communications presents a greater challenge with the brand-based comparative approach, for example, consumer response to a proposed new advertising campaign. In this case, story boards and animatic or photomatic versions of an ad could be used rather than a finished ad to allow for the necessary disguise of the brand. Although this approach should work well with "informational" type ads, it probably would be less appropriate for "transformational" type ads, where production values are a critical ingredient in achieving communication goals. Also, such an approach would only capture the effects of brand knowledge on consumer response to creative and message strategies and not media weight.

Critique

The main advantage to a brand-based comparative approach is that, because it holds all aspects of the marketing program fixed for the brand, it isolates the value of a brand in a very real sense. Understanding exactly how knowledge of the brand affects consumer responses to prices, advertising, and other factors is extremely useful in developing strategies in these different areas. At the same time, there is almost an infinite variety of marketing activities that potentially could be studied so that the totality of what is learned will depend on how many different applications are examined.

Brand-based comparative methods are particularly applicable when the marketing activity under consideration represents a change from past marketing of the brand, such as a new sales or trade promotion, ad campaign, or proposed brand extension. If the marketing activity under consideration is already strongly identified with the brand (e.g., an ad campaign that has been running for years), it may be difficult to attribute some aspect of the marketing program to a fictitiously named or unnamed version of the product or service in a believable fashion.

Thus, a crucial consideration with the brand-based comparative approach is the experimental realism that can be achieved when some aspect of the marketing program is attributed to a fictitiously named or unnamed version of the product or service. There will necessarily be a tradeoff involving a sacrifice of some realism in order to gain sufficient control to be able to isolate the effects of brand knowledge. Detailed concept statements of the particular marketing activity under consideration can be employed in some situations when it may be otherwise difficult for consumers to examine or experience that element of the marketing program without being aware of the brand.

Thus, concept statements may be useful in assessing customer-based brand equity when consumers make some type of product evaluation or respond to a proposed price or distribution change. For example, consumers could be asked to judge a proposed new product when it is either introduced by the firm as a brand extension or, alternatively, introduced by an unnamed firm in that product market. Similarly, consumers could be asked acceptable price ranges and store locations for the brand name product or a hypothetical unnamed version. Nevertheless, a concern with brand-based comparative approaches is that the simulations and concept statements that are used may highlight those particular characteristics that are mentioned or featured and make them more salient than they would otherwise be, distorting the results.

MARKETING-BASED COMPARATIVE APPROACHES

Marketing-based comparative approaches hold the brand fixed and examine consumer response based on changes in the marketing program.

Applications

There is a long academic and industry tradition exploring price premiums with these types of comparative approaches. In the mid-1950s, Edgar Pessemier developed a dollarmetric measure of brand commitment that involved a step-by-step increase of the price difference between the brand normally purchased and an alternative brand.[3] Pessemier plotted the percentage of consumers who switched from their regular brand as a function of the brand price increases to reveal brand-switching and loyalty patterns. Variations of this approach have been adopted by a number of marketing research suppliers to derive similar types of demand curves—Branding Brief 9–1 describes the results of ad agency DDB Needham's pricing studies—and many firms now try to assess price sensitivity and thresholds for different brands. For example, Intel routinely surveys computer shoppers to find out how much of a discount they would require before switching to a personal computer that did not have an Intel microprocessor in it, or, conversely, what premium they would be willing to pay to buy a personal computer with an Intel microprocessor in it.

Marketing-based comparative approaches can be applied in other ways. Consumer response to different advertising strategies, executions or media plans can be assessed through multiple test markets. For example, IRI's electronic test markets (see Branding Brief 6–1) and other such research methodologies can permit tests of different advertising weights or repetition schedules as well as ad copy tests. By controlling for other factors, the effects of the brand and product can be isolated. Recall from chapter 2 how Anheuser-Busch conducted an extensive series of test markets that revealed that Budweiser beer had such a strong image with consumers that advertising could be cut, at least in the short run, without hurting sales performance.

Potential brand extensions can also be explored in this fashion by collecting consumer evaluations to a range of concept statements describing brand extension candidates. For example, Figure 9–1 displays the results of a consumer survey examining reactions to possible extensions of the Planters nuts brand. Contrasting those extensions that consumers approve with those that they disapprove provides some indication of the equity of the brand involved. In this example, the survey results would seem to suggest that consumers expect any Planters brand extension to be "nut-related." Appropriate product characteristics for a possible Planters brand extension

---

DDB Needham's Pricing Studies

James Crimmins reports that DDB Needham takes the consumer perspective to look at brand value.[a] He maintains that brand value has three dimensions:

- The amount of value added by a brand name in a category
- The breadth of the added value, that is, the range of product categories in which the brand name can add value
- The content of the added value, that is, the specific qualities that are implied by the brand name that serve as the reasons why consumers choose the brands

Crimmins argues that marketers often measure the content of the brand name but rarely measure the amount or breadth of brand value. He defines the amount of value added by a brand as the ratio of its price to its competitor's price when both products are equally desirable to consumers, minus one. In other words, if brand A and brand B are equally desirable when brand A costs $1.20 and brand B costs $1.00, then the amount of relative value added by brand A is 20 percent, as follows:

$$\$1.20/\$1.00 - 1 = 20\%$$

DDB Needham implements this approach by offering consumers a series of choices among five or six brands where only the price of the target brand is changed to become the lowest and highest in the choice set while all other prices stay constant.

In applying this methodology, DDB Needham has measured the value added by brand names in a wide range of categories. They found that across thirteen categories, the median amount of value added by the number-one brand relative to a store brand was around 40 percent although this number varied widely from a high of 113 percent to a low of 19 percent. They also examined the value added of the number-one brand versus the number-two brand across fourteen product categories and found that the typical number one brand is worth around 10 percent more than its next biggest competitor. DDB Needham also used this methodology to examine the breadth of a brand.

---

[a]James C. Crimmins, "Better Management of Brand Value," *Journal of Advertising Research* (July/August 1992), pp. 11–19.

---

would seem to be "crunchy," "sweet," "salty," "spicy," and "buttery." In terms of what parts of the store where consumers would expect to find new Planters products, the snack and candy sections seem most likely. On the other hand, consumers do not seem to expect to find new Planters products in the breakfast food aisle, bakery product section, refrigerated section or frozen food section.

Average Scale Rating[a]	Proposed Extensions
10	Peanuts
9	Snack mixes, nuts for baking
8	
7	Pretzels, chocolate nut candy, caramel corn
6	Snack crackers, potato chips, nutritional granola bars
5	Tortilla chips, toppings (ice cream/dessert)
4	Lunchables/lunch snack packs, dessert mixes (cookie/cake/brownie)
3	Ice cream/ice cream bars, toppings (salad/vegetable)
2	Cereal, toaster pastries, oriental entrees/sauces, stuffing mix, refrigerated dough, jams/jellies
1	Yogurt

[a]Consumers rated proposed extensions on 11-point scale anchored by:
  0 = Definitely would *not* expect Planters to sell it
10 = Definitely would expect Planters to sell it.

FIGURE 9-1   Reactions to Proposed Planters Extensions

Critique

The main advantage with the marketing-based comparative approach is the ease of implementation. Virtually any proposed set of marketing actions can be compared for the brand. At the same time, the main drawback of the comparative approach is that it may be difficult to discern whether consumer response to changes in the marketing stimuli are being caused by brand knowledge or more generic product knowledge. In other words, it may be that for *any* brand in the product category, consumers would be willing or unwilling to pay certain prices, accept a particular brand extension, and so on. One way to determine whether consumer response is specific to the brand is to conduct similar tests of consumer response with competitive brands. We next describe a statistical technique well-suited to do just that.

CONJOINT ANALYSIS

Conjoint analysis is a survey-based multivariate technique that enables marketers to profile the consumer buying decision process with respect to products and brands.[4] Specifically, by asking consumers to express preferences or make choices among a number of carefully designed different product profiles, marketing researchers can determine the tradeoffs consumers are making between various brand attributes and thus the importance that consumers are attaching to those attributes.[5] Each profile shown to consumers is made up of a set of attribute levels. The particular attribute levels chosen for any one profile are made on the basis of experimental design principles to satisfy certain mathematical properties. The value that consumers attach to each attribute level, as statistically derived by the conjoint formula, is called a *part worth*. The part worths can be used in various ways to estimate how consumers would value a new combination of the attribute levels.

In particular, one attribute that can be included is the brand name. The part worth for the "brand name" attribute would then reflect its value. One classic study of conjoint analysis was reported by Green and Wind.[6] This study concerned consumer evaluations of a spot-remover product. Five attributes were studied: (1) package design, (2) brand name, (3) price, (4) Good Housekeeping seal, and (5) money-back guarantee. Figure 9–2 contains the eighteen profiles that made up the experimental design. Figure 9–3 shows the results of the statistical analyses to determine the part worths.

Adweek magazine recently commissioned conjoint studies in five broad categories: credit cards, adult ready-to-eat cereals, soft drinks, airlines, and automobiles. While some findings might seem somewhat surprising, other findings were more predictable. For example, as might be expected, Coke Classic and Pepsi were evaluated almost equally. Branding Brief 9–2 describes a highly successful application of conjoint analysis in the development of the Courtyard by Marriott hotel chain.

Applications

There are a number of different possible applications of conjoint analysis. Ogilvy & Mather ad agency has used a Brand/Price Tradeoff methodology as a means of assessing advertising effectiveness and brand value.[7] Brand/Price Tradeoff is a simplified version of conjoint measurement with just two variables—brand and price. Consumers are faced with a series of simulated purchase choices between different combinations of brands and prices. Each choice triggers an increase in the price of the selected brand, forcing the consumer to trade off between choosing a preferred brand and paying less. In this way, consumers reveal how much their brand loyalty is worth and, conversely, which brands they would relinquish for a lower price

Other variations and applications of conjoint analysis have been applied by academic researchers with an interest in brand image and equity.[8] For example, academic researchers Rangaswamy, Burke, and Oliva use conjoint analysis to explore how brand names interact with physical product features to affect the extendability of brand names to new product categories.[9] Barich and Srinivasan apply conjoint analysis to corporate image programs to show how it can be used to: (1) determine the company attributes that are relevant to customers; (2) rank the importance of those attributes; (3) estimate the costs of making improvements (or correcting customer perceptions); and (4) prioritize image goals so that the improvements in perceptions obtain the maximum benefit, in terms of customer value, for the resources spent.[10]

Critique

The main advantage of the conjoint-based approach is that it allows for both different brands and different aspects of the product or marketing program (product composition, price, distribution outlets, etc.) to be simultaneously studied. Thus, information about consumers' response to different marketing activities can be uncovered for both the focal and competing brands. One of the disadvantages of conjoint analysis is that marketing profiles may be presented to consumers that violate their expectations based on what they already know about brands. Thus, if conjoint analysis

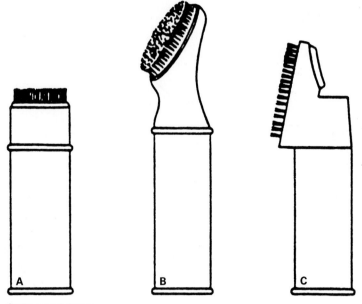

Orthogonal Array

	Package design	Brand name	Price	Good Housekeeping seal?	Money-back guarantee?	Respondent's evaluation (rank number)
1	A	K2R	$1.19	No	No	13
2	A	Glory	1.39	No	Yes	11
3	A	Bissell	1.59	Yes	No	17
4	B	K2R	1.39	Yes	Yes	2
5	B	Glory	1.59	No	No	14
6	B	Bissell	1.19	No	No	3
7	C	K2R	1.59	No	Yes	12
8	C	Glory	1.19	Yes	No	7
9	C	Bissell	1.39	No	No	9
10	A	K2R	1.59	Yes	No	18
11	A	Glory	1.19	No	Yes	8
12	A	Bissell	1.39	No	No	15
13	B	K2R	1.19	No	No	4
14	B	Glory	1.39	Yes	No	6
15	B	Bissell	1.59	No	Yes	5
16	C	K2R	1.39	No	No	10
17	C	Glory	1.59	No	No	16
18	C	Bissell	1.19	Yes	Yes	1*

*Highest ranked

FIGURE 9–2 Product Profiles for Conjoint Analysis Application

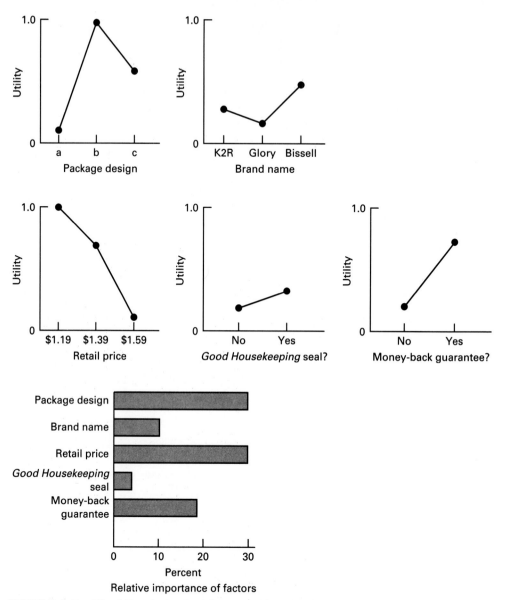

FIGURE 9–3 Part Worth Results for Conjoint Analysis Application

---

BRANDING BRIEF 9-2

Building a Better Mousetrap[a]

One powerful application of conjoint analysis is the recent design and introduction of the new hotel chain, Courtyard by Marriott.[b] The Marriott company was founded as a root beer stand in 1927 by J. Willard Marriott, Sr., and its early business ventures were in family restaurant business. Marriott built its first hotel in 1957. While most hotel chains grow through franchising, Marriott designed, built, financed, and managed its own hotels, selling ownership to limited partnerships or institutions. Growing quickly in the following decades, by the early 1980s, Marriott had become the single largest operator of hotel rooms in the United States, and its lucrative management contracts made Marriott one of the industry's most profitable companies.

Because the market was expanding, Marriott concentrated on operations and, like most competitors, did little consumer research or extensive marketing programs. Marriott was centrally driven and run, literally, by the book—a dozen or so encyclopedic tomes that detailed everything from how to clean the rooms to how to prepare the food in the restaurants. In the early 1980s, however, Marriott became concerned that it was running out of good sites to place the standard design Marriott Hotel—a 300- to 400-room, full-service facility located near an airport or large suburban population center—at a high enough rate of growth. In search of new markets, Marriott felt it needed to shift from a purely operations-driven company to a marketing-oriented company. As part of this shift, Marriott bolstered its marketing staff, devised new promotional and compensation plans to keep its best people selling, started a frequent-guest bonus program, automated hotel operations to allow more efficient tracking of guests, and tried to find ways to "jazz up" Marriott's staid image.

Marriott also made a decision to develop a new hotel chain for the segment of travelers who were not satisfied with current offerings. Two *a priori* segments were identified: business travelers (who travel at least six times a year and stay in mid-level hotels or motels) and pleasure travelers (who travel at least twice a year and stay in hotels or motels). Marriott management faced a difficult decision: What type of hotel facilities and services should Marriott design and offer to attract these travelers away from competitive facilities? To answer this question, Marriott conducted an extensive three-year research project. The centerpiece of the project was one of the most complex conjoint studies conducted to date. In this study, seven sets of attributes were examined: (1) external factors, (2) rooms, (3) food-related services, (4) lounge facilities, (5) services, (6) leisure-time facilities, and (7) security factors.

The research indicated that room quality and outdoor surroundings mattered most to a would-be guest so Marriott tried to keep Courtyard's rooms as close as possible in quality to its full-service rooms, while throwing in a landscaped courtyard with serpentine walkways and a swimming pool. To reduce costs, a Courtyard hotel has a tiny lobby and lounge, just one restaurant, several small meeting rooms, and no doorman, bellman, or room service. The Courtyard by Marriott chain has been a huge success, and the chain grew to 300 hotels by 1994 (with sales exceeding $1 billion).

---

[a]Steve Schwartz, "How Marriott Changes Hotel Design to Tap Midpriced Market" *Wall Street Journal* (September 18, 1985), pp. 1, 22.

[b]Jerry Wind, Paul E. Green, Douglas Shifflet, and Marsha Scarbrough, "*Courtyard by Marriott:* Designing a Hotel Facility with Consumer-Based Marketing Models," *Interfaces,* 19 (1) (January–February 1989), pp. 25–47.

is employed, care must be taken that consumers do not evaluate unrealistic product profiles or scenarios.

Holistic Methods

Comparative methods attempt to approximate specific benefits of brand equity. *Holistic methods* attempt to place an overall value for the brand in either abstract utility terms or concrete financial terms. Thus, holistic methods attempt to "net out" various considerations to determine the unique contribution of the brand. The *residual approach* attempts to examine the value of the brand by subtracting out consumers' preferences for the brand based on physical product attributes alone from their overall brand preferences. The *valuation approach* attempts to place a financial value on brand equity for accounting purposes, mergers and acquisitions, or other such reasons. We describe each of these two approaches in turn.

RESIDUAL APPROACHES

The rationale behind residual approaches is a view that brand equity is what remains of consumer preferences and choices after subtracting physical product effects. A basic tenet behind these approaches is that it is possible to infer the relative valuation of brands through the observation of consumer preferences and choices *if* as many sources of measured attribute values are taken into account as possible. Specifically, several researchers have defined brand equity as the incremental preference over and above that which would result for the product without brand identification. According to this view, brand equity would then be calculated by attempting to subtract out preference for objective characteristics of the physical product from overall preference.[11]

Kamakura and Russell propose a scanner-based measure of brand equity model that employs consumer purchase histories from supermarket scanner data to estimate brand equity through a residual approach.[12] Specifically, their model attempts to explain the choices observed from a panel of consumers as a function of the store environment (actual shelf prices, sales promotions, displays, etc.), the physical characteristics of available brands, and a residual term dubbed brand equity. By controlling for other aspects of the marketing mix, their approach attempts to estimate that aspect of

brand preference that is unique to a brand and not currently duplicated by competitors. The output of their model is estimates of benefit segments, cross price elasticities for segments and the entire market, and equity measures for each brand. They illustrate their approach with an application to the laundry detergent market. Their analysis shows that brand equity is closely related to order of entry of brands and their cumulative advertising expenditures.

Swait, Louviere, and their colleagues have proposed a related approach to measuring brand equity that designs choice experiments that account for brand name, product attributes, brand image, and differences in consumer sociodemographic characteristics and brand usage.[13] They define the *equalization price* as the price that equates the utility of a brand to the utilities that could be attributed to a brand in the category where no brand differentiation occurred. Equalization price can be seen as a proxy for brand equity. They illustrate their approach with applications to the deodorant, athletic shoe, and jeans markets.

Park and Srinivasan have proposed perhaps the most comprehensive residual methodology to measure brand equity based on the multiattribute attitude model.[14] Their approach reveals the relative sizes of different bases of brand equity by dividing it into two components: attribute-based and non-attribute-based. The *attribute-based component* of brand equity is the difference between subjectively perceived attribute values and objectively measured attribute values. Objectively measured attribute values are collected from independent testing services such as Consumer Reports or acknowledged experts in the field. The *non-attribute-based component* of brand equity is the difference between subjectively perceived attribute values and overall preference and reflects the consumer's configural appraisal of a brand that would go beyond the assessment of the utility of individual product attributes. Park and Srinivasan propose a survey procedure to collect information to estimate these different perception and preference measures.

To demonstrate their approach, they conducted a national survey of current users of toothpaste or mouthwashes. Objective attribute ratings were collected from a survey of 120 dentists. Figure 9–4 contains the study results. On the basis of this measurement procedure, the researchers concluded that Crest had a positive equity of 21.6 cents while the baseline store brand had a negative equity of 33.4 cents. The researchers also concluded that the non-attribute-based component of brand equity showed larger variation across brands than the attribute-based components.

Critique

Residual approaches provide a useful benchmark to interpret brand equity. In particular, they may be useful for situations when approximations of brand equity are necessary and thus may also be valuable to researchers interested in a financially oriented perspective on brand equity. The disadvantages of these approaches is that they are most appropriate for brands characterized with a predominance of product-related attribute associations because they are unable to distinguish between different types of non-product-related attribute associations. Consequently, its diagnostic value for strategic decision making in other cases is much more limited.

More generally, note also that this approach takes more of a "static" view of brand equity by attempting to identify sources of consumer preferences in order to uncover the contribution by the brand. This approach contrasts sharply with the

Aggregate-Level Brand Equity Measures (in cents)			
Brands	*Brand Equity*	*Attribute- Based*	*Nonattribute- Based*	*Market Share (%)[a]*
Toothpastes				
Crest	21.6	4.8	16.9	36.9
Colgate	17.1	2.2	14.9	23.7
Aquafresh	−3.7	−3.5	−.2	10.6
Close-Up	−1.6	3.0	−4.6	9.1
Store brand	−33.4	−6.5	−27.0	1.0
Mouthwashes				
Scope	28.7	1.9	26.8	32.1
Listerine	−.3	−1.2	.9	29.4
Close-Up	.5	−.2	.8	1.0
Plax	−5.9	2.7	−8.6	10.7
Colgate	1.4	.5	.9	1.5
Store brand	−24.4	−3.6	−20.8	4.0

[a]Based on the last brand purchased

FIGURE 9-4 Results of Park and Srinivasan Study

"process" view advocated with the customer-based brand equity framework, as reflected by the brand-based and marketing-based comparative approaches, which stress looking at consumer response to the marketing of a brand and attempting to uncover the extent to which that *response* is affected by brand knowledge. Consumer response is defined in terms of perceptions, preferences, and behaviors and, most importantly, with respect to a variety of marketing activities. That is, it goes beyond attempting to dissect consumer preferences to the product itself to assess how consumers respond to the marketing of a brand and, especially, new marketing activity supporting it.

This distinction is also relevant for the issues of "separability" in brand valuation raised by various researchers. For example, Barwise and his colleagues note that marketing efforts to create an extended or augmented product (e.g., extra features or service plus other means to enhance brand value) "raises serious problems of separating the value of the brand name and trademark from the many other elements of the 'augmented' product."[15] According to customer-based brand equity, those efforts could affect the favorability, strength, and uniqueness of various brand associations, which would, in turn, affect consumer response to *future* marketing activities. For example, imagine that a brand becomes known for providing extraordinary customer service because of certain policies and favorable advertising, publicity, and/or word of mouth (e.g., as with Nordstrom department stores). These favorable perceptions of customer service and the favorable attitudes they engender could create customer-based brand equity by affecting consumer response to a price policy (e.g., a willingness to pay higher prices), a new ad campaign (e.g., the acceptance of an ad illustrating customer satisfaction), or a brand extension (e.g., interest in trying a new type of retail outlet).

VALUATION APPROACHES

Rationale

The ability to value and put a price tag on a brand's value may be useful for a number of reasons:

1. *Mergers and acquisitions:* Both to evaluate possible purchases as well as to facilitate disposal
2. *Brand licensing:* Internally for tax reasons and to third parties
3. *Fund raising:* As collateral on loans or for sale or leaseback arrangements
4. *Brand management decisions:* To allocate resources, develop brand strategy, or prepare financial reports

For example, many companies appear as attractive acquisition candidates because of the strong competitive positions of their brands and their reputation with consumers. Unfortunately, the value of the brand assets in many cases are largely excluded from the company's balance sheet and therefore of little use in determining value. As one commentator put it, "The worth of a strong brand is rarely represented fully in a company's stock price. It doesn't appear on a balance sheet. But it's the motor behind the numbers, the fuel that drives consumers to the marketplace and helps them make choices."[16]

It has been argued that adjusting the balance sheet to reflect the true value of a company's brands permits a more realistic view and allows assessment of the purchase premium to book value that might be earned from the brands after acquisition. Such a calculation, however, would require estimates of capital required by brands and the expected after-acquisition return on investment (ROI) of a company.

Separating out the percentage of revenue or profits that is attributable to brand equity is a difficult task.[17] In the United States, there is no conventional accounting method for doing so. Thus, despite the fact that expert analysts estimate the value of the Coca-Cola name to approach $45 *billion*, it appears in the owner's books as only $25 *million*. In other countries, however, there has been more movement in the direction of attempting to capture that value. How do you calculate the financial value of a brand? In this section, after providing some accounting background and historical perspective, we critically evaluate several such approaches.

Accounting Background

The assets of a firm can be classified as either tangible or intangible. *Tangible assets* include: (1) property, plant, and equipment; (2) current assets (inventories, marketable securities, and cash); and (3) investments in stocks and bonds. The value of tangible assets can be estimated using accounting book values and reported estimates of replacement costs. *Intangible assets*, on the other hand, are defined as any factors of production or specialized resources that permit the company to earn cash flows in excess of the return on tangible assets. In other words, intangible assets augment the earning power of a firm's physical assets. Intangible assets are typically lumped by accountants under the heading of goodwill and include things like patents, trademarks, and licensing agreements, as well as "softer" considerations such as the skill of the management and customer relations.

Also, in an acquisition, the goodwill item often includes a premium paid to gain control that, in certain instances, may even exceed the value of tangible and intangible assets. Despite the fact that these various types of intangibles are so disparate in nature, they are all swept together under the term "goodwill." In Britain and certain other countries, it has been common to write off against reserves the goodwill element of an acquisition but tangible assets, on the other hand, are transferred straight to the acquiring company's balance sheet.

Historical Perspectives

Brand valuation's recent past started with Rupert Murdoch's News Corporation which included a valuation of some of its magazines on its balance sheets in 1984, as permitted by Australian accounting standards. The rationale was that the "goodwill" element of publishing acquisitions—the difference in value between net assets and the price paid—was often enormous and negatively impacting the balance sheet. The recognition that the titles themselves contained much of the value of the acquisition was used to justify placing them on the balance sheet, improving the debt/equity ratio as a result and allowing News Corp. to get some much needed cash to finance the further acquisitions of some foreign media companies.

In the United Kingdom, Grand Metropolitan was one of the first British companies to place a dollar value on the brands it owned and to put that value on its balance sheet. When Grand Met acquired Heublein distributors, Pearle eye care, and Sambuca Romana liqueur in 1987, it placed the value of some of its brands—principally Smirnoff—on the balance sheet for roughly $1 billion. In doing so, Grand Met used one of two different methods. If a company consisted of primarily one brand, it figured the value of the brand was 75 percent of the purchase price, while if the company had many brands, it used a multiple of an income figure.

British firms used brand values primarily to boost their balance sheets. By recording their brand assets, the firms maintained that they were attempting to bring their shareholder funds nearer to the market capitalization of the firm. Accounting firms in favor of valuing brands put forth arguments such as that it was a way to strengthen the presentation of a company's accounts; to record hidden assets so that they were disclosed to company's shareholders; to enhance a company's shareholders' funds to improve its gearing ratios; to provide a realistic basis for management and investors to measure a company's performance; and to reveal detailed information on brand strengths so that management could formulate appropriate brand strategies. In practical terms, recording brand values as intangible assets from the firm's perspective increased the asset value of the firm.

Actual practices have varied from country to country. When Grand Met acquired Pillsbury for $5.7 billion in January 1989, it revalued Pillsbury's intangible assets to add $2.4 billion to its intangible assets. Unlike a U.S. company, Grand Met did not intend to write down those intangible assets (unless permanently impaired). Grand Met (separate from intangible assets) also adjusted its goodwill account by a substantial amount as a result of the Pillsbury acquisition.[18]

In the United Kingdom, Martin Sorrell improved the balance sheet of WPP by attaching brand value to its primary assets, including J. Walter Thompson Co., Ogilvy & Mather, and Hill & Knowlton, stating in the annual report that:[19]

Intangible fixed assets comprise certain acquired separable corporate brand names. These are shown at a valuation of the incremental earnings expected to arise from the ownership of brands. The valuations have been based on the present value of notional royalty savings arising from [ownership] and on estimates of profits attributable to brand loyalty.

In the United States, generally accepted accounting principles, due to blanket amortization principals, would mean that to place a brand on the balance sheet would require amortization of that asset for up to forty years. Such a charge would severely hamper firm profitability, and as a result firms avoid such accounting maneuvers. On the other hand, certain other countries (including Canada, Germany, and Japan) have gone beyond tax deductibility of brand equity to permit some or all of the goodwill arising from an acquisition to be deducted for tax purposes.

General Approaches

In determining the value of a brand in an acquisition or merger, a number of approaches are possible:[20]

Cost Approach   This view maintains that brand equity is the amount of money that would be required to reproduce or replace the brand (including all costs for research and development, test marketing, advertising, etc.). One commonly noted criticism of approaches involving historic or replacement cost is that it rewards past performance in a way that may bear little relation to future profitability—that is, many brands with expensive introductions have been unsuccessful. It obviously is easier to estimate costs of tangible assets than intangible assets but the latter often may lie at the heart of brand equity.

Market Approach   According to this view, brand equity can be thought of as the present value of the future economic benefits to be derived by the owner of the brand asset. In other words, the amount an active market would allow such that the brand asset would be exchanged between a willing buyer and seller. The main problem with this approach is the lack of open market transactions for brand assets.

Simon and Sullivan, however, have developed a technique for estimating a firm's brand equity derived from financial market estimates of brand-related profits.[21] They define brand equity as the incremental cash flows that accrue to branded products over and above the cash flows that would result from the sale of unbranded products. To implement their approach, they begin by estimating the current market value of the firm. The market value of the firm's securities are then assumed to provide an unbiased estimate of the future cash flows that are attributable to all of the firm's assets. Their methodology attempts to extract the value of a firm's brand equity from the value of the firm's other assets. The result is an estimate of brand equity that is based on the financial market valuation of the firm's future cash flows.

Their rationale is as follows. They assume that the financial market value of a firm is based on the aggregate earning power of both tangible and intangible assets. They also make the "efficient-market" assumption that in a well-functioning capital market, securities prices provide the best available unbiased estimate of the value of a company's assets. In other words, the financial market's valuation of the firm incorporates the expected value of future cash flows and returns.

From these basic premises, Simon and Sullivan derive their methodology to extract the value of brand equity from the financial market value of the firm. The total asset value of the firm is defined as the sum of the market value of common stock, preferred stock, long-term debt, and short-term debt. The value of intangible assets is captured in the ratio of the market value of the firm to the replacement cost of its tangible assets. Three categories of intangible assets are defined: (1) brand equity, (2) nonbrand factors that reduce the firm's costs relative to competitors (e.g., R&D and patents), and (3) industry-wide factors that permit monopoly profits such as regulation. By considering factors such as the age of the brand, order of entry in the category, and current and past advertising share, Simon and Sullivan then provide estimates of brand equity.

Figure 9–5 displays their estimates of brand equity for some selected food companies. According to this analysis, the high estimated brand equity of Tootsie Roll suggests that even though it may be relatively easy to develop a "me-too" candy product, a considerable amount of the profits ascribed to Tootsie Roll accrue directly from its strong brand name. Simon and Sullivan conduct an in-depth analysis tracing the brand equity of Coca-Cola and Pepsi over three major events in the soft drink industry from 1982 to 1986, e.g., showing how the introduction of Diet Coke increased the equity of Coca-Cola and decreased the equity of Pepsi.

Branding Brief 9–3 describes the findings of some other studies that have studied the relationship of brand equity to the stock market.

Income Approach   The third approach to determining the value of a brand argues that brand equity is the discounted future cash flow from the future earnings stream for the brand. Three such income approaches are:

1. Capitalizing royalty earnings from a brand name (when these can be defined)
2. Capitalizing the premium profits that are earned by a branded product (by comparing its performance with that of an unbranded product)
3. Capitalizing the actual profitability of a brand after allowing for the costs of maintaining it and the effects of taxation

Company	Brand Equity
Anheuser-Busch	35
Brown-Foreman	82
Cadbury-Schwepps	44
Campbells	31
Dreyer's Ice Cream	151
General Mills	52
Heinz	62
Kellogg	61
Pillsbury	30
Quaker	59
Ralston-Purina	40
Sara Lee	57
Seagram	73
Smucker	126
Tootsie Roll	148

FIGURE 9–5 Simon and Sullivan's Measured Brand Equity for Food Product Companies (as a percent of firm replacement value)

The Stock Market's View of Brand Equity

Several researchers have studied how the stock market reacts to the brand equity for companies and products. For example, David Aaker and Robert Jacobson examined the association between yearly stock return and yearly brand equity changes (as measured by EquiTrend's perceived quality rating of brand equity) for 34 companies during the years of 1989 to 1992.[a] They also compared the accompanying changes in current-term return on investment (ROI). They found that, as expected, stock market return was positively related to changes in ROI. Interestingly, they also uncovered a strong positive relationship between brand equity and stock return. Firms who experienced the largest gains in brand equity saw their stock return average 30 percent. Conversely, those firms with the largest losses in brand equity saw stock return average a negative 10 percent. The researchers concluded that investors can and do learn about changes in brand equity—not necessarily through EquiTrend studies (which may have little exposure to the financial community) but by learning about a company's plans and programs.

Adopting an event study methodology, Lane and Jacobson were able to show that stock market participant's response to brand extension announcements, consistent with the tradeoffs inherent in brand leveraging, depend interactively and nonmonotoically on brand attitude and familiarity.[b] Specifically, the stock market responded most favorably to extensions of high-esteem, high-familiarity brands and to low-esteem, low-familiarity brands (in the latter case, presumably because there was little to risk and much to gain with extensions). The stock market reaction was less favorable (and sometimes even negative!) for extensions of brands where consumer familiarity was disproportionately high compared to consumer regard and to extensions of brands where consumer regard was disproportionately high compared to familiarity.

---

[a]David A. Aaker and Robert Jacobson, "The Financial Information Content of Perceived Quality," *Journal of Marketing Research*, 31 (May 1994), pp. 191–201.
[b]Vicki Lane and Robert Jacobson, "Stock Market Reactions to Brand Extension Announcements: The Effects of Brand Attitude and Familiarity," *Journal of Marketing*, 59 (January 1995), pp. 63–77.

As a very rough guideline, Chevron's Lew Winters reports that accountants are inclined to price a brand at four to six times the annual profit realized from the sale of the product bearing the brand name to be acquired.

Interbrand

Probably the premier brand valuation firm, Interbrand evaluated a number of different approaches in developing its brand valuation methodology. Its goal was to identify an approach that: (1) incorporated marketing, financial, and legal aspects; (2) followed fundamental accounting concepts; (3) allowed for regular revaluation on a consistent basis; and (4) was suitable for acquired and home-grown brands.

Interbrand decided to approach the problem of brand valuation by assuming that the value of a brand, like the value of any other economic asset, was the present worth of the benefits of future ownership.[22] Thus, to estimate brand value, they felt it was necessary to identify projected future earnings for the brand and the discount rate to adjust these earnings for inflation and risk. Specifically, based on all of these criteria, Interbrand developed a two-step method of calculating brand value: (1) identifying the true brand earnings and cash flow, and (2) capitalizing the earnings by applying a multiple to historic earnings as a discount rate to future cash flow.[23] Both steps require a number of different actions, as described next.

Brand Earnings   Interbrand believes that arriving at a measure of profitability is more complicated than merely applying a simple discount rate or multiplier to the post-tax profits of the brand-owning company for two main reasons. First, Interbrand maintains that not all of the profitability of a brand can necessarily be applied to the valuation of that brand. A brand may essentially be a commodity or derive much of its profitability from non-brand-related considerations (e.g., its distribution system). The elements of profitability that do not result from the brand's identity must therefore be excluded. Second, because the valuation may be adversely affected by using a single, possible unrepresentative year's profit, a three-year weighted average of historical profit is used.

A number of additional issues must be taken into consideration in calculating brand earnings: determining brand profits, the elimination of private label production profits, remuneration of capital, and so on. In recognition of these considerations, brand earnings are calculated by subtracting a number of quantities from brand sales: (1) costs of brand sales, (2) marketing costs, (3) variable and fixed overheads (including depreciation and central overhead allocation), (4) remuneration of capital charge (a 5% to 10% rental charge on the replacement value of the capital employed in the line of production), and (5) taxation.

Brand Strength   To adjust these earnings, Interbrand conducts an in-depth assessment of brand strength. Brand strength is reflected in a number of factors: historic and forecast, quantitative and qualitative, objective and subjective, and micro and macro. Assessing brand strength involves a detailed review of the brand, its positioning, the market in which it operates, competition, past performance, future plans, risks to the brand, and other considerations. Specifically, to determine brand strength, Interbrand evaluates brands on the basis of seven factors.[24]

1. *Leadership:* The brand's ability to influence its market and be a dominant force with a strong market share such that it can set price points, command distribution, and resist competitive invasions. A brand that leads its market or market sector is a more stable and valuable property than a brand lower down the order.

2. *Stability:* The ability of the brand to survive over a long period of time based on consumer loyalty and past history. Long-established brands that have become part of the "fabric" of their markets are particularly valuable.

3. *Market:* The brand's trading environment in terms of growth prospects, volatility, and barriers to entry. Brands in markets such as foods and drinks are intrinsically more valu-

able than brands in, for example, high tech or clothing areas as these latter markets are more vulnerable to technological or fashion changes.

4. *Geographic spread:* The ability of the brand to cross geographic and cultural borders. Brands that are international are inherently more valuable than national or regional brands.

5. *Trend:* The ongoing direction and ability of the brand to remain contemporary and relevant to consumers.

6. *Support:* The amount and consistency of marketing and communication activity. Those brand names that have received consistent investment and focused support must be regarded as more valuable than those that have not. While the amount spent in supporting a brand is important, the quality of this support is equally significant.

7. *Protection:* The brand owner's legal titles. A registered trademark is a statutory monopoly on a name, device, or a combination of these two. Other protection may exist in common law, at least in certain countries. The strength and breadth of the brand's protection is critical in assessing its worth.

Interbrand administers a detailed questionnaire to collect the information. Branding Brief 9–4 provides an example of how four different brands might be scored.

The brand strength is a composite of seven weighted factors, each of which is scored according to established guidelines (see Figure 9–6). The scores are weighted and the resulting total, known as the brand strength score, is expressed as a percentage. This score is in turn converted to an earnings multiple to be used against the brand-related profits. Certain adjustments are made to create a weighted average of post-tax brand profitability against which the brand multiplier is applied. Interbrand notes that the relationship between brand strength and brand value follows a normal distribution and is represented by a classic "S" curve as a result of the following factors:[25]

- As a brand's strength increases from virtually zero (an unknown or new brand) to a position as a number three or four brand in a national market the brand value increases gradually.
- As a brand moves into the number one or two position in its market and/or becomes internationally known, there is an exponential effect on its brand value.
- Once a brand is established as a powerful world brand its value no longer increases at the same exponential rate even if market share internationally is improved.

Financial World

Financial World magazine provides annual estimates of brand equity of leading brands on the basis of a formula very similar to that of Interband. To illustrate, it begins with company sales and, based on expert estimates of margins, the resulting operating profits. Next, it deducts from operating profits an amount equal to what would be earned on a basic unbranded or generic version of the product. For example, it estimates, again based on expert opinion, the amount of capital required to generate a brand's sales, multiplies that amount by the net return on that capital (e.g., they assume a generic version of the product would generate a 5% net return on capital employed), and subtracts that figure from operating profits to determine the profit attributable to the brand name alone. After adjusting on the basis of taxes, the remainder is deemed net brand-related profits. Finally, *Financial World* assigns a multiple based on Interbrand's seven-factor model of brand strength outlined above. The stronger the brand, the higher the multiple, ranging from 6 to 20. Branding Brief 9–5

BRANDING BRIEF 9-4

Interbrand Applications

Birken provides the following example of how four brands could be scored for brand strength by the Interbrand method.

Brand A   This is a leading international toiletries brand operating in a "mainstream" and stable market sector. The brand has been established for many years and is a brand leader or a strong number two in all its major international markets.

Brand B   This is a leading food brand that operates in a traditional and stable market but one where tastes are slowly changing with a move away from traditional products and towards convenience foods. The brand has limited export sales and its trademark protection, though quite strong, is based mainly on common law rather than registered rights.

Brand C   This is a secondary but aspiring national soft drink brand launched just five years ago. The market is very dynamic and growing strongly. The brand has been very heavily supported and much has been achieved; it is, however, still early days. Even though export sales are still very small, the brand name, "get up," and positioning have all been developed with international markets in mind. The brand still has some trademark registration problems in its home market.

Brand D   This is an established but quite regional brand in a highly fragmented yet stable market.

Based on these profiles, the following scores might be given by Interbrand on the seven strength factors:

	Maximum Score	Brand A	Brand B	Brand C	Brand D
Leadership	25	18	19	9	6
Stability	15	11	10	7	11
Market	10	7	6	8	6
Internationality	25	17	5	2	0
Trend	10	6	6	7	5
Support	10	8	7	7	4
Protection	5	5	3	4	3
Total	100	72	56	44	35

---

shows how this procedure resulted in a brand value for Coke in 1993 of $33.4 billion and also displays *Financial World*'s "Top Twenty" from 1996 (by which time Coke was estimated to have a brand value of $43.4 billion).

In summary, brand valuation and the "brands on the balance sheet" debate are controversial subjects. The advantage of the Interbrand and *Financial World* valua-

---

Leadership (25%)
Market share
Awareness
Positioning
Competitor profile

Stability (15%)
Longevity
Coherence
Consistency
Brand identity
Risks

Market (10%)
What is the market?
Nature of the market
   (e.g., volatility)
Size of market
Market dynamics
Barriers to entry

Internationality (25%)
Geographical spread
International positioning
Relative market share
Prestige
Ambition

Trend (10%)
Long term market share performance
Projected brand performance
Sensibility of brand plans
Competitive actions

Support (10%)
Consistency of message
Consistency of spend
Above versus below line
Brand franchise

Protection (5%)
Trademark registration
   and registrability
Common law
Litigation/disputes

FIGURE 9-6 Interbrand Brand Strength Attributes

tion approaches is that they are very generalizable and can be applied to virtually any type of brand or product. Nevertheless, many marketing experts feel it is impossible to reduce the richness of a brand to a single, meaningful number, and that any formula is too much of an abstraction and too arbitrary. Thus, the primary disadvantage of these and other similar valuation approaches is that they make a host of potentially oversimplified assumptions to arrive at one measure of brand equity. For example, Sir Michael Perry, chairman of Unilever, objects for philosophical reasons:[26]

> The seemingly miraculous conjuring up of intangible asset values, as if from nowhere, only serves to reinforce the view of the consumer skeptics, that brands are just high prices and consumer exploitation. At Unilever, we have consistently rejected this approach.

At the heart of much of the criticism is the issue of separability. An *Economist* editorial put it this way:[27] "Brands can be awkward to separate as assets. With Cadbury's Dairy Milk, how much value comes from the name Cadbury? How much from Dairy Milk? How much merely from the product's (replicable) contents or design?"

BRANDING BRIEF 9-5

Financial World Calculation of the Value of the Coca-Cola Brand

Financial World began its calculation of the value of the Coca-Cola brand in 1993 with the worldwide sales figure for the Coca-Cola brand family of $9 billion. Based on estimates of consultants and beverage experts, they assumed that Coke's operating margin was around 30 percent, resulting in operating profits for the Coke brand of $2.8 billion. Although Coke's extensive bottling and distribution system generated another $27 billion in revenues and $3 billion in operating profits, because the numbers did not reflect the value added by Coke directly, they were not taken into consideration in valuing the Coca-Cola brand.

With Coke's product-related profits in place, *Financial World* next deducted from these operating profits an amount equal to what could be expected to be earned on a basic or generic version of the product. To do so, it assumed, based on analysts' calculations, that it requires on average 60 cents worth of capital—which is generally a little higher than net property, plant and equipment plus net working capital—to produce each dollar of sales. Thus, *Financial World* calculated the capital used in production for Coke to be $5.5 billion. They next assumed that a 5 percent net return on employed capital after inflation could be expected from a similar non-branded product and therefore deducted 5 percent of Coke's capital employed ($273 million) from the $2.7 billion in operating profits to obtain the profit attributable to the brand name alone.

The resulting adjusted operating profit figure was $2.4 billion. After adjusting for taxes, the remainder was deemed to be net brand-related profits. The final adjustment was made on the basis of brand strength. Brand strength was calculated based on Interbrand's definition and seven components. Consistent with Interbrand's approach, the brand strength multiplier takes on values ranging from 9 to 20. Coke was assigned the highest multiple, resulting in a brand value of $33.4 billion. In 1996, that figure rose to $43.43 billion, and Coke became *Financial World*'s second most valuable brand. The value of *Financial World*'s entire top twenty from that year is as follows:

	Brand Value (million)		*Brand Value (million)*
1. Marlboro	$44,614	11. Gillette	$10,292
2. Coca-Cola	43,427	12. Motorola	9,624
3. McDonald's	18,920	13. GE	9,304
4. IBM	18,491	14. Pepsi	8,895
5. Disney	15,358	15. Sony	8,800
6. Kodak	13,267	16. Hewlett-Packard	8,111
7. Kellogg's	11,409	17. Frito-Lay	7,786
8. Budweiser	11,026	18. Levi's	7,376
9. Nescafe	10,527	19. Nike	7,267
10. Intel	10,499	20. Campbell's	6,464

To make a sports analogy, extracting brand value may be as difficult as determining the value of the coach to a team's performance.

As a result of these criticisms, the climate towards brand valuation has changed. In 1989, Britain's Accounting Standards Committee ruled that companies could only value brands if they were acquired in a takeover and if only they were then depreciated over twenty years against profits—adopting the more conservative American practice of gradually writing off goodwill (brands and all). The International Accounting Standards Committee is also grappling with the issue.

Review

In this chapter, we considered the two main ways to measure the benefits or outcomes of brand equity—comparative methods (a means to better assess the effects of consumer perceptions and preferences on aspects of the marketing program) versus holistic methods (an attempt to come up with an estimate of the overall value of the

---

Comparative methods involve experiments that examine consumer attitudes and behavior towards a brand to more directly assess the benefits arising from having a high level of awareness and strong, favorable, and unique brand associations.

> *Brand-based comparative approaches* use experiments in which one group of consumers responds to an element of the marketing program when it is attributed to the brand and another group responds to that same element when it is attributed to a competitive or fictitiously named brand.

> *Marketing-based comparative approaches* use experiments where consumers respond to changes in elements of the marketing program for the brand or competitive brands.

> *Conjoint analysis* is a survey-based multivariate technique that enables marketers to profile the consumer buying decision process with respect to products and brands.

Holistic methods attempt to place an overall value for the brand in either abstract utility terms or concrete financial terms. Thus, holistic methods attempt to "net out" various considerations to determine the unique contribution of the brand.

> The *residual approach* attempts to examine the value of the brand by subtracting out consumers' preferences for the brand based on physical product attributes alone from their overall brand preferences.

> The *valuation approach* attempts to place a financial value on the brand for accounting purposes, mergers and acquisitions, or other such reasons.

FIGURE 9-7 Measures of Outcomes of Brand Equity

brand). Figure 9–7 summarizes the different approaches. The two approaches can be seen as complementary. In fact, understanding the particular range of benefits for a brand on the basis of comparative methods may be useful as inputs in estimating the overall value of a brand by holistic methods. Chapter 10 considers how these measures can be further supplemented by measures of sources of brand equity as part of a brand equity measurement system.

Discussion Questions

1. Choose a product. Conduct a branded and unbranded experiment. What do you learn about the equity of the brands in that product class?
2. Can you identify any other advantages or disadvantages with the comparative methods?
3. What do you think of the Interbrand methodology? What do you see as its main advantages and disadvantages?

Notes

1. Peter Farquhar and Yuji Ijiri make several other distinctions in classifying brand equity measurement procedures. They describe two broad classes of measurement approaches to brand equity: Separation approaches and integration approaches. *Separation approaches* view brand equity as the "value added" to a product. Farquhar and Ijiri categorize separation approaches into residual methods and comparative methods:

   1) *Residual methods* determine brand equity as what remains after subtracting physical product effects.

   2) *Comparative methods* determine brand equity by comparing the branded product with an unbranded product or an equivalent benchmark.

   Integration approaches, on the other hand, typically define brand equity as a composition of basic elements. Farquhar and Ijiri categorize integration approaches into association and valuation methods:

   1) *Valuation methods* measure brand equity by its cost or value as an intangible asset for a particular owner and intended use.

   2) *Association methods* measure brand equity in terms of the favorableness of brand evaluations, the accessibility of brand attitudes, and the consistency of brand image with consumers.

   The previous chapter described techniques that could be considered association methods. In this chapter, we consider techniques related to the other three categories of methods.

2. B. G. Yovovich, "What is Your Brand Really Worth," *Adweek's Marketing Week* (August 8, 1988), pp. 18–24.

3. Edgar Pessemier, "A New Way to Determine Buying Decisions," *Journal of Marketing*, 24 (1959), pp. 41–46.

4. Paul E. Green and V. Srinivasan, "Conjoint Analysis in Consumer Research: Issues and Outlook," *Journal of Consumer Research,* 5 (1978), pp. 103–123 and Paul E. Green and V. Srinivasan, "Conjoint Analysis in Marketing: New Developments with Implications for Research and Practice," *Journal of Marketing*, 54 (1990), pp. 3–19

5. For more details see Betsy Sharkey, "The People's Choice" *Adweek* (November 27, 1989), pp. 6–10.

6. Paul E. Green and Yoram Wind, "New Ways to Measure Consumers' Judgments," *Harvard Business Review,* 53 (July–August 1975), pp. 107–11.

7. Max Blackstone, "Price Trade-Offs as a Measure of Brand Value," *Journal of Advertising Research* (August/September, 1990), pp. RC3–RC6.

8. For some discussion, see Jordan Louviere and Richard Johnson, "Measuring Brand Image with Conjoint Analysis and Choice Models," in Lance Leuthesser (ed.), *Defining, Measuring, and Managing Brand Equity: A Conference Summary,* Marketing Science Institute Report # 88-104.

9. Arvind Rangaswamy, Raymond R. Burke, and Terence A. Oliva, "Brand Equity and the Extendibility of Brand Names," *International Journal of Research in Marketing*, 10 (March 1993), pp. 61–75. See also Moonkyu Lee, Jonathan Lee, and Wagner A. Kamakura, "Consumer Evaluations of Line Extensions: A Conjoint Approach," in *Advances in Consumer Research*, 23 (1996), pp. 289–295.

10. Howard Barich and V. Srinivasan, "Prioritizing Marketing Image Goals under Resource Constraints," *Sloan Management Review* (Summer 1993), pp. 69–76.

11. V. Srinivasan, "Network Models for Estimating Brand-Specific Effects in Multi-Attribute Marketing Models," *Management Science*, 25 (January 1979), pp. 11–21.

12. Wagner A. Kamakura and Gary J. Russell, "Measuring Brand Value with Scanner Data," *International Journal of Research in Marketing*, 10 (1993), pp. 9–22.

13. Joffre Swait, Tulin Erdem, and Jordan Louviere, and Chris Dubelar, "The Equalization Price: A Measure of Consumer-Perceived Brand Equity," *International Journal of Research in Marketing,* 10 (1993), pp. 23–45.

14. Chan Su Park and V. Srinivasan, "A Survey-Based Method for Measuring and Understanding Brand Equity and its Extendability," *Journal of Marketing Research*, 31 (May 1994), pp. 271–288.

15. Patrick Barwise (with Christopher Higson, Andrew Likierman and Paul Marsh), "Brands as 'Separable Assets,'" *Business Strategy Review* (Summer 1990), p. 49.

16. Betsy Sharkey, "The People's Choice," *Adweek* (November 27, 1989), pp. M.R.C. 8.

17. Joanne Lipman, "British Companies Value U.S. Brand Names—Literally," *Wall Street Journal* (February 9, 1989), p. B-6 and Laurel Wentz, "WPP Considers Brand Valuation," *Advertising Age* (January 16, 1989), p. 24.

18. David M. Fredricks, "Branded Assets: The Issue of Measurement," ARF Fourth Annual Advertising and Promotion Workshop, February 12–13, 1992.

19. Quoted in "What's a Brand Worth?" editorial, *Advertising Age* (July 18, 1994).

20. Lew Winters, "Brand Equity Measures: Some Recent Advances," *Marketing Research* (December 1991), pp. 70–73; Gordon V. Smith (1988), *Corporate Valuation—A Business and Professional Guide.* New York: John Wiley & Sons, Inc.

21. Carol J. Simon and Mary W. Sullivan, "Measurement and Determinants of Brand Equity: A Financial Approach," *Marketing Science,* 12 (1) (Winter 1993), pp. 28–52.

22. Michael Birkin, "Assessing Brand Value," *Brand Power*, ed. Paul Stobart. Washington Square, NY: NY University Press, 1994.

23. Simon Mottram, "The Power of the Brand," ARF Brand Equity Conference, February 15–16, 1994.

24. John Murphy, *Brand Valuation*, Hutchinson Business Books: London, 1989; Jean-Noel Kapferer, *Strategic Brand Management*, Kogan Page Limited: London, 1992; Noel Penrose

and Martin Moorhouse, "The Valuation of Brands," *Trademark World*, Issue Seventeen, February 1989; Tom Blackett, "The Role of Brand Valuation in Marketing Strategy," *Marketing Research Today*, 17(4) (November 1989), pp. 245–248.

25. Michael Birkin, "Assessing Brand Value," *Brand Power*, ed. Paul Sobart, Washington Square, NY: NY University Press, 1994.

26. Diane Summers, "IBM Plunges in Year to Foot of Brand Name Value League," *Financial Times* (July 11, 1994), p. 1.

27. "On the Brandwagon," *The Economist* (January 20, 1990), p. 17.

C H A P T E R

Brand Equity Measurement System

Preview

To measure brand equity, ideally, it would be possible to create a "brand equity index," one easily calculated number that would summarize the "health" of the brand and that would capture completely its brand equity. But just as a thermometer measuring body temperature provides only one indication of how healthy a person is, so does any one measure of brand equity provide only one indication of the "health" of a brand. Brand equity is a multidimensional concept and complex enough so that many different types of measures are required. Multiple measures increase the diagnostic power of marketing research and the likelihood that managers will better understand what is happening to their brands and, perhaps more importantly, why.

In arguing that researchers should employ multiple measures of brand equity, Chay draws an interesting comparison between measuring brand equity and determining the performance of an aircraft in flight:

> The pilot of the plane has to consider a number of indicators and gauges as the plane is flown. There is the fuel gauge, the altimeter, and a number of other important status indicators. All of these dials and meters tell the pilot different things about the health of the plane. There is no one gauge that summarizes everything about the plane. The plane needs the altimeter, compass, radar, and the fuel gauge. As the pilot looks at the instrument cluster, he has to take all of these critical indicators into account as he flies.

Chay concludes by noting that the gauges on the plane that together measure its health in flight are analogous to the multiple measures of brand equity that are necessary to collectively assess the health of a brand.

In this chapter, we consider how to develop and implement a brand equity measurement system. A *brand equity measurement system* is a set of research procedures designed to provide timely, accurate, and actionable information for marketers on brands so that they can make the best possible tactical decisions in the short run and strategic decisions in the long run. The goal in developing a brand equity measurement system is to be able to achieve a full understanding of the sources and outcomes of brand equity and be able to, as much as possible, relate the two. Chapter 8 reviewed research methods to measure sources of brand equity (i.e., the depth and breadth of brand awareness and strength, favorability, and uniqueness of brand associations). Chapter 9 reviewed research methods to measure outcomes of brand equity (i.e., seven key benefits that potentially may result from creating these sources of brand equity). In this chapter, suggestions are offered as to how marketers can uncover and track the sources and outcomes of their brand equity and effectively implement a brand equity measurement system using these research methods.

The ideal brand equity measurement system would provide complete, up-to-date, and relevant information on the brand and all its competitors to relevant decision makers within the organization. Introducing a brand equity measurement system requires enacting the following three steps:

1. Conducting brand audits.
2. Designing brand tracking studies.
3. Establishing a brand equity management system.

The remainder of the chapter outlines each of these steps in detail.

Conducting Brand Audits

To learn what consumers know about brands and products so that they can make informed strategic decisions, marketers should first conduct a brand audit to profile consumer knowledge structures. A *brand audit* is a comprehensive examination of a brand in terms of its sources of brand equity. In accounting, an audit involves a systematic inspection of accounting records involving analyses, tests, and confirmations.[1] The outcome of an accounting audit is an assessment of the financial health of the firm. An outside accounting firm serves as the auditor and checks the accuracy, fairness, and general acceptability of accounting records, rendering its opinion in the form of a report.

A similar concept has been suggested for marketing. A marketing audit has been defined as a "comprehensive, systematic, independent, and periodic examination of a company's—or business unit's—marketing environment, objectives, strategies, and activities with a view of determining problem areas and opportunities and recommending a plan of action to improve the company's marketing performance."[2] The marketing audit process has been characterized as a three-step procedure where the first step is agreement on objectives, scope, and approach; the second step is data collection; and the third and final step is report preparation and presentation. Thus, the marketing audit is an internal company-focused exercise to make sure that marketing operations are efficient and effective.

A brand audit, on the other hand, is a more external consumer-focused exercise that involves a series of procedures to assess the health of the brand, uncover its sources of brand equity, and suggest ways to improve and leverage its equity. A brand audit requires understanding sources of brand equity from the perspective of both the firm and the consumer. From the perspective of the firm, it is necessary to understand exactly what products and services are currently being offered to consumers and how they are being marketed and branded. From the perspective of the consumer, it is necessary to dig deeply into their minds and tap perceptions and beliefs to uncover the true meaning of brands and products.

The brand audit can be used to set strategic direction for the brand. Are the current sources of brand equity satisfactory? Do certain brand associations need to be strengthened? Does the brand lack uniqueness? What brand opportunities exist and what potential challenges exist for brand equity? As a result of this strategic analysis, a marketing program can be put into place to maximize long-term brand equity. A brand audit should be conducted whenever important shifts in strategic direction are contemplated. Moreover, conducting brand audits on a regular basis (e.g., annually) allows marketers to keep their "fingers on the pulse" of their brands so that they can be more proactively and responsively managed. As such, they are particularly useful background for managers as they set up their marketing plans.

Brand audits can have profound implications on the strategic direction for brands and their resulting performance.[3] As a result of a brand audit, luxury goods marketer Alfred Dunhill refined its classic "English" appeal—which has been especially valuable in Asia—to also take on more of a dynamic, international flavor. In Europe, the results of a brand audit led Polaroid to decide to try to change its conventional photography image to emphasize the "fun side" of its cameras. Polaroid learned from research that its cameras could be seen as a social stimulant and catalyst, provoking fun moments in people's lives, a theme that has been picked up in advertising and that has suggested the creation of new distribution strategies.

The brand audit consists of two steps: the brand inventory and the brand exploratory. Each is discussed in turn.

BRAND INVENTORY

The purpose of the *brand inventory* is to provide a current, comprehensive profile of how all the products and services sold by a company are marketed and branded. Profiling each product or service requires that all associated brand elements be identified as well as the supporting marketing program. In other words, it is necessary to catalog for each product or service sold: (1) the names, logos, symbols, characters, packaging, slogans, or other trademarks used, and (2) the inherent product attributes or characteristics of the brand and the pricing, communications, distribution policies, and any other relevant marketing activity related to the brand. This information should be summarized in both visual and verbal form.

The outcome of the brand inventory should be an accurate, complete, and timely profile of how all the products and services sold by a company are branded in terms of which brand elements are employed (and how) and the nature of the supporting marketing program. As part of the brand inventory, it is also advisable to profile competitive brands, in as much detail as possible, in terms of their branding and marketing efforts. Such information is useful in determining points of parity and points of difference.

Rationale
The brand inventory is a valuable first step in the brand audit for several reasons. First, it helps to suggest what consumers' current perceptions *may* be based on. In other words, consumer associations are typically—although not necessarily always—rooted in the reality of how products and services are branded according to the particular brand elements employed and the *intended* meaning attached to them through the supporting marketing program. Thus, the brand inventory provides useful information for interpreting followup research activity such as the brand exploratory, which collects actual consumer perceptions toward the brand.

Although the brand inventory is primarily a descriptive exercise, some useful analysis can be conducted too, and the brand inventory may provide some initial insights into how brand equity may be better managed. For example, the consistency of all the different products or services sharing a brand name can be assessed. Are the brand elements used in a consistent basis or are there many different variations and versions of the brand name, logo, and other elements for the same product (perhaps for no obvious reason) depending on which geographical market it is being sold in or which market segment it is being targeted to, for example? Similarly, are the supporting marketing programs logical and consistent across related brands? As firms expand their products geographically and extend them into other categories, it is common for deviations—sometimes significant in nature—to emerge in the appearance of brands and how they are being marketed across markets and products. A thorough brand inventory should be able to reveal the extent of brand consistency.

At the same time, a brand inventory can also reveal a lack of perceived differences among different products sharing the brand name—perhaps as a result of line extensions—that are designed to differ on one or more key dimensions. Creating sub-brands with distinct positionings is often a marketing priority and a brand inventory may help to uncover undesirable redundancy and overlap that could potentially lead to consumer confusion or retailer resistance.

The Disney Experience

In the late 1980s, Disney became concerned that some of its characters (Mickey Mouse, Donald Duck, etc.) were being used inappropriately and becoming overexposed. To investigate the severity of the problem, Disney undertook an extensive brand inventory. First, they compiled a list of all Disney products that were available (licensed and company manufactured) and all third-party promotions (complete with point-of-purchase displays and relevant merchandising) from stores across the country and all over the world. At the same time, Disney also launched its first major consumer research study to investigate how consumers felt about the Disney brand.

The results of the brand inventory were a revelation to senior management. The Disney characters were on so many products and marketed in so many ways that it was difficult to understand how or why many of the decisions had been made in the first place. The consumer study only reinforced Disney's concerns. Because of the broad exposure of the characters in the marketplace, many consumers had begun to feel that Disney was exploiting its name. For example, Disney characters were used in a promotion of Johnson Wax, a product that would seemingly leverage almost nothing of value from the Disney name. Consumers even felt that Disney exploited itself when its characters were linked with well-liked premium brands such as Tide laundry detergent. In this case, consumers felt that the characters added little value to the product and, worse yet, the characters involved children in a purchase decision that they would typically ignore.

If consumers reacted so negatively with a strong brand like Tide, imagine how they reacted when they saw the hundreds of other Disney licensed products or joint promotions! Because of its aggressive marketing efforts, Disney had written contracts with many of its "park participants" for co-promotions or licensing arrangements. Disney characters were selling everything from diapers to cars to McDonald's hamburgers. Disney learned in the consumer study, however, that consumers did not differentiate between all of the product endorsements. "Disney was Disney" to consumers, whether they saw the characters in films, records, theme parks, or consumer products. Consequently, *all* products and services that used the Disney name or characters had an impact on Disney's brand equity. Consumers reported that they resented the large number of endorsements because they felt that they had a special, personal relationship with the characters and with Disney that should not be handled so carelessly.

As a result of the brand inventory and the consumer research study, Disney moved quickly to establish a brand equity team to better manage the brand franchise and more selectively evaluate licensing and other third-party promotional opportunities. One of the mandates of this team was to ensure that a consistent image for Disney—reinforcing their key association of wholesome, fun family entertainment—was conveyed by all third-party products and services. For example, Disney was approached to co-brand a mutual fund in Europe that was designed for families as a way for parents to save for the college expenses of their children. The opportunity was declined despite the consistent "family" association because Disney believed that a connection with the financial community or banking suggested other associations that were inconsistent with its brand image.

BRAND EXPLORATORY

Although the supply-side view of the brand as revealed by the brand inventory is useful, *actual* consumer perceptions, of course, may not necessarily reflect the consumer perceptions that were intended to be created by the marketing program. Thus, the second step of the brand audit is to provide detailed information as to what consumers think of the brand by means of the brand exploratory, particularly in terms of brand awareness and the strength, favorability, and uniqueness of brand associations. The *brand exploratory* is research activity directed to understand what consumers think and feel about the brand and its corresponding product category to identify sources of brand equity.

Preliminary Activities

Several preliminary activities are useful for the brand exploratory. First, in many cases, a number of prior research studies may exist and be relevant. It is important to dig through company archives to uncover reports that may have been buried and perhaps even long forgotten, but that contain insights and answers to a number of important questions or suggest new questions that may still need to be posed. These studies should be carefully reviewed and summarized as to the insights they yield into sources and outcomes of brand equity.

Second, it is also useful to interview internal personnel to gain an understanding of their beliefs about consumer perceptions for the brand and competitive brands. Past and current marketing managers may be able to share some wisdom not necessarily captured in prior research reports. For example, in Australia in the early 1970s, Lever used a "brightness" positioning for Omo laundry detergent—brightness both in terms of the clothes washed in Omo and the intelligence of women who used the product.[4] By being one of the first laundry detergents to show women in a modern light (and not just as being "chained" to their kitchens and utility rooms), Omo became the market leader. In the early 1980s, however, Lever abandoned the brightness theme and promoted other product qualities such as softness and whiteness. Its market share slipped from 18.5 percent in 1978 to 11 percent in 1987. By reacquainting themselves with the brand's past, Lever's management realized that Omo's core benefit truly was "brightness." As a result, Lever launched a new campaign in 1988 to revive the brand by reminding consumers of Omo's brightness heritage.[5]

The diversity of opinion that typically emerges from these internal interviews about the brand serves several functions, for example, increasing the likelihood that useful insights or ideas will be generated, as well as pointing out any inconsistencies or misconceptions that may exist internally for the brand. Although these preliminary activities may yield some useful findings and suggest certain hypotheses, they are often incomplete. As a result, additional research is often required to better understand how customers shop for and use products and services and what they think of various brands. To allow a broad range of issues to be covered and to permit certain issues to be pursued in greater depth, the brand exploratory often employs qualitative research techniques. Chapter 8 reviewed a number of these different approaches, as summarized in Figure 10–1.

Interpreting Qualitative Research

In choosing the range of possible qualitative research techniques to include in the brand exploratory, Gardner and Levy note:

> The emphasis in such research must necessarily be given to skill in interpretation and to reaching a coherent picture of the brand. The researchers must allow their respondents sufficient self-expression so that the data are rich in complex evaluations of the brand. In this way, the consumer's thoughts and feelings are given precedence rather than the preconceptions of the researchers, although these are present too in hypotheses and questions.[6]

Levy identifies three criteria by which a qualitative research program can be classified and judged: direction, depth, and diversity.[7] For example, any projective technique varies, respectively, in terms of the nature of the stimulus information involved (e.g., related to the person or the brand), the extent to which responses are more superficial and concrete in meaning versus deeper and more abstract in meaning

---

Free Association
Adjective Ratings and Checklists
Projective Techniques
Photo Sorts
Bubble Drawings
Story-Telling
Personification Exercises
Role-Playing

———
[a]Judie Lannon and Peter Cooper, "Humanistic Advertising: A Holistic Cultural Perspective," *International Journal of Advertising,* 2 (1983), pp. 195–213.

FIGURE 10-1 Summary of Qualitative Techniques[a]

(and thus requiring more interpretation), and how it relates to the information gathered by other projective techniques.

In Figure 10–1, the tasks at the top of the list involve very specific questions whose answers may be easier to interpret. The tasks on the bottom of the list (e.g., personification exercises and role-playing) involve potentially much richer questions but ones that are also much harder to interpret. According to Levy, the more specific the question, the narrower the range of information given by the respondent. When the stimulus information in the question is more open-ended and responses are freer or less constrained, the information provided tends to be greater. The more abstract and symbolic the research technique that is employed, however, the more important it is to follow up with probes and other questions that explicitly reveal the motivation and reasons why behind consumers' responses.

Ideally, qualitative research conducted as part of the brand exploratory would vary in direction and depth as well as in the diversity of the techniques involved. Regardless of which techniques were actually employed, the challenge with qualitative research is to provide accurate interpretation—going beyond what consumers explicitly state to determine what they implicitly mean.

Conducting Quantitative Research

Qualitative research is suggestive but a more definitive assessment of the depth and breadth of brand awareness and the strength, favorability, and uniqueness of brand associations often requires a quantitative phase of research. Chapter 8 reviewed a number of different quantitative approaches to provide better approximations of consumer brand knowledge structures, as summarized in Figure 10–2. The guidelines for the quantitative phase of the exploratory are relatively straightforward. All potentially salient associations identified by the qualitative research phase should be assessed according to strength, favorability, and uniqueness. Both specific brand beliefs and overall attitudes and behaviors should be examined to reveal potential sources and outcomes of brand equity. Additionally, the depth and breadth of awareness of

FIGURE 10-2 Summary of Quantitative Measures

1. *AWARENESS*
   - Recognition
   - Recall by product category cue
   - Recall by sub-category cue
   - Recall by usage situation cue

2. *IMAGE*
   - Open-ended associations
   - Attribute and benefit beliefs
   - Overall attitudes
   - Perceived quality and satisfaction
   - Reported past usage and intended future usage
   - Perceptions of the company behind the brand
   - Price perceptions

3. *BACKGROUND MEASURES*

the brand should also be assessed by employing various cues. Typically, it is necessary to conduct similar types of research for competitors to better understand their sources of brand equity and how they compare to the target brand.

Much of the discussion of qualitative and quantitative measures has concentrated on associations to the brand name element of the brand—that is, what do consumers think about the brand when given its name as a probe? Other brand elements could and should be studied in the brand exploratory as they may trigger other meanings and facets of the brand. Consumers can be asked what inferences they make about the brand on the basis of the product packaging and logo alone—for example, "What would you think about the brand on the basis of just its packaging alone?" Even more specific aspects of the brand elements could be explored—for example, the label on the package or the shape of the package itself—to uncover their role in creating brand associations and thus sources of brand equity. The more it is the case that other brand elements are present and visible when consumers make brand and product decisions (e.g., at the point of purchase), the more important it is to employ all relevant brand elements as stimuli. In the process of examining other brand elements, it is also important to determine which of these elements most effectively represents and symbolizes the brand as a whole.

BRAND POSITIONING AND THE SUPPORTING MARKETING PROGRAM

The brand exploratory should uncover the current knowledge structures for the core brand and its competitors as well as potential sources of brand equity. This information can provide the basis for the brand positioning (see chapter 3). Brand positioning requires analysis of that information to determine the desired brand awareness and brand image and the necessary points of parity and points of difference with respect to competitors. Moving from the current brand image to the desired brand image typically involves decisions to add new associations, strengthen existing ones, or weaken or eliminate undesirable ones in the minds of consumers. John Roberts, a leading marketing academic in Australia, sees the challenge in achieving the ideal positioning for a brand in being able to achieve congruence among: (1) what customers currently believe about the brand (and thus find credible), (2) what customers will value in the brand, (3) what the firm is currently saying about the brand, and (4) where the firm would like to take the brand (See Figure 10–3.)

A number of different internal management personnel can be part of the planning and positioning process (brand, marketing research, and production managers),

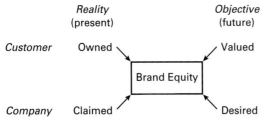

FIGURE 10-3 Roberts' Positioning Considerations for Managing Brand Equity

as well as relevant outside marketing partners such as ad agency representatives. Once marketers have a good understanding from the brand audit of current brand knowledge structures for their target consumers and have decided on the desired brand knowledge structures for optimal positioning, additional research still may be necessary to test out the viability of alternative tactical programs to achieve that positioning. There may be a number of different possible marketing programs that, at least on the surface, may be able to achieve the same goals, and additional research may be useful to assess their relative effectiveness and efficiency.

Finally, once the proper marketing programs are put in place, they can be evaluated as to their ability to achieve the relevant goals. In other words, to what extent does the marketing activity for the brand actually create the desired levels of brand awareness and brand image with consumers? The next section describes how tracking studies can be designed to monitor the ability of the marketing program to create sources and outcomes of brand equity.

Designing Brand Tracking Studies

Brand audits provide in-depth information and insights that are essential for setting long-term strategic direction for the brand. In terms of more short-term tactical considerations, less detailed brand-related information should be collected as a result of conducting tracking studies. *Tracking studies* involve information collected from consumers on a routine basis over time. Tracking studies typically employ quantitative measures to provide marketers with current information as to how their brands and marketing programs are performing on the basis of a number of key dimensions identified by the brand audit or other means.

Tracking studies play an important function for managers by providing consistent baseline information to facilitate their day-to-day decision making. As more marketing activity surrounds the brand—new products are introduced as brand extensions, an increasing variety of communication options are incorporated into marketing communications programs supporting the brand, and so on—it becomes difficult and expensive to research each individual marketing action. Tracking studies provide valuable diagnostic insights into the collective effects of a host of marketing actions on the equity of the brand. Regardless of how few or many changes are made in the marketing program over time, it is important to monitor the health of the brand so that proper adjustments can be made if necessary.

A number of issues must be addressed in implementing a brand equity tracking system. Here we will address what measures should be employed in tracking studies, how tracking studies should be implemented, and how tracking studies should be interpreted.

WHAT TO TRACK

As noted above, chapter 8 reviewed a number of quantitative measures of brand knowledge structures that may be useful for tracking purposes. Although this section presents some general tracking guidelines based on these measures, it should be recognized that it is usually necessary to customize tracking surveys to address the specific issues faced by the brand(s) in question. To a great extent, each brand faces a unique situation that must be reflected in different types of questions in its tracking survey.

Product-Brand Tracking

Tracking an individually branded product involves measuring brand awareness and image for the particular brand. In terms of brand awareness, both recall and recognition measures should be collected. In general, awareness measures should move from more general to more specific questions. Thus, it may make sense to first ask consumers what brands come to mind in certain situations, to next ask for recall of brands on the basis of various product category cues, and to then finish with tests of brand recognition (if necessary).

As with brand awareness, it is usually desirable that a range of more general to more specific measures be employed in brand tracking surveys to measure brand image, especially in terms of specific perceptions (what consumers think characterizes the brand) and evaluations (what the brands mean to consumers). A number of specific brand associations typically exist for the brand, depending on the richness of consumer knowledge structures, that could potentially be tracked over time. The most important specific brand associations are those attribute and benefit beliefs that serve as the basis of the brand positioning in terms of key points of parity and points of difference with competitive brands, such as performance-related attributes and benefits like convenience, ease of use, and so on. Certainly those specific brand associations that make up the potential sources of brand equity should be assessed on the basis of strength, favorability, and uniqueness *in that order*. Unless associations are strong enough so that they are likely to be recalled, their favorability does not matter, and unless associations are sufficiently favorable enough to be a decision consideration, uniqueness does not matter. Ideally, measures of all three dimensions would be collected but perhaps for only certain associations and only some of the time (e.g., favorability and uniqueness may only be measured once a year for three to five key associations).

Given that brands often compete at the augmented product level (see chapter 1), it is important to measure *all* associations that may distinguish competing brands. Thus, measures of specific, lower-level brand associations should include all potential sources of brand equity—product-related and non-product-related attributes and functional, experiential, and symbolic benefits. Because they often represent key points of parity or points of difference, it is particularly important to track benefit associations. To better understand any changes in benefit beliefs for a brand, however, it may be necessary to also measure the corresponding attribute beliefs that underlie those benefits. In other words, changes in descriptive attribute beliefs may help to explain changes in more evaluative benefit beliefs for a brand.

At the same time, it is also important to track more general, higher-order brand associations and outcome measures. Chapter 8 outlined various measures of brand attitudes, intentions, and behavior. After asking for overall opinions, consumers can be asked if they have changed their attitudes, intentions, and/or behavior in recent weeks or months, and if so, why they did so.

Branding Brief 10–1 provides an illustrative example of a tracking survey for the new brand of Miller beer.

Sample Brand Tracking Survey

To illustrate how brand tracking surveys might be conducted, consider the situation faced by Miller Brewing Co. Miller has an extensive brand portfolio, including a separate company, Plank Road Brewery, that they created to spin out non-Miller identified beers (see Figure 10–4 for an example of Miller's brand hierarchy). In 1996, Miller introduced a new flagship brand of beer, Miller beer.[a] Packaged with a distinctive red label and eagle logo, Miller beer was positioned as premium, mainstream beer with a "full, rich flavor" as a result of using the "hearts of the hops." Designed to compete head-on with Budweiser, the goal behind Miller beer was to strike a balance between taste and drinkability to meet what they felt was "the changing taste of today's beer drinkers." Initial ads exhorted drinkers to "Reach for what's out there" as images flashed by of young men riding motorcycles, hang-gliding over meadows, and kicking back on clapboard porches in the American heartland. As the vice president of marketing for Miller Brewing noted, "The new Miller beer will stand for possibilities" and reflect a "sea of change" in the emotions of young adults toward "forward-thinking optimism" and away from an "agenda of denial."

Assume that Miller Brewing was interested in designing a short tracking survey to be conducted over the phone for their new Miller beer. How might you set it up? Although there are a number of different types of questions, it might take the following form:

"We are conducting a short phone interview concerning consumer opinions about beer." [Establish legal drinking age.]

Brand Awareness and Usage

1. What brands of beer are you aware of?
2. Which brands of beer would you consider buying?
3. Have you bought any beer in the last week? Which brands?
4. If you were to buy beer for this coming weekend, which brand of beer would you buy?

Brand Image

We want to ask you some general questions about a particular brand of beer, Miller beer.

Have you heard of this beer? [Establish familiarity.]
Have you tried this beer? [Establish trial.]

5. When I say Miller beer, what are the first associations that come to your mind? Anything else?

We are interested in your overall opinion of Miller beer.

6. How favorable is your attitude toward Miller beer?
7. How well does Miller beer satisfy your needs?
8. How likely would you be to recommend Miller beer to others?

9. How good a value is Miller beer?
10. Is Miller beer worth a premium price?
11. What do you like best about Miller beer?
12. What is most unique about Miller beer?

We now would like to ask some specific questions about Miller beer. Please indicate your agreement with the following statements.

13. Miller beer . . .
    a) Is smooth and easy to drink
    b) Has a rich, full-bodied flavor
    c) Has a less bitter aftertaste
    d) Appeals to men
    e) Appeals to young adults
    f) Fun to drink with friends
    g) Represents positive, optimistic thinking

Corporate Image

We now want to ask you some questions about Miller Brewing Co., makers of Miller beer. Please indicate your agreement with the following statements.

14. Miller Brewing is . . .
    a) Innovative
    b) Trustworthy
    c) Likable
    d) Concerned about its customers
    e) Concerned about society as a whole

----

[a] Sally Goll Beatty, "Miller's Flagship Brew Sails on 'Sea Change' of Attitudes," *Wall Street Journal* (February 1, 1996), p. B7. Richard A. Melcher, "Is It Finally Miller Time?" *Business Week* (February 12, 1996), p. 37.

Corporate or Family Brand Tracking

In the case of a family or corporate brand, some additional questions may be warranted. Although many of these types of questions could be included in tracking studies for individual products for the brand, there may also be justification for tracking the corporate or family brand separately and/or concurrently with individual products. A number of specific measures of corporate brand associations are possible, including some of the following (illustrated with the GE corporate brand):

- How expert is GE at what they do?
- How well-managed is GE?
- How easy is it to do business with GE?
- How innovative is GE?

FIGURE 10-4 Miller Brand Hierarchy

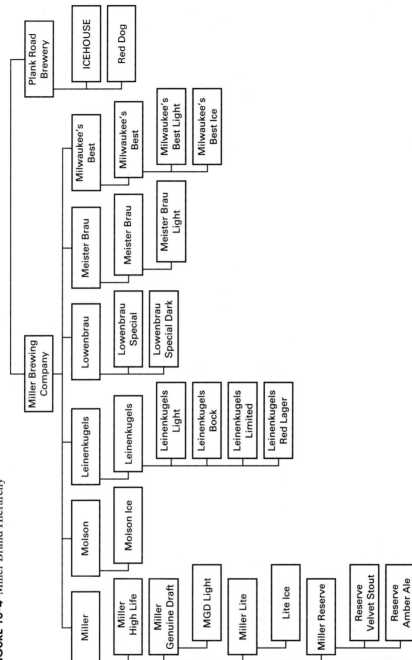

- How much do you trust GE?
- How likable is GE?
- How concerned is GE with their customers?
- How approachable is GE?
- How accessible is GE?
- How much respect do you have for GE?
- How much do you admire GE?
- How much do you like doing business with GE?

The actual questions used should reflect the level and nature of experience that the particular group of respondents would be likely to have had with the company.

A number of firms track corporate image. As an example, Dupont has tracked the following broad measures of corporate image:[8]

- Outstanding American companies (unaided)
- Outstanding companies on eleven different attributes (unaided)
- Rating on those attributes
- Outstanding companies in eight different industries (unaided)
- Association with those industries
- Ratings in associated industries
- Familiarity with products and services
- Likelihood of investing in stock
- Feeling about friend accepting employment

When a brand is identified with multiple products, as with a corporate or family branding strategy, one important issue is which particular products the brand reminds consumers of. An important related consideration is which particular products are most influential in affecting consumer perceptions about the brand. To identify which products are most closely linked to the brand, consumers could be probed as to which products they associate with the brand on an unaided basis (e.g., "What products come to mind when you think of the Nike brand?") or aided basis by listing sub-brand names (e.g., "Are you aware of Nike Air Flight basketball shoes? Nike Challenge Court tennis apparel? Nike Air Max running shoes?"). To better understand the dynamics between the brand and its corresponding products, consumers can be probed as to their relationship ("There are many different products associated with Nike. Which ones are most important to you in formulating your opinion about the brand?").

Choice of Brand Elements

In all of these tracking studies, one question is, Which elements of the brand should be used? In general, the brand name is always used in tracking but, as noted in chapter 4, it may also make sense to employ other brand elements, such as a logo or symbol, in probing brand structures, especially if they can play a visible and important role in the decision process.

HOW TO CONDUCT TRACKING STUDIES

Conducting tracking studies requires decisions about who to track, as well as when and where to track.

Who to Track

As chapter 3 noted, there are a number of possible segmentation schemes that can be profitably incorporated into tracking approaches. Tracking often concentrates on current customers, but it can also be informative to monitor non-users of the brand or even the product category as a whole. For example, it often can be insightful to track those customers loyal to the brand versus those who are loyal to other brands or who switch among brands. Among current customers of the brand, it is often informative to distinguish between heavy and light users of the brand. Dividing up the market typically requires different questionnaires (or at least sections of a questionnaire) to better capture the specific issues associated with each segment.

For example, Miles Laboratory collects much data on the image of its flagship product, Alka Seltzer. The data has revealed marked differences in the product image for users versus non-users. For example, users of Alka Seltzer regard effervescence as a highly convenient feature of the brand. In contrast, non-users regard effervescence as highly *in*convenient. Desired benefits for Alka Seltzer also vary by type of user. Heavy users claim "efficacy" and "speed of relief" as the most valued attributes. Light users, on the other hand, value "gentleness" and "no side effects" more highly. Recognizing that effervescence is a key source of the brand equity for Alka Seltzer, it is tracked closely. Because of the strategic importance of this association, they deliberated carefully before introducing a liquid gel version of the product and keenly watched subsequent consumer reaction.

Other types of customers can be monitored, too. For example, it is often useful to track channel members and other intermediaries closely to understand their perceptions and actions toward the brand. Of particular interest is their image of the brand and the manner by which they feel they may be or could be helping or hurting its equity. Retailers can be asked direct questions such as, "Do you feel that products in your store sell faster if they have the [brand name] on it? Why?" Similarly, it also may be important to track employees to better understand their beliefs about the brand and how they feel they currently are contributing to its equity or possibly could be contributing to its equity in the future. Such tracking may be especially important with service organizations where employees play such profound roles in affecting brand equity.

When and Where to Track

It is necessary to decide how frequently tracking information should be collected. One useful tracking approach to monitor brand associations involves *continuous tracking studies* where information is collected from consumers on a continual basis over time. The advantage of continuous tracking is that it "smooths out" aberrations or unusual marketing activities or events (e.g., a splashy new ad campaign or an unlikely occurrence in the marketing environment) to provide a more representative set of baseline measures.

There are a host of different ways to conduct these types of studies. The frequency of such tracking studies, in general, depends on the frequency of product purchase—durable goods are typically tracked less frequently because they are purchased less often—and the consumer behavior and marketing activity in the product category. Many companies conduct a certain number of interviews of different consumers every week, or even every day, and assemble the results on a rolling or moving average basis for monthly or quarterly reports. For example, marketing research tracking pioneer Millward Brown Inc. usually interviews 100 people a week and looks at the data through a rolling four-week window in its "Advanced Tracking Program." Typically, these involve short phone interviews (e.g., 10 to 20 minutes in length) that include measures of brand perceptions and preferences, as well as background demographic and usage measures. A short (12-minute) interview for a typical consumer product administered over the phone to 50 nationally representative consumers weekly can cost roughly $125,000 to $150,000 annually.

When the brand has more stable and enduring associations, tracking can be conducted on a less frequent basis. Nevertheless, even if it were the case that the marketing of a brand may not appreciably change over time, it is still important to track brands, if for no other reason, because competitive entries can change consumer perceptions of the whole dynamics within the market. For example, when MCI entered the telecommunications market, it took on the persona of a "young, brash guy, just out of school, aggressively making his mark." As a result, in the eyes of consumers, AT&T took on much more of a persona as an "older, conservative banker type, staid and traditional in conducting business" even though its marketing program had not changed.

Finally, on a global basis, it is important to recognize the stage of the product or brand life cycle in deciding on the frequency of tracking—opinions of consumers in mature markets may not change much whereas emerging markets may shift quickly and perhaps even in unpredictable ways.

HOW TO INTERPRET TRACKING STUDIES

Assessing Measures

For tracking measures to yield actionable insights and recommendations, it is important that they are as reliable and sensitive as possible. One problem with many traditional measures of marketing phenomena is that they do not change much over time. Although this stability may reflect the fact that the underlying strength, favorability, and uniqueness of brand associations and levels of awareness do not change much, in other cases it may also be that one or more of those dimensions may have changed to some extent but the measures themselves are not sensitive enough to detect these more subtle shifts. To develop sensitive tracking measures, it may be necessary to phrase questions in a more comparative (e.g., "compared to other brands, how much . . .") or temporal (e.g., "compared to one month/one year ago, how much . . .") manner.

Another challenge in interpreting tracking studies is to decide on appropriate cutoffs. For example, what is a sufficiently high level of awareness? When are associations sufficiently strong, favorable, and unique? To some extent, these targets need to be driven by competitive considerations and the nature of the category. In some low-involvement categories (e.g., light bulbs), it may be difficult to carve out a very distinct image, as compared to higher-involvement products (e.g., cars or computers). Along these lines, it may be important to allow for and monitor the number of respondents who indicate that they "don't know" or have "no response" with respect to the brand tracking measures—the more of these types of answers that are evident, the less consumers would seem to care.

Relating Measures

One of the most important tasks in conducting brand tracking studies is to identify the determinants of brand equity. It is critical that marketers identify as many as possible of the brand associations that potentially can serve as sources of brand equity, and which ones actually influence consumer attitudes and behavior and create value for the brand. In other words, what are the real "value drivers" for a brand—those tangible and intangible points of difference that influence and determine consumers' product and brand choices? Similarly, it is also important that the marketing activities that are most effectively impacting brand knowledge are identified, too, especially with respect to consumer exposure to advertising and other communication mix elements. Carefully monitoring and relating key sources and outcome measures of brand equity should help to address these issues.

Establishing a Brand Equity Management System

Brand audits and brand tracking studies can provide a huge reservoir of information concerning how to best build and measure brand equity. Nevertheless, the potential value of these research efforts will not be realized unless proper internal structures and procedures are put into place within the organization to capitalize on the usefulness of the brand equity concept and the information that is collected with respect to it. Although a brand equity measurement system does not ensure that "good" decisions about the brand will always occur, it should increase the likelihood that they do and, if nothing else, should at least decrease the likelihood that "bad" decisions about the brand will be made.

Embracing the concept of branding and brand equity, many firms have launched task forces to consider how the concept can be best factored into the organization. Interestingly, perhaps one of the biggest threats to brand equity comes from *within* the organization and the fact that too many marketing managers for too many brands remain on the job for only a limited period of time. As a result of these short-term assignments, marketing managers may adopt a short-term perspective, leading to an overreliance on "quick fix" sales-generating tactics such as line and category extensions, sales promotions, and so on. Because of a lack of understanding and appreciation of the brand equity concept, some critics maintain that these managers are essentially running the brand "without a license."

To counteract these and other potential forces within an organization that may lead to ineffective long-term management of brands, it may be necessary to put a brand equity management system into place. A *brand equity management system* is defined as a set of organizational processes designed to improve the understanding and use of the brand equity concept within a firm. Three major steps should be taken organizationally to implement a brand equity management system: (1) brand equity charters, (2) brand equity reports, and (3) brand equity responsibilities. We discuss each of these in turn.

BRAND EQUITY CHARTER

The first step in establishing a brand equity management system is to formalize the company view of brand equity into a document, the brand equity charter, that provides relevant guidelines to marketing managers within the company as well as key marketing partners outside the company (e.g., ad agency personnel). This document should:

1. Define the firm's view of the brand equity concept and explain why it is important.

2. Describe the scope of key brands in terms of associated products and the manner by which they have been branded and marketed (as revealed by historical company records as well as the most recent brand inventory).

3. Specify what the actual and desired equity is for a brand at all relevant levels of the hierarchy at both the corporate level and at the individual product level. A range of relevant associations should be defined, including those attributes, benefits, and attitudes that constitute points of parity and points of difference.

4. Explain how brand equity is measured in terms of the tracking study and the resulting brand equity report.

5. Suggest how brand equity should be managed in terms of some general strategic guidelines (e.g., stressing consistency in marketing programs over time).

6. Outline how marketing programs should be devised in terms of some specific tactical guidelines (e.g., ad evaluation criteria, brand name choice criteria). The proper treatment of the brand in terms of trademark usage, packaging, and communications also should be specified.

For example, GE has an "identity program document" that defines the GE brand as it should appear in all GE marketing communications. After providing a short history of branding and the importance of brands, the document summarizes research concerning the value of the GE brand, identifies the brand's core promise ("better living"), personality, and values and provides guidelines as to how the brand should be managed. Guidelines stress consistency and discipline and are summarized by a checklist of questions that force GE marketing decision makers to specify key product features and sales propositions and how they relate to the core benefit promise of "better living."

Although parts of the brand equity charter may not change from year to year, it should nevertheless be updated on an annual basis to provide a current brand profile and identify new opportunities and potential risks for the brand to decision makers. As new products are introduced, brand programs change, and other marketing initiatives take place, it is important that they be reflected adequately in the brand equity charter. Many of the in-depth insights that emerge from brand audits belong in the charter.

Procter & Gamble's Experience

Procter & Gamble puts together a brand equity statement for each of its brands. P&G has divided its definition of brand equity into two parts, strategic equities and executional equities. *Strategic equities* refer to those equities—typically product-related—that the brand wants to build for the long run. The brand may or may not possess these currently, but they represent the ultimate goal for the brand. *Execu-*

tional equities refers to those equities that the brand already owns and that help to support strategic equities. Executional equities are usually related to other marketing mix elements such as advertising and promotion or other brand elements such as packaging. P&G places much importance on clearly defining each of these equity dimensions so that every brand manager understands his or her goals within and between product categories.

For example, Cheer laundry detergent has had at its core the strategic equity of "fabric care" and the benefit of "protecting clothes so that they can be worn longer"—an association unique to the product category and one that does not conflict with the core strategic equity for P&G's leading laundry detergent brand, Tide, of "superior cleaning ability." Another aspect of Cheer's strategic equity is the brand's personality and user imagery. As distinct from the historical image of Tide as a detergent brand for consumers who take pride in "doing laundry right," Cheer has a less serious appeal and is for consumers who are more likely to believe "it's important, but it's only laundry." In terms of executional equities, P&G has run a successful ad campaign for a number of years for Cheer dubbed "Live Demo" that shows a tuxedoed man silently demonstrating the cleaning ability of Cheer in a clever musically themed commercial. The character and typical script for these ads thus represents a key executional equity for P&G.

BRAND EQUITY REPORT

The second step in establishing a brand equity management system is to assemble the results of the tracking survey and other relevant performance measures for the brand into a brand equity report to be distributed to management on a regular basis (monthly, quarterly, or annually). Much of the information relevant to the report may already exist within or be collected by the organization. Yet, the information may have been otherwise presented to management in disjointed chunks such that a more holistic understanding is not possible. The brand equity report attempts to effectively integrate all these different measures.[9]

The Brand Equity Report should provide descriptive information as to *what* is happening with a brand as well as diagnostic information as to *why* it is happening. It should include all relevant internal and external measures of brand performance and sources and outcomes of brand equity. In particular, one section of the report should summarize consumer perceptions on key attribute or benefit associations, preferences, and reported behavior as revealed by the tracking study. Another section of the report should include more descriptive market level information such as:

1. Product shipments and movement through channels of distribution
2. Relevant cost breakdowns
3. Price and discount schedules where appropriate
4. Sales and market share information broken down by relevant factors, such as geographic region, type of retail account or customer
5. Profit assessments

With advances in computer technology, it will be increasingly easy for firms to place the information that makes up the brand equity report on-line so that it can be accessible to managers through the firm's intranet or some other means. For example, Ocean Spray Cranberries, Inc., assisted by Duke University's John McCann and John Gallagher, created a "Marketplace Insight Web" that was designed to "... provide access to consumer and customer insights which help decision makers better understand and influence the marketplace. Content covers products, markets, accounts, and the marketing mix elements which impact our business." The first-level menu of the system allows users to link to additional information on advertising, coupons, distribution, pricing, trade promotion, products, markets, and retailers. In each case, relevant research information is presented with additional links for cross reference or to elaborate on technical or definitional aspects of the research. For example, the Advertising Insights link has further links to video versions of three of Ocean Spray's TV ads, as well as the original ASI copy test results and quarterly topline reports from the Millward Brown continuous tracking studies. The site is password-protected in a manner so that outside parties can access relevant information. Thus, Ocean Spray's Marketplace Insight Web allows marketing decision makers to instantaneously obtain brand-relevant data and background information.

BRAND EQUITY RESPONSIBILITIES

Finally, to develop a brand equity management system that will maximize long-term brand equity, it is important that organizational responsibilities and processes with respect to the brand are clearly defined. In this section, we consider issues internal to the firm related to assigning responsibilities and duties for properly managing brand equity, as well as issues external to the firm as to the proper roles of marketing partners.

Overseeing Brand Equity

To provide central coordination, a position of Vice President or Director of Strategic Brand Management or Brand Equity Management should be established within the organization. The person in that position would be responsible for overseeing the implementation of the brand equity charter and brand equity reports to make sure that, as much as possible, product and marketing actions across divisions and geographical boundaries are done in a way that reflect the spirit of the brand equity charter and the substance of the brand equity reports so as to maximize the long-term equity of the brand. A natural place to house such oversight duties and responsibilities would be in a corporate marketing group with a senior management reporting relationship.

Even strong brands need to be watched carefully to prevent managers from overconfidently believing that it is acceptable to "make one little mistake" or "let one slide" with respect to the equity of the brand. A number of top companies—Colgate-Palmolive, Canada Dry, Quaker Oats, Pillsbury, Coca-Cola, and Nestlé Foods—have already created such brand equity "gatekeepers" for some or all of their brands.[10] IBM recently put a team in place to be in charge of the research that involves brand equity. Their task has been to discover what associations exist for the corporate brand and then determine which ones are undesirable, and therefore should be pruned, and which other ones are desirable and should be nurtured in order to take the brand image to where the firm wants it to be in the future. This group has had input into a wide variety of areas—including the general look and feel of products—

to ensure that the products reinforced the brand equity as much as possible. The team also has had responsibility for communicating the brand equity message throughout IBM's many divisions and arbitrating any disputes that might arise among groups concerning brand equity.

Organizational Design and Structures

In a general sense, the marketing function must be organized within the firm in a way to optimize brand equity. Several trends have emerged in organizational design and structure that reflect the growing recognition of the importance of the brand and the challenges of managing its equity carefully. For example, an increasing number of firms are embracing brand management. Firms from more and more industries—such as the automobile, health-care, pharmaceutical, computer software, and computer hardware industries—are introducing brand managers into their organizations. Often, they have hired managers from top packaged goods companies, adopting some of their same marketing practices with respect to brands as a result. Interestingly, packaged goods companies continue to evolve the brand management system, as reflected by the following two developments.

Category Management   Procter & Gamble, pioneers of the brand management system, and several other top firms have made a significant shift in recent years to incorporate category management.[11] Previously, senior management at P&G included a handful of divisional marketing vice-presidents, responsible for three to six product categories and twelve to eighteen brands. With its new category emphasis starting in the late 1980s, a general manager was assigned to each of the 40 or so product categories in which P&G competed (e.g., laundry detergents, dishwashing detergents, and specialty products) and given direct profit responsibility. The duties of individual brand managers, however, were essentially unchanged.

Although in some ways counter to management trends toward downsizing the organization and reducing management levels,[12] P&G cites a number of advantages to the new organizational structure. By fostering internal competition among brand managers, the traditional brand management system created strong incentives to excel. However, these inducements came at the cost of internal coordination as brand managers sometimes contested corporate resources—such as ad spending dollars and manufacturing capacity—and failed to synchronize their programs. Whereas a smaller share category might have become relatively neglected before (e.g., in product categories such as "hard surface cleaners"), the new scheme was designed to ensure that all categories would be able to receive adequate resources. Thus, category management was seen as a means to provide better management of brand portfolios to increase the similarity, where appropriate, as well as the differences of brands in categories. As academic validation, Zenor provides a game theoretic analysis and empirical demonstration of the profit advantages of coordinating prices and other marketing activity for a firm's different products and brands through category management.[13]

Another often-cited rationale for placing more emphasis on category management is the increasing power of the trade. Because the retail trade has tended to think in terms of product categories and the profitability derived from different departments and sections of their stores, P&G felt it only made sense for them to deal with the trade along similar lines. Retailers such as Wal-Mart and regional grocery chains such as Dominick's have embraced category management themselves as a means to define a particular product category's strategic role within the store—for example, in terms of its ability to generate store traffic or help provide a particular consumer image—and to address such operating issues as logistics, the role of private label products, and the tradeoffs between offering product variety and avoiding inefficient duplication.[14]

Geographical Marketing Initiatives   Another important issue is how to best organize the marketing effort geographically to manage brand equity. As an interesting example, Miller Brewing recently reorganized its sales and marketing function through a program dubbed "Service 2000." Under Service 2000, Miller divided the United States into 19 major market areas, based on volume, chain configuration, geography, and unique legalities. The areas were then grouped into Eastern, Southern, and Western regions. Each region is to be managed by multifunctional teams that are given authority for tactical marketing issues related to price promotions, merchandising, sales, and tailored local marketing programs, as well as responsibility for profit and loss. At the same time, a franchise group in Miller's Milwaukee headquarters was set up to strategically manage long-term equities and make decisions related to packaging, national advertising, and so on. Thus, Miller's new marketing scheme can be seen as an attempt to best blend the regional and national needs of its brands.

In summary, firms are attempting to redesign their marketing organizations to better reflect the challenges faced by their brands. Interestingly, at the same time, because of changing job requirements and duties, the traditional marketing department is disappearing from a number of companies who are exploring other ways to conduct their marketing functions through business groups, multidisciplinary teams, and so on.[15] The goal in these new organizational schemes is to improve internal coordination and efficiencies as well as external focus with respect to retailers and consumers. Although these are laudable goals, clearly one of the challenges with these new designs is to ensure that the equity of brands is preserved and nurtured and not neglected due to a lack of oversight.

Managing Marketing Partners

Because the performance of a brand will also depend on the actions taken by outside suppliers and marketing partners, it is important that these relationships be managed carefully. Increasingly, firms have been consolidating their marketing partnerships and reducing the number of their outside suppliers. This trend has been especially apparent with global advertising accounts where a number of firms have placed most, if not all, of their business with one agency, for example, Colgate-Palmolive with Young & Rubicam, IBM with Ogilvy & Mather, and Reebok with Leo Burnett. A number of factors affect the decision of how many outside suppliers to hire in any one area—cost efficiencies, organizational leverage, creative diversification, and so on. From a branding perspective, one advantage of dealing with one major supplier such as an ad agency is the potentially greater consistency that might be produced in the understanding and treatment of a brand.

Other marketing partners can also play an important role. For example, chapter 5 described the importance of channel members and retailers in enhancing brand equity and the need for cleverly designed "push" programs.

Brand Investments

One of the important roles taken by senior management is the determination of marketing budgets and where and how company resources will be allocated within the organization. It is important that a brand equity management system be able to inform and provide input to those decision makers so that they are able to recognize the short-term and long-term ramifications of their decisions for brand equity. Decisions concerning which brands to invest in and whether to implement brand-building marketing programs or instead to leverage brand equity through brand extensions, reduced communication expenditures, and so on should reflect the current and desired state of the brand as revealed through brand tracking or other programs.

Review

In this chapter, we introduced the concept of a *brand equity measurement system,* which is defined as a set of research procedures designed to provide timely, accurate, and actionable information for marketers on brands so that they can make the best possible tactical decisions in the short run as well as strategic decisions in the long run. Implementing a brand equity measurement system involves three steps:

1. Conducting the brand audit.
2. Designing brand tracking studies.
3. Establishing a brand equity management system.

A *brand audit* is an external consumer-focused exercise that involves a series of procedures to assess the health of the brand, uncover its sources of brand equity, and suggest ways to improve and leverage its equity. A brand audit requires understanding sources of brand equity from the perspective of both the firm and the consumer. From the perspective of the firm, it is necessary to understand exactly what products and services are currently being offered to consumers and how they are being marketed and branded. From the perspective of the consumer, it is necessary to dig deeply into the minds of consumers and tap their perceptions and beliefs to uncover the true meaning of brands and products.

The brand audit consists of two steps: the brand inventory and the brand exploratory. The purpose of the *brand inventory* is to provide a complete, up-to-date profile of how all the products and services sold by a company are marketed and branded. Profiling each product or service requires that the associated brand elements must be identified as well as the supporting marketing program. The *brand exploratory* is research activity directed to understand what consumers think and feel about the brand to identify sources of brand equity.

The brand audit can be used to set strategic direction for the brand. As a result of this strategic analysis, a marketing program can be put into place to maximize long-term brand equity. Tracking studies then can be conducted employing quantitative measures to provide marketers with current information as to how their brands are performing on the basis of a number of key dimensions identified by the brand audit. *Tracking studies* involve information collected from consumers on a routine basis over time. Tracking studies provide valuable tactical insights into the short-term effectiveness of marketing programs and activities. Whereas brand exploratories measure "where the brand has been," tracking studies measure "where the brand is" and whether marketing programs are having their intended effects.

To implement a brand equity measurement system, three major changes must occur as part of a brand equity management system. First, the company view of brand equity should be formalized into a document, the *brand equity charter*. This document serves a number of purposes: It chronicles the company's general philosophy with respect to brand equity; summarizes the activity and outcomes related to brand audits, brand tracking, and other such sources; outlines guidelines for brand strategies and tactics; and documents proper treatment of the brand. The charter should be updated annually to identify new opportunities and risks and to fully reflect information gathered by the brand inventory and brand exploratory as part of any brand audits. Second, the results of the tracking survey and other relevant outcome measures should be assembled into a *brand equity report* that is distributed to management on a regular basis (monthly, quarterly, or annually). The brand equity report should provide descriptive information as to *what* is happening within a brand as well as diagnostic information as to *why* it is happening. Finally, senior management must be assigned to oversee how brand equity is treated within the organization. The people in that position would be responsible for overseeing the implementation of the brand equity charter and brand equity reports to make sure that, as much as possible, product and marketing actions across divisions and geographical boundaries are done in a way that reflect the spirit of the charter and the substance of the reports so as to maximize the long-term equity of the brand.

In an alternative—albeit complementary—view of how firms should incorporate the brand equity concept into their marketing research and planning, Branding Brief 10–2 describes how one of the world's best ad agencies, Ogilvy & Mather, incorporates branding issues in the services they provide their clients.

Closing Thoughts

Perhaps the dominant theme of this and the previous two chapters on measuring sources and outcomes of brand equity is the importance of employing multiple measures and research methods to capture the richness and complexity of brand equity.[16] No matter how well conducted, single measures of brand equity run the risk of missing important dimensions of brand equity. Recall the problems encountered by Coca-Cola from their overreliance on blind taste tests, described in Branding Brief 1–1. In explaining the new Coke debacle, Randy Scruggs of Miles Laboratories makes an interesting analogy concerning the effects of Coca-Cola's focus on a single measure to assess consumer response to new Coke to the interpretation that someone might give when viewing a pencil head-on from the end with the eraser. From that perspective, a pencil might look like a circle. If one were to look through a magnifying glass—akin to Coke's 190,000 taste tests—he or she would be even more convinced that what they were looking at was a circle! Only if one were to look at the pencil from other angles

Managing Brands at Ogilvy & Mather

Ogilvy & Mather (O&M), one of the world's largest agencies, manages its clients' brands by a five-step process called *brand stewardship*. The five steps include:

1. Information gathering
2. The Brand Audit
3. The Brand Probe
4. The BrandPrint
5. The Brand Check.

The first step is information gathering, where all existing knowledge of the brand is reviewed (facts about product details, consumers, competition, and the marketing environment). The second step is the Brand Audit, which is defined as an "exhaustive effort to set down, in black and white, the intangible cluster of feelings, impressions, connections, opinions, flashes of memory, hopes, and satisfactions . . . and yes, criticisms and disappointments . . . which blend together to form the consumer's perception of your Brand." The audit is based on the information gathered in step 1. The final version of the audit becomes the raw material for the BrandPrint, described in step 4.

If O&M is unable to answer the brand audit questions from existing sources of information, they then commission a piece of research to provide the insight and understanding necessary to be able to answer the Brand Audit. The Brand Probe is described as a four-stage research program that explores the thoughts and attitudes of a wide sample of interested people (brand loyal consumers, representatives from the client and agency, and other marketing companies working with the agency).

After all of this preliminary research is completed, O&M writes the BrandPrint, which they define as "a vivid statement of the unique relationship that exists between the consumer and a brand." According to O&M, a good BrandPrint should be "distinctive, linked, clear, colloquial, colorful, appealing, and flexible in use." The BrandPrint's role in the fourth step is to be used as a tool to guide marketing and especially advertising decisions. The fifth and final step is the Brand Check, conducted once a year, to ensure that "every aspect of a brand, its product performance, its physical characteristics, its packaging, all its communications, etc. reflect the nature of and remain true to the brand consumer relationship as articulated in the BrandPrint."

As is clear from this description, Ogilvy is on the forefront of bringing branding issues and perspectives to the development of advertising and other communications.

and perspectives would it be clear that the object was multidimensional and had shape. Thus, as this analogy suggests, a single measure only provides at best a one- or two-dimensional view of a brand. To extend the Scruggs' analogy, measuring the volume of a pencil may reveal something about its size but it would say nothing about how well the pencil writes or how comfortable it would be to hold. Thus, any one measure of a multidimensional concept such as brand equity necessarily overlooks or distorts important information.

Consistent with this view, according to the definition of customer-based brand equity, no single number or measure fully captures brand equity.[17] Rather, brand equity should be thought of as a multidimensional concept that depends on what knowledge structures are present in the minds of consumers and what actions a firm can take to capitalize on the potential offered by these knowledge structures. Thus, there are many different sources of brand equity and many different possible outcomes of brand equity that may arise as a result depending on the skill and ingenuity of the marketers involved. Different firms may be more or less able to maximize the potential value of a brand according to the type and nature of marketing activities. As Wharton's Peter Fader says:

> The actual value of a brand depends on its fit with buyer's corporate structure and other assets. If the acquiring company has manufacturing or distribution capabilities that are synergistic with the brand, then it might be worth paying a lot of money for it. Paul Feldwick, a British executive, makes the analogy between brands and properties on the Monopoly game board. You're willing to pay a lot more for Marvin Gardens if you already own Atlantic and Ventnor Avenues!

Accordingly, the customer-based brand equity framework emphasizes the importance of employing a range of research measures and methods to fully capture the multiple potential sources and outcomes of brand equity.

Discussion Questions

1. Disney recently entered a long-term agreement with McDonald's that included, among other things, joint promotions. From Disney's perspective and what you know about the two brands, was this the right decision? Is there any downside? Would you want to conduct any research to inform the decision? What kind?
2. Consider the Miller Beer tracking survey presented in Branding Brief 10–1. What might you do differently? What questions would you change or drop? What questions might you add? How might this tracking survey differ from those used for other products?

Notes

1. Sidney Davidson, James Schindler, Clyde P. Stickney, and Roman Weil, *Financial Accounting: An Introduction to Concepts, Methods, and Uses.* Hinsdale, IL: Dryden Press, 1976.
2. Phillip Kotler, William Gregor, and William Rogers, "The Marketing Audit Comes of Age," *Sloan Management Review*, 18 (2) (Winter, 1977), pp. 25–43.

3. Laurel Wentz, "Brand Audits Reshaping Images," *Ad Age International* (September 1996), pp. 38–41.

4. Neil Shoebridge, "Lintas Offers Solution to Brand Value Controversy," *Business Review Weekly* (March 9, 1990), pp. 78–80.

5. There's not always a happy ending with changes in branding strategies. Despite this return to its positioning roots, according to Professor John Roberts from the Australian Graduate School of Management, Omo really hasn't bounced back since 1988 for three main reasons. First, although it returned to its "brighter" benefit proposition in principle, it didn't necessarily have the internal discipline to stick with it in practice. For example, Omo offered two seemingly inconsistent variants ("Free" and "With Enzymes") side by side on the shelf. Second, it was out-innovated. For example, one competitor, Radiant, came out with a clear bottle and a pourable powder. Another competitor, Bio-Z, came out with an enzyme power promise that left Omo looking old-fashioned. Third, as Lever innovated across its whole laundry detergent brand portfolio (e.g., Omo, Drive, and Surf), the differences within brand names became more pronounced than the differences across brand names but within product forms and package styles.

6. Burleigh B. Gardner and Sidney J. Levy, "The Product and the Brand," *Harvard Business Review* (March–April 1955), pp. 33–39.

7. Sidney J. Levy, "Dreams, Fairy Tales, Animals, and Cars," *Psychology and Marketing*, 2 (2) (Summer 1985), pp. 67–81.

8. John B. Frey, "Measuring Corporate Reputation and its Value," presentation given at Marketing Science Conference at Duke University, March 17, 1989.

9. Joel Rubinson, "Brand Strength Means More Than Market Share," ARF Fourth Annual Advertising and Promotion Workshop, February 12–13, 1992.

10. Betsy Spethman, "Companies Post Equity Gatekeepers," *Brandweek* (May 2, 1994), p. 5.

11. Zachary Schiller, "The Marketing Revolution at Procter & Gamble," *Business Week* (July 25, 1988), pp. 72–76. Laurie Freeman, "P&G Widens Power Base: Adds Category Managers," *Advertising Age*, Vol. 58, p. 1, October 12, 1987.

12. John Byrne, "The Horizontal Corporation," *Business Week* (December 20, 1993), pp. 76–81.

13. Michael J. Zenor, "The Profit Benefits of Category Management," *Journal of Marketing Research*, 31 (May 1994), pp. 202–213.

14. Gerry Khermouch, "Brands Overboard," *Brandweek* (August 22, 1994), pp. 25–39.

15. "The Death of the Brand Manager," *The Economist* (April 9, 1994), pp. 67–68.

16. This chapter benefited from perceptive comments made in interviews with Laurie Lang (Disney), Chris Lowe (Coca-Cola), Glenda Green (DuPont), Fred Nordeen, Scott Barnham, and James Taylor (Miller Brewing), Jim VanEcko (John Hancock), Cary Rosenzweig and Ross Love (Procter & Gamble), Pat Crane (Kodak), Lew Winters (Chevron), Phil Davies (Prudential), Wayne McCullough and Charlie Pankenier (IBM), and Randy Scruggs (Miles).

17. For an interesting empirical application, see Manoj K. Agarwal and Vithala Rao, "An Empirical Comparison of Consumer-Based Measures of Brand Equity," *Marketing Letters*, 7 (3) (1996), pp. 237–247.

CHAPTER

Branding Strategies

Preview

Parts II and III of the book examined strategies to build and measure brand equity. In this fourth part, we take a broader perspective and consider how to create, maintain, and enhance brand equity under various situations and circumstances. We begin in chapter 11 by considering issues related to branding strategies and how brand equity can be maximized across all the different brands and products that might be sold by the firm. The branding strategy of a firm concerns which brand elements a firm chooses to apply across the products it offers for sale. As noted in chapter 2, many firms employ complex branding strategies. For example, brand names may consist of multiple brand name elements (e.g., Toyota Camry V6 XLE) and may be applied across a range of products (e.g., Toyota cars and trucks). What is the best way to characterize a firm's branding strategy under such instances? What guidelines exist to choose the right combinations of brand names and other brand elements to optimally manage brand equity across the entire range of a firm's products?

Chapter 11 begins by describing two important strategic tools. The brand-product matrix and the brand hierarchy—by defining various relationships among brands and products—help to formulate branding strategies. We next suggest some guidelines as to how to best design branding strategies, devoting special attention to the role of the corporate brand and corporate image dimensions. Finally, we consider a number of different issues in implementing branding strategies, including issues in designing the brand hierarchy and the supporting marketing program. Guidelines are provided concerning the number of levels of the hierarchy to use, how brands from different levels of the hierarchy can be combined, if at all, for any one particular product, and how any one brand can be linked, if at all, to multiple products. Subsequent chapters examine issues related to introducing and naming new products such as brand extensions (chapter 12), managing brands over time (chapter 13), and managing brands over geographical boundaries, cultures, and market segments (chapter 14).

Brand-Product Matrix

DEFINITIONS

To characterize the product and branding strategy of a firm, one useful tool is the brand-product matrix. The *brand-product matrix* is a graphical representation of all the brands and products sold by the firm. The matrix (or grid) has the brands of a firm as rows and the corresponding products as columns (see Figure 11–1).

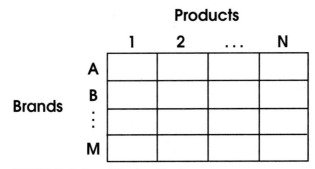

FIGURE 11-1 Brand-Product Matrix

The rows of the matrix represent *brand-product relationships* and capture the brand extension strategy of the firm in terms of the number and nature of products sold under the brands of the firm. A *brand line* consists of all products—original as well as line and category extensions—sold under a particular brand. Thus, a brand line would be one row of the matrix. As chapter 12 discusses, a potential new product extension for a brand must be judged by how effectively it leverages existing brand equity from the parent brand to the new product, as well as how effectively the extension, in turn, contributes to the equity of the parent brand. In other words, what is the level of awareness likely to be and what is the expected strength, favorability, and uniqueness of brand associations of the particular extension product? At the same time, how does the introduction of the brand extension affect the prevailing levels of awareness and the strength, favorability, and uniqueness of brand associations of the parent brand as a whole?

The columns of the matrix, on the other hand, represent *product-brand relationships* and capture the brand portfolio strategy in terms of the number and nature of brands to be marketed in each category. The *brand portfolio* is the set of all brands and brand lines that a particular firm offers for sale to buyers in a particular category. Thus, a brand portfolio would be one particular column of the matrix. Different brands may be designed and marketed to appeal to different market segments. Brands also can take on very specialized roles in the portfolio—as flanker brands to protect more valuable brands, as low-end entry-level brands to expand the customer franchise, as high-end prestige brands to enhance the worth of the entire brand line, or as cash cows to "milk" all potentially realizable profits, as will be described below.

One final set of definitions is useful.[1] A *product line* is a group of products within a product category that are closely related because they function in a similar manner, are sold to the same customer groups, are marketed through the same type of outlets, or fall within given price ranges. A product line may be composed of different brands or a single family brand or individual brand that has been line extended. A *product mix* (or product assortment) is the set of all product lines and items that a particular seller makes available to buyers. Thus, product lines represent different sets of columns in the brand-product matrix that, in total, make up the product mix. A *brand mix* (or brand assortment) is the set of all brand lines that a particular seller makes available to buyers.

The *branding strategy* for a firm reflects the number and nature of common and distinctive brand elements applied to the different products sold by the firm. In other words, brand strategy involves deciding which brand elements will be applied to which products and the nature of new and existing brand elements to be applied to new products. A branding strategy for a firm can be characterized according to its *breadth* (in terms of brand-product relationships and brand extension strategy) and its *depth* (in terms of product-brand relationships and the brand portfolio or mix). For example, a branding strategy can be seen as both deep and broad if the firm has a large number of brands, many of whom have been extended into various product categories. Although we next briefly consider some basic considerations concerning the breadth of a branding strategy and brand extensions, we devote chapter 12 to considering these issues in greater detail. Following this discussion, the remainder of this section does, however, outline some of the key issues associated with the depth of a branding strategy and brand portfolios.

BREADTH OF A BRANDING STRATEGY

The breadth of a branding strategy concerns the number and nature of different products linked to the brands sold by a firm. There are a number of considerations concerning the product mix and which products the firm should manufacture and/or sell. Strategic decisions have to be made concerning how many different product lines the company should carry (the breadth of the product mix), as well as how many variants should be offered in each product line (the depth of the product mix).

Breadth of Product Mix

Lehmann and Winer provide an in-depth consideration of factors affecting product category attractiveness.[2] They note that three main sets of factors determine the inherent attractiveness of a product category: aggregate market factors, category factors, and environmental factors (see Figure 11–2).

1. *Aggregate market factors* concern those descriptive characteristics of the market itself. All else equal, a category is considered attractive if it is: (a) relatively large (as measured both in units and dollars); (b) fast-growing (both in current and projected terms) and in the growth stage of the product life cycle; (c) non-cyclical and non-seasonal in sales patterns; and (d) characterized by relatively high, steady profit margins.

2. *Category factors* relate to those underlying structural factors affecting the category. In general, a category is considered attractive if it is the case that: (a) the threat of new entrants is low (e.g., due to barriers of entry from economies of scale, product differentiation, capital requirements, switching costs, or distribution systems); (b) bargaining power of buyers is low (e.g., when the product bought is a small percentage of buyers' costs or sharply differentiated or when buyers are earning high profits, lack information about competitive offerings, or are unable to integrate backwards); (c) current category rivalry is low (e.g., when there are few or an imbalance in competitors in fast growing markets); (d) few close product substitutes exist in the eyes of consumers; and (e) the market is operating at or near capacity.

3. *Environmental factors* address those external forces unrelated to the product's customers and competitors that affect marketing strategies. A host of technological, political, economic, regulatory, and social factors will impact the future prospects of a category and should be forecasted.

I. **AGGREGATE MARKET FACTORS**
Market size
Market growth
Stage in product life cycle
Sales cyclicity
Seasonality
Profits

II. **INDUSTRY FACTORS**
Threat of new entrants
Bargaining power of buyers
Bargaining power of suppliers
Current industry rivalry
Pressures from substitutes
Industry capacity

III. **ENVIRONMENTAL FACTORS**
Technological
Political
Economic
Regulatory
Social

FIGURE 11-2 Category Attractiveness Criteria

All of these factors relate in some way to consumers, competition, and the marketing environment and must be assessed to determine the inherent attractiveness of a product category or market. The ultimate decision for a firm to enter such markets, however, must also take into account fundamental considerations related to the firm's capabilities and abilities as well as its strategic objectives and goals.

The actual names chosen for the products to enter these different markets will depend on the branding strategy adopted, as described in chapter 12. For example, although Xerox saw the organizational and marketing imperative to move into office automation and computing, they chose to brand their first computers with the Xerox name. Because of the near-generic qualities of its name—virtually synonymous with photocopying—it is perhaps not surprising that consumers balked. Print ads announcing that, "Here's a Xerox that does not even make a copy" may have raised questions in consumers' minds as to how—or even if!—the computer worked.

Depth of Product Mix

Once broad decisions concerning appropriate product categories and markets in which to compete have been made, decisions concerning the optimal product line strategy must also be made. Product line analysis requires a clear understanding of the market and cost interdependencies between products.[3] Specifically, product line analysis involves examining the percentage of sales and profits contributed by each item or member in the product line. The ability of each item in the product line to withstand competition and address consumer needs also needs to be assessed. At its simplest, a product line is too short if the manager can increase long-term profits by adding items; the line is too long if the manager can increase profits by dropping items.[4] Increasing the length of the product line by adding new variants or items typically expands market coverage and therefore market share but also increases costs. From a branding perspective, longer product lines also may decrease the consistency of the associated brand image if the same brand is used.

For example, although a raging success in the 1980s, Laura Ashley found its sales wilting in the 1990s. The brand meant different things to different people—unfortunately, many of these people worked at Laura Ashley! Stores in the United States and Europe offered vastly different product lines. Designers and buyers were scattered all over the world and introduced hundreds of clothing styles—many of which clashed with the English country fashions for which Laura Ashley had become famous. The chain's vast range of product lines—which included adult clothes, children's clothes, and home furnishings—were tilled with weak sellers and duplicate styles. Eighty-two percent of the company's sales came from just 22 percent of the merchandise. New management pared down the brands, eliminating 30 percent of the clothing styles and 20 percent of the home furnishing lines. They also consolidated design, buying, and merchandise and took steps to create a more common store design and format.[5]

Given that product policy has been set for a firm in terms of product boundaries (i.e., appropriate product categories and product lines), then the proper branding strategy must be decided upon in terms of which brand elements should be used for which products. Specifically, decisions must be made as to which products to attach to any one brand as well as how many brands to support in any one product category. The former decision concerns brand extensions and will be discussed in detail in the next chapter; the latter decision concerns brand portfolios, which we address next. Branding Brief 11–1 describes Kodak's experiences in stretching its brand name.

DEPTH OF A BRANDING STRATEGY

The depth of a branding strategy concerns the number and nature of different brands marketed in the product class sold by a firm. Why might a firm have multiple brands in the same product category? The primary reason relates to market coverage. Although originally pioneered by General Motors, Procter & Gamble is widely recognized as popularizing the practice of multiple branding. P&G became proponents of multiple brands after recognizing that introducing its Cheer detergent brand as an alternative to its already successful Tide detergent resulted in higher combined product category sales.

The main reason to adopt multiple brands is to pursue multiple market segments. These different market segments may be based on all types of considerations—different price segments, different channels of distribution, or different geographical boundaries. Figure 11–3 displays Seiko's different brands based on price segments. As another example, as part of a plan to upgrade Holiday Inn Worldwide, the hotel chain broke its domestic hotels into five separate chains to tap into five different benefit segments—the upscale Crowne Plaza, the traditional Holiday Inn, the budget Holiday Inn Express, and the business-oriented Holiday Inn Select and Holiday Inn Suites & Rooms.[6] Marriott had already adopted a very similar strategy, and other hotel chains have similarly followed suit.

Stretching the Kodak Brand[a]

Although Kodak has maintained its domination of the photo film market, it watched its market share drop in the first half of the 1990s from between 75 percent and 80 percent to 70 percent because of increased competition from low-priced products from Fuji Photo Film Co. and Konica Corp. To boost sales, Kodak decided to revamp its brand offerings by introducing its first economy brand, Funtime, and a new premium brand, Royal Gold.

This wasn't the first time Kodak had made a major branding move. In 1988, Kodak replaced its highly successful line of VR-G films with a new name and look with a global redesign. The VR-G line of 35mm color-print amateur film, originally introduced in 1985, targeted the fastest-growing market for film and represented about 70 percent of the total color-negative exposures in the United States. Called Kodacolor "Gold," the packages prominently displayed the new name in gold-colored foil against a black background. The "Gold" name was chosen to connote quality and cachet and, by uniformly applying it across the world, was designed to ease distribution and packaging complexities

Funtime was intended to compete with private label knockoffs and low-priced competitors. Priced about 20 percent lower than Kodak's flagship Gold brand, Funtime was not to be advertised and to be sold in limited quantities only twice a year—in the spring and the fall—in all of Kodak's traditional outlets. Funtime was offered in the two most popular speeds of 100 and 200 and in multipacks of two 24-exposure rolls and another one of four rolls—three 24-exposure rolls with one 36-exposure roll. Royal Gold was a replacement for Kodak's Ektar premium brand and was priced at 20 percent to 25 percent more than Gold but less than what Ektar was sold for. Advertising for Royal Gold was to communicate the brand's quality and value and expand the target market from professionals and serious amateurs to a broader audience. To facilitate finding negatives from which to create reprints or enlargements, Royal Gold also offered a small indexing print illustrating all photos from each roll of film. Royal Gold came in speeds of 25, 100, 400, and 1000.

Recognizing that consumers take pictures for different reasons at different occasions, Kodak hoped that the new brand portfolio would satisfy consumers' picture-taking habits. As one Kodak executive explained:

> We now have Royal Gold film, for those very special memories—the birth of a baby, graduations, etc. We continue to offer Gold film, for capturing those unexpected moments—the baby smiling, the father and son playing catch in the backyard. And now we will offer a special promotion twice a year, featuring a modified version of Gold film at a slightly higher price than our other films.

Kodak's new branding strategy seemed to meet with mixed results. The Royal Gold brand "exceeded sales expectations" in 1994 and, as a result, received increased advertising support. Funtime sales, however, were below expectations and prompted a number of changes. Critics maintained that the packaging did not signal "film" clearly enough and was priced too closely to the Gold line. Kodak decided to market its economy film under a new name to discount warehouses and mail order firms, retailers where Funtime had been least successful. The company also made the brand available throughout the year to these mass merchants, also giving the product a new package and label that picked up the theme of "photos for the fun of it." Kodak continued to sell Funtime as before in retail outlets such as drugstores where sales were stronger. Kodak also decided to offer more multipack deals on its full-price lines.

[a]Clare Ansberry, "Kodak Revamping Its 35mm Color Film to Cash In on Marketing Cachet of Gold," *Wall Street Journal* (April 25, 1988), p. 32; Wendy Bounds, "Kodak Develops Economy-Brand Film That Is Focused on Low-Priced Rivals," *Wall Street Journal* (January 26, 1994), p. A-3; Wendy Bounds, "Kodak to Change Marketing Strategy for Low-End Film," *Wall Street Journal* (December 9, 1994), p. B-3; Gerry Khermouch, "As Royal Gold Ads Kick in, Kodak Plans Funtime Recast," *Brandweek* (June 20, 1994), p. 3; Robert J. Dolan, "Eastman Kodak Company: Funtime Film," Harvard Business School Case 9-594-111. May 8, 1995. Boston, MA.

In many cases, multiple brands have to be introduced by a firm because any one brand is not viewed equally favorably by all the different market segments that the firm would like to target. For example, Ford chose to acquire Jaguar to appeal to the luxury car market segment that might have been less likely to be receptive to a new high-end entry with a Ford name. Interestingly, despite Jaguar's strong brand equity, some critics still believe Ford paid too much for the brand—estimated to be $2.6 billion in purchase price (with an additional investment of $2.0 billion or so to upgrade Jaguar's quality and technology to world-class standards).[7]

Some other reasons for introducing multiple brands in a category that have been put forth include:[8]

1. To increase shelf presence and retailer dependence in the store
2. To attract consumers seeking variety who may otherwise have switched to another brand
3. To increase internal competition within the firm
4. To yield economies of scale in advertising, sales, merchandising, and physical distribution

FIGURE 11-3 Seiko's Segmentation of the Watch Market[a]

Segment	Seiko Brands
Luxury brands (e.g., Rolex, Piaget, Cartier)	Lassale
Up-market brands (e.g., Omega, Longines)	Credor, Seiko
Mid-price brands (e.g., Bulova, Tissot, Citizen)	Seiko, Pulsar
Mass-market brands (e.g., Swatch, Timex)	Pulsar, Lorus
Commodity watches (Hong Kong LCDs)	

[a]Adapted from Helen Chase Kimball and Christine Pinson, Swatch, Fountainbleau: INSEAD, Case 589-005, 1987.

In designing the optimal brand portfolio, marketers generally need to trade off market coverage and these other considerations with costs and profitability. As with a product line, a portfolio is too big if profits can be increased by dropping brands; a portfolio is not big enough if profits can be increased by adding brands. In other words, any brand should be clearly differentiated and appealing to a sizable enough marketing segment to justify its marketing and production costs. Brand lines with poorly differentiated brands are likely to be characterized by much cannibalization and require appropriate "pruning."[9] For example, Nabisco announced that it was going to adopt a more cautious new product strategy after it appeared that the introduction of too many line extensions that consumers saw as offering too few differences depressed earnings. The firm also believed that an overreliance on new product extensions also distracted them from providing adequate support to their "tried and true" brands like Ritz crackers, Fig Newtons, and Oreo cookies.[10]

Besides these considerations, there are a number of specific roles that brands can play as part of a brand portfolio. Figure 11–4 summarizes some of the different functions and roles that brands might take.

Flankers

An increasingly important role for certain brands is as protective flanker or "fighter" brands. The purpose of flanker brands typically is to create stronger points of parity with competitors' brands so that more important (and more profitable) flagship brands can retain their desired positioning. In particular, as noted in chapter 5, many firms are introducing discount brands as flanker brands to better compete with store brands and private labels and protect their higher-priced brand companions. For example, Philip Morris has introduced a discount brand of cigarettes, Basic, which lives up to its name as a "no-frills" flanker brand designed to protect Marlboro and preserve its premium price position. Backed by the slogan, "It tastes good. It costs

FIGURE 11-4 Possible Special Roles of Brands in the Brand Portfolio

1. To attract a particular market segment not currently being covered by other brands of the firm.
2. To serve as a flanker and protect flagship brands.
3. To serve as a cash cow and be milked for profits.
4. To serve as a low-end entry-level product to attract new customers to the brand franchise.
5. To serve as a high-end prestige product to add prestige and credibility to the entire brand portfolio.
6. To increase shelf presence and retailer dependence in the store.
7. To attract consumers seeking variety who may otherwise have switched to another brand.
8. To increase internal competition within the firm.
9. To yield economies of scale in advertising, sales, merchandising, and physical distribution.

less," one print ad showed a simple scene of the cigarette pack with a pair of blue jeans and the headline, "Your basic fashion." Another ad paired the cigarette with a Walkman-like personal stereo and the headline, "Your basic concert."

In designing these fighter brands, marketers must walk a fine line. Fighter brands must not be designed to be so attractive that they take sales away from their higher-priced comparison brands or referents. At the same time, if fighter brands are seen as connected as an extension to other brands in the portfolio in any way (e.g., by virtue of a common branding strategy), then fighter brands must not be designed so cheaply such that they would reflect poorly on these other brands.

Cash Cows

On the other hand, some brands may be kept around despite dwindling sales because they still manage to hold onto a sufficient number of customers and maintain their profitability with virtually no marketing support. These "cash cows" brands can be effectively "milked" by capitalizing on their reservoir of existing brand equity. For example, despite the fact that technological advances have moved much of their market to their newer Sensor brand of razors, Gillette still sells their older Trac II and Atra brands. Because withdrawing these brands may not necessarily result in customers switching to another Gillette brand, it may be more profitable for Gillette to keep the brands in their brand portfolio for razor blades. As another example, Unilever's Lux beauty bar, which hasn't advertised in years, still generates over $10 million in profits.[11]

Low-End Entry-Level or High-End Prestige

Many brands introduce line extensions or brand variants in a certain product category that vary in price and quality. These sub-brands leverage associations from other brands while distinguishing themselves on the basis of their price and quality dimensions. In this case, the endpoints of the brand line often play a specialized role.

The role of a relatively low-priced brand in the brand portfolio often may be as a means of attracting customers to the brand franchise. Retailers like to feature these "traffic builders" because they often are able to "trade up" customers to a higher-priced brand. For example, BMW introduced certain models into its 3-series automobiles in part as a means of bringing new customers into its brand franchise with the hope of later "moving them up" to higher-priced models when they later decided to trade in their cars. Similarly, Mercedes plans to attract younger car buyers through its new A-Class, the smallest car it has ever made.

On the other hand, the role of a relatively high-priced brand in the brand family often is to add prestige and credibility to the entire brand portfolio. For example, one analyst argued that the real value to Chevrolet of its Corvette high performance sports car was in ". . . its ability to lure curious customers into showrooms and at the same time help improve the image of other Chevrolet cars. It does not mean a hell of a lot for GM profitability, but there is no question that it is a traffic builder."[12] Corvette's technological image and prestige was hoped to cast a halo over the entire Chevrolet line.

In short, brands can play a number of different roles within the brand portfolio based on considerations related to consumers, the competition, and/or the company. Brands may expand coverage, provide protection, extend an image, or fulfill a variety of other roles for the firm. In all brand portfolio decisions, the basic criteria are simple, even though their application can be quite complicated: Each brand name product must have a well-defined role of what it is supposed to do for the firm and, as such, a well-defined positioning as to what benefits or promises it offers consumers, as encapsulated in the associations that it owns in customers' minds.

Brand Hierarchy

DEFINITIONS

The brand-product matrix helps to highlight the range of products and brands sold by a firm. As described, it assumes each product is given one brand name. In many cases, a firm may want to make connections across products and brands to show consumers how these products and brands may be related. As a result, brand names of products are typically not restricted to one name but often consist of a combination of multiple brand name elements. For example, an IBM ThinkPad 760 notebook personal computer consists of three different brand name elements, "IBM," "ThinkPad," and "760." Some of these brand name elements may be shared by many different products; other brand name elements are limited to a more restricted range of products. For example, whereas IBM uses its corporate name to brand many of its products, ThinkPad designates a certain type of computer (i.e., one that is portable as opposed to desktop); and 760 identifies a particular model of ThinkPad (i.e., one with a 100MHz or higher Pentium microprocessor, a 810MB or higher hard disk, and 8MB or 16MB upgradable RAM in memory with a 11.3" or higher SVGA screen).

A *brand hierarchy* reveals an explicit ordering of brand elements by displaying the number and nature of common and distinctive brand elements across the firm's products. By capturing the potential branding relationships among the different products sold by the firm, a brand hierarchy is a useful means to graphically portray a firm's branding strategy. Specifically, a brand hierarchy is based on the realization that a product can be branded in different ways depending on how many new and existing brand elements are used and how they are combined for any one product. Because certain brand elements are used to make more than one brand, a hierarchy can be constructed to represent how (if at all) products are nested with other products because of their common brand elements. Some brand elements may be shared by many products (e.g., Ford); other brand elements may be unique to certain products (e.g., Explorer).

As with any hierarchy, moving from the top level to the bottom level of the hierarchy typically involves more entries at each succeeding level or, in this case, more brands. There are different ways to define brand elements and levels of the hierarchy. For example, Figure 11–5 displays a classification system developed by one of Europe's leading branding experts, Jean-Noel Kapferer. Perhaps the simplest representation of possible brand elements and thus potential levels of a brand hierarchy, from top to bottom, might be as follows:

1. Corporate (or company) brand
2. Family brand

3. Individual brand

4. Modifier (designating item or model)

The highest level of the hierarchy technically always involves one brand—the *corporate or company brand*. For legal reasons, the company or corporate brand is almost always present somewhere on the product or package, although it may be the case that the name of a company subsidiary may appear instead of the corporate name. For example, Quaker Oats used the name of its Fisher-Price subsidiary for years on its toys. For some firms, the corporate brand is virtually the only brand used (e.g., as with General Electric and Hewlett Packard). Some other firms combine their corporate brand name with family brands or individual brands (e.g., conglomerate ITT's different business units are branded ITT Hartford, ITT Automotive, ITT Sheraton, ITT Defense & Electronics, ITT Financial, ITT Fluid Technology, and ITT Communications and Information). Finally, in some other cases, the company name is virtually invisible and, although technically part of the hierarchy, receives virtually no attention in the marketing program (e.g., although perhaps an obvious example, Philip Morris chooses not to use its name with Kraft foods and brands from other subsidiaries).

At the next lower level, a *family brand* is defined as a brand that is used in more than one product category but is not necessarily the name of the company or corporation itself. For example, ConAgra's Healthy Choice family brand is used to sell a wide spectrum of food products, including frozen microwave entrees, packaged cheeses, packaged meats, sauces, and ice cream. Other family brands boasting over a billion

FIGURE 11-5 Kapferer's Branding System[a]

---

1. *Product brand:* Assign an exclusive name to a single product to accord its own individual positioning (e.g., Procter & Gamble's Ariel, Tide, and Dash laundry detergents).

2. *Line brand:* Extend the specific concept across different products, allowing for cross-branding (e.g., Renault automobiles).

3. *Range brand:* Bestow a single name and promise on a group of products having the same ability (Green Giant foods).

4. *Umbrella brand:* Support products in different markets, each with its own communication and individual promise (e.g., Canon cameras, photocopiers, and office equipment).

5. *Source brand:* Identical to an umbrella brand but the products are directly named (e.g., Yves Saint Laurent with Jazz perfumed deodorant and various brands of clothes).

6. *Endorsing brand:* Give approval to a wide diversity of products grouped under product brands, line brands, or range brands (e.g., General Motors cars).

---

[a]Jean-Noel Kapferer, *Strategic Brand Management*. London, England: Kogan-Page, 1992.

dollars in annual sales include Seagram's Tropicana juices and Anheuser-Busch's Budweiser beer. Most firms typically only support a handful of family brands. If the corporate brand is applied to a range of products, then it functions as a family brand, too, and the two levels collapse to one for those products.

An *individual brand,* on the other hand, is defined as a brand that has been restricted to essentially one product category, although it may be used for several different product types within the category. For example, in the "salty snack" product class, Frito-Lay offers Fritos corn chips, Doritos tortilla chips, Lay's and Ruffles potato chips, and Rold Gold pretzels. Each brand has a dominant position in its respective product category within the broader salty snack product class. A *modifier* is a means to designate a specific item or model type or particular version or configuration of the product. Thus, many of Frito-Lay's snacks come in both full-flavor or low fat "Better For You" forms. Similarly, Land O' Lakes offers "whipped," "unsalted," and "regular" versions of its butter. Yoplait yogurt comes as "light," "custard style," or "original" flavors.

An example originally suggested by Peter Farquhar, Paul Herr, and their colleagues helps to illustrate some of the issues involved in portraying and interpreting a brand hierarchy.[13] They note how General Motors' Chevrolet Camaro Z28 sports car can be represented as a brand that combines a corporate brand (General Motors), a family brand (Chevrolet), an individual brand (Camaro), and a model type (Z28). Figure 11–6 displays an abridged version of a brand hierarchy that shows how that particular car model can be characterized within General Motors' branding strategy. It is important to note that, as this example suggests, different levels of the hierarchy may receive different emphasis in developing a branding strategy, or perhaps essentially none. For example, General Motors traditionally chose to downplay its corporate name in branding its cars, although it recently has played a more important role in its supporting marketing activities. As will be discussed below, such shifts in emphasis are an attempt by the firm to harness the positive associations and mitigate against the negative associations of different brands in different contexts. There are a number of ways to place more or less emphasis on the different elements that combine to make up the brand.

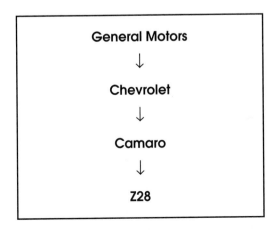

FIGURE 11-6 Example of General Motors Brand Hierarchy

BUILDING EQUITY AT DIFFERENT HIERARCHY LEVELS

Before considering how the brand hierarchy can help to formulate branding strategies, it is worthwhile to first examine some of the specific issues in building brand knowledge structures—and thus brand equity—at each of the different levels of the brand hierarchy.

Corporate or Company Brand Level

For simplicity, we refer to a corporate and company brand interchangeably, recognizing that consumers may not necessarily draw a distinction between the two (i.e., the fact that corporations are potentially more encompassing and may subsume multiple companies). A *corporate image* can be thought of as the associations that consumers have in memory to the company or corporation making the product or providing the service as a whole. Corporate image is a particularly relevant concern when the corporate or company brand plays a prominent role in the branding strategy adopted.

More generally, some marketing experts believe that a factor increasing in importance in consumer purchase decisions is consumer perceptions of a firm's whole role in society, for example, how a firm treats its employees, shareholders, local neighbors, and others. As Procter & Gamble's one-time CEO Ed Artz remarked, "Consumers now want to know about the company, not just the products."[14] Similarly, as the head of a large ad agency put it: "The only sustainable competitive advantage any business has is its reputation."[15] Consistent with this reasoning, a large national U.S. study of consumers indicated that 89 percent of the sample reported that the reputation of the company often determined which products they would buy. Moreover, 71 percent of the sample indicated that "the more they know about a company, the more favorable (they) feel toward it." Interestingly, 80 percent of the sample reported that they saw charitable donations as an indication that companies were "more likely to be concerned with satisfying their customers."[16]

A realization that consumers may be interested in issues beyond product characteristics and associations has prompted much marketing activity to establish the proper corporate image. A corporate image will depend on a number of factors, such as: (1) the products a company makes, (2) the actions it takes, and (3) the manner with which it communicates to consumers. Barich and Kotler identify a host of specific determinants of company image (see Figure 11–7).[17] As Ralph Larson, CEO at Johnson & Johnson observes, "Reputations reflect behavior you exhibit day in and day out through a hundred small things. The way you manage your reputation is by always thinking and trying to do the right thing every day."

In establishing a corporate image, a corporate brand may evoke associations wholly different from an individual brand, which is only identified with a certain product or products. For example, a corporate brand name may be more likely to evoke associations of common products and their shared attributes or benefits, people and relationships, programs and values, and corporate credibility, as will be discussed in more detail in a later section of the chapter.

Branding Brief 11-2 describes a closely related concept—corporate reputation—and how it may be looked at from the perspective of other firms. We next consider brand image issues at the other three levels of the brand hierarchy.

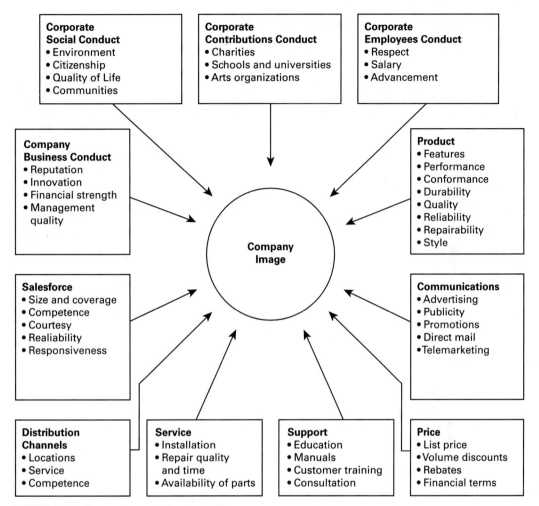

Corporate Social Conduct	**Corporate Contributions Conduct**	**Corporate Employees Conduct**
• Environment	• Charities	• Respect
• Citizenship	• Schools and universities	• Salary
• Quality of Life	• Arts organizations	• Advancement
• Communities		

Company Business Conduct
• Reputation
• Innovation
• Financial strength
• Management quality

Product
• Features
• Performance
• Conformance
• Durability
• Quality
• Reliability
• Repairability
• Style

Company Image

Salesforce
• Size and coverage
• Competence
• Courtesy
• Realiability
• Responsiveness

Communications
• Advertising
• Publicity
• Promotions
• Direct mail
•Telemarketing

Distribution Channels
• Locations
• Service
• Competence

Service
• Installation
• Repair quality and time
• Availability of parts

Support
• Education
• Manuals
• Customer training
• Consultation

Price
• List price
•Volume discounts
• Rebates
• Financial terms

FIGURE 11-7 Determinants of Corporate Image

Family Brand Level

Family brands, like corporate or company brands, are brands applied across a range of product categories. The main difference is that because a family brand may be distinct from the corporate or company brand, company-level associations may be less likely to be salient. Other authors sometimes refer to these types of brands as "range" brands or "umbrella" brands.

Family brands may be used instead of corporate brands for several reasons. As products become more dissimilar, it may be harder for the corporate brand to be used and still retain any product meaning. If the corporate brand is linked to a wide variety of products with little product similarity, it may difficult for the corporate brand to effectively link the disparate products and serve as an umbrella brand. As noted in chapter 7, Beatrice was unable to create a meaningful corporate brand around its heterogeneous collection of products. Distinct family brands, on the other hand, can be

---

Corporate Reputations:
America's Most Admired Companies[a]

Every year *Fortune* magazine conducts a comprehensive survey of business perceptions of the companies with the best corporate reputations. The 1994 survey included 395 companies in 41 industry groups that appeared in the 1994 Fortune 500 industrial and Fortune 500 service directories. More than 10,000 senior executives, outside directors, and financial analysts were asked to rate the ten largest companies (or sometimes fewer) in their own industries. They measured the contenders by eight attributes: quality of management; quality of products or services; innovativeness; long-term investment value; financial soundness; ability to attract, develop, and keep talented people; responsibility to the community and the environment; and wise use of corporate assets. Interestingly, in ranking the eight attributes in terms of importance, respondents listed "quality of management" and "quality of products and services" ahead of the three more financial measures.

In compiling their rankings, the *Fortune* writers credited the stability of the top companies—eight of the Top Ten companies had made the same list the previous year, and Rubbermaid was No. 1 the second year in a row—due to the fact that it had "mastered the art of maintaining continuity while fostering a state of perpetual renewal." They also note that:

> If there is one characteristic that sets the top-ranking companies of the Most Admired apart, it is their robust cultures. The culture of a company, a good proxy for character in a person, drives reputation. And like character, culture guides and defines its host body, allowing it to anticipate change and grow while remaining true to some core self.

Fortune's Top Ten Most Admired companies and their ratings are as follows:

Rank	Company	Score	Quality of management	Quality of products or services	Financial soundness	Value as long-term investment
1	Rubbermaid	8.65	8.99	9.13	8.72	8.44
2	Microsoft	8.42	8.90	8.31	9.15	8.46
3	Coca-Cola	8.39	8.82	8.49	9.08	8.78
4	Motorola	8.38	8.73	9.01	8.31	8.59
5	Home Depot	8.24	8.97	8.40	8.38	8.02
6	Intel	8.17	8.50	8.74	8.37	7.92
7	Procter & Gamble	8.13	8.69	8.76	8.67	8.21
8	3M	8.09	8.40	8.50	8.23	7.87
9	UPS	8.05	8.69	8.46	8.63	8.25
10	Hewlett-Packard	8.04	8.50	8.50	8.40	7.99

Rank	Company	Use of corporate assets	Innovativeness	Community or environmental responsibility	Ability to attract, develop, and keep talented people
1	Rubbermaid	8.39	9.03	8.22	8.27
2	Microsoft	8.05	8.49	6.99	9.02
3	Coca-Cola	8.30	7.44	7.77	8.49
4	Motorola	8.09	8.77	7.19	8.38
5	Home Depot	8.07	8.53	7.35	8.19
6	Intel	7.78	8.82	6.93	8.27
7	Procter & Gamble	7.68	8.00	7.03	7.99
8	3M	7.59	8.52	7.63	7.95
9	UPS	7.80	7.47	7.36	7.75
10	Hewlett-Packard	7.79	7.83	7.27	8.08

Fortune's next 10 included the following:

Rank	Company	Score
11	United HealthCare	7.92
12	Gillette	7.91
13	Boeing	7.88
14	General Electric	7.84
15	Albertson's	7.83
16	Levi Strauss	7.82
17	Johnson & Johnson	7.81
18	Corning	7.76
19	AT&T	7.68
20	Fluor	7.64

[a]Rahul Jacob, "Corporate Reputations," *Fortune* (March 6, 1995), pp. 54–94.

circumscribed to evoke a specific set of associations across a group of related products. As with corporate brands, these associations may relate to common product attributes, benefits, and attitudes and, perhaps to a lesser extent, people and relationships, programs and values, and corporate credibility.

Family brands can be an efficient means to link common associations to multiple, but distinct products. The cost of introducing a related new product can be lower and the likelihood of acceptance can be higher when an existing family brand is used to brand a new product. On the other hand, if the products linked to the family brand and their supporting marketing programs are not carefully considered and designed, the associations to the family brand may become weaker and less favorable. Moreover, the failure of one product may have more adverse ramifications on other products sold by the firm under the same brand by virtue of the common brand identification.

Individual Brand Level

Individual brands are restricted to essentially one product category, although multiple product types may be offered on the basis of different models, package sizes, or flavors. Much of the earlier focus of the book has been on individual brands. Chapter 3 described the range of different types of attribute, benefit, and attitude associations that can be linked to a brand. The main advantage to creating individual brands is that the brand and all its supporting marketing activity can be customized and tailored to meet the needs of a specific customer group. Thus, the name, logo, and other brand elements, as well as product design, marketing communication programs, and pricing and distribution strategies can all be designed to focus on a certain target market. Moreover, if the brand runs into difficulty or fails, the risk to other brands and the company itself is minimized. The disadvantage to solely creating individual brands, however, is the difficulty, complexity, and expense involved in developing separate marketing programs to build sufficient brand equity. We outline more of the pros and cons of individual brands versus corporate or family brands in considering brand extensions in chapter 12.

Modifier Level

Regardless of whether corporate, family, or individual brands are employed, it is often necessary to further distinguish brands according to the different types of items or models involved. Adding a modifier often can signal refinements or differences in the brand related to factors such as quality levels (e.g., Johnnie Walker Red Label, Black Label, and Gold Label Scotch Whiskey), different attributes (e.g., Wrigley's Spearmint, Doublemint, and Juicy Fruit flavors of chewing gum), or different functions (e.g., Kodak's 100, 200, and 400 speed film).[18] Brand modifiers can play an important organizing role in communicating how different products within a category that share the same brand name differ on one or more significant attribute or benefit dimensions. Thus, one of the uses of brand modifiers is to show how one brand variation relates to others in the same brand family. As such, brand modifiers play an important role in ensuring market coverage within a category for the company as a whole. Modifiers help to make products more understandable and relevant to consumers or even the trade. Farquhar, Herr, and their colleagues note how modifiers can even become strong trademarks if they are able to develop a unique association with the parent brand, citing as examples the fact that only Uncle Ben has "Converted Rice" and only Orville Redenbacher sells "Gourmet Popping Corn."[19]

CORPORATE IMAGE DIMENSIONS

Thus, different types of associations may become linked to different levels of brands. Before considering some of the decisions needed to set up a brand hierarchy, it is worthwhile to consider in more detail the types of associations that may exist at the corporate or company brand level—or perhaps even the family brand level—given their potential importance and relative lack of attention in the text up until now. In this section, we highlight some of the different types of associations that are likely to be linked to a corporate brand and that potentially can impact brand equity (see Figure 11–8).[20]

1. **Common Product Attributes, Benefits, or Attitudes**
   - Quality
   - Innovativeness

2. **People and Relationships**
   - Customer orientation

3. **Values and Programs**
   - Concern with environment
   - Social responsibility

4. **Corporate Credibility**
   - Expertise
   - Trustworthiness
   - Likability

FIGURE 11–8 Some Important Corporate Image Associations

Common Product Attributes, Benefits, or Attitudes

As with individual brands, a corporate or company brand may evoke product-related or non-product-related attribute or benefit associations as well as attitude associations. Thus, a corporate brand may evoke a strong association with consumers to a product attribute (e.g., Hershey with "chocolate"), type of user (e.g., BMW with "yuppies"), usage situation (e.g., Club Med with "fun times"), or attitude (e.g., Sony with "quality").

If a corporate brand is linked to products across diverse categories, then some of its strongest associations are likely to be those intangible attributes, abstract benefits, or attitudes that span each of the different product categories. For example, companies may be associated with products or services that solve particular problems (e.g., Black and Decker), bring excitement and fun to certain activities (e.g., Nintendo), are built with the highest quality standards (e.g., Motorola), contain advanced or innovative features (e.g., Rubbermaid), or represent market leadership (e.g., Hertz). Two specific product-related corporate image associations—high quality and innovation—deserve special attention, as follows.

A *high quality corporate image association* involves the creation of consumer perceptions that a company makes products of the highest quality. A number of different organizations rate products (e.g., J.D. Powers, *Consumer Reports,* and various trade publications for automobiles) and companies (e.g., Malcolm Baldrige award) on the basis of quality. As chapter 3 points out, consumer surveys often reveal that quality is one of, if not the most important decision factors for consumers. Ford Motor Company is an example of a firm that has attempted to create a high quality corporate image through its marketing program (see Figure 11–9).

An *innovative corporate image association* involves the creation of consumer perceptions of a company as developing new and unique marketing programs, especially with respect to product introductions or improvements. Being innovative is seen in part as being modern and up-to-date, investing in research and development, em-

FORD DESIGNERS FROM LEFT TO RIGHT:
—— SUSAN K. WESTFALL, DAVID HILTON, GARY BRADDOCK, SOO KANG, PAUL ARNONE, AARON WALKER ——

FIGURE 11-9 Sample Ford Ad

IF YOU WANT TO KNOW WHAT CARS AND TRUCKS WILL BE LIKE IN 2005 TALK TO SOME OF THE PEOPLE WHO LIVE THERE.

AT Ford Motor Company, our young designers help keep us in touch with the future, SHARING THEIR VIEWS of the world they'll be inheriting and the vehicles they envision there. ∞ To widen their horizons even further, we provide them with access to other Ford design studios from Turin, Italy to Melbourne, Australia, all of which are linked electronically. In this "GLOBAL STUDIO" environment, these men and women of the computer age use the latest tools and technologies to design vehicles for people living in a RAPIDLY CHANGING WORLD. ∞ At Ford, this is one way our young designers make sure that our customers get what they want, before they even know they want it. To us, that's what quality is all about.

· FORD · FORD TRUCKS · *Ford* · LINCOLN · MERCURY ·

QUALITY IS JOB 1.

FIGURE 11-9 Sample Ford Ad (*continued*)

ploying the most advanced manufacturing capabilities, and introducing the newest product features. An image priority for many Japanese companies—from consumer product companies such as Kao to more technically oriented companies such as Canon—is to be perceived as innovative.[21]

Perceived innovativeness is also a key competitive weapon and priority for firms in other countries. In Europe, firms like Michelin ("Driving Tire Science") and Philips electronics ("Let's Make Things Better") attempt to distinguish themselves on their ability to innovate and successfully invent new products. In the United States, 3M has created a strong culture that emphasizes innovation, mandating that 30 percent of sales comes from products introduced within the previous four years. The company rewards entrepreneurial activity and innovation, and employees are encouraged to spend up to 15 percent of their time thinking up new product ideas. To reflect this corporate philosophy, 3M's advertising slogan has been, "Innovation working for you." 3M's branding strategy uses its corporate name to endorse a diverse range of products (e.g., overhead projectors, cameras, medical adhesives, and Post-It notes). Similarly, 3M's strong Scotch family brand also has been used on a whole host of products, including video cassettes, photographic films, and fabric protectors.[22]

People and Relationships

Corporate image associations may reflect characteristics of the employees of the company. Although this is a natural positioning strategy for service firms such as airlines (e.g., Delta), rental cars (e.g., Avis), and hotels (e.g., Doubletree), manufacturing firms such as DuPont, Philips, and others have also focused attention on their employees in communication programs. The rationale for such a positioning is that the traits exhibited by employees will directly or indirectly have implications for consumers about the products the firm makes or the services they provide. For example, General Motors recently ran a high-profile corporate ad campaign whose purpose—in addition to improving perceptions of product quality—was to change consumer perceptions of the company as arrogant and out-of-touch with customers.[23] Relatedly, General Motors also created an entire car division, Saturn, which advertises itself as a "Different Kind of Car Company," in an attempt to build unique relationships with consumers. All of these marketing efforts are designed to humanize its employees and signal to customers their enhanced importance to the firm.

Retail stores also derive much brand equity from employees within the organization. For example, growing from its origins as a small shoe store, Seattle-based Nordstrom became one of the nation's leading fashion specialty stores through a commitment to quality, value, selection, and, especially, service. Legendary for its "personalized touch" and willingness to go to extraordinary lengths to satisfy its customers, much of the source of Nordstrom's brand equity results in a large part from the efforts of its salespeople and the relationships they develop with consumers.

Thus, a *customer-focused corporate image association* involves the creation of consumer perceptions of a company as responsive to and caring about its customers. In such cases, consumers believe that "their voice will be heard" and that the company is not attempting to be exploitative. Thus, a company seen as customer-focused is likely to be described as "listening" to customers and having their best interests in mind. Often this philosophy is reflected all through the marketing program and communicated through advertising, as in USAir's slogan, "USAir Begins with You."

Values and Programs

Corporate image associations may reflect values and programs of the company that do not always directly relate to the products that they sell. In many cases, these efforts are publicized through marketing communication campaigns. Firms can run corporate image ad campaigns as a means to describe to consumers, employees, and others the philosophy and actions of the company with respect to organizational, social, political, or economic issues. For example, a focus of many recent corporate advertising campaigns has been on company programs and activities designed to address environmental issues and communicate social responsibility, which we highlight next.

An *environmentally concerned corporate image association* involves the creation of consumer perceptions of a company as developing marketing programs to protect or improve the environment and make more effective use of scarce natural resources. Concern for the environment is a growing social trend that is reflected in attitudes and behavior of both consumers and corporations. For example, one survey found that 83 percent of American consumers said they prefer buying environmentally safe products.[24] Another survey found that 23 percent of American consumers now claim to make purchases based on environmental considerations.[25]

On the corporate side, a host of "green marketing" initiatives have been undertaken with environmental overtones. For example, Chevron' s highly visible "People Do" ad campaign has attempted to transform consumers' negative perceptions of oil companies and their effects on the environment by describing specific Chevron programs designed to save wildlife, preserve seashores, and provide other such benefits. Procter & Gamble has begun to advertise more in recent years its support of environmental efforts such as recycling plastic detergent bottles and composting disposable diapers. McDonald's dropped its polystyrene package and began testing numerous other changes to become more environmentally sensitive. "Green marketing" programs, however, have not been entirely successful. Branding Brief 11–3 describes some of the "ups and downs" of green marketing.

A *socially responsible corporate image association* involves creation of consumer perceptions of a company as contributing to community programs, supporting artistic and social activities, and generally attempting to improve the welfare of society as a whole. The 1980s saw the advent of "cause-related marketing." Formally, *cause-related marketing* has been defined as "the process of formulating and implementing marketing activities that are characterized by an offer from the firm to contribute a specified amount to a designated cause when customers engage in revenue-providing exchanges that satisfy organizational and individual objectives."[26] As Varadarajan and Menon note, the distinctive feature of cause-related marketing is the firm's contribution to a designated cause being linked to customers' engaging in revenue-producing transactions with the firm.

Many observers credit American Express for raising awareness of the mutual benefits of cause-related marketing through its 1983 campaign to help restore the Statue of Liberty. Donating a penny for every credit-card transaction and a dollar for each new card issued, American Express gave $1.7 million to the Statue of Liberty–Ellis Island Foundation. In the process, transactions for American Express rose 30 percent, and new cards issued increased by 15 percent during this period. In the next five years, American Express supported more than 70 different causes in 18 countries,

---

Green Marketing Challenges and Opportunities[a]

Although environmental issues have long affected marketing practices, especially in Europe, their salience has increased in recent years. The well-publicized Earth Day activities in the United States in April 1990 led to a explosion of "environmentally friendly" products and marketing programs. The "green marketing" movement was born, and firm after firm appeared to try to capitalize on consumers' perceived increased sensitivity to environmental issues. Despite reported public interest in greater environmental responsibility, however, many of these new products and programs were unsuccessful. What obstacles did the green marketing movement encounter?

OVEREXPOSURE AND LACK OF CREDIBILITY

So many companies made environmental claims that the public became skeptical of their validity. Government investigations into some "green" claims (e.g., the degradability of trash bags) and media reports of the spotty environmental track records behind others only increased consumers' doubts. This backlash resulted in many consumers deeming environmental claims as marketing gimmicks.

CONSUMER BEHAVIOR

As with many well-publicized social trends, the underlying reality is often fairly complex and does not always fully match public perceptions. Attitudes toward the environment were no exception. Several studies conducted at that time helped to put consumers' attitudes toward the environment in perspective.

A 1991 Roper study found that to buy products that would cause one-third less pollution, the average price increases consumers were willing to pay for otherwise identical products in eight categories—gasoline, paper, plastics, aerosols, detergents, and autos—was 6.6 percent. One-third of the sample was not willing to pay *anything* more. The study concluded that the products needed to achieve a point of parity on quality and price and credible environmental claims for green marketing to work. A Syracuse University study also found that the proper price and quality were the key to successful green marketing strategies. Two-thirds of its sample believed that the badge of "environmental correctness" should not result in higher prices—"environmentally safe products shouldn't have to cost more because they use natural ingredients." The study revealed that environmental appeals were more likely to be effective for certain market segments (e.g., 31- to 45-year-old women) and in certain product categories (e.g., cleaners, detergents, fabric softeners, diapers, aerosol sprays, paints, and canned tuna).

The main conclusion that could be drawn from these and other studies is that consumers as a whole may not be willing to pay a premium for environmental benefits, although there may be a certain market segment that will. Most consumers appear unwilling to give up the benefits of other options to choose green products. For example, some consumers dislike the performance, appearance, or texture of recycled paper and household products. Similarly, some consumers are unwilling to give up the convenience of disposable products such as diapers.

POOR IMPLEMENTATION

In jumping on the green marketing bandwagon, many firms did a poor job implementing their marketing program. Products were poorly designed in terms of their environmental worthiness, overpriced, and inappropriately promoted. For example, Starch, a well-known research supplier, surveyed thousands of magazine readers to study 300 "green" ads that appeared in 186 magazines since 1991. Their analysis revealed that the main mistake with those ads that tested as "unpersuasive" was that they forget to emphasize "what's in it for me" to the consumer—they failed to make the connection between what the company was doing for the environment and how it affected individual consumers. Starch's study conclusion was that firms should be specific about product benefits in their ads.

POSSIBLE SOLUTIONS

The environmental movement in Europe or Japan has a longer history and firmer footing. In Europe, many of Procter & Gamble's basic household items, including cleaners and detergents, are available in refills that come in throwaway pouches. P&G says U.S. customers probably would not take to the pouches. In the United States, firms continue to strive to meet the wishes of consumers concerning the environmental benefits of their products, while maintaining necessary profitability. One expert in the field offers the following recommendations:

1. Green your product before forced to.
2. Communicate environmental aspects of products, especially recycled content.
3. Deliver on performance and price.
4. Dramatize environmental benefits.
5. Stress direct, tangible benefits.
6. Be consistent, thorough.

---

[a]Joanne Lipman, "Environmental Theme Hits Sour Notes," *Wall Street Journal* (May 3, 1990), p. B-6.

ranging from the preservation of the national bird of Norway to the protection of the Italian coastline.

During this time, American Express' competitors also followed suit: Visa created a transaction-based donation program to support the 1988 Olympics (see chapter 7); and MasterCard tied use of its credit card to donations to six charitable organizations with its "Make A Difference" campaign. Other companies became involved, too, sponsoring charitable activities such as the Special Olympics, Live Aid, and Hands Across America. Despite some drop in interest during tighter economic times, companies in recent years have again looked to cause marketing as a means of differentiating themselves. For example, in its first national media campaign for a philanthropic cause since its Statue of Liberty campaign, American Express initiated the "Charge Against Hunger" campaign in 1993. The campaign, which raised $5 million in its first year, contributes three cents to feed the hungry every time members use their American Express cards during the months of November and December.[27] American Express also has been supporting the arts at the local community level, publicizing its efforts with ads praising the charitable cause while underscoring the convenience of using the American Express card.

Cause marketing comes in many forms.[28] Although often associated with advertising and promotional activities, it may also involve product development. For example, Levi-Strauss introduced Naturals, a line of cotton jeans whose brown color is inherent in the fiber rather than produced through chemical dyeing; Dannon launched a new line of yogurts that tied in with the National Wildlife Federation; and Scott Paper introduced Helping Hands toilet paper, napkins, and other products that donated a nickle for every purchase to groups such as the March of Dimes.

Some firms have used cause marketing very strategically to gain a marketing advantage. Branding Brief 7–1 described how the Body Shop adopted cause-related marketing as the essence of its brand positioning. Ben & Jerry's ice cream is another firm that has created a strong association as a "do-gooder" through various other products and programs—such as its Rain Forest Crunch ice cream—and by donating 7½ percent of pre-tax profits to various causes. Toyota has run an extensive print ad campaign with the slogan "Investing in the Things We All Care About" to show how it has invested in local U.S. communities (see Figure 11–10). For Toyota, this campaign may go beyond cause marketing and be seen as a means to help the brand create a vital point of parity on "country of origin" with respect to domestic car companies.

As with green marketing, which can be seen as closely related to cause marketing, the danger is that the promotional efforts behind a cause marketing program could backfire if cynical consumers question the link between the product and the cause and see the firm as being self-serving and exploitative as a result. The hope is that cause marketing strikes a chord with consumers and employees, improving the image of the company and energizing these constituents to act. With near-parity products, some marketers feel a strongly held point of difference on the basis of community involvement and concern may in some cases be the best way—and perhaps the only way—to uniquely position a product.

Perhaps the most important benefit of cause-related marketing is that by humanizing the firm, consumers may develop a strong, unique bond with the firm that transcends normal marketplace transactions. A dramatic illustration of such benefits is with McDonald's, whose franchises have long been required to stay close to local communities and whose Ronald McDonald Houses for sick children concretely symbolize their "do-good" efforts. When whole blocks of businesses were burned and looted in the 1992 South Central Los Angeles riots, one McDonald's executive observed, "We literally had people standing in front of some restaurants saying, 'No, don't throw rocks through this window—these are the good guys.'" When the dust cleared, all sixty McDonald's restaurants in South Central were spared.

Some of our most **SUCCESSFUL** research and **DEVELOPMENT** programs **HAVE NOTHING** to do with cars.

AT TOYOTA, improving the quality of life is as important to us as improving the quality of our vehicles. That's why, for the last 20 years, we've been supporting American community projects that are as diverse and exciting as the people who participate in them. This year alone, we're investing more than $12 million in organizations ranging from the National Science Teachers Association to the United Negro College Fund to educational PBS programming, such as "Where in the World Is Carmen Sandiego?" To us, a successful business shouldn't just try to make a profit, it should try to make a difference as well.

INVESTING IN THE THINGS WE ALL CARE ABOUT. **TOYOTA**

For more information about Toyota in America write Toyota Motor Corporate Services, 9 West 57th Street, Suite 4900-C10, New York, NY 10019.

FIGURE 11-10 Sample Toyota Ad

Corporate Credibility

Besides all the associations noted above, consumers may form more abstract beliefs about the company. For example, as chapter 3 described with respect to an individual brand, consumers may form perceptions of the personality of a corporate brand. For example, one major utility company was described by customers as "male, 35 to 40 years old, middle class, married with children, wearing a flannel shirt and khaki pants who would be reliable, competent, professional, intelligent, honest, ethical, and business-oriented." On the downside, the company was also described by these same customers as "distant, impersonal, and self-focused," suggesting an important area of improvement in its corporate brand image.

A particularly important set of abstract associations to a corporate brand is corporate credibility. *Corporate credibility* refers to the extent to which consumers believe that a firm can design and deliver products and services that satisfy customer needs and wants. Thus, corporate credibility relates to the reputation that the firm has achieved in the marketplace.

Corporate credibility, in turn, depends on three factors:

1. *Corporate expertise:* The extent to which a company is seen as able to competently make and sell its products or conduct its services.

2. *Corporate trustworthiness:* The extent to which a company is seen as motivated to be honest, dependable, and sensitive to customer needs.

3. *Corporate likability:* The extent to which a company is seen as likable, attractive, prestigious, dynamic, and so on.

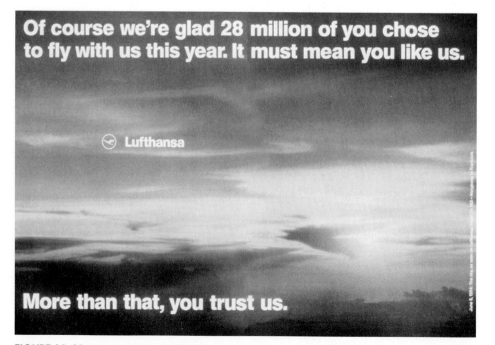

FIGURE 11-11 Sample Lufthansa Ad

FIGURE 11-12 Sample Chevron Ad

Figures 11–11 and 11–12 show examples of ads designed to emphasize corporate brand credibility.

In terms of consequences, a number of other characteristics can also be related to these three dimensions, such as success and leadership. Creating a firm with a strong and credible reputation may offer benefits beyond the consumer response in the marketplace. A highly credible company may also be treated more favorably by other external constituencies such as government or legal officials. It also may be possible to attract better-qualified employees as a result. For example, Wendy's has used the folksy image of its popular CEO and advertising spokesperson, Dave Thomas, as a means to attract employees. In-store signs solicit job applications by displaying his picture with a headline caption that reads, "Would Dave Be Great to Work With or What?"

A highly credible company may also help to motivate existing employees to be more productive and loyal. As one Shell Oil employee remarked as part of some internal corporate identity research, "If you're really proud of where you work, I think you put a little more thought into what you did to help get them there. . . ." A strong corporate reputation can help a firm survive a brand crisis and avert public outrage that could potentially depress sales, encourage unionism, or block expansion plans. As Harvard's Steve Greyser notes, "Corporate reputation . . . can serve as a capital account of favorable attitudes to help buffer corporate trouble."

Keller and Aaker experimentally showed how different corporate image strategies—being innovative, environmentally concerned, or community-involved—can differentially affect corporate credibility and strategically benefit the firm by increasing the acceptance of brand extensions as a result.[29] Specifically, they showed how environmentally concerned and community-involved corporate images affected perceptions of corporate trustworthiness and likability but not corporate expertise. Interestingly, an innovative corporate image was not only seen as expert but also as trustworthy and likable. Because only an innovative corporate image affected perceptions of corporate expertise, however, it was the only image type to affect perceptions of the fit and quality of a proposed extension. The other two image types, although perhaps useful in other contexts, were not as much of an asset in facilitating new product acceptance. In related research, Goldberg and Hartwick also showed that consumers were more accepting of extreme ad claims (e.g., "best in the category") from companies with more credible reputations.[30]

In short, all types of associations may become linked to a corporate brand that transcends physical product characteristics. These intangible associations may provide valuable sources of brand equity and serve as critical points of parity or points of difference. Companies also have a number of means—indirect or direct—of creating these associations. In doing so, it is important that companies "talk the talk *and* walk the walk" by communicating to consumers as well as backing up their claims with concrete programs that consumers can easily understand or even experience.

Designing a Branding Strategy

Given the different possible levels of a branding hierarchy, a firm has a number of branding options available to it, depending on how each level is employed, if at all. There is no uniform agreement as to one type of branding strategy that should be

CHAPTER 11   Branding Strategies   **429**

adopted by all firms for all products. LaForet and Saunders conducted a content analysis of the branding strategies adopted by twenty key brands sold by each of twenty of the biggest suppliers of grocery products to Tesco and Sainsbury, Britain's two leading grocery chains.[31] They categorized the brand strategy adopted by each brand into a classification scheme that can be seen as essentially a refinement of the four-level brand hierarchy described above. As Figure 11–13 shows, a variety of branding approaches were employed. The authors note how different companies within the same market could adopt sharply contrasting strategies, offering the following example:[32]

> For a long time Cadbury, Mars, and Nestle have competed in the confectionery market. They often match each other brand for brand but their branding strategies are quite different. While Cadbury led with the Cadbury name and colors across virtually all their products, such as Cadbury's Dairy Milk, Cadbury's Milk Tray, Cadbury's Flake, etc. Mars led with their brands such as Mars Bars, Snickers, and Twix with no corporate endorsement. Until recently, Nestle Rowntree pursued a branded approach like Mars, but now the Nestle name has started to appear upon the once independently branded products.

Even within any one firm, different branding strategies may be adopted for different products. For example, although Miller has used its name across its different types of beer over the years with various sub-brands (e.g., Miller High Life, Miller Lite, and Miller Genuine Draft), it carefully branded its no-alcohol beer substitute as Sharp's with no overt Miller identification. Similarly, although Toyota adopted a branding strategy that used its corporate name combined with individual brand names and modifiers for most of its cars and trucks, it chose to brand its top-of-the-line cars as Lexus, deliberately avoiding using the Toyota name.

Thus, it is important to note that *the brand hierarchy may not be symmetric.* Because of considerations related to corporate objectives, consumer behavior, or com-

FIGURE 11-13 Breakdown of Brand Types

Percent of Occurence	*Branding Strategy*
	I. **Corporate dominant**
5	1. *Corporate brands:* Corporate name used
11	2. *House brands:* Subsidiary name used
	II. **Mixed brands**
38.5	3. *Dual brands:* Two or more names given equal prominence
13.5	4. *Endorsed brands:* Brand endorsed by corporate or house identity
	III. **Brand dominant**
19	5. *Mono brands:* Single brand name used
13	6. *Furtive brands:* Single brand name used and corporate identity undisclosed

petitive activity, there may sometimes be significant deviations in branding strategy and how the brand hierarchy is organized for different products or for different markets. Brand elements may receive more or less emphasis, or not be present at all, depending on the particular products and markets involved. For example, in appealing to an organizational market segment where the DuPont brand name may be more valuable, it receives more emphasis than associated sub-brands. In appealing to a consumer market segment, a sub-brand such as Dacron may be more meaningful and thus receive relatively more emphasis (see Figure 11–14).

How does a firm use different levels of the brand hierarchy to build brand equity? Brand elements at each level of the hierarchy may contribute to brand equity through their ability to create awareness and foster strong, unique, and favorable brand associations for products. Therefore, the challenge in setting up the brand hierarchy and arriving at a branding strategy is to:

1. Design the proper brand hierarchy in terms of the number and nature of brand elements to use at each level.
2. Design the optimal supporting marketing program in terms of creating the desired amount of brand awareness and type of brand associations at each level.

A number of specific issues arise in designing and implementing a branding strategy with respect to these two areas.

DESIGNING THE BRAND HIERARCHY

Designing a brand hierarchy involves decisions related to:

1. The number of levels of the hierarchy to use in general
2. How brand elements from different levels of the hierarchy are combined, if at all, for any one particular product
3. How any one brand element is linked, if at all, to multiple products

We consider issues related to these three main decisions in turn and also suggest ways to simplify and organize the hierarchy and designate products.

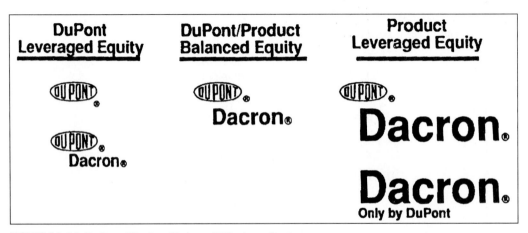

FIGURE 11-14 DuPont "Product Endorsed" Business Strategy

Number of Levels of the Brand Hierarchy

The first decision to make in defining a branding strategy is, broadly, which level or levels of the branding hierarchy should be used. In general, most firms choose to use more than one level for two main reasons. Each successive branding level used allows the firm to communicate additional, specific information about its products. Thus, developing brands at lower levels of the hierarchy allows the firm flexibility in communicating the uniqueness about its products. At the same time, developing brands at higher levels of the hierarchy such that the brand is applied across multiple products is obviously an economical means of communicating common or shared information and providing synergy across the company's operations, both internally and externally.

The practice of combining an existing brand with a new brand to brand a product is called *sub-branding,* as the subordinate brand is a means of modifying the superordinate brand. Sub-branding often combines the company or family brand name with individual brands and even model types. Extending our earlier example, ThinkPad can be seen as a sub-brand to the IBM name with 760 as a second-level sub-brand to further modify the meaning of the product. As suggested above, a sub-brand, or hybrid branding, strategy offers two potential benefits in that it can both

1. Facilitate access to associations and attitudes to the company or family brand as a whole and, at the same time,
2. Allow for the creation of specific brand beliefs.

Thus, using the IBM name allows access to global associations that consumers may have towards the company, such as reliable, trustworthy, and good quality. Introducing different sub-brands—most recently Aptiva (which replaced PS/1 as its main home and small business PCs) and ThinkPad (for its portable PCs)—allows IBM to develop distinct brand images at the same time.

As another example, Volvo has strong brand associations for making safe, reliable cars especially well-suited for parents with young children. In attempt to create a sporty image for their sleek new Volvo 850 models, they created a stylish $20 million ad campaign to give the sub-brand a more contemporary and exciting look. In an ideal world, Volvo would retain all of its previous associations but consumers would, in effect, create a mental "asterisk" for the 850 that involved the addition of different associations. Volvo's ability to create such mental structures will depend on the design of its marketing program and consumers' willingness to compartmentalize sub-brands in that fashion.

As another example, Hershey's chocolate has a traditional, homespun image, as reflected by its 20-plus-year-old advertising slogan, "Hershey's. The Great American Candy Bar." As a result of a clever ad campaign that transforms the teardrop-shaped, foil-wrapped Hershey's Kisses into animate objects and places them in amusing, product-relevant situations, however, the Kisses sub-brand has a much more playful and fun brand image. For example, one such ad showed five Kisses tap dancing, with the voice-over saying, "Why are Hershey's Kisses wrapped in foil? So you can hear them tap dance." The successful Hershey's Kisses sub-brand led to a further extension, Hershey's Hugs (a Hershey's Kiss with an outside layer of white chocolate).

Thus, sub-branding creates a stronger connection to the company or family brand and all the associations that come along with that. As an illustration, consider the cereal category, where Kellogg's has adopted a sub-branding strategy while other manufacturers (e.g., Post) have adopted more of an endorsement strategy. These different strategies have had profound implications on consumers' identification of and associations with certain cereal brands. For example, one research study revealed that when consumers were asked to identify the makers of each cereal from a list of ten cereals, Kellogg's were mismatched or unidentified only 14 percent of the time, but Post cereals were not correctly matched 56 percent of the time. Moreover, when consumers were asked whether having the name of various manufacturers would have a positive, neutral, or negative effect on their likelihood of purchasing a new cereal product, over half of the sample claimed that the Kellogg's name would encourage them to make the purchase, but only a little over a quarter of the sample felt the same way towards the Post name. Apparently, through its sub-branding strategy and marketing activities, Kellogg's has done a more effective job both connecting its corporate name to its products and creating favorable associations to its corporate name. As a result, Kellogg's has become a strong umbrella brand for its individual products.

At the same time, developing sub-brands allows for the creation of brand-specific beliefs. This more detailed information can help customers better understand how products vary and which particular product may be the right one for them. Sub-brands also help to organize selling efforts so that salespeople and retailers have a clear picture as to how the product line is organized and how it might best be sold. For example, one of the main advantages to Nike of continually creating sub-brands in its basketball line (e.g., Air Jordan, Air Flight, Air Force) has been to generate retail interest and enthusiasm.

In general, the desired number of levels of the brand hierarchy depends on the complexity of the product line or product mix associated with a brand and thus the combination of shared and separate brand associations that the company would like to link to any one product in its product line or mix. With relatively simple, low involvement products, such as light bulbs, batteries, and chewing gum, the branding strategy often consists of an individual or perhaps family brand combined with modifiers that describe differences in product features. For example, with a fairly simple product such as batteries, Eveready has two main brands (Energizer and Classic "9 Lives") combined with a voltage designation (AAA, AA, C, D, etc.). With a complex set of products—such as cars, computers, or other durable goods—more levels of the hierarchy are necessary. Regardless of the complexity involved, it is difficult to brand a product with more than three levels of brand names without overwhelming or confusing consumers. In such cases, a better approach might be to introduce multiple brands at the same level (e.g., multiple family brands) and expand the depth of the brand portfolio.

Combining Brand Elements from Different Levels

If multiple brand elements from different levels of the brand hierarchy are combined to brand new products, it is necessary to decide how much emphasis should be given to each brand element. For example, if a sub-brand strategy is adopted, how much prominence should individual brands be given at the expense of the corporate or family brand?

When multiple brands are used, each brand element can vary in the relative emphasis it receives in the combined brand. The *prominence* of a brand element refers to its relative visibility as compared to other brand elements. For example, the prominence of a brand name element depends on several factors, such as its order, size, and appearance, as well as its semantic associations. A brand name should generally be more prominent when it appears first, is larger, and looks more distinctive. For example, assume Pepsi has adopted a sub-branding strategy to introduce a new vitamin-fortified cola, combining its corporate family brand name with a new individual brand name (e.g., "Vitacola"). The Pepsi name could be made more prominent by placing it first and making it bigger—**PEPSI** *Vitacola*. On the other hand, the individual brand could be made more prominent by placing it first and making it bigger—*Vitacola* **BY PEPSI.**

Along these lines, Gray and Smeltzer define *corporate/product relationships* as the approach a firm follows in communicating the relationship of its products to one another and to the corporate entity. They identify five possible categories (with illustrative examples):[33]

1. *Single entity.* One product line or set of services are offered such that the image of the company and the product tend to be one and the same (e.g., Federal Express).

2. *Brand-dominance.* The strategic decision is made not to relate brand and corporate names (e.g., Philip Morris makes little connection to Marlboro, Merit, and other cigarettes).

3. *Equal dominance.* Separate images are maintained for products but each is also associated with the corporation. Neither the corporate nor the individual brand names dominate (e.g., at the company level, General Motors with its different car divisions and individual brands—Buick LeSabre, Buick Electra, Buick Riviera, etc.).

4. *Mixed dominance.* Sometimes the individual product brands are dominant and sometimes the corporate name is dominant, and in some cases, they are used together with equal emphasis (e.g., the German firm Bosch uses its corporate name on some of the products it manufactures but not on others, such as Blaupunkt radios).

5. *Corporate dominance.* Corporate name is supreme and applied across a range of product lines, and communications tend to reinforce the corporate image (e.g., Xerox).

The relative prominence of the brand elements determines which element(s) becomes the primary one(s) and which element(s) becomes the secondary one(s). In general, primary brand elements should be chosen to convey the main product positioning and points of difference. Secondary brand elements are often chosen in more of a supporting role to convey a more restricted set of associations such as points of parity or perhaps an additional point of difference. A secondary brand element may also facilitate awareness. Thus, with the Canon Rebel 35mm camera, the primary brand element is the Rebel name, which reinforces the youthful, active lifestyle that makes up the desired user and usage imagery for the camera. The Canon name, on the other hand, is more of a secondary brand element that ideally would convey credibility, quality, and professionalism.

The relative prominence of the individual brand compared to the corporate brand should affect perceptions of product distance and the type of image created for the new product. If the corporate or family brand is made more prominent, then its associations are more likely to dominate. If the individual brand is made more prominent, on the other hand, then it should be easier to create a more distinctive brand image. In this case, the corporate or family brand is signaling to consumers that the new product is not as closely related to its other products that share that name. As a result, consumers should be less likely to transfer corporate or family brand associations. At the same time, the success or failure of the new product should, because of the greater perceived distance involved, be less likely to affect the image of the corporate or family brand. With a more prominent corporate or family brand, however, feedback effects are probably more likely to be evident. Chapter 12 discusses these issues in more detail.

To illustrate how relative prominence can affect the resulting image of a product, in the Pepsi Vitacola example above, assume that Pepsi was the more prominent brand element as compared to Vitacola. By making the corporate and family brand prominent, the new product would take on many of the associations that would be in common with other Pepsi-branded products (e.g., cola). If the Vitacola brand were more prominent, however, then the new product would most likely take on a much more distinct positioning. In this case, the Pepsi name would function more for awareness and perhaps only transfer broader, more abstract associations such as perceived quality or brand personality.

Finally, in some cases, the brand elements may not be explicitly linked at all. A *brand endorsement strategy* is when a brand element appears on the package, signage, or product appearance in some way but is not directly included as part of the brand name. Often this distinct brand element is the corporate brand name or logo. For example, General Mills places its "Big G" logo on its cereal packages but retains distinct brand names such as Cheerios and Wheaties. As noted above, Kellogg's, on the other hand, adopts a sub-brand strategy with its cereals that combines the corporate name with individual brands—Kellogg's Corn Flakes and Kellogg's Special K. The brand endorsement strategy presumably establishes the maximum distance between the corporate or family brand and the individual brands, suggesting that it would yield the smallest transfer of brand associations to the new product but, at the same time, minimize the likelihood of any negative feedback effects.

Linking Brand Elements to Multiple Products

The previous discussion highlighted how different brand elements may be applied to a particular product (i.e., "vertical" aspects of the brand hierarchy). Next, we consider how any one brand element can be linked to multiple products (i.e., "horizontal" aspects of the brand hierarchy). There are many different ways to connect a brand element to multiple products. The simplest way is literally to use the brand element "as is" across the different products involved. Other possibilities exist by adapting the brand, or some part of it, in some fashion to make the connection. For example, a common prefix or suffix of a brand name may be adapted to different products. Hewlett-Packard capitalized on its highly successful LaserJet computer printers to introduce a number of new products using the "Jet" suffix—the DeskJet, PaintJet, ThinkJet, and OfficeJet printers. Sony has designated its portable audio equipment with a "Man" suffix—Walkman personal stereos and Discman portable CD players. McDonald's has used its "Mc" prefix to introduce a number of products—Chicken McNuggets, Egg McMuffin, and the McRib sandwich. Initials can sometimes be used if multiple names make up the brand name, as with a designer name such as Donna Karan's DKNY brand, Calvin Klein's CK brand, and Ralph Lauren's Double RL brand.

A relationship between a brand and multiple products can also be made with common symbols. For example, corporate brands often place their corporate logo more prominently on their products than their name (e.g., Nabisco), creating a strong brand endorsement strategy. Nestlé ran an advertising campaign in 1993 that attempted to create greater awareness and understanding of its corporate brand. The ads contained the slogan "makes the very best"—a subtle variation of their well-known "makes the very best chocolate" slogan—and prominently displayed a logo of a nest with a mother and two baby birds. Although the founder's name, Nestlé, in fact means little nest, their hope in using the symbol was to communicate more abstract associations of warmth, family, and shelter. The symbol was to be used on all packages as a means to unite a diversified set of products with vastly different names (see Figure 11–15). As another example, Anheuser-Busch used the symbol of the eagle—

FIGURE 11–15 Nestlé Corporate Logo Ad

ALL OVER THE WORLD THIS IS A SYMBOL FOR WARMTH, FAMILY AND SHELTER.

In 1867, a man named Henri Nestlé began to build a food company.

His name, which means "little nest," has since become synonymous with food, family and quality throughout the world.

Today, that symbol can be found on the back of many well-known products.

Great-tasting Nestlé brands that include Stouffer's, Contadina, Libby's, Taster's Choice, Hills Bros, Carnation and more.

AND NESTLÉ.

And thanks to an unparalleled international network of Nestlé research and development centers, you have our assurance the products we introduce in the future will be as good as the ones we make today.

It's also why this little bird's nest represents 125 years of Nestlé quality. As well as the very best.

Nestlé
Makes the very best.

FIGURE 11-15 Nestlé Corporate Logo Ad (*continued*)

prominent in the logo used on its Budweiser beer and elsewhere—to introduce an entire line of Eagle branded snacks (although they eventually sold the line off after disappointing sales).

Simplifying the Hierarchy

Often it is desirable to have a logical ordering among brands in a product line to communicate how the different brands are related and to simplify consumer decision making. The relative ordering may be communicated to consumers though colors (e.g., American Express offers Green, Gold, and Platinum Cards), numbers (e.g., BMW offers their 3, 5, and 7 series cars), or other means. Branding Brief 11–4 describes how Acura is attempting to rename its product line to create more structure. Such a branding strategy is especially important in developing brand migration strategies as to how customers should switch among the brands offered by the company, if at all, over their lifetime (see chapter 13).

A second issue concerns the relative emphasis received by different products making up the brand hierarchy. If a corporate or family brand is associated with multiple products, which product should be the core or "flagship" product? What should represent "the brand" to consumers? Which product do consumers think best represents or embodies the brand? Understanding these brand "drivers" is important in identifying sources of brand equity and therefore how to best fortify and leverage the brand.

Designating Products

Although not considered a brand element per se, the product descriptor chosen to describe the actual branded product may be an important ingredient of branding strategy. The product descriptor helps consumers understand what the product is and does and also helps to define the relevant competition in consumers' minds. In some cases, it may be hard to actually succinctly describe what the product is, especially in the case of a new product with unusual functions. For example, one of the branding challenges at Intuit, makers of the highly successful Quicken software package, is describing what exactly Quicken *is*. Although labeled as "personal financial software," this may not be a product category descriptor with which consumers have much familiarity. Consequently, a problem may arise if Intuit launches brand extensions under the Quicken name. Unless carefully differentiated, consumers could become confused as to what distinguishes different products sharing the same Quicken name and which product was the "original" one. Introducing a truly new product with a familiar product name may facilitate basic familiarity and comprehension but perhaps at the expense of a richer understanding of how the new product is different from closely related, already existing products.

DESIGNING SUPPORTING MARKETING PROGRAMS

At the same time that the broad parameters of the brand hierarchy are put into place as to how brand elements relate to particular products, decisions also have to be made concerning how to design the supporting marketing program in a way that best reflects the desired content and structure of the brand hierarchy. In doing so, decisions have to be made concerning the planned or desired image at each brand hierarchy

Renaming the Acura Brand Portfolio[a]

Honda grew from humble origins to become a top import competitor in the United States. Recognizing that future sales growth would come from more up-scale customers, Honda set out in the early 1980s to compete with European luxury cars. Deciding that the functional Honda image of making dependable, economical cars was short on pizzazz and therefore would not appeal to that market, Honda embarked on a different strategy, setting up the new Acura division. Matching the quality, performance, and luxury of the European imports but costing thousands less, the $10,000 Acura Integra and $20,000 Acura Legend were introduced in 1986. Careful to eschew its corporate name, Acuras were sold through a different dealer network. Acura sold 52,000 cars that first year, most of them Legends. By the time Lexus and Infiniti entered the market in 1989, Acura was selling 142,000 cars and receiving top marks in customer satisfaction.

Rapidly rising sticker prices—due in part to a strengthening yen—and increased competition eroded sales such that Honda barely topped 100,000 cars in 1993. With its market leadership threatened and its customer base splintering—the typical Integra buyer made $57,000 or half that of the average Legend buyer—Honda felt it needed a dramatic marketing move. Research indicated that its Legend, Integra, and Vigor sub-brand names did not communicate luxury and order in the product line as well as the alphanumeric branding scheme of its competitors—BMW, Mercedes, Lexus, and Infiniti. Honda decided that the strength of the brand should lie in the Acura name. Thus, despite the fact that nearly $600 million had been spent on advertising those Acura sub-brands over the past eight years to build their equity, Honda announced a new alphanumeric numbering system in the winter of 1995 to be supported by $100 million in advertising. The ads retained the upscale theme, "Some Things Are Worth the Price."

The new $30,000 TL (for Touring Luxury) sedan series, designed to replace the Vigor, was the first rebranded model to hit dealers in mid-March of that year. Two models were introduced, the 2.5 TL and the 3.2 TL, designating the two engine sizes, a 2.5-liter five-cylinder engine and a 3.2-liter six-cylinder engine. Acura also introduced AcuraCare, a long-term service contract, to cover sales of their new models. The NSX sports car, whose strong sales hastened the switch, retained its name. Two additional models were to be introduced in the following eighteen months. The following year, Acura rolled out a replacement for its top-of-the-line Legend model (the 3.5 RL luxury sedan) and a new line priced in the mid-$20,000 range, which was its first U.S.-built model and which was positioned below the TL but above the Integra models (the 2.2 CL and 3.0 CL luxury sports coupes). They also introduced the SLX sports utility vehicle.

---

[a]Stewart Toy, "The Selling of Acura—A Honda That's Not a Honda," *Business Week* (March 17, 1986), p. 93; Fara Werner, "Remaking of a Legend," *Brandweek* (April 25, 1994), pp. 23–28; Neal Templin, "Japanese Luxury-Car Makers Unveiling Cheaper Models in Bid to Attract Buyers," *Wall Street Journal* (February 9, 1995), p. A-4; T. L. Stanley and Kathy Tryer, "Acura Plays Numbers Game to Fortify Future," *Brandweek,* February 20, 1995, p. 3; T. L. Stanley, "Acura Rolls TL, New Nameplate Position with $40M in Ad Fuel," *Brandweek,* (March 20, 1995), p. 4.

level and any necessary adjustments that should be made to the marketing program to support the new image.

Desired Awareness and Image at Each Hierarchy Level

Once multiple brand levels are chosen, the question becomes, how much awareness and what types of associations are to be created for brand elements at each level? Achieving the desired level of awareness and strength, favorability, and uniqueness of brand associations may take some time and involve a considerable change in consumer perceptions. Marketing programs must be carefully designed, implemented, and evaluated. Assuming some type of sub-branding strategy is adopted involving two or more brand levels, two general principles—relevance and differentiation—should guide the brand knowledge creation process at each level, as follows.

Relevance   The first principle is based on the advantages of efficiency and economy. In general, it is desirable to create associations that are relevant to as many brands nested at the level below as possible, especially at the corporate or family brand level. The more an association has some value in the marketing of products sold by the firm, then the more efficient and economical it is to consolidate this meaning into one brand that becomes linked to all these products. For example, Nike's slogan ("Just Do It") reinforces a key point of difference for the brand—performance—that is relevant to virtually all the products Nike sells. The more abstract the association, in general, the more likely it is to be relevant in different product settings. Thus, benefit associations are likely to be extremely advantageous associations because they potentially can "cut across" so many product categories.

Differentiation   The second principle is based on the disadvantages of redundancy. In general, it is desirable to distinguish brands at the same level as much as possible. If two brands cannot be easily distinguished, then it may be difficult for retailers or other channel members to justify supporting both brands. It may also be confusing for consumers to make choices between them. For example, Tropicana's orange juice sub-brands have included its flagship Pure Premium (which comes in several flavors including Ruby Red Orange) as well as Grovestand ("The Taste of Fresh Squeezed"), and Season's Best (100% pure orange juice from concentrate with vitamins added) extensions, which also come in different varieties and packaging. Certainly on the basis of the names and positionings, there would seem to be the potential for consumer confusion as to how the different variety of juices differ and which Tropicana juice is the right product for them.

Although the principle of differentiation is especially important at the individual brand or modifier levels, it is also valid at the family brand level. For example, one of the criticisms of marketing at General Motors is that GM has failed to adequately distinguish its family brands of automobiles (see Branding Brief 11–5). Ford Motor Co. has faced similar problems with its Mercury family brand, prompting the second largest U.S. car maker to embark on the largest advertising and promotional campaign that has ever been conducted for the brand. Designed to transform the Mercury image from that of "slightly more expensive versions of Fords," one ad shows the redesigned Mercury Sable winding through scenic locations while soft, contemporary

General Motors' Branding Challenges

In the early 1920s, Alfred P. Sloan of the General Motors Corporation decreed that his company would not make a single, universal automobile—as did his main competitor, Ford, with its Model T—but would instead offer a line of automobiles: "A car for every purse and purpose."[a] This philosophy led to the creation of the Cadillac, Oldsmobile, Buick, Pontiac, and Chevrolet divisions. Thus, General Motors branding strategy traditionally has been to create different divisions and automobiles that would appeal to distinctly unique market segments on the basis of price, product design, user imagery, and other factors.

Over the years, the marketing overlap between the five main GM divisions slowly increased and their distinctiveness diminished as each division attempted to offer cars for everybody. Finally, by the mid-1980s, GM offered many of its basic body types under multiple brand names. For example, under pressure to reduce costs, GM sold one body type (the J-body), with only minor physical differentiation, under *five* different brand names. In fact, advertisements for Cadillac in the 1980s actually stated "Motors for a Cadillac may come from other divisions, including Buick and Oldsmobile." Furthermore, not only were the cars sold in the same basic type of distribution channel, in some cases, more than one GM brand could be sold through the same dealership (e.g., Oldsmobile and Cadillac).[b]

Recognizing that consumer confusion over product design, brand image, and the marketing of the different brands was hampering sales, GM set out in 1990 to draw sharper differences in the marketplace among its name plates. At the same time, a corporate image ad campaign was launched to dispel customer concerns of slipping GM quality—and motivate its own 608,000 employee work force—through ads touting "Putting Quality on the Road."

The different divisions attempted to clear up their blurry images by adopting new brand positions:[c]

Division	Brand Positioning
Chevrolet	Value-priced entry level
Saturn	One-price, customer-oriented service
Pontiac	Sporty, performance-oriented for young people
Oldsmobile	Medium-priced larger cars
Buick	Premium and "near-luxury"
Cadillac	Top-of-the-line standard of luxury

In laymen's terms, Chevrolet was supposed to build lower-price, quality cars; Pontiac was to concentrate on performance; Olds was supposed to excel in engineering; Buick was to emphasize highway comfort; and Cadillac was to represent the best. GM went back to basics to regain some of its lost equity. For example, GM abandoned attempts to make the Chevrolet brand look trendsetting and foreign and returned to images of "America, hot dogs, and apple pie" through the highly successful "Heartbeat of America" ad campaign.

Turning around the divisions has been a challenge for GM. Despite improved performances from Pontiac and the newly introduced Saturn division, the bottom and top of the lines, Chevrolet and Cadillac, have struggled. Chevrolet was criticized by some as having too many overlapping products—from a $7000 Geo Metro to a $65,000 Corvette ZR-1—and a muddled marketing strategy.[d] Cadillac suffered from intense foreign competition and a disastrous foray with the downsized Cimarron model (see chapter 12).

After being hired from Bausch and Lomb in December 1995, Ronald Zarella reemphasized the importance of branding at GM, stating that GM's future depended as much on good marketing as good products: "There's a belief in this industry that product is everything—and it's not." Zarella decided that GM's 65 car and truck models should be marketed more as individual brands to specific market segments with less emphasis on their divisions. Accordingly, he placed 29 brand managers in charge of creating clear and distinct images for the brands.[e] Plans were initiated to replace one-fourth of their auto lineup. Another sign of changing brand strategies at GM was the marketing program for the high end Aurora: More emphasis was placed on the Aurora nameplate than on the division. The Oldsmobile name can only be found in one place on the car (on a "trim plate" above the radio on the dashboard), and the expensive introductory advertising campaign only mentioned the Oldsmobile name once.[f]

---

[a]Alfred P. Sloan, *My Years With General Motors*. Garden City, NY: Doubleday & Company, Inc., 1964, p. 67 as quoted in William M. Weilbacher, *Brand Marketing: Building Winning Brand Strategies That Deliver Value and Customer Satisfaction*. Lincolnwood, IL: NTC Business Books, 1993.

[b]Adrian B. Ryans, Roger A. More, and John S. Hulland, "Profitable Multibranding," working paper, Western Business School, The University of Western Ontario.

[c]Jerry Flint, "'A Brand is Like a Friend,'" *Forbes* (November 14, 1988), pp. 267–270; Mark Landler, "Shirley Young: Pushing GM's Humble-Pie Strategy," *Business Week* (June 11, 1990), pp. 52–53.

[d]Neal Templin, "Chevy, a Bit Rusty and Slowing Down, Finds Itself Boxed in by GM's Problems," *Wall Street Journal* (April 24, 1992), p. B-1.

[e]Micheline Maynard, "Marketing Over Matter: GM Keys on Brand Advertising," *USA Today* (October 20, 1995), p. B-2.

[f]Kevin Goldman, "GM's Oldsmobile Lets Aurora Drive Solo," *Wall Street Journal* (September 14, 1994), p. B-10.

---

music plays in the background and a narrator asks viewers to, "Imagine yourself in a Mercury."

Adjustments to the Marketing Program

When a firm moves away from a simple "single brand–single product" branding strategy to adopt more complex branding strategies—perhaps involving multiple brand extensions, multiple brands, and/or multiple levels of the hierarchy used to brand any one product—certain adjustments may be necessary in the supporting marketing program. For example, as noted above, different brands can play different roles and therefore require quite different marketing mixes. Consequently, product design, pricing policies, distribution plans, and marketing communication campaigns may differ significantly depending on the role of the brand and its interdependencies with other brands. In general, many of the principles in developing supporting marketing programs to build brand equity from chapters 5 to 7 still apply. In this section, we highlight some of the adjustments in the supporting marketing program that may be necessary as a result of having interrelated brands and products.

Communication Strategies   As noted above, assuming multiple levels of a branding hierarchy are employed, different levels of awareness and image may be desired at each level. In particular, if a sub-brand strategy is adopted, it may make sense to create a marketing communication campaign at the corporate, company, or family brand levels to complement more product-specific or individual brand marketing communication campaigns (as were reviewed in chapter 6). As part of this "higher-level" campaign, companies may employ the full range of marketing communication options, including advertising, public relations, promotions, and sponsorship. Two potentially useful marketing communication strategies to build brand equity at the corporate brand or family brand level are discussed here.

Corporate image campaigns are designed to create associations to the corporate brand as a whole and, consequently, tend to ignore or downplay individual products or sub-brands in the process.[34] As would be expected, some of the biggest spenders on these kinds of campaigns are those well-known firms who prominently use their company or corporate names in their branding strategies, for example, Ford, AT&T, IBM, Dow, GTE, Hewlett-Packard, and American Express. More firms are now running these types of non-product-specific ads—especially retail and service brands who commonly use their corporate names—in part due to the fact that so many products have become linked to their family or corporate brands over time through brand extensions. For example, Pizza Hut recently launched a corporate image campaign with ads that mixed vignettes of kids and families with lilting music and the voice-over of actor Jason Robards announcing, "If your pizza's not right, it's free." The tag line proclaims, "You'll Love the Stuff We're Made Of."

Corporate image campaigns have been criticized by some in the past as an ego-stroking waste-of-time. To maximize the probability of success, objectives of a corporate image campaign must be clearly defined *and* results must be carefully measured against these objectives. There are a number of different possible objectives in a corporate image campaign:

1. Build awareness of the company and the nature of its business.
2. Create favorable attitudes and perceptions of company credibility.
3. Link beliefs that can be leveraged by product-specific advertising.
4. Make favorable impression on financial community.
5. Motivate present employees and attract better recruits.
6. Influence public opinion on issues.

In terms of building customer-based brand equity, the first three objectives are particularly critical, that is, the extent to which a corporate image campaign can enhance awareness and create a more positive image of the corporate brand that will influence consumer evaluations and increase the equity associated with individual products and any related sub-brands. In certain cases, however, the latter three objectives can take on greater importance. Because the first three objectives are the ones most directly related to building customer-based brand equity, we highlight notable examples for each of these objectives:

1. *Building awareness of the company and its nature of business.* After finding that half of its potential customers thought it still made appliances—despite the fact that they sold off their refrigerator line in 1974, their light bulb line in 1984, and so on—Westinghouse launched a 3-year corporate brand program in 1989 to showcase its current lines of business—defense electronics, waste management, broadcasting, and financial services. They did decide to bring back their old corporate slogan, however, "You Can Be Sure If It Is Westinghouse." Westinghouse faced a new branding challenge after its 1995 acquisition of CBS in terms of what they would name the broadcasting side of the business.

2. *Building company trustworthiness and credibility.* Johnson & Johnson recently launched an ad campaign to promote the trustworthiness of the corporate brand. The commercials featured many "warm and fuzzy" shots of families. Johnson & Johnson products were not emphasized, although their baby powder, Band-Aids, and Reach toothbrush products were shown in passing. The ad concluded with the words: "Over the years, Johnson & Johnson has taken care of more families than anyone else."

3. *Creating corporate image associations that can be leveraged by product-specific advertising.* DuPont has run corporate advertising campaigns since 1936. Originally, its corporate ads contained the slogan, "Better Things for Better Living Through Chemistry," although the chemistry reference was later dropped because it was seen as too confining and restrictive. In its corporate advertising, DuPont attempts to feature products that it believes connect in a constructive, positive way with public issues and have the potential to make a difference in people's lives. DuPont wants to be seen by the general public—as well as opinion leaders in education, business, and government—as "an innovative, responsible, and responsive industry leader." At the same time, DuPont runs comprehensive marketing campaigns supporting its individual products (e.g., recall the discussion of the Stainmaster brand from chapter 5 and the Lycra brand in chapter 7). A research study analyzing consumer response to its various advertising campaigns revealed some important synergies between its corporate image and individual product ad campaigns. For example, one study revealed that consumers with a more favorable corporate image of DuPont were more likely to respond favorably to the claims made in an ad for Stainmaster and buy the product.[35]

Thus, corporate image campaigns focus on characteristics or aspects of the brand as a whole. These broader image campaigns may also be employed at the family brand level. A second marketing communication strategy to build brand equity at the corporate brand or family brand level is with brand line campaigns. *Brand line campaigns* emphasize the breadth of products associated with the brand. Unlike a corporate image campaign that presents the brand in abstract terms with perhaps few, if any, references to specific products, brand line campaigns refer to the range of products associated with a brand line. By showing consumers the different uses or benefits of the multiple products offered by a brand, brand line ads may be particularly useful in building brand awareness, clarifying brand meaning and suggesting additional usage applications. Brand line promotions can achieve similar goals. For example, unified brand line promotions have been run for Thomas' English Muffins, Bagels, and Pita Bread (see Figure 11–16), as well as for many other brands.

FIGURE 11-16 Examples of Umbrella Brand Promotions

Even when individual brands are used, umbrella ads that encompass multiple brands may serve a purpose. For example, in several advertising campaigns in 1995, Procter & Gamble promoted category-wide product benefits for its brands such as the sanitary power of its dishwashing detergents and the waste-reduction advantages of "ultra" laundry detergents.[36] In both cases, the benefit is a point of difference—compared to lower-priced competitors—shared by all P&G brands in the category.

Review

A key aspect of managing brand equity is the proper branding strategy. Brand names of products typically do not consist of only one name but often consist of a combination of different brand names and other brand elements. A *branding strategy* for a firm identifies which brand elements a firm chooses to apply across the various products it sells. This chapter described two important tools to help formulate branding strategies—the brand-product matrix and the brand hierarchy. Combining these tools with customer, company, and competitive considerations can help a marketing manager formulate the optimal branding strategy.

The *brand-product matrix* is a graphical representation of all the brands and products sold by the firm. The matrix or grid has the brands for a firm as rows and the corresponding products as columns. The rows of the matrix represent brand-product relationships and capture the brand extension strategy of the firm with respect to a brand. Potential extensions must be judged by how effectively they leverage existing brand equity to a new product, as well as how effectively the extension, in turn, contributes to the equity of the existing parent brand. The columns of the matrix represent product-brand relationships and capture the brand portfolio strategy in terms of the number and nature of brands to be marketed in each category.

A branding strategy can be characterized according to its breadth (i.e., in terms of brand-product relationships and brand extension strategy) and its depth (i.e., in terms of product-brand relationships and the brand portfolio or mix). The breadth of the branding strategy concerns the product mix and which products the firm should manufacture and/or sell. Issues concerning how many different product lines the company should carry (i.e., the breadth of the product mix), as well as how many variants should be offered in each product line (i.e., the depth of the product mix) were reviewed. The depth of the branding strategy concerns the brand portfolio and the set of all brands and brand lines that a particular seller offers for sale to buyers. A firm may offer multiple brands in a category to attract different—and potentially mutually exclusive—market segments. Brands also can take on very specialized roles in the portfolio—as flanker brands to protect more valuable brands, as low-end entry-level brands to expand the customer franchise, as high-end prestige brands to enhance the worth of the entire brand line, or as cash cows from which to milk all potentially realizable profits. Companies must be careful to understand exactly what each brand should do for the firm and, more importantly, what they want it to do for the customer.

A *brand hierarchy* reveals an explicit ordering of all brand names by displaying the number and nature of common and distinctive brand name elements across the firm's products. By capturing the potential branding relationships among the different products sold by the firm, a brand hierarchy is a useful means to graphically portray a firm's branding strategy. One simple representation of possible brand elements and thus potential levels of a brand hierarchy is (from top to bottom): (1) corporate (or company) brand, (2) family brand, (3) individual brand, and (4) modifier.

A number of specific issues arise in designing the brand hierarchy. Brand elements at each level of the hierarchy may contribute to brand equity through their ability to create awareness and foster strong, unique, and favorable brand associations. The challenge in setting up the brand hierarchy and arriving at a branding strategy is: (1) to design the proper brand hierarchy in terms of the number and nature of brand elements to use at each level and (2) to design the optimal supporting marketing program in terms of creating the desired amount of brand awareness and type of brand associations at each level.

In terms of designing a brand hierarchy, the number of different levels of brands that will be employed and the relative emphasis or prominence that brands at different levels will receive when combined to brand any one product must be defined. In general, the number of levels employed typically are two or three. One common strategy to brand a new product is to create a sub-brand where an existing company or family brand is combined with a new individual brand. When multiple brand names are used, as with a sub-brand, the relative visibility of a brand element as compared to other brand elements determines its prominence. Brand visibility and prominence will depend on factors such as the order, size, color, and other aspects of physical appearance of the brand. To provide structure and content to the brand hierarchy, the specific means by which a brand is used across different products and, if different brands are used for different products, the relationship among those brands also must be made clear to consumers.

In terms of designing the supporting marketing program in the context of a brand hierarchy, the desired awareness and image at each level of the brand hierarchy for each product must be defined. In a sub-branding situation, the desired awareness of a brand at any level will dictate the relative prominence of the brand and the extent to which associations linked to the brand will transfer to the product. In terms of building brand equity, determining which associations to link at any one level should be based on principles of relevance and differentiation. In general, it is desirable to create associations that are relevant to as many brands nested at the level below and to distinguish any brands at the same level. Corporate or family brands can establish a number of valuable associations that can help to differentiate the brand such as common product attributes, benefits, or attitudes; people and relationships; programs and values; and corporate credibility. A corporate image will depend on a number of factors, such as the products a company makes, the actions it takes, and the manner with which it communicates to consumers. Communications may focus on the corporate brand in the abstract or on the different products making up the brand line.

Discussion Questions

1. Pick a company. As completely as possible, characterize its brand portfolio and brand hierarchy. How would you improve its branding strategies?
2. Do you think the Nestlé corporate image campaign described in the chapter will be successful? Why or why not? What do you see as key success factors for a corporate image campaign?

3. Contrast the branding strategies and brand portfolios of market leaders in two different industries. For example, contrast the approach by Anheuser-Busch and its Budweiser brand with that of Kellogg in the ready-to-eat cereal category.

4. What are some of the product strategies and communication strategies that General Motors could use to further enhance the level of perceived differentiation between its divisions?

Notes

1. Philip Kotler, *Marketing Management*, 9th ed. Upper Saddle River, NJ: Prentice Hall, 1997.
2. Donald R. Lehmann and Russell S. Winer, "Category Attractiveness Analysis," (Chapter 4) and "Market Potential and Forecasting" (Chapter 7), *Product Management*. Burr Ridge, IL: Irwin, 1994.
3. Glen L. Urban and Steven H. Star, *Advanced Marketing Strategy: Phenomena, Analysis, and Decisions*. Upper Saddle River, NJ: Prentice Hall, 1991.
4. Philip Kotler, *Marketing Management*, 9th ed. Upper Saddle River, NJ: Prentice Hall, 1997.
5. Tara Parker-Pope, "Laura Ashley's Chief Tries to Spruce Up Company That Isn't Dressing for Success," *Wall Street Journal* (September 22, 1995), p. B-1.
6. David Greising, "Major Reservations," *Business Week* (September 26, 1994), p. 66.
7. Patrick Barwise and Thomas Robertson, "Brand Portfolios," *European Management Journal*, 10 (3) (September 1992), pp. 277–285.
8. Philip Kotler, *Marketing Management*, 9th ed. Upper Saddle River, NJ: Prentice Hall, 1997. Patrick Barwise and Thomas Robertson, "Brand Portfolios," *European Management Journal*, 10 (3) (September 1992), pp. 277–285.
9. For a methodological approach for assessing the extent and nature of cannibalization, see Charlotte H. Mason and George R. Milne, "An Approach for Identifying Cannibalization within Product Line Extensions and Multi-Brand Strategies," *Journal of Business Research*, 31 (1994), pp. 163–170.
10. Yumiko Ono, "Nabisco Favors Tried and True Over New Lines," *Wall Street Journal* (June 28, 1996), pp. B1–3.
11. David A. Aaker, *Managing Brand Equity*. New York: Free Press, 1991.
12. Paul W. Farris, "The Chevrolet Corvette," Case UVA-M-320, The Darden Graduate Business School Foundation, University of Virginia, Charlottesville, Virginia, 1995.
13. Peter H. Farquhar, Julia Y. Han, and Paul M. Herr, and Yuji Ijiri, "Strategies for Leveraging Master Brands," *Marketing Research* (September 1992), pp. 32–43.
14. Alecia Swasy, "P&G To Tout Name Behind the Brands," *Wall Street Journal* (December 12, 1991), B1–B3.
15. Laurel Cutler, vice-chairman of FCB/Leber Katz Partners, a New York City advertising agency quoted in Susan Caminit, "The Payoff from a Good Reputation," *Fortune* (March 6, 1995), p. 74.
16. Lydia Demworth, "Consumers Care About Corporate Images," *Psychology Today* (September 1989), p. 14.
17. Howard Barich and Philip Kotler, "A Framework for Image Management," *Sloan Management Review* (Winter 1991), pp. 94–104.
18. Much of this section—including examples—is based on an excellent article by Peter H. Farquhar, Julia Y. Han, and Paul M. Herr, and Yuji Ijiri, "Strategies for Leveraging Master Brands," *Marketing Research* (September 1992), pp. 32–43.

19. Peter H. Farquhar, Julia Y. Han, Paul M. Herr, and Yuji Ijiri, "Strategies for Leveraging Master Brands," *Marketing Research* (September 1992), pp. 32–43.

20. Several excellent reviews of corporate images are available. See, for example, Grahame R. Dowling, *Corporate Reputations*. Melbourne, Australia: Longman Professional, 1994; and James R. Gregory, *Marketing Corporate Image*. Lincolnwood, IL: NTC Business Books, 1991.

21. Masashi Kuga, "Kao's Strategy and Marketing Intelligence System," *Journal of Advertising Research*, 30 (April/May 1990), pp. 20–25.

22. John Murphy, *Brand Strategy*. Upper Saddle River, NJ: Prentice Hall, 1990, p. 54.

23. Jacqueline Mitchell, "GM's New Ads Focus on Humility, Client's Importance," *Wall Street Journal* (March 10, 1994), p. B-6.

24. Judann Dagnoli, "Consciously Green," *Advertising Age* (September 19, 1991), p. 14.

25. Lawrence E. Joseph, "The Greening of American Business," *Vis a Vis* (May 1991), p. 32.

26. P. Rajan Varadarajan and Anil Menon, "Cause-Related Marketing: A Coalignment of Marketing Strategy and Corporate Philanthropy," *Journal of Marketing*, 52 (July 1988), pp. 58–74.

27. Greg Goldin, "Cause-Related Marketing Grows Up," *Adweek* (November 17, 1987), pp. 20–22; and Ronald Alsop, "More Firms Push Promotion Aimed at Consumers' Hearts," *Wall Street Journal* (August 29, 1985), p. 23.

28. Yumiko Ono, "Do-Good Ads Aim for Sales That Do Better," *Wall Street Journal* (September 2, 1994), p. B-8.

29. Kevin Lane Keller and David A. Aaker, "Managing the Corporate Brand: The Effects of Corporate Marketing Activity on Consumers Evaluations of Brand Extensions," Marketing Science Institute working paper # 97-106, Cambridge, MA, 1997.

30. Marvin E. Goldberg and Jon Hartwick, "The Effects of Advertiser Reputation and Extremity of Advertising Claim on Advertising Effectiveness," *Journal of Consumer Research*, 17 (September 1990), pp. 172–179.

31. Sylvie LaForet and John Saunders, "Managing Brand Portfolios: How the Leaders Do It," *Journal of Advertising Research* (September/October 1994), pp. 64–76.

32. Sylvie LaForet and John Saunders, "Managing Brand Portfolios: How the Leaders Do It," *Journal of Advertising Research* (September/October 1994), pp. 64–76.

33. Edmund Gray and Larry R. Smeltzer, "Corporate Image—An Integral Part of Strategy," *Sloan Management Review* (Summer 1985), pp. 73–78.

34. For a review of current and past practices, see David W. Schumann, Jan M. Hathcote, and Susan West, "Corporate Advertising in America: A Review of Published Studies on Use, Measurement, and Effectiveness," *Journal of Advertising*, 20 (3) (September 1991), pp. 35–56.

35. "Dupont: Corporate Advertising," Harvard Business School Case # 9-593-023. December 28, 1992. Cambridge, MA. John B. Frey, "Measuring Corporate Reputation and its Value," presentation given at Marketing Science Conference at Duke University, March 17, 1989.

36. Fara Warner, "P&G, Breaking With Tradition Promotes Products as a Category," *Wall Street Journal* (April 25, 1995), p. B8.

CHAPTER **12**

Introducing and Naming New Products and Brand Extensions

449

Preview

Chapter 11 reviewed several key concepts in developing a firm's branding strategy. Two useful tools were introduced: the brand-product matrix—a graphical means of representing the products and brands marketed by a firm—and the brand hierarchy—a visual means to portray relationships among various brand elements. In this chapter, we consider in more detail the role of new product strategy in creating, maintaining, and enhancing brand equity. Specifically, we develop guidelines to facilitate the introduction and naming of new products and brand extensions.

To provide some historical perspective, for years firms tended to follow the lead of Procter & Gamble, Coca-Cola, and other major consumer goods marketers who essentially avoided introducing any new products using an existing brand name. Over time, tight economic conditions, a need for growth, and other factors forced firms to rethink their "one brand–one product" policies. Recognizing that one of their most valuable assets is their brands, many firms have since decided to leverage that asset by introducing a host of new products under some of their strongest brand names.

Because brand extensions have only recently become so prevalent, to some extent, "rules" guiding brand extension strategy are still emerging. Nevertheless, a flurry of academic research activity and some notable marketplace successes and failures are providing insight as to best management practices. The chapter begins by describing some basic brand extension issues and outlining the main advantages and disadvantages of brand extensions. The chapter then presents a simple model of how consumers evaluate brand extensions. The chapter concludes by summarizing research findings and offering managerial guidelines concerning the proper means to introduce and name new products and brand extensions.

New Products and Brand Extensions

As background, it is worthwhile to first consider the sources of growth for a firm. One useful perspective is offered by Ansoff's product/market expansion grid. As shown in Figure 12–1, growth strategies can be categorized as to whether they involve existing or new products and whether they target existing or new customers or markets. As evidenced by this framework, although existing products can be used to further penetrate existing customer markets or expand into new customer markets (the focus of chapter 13), new product introductions are often vital to the long-run success of a firm.

As noted in chapter 11, a number of factors related to consumer behavior, corporate capabilities, and competitive actions will affect the successful development of a new product or market. Branding Brief 12–1 describes the challenges faced as Clorox attempted to introduce a new product into the frozen foods category. A discussion of all of the issues involved in effectively managing the development and introduction of new products is beyond the scope of this chapter. In this section, however, we will address some brand equity implications of new products.[1]

To facilitate the discussion, it is useful to establish some terminology. When a firm introduces a new product, it has three main choices as to how to brand it:

1. It can develop a new brand, individually chosen for the new product.
2. It can apply one of its existing brands in some way.
3. It can use a combination of a new brand with an existing brand.

A *brand extension* is when a firm uses an established brand name to introduce a new product (approaches 2 or 3). When a new brand is combined with an existing brand (approach 3), the brand extension can also be called a *sub-brand*. An existing brand that gives birth to a brand extension is referred to as the *parent brand*. As noted in

FIGURE 12–1 Ansoff Growth Share Matrix

	Current Products	**New Products**
Current Markets	Market Penetration Strategy	Product Development Strategy
New Markets	Market Development Strategy	Diversification Strategy

Trying to Warm up Sales for Hidden Valley Ranch Frozen Entrees[a]

Each year, thousands of new products are introduced and fail. Many probably deserve to do so because they do not really satisfy new consumer needs or wants, are poorly designed, and/or are inadequately marketed. Nevertheless, sometimes products that probably should survive fail to do so.

One such product might have been Hidden Valley Ranch frozen microwave entrees, introduced by Clorox. Hidden Valley Ranch entrees took advantage of novel microwave technology. Instead of simply thawing and reheating precooked fare, Hidden Valley Ranch entrees effectively turned the microwave into a steamer. Consumers had to add water—a paper measuring cup was included—but the result was "crisp vegetables, al dente pasta, tasty meats, and flavorful sauces." Despite some clear advantages, however, the product ultimately failed in test markets. Critics identified a number of possible explanations as to why consumers had such a lukewarm response to the new product concept. Their analysis helps to illuminate some of the potential difficulties in successfully introducing new food products.

Highly competitive category. One of the most crowded supermarket categories—and costly to enter—is frozen foods. Driven by the swift adoption of microwave technology, "heat-and-eat" foods quickly became a $4 billion-a-year market. But with demand slowing and an avalanche of new products, supermarket retailers were constantly assessing the most effective allocation of their precious freezer space. Four strong competitors—ConAgra, Kraft General Foods, Stouffers, and Campbell Soup—had gained preeminent positions in this battle for shelf space and aggressively protected their turf with deep discounts and other marketing activity.

Consumer reluctance. Although steam cooking had its appeal and benefits, it did require consumers to invest some effort—adding water and stirring cooked ingredients—perhaps more than many consumers in this market might have been willing to expend. Moreover, alongside its competition, Hidden Valley's package appeared to be smaller and to contain less food—because it was designed to make better use of limited freezer space and, as a result of the steaming technology, needed to have a certain package size, weight, and shape.

Confusing brand name. Despite the positive attitudes consumers held toward the Hidden Valley Ranch brand, most people equated the name with salad dressing and did not find the brand as relevant as a frozen food. Spotty promotional and advertising support for the brand only compounded the problem, especially given the large sums spent by competitors.

Clorox's experience with Hidden Valley Ranch frozen entrees is a clear demonstration of how difficult it is to introduce new products and how new products must be carefully designed *and* marketed.

---

[a]Richard Gibson, "Novel Microwave Dinners Are Tasty—And Likely to Fail Without a Quick Fix," *Wall Street Journal* (July 12, 1991), p. B1.

chapter 11, if the parent brand is already associated with multiple products through brand extensions, then it may also be called a *family brand*.

Brand extensions can be broadly classified into two general categories:[2]

1. A *line extension* is when the parent brand is used to brand a new product that targets a new market segment within a product category currently served by the parent brand. A line extension often involves a different flavor or ingredient variety, a different form or size, or a different application for the brand, such as Head & Shoulders Dry Scalp shampoo.

2. A *category extension* is when the parent brand is used to enter a different product category from that currently served by the parent brand, such as Swiss Army watches.

Most new products are line extensions. In 1990, 63 percent of products introduced were line extensions, and another 18 percent were category extensions. Moreover, as Figure 12–2 shows, many of the most successful new products, as rated by various sources, are extensions. Nevertheless, many new products are introduced each year as new brands. The last decade has seen highly successful launches of such new brands as Surf laundry detergent, Salon Selectives shampoo and conditioners, and Teddy Graham cookies. Branding Brief 12–2 describes one of the most successful packaged goods launches in recent years, Lever 2000 soap.

Brand extensions can come in all forms. For example, one well-known branding expert, Edward Tauber, identifies the following seven general strategies to establish a category—or what he calls a franchise—extension:

1. *Introduce the same product in a different form:* For example, Ocean Spray Cranberry juice cocktail and Jell-O Pudding Pops.

2. *Introduce products that contain the brand's distinctive taste, ingredient, or component:* For example, Philadelphia Cream Cheese salad dressing and Haagen-Dazs Cream liqueur.

FIGURE 12–2 Best New Products in 1994

Business Week	RCA Digital Satellite System
Packard Bell multimedia computers	Chrysler Cirrus automobile
Oldsmobile Aurora automobile	HP OfficeJet printer
Bose WAVE radio	Chevy Blazer sports-utility vehicle
SportsTrax pager	
Dante II robot	*Fortune*
Seiko MessageWatch	Wonderbra
Taylor Made mid-size woods golf clubs	Mighty Morphin Power Rangers
Mosiac Internet software program	Oldsmobile Aurora
Nokia 2100 series digital mobile phones	RCA DSS
Lotus Notes software	Baby Think It Over dolls
Nikon N-50 35mm SLR camera	Black & Decker SnakeLight
Myst CD-ROM game	Mosiac Internet software program
Sony SLV-770HF VCRs	Svelte cellulite removal
Donkey Kong Country computer game	Myst CD-ROM game
Power Macintosh personal computer	"The Lion King" movie

BRANDING BRIEF 12-2

Sudsing up a Winner with Lever 2000[a]

Despite the difficulty in launching a new product, marketers occasionally "strike gold." One such winner was Lever Brothers' Lever 2000. Its phenomenal sales achievements provides some lessons as to what it takes to succeed with a new product.

Lever 2000 is a "triple threat" bath soap that moisturizes, deodorizes, and kills bacteria. The product's origin can be traced to the early 1980s when marketing researchers uncovered the fact that consumers were dissatisfied in choosing between moisturizing bars, such as Dove, which they felt did not effectively deodorize, and deodorant bars, such as Dial, which they felt could dry their skin. To fill this void, Lever's research and development technicians devised a patented process to combine moisturizing and deodorizing properties into one bar.

Wanting to choose a name that reflected its revolutionary qualities, the firm arrived at Lever 2000. After fumbling around with futuristic images for its advertising, Lever's ad agency, J. Walter Thompson, came up with a more user- and usage-relevant advertising theme reflected by the tag line, "Presenting some of the 2000 body parts you can clean with new Lever 2000." Introductory ads had a playful tone and were somewhat racy, showing plenty of skin as both men and women were shown lathering up in the shower. Lever's marketing program also involved extensive sampling, massive distribution, and deep discounts. Roughly half of all U.S. households received samples, and initial coupons knocked off 75 cents off the average $1.69 retail price for two 5-ounce bars.

Buoyed by repeat rates hitting the 40 percent range, even after the heavy discounts ended, Lever quickly became the No. 2 deodorant soap in dollar volume. Within six months after its 1991 national rollout, Lever 2000 had achieved a remarkable 8.4 percent share of the $1.5 billion bar soap market.

---

[a]Christopher Power, "Everyone is Bellying Up to This Bar," *Business Week* (January 27, 1992), p. 84.

---

3. *Introduce companion products for the brand:* For example, Coleman camping equipment and Duracell Durabeam flashlights.

4. *Introduce products relevant to customer franchise of the brand:* For example, Gerber insurance and Visa traveler's checks.

5. *Introduce products that capitalize on the firm's perceived expertise:* For example, Honda lawn mowers and Canon photocopy machines.

6. *Introduce products that reflect the brand's distinctive benefit, attribute, or feature owned:* For example, Lysol's "deodorizing" household cleaning products and Ivory's "mild" cleaning products.

7. *Introduce products that capitalize on the distinctive image or prestige of the brand:* For example, Calvin Klein clothes and accessories and Porsche sunglasses.

Later in the chapter we will consider brand extension strategies more systematically. Next, however, we outline some of the main advantages and disadvantages of brand extensions.

Advantages of Extensions

For most firms, the question is not whether the brand should be extended, but when, where, and how the brand should be extended. Well-planned and implemented extensions offer a number of advantages to marketers. These advantages can broadly be categorized as those that facilitate new product acceptance and those that provide feedback benefits to the parent brand or company as whole (see Figure 12–3), as follows.

FACILITATE NEW PRODUCT ACCEPTANCE

The high failure rate of new products is well documented. Marketing analysts put the success rate of new products as perhaps only 2 out of 10, or maybe even as low as 1 out of 10. As noted above, new products can fail for a number of reasons. Robert McMath—who oversees a collection of over 75,000 once-new consumer products called the New Products Showcase and Learning Center in Ithaca, New York—identifies nine main reasons for product failure:[3]

1. Market was too small (insufficient demand for type of product).
2. Poor match for company.

FIGURE 12-3 Advantages of Brand Extension

Facilitate New Product Acceptance

Reduce risk perceived by customers

Increase the probability of gaining distribution and trial

Increase efficiency of promotional expenditures

Reduce costs of introductory and followup marketing programs

Avoid cost of developing a new brand

Allow for packaging and labeling efficiencies

Permit consumer variety-seeking

Provide Feedback Benefits to the Parent Brand and Company

Clarify brand meaning

Enhance the parent brand image

Bring new customers into brand franchise and increase market coverage

Revitalize the brand

Permit subsequent extensions

3. Justified on inadequate or inaccurate marketing research or ignored research results.

4. Too early or too late in researching market (failure to capitalize on its marketing window).

5. Insufficient return on investment (poor profit margins and high costs).

6. Not new, not different (a poor idea that really offered nothing new).

7. Did not go hand in hand with familiarity.

8. Credibility not confirmed on delivery.

9. Consumers could not recognize.

Brand extensions can certainly suffer from some of the same shortcomings faced by any new product. Nevertheless, a new product introduced as a brand extension may be more likely to succeed, at least to some degree, by offering the following advantages.

Reduced Risk Perceived by Customers

As chapter 2 noted, one of the advantages of a well-known and well-liked brand is that consumers form expectations over time concerning its performance. Similarly, with a brand extension, consumers can make inferences and form expectations as to the likely composition and performance of a new product based on what they already know about the brand itself and the extent to which they feel this information is relevant to the new product.[4] For example, when Sony introduced a new personal computer tailored for multimedia applications, consumers may have been more likely to feel comfortable with its anticipated performance because of their experience with and knowledge of other Sony products than if the product had been branded by Sony as something completely new.

One research study examining factors affecting new product acceptance found that the most important factor for predicting initial trial of a new product was the extent to which a known family brand was involved.[5] Extensions from well-known corporate brands such as General Electric, Hewlett-Packard, Motorola, or others may communicate longevity and sustainability. Although corporate brands may lack specific product associations because of the breadth of products attached to their name, their established reputation for being able to introduce quality products and "stand behind" them may be an important risk reducer for consumers.[6] Thus, perceptions of corporate credibility in terms of expertise and trustworthiness can be valuable associations in introducing brand extensions.[7] Similarly, although widely extended supermarket family brands such as Betty Crocker, Green Giant, Del Monte, and Pepperidge Farm may lack specific product meaning, they may still stand for product quality in the minds of consumers and, by reducing perceived risk, facilitate the adoption of brand extensions.

Increase the Probability of Gaining Distribution and Trial

Because of the potentially increased consumer demand resulting from introducing a new product as an extension, it may be easier to convince retailers to stock and promote a brand extension. For example, a study by Stanford's David Montgomery indicated that brand reputation was a key screening criterion by gatekeepers making new product decisions at supermarkets.[8]

Increase Efficiency of Promotional Expenditures

From a marketing communications perspective, one obvious advantage of introducing a new product as a brand extension is that the introductory campaign does not have to create awareness of both the brand and the new product but instead can concentrate on only the new product itself. In general, it should be easier to add a link from a brand already existing in memory to a new product than it is to have to first establish the brand in memory and then also link the new product to it.[9] As a dramatic illustration of the marketing communication efficiencies of brand extensions, when General Mills launched its fourth Cheerios extension—Frosted Cheerios—the brand was able to achieve a .44 percent market share in the extremely competitive cereal category in its very first week of sales with essentially *no* advertising or promotion. Sheerly on the basis of its name and product concept, demand for the sweetened oat cereal was so high that most supermarkets were forced to limit the number of boxes that could be purchased.

Several research studies document this extension benefit. One study of 98 consumer brands in 11 markets found that successful brand extensions spent less on advertising than did comparable new-name entries.[10] A comprehensive study by Indiana University's Dan Smith found similar results, indicating that the average advertising/sales ratio for brand extensions was 10 percent, as compared to 19 percent for new brands. His study identified some underlying factors moderating this extension advantage. The difference in advertising efficiency between brand extensions and new brands was shown to increase:

- As fit with other products affiliated with the parent brand increased
- As the new product's relative price compared to competitor's increased
- As distribution intensity increased

On the other hand, the difference in advertising efficiency between brand extensions and new brands was shown to decrease:

- When the new product was comprised primarily of search attributes (i.e., when product quality could be judged through visual inspection)
- As the new product became established in the market
- As consumers' knowledge of the new product category increased[11]

Reduce Costs of Introductory and Follow-Up Marketing Programs

Because of these "push" and "pull" considerations in distribution and promotion, it has been estimated that a firm can save 40 percent to 80 percent on the estimated $30 to $50 million it can cost to launch a new supermarket product nationally in the United States. Moreover, other efficiencies can result after the launch. As one such example, when a brand becomes associated with multiple products, advertising can become more cost effective for the family brand as a whole. For example, in 1988, Jaguar introduced its first substantially improved automobile model in sixteen years, adopting new technology to improve reliability although still retaining the classic Jaguar look. The resulting marketing program, which included a lavish ad campaign, increased demand for *all* new Jaguars. Even older Jaguars found their resale market value enhanced.[12]

Avoid Cost of Developing a New Brand

As chapter 4 indicated, developing new brand elements is an art and science. To conduct the necessary consumer research and employ skilled personnel to design high quality brand names, logos, symbols, packages, characters, and slogans can be quite expensive, and there is no assurance of success. As the number of available—and appealing—brand names keeps shrinking, legal conflicts are more likely to result. Despite the fact that they had conducted a trademark search, Cosmair's L'Oreal division was successfully sued for $2.1 million when a court decided that the name they had chosen to introduce a new green and purple hair dye, Zazu, infringed on the name of a line of shampoos sold by a Hinsdale, IL hairstyling salon called ZaZu Designs.[13]

Allow for Packaging and Labeling Efficiencies

Similar or virtually identical packages and labels for extensions can result in lower production costs and, if coordinated properly, more prominence in the retail store by creating a "billboard" effect. For example, Stouffers offers a variety of frozen entrees with identical orange packaging that increases their visibility when stocked together in the freezer. A similar billboard effect is evident with other supermarket brands such as with Coca-Cola soft drinks and Campbell soup.

Permit Consumer Variety-Seeking

By offering consumers a portfolio of brand variants within a product category, consumers who need a change because of boredom, satiation, or whatever can switch to a different product type if they so desire one without having to leave the brand family. Even without such underlying motivations, by offering a complement of line extensions, customers may be encouraged to use the brand to a greater extent or in new ways than otherwise may have been the case. Moreover, to even effectively compete in some categories, it may be necessary to have multiple items that together form a cohesive product line.

As an example of the benefits of expansive market coverage, consider the low-priced family brand, Suave, sold by Helene-Curtis. Suave includes a variety of personal care products such as shampoo, baby products, skin cream, and so on. Given the amount of brand switching and the large number of brands kept in inventory by consumers with personal care products in general and shampoos in particular, the ability of Suave to offer a full product line is a competitive advantage. By continually line extending, Suave keeps up with any new market trend or shift in consumer demand.[14] Adopting a "follower" strategy, whenever a new type of product becomes successful, Helene-Curtis introduces a similar version under the Suave name designed to match it. Suave's advertising slogan has been, "With All Suave Products, Great Performance Doesn't Have to Cost a Fortune." Suave's well-defined brand image and branding strategy has resulted in high degrees of consumer loyalty and market share for the brand.

PROVIDE FEEDBACK BENEFITS TO THE PARENT BRAND

Besides facilitating acceptance of new products, there are a number of ways that brand extensions can also provide positive feedback to the parent brand, as follows.

Clarify Brand Meaning

Extensions can help to clarify the meaning of a brand to consumers and define the kinds of markets in which it competes. Thus, through brand extensions, brands such as Hunts means "tomato," Clairol means "hair coloring," Gerber means "baby care," Nabisco means "baked cookies and crackers," and Chun King means "Chinese food" with consumers. Figure 12–4 shows how other brands that have introduced multiple brand extensions may have broadened their meaning with consumers.

A fascinating example of attempting to broaden product meaning is Xerox.[15] Realizing that electronic copies of documents were increasingly replacing traditional paper copies (where the brand had originally made its name), Xerox expanded its product line from office copiers to include other products such as digital printers, scanners, and word processing software. Xerox embarked on an ambitious advertising and marketing campaign to change its image with consumers to better reflect its new capabilities. A new logo was designed for all Xerox advertising, marketing materials, and products. The new logo consisted of a stylized red "X" with squares missing from its upper right arm. The new logo was intended to convey a digital appearance and symbolize the company's commitment to technology. An accompanying ad campaign adopted the slogan, "The Document Company" (see Figure 12–5).

Marketing Myopia   Such broader meaning often is necessary so that firms avoid "marketing myopia" and do not mistakenly draw narrow boundaries around their brand, missing market opportunities or making themselves vulnerable to well-planned competitive strategies. Thus, as Harvard's Ted Levitt pointed out in a pioneering article, railroads are not just in the "railroad" business but also the "transportation" business.[16] In other words, railroads do not necessarily compete with other railroads so much as with other forms of transportation. Thinking more broadly about product meaning can easily result in different marketing programs and new product opportunities.

FIGURE 12-4 Expanding Brand Meaning Through Extensions

Brand	Original Product	Extension Products	New Brand Meaning
Weight Watchers	Fitness centers	Low calorie foods	Weight loss and maintenance
Sunkist	Oranges	Vitamins, juices	Good health
Crayola	Crayons	Markers, paints, pens, pencils, clay	Colorful crafts for kids
Aunt Jemima	Pancake mixes	Syrups, frozen waffles	Breakfast foods

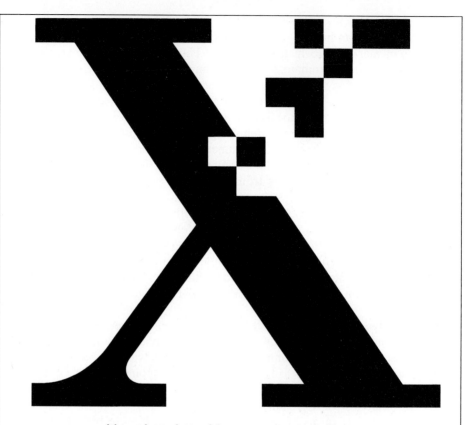

It's not just a letter. It's a way to get work done.

The letter is X. The company is Xerox. And the story is all about change.

Change is something we're comfortable with at Xerox. It's what we've been doing since the day we created the first copier, and changed forever the way people work with documents.

Indeed, we've built our business by following the document wherever it takes us. Today, few things in business change as fast as the document. It begins on a computer screen. It moves around the world on interactive, electronic networks. It exists in multimedia environments. It can be scanned, stored, retrieved, revised, distributed, printed and published where, when and how you want it.

In short, the document is constantly moving from digital form to paper, and back again. Which is why now, more than ever, our mission as The Document Company is clear: to put together the innovative document services you need—the sys-

tems, solutions, products and people—to make your business more productive.

It is also why this new "digitized" X is more than a letter to us. It is a symbol of change and vitality in the newly emerging digital world. It represents everything we do to help you get your work done, and make your life at work a little more satisfying and rewarding.

We'll be using this new symbol in many different ways, so keep your eyes open for it.

For us, it signals the next step in a long Xerox tradition of taking the first step into the future. And in a world that won't stop changing, that's still the most productive step anyone can take.

THE
DOCUMENT
COMPANY
XEROX
Worldwide Sponsor

THE DOCUMENT COMPANY
XEROX

FIGURE 12–5 Sample Xerox Ad

For example, Steelcase's slogan, "A Smarter Way to Work," reflects the fact that it defines its business as more than manufacturing desks, chairs, file cabinets, and credenzas but as "helping to enhance office productivity." As one ad states:

> At the risk of sounding esoteric, we sell knowledge. Ideas. Advice. Because creating effective workspaces is a much bigger issue than fitting another person in this corner. Or buying just another office system. It's completely rethinking your office space from top to bottom. . . . furniture can help make your people and your company more productive, more efficient and more profitable, no matter what business you're in. . . . the simple truth is: Space is a tool (albeit, an often overlooked tool) as valuable and powerful as any technological breakthrough. And nobody knows more about how furniture can make your space more dynamic than Steelcase and its dealers.

For some brands, creating broader meaning is critical and may be the only way to expand sales. The growers cooperative, Ocean Spray Cranberries, Inc., once found itself in such a position. During the 1960s and 1970s, it had been essentially a single-purpose, single-usage product: Consumption of cranberries was almost entirely confined to the serving of cranberry sauce as a side dish with Thanksgiving and Christmas holiday dinners. After a pesticide scare one Thanksgiving drastically cut sales and almost put its growers out of business, the cooperative embarked on a program to diversify and create a year-round market by producing cranberry-based juice drinks and other products. After introducing Ocean Spray Cranberry Juice Cocktail and cranberry-flavored drinks like Cranapple and Crangrape, they eventually even introduced a line of Ocean Spray Refreshers juices with *no* cranberry link at all. This ambitious brand extension program over a twenty-year period, supported by ads exhorting consumers to "Crave the Wave," has broadened the meaning of Ocean Spray to connote "good tasting fruit juice drinks that are good for you."[17]

In some cases, it is advantageous to establish a portfolio of related products that completely satisfy consumer needs in a certain area. For example, the $3 billion oral care market is characterized by a number of mega brands (e.g., Colgate and Crest) that compete in multiple segments with multiple product offerings (see sample Oral B promotion in Figure 12–6). Although these different brands were limited to a few specific products at one time, they have broadened their meaning through brand extensions to represent "complete oral care." Similarly, many specific-purpose cleaning products have broadened their meaning to become seen as more multi-purpose (e.g., Lysol and Comet).

Enhance the Parent Brand Image

According to the customer-based brand equity model, one desirable outcome from a successful brand extension is that it may enhance the parent brand image by strengthening an existing brand association, improving the favorability of an existing brand association, and/or adding a new brand association.

One common way that a brand extension affects the parent brand image is by establishing its core brand associations. *Core brand associations* are those attribute and benefits that come to characterize all the products in the brand line and, as a result, with which consumers often have the strongest associations. For example, Nike has expanded from running shoes to other athletic shoes, athletic clothing, and ath-

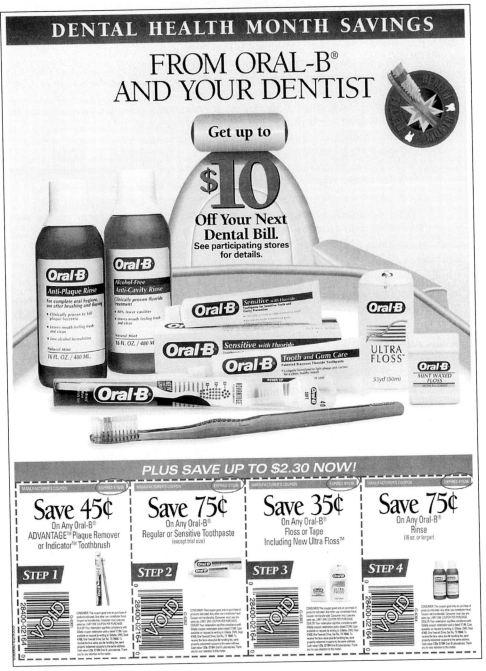

FIGURE 12-6 Sample Oral B Promotion

letic equipment, strengthening its associations to "peak performance" and "sports" in the process.

Another type of association that may be improved by successful brand extensions is consumer perceptions of the credibility of the company behind the extension. For example, Keller and Aaker showed that a successful corporate brand extension led to improved perceptions of the expertise, trustworthiness, and likability for the company.[18]

Bring New Customers into the Brand Franchise and Increase Market Coverage

Line extensions can benefit the parent brand by expanding market coverage, such as by offering a product benefit that heretofore may have prevented consumers from trying the brand. For example, when Tylenol introduced a capsule form of its acetaminophen pain reliever, it was able to attract consumers who had difficulty swallowing tablets and therefore might have otherwise avoided the brand.

By creating "news" and bringing attention to the parent brand, its sales may also increase. For example, although the market share of regular powdered Tide—which once was at 27 percent—had slipped to 21 percent in the early 1980s, the introduction of Liquid Tide and Multi-Action Tide (a combined detergent, whitener, and fabric softener) resulted in market share increases of 2 percent to 4 percent for the flagship Tide parent brand by 1986.

Revitalize the Brand

Sometimes brand extensions can be a means to renew interest and liking for the brand. For example, Miller Brewing's 1996 introduction of a new brand extension—Miller Beer—as its new flagship premium beer brand was intended in part to revitalize the Miller brand franchise (see Branding Brief 10–1). The original flagship premium beer brand, Miller High Life, had in effect become a "fighter" brand over the years by virtue of steep price discounts. One of Miller Brewing's previous brand extensions, Miller Genuine Draft, had helped to change the image of the Miller brand by providing a contrast to the problematic perception of "lightness" about the brand held by many consumers.

Permit Subsequent Extensions

One benefit of a successful extension is that it may also serve as the basis for subsequent extensions. For example, Levi-Strauss' successful extension, Levi's Dockers (100 percent cotton pants) led to the subsequent introduction of Dockers Authentics, a slightly more upscale pants line, and the introduction of Dockers into other clothing categories. Similarly, Goodyear's successful introduction of their Aquatred tires subbrand led to the introduction of Eagle Aquatred for performance vehicles with either wider wheels (e.g., the Ford Mustang) or a luxury image (e.g., the Cadillac Seville).

Disadvantages of Brand Extensions

Despite these potential advantages, there a number of potential disadvantages to brand extensions (see Figure 12–7).

Can confuse or frustrate consumers
Can encounter retailer resistance
Can fail and hurt parent brand image
Can succeed but cannibalize sales of parent brand
Can succeed but diminish identification with any one category
Can succeed but hurt the image of parent brand
Can dilute brand meaning
Can forgo the chance to develop a new brand

FIGURE 12-7 Disadvantages of Brand Extension

CAN CONFUSE OR FRUSTRATE CONSUMERS

The different varieties of line extensions may confuse and perhaps even frustrate consumers as to which version of the product is the "right one" for them. As a result, they may reject new extensions for "tried and true" favorites or all-purpose versions that claim to supersede more specialized product versions. Moreover, because of the large number of new products and brands continually being introduced, many retailers physically just do not have enough shelf or display space to stock them all. Consequently, some consumers may be disappointed when they are unable to find an advertised brand extension if a retailer is unable or unwilling to stock it.

CAN ENCOUNTER RETAILER RESISTANCE

On average, the number of consumer packaged-goods SKUs (stock-keeping units) grew 16 percent each year from 1985 to 1992, while at the same time retail shelf space expanded by only 1.5 percent each year. Many brands now come in a multitude of different forms. For example, Procter & Gamble has introduced a dozen different varieties of Pampers. Campbell's has introduced a number of different lines of soup—including Manhandler, Home Cookin', Chunky, Homestyle, Healthy Request, Creamy Natural, Soup Du Jour, and Cookbook Classics—and offers more than 100 flavors in all.

As a result, it has become virtually impossible for a grocery store or supermarket to offer *all* the different varieties available across *all* the different brands in any one product category. Moreover, retailers often feel that many line extensions are merely "me-too" products that duplicate existing brands in a product category and should not be stocked anyway even if there were space. Attacking brand proliferation, a year-long Food Marketing Institute (FMI) study showed that retailers could reduce their stock-keeping units by 5 percent to 25 percent in certain product categories without hurting sales or consumer perceptions of the variety offered by their store.[19] The FMI "product variety" study recommended that retailers systematically identify duplicated and slow-moving items and eliminate them to maximize profitability.

CAN FAIL AND HURT PARENT BRAND IMAGE

The worst possible scenario with an extension is that not only does it fail, but it harms the parent brand image somehow in the process. Unfortunately, these negative feedback effects can sometimes happen.

Consider General Motor's experience with the Cadillac Cimarron.[20] This model, introduced in the early 1980s, was a "relative" of models in other GM lines such as the Pontiac 2000 and Chevrolet Cavalier. The target market was less affluent buyers seeking a small luxury car who wanted, but could not really afford, a full-size Cadillac. Not only was the Cadillac Cimarron unsuccessful at generating new sales with this market segment, but existing Cadillac owners hated it. They felt it was inconsistent with the large size and prestige image they had expected from Cadillac. As a result, Cadillac sales dropped significantly in the mid-1980s. Looking back, one GM executive offered the following insights:

> The decision was made purely on the basis of short-sighted profit and financial analysis, with no accounting for its effect on long-run customer loyalty or, if you will, equity. A typical financial analysis would argue that the Cimarron will rarely steal sales from Cadillac's larger cars, so any sale would be one that we wouldn't have gotten otherwise. The people who were most concerned with such long-range issues raised serious objections but the bean counters said, "Oh no, we'll get this many dollars for every model sold." There was no thinking about brand equity. We paid for the Cimarron down the road. Everyone now realizes that using the model to extend the name was a horrible mistake.

Even if an extension initially succeeds, by linking the brand to multiple products, the firm increases the risk that an unexpected problem or even tragedy with one product in the brand family can tarnish the image of some or all of the remaining products. For example, starting in 1986, the Audi 5000 car suffered from a tidal wave of negative publicity and word-of-mouth as it was alleged to have a "sudden acceleration" problem that resulted in an alarming number of sometimes fatal accidents. Even though there was little concrete evidence to support the claims—resulting in Audi, in a public relations disaster, attributing the problem to the clumsy way that Americans drove the car—Audi's U.S. sales declined from 74,000 in 1985 to 21,000 in 1989. As might be expected, the damage was most severe for sales of the Audi 5000 but the adverse publicity also "spilled over" to affect the 4000 model, and to a lesser extent, the Quattro model. The Quattro might have been relatively more insulated from negative repercussions because it was more distanced from the 5000 by virtue of its more distinct branding and advertising strategy.[21]

Understanding when unsuccessful brand extensions may damage the parent brand is important, and we develop a conceptual model and describe some important findings below to address the topic. On a more positive note, however, it should be recognized that one reason why an unsuccessful brand extension may not necessarily damage the parent brand is for the very reason that the extension may have been unsuccessful in the first place—hardly anyone may have even heard of it! Thus, the "silver lining" in the case when a brand extension fails as a result of an inability to secure adequate distribution or a failure to achieve sufficient brand awareness is that the parent brand is more likely to survive relatively unscathed. Product failures, where the extension is found to be inadequate in some way on the basis of performance, however, are more likely to negatively impact parent brand perceptions than these "market" failures.

CAN SUCCEED BUT CANNIBALIZE SALES OF PARENT BRAND

Even if sales of a brand extension are high and meet targets, it is possible that this revenue may have merely resulted from consumers switching to the extension from existing product offerings of the parent brand, in effect "cannibalizing" the parent brand by decreasing its sales. Line extensions are often designed to establish points of parity with current offerings competing in the parent brand category, as well as to create additional points of difference in other areas (e.g., low fat food versions). These types of line extensions may be particularly likely to result in cannibalization. Oftentimes, however, such intra-brand shifts in sales may not necessarily be so undesirable, as they can be thought of as a form of "preemptive cannibalization." In other words, consumers might have switched to a competing brand instead of the line extension if it had not been introduced into the category.

For example, Diet Coke's point of parity of "good taste" and point of difference of "low calories" undoubtedly resulted in some of its sales coming from regular Coke drinkers. In fact, although U.S. sales of Coca-Cola's cola products remained flat from 1980 to 1986 at 1.3 million cases, sales in 1980 came from Coke alone whereas sales in 1986 also received significant contributions from Diet Coke, Cherry Coke, and decaffeinated forms of Coke. Without the introduction of those extensions, however, some of Coke's sales might have just gone to competing Pepsi products or other soft drinks or beverages instead.

CAN SUCCEED BUT DIMINISH IDENTIFICATION WITH ANY ONE CATEGORY

One risk with linking multiple products to a single brand is that the brand may not be as strongly identified with any one product. Thus, brand extensions may obscure the identification of the brand with its original categories, reducing brand awareness.[22] For example, when Cadbury became linked in the United Kingdom to mainstream food products such as Smash instant potatoes, marketers of the brand may have run the risk of weakening its association to fine chocolates. Pepperidge Farm is another brand that has been accused by marketing critics of having been extended so much (e.g., into soups) that the brand has lost its original meaning as "delicious, high-quality cookies."

This potential drawback has been popularized by the vociferous business consultants, Al Reis and Jack Trout, who in 1981 introduced the notion of the "line extension trap." They provide a number of examples of brands that, at the time, they believe "overextended." One such example was Scott Paper, which Ries and Trout believe became overextended when its name was expanded to encompass ScotTowels paper towels, ScotTissue bath tissue, Scotties facial tissues, Scotkins, and Baby Scot diapers.[23] Interestingly, in early 1995, Scott decided to attempt to more effectively unify its product line by renaming ScotTowels as Scott Clean and ScotTissue as Scott 1000, adding a "breezy" blue logo on both packages. In perhaps a risky move, Scott also decided to phase out local brand names in 80 foreign countries where Scott garnered almost half its sales, including Andrex, their top-selling British bath tissue.[24] Scott's hope was that the advantages of brand consolidation and global branding would offset the disadvantages of losing local brand equity.

Some notable—and fascinating—counterexamples to these dilution effects exist, however, in terms of firms who have branded a heterogeneous set of products and still achieved a reasonable level of perceived quality in the minds of consumers in each. As chapter 11 notes, many Japanese firms have adopted a corporate branding strategy with a very broad product portfolio. For example, Yamaha has developed a strong reputation selling an extremely diverse brand line that includes motorcycles, guitars, and pianos! Mitsubishi uses its name to brand a bank, cars, and aircraft. Canon has successfully marketed cameras, photocopiers, and office equipment. The large Japanese consumer products firm Kao sells everything from laundry detergent to computer floppy disks. In a similar vein, the founder of Virgin Records, Richard Branson, has recently embarked on an ambitious, and perhaps risky, brand extension program (see Branding Brief 12–3). In all these cases, it seems the brand has been able to secure a dominant association to quality in the minds of consumers without strong product identification that might otherwise limit it.

CAN SUCCEED BUT HURT THE IMAGE OF PARENT BRAND

If the brand extension has attribute or benefit associations that are seen as inconsistent or perhaps even conflicting with the corresponding associations for the parent brand, consumers may change their perceptions of the parent brand as a result. For example, Farquhar notes that when Domino's Pizza entered into a licensing agreement to sell fruit-flavored bubble gum, it ran the risk of creating a "chewiness" association that could negatively impact their flagship pizza products!

As another example, chapter 4 described Miller Brewing's difficulty in creating a "hearty" association to its flagship Miller High Life beer brand in part because of the clear bottle—as compared to Budweiser's dark bottle—and other factors such as its advertising heritage as the "champagne of bottled beer." It has often been argued that the early success of the Miller Lite light beer extension—market share soared from 9.5 percent in 1978 to 19 percent in 1986—only exacerbated the tendency of consumers to think of Miller High Life as "watery" tasting and not a full-bodied beer. These unfavorable perceptions were thought to have helped to contribute to the sales decline of Miller High Life (e.g., whose market share slid from 21 percent to 12 percent during that same eight-year period).

CAN DILUTE BRAND MEANING

The potential drawbacks from a lack of identification with any one category and a weakened image may be especially evident with high quality or prestige brands. For example, in its prime, the Gucci brand symbolized luxury, status, elegance, and qual-

---

BRANDING BRIEF 12-3

Are There Any Boundaries to the Virgin Brand Name?[a]

Perhaps the most extensive brand extension program in recent years has been undertaken by Richard Branson with his Virgin brand. Born in 1951, Branson started a teen magazine at age 16, a record retailing chain at age 19, and a record label at age 21. In 1984, he even launched an airline, Virgin Atlantic Airways. When Branson sold his label to Thorn-EMI in 1992 for $900 million, he personally pocketed $515 million on the deal and made millions more when he sold majority control of his Virgin record retailing chain and his Virgin computer games business.

After licensing the use of the Virgin name to European startup airlines who were flying the London/Athens and London/Dublin routes, Branson decided to expand the range of products carrying the Virgin brand. He has since licensed the Virgin name for use on personal computers and has set up joint ventures to market Virgin vodka and Virgin cola. The Virgin cola is manufactured in a 50-50 joint venture with partner Cott Corp. from Canada who supplies private label colas in the U.S. market. Priced 25 percent to 33 percent below Coke and Pepsi and advertised as "The Unreal," Virgin cola captured between 10 percent to 15 percent of the market within months after being introduced in Britain. Other product introductions with the Virgin name have included financial services, radio stations, bridal services, and movie theaters.

Some critics question the strategy of such broad brand expansion, believing that Virgin consumer products will do little more than generate publicity for Virgin airlines. They also caution of overexposure, even with the young, hip audience the Virgin brand has attracted. For example, Clive Chajet, chairman of the well-known New York marketing agency, Lippincott & Margulies, remarked: "I would imagine the risk is that the Virgin brand name can come to mean everything to everybody, which in turn means it becomes nothing to nobody."

Although some critics draw a comparison to the trials and tribulations of Swatch, the popular Swiss watchmaker, who unsuccessfully tried to apply its name to sell clothing, bags, and other items, Virgin officials prefer the comparison to Japanese firms such as Yamaha and Mitsubushi who have achieved wideranging success. Ever expanding, Branson subsequently announced his plans to introduce the cola into Hong Kong, Japan, China, and elsewhere, as well as also launching Virgin Water—in bubbly and non-bubbly form—and a new fizzy lime beverage in Asian markets after first being introduced in Britain. He also set his sights on the huge American market.

---

[a]Peter Fuhrman, "Brand-Name Branson," *Forbes* (January 2, 1995), pp. 41–42; Tara Parker Pope, "Can the Virgin Name Sell Cola, Computers, Vodka, and More?," *Wall Street Journal* (October 14, 1994), p. B-3; Miriam Jordan, "Virgin's Air Chief to Offer 'Unreal' Cola in Hong Kong, Japan, China by Dec. 31," *Wall Street Journal* (February 23, 1988), p. 36.

ity. By the 1980s, however, the label had become tarnished from sloppy manufacturing, countless knockoffs, and even a family feud among the managing Gucci brothers. The product line consisted of 22,000 items, distributed extensively across all types of department stores. Not only were there too many items, some items did not even fit the Gucci image, for example, a cheap canvas pocketbook with the double-G logo that was easily copied and sold on a counterfeit basis "on the street" for $35. Sales only recovered when Gucci refocused the brand, paring the product line to 7000 high-end items and selling them through its own company-owned outlets. Backed by an ad campaign stressing enduring value, Gucci's hot U.S. seller in 1994 was a $995 calfskin knapsack—triple the price of the quintessential 1980s Gucci bag—with the Gucci name discreetly etched on metal grommets near the drawstrings.

CAN FORGO THE CHANCE TO DEVELOP A NEW BRAND

One easily overlooked disadvantage to brand extensions is that by introducing a new product as a brand extension, the firm forgoes the chance to create a new brand with its own unique image and equity. For example, consider the advantages to Disney for having introduced Touchstone films (which attracted an audience interested in movies with more adult themes and situations than Disney's traditional family-oriented releases), to Levi's for having introduced Dockers pants (which attracted a customer segment interested in casual pants), and to General Motors for having introduced Saturn (which attracted consumers weary of "the same old cars sold the same old way"). Each of these brands created its own associations and images and tapped into markets completely different from those that currently existed for other brands sold by the company. Thus, introducing a new product as a brand extension can have significant and potentially hidden costs in terms of lost opportunities of creating a new brand franchise.

Understanding How Consumers Evaluate Brand Extensions

What determines whether a brand extension is able to capitalize on these potential advantages and avoid, or at least minimize, these potential disadvantages? Figure 12–8 displays some examples of successful and unsuccessful brand extensions. The difficulty in introducing a brand extension can be recognized by noting how many even leading marketing companies have failed, despite their best intentions, in launching a brand extension. To illustrate, Branding Brief 12–4 describes Seven-Up Co.'s struggles with the introduction of its 7Up Gold soft drink extension.

In this section, we examine how consumers evaluate brand extensions. We develop some simple conceptual notions to help a marketing manager better forecast and improve the potential odds for success of a brand extension.[25]

MANAGERIAL ASSUMPTIONS

In analyzing potential consumer response to a brand extension, it useful to start with a "baseline case" where it is assumed that consumers are evaluating the brand extension based *only* on what they already know about the parent brand and the extension cate-

"SUCCESSFUL" CATEGORY EXTENSIONS	"UNSUCCESSFUL" CATEGORY EXTENSIONS
Ivory shampoo & conditioner	Campbell's tomato sauce
Vaseline Intensive Care skin lotion	LifeSavers chewing gum
Hershey chocolate milk	Dunkin' Donut cereal
Jell-O Pudding Pops	Harley Davidson wine coolers
Visa traveler's cheques	Hidden Valley Ranch frozen entrees
Sunkist orange soda	Bic perfumes
Colgate toothbrushes	Xerox computers
Mars ice cream bars	Kleenex diapers
Arm & Hammer toothpaste	Clorox laundry detergent
Bic disposable lighters	Levi's Tailored Classics suits
Aunt Jemima pancake syrup	Nautilus athletic shoes
Honda lawnmowers	Domino's fruit-flavored bubble gum

FIGURE 12-8 Examples of Category Extensions

gory and before any advertising, promotion, or detailed product information would be made available. This baseline case provides the "cleanest" test of the extension concept itself and provides managers with guidance as to whether to proceed with an extension concept and, if so, what type of marketing program might be necessary.

In evaluating a brand extension under these baseline conditions, consumers can be expected to use their existing brand knowledge, as well as what they know about the extension category, to try to infer what the extension product might be like. In order for these inferences to result in favorable consumer evaluations of an extension, four basic assumptions must generally hold true:

1. *Consumers have some awareness of and positive associations about the parent brand in memory.* That is, unless there exists some type of potentially beneficial consumer knowledge about the parent brand, it is difficult to expect consumers to form favorable expectations of an extension.

2. *At least some of these positive associations will be evoked by the brand extension.* As will be discussed below, a number of different factors will determine which parent brand associations are evoked when consumers evaluate an extension. In general, consumers are likely to infer associations similar in strength, favorability, and uniqueness to the parent brand when the brand extension is seen as being similar or close in "fit" to the parent brand.

3. *Negative associations are not transferred from the parent brand.* Ideally, any negative associations that do exist for the parent brand would be "left behind" and not play a prominent role in the evaluation of the extension.

4. *Negative associations are not created by the brand extension.* Finally, it must be the case that any attributes or benefits that are viewed positively, or at least neutrally, by consumers with respect to the parent brand are not seen as a negative in the extension context. Consumers must also not infer any new attribute or benefit associations that did not characterize the parent brand but that they see as a potential drawback to the extension.

BRANDING BRIEF 12-4

7Up Fails to Strike Gold in the Cola Market[a]

Seven-Up has struggled for years to properly position its flagship lemon-lime beverage and compete with the powerful Coke and Pepsi cola brands. To grow sales of the brand, it embarked on a brand extension program, introducing Cherry 7Up in 1987. Buoyed by its success—the product gained 1.7 percent market share in its first year—Seven-Up Co. decided to launch another new brand extension, 7Up Gold, in 1988. 7Up Gold was an amber-colored, spicy, caffeinated drink flavored with cinnamon, ginger, and lemon-lime, tasting something like a cross between ginger ale and Dr. Pepper. More robust, masculine, and darker than regular 7Up, the new product was intended to fill in the "missing link" in the company's product offerings.

In many ways, Seven-Up executed a traditional introductory marketing program to launch the product. It first tested the flavor to ensure its consumer likability. It strategically selected a brand name that combined the established 7Up name—for reassurance—with the "Gold" modifier to connote high quality (but which was intended to still be ambiguous enough to reflect its unusual taste). They backed the brand with a $10 million introductory advertising campaign. Initial network television ads used the theme song "Wild Thing," as performed by the Troggs, and showed images of boisterous partygoers and drag-racing soda cans raising clouds of spray. The ads contained the tag line "The Wild Side of 7Up."

What went wrong? In the first place, the company chose to introduce the product quickly without any test marketing to understand consumer reaction to the marketing program as a whole. Unfortunately, as one Seven-Up executive stated,

> The product was misunderstood by the consumer. People had a clear view of what 7Up products should be—clear and crisp, and clean and no caffeine. 7Up Gold is darker and it does have caffeine so it doesn't fit the 7Up image.

Prophetically, the product failed to attract the lucrative teen market or an equally powerful group of consumers—mothers of young children.

Although sales initially looked promising, they quickly began to drop precipitously. Even more worrisome to Seven-Up management, sales of Cherry 7Up also started to slip, as 7Up Gold began to drain away advertising and marketing resources. With market share hovering at only one-tenth of one percent—well below its 1 percent target—Seven-Up was forced to discontinue the product.

---

[a]Douglas C. McGill, "7Up Gold: The Failure of a Can't Lose Plan," *New York Times* (February 11, 1989); Jennifer Lawrence, "Seven-Up Puts New Fizz in Ads," *Advertising Age* (October 17, 1988), p. 34; Marj Charlier, "Seven-Up, Despite Market Glut, Plans to Launch New Soft Drink," *Wall Street Journal* (February 23, 1988), p. 36.

The more that these four assumptions hold true, the more likely it is that consumers will form favorable attitudes toward an extension. We next examine some factors that influence the validity of these assumptions as well as consider in more detail how a brand extension, in turn, impacts brand equity.

BRAND EXTENSIONS AND BRAND EQUITY

The ultimate success of an extension will depend on its ability to both achieve some of its own brand equity in the new category as well as contribute to the equity of the parent brand. We examine each consideration in turn.

Creating Extension Equity

In terms of creating equity for the brand extension itself, as with the parent brand, the extension must also have a sufficiently high level of awareness and some strong, favorable, and unique associations. Brand awareness will depend primarily on the marketing program and resources devoted to "spreading the word" about the extension. As chapter 11 described, it will also obviously depend on the type of branding strategy adopted—the more prominently an existing brand that has already achieved a certain level of awareness and image is used to brand an extension, the easier it should be to create awareness of and an image for the extension in memory.

Initially creating a positive image for an extension will depend primarily on three consumer-related factors:

1. How *salient* parent brand associations are in the minds of consumers in the extension context, that is, what information comes to mind about the parent brand when consumers think of the proposed extension and the strength of those associations.

2. How *favorable* any inferred associations are in the extension context, that is, whether this information is seen as suggestive of the type of product or service that the brand extension would be and whether these associations would be viewed as good or bad in the extension context.

3. How *unique* any inferred associations are in the extension category, or how these perceptions compare to those of competitors.

As with any brand, successful brand extensions must achieve desired points of parity and points of difference. Without powerful points of difference, the brand risks becoming an undistinguished "me-too" entry, vulnerable to well-positioned competitors.[26] Tauber refers to "competitive leverage" as the set of advantages that a brand conveys to an extended product in the new category—"when consumers, by simply knowing the brand, can think of important ways that they perceive that the new brand extension would be better than competing brands in the category."[27]

At the same time, it is also necessary to establish any required points of parity. The more dissimilar the extension product is to the parent brand, the more likely it is that points of parity will become a positioning priority. For example, when Johnson & Johnson test-marketed a brand of aspirin for babies, despite the fact that the Johnson & Johnson name is virtually synonymous with baby products, the product failed. As it turned out, parents were just as concerned with getting fevers down quickly as they were with the safety and gentleness of an aspirin—Johnson & Johnson's key point of difference and core benefit association with their existing baby products. Thus, the lack of a necessary point of parity association doomed the product.

Contributing to Parent Brand Equity

To contribute to parent brand equity, an extension must strengthen or add favorable and unique associations to the parent brand as well as not diminish the strength, favorability, or uniqueness of any already existing associations for the parent brand.

The effects of an extension on consumer brand knowledge will depend on three factors:

1. How *compelling* the evidence is concerning the corresponding attribute or benefit association in the extension context, that is, how unambiguous or easily interpretable the information is concerning product performance or imagery for that association.

2. How *relevant* or diagnostic the extension evidence is concerning the attribute or benefit for the parent brand, or, how much evidence on product performance or imagery in one category is seen as predictive of product performance or imagery for the brand in other categories.

3. How *strongly* existing attribute or benefit associations are held in consumer memory for the parent brand, that is, how potentially easy an association might be to change.

According to these factors, feedback effects that change brand knowledge are most likely when consumers view information about the extension as equally revealing about the parent brand and when they only hold a weak association about the parent brand with respect to that information. The nature of the feedback effects will depend on the nature of the actual information: An unfavorable extension evaluation can lead to negative feedback effects, whereas a favorable extension evaluation can lead to positive feedback effects. Note that negative feedback effects are not just restricted to product-related performance associations. As noted above, if a brand has a favorable "prestige" image association, then a "vertical" extension such as offering a new version of the product at a lower price may be viewed disapprovingly or even resented by the existing consumer franchise.

Selected Extension Research Findings

Although these two basic models provide some general insight into the effects of brand extensions on brand equity, more specific guidance is necessary. Fortunately, brand extension research has received much research attention from academics in recent years. Some of the important research conclusions that have emerged are summarized in Figure 12–9 and described in detail below.

1. *Successful brand extensions occur when the parent brand is seen as having favorable associations and there is a perception of fit between the parent brand and the extension product.* To better understand the process by which consumers evaluate a brand extension, many academic researchers have adopted a "categorization" perspective. Categorization research has its roots in psychological research, which shows that people do not evaluate each new stimulus to which they are exposed deliberately and individually, but often in terms of whether it can be classified as a member of a previously defined category, as illustrated by the following example.

1. Successful brand extensions occur when the parent brand is seen as having favorable associations and there is a perception of fit between the parent brand and the extension product.

2. There are many bases of fit: product-related attributes and benefits, as well as non-product-related attributes and benefits related to common usage situations or user types.

3. Depending on consumer knowledge of the categories, perceptions of fit may be based on technical or manufacturing commonalties or more surface considerations such as necessary or situational complementarity.

4. High quality brands stretch farther than average quality brands, although both types of brands have boundaries.

5. A brand that is seen as prototypical of a product category can be difficult to extend outside the category.

6. Concrete attribute associations tend to be more difficult to extend than abstract benefit associations.

7. Consumers may transfer associations that are positive in the original product class but become negative in the extension context.

8. Consumers may infer negative associations about an extension, perhaps even based on other inferred positive associations.

9. It can be difficult to extend into a product class that is seen as easy-to-make.

10. A successful extension can not only contribute to the parent brand image but also enable a brand to be extended even farther.

11. An unsuccessful extension hurts the parent brand only when there is a strong basis of fit between the two.

12. An unsuccessful extension does not prevent a firm from "backtracking" and introducing a more similar extension.

13. Vertical extensions can be difficult and often require sub-branding strategies.

14. The most effective advertising strategy for an extension is one that emphasizes information about the extension (rather than reminders about the parent brand).

FIGURE 12-9 Research Findings Concerning Brand Extensions

Assume that you went to a party and found yourself in a conversation with an athletic-looking person who was casually dressed in sportswear and seemed to only want to talk about sports—what he or she read in the paper, saw on television, and was involved with as a participant. You might have a mental category of a "sports fanatic" as someone who looked like a "jock" and only read the sports section of the newspaper, watched sports on television, and talked sports with friends and family. As a result of this knowledge, you might quickly categorize that person as a "sports fanatic," and your evaluation of that person would probably depend on how you felt about the category of sports fanatics in general. As opposed to this "categorical processing," assume that you went up to another person at the party. This extremely pale person was dressed in a very fashionable "punk" manner yet, at the same time, also seemed to only want to talk about sports. Because of his or her appearance, this other person might not fit so neatly into your category of "sports fanatic," so that you would have to form your evaluation in a more detailed fashion, that is, by "piecemeal processing" where you would have to construct an attitude based on all the different considerations involved.

Applying categorization notions in a marketing context, it could be argued that consumers use their categorical knowledge of brands and products to simplify, structure, and interpret their marketing environments.[28] For example, it has been argued that consumers see brands as categories that over time have come to be associated with a number of specific attributes based on the attributes associated with the different products that represent individual members of the brand category. For example, Ivory might be associated with "soap," "mildness," and "quality" as a result of its soap, shampoo and conditioner, dishwashing liquid, and laundry detergent products.[29]

According to a categorization perspective, if a brand were to introduce an extension that was seen as closely related or similar to the brand category, then consumers could easily transfer their existing attitude about the parent brand to the extension. On the other hand, if consumers were not as sure about the similarity, then consumers might be expected to evaluate the extension in a more detailed, piecemeal fashion. In this case, the favorability of any specific associations that would be inferred about the extension would be the primary determinant of extension evaluations.[30]

Thus, a categorization view of how consumers evaluate brand extensions is that it is a two-step process. First, consumers determine whether in their minds there is a "match" between what they know about the parent brand and what they believe to be true about the brand extension. Second, if the match is good, then consumers might be expected to transfer their existing parent brand attitudes to the extension. Otherwise, consumers might be more likely to evaluate the brand in a more piecemeal fashion. With this latter type of processing, consumer evaluations would depend on the strength, favorability, and uniqueness of salient brand associations in the extension context. Consistent with these notions, Aaker and Keller collected consumer reactions to twenty proposed extensions from six well-known brands and found that both a perception of fit between the original and extension product categories and a perception of high quality for the parent brand led to more favorable extension evaluations.[31]

Thus, in general, brand extensions are more likely to be favorably evaluated by consumers if they see some bases of "fit" or similarity between the proposed extension and parent brand.[32] A lack of fit may doom a potentially successful brand extension. For example, Bausch & Lomb built a strong reputation in eyewear and eye care by successfully introducing contact lenses, cleaning products, and related items. After buying an oral-care business, it introduced a line of no alcohol mouthwashes that, although primarily branded as "Clear Choice," were clearly identified as coming from Bausch and Lomb. Consumers evidently found the combination of eye care and mouthwashes as too incongruent and, after disappointing earnings that resulted in a one-time $75 million charge to its oral-care division, Bausch and Lomb decided to sell the division.

2. *There are many bases of fit: product-related attributes and benefits, as well as non-product-related attributes and benefits related to common usage situations or user types.* Any association held in memory by consumers about the parent brand may serve as a potential basis of fit. As chapter 3 noted, many different types of associa-

tions may become linked to the brand. Therefore, brand extensions may be seen as similar or close in "fit" to the parent brand in many ways. Most academic researchers typically assume that similarity judgments are a function of salient shared associations between the parent brand and the extension product category. Specifically, the more common and fewer distinctive associations that exist, the greater the perception of overall similarity. These similarity judgments could be based on product-related attributes or benefits, as well as non-product-related attributes or benefits.[33] Consumers may also use attributes for a prototypical brand or a particular "exemplar" as the standard of reference for the extension category and form their perceptions of fit with the parent brand on that basis.

To demonstrate how fit does not have to be based on product-related associations alone, Park, Milberg, and Lawson have distinguished between fit based on "product-feature-similarity"—as described above—and on "brand-concept-consistency."[34] They define *brand concepts* as the brand-unique image associations that arise from a particular combination of attributes, benefits, and the marketing efforts used to translate these attributes into higher order meanings (e.g., high status). *Brand-concept-consistency* is defined in terms of how well the brand concept accommodates the extension product. The important point these researchers make is that different types of brand concepts from the same original product category may meet with varying degrees of acceptance extending into the same category, even when product-feature-similarity is high.

Park and his co-authors further distinguish between *function-oriented brands,* whose dominant associations relate to product performance (e.g., Timex watches), and *prestige-oriented brands,* whose dominant associations relate to consumers' expression of self-concepts or images (e.g., Rolex watches). Experimentally, they showed that the Rolex brand could more easily extend into categories such as grandfather clocks, bracelets, and rings than the Timex brand; but, on the other hand, Timex could more easily extend into categories such as stopwatches, batteries, and calculators than Rolex. In the former case, there was high brand-concept-consistency for Rolex that overcame a lack of product feature similarity; in the latter case there was enough product feature similarity to favor a function-oriented brand such as Timex.

Broniarczyk and Alba provide another compelling demonstration of the importance of recognizing salient brand associations. They show that a brand that may not even be as favorably evaluated as a competing brand in its category—depending on the particular parent brand associations involved—may be more successfully extended into certain categories. For example, although Close-Up toothpaste was not as well-liked by their sample as Crest toothpaste, a proposed Close-Up breath mint extension was evaluated more favorably than one from Crest. Alternatively, a proposed Crest toothbrush extension was evaluated more favorably than one from Close-Up.[35]

Broniarczyk and Alba also showed that a perceived lack of fit between the parent brand's product category and the proposed extension category could be overcome if key parent brand associations were salient and relevant in the extension category. For example, Froot Loops cereal—which has strong brand associations to "sweet," "flavor," and "kids"—was better able to extend to dissimilar product categories such as lollipops and popsicles than to even similar product categories such as waffles and hot cereal because of the relevance of its brand associations in the dissimilar extension category. The reverse was true for Cheerios cereal, however, which had a "healthy grain" association that was only relevant in similar extension product categories.

These research studies and others demonstrate the importance of taking a broader perspective of categorization and fit. For example, Bridges refers to "category coherence." Coherent categories are those whose members "hang together" and "make sense." According to Bridges, to understand the rationale for a grouping of products in a brand line, a consumer needs "explanatory links" that tie the products together and summarize their relationship. For example, the physically dissimilar toy, bath care, and car seat products in the Fisher-Price product line can be united by the link "products for children."[36]

3. *Depending on consumer product knowledge, perceptions of fit may be based on technical or manufacturing commonalties or more surface considerations such as necessary or situational complementarity.* Fit perceptions can also be based on other considerations than attributes or benefits. Taking a demand side and supply side perspective of consumer perceptions, the Aaker and Keller study showed that perceived fit between the parent brand and extension product could be related to the economic notions of perceived substitutability and complementarity in product use (from a demand side perspective), as well as the perceived ability of the firm to have the skills and assets necessary to make the extension product (from a supply side perspective). Thus, Honda's perceived expertise in making motors for lawn mowers, cars, and other equipment may help perceptions of fit for any other machinery with small motors that Honda may want to introduce. Similarly, expertise with small disposable products offers numerous opportunities for Bic. On the other hand, there are other extension examples with little manufacturing compatibility but usage complementarity instead, such as Colgate's extension from toothpaste to toothbrushes or Duracell's extension from batteries to flashlights.

These perceptions of fit, however, may depend on how much consumers know about the product categories involved. As demonstrated by Muthukrishnan and Weitz, knowledgeable, "expert" consumers are more likely to use technical or manufacturing commonalties to judge fit, considering similarity in terms of technology, design and fabrication, and the materials and components used in the manufacturing process. Less knowledgeable "novice" consumers, on the other hand, are more likely to use superficial, perceptual considerations such as common package, shape, color, size, or usage.[37] Specifically, they experimentally showed that less knowledgeable consumers were more likely to see a basis of fit between tennis racquets and tennis shoes than tennis racquets and golf clubs, despite the fact that the latter actually share more manufacturing commonalties. The effects for more knowledgeable consumers, on the other hand, were reversed, as they recognized the technical synergies that would be involved in manufacturing tennis racquets and golf clubs.

Relatedly, Broniarczyk and Alba also showed that perceptions of fit on the basis of brand-specific associations were contingent on consumers having the necessary knowledge about the parent brand. Without such knowledge, consumers tended again to rely on more superficial considerations, such as their level of awareness for the brand or overall regard for the parent brand, in forming extension evaluations.[38]

4. *High quality brands stretch farther than average quality brands, although both types of brands have boundaries.* High quality brands are often seen as more credible,

expert, and trustworthy at what they do. As a result, even though consumers may still believe a relatively distant extension does not really fit with the brand, they may be more willing to give a high quality brand the "benefit of the doubt." When a brand is seen as more average in quality, however, such favorable source attributions may be less forthcoming, and consumers may be more likely to question the ability or motives of the company involved.[39] Thus, one important benefit of building a strong brand is that it can be extended more easily into more diverse categories.[40] For example, Procter & Gamble has capitalized on a strong association with "mildness" and "quality" for its Ivory brand to successfully extend into a diverse set of product categories, including the extremely competitive hair care category where it was able to gain an impressive 8 percent market share with Ivory brand shampoo and 10 percent market share with Ivory brand conditioner in the first year.

Regardless, all brands have boundaries, as a number of observers have persuasively argued by pointing out potentially ridiculous, and even comical, hypothetical brand extension possibilities. For example, as Tauber states, few consumers would want Jell-O shoelaces or Tide frozen entrees!

5. *A brand that is seen as prototypical of a product category can be difficult to extend outside the category.* As a caveat to the previous conclusion, if a brand is seen as representing or exemplifying a category too much, it may be difficult for consumers to think of the brand in any other way. Farquhar and Herr forcefully make this point, citing the difficulties of such market leaders as Planters nuts, Country Time lemonade, and Tabasco hot sauce to successfully expand outside their categories.[41] Perhaps the most extreme example of this caveat is with brands like Thermos and Kleenex, which lost their trademark distinctiveness and became generic terms for the categories.

To illustrate the difficulty that a prototypical brand may have in extending, consider Clorox, a well-known brand whose name is virtually synonymous with bleach. In 1988, Clorox took on consumer goods giants Procter & Gamble and Unilever by introducing the first bleach with detergent. After pouring $225 million to develop and distribute its detergent products over the next three years, Clorox was only able to achieve a 3 percent market share. Despite being beaten to market, P&G's subsequently introduced Tide With Bleach was able to achieve a 17 percent market share. Reluctantly, Clorox chose to exit the market. Although a number of factors may have driven that decision, Clorox's failure can certainly be attributed in part to the fact that consumers could only think of Clorox in a very limited sense as a bleach product. Clorox has successfully extended its brand into household cleaning products (e.g., toilet bowl cleaners) where the bleach ingredient is seen as more relevant.

Also note that Clorox's extension failure may have also been a result of the fact that with a combined "laundry detergent with bleach" product, laundry detergent is seen by consumers as the primary ingredient and bleach is seen as the secondary ingredient. As a result, a laundry detergent extension (such as Tide With Bleach) might be expected to have an advantage over a bleach extension (such as Clorox) when entering the combined laundry detergent with bleach category.[42] A similar type of interpretation might explain why Aunt Jemima was successful in introducing a pancake syrup extension from its well-liked pancake mix product but why Log Cabin was less successful in introducing a pancake mix extension from its well-regarded pancake syrup product—pancake mix is seen as a more dominant ingredient than pancake syrup in breakfast pancakes.

Numerous other examples exist of category leaders who have failed in introducing brand extensions. Bayer, a brand synonymous with aspirin, ran into a stumbling block introducing the Bayer Select line of specialized painkillers.[43] Chiquita was unsuccessful in its attempt to move beyond its strong "banana" association with its failed frozen juice bar extension.[44] Country Time could not overcome its "lemonade" association to introduce an apple cider.

Farquhar, Herr, and their colleagues have developed an interesting approach to generating brand extension possibilities for prototypical brands and market leaders.[45] They define a master brand as an established brand so dominant in customer's minds that it "owns" a particular association—the mention of a product attribute or category, a usage situation, or a customer benefit instantly brings a master brand to mind. Other examples of master brands according to these researchers, in addition to those noted above, include Arm & Hammer baking soda, Band-Aid adhesive bandages, Bacardi rum, Alka-Seltzer antacid, Jell-O gelatin, Campbell's soup, Crayola crayons, Morton salt, Lionel toy trains, Philadelphia cream cheese, and Vaseline petroleum jelly.

Recognizing that the exceptionally strong associations of a master brand often make it difficult to extend it directly to other product categories, they propose strategies to extend master brands *indirectly* by leveraging alternative master brand associations that come from different parts of the brand hierarchies. Specifically, they describe the brand-leveraging compass to illustrate four principal directions for leveraging master brands.

1. *Sub-branding* introduces a new element into the brand hierarchy below the level of the master brand to refine or modify its meaning (e.g., DuPont Stainmaster carpet).

2. *Super-branding* adds new elements to an existing brand hierarchy above the level of the master brand, typically to suggest some product improvement (e.g., Eveready Energizer batteries).

3. *Brand-bundling* or "cross branding" fortifies a master brand through associations with other brands, including cooperative or co-branding (e.g., Citibank AAdvantage Visa card).

4. *Brand-bridging* uses the master brand to endorse a new brand as the company attempts to move to a more distant product category (e.g., T/Gel therapeutic shampoo was initially endorsed by Neutrogena).

These strategies, all of which have been discussed in prior chapters, are suggested as different means to shield the parent or master brand by creating some distance to the extension and finding other ways to build brand equity for the extension by incorporating additional brands or brand elements.

6. *Concrete attribute associations tend to be more difficult to extend than abstract benefit associations.* The limits to extension boundaries potentially faced by market leaders may be exacerbated by the fact that, in many cases, brands that are market leaders have strong concrete product attribute associations. In some cases, these attribute associations may even be reinforced by their names (e.g., Liquid Paper, Cheez Whiz, and Shredded Wheat).[46] In general, concrete attribute associations may not transfer as broadly to extension categories than more abstract attribute associations. For example, the Aaker and Keller study showed that consumers dismissed a hypothetical Heineken popcorn extension as potentially tasting bad or like beer; a hypo-

thetical Vidal Sassoon perfume extension as having an undesirably strong shampoo scent; and a hypothetical Crest chewing gum extension as tasting like toothpaste or, more generally, tasting unappealing. In each case, consumers inferred a concrete attribute association with an extension that was technically feasible even though common sense might have suggested that a manufacturer logically would not be expected to introduce a product with such an attribute.

More abstract associations, on the other hand, may be seen as more relevant across a wide set of categories because of their intangible nature. For example, the Aaker and Keller study also showed that the Vuarnet brand had a remarkable ability to be exported to a disparate set of product categories—sportswear, watches, wallets, and even skis. In these cases, complementarity may have led to an inference that the extension would have the "stylish" attribute associated with the Vuarnet name, and such an association was valued in the different extension contexts.

Several caveats should be noted, however, concerning the relative extendability of concrete and abstract associations. First, concrete attributes can be transferred to some product categories. For example, if the parent brand has a concrete attribute association that is highly valued in the extension category because it creates a distinctive taste, ingredient, or component, an extension on that basis can often be successful.[47] According to Farquhar and Herr, examples of such extensions might include Philadelphia Cream Cheese salad dressing, Tylenol sinus medication, Haagen-Dazs cream liqueur, Oreo cookies and cream ice cream, and Arm & Hammer carpet deodorizer.[48]

Second, abstract associations may not always transfer easily. This second caveat emerged from a study conducted by Bridges.[49] She examined the relative transferability of product-related brand information when it was either represented as an abstract brand association or when it was represented as a concrete brand association. For example, one such comparison contrasted the relative transferability of a watch characterized by dominant concrete attribute associations such as "water-resistant quartz movements, a time-keeping mechanism encased in shockproof steel covers, and shatterproof crystal" to a watch characterized by dominant abstract attribute associations such as "durable." Although she expected the abstract brand representation to fare better, she found that, for several reasons, the two types of brand images extended equally well into a dissimilar product category (e.g., handbags). Perhaps the most important reason for this was that consumers did not believe the abstract benefit would have the same meaning in the extension category (i.e., durability does not necessarily "transfer" because durability for a watch is not the same as durability for a handbag).

7. *Consumers may transfer associations that are positive in the original product class but become negative in the extension context.* Because of different consumer motivations or product usage in the extension category, a brand association may not be as highly valued as it was in the original product context. For example, when Campbell's test marketed a tomato sauce with the Campbell's name, it flopped. Apparently, Campbell's strong associations to soup signaled to consumers that the new product would be watery. To give the product more credibility, Campbell's changed the name to the Italian-sounding "Prego," and the product has gone on to be a big success.

8. *Consumers may infer negative associations about an extension, perhaps even based on other inferred positive associations.* Even if consumers transfer positive associations from the parent brand to the extension, they may still infer other negative associations. For example, the Bridges study also showed that even if consumers

thought that a proposed handbag extension from a hypothetical maker of durable watches also would be durable, they often assumed that it would not be fashionable, too, helping to contribute to low extension evaluations.[50]

9. *It can be difficult to extend into a product class that is seen as easy-to-make.* Some seemingly appropriate extensions may be dismissed because of the nature of the extension product involved. If the product is seen as comparatively easy-to-make—such that brand differences are hard to come by—then a high-quality brand may be seen as incongruous or, alternatively, consumers may feel that the brand extension will attempt to command an unreasonable price premium and be too expensive.

For example, Aaker and Keller showed that hypothetical extensions such as Heineken popcorn, Vidal Sassoon perfume, Crest shaving cream, and Haagen-Dazs cottage cheese received relatively poor marks from experimental subjects in part because *all* brands in the extension category were seen as being about the same in quality, suggesting that the proposed brand extension was unlikely to be superior to existing products. The failure of designers such as Bill Blass and Gloria Vanderbilt to introduce certain products such as chocolates and perfume under their names may be in part a result of these perceptions of incongruity, lack of differentiation, and unwarranted price premiums.

When the extension category is seen as difficult to make, on the other hand, such that brands potentially vary a great deal in quality, there is a greater opportunity for a brand extension to differentiate itself, although consumers may also be less sure as to what exactly will be the quality level of the extension.[51]

10. *A successful extension not only can contribute to the parent brand image but may also enable a brand to be extended even farther.* As noted above, a successful brand extension can change the meaning and image of a brand. An extension can help the image of the parent brand by improving the strength, favorability, or uniqueness of its associations. For example, Keller and Aaker showed that when consumers did not already have strongly held attitudes, the successful introduction of a brand extension improved evaluations of a parent brand that was originally perceived only to be of average quality. Finally, the associations that become linked to the parent brand by virtue of the extension product category also may help clarify the basic core benefits for the brand. For example, one of Australia's leading cereal brands, Uncle Toby's, was able to broaden its meaning to be seen as a "healthy breakfast and snack food" by introducing meusli bars and other products.

If an extension changes the image and meaning of the brand, then subsequent brand extensions that otherwise may not have seemed appropriate to consumers may make more sense and be seen as a better fit. For example, Keller and Aaker showed that by taking "little steps," that is, by introducing a series of closely related but increasingly distant extensions, it may be possible for a brand to ultimately enter product categories that would have been much more difficult, or perhaps even impossible, to have entered directly.[52]

The Dunhill brand provides an excellent example of gradually extending a brand to transform its meaning.[53] For all practical purposes, Dunhill started as a cigarette brand that was first extended into smoking accessories (e.g., pipes, pouches, and lighters). After establishing itself there, the brand was then extended into other male accessories (e.g., belts, desktop items, cufflinks, and clothing). Most recently, the brand has been extended yet again into male fragrances and mainstream fashion items. As a result of all of this extension activity, the Dunhill brand now not only represents a leading cigarette brand but also "luxury products and accessories for both men and women."

Relatedly, Dacin and Smith have shown that if the perceived quality levels of different members of a brand portfolio are more uniform, then consumers tend to make higher, more confident evaluations of a proposed new extension.[54] They also showed that a firm that had demonstrated little variance in quality across a diverse set of product categories was better able to overcome perceptions of lack of extension fit. In other words, it is as if consumers in this case think, "whatever they do, they tend to do well."

11. *An unsuccessful extension hurts the parent brand only when there is a strong basis of fit between the two.* The general guideline emerging from academic research and industry experience is that an unsuccessful brand extension potentially can damage the parent brand only when there is a high degree of similarity or "fit" involved, such as in the case of a failed line extension in the same category. For example, Roeder John and Loken found that perceptions of quality for a parent brand in the health and beauty aids area decreased with the hypothetical introduction of a lower-quality extension in a similar product category (i.e., shampoo). Quality perceptions of the parent brand were unaffected, however, when the proposed extension was in a dissimilar product category (i.e., facial tissue).[55] Similarly, Keller and Aaker as well as Romeo found that unsuccessful extensions in dissimilar product categories did not affect evaluations of the parent brand.[56] When the brand extension is farther removed, it seems easier for consumers to "compartmentalize" the brand's products and disregard its performance in what is seen as an unrelated product category.

12. *An unsuccessful extension does not prevent a firm from "backtracking" and introducing a more similar extension.* The Keller and Aaker study also showed that unsuccessful extensions do not necessarily prevent a company from retrenching and later introducing a more similar extension. For example, in the early 1980s, Levi-Strauss attempted to introduce its Tailored Classics line of men's suits. Levi's Tailored Classics was targeted to independent-thinking "clothes horses," dubbed by research as the "Classic Individualist." Although the suit was not supposed to need tailoring, to allow for the better fit necessary for these demanding consumers, Levi's designed the suit slacks and coat to be sold as "separates." They chose to price these wool suits quite competitively and to distribute them through their existing department store accounts as opposed to specialty stores where the classic individualist traditionally shopped.

Despite a determined marketing effort, the product failed to achieve its desired sales goals. This failure can probably be attributed to a number of factors—problems with the chosen target market, distribution channels, product design, plus others—but perhaps the most fundamental problem was the lack of fit with the Levi's brand image and the image needed for the extension product and desired by the target market. Levi's had an informal, rugged, outdoor image that was inconsistent with the self-image of the classic individualist and the image they sought from their suits. Despite the ultimate withdrawal and failure of the product, Levi's—including some of the same marketing managers!—later were able to execute one of the most successful apparel launches ever—Levi's Dockers pants.

As Levi's experiences with brand extensions illustrate, failure does not doom a firm to never be able to introduce any extensions—certainly not for a brand with as much equity as Levi's. An unsuccessful extension does, however, create almost a "perceptual boundary" of sorts in that it reveals the limits to the brand in the minds of consumers. It does not preclude, however, a firm from later introducing an extension with a higher degree of fit, as was the case with Levi's.

13. *Vertical extensions can be difficult and often require sub-branding strategies.* For market reasons or competitive considerations, it may be desirable for the firm to introduce a lower-priced version of a product. As noted above, such a product could be introduced as its own brand and function essentially as a fighter brand. Alternatively, the existing brand could be stretched downward by vertically extending. The danger with such an extension strategy, however, is that the parent brand image could be cheapened or tarnished in some way.

As a result, most firms adopt sub-branding strategies as a means to distinguish their lower-priced entries. For example, Gillette introduced the Good News brand as a line of inexpensive personal care products such as disposable razors. United Airlines introduced Shuttle by United as an inexpensive short-haul carrier to compete with no-frills Southwest Airlines in the lucrative West Coast market. Courtyard by Marriott was a lower-priced version of the regular Marriott and upscale Marriott Marquis hotel chains. Such extension introductions clearly must be handled carefully—typically the parent brand plays much more of a secondary role. Branding Brief 12–5 describes how Waterford successfully introduced a new sub-brand to revive its brand sales.

An even more difficult vertical extension is an upward brand stretch.[57] In general, it is difficult to sufficiently change people's impressions of the brand to justify a significant upward extension. Consider Gallo, which stubbornly refused for years to put any other brand on the label of their better vintages besides their Gallo brand. Despite repeated ad campaigns that promised that some new varietal would "change the way you think about Gallo," as when they introduced White Grenache, many consumers continued to think of the brand as they did before—as a relatively inexpensive jug wine.[58]

This concern about the unwillingness of consumers to update their brand knowledge was what led Honda, Toyota, and Nissan to introduce their luxury car models as separate nameplates (Acura, Lexus, and Infiniti, respectively). As it turns out, product improvements to the upper ends of their brand lines since the introduction of these new car nameplates may have made it easier to bridge the gap with their brands into the luxury market. In fact, the top end of the Toyota product line, the Camry, was so close in quality to the Lexus that one of Lexus' main competitors, BMW, chose to introduce a hard-hitting campaign equating the two.

At the same time, it is possible to use certain brand modifiers to signal a noticeable, although presumably not dramatic, quality improvement—for example, Ultra Dry Pampers, Extra Strength Tylenol, or PowerPro Dustbuster Plus. As noted earlier, Farquhar, Herr, and their colleagues note that this means of indirect extensions, or "super-branding" may be less risky than direct extensions when moving a master brand up-market[59] They recommend veiling the master brand from the customer's view. The idea would be for the new super-brand to draw attention to itself and the merits of the product and later unveil the super-brand's link to the "hidden master brand" to provide familiar reassurance to consumers. They caution that a premature connection with the master brand can generate skepticism and indecision, citing as supporting evidence Coleman's success at introducing up-market camping equipment first as Peak 1 and then only later making the Coleman connection.

Shining up the Waterford Image[a]

When Waterford Wedgewood, the well-known Irish maker of Waterford crystal and Wedgewood china, went through a late 1980s sales slump, the company's fortunes were turned around as the result of its first brand introduction in 200 years. Marquis by Waterford, a new brand of crystal, was a calculated risk by the company to revitalize the brand.

Priced 20 percent less than traditional Waterford, company officials maintain that the key to the success of Marquis was keeping it sufficiently different from traditional Waterford while still allowing the new brand to benefit by association from the Waterford name. Therefore, Marquis had to be seen as "cheaper" but not "cheap." The company also gave Marquis a distinctively different design—one that was simpler and lighter-looking than traditional Waterford. The best-selling Marquis line, for instance, carries a distinctive gold trim. In its advertising, it positions Marquis for younger consumers, particularly younger brides. Meanwhile, the company freshened up the original Waterford products as well, introducing colored crystal, new limited-edition sculpted pieces and new designs, such as the Doors of Dublin, which reflected its Irish tradition.

Marquis became the sixth largest seller in the U.S. premium crystal segment. More importantly, Marquis did not detract from the flagship brand—sales of traditional Waterford were up 16 percent in the last year, and it is the top-selling premium brand.

---

[a]Judith Valente, "A New Brand Restores Sparkle to Waterford," *Wall Street Journal* (November 10, 1994), pp. B1, B4.

"Vertical" extensions can be especially tricky for prestige brands. In such cases, firms must often maintain a difficult balance between availability and scarcity such that people always aspire to be a customer and not feel excluded. By launching ambitious marketing campaigns with such offerings as "How to Buy a Diamond," and "Pearl Authority," the upscale retail chain Tiffany's has attempted to convince buyers of the quality of its products and the fact that they are attainable. With an average retail price of goods sold of around $250, Tiffany's has managed to maintain its lofty image while also drawing a wider array of customers.[60]

14. *The most effective advertising strategy for an extension is one that emphasizes information about the extension (rather than reminders about the parent brand).* A number of studies have shown that the information provided about brand extensions, by triggering selective retrieval from memory, may "frame" the consumer decision process and affect extension evaluations. In general, the most effective strategy appears to be one that recognizes the type of information that is already salient for the brand in the minds of consumers when they first consider the proposed extension and highlights additional information that would otherwise be overlooked or misinterpreted.

For example, the Aaker and Keller study found that cueing or reminding consumers about the quality of a parent brand did not improve evaluations for poorly rated extensions. Because the brands they studied were well known and well liked, such reminders may have been unnecessary. Elaborating briefly on specific extension attributes about which consumers were uncertain or concerned, however, did lead to more favorable evaluations. To illustrate, one of their poorly rated extension concepts was for McDonald's photo processing that in some cases conjured up undesirable "greasy photo" associations and that consumers felt was incongruent for McDonald's. If consumers were told that the extension was "from the providers of fast, inexpensive, and convenient service," then their extension evaluations were essentially unchanged. On the other hand, if consumers were told that the extension was "physically separated from the food service and used a well-established camera retailer to process the film," then ratings significantly improved. Even so, the extension concept still was not as well received as other, perhaps more logical, hypothetical McDonald's extensions such as McDonald's frozen french fries and McDonald's theme parks. This finding and those in other categories suggest that by clarifying the nature of an important attribute of the new product, the elaboration appeared to be effective in inhibiting negative inferences and in reducing the salience of consumer's concerns about the firm's credibility in the extension context.

Bridges found that providing information could improve perceptions of fit in two cases when consumers perceived low fit between the brand and the extension. First, when the parent brand and the extension shared physical attributes but the parent brand image was non-product-related and based on abstract user characteristics, consumers tended to overlook an obvious explanatory link between the parent brand and extension on the basis of shared product features (e.g., a tennis shoe with a high-fashion image attempting to extend to work boots was not evaluated favorably). Information that raised the salience of the physical relationship relative to distracting non-product-related associations—a "relational" communication strategy—improved extension evaluations (e.g., when subjects were told the work boots would have leather uppers similar to those used in the tennis shoes). Second, when the parent brand and the extension only shared non-product-associations and the parent brand image was product-related, consumers often made negative inferences on the basis of existing associations (e.g., a tennis shoe with an image for durability attempting to extend to swimsuits was seen as being unfashionable). In this case, providing information that established an explanatory link on an entirely new, "reassuring" association—an "elaborational" communication strategy—improved extension evaluations (e.g., when subjects were told the swimsuits would also be fashionable).[61]

Evaluating Brand Extension Opportunities

Academic research and industry experience have revealed a number of principles concerning the proper way to introduce brand extensions. Brand extension strategies must be carefully considered by systematically conducting the following five steps. Managerial judgment *and* consumer research should be employed to help make *each* of these decisions (see Figure 12–10).

1. Define actual and desired consumer knowledge about the brand.
2. Identify possible extension candidates.
3. Evaluate extension candidate potential.
4. Design marketing campaign to launch extension.
5. Evaluate extension success and effects on parent brand equity.

FIGURE 12-10 Steps in Successfully Introducing Brand Extensions

DEFINE ACTUAL AND DESIRED CONSUMER KNOWLEDGE ABOUT THE BRAND

Chapter 8 outlined qualitative and quantitative measures of consumer brand knowledge structures in detail. In particular, it was noted there that it is critical to fully understand the depth and breadth of awareness of the parent brand and the strength, favorability, and uniqueness of its associations. Moreover, before any extension decisions are contemplated, it is also important that the desired knowledge structures have been fully articulated. Specifically, what is to be the basis of positioning and core benefits satisfied by the brand? Profiling actual and desired knowledge structures helps to identify possible brand extensions as well as help to guide decisions concerning their likely success. It is important to understand where the brand would like to be taken over the long run in evaluating an extension. Because the introduction of an extension potentially changes brand meaning, consumer response to all subsequent marketing activity may be affected as a result.

IDENTIFY POSSIBLE EXTENSION CANDIDATES

Chapter 11 described a number of criteria related to the consumer, firm, and competition in choosing which products and markets a firm should enter. With respect to consumer factors, to identify potential brand extensions, marketers should consider parent brand associations—especially as they relate to brand positioning and core benefits—and product categories that might seem to fit with that brand image in the minds of consumers. Possible category extension candidates can be generated through managerial brainstorming sessions as well as consumer research. Although consumers are generally better able to react to an extension concept than suggest one, it still may be instructive to ask consumers what products the brand should consider offering if it were to introduce a new product.

One or more associations can often serve as the basis of fit. Figure 12–11 displays an analysis by Ed Tauber of possible extensions of the Vaseline Intensive Care brand by recognizing the range of associations held by consumers. As another example, Beecham marketed Lucozade in Britain for years as a glucose drink to combat dehydration and other maladies of sick children. By introducing new flavor formulas, packaging formats, and other changes, Beecham was able to capitalize on the association of the brand as a "fluid replenisher" to transform its meaning to "a healthy sports drink for people of all ages." Reinforced by ads featuring the famous British Olympic decathlete Daley Thompson, sales and profits for the brand increased

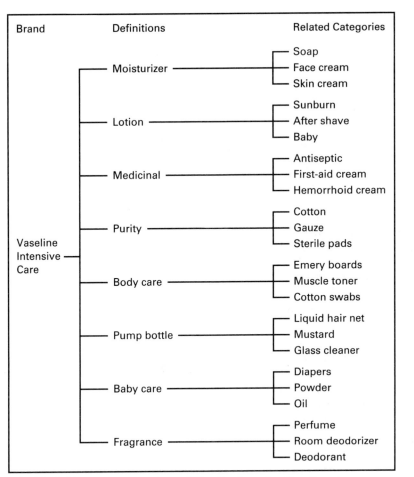

FIGURE 12-11 Possible Extensions of Vaseline Intensive Care Brand

dramatically. Thus, by recognizing that Lucozade did not have to be just a pharmaceutical product but could be repositioned through brand extensions and other marketing activity as a healthy and nutritious drink, Beecham was able to credibly transform the brand.[62]

EVALUATE EXTENSION CANDIDATE POTENTIAL

In forecasting the success of a proposed brand extension, it is necessary to assess—through judgment and research—the likelihood that the extension would realize the advantages and avoid the disadvantages of brand extensions as summarized in Figures 12–3 and 12–5. As with any new product, analysis of consumer, corporate, and competitive factors can be useful in doing so, as follows.

Consumer Factors

Evaluating the potential success of a proposed brand extension requires an assessment of its ability to achieve its own brand equity, as well as the likelihood of it possibly affecting the existing brand equity for the parent brand. First, marketers must forecast the strength, favorability, and uniqueness of *all* associations to the brand extension. In other words, what will be the salience, favorability, or uniqueness of parent brand associations in the proposed extension context? Similarly, what will be the strength, favorability, and uniqueness of any other inferred associations?

To narrow down the list of possible extensions, consumer research is often needed (see chapter 9 for a review). Consumers may be probed directly (e.g., "How well does the proposed extension 'fit' with the parent brand?" or "Would you expect such a new product from the parent brand?"). Consumers may even be asked what products they believe are currently attached to the brand—if a majority of consumers believe a proposed extension product is already being sold under the brand, then there would seem to be little risk involved in introducing it, at least in terms of initial consumer reaction. To better understand consumers' perceptions of a proposed extension, consumer research is often employed using open-ended associations (e.g., "What comes into your mind when you think of the brand extension?" or "What are your first impressions in hearing that the parent brand is introducing the extension?"), as well as ratings scales based on reactions to concept statements.

Possible Pitfalls   There are several common pitfalls to avoid in evaluating brand extension potential. One major mistake in evaluating extension opportunities is failing to take *all* of consumers' brand knowledge structures into account. Often marketers mistakenly focus on one or perhaps a few brand associations as a potential basis of fit and ignore other possibly more important brand associations in the process. For example, the French company Société Bic, by emphasizing inexpensive disposable products, was able to create markets for nonrefillable ballpoint pens in the late 1950s; disposable cigarette lighters in the early 1970s; and disposable razors in the early 1980s. They unsuccessfully tried the same strategy in marketing Bic perfumes in the United States and Europe in 1989. The perfumes—two for women ("Nuit" and "Jour") and two for men ("Bic for Men" and "Bic Sport for Men")—were packaged in quarter-ounce glass spray bottles that looked like fat cigarette lighters and sold for $5 each. The products were displayed on racks in plastic packages at checkout counters throughout Bic's extensive distribution channels, which included 100,000 or so drugstores, supermarkets, and other mass merchandisers. At the time, a Bic spokeswoman described the new products as extensions of the Bic heritage—"high quality at affordable prices, convenient to purchase, and convenient to use."[63] The brand extension was launched with a $20 million advertising and promotion campaign containing images of stylish people enjoying themselves with the perfume and using the tagline, "Paris in your pocket." Nevertheless, Bic was unable to overcome its lack of cache and negative image associations and, by failing to achieve a critical point of parity, the extension was a failure.

Another major mistake in evaluating brand extensions is overlooking how literal consumers can be in evaluating brand extensions. Although consumers ultimately care about benefits, they often notice and evaluate attributes—especially concrete ones—in reacting to an extension. Brand managers, though, tend to focus on perceived benefits in predicting consumer reactions and, as a result, may overlook some potentially damaging attribute associations. For example, as noted above, Aaker and

Keller's study showed how consumers thought that a hypothetical Heineken popcorn extension would taste like beer, a hypothetical Crest chewing gum extension would taste like toothpaste, and a proposed Vidal Sassoon perfume would smell like the shampoo.

Corporate and Competitive Factors

Marketers must not only take a consumer perspective in evaluating a proposed brand extension but also must take a broader corporate and competitive perspective. How effectively are the corporate assets leveraged in the extension setting? How relevant are existing marketing programs, perceived benefits, and target customers in the extension context? What are the competitive advantages to the extension as perceived by consumers and possible reactions initiated by competitors as a result?

Too many extension products and strongly entrenched competition can put a strain on company resources. For example, Church & Dwight in the 1980s decided to extend its Arm & Hammer baking soda brand and its familiar yellow box into a variety of new product categories—toothpaste, carpet deodorizer, air freshener, antiperspirant, and so on. Despite some early successes, the company had one of its worst years ever in 1994 as earnings fell 77 percent from the previous year. What happened? The market share of two of their more promising product introductions—toothpaste and laundry detergent—fell sharply when, after observing increased consumer acceptance of baking soda-based products, packaged goods giants such as Procter & Gamble, Unilever, and Colgate-Palmolive aggressively introduced their own baking soda versions of these products. Priced higher and with less advertising support, the market share of Arm & Hammer's products dropped. Church & Dwight management admitted that, "it was too much for a company of our size to introduce so many new products in one year . . ." and vowed to focus in the short-run on existing products.

Too many new products have also been thought to pose a problem at times for Pepsi.[64] In the early 1990s it embarked on an aggressive multi-brand strategy, expanding its brand offerings from 14 to 60 by introducing fruit juices (jointly with Ocean Spray), iced teas (jointly with Lipton), flavored waters, and sports drinks (All Sport). These brands met with mixed success, but their one major line extension introduced in 1993, Crystal Pepsi, was a decided flop. A number of factors are thought to have contributed to its failure—wrong taste, wrong name, wrong packaging, and wrong advertising. With hints of cinnamon, ginger, and pepper, Crystal Pepsi, despite its name, had a decidedly non-cola flavor. Perhaps the biggest worry for Pepsi during this episode was that its flagship cola brands lost market share to Coca-Cola, raising concerns that the flurry of new products had diverted Pepsi's attention from its core brands.

DESIGN MARKETING PROGRAMS TO LAUNCH EXTENSION

Too often extensions are used as a shortcut means of introducing a new product, and insufficient attention is paid to developing a branding and marketing strategy that will maximize the equity of the brand extension, as well as enhance the equity of the parent brand. As is the case with a new brand, building brand equity for a brand extension requires choosing brand elements, designing the optimal marketing program to launch the extension, and leveraging secondary associations.

Choosing Brand Elements

By definition, a brand extension retains one or more elements from an existing brand. It is also important that marketers realize that brand extensions do not necessarily have to only leverage a brand name but other brand elements, too. For example, companies such as Heinz and Campbell Soup have implemented package designs that attempt to both distinguish different line extensions or brand types but reveal their common origin at the same time.[65]

In some cases, packaging is such a critical component of equity for the brand that it is hard to imagine an extension without the same package design elements. Brands in such cases are in a real dilemma because if they choose to use the same type of packaging, they run the risk that the extension is not well distinguished. On the other hand, if they choose to use a different type of packaging, a key source of brand equity may be left behind. For example, Tanqueray gin has a distinctive green bottle with red trim that had been the centerpiece of its print ads during the 1980s. To distinguish its new Tanqueray vodka extension, it chose to use a silver bottle that, although stylish, failed to leverage its key packaging equities.

Kapferer describes the experiences of Kodak when it began marketing alkaline batteries under the Ultra Life brand name in 1985. Instead of using its familiar yellow and red colors for packaging as with other Kodak products, the new battery had its own look and identity with the Kodak name only appearing in small type. After disappointing sales, Kodak changed the packaging to give more emphasis to the Kodak name and return to the more familiar Kodak look, with an immediate increase in sales.[66]

Thus, a brand extension can retain or modify one or more brand elements from the parent brand as well as adopt its own brand elements. In creating new brand elements for an extension, the same guidelines should be followed with the development of any brand as were described in chapter 4 in terms of memorability, meaningfulness, protectability, adaptability, and transferability. New brand elements are often necessary to help to distinguish the brand extension from the parent brand to build its awareness and image. As chapter 11 noted, the relative prominence of existing parent brand elements and new extension brand elements will dictate the strength of transfer from the parent brand to the extension as well as the feedback from the extension to the parent brand.

Designing the Optimal Marketing Program

The marketing program for a brand extension must consider the same guidelines in building brand equity that were described in chapters 5 and 6. In terms of designing the supporting marketing program, product-related and non-product-related associations often must be created, consumer perceptions of value must guide pricing decisions, distribution strategies must blend push and pull considerations, and marketing communications should be integrated by mixing and matching communication options.

In terms of properly positioning a brand extension, the less similar the extension is to the parent brand, the more important typically it is to establish necessary and competitive points of parity. The points of difference for a category extension in many cases directly follow from the points of difference for the parent brand and are easily perceived by consumers. Thus, when Ivory soap was extended into shampoo and conditioners, its key "gentleness" point of difference presumably transferred easily. It would seem that the bigger challenge would have been to reach parity in the minds of consumers with category considerations related to glamour and how the shampoo made someone look and feel. Thus, with category extensions, points of parity are often critical. With line extensions, on the other hand, it is often the case that a new association has to be created that can serve as an additional point of difference and help to distinguish the extension from the parent brand, too.

For line extensions, to minimize possible cannibalization or confusion, it is important that consumers understand how the new product relates to existing products. For example, in Australia, General Motors sells its cars under the Holden name. For some time, GM marketed only one car—the Holden Gemini—in the small car market segment there. When it decided to introduce a second car, the Holden Astra, consumers thought the car was intended to replace Holden's existing Gemini model. Without explicit communication as to the relationship among the products, consumers began to think of the Gemini as an outdated model.[67]

Miles Laboratories Inc. ran into a similar problem with its Alka-Seltzer Plus cold medicine. At first, consumers perceived it as simply a more potent form of regular Alka-Seltzer, resulting in less than effervescent sales. Consequently, the company shrank the Alka-Seltzer part of the name on the cold medicine package and began running more distinctive ads. Whereas regular Alka-Seltzer ads would show office workers suffering from stress huddled around a water cooler, the new Alka-Seltzer Plus ads featured testimonials from residents of frigid Winter Harbor, Maine. The brand's fortunes turned around as a result.

Leveraging Secondary Brand Associations

In general, brand extensions will often leverage the same secondary associations as the parent brand, although there may be instances where competing in the extension category requires some additional fortification such that linking to other entities may be desirable. A brand extension differs in that, by definition, there is always some leveraging of another brand or company. The extent to which these other associations become linked to the extension, however, depends on the branding strategy that is adopted and how the extension is branded. As noted above, the more common are the brand elements and the more prominence they receive, the more likely it is that parent brand associations will transfer.

EVALUATE EXTENSION SUCCESS AND EFFECTS ON PARENT BRAND EQUITY

The fifth and final step in evaluating brand extension opportunities involves assessing the extent to which an extension is able to achieve its own equity as well as contribute to the equity of the parent brand. A number of decisions have to be made concerning the introduction of a brand extension. Thus, a number of factors will affect the success of an extension. Branding Brief 12–6 describes a perceptive analysis of line extensions by Quelch and Kenny. In other related research, Reddy, Holak, and Bhat studied the determinants of line extension success using data on 75 line extensions of 34 cigarette

---

BRANDING BRIEF 12-6

Guidelines for Profitable Line Extensions

In a perceptive and illuminating analysis, Quelch and Kenney persuasively argue that unchecked product-line expansion can weaken a brand's image, disturb trade relations, and disguise cost increases.[a] In describing the lure of line extensions, Quelch and Kenny began by noting seven factors that explain why so many companies have aggressively pursued a line extension strategy:

1. *Customer segmentation.* Line extensions are seen as a low-cost, low-risk way to meet the needs of target market segments. They can be increasingly refined due to sophisticated marketing research, advertising media, and direct marketing practices.

2. *Consumer desires.* More consumers than ever are switching brands and making in-store purchase decisions. A full brand line can offer "something for everyone" and attracts consumer attention.

3. *Pricing breadth.* Line extensions give marketers the opportunity to offer a broader range of price points in order to capture a wider audience.

4. *Excess capacity.* Many companies have added faster production lines without retiring older ones. These already existing manufacturing capabilities can often be easily modified to produce line extensions.

5. *Short-term gain.* Many managers believe line extensions offer immediate rewards with minimal risk. Similar to sales promotions, line extensions are seen as a dependable, "quick fix" to improve sales.

6. *Competitive intensity.* Many managers also believe that extensions can expand the retail shelf space for the category, or at least that amount devoted to the brand itself. Frequent line extensions are often used by major brands to raise the admission price to the category for newly branded or private-label competitors and to drain the limited resources of third- and fourth-place brands.

7. *Trade pressure.* The proliferation of different types of retail channels—often demanding their own special versions of the brand to suit their marketing needs or to reduce price-shopping by consumers—necessitates a more varied product line.

Quelch and Kenny continue by noting that, although it is easy to understand why line extensions have been so widely embraced against such a backdrop, managers are also discovering problems and risks from brand proliferation.

1. *Weaker line logic.* Because managers often extend a line without removing any existing items, the strategic role of each item becomes muddled. As a result, retailers may fail to stock the entire line or even appropriate items. A disorganized product line may result in consumers seeking out a simple, all-purpose product as a result.

2. *Lower brand loyalty.* Although line extensions can help a single brand satisfy a consumer's diverse needs, they can also motivate customers to seek variety and, hence, indirectly encourage brand switching. If line extensions result in cannibalization, a suboptimal shift in marketing support, or a blurring in image, the long-term health of the brand franchise will be weakened.

3. *Underexploited ideas.* Some important new products justify the creation of a new brand and potential long-term profits may suffer if such products are introduced as an extension.

4. *Stagnant category demand.* A review of several product categories—pet food, crackers and cookies, catsup, coffee, shampoo and conditioner, cake mix and frosting, and spaghetti sauce—reveals that line extensions rarely expand total category demand.

5. *Poorer trade relations.* An explosion of line extensions in virtually every product category has put a squeeze on available shelf space. Retailers have responded to this brand proliferation by rationing shelf space, stocking slow-moving items only when promoted by their manufacturers, and charging manufacturers slotting fees to obtain shelf space for new items and failure fees for items that fail to meet target sales within two or three months. As manufacturer's credibility has declined, retailers have allocated more shelf space to their own private label products. Competition among manufacturers for limited shelf space has escalated overall promotion expenditures and shifted margin to increasingly powerful retailers.

6. *More competitor opportunities.* By spreading marketing efforts across a range of line extensions, some of the most popular entries in the brand line may be vulnerable to well-positioned and supported competitors.

7. *Increased costs.* Although marketers can correctly anticipate many of the increased costs of extensions, other possible complications may be overlooked, such as fragmentation of the marketing effort and dilution of the brand image; increased production complexities resulting from shorter production runs and more frequent line changeovers; more errors in forecasting demand and increased logistics complexity; increased supplier costs; and distraction of the research and development group from new product development. As a result of these considerations, unit costs for multi-item lines can be 25 percent to 45 percent higher than the theoretical cost of producing only the most popular item in the line.

8. *Hidden costs.* Although these increased costs may make it difficult for a line extension to increase demand enough or command a high enough margin to achieve profitability, they remain "hidden" for several reasons. Traditional cost accounting systems allocate overheads to items in proportion to their sales, which can overburden the high sellers and undercharge the slow movers. Although price increases have been used by many to offset cost increases, this practice has become more difficult in the low inflationary environment that has characterized many countries in recent years. Finally, because line extensions are added one at a time, it is easy to overlook broader cost considerations that may affect or are affected by the entire brand line.

Quelch and Kenny conclude their analysis by offering eight directives to help marketing managers improve their product-line strategies:

1. *Improve cost accounting.* Study, in detail, the absolute and incremental costs associated with the production and distribution of each stock-keeping unit (SKU) from the beginning to the end of the value chain, accounting for timing of demand. Target underperforming SKUs and consider the incremental sales, costs, and savings of adding a new SKU.

2. *Allocate resources to winners.* To avoid undersupporting new, up-and-coming SKUs and oversupporting long-established SKUs whose appeal may be weaken-

ing, use an accurate activity-based cost-accounting system combined with an annual zero-based appraisal of each SKU to ensure a focused product line that optimizes the company's use of manufacturing capacity, advertising and promotion dollars, sales-force time, and available retail space.

3. *Research consumer behavior.* Make an effort to learn how consumers perceive and use each SKU, especially in terms of loyalty and switching patterns among SKUs. Identify core items that have a long-standing appeal to loyal heavy users and other items that reinforce and expand usage among existing customers. Consider a third set of SKUs to attract new customers or to persuade multibrand users to buy more from the same line more often.

4. *Apply the line logic test.* Ensure that everyone who may affect the success of the marketing program (e.g., salespeople) is able to state in one sentence the strategic role that a given SKU plays in the brand line. Similarly, ensure that the consumer is able to understand quickly which SKU fits his or her needs.

5. *Coordinate marketing across the line.* Adopt consistent and logical pricing and packaging to simplify understanding of the brand line by salespeople, trade partners, customers, and others.

6. *Work with channel partners.* To improve trade relations and new product acceptance, set up multifunctional teams to screen new product ideas and arrange in-store testing with leading trade customers in order to research, in advance, the sales and cost effects of adding new SKUs to the brand line.

7. *Expect product-line turnover.* Foster a climate in which product-line deletions are not only accepted but also encouraged.

8. *Manage deletions.* If items identified as unprofitable cannot be quickly and easily restored to profitability, develop a deletion plan that addresses customers' needs while managing costs.

---

[a] John A. Quelch and David Kenny, "Extend Profits, Not Product Lines," *Harvard Business Review* (September-October 1994), pp. 153–60. See also the commentary on this article and the issue of product line management in "The Logic of Line Extensions," *Harvard Business Review* (November-December 1994), pp. 53–62.

brands over a 20–year period.[68] The major findings from their study reinforce many of the above conclusions, indicating that:

1. Line extensions of strong brands are more successful than extensions of weak brands.

2. Line extensions of symbolic brands enjoy greater market success than those of less symbolic brands.

3. Line extensions that receive strong advertising and promotional support are more successful than those extensions that receive meager support.

4. Line extensions entering earlier into a product subcategory are more successful than extensions entering later, but only if they are extensions of strong brands.

5. Firm size and marketing competencies also play a part in an extension's success.

6. Earlier line extensions have helped in the market expansion of the parent brand.

7. Incremental sales generated by line extensions may more than compensate for the loss in sales due to cannibalization.

Review

This chapter examined the role of brand extensions in managing brand equity. Brand extensions are when a firm uses an established brand name to introduce a new product. Brand extensions can be distinguished as to whether the new product is being introduced in a product category currently served by the parent brand (i.e., line extension) or a completely different product category (i.e., category extension). Brand extensions can come in all forms. Brand extensions offer many potential benefits but also can pose many problems. This chapter outlined these pros and cons (see Figures 12–3 and 12–5) and offered some simple conceptual guidelines to maximize the probability of extension success.

The basic assumption with brand extensions is that consumers have some awareness of and positive associations about the parent brand in memory and at least some of these positive associations will be evoked by the brand extension. Moreover, negative associations are not transferred from the parent brand or created by the brand extension. The ability of the extension to establish its own equity will depend on the salience of parent brand associations in the minds of consumers in the extension context and the resulting favorability and uniqueness of any inferred associations. The ability of the extension to contribute to parent brand equity will depend on how compelling the evidence is concerning the corresponding attribute or benefit association in the extension context, how relevant or diagnostic the extension evidence is concerning the attribute or benefit for the parent brand, and how strong existing attribute or benefit associations are held in consumer memory for the parent brand.

A number of important research findings concerning brand extensions were summarized (see Figure 12–9) concerning factors affecting the acceptance of a brand extension as well as the nature of feedback to the parent brand. The chapter concluded by outlining a process to evaluate brand extension opportunities. It was argued that brand extension strategies need to be carefully considered by using managerial judgment and consumer research to systematically conduct the following steps: (1) define actual and desired consumer knowledge about the brand, (2) identify possible extension candidates, (3) evaluate extension candidate potential, (4) design marketing programs to launch extensions, and (5) evaluate extension success and effects on parent brand equity.

Discussion Questions

1. Pick a brand extension. Use the models presented in the chapter to evaluate its ability to achieve its own equity as well as contribute the equity of a parent brand. If you were the manager of that brand, what would you do differently?
2. Do you think a brand like Xerox will be able to transform its product meaning? What are the arguments for or against?

Notes

1. For more comprehensive treatments, see Glen Urban and John Hauser, *Design and Marketing of New Products.* Upper Saddle River, NJ: Prentice Hall, 1980.

2. Peter Farquhar, "Managing Brand Equity," *Marketing Research*, 1 (September 1989), pp. 24–33.

3. Robert M. McGrath, "The Vagaries of Brand Equity," ARF Fourth Annual Advertising and Promotion Workshop," February 12–13, 1992.

4. Byung-Do Kim and Mary W. Sullivan, "The Effect of Brand Experience on Extension Choice Probabilities: An Empirical Analysis," working paper, October 1995, University of Chicago, Graduate School of Business.

5. Henry J. Claycamp and Lucien E. Liddy, "Prediction of New Product Performance: An Analytical Approach," *Journal of Marketing Research* (November 1969), pp. 414–420.

6. Kevin Lane Keller and David A. Aaker, "The Effects of Sequential Introduction of Brand Extensions," *Journal of Marketing Research*, 29 (February 1992), pp. 35–50. John Milewicz and Paul Herbig, "Evaluating the Brand Extension Decision Using a Model of Reputation Building," *Journal of Product & Brand Management*, 3 (1) (1994), pp. 39–47.

7. See also Jonlee Andrews, "Rethinking the Effect of Perceived Fit on Customers' Evaluations of New Products," *Journey of the Academy of Marketing Science*, 23 (1) (1995), pp. 4–14.

8. David B. Montgomery, "New Product Distribution: An Analysis of Supermarket Buyer Decisions," *Journal of Marketing Research*, 12 (3) (1978), pp. 255–264.

9. David A. Aaker and Ziv Carmon, "The Effectiveness of Brand Name Strategies at Creating Brand Recall," working paper, University of California at Berkeley, July 1992.

10. Mary W. Sullivan, "Brand Extensions: When to Use Them," *Management Science*, 38 (6) (June 1992), pp. 793–806.

11. Daniel C. Smith, "Brand Extension and Advertising Efficiency: What Can and Cannot Be Expected," *Journal of Advertising Research* (November/December 1992), pp. 11–20. See also, Daniel C. Smith and C. Whan Park, "The Effects of Brand Extensions on Market Share and Advertising Efficiency," *Journal of Marketing Research*, 29 (August 1992), pp. 296–313.

12. Mary W. Sullivan, "Measuring Image Spillovers in Umbrella-branded Products," *Journal of Business,* 63 (3) (1990), pp. 309–329.

13. Ronald Alsop, "It's Slim Pickings in Product Name Game," *Wall Street Journal* (November 29, 1988), p. B1

14. Laurie Freeman, "Helene Curtis Relies on Finesse," *Advertising Age* (July 14, 1986), p. 2.

15. Kevin Goldman, "Xerox Touts Array of Products to Broaden Image Beyond Copiers," *Wall Street Journal* (August 4, 1994), p. B-12; Tim Smart, "Can Xerox Duplicate Its Glory Days?," *Business Week* (October 4, 1993), pp. 56–58; Subrata N. Chakravarty, "Back in Focus," *Forbes* (June 6, 1994), pp. 72–76.

16. Theodore Levitt, "Marketing Myopia," *Harvard Business Review* (July/August, 1960), pp. 45–56.

17. Harold Thorkilsen, "Manager's Journal: Lessons of the Great Cranberry Crisis," *Wall Street Journal* (December 21, 1987), p. 20.

18. Kevin Lane Keller and David A. Aaker, "The Effects of Sequential Introduction of Brand Extensions," *Journal of Marketing Research*, 29 (February 1992), pp. 35–50.

19. Ira Teinowitz and Jennifer Lawrence, "Brand Proliferation Attacked," *Advertising Age* (May 10, 1993), p. 1, 48. The product categories studied were spaghetti sauce, toilet tissue, pet food, salad dressing, cereal, and toothpaste.

20. B.G. Yovovich, "Hit and Run: Cadillac's Costly Mistake," *Adweek's Marketing Week* (August 8, 1988), p. 24.

21. Mary W. Sullivan, "Measuring Image Spillovers in Umbrella-branded Products," *Journal of Business,* 63 (3) (1990), vol. 63, no. 3, pp. 309–329.

22. Mareen Morrin, "The Effects of Brand Extensions on Consumer Knowledge Structures and Memory Retrieval Processes," working paper, July 1996, Boston University.

23. Al Ries and Jack Trout, *Positioning: The Battle for Your Mind*, New York: McGraw-Hill Book Company, 1985.

24. Joseph Weber, "Scott Rolls Out a Risky Strategy," *Business Week* (May 22, 1995), p. 48.

25. For a review of some of the early brand extension literature, see Elyette Roux and Frederic Lorange, "Brand Extension Research: A Typology," working paper DR 92033, CER-ESSEC (Centre d'Etudes et de Recherche de l'ESSEC), Cergy Pontoise Cedex, France, 1993.

26. Kalpesh Kaushik Desai, Wayne D. Hoyer, and Rajendra Srivastava, "Evaluation of Brand Extension Relative to the Extension Category Competition: The Role of Attribute Inheritance from Parent Brand and Extension Category," working paper, State University of New York at Buffalo, 1996.

27. Edward M. Tauber, "Brand Leverage: Strategy for Growth in a Cost-Control World," *Journal of Advertising Research* (August/September 1988), pp. 26–30.

28. Mita Sujan, "Nature and Structure of Product Categories," working paper, Pennsylvania State University. Joan Myers-Levy and Alice M. Tybout, "Schema Congruity as a Basis for Product Evaluation," *Journal of Consumer Research*, 16 (June 1989), 39–54.

29. Deborah Roedder John and Barbara Loken, "Diluting Brand Beliefs: When do Brand Extensions Have a Negative Impact?" *Journal of Marketing* (July 1993), pp. 71–84.

30. David Boush and Barbara Loken, "A Process Tracing Study of Brand Extension Evaluations," *Journal of Marketing Research*, 28 (February 1991), pp. 16–28. Cathy L. Hartman, Linda L. Price, and Calvin P. Duncan, "Consumer Evaluation of Franchise Extension Products: A Categorization Processing Perspective," *Advances in Consumer Research,* 17 (1990), pp. 120–26.

31. David A. Aaker and Kevin Lane Keller, "Consumer Evaluations of Brand Extensions," *Journal of Marketing*, 54 (January 1990), pp. 27–41.

32. David Boush, Shannon Shipp, Barbara Loken, Ezra Gencturk, Susan Crockett, Ellen Kennedy, Betty Minshall, Dennis Misurell, Linda Rochford, and Jon Strobel, "Affect Generalization to Similar and Dissimilar Line Extensions," *Psychology and Marketing,* 4 (Fall 1987), pp. 225–41.

33. Deborah MacInnis and Kent Nakamoto, "Cognitive Associations and Product Category Comparisons: The Role of Knowledge Structures and Context," working paper, University of Arizona, 1990.

34. C. Whan Park, Sandra Milberg, and Robert Lawson, "Evaluation of Brand Extensions: The Role of Product Level Similarity and Brand Concept Consistency," *Journal of Consumer Research,* 18 (September 1991), pp. 185–93.

35. Susan M. Broniarczyk and Joseph W. Alba, "The Importance of the Brand in Brand Extension," *Journal of Marketing Research*, 31 (May 1994), pp. 214–228. Incidentally, although a Crest toothpaste was not available at the time that the study was conducted, one was later in fact introduced as Crest Complete.

36. See also Bernd H. Schmitt and Laurette Dube, "Contextualized Representations of Brand Extensions: Are Feature Lists or Frames the Basic Components of Consumer Cognition?," *Marketing Letters*, 3(2) (1992), pp. 115–26.

37. A.V. Muthukrishnan and Barton A. Weitz, "Role of Product Knowledge in Brand Extensions," in *Advances in Consumer Research,* Rebecca H. Holman and Michael R. Solomon, eds. Provo, UT: Association for Consumer Research, 18 (1990), pp. 407–13.

38. Susan M. Broniarczyk and Joseph W. Alba, "The Importance of the Brand in Brand Extension," *Journal of Marketing Research,* 31 (May 1994), pp. 214–228.

39. Kevin Lane Keller and David A. Aaker, "The Effects of Sequential Introduction of Brand Extensions," *Journal of Marketing Research*, 29 (February 1992), pp. 35–50.

40. See also Arvind Rangaswamy, Raymond Burke, and Terence A. Oliva, "Brand Equity and the Extendibility of Brand Names," *International Journal of Research in Marketing,* 10 (March 1993).

41. See, for example, Peter H. Farquhar and Paul M. Herr, "The Dual Structure of Brand Associations," in David A. Aaker and Alexander L. Biel (eds.), *Brand Equity and Advertising: Advertising's Role in Building Strong Brands,* (pp. 263–77). Hillsdale, NJ: Lawrence Erlbaum Associates, Inc., 1993.

42. Robert D. Hof, "A Washout for Clorox?," *Business Week* (July 9, 1990), pp. 32–33. Alicia Swasy, "P&G and Clorox Wade Into Battle Over the Bleaches," *Wall Street Journal* (January 16, 1989), p. 5. Maria Shao, "A Bright Idea that Clorox Wishes It Never Had," *Business Week* (June 24, 1991), pp. 118–119.

43. Ian M. Lewis, "Brand Equity or Why the Board of Directors Needs Marketing Research," ARF Fifth Annual Advertising and Promotion Workshop, February 1, 1993.

44. Stephen Phillips, "Chiquita May Be a Little Too Ripe," *Business Week* (April 30, 1990), p. 100.

45. Peter H. Farquhar, Julia Y. Han, Paul M. Herr, and Yuji Ijiri, "Strategies for Leveraging Master Brands," *Marketing Research* (September 1992), pp. 32–43.

46. Peter H. Farquhar, Julia Y. Han, Paul M. Herr, and Yuji Ijiri, "Strategies for Leveraging Master Brands," *Marketing Research* (September 1992), pp. 32–43.

47. Peter H. Farquhar, Julia Y. Han, Paul M. Herr, and Yuji Ijiri, "Strategies for Leveraging Master Brands," *Marketing Research* (September 1992), pp. 32–43

48. Peter H. Farquhar, Julia Y. Han, Paul M. Herr, and Yuji Ijiri, "Strategies for Leveraging Master Brands," *Marketing Research* (September 1992), pp. 32–43.

49. Sheri Bridges, "A Schema Unification Model of Brand Extensions," unpublished doctoral dissertation, Graduate School of Business, Stanford University, 1990.

50. Sheri Bridges, "A Schema Unification Model of Brand Extensions," unpublished doctoral dissertation, Graduate School of Business, Stanford University, 1990.

51. Frank Kardes and Chris Allen, "Perceived Variability and Inferences About Brand Extensions," in *Advances in Consumer Research,* Rebecca H. Holman and Michael R. Solomon, eds. Provo, UT: Association for Consumer Research, 18 (1990), pp. 392–398.

52. See also, Sandy D. Jap, "An Examination of the Effects of Multiple Brand Extensions on the Brand Concept," in *Advances in Consumer Research*, 20 (1993), pp. 607–611.

53. John M. Murphy, *Brand Strategy*, Upper Saddle River, NJ: Prentice Hall, 1990.

54. Peter Dacin and Daniel C. Smith, "The Effect of Brand Portfolio Characteristics on Consumer Evaluations of Brand Extensions," *Journal of Marketing Research*, 31 (May 1994), pp. 229–242. See also, David Boush and Barbara Loken, "A Process Tracing Study of Brand Extension Evaluations," *Journal of Marketing Research*, 28 (February 1991), pp. 16–28, and Niraj Dawar, "Extensions of Broad Brands: The Role of Retrieval in Evaluations of Fit," *Journal of Consumer Psychology*, 5 (2) (1996), pp. 189–207.

55. Deborah Roedder John and Barbara Loken, "Diluting Brand Beliefs: When Do Brand Extensions Have a Negative Impact?," *Journal of Marketing*, 57 (Summer 1993), p. 71.

56. Jean B. Romeo, "The Effect of Negative Information on the Evaluation of Brand Extensions and the Family Brand," in *Advances in Consumer Research*, Rebecca H. Holman and Michael R. Solomon, eds., Provo, UT: Association for Consumer Research, 18 (1990), pp. 399–406.

57. For related research, see Carol M. Motely and Srinivas K. Reddy, "Moving Up or Down: An Investigation of Repositioning Strategies," Working Paper 93–363, University of Georgia, Athens, GA, 1993 and Carol M. Motely, "Vertical Extensions: Strategies for Changing Brand Prestige," working paper, University of Georgia, Athens, GA, 1993.

58. Joshua Levine, "Pride Goeth Before a Fall," *Forbes* (May 29, 1989), p. 306.

59. Peter H. Farquhar, Julia Y. Han, and Paul M. Herr, and Yuji Ijiri, "Strategies for Leveraging Master Brands," *Marketing Research* (September 1992), pp. 32–43.

60. Lori Bongiorno, "How Tiffany's Took the Tarnish Off," *Business Week* (August 26, 1996), pp. 67–69.

61. Sheri Bridges, "A Schema Unification Model of Brand Extensions," unpublished doctoral dissertation, Graduate School of Business, Stanford University, 1990.

62. John M. Murphy, *Brand Strategy*. Upper Saddle River, NJ: Prentice Hall, 1990.

63. Andrea Rothman, "France's Bic Bets U.S. Consumers Will Go for Perfume on the Cheap," *Wall Street Journal* (January 12, 1989), p. B6.

64. Laura Zinn, "Does Pepsi Have Too Many Products?," *Business Week* (February 14, 1994), pp. 64–68.

65. John M. Murphy, *Brand Strategy*. Upper Saddle River, NJ: Prentice Hall, 1990.

66. Jean-Noel Kapferer, *Strategic Brand Management*. New York: Free Press, 1992.

67. Max Sutherland and Bruce Smith, "Communicating Kinship: Beware Mistaken Identity in Brand Extensions," *The Journal of Brand Management*, 1(2), pp. 90–93.

68. Srinivas K. Reddy, Susan L. Holak, and Sbodh Bhat, "To Extend or Not to Extend: Success Determinants of Line Extensions," *Journal of Marketing Research*, 31 (May 1994), pp. 243–262. For some conceptual discussion, see Kalpesh Kaushik Desai and Wayne D. Hoyer, "Line Extensions: A Categorization and an Information Processing Perspective," in *Advances in Consumer Research*, 20 (1993), pp. 599–606.

CHAPTER **Managing Brands Over Time**

Preview

As noted in chapter 1, one of the challenges in managing brands is the many changes that have occurred in the marketing environment in recent years. Undoubtedly, the marketing environment will continue to evolve and change, often in very significant ways, in the coming years. Shifts in consumer behavior, competitive strategies, government regulations, or other aspects of the marketing environment can profoundly impact the fortunes of a brand. Besides these external forces, the firm itself may engage in a variety of activities and changes in strategic focus or direction that may necessitate minor or major adjustments in the way that its brands are being marketed. Consequently, effective brand management requires proactive strategies designed to at least maintain, if not actually enhance, customer-based brand equity in the face of all of these different forces.

In this chapter, we consider how to best manage brands over time. Effective brand management requires taking a long-term view of marketing decisions. Any action that a firm takes as part of its marketing program has the potential to change consumer knowledge about the brand in terms of some aspect of brand awareness or brand image. These changes in consumer brand knowledge from current marketing activity also will have an indirect effect on the success of *future* marketing activities. Thus, from the perspective of customer-based brand equity, it is important when making marketing decisions to consider how the changes in brand awareness and image that could result from those decisions may help or hurt *subsequent* marketing decisions (see Figure 13–1). For example, the frequent use of sales promotions involving temporary price decreases may create or strengthen a "discount" association to the brand, with potentially adverse implications on customer loyalty and responses to future price changes or non-price-oriented marketing communication efforts. Unfortunately, marketers may have a particularly difficult time trying to anticipate future consumer response: If the new knowledge structures that will influence future consumer response do not exist until the short-term marketing actions actually occur, how can future consumer response be realistically simulated to permit accurate predictions?

The main assertion of this chapter is that brand equity must be actively managed over time by reinforcing the brand meaning and, if necessary, by making adjustments to the branding program to identify new sources of brand equity. In considering these two topics, we consider a number of different issues, including the advantages of maintaining brand consistency, the importance of protecting sources of brand equity, tradeoffs in fortifying versus leveraging brands, and different possible brand revital-

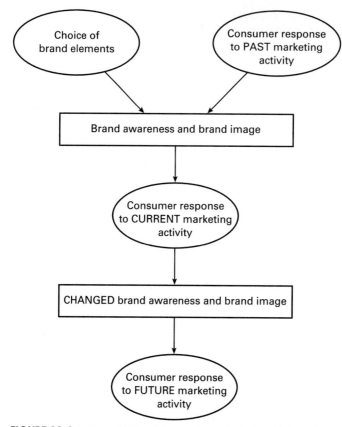

FIGURE 13-1 Understanding the Long-Term Effects Of Marketing Actions on Brand Equity

ization strategies. We also discuss several special topics, such as issues in changing a corporate name and how to manage a brand crisis, as well as brand portfolio issues related to brand migration strategies and retiring brands.

Reinforcing Brands

How should brand equity be reinforced over time? How can marketers make sure that consumers have the desired knowledge structures such that their brands continue to have the necessary sources of brand equity? In a general sense, brand equity is reinforced by marketing actions that consistently convey the meaning of the brand to consumers—in terms of brand awareness and brand image—as follows:

1. *What products does the brand represent; what benefits does it supply; and what needs does it satisfy?* For example, Nutri-Grain has expanded from cereals into granola bars and other products, cementing its reputation as "makers of healthy breakfast and snack foods."

2. *How does the brand make those products superior? What strong, favorable, and unique brand associations exist in the minds of consumers?* For example, through product development and the successful introductions of brand extensions, Black and Decker is now seen as offering "innovative designs" in its small appliance products.

Both of these issues—brand meaning in terms of products, benefits, and needs as well as in terms of product differentiation—depend on the firm's general approach to product development, branding strategies and other strategic concerns, as was discussed in chapters 11 and 12. In this section, we review some other important considerations concerning brand reinforcement.

MAINTAINING BRAND CONSISTENCY

Without question, the most important consideration in reinforcing brands is the consistency of the marketing support that the brand receives—in terms of both the amount and the nature of marketing support. Brand consistency is critical to maintaining the strength and favorability of brand associations. Brands that receive inadequate support in terms of shrinking research and development and marketing communication budgets run the risk of becoming technologically disadvantaged or even obsolete, as well as out-of-date, irrelevant, or forgotten.

Market Leaders and Failures

From the perspective of maintaining consumer loyalty, inadequate marketing support is an especially dangerous strategy when combined with price increases. Once the comfortable leader in its market, Tampax lost market share to brands from Playtex and Johnson & Johnson when its prices were raised while its ad spending was simultaneously cut. To recover lost ground, management was eventually forced to quickly introduce a $20 million ad campaign for the brand that promoted, "Trust is Tampax Tampons."[1] Another example of the downside of failing to adequately support a brand occurred in the oil and gas industry. In the late 1970s, consumers had an extremely positive image of Shell Oil and saw clear differences between the brand and its major branded competitors. In the early 1980s, for various reasons, Shell went through a period of time where it cut back considerably on its advertising and marketing support for the brand. As a result, Shell no longer enjoys the same special status in the eyes of consumers and is now seen as much more similar to other oil companies.

In terms of qualitative aspects of positioning, an even cursory examination of the brands that have maintained market leadership for the last 50 or 100 years or so is a testament to the advantages of staying consistent. Brands like Budweiser, Coca-Cola, Hershey, and others have been remarkably consistent in their strategies once they achieved a preeminent market leadership position. For example, Philip Morris has single-mindedly focused its marketing communications for its Marlboro cigarettes brand on a western cowboy image. Ironically, Marlboro was once a brand that was targeted to women. In the roaring twenties, Marlboro cigarettes were made with a rose-colored tip so that the red imprint of women's lipstick would not show. The brand at that time was backed by ads with the slogan, "Mild as May." When filtered cigarettes became popular in the 1950s, Philip Morris decided to reposition the struggling brand. Packaging was redesigned to include the trademark red and white graphics and the innovative fliptop box. An authentic western image was achieved by using real cowboys from Western ranches in its ads. Since the mid-1970s, Marlboro has been America's No. 1 cigarette brand. The romantic images of the rugged cowboy have since been taken worldwide and even successfully transferred to billboards and print ads when Marlboro's cigarette commercials were banned from television and radio.[2]

Perhaps an even more compelling demonstration of the benefits of consistency is to consider the fortunes of those brands that have been inconsistent in their marketing programs by constantly repositioning, changing ad agencies, and other actions. For example, since its highly successful mid-1970s "Have It Your Way" campaign that touted the uniqueness and quality of its hamburgers, Burger King suffered through twenty years of false starts and wrong turns in brand support (see Figure 13–2). The disastrous $40 million Herb campaign in 1985—featuring a nerd-like character who was supposed to be the only person in America never to have tasted a Whopper—was pulled after only three months. While watching its market share of the total fast food market drop, Burger King has gone through a number of company presidents, marketing directors, and ad agencies. Eventually, Burger King advertising returned to perhaps its strongest and most favorable brand association—the popular Whopper hamburger—in a new campaign themed, "Get Your Burger's Worth."

Michelob is another brand that failed to turn around sales while enduring numerous repositionings. Celebrating its 100th year anniversary in 1996, Michelob has always been positioned as an upscale, super-premium beer. In the 1970s, Michelob ran ads featuring successful young professionals that confidently proclaimed, "Where You're Going, It's Michelob." Moving away from the strong user imagery of that campaign, the next ad campaign trumpeted, "Weekends Were Made for Michelob." Later, to bolster sagging sales, the ad theme was switched to, "Put a Little Weekend in Your Week." In the mid-1980s, yet another campaign was launched, featuring laid-back rock music and stylish shots of beautiful people, that proclaimed, "The Night Belongs to Michelob." None of these campaigns could stop a sales slide. Finally, another ad campaign was introduced in 1994, "Some Days Are Better than Others," which ex-

Years	Slogan
1974–76	Have it your way
1976–78	America loves burgers and we're America's Burger King
1978	Best darn burger
1979–82	Make it special, make it Burger King
1982–85	Battle of the burgers: Aren't you hungry for Burger King now?
1985	Search for Herb
1986	This is a Burger King town
1987	The best food for fast times
1987–89	We do it like you'd do it
1989–91	Sometimes you've gotta break the rules
1991	Your way. Right away
1992–93	BK Tee Vee: I love this place
1994	Get your burger's worth

FIGURE 13–2 Burger King's Ad History

plained to consumers, "A Special Day Requires a Special Beer." The slogan was later modified to, "Some Days Were Made for Michelob." Pity the poor consumer. Previous ad campaigns just required that they look at a calendar or out a window to decide whether it was the right time to drink Michelob—now they had to figure out how well their day was going! After so many different messages, consumers could hardly be blamed if they had no idea when they were supposed to drink the beer. Through all of this, sales performance for Michelob suffered. Sales in 1994 were 2.3 million barrels, as compared to a 1980 peak of 8.1 million barrels.[3]

Consistency and Change

Consistency does *not* mean, however, that marketers should avoid making any changes in the marketing program. On the contrary, the opposite can be quite true—being consistent in managing brand equity may require numerous tactical shifts and changes in order to maintain the strategic thrust and direction of the brand. As earlier chapters in the book described, there are many ways that brand awareness and brand image can be created, maintained, or improved through properly designed marketing programs. The tactics that may be most effective for a particular brand at any one time can certainly vary from those that may be most effective for the brand at another time. As a consequence, prices may move up or down, product features may be added or dropped, ad campaigns may employ different creative strategies and slogans, different brand extensions may be introduced or withdrawn, and so on over time in order to create the *same* desired knowledge structures in consumers' minds. Nevertheless, despite these different types of changes in marketing programs, the strategic positioning of many leading brands has remained remarkably consistent over time. A contributing factor to the success of these brands is that despite these tactical changes, certain key elements of the marketing program are always retained and continuity has been preserved in brand meaning over time.

For example, over the years, McDonald's has employed many different slogans and ad campaigns. Nevertheless, these advertising efforts all reflect the core values and associations for the brand. For example, McDonald's 1995 ad theme, "Have You Had Your Break Today?" is a throw-back to its 1970s ad campaign, "You Deserve A Break Today." The new slogan can be seen as a clever attempt to capitalize on the good feelings and product meaning embedded in the old slogan—reminding consumers of the efficiency, convenience, and friendliness of McDonald's service—while providing a new twist and stronger call to action.

Similarly, many brands have kept a key creative element in their marketing communication programs over the years and, as a result, have effectively created some "advertising equity." For example, Nestea iced tea has used the "Nestea Plunge" in ads and promotions for years. Jack Daniels bourbon whiskey has stuck with rural scenes of its Tennessee home and the slogan, "Charcoal Mellowed Drop by Drop" literally for decades. Recognizing the latent value of their past advertising, new ad campaigns have seen the return of such advertising icons as Colonel Sanders for Kentucky Fried Chicken, Charlie the Tuna for Starkist tuna, American Touristter's luggage-thumping gorilla, the percolating Maxwell House coffee and sing-song Oscar Mayer wiener jingles, the Culligan lady who shouts "Hey, Culligan Man!" for the bottled water, the little girl in the Shake 'n' Bake coating ad who proudly proclaims "An' I Halped," and so on.

These ads should have a ring of familiarity to baby boom consumers, serving as a pleasant reminder of younger, perhaps simpler days. Dubbed "retro-branding" or "retro-advertising" by some marketing pundits, it is also a means to tie in with past advertising that was, and perhaps could still be, a key source of brand equity. Most importantly, it may activate and strengthen brand associations that would be virtually impossible to recreate with new advertising today. One of the most creative advertising agencies of the 1990s, San Francisco's Goodby, Silverstein & Partners, in designing a new ad campaign for Porsche automobiles, decided to return to a line not used in advertising for the brand in fifteen years: "Porsche: There Is No Substitute." Agency founder Jeff Goodby explained the decision with the following logic, "Everybody remembers that line. It's the line Tom Cruise said in 'Risky Business.' As soon as we put it back in the ads, people just assumed Porsche had been using it all along. It was that familiar."[4] Similarly, Foster Grant recently returned to its "Who's That Behind Those Foster Grants?" slogan after every participant in their focus groups said they remembered it.

From an awareness standpoint, such efforts obviously make sense. At the same time, it is important to determine whether these old advertising elements have enduring meaning with older consumers and, at the same time, can be made to seem relevant to younger consumers. More generally, the entire marketing program should be examined to determine which elements are making a strong contribution to brand equity and therefore must be protected, as discussed next.

PROTECTING SOURCES OF BRAND EQUITY

Consistency, therefore, should be viewed in terms of strategic direction and not necessarily the particular tactics employed by the supporting marketing program for the brand at any one point in time. Unless there is some change with either consumers, competition, or the company that makes the strategic positioning of the brand less powerful—for example, changes that somehow make the points of difference or points of parity for the brand less desirable or deliverable—there is likely to be little need to deviate from a successful positioning. Although brands should always look for potentially powerful new sources of brand equity, a top priority under those circumstances is to preserve and defend those sources of brand equity that already exist.

For example, a few years back, Procter & Gamble made a minor change in the formulation of its Cascade automatic dishwashing detergent, primarily for cost-savings reasons. As a result, the product was not quite as effective as it previously had been under certain, albeit very atypical water conditions. After discovering the fact, one of its chief competitors, Lever Brothers, began running comparative ads for its Sunlight brand featuring side-by-side glasses that claimed, "Sunlight Fights Spots Better Than Cascade." Since the consumer benefit of "virtually spotless" is a key brand association and source of brand equity for Cascade, P&G reacted swiftly. They immediately returned Cascade to its original formula and contacted Lever Brothers to inform them of the change, effectively forcing them to stop running the new Sunlight ads on legal grounds. As this episode clearly demonstrates, Procter & Gamble fiercely defends the equity of its brands, perhaps explaining why so many of P&G's brands have had such longevity.

As another example, consider the public relations problems encountered by Intel Corp. with the "floating decimal" problem in their Pentium microprocessors in December 1994. Although the flaw in the chip resulted in miscalculation problems in only extremely unusual and rare instances, Intel was probably at fault—as company executives now admit—for not identifying the problem and proposing remedies to consumers more quickly. Once the problem became public, Intel endured an agonizing six-week period where the company was the focus of media scrutiny and criticism for its reluctance to publicize the problem and its failure to offer replacement chips. Two key sources of brand equity for Intel microprocessors like the Pentium, emphasized throughout its marketing program, are "power" and "safety." Although consumers primarily think of safety in terms of upgradability, the perceptions of financial risk or other problems that might result from a potentially flawed chip certainly should have created a sense of urgency within Intel to protect one of its prize sources of brand equity. Eventually, Intel recapitulated and offered a replacement chip. Perhaps not surprisingly, only a very small percentage of consumers—an estimated 1 percent to 3 percent—actually requested a replacement chip, suggesting that it was Intel's stubbornness to act and not the defect per se that rankled so many consumers. In a later section in this chapter, we will consider in more detail how to handle a brand crisis.

Ideally, key sources of brand equity would be of enduring value. If so, these brand associations should be guarded and nurtured carefully. Unfortunately, their value can easily be overlooked as marketers attempt to expand the meaning of their brands and add new product-related or non-product-related brand associations. We consider these types of tradeoffs in the next section.

FORTIFYING VERSUS LEVERAGING

As chapters 4 through 7 described, there are a number of different ways to raise brand awareness and create strong, favorable, and unique brand associations in consumer memory to build customer-based brand equity. In managing brand equity, it is important to recognize tradeoffs between those marketing activities that attempt to fortify and further contribute to brand equity versus those marketing activities that attempt to leverage or capitalize on existing brand equity to reap some financial benefit.

As noted in chapter 2, the advantage of creating a brand with a high level of awareness and a positive brand image is that many benefits may result to the firm in terms of cost savings and revenue opportunities. Marketing programs can be designed that primarily attempt to capitalize on or perhaps even maximize these benefits, such as by reducing advertising expenses, seeking increasingly higher price premiums, or introducing numerous brand extensions. The more that there is an attempt to realize or capture brand equity benefits, however, the more likely it is that the brand and its sources of equity may become neglected and perhaps diminished in the process. In other words, marketing actions that attempt to leverage the equity of a brand in different ways may come at the expense of other activities that may help to fortify the brand by maintaining or enhancing its awareness and image.

At some point, failure to fortify the brand will diminish brand awareness and weaken brand image. *Without these sources of brand equity, the brand itself may not continue to yield benefits which are as valuable.* Recall the problems encountered by Tampax and Shell from inconsistent advertising support noted earlier in the chapter.[5] As another example, H. J. Heinz Co. severed ties with its long-time ad agency, Leo Burnett, as part of a shift to heavier dependence on trade and price promotion and less emphasis on advertising and other brand investment alternatives. The apparent lack of certain brand-building marketing activities caused some critics to charge that Heinz ". . . has reduced many of their brands to commodity status."[6]

Just as a failure to properly maintain a car eventually affects its performance, neglecting a brand, for whatever reason, can similarly catch up with marketers. As Coors Brewing devoted increasing attention in its marketing on growing the equity of less established brands (e.g., Coors Light beer) and introducing new products (e.g., Zima clear malt beverage), ad support for the flagship Coors beer slipped from a peak of about $43 million in 1985 to a meager $4 million by 1993. Perhaps not surprisingly, sales of Coors beer dropped in half from 1989 to 1993. In launching a new ad campaign to prop up sales, Coors returned to its iconoclastic, independent Western image. Marketers at Coors now admit they did not give the brand the attention it deserves, "We've not marketed Coors as aggressively as we should have in the past ten to fifteen years."[7] Branding Brief 13–1 describes how Borden's brands similarly suffered from a lack of marketing support over time.

FINE-TUNING THE SUPPORTING MARKETING PROGRAM

Although the specific tactics and supporting marketing program for the brand are more likely to change than the basic positioning and strategic direction for the brand, brand tactics also should only be changed when there is evidence that they are no longer making the desired contributions to maintaining or strengthening brand equity. For example, Dove soap has been advertised in a remarkably consistent fashion over the years, even across geographical boundaries (see chapter 14). Dove is positioned as a beauty bar with one-quarter cleansing cream that "creams skin while it washes." Dove advertising has consistently been positioned to consumers on a performance basis with the slogan "Dove Doesn't Dry Your Skin." For years, advertising has always been trial-oriented, using consumer testimonials to vouch for the quality of the product (e.g., "Take the 7-Day Dove Test").

Reinforcing brand meaning may depend on the nature of brand associations involved. Branding Brief 13–2 outlines one perspective on different ways to manage brand concepts. Several specific considerations play a particularly important role in reinforcing brand meaning in terms of product-related and non-product-related associations, as follows.

Product-Related Associations

For brands whose core associations are primarily product-related attributes and/or functional benefits, innovation in product design, manufacturing, and merchandising is especially critical to maintaining or enhancing brand equity. For example, after Timex watched brands like Casio and Swatch gain significant market share by emphasizing digital technology and fashion (respectively) in their watches, they made a number of innovative marketing changes. Within a short period of time, Timex introduced Indiglo glow-in-the-dark technology, showcased popular new models such as the Ironman in mass media advertising, and launched new Timex stores to

---

Milking the Borden Cash Cow[a]

Borden Inc. shows some of the dire consequences that may result from mismanaging brand portfolios and failing to properly manage brand equity over time. Borden sells a vast range of grocery products—dairy (Meadow Gold milk and Lady Borden ice cream), pasta (Cremette, Anthony's pasta, and Classico sauce), snacks (Lays, Wise potato chips, and Cheez Doodles in North America and Rileys and Groovers chips in England) and others (Cracker Jack and ReaLemon lemon juice)—as well as some nonfood consumer products (Elmer's and Krazy Glue) and chemicals. This diverse brand portfolio and the marketing programs designed to support these brands resulted in major problems for Borden.

Between 1986 and 1991, Borden spent more than $2 billion on 91 acquisitions of mostly regional and niche brands in diverse product categories from pasta to potato chips. Unfortunately, the company found combining all those brands a formidable task, exacerbated by its increasingly debt-laden balance sheet. While experiencing double digit earnings increases throughout the 1980s, Borden's profits began to slide starting in 1991. The company's vast collection of tiny brands in disparate categories made any cohesive marketing program difficult and expensive. Operating with a collection of unintegrated businesses, Borden was less efficient than many large rivals and lacked their marketing clout.

For example, company officials now admit that Borden's brands lost their consumer cachet in part because of the company's decentralized approach to advertising—virtually all of the new brands that were acquired retained their own agencies. Many of the regional brands were inexpensive to buy, but had weak images that needed impactful advertising to grow. Preoccupied by financial matters and plant modernization, the company only spent 2.5 percent of its food sales on advertising, considerably less than major competitors such as Hershey Foods and CPC International. Smaller regional brands became overshadowed by stronger competition and even some of the company's biggest brands began to falter.

In 1992, Borden made a number of marketing changes to revitalize its brands. As the company's CEO at the time observed, "We can sell more product by revitalizing the equity in our name, our slogan, and our Elsie." Elsie the cow, their famous brand symbol, returned to TV advertising in 1992 after being put out to pasture twenty years ago, as did the slogan, "If It's Borden, It's Got to Be Good," plastered all over its products. Marketing efforts were centralized at administrative headquarters and plans were put into place to eliminate or sell many of Borden's small regional businesses while focusing its efforts on building its national brands. Unfortunately, implementation proved difficult. For example, on the basis of research showing that 97 percent of consumers recognized Borden as a leading milk brand, Borden kept its prices steady despite a steep drop of as much as a third in raw milk prices. Because many consumers believe "milk is milk," the premium-pricing strategy adversely impacted sales. In pasta, revitalization efforts concentrated on their leading national brand Creamette. Misguided advertising did more to boost pasta consumption as a category, however, than affect Creamette's brand image. Neglected, sales of its strong regional brands such as Prince in the Northeast and Anthony's in the West suffered.

Thus, despite these changes, profits continued to slide, particularly in Borden's dairy and snacks business. Finally, after a change in top-management and continued weak performance, the company, and any of its parts, were put up for sale. After a long waiting period, Borden was finally bought in late 1994 by Kohlberg Kravis Roberts & Co., the New York leveraged buyout firm that owned RJR Nabisco Holdings, Safeway Stores, and Stop & Shop, in an all-stock, no-cash deal.

---

[a]Elizabeth A. Lesley, "Borden Faces Facts: It's Time To Shed the Flab," *Business Week* (November 9, 1992), p. 44. Elizabeth Lesley, "Why Things Are So Sour at Borden," *Business Week* (November 22, 1993), pp. 78–86. Elizabeth Lesley, "The Carving of Elsie, Slice by Slice," *Business Week* (January 17, 1994), p. 29. Laura Zinn, "Elsie May Be Ailing, But KKR is Thinking Whipped Cream," *Business Week* (September 26, 1994), p. 55.

showcase their products. Timex also bought the Guess and Monet watch brands to distribute through upscale department stores and expand its brand portfolio. These innovations in product design and merchandising have significantly revived the brand's fortunes.[8]

Hasbro Inc. is another company that has attempted to use product introductions and innovations to keep its brand lines fresh. Hasbro's formula for success is to take well-known but perhaps stagnant-selling brands—for example, Cabbage Patch dolls, Nerf foam toys, G.I. Joe action figures, Tonka trucks, and Teddy Ruxpin talking bears—spruce them up with new offerings and features and step up their advertising support. New models such as Crimp 'N' Curl Cabbage Patch dolls; Nerf slingshots, bow-and-arrows, and footballs that whistle through the air; and a new 12-inch high, limited "Hall of Fame" edition G.I. Joe helped to revitalize each of those brand franchises. At the same time, Hasbro also brings out new toy lines in hopes of finding the "hot" new hit. This diversification strategy of combining stable, dependable brands with exciting, new ones is intended to yield a steadier profit picture for the company.[9]

Failure to innovate can have dire consequences. For example, Schwinn Bicycle once owned the children's bike market with famous models such as the Phantom (a 1950s workhorse with balloon tires) and the Varsity (a 10-speed stalwart of the 1970s). Unfortunately, its market share, which peaked at 25 percent in the 1960s, slipped to single digits by the early 1990s. The problem? In part, Schwinn was slow to adjust to changing consumer tastes and take aggressive new rivals seriously. While other companies won over biking enthusiasts with lighter, sleeker models in the early 1980s, Schwinn continued to crank out its durable, but bulky, standbys. As one custom bicycle dealer observed, "Schwinn never spent the money on research and development

Brand Concept Management

In an award-winning article, C. W. Park, Bernie Jaworski, and Debbie MacInnis present a normative framework termed brand concept management (BCM) for selecting, implementing, and controlling brand image over time to enhance market performance.[a] The framework consists of a sequential process of selecting, introducing, elaborating, and fortifying a brand concept. The brand concept guides positioning strategies, and hence the brand image, at each of these stages. The method for maintaining this concept-image linkage depends on whether the brand concept is functional, symbolic, or experiential.

A brand concept is defined in terms of firm-selected brand meaning derived from basic consumer needs. An important factor in influencing the selection of a brand concept is the different types of consumer needs that might prevail, as follows:

1. Functional needs are defined as those that involve the search for products that solve consumption-related problems (e.g., solve a current problem, prevent a potential problem, resolve conflict, or restructure a frustrating situation). A brand with a *functional concept* is defined as one designed to solve externally generated consumption needs.

2. Symbolic needs are defined as desires for products that fulfill internally generated needs for self-enhancement, role position, group membership, or ego identification. A brand with a *symbolic concept* is one designed to associate the individual with a desired group, role, or self-image.

3. Experiential needs are defined as desires for products that provide sensory pleasure, variety, and/or cognitive stimulation. A brand with an *experiential concept* is designed to fulfill these internally generated needs for stimulation or variety.

Once a broad needs-based concept has been selected, it can be used to guide positioning decisions. For each of the three management stages, positioning strategies need to be implemented that enable consumers to understand a brand image (introduction), perceive its steadily increasing value (elaboration), and generalize it to other products produced by the firm (fortification). Specifically, the *introductory stage* of BCM is defined as a set of activities designed to establish a brand image/position in the marketplace during the period of market entry. During the *elaboration stage,* positioning strategies focus on enhancing the value of the brand's image so that its perceived superiority in relation to competitors can be established or sustained. At the final stage of BCM, the *fortification stage,* the aim is to link an elaborated brand image to the image of other products produced by the firm in different product classes.

The specific positioning strategies implemented at the introduction, elaboration, and fortification stages depend on the concept type. Figure 13–3 displays examples of brands with different concepts and the implications for brand concept management according to Park and his co-authors.

---

[a]C. Whan Park, Bernard J. Jaworski, and Deborah J. MacInnis, "Strategic Brand Concept—Image Management," *Journal of Marketing*, 50 (October 1986), pp. 135–145.

Examples of Brands with Functional Concepts		
Concept Introduction	*Concept Elaboration*	*Concept Fortification*

Clorox Bleach (whiter and brighter clothes)

In 1913 Clorox liquid bleach introduced to the market	Problem-solving generalization strategy[a]	Clorox Pre-Wash soil and stain remover used prior to laundering clothes
	Product usage extended from cottons to synthetic fibers	Tackle cleaner, a fresh-scented, all-purpose household cleaner[b]

Vaseline Petroleum Jelly (general purpose medicinal cream)

1869 Vaseline Petroleum Jelly introduced to the market as a lubricant and as a skin balm for burns	Problem-solving generalization strategy
	 Produce usage extended to multiple-usage situations: preventing diaper rash, removing eye makeup, lip balm
		Vaseline health and beauty related products:
		   Vaseline Intensive Care Lotion
		   Intensive Care Bath Beads
		   Vaseline Constant Care
		   Vaseline Dermatology Formula
		 Vaseline baby care products:
		   Wipe 'N Dipes
		   Vaseline Intensive Care Baby Lotion
		   Vaseline Intensive Care Baby Shampoo
		   Vaseline Intensive Care Baby Powder

[a]Clorox did not follow this strategy. This strategy would be consistent with the proposed elaboration approach.

[b]Tackle cleaner should have been linked more clearly to the Clorox concept. One method to accomplish this link would be to use family names.

Examples of Brands with Symbolic Concepts		
Concept Introduction	*Concept Elaboration*	*Concept Fortification*

Lenox China ("A World Apart," "Let It Express Your World")

Almost a century ago, the Lenox Company introduced a line of fine china	Market shielding A tightly controlled marketing mix to preserve the status concept	Lenox crystal Lenox silverplated holloware Candles Jewelry

Brooks Brothers (attire for the conservative, professional gentleman)

In 1818 Brooks Brothers introduced a "gentleman's suit"	Market shielding A tightly controlled marketing mix to shield the market (e.g., only 26 stores in the United States and carefully controlled in-store merchandising)	Brooks Brothers shoes Brooks Brothers cologne Brooks Brothers hats Brooks Brothers valet stands

FIGURE 13–3 Examples of Brand Concept Management

Examples of Brands with Experiential Concepts		
Concept Introduction	*Concept Elaboration*	*Concept Fortification*

Barbie Doll (the sophisticated teenager)

Barbie Doll was introduced to the market in 1959	Brand accessory strategy Accessories like outfits, houses, furniture, cars, jewelry for Barbie, Ken	Barbie Magazine Barbie Game Barbie Boutique

Lego Building Blocks (unbreakable safe toy emphasizing creativity and imagination)

Lego Building Blocks for 3- to 8-year-olds introduced in 1960	Brand accessory strategy Accessories like minifigures, trees, signs, idea books, storage cases Accessories like large bricks for 1- to 5-year-olds that can link with the smaller bricks when the child gets older Expert builder sets for ages 7–12 with items such as wheels, gears, axles, toggle joints, and connectors	Do-it-yourself furniture[a] such as Lego chairs, couches, desks, bookshelves

[a]Suggested; not actual fortification strategy for Lego.

FIGURE 13-3 Examples of Brand Concept Management (*continued*)

or planned for the long-term, like so many American companies. Except for their name, they really have nothing to sell."[10]

Schwinn is not alone. Smith Corona, after struggling to sell its typewriters and word processors in a booming personal computer market, finally filed for bankruptcy. As one industry expert observed: "Smith Corona never realized they were in the document business, not the typewriter business. If they had understood that, they would have moved into software."[11] Jiffy Pop popcorn, made to be cooked over a stove, was made virtually obsolete by the widespread adoption of the microwave oven. Jiffy Pop eventually introduced Microwave Jiffy Pop but not before it was too late to save the brand. Ultimately, it was discontinued.[12]

Thus, product innovations are critical for performance-based brands whose sources of brand equity primarily rest in product-related associations. Branding Brief 13–3 describes the sales setbacks encountered by Bacardi from failing to innovate. In some cases, product advances may involve brand extensions based on a new or improved product ingredient or feature, for example, Sony televisions with special Trinitron color tubes, Oreo Double Stuff cookies with extra filling, and Ziploc Gripper Zipper storage bags.[13] In fact, in many categories, a strong family sub-brand has emerged from product innovations associated with brand extensions, such as Wilson Hammer wide-body tennis racquets. In other cases, product innovations may center on existing brands. For example, General Mills "Big G" cereal division strives to im-

---

BRANDING BRIEF 13–3

Bacardi's Sour Sales Slide[a]

Bacardi rum, although still the largest liquor brand in the United States in terms of sales, suffered one of the worst sales drops in modern spirits history, losing over two million cases in sales as their sales decreased from 8.7 million cases in 1991 to 6.4 million cases in 1992. The reasons behind Bacardi's sales slide during this period provides perhaps a textbook example of how *not* to build brand equity over time.

Through the 1950s and 1960s, sales of Bacardi in the United States exploded as young drinkers adopted rum and Coke as an easy, fun alternative to the martinis and scotches drunk by their parents. Although the brand enjoyed uninterrupted growth for nearly three decades, there was little innovation in its supporting marketing program during that time. With an onset of "cola fatigue" and the growing popularity of juice-based drinks, however, Bacardi has found it increasingly difficult to compete. Not only has the "mixable" crown been lost to vodka, but Bacardi faces stiff competition in its own market. Seagram's Captain Morgan Spiced Rum, launched in 1983, successfully implemented the type of marketing program that Bacardi had avoided, infusing its drink with a sweeter taste and promoting the brand with Captain Morgan and the Morganettes (a pirate character with female companions) to young drinkers in popular night spots. Other competitors also introduced trendy, flavored products such as Absolut Kurant and Stolchnaya Ohranj—currant and orange vodkas, respectively—to entice young drinkers. Through it all, Bacardi stubbornly refused to expand its product portfolio.

In addition to these developments, a series of price increases and a federal excise tax increase between 1988 and 1991 resulted in the price of a 750 milliliter (22.5 fluid ounce) bottle increasing from $7.50 to as much as $10.99 and also contributed to the dismal sales performance in 1992. To stop the slide in sales, Bacardi management aggressively cut prices, doubled spending to launch a new print ad campaign, began on-premise promotions in big-city bars, and introduced a new flavored, spiced rum (Bacardi Spice) and lemon-flavored rum targeted at vodka drinkers (Bacardi Limón). Bacardi management also began to explore entering other product categories (Scotch and low-alcohol products) and new markets in Eastern Europe, Latin America, and the Far East. To many observers, however, the Bacardi brand had become dangerously out of touch with younger consumers, and the question remains as to whether it can recapture its preeminent position.

---

[a]Adapted from Suein L. Hwang, "As Rivals Innovate, Old-Line Bacardi Becomes a Chaser," *Wall Street Journal* (July 6, 1994), p. B4.

prove at least a third of its nearly two dozen brand lines each year, most recently reformulating Cheerios and Wheaties.[14]

At the same, it is important not to change products too much, especially if the brand meaning to consumers is wrapped up in the product design or makeup. Recall the strong consumer resistance encountered by new Coke described in chapter 2. As another example, Revlon also underestimated how passionately consumers can feel about well-established brands and how much they can resent any tampering with the products themselves. To better appeal to younger women, Revlon reformulated the heavy floral scent of its 30-year-old Intimate fragrance to a lighter, less sweet scent. Longtime customers protested, forcing the company to reintroduce the old formulation as "Intimate the Original" while continuing to market the reformulated new Intimate.

In making product changes to a brand, it is important that loyal consumers feel that a reformulated product is a *better* product but not necessarily a *different* product. The timing of the announcement and introduction of a product improvement is also important: If the brand improvement is announced too soon, consumers may cease to buy existing products; if the brand improvement is announced too late, competitors may have already taken advantage of the market opportunity with their own introductions.

Non-Product-Related Associations

For brands whose core associations are primarily non-product-related attributes and symbolic or experiential benefits, relevance in user and usage imagery is critical. For example, Maybelline found itself slipping behind Cover Girl in 1985 as sales leader in the mass-market cosmetics business. To respond, Maybelline made a number of changes, including introducing a number of easy-to-use beauty tools—Perfect Pen (an eye liner with a tip like a felt pen) and Plush Brush (a powder blush that comes in an hourglass-shaped tube). Perhaps the biggest contributor to Maybelline's comeback, however, was a new $50 million ad campaign designed to transform its image as a tired, low-priced brand to one used by smart, sophisticated women. The stylish ads contained sexier models, jazzier music, and the new slogan, "Smart. Beautiful. Maybelline."

Because of their intangible nature, non-product-related associations may be potentially easier to change, for example, through a major new advertising campaign that communicates a different type of user or usage situation. Nevertheless, ill-conceived or too-frequent repositionings can blur the image of a brand and confuse or perhaps even alienate consumers. For example, Pepsi-Cola's fresh, youthful appeal has been a key point of difference versus Coca-Cola. Moving away from its "Choice of a New Generation" slogan, Pepsi launched a new campaign with the slogan "Gotta Have It" during the 1992 Super Bowl. The ads, showing young and old Pepsi drinkers, were an attempt to expand the "Pepsi Generation" to include older age groups. With little indication of sales success, Pepsi returned to its more familiar and powerful positioning, introducing new ads with the snappy tag line, "Be Young. Have Fun. Drink Pepsi."[15] More recently, Pepsi perhaps again ran the risk of straying away from a key source of equity with the introduction of its latest ad theme, "Nothing Else Is a Pepsi," before returning to a youthful appeal with the slogan, "Generation Next."

Another example of a too hasty departure from advertising equity occurred with Miller Lite light beer. As described in chapter 3, Miller Lite was advertised for years with the slogan, "Tastes Great. Less Filling.," in humorous ads featuring famous re-tired athletes. In part to revive fading brand sales, a new ad campaign was launched in 1992. A dramatic departure from previous advertising, the new campaign, featuring fashionable young people, contained the slogans, "C'mon, Let Me Show You Where It's At" and "It's It and That's That." When the slide in brand sales continued, Miller reversed its field to create a new campaign, much more faithful to its original position-ing. The "Combinations" campaign showed Miller Lite drinkers disagreeing over which of two completely different events to watch on TV. After banging their TV set with a bottle of Lite beer, the two events became combined into one "wacky" specta-tor sport—"Sumo High Dive," "Recliner Chair Ski Jump," "Wiener Dog Winter Na-tionals," and "Big Lawyer Round-Up." The new ad tagline, echoing the past, became, "Great Taste. Less Filling. Can Your Beer Do This?" More recently, Miller Lite adopted yet-another slogan, "Life is Good," although retaining some of the stylistic characteristics of the Combinations campaign. The return to advertising form has seen a comeback in sales, although Miller chose to introduce a quirky, controversial ad campaign featuring a fictitious copywriter, Dick, in 1997.

It is particularly dangerous to flip-flop between product-related and non-product-related associations because of the fundamentally different marketing and advertising approaches each entails. For example, consider the dramatic change in positioning for Cutty Sark Blended Scots Whiskey. In the late 1980s, lifestyle oriented print ads were run for the brand. For example, one ad showed two stylish men dressed in tuxedoes relaxing and sharing a joke together under the headline "When You Live A Cutty Above." A few years later, ads for the brand showed it in a completely differ-ent light. Underneath a large shot of a clear glass containing a scotch and soda on the rocks, the ad read:

> This is a glass of Cutty Sark.
> It won't make you hip. It won't make you successful.
> And it won't change your life.
> And if you drink it simply because you like the way it tastes,
> your life's pretty good already.

The new campaign would seem to almost directly refute the old campaign, running the risk of confusing or perhaps even alienating existing customers! Interestingly, ad-vertising for Heineken beer made almost the exact *opposite* switch in positioning. Earlier ads showed simple scenes of the bottle or people peacefully drinking the beer, backed by the slogan, "Just being the best is enough." More recent ads, in an attempt to make the brand more "hip" and contemporary, are much artier—featuring the bright red star logo—and have a much more prominent lifestyle component.

Significant repositionings may be dangerous for other reasons, too. Brand images can be extremely sticky, and once consumers form strong brand associations, they may be difficult to change. Consumers may choose to ignore or just be unable to remember the new positioning when strong, but different, brand associations already exist in memory.[16] Club Med has attempted for years to transcend its image as a vacation romp for swingers to attract a broader cross-section of people. Branding Brief 13–4 describes the problems encountered by American Express as it has attempted to update and fine-tune its image.

Do You Know My New Ad Campaign?:
Repositioning the American Express Card[a]

Marketing has long played a key role at American Express, whose chairman stated in 1985, "Marketing is our top priority." The Travel Related Services group, which handles credit cards, traveler's checks, and other travel services, has received the bulk of the company's marketing expenditures. Introduced in 1958, American Express revolutionized the credit card business through a combination of generous credit limits and clever advertising touting the card as the ultimate icon of wealth, prestige, and high-class consumption. American Express and its famous centurion effectively positioned itself as an upscale alternative to MasterCard and Visa. Long-time ad agency Ogilvy & Mather created successful ad campaigns such as "Do You Know Me?" which began in 1974 and featured famous—but not always easily recognizable—entertainers (Mel Blanc, Benny Goodman, Luciano Pavarotti), athletes (Jesse Owens, Pele, Rusty Staub), executives (George Gallup, Roy Jacuzzi), and politicians (Sam Ervin, William Miller). All ads used the same format with the celebrity uttering that famous line before touting the virtues of his or her American Express card. The campaign was later adapted to run in Europe. Sensing a change in consumer attitudes, the "Interesting Lives" campaign, which started in 1984, redefined prestige to mean "leading an interesting, varied, and unexpectedly rich life" and positioned the card as indispensable to a new, younger audience. The much praised "Portraits" print campaign (described in chapter 6) with its striking photos of celebrity cardholders and theme of "Membership Has Its Privileges" further cemented American Express upscale image and cachet.

Dramatic changes in the credit card market in recent years, however, have had an adverse impact on American Express' fortunes. Competitors have engaged in a fierce marketplace battle. Visa has hammered home its key points of difference—convenience, acceptability, and availability—in hard-hitting comparative ads showing different places around the world that "Don't Take American Express" while at the same time stressing that with Visa, "It's Everywhere You Want To Be" (see chapter 7). MasterCard has focused on creating points of difference related to practicality, value, and added services in ads that exhort consumers to "Master the Moment." The American Express card has always been marketed as high-prestige and expensive—at one time, it cost $55 a year for a green card, $85 for a gold card, and $300 for a top-end platinum card. Although its corporate card business has remained strong, many individuals decided that prestige and other benefits did not justify the price premium. As a result, its share of the U.S. credit card billings dropped to under 20 percent in 1993 from a 1983 peak of 33 percent.

American Express advertising and product changes over the years have met with mixed success. After firing long-time ad agency Ogilvy & Mather in 1991, American Express embarked on a new set of ads that presented the card literally as an icon, placing it in exaggerated large size in unusual settings (e.g., as a statue on Easter Island, a bridge over a water hazard on a golf course, and as a window on a train). Widely derided as off-strategy, the agency that created the ads was eventually replaced by Ogilvy & Mather. Many critics maintain that Ogilvy & Mather was unduly vilified to start with—American Express' main problem was with its products. For example, to better compete with Visa in retail stores, American Express introduced the Optima Card in 1987, which carried an interest rate of 13.5%, comparatively low for the time. Weak credit standards, however, led to massive loan write-offs—$155 million in losses in 1991 from poor credit decisions.

Recently, ad campaigns have attempted to make the ad seem more relevant in a popular and humorous ad campaign featuring comedian Jerry Seinfeld. Recognizing the need to expand its brand portfolio in consumer cards, American Express has also introduced several new credit cards. In September 1994, after nearly 4000 consumer interviews, American Express launched the Optima True Grace Card. Unlike other credit cards, the True Grace Card did not start charging interest until 25 days after the close of each monthly account cycle, even if the card holder carried over the balance. The brand has been supported by a $50 million marketing campaign featuring ads showing home decorating expert Martha Stewart facetiously cutting up her bank cards and using them to retile her pool. Low interest rates and waived annual fees with minimum usage were also included. Late in 1995, American Express introduced a co-branded card under its Optima brand with Delta Airlines—the Delta SkyMiles Card from American Express. Plans were made to introduce ten to fifteen additional niche cards in the following years. A major corporate brand campaign was introduced in 1996 with the umbrella theme "Do More," reinforced in ads for their travel ("Find More"), financial ("Prepare More"), and card ("Whatever More") services.

Many challenges remain for American Express. Nevertheless, American Express has gained a broader view of their brand equity. A top American Express executive recently described his view of the brand as follows:

> The brand has been remarkably resilient. It stands as an icon for safety, security, trust, and global service. On another level it stands for "people like me." It has stood in the past for prestige and I think it still does, but prestige defined differently than has historically been the case. It clearly is characterized by a sense of affiliation and belonging and of special access, privilege.

[a]Joanne Lipman, "Ogilvy Angles Hard to Win Back American Express Card Account," *Wall Street Journal* (March 4, 1992), p. B-5. Kim Foltz, "A Green Giant Is on the Move," *Newsweek* (October 28, 1985), pp. 58–59. Leah Nathans Spiro, "Is This Amex' Trump Card?," *Business Week* (October 24, 1994), pp. 32–33. John McManus and Terry Lefton, "Amex's Card Shark," *Brandweek* (May 23, 1994), pp. 26–35. Linda Grant, "Why Warren Buffett's Betting Big on American Express," *Fortune* (October 30, 1995), pp. 70–84.

For dramatic repositioning strategies to work, convincing new brand claims must be presented in a compelling fashion. One brand that successfully shifted from a primarily non-product-related image to a primarily product-related image is BMW. Uniformly decreed as the quintessential "yuppie" vehicle of the 1980s, sales of the brand dropped almost in half from 1986 to 1991 as new Japanese competition emerged and a backlash to the "Greed Decade" set in. Convinced that high status was no longer a sufficiently desirable and sustainable position, marketing and advertising efforts switched the focus to BMW's product developments and improvements, such as the responsive performance, distinctive styling, and leading-edge engineering of the cars. These efforts, showcased in well-designed ads, helped to diminish the "yuppie" association, and sales by 1995 approached their earlier peak.[17]

In summary, reinforcing brand equity requires consistency in the amount and nature of the supporting marketing program for the brand. Although the specific tactics may change, the key sources of equity for the brand should be preserved and amplified where appropriate. Product innovation and relevance is paramount in maintaining continuity and expanding the meaning of the brand. We next consider situations where more drastic brand actions are needed.

Revitalizing Brands

At the beginning of the chapter, it was noted that changes in consumer tastes and preferences, the emergence of new competitors or new technology, or any new development in the marketing environment could potentially affect the fortunes of a brand. In virtually every product category, there are examples of once prominent and admired brands that have fallen on hard times or, in some cases, even completely disappeared. Nevertheless, a number of these brands have managed to make impressive comebacks in recent years as marketers have breathed new life into their customer franchises. Brands such as Harley Davidson, Ford Mustang, Atari, and Chrysler have all seen their brand fortunes successfully turned around to varying degrees. Branding Brief 13–5 describes how RCA restored the status of its brand. Some of the stories behind other brands who have successfully made comebacks include the following:

1. *Hush Puppies*. Hush Puppies' suede shoes, symbolized by the cuddly, rumpled, droopy-eyed dog, was a kid's favorite in the 1950s and 1960s. Changes in fashion trends and a series of marketing mishaps, however, eventually resulted in an out-of-date image and diminished sales. Wolverine World Wide, makers of Hush Puppies, made a number of marketing changes in the early 1990s to reverse the sales slide. New product designs and numerous off-beat color combinations (e.g., bright shades of green, purple, and pink) enhanced the brand's fashion appeal. Increased expenditures backed an ad campaign featuring youthful, attractive people wearing the shoes and the tag line, "We Invented Casuals." Popular designers began to use the shoes in their fashion shows. The brand even got a boost when the actor Tom Hanks wore a pair of old Hush Puppies in the final scene of *Forrest Gump*. As a result of all these developments, and a concerted program to engage retailer interest, the brand has now reappeared in fashionable department stores and sales and profits have skyrocketed.[18]

RCA: Updating a Brand Icon[a]

Radio Corporation of America (RCA) was the inventor of television on a commercial basis. For forty years, RCA dominated the U.S. television market. Unfortunately, while the consumer electronics market exploded in size and diversity in the 1970s and 1980s, RCA failed to innovate. Missing the market in video cassette recorders and camcorders with young, affluent customers, RCA risked being left behind by well-designed, high-technology products. Unless something was done, RCA could be left with an aging customer base and obsolete product offerings. Acquired by French electronics group Thomson in 1987, new management set out to revitalize the brand.

Perhaps the main problem faced by RCA was in fact its heritage. RCA was seen by consumers as a manufacturing-led company, producing low-technology, large-scale, mid-range TVs. Consumers—especially younger ones—thought of the brand in terms of ornate, wooden cabinets in their grandparents' house! RCA was certainly not seen as relevant to the videophiles segment. The brand had been severely underadvertised and because of the lack of new features, retailers and their salespeople were not interested in pushing the brand.

Rather than attack its Japanese competition head on with new technology and features, RCA took a slightly different angle. RCA decided to concentrate on technological innovation that would make the product easier to use, investing $300 million in research and development to enhance both the usage and styling of its products. Its new ad campaign had multiple objectives. Its goal was to reposition RCA by using its heritage as an entertainment provider. Doing so would distinguish it from competition and also reassure existing customers of the constancy of the RCA product. Additionally, a successful campaign would update the brand image among a younger target market, create visibility for other RCA video products besides televisions, and inspire trade support.

RCA reinvigorated the brand through dramatic product innovations (e.g., RCA branded its larger-screen televisions, "Home Theatre") and a modern-looking new ad campaign (see Figure 13–4). Ads featured the longtime (over 100 years old!) RCA Dalmatian icon, "Nipper," providing breakthrough, instantaneous recognition; but these ads also provided a break from the past. The new dimension of change was portrayed by giving Nipper a young son, "Chipper," who could represent the forward-looking RCA, a clever means to build on—but distinguish itself from—past advertising efforts. As a top executive at RCA's ad agency noted, "Consumers easily attached perceptions of 'new' and 'state of the art' to the pup and felt comfortable and reassured with Nipper." The dual symbol achieved the perfect image balance for the new RCA. Their new ad slogan, "Changing Entertainment. Again.", further reinforced the balance of new and old, change and heritage.

---

[a]Nicholas Lind, "RCA Consumer Electronics: Making the Most of Your Heritage," in *Great Advertising Campaigns*, London: Kogan Page, 1993.

FIGURE 13-4 Sample RCA Home Theatre Ad

2. *Adidas*. The one-time standard of athletic footwear, Adidas saw its leading market position overtaken by rivals Nike and Reebok as the company became mired in outdated business practices and internal squabbles. New management, headed by a former chief executive at Saatchi & Saatchi ad agency, began efforts to turn the brand around in 1993. Adidas decided to concentrate its efforts on the lucrative—but fickle—teenage market with the hope that this group might choose to reject brands adopted by their parents and others to create their own identity. New performance-oriented products, advertising, and athlete sponsors targeted a young, urban audience. Additional promotional efforts capitalized on the World Cup soccer tournament in the United States. Complementing this "pull" effort, Adidas also attempted to increase its share of shelf space in stores. As a result, Adidas increased its share of the $8 billion athletic shoe market to 5 percent from 2 percent in just four years, and has become the number four sneaker company in the United States, challenging number three Fila.[19]

3. *Quaker State*. Quaker State was an industry titan in motor oil that had fallen on hard times in recent years. Rival brands like Pennzoil and Castroil used discounts and rebates in the mid-1980s to lure distributors and customers away and steal the top spots in the market. Stubbornly sticking to its higher prices, Quaker State was losing 1.5 points of market share a year. Hiring a top marketer from Campbell as chairman in early 1993, the marketing program went back to basics. Quaker State's dark logo was spruced up with brighter colors and new lettering, and the motor oil was repackaged in bright green bottles. The name change of Quaker State's Minit-Lube drive-through chain to Q-Lube was accelerated to emphasize the brand tie-in. Ad spokesman Burt Reynolds was fired, and new ad agency Chiat-Day created a much more product-focused campaign with the slogan, "An Intelligent Oil for a Longer Engine Life." New extensions were introduced and rebates were launched to prop up moribund brands. Within two years, the brand had gained three market share points and become a solid number two player in the market.[20]

4. *Ovaltine*. At one time, Ovaltine was dominant in the milk modifier business, becoming a household name from its sponsorships of the exploits of superhero Captain Midnight on radio and TV starting in the 1940s. Forgotten and ignored, Ovaltine staged a comeback in 1992 backed by a new ad campaign touting the powder as a means of turning ordinary milk into a delicious vitamin-rich, chocolate-flavored drink. Blending nostalgia with nutrition as key points of difference, sales surged.[21]

As these examples illustrate, brands sometimes have had to "return to their roots" to recapture lost sources of equity. In other cases, the meaning of the brand has had to fundamentally change to regain lost ground and recapture market leadership. Reversing a fading brand's fortunes thus requires either that lost sources of brand equity are recaptured or that new sources of brand equity are identified and established. Regardless of which approach is taken, brands on the comeback trail have to make more "revolutionary" changes than the "evolutionary" changes to reinforce brand meaning that were described above.

Often, the first place to look in turning around the fortunes of a brand is to understand what the sources of brand equity were to begin with. As Ogilvy & Mather's Norman Berry says:[22]

> The brands most likely to respond to revitalization efforts are those that have clear and relevant values that have been left dormant for a long time, have not been well expressed in the marketing and communications recently, have been violated by product problems, cost reductions, and so on. *Where there is evidence that these values exist and that they were indeed a part of the brand's magnetism during healthier days, then*

chances of revitalization are good. If you find that the brand really does not have any strong values, chances are that the product or business strength in the past was a function simply of performance and spending characteristics and that, in fact, according to our definition, it never really became a *true brand*. Bringing these brands back to life is more like starting from scratch. It really isn't revitalization.

In profiling brand knowledge structures to guide repositioning, it is important to accurately and completely characterize the breadth and depth of brand awareness and the strength, favorability, and uniqueness of brand associations held in consumer memory. A comprehensive brand equity measurement system as outlined in chapter 10 should be able to reveal the current status of these sources of brand equity. If not, or to provide additional insight, a special brand audit may be necessary. Of particular importance is the extent to which key brand associations are still adequately functioning as points of difference or points of parity and properly positioning the brand. Are positive associations losing their strength or uniqueness? Have negative associations become linked to the brand, perhaps due to some type of changes in the marketing environment? Decisions must then be made as to whether to retain the same positioning or to create a new positioning and, if so, which positioning to adopt. The positioning considerations outlined in chapter 3 can provide useful insights as to the desirability and deliverability of different possible positionings based on company, consumer, and competitive considerations.

With an understanding of the current and desired brand knowledge structures in hand, the customer-based brand equity framework again provides guidance as to how to best refresh old sources of brand equity or create new sources of brand equity to achieve the intended positioning. According to the model, two such approaches are possible:

1. Expand the depth and/or breadth of brand awareness by improving consumer recall and recognition of the brand during purchase or consumption settings.

2. Improve the strength, favorability, and uniqueness of brand associations making up the brand image. This approach may involve programs directed at existing or new brand associations.

Strategically, lost sources of brand equity can be refurbished and new sources of brand equity can be established in the same three main ways that sources of brand equity are created to start with—by changing brand elements, changing the supporting marketing program, and/or leveraging new secondary associations. In the remainder of this section, we consider several alternative strategies to affect the awareness and image of an existing brand to refresh old sources or create new sources of brand equity.

EXPANDING BRAND AWARENESS

With a fading brand, often it is not the *depth* of brand awareness that is a problem—consumers can still recognize or recall the brand under certain circumstances. Rather, the *breadth* of brand awareness is the stumbling block—consumers only tend to think of the brand in very narrow ways. Therefore, as was suggested in chapter 3, one powerful means of building brand equity is to increase the breadth of brand awareness, making sure that consumers do not overlook the brand and think of purchasing or consuming it in those situations where the brand can satisfy consumers' needs and wants.

In this section we consider strategies to increase usage of and find new uses for the brand. Assuming a brand has a reasonable level of awareness and a positive brand image, perhaps the most appropriate starting point to creating new sources of brand equity is with ways that increase usage. In many cases, approaches to increase usage represent the "path of least resistance" because they do not involve potentially difficult and costly changes in brand image or positioning as much as potentially easier-to-implement changes in brand salience and awareness.

Usage can be increased by either increasing the level or quantity of consumption (i.e., "how much the brand is used") or increasing the frequency of consumption (i.e., "how often the brand is used"). In general, it is probably easier to increase the number of times a consumer uses the product than it is to actually change the amount used at one time. Consumption amount is more likely to be a function of the particular beliefs that the consumer holds as to how the product is best consumed. A possible exception to that rule is for more "impulse" consumption products whose usage increases when the product is made more available, such as soft drinks and snacks.

Wansink defines *usage variant products* as products that have elastic demand functions because they have a high degree of substitutability or because they are able to create their own demand when salient, for example, food and household cleaning products.[23] For these types of products, marketing strategies to increase consumer stockpiling—promotions or changes in packaging—may increase the salience and thus usage of the product. For example, larger package sizes and price discounts, by lowering the perceived unit cost of the product, have been shown to accelerate usage.[24] Another potential way to increase the quantity used is to reduce the undesirable consequences of an increased usage level.[25] For example, a shampoo designed to be gentle enough for daily use may alleviate concerns from those consumers who believe that frequent hair washing is undesirable and therefore eliminate their tendency to conserve the amount of product they use.

Increasing frequency of use, on the other hand, involves either identifying additional or new opportunities to use the brand in the same basic way or identifying completely new and different ways to use the brand. Increasing frequency of use is a particularly attractive option for large market-share brands who are leaders in their product category. We consider both of these approaches to increasing the frequency of product usage in turn.

Identifying New or Additional Usage Opportunities

In some cases, the brand may be seen as useful only in certain places and at certain times, especially if it has strong brand associations to particular usage situations or user types. In general, to identify additional or new opportunities for consumers to use the brand more—albeit in the same basic way—a marketing program should be designed to include both:

1. Communications to consumers as to the appropriateness and advantages of using the brand more frequently in existing situations or in new situations.
2. Reminders to consumers to actually use the brand as close as possible to those situations.

For many brands, increasing usage may be as simple as improving top-of-mind awareness through reminder advertising (e.g., as with V-8 vegetable juice and its famous "Wow! I Could Have Had a V-8" ad campaign). In other cases, more creative types of retrieval cues may be necessary. These reminders may be critical as consumers often adopt "functional fixedness" with a brand such that it can be easily ignored in nontraditional consumption settings.

For example, some brands are seen as only appropriate for special occasions. An effective strategy for those brands may be to redefine what it means for something to be "special." For example, Chivas Regal ran a print ad campaign for its Blended Scotch in 1988 with the theme, "What are you saving the Chivas for?" The ads, showing different people in different scenes, included headlines such as: "Sometimes life begins when the baby sitter arrives"; "Your Scotch and soda is only as good as your Scotch and soda"; and "If you think people might think you order Chivas to show off, maybe you're thinking too much." Similarly, Nabisco's strategy of making Grey Poupon mustard a premium brand—supported by popular TV commercials showing stuffy aristocrats passing the product through the windows of their Rolls-Royces—worked a little too well: Consumers tended to reserve it for special occasions. A new ad campaign encouraging broader usage of the brand suggested "Poupon the Potato Salad" and "Class Up the Cold Cuts."[26] For either of these campaigns to "work," however, it is essential that the brand is able to retain its "premium" brand association, a key source of equity, but also be able to convince consumers to adopt broader usage habits at the same time.

Another potential opportunity to increase frequency of use is when consumers' *perceptions* of their usage differ from the *reality* of their usage. For many products with relatively short life spans, consumers may fail to replace the product in a timely manner because of a tendency to underestimate the length of productive usage.[27] One strategy to speed up product replacement is to tie the act of replacing the product to a certain holiday, event, or time of year. For example, several brands have run promotions tied in with the springtime switch to daylight savings time (e.g., Oral-B toothbrushes). Another strategy might be to provide consumers with better information as to either when the product was first used or would need to be replaced or the current level of product performance. For example, batteries now offer built-in gauges that show how much power they have left.

Finally, perhaps the simplest way to increase usage is when actual usage of a product is less than the optimal or recommended usage. In this case, consumers must be persuaded of the merits of more regular usage, and any potential hurdles to increased usage must be overcome. In terms of the latter, product designs and packaging can make the product more convenient and easier to use.

Identifying New and Completely Different Ways to Use the Brand

The second approach to increase frequency of use for a brand is to identify completely new and different usage applications. For example, food product companies have long advertised new recipes that use their branded products in entirely different ways. After years of sales declines of 3 percent to 4 percent annually, sales of Cheez-Whiz rose 35 percent when the brand was backed by a new ad campaign promoting

The First Thing To Put Under Your Tree Is A Little Clorox® Bleach.

It's an environmentally friendly way to extend the life of your fresh-cut tree.

If you want to help keep your newly-cut tree fresh and green, here's how to give it added life over the holidays.

As soon as you've placed the tree in its stand, fill it with a solution of 2 teaspoons of Clorox Bleach in 1/2 gallon of hot water. (For even better results, add 1 cup corn syrup and 1/8 cup powdered chelated iron, available from your local nursery.) Be sure to refresh it frequently as the solution is absorbed. And avoid spilling, which may discolor floorcoverings.

You can also keep holiday floral arrangements looking fresh simply by adding 1/4 teaspoon (20 drops) of Clorox Bleach to each quart of water used in your vase.

With all that holiday cooking, your disposal is working overtime. Sometimes those odors linger longer than holiday memories.

Pouring Clorox Bleach down your sink is an easy way to get rid of odors in the disposal. As the diagram shows, it's also an environmentally friendly way, because Clorox Bleach breaks down to little more than salt and water after use.

It's nice to know that a little Clorox Bleach can add life to a cut tree, freshen a drain and be kind to the environment as well.

The Simple Solution For A Healthy Home.

FIGURE 13–5 Sample Clorox Ad

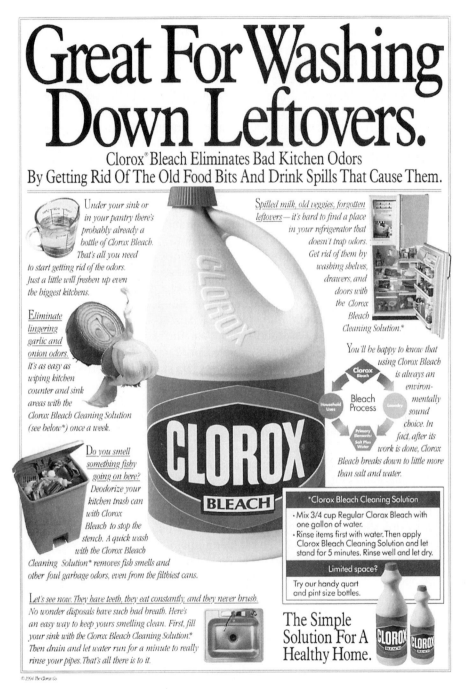

FIGURE 13–5 Sample Clorox Ad (*continued*)

the product as a cheese sauce accompaniment to be used in the microwave oven.[28] Perhaps the classic example of finding creative new usage applications for a product is Arm & Hammer baking soda, whose deodorizing and cleaning properties have led to a number of new uses for the brand.

Other brands have taken a page from Arm & Hammer's book: Clorox has run ads stressing the many benefits of its bleach, for example, how it eliminates kitchen odors (see Figure 13–5); Wrigley's chewing gum has run ads touting their product as a substitute for smoking (see Figure 13–6); and Tums has run ads for its antacid promoting its benefits as a calcium substitute (see Figure 13–7). New usage applications may require more than just new ad campaigns. Often, new uses can arise from new packaging. For example, Arm & Hammer introduced a "Fridge-Freezer Pack" (with freshflo vents) for their natural baking soda that was especially designed to better freshen and deodorize refrigerators and freezers. Maxwell House Filter Pack Singles and Folgers Coffee Singles were both an attempt to accommodate consumers' desires to drink ground roast coffee without brewing an entire pot.

Wansink describes a number of different ways to identify and communicate new usage situations.[29] An obvious starting point for generating potential expansion opportunities is with brainstorming meetings or focus groups involving loyal or heavy users and less loyal or light users. Contrasting the preferences and behaviors of the two groups can yield insights into potential barriers in perceptions and usage that must be overcome, as well as opportunities for further growth. Additionally, he also notes how perceptions of potentially related products and situations could be uncovered through cluster analysis or other multivariate statistical approaches.

Wansink further argues that successful media strategies for expansion ad campaigns are often based on clever targeting and timing. He notes how small share brands can more affordably target users of their brands by advertising new uses on their packages and labels. For example, Trix cereal used a side panel to note complementary products (e.g., ice cream, yogurt, and trail mix) on which Trix could be sprinkled. Murphy's Oil Soap printed a series of different usage ideas under peel-off stickers that had been affixed to its spray bottles. Similarly, Roy Rogers restaurants used its paper placemats to advertise eight situations, such as parties, picnics, and meetings, where customers could eat their carry-out chicken. In terms of timing, Wansink notes that advertising exposure ideally would coincide with situations when brand choice and usage has the highest likelihood of being made. For example, Campbell schedules radio ads for its soups to be broadcast just prior to lunch and dinner to be top-of-mind at the most opportune moment.

IMPROVING BRAND IMAGE

Although changes in brand awareness are probably the easiest means of creating new sources of brand equity, more fundamental changes are often necessary. A new marketing program may be necessary to improve the strength, favorability, and uniqueness of brand associations making up the brand image. As part of this repositioning— or recommitment to the existing positioning—any positive associations that have faded may need to be bolstered, any negative associations that have been created may have to be neutralized, and additional positive associations may have to be created.

FIGURE 13–6 Sample Wrigley's Ad

Two Tums a day can help prevent osteoporosis.

Because Tums* is jam-packed with calcium. And calcium is one of the very best lifelong defenses against the pain and brittle bones and stooped back that can come from osteoporosis.

It doesn't only happen to "somebody else."

It's tragic that 20 million American women suffer from a disease that *can be prevented*! We urge you to ask your doctor about osteoporosis and risk factors such as age, race and family history. He may recommend exercise or other therapy. But key in preventing osteoporosis is getting enough calcium from your diet – from adolescence right through menopause. The chart shows most of us don't come close!

A superior kind of calcium.

The best source of extra calcium is Tums; Tums calcium is *calcium carbonate*, which is highly concentrated and as easily absorbed as milk*. And Tums costs less than other supplements. For the same amount of calcium, Caltrate*† or Os-cal*† charge almost twice as much.

Two Tums a day every day.

Since each Tums contains 200 milligrams of calcium, two tablets every day will close a 400-milligram gap. They come in six refreshing flavors and they're chewable. You can take them anywhere!

*American Journal of Clinical Nutrition, 1988.   †Registered trademarks of other companies. ©1992 SmithKline Beecham.

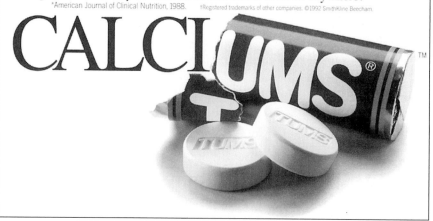

FIGURE 13-7 Sample Tums Ad

Repositioning the Brand

In some cases, repositioning the brand requires establishing more compelling points of difference. This may just require reminding consumers of the virtues of a brand that they have begun to "take for granted." Recall how the new Coke debacle described in chapter 2, in a round-about way, accomplished just that. Along these lines, Kellogg's Corn Flakes ran a successful ad campaign with the slogan, "Try Them Again For the First Time." Wonder Bread is similarly trying to "walk consumers down memory lane" in new ads. In some of these cases, a key point of difference may turn out to be nostalgia and heritage as much as any product-related difference.

Other times, a brand needs to be repositioned to establish a point of parity on some key image dimensions. A common problem for established, mature brands is that they must be made more contemporary by creating relevant usage situations, a more contemporary user profile, or a more modern brand personality. Heritage brands that have been around for years may be seen as trustworthy but also boring, uninteresting, and not that likable. Updating a brand may involve some combination of new products, new advertising, new promotions, or new packaging. For example, the 165-year old regional beer, Yuengling, saw its sales virtually double by introducing lighter and fuller-flavored versions; new labels that gave the beer an arty, nostalgic look; and new promotions that tapped into regional pride by focusing on the brewery's place in Pennsylvania history. The new image permitted higher prices and allowed the brand to gain more high-end, on-premise accounts.[30]

Sometimes negative product-related associations emerge because of changes in consumer tastes. For example, Del Monte, makers of canned fruits and vegetables, found that its sales steadily declined after a peak in 1969. Even worse, its loyal buyers were aging—the typical buyer was a female over the age of 55—and not being replaced by younger ones. The problem was that younger consumers saw Del Monte products as being old-fashioned, inconvenient, and laden with additives and preservatives. In 1994, the company launched its first ad campaign in ten years to dispel negative associations that had been created. Attempting to make canned foods more relevant and contemporary, the campaign targeted "emerging families"—those consumers beginning a career, starting a household, getting married, and having children—who would presumably be more likely to reevaluate their eating habits.[31]

Changing Brand Elements

Often one or more brand elements must be changed to either convey new information or to signal that the brand has taken on new meaning because the product or some other aspect of the marketing program has changed. Although the brand name is typically the most important brand element, it is often the most difficult to change. Nevertheless, names can be dropped or combined into initials to reflect shifts in marketing strategy or to ease pronounceability and recall. Shortened names or initials also can disguise potentially negative product associations. For example, in an attempt to convey a healthier image, Kentucky Fried Chicken's name was abbreviated to the initials KFC. KFC also introduced a new logo incorporating the visual character symbol of Colonel Sanders as a means to maintain tradition but also modernize its appeal. Brand names may be changed for other reasons. Federal Express chose to officially shorten its name to FedEx and introduce a new logo in response to what consumers actually were calling the brand (see Figure 13–8). Company officials also thought that

FIGURE 13-8 Sample Federal Express Ad

the name sounded more technological and innovative and would be easier to pronounce and recall in other countries.[32]

Other brand elements are easier to change and may need to be, especially if they play an important awareness or image function. Chapter 4 described how packaging, logos, and characters can be modified and updated over time. An important point noted there is that changes generally should be moderate and evolutionary in nature, and great care should be taken to preserve the most salient aspects of the brand elements. For example, when General Electric decided it wanted to communicate a fresh, "hi-tech" look to the public—but not lose the valuable equity it had accrued in their name at the same time—it chose to rename the company as GE with virtually no loss in equity. Later in the chapter, we consider in more detail issues concerning changing corporate names and other brand elements.

ENTERING NEW MARKETS

Positioning decisions require a specification of the target market and nature of competition to set the competitive frame of reference. The target markets for a brand typically do not constitute all possible segments that potentially make up the entire market. In some cases, the firm may have other brands that target these remaining market segments. In other cases, however, these market segments represent potential growth targets for the brand. Effectively targeting these other segments, however, typically requires some changes or variations in the marketing program—especially in advertising and other communications—and the decision as to whether to target these segments ultimately depends on a cost-benefit analysis. Chapter 3 introduced some basic segmentation issues, and chapter 14 considers some specific segmentation issues in the context of global brands as well as geographical and other factors. Here we highlight a few key segmentation issues as they relate to brand revitalization.

To grow the brand franchise, many firms have reached out to new customer groups to build brand equity. One classic example of this approach was with Procter & Gamble's Ivory soap who revived its brand franchise by promoting Ivory as a pure and simple product for adults instead of just for babies. Johnson & Johnson baby shampoo achieved success by virtue of a similar strategy, promoting the gentleness and everyday applicability of its shampoo to an adult audience. After a century of fighting tooth-and-nail with arch rival Arrow, Van Heusen finally was able to take over the top spot in the dress shirt market in 1991. By devoting half of its $8 million budget to advertise directly to women in women's magazines, Van Heusen was able to influence key decision makers in the men's dress shirt purchase—women buy an estimated 60 percent to 70 percent of men's shirts! After seeing the success of this strategy, Arrow—which had earlier survived a difficult transformation to selling bolder colors and busier patterns at higher prices—also began a more aggressive advertising campaign to brand its shirts, especially with women.[33]

Segmenting on the basis of demographic variables or other means and identifying neglected segments is thus one viable brand revitalization option. For example, Royal Crown Cola finds itself in a difficult situation competing with soft drink giants, Coke and Pepsi. Knowing that a frontal assault was financially impossible, it sought to identify a weak spot in the strong brand images of their competitors. It decided that the sheer size of Coke and Pepsi meant that certain audiences were likely to feel overlooked or ignored. Royal Crown chose to target 18- to 29-year-olds, who they felt were an important, less brand loyal segment. New ads encouraged these consumers to "Shake Things Up."[34]

In some cases, just retaining existing customers who would eventually move away from the brand or recapturing lost customers who no longer use the brand can be a means to increase sales. Brands like Kellogg's Frosted Flakes cereal, Oreo cookies, and Keds tennis shoes have run ad campaigns targeting adults who presumably quit using the product long ago. Some of these ads use themes and appeals to nostalgia or heritage. Others attempt to make the case that the product's enduring appeal is still relevant for users today. The importance of retaining current customers can be recognized by calculating the lifetime value of customers. One study noted that a purchaser of automobiles will spend more than $500,000 on cars during his or her lifetime but that it costs five times as much to sell an automobile to a new customer as it does to sell to a satisfied existing customer.[35]

Attracting a new market segment can be deceptively difficult. Nike, Gillette, and other marketers have struggled for years to find the right blend of products and advertising to make their brands—which have more masculine-oriented images—appear relevant and appealing to women. Creating marketing programs to appeal to women has become a priority of makers of products from cars to computers. Marketers have also introduced targeted new marketing programs to different racial groups (e.g., African Americans, Asian Americans, and Hispanic Americans), age groups, and income groups. Attracting emerging new market segments based on more cultural dimensions may require different messages, creative strategies, and media.[36]

Of course, one strategic option to revitalize a fading brand is just to more or less abandon the consumer group that supported the brand in the past to target a completely new market segment. Gillette decided Dippity-Do hair gel carried too much negative baggage to appeal to those women who used it in the 1960s but who now associated it with out-of-fashion bouffant hairdos and flips. Rather than targeting middle-aged consumers, Gillette chose to start with a clean slate by targeting a new generation of younger consumers and repositioning the brand as a fun, hip product through advertising in teen magazines.[37] Similarly, the hair conditioner, Brylcreem, which gave teenagers the slicked-back look in the 1950s, saw its sales go limp in the 1960s when the Beatles popularized a "mop-top" look and bangs. To revive the brand, product packaging has since been modernized and a clear Brylcreem Power Gel introduced to appeal to a younger audience.[38]

Adjustments to the Brand Portfolio

Managing brand equity and the brand portfolio requires taking a long-term view of the brand. As part of this long-term perspective, it is necessary that the role of different brands and the relationships among different brands in the portfolio be carefully considered over time. In particular, a brand migration strategy needs to be designed and implemented so that consumers understand how various brands in the portfolio can satisfy their needs as they potentially change over time or as the products and brands themselves change over time. Managing brand transitions is especially important in rapidly changing, technologically intensive markets.

MIGRATION STRATEGIES

As noted in chapter 11, brands can play special roles that facilitate the migration of customers within the brand portfolio. For example, entry-level brands are often critical in bringing in new customers and introducing them to the brand offerings. Ideally, brands would be organized in consumers' minds so that they at least implicitly knew how they could switch among brands within the portfolio as their needs or desires changed. For example, a corporate or family branding strategy where brands are ordered in a logical manner could provide the hierarchical structure in consumers' minds to facilitate brand migration. Car companies are quite sensitive to this issue, and brands like BMW with its 3-, 5-, and 7-series numbering systems to denote increasingly higher levels of quality are good examples of such a strategy. Chrysler recently designated Plymouth as its "starter" car line such that Plymouth owners would then be expected to trade up in later years to higher-priced Chrysler models.

ACQUIRING NEW CUSTOMERS

All firms face tradeoffs in their marketing efforts to attract new customers versus retaining existing ones. In mature markets, trial is generally less important than building loyalty and retaining existing customers. Nevertheless, some customers inevitably—even if only by natural causes—leave the brand franchise. Consequently, it is imperative that the firm proactively develop strategies to attract new customers, especially younger ones. The marketing challenge in acquiring new customers, however, lies in making a brand seem relevant to customers from potentially vastly different generations and cohort groups or lifestyles (see Figure 13–9).[39] This challenge is exacerbated when the brand has strong personality or user image associations that tie the brand to one particular consumer group.

Unfortunately, even as younger consumers age, there is no guarantee they will have the same attitudes and behaviors of older consumers who preceded them. In 1996, the first wave of post-World War II baby boomers celebrated their fiftieth birthdays and officially entered the "senior market." Many experts forecast that this group will demand that companies embrace their own unique values in marketing their products and services. As one demographic expert says, "Nothing could be further from the truth than saying boomers will be like their parents." Because there can be no expectations that younger consumers will necessarily view brands and products in the same way as older consumers who preceded them, proactive strategies must be put in place to both acquire new customers and retain existing ones.

The response to the challenge of marketing across generations and cohort groups has taken all forms. Some marketers have attempted to cut loose from the past. For example, Procter & Gamble's Old Spice has had to wrestle with the problem of being seen as "your father's aftershave" by young male consumers. As one P&G marketing executive notes, "We recognize the need to change and bring in a new generation of young users. At the same time, we don't want to alienate the users we already have." To revitalize the brand, a new campaign backed by heavy spending was

The G.I. Generation

Born: 1912–21
Age in 1995: 74–83
% of Adult Population: 7% (13 million)
Money Motto: Save for a Rainy Day
Sex Mindset: Intolerant
Favorite Music: Big Band

The Depression Cohort

People who were starting out in the Depression era were scarred in ways that remain with them today—especially when it comes to financial matters like spending, saving, and debt. The Depression cohort was also the first to be truly influenced by contemporary media: radio and especially motion pictures.

The Depression Generation

Born: 1922–27
Age in 1995: 68–73
% of Adult Population: 6% (11 million)
Money Motto: Save a lot, spend a little
Sex Mindset: Ambivalent
Favorite Music: Swing

The World War II Cohort

People who came of age in the forties were unified by the shared experience of a common enemy and a common goal. Consequently, this group became intensely romantic. A sense of self-denial that long outlived the war is especially strong among the 16 million veterans and their families.

The Silent Generation

Born: 1928–45
Age in 1995: 50–67
% of Adult Population: 21% (41 million)
Money Motto: Save some, spend some
Sex Mindset: Repressive
Favorite Music: Frank Sinatra

The Postwar Cohort

Members of this 18-year cohort, the war babies, benefited from a long period of economic growth and relative social tranquillity. But global unrest and the threat of nuclear attack sparked a need to alleviate uncertainty in everyday life. The youngest subset, called the cool generation, were the first to dig folk rock.

The Woodstock Generation

Born: 1946–54
Age in 1995: 41–49
% of Adult Population: 17% (33 million)
Money Motto: Spend, borrow, spend
Sex Mindset: Permissive
Favorite Music: Rock & roll

The Boomers I Cohort

Vietnam is the demarcation point between leading-edge and trailing-edge boomers. The Kennedy and King assassinations signaled an end to the status quo and galvanized this vast cohort. Still, early boomers continued to experience economic good times and want a lifestyle at least as good as their predecessors'.

FIGURE 13-9 Profiling Consumer Generations and Cohorts

Zoomers

Born: 1955–65
Age in 1995: 30–40
% of Adult Population: 25% (49 million)
Money Motto: Spend, borrow, spend
Sex Mindset: Permissive
Favorite Music: Rock & roll

Baby-Busters

Born: 1966–76
Age in 1995: 19–29
% of Adult Population: 21% (41 million)
Money Motto: Spend? Save? What?
Sex Mindset: Confused
Favorite Music: Grunge, rap, retro

The Boomers II Cohort

It all changed after Watergate. The idealistic fervor of youth disappeared. Instead, the later boomers exhibited a narcissistic preoccupation that manifested itself in things like the self-help movement. In this dawning age of downward mobility, debt as a means of maintaining a lifestyle made sense.

The Generation X Cohort

The slacker set has nothing to hang onto. The latchkey kids of divorce and day care are searching for anchors with their seemingly contradictory "retro" behavior: the resurgence of proms, coming-out parties, and fraternities. This political conservatism is motivated by a "What's in it for me?" cynicism.

FIGURE 13-9 Profiling Consumer Generations and Cohorts (*continued*)

launched in 1993. The new TV ads eliminated the trademark "whistling sailor" character to show—via rapid-fire editing—active, contemporary men. Old Spice also became a sponsor for several AVP volleyball tournaments. On the product side, P&G put heavy support behind its fast-selling and more youthfully positioned Old Spice High Endurance deodorant.[40]

Perhaps the brand that attempted the cleanest break from its past in recent years was Oldsmobile with its lavish, $100 million-plus ad campaign in 1988. With the theme, "This is Not Your Father's Oldsmobile," each ad featured an icon from the 1960s—such as Star Trek's William Shatner, TV game-show host Monty Hall, the Beatle's Ringo Starr, astronaut Scott Carpenter, and actress Priscilla Presley—paired with one of their children. The ads showed the celebrity parent being driven away in an Oldsmobile by his or her child. With the average age of an Oldsmobile buyer at 51 years old, the purpose of the ads was to redefine user and usage imagery and make the brand relevant for a new market. Although the ads were among the best-remembered of the year—especially among the target consumers aged 35–44—sales continued to slide even after the campaign was introduced. Ultimately, it was withdrawn from the air. Critics faulted the campaign for drawing attention to the dowdiness of the brand's image. Others defended the campaign by noting that: (1) auto sales were generally soft during that period; (2) Oldsmobile's models were relatively high priced for younger buyers; and, most importantly, (3) Oldsmobile's models really hadn't changed all that much anyway. Subsequent efforts to revive the brand similarly stuttered, and Oldsmobile sales have shrunk from 1.1 million cars and trucks in 1986 to under 400,000 in 1995. The company announced plans in 1996 to cut the number of dealers selling Oldsmobiles in half.

General Motors has experienced similar problems with its Buick and Cadillac divisions. For example, Cadillac sales, which reached a peak of over 350,000 cars in 1978, dipped to roughly 175,000 in 1995. The average age of Cadillac buyers at that time was 65 years old but the average age of the entry-level luxury car owner was about 44 years old. This younger market segment did not view Cadillac as a symbol of American affluence and success as much as their parents did. To attract younger consumers, Cadillac introduced the entry-level Catera, a clone of the Opel Omega MV6 sold by GM in Europe, advertised as "the caddy that zigs." Cadillac also targeted younger consumers with its older Seville models. To retain existing older customers, however, Cadillac only did a modest makeover of its Sedan de Ville models—redesigned primarily to satisfy its most loyal customers—and retained the expansive Fleetwood models. Similar demographic problems plague the Buick line, too, causing one dealer to complain, "Our customers are going out the back door and nobody's coming in the front door."[41]

Other brands have attempted to develop more inclusive marketing strategies to include both new and old customers. Some alternative approaches that attempt to broaden the marketing program and attract new customers as well as retain existing ones are as follows.

Multiple Marketing Communication Programs

One approach to attract a new market segment for a brand and satisfy current segments is to create separate advertising campaigns and communication programs for each segment. For example, Dewars launched the "Authentic" and "Profiles" campaigns—each directed to a different market segment. The "Authentic" campaign focused on the brand heritage in terms of its product quality and Scottish roots and was focused on an older segment, including existing customers. The "Profiles" campaign took a completely different tack, literally profiling younger users of the brand to make the brand seem relevant and attractive to a younger audience. Different media buys then attempted to ensure that the appropriate campaign was seen by the relevant market segment.

Similar approaches have been adopted by beer companies. For example, at one time Anheuser-Busch ran a mass market ad campaign to build on-premise consumption of its Bud Lite light beer ("Don't Just Ask for a Light . . .") while at the same time employing the laconic dog, Spuds Mackenzie, and his attractive female background singers, the Spudettes, in ads targeted to young adults. Similarly, Anheuser-Busch recently ran ads for its flagship brand of beer, Budweiser, showing youthful, 20-something-year-olds relaxing and enjoying the beer in pool halls and other places while at the same time a mass market ad campaign was run with the more traditional theme, "Proud to Be Your Bud." The increased effectiveness of targeted media makes multiple targets more and more feasible. The obvious drawback to this approach is the expense involved and the potential blurring of images if there is too much media overlap among target groups and if the respective ad positionings are seen as incompatible.

Brand Extensions and Sub-Brands

Another approach to attract new customers to a brand and keep the brand modern and up-to-date is to introduce a line extension or establish a new sub-brand. These new product offerings for the brand can incorporate new technology or features to satisfy the needs of new customers as well as satisfy the changing desires of existing customers. For example, Haagen-Dazs successfully introduced its ingredient-laden Extraas sub-brand, with flavors like Cappucino Commotion and Carrot Cake Passion, to give its brand a more youthful appeal and to better compete with Ben & Jerry's, whose products had a stronger draw with younger consumers.[42] Similarly, Aqua Velva introduced its Ice Sport aftershave sub-brand to appeal to a younger audience.

New Distribution Outlets

In some cases, attracting a new market segment may be as simple as making the product more available to that group. For example, the sunglasses industry, which grew sales from $100 million in 1972 to $2.5 billion fifteen years later, benefited from social and fashion trends but also a shift in distribution strategies. Sunglasses used to be sold mostly by opticians; however, in the 1970s, Sunglass Hut and other companies moved into malls, sporting-goods stores, and campuses, building strong loyalty with teenagers and college students in the process.

RETIRING BRANDS

Because of dramatic or adverse changes in the marketing environment some brands are just not worth saving. Their sources of brand equity may have essentially dried up, or, even worse, damaging and difficult-to-change new associations may have been created. At some point, the size of the brand franchise—no matter how loyal—fails to justify the support of the brand. In the face of such adversity, decisive management actions are necessary to properly retire or "milk" the brand.

Several options are possible to deal with a fading brand. A first step in retrenching a fading brand is to reduce the number of its product types (e.g., package sizes or variations). Such actions reduce the cost of supporting the brand support and allow the brand to put its "best foot forward." Under these reduced levels of support, a brand may more easily hit profit targets. Relatedly, if a sufficiently large and loyal enough customer base exists, marketing support can be virtually eliminated all together as a means to milk or harvest brand profits from these "cash cows." For example, as noted in chapter 11, Unilever's Lux Beauty Bars, despite not having received any advertising support for fifteen years, still retains almost 3 percent market share from sales to consumers who became loyal to the brand in years past. As a result, Lux contributes over $10 million in gross profits to Unilever.[43]

In some cases, on the other hand, the brand is beyond repair and more drastic measures have to be taken. One possible option for fading brands is to consolidate them into a stronger brand. For example, Procter & Gamble merged White Cloud and Charmin toilet paper, eliminating the White Cloud line in 1992. P&G also merged Solo and Bold detergents. With shelf space at a premium, brand consolidation will increasingly be seen as a necessary option to create a stronger brand, cut costs, and focus marketing efforts.[44] Finally, a more permanent solution may be to discontinue the product all together. The marketplace is littered with brands that either failed to establish an adequate level of brand equity or found that its sources of brand equity disappeared because of changes in the marketing environment.

Obsoleting Existing Products

How do you decide which brands to attempt to revitalize or at least milk and which ones to obsolete? Beecham chose to abandon such dying brands as 5-Day deodorant pads, Rose Milk skin care lotion, and Serutan laxative, but attempted to resurrect Aqua-Velva aftershave, Geritol iron and vitamin supplement, and Brylcreem hair styling products. The decision to retire a brand depends on a number of factors. Aaker outlines a number of strategic questions that can be raised as to whether to invest in fading brand (see Figure 13–10).[45]

Fundamentally, the issue is the existing and latent equity of the brand. As the head of consumer package goods giant Unilever commented in explaining his company's decision to review about 20 percent of its brands and lines of businesses for possible sell-offs: "If businesses aren't creating value, we shouldn't be in them. It's like having a nice garden which gets weeds. You have to clean it up, so the light and air get in to the blooms which are likely to grow the best."[46]

FIGURE 13–10 Investment Decisions in a Declining Industry

MARKET PROSPECTS

1. Is the rate of decline orderly and predictable?
2. Are there pockets of enduring demand?
3. What are the reasons for the decline—is it temporary? Might it be reversed?

COMPETITIVE INTENSITY

4. Are there dominant competitors with unique skills or assets?
5. Are there many competitors unwilling to exit or contract gracefully?
6. Are customers brand-loyal? Is there product differentiation?
7. Are there price pressures?

BRAND STRENGTH AND ORGANIZATIONAL CAPABILITIES

8. Is the brand strong? Does it enjoy high recognition and positive, meaningful associations?
9. What is the market share position and trend?
10. Does the business have some key sustainable competitive advantages with respect to key segments?
11. Can the business manage a milking strategy?
12. Is there synergy with other businesses?
13. Does the brand fit with current firm's strategic thrust?
14. What are the exit barriers?

Special Topics

In this section, we address two key issues to managing brands over time—implementing corporate name changes and managing a brand crisis.

CORPORATE NAME CHANGES

Reasons Why

As chapter 11 noted, corporate brand names and corporate images can perform a variety of functions to multiple audiences or target markets. Consequently, corporate names may have to be changed for a number of different reasons. More than 1100 private and public U.S. companies changed their names in 1994, according to a leading corporate-identity consulting firm.[47] The main reason that corporations change their names is as a result of mergers and acquisitions with other businesses. In such cases, a completely new name may be chosen to signal new capabilities. For example, when Sperry and Burroughs merged, they became Unisys (a Latin cognate that was designed to suggest information systems). In other cases, a new corporate name arising from a merger or acquisition may just be based on some combination of the two existing corporate names. For example, when Glaxo and Burroughs Wellcome merged they became Glaxo Wellcome, Lockheed and Martin Marrietta became Lockheed Martin, and so on.

Relatedly, another reason corporate names may need to be changed is because of divestitures, leveraged buyouts, or sale of assets. For example, when the 155-year old farm equipment and truck maker, International Harvester Co., sold its agricultural equipment operations along with its name and the IH logo in 1984, it legally was required to change its name within five years. After much research, the new name Navistar was chosen, with "Navi" coming from the Latin word for leading or navigating and "star" signifying a heavenly body or outstanding performer. Although some critics faulted the name for sounding more like a company with interests in marine equipment or space flight than trucks, Navistar marketing executives note that the name was deliberately chosen to be flexible and permit room for growth in the future.[48]

Another reason the corporate name may need to be changed is because of public misperceptions about the nature of the company's business. For example, Europe's third-biggest food company, BSN, renamed its company after its Danone brand—a hugely successful fresh dairy products subsidiary (second only to Coca-Cola in terms of branded sales in Europe)—because many consumers didn't know what the old name stood for. Moreover, BSN was already used by other companies in other countries—a bank in Spain, a textile firm in the United States, and a television station in Japan.[49]

Finally, significant shifts in corporate strategy may necessitate name changes. For example, US Steel changed its name to USX to downplay the importance of steel and metal in their product mix. Allegheny Airlines changed its name to USAir when it moved from a regional to a national carrier, and later to US Airways when it wanted a more global presence.

Guidelines

In changing the corporate name, the assumption is that the existing brand associations do not have the desired strength, favorability, and uniqueness and that a new name can be chosen—perhaps in combination with a corporate image campaign—that better conveys the desired brand image. Name changes are typically complicated, time-consuming, and expensive, however, and only should be undertaken when compelling marketing or financial considerations prevail and a proper supporting marketing program can also be put into place. A new corporate name cannot hide product or other marketing deficiencies. A company with little consumer exposure may spend as much as $5 million on research, advertising, and other marketing costs (e.g., new signs, stationery, business cards, and so on) to change its identity, but a company with a high public profile may have to spend up to $100 million.[50]

Many of the same issues in choosing brand names discussed in chapter 4 are relevant in choosing or changing a corporate name. Thus, candidate names should be evaluated in terms of memorability, meaningfulness, protectability, adaptability, and transferability. The importance of the corporate name will depend on the corporate branding strategy that is adopted and the marketing objectives with respect to different target markets. If the financial community is a priority, a different name may be chosen than if the consumer market is the priority. For example, if the financial community is a priority, corporate names may be changed to highlight a particular brand or company (e.g., Consolidated Foods Corporation switched to Sara Lee Corporation; Castle & Cooke, Inc. switched to Dole Food Company; and United Brands Company switched to Chiquita Brands International). If the consumer market is the primary objective, then names may be chosen to reflect or be suggestive of certain product characteristics, benefits, or values.

One of the biggest name change fizzles ever occurred with UAL, the parent company of United Airlines. In 1987, UAL was no longer just an airline but a $9 billion business that owned Hertz car rental, as well as Westin and Hilton International hotels. It was decided that a new name was necessary to convey the identity of a travel company that offered one-stop shopping. After extensive research, the name "Allegis" was chosen, a compound of "allegiance" and "aegis." Public reaction was decidedly negative. Critics maintained that the name was difficult to pronounce, pretentious-sounding, and had little connection with travel services. Real estate developer Donald Trump, formerly a major UAL shareholder, said the new name was "better suited to the next world class disease." After six weeks and $7 million in research and promotion expenditures, the company decided to shed its car rental and hotel businesses and rename the surviving company as United Airlines Inc.[51]

Many name changes seem to follow trends—one corporate identity specialist notes that although businesses took on exotic-sounding animal-like names in the 1950s and 1960s, high-tech sounding names became popular in the 1970s and 1980s.[52] "Star" became a commonly used prefix, and names with "X" also became popular as a means to signal excellence. A new corporate brand name and other supporting brand elements, however, should be chosen systematically in the same careful way that any brand name is chosen. Moreover, once a new name is chosen, substantial efforts must be undertaken to "sell" the new name to employees, customers, suppliers, investors, and the public at large.[53] Because of a resistance to change, initial reaction to a new name is almost always negative. For example, when New York Telephone and New

England Telephone changed its name to NYNEX, critics attacked the name as sounding too much like medicine or Ex-Lax (a well-known laxative).[54] Over time though, if properly chosen and handled, new names gain familiarity and acceptance. Effective implementation requires guidelines that encourage uniformity and consistency in appearance and usage of the brand, and these rules should be included as part of a revised Brand Charter (see chapter 10).

MANAGING A BRAND CRISIS

Although Exxon spent millions of dollars advertising its gasoline and crafting its brand image over the years, it had essentially ignored marketing its corporate identity and image. This decision came back to haunt the company in the weeks following March 24, 1989. That morning, the Exxon Valdez tanker hit a reef in Prince William Sound, Alaska, resulting in some 11,000,000 gallons of oil spilling into the waters of the Alaska shore. The oil spill wreaked devastation on the fish and wildlife of some 1300 square miles of the previously unspoiled Sound. Top Exxon officials declined to comment publicly for almost a week after the incident, and the public statements that were eventually made sometimes appeared to contradict information from other sources involved in the situation (e.g., the severity of the spill) or assigned blame for the slow cleanup efforts to other parties (e.g., the U.S. Coast Guard). Exxon received withering negative press and was the source of countless jokes on late night talk shows. In frustration and anger, some of Exxon's consumers began literally to tear up their Exxon credit cards. On April 3, ten days after the accident, Exxon's chairman ran an open letter to the public in the form of a full-page message expressing Exxon's concern and justifying its actions to address the situation.[55]

Marketing managers must assume that at some point in time, some kind of brand crisis will arise. Diverse brands such as Jack in the Box restaurants, Firestone tires, E.F. Hutton brokerage firms, USAir airlines, and Suzuki Samurai sport-utility vehicles have all experienced a serious, potentially crippling brand crisis. In general, the more that brand equity and a strong corporate image has been established—especially with respect to corporate credibility and trustworthiness—the more likely it is that the firm can weather the storm. Careful preparation and a well-managed crisis management program, however, is also critical. Most experts would agree that the Exxon incident is a good example of how *not* to handle a brand crisis. Chapter 2 described Johnson & Johnson's nearly flawless handling of the Tylenol product tampering incident. As noted there, the two keys to effectively managing a crisis is that the response by the firm is seen by consumers as both swift *and* sincere, as follows.

First, in terms of swiftness, the longer it takes a firm to respond to a marketing crisis, the more likely it is that consumers can form negative impressions as a result of unfavorable media coverage or word-of-mouth. Perhaps even worse, consumers may find out that they do not really like the brand that much after all and permanently switch to alternative brands or products. For example, Perrier was forced to halt production worldwide and recall all of its existing bottles in February 1994 when traces of benzene, a known carcinogen, was found in excessive quantities in the bottled water. Over the course of the next few weeks, several explanations were offered as to how the contamination occurred, creating confusion and skepticism. Perhaps even more damaging, the product itself was off the shelves until May 1994. Despite an expensive relaunch featuring ads and promotions, the brand struggled to regain lost market share, and a full year later found its sales less than half of what they once had been. Part of the problem was that during the time the product was unavailable, consumers and retailers found satisfactory substitutes (e.g., waters such as Saratoga, San Pellegrino, and so on). With its key "purity" association tarnished—the brand had been advertised as the "Earth's First Soft Drink" and "It's Perfect. It's Perrier."—the brand had no other compelling points of difference over these competitors.[56] Finally, compounding the problems arising from its marketing crisis, the brand was gaining an increasingly stodgy image and was seen as much more appealing to the over-45 consumer market and much less appealing to those consumers under 25 years old. Eventually, the company was taken over by Nestle SA.

Second, swift actions must also come across as sincere to consumers. The more sincere the response by the firm—in terms of public acknowledgment of the severity of the impact on consumers and a willingness of the firm to take whatever steps are necessary and feasible to solve the crisis—the less likely it is that consumers will form negative attributions to the firm's behavior. For example, although Gerber had established a strong image of trust with consumers, baby food is a product category characterized by an extremely high level of involvement and need for reassurance. When consumers reported finding shards of glass in some jars of its baby food, although Gerber tried to reassure the public that there were no problems in its manufacturing plants, it adamantly refused to have its baby food withdrawn from grocery-food stores. Some consumers clearly found Gerber's response unsatisfactory as their market share slumped from 66 percent to 52 percent within a couple of months. As one company official admits, "Not pulling our baby food off the shelf gave the appearance that we aren't a caring company."[57]

Brand crises are so difficult to manage because, despite its best efforts, it is difficult for the firm to be in control of the situation. To some extent, the firm is at the mercy of public sentiment and media coverage, which it can attempt to direct and influence, but which sometimes can take on a "life of its own." Swift and sincere words and actions, however, often can go a long way towards defusing the situation. As one commentator notes:[58]

> No one strategy works in every crisis. There are too many variables—the news play, the marketplace, public sympathy or antipathy, whether the company cleans house as well as its image. . . . Reality still counts. But simple honesty—"We've got a problem and we're doing X, Y, and Z about it"—is inevitably the last resort.

Review

Effective brand management requires taking a long-term view of marketing decisions. A long-term perspective of brand management recognizes that any changes in the supporting marketing program for a brand may, by changing consumer knowledge, affect the success of future marketing programs. Additionally, a long-term view necessitates proactive strategies designed to maintain and enhance customer based brand equity over time in the face of external changes in the marketing environment and internal changes in a firm's marketing goals and programs. In this chapter, we considered how to reinforce, revitalize, and retire brands and examined a number of specific topics in managing brands over time.

REINFORCING BRANDS

Brand equity is reinforced by marketing actions that consistently convey the meaning of the brand to consumers in terms of: (1) what products the brand represents, what core benefits it supplies, and what needs it satisfies, and (2) how the brand makes those products superior and which strong, favorable, and unique brand associations should exist in the minds of consumers. The most important consideration in reinforcing brands is the consistency of the marketing support that the brand receives, both in terms of the amount and nature of that support. Consistency does not mean that marketers should avoid making any changes in the marketing program and, in fact, many tactical changes may be necessary to maintain the strategic thrust and direction of the brand. Unless there is some change in the marketing environment, however, there is little need to deviate from a successful positioning. In such cases, the critical points of parity and points of difference that represent sources of brand equity should be vigorously preserved and defended.

Reinforcing brand meaning depends on the nature of the brand association involved. For brands whose core associations are primarily product-related attributes and/or functional benefits, innovation in product design, manufacturing, and merchandising is especially critical to maintaining or enhancing brand equity. For brands whose core associations are primarily non-product-related attributes and symbolic or experiential benefits, relevance in user and usage imagery is especially critical to maintaining or enhancing brand equity. In managing brand equity, it is important to recognize the tradeoffs that exist between those marketing activities that fortify the brand and reinforce its meaning and those that attempt to leverage or borrow from its existing brand equity to reap some financial benefit. At some point, failure to fortify the brand will diminish brand awareness and weaken brand image. Without these sources of brand equity, the brand itself may not continue to yield as valuable benefits.

REVITALIZING BRANDS

Revitalizing a brand requires either that lost sources of brand equity are recaptured or that new sources of brand equity are identified and established. According to the customer-based brand equity framework, two general approaches are possible: (1) expand the depth and/or breadth of brand awareness by improving brand recall and recognition of consumers during purchase or consumption settings, and (2) improve the strength, favorability, and uniqueness of brand associations making up the brand image. This latter approach may involve programs directed at existing or new brand associations.

With a fading brand, the depth of brand awareness is often not as much of a problem as the breadth—consumers tend to think of the brand in very narrow ways. Strategies to increase usage of and find new uses for the brand were reviewed. Although changes in brand awareness are probably the easiest means of creating new sources of brand equity, a new marketing program often may have to be implemented to improve the strength, favorability, and uniqueness of brand associations. As part of this repositioning, new markets may have to be tapped. The challenge in all of these efforts to modify the brand image is to not destroy the equity that already exists.

As part of the long-term perspective in managing a brand portfolio, it is necessary that the role of different brands and the relationships among different brands in the portfolio be carefully considered over time. In particular, a brand migration strategy needs to be designed and implemented so that consumers understand how various brands in the portfolio can satisfy their needs as they potentially change over time or as the products and brands themselves change over time. A number of different possible strategies designed to both acquire new customers and retain existing ones were reviewed. Different possible strategies to retire those brands whose sources of brand equity had essentially "dried up" or who had acquired damaging and difficult-to-change associations were also discussed. The chapter concluded by providing rationale and guidelines for corporate name changes and how to effectively manage a brand crisis. It was noted that effective crisis management requires swift and sincere actions.

In closing, the importance of the material in this chapter can be seen through the words of one marketing commentator who has an interesting view of how to think about managing brands over time:

> Brands are like ships. You could fill a book with analogies. One key common denominator is that brands, once they gain momentum, overtake agility. A brand heading in the right direction absorbs a lot of mishandling before it stops dead in the water, or goes off course. A brand heading south takes effort and time to turn around. Think through all of the similarities and you'll soon find yourself wondering why brands aren't staffed like ships. True most brands have a captain, several admirals, and assorted crew to run the engines and polish the brass. But all too few brands have a navigator whose job is to keep the ship on course towards a destination that is far over the horizon. This is especially scary when you consider your USS Brand will undergo several complete crew changeovers before reaching anything remotely resembling a safe port, and that it sails in oceans studded with the perils of changing winds, tides, and currents, to say nothing of enemy subs and icebergs appearing out of the fog.

Discussion Questions

1. Pick a brand. Assess its efforts to manage brand equity in the last five years. What actions has it taken to be innovative and relevant? Can you suggest any changes to its marketing program?
2. Identify a fading brand. What suggestions can you offer to revitalize its brand equity? Try to apply the different approaches suggested in the chapter. Which strategies would seem to work best?

Notes

1. Laura Bird, "Tambrands Plans Global Ad Campaign," *Wall Street Journal* (June 22, 1993), p. B-8.
2. Ronald Alsop, "Enduring Brands Hold Their Allure By Sticking Close to Their Roots," *Wall Street Journal Centennial Edition* (June 23, 1989), p. B4.

3. Kevin Goldman, "Michelob Tries to Rebottle Its Old Success," *Wall Street Journal* (September 28, 1995), p. B-8.

4. John Flina, "Madison Avenue Flashback," *San Francisco Examiner* (June 11, 1995), p. B-1.

5. For an empirical examination of the power of sustained advertising, see Cathy J. Cobb-Walgren, Cynthia A. Ruble, and Naveen Donthu, "Brand Equity, Brand Preference, and Purchase Intent," *Journal of Advertising*, 24 (3) (Fall 1995), pp. 25–40.

6. Andy Wallenstein and Michael Wilke, "How Heinz Evolved into a Lean Giant," *Advertising Age* (February 13, 1995), p. 4.

7. Marj Charlier, "Coors Pours on Western Themes to Revive Flagship Beer's Cachet," *Wall Street Journal* (August 2, 1994), p. B-6.

8. Chris Roush, "At Timex, They're Positively Glowing," *Business Week* (July 12, 1993), p. 141.

9. Joseph Pereira, "Hasbro Enjoys Life Off the Toy-Market Roller Coaster," *Wall Street Journal* (May 5, 1992), p. B-4. Keith H. Hammonds, "'Has-Beens Have Been Very Good to Hasbro," *Business Week* (August 5, 1991), pp. 76–77.

10. Timothy L. O'Brien, "Beleaguered Schwinn Seeks Partner to Regain Luster," *Wall Street Journal* (May 20, 1992), p. B-2.

11. Jonathan Auerbach, "Smith Corona Seeks Protection of Chapter 11," *Wall Street Journal* (July 6, 1995), p. A-4.

12. Bruce Horovitz and Melanie Wells, "Long After Their Sales Stop Sizzling, Some Brand Names Linger In . . . Product Purgatory," *USA Today* (May 2, 1995), p. B-1.

13. Peter H. Farquhar, "Managing Brand Equity," *Marketing Research*, 1 (September 1989), pp. 24–33.

14. Richard Gibson, "Classic Cheerios and Wheaties Reformulated," *Wall Street Journal* (August 31, 1994), p. B1.

15. Michael J. McCarthy, "Pepsi is Returning to Original Focus: Its Profitable Younger Generation," *Wall Street Journal* (January 22, 1993), p. B6.

16. Kevin Lane Keller, Susan Heckler, and Michael J. Houston, "The Effects of Brand Name Suggestiveness on Recall of Advertising Effects," *Journal of Marketing*, January 1998, in press..

17. Raymond Serafin, "BMW: From Yuppie-Mobile to Smart Car of the '90s," *Advertising Age* (October 3, 1994), p. S-2.

18. Oscar Suris, "Ads Aim to Sell Hush Puppies to New Yuppies," *Wall Street Journal* (July 28, 1993), pp. B1, B6; Keith Naughton, "Don't Step on My Blue Suede Hush Puppies," *Business Week* (September 11, 1995), pp. 84–86; Cyndee Miller, "Hush Puppies: All of a Sudden They're Cool," *Marketing News* (February 12, 1996), p. 10.

19. Kevin Goldman, "Adidas Tries to Fill Its Rivals' Big Shoes," *Wall Street Journal* (March 17, 1994), p. B-5. Joshua Levine, "Adidas Flies Again," *Forbes* (March 25, 1996), pp. 44–45.

20. Matt Murray, "How the Man From Campbell Taught Quaker State to Market Oil Like Soap," *Wall Street Journal* (July 14, 1995), pp. B1, B4.

21. Richard Gibson, "Stirring Memories Gives Ovaltine a Lift," *Wall Street Journal* (December 3, 1992), p. B-1.

22. Norman C. Berry, "Revitalizing Brands," *The Journal of Consumer Marketing*, 5 (3) (Summer 1988), pp. 15–20.

23. Brian Wansink, "Can Package Size Accelerate Usage Volume?," *Journal of Marketing*, 60 (3) (July 1996), pp. 1–14.

24. Brian Wansink, "Can Package Size Accelerate Usage Volume?," *Journal of Marketing*, 60 (3) (July 1996), pp. 1–14.

25. David A. Aaker, *Managing Brand Equity*. New York: Free Press, 1991.

26. Laura Bird, "Grey Poupon Tones Down Tony Image," *Wall Street Journal* (July 22, 1994), p. B-3.

27. John D. Cripps, "Heuristics and Biases in Timing the Replacement of Durable Products," *Journal of Consumer Research*, 21 (September 1994), pp. 304–318.

28. Ronald Alsop, "Giving Fading Brands a Second Chance," *Wall Street Journal* (January 24, 1989), p. B-1.

29. Brian Wansink, "Advertising Strategies to Increase Usage Frequency," *Journal of Marketing*, 60 (1) (January 1996), pp. 31–46.

30. Marj Charlier, "Yuengling's Success Defies Convention," *Wall Street Journal* (August 26, 1993), p. B-1.

31. Kevin Goldman, "Del Monte Tries to Freshen Its Market," *Wall Street Journal* (October 20, 1994), p. B-4.

32. Tim Triplett, "Generic Fear to Xerox is Brand Equity to FedEx," *Marketing News* (August 15, 1994), pp. 12–13.

33. Teri Agins, "Women Help Van Heusen Collar Arrow," *Wall Street Journal* (May 22, 1992), p. B-1.

34. Eleena de Lisser, "Royal Crown Girds to Battle Its Giant Rivals," *Wall Street Journal* (March 1, 1994), p. B-1.

35. David W. Stewart, "Advertising in a Slow-Growth Economy," *American Demographics* (September 1994), pp. 40–46.

36. David W. Stewart, "Advertising in a Slow-Growth Economy," *American Demographics* (September 1994), pp. 40–46.

37. Ronald Alsop, "Giving Fading Brands a Second Chance," *Wall Street Journal* (January 24, 1989), p. B-1.

38. Bruce Horovitz and Melanie Wells, "Long After Their Sales Stop Sizzling, Some Brand Names Linger In . . . Product Purgatory," *USA Today* (May 2, 1995), p. B1.

39. Adapted from Faye Rice, "Making Generational Marketing Come of Age," *Fortune* (June 26, 1995), pp. 110–114.

40. Kevin Goldman, "Old Spice's Familiar Sailor is Lost at Sea," *Wall Street Journal* (September 10, 1993), p. B-2.

41. Oscar Suris, "Cadillac's Sedan de Ville Spurns Youth," *Wall Street Journal* (August 10, 1993), p. B-1. Gabriella Stern, "As Old Cadillac Buyers Age, the GM Division Fights to Halt Slippage," *Wall Street Journal* (August 25, 1995), p. A-1. Gabriella Stern, "Buick Confronts Its Fuddy-Duddy Image," *Wall Street Journal* (June 19, 1995), p. B-1.

42. Julie Liesse, "Haagen-Dazs Spoons Up a Revival," *Advertising Age* (August 22, 1994), p. 38.

43. David A. Aaker, *Managing Brand Equity*. New York: Free Press, 1991.

44. Jennifer Reingold, "Darwin Goes Shopping," *Financial World* (September 1, 1993), p. 44.

45. David A. Aaker, *Managing Brand Equity*. New York: Free Press, 1991.

46. Tara Parker-Pope, "Unilever Plans a Long-Overdue Pruning," *Wall Street Journal* (September 3, 1996), p. A13.

47. Dottie Enrico, "Companies Play Name-Change Game," *USA Today* (December 28, 1994), p. 4B.

48. Associated Press, "Corporately Speaking, There's a Lot in a Name," pp. C-1, C-3.

49. "BSWho?," Editorial, *The Economist* (May 14, 1994), p. 70.

50. Dottie Enrico, "Companies Play Name-Change Game," *USA Today* (December 28, 1994), p. 4B.

51. Associated Press, "Allegis: A $7 Million Name is Grounded," *San Francisco Examiner* (June 16, 1987), p. C-9.

52. Bernice Kanner, "The New Name Game," *New York* (March 16, 1987), pp. 16, 19.

53. Amanda Bennett, "Firms Grapple to Find New Names As Images and Industries Change," *Wall Street Journal* (November 17, 1986), p. 36.

54. Bernice Kanner, "The New Name Game," *New York* (March 16, 1987), pp. 16, 19.

55. Nancy Langford and Steven A. Greyser, "Exxon: Communications After Valdez," Harvard Business School Case #593-014. Boston, MA. September 30, 1992 and October 18, 1995.

56. Norman Klein and Stephen A. Greyser, "The Perrier Recall: A Source of Trouble," Harvard Business School Case #9-590-104, April 10, 1990 and "The Perrier Relaunch," Harvard Business School Case #9-590-130. Boston, MA. June 27, 1990.

57. Ronald Alsop, "Enduring Brands Hold Their Allure By Sticking Close to Their Roots," *Wall Street Journal Centennial Edition* (June 23, 1989), p. B4.

58. Leslie Savan, "Selling a Sullied Product," *San Francisco Chronicle* (August 17, 1986), p. 5.

CHAPTER

14 Managing Brands over Geographical Boundaries, Cultures, and Market Segments

Preview

An important consideration in managing brand equity is recognizing and accounting for different types of consumers in developing branding and marketing programs. Previous chapters have considered how and why marketers may need brand portfolios to satisfy different market segments and may need to develop brand migration strategies to attract new customers and retain existing customers through brand and family life cycles. In this chapter, we examine in more detail the implications of differences in consumer behavior and the existence of different types of market segments on managing brand equity. We pay particular attention to international issues and global branding strategies.

Specifically, after discussing the basic rationale for taking brands abroad, we discuss some pros and cons of developing a standardized global marketing program for a brand. Next, we outline four major decisions in developing a global marketing program for a brand:

- Deciding which markets to enter
- Deciding how to enter the market
- Deciding on the marketing program
- Deciding on the marketing organization

The chapter concludes by considering specific strategic and tactical issues in building customer-based brand equity over geographical boundaries, cultures, and market segments. The basic contention of this chapter is that in building brand equity, it is often necessary to create different marketing programs to satisfy different market segments by:

1. Identifying differences in consumer behavior (i.e., how consumers purchase and use products and what they know and feel about brands)

2. Adjusting the branding program accordingly (i.e., through the choice of brand elements, the nature of the supporting marketing program, and leverage of secondary associations)

The chapter describes how these two activities are influenced by international, regional, and other nongeographical demographic or cultural factors.

Rationale for Going Abroad

A number of well-known global brands have derived much of their sales and profits from nondomestic markets for years, Coca-Cola, Shell, Bayer, Rolex, Marlboro, and Mercedes-Benz to name a few. Recent years have seen the successful introduction of brands such as Apple computers, Gillette Sensor razors, L'Oreal cosmetics, Pert shampoo, and Nescafe instant coffee onto the global landscape. Figure 14–1 contains

FIGURE 14-1 Household Words by 2000?

Brand (Country)	Products
Acer (Taiwan)	Personal computers
Aveda (U.S.)	Hair and skincare products and cosmetics
Body Shop (U.K.)	Personal care products
BT (U.K.)	Telephone service
Compuserve (U.S.)	Online services
Daewoo (Korea)	Automobiles
Danone (France)	Yogurt
Discovery Channel (U.S.)	Satellite-delivered documentary channel
Dr Pepper (U.S.)	Soft drink
Episode (Hong Kong)	Upmarket women's apparel chain
Ericsson (Sweden)	Mobile phones
ESPN (U.S.)	Satellite-delivered sports network
The Gap (U.S.)	Apparel
Gateway 2000 (U.S.)	Mail-order personal computers
International Data Group (U.S.)	Computer magazine, research, and exhibitions
LG (formerly Goldstar—Korea)	Consumer electronics
Lotus Notes (U.S.)	Computer software
Marie Claire (France)	Women's monthly magazine
Nine West (U.S.)	Women's shoes
Orangina (France)	Soft drink
Planet Hollywood (U.S.)	Restaurant chain
Samsung (Korea)	Consumer electronics
Singapore Airlines (Singapore)	Airline
Virgin (U.K.)	Airline, retail, and consumer products

the results of a recent survey of marketing experts forecasting twenty-five emerging new global brands.[1]

The success of these brands has provided encouragement to many firms to market their brands abroad. A number of other forces have also contributed to the growing interest in global marketing, including:

1. Perception of slow growth and increased competition in domestic markets
2. Belief in enhanced overseas growth and profit opportunities
3. Desire to reduce costs from economies of scale
4. Need to diversify risk
5. Recognition of global mobility of customers

In more and more product categories, the ability to establish a global profile is becoming virtually a prerequisite for success. For example, with U.S. liquor consumption steadily declining, many American producers have stepped up their marketing efforts abroad, riding the fortunes of brands such as Jim Beam, Jack Daniels, and Southern Comfort in overseas markets. As one observer notes, "Spirits companies now view themselves as global marketers. If you want to be a player, you have to be in America, Europe, and the Far East. You must have world-class brands, a long-term perspective, and deep pockets."[2]

Ideally, the marketing program for a global brand would consist of one product formulation, one package design, one advertising program, one pricing schedule, one distribution plan, and so on that would be the most effective and efficient possible option for each and every country in which the brand was sold. Unfortunately, such a uniformly optimal strategy is rarely possible. As one global marketer put it:[3]

> Multi-country marketers must do the same work as the local ones. They must find ways to market a product to a person, to make that product relevant to that person. In addition to maintaining a focus on the individual needs of one market, the global marketer must simultaneously be aware of the needs of other potential markets. Micro and macro. Zoom and wide angle lens. This duality of focus is the source of both the challenge and the economies for multi-country marketing.

Before considering the decisions to be made in developing a global marketing program for a brand and the factors affecting the tradeoff between standardization and customization, it is useful to first consider some of the main advantages and disadvantages of creating standardized supporting marketing programs on a global basis.

Advantages of Global Marketing Programs

A number of potential advantages have been put forth concerning the development of a global marketing program (see Figure 14–2). In general, the more standardized the marketing program—the less the marketing program varies from country to country—the greater the extent to which these different advantages will actually be realized.

Economies of scale in production and distribution
Lower marketing costs
Power and scope
Consistency in brand image
Ability to leverage good ideas quickly and efficiently
Uniformity of marketing practices

FIGURE 14-2 Advantages of Global Marketing Programs

ECONOMIES OF SCALE IN PRODUCTION AND DISTRIBUTION

From a supply-side or cost perspective, the primary advantage of a global marketing program is the manufacturing efficiencies and lower costs that derive from higher volumes in production and distribution. The more that strong experience curve effects exist—such that the cost of making and marketing a product declines sharply with increases in cumulative production—the more economies of scale in production and distribution will be realized from a standardized global marketing program.

LOWER MARKETING COSTS

Another set of cost advantages can be realized from uniformity in packaging, advertising, promotion, and other marketing communication activities. For example, Colgate-Palmolive introduced its tartar control toothpaste in over forty countries by letting country managers choose one of two ads (e.g., the U.S. version was dubbed "The Wall" and showed little men building a wall of tartar on giant teeth). They believe that every country where the same ad was run saved one to two million dollars in production costs.[4] In particular, the more uniform the branding strategy adopted across countries, the more potential cost savings that should prevail. Along these lines, a global corporate branding strategy (e.g., as with Sony) is perhaps the most efficient means of spreading marketing costs across both products and countries.

POWER AND SCOPE

A global brand profile may communicate credibility to consumers. Consumers may believe that selling in many diverse markets is an indication that a manufacturer has gained much expertise and acceptance. The fact that the brand is widely available may signal that the product is high quality and convenient to use. A prominent international profile may be especially important for certain service brands. For example, Avis assures its customers that they can receive the same high quality service renting its cars anywhere in the world, further reinforcing a key benefit promise embodied in their slogan, "We Try Harder." Relatedly, uniform campaigns across borders may enhance country-of-origin effects for those brands who rely on such associations. For example, Japanese consumers buying European cars in Japan may be particularly responsive to the cosmopolitan image conveyed by European-style branding and communication strategies for those cars.

CONSISTENCY IN BRAND IMAGE

Maintaining a common marketing platform all over the world helps to maintain the consistency of brand and company image. This consideration becomes particularly important in those markets where there is much customer mobility or where media exposure transmits images across national boundaries. For example, Gillette Sensor sells functional superiority and an appreciation of human character and aspirations worldwide. Services often desire to convey a uniform image due to consumer movements. For example, American Express communicates the prestige and utility of its card and the convenience and ease-of-replacement of its travelers' checks worldwide.

ABILITY TO LEVERAGE GOOD IDEAS QUICKLY AND EFFICIENTLY

One global marketer notes that globalization also can result in increased sustainability and "facilitate continued development of core competencies with the organization . . . in manufacturing, in R&D, in Marketing and Sales, and in less talked about areas such as Competitive Intelligence . . . all of which enhance the company's ability to compete."[5] Rank Xerox, the 80 percent owned subsidiary of Xerox that sells billions of dollars worth of copiers, document processors, and services, initiated a "plug-and-play" benchmarking project in an attempt to spread best marketing practices. Gathering sales data and making country-by-country comparisons, Xerox easily found eight cases in which one country outperformed the others and documented how it was being done. For example, France sold five times more color copiers than its sister divisions. By copying France's practices in selling color copiers—chiefly by improving sales training and making sure that color copiers were pushed through dealer channels as well as direct sales—Switzerland increased its unit sales of color copiers by 328 percent, Holland by 300 percent, Norway by 152 percent, and so on.[6]

UNIFORMITY OF MARKETING PRACTICES

Finally, a standardized global marketing program may simplify coordination and provide greater control for how the brand is being marketed in different countries, especially with respect to product quality. For example, Colgate-Palmolive has been a highly successful global marketer for years because of its tight focus on marketing strategies and objectives.[7] Colgate's "bundle books" contain, down to the smallest details, everything that Colgate knows about any given brand and that a country or regional manager needs to know about how to effectively market a particular product, including the product attributes, its formulas, ingredient sourcing information, market research, pricing positions, graphics, even advertising, public relations, and point-of-sales materials. With a bundle book, a Colgate manager in any one of the 206 countries and territories where Colgate sells its products can project the Colgate brand exactly like every one of his or her counterparts. As one executive noted, "As the smallest among our major competitors, we are trying to make sure that we maximize our resources. By having tightly controlled brands, we can leverage across borders rapidly."

Disadvantages of Global Marketing Programs

A number of potential disadvantages of a standardized global marketing program have also been raised (see Figure 14–3). Perhaps the most compelling criticism is that standardized global marketing programs often ignore fundamental differences across countries and cultures. Critics claim that designing one marketing program for all possible markets often results in unimaginative and ineffective strategies geared to the "lowest common denominator." Possible differences across countries come in a variety of forms, as follows.

DIFFERENCES IN CONSUMER NEEDS, WANTS, AND USAGE PATTERNS FOR PRODUCTS

Because of differences in cultural values, economic development, and other factors across nationalities, consumer behavior with respect to many product categories are fundamentally different. For example, the French eat four times more yogurt than the British; the British consume eight times more chocolate than the Italians; and Americans drink eleven times more soft drinks than consumers abroad.[8] Product strategies that work in one country may not work in another. Recently, Disney entered a licensing agreement with Tupperware to sell in Japan. Although marketing research suggested it was a good idea, the product failed miserably. Apparently the problem was in the politeness of the Japanese housewives. Although they said they would attend Tupperware parties—and did in fact come and buy products at parties—they resented the people who hosted the party and the company for putting them into that situation.

DIFFERENCES IN CONSUMER RESPONSE TO MARKETING MIX ELEMENTS

Consumers in different parts of the world can vary in their attitudes and opinions concerning marketing activity.[9] For example, countries vary in their general attitudes toward advertising as an institution. Research has shown that Americans, in general,

FIGURE 14–3 Disadvantages of Global Marketing Programs

Differences in consumer needs, wants, and usage patterns for products
Differences in consumer response to marketing mix elements
Differences in brand and product development and the
   competitive environment
Differences in the legal environment
Differences in marketing institutions
Differences in administrative procedures

tend to be fairly cynical toward advertising while Japanese view it much more positively. Research has also shown differences in advertising style between the two countries: Japanese ads tend to be softer and more abstract in tone, whereas American ads tend to be richer in product information. Price sensitivity, promotion responsiveness, and sponsorship support, all may differ by the country involved. These differences in response to marketing activity may also be reflected in differences in consumer behavior and decision making. For example, in a comparative study of brand purchase intentions for Korean and U.S. consumers, Lee and Green found that the purchase intentions of Americans were twice as likely to be affected by their product beliefs and attitudes toward the brand itself whereas Koreans were eight times more likely to be influenced by social normative beliefs and what they felt others would think about the purchase.[10]

DIFFERENCES IN BRAND AND PRODUCT DEVELOPMENT AND THE COMPETITIVE ENVIRONMENT

Products may be at different stages of their life cycle in different countries. Moreover, the perceptions and positionings of particular brands may also differ considerably across countries. Figure 14–4 shows the results of a comprehensive study of the leading brands in the United States, Japan, and Europe conducted by Landor Associates in 1990.[11] Brands are ranked according to their "share of mind"—a measure of awareness—and "esteem"—a measure of attitudes. Relatively few brands appear on all three lists, suggesting that, if nothing else, consumer perceptions of even top brands can vary significantly by geographical region. The nature of competition may also differ. Europeans tend to have more competitors because shipping products across borders is easy. For example, Procter & Gamble competes in France against Italian, Swedish, and Danish companies in many categories.[12]

DIFFERENCES IN THE LEGAL ENVIRONMENT

Different kinds of regulatory hurdles exist in different countries. One of the challenges in developing a global ad campaign is the maze of constantly changing legal restrictions that exist from country to country. For example, at one time, laws in Venezuela, Canada, and Australia stipulated that commercials had to be physically produced in the native country. Poland required commercial lyrics to be sung in Polish. Advertising restrictions have been placed on the use of children in commercials in Austria, heroic figures in cigarette ads in the United Kingdom (e.g., prohibiting even the use of the Marlboro Man), comparative ads in Singapore, and toy soldiers with either machine guns or tanks in Germany. Note the challenges posed by the following example.

> At the J. Walter Thompson ad agency, executives point to a 30-second cereal commercial produced for British TV to show how much regulations in Europe alone can sap an ad. References to iron and vitamins would have to be deleted in the Netherlands; a child wearing a Kellogg's T-shirt would be edited out in France where children are forbidden from endorsing products on TV. And in Germany, the line, "Kellogg makes its corn flakes the best they've ever been" would be axed because of rules against making competitive claims. After the required changes, the commercial would be about five seconds long.[13]

FIGURE 14–4 Top 25 Brands in the United States, Europe, Japan, and Worldwide

	UNITED STATES	Rank SOM	Esteem	EUROPE	Rank SOM	Esteem	JAPAN	Rank SOM	Esteem	WORLD	Rank SOM	Esteem
	Brand	SOM	Esteem	Brand	SOM	Esteem	Brand	SOM	Esteem	Brand	SOM	Esteem
1	Coca-Cola	1	5	Coca-Cola	1	10	Sony	1	4	Coca-Cola	1	6
2	Campbell's	6	1	Sony	3	1	National	4	9	Sony	4	1
3	Disney	10	2	Mercedes-Benz	8	3	Mercedes-Benz	50	2	Mercedes-Benz	12	2
4	Pepsi-Cola	4	11	BMW	11	2	Toyota	9	18	Kodak	5	9
5	Kodak	8	4	Philips	2	6	Takashimaya	5	25	Disney	8	5
6	NBC	3	16	Volkswagen	4	7	Rolls Royce	100	1	Nestlé	7	14
7	Black & Decker	15	3	Adidas	6	9	Seiko	21	14	Toyota	6	23
8	Kellogg's	9	7	Kodak	7	8	Matsushita	18	20	McDonald's	2	85
9	McDonald's	2	84	Nivea	5	14	Hitachi	6	44	IBM	20	4
10	Hershey's	22	6	Porsche	18	4	Suntory	8	42	Pepsi-Cola	3	92
11	Levi's	18	10	Volvo	16	12	Porsche	118	3	Rolls Royce	23	3
12	GE	14	14	Colgate	9	24	Kirin	17	32	Honda	9	22
13	Sears	5	79	Rolls Royce	28	5	Hotel New Otani	78	8	Panasonic	17	10
14	Hallmark	32	9	Levi's	21	13	Fuji TV	7	81	Levi's	16	8
15	Johnson & Johnson	35	8	Ford	15	31	Snow Brand Milk	19	45	Kleenex	13	16
16	Betty Crocker	26	12	Jaguar	38	11	Imperial Hotel	109	7	Ford	10	24
17	Kraft	24	13	Fanta	10	51	Coca-Cola/Coke	3	119	Volkswagen	11	26
18	Kleenex	20	19	Nescafé	13	56	Mitsukoshi	20	48	Kellogg's	14	30
19	Jell-O	16	26	Black & Decker	25	20	Japan Travel Bureau	13	63	Porsche	27	11
20	Tylenol	28	18	Esso	17	42	Disney	55	19	Polaroid	15	44
21	AT&T	12	62	Michelin	29	21	Aunomoto	12	74	BMW	32	12
22	Crest	31	28	Lego	41	15	Kikkoman	14	70	Colgate	21	51
23	Duracell	39	20	Bosch	43	16	All-Nippon-Airlines	28	49	Seiko	33	15
24	IBM	46	17	Peugeot	19	50	Honda	30	50	Nescafé	19	64
25	Fruit of the Loom	25	41	Audi	36	22	Yamaha	38	34	Canon	35	17

Although some of these laws have been or will be relaxed in the near future, numerous legal differences still exist.

DIFFERENCES IN MARKETING INSTITUTIONS

Some of the basic marketing infrastructure may differ from country to country, making implementation of the same marketing strategy difficult. For example, channels of distribution and retail practices, media availability and costs, and so on all may vary significantly. When DuPont set out to implement a global tracking system for its various brands, efforts were hampered by the fact that the level of sophistication of local marketing research companies varied considerably for the forty primary countries in which DuPont operated. The penetration of television sets, telephones, and supermarkets, for example, all may vary considerably, especially with respect to developing countries (e.g., Bangladesh).

DIFFERENCES IN ADMINISTRATIVE PROCEDURES

In practice, it may be difficult to achieve the control necessary to implement a standardized global marketing program. Local offices may resist having their autonomy threatened. Local managers may suffer from the "not invented here" syndrome and raise objections—rightly or wrongly—as to the fact that the global marketing program misses some key dimension of the local market. Local managers who feel that their autonomy has been reduced may lose motivation and feel doomed to failure.

Global Branding Decisions

As the previous discussion suggests, although firms are increasingly adopting an international marketing perspective to capitalize on market opportunities, a number of possible pitfalls exist. In particular, marketers have encountered some difficult-to-overcome obstacles in developing successful standardized global marketing programs. Before considering the issue of standardization in more detail, it is useful to provide a broader context as to the development of a global marketing program for a brand. Kotler identifies four key decisions that must be made in developing a global marketing program:[14]

1. Deciding which markets to enter
2. Deciding how to enter the market
3. Deciding on the marketing program
4. Deciding on the marketing organization

In making these decisions, marketers attempt, in a general sense, to maximize the probability of realizing the advantages of a global marketing program while minimizing the probability of suffering from any potential disadvantages of globalization. After briefly examining each of these decisions, we consider how to develop global brands and build customer-based brand equity on a global basis.[15]

SELECTING GLOBAL MARKETS

The first decision in developing a global marketing program is to decide which markets to enter. In general, the factors influencing the selection of a new geographical market to enter is similar to the factors affecting the decision to enter any new market, as outlined in chapter 11. Marketers must evaluate the attractiveness of the market, the possible competitive advantages that can be obtained in the market, the manufacturing and marketing costs of servicing the market, the level of risk involved in the market, and so on. In making these evaluations, it is necessary to appraise a number of factors related to the economic, cultural, demographic, political, and legal environments of the country (see Figure 14–5).[16]

In making these deliberations and selecting global markets for entry, it is important to bear in mind two strategic considerations. The first issue is whether the marketing capabilities of the corporation are transportable into the new market. This assessment will revolve around a calibration of customers' needs, perceptions, and so on, as well as an evaluation as to whether the company's strengths, as they could be applied in the new market, would be sufficient to generate sources of brand equity and provide competitive advantages there. One of the major pitfalls that global marketers can fall into is a mistaken belief that their strong position in a domestic market would easily—or even automatically!—translate into a strong position in a foreign market, especially with respect to the brand associations held by consumers. Thus, they fail to realize that in their own country, they are building on a foundation of per-

FIGURE 14-5 Global Environment Choice Criteria

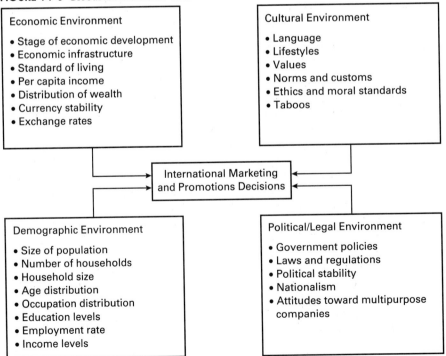

haps decades of carefully compiled associations in customers' minds. For example, when Hershey's chocolate decided to export to Australia in 1988—in part because of that country's attractive per capita chocolate consumption rates—they used American-style advertising, including ads with "the girl with the Hershey's smile." Although such a campaign would have most likely elicited strong and favorable associations from American consumers who had a long history with the brand, it meant little to Australian consumers who lacked this prior experience.[17]

The second issue is the need for an understanding of the broader objectives of the company and how they might be met by entering in the new market (e.g., to divert a competitor's attention, to leverage off its domestic fixed costs, or to gain a reputation internationally). Thus, it is not only necessary with global branding to work out what customers would want from the brand in the new market, it is also important to work out what the company wants from entering that specific market.

DEVISING GLOBAL MARKET ENTRY STRATEGIES

The second decision in developing a global marketing program is to decide how to enter the market. Much of the information gathered in deciding whether to enter a market can be useful in determining how to best enter the chosen markets. Barwise and Robertson identify three alternative ways to enter a new global market:[18]

1. By exporting existing brands of the firm into the new market, i.e., introducing a "geographic extension"
2. By acquiring existing brands already sold in the new market but not owned by the firm
3. By creating some form of brand alliance with another firm (e.g., joint ventures, partnerships, or licensing agreements)

They also identify three key criteria—speed, control, and investment—by which the different entry strategies can be judged. According to Barwise and Robertson, as Figure 14–6 displays, there are tradeoffs among the three criteria such that no one strategy dominates. For example, the major problem with geographic extensions is speed. Because most firms do not have the necessary financial resources and marketing experience to roll out products to a large number of countries simultaneously, global expansion can be a slow, market-by-market process. Brand acquisitions, on the other hand, can be expensive and often more difficult to control than is typically assumed. Brand alliances may offer even less control although are generally much less costly.

The choices among these different entry strategies depend in part on how the resources and objectives of the firm match up with costs and benefits of each strategy. For example, for a roughly ten year period starting in 1984, Nestlé spent $18 billion on

FIGURE 14–6 Market Entry Strategies Tradeoffs

Strategy	Criteria for Evaluation		
	Speed	*Control*	*Investment*
Geographical extension	Slow	High	Medium
Brand acquisition	Fast	Medium	High
Brand alliance	Moderate	Low	Low

acquisitions in different countries, including such major brands as Carnation, dairy (and other) products (U.S.), Perrier, mineral water (France), Stouffers, frozen foods (U.S.), Rowntree, confectionery (U.K.), and Buitoni-Perugina, pasta and chocolate (Italy). Although Nestlé now owns 8000 worldwide brands, only 750 of these brands are registered in more than one country and only 80 brands are registered in more than ten countries. Nestlé has adopted a strategy to have local brands run by regional managers—generally only product technology "goes global."

Thus, major acquisitions yield valuable economies of scale to Nestlé in developed markets. In less developed markets, however, they adopt a different strategy. Their entry strategy there is to manipulate ingredients or processing technology for local conditions and then apply the appropriate brand name, for example, existing brands like Nescafe coffee in some cases or new brands such as Bear brand condensed milk in Asia in other cases. Nestlé strives to get into markets first and is patient—the company negotiated for more than a decade to enter China.[19] To limit risks and simplify their efforts in new markets, Nestlé attacks with a handful of labels, selected from a set of eleven strategic brand groups. Nestlé then concentrates its advertising and marketing money on just two or three brands.[20]

Procter & Gamble has applied a similar entry strategy in new markets, first entering categories in which it excels, such as diapers, detergents, and sanitary pads, building its infrastructure and then bringing in other categories such as personal care or health care.[21] Heineken's sequential strategy has been slightly different in nature. They first enter a new market by exporting to build brand awareness and image. If the market response is deemed satisfactory, the company will then license its brands to a local brewer in hopes of expanding volume. If that relationship is successful, Heineken may then take an equity stake or forge a joint venture. In doing so, Heineken piggybacks sales of its high-priced Heineken brand with an established local brand.[22] Heineken's takeover of DB Breweries in New Zealand is a successful example of such a strategy with both supply-side and demand-side benefits in terms of improved efficiency in marketing and production and a stronger customer franchise.

Joint ventures are a common entry strategy and are often seen as a fast and convenient way to enter complex foreign markets. Fuji Xerox has been a highly successful joint venture in Japan that has even outperformed Xerox's U.S. parent company. Joint ventures have been popular in Japan where convoluted distribution systems, tightly knit supplier relationships and close business–government cooperation have long encouraged foreign companies to link up with knowledgeable local partners.[23] Blockbuster entered Japan with a joint venture with one of that country's best known retailers, Den Fujita, who also runs McDonald's (Japan) and has a stake in Toys 'R Us in Japan. Blockbuster also negotiated joint ventures in France, Germany, and Italy.[24] Pier 1 has similarly expanded through joint ventures and licensing accords.[25] Pepsi has ownership positions via joint ventures and five outright acquisitions in 40 percent of its bottling networks outside North America.[26] Branding Brief 14–1 describes the launch of Cereal Partners Worldwide, a joint venture between Nestlé and General Mills.

Finally, in some cases, mergers or acquisitions result from a desire to command a higher global profile. For example, U.S. baby food maker Gerber agreed to be acquired by Swiss drug maker Sandoz, in part, because of a need to establish a stronger

Cereal Partners Worldwide[a]

For years, while Kellogg's made some of the characters behind its cereals (Toucan Sam, Tony the Tiger, and Snap, Crackle, and Pop) household names in Europe, General Mills chose to ignore overseas markets to concentrate on domestic concerns. In 1992, General Mills decided that its well-known cereal brands such as Cheerios, Wheaties, Golden Grahams, Trix, and Lucky Charms needed to grow their sales, at least in part by looking at new markets. International markets offered a golden opportunity for growth. Europeans on average eat just three pounds of cereal a year per capita, compared with ten pounds in the United States. Starting from a small base, sales volume in some markets, such as Spain and Portugal, have been growing at 20 percent to 50 percent a year, versus 5 percent in the United States. The challenge? How to overcome Kellogg's 70-year head start and strong presence in the $3.5 billion European cereal market. Deciding that the few available takeover candidates were overpriced and that building factories and distribution channels from scratch would have taken too long and be too risky, General Mills' solution was to adopt an unusual entry strategy for a packaged goods company—a joint venture.

Cereal Partners Worldwide (CPW) is a joint venture between General Mills and Nestlé. Nestlé, the world's largest food company, possessed much brand equity and a strong distribution system but lacked any cereal brands. As part of the agreement, General Mills supplied Nestlé with its product formulations, technology, and cereal-making expertise. Nestlé, using three of its existing cereal plants in Europe, would then produce some of the thirty or so cereal brands that General Mills made in North America. Nestlé's corporate name would then appear across the entire product line with the General Mills or Nestlé brand used to identify individual items. In 1990, the venture acquired the cereals business from Ranks Hovis McDougall PLC for roughly $165 million. With brands such as Shreddies and Shredded Wheats, they obtained an instant 15 percent market share in the United Kingdom. General Mills set aside most of Nestlé's weaker brands to roll out its familiar American standbys while adding the Nestlé trademark to the packages. They also directed a complete makeover of Nestlé's Chocapic cereal.

In any brand alliance, there are risks involved. It is rare that partnerships are equal. One partner may split off, and with the knowledge gained from the other, become an even stronger competitor. General Mills felt that the benefits outweighed the costs and even chose to enter into another European joint venture in 1992 with PepsiCo. Snack Ventures Europe started with revenues of around $641 million, split 60 percent PepsiCo and 40 percent General Mills. General Mills' rationale again was to combine strengths with another consumer goods giant. In this case, General Mills was good at making products that were extruded into distinct shapes (e.g., Bugles snacks) while PepsiCo dominated the snack business. Moreover, General Mills was stronger in Northern Europe while PepsiCo was stronger in Southern Europe.

---

[a]Adapted from Lois Therrien, "Cafe Au Lait, A Croissant—And Trix," *Business Week* (August 24, 1992), pp. 50–51, and Richard Gibson, "General Mills Would Like to Be Champion of Breakfasts in Europe," *Wall Street Journal* (December 1, 1989), p. 6.

presence in Europe and Asia where Sandoz has a solid base. Sandoz, on the other hand, was attracted by Gerber's 73 percent market share in the United States. Although the acquisition was seen as potentially beneficial for both marketing efforts, some observers still questioned the $3.3 billion price Sandoz bid as part of the acquisition.[27]

As these examples illustrate, different entry strategies have been adopted by different firms, or even by the same firm in different countries. These entry strategies also may evolve over time. For example, in Australia, Coca-Cola not only produces and sells its global brands such as Coke, Fanta, and Sprite, it has also taken over a number of local brands through acquisitions. One of Coca-Cola's objectives with these acquisitions is to slowly migrate demand from the local brands to global brands, thus capitalizing on economies of scale.

Next, we consider how to design the particular marketing programs for different countries assuming that a geographic extension or exporting strategy is adopted.

DESIGNING GLOBAL MARKETING PROGRAMS

The third decision in developing a global marketing program for a brand is to decide on the actual nature of the program. In this section, we consider a number of different issues, such as the controversy over standardization versus customization strategies, factors that would favor one strategy over another, successful examples of each type of strategy, and the changing landscape for global brands.

Standardization versus Customization

Perhaps the most fundamental issue in developing a global marketing program is the extent to which the marketing program should be standardized across countries. Perhaps the biggest proponent of standardization is the legendary Harvard professor, Ted Levitt. In a controversial 1983 article, Levitt argued that companies needed to learn to operate as if the world were one large market—ignoring superficial regional and national differences:[28]

> A thousand suggestive ways attest to the ubiquity of the desire for the most advanced things that the world makes and sells—goods of the best quality and reliability at the lowest price. The world's needs and desires have been irrevocably homogenized. This makes the multinational corporation obsolete and the global corporation absolute. . . .
>
> But although companies customize products for particular market segments, they know that success in a world with homogenized demand requires a search for sales opportunities in similar segments across the globe in order to achieve the economies of scale necessary to compete.

According to Levitt, because the world is shrinking—due to leaps in technology, communications, and so on—well-managed companies should shift their emphasis from customizing items to offering globally standardized products that are advanced, functional, reliable, and low-priced for all.

Levitt's strong position elicited an equally strong response. Carl Spielvogel, chairman and chief executive of ad agency Backer Spielvogel Bates Worldwide, replied, "There are about two products that lend themselves to global marketing—and one of them is Coca-Cola." Other critics pointed out that even Coca-Cola did not standardize its marketing and noted the lack of standardization in other global brands such as McDonald's, Marlboro, and others, as follows:

1. *Coca-Cola:* For legal reasons Diet Coke is called Coca-Cola Light in Europe, and the particular artificial sweeteners and packaging for Diet Coke can differ in different parts of the world, too. Over the years, Coke's ads have been adapted or developed specially for different countries. For example, Coke's famous "Mean Joe" Green TV ad from the United States—where the tired, weary football star reluctantly accepts a Coke from an admiring young fan and then unexpectedly tosses him his jersey in appreciation—was shot in a number of different countries in exactly the same format using famous athletes from those regions (e.g., ads in South America used the Argentine soccer star, Maradonna, while those in Asia used the Thai soccer star, Niat). Even Coke's global ad campaigns, such as the 1992 Winter Olympics singalong, was dubbed into twelve languages before being beamed to 3.8 billion viewers in 131 countries. Local managers are actually assigned responsibility for sales and distribution programs of Coke products to reflect the marked differences in consumer behavior across countries. For example, in Spain, Coke has been used as a mixer, even for wine; in Italy, with meals in place of wine or cappuccino; and in China, for special government functions. Finally, Coca-Cola failed when it tried to export its Georgia Coffee, a canned drink popular in Japan, to other countries.

2. *McDonald's:* Another famous global marketer, McDonald's, has also modified and adapted its successful formula of "food, fun, and families" in going overseas. Although the Big Mac and Ronald McDonald appear worldwide, McDonald's customizes other aspects of its marketing program. They serve beer in Germany, wine in France, and coconut, mango, and tropical mint shakes in Hong Kong. Hamburgers are made with different meat and spices in Japan, and McSpaghetti is offered in the Philippines. McDonald's first Indian restaurant in New Delhi featured a lamb burger, "Maharaja Mac," and offered no beef products on the menu. McDonald's joint venture partners, who typically run the franchises abroad, take much of the responsibility for their own local marketing.[29]

3. *Marlboro:* Even Marlboro cigarettes, often cited as a prime example of globalization, has introduced some flexibility into its marketing program. Traditionally, a creative team of Marlboro's ad agency, Leo Burnett, met in the United States to create its yearly pool of "Marlboro Man" television commercials to be run in those countries where such advertising was permitted. Starting in 1987, however, more nationalistic views were allowed. Creative people in twenty-five main Marlboro markets submitted ideas for a new campaign. After some review, five commercials were approved and produced, and each country was able to choose which versions of the ad to run.

The experiences of these top marketers have also been shared by others who found out—in many cases, the hard way—that differences in consumer behavior still prevail across countries. When Pillsbury decided to introduce a canned sweet corn as a global launch of its Green Giant brand of vegetables, it was surprised to find that, instead of being eaten as a hot side dish as intended, the French added it to salad and ate it cold, the British used it as a sandwich and pizza topping, and Japanese children ate it as an afterschool treat.[30] When General Foods attempted to make its Tang powdered orange drink into a world brand, they found that the Germans did not like the name, the British did not like the taste, and the French did not typically drink orange juice for breakfast. To crack those markets, they had to rename the drink Seefrisch in Germany, sell a tarter-tasting Tang in Britain, and reposition the product as an all-day, fun, family drink in France.[31]

In summary, it is difficult to identify any one company applying the global marketing concept in the *strict* sense—selling an identical brand exactly the same way, everywhere. Branding Brief 14–2 describes the problems Parker Pen faced when it attempted to standardize its marketing program worldwide. Many firms have been forced to tailor products and marketing programs to different national markets. For example, Heinz ketchup has a slightly sweet taste in the United States but is spicier in certain European countries where it is available in hot, Mexican, and curry flavors. Ketchup usage varies by country, too. In Greece, it is poured on pasta, eggs, and cuts of meat. In Japan, it is promoted as an ingredient to Western-style foods such as omelets, sausages, and pasta. Heinz has downplayed its American heritage in certain countries, such as Sweden, where ketchup is used to accompany traditional meatballs and fishballs. In fact, Swedes thought the brand was German because of the name. In Germany, however, American themes work well and have been used in advertising.[32]

Standardization *and* Customization

Increasingly, marketers are blending global objectives with local or regional concerns. Industry branding pundit Larry Light maintains the correct view of global marketing is:[33]

> Think globally. Compete locally. Sell personally.

In effect, a hierarchy of brand associations must be defined in a global context that defines which associations are to be held by consumers in all countries and which are to be held only in certain countries. At the same time, decisions have to be made as to how these associations should be created in different markets to account for different consumer perceptions, tastes, and environments. Thus, marketers must be attuned to similarities *and* differences across markets.

Consistent with this view, Procter & Gamble's strategy is to make global plans, replan for each region, and execute locally. Ad agencies such as Grey Advertising talk about "Global Vision with a Local Touch." From these perspectives, transferring products across borders may mean consistent positioning for the brand, but not necessarily the same exact brand name and marketing program in each market. Similarly, packaging may have the same overall look, but be tailored as required to fit the local populace and market needs.

In short, centralized marketing strategies that preserve local customs and traditions at the same time can be a boon for products sold in more than one country—even in diverse cultures. Fortunately, firms have improved their capabilities to tailor products and programs to local conditions: ". . . [New technologies] have the important attribute of allowing customized or tailored product offerings reflecting local con-

BRANDING BRIEF 14-2

Parker Pen's Global Misadventures[a]

One of the most spectacular failures of global marketing was Parker Pen's misguided foray into standardizing their global marketing program in 1984. Parker was one of the world's best known brands. It sold writing instruments in 154 countries and decided to bring virtually every one of them under the "global marketing" umbrella. Its plan was to centralize and standardize all aspects of the marketing program—packaging, pricing, promotional materials, and especially advertising. This "one look, one voice" approach to global marketing was to be orchestrated completely from the company's U.S. headquarters in Janeville, Wisconsin.

Parker's plans were a result of increasing dissatisfaction with the brand's performance in the 1960s and 1970s. Aggressive marketing of inexpensive Japanese disposable pens and direct competition from A.T. Cross's upscale pens had eaten into the sales of Parker's high-priced pens. Production facilities were out of date, and new product development was stagnant. Marketing was largely left to local operations who often introduced their own products and worked with their own ad agencies. New management in 1982 moved quickly to revive the fortunes of the brand, trimming the payroll, chopping the product line to 100, consolidating and overhauling manufacturing operations to make it state-of-the-art.

As part of the new strategy, management also set in motion plans to create a standardized global marketing plan. They assigned the worldwide account to Ogilvy & Mather. In the process, they fired longtime agencies such as Lowe Howard-Spink in London whose almost legendary U.K. advertising campaigns helped to make it the most profitable market for Parker. Also, because 65 percent of the business consisted of pens sold under $3, Parker management decided to attack the low end of the market with pens such as the roller-ball Vector that sold for $2.98. Parker's intention was to participate in every viable segment of the writing instrument business. Product merchandising was changed to employ new, uniform graphics with a striking black motif.

Problems emerged almost from the start. As demand for the new roller-ball and other products was picking up, the new automated manufacturing lines were not working, resulting in higher than expected labor costs and defective products. To make matters worse, production managers at the plant, bristling at the new marketing orientation, were uncooperative. Perhaps the biggest problem occurred with advertising. The new management decreed that "Advertising for Parker pens [no matter model or mode] will be based on a *common* creative strategy and positioning . . . The worldwide advertising theme, 'Make your mark with a Parker,' has been adopted . . . [It] will utilize similar graphic layout and photography. It will utilize an agreed-upon typeface. It will utilize the approved Parker logo/graphic design. It will be adapted from centrally supplied materials . . ." Although resistant to the notion of standardization, Ogilvy & Mather finally complied, creating a common ad for all countries that contained long copy, horizontal layout, illustrations in precisely the same place, the Parker logo at the bottom, and the "Make Your Mark with a Parker" tag line at the bottom right.

As one management critic observed, "It was the lowest-common-denominator advertising. It tried to say something to everybody and it didn't say anything to anybody." Consumers ignored the campaign, fueling the frustration of country marketing managers. Another critic pointed out that the new strategy of producing low cost pens for the world was wrong because it ran against Parker tradition and image. Moreover, when the dollar appreciated against other currencies, the products became priced out of the market. With sales and profits plummeting, the new management team was banished within a year, and the authority of country managers was reinstated. Parker's writing instruments business was sold soon thereafter to an investment group for $100 million.

Parker Pen's global misadventure is in stark contrast to the global achievements of one of their American-based competitors, A.T. Cross. Cross pens and pencils are now sold in more than 150 countries. The cherished possession of many business executives, Cross started exporting its product in 1965 by using foreign distributors. Once Cross felt it knew "the lay of the land," it established its own full-time sales force and began to tackle bigger markets. The first beachhead in Europe was Ireland where they also spent double the previous year's sales in advertising to build awareness. Eventually, the brand became the country's top seller. Similar large investments in West Germany also paid big dividends.

Moving to the next stage of its strategy, Cross decided to tailor the product, as necessary, for overseas markets. A team of engineers was sent around the world to better understand what each country might prefer. They learned, for example, that in Thailand, the product did not write as evenly as it should have. Investigating the problem, Cross engineers discovered that Thailand's hot, humid climate was causing the ink to absorb too much moisture, throwing off the flow. As a solution, they came up with a new refill design for all pens sold in the tropics, and Far East sales went up. Cross even decided to develop products purely for foreign markets, introducing fountain pens in many European countries where such products are seen as status symbols. This attention to consumers and product design and quality (e.g., Cross offers a lifetime guarantee) has resulted in a 50 percent share of the U.S. market for upper-end writing instruments and a leadership position in dozens of countries.

[a]This section is based on two excellent articles: Joseph M. Winski and Laurel Wentz, "Parker Pen: What Went Wrong?," *Advertising Age* (June 2, 1986), p. 1, and Mark Patinkin, "Cross Pen Succeeds by Doing Its Homework," Scripps Howard News, with an excerpt from Ira Magaziner's *The Silent War*. New York: Random House, 1989.

ditions at much lower costs. The need to standardize products worldwide is diminishing."[34] The implication is that there is a decreasing concentration of activities made possible by flexible manufacturing technology, as well as an increasing ability for coordination made possible by advances in information systems and telecommunications.

Factors Favoring Greater Standardization

In terms of designing global marketing programs, much has been written concerning the circumstances favoring standardization over customization. Some of the commonly observed factors suggested as favoring the use of a more standardized global marketing program include:

1. Common customer needs
2. Global customers and channels
3. Favorable trade policies and common regulations
4. Compatible technical standards
5. Transferable marketing skills

One industry observer offered the following three criteria as essential for the development of a global brand:[35]

1. Basic positioning and branding that can be applied globally
2. Technology that can be applied globally, with local tailoring
3. Capabilities for local implementation

Reinforcing these points, the head of Grey Advertising, one of the world's largest ad agencies, maintained that there are two key considerations in implementing a global marketing program.[36] First, market development and the competitive environment must be at similar stages from country to country. This criterion may be easier to satisfy with new products (e.g., as was the case with personal computers for Intel and their "Intel Inside" microprocessor campaign). As the head of another large ad agency noted:

> There is more hope for a brand yet to be developed going global than for taking current products and making them global brands, because you can't change the structure through which existing brands are being marketed. But you can create the structure for a brand that is in development. And it is that structure that determines the outcome, because without that, and a paralleling agency structure, you just have a marketing mess on your hands.[37]

The second key consideration is that consumer target markets should be alike, and consumers must share the same desires, needs, and uses for the product. Harvard's Stephen Greyser claims, "The fulcrum of global marketing rests on whether the consumer or customer segment is similar across countries seeking the same values in physical performance or psychological satisfactions or both."[38] In other words, according to Greyser, brand image must be relevant to consumers in both a product-related and non-product-related sense. As the head of a large multinational advertising agency observed:

It may sound simplistic but making the brand relevant can actually be particularly tricky when it comes to global marketing. Since brand perception alters according to past experience, a marketer needs to understand the likely perceptions and experiences of consumers in individual markets.[39]

What types of products are difficult to sell through standardized global marketing programs? Many experts note that foods and beverages that have years of tradition and entrenched preferences and tastes can be particularly difficult to sell in a standardized global fashion. For example, when Campbell Soup introduced its condensed soup into the United Kingdom in the late 1960s, Heinz's non-condensed soup was considered the category standard. Consumers there had to be convinced that adding liquid would not water the soup down. Similarly, Unilever has found that standard preferences are more common across countries in cleaning products such as detergents and soaps than with food products. Health and beauty-related products are often seen as very culture-bound and difficult to standardize. For all their huge inroads in American markets, Japanese marketers have not had much success selling consumer products such as toothpaste, cosmetics, and bath soaps there.

More generally, the following types of products and brands are often noted as likely candidates for global campaigns that are able to retain a similar marketing strategy worldwide:

1. *High technology products—such as televisions, VCRs, watches, computers, cameras, and automobiles—with strong functional images* (because the products tend to be universally understood and are not typically part of the cultural heritage).

2. *High image products—such as cosmetics, clothes, jewelry, and liquor—with strong associations to fashionability, sensuality, wealth, or status* (because they can appeal to the same type of market worldwide).

3. *Services and business-to-business products that emphasize corporate images in their global marketing campaigns* (e.g., airlines and banks).

4. *Retailers that sell to upper class individuals or that specialize in a salient, but unfulfilled need.* For example, by offering a wide variety of toys at affordable prices, Toys 'R Us transformed the European toy market by getting Europeans to buy toys for children any time of the year, and not just Christmas, and forcing competitors to level prices across countries.

5. *Brands positioned primarily on the basis of their country-of-origin* (e.g., Foster's beer).[40]

6. *Products that do not need customization or other special products to be able to function properly.* ITT found that stand-alone products such as heart pacemakers could be sold easily the same way worldwide, but integrated products such as telecommunications equipment have to be tailored to function within local phone systems.[41]

Examples of Standardized and Customized Global Marketing

What are some notable examples of *standardized* marketing? Procter & Gamble used the same slogan for their Pampers diapers—"Even When They're Wet, They're Dry"—in 58 countries. In 1991, Seagrams unveiled an ambitious $40 million global billboard campaign for Chivas Regal scotch, which they hailed as a success. Unilever's Impulse body spray offers a dual benefit of deodorant and fragrance to 40 countries by employing the same advertising concept—"boy meets girl"—which they believe is universally relevant and meaningful. L'Oreal is offered to women all over as a reward,

"It's Expensive and I'm Worth It." Pert Plus (Wash & Go in some countries) 2-in-1 shampoo and conditioner offers convenience and ease of use in all countries in which it is marketed. Although Snuggle goes by different names in different countries (e.g., Kuschelweich in Germany, Coccolino in Italy, and Mimosin in France), the teddy bear symbol is the same.[42]

What are some more notable examples of brands with *differentiated* global marketing strategies? Although Heineken is seen as an everyday brand in the Netherlands, it is considered a "top-shelf" brand almost everywhere else. For example, a case of Heineken costs almost twice as much in the United States as a case of the most popular American beer, Budweiser.[43] For a long time, its slogan in the United Kingdom and other countries—"Heineken Refreshes the Parts Other Beers Can't Reach"—was different from its U.S. positioning. Although advertising for Nescafe, the world's largest brand of coffee, generally stresses the taste, aroma, and warmth of shared moments, the brand was successfully positioned in Thailand as a way to relax from the pressures of daily life.[44] In Russia, Procter & Gamble decided to roll out three new detergent brands at three price points: its major international detergent, Ariel, as a premium brand; its Eastern European brand, Tix, as a mid-priced brand; and its American stalwart, Tide, as an economy brand. P&G justified marketing Tide differently from in the United States by maintaining that although the Tide name had some residue of awareness in the Russian market, little specific knowledge existed. Accordingly, it was felt that its formula, pricing, and positioning could be completely different from that in the United States.[45]

Changing Landscape for Global Brands

Finally, it should be noted that the landscape for global brands is dramatically changing, especially with respect to younger consumers. Due to increased consumer mobility, better communication capabilities, and expanding transnational entertainment options, lifestyles are fast becoming more similar across countries within sociodemographic segments than they are within countries across sociodemographic segments. Because of the growth of global media such as MTV, a teenager in Paris may have more in common with a teenager in London, New York, Sydney, or almost any other major city in the world than with his or her own parents. This younger generation may be more easily influenced by trends and broader cultural movements fueled by worldwide exposure to movies, television, and other media than ever before. Certainly one consequence of this trend is that those brands who are able to tap into the global sensibilities of the youth market may be better able to adopt a standardized branding program and marketing strategy.

ORGANIZING THE GLOBAL MARKETING EFFORT

The fourth and final decision in developing a global marketing program is to decide on the most appropriate organizational structure for managing global brands. In general, there are three main approaches to organizing for the global marketing effort:

1. Centralization at home office or headquarters
2. Decentralization of decision making to local foreign markets
3. Some combination of centralization and decentralization

Companies vary as to which approach they adopt in organizing the global marketing effort. In general, firms tend to adopt a combination of centralization and decentralization. One area of centralization is with advertising. As noted in chapter 10, firms increasingly are consolidating their worldwide ad accounts and shifting most or all of their advertising billings to agencies with extensive global networks. Firms are making these moves as a means to reduce costs and increase efficiency and control. Nevertheless, Braun and Levi-Strauss's regional managers have been able to bar a global campaign from being run in their area. Unilever's regional managers who seek to substitute their own campaigns, however, must produce research showing that the global plan is inappropriate. Coke and Procter & Gamble take the middle ground, developing a global communications program but testing them and fine-tuning them in meetings with regional managers.[46]

Building Global Customer-Based Brand Equity

The previous section considered the four major decisions that must be made in developing a global branding strategy. In this section, we delve in greater depth into how to best build strong global brands. In terms of building global customer-based brand equity, the basic tactics already discussed in Part II of the text still apply. In particular, it is necessary to create brand awareness and a positive brand image in each country in which the brand is sold. As noted above, the means by which sources of brand equity are created may differ from country to country, or the actual sources of brand equity themselves may vary across countries in terms of the particular attribute or benefit associations that make up the points of parity and points of difference. Nevertheless, it is critically important in each country that there are sufficient levels of brand awareness and strong, favorable, and unique brand associations to provide sources of brand equity.

The danger in entering new markets is that marketers take "short cuts" and fail to build the necessary sources of brand equity by inappropriately exporting marketing programs from other countries or markets in which the brand has already established a great deal of equity. Many companies have learned this lesson the hard way. For example, in 1990, Pepsi bought the rights to bottle and sell its soft drink to German retailers. Pepsi attempted to match Coke's high prices in the market without sufficient "pull" from brand-building activities and merchandising and without sufficient "push" from a strong distribution network with the right kind of trucks, coolers, or other facets. Pepsi so alienated two major German retailers, Tengelmann and Asko, that it actually lost distribution in those stores for a couple of years. The brand languished with a market share under 5 percent as a result and has only recently started to bounce back.[47]

Building brand equity in a global context must be a carefully designed and implemented process. As noted above, the generally accepted strategy is to find ways to best balance local adaptation and global standardization. In many, if not most, markets, the cost savings of standardization may not outweigh the revenue potential from tailoring programs in some fashion to different groups of consumers.[48] Each aspect of the marketing program is a candidate for globalization. Which elements of the marketing program should be standardized, and to what degree? In a basic sense, cost and revenue considerations should be the primary considerations in deciding which elements of the marketing program should be adapted for which country.

Riesenbeck and Freeling advocate a mixed strategy, standardizing the "core aspects" of the brand (i.e., those that provide its main competitive edge), but allowing local adaptation of "secondary aspects." According to their approach, branding, positioning, and product formulation are more likely to be standardized; advertising and pricing less so; and distribution is most often localized.[49] Branding Brief 14–3 describes how leading marketing strategists Quelch and Hoff believe global marketing should be customized.

We next consider some specific considerations for the three main approaches for building global brand equity.

CHOOSING BRAND ELEMENTS

As chapter 4 pointed out, in assembling the brand elements that make up the brand, an important consideration is their geographical transferability. As Figure 4–2 showed, a number of brands have encountered resistance because of difficulty in translating their name, packaging, slogans, or other brand elements to another culture. In general, nonverbal brand elements such as logos, symbols, and characters are more likely to directly transfer effectively—at least as long as their meaning is visually clear—than verbal brand elements that may need to be translated into another language. Nonverbal brand elements are more likely to be helpful in creating brand awareness than brand image, however, which may require more explicit meaning and direct statements.

Even nonverbal elements can encounter translation problems. For example, certain colors have strong cultural meaning. Marketing campaigns using various shades of green in advertising, packaging, and other marketing programs ran into trouble in Malaysia where these colors symbolize death and disease.[50] In some cases, verbal elements can be translated into native languages without much appreciable loss in meaning. For example, Coke's "Can't Beat the Feeling" slogan was translated to the equivalent of "I Feel Coke" in Japan, "Unique Sensation" in Italy, and "The Feeling of Life" in Chile. Germany proved a problem—no translation really worked—so the slogan was kept in English because of the relatively large bilingual audience there.

Because of a desire to standardize globally, however, many firms have attempted to create more uniform brand elements. Pursuing a global branding strategy, Mars chose to replace its Treets and Bonitos brands with the M&M's brand worldwide and changed the name of its third largest U.K. brand—Marathon—to the Snickers name used in the rest of Europe and the United States.[51] To create a stronger global brand, PepsiCo pulled together its dozens of company-owned brands of potato chips—previously sold under different names—and began to market them abroad all under a more uniform Lay's logo. They also boosted advertising and improved quality to enhance the brand image at the same time.[52]

DEVELOPING SUPPORTING MARKETING PROGRAMS

Perhaps the most adaptable aspect in going global is the supporting marketing program. A number of possible changes may be adopted across countries, as follows:

Customizing Global Marketing

John Quelch, with his co-author Edward Hoff, wrote an insightful piece on how to develop global marketing strategies.[a] The central tenet to their approach is that the big issue faced by marketers is not whether to go global, but how to tailor the global marketing concept to fit each business and how to make it work:

> Too often, executives view global marketing as an either/or proposition—either full standardization or local control. But when a global approach can fall anywhere on a spectrum from tight worldwide coordination on programming details to loose agreement on a product idea, why the extreme view? In applying the global marketing concept and making it work, flexibility is essential. Managers need to tailor the approach they use to each element of the business system and marketing program.

Quelch and Hoff examine four dimensions of global marketing—business functions, products, marketing mix elements, and countries—in light of the degree of standardization or adaptation that is appropriate. In doing so, they make a number of valuable observations, such as the following:

1. Marketing is usually one of the last functions to be centrally directed because it is difficult to measure its effectiveness.
2. Products that enjoy high scale economies or are not highly culture bound are easier to market globally than others.
3. For most products, the appropriate degree of standardization varies from one element of the marketing mix to another.
4. Strategic elements like product positioning are more easily standardized than execution-sensitive elements like sales promotions.
5. The extent to which a decentralized multinational wishes to pursue global marketing will often vary from one country to another.
6. Because large markets with strong local management are often less willing to accept global programs, headquarters should make standard marketing programs reflect the needs of large rather than small markets.

Quelch and Hoff note that the challenge in implementing a global marketing program is the extent of the gap between the current and desired levels of program adaptation or standardization on the four dimensions. Although the urgency with which a gap must be closed depends on factors such as a company's strategy and financial performance, competitive pressures, technological change, and converging consumer values, Quelch and Hoff caution against moving forward too far too fast, describing how headquarters can intervene with local offices by informing, persuading, coordinating, approving, and directing. They conclude their recommendations by making five suggestions as to how to motivate and retain talented country managers when making the shift to global marketing:

1. Encourage field managers to generate ideas.

2. Ensure that the field manager participates in the development of the marketing strategies and programs for global brands.

3. Maintain a product portfolio that includes, where scale economies permit, local as well as regional and global brands.

4. Allow country managers continued control of their marketing budgets so they can respond to local customer needs and counter local competition.

5. Emphasize the general management responsibilities of country managers that extend beyond the marketing function.

To illustrate these ideas, Quelch and Hoff contrast global marketing between Coca-Cola and Nestlé (see Figures 14–7 and 14–8).

---

[a]John A. Quelch and Edward J. Hoff, "Customizing Global Marketing," *Harvard Business Review,* 64 (3) (May–June, 1986), pp. 59–68.

Product Features

Many marketers believe that only certain products can be marketed similarly—in some places—and only after variables like marketing mix and culture are fully analyzed, understood, and incorporated into the marketing program. A global marketing pioneer, Procter & Gamble often learned this lesson the hard way. For example, when P&G entered the Japanese market with Pampers disposable diapers in 1977, it believed a "baby was a baby" and tried to sell the same diaper to Japanese parents that it sold in the United States. Although it met with great success initially, its growth slowed. When a Japanese competitor entered the market with a new design that included reusable parts, its market share dropped from 90 percent to under 10 percent. The problem was that P&G failed to recognize that Japanese housewives did their laundry daily—not weekly as in American households—and were using the disposables only at night. After introducing smaller, thinner diapers better suited to Japanese babies, they regained market share.[53]

As another example, when P&G introduced Vizir liquid detergent in Europe in the early 1980s, the product flopped because they didn't recognize that European washing machines were not designed to accept liquid detergents. The product fared better when it was sold with a reusable dispensing ball that sat atop the wash load.[54] Learning from its mistakes, many of Procter & Gamble's mainstay products are now changed to suit different markets. The smell of Camay soap, the flavor of Crest toothpaste, and the formula of Head and Shoulders shampoo now all vary by country.

One reason why so many companies ran into trouble initially going overseas is that they unknowingly—or perhaps even deliberately—overlooked differences in consumer behavior. Because of the relative expense and sometimes unsophisticated nature of the marketing research industry in smaller markets, many companies chose to forgo basic consumer research to put products on the shelf to "see what would happen." As a result, they sometimes became aware of these consumer differences only after the fact. To better understand consumer preferences and avoid these types of mistakes, marketers may need to conduct research into local markets. For example,

Exhibit I

Global marketing planning matrix:
how far to go

		Adaptation		Standardization	
		Full	Partial	Partial	Full
Business functions	Research and development			Nestlé	Coca-Cola
	Finance and accounting			Nestlé	Coca-Cola
	Manufacturing		Nestlé	Coca-Cola	
	Procurement	Nestlé		Coca-Cola	
	Marketing		Nestlé		Coca-Cola
Products	Low cultural grounding / High economies or efficiencies				Coca-Cola
	Low cultural grounding / Low economies or efficiencies				
	High cultural grounding / High economies or efficiencies		Nestlé		
	High cultural grounding / Low economies or efficiencies				
Marketing mix elements	Product design			Nestlé	Coca-Cola
	Brand name			Nestlé	Coca-Cola
	Product positioning		Nestlé		Coca-Cola
	Packaging			Coca-Cola	
	Advertising theme		Nestlé		Coca-Cola
	Pricing		Nestlé	Coca-Cola	
	Advertising copy	Nestlé			Coca-Cola
	Distribution	Nestlé	Coca-Cola		
	Sales promotion	Nestlé	Coca-Cola		
	Customer service	Nestlé	Coca-Cola		
Countries Region 1	Country A			Nestlé	Coca-Cola
	Country B			Nestlé	Coca-Cola
Region 2	Country C		Nestlé		Coca-Cola
	Country D		Nestlé		Coca-Cola
	Country E	Nestlé			Coca-Cola

Nestlé   Coca-Cola

FIGURE 14–7 Contrasting Coca-Cola's and Nestlé's Global Marketing Planning

Exhibit II   Global marketing planning matrix: how to get there

		Informing	Persuading	Coordinating	Approving	Directing
Business functions	Research and development	■	■	■	■	■
	Finance and accounting	■	■	■	■	■
	Manufacturing	▨	▨	■	■	
	Procurement	▨		■		
	Marketing	▨	■	▨	■	■
Products	Low cultural grounding High economies or efficiencies	■	■	■	■	
	Low cultural grounding Low economies or efficiencies					
	High cultural grounding High economies or efficiencies	▨	▨	▨		
	High cultural grounding Low economies or efficiencies					
Marketing mix elements	Product design	■	■	■	■	■
	Brand name	■	■	■	■	■
	Product positioning	■	■	■	■	■
	Packaging	■	■	■	■	
	Advertising theme	▨	■	■	■	■
	Pricing	▨	▨	■	■	
	Advertising copy	▨	▨	■		
	Distribution	■	■			
	Sales promotion	▨	■			
	Customer service	▨	■			
Countries Region 1	Country A				▨	■
	Country B			▨		■
Region 2	Country C			▨		■
	Country D		▨			■
	Country E	▨				■

▨ Nestlé   ■ Coca-Cola

FIGURE 14-8 Contrasting Coca-Cola's and Nestlé's Global Marketing Implementation

Japanese firms often hire local marketing experts to help design their products to better suit local tastes.[55]

In fact, in many cases marketing research reveals that product differences are just not justified for certain countries. At one time, Palmolive soap was sold globally, although with 22 different fragrances, 17 different packages, 9 different shapes, and with numerous different positionings. After marketing analyses to reap the benefits of global marketing, they now just employ 7 fragrances, 1 core packaging design, and 3 main shapes, all executed around two related positionings (one for developed markets and one for developing markets).[56] Branding Brief 14–4 describes how UPS has attempted to adapt its service for the European market.

From a corporate perspective, one obvious solution to the tradeoff between global versus local brands is to sell both types of brands as part of the brand portfolio in a category. Even companies that have succeeded with global brands maintain that standardized international marketing programs work only with some products, in some places, and at some times, and will never totally replace brands and ads with local appeal.[57] For example, while Coca-Cola sells Coke to a growing group of consumers in Asia who see it as a new and exciting taste, it also sells local brands there such as "Seasons" in Singapore, which has flavors such as "Waterchestnut Drink" and "Grass Jelly Drink." This combination of local and global brands enables Coca-Cola to exploit the benefits of global branding and global trends in tastes while also tapping into traditional domestic markets at the same time.

Prices

In designing a global pricing strategy, the value pricing principle from chapter 5 still generally applies. Thus, it is necessary to understand in each country what consumer perceptions of the value of the brand are, their willingness to pay, and their elasticities with respect to price changes. Sometimes differences in these considerations permit differences in pricing strategies. For example, brands such as Levi's, Heineken, and Perrier have been able to command a much higher price outside their domestic market because they have a distinctly different brand image—and thus sources of brand equity—in other countries that consumers place more value on. In addition to these consumer differences across countries, differences in distribution structures, competitive positions, and tax and exchange rates all may justify differences in prices.

Unfortunately, setting drastically different prices across countries is becoming more difficult.[58] Pressures for international price alignment have arisen, in part, because of increasing numbers of legitimate imports and exports and the ability of retailers and suppliers to exploit price differences through "gray imports" across borders. This problem is especially acute in Europe where price differences are often large—prices of identical car models may vary by 30 percent to 40 percent—and ample opportunity exists to ship or shop across national boundaries.

In such cases, Hermann Simon, a German expert on pricing, recommends creating an international "price corridor" that takes into account both the inherent differences between countries and alignment pressures. Specifically, the corridor is calculated by company headquarters and its country subsidiaries by considering market data for the individual countries, price elasticities in the countries, parallel imports resulting from price differentials, currency exchange rates, costs in countries and arbi-

---

BRANDING BRIEF 14-4

UPS's European Express[a]

Over the last decade, United Parcel Service of America has spent $1 billion to buy sixteen delivery businesses, put brown uniforms on 25,000 Europeans, and spray its brown paint on 10,000 delivery trucks in the process of becoming the largest delivery company in Europe. UPS had to overcome a number of obstacles along the way. French drivers were outraged that they could not have wine with lunch; British drivers protested when their dogs were banned from delivery trucks; Spaniards were dismayed when they realized the brown UPS trucks resembled the local hearses; and Germans were shocked when brown shirts were required for the first time since 1945.

Hampering the spread of services and service-related jobs in Europe is the reluctance there to part with traditional ways of doing business, such as state-owned monopolies and rigid work practices (e.g., resisting part-time work and providing stronger employment protection and higher non-wage costs than enjoyed by workers in the United States). The standards of service, like the techniques for providing it, are well below American levels. For example, Manpower Inc. virtually created the temporary help business in Europe and derives more than 40 percent of its world-wide revenues there. Although UPS operations are basically the same, the company faces problems that may be less common or even nonexistent in the United States—truck restrictions on weekends and holidays, low bridges and tunnels, widely varying weight regulations, terrible traffic, and in some places, limited highway systems and primitive airports and night curfews.

Marketing challenges abound. In Europe, UPS is still building awareness, hampered by the fact that it has only been advertising for the last six years and has been using country-specific advertising. On the supply side, UPS is also building up its European infrastructure there and trying to drive sales to reach critical mass. In a competitive marketplace, battling with FedEx, TNT, and DHL, UPS will need to make all the right moves to survive.

---

[a]Adapted from Dana Milbank, "Can Europe Deliver?," *Wall Street Journal* (September 30, 1994), p. R15. Alan Saloman, "Delivering a Market Battle," *Advertising Age.*

---

trage costs between them, and data on competition and distribution. No country is then allowed to set its price outside the corridor: Countries with lower prices have to raise them, and countries with higher prices have to lower them. Another possible strategy suggested by Simon is introduce different brands in high-price, high-income countries and in low-price, low-income countries, depending on the relative cost tradeoffs of standardization versus customization.

In Asia, many American brands command hefty premiums over inferior home-grown competitors as consumers in these countries strongly associate the United States with high-quality consumer products.[59] In assessing the viability of Asian markets, because of the large consumer population involved, it is important not to just look at average income but to also consider the distribution of incomes. For example, although the average annual income in India is maybe only $330, some 60 million people can still afford the same types of products that might be sold to middle-class Europeans. In China, Gillette recently introduced Oral-B toothbrushes at 90 cents, as compared to locally produced toothbrushes sold at 19 cents. Gillette's reasoning is that even if they only gained 10 percent of the Chinese market, it still would sell more toothbrushes there than they were currently selling in the U.S. market.

Channels

In many cases, distribution is the key to the success of a global marketing program. For example, foreign companies have struggled for years to break into Japan's rigid distribution system that locks out many foreign goods. China's primitive logistics—poor roads, jammed rivers, and clogged railways—and inexperienced, indifferent, and often corrupt middlemen present a different kind of challenge.[60]

As in domestic markets, it is often desirable to blend "push" and "pull" strategies to build brand equity. This is certainly true in global markets and can present special challenges. Concerned about poor refrigeration in European stores, Haagen-Dazs ended up supplying thousands of free freezers to retailers across the continent.[61] Although Coca-Cola cultivates an All-American nice-guy image overseas—through its cheery advertising and merchandising—it has been hard-nosed about achieving adequate distribution coverage and support. Coca-Cola has wielded both "carrots" and "sticks" in its distribution strategy, balancing rewards and punishments with its overseas bottling partners and retailers.[62]

In some cases, distribution channels have to be built from scratch. For example, after thirteen years of negotiations, Nestlé was finally invited into the Heilongjiang province of China in 1987 to boost milk production. Soon thereafter, Nestlé opened a powdered milk and baby cereal plant in China. They deemed the overburdened local trains and roads undependable to collect milk and deliver finished goods. Nestlé chose to establish its own distribution network known as "milk loads" between 27 villages in the region and factory collection points called "chilling centers" where farmers could push wheelbarrows, pedal bicycles, or walk to have their milk weighed and analyzed. Production has exploded as a result.[63]

Marketing Communication Program

Perhaps the most adaptable element of a global branding program is marketing communications. In this section, we consider some key issues in developing a global marketing communication program concerning advertising message, execution, and media, and promotion and sponsorship.

Advertising Message   In going abroad, because the brand is often at an earlier stage of development, it may be necessary to first establish awareness and key points of parity. Once brand awareness and points of parity category considerations have been established, then additional competitive considerations may come into the picture.

For example, when Kellogg's first introduced its corn flakes into the Brazilian market in 1962, cereal was eaten as a dry snack by Brazilians—like Americans eat potato chips—as many Brazilians did not eat breakfast at all. As a result, the ads there centered on the family and breakfast table—much more so than in the United States.

As in other Latin American countries where big breakfasts are not part of the meal tradition, Kellogg's task has been to inform consumers of the "proper" way to eat cereal with cold milk in the morning.[64] Similarly, a challenge to Kellogg's in increasing the relatively low per capita consumption of ready-to-eat breakfast cereals in Asia is the low consumption of milk products and the positive distaste with which drinking milk is held in many Asian countries.

Advertising Execution   In going global, it is important to recognize that although the brand positioning may be the same in different countries, creative strategies in advertising may have to differ. Thus, even if a basic positioning is adopted everywhere, it may be adapted and translated as appropriate into local markets. For example, Dove soap adopts the same basic positioning worldwide—based on the fact that it contains one-quarter cleansing cream—but has used testimonials where pretty, thirty-ish women praise the brand's skin-softening virtues in their own languages in countries such as Australia, France, Germany, and Italy.[65]

Different countries can be characterized as being more or less receptive to different creative styles. For example, humor is more common in United States and United Kingdom ads than, say, in German ads. European countries such as France and Italy are more tolerant of sex appeal and nudity in advertising. William Wells, former ad agency executive at DDB Needham, makes the general distinction in advertising response between *high context* cultures, where the meaning of a message cannot be understood without its context, from *low context* cultures, where the meaning of a message can be isolated from the context in which it occurs and understood as an independent entity, as follows:[66]

> High context cultures—much of the Middle East, Asia, and Africa, for example—are relational, holistic, integrative, intuitive, and contemplative, while the low-context cultures found in North America and much of Western Europe are logical, analytical, linear, and action-oriented. In high context cultures, emphasis is placed on interpersonal relationships between communicators, nonverbal expression, physical setting, and social circumstances. Low context cultures tend to stress clearly articulated spoken or written messages.

Relatedly, Roth found that in countries with high individualism (e.g., European countries), brand images that emphasized functional, variety, novelty, or experiential needs were more effective than social image strategies that emphasized group membership and affiliation benefits. On the other hand, cultures with low individualism (e.g., Asian countries) were more amenable to social image strategies than sensory brand images. Roth also found that in low power distance cultures (e.g., Germany, Netherlands, and Argentina) in which people are not highly focused on social roles and group affiliation, functional brand images that deemphasize the social, symbolic, sensory, and experiential benefits of products were most appropriate. On the other hand, for countries with a high degree of power distance (e.g., China, France, and Belgium) in which people are more concerned with prestige, wealth, and class differences, Roth found that social and/or sensory needs were more appropriate.[67]

In terms of a concrete example, Procter & Gamble found that although their U.S. ads for Camay soap could be effectively adapted for other countries, they turned out to be a disaster in Japan. Specifically, Camay traditionally has been advertised as a luxury soap that makes a woman's skin feel soft and smell sweet, allowing her to feel more attractive as a result. Ads in other countries showed a beautiful woman bathing blissfully in a bathtub of suds. In ads for France, Italy, and Venezuela, her husband came into the bathroom and talked to her while she was bathing. In Japan, the ads also featured a man entering the bathroom and gently touching the woman's skin and complimenting her while she bathed. Although these ads might perhaps be seen as sensual in other countries, such behavior could be considered rude and in bad taste in Japan—even the idea of a man being in the same bathroom with a female can be seen as taboo there. As a result of negative public reaction, the Japanese ad for Camay was changed to show a beautiful European-looking woman—alone—in a European style bath.

Advertising Media   Numerous media options exist globally. Although commercial television time has been limited worldwide, the penetration of satellite and cable TV has expanded the broadcast media options available. As a result, it is easier to simultaneously air the same TV commercial in many different countries. American cable networks such as CNN (seen by 78 million households in 100 countries) and MTV (seen by 210 million households in 78 countries) and other networks such as Sky TV in Commonwealth countries and Star TV in Asia have increased advertisers' global reach. *Fortune, Time, Newsweek,* and other magazines have printed foreign editions in English for years. Increasingly, other publishers are starting or adding local-language editions, either by licensing their trademarks to local companies, entering into joint ventures or creating wholly owned subsidiaries, e.g., *Rolling Stone* in French; *Esquire* in Italian, German, and Japanese; *Fortune* in Italian; and *Life* in German.[68] *Elle* has nineteen editions targeting the same demographic group but tailored to the country where it is published.

Each country has its own unique media challenges and opportunities. For example, when Colgate-Palmolive decided to further penetrate the 630 million or so people that live in rural India, it had to overcome the fact that more than half of all Indian villagers are illiterate, and only one-third live in households with television sets. Their solution was to create half-hour infomercials carried through the countryside in video vans.[69]

Promotion and Sponsorship   Chapters 6 and 7 described some of the issues in developing sponsorship programs. It was noted there that sponsorship programs have a long tradition in many countries outside the United States because of a historical lack of advertising media there. Increasingly sponsorship can now become executed on a global basis and entertainment and sports sponsorship can be an especially effective way to reach a younger audience. For example, Nestlé has run worldwide promotional tie-ins with Disney movies such as the Lion King. Mars has become a worldwide sponsor of the World Cup and Olympics.

LEVERAGING SECONDARY BRAND ASSOCIATIONS

The third way to build global brand equity, leveraging secondary brand associations, is probably the most likely to *have* to be changed across countries. Because the meaning of various entities that may be linked to a brand may take on very different meanings in different countries—the fact that different knowledge exists for a certain person, place, or thing—secondary associations may have to be leveraged differently in different countries. For example, American companies such as Coca-Cola, Levi-Strauss, and Nike gain an important source of equity in going overseas by virtue of their American heritage that is not as much of an issue or asset in their domestic market. Harley-Davidson has aggressively marketed its classic American image—customized for different cultures—to generate a quarter of its sales from abroad. Chapter 7 reviewed how country of origin, as in these cases, could be leveraged to build brand equity. Thus, in developing global brands, it is important to consider how secondary associations may vary in their strength, favorability, and uniqueness and may therefore play a different role in building brand equity.

Building Brand Equity across Other Market Segments

The above discussion concentrated on market segmentation based on national boundaries. Many of the principles discussed concerning building brand equity are equally valid for market segments based on other criteria. In this section, we briefly consider several other segmentation plans and their implications for branding and marketing strategy.

REGIONAL MARKET SEGMENTS

Regionalization is an important recent trend that, perhaps on the surface, seems to run counter to the globalization trend. Although marketers have developed different marketing programs for different geographical regions of a country for years, "regional marketing" received a boost in the United States with Campbell's well-publicized move to a regionalized marketing plan. Starting in the 1980s, Campbell's began to tailor its soup products, advertising, promotion, and sales efforts to fit different regions of the country—and even individual neighborhoods within cities. Dividing the United States into 22 regions, a combined sales and marketing force received marketing strategy and media buying information and was given an ad and trade promotion budget.[70] Some examples of tailored Campbell's programs during this time included a car giveaway in Pittsburgh tied to a local TV station; short film spots for Campbell's dip soups and its brand-name mushrooms in two Sacramento cinemas; soup billboards atop a ski lift in upstate New York; and a Spanish radio and giveaway campaign for V-8 juice in Northern California.[71] In a similar spirit, Pepsi divided its U.S. operations into four regional companies to gear its marketing locally.

Around the same time, Joel Garreau published *The Nine Nations of North America*, which argued that North America was divided into nine "nations," regions populated by people sharing distinct values, attitudes, and styles. These differences were found to manifest themselves in market behavior. As one observer noted:[72]

> . . . people are different in different parts of the country. For example, Northeasterners and Midwesterners prefer chicken noodle and tomato soups, but in California, cream of mushroom is number one. Pepper pot soup sells primarily in the Philadel-

phia area, and cream of vegetable on the West Coast. People in the Southwest drive more pickup trucks, people in the Northeast more vans, and Californians like high-priced imported cars such as BMWs and Mercedes Benzes. Texans drive big cars, New Yorkers like smaller ones. New Hampshirites drink more beer per capita than other Americans. The anxious denizens of Atlanta consume more aspirin and antacids a head, and sweet-toothed Mormons of Salt Lake City eat more candy bars and marshmallows.

Interest in regional marketing has been driven by a number of factors: a realization that mass markets are splintering, an availability of computerized sales data from supermarket scanners that reveal pockets of sales strengths and weaknesses in different parts of the country, and an opportunity to employ marketing communications that now permit more focused targeting of consumer groups defined along virtually any lines. The shift from national advertising to sales promotions, in particular, necessitated a more market-by-market planning. Different battles are now being fought between brands in different regions of the country. Anheuser-Busch and Miller Brewing have waged a fierce battle in Texas where nearly one in ten beers sold in the United States is drunk. Anheuser has made sizable inroads in recent years through special ad campaigns, displays, and sales strategies. As one observer noted, "Texans believe it's a whole different country down here. They don't want you to just slap an armadillo in a TV spot."[73]

Regional marketing must be done carefully and is not without its drawbacks.[74] Modifying products can lead to production headaches. For example, when Campbell's set out to make a spicier version of its nacho cheese soup for the west and southwest United States, so many jalapeno peppers were added that it created a gas cloud during manufacturing that made it virtually impossible for its factory workers to overcome! Marketing efficiency may suffer and costs may rise with regional marketing. Moreover, regional campaigns may force local producers to become more competitive or can blur a brand's national identity.

OTHER DEMOGRAPHIC AND CULTURAL SEGMENTS

Any market segment, however defined, may be considered as a candidate for a specialized marketing and branding program. For example, chapter 3 noted how consumers may be categorized according to demographic dimensions such as age, income, gender, and race, as well as psychographic considerations. These more descriptive factors often are related to more fundamental behavioral considerations as to how different types of consumers shop for products or think about brands. These differences in attitudes and behavior with respect to products and brands can often serve as the rationale for a separate branding and marketing program. The segmentation decision ultimately rests on cost and benefit considerations as to the costs of customizing marketing efforts versus the benefits of a more targeted focus.

For example, chapter 13 described how important it is for marketers to consider age segments and how younger consumers can be brought into the consumer franchise. As another example, the Hispanic market in the United States is estimated to have $220 billion in purchasing power. Various firms have created specialized marketing programs with different products, advertising, promotions, and so on to better reach and persuade this market. For example, Kraft launched a brand of fast-melting

---

Marketing to African Americans[a]

Census and marketing surveys have revealed the buying power of the African American community. Representing approximately 12 percent of the population, their expenditures approach $300 billion in sales. Despite that fact, only $736 million were spent to specifically target the African American market in 1990, compared to $51 billion in total advertising dollars—only a little over 1 percent of the total. Although much marketing has targeted baby boomers, the elderly, and other demographic or psychographic groups, many critics argue that the African American market has not been effectively targeted by many companies. Marlene Rossman, author of *Multicultural Marketing,* makes the following argument:

> Whether it is a poverty myth, the fear of venturing into an unknown market, or just plain ignorance that holds back mainstream markets, the fact is not enough goods and services are being targeted to the African American market and its segments. Many businesses that are struggling to stay afloat continue to target the same overtapped general market when going after black consumers could make the difference between breaking even and increased market share and profits.

Because almost all African Americans speak English as their first and primary language and watch much network television, many companies rely on their general marketing campaigns to reach these consumers. Black media executives such as Thomas Burrell, chairman of Burrell Advertising in Chicago, the largest black-owned agency in the United States, maintains that such an approach is a mistake: "Black people aren't dark-skinned white people. We have different preferences and customs, and we require special effort."

African Americans can be found in virtually every conceivable income, education, and geographic segment. At the same time, they often have unique attitudes and behaviors that distinguish them from other groups. Many observers note the important role of religion, church, and family with African Americans. As a result of their historical experiences, African Americans are often thought to exhibit a strong togetherness and pride in their heritage. In terms of buying habits, African Americans spend a disproportionate amount of their income on apparel, footwear, and home electronics. For example, recognizing that African Americans often prefer larger helpings of sugar, cream, or nondairy creamer in their coffee, CoffeeMate began marketing to African Americans more specifically through black radio, magazines, and billboards, with a corresponding increase in sales.

Alcohol and tobacco companies were some of the first firms to develop campaigns targeted specifically to African American consumers, in recognition of different product preferences held by these consumers (e.g., a disproportionate amount of purchases of menthol cigarettes, certain types of hard liquors—brandy, scotch, and cognac—and malt liquor beers than the general population). The marketing efforts of some of these early pioneers, however, were controversial. Colt 45's suggestive ad campaign—portraying actor Billy Dee Williams romancing a young woman to drink the malt liquor while the tag line proclaimed, "The power of Colt 45. It works every time."—was roundly criticized as being in poor taste.

Other marketing campaigns attempt to address African Americans through existing campaigns in some way. Several possible shortcomings have been noted by marketing critics. Ads may fall prey to what African Americans decry as "eleventh man black tokenism," that is, when an African American is stuck in the back of a crowd in an ad in what is seen as a blatant appeal to the African American audience. Other mistakes pointed out by marketing critics are to simple-mindedly replace white actors with black actors or run the same ads on black media vehicles. For example, because a large proportion of their travelers are African Americans, Greyhound decided to promote its low cross-country fares on urban contemporary radio stations that appealed to that group. Because they used the same ad as was being run for the mass market, the music in the background was country and western, "turning off and tuning out" many of the black listeners. Similarly, Mattel several years ago put out a "black Barbie" in an attempt to attract African American consumers, but the doll was simply a "white Barbie" (e.g., same facial features) painted one shade of brown and with straight, brown hair.

In terms of building brand equity, the challenge is how to create relevant marketing programs and communication campaigns to African American consumers, and accurately portray brand personality and user and usage imagery. Along these lines, one president of a black-owned ad agency asserted that the formula for marketing to blacks consists of relevance, recognition, and respect. Several guidelines should be adhered to:

> First, it is important to recognize the diversity of the African American market—just as in the mass market, there is great variety in lifestyle across different geographic and psychographic segments in the African American market. For example, Cover Girl advertises its ten different shades of makeup designed for African Americans, from Cappucino Cream to Rich Mahogany. Such understanding clearly requires properly conducting and interpreting marketing research.

> Second, design marketing campaigns that are relevant to the lifestyles of African Americans and reflect their consumer sensibilities. One survey indicated that 60 percent of black consumers feel that most television and print ads "are designed only for white people." What types of messages should be sent? Rossman makes the following argument: "When marketing to African Americans, keep in mind that they value self-image style, and personal elegance. . . . African Americans are trendsetters. . . . African Americans often want to define their own style rather than follow what the establishment dictates."

> Finally, explore media that specifically targets African Americans, e.g., cable's Black Entertainment Television (BET); *Ebony, Essence, Black Enterprise,* and other magazines and newspapers; and urban contemporary and other types of radio stations. Even general media should be bought differently. A 1992 study by BBDO ad agency revealed that none of the top ten

programs most watched by blacks were on the list of the top ten shows most watched by the general market.

The challenge is to target African Americans in a way to build brand equity without fostering stereotypes, offending sensibilities, or lumping segments together. As with global brand programs, standardization and customization should be blended as appropriate.

[a]Based on material from Marlene Rossman, *Multicultural Marketing: Selling to a Diverse America*, New York: AMACOM, 1994, and Barbara Lloyd, *Capitalizing on the American Dream: Marketing to America's Ethnic Minorities*, Stanford Business School independent study, 1990.

white cheese and rich cream called Valle Lindo ("beautiful valley") backed with ads airing on Spanish language television and radio stations especially for Hispanic consumers.[75] Branding Brief 14–5 describes marketing efforts to build brand equity with African Americans.

Beyond the expense involved, one major concern raised by marketing critics in creating separate marketing campaigns for different demographic groups is that some consumers may not like the fact that they are being targeted because they are "different" as that only reinforces their image or stereotype as outsiders or a minority. Moreover, consumers *not* in the market segment targeted may feel more alienated or at least distanced from the company and brand as a result.

Review

Increasingly, it is imperative that marketers properly define and implement a global branding strategy. A number of factors are encouraging firms to sell their products and services abroad. Some advantages of a global marketing program are economies of scale in production and distribution, lower marketing costs, communication of power and scope, consistency in brand image, an ability to leverage good ideas quickly and efficiently, uniformity of marketing practices, and thus greater competitiveness. The more standardized the marketing program, in general, the more that these different advantages will actually be realized. At the same time, the primary disadvantage of a standardized global marketing program is that it may potentially ignore important differences across countries in consumer needs, wants, and usage patterns for products; consumer response to marketing mix elements; product development and the competitive environment, legal environment, marketing institutions, and administrative procedures.

In developing a global marketing program, marketers attempt to obtain as many of these advantages as possible while minimizing any of these possible disadvantages. Specifically, the four major decisions in developing a global marketing program are deciding which markets to enter, how to enter markets, how to design marketing programs, and how to organize the marketing effort. Market entry decisions depend on considerations such as the inherent attractiveness of the market, the possible competitive advantages in the market, the manufacturing and marketing costs of servicing the market, the level of risk involved in the market, and so on. The three main strategies to enter new markets are to export existing brands and products; to acquire an already existing brand; or to create some form of brand alliance with another firm (e.g., joint venture). These three entry strategies vary in terms of speed, control, and investment.

Building global customer-based brand equity means creating brand awareness and a positive brand image in each country in which the brand is sold. A number of issues in creating a standardized marketing program were noted. It is difficult to identify any one company applying the global marketing concept in the strictest sense. Increasingly, marketers are blending global objectives with local or regional concerns. The means by which brand equity is built may differ from country to country or the actual sources of brand equity themselves may vary across countries in terms of specific attribute or benefit associations. Nevertheless, there must be sufficient levels of brand awareness and strong, favorable, and unique brand associations in each country in which the brand is sold to provide sources of brand equity. In doing so, it is necessary to:

1. Identify differences in consumer behavior (i.e., how consumers purchase and use products and what they know and feel about brands).
2. Adjust the branding program accordingly (i.e., through the choice of brand elements, nature of the supporting marketing program, and leverage of secondary associations).

The chapter reviewed material concerning how to best modify the branding program to adapt to differences in consumer behavior through different product features, prices, channels, and marketing communication programs. The chapter concluded by considering other possible segmentation bases.

Discussion Questions

1. Pick a brand that is marketed in more than one country. Assess the extent to which the brand is marketed on a standardized versus customized basis.
2. How aware are you of the country of origin of different products you own? Which products do you care about their country of origin? Why? For those imported brands that you view positively, find out and critique how they are marketed in their home countries.

Notes

1. "AAI Picks Next Major Marketers," *Advertising Age International* (September 18, 1995), p. 1.
2. James S. Hirsch, "U.S. Liquor Makers Seek Tonic in Foreign Markets," *Wall Street Journal* (October 24, 1989), p. 1.
3. Maureen Marston, "Transferring Equity Across Border," ARF Fourth Annual Advertising and Promotion Workshop, February 12–13, 1992.
4. Edward Meyer, "Consumers Around the World: Do They Have the Same Wants and Needs?," *Management Review* (January 1985), pp. 26–29.
5. Ian M. Lewis, "Key Issues in Globalizing Brands: Why There Aren't Any Global OTC Medicine Brands," talk given at *Third Annual Advertising and Promotion Workshop,* Advertising Research Foundation, February 5–6, 1991.

6. Thomas A. Stewart, "Beat the Budget and Astound Your CFO," *Fortune* (October 28, 1996), pp. 187–189.

7. Sharen Kindel, "A Brush with Success: Colgate Palmolive Company," *Hemisphere* (September 1996), p. 15.

8. Patricia Sellers, "Pepsi Opens a Second Front," *Fortune* (August 8, 1994), pp. 70–76; Patrick Barwise and Thomas Robertson "Brand Portfolios," *European Management Journal,* 10 (3) (September 1992), pp. 277–285.

9. Dawar and Parker, however, show how the use of brand name as an important signal of quality occurs in various countries. See Niraj Dawar and Philip Parker, "Marketing Universals: Consumers' Use of Brand Name, Price, Physical Appearance, and Retailer Reputation as Signals of Quality," *Journal of Marketing*, 58 (April 1994), pp. 81–95.

10. Lee and Green, *Journal of International Studies*, 1991.

11. Stewart Owen, "The Landor ImagePower Survey: A Global Assessment of Brand Strength," Chapter 2 of *Brand Equity and Advertising*, editors David A. Aaker and Alexander L. Biel, Hillsdale, NJ: Lawrence Erlbaum Associates, 1993, pp. 11–30. The European countries were Belgium, France, West Germany, Italy, the Netherlands, Spain, Sweden, and the United Kingdom.

12. Dennis Chase, "A Global Comeback," *Advertising Age* (August 20, 1987), pp. 142–214.

13. Ronald Alsop, "Countries Different Ad Rules Are Problem for Global Firms," *Wall Street Journal* (September, 27, 1984), p. 33.

14. Philip Kotler, *Marketing Management*, 9th ed. Upper Saddle River, NJ: Prentice Hall, 1997.

15. For more information on global marketing strategies, especially with respect to the first two decisions, see George S. Yip, *Total Global Strategy*. Upper Saddle River, NJ: Prentice Hall, 1996.

16. George E. Belch and Michael Belch, *Introduction to Advertising and Promotion Management: An Integrated Marketing Communications Perspective*, 3rd ed. Chicago: Richard Irwin, 1995.

17. Neil Shoebridge, "Sweet Dream Fails in Australia," *Business Review Weekly* (January 15, 1988), p. 54.

18. Patrick Barwise and Thomas Robertson, "Brand Portfolios," *European Management Journal,* 10 (3) (September 1992), pp. 277–285.

19. Carla Rapoport, "Nestlé's Brand Building Machine," *Fortune* (September 19, 1994), pp. 147–156.

20. Carla Rapoport, "Nestlé's Brand Building Machine," *Fortune* (September 19, 1994), pp. 147–156.

21. Jennifer Lawrence and Dagmar Mussey, "P&G Accelerates International Pace," *Advertising Age* (March 21, 1994), p. I-3.

22. Julia Flynn, "Heineken's Battle to Stay Top Bottle," *Business Week* (August 1, 1994), pp. 60–61.

23. David P. Hamilton, "United It Stands. Fuji Xerox is a Rarity in World Business: A Joint Venture that Works," *Wall Street Journal* (September 26, 1996), R19.

24. Gail DeGeorge, "They Don't Call It Blockbuster for Nothing," *Business Week* (October 19, 1992), pp. 113–114.

25. Stephanie Anderson Forest, "A Pier 1 in Every Port?," *Business Week* (May 31, 1993), p. 81.

26. Patricia Sellers, "Pepsi Opens a Second Front," *Fortune* (August 8, 1994), pp. 70–76.

27. Richard Gibson, "Gerber Missed the Boat In Quest to Go Global, So It Turned to Sandoz," *Wall Street Journal* (May 24, 1994), pp. A1, A4.

28. Theodore Levitt, "The Globalization of Markets," *Harvard Business Review* (May-June 1983), pp. 92–102.

29. Joanne Lipman, "Marketers Turn Sour on Global Sales Pitch Harvard Guru Makes," *Wall Street Journal* (May 12, 1988), p. 1; and Julie Skur Hill and Jospeh M. Winski, "Goodbye Global Ads," *Advertising Age* (November 16, 1987), pp. 22, 36.

30. Joanne Lipman, "Marketers Turn Sour On Global Sales Pitch Harvard Guru Makes," *Wall Street Journal* (May 12, 1988), p. 1; and Tara Parker-Pope, "Custom-Made. The Most Successful Companies Have to Realize a Simple Truth: All Consumers Aren't Alike" *Wall Street Journal* (September 26, 1996), pp. R22–23.

31. George Anders, "Ad Agencies and Big Concerns Debate World Brands' Value," *Wall Street Journal* (June 14, 1984), p. 33.

32. Gabriella Stern, "Heinz Aims to Export Taste for Ketchup," *Wall Street Journal* (November 20, 1992), p. B-1.

33. Larry Light, "Brand Equity: New Challenges and Issues for the Nineties," talk given at *Third Annual Advertising and Promotion Workshop*, Advertising Research Foundation, February 5–6, 1991.

34. Michael Porter, *Competitive Advantage* (pp. 4–5). New York: Free Press, 1985.

35. Ian M. Lewis, "Key Issues in Globalizing Brands: Why There Aren't Any Global OTC Medicine Brands," talk given at *Third Annual Advertising and Promotion Workshop*, Advertising Research Foundation, February 5–6, 1991.

36. Edward H. Meyer, "Consumers Around the World: Do they Have the Same Wants and Needs?," *Management Review* (January 1985), pp. 26–29.

37. Fred Gardner, "BBDO Thinks Beyond Global Options," *Marketing & Media Decisions* (December 1984), pp. 52–53.

38. Stephen A. Greyser, "Let's Talk Sense About Global Marketing," speech given to Asian Advertising Congress, Bangkok, July 1986.

39. Rebecca Fanin, "JWT's Global Mandate: Keep It Local," *Marketing & Media Decisions* (December 1984), pp. 49–50.

40. Rebecca Fanin, "What Agencies Really Think of Global Theory," *Marketing & Media Decisions* (December 1984), pp. 74–82.

41. George Anders, "Ad Agencies and Big Concerns Debate World Brands' Value," *Wall Street Journal* (June 14, 1984), p. 33.

42. Asihish Banerjee, "Global Campaigns Don't Work; Multinationals Do," *Advertising Age* (April 18, 1994), p. 23.

43. Julia Flynn, "Heineken's Battle to Stay Top Bottle," *Business Week* (August 1, 1994), pp. 60–62.

44. Carla Rapoport, "Nestlé's Brand Building Machine," *Fortune* (September 19, 1994), pp. 147–156.

45. Jennifer Lawrence and Dagmar Mussey, "P&G Accelerates International Pace," *Advertising Age* (March 21, 1994), p. I-3.

46. Ken Wells, "Global Campaigns, After Many Missteps, Finally Pay Dividends," *Wall Street Journal* (August 27, 1992), p. A-1.

47. Patricia Sellers, "Pepsi Opens a Second Front," *Fortune* (August 8, 1994), pp. 70–76.

48. Hubert Gatignon and Piet Vanden Abeele, "To Standardize or Not to Standardize: Marketing Mix Effectiveness in Europe," MSI Report No. 95-109, Cambridge, MA. 1995.

49. Hajo Riesenbeck and Anthony Freeling, "How Global Are Global Brands?," *McKinsey Quarterly*, #4, pp. 3–18; as referenced in Patrick Barwise and Thomas Robertson, "Brand

Portfolios," *European Management Journal,* 10 (3) (September 1992), pp. 277–285. See also, Dennis M. Sandler and David Shani, "Brand Globally but Advertise Locally?: An Empirical Investigation," *Journal of Product & Brand Management,* 2 (2) (1993), pp. 59–71; Hubert Gatignon and Piet Vanden Abeele, "To Standardize or Not to Standardize: Marketing Mix Effectiveness in Europe," Marketing Science Institute Report 95-109; Saeed Samiee and Kendall Roth, "The Influence of Global Marketing Standardization on Performance," *Journal of Marketing,* 56 (April 1992), pp. 1–17; and David M. Szymanski, Sundar G. Bharadwaj, and P. Rajan Varadarajan, "Standardization versus Adaptation of International Marketing Strategy: An Empirical Investigation," *Journal of Marketing,* 57 (October 1993), pp. 1–17.

50. George E. Belch and Michael Belch, *Introduction to Advertising and Promotion Management: An Integrated Marketing Communications Perspective*, 3rd ed. Chicago: Richard Irwin, 1995.

51. Patrick Barwise and Thomas Robertson, "Brand Portfolios," *European Management Journal,* 10 (3) (September 1992), pp. 277–285.

52. Robert Frank, "Potato Chips To Go Global—Or So Pepsi Bets," *Wall Street Journal* (November 30, 1995), p. B-1.

53. Julie Skur Hill and Jospeh M. Winski, "Goodbye Global Ads," *Advertising Age* (November 16, 1987), p. 22.

54. Julie Skur Hill and Jospeh M. Winski, "Goodbye Global Ads," *Advertising Age* (November 16, 1987), p. 22.

55. Douglas R. Sease, "Japanese Firms Use U.S. Designers to Tailor Products to Local Tastes," *Wall Street Journal* (March 4, 1986), p. 1.

56. Maureen Marston, "Transferring Equity Across Border," ARF Fourth Annual Advertising and Promotion Workshop, February 12–13, 1992.

57. Joanne Lipman, "Marketers Turn Sour On Global Sales Pitch Harvard Guru Makes," *Wall Street Journal* (May 12, 1988), p. 1.

58. Hermann Simon, "Pricing Problems in a Global Setting," *Marketing News* (October 9, 1995), p. 4.

59. Rahul Jacob, "Asia, Where Big Brands Are Blooming," *Business Week* (August 23, 1993), p. 55.

60. Craig S. Smith, "Doublemint in China: Distribution Isn't Double the Fun," *Wall Street Journal* (December 5, 1995), p. B-1.

61. Mark Maremont, "They're All Screaming for Haagen-Dazs," *Business Week* (October 4, 1991), p. 121.

62. Michael J. McCarthy, "As a Global Marketer, Coke Excels by Being Tough and Consistent," *Wall Street Journal* (December 19, 1989), p. 1.

63. Carla Rapoport, "Nestlé's Brand Building Machine," *Fortune* (September 19, 1994), pp. 147–156.

64. Julie Skur Hill and Jospeh M. Winski, "Goodbye Global Ads," *Advertising Age* (November 16, 1987), p. 22.

65. Ken Wells, "Global Campaigns, After Many Missteps, Finally Pay Dividends," *Wall Street Journal* (August 27, 1992), p. A-1.

66. William Wells, "Global Advertisers Should Pay Heed to Contextual Variations," *Marketing News* (February 13, 1987), p. 18.

67. Martin S. Roth, "The Effects of Culture and Socioeconomics on the Performance of Global Brand Image Strategies," *Journal of Marketing Research*, 32 (May 1995), pp. 163–175.

68. Joann S. Lublin, "More U.S. Magazines to Travel Abroad," *Wall Street Journal* (January 18, 1990), p. B-1.

69. Miriam Jordan, "In Rural India, Video Vans Sell Toothpaste and Shampoo," *Wall Street Journal* (January 10, 1996), p. B1, B5.

70. Christine Dugas, "Marketing's New Look," *Business Week* (January 26, 1987), pp. 64–69.

71. Peter Oberlink, "Regional Marketing Starts Taking Hold," *Adweek* (April 6, 1987), pp. 36–37.

72. Thomas Moore, "Different Folks, Different Strokes," *Fortune* (September 16, 1985), pp. 65, 68.

73. Michael J. McCarthy, "In Texas Beer Brawl, Anheuser and Miller Aren't Pulling Punches," *Wall Street Journal* (December 5, 1996), pp. A1, A12.

74. Alix M. Freedman, "National Firms Find That Selling to Local Tastes is Costly, Complex," *Wall Street Journal* (February 9, 1987), p. 1.

75. Yumiko Ono, "Kraft Hope Hispanic Market Says Cheese," *Wall Street Journal* (December 13, 1995), p. B-5.

CHAPTER
15

Closing
Observations

Preview

After introducing branding and the concept of brand equity and outlining the customer-based brand equity framework in Part I of the text, previous chapters addressed how to build (Part II), measure (Part III), and manage (Part IV) customer-based brand equity. In Part V, we consider some implications and applications of the customer-based brand equity framework. Specifically, in this final chapter, we provide some closing observations concerning strategic brand management. We first briefly review the customer-based brand equity framework. Next, we highlight managerial guidelines and key themes that emerged in previous chapters. After summarizing success factors for branding, we then consider some special topics by applying the customer-based brand equity framework to address specific strategic brand management issues for different types of products. To provide additional perspective, we also relate the customer-based brand equity framework to several other popular views of brand equity. The chapter concludes by considering the future of branding.

Strategic Brand Management Guidelines

SUMMARY OF CUSTOMER-BASED BRAND EQUITY FRAMEWORK

Strategic brand management involves the design and implementation of marketing programs and activities to build, measure, and manage brand equity. Before reviewing some guidelines for strategic brand management, it is useful to briefly summarize—one last time!—the customer-based brand equity framework.

The rationale behind the framework is to recognize the importance of the customer in the creation and management of brand equity. As one top marketing executive put it: "Consumers own brands and your brand is what consumers will permit you to have." Consistent with this view, customer-based brand equity was defined in chapter 2 as the differential effect that consumers' brand knowledge has on their response to the marketing of that brand. A brand is said to have positive customer-based brand equity when customers react more favorably to a product and the way it is marketed when the brand is identified as compared to when it is not (e.g., when it is attributed to a fictitiously named or unnamed version of the product).

The basic premise with customer-based brand equity is that the power of a brand lies in the minds of consumers and what they have experienced and learned about the brand over time. More formally, brand knowledge was described in chapter 3 in terms of an associative network memory model as a network of nodes and links where the brand can be thought of as being a node in memory with a variety of different types of associations potentially linked to it. Brand knowledge can be characterized in terms of two components: brand awareness and brand image. Brand awareness is related to the strength of the brand node or trace in memory as reflected by consumers' ability to recall or recognize the brand under different conditions. Brand awareness can be characterized by depth and breadth. The depth of brand awareness relates to the likelihood that the brand can be recognized or recalled. The breadth of brand awareness relates to the variety of purchase and consumption situations in which the brand comes to mind. Brand image is defined as consumer perceptions of and preferences for a brand, as reflected by the various types of brand associations held in consumers' memory. Brand associations come in many forms, although a useful distinction can be made between attributes (i.e., what a product is or has), benefits (i.e., what a product has to offer consumers), and attitudes (i.e., consumers' overall evaluations of a product).

Sources of Brand Equity

Customer-based brand equity occurs when the consumer has a high level of awareness and familiarity with the brand and holds some strong, favorable, and unique brand associations in memory. In some cases, brand awareness alone is sufficient to result in more favorable consumer response, for example, in low-involvement decision settings where consumers lack motivation and/or ability and are willing to base their choices merely on familiar brands. In other cases, the strength, favorability, and uniqueness of the brand associations play a critical role in determining the differential response making up the brand equity. These three critical dimensions of brand associations are determined by the following factors:

1. *Strength.* The strength of a brand association is a function of both the amount or quantity of processing that information initially receives and the nature or quality of that processing. The more deeply a person thinks about brand information and relates it to existing brand knowledge, the stronger are the resulting brand associations. Relatedly, two factors facilitating the strength of association to any piece of brand information are the personal relevance of the information and the consistency with which this information is presented over time.

2. *Favorability.* Favorable associations for a brand are those associations that are desirable to customers and are successfully delivered by the product and conveyed by the support-

ing marketing program for the brand. Associations may relate to the product or other intangible, non-product-related aspects (e.g., usage or user imagery). Not all brand associations, however, will be deemed important and viewed favorably by consumers, nor will they be equally valued across different purchase or consumption situations.

3. *Uniqueness.* Finally, to create the differential response that leads to customer-based brand equity, it is important to associate unique, meaningful points of difference to the brand to provide a competitive advantage and a reason why consumers should buy it. For other brand associations, however, it may be sufficient that they are seen as comparable or roughly equal in favorability to competing brand associations. These associations function as points of parity in consumers' minds to establish category membership and negate potential points of difference for competitors. In other words, these associations are designed to provide no reason why not consumers should choose the brand.

Figure 15–1 summarizes these broad conceptual guidelines as to how to create desired brand knowledge structures. These guidelines can provide general motivation and direction in designing tactical programs and activities to build brand equity.

Outcomes of Brand Equity

Assuming a positive brand image is created by marketing programs that are able to register the brand in memory and link it to strong, favorable, and unique associations, a number of benefits for the brand may be realized, as follows:

- Greater loyalty
- Less vulnerability to competitive marketing actions
- Less vulnerability to marketing crises
- Larger margins
- More inelastic consumer response to price increases
- More elastic consumer response to price decreases
- Greater trade cooperation and support
- Increased marketing communication effectiveness
- Possible licensing opportunities
- Additional brand extension opportunities

FIGURE 15–1 Determinants of Desired Brand Knowledge Structures

1. *Depth of brand awareness* is determined by the ease of brand recognition and recall.

2. *Breadth of brand awareness* is determined by the number of purchase and consumption situations for which the brand comes to mind.

3. *Strong brand associations* are created by marketing programs that convey relevant information to consumers in a consistent fashion at any one point in time, as well as over time.

4. *Favorable brand associations* are created when marketing programs effectively deliver product-related and non-product-related benefits that are desired by consumers.

5. *Unique brand associations* that are also strong and favorable create points of difference that distinguish the brand from other brands. Brand associations that are not unique, however, can create valuable points of parity to establish necessary category associations or to neutralize competitive points of difference.

TACTICAL GUIDELINES

Figures 2–8 to 2–10 in chapter 2 summarized the chief ingredients to the customer-based brand equity framework in terms of how to build, measure, and manage brand equity. More specific themes and recommendations were developed in subsequent chapters, as follows.

Building Brand Equity

Tactically, brand equity can be built in three major ways: (1) through the initial choice of the brand elements making up the brand, (2) through the design of the supporting marketing program, and (3) through the leverage of secondary associations by linking the brand to other entities (a company, geographical region, other brand, person, event, and so on). Guidelines emerged in chapters 4 through 7 for each of these three different types of approaches, as summarized in Figure 15–2.

Themes   A dominant theme across many of these different ways to build brand equity is the importance of complementarity and consistency. *Complementarity* involves choosing different brand elements and different supporting marketing activities and programs such that the potential contribution to brand equity of one particular brand element or marketing activity compensates for the shortcomings of other elements

FIGURE 15–2 Guidelines for Building Brand Equity

1. Mix and match brand elements—brand names, logos, symbols, characters, slogans, jingles, and packages—by choosing different brand elements to achieve different objectives and by designing brand elements to be as mutually reinforcing as possible.

2. Ensure a high level of perceived quality and create a rich brand image by linking tangible and intangible product-related and non-product-related associations to the brand.

3. Adopt value-based pricing strategies to set prices and guide discount pricing policy over time that reflect consumers' perceptions of value and willingness to pay a premium.

4. Consider a range of direct and indirect distribution options and blend brand-building "push" strategies for retailers and other channel members with brand-building "pull" strategies for consumers.

5. Mix marketing communication options by choosing a broad set of communication options based on their differential ability to impact brand awareness and create, maintain, or strengthen favorable and unique brand associations. Match marketing communication options by ensuring consistency and directly reinforcing some communication options with other communication options.

6. Leverage secondary associations to compensate for otherwise missing dimensions of the marketing program by linking the brand to other entities such as companies, channels of distribution, other brands, characters, spokespeople or other endorsers, or events that reinforce and augment the brand image.

and activities. For example, some brand elements may be designed primarily to enhance awareness (e.g., through a memorable brand logo), whereas other brand elements may be designed primarily to facilitate the linkage of brand associations (e.g., via a meaningful brand name). Similarly, an ad campaign may be designed primarily to create a certain point-of-difference association, whereas a retail promotion may be designed primarily to create vital point-of-parity associations. Finally, certain other entities may be linked to the brand to leverage secondary associations and provide otherwise missing sources of brand equity.

Thus, it is important that a varied set of brand elements and marketing activities and programs be strategically put into place to create the desired level of awareness and type of image to provide necessary sources of brand equity. At the same time, a high degree of consistency across these elements helps to create the highest level of awareness and the strongest and most favorable associations possible. *Consistency* involves ensuring that diverse brand and marketing mix elements share a common core meaning, perhaps in some cases literally containing or conveying the same information. For example, brand elements may be designed to convey a certain benefit association that is further reinforced by a highly integrated, well-branded marketing communications program.

Measuring Brand Equity

According to the definition of customer-based brand equity, brand equity can be measured indirectly, by measuring the potential sources of brand equity, and directly, by measuring the possible outcomes of brand equity. Measuring sources of brand equity involves profiling consumer knowledge structures in terms of breadth and depth of awareness and strength, favorability, and uniqueness of brand associations. Measuring outcomes of brand equity involves approximating the various benefits realized from creating these sources of brand equity.

Organizationally, it is important to properly design and implement a brand equity measurement system. A brand equity measurement system was defined as a set of research procedures that is designed to provide timely, accurate, and actionable information for marketers about their brands so that they can make the best possible tactical decisions in the short run as well as strategic decisions in the long run. Implementing a brand equity measurement system involves three steps: (1) conducting brand audits, (2) designing brand tracking studies, and (3) establishing a brand equity management system. Guidelines in each of these areas are summarized in Figure 15–3.

Themes   The dominant theme in measuring brand equity is the need to employ a full complement of research techniques and processes that capture as much as possible the richness and complexity of brand equity. Multiple techniques and measures are necessary to tap into all the various sources and outcomes of brand equity. Simplistic approaches to measuring brand equity, for example, by attempting to estimate the equity of a brand with only one number, are potentially fraught with error and lack diagnostic or prescriptive power. Multiple processes are necessary to help interpret brand equity research and ensure that actionable information is provided to the right people at the right time.

1. Formalize the firm's view of brand equity into a document, the brand equity charter, that provides relevant branding guidelines to marketing managers.

2. Conduct brand inventories to profile how all of the products sold by a company are branded and marketed and conduct brand exploratories to understand what consumers think and feel about a brand as part of periodic brand audits to assess the health of brands, understand their sources of brand equity, and suggest ways to improve and leverage that equity.

3. Conduct consumer tracking studies on a routine basis to provide current information as to how brands are performing with respect to the key sources and outcomes of brand equity as identified by the brand audit.

4. Assemble results of tracking survey and other relevant outcome measures into a brand equity report to be distributed on a regular basis to provide descriptive information as to what is happening with a brand as well as diagnostic information as to why it is happening.

5. Establish a person or department to oversee the implementation of the brand equity charter and brand equity reports to make sure that, as much as possible, product and marketing actions across divisions and geographical boundaries are done in a way that reflect the spirit of the Charter and the substance of the Report so as to maximize the long-term equity of the brand.

FIGURE 15-3 Guidelines for Measuring Brand Equity

Managing Brand Equity

Finally, managing brand equity requires taking a broader, long-term perspective of brands. First, a *broad view* of brand equity is critically important, especially when firms are selling multiple products and multiple brands in multiple markets. In such cases, brand hierarchies must be created that define common and distinct brand elements among various nested products. New product and brand extension strategies also must be designed to determine optimal brand and product portfolios. Finally, these brands and products must be effectively managed over geographical boundaries and target market segments by creating brand awareness and a positive brand image in each market in which the brand is sold.

Second, a *long-term view* of brand equity is necessary because of the implications that changes in current marketing programs and activities and the marketing environment have on consumers' brand knowledge structures and thus their response to *future* marketing programs and activities. Managing brands over time requires reinforcing the brand meaning and adjusting the branding program as needed. For brands whose equity has eroded over time, a number of revitalizing strategies are available. Figure 15-4 highlights some important guidelines for managing brand equity.

Themes   The dominant theme in managing brand equity is the need to consider brands from a broad, corporate perspective in a top-down as well as a bottom-up fashion. Building brands in a *bottom-up* fashion means that marketing managers primarily

1. Define the brand hierarchy in terms of the number of levels to use and the relative prominence that brands at different levels will receive when combined to brand any one product.

2. Create global associations relevant to as many brands nested at the level below in the hierarchy as possible but sharply differentiate brands at the same level of the hierarchy.

3. Introduce brand extensions that complement the product mix of the firm, leverage parent brand associations, and enhance parent brand equity.

4. Clearly establish the roles of brands in the brand portfolio, adding, deleting, and modifying brands as necessary.

5. Reinforce brand equity over time through marketing actions that consistently convey the meaning of the brand in terms of what products the brand represents, what benefits it supplies, what needs it satisfies, and why it is superior to competitive brands.

6. Enhance brand equity over time through innovation in product design, manufacturing, and merchandising and continued relevance in user and usage imagery.

7. Identify differences in consumer behavior in different market segments and adjust the branding program accordingly on a cost-benefit basis.

FIGURE 15-4 Guidelines for Managing Brand Equity

direct their marketing activities to brand individual products for particular markets—with relatively little regard for other brands and products sold by the firm or for other markets in which their brands and products may be sold. Although such close, detailed brand supervision can be advantageous, creating brand equity for every different possible product and market in this way can be an expensive and difficult process and, most importantly, ignores possible synergies that may be obtainable.

A *top-down* branding approach, on the other hand, involves marketing activities that capture the "big picture" and recognize the possible synergies across products and markets to brand products accordingly. Such a top-down approach would seek to find common products and markets that could share marketing programs and activities for brands and only develop separate brands and marketing programs and activities as dictated by the consumer or competitive environment. Unfortunately, if left unmanaged, firms tend to follow the bottom-up approach, resulting in many brands marketed inconsistently and incompatibly. Managing brands in a top-down fashion requires centralized and coordinated marketing guidance and actions from high-level marketing supervisors.

The other major theme for managing brand equity is the importance of moderate levels of change in the marketing program over time. Without some modifications of the marketing program, a brand runs the risk of becoming obsolete or irrelevant to consumers. At the same time, dramatic shifts back and forth in brand strategies run the risk of confusing or alienating consumers. Thus, a consistent thread of meaning—that consumers can recognize—should run through the marketing program that reflects the key sources of equity for the brand and its core brand associations. In other words, changes in the product and how it is priced, advertised, promoted, or distrib-

To build strong brands and maximize their equity, marketing managers must:

1. Understand what brands mean to consumers and develop products that are appropriate to the brand and address the needs of the target market.
2. Properly position brands by achieving necessary and desired points of parity and points of difference.
3. Provide superior delivery of desired benefits all through the marketing program.
4. Maintain innovation in design, manufacturing, and marketing and relevance in brand personality and imagery.
5. Establish credibility and be seen as expert, trustworthy, and likable.
6. Communicate with a consistent voice at any one point in time and over time.
7. Employ a full range of complementary brand elements and supporting marketing activities.
8. Design and implement a brand hierarchy and brand portfolio that puts brands in the proper context with respect to other brands and other products sold by the firm.

FIGURE 15-5 Characteristics of Strong Brands

uted may be needed to preserve or enhance sources of brand equity over time but these changes should illuminate and not obscure key brand associations.

What Makes a Strong Brand?

With the above discussion as background, we can provide some perspective on what makes a strong brand. Figure 15–5 summarizes guidelines for marketing managers to create a strong brand.

On the flip side of the coin, what are the common branding mistakes that prevent firms from creating strong, powerful brands? In contrast to the previous list, some of the more common branding problems include (see Figure 15–6):

1. *Failure to fully understand the meaning of the brand.* Given that consumers "own" brands, it is critical to understand what consumers think and feel about brands and then plan and implement marketing programs accordingly. Too often, managers convince themselves of

FIGURE 15-6 Five Deadly Sins of Brand Management

1. Failure to understand the full meaning of the brand.
2. Failure to adequately support the brand.
3. Failure to be patient with the brand.
4. Failure to adequately control the brand.
5. Failure to properly balance consistency and change with the brand.

the validity of marketing actions—for example, a new brand extension, ad campaign, or price hike—based on a mistaken belief of what consumers know or what marketers would like them to know about the brand. Relatedly, managers often ignore the full range of associations, both tangible and intangible, that may characterize the brand.

2. *Failure to adequately support the brand.* Creating and maintaining brand knowledge structures requires marketing investments. Too often, managers want to get "something for nothing" by building brand equity without a willingness to provide proper marketing support or, once brand equity has been built, expecting the brand to remain strong despite the lack of further investments.

3. *Failure to be patient with the brand.* Brand equity must be carefully and patiently built "from the ground up." A firm foundation for brand equity requires that consumers have the proper depth and breadth of awareness and strong, favorable, and unique associations in memory. Too often, managers want to take short cuts and bypass more basic branding considerations—such as achieving the necessary level of brand awareness—to concentrate on "flashier" aspects of brand building related to its image.

4. *Failure to adequately control the brand.* Brand equity must be understood by all employees of the firm and actions must be taken to reflect a broader corporate perspective as well as a more specific product perspective. Too often, decisions are made haphazardly without a true understanding of the current and desired brand equity and without a recognition of the impact of these decisions on other brands or brand-related activities.

5. *Failure to properly balance consistency and change with the brand.* Managing a brand necessitates striking the difficult but crucial balance between maintaining continuity in marketing activities and implementing changes to update the product or image of a brand. Too often, managers are "left behind" as a result of not making adjustments in their marketing programs to reflect changes in the marketing environments or, alternatively, make so many changes that the brand becomes a "moving target" without any meaning to consumers.

Special Applications

Although conventional use of the term "product" might be seen as representing only "physical goods," product was deliberately defined broadly in chapter 1 to encompass not only physical goods but also services, retail stores, people, organizations, places, or ideas. Chapter 1 provided examples of how each of these different types of products could be branded. Accordingly, the term "product" was used throughout the text in a broad sense, and the themes and guidelines for building, measuring, and managing brand equity presented above should be appropriate for virtually all types of products. Nevertheless, it is worthwhile to consider in greater detail some specific strategic brand management issues for some of these different types of products. In this section, additional guidelines are suggested for the following five special cases: (1) industrial (or business-to-business) products, (2) high technology products, (3) services, (4) retailers, and (5) small businesses.

INDUSTRIAL GOODS

Physical goods can be classified in various ways. For example, one classification based on consumer shopping habits distinguishes between the following:[1]

1. *Convenience goods.* Goods that the customer usually purchases frequently, immediately, and with a minimum of effort (e.g., chewing gum, candy bars, and soft drinks).

2. *Shopping goods.* Goods that the customer, in the process of selection and purchase, characteristically compares on such bases as suitability, quality, price, and style (e.g., furniture, clothing, and major appliances).

3. *Specialty goods.* Goods with unique characteristics and/or brand identification for which a significant group of buyers are habitually willing to make a special purchasing effort (e.g., specific brands and types of luxury goods, cars, and audio and video equipment).

Another classification is based on durability: *Nondurable goods* are goods that normally are consumed in one or a few uses; *durable goods* are tangible goods that normally survive many uses. Although the concepts and guidelines that were reviewed above may be particularly appropriate for nondurable goods, it is also true—as was demonstrated throughout the text—that they are equally valid to durable goods. As a further example in a durable goods context, Branding Brief 15–1 shows how branding principles and the concept of brand personality were applied by Whirlpool in marketing its major appliances.

Finally, an additional physical goods classification is based on the nature of the customer buying the product: *Consumer goods* are typically bought by an individual or family for personal or home use whereas *industrial goods* are typically bought by an organization for business or commercial use. Because industrial goods usually involve business-to-business marketing practices, it is worthwhile to consider branding principles for industrial goods in more detail.

There are many different types of industrial goods, such as:[2]

- Raw materials and manufactured materials and parts that enter the manufacturer's product completely
- Long-lasting capital installations and equipment that facilitate developing and/or managing finished products
- Short-lasting supplies and services that facilitate developing and/or managing finished products

Regardless of the particular type of industrial goods sold, some basic branding guidelines can be offered (see Figure 15–7), as follows.

Adopt a Corporate Branding Strategy and Well-Defined Brand Hierarchy

Because companies selling industrial goods are often characterized by a large and complex number of product lines and variations, it is important that a logical and well-organized brand hierarchy be devised. In particular, because of the breadth and complexity of their product mix, companies selling industrial goods are more likely to emphasize corporate or family brands. It is especially important that these corporate or family brands convey credibility and possess favorable global associations. Corporate credibility is often a primary risk-reduction heuristic adopted by industrial buyers. For years, one of the key sources of brand equity for IBM was the fact that a marketplace perception existed that ". . . you'll never get fired for buying IBM." Once that special cachet faded, the brand found itself in a much more competitive situation. In completing the brand hierarchy for industrial goods, for clarity and differentiation, individual brands and modifiers often take on descriptive product meaning. Thus, a

---

Branding Appliances

To illustrate how branding principles may apply to durable goods, consider research by Whirlpool who conducted a study of appliances to identify the personalities of Whirlpool's corporate brands and those of competitors.[a] A series of research approaches were employed in the study. First, consumers in focus groups cut out pictures to show what the brand would look like as a person, explaining to a facilitator their beliefs and feelings about each brand. Next, another group of consumers completed four different tasks: (1) a 70-item adjective check list to describe each brand; (2) classification of brands as masculine or feminine; (3) comparison of brands to types of work, music, hobbies and reading material; and (4) comparison of brands to eras (thirties to the nineties).

The findings indicated that significantly distinct branding personalities prevailed even in the appliance category. For example, although Whirlpool and its high-end KitchenAid brand were both seen as "feminine" brands, very different profiles emerged.

> Whirlpool was described as gentle, sensitive, quiet, good-natured, flexible, modern, cheerful, and creative. Personified, the brand was seen as a modern, family-oriented woman who lived the best of suburban life. She would be a good friend and neighbor, action-oriented and successful, attractive and fashionable, but not flashy. Whirlpool was associated with jazz and rock music, sailing and the seventies.
>
> KitchenAid was described as sophisticated, glamorous, wealthy, elegant, fashionable, and innovative. Personified, the brand was seen as a modern professional woman who was competent, aggressive, and smart and who worked hard to get the better things in life. KitchenAid was associated with classical music and theater, sailing, jazz, and science and the eighties and nineties.

In terms of implications, the personality traits give product designers and marketers some direction and focus. Consequently, the brand can be established more forcefully in all communications and be more effectively differentiated in product design. For Whirlpool, the feminine perception suggested possible colors and styles of appliances and resulted in the use of female announcers for the commercial voice-overs.

Whirlpool's recent marketing challenge has been to take its products and brands global. Whirlpool's $1 billion purchase of N. V. Philips's floundering European appliance business in 1989 catapulted Whirlpool into the number-one position in the worldwide appliance business. Whirlpool's strong reputation is relatively unknown in Europe, however, and the purchase agreement only gives them the right to use the Philips name until 1999. A $110 million ad campaign was launched in 1991 to boost consumer recognition while gradually phasing in the Whirlpool name. Whirlpool also set its sights on other countries, especially developing countries where it has introduced specially designed compact washing machines through joint-venture agreements. By 1996, Whirlpool made appliances in twelve countries and sold them in 140. Despite these efforts,

Whirlpool encountered some difficulties in its marketing in 1996: weak demand in Europe, high startup costs in Asia, the botched launch of a new refrigerator line, and a challenge from General Electric in its home market. Nevertheless, management has stuck to its globalization strategy and a belief that Whirlpool's technological edge and ability to standardize will eventually overcome these challenges: "Maintaining a global presence is absolutely the correct way to create long-term shareholder value."

---

[a]Tim Triplett, "Brand Personality Must Be Manged or It Will Assume a Life of Its Own," *AMA Marketing News* 28 (10) (May 9, 1994): p. 9. Bill Vlasic, "Did Whirlpool Spin Too Far Too Fast," *Business Week* (June 24, 1996), pp. 134–136. Carl Quintanilla, "Whirlpool, Hurt in Europe, Sees Steep Decline in Operating Profit," *Wall Street Journal* (September 30, 1996), p. B4.

particularly effective branding strategy for industrial goods is to create sub-brands by combining a well-known and respected corporate name with descriptive product modifiers. Branding Brief 15–2 describes some of the branding challenges faced by CSR, a leading supplier of building and construction materials in Australia and North America.

Link Non-Product-Related Associations

Developing supporting marketing programs to build brand equity for industrial goods can be different from consumer goods in that, given the nature of the organizational buying process, product-related associations may play a relatively more important role as compared to non-product-related associations. Nevertheless, even non-product-related associations can be useful in terms of the credibility or other perceptions of the firm, as well as the prestige or type of company that uses the firm's products. Many industrial firms distinguish themselves on the basis of the customer service they provide in addition to the quality they place in their products. For exam-

FIGURE 15–7 Additional Guidelines for Industrial Products

1. Adopt a corporate or family branding strategy.
2. Establish strong perceptions of company credibility.
3. Clearly label and differentiate individual products, perhaps using descriptive names.
4. Link non-product-related associations.
5. Employ a full range of marketing communication options that combine direct "hard-sell" messages with more indirect "image-related" messages that convey who and what the company is all about.
6. Consider leveraging other companies that are customers as a means to create secondary associations.
7. Define market segments carefully and develop appropriate branding and marketing programs.

BRANDING BRIEF 15-2

Building Corporate Brand Equity: The CSR Challenge

The main branding challenge faced by Australia's CSR Limited is one faced by many expanding industrial firms: how to create the proper brand hierarchy to reflect a vastly changed—and still changing—line of business. CSR's history in Australia goes back decades. The company was originally named Colonial Sugar Refinery and its early reputation was formed as a sugar company. Through the years, the CSR brand became synonymous with sugar. The company began to sell by-products of its sugar cane starting in 1936 when waste sugar cane fibre was used to manufacture and sell wallboards known as "Cane-ite." Over the years, CSR found itself moving outside the sugar business. By the mid-1990s, through product development and acquisition, nearly 90 percent of its assets and 80 percent of its profits were in the building and construction materials. CSR had become one of the top ten companies in Australia. The eight business units making up their building and construction materials business ranged in sales from $200 million to $1.5 billion and included:

1. Readymix pre-mixed concrete
2. Gyprock plaster boards and drywall
3. Hebel lightweight aerated concrete blocks and reinforced panels
4. Monier clay and concrete roof tiles
5. PGH bricks
6. Bradford insulation
7. CSR softwoods timber
8. CSR wood panels (hard board, particle board, medium density fibreboard and decorative laminates)

CSR faces a number of branding and marketing challenges. The majority of its building and construction products acquired over the years were branded under its former manufacturers' name. Many of these products are seen as commodities by customers, leading to an over-emphasis on price as a basis of competing. Finally, the different products and brands had been traditionally marketed relatively independently of each other.

How should CSR best exploit brand synergies? They sell virtually all the "ingredients" to construct a house, commercial building, or almost any type of structure. How should they "package" their different brands so that the "whole is greater than the sum of the parts"? Along these lines, CSR has already developed "Homescape Selection Centres" to allow consumers 1-stop shopping. Homescape centres are seen as a means of increasing consumer confidence in their choice of building supplies and materials by allowing them to see the full range of offerings. How far should CSR push such a concept? Should it get involved in the actual installation of these products? How should it deal with its intermediaries, e.g., builders and contractors?

Second, and relatedly, should a brand umbrella be placed over these different businesses? A circular red logo was developed that placed the CSR name in the middle surrounded by the slogan, "Building in Quality" along the outside border. The logo was placed alongside all the different brands, and the CSR name was placed. Was this sufficient? Did this create an adequate connection? To many Australians, CSR still meant sugar—a stark contrast from building supplies and material. Should the sugar company be spun off? Should another brand be introduced to encompass the other, more similar products? Alternatively, should a strong sub-brand be introduced under the CSR name that accomplished a similar thing? Finally, could CSR adopt an ingredient branding strategy for its individual brands? What would the supporting marketing program look like?

Thus, CSR must address some fundamentally important branding issues that will affect their corporate brand equity as well as the equity of the individual products they sell. Its decisions in these different areas will go a long way in determining their success in the coming years.

ple, Premier Industrial Corp. charges up to 50 percent more than competitors for every one of the 250,000 industrial parts it stocks and distributes because of its strong commitment to customer service, as exemplified by the following anecdote:[3]

> Early one afternoon in late 1988, Premier Industrial Corp. got a call from the manager of a Caterpillar Inc. tractor plant in Decatur, Illinois. A $10 electrical relay had broken down, idling an entire assembly line. A sales representative for Premier located a replacement at the company's Los Angeles warehouse and rushed it to a plane headed for St. Louis. By 10:30 that night, a Premier employee had delivered the part, and the line was up and running. "You can't build tractors if you can't move the line," remarked the Caterpillar purchasing analyst. "They really saved us a bundle of money."

As further illustration, creative changes in customer service have similarly built brand equity and allowed Armstrong World Industries to charge higher prices for its floor tiles and Weyerhaeuser's wood-products division to command premiums for its commodity-like two-by-fours.

Employ Full Range of Marketing Communication Options

Another difference between industrial and consumer products is the manner by which they are sold, as a different marketing communication mix exists with industrial products than with consumer products (see Figure 15–8). Because of the well-defined target market and complex nature of product decisions, marketing communications tend to convey more detailed product information in a more direct or face-to-face manner. Thus, personal selling plays an important role. At the same time, other communication options can be employed to enhance awareness or the formation of brand associations.

1. Media advertising (TV, radio, newspaper, magazines)
2. Trade journal advertising
3. Directories
4. Direct mail
5. Brochures and sales literature
6. Audiovisual presentation tapes
7. Giveaways
8. Sponsorship or event marketing
9. Exhibitions, trade shows, and conventions
10. Publicity or public relations

FIGURE 15-8 Alternative Communication Options: Business-to-Business Market

Leverage Equity of Other Companies

Secondary associations can be leveraged differently for industrial brands. For example, one commonly adopted means of communicating credibility is to identify other companies that are customers for the firm's products or services (see Figure 15–9). The challenge in communicating this endorsement through advertising, however, is ensuring that the other companies used as endorsers do not distract from the message about the advertised company and its brands. Even countries can be used in an endorsement strategy. For example, Interlock Industries—a New Zealand firm that specials in window hardware—has used the fact that it is the only foreign company in its industry to sell in Japan as an endorsement strategy to sell its products to firms in other countries.

Segment Customers Carefully

Finally, as with any brand, it is important to understand how different customer segments view products and brands. With selling industrial goods, however, the different customer segments may exist *within* organizations as well as *across* organizations. Depending on the perceptions and preferences of the organizational segments involved—for example, engineers, brand or marketing managers, accountants, or purchasing managers—the particular associations that serve as sources of brand equity may differ. It may be particularly important to achieve points of parity with these different constituencies so that a key point of difference may come into play. U.K. branding experts de Chernatony and McDonald put it this way:[4]

> In consumer marketing, brands tend to be bought by individuals, while many people are involved in organizational purchasing. The brand marketer is faced with the challenge of not only identifying which managers are involved in the purchasing decision, but also what brand attributes are of particular concern to each of them. The various benefits of the brand, therefore, need to be communicated to all involved, stressing the relevant attributes to particular individuals. For example, the brand's reliable delivery may need to be stressed to the production manager, its low life-cycle costs to the accountant, and so on.

FIGURE 15–9 Leveraging Another Company's Equity Through Advertising

HIGH-TECH PRODUCTS

One other special category of physical goods, potentially sold to both consumer and industrial customers, is technologically intensive, high-tech products. The main distinguishing feature of high-tech products is the fact that the products themselves change so rapidly over time due to technological innovations and R&D breakthroughs. Branding Brief 15–3 describes branding developments for Microsoft, one of the fastest growing and most successful corporate brands of the past decade. It should be recognized that high-tech products are not restricted to computer- or microprocessor-related products. Technology has played an important role in the branding and marketing of products as diverse as razor blades for Gillette and athletic shoes for Nike.

The short product life cycles for high-tech products have several significant branding implications (see Figure 15–10 for specific guidelines). First, it puts a premium on creating a corporate or family brand with strong credibility associations. Because of the often complex nature of high-tech products and the continual introduction of new products or modifications of existing products, consumer perceptions of the expertise and trustworthiness of the firm are particularly important. In a high-tech setting, trustworthiness also relates to consumers' perceptions of the firm's longevity and "staying power."

Leverage Secondary Associations of Quality

Lacking ability to judge the quality of high-tech products, consumers may use brand reputation as a means to reduce risk. This lack of ability by consumers to judge quality also means that it may be necessary to leverage secondary associations to better communicate product quality. Third-party endorsements from top companies, leading consumer magazines, or industry experts may help to achieve the necessary perceptions of product quality. To be able to garner these endorsements, however, will typically necessitate demonstrable differences in product performance, suggesting the importance of innovative product development over time.

Link Non-Product-Related Associations

Non-product-related associations related to brand personality or other imagery may be important, too, however, especially in distinguishing near-parity products. For example, consider the ad campaign by Matrix Integrated System, which makes two

FIGURE 15–10 Additional Guidelines for High-tech Products

1. Adopt a sub-branding strategy that combines a corporate or family brand with individual brands.
2. Selectively introduce new products as new brands and clearly identify the nature of brand extensions.
3. Carefully review the brand portfolio and update as needed over time.
4. Establish strong perceptions of company credibility and other important corporate image associations.
5. Consider leveraging other companies who are customers for secondary associations or third party endorsements as a signal of quality.

Building the Microsoft Brand[a]

One of the more revered (and perhaps feared!) brands of the 1990s is Microsoft, which has become the undisputed personal computer software leader. Recognizing the importance of branding, Microsoft has engaged in a number of activities to enhance its brand equity and market value. Microsoft's software products are designed to be technologically advanced, reliable, easy-to-use, and reasonably priced. Microsoft has used classic package-goods marketing techniques— TV, print, and outdoor advertising, direct response with toll-free 800 numbers, specially designed packaging, and sophisticated merchandising—to sell its products. Microsoft has found sampling particularly useful, for example, 50,000 free videos were distributed in the winter of 1994 to demonstrate how a dozen different software titles could be used. Complementing this consumer pull strategy is an intensive push strategy targeting such large retail chains as Egghead Software and CompUSA.

   In terms of branding strategy, Microsoft has adopted a sub-brand strategy to brand its products, combining the Microsoft corporate name with family brand or individual brands. At the corporate brand level, Microsoft has attained a high degree of credibility and respect. To better craft its image, it launched a $100 million global image campaign—created by Nike's ad agency Weiden & Kennedy—in 1995. The TV and print ads, showing a diverse group of computer owners using the software, contained the tag line, "Where Do You Want to Go Today?" Seventy-five percent of the budget was spent on consumer markets and 25 percent on the trade; half the budget was spent in the United States and the other half in the United Kingdom, Germany, France, and Australia. Microsoft has linked its corporate name to many different sub-brands. Microsoft Office packages word-processing, spreadsheet, presentation, and database software under the umbrella theme, "software that works for you." Microsoft Home is the consumer division and sells its product with its own logo and brand name. Microsoft Home software includes titles in four broad areas—reference, entertainment, personal productivity, and children's creativity—and such popular items as the movie guide Cinemania and the multimedia encyclopedia Encarta.

   Initially, Microsoft used a numerical modifier for technological advances to its Windows computer operating system software but decided in 1994 to brand the followup to Windows 3.1 and MS-DOS as Windows95 (while retaining the flag-shaped Windows logo to maintain a connection). They launched Windows95 on August 24, 1995 in a $200 million marketing and advertising extravaganza designed to gain awareness and acceptance. For a multimillion dollar payment, Mick Jagger and Keith Richards of the Rolling Stones allowed commercial use for the first time of one of their copyrighted songs, "Start Me Up," which became the theme song in a splashy introductory TV ad campaign. Other U.S. marketing activities included print ads, billboards, a half-hour "big event" infomercial, and lavish press conferences. Later international events were even more ambitious. In Australia, a four-story Windows95 box sailed on a barge in the Sydney harbor. In Britain, Microsoft painted farmer fields with the product logo so it would be visible from aircraft. In Poland, Microsoft took journalists down in a submarine to show them what it would be like to live "in a world without Windows."

In recent years, other marketing efforts have concentrated on its on-line service, The Microsoft Network, and its Microsoft NT for network computing. Microsoft has its eye on dominating the emerging information highway with software that runs everything from interactive video systems to computerized home banking.

---

[a]Tim Clark, "Microsoft Reboots Future Marketing," *Advertising Age* (April 26, 1994), p. 64. Don Clark, "Windows 95 Buzz Will Get Even Louder," *Wall Street Journal* (August 18, 1995), p. B1.

machines that are key equipment in the semiconductor manufacturing business—an etcher and a stripper.[5] In a clever play-on-words on the "stripper" product name, they launched a new ad campaign in 1990 that showed seven of their top executives wearing only loud boxer shorts, undershirts, shoes, socks, and large ostrich-feather boas under a headline proclaiming, "The Least Sexy but the Hardest Working Strippers in the Business." Building on Matrix's reputation and commitment to service, the unconventional ad was noted as one of the top high-tech campaigns of that year.

Carefully Design and Update Brand Portfolios and Hierarchies

Another implication of the abbreviated nature of product life cycles with high-tech marketers is the importance of optimally designing brand portfolios and brand hierarchies. Several issues are relevant here. First, brand extensions are a common high-tech branding strategy. With new products continually emerging, it would be prohibitively expensive to brand them with new names in each case. Typically, names for new products are given modifiers from existing products—numerical (Microsoft Word 6.0), time-based (Microsoft Windows 95), and so on—*unless* they represent dramatic departures or marked product improvements for the brand, in which case a new brand name might be employed. Using a new name for a new product is a means to signal to consumers that this particular generation or version of a product is a major departure and significantly different from prior versions of the product.

Thus, family brands are an important means of grouping products. Individual items or products within those brand families must be clearly distinguished, however, and brand migration strategies must be defined that reflect product introduction strategies and consumer market trends. Other brand portfolio issues relate to the importance of retaining some brands. Too often, high-tech firms continually introduce new sub-brands, making it difficult for consumers to develop product or brand loyalty.

SERVICES

Kotler defines a service as "any act or performance that one party can offer to another that is essentially intangible and does not result in the ownership of anything."[6] Services come in many different forms. Although the production of services is not necessarily tied to a physical product, they can often accompany goods in some way.

Kotler maintains that company service offerings can really be placed on a continuum that includes five levels:

1. *Pure tangible good* (e.g., a toothpaste)
2. *Tangible good with accompanying services* (e.g., an automobile)
3. *Hybrid* (e.g., a restaurant)
4. *Major service with accompanying minor goods and services* (e.g., an airline)
5. *Pure service* (e.g., a hair stylist)

In terms of where offerings are placed on the continuum, pure services can be distinguished from pure tangible goods along four dimensions:

1. *Tangibility:* Unlike physical goods, services cannot be seen, tasted, felt, heard, or smelled before they are bought.
2. *Separability:* Unlike physical goods, services are typically produced and consumed simultaneously.
3. *Variability:* Unlike physical goods, services depend more on exactly who provides them and where they are provided.
4. *Perishability:* Unlike physical goods, services cannot be stored.

These four dimensions pose challenges to the marketing of services. To overcome these potential marketing problems, service firms can take a number of actions. For example, potential perishability problems can be addressed on the demand side by marketing actions such as differential pricing, the cultivation of non-peak demand, complementary services, and reservation systems. Potential perishability problems can be addressed on the supply side by marketing actions such as part-time employee staffing, peak-time efficiency routines, increased consumer participation, shared services, and facilities for future expansion.[7]

Maximize Service Quality

From a branding perspective, one challenge with services is their intangible nature (see Figure 15–11 for some specific guidelines). One consequence of this intangibility is that consumers may have difficulty forming their quality evaluations and may end up basing those evaluations on considerations other than factors directly related to their service experiences. Specifically, researchers have identified a number of dimensions of service quality.[8]

1. *Tangibles:* Physical facilities, equipment, and appearance of personnel
2. *Reliability:* Ability to perform the promised service right the first time (standardized facilities and operations)
3. *Responsiveness:* Willingness to help customers and provide customer service
4. *Competence:* Knowledge and skill of employees
5. *Trustworthiness:* Believability and honesty (ability to convey trust and confidence)
6. *Empathy:* Caring, individualized attention provided
7. *Courtesy:* Friendliness of customer contact
8. *Communication:* Keeping customers informed in language they can understand and listening to what they say

1. Maximize service quality by recognizing the myriad ways to impact consumer service perceptions.

2. Create strong, favorable, and unique associations to the corporation as a whole, especially if adopting a corporate branding strategy.

3. Design corporate communication programs that augment consumers' service encounters and experiences.

4. Employ a full range of brand elements to enhance brand recall and signal more tangible aspects of the brand.

5. Establish a brand hierarchy by creating distinct family brands or individual brands as well as meaningful ingredient brands.

FIGURE 15-11 Additional Guidelines for Services

Thus, service quality perceptions depend on a number of specific associations that vary in how directly they relate to the actual service experience. In terms of creating service offerings that excel on these various dimensions, academic researchers Berry, Parasuraman, and Zeithaml offer ten lessons that they maintain are essential for improving service quality across service industries (see Figure 15–12).[9]

Create and Communicate Strong Organizational Associations

Organizational associations—such as perceptions about the people who make up the organization and who provide the service—are likely to be particularly important brand associations that may affect evaluations of service quality directly or indirectly. One particularly important association is company credibility and perceived expertise, trustworthiness, and likability. Consequently, service firms must design marketing communication and information programs so that consumers learn more about the brand than the information they glean from their service encounters alone. These programs may involve advertising, direct mail, and so on that may be particularly effective at helping the firm to develop the proper brand personality.

Employ a Full Range of Brand Elements

Intangibility also has implications for the choice of brand elements. Because service decisions and arrangements are often made away from the actual service location itself (e.g., at home or at work), brand recall becomes critically important. In such cases, an easy-to-remember and pronounce brand name may become critically important. Because a physical product does not exist, packaging in a literal sense is not really relevant, although the physical facilities of the service provider can perhaps be seen as the external "packaging" of a service (e.g., through its primary and secondary signage, environmental design and reception area, apparel, collateral material, and so on). Other brand elements—logos, symbols, characters, and slogans—must then "pick up the slack" and complement the brand name to build brand awareness and brand image. These other brand elements often attempt to make the service and some of its key benefits more tangible, concrete, and real—the "friendly skies" of United, the "good hands" of Allstate, and the "bullish" nature of Merrill Lynch.

1. *Listening:* Understand what customers really want through continuous learning about the expectations and perceptions of customers and non-customers (e.g., by means of a service quality information system).

2. *Reliability:* Reliability is the single most important dimension of service quality and must be a service priority.

3. *Basic service:* Service companies must deliver the basics and do what they are supposed to do—keep promises, use common sense, listen to customers, keep customers informed, and be determined to deliver value to customers.

4. *Service design:* Develop a holistic view of the service while managing its many details.

5. *Recovery:* To satisfy customers who encounter a service problem, service companies should encourage customers to complain (and make it easy for them to do so), respond quickly and personally, and develop a problem resolution system.

6. *Surprising customers:* Although reliability is the most important dimension in meeting customers' service expectations, process dimensions (e.g., assurance, responsiveness, and empathy) are most important in exceeding customer expectations, such as by surprising customers with uncommon swiftness, grace, courtesy, competence, commitment, and understanding.

7. *Fair play:* Service companies must make special efforts to be fair and to demonstrate fairness to customers and employees.

8. *Teamwork:* Teamwork is what enables large organizations to deliver service with care and attentiveness by improving employee motivation and capabilities.

9. *Employee research:* Conduct research with employees to reveal why service problems occur and what companies must do to solve problems.

10. *Servant leadership:* Quality service comes from inspired leadership throughout the organization; from excellent service-system design; from the effective use of information and technology; and from a slow-to-change, invisible, all-powerful, internal force called corporate culture.

FIGURE 15–12 Recommendations for Improving Service Quality

Establish a Brand Hierarchy

Finally, services also must consider developing a brand hierarchy and brand portfolio that permits positioning and targeting of different market segments. Classes of service can be branded vertically on the basis of price and quality. Vertical extensions often require sub-branding strategies where the corporate name is combined with an individual brand name or modifier. In the hotel and airlines industry, brand lines and portfolios have been created by brand extension and introductions. For example, United Airlines brands its business class service as Connoisseur Class, its frequent flier program as Mileage Plus, and its discount West Coast airlines as Shuttle by United. As another example, Hilton Hotel has introduced Hilton Garden Inns to target budget-conscious business travelers and compete with the popular Courtyard by Marriott chain.

RETAILERS

Chapters 5 and 7 reviewed a number of issues concerning how retailers and other channel intermediaries may affect the brand equity of the products they sell as well as how they may create their own brand equity. Fundamentally, retailers create their own brand equity by establishing awareness and associations to their product assortment (breadth and depth), pricing and credit policy, and quality of service. For example, Wal-Mart has become a premiere U.S. retail brand by becoming seen as the low-price, high-value provider of a host of everyday consumer products. Consumers may form these associations in many ways—on the basis of personal experience, word-of-mouth, or through advertisements or other indirect means. In building brand equity for a retailer, several guidelines are particularly relevant (see Figure 15–13).

Create Brand Hierarchies

First, it is important to create a brand hierarchy by branding the store as a whole, as well as individual departments, classes of service, or any other noteworthy aspect of the retail service or shopping experience. Establishing a brand hierarchy helps to create synergies in brand development. Retailers also must consider brand portfolio issues and what other retail stores or chains should be introduced to provide more complete market coverage. For example, Wal-Mart introduced another retail chain, Sam's Club, to tap into the growing discount or warehouse retail market.

Similarly, individual departments can take on their own unique set of associations that appeal to a particular target market. For example, Nordstrom has clothing departments such as Point of View, Plum Avenue, The Brass Connection, Town Square, Encore, Individualist, and The Rail, each designed with distinct images and positionings. These departments may be branded by the retailer or even as "ingredient brands," designed and supported by a national manufacturer (e.g., as with Polo shops in major department stores that only sell that Ralph Lauren brand).

Enhance Manufacturer's Brand Equity

As a second guideline, retailers should exploit as much as possible the brand equity of the brands they sell by communicating and demonstrating their points of difference and other strong, favorable, and unique brand associations. Manufacturers often employ "push" strategies that involve various programs to encourage retailers

FIGURE 15-13 Additional Guidelines for Retailers

1. Create a brand hierarchy by branding the store as a whole, as well as individual departments, classes of service, or any other aspects of the shopping experience.
2. Exploit the brand equity of product offerings by communicating and demonstrating points of difference and other strong, favorable, and unique brand associations.
3. Establish brand equity at all levels of the brand hierarchy by offering added value in the selection, purchase, or delivery of product offerings.
4. If selling own store or private labels, do not "overbrand" by employing too many brands.

to better support their brands. By cooperating with and perhaps even enhancing these programs to better communicate the value and equity of the brands sold, retailers should be able to sell these products at higher prices and margins, generating greater profits as a result.

Establish Retailer's Brand Equity

Third, retailers must establish brand equity at all levels of the brand hierarchy by offering added value in the selection, purchase, or delivery of product offerings. Thus, retailers must create their own strong, favorable, and unique associations that go beyond the products they sell. Sharper Image has created a niche as a seller of creative, upscale products and gadgets. Victoria's Secret has gained notoriety as a provider of stylish, feminine clothing. Costco and Price Club created strong discount associations.

Some of the most successful retail brands in recent years have been warehouse stores or "category killers" that have created strong associations to a certain set of products. Home Depot captured a huge chunk of the home-improvement and hardware store business by selling thousands of items through skilled and helpful salespeople and a "no questions asked" return policy. Other category killers include retailers such as Toys 'R Us, Linens 'N Things, and Circuit City. One advantage these chains have is the sharp positioning they are able to create in the minds of consumers.

To communicate these broader associations, retail strategies are often reflected in image campaigns that focus more on the advantages to consumers of shopping at and buying from the stores in general, as compared to the promotions on specific sale items. For example, Radio Shack now advertises that it is the "consumer-friendly" provider of electronic parts, accessories, and specialty equipment through a campaign with a slogan, "You've Got Questions. We've Got Answers."

Avoid Overbranding

Finally, if a retailer is selling its own private labels, it is important not to "overbrand" by employing too many brands. Retailers are particularly susceptible to "bottom-up branding" where each department creates its own set of brands. For example, Nordstrom found itself in the position of having to support scores of different brands across its different departments, sometimes with little connection across them. Recall from chapter 5 that one advantage of store brands, however, is that they often represent associations, such as value, that transfer across categories. The greater the extent to which an abstract association—value, fashionability, and so on—can be seen as desirable and deliverable across categories, the more likely it is that efficiencies can be gained by concentrating on a few major brands. To illustrate the importance of private labels to retailers, Branding Brief 15–4 describes how brand equity was built at The Gap.

SMALL BUSINESSES

Building brands for a small business is a challenge because of the limited resources and budgets typically involved. Unlike major brands that often have more resources at their disposal, small businesses usually do not have the luxury to make mistakes and must design and implement marketing programs much more carefully. Nevertheless, there are numerous success stories of entrepreneurs who have built their brands up essentially from scratch to become powerhouse brands.

Building the Gap Brand[a]

Donald Fisher founded the Gap in San Francisco in 1969 after recognizing the need for a store that sold jeans in a variety of colors and sizes. Naming the store after the "generation gap," Fisher targeted baby boomers who had embraced jeans in general—and Levi's in particular—as the uniform of their generation. Early television ads touted the variety of Levi's products available and used the theme, "Fall into the Gap."

As the popularity of Gap stores increased, Fisher broadened the merchandise assortment by adding a limited number of Gap brand products and as many as fifteen other national brands. Gap brand jeans were essentially a knock-off of Levi's with similar stitching and patch designs. New products catered to the aging baby boom audience while attempting to retain its traditionally young customer base. As Levi-Strauss expanded its distribution base to include department stores and discount chains, the Gap began to experience increased price pressure. To avoid shrinking margins and to tap into a more affluent market than students, Fisher decided to upgrade the Gap image. Aided by Mickey Drexler, who had successfully turned around Ann Taylor, Fisher began the process of transformation in 1983.

In a bold move, Drexler dropped all non-Gap merchandise except for Levi's and introduced a new look to Gap brand merchandise—more colorful sweaters, jerseys, and shirts—to appeal to an increasingly older and affluent market. Eschewing trendy fashions, Gap brand clothing was positioned as causal, functional, and "basic with attitude." High-quality cotton fabrics sold at moderate prices combined to help create a no-nonsense value perception of Gap clothes with customers. Gap sales grew through the 1980s, cracking the $1 billion mark in sales in 1987. The highly successfully "Individuals of Style" campaign—a series of black and white photos of diverse personalities from jazz giant Miles Davis to country singer k. d. lang in very down-to-earth poses and setting, all comfortably wearing their Gap clothes with other clothes—helped to give the brand a fresh new look.

Gap's dramatic turnaround in the mid-1980s solidified its customer franchise—especially among women—and established its own brand equity, permitting further expansion. The brand had become strongly associated with quality, comfort, and everyday styles. Gap's relaxed image fit well with the more conservative, reserved lifestyles at the turn of the decade. Gap expanded its clothing offerings to include new fashions and styles (including prints and plaids) and new fabrics, as well as new clothing categories such as blazers and outerwear, boxer shorts, footwear, swim suits and swim trunks, hats, and handbags.

The Gap has also expanded beyond its flagship stores through acquisitions and extensions. The Gap bought Banana Republic and its unique travel and safari-themed stores and catalogues. GapKids is a highly successful extension introduced in 1986. Riding the wave of the baby boom "echo" to successfully open 350+ stores by 1995, GapKids accounts for more than approximately 16 percent of Gap's annual earnings. In March 1994, Gap introduced Old Navy

Clothing stores to sell Gap-like men's, women's, and children's apparel at lower prices in large warehouse-style outlets (e.g., Old Navy jeans would sell for $22 whereas Gap jeans would sell for $34). Plans were to introduce 60 to 70 Old Navy stores each year.

The Gap faces a number of opportunities and challenges in the coming years. As the brand has gained more lifestyle associations, it has even introduced non-apparel products such as GapScents, a collection of bath and body products (with fragrances called grass, day, heaven, and earth), launched in a subset of Gap stores in 1994. It must selectively extend the Gap name into appropriate categories. It must successfully distinguish the different brands in its portfolio, especially Old Navy and the Gap where the risk of cannibalization is potentially great. Finally, they must keep the Gap brand contemporary and relevant in the fickle, fast-changing fashion business. A troubling sign there is that whereas 90 percent of teens in Leo Burnett's biannual "What's Hot Among Kids" survey said Gap clothes were "cool" in 1992, only two-thirds agreed with that designation two years later.

---

[a]The Gap, HBS Case N9-593-043. Christina Duff, "Bobby Short Wore Khakis—Who's He and Who Cares?" *Wall Street Journal* (February 16, 1995), p. A1.

For example, consider the story of Starbucks coffee.[10] From nine Seattle stores in 1987, Starbucks has expanded to over 600 stores all over the United States. Starbucks company-owned gourmet coffee bars roast their own coffee and cater to an espresso-drinking audience that appreciates its "hip" image and the quality service that results from employees' twenty-four hours of classroom training. Starbucks has expanded its distribution to sell through new outlets (e.g., direct mail) and with new partners (e.g., United Airlines) and expanded its product line to include Frapuccino (i.e., a cold blend of ice, milk, and coffee) and coffee ice cream (in a joint venture with Dreyer's Grand Ice Cream).

Figure 15–14 displays some specific branding guidelines for small businesses, as follows.

Focus Creatively Designed Branding and Marketing Programs

In general, because limited resources may be placed behind the brand, both focus and consistency in marketing programs are critically important. To compensate for fewer funds, creativity is paramount, finding new ways to market new ideas about products to consumers. Strategically, it may be necessary to emphasize building one or two strong brands that rely on only one or two key associations as points of difference. Along these lines, employing a corporate branding strategy can be an efficient means to build brand equity, although the focus may just be on a major family brand. For example, Intuit concentrated its marketing efforts on building the Quicken brand name of software. To overcome resource constraints from limited budgets, creativity in design and execution is also invaluable.

1. Emphasize building one or two strong brands.

2. Focus a creatively designed marketing program on one or two key brand associations to serve as sources of brand equity.

3. Employ a well-integrated set of brand elements that enhance both brand awareness and brand image.

4. Design brand-building "push" campaigns and creative "pull" campaigns that capture attention.

5. Leverage as many secondary associations as possible.

FIGURE 15-14 Additional Guidelines for Small Businesses

Employ a Well-Integrated Set of Brand Elements

Tactically, it is important for small businesses to maximize the contribution of each of the three main ways to build brand equity. First, a distinctive, well-integrated set of brand elements should be developed that enhances both brand awareness and brand image. For example, Seattle's Wall Data makes connectivity software between desktop and host computers (various mainframes) that allows users to avoid rebooting or reconfiguring. Wall Data cleverly branded its family of software products "Rumba" and combined that name with a character symbol of a man and woman dancing cheek-to-cheek (see Figure 15–15). They used the slogan, "Get Connected" in advertising, promotional materials, and packaging. To further build awareness and image, they even hosted rumba dance lessons at trade shows! The success of the Rumba product line has permitted the introduction of a new set of software products, branded "Salsa."

Thus, brand elements ideally should be as memorable and meaningful, with as much creative potential as possible. Innovative packaging can be a substitute for ad campaigns by capturing attention at the point of purchase. For example, Smartfood introduced its first product without any advertising by means of both a unique package that served as a strong visual symbol on the shelf as well as an extensive sampling program that encouraged trial.

Design Brand-Building "Push" Campaigns and Creative "Pull" Campaigns

Small businesses must design creative push and pull programs that capture the attention of consumers and other channel members alike. Clearly, this is a sizable challenge on a limited budget. Unfortunately, without a strong pull campaign creating product interest, retailers may not feel enough motivation to stock and support the brand. Conversely, without a strong push campaign that convinces retailers of the merits of the product, it may fail to achieve adequate support or not even be stocked at all. Thus, push and pull marketing programs ideally would be creatively designed and integrated, employing the most cost-effective tools available, to increase the visibility of the brand and get both consumers and retailers talking about the brand.

Because small businesses often must rely on word-of-mouth to create strong, favorable, and unique brand associations, public relations and low-cost promotions and

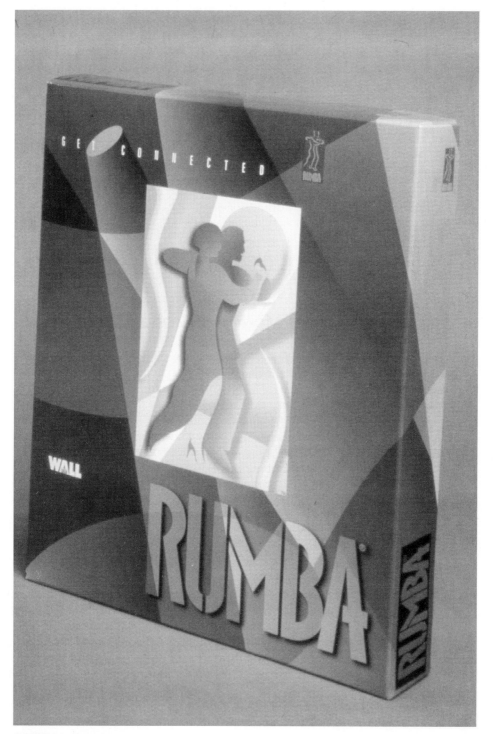

FIGURE 15–15 Rumba Logo

sponsorship can be inexpensive means to enhance brand awareness and brand image. For example, Noah Alper, co-founder of Noah's Bagels, reached out to the Jewish community and transplanted New Yorkers in Northern California through well-publicized events and appearances that promoted the "authentic" nature of the bagel chain. Marketers of the PowerBar, a nutrient-rich, low-fat "energy bar," used selective sponsorship of top marathon runners, cyclists, and tennis players and events like the Boston Marathon to raise awareness and improve image. Selective distribution that targets opinion leaders can also be a cost-effective means to implement a "push" strategy. For example, brands like Perrier bottled water and Paul Mitchell and Nexus shampoos were initially introduced to a carefully selected set of outlets before broadening distribution.

Leverage as Many Secondary Associations as Possible

Finally, the third way for small businesses to build brand equity is to leverage as many secondary associations as possible. Secondary associations are often a cost-effective, shortcut means to build brand equity. Any entity with potentially relevant associations should be considered, especially those that help to signal quality.

Comparisons with Other Models of Brand Equity

The above discussion highlights different specific applications of the customer-based brand equity framework. To provide additional perspective on brand equity, it is useful to briefly review other proposed frameworks. A number of views of brand equity have been put forth by both academics and practitioners. By far the most comprehensive and well-known academic treatment of brand equity, with aspects relevant to both a financial and strategic perspective, is by David Aaker from the University of California at Berkeley.[11] On the practitioner side, one of the leading industry approaches to brand equity is a well-publicized model, BrandAsset Valuator, by the Young & Rubicam ad agency. Both of these views of brand equity complement the customer-based brand equity (CBBE) framework reviewed in this book and yield diagnostic information and insights to improve strategic decisions concerning the brand, as reviewed next.

THE AAKER MODEL

Aaker defines brand equity as a set of five categories of brand assets and liabilities linked to a brand, its name, and symbol, that add to or subtract from the value provided by a product or service to a firm and/or to that firm's customers. These categories of brand assets are: (1) brand loyalty, (2) brand awareness, (3) perceived quality, (4) brand associations, and (5) other proprietary assets (e.g., patents, trademarks, and channel relationships). These assets provide various benefits and value, as shown in Figure 15–16.

Aaker describes a number of issues in building, measuring, and managing brand equity. A summary of guidelines emerging from his framework can be found in Figure 15–17. According to Aaker, a particularly important concept for building brand equity is the concept of brand identity. Aaker defines brand identity as:[12]

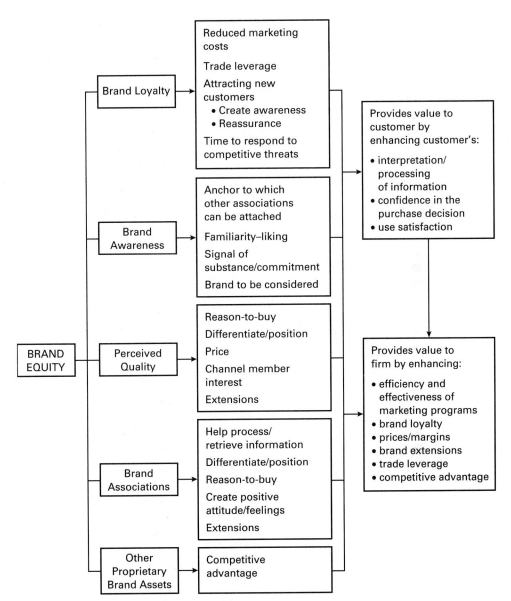

FIGURE 15-16 Aaker's Brand Equity Model

. . . a unique set of brand associations that the brand strategist aspires to create or maintain. These associations represent what the brand stands for and imply a promise to customers from the organization members. Brand identity should help establish a relationship between the brand and the customer by generating a value proposition involving functional, emotional, or self-expressive benefits.

Brand identity consists of twelve dimensions organized around four perspectives—the brand-as-product (product scope, product attributes, quality/value, uses, users, coun-

1. **Brand identity.** Have an identity for each brand. Consider the perspective of the brand-as-person, brand-as-organization, and brand-as-symbol, as well as the brand-as-product. Identify the core identity. Modify the identity as needed for different market segments and products. Remember that an image is how you are perceived, and an identity is how you aspire to be perceived.

2. **Value proposition.** Know the value proposition for each brand that has a driver role. Consider emotional and symbolic benefits as well as functional benefits. Know how endorser brands will provide credibility. Understand the customer/brand relationship.

3. **Brand position.** For each brand, have a brand position that will provide clear guidance to those implementing a communication program. Recall that a position is the part of the identity that is actively communicated.

4. **Execution.** Execute the communication program so that it not only is on target with the identity and position but achieves brilliance and durability. Generate alternatives and consider options beyond media advertising.

5. **Consistency over time.** Have as a goal a consistent identity, position, and execution over time. Maintain symbols, imagery, and metaphors that work. Understand and resist organizational biases toward changing the identity, position, and execution.

6. **Brand system.** Make sure the brands in the portfolio are consistent and synergistic. Know their roles. Have or develop silver bullets to help support brand identities and positions. Exploit branded features and services. Use sub-brands to clarify and modify. Know the strategic brands.

7. **Brand leverage.** Extend brands and develop co-branding programs only if the brand identity will be both used and reinforced. Identify range brands and, for each, develop an identity and specify how that identity will be different in disparate product contexts. If a brand is moved up or down, take care to manage the integrity of the resulting brand identity.

8. **Tracking brand equity.** Track brand equity over time, including brand awareness, perceived quality, brand loyalty, and especially brand associations. Have specific communication objectives. Especially note areas where the brand identity and positioning and communication objectives are not reflected in the perceptions of the brand.

9. **Brand responsibility.** Have someone in charge of the brand who will create the identity and positions and coordinate the execution over organizational units, media, and markets. Beware when a brand is being used in a business where it is not the cornerstone.

10. **Invest in brands.** Continue investing in brands even when the financial goals are not being met.

FIGURE 5-17 Aaker's 10 Guidelines for Building Strong Brands

try of origin), brand-as-organization (organizational attributes, local versus global), brand-as-person (brand personality, brand-customer relationships), and brand-as-symbol (visual imagery/metaphors and brand heritage).

Brand identity structure includes a core and extended identity. The core identity—the central, timeless essence of the brand—is most likely to remain constant as the brand travels to new markets and products. The extended identity includes brand identity elements, organized into cohesive and meaningful groups.

A particularly important concept for managing brand equity according to Aaker is the concept of brand systems. Aaker emphasizes that a key to managing brands in an environment of complexity is to consider them not just as individual performers but as members of a system of brands that must work together to support one another. He notes that the goals of the system are qualitatively different from the goals of individual brand identities and include: (1) exploit commonalties to generate synergy, (2) reduce brand identity damage, (3) achieve clarity of product offerings, (4) facilitate change and adaptation, and (5) allocate resources. Aaker also notes that many brands within a system usually fall into a natural hierarchy and may play different roles in the system—endorser, driver, strategic brands, silver bullets, branded benefits, and sub-brand roles.

Aaker identifies and reviews a number of other branding concepts and identifies classic marketing successes and failures. Aaker's view of brand equity provides many useful insights. One of the advantages of his treatment is that he identifies a host of useful marketing principles and anecdotes to illustrate his points about branding. Many ingredients and implications of his framework parallel those that emerge from the customer-based brand equity framework described in his book. In particular, both approaches take a customer-oriented perspective to emphasize the importance of brand awareness and associations. Despite this commonality, some important differences exist. The primary difference is that the CBBE framework is based on a more detailed and fully articulated conceptual foundation. A much stronger focus on consumers and their brand knowledge structures permits a more definitive set of recommendations and guidelines concerning how to build, measure, and manage brand equity. Nevertheless, Aaker's model complements the CBBE framework presented here, reinforcing some key points and highlighting some others.

THE YOUNG AND RUBICAM "BRANDASSET VALUATOR"™ MODEL

Young & Rubicam (Y&R), one of the world's largest worldwide advertising agencies, has conducted the most extensive research program on global branding to date. In the first wave alone, almost 45,000 adult consumers in 27 countries were interviewed, beginning in October 1993 and continuing through 1996. Specifically, consumers were interviewed in the Americas (Brazil, Canada, Mexico, United States), Western Europe (France, Germany, Great Britain, Italy, Netherlands, Spain), Central and Eastern Europe (Poland, Hungary, Czech Republic, Russia), Asia and the Pacific (Australia, Japan, People's Republic of China, Thailand), and Africa (South Africa).

More recently, fieldwork has been initiated on a second worldwide wave, which includes additional countries, a more extensive set of brands, additional questionnaire items about emotional connections between consumers and brands, and, for the first time, teen respondents. This most recent worldwide wave measures over 8,500 brands in total, about 500 of which are global in nature.

In the interviews, Y&R chose to have respondents evaluate brands in a category-free context to deliberately encourage thoughts about a brand in relation to *all* brands rather than to a narrowly defined category, as would be done in a traditional consumer study. In the most recent wave, each brand is rated on 64 different items tapping a variety of perceptual dimensions. Additional measures include Current Usage, Future Usage Intent, Media Habits and Attitudes, as well as psychographics and demographics.

Four Pillars

Using these data, Y&R has developed an empirically-based theory of brand-building which they call the BrandAsset Valuator™. According to this model, successful brands are built through a very specific progression of consumer perceptions: first Differentiation, then Relevance, next Esteem, and, finally, Knowledge.

Y&R explains their model as follows. Differentiation measures the perceived distinctiveness of the brand. It is within Differentiation that consumer choice, meaning, brand essence, and potential margin reside. Relevance measures a brand's personal appropriateness among consumers and is strongly tied to household penetration. Relevance alone is *not* the key to brand success according to Y&R. Rather, Relevance together with Differentiation represents *Brand Strength,* which Y&R identifies as an important leading indicator of future performance and potential. Relevant Differentiation—being both different from other brands and personally appropriate to the consumer—is viewed by Y&R as the central challenge for all brands.

If a marketer is successful in creating Relevant Differentiation, according to Y&R, consumers will hold the brand in high regard and show high levels of Esteem. Ultimately, if a brand has established Relevant Differentiation, and consumers have high Esteem, then the final pillar of Knowledge develops. Y&R notes that Knowledge is much deeper than brand awareness and captures the consumer's intimate understanding of the brand and what it stands for. Combining Esteem and Knowledge creates *Brand Stature,* an indication of a brand's current presence.

Y&R believes that the examination of the relationships between these four measures—a brand's "pillar pattern"—reveals much about the current and future status of a brand. New brands that have just been launched show low levels on all four measures. Strong new brands tend to show higher levels of Differentiation, lower levels of Relevance, still lower levels of Esteem, and quite low levels of current Knowledge. Leadership brands show high levels on all four measures. Finally, declining brands show high Knowledge levels relative to lower Esteem levels, even lower levels of Relevance, and quite low levels of Differentiation.

PowerGrid

Y&R has integrated the two fundamental dimensions of Brand Strength and Brand Stature into a visual analytic device which they call the PowerGrid, as shown in Figure 15–18, which depicts the cycle of brand development—and characteristic pillar patterns—in successive quadrants. According to Y&R, brands generally begin life in the lower left corner, where they first establish their Relevant Differentiation, their reason for being. Most of the movement from there is upward. Differentiation starts

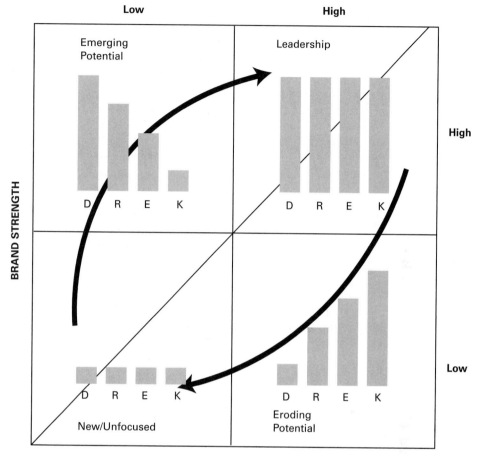

FIGURE 15-18 The PowerGrid Shows How Brands Grow and Decline

the process of growth, then Relevance, while the brand is not yet held in Esteem or widely known. Enough Brand Strength boosts the brand into the upper left quadrant. Y&R believes this quadrant represents tremendous emerging potential for a brand. Brand Strength is still building and the challenge here is to translate this Brand Strength into Brand Stature. Specialist brands that appeal to focused target groups tend to remain in this quadrant. Or, this upper left quadrant can be the base from which to launch an attack. Current brand leaders need to recognize the brands here as their emerging competition.

Y&R notes that the upper right area—the Leadership Quadrant—is populated by brand leaders and the strongest brands—those brands that have both high levels of Brand Strength and Brand Stature. Y&R also notes that there are both older *and* relatively younger brands in this upper right quadrant which they interpret as meaning that maintaining brand leadership is not a function of age, but rather a reflection of Brand Strength and Brand Stature. They also see this pattern as meaning that brands can hold a position of power, virtually forever, if managed properly—i.e., there is no inevitability to brand decline. Conversely, if a brand has lower Brand Strength than it has Brand Stature, that is often a sign of potential weakness. Brands that fail to maintain their Brand Strength—their Relevant Differentiation—begin to fade. Y&R observes that these brands frequently end up being drawn into price wars and are extremely vulnerable to the threat of Private Label brands. Finally, if unattended for a long enough period, their Brand Stature will also begin to fall. Figure 15–19 presents examples of brands in each of these four quadrants of the PowerGrid.

Finally, Y&R notes that a brand's health—in terms of Brand Strength and Brand Stature—may vary by countries. For example, Figure 15–20 displays three brands. Each point on the PowerGrid for these brands corresponds to the perceptions among consumers in a particular country. Note how Calvin Klein varies tremendously in brand development across various countries, suggesting that different marketing strategies and programs may have to be adopted in different parts of the world for that brand. On the other hand, Coca-Cola shows a remarkable level of consistency in

FIGURE 15-19 Examples of Brands in the Four Quadrants of the Y&R PowerGrid

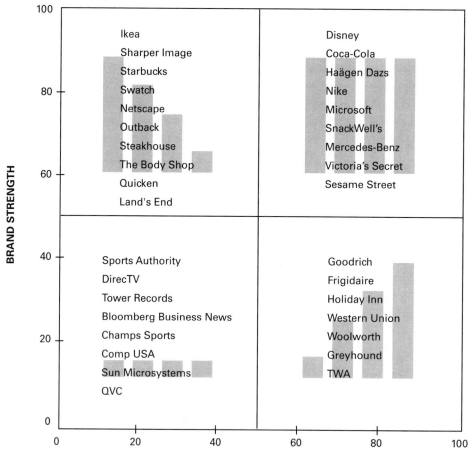

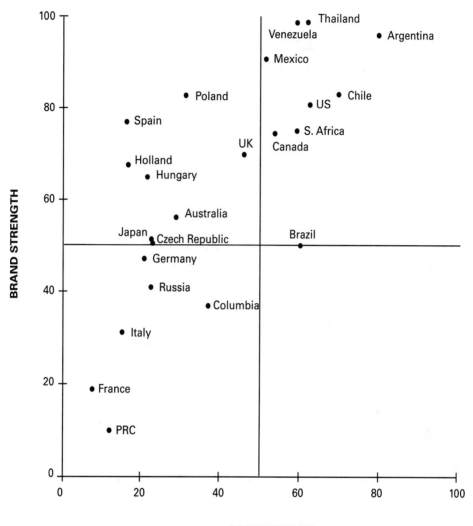

FIGURE 15–20a PowerGrid for Calvin Klein around the World among Total Population

brand development around the world. Disney appears to fall somewhere between the other two in its developmental level across markets.

Critique

There is a high degree of commonality between Y&R's BrandAsset Valuator™ Model and the CBBE framework, as shown by the similarity between the four pillars and key elements of the CBBE framework:

Knowledge relates to CBBE's awareness and familiarity

Esteem relates to CBBE's favorability of brand associations

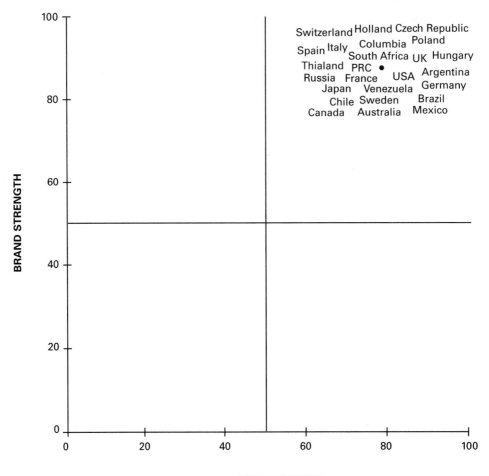

FIGURE 15-20b PowerGrid for Coca-Cola around the World among Total Population

Relevance relates to CBBE's strength of brand associations

Differentiation relates to CBBE's uniqueness of brand associations.

One chief benefit of the BrandAsset Valuator™ model is that it identifies which fundamental "brandedness" dimensions require support, investment, or corrective action. It also provides a metric that is inherently comparative, showing marketers the standing of their brands on key dimensions of health relative to all other brands across a wide variety of categories and a vast array of countries. This ability is especially valuable since marketers typically focus on their brand's category, often neglecting the reality that consumers may be buying across categories. BrandAsset Valuator™ enables cross-category and cross-country insights that would not be possible from a more traditionally designed study of consumer perceptions.

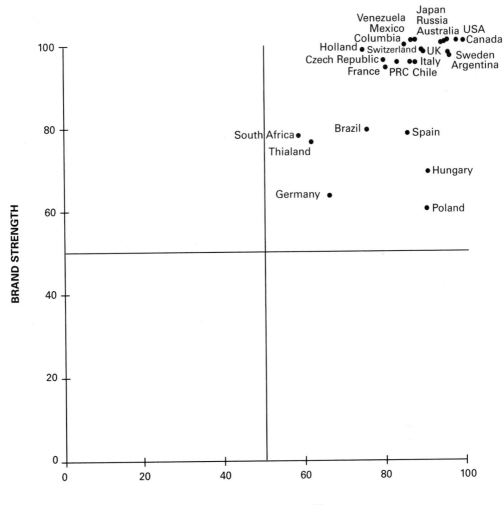

FIGURE 15-20c PowerGrid for Disney around the World among Total Population

However, it should be noted that Y&R's model and measurement system trades product specificity for cross-category generality. By necessity, many if not most of the measures have been designed to be broadly applicable across brands that represent a wide variety of product- and service-offerings. Thus, the model tends to operate at the strategic rather than tactical level, is abstract in nature, and is not directly related to category dynamics. As a result, the Y&R model is best used as a strategic planning tool. In contrast, the CBBE framework is complementary to Y&R's approach and is especially applicable at the category level, permitting much more detailed tactical insights on how to build, measure, and manage brand equity. Nevertheless, the Y&R model represents a landmark study in terms of marketers' ability to understand what drives top brands and how to energize, maintain, or reverse the decline of brands.

Future Prospects

Our journey to understand strategic brand management is about over, but it is worth considering one final question—"How will branding change in the coming years? What will make a successful '21st century brand'?" In this final section, we will speculate as to how branding and the principles of building, measuring, and managing brand equity espoused in this text might evolve and change over time.

ROLE OF BRANDS

In a general sense, the importance of branding seems unlikely to change for one important reason. It seems highly likely that consumers will continue to value the functions provided by brands. In a seemingly more and more complex world, well-managed brands can simplify, communicate, reassure, and provide important meaning to consumers.

BUILDING BRAND EQUITY

The basic principles of choosing brand elements to build brand equity should continue to hold in the coming years. In other words, creating strong brands will still involve combining brand elements in a consistent and complementary fashion so that, collectively, the brand is memorable, meaningful, transferable, and protectable. Thus, smart marketers will employ the full repertoire of brand elements to choose vivid brand names that suggest some concrete or abstract benefit, visually reinforced by a logo, symbol, or character, and verbally reinforced by a slogan or jingle that enhances awareness and image.

In a cluttered, competitive marketplace with distracted or disinterested consumers, however, those brand elements that make up the brand will have to do more and more of the "selling job." In a time-compressed marketing world, the fact that a brand name can be noticed and its meaning registered or activated in memory within just a few seconds is a tremendous asset. Creating a powerful brand with inherent marketing value to build awareness and image, as well as serve as a strong foundation to link associations, can provide a firm with a strong competitive advantage.

Although the general branding principles will apply in designing a twenty-first-century brand, what may change, however, are some of the means to create strong brands. The brand elements that are chosen will increasingly involve verbal and visual elements that creatively and dramatically help to build brand equity. Meaningful brands with creative potential will benefit from multiple sensory presentations. Brands have long used auditory branding devices, for example, the three-note Nabisco jingle, the percolating Maxwell House jingle, and the NBC jingle. Movie studios have always been able to take advantage of their cinematic exposure to use sight, sound, and motion to present their brands (e.g., Universal's spinning globe, Paramount's mountain peak, and MGM's roaring lion). With increased technical abilities and improved special effects, marketers will now be able to create brand elements that come to life and capture consumer attention, an important quality given the need to communicate and sell through brands in current markets. Thus, the static images of brands with which marketers are used to dealing will be supplemented by multidimensional forms that play a more important role in audio and video presentations of the brand.

For example, perhaps one of the strongest brands to emerge in the last decade has been Intel and its Intel Inside microprocessor brand. There are a number of success factors for the brand, but one extremely worthwhile decision Intel made in its introductory television campaign was to end its ads with a picture of the "Intel Inside" logo dramatically flashing and swirling on the TV screen—almost literally "Intel in your face"—while the voice-over announced: "The computer inside." This branding device captured consumers' attention at a critical moment in the ad, helping to both build awareness of the Intel brand and linking it to the communication effects engendered by the ad—a major challenge in today's difficult media environment.

Thus, a twenty-first-century brand will consider how to take advantage of different media to customize the brand presentation so that each brand element more effectively contributes to brand equity through enhanced awareness and image *and* brand elements more effectively reinforce each other so that they become more consistent and cohesive as a result. Finally, as with the Intel example, smart marketers in the twenty-first-century will attempt to find ways to make sure that strong brand associations are created to all possible marketing effects. In particular, it will be necessary to carefully and imaginatively consider how the brand itself will be effectively integrated into the marketing program to maximize its contribution to brand equity. In other words, the issue will not just be which brand elements are chosen to represent the brand but instead how these brand elements will actually be used in the marketing program. As the Intel example revealed, it is necessary to go beyond traditional approaches to find creative solutions to increasing the prominence of the brand in marketing strategies.

Strong brands in the twenty-first century also will rise above other brands by better understanding the needs, wants, and desires of consumers to create marketing programs that fulfill and even surpass consumer expectations. Successful brands will have a rich but internally cohesive brand image whose associations are highly valued to consumers. Marketing programs will seamlessly reinforce these associations through product, pricing, and distribution strategies, and communication strategies that consistently and creatively inform and remind consumers of what the brand has to offer. Consumers will have a clear picture of what the brand represents and why it is special. Consumers will view these brands as "old friends" and value their dependability and superiority. Managers of these brands will engage in dialogue with consumers, listening to their product joys and frustrations, and establishing a rapport and relationship that transcends mere commercial exchanges.

MEASURING BRAND EQUITY

Marketers of successful twenty-first-century brands will create formalized measurement approaches and processes that ensure that they continually and exhaustively monitor their sources of brand equity and those of competitors. As part of this process, managers will develop a greater understanding of how different marketing actions affect their sources and outcomes of brand equity. Thus, marketers of successful twenty-first-century brands will go beyond piecemeal research projects (e.g., periodic advertising campaign evaluations) to devise new and original ways to obtain accurate, comprehensive, and up-to-date information on the status of their brands. By maintaining close contact with their brands, managers will be better able to understand just what "makes their brand tick." By achieving greater accountability in marketing activities and programs, it will be possible for managers to better optimize their brand investments, putting money behind the right brands in the right ways at the right time.

MANAGING BRAND EQUITY

Marketers of successful twenty-first-century brands will continually evolve and adapt every aspect of their marketing programs to enhance brand equity. These marketers will develop a deep understanding of what makes their brand successful, retaining enduring core elements while modifying peripheral elements that fail to add value or unnecessarily absorb costs. Marketers of successful twenty-first-century brands also will appreciate how their brands fit in with respect to other brands sold by the firm. They will capitalize on and judiciously exploit the potential of their brand in product development and brand extensions while at the same time recognizing its limits and boundaries.

Review

The challenges and complexities of the modern marketplace make efficient and effective marketing an imperative. The concept of brand equity has been put forth as means to focus marketing efforts. The businesses that win in the twenty-first century will be those that have marketers who successfully build, measure, and manage brand equity. This final chapter reviewed some of the important guidelines put forth in this text to help in that endeavor. Effective brand management requires consistent actions and applications of these guidelines across all aspects of the marketing program. Nevertheless, to some extent, rules are sometimes made to be broken, and these guidelines should be viewed only as a point of departure in the difficult process of creating a world-class brand. Each branding situation and application is unique and requires careful scrutiny and analysis as how to best apply, or perhaps in some cases, ignore these various recommendations and guidelines. Smart marketers will capitalize on every tool at their disposal, and devise ones that are not, in their relentless pursuit of achieving brand pre-eminence.

Discussion Questions

1. What do you think makes a strong brand? Can you add any criteria to the list provided?
2. What do you see as the future of branding? How will the role of brands change and what different strategies might emerge as to how to build, measure, and manage brand equity?

Notes

1. Philip Kotler, *Marketing Management: Analysis, Planning, and Control*, 8th ed. Upper Saddle River, NJ: Prentice Hall, 1994.

2. Philip Kotler, *Marketing Management: Analysis, Planning, and Control*, 8th ed. Upper Saddle River, NJ: Prentice Hall, 1994.

3. Stephen Philips and Amy Dunkin, "King Customer," *Business Week* (March 12, 1990), pp. 88–94.

4. Leslie de Chernatony and Malcom H.B. McDonald, *Creating Powerful Brands*. Oxford: Butterworth-Heinemann, 1992.

5. Chiori Santiago, "A Good Ad is Hard to Find, " *SF* (August 1991), pp. 72–75.

6. Philip Kotler, *Marketing Management: Analysis, Planning, and Control*, 8th ed. Upper Saddle River, NJ: Prentice Hall, 1994.

7. Philip Kotler, *Marketing Management: Analysis, Planning, and Control*, 8th ed. Upper Saddle River, NJ: Prentice Hall, 1994.

8. A. Parasuraman, Valarie A. Zeithaml, Leonard L. Berry, "A Conceptual Model of Service Quality and Its Implications for Future Research," *Journal of Marketing* (Fall 1985), pp. 41–50.

9. Leonard L. Berry, A. Parasuraman, and Valarie A. Zeithaml, "Ten Lessons for Improving Service Quality," Marketing Science Institute Report 93-104, May 1993, Cambridge, MA.

10. Dori Jones Yang, "The Starbucks Enterprise Shifts into Warp Speed," *Business Week* (October 24, 1994), pp. 76–79.

11. Aaker's model has been written up in two popular books, *Building Strong Brands*. New York: Free Press, 1995, and *Managing Brand Equity*. New York: Free Press, 1991.

12. David A. Aaker, *Building Strong Brands*. New York: Free Press, 1995.

13. This summary is based on a talk by Stuart Agres, "Leading and Lagging Indicators of Brand Health," at the Marketing Science Institute Conference titled "Brand Equity and the Marketing Mix: Creating Customer Value," March 3, 1995, Tucson, AZ.

Levi's Dockers: Creating a Sub-brand[1]

Introduction

In the spring of 1985, Levi Strauss & Co. (LS&Co.) was basking in the glow of the company's highly successful "501 Blues" jeans ad campaign. The innovative ad campaign, focusing on the individuality of young Levi's jeans wearers, had recaptured the essence of LS&Co.'s image and core values. The success of the 501 campaign was critical to LS&Co. as the centerpiece of its "back to basics" strategy following a series of less successful forays into the casual clothes market earlier in the decade. Confident in the wake of 501's success, the company was contemplating next steps when research revealed what company executives now refer to as the "scariest graph" the company had ever seen—jeans purchased per capita by age. In short, the company's bread-and-butter customer for the last 30 years—the American male teenager—was now 25–49 and was moving out of the jeans market at an alarming rate. This one chart revealed the greatest marketing challenge in LS&Co.'s 130 year history: How to keep the aging baby boomer in the Levi's brand franchise even though he or she now bought fewer of the traditional Levi's products.

The Origins of Levi Strauss & Co. and Levi's 501 Jeans

In 1849, a poor Bavarian immigrant named Levi Strauss landed in San Francisco, California at the invitation of his brother-in-law, David Stern, owner of a dry goods business. This dry goods business would later become known as Levi Strauss & Co. Strauss quickly learned that the gold miners were seeking a durable pair of pants that could withstand their rugged lifestyle. To meet their needs, Strauss designed a pair of pants from a heavy brown canvas-like material—the world's first pair of "jeans."

A-1

Levi's pants quickly became an indispensable part of the miner's uniform, gaining a reputation for being as tough and rugged as the people who wore them. Strauss called his pants "waist high overalls"—the miners called them "those pants of Levi."

Strauss soon switched to a sturdier fabric called "serge de Nimes," made in Nimes, France, to make his pants. The fabric name was later shortened to "denim", and indigo dye was added to give the jeans their blue color. In 1873, rivets were added to strengthen pockets, which had been unable to hold up under the weight of the miners' gold nuggets, along with the patented double arcuate pattern sewn into the back hip pocket—America's first apparel trademark—and the "Two Horse Brand" leather patch. By the 1890s, the popularity of LS&Co.'s jeans and other dry goods had spread, and to keep better track of the expanding product line, LS&Co. adopted a new inventory system. Levi's jeans were assigned the lot number "501" and given that number as their name.

In 1902, the unmarried Levi Strauss died, leaving the $10 million business to his four nephews. In 1919 Walter Haas Sr., the son-in-law of Sigmund Stern (who would serve as LS&Co.'s president from 1921 to 1928), was invited to join the company. Haas set out to cut costs, update the bookkeeping system, and promote the Levi's brand name through advertisements, effectively transforming the grassroots enterprise into a modern firm.

Sales of Levi's 501 jeans grew through the 1900s. During the 1930s, Levi's jeans' popularity burgeoned as Western movies began to glamorize blue jeans, establishing 501's Western mystique. Levi's jeans became an even more valuable product during World War II, when the government declared them an essential commodity available primarily to defense workers.

In the 1950s, appearances by teenage idols James Dean and Marlon Brando wearing jeans in the motion pictures *Rebel Without a Cause* and *The Wild Ones* captivated an entire post-war baby boom generation. LS&Co. abandoned the wholesale dry goods business and concentrated exclusively on selling its own brand of clothes to a generation that represented millions of potential customers. By 1959, Levi's sales' volume totaled $46 million. The love affair with Levi's jeans continued into the 1960s as students continued to wear 501's as a form of self-expression. The Levi's brand name became synonymous with jeans. By the time of the Woodstock rock festival in 1969, Levi's jeans were the essential fashion for the emerging baby boom generation. What had originally been a tough pair of pants had become a symbol of freedom, adventure, and independence. Levi's 501 jeans had become an icon.

Diversification: 1970–1984

For nearly 30 years since World War II, LS&Co. had serviced a seemingly "bottomless" jeans market. Through the fifties and sixties, the company doubled sales every three to four years. By the end of the 1960s, the company's operations included jeans, cords, slacks and sportswear for men, as well as a range of apparel for women and children. In 1968, new operating divisions for youth wear, sportswear, and accessories were created. The Levi's for Gals marketing unit was expanded into a full-fledged women's wear division. In addition, Levi Strauss International was formed as a subsidiary, enabling the company to parlay its legendary All-American image to foreign consumers eager to own a piece of Americana. With all this growth activity, LS&Co.'s worldwide sales in 1969 totaled some $251 million.

The rapid expansion necessitated further capital. In 1971, the company was taken public with an initial public offering of $47.50 per share. LS&Co.'s sales continued to experience rapid growth as baby boomer teens entered college. By 1975, sales had reached $1 billion, rising to $2 billion in 1979. During this time the company's flagship product—501 jeans—remained its top-selling product, and LS&Co. continued to hold nearly a third of the U.S. jeans market. Production expanded locally and abroad to meet continuing demand. Nonetheless, given the slow growth among its primary market—the 12–24 year olds—cash-rich LS&Co. considered alternative actions to hedge against an expected decline in the jeans market in the 1980s.

In the early 1980s, LS&Co. adopted a strategy to expand beyond the core jeans lines to utilize the Levi's name on non-jeans. "We are not going to forget the gal we brought to the dance," explained Robert Haas, then the company's Executive Vice-President and COO and great-great grand-nephew of the company's founder. "We want to reemphasize our central nature. But we want to bring out flanking products in our basic industries, to make them more exciting."[2] LS&Co. introduced new product lines, covering a broad range of family clothing needs. Many of these came from within the company's existing divisions. Product lines included denim and corduroy jeans for men, women, and children; Action Suits and Tailored Classic blazers and slacks for professional men; and Activewear for sports participants—skiers, tennis players, and the general outdoors person. Counting colors, styles and sizes, the company was offering thousands of different pants, skirts, vests, shirts, blazers, shorts, and blouses—even maternity jeans and jumpers.

An acquisition strategy was also implemented to provide for further growth. LS&Co.'s acquisition in 1979 of Koracorp Industries, a $185 million California clothing manufacturer, immediately doubled Levi's women's wear sales. Koracorp businesses included: Koret of North America women's wear, Byer-Rolnick hats, Oxxford men's suits, and a European-based children's wear division. Other LS&Co. acquisitions included Resistol hats, Rainfair industrial clothing, and Frank Shorter running gear. The company also established numerous licensing agreements for products including casual shoes and socks bearing the Levi's brand, as well as with designers, including Perry Ellis America, Alexander Julian, and Andrew Fezza, to broaden LS&Co.'s scope of business into more fashionable clothing segments. New internally generated labels—David Hunter men's sportswear division and the Roegiers' Tourage SSE collection of men's casual wear—were the only lines that did not carry the Levi's logo. As a result of this vigorous diversification and acquisition strategy, LS&Co. owned apparel businesses that offered products to suit almost any lifestyle.

To accommodate this growth, the company reorganized its operational structure. The U.S. division was divided into four major groups—Jeanswear, Womenswear, Menswear, and Youthwear—each with its own president and organization. Within these major groups were a total of seventeen marketing units, each with its own sales force. Key company executives were moved from the jeans business to manage these new non-jeans apparel groups.

Levi Strauss & Co.'s Communications Strategy

Historically, LS&Co. advertisements had focused almost exclusively on the quality of Levi's jeans for men. The ads, whether print or TV, had emphasized the quality, durability, and timeless nature of Levi's jeans for men. Western gold miner themes dominated the tone of the early ads. Beginning in the 1970s, however, LS&Co. shifted its advertising strategy to reflect the company's change in product focus. LS&Co. largely replaced its traditional western, miner, or prospector image with more contemporary, psychedelic, "hip" imagery of the day. With the help of its long-time advertising agency, Foote, Cone & Belding, the company adopted the "alteration of reality" creative technique and developed a series of animated ads produced with the use of state-of-the-art, computer-generated imagery. In an effort to leverage the Levi's brand name and quality image, these ads emphasized the diversity, variety, and fashionability of Levi's non-jeans products. Ad tag lines included: "Levi's don't have to be blue—they just have to be good"; "Quality never goes out of style"; and "We put a little blue jean in everything we make." At the same time, even though they were diversifying dramatically, the company also wanted to ensure that American men understood that LS&Co. still sold its traditional jeans as work clothes for men. Consequently, the company produced some ads that focused exclusively on men's jeans, retaining the traditional emphasis on jeans as the quality, good-value pant for hard-working American men.

When LS&Co. reorganized its corporate structure, each division became responsible for its own advertising strategy. As a result, the focus of the company's ads shifted to target specific groups rather than selling products across divisions. Ads were created to address multiple audiences simultaneously, and multiple product lines often were promoted in one commercial. Many of the men's jeans ads targeted Levi's jeans and cords, emphasizing the variety of colors and styles available. These ads moved away from the psychedelic imagery of the early 1970s to a high-tech, "space-age" feel. Regular denim jeans continued to focus on the basic qualities associated with Levi's jeans in an effort to reach working men.

Although LS&Co.'s advertising focused primarily on selling to men, expansion of its women's wear and youth apparel lines resulted in more advertising dollars being allocated to these two consumer groups. To sell its array of new apparel lines, LS&Co. expanded its advertising budget dramatically beginning in 1978. By 1982, the advertising budget had grown to $100 million.[3] In addition, the mix of advertising media significantly changed, with national media spending rising from $6.4 million in 1976 to $19.7 million in 1978 and $28.7 million in 1980. Network TV as an advertising medium grew the most dramatically, from $1.8 million in 1976 to $15 million in 1980.[4]

Back to Basics

Initially LS&Co.'s diversification efforts produced promising results. Starting in 1980, however, LS&Co. began a three-year earnings decline. Between 1980 and 1982, LS&Co.'s sales fell 10 percent and net income dropped 76 percent. Although sales and earnings rebounded in 1983 as a result of expanding retail distribution to include Sears and J. C. Penney, they slipped again in 1984. Many of their non-jeans lines struggled in the face of more established competition. Concern arose that the failure of a number of non-jeans products could adversely impact the cachet associated with its jeans. LS&Co. management had learned that while the Levi's brand was the company's most powerful asset, it also had its limitations in terms of the products with which it could be identified. With the decline in sales, the company began to consider further expanding its distribution to accounts like Wal-Mart and K-Mart. Reflecting back on the years, Robert Haas described the situation as follows:

> We had diversified too much. We produced everything from hats to $2000 suits, but we no longer stood for anything. We had lost our focus on our core products. Our retail relations had sunk to a point of hostility.[5]

In October 1984, Tom Tusher, president of Levi Strauss International, was named Executive Vice-President and Chief Operating Officer. At the employee meeting in which his appointment was announced, he indicated his first decision—LS&Co. would not expand its distribution but would rather concentrate on changing product focus and rebuilding relations with its department and specialty store accounts. Thus, under Tusher's direction, the company instituted plans to improve relations with its retailers and refocus the Levi's brand name and image to bolster sagging sales.

For Tusher and Haas, LS&Co.'s main objective was to preserve the company's "important values and traditions." To achieve this objective, LS&Co. planned to move away from non-core products and reemphasize its basic jeans and corduroy lines, which comprised almost two-thirds of revenues, as the company's mainstays throughout the 1990s and "to grow the company from the bottom line—through greater efficiency, penetrating market segments more effectively and through cost savings."[6]

Retail Relations

Because of the average growth of 20 percent a year during the 1960s and 1970s, demand for Levi's products exceeded supply. As a result, the company's products had been sold on allocation, and LS&Co could dictate to retailers how much product they would receive. Content primarily with achieving higher levels of manufacturing, the company had become inwardly focused. As Robert Haas explained, "We were in the driver's seat, and it created arrogant behavior on our part and resentment from retailers."[7] In the early 1980s, many long-term retail customers, upset when LS&Co. decided to allow Sears and J. C. Penney to sell its products, rebelled by reducing orders or, as R. H. Macy did, by dropping the Levi's line altogether.[8] Retailers saw LS&Co. as aloof and inflexible.

In an effort to improve relations with retailers, the company made a conscious effort to provide better service. LS&Co. expanded its retailer co-op advertising budget and its participation in retailer-driven promotions. Other changes were instituted later. For example, the company began to offer retailers volume discounts for the first time and agreed to exchange unsold goods for other products. To help small retailers,

LS&Co. established a toll-free number to order items in small lots, rather than waiting for a LS&Co. sales representative to visit. The company also created an innovative computer system, LeviLink, so that its retailers could track sales and deliveries.

Strengthening the Brand Image

Next, LS&Co. focused its marketing efforts on strengthening the Levi's brand. In mid-1985, after reporting a $114 million loss, the company was taken private through a $1.65 billion leveraged buyout, the largest LBO ever at the time. The strategic direction outlined by Tusher in late 1984—shifting the focus back to the core product businesses—began to be implemented. Consistent with the core product focus and as a means to pay down debt, non-core businesses were sold or discontinued: Rainfair in 1984, Resistol in 1985, Koret of North America, Oxxford, and Frank Shorter in 1987. LS&Co. also discontinued its licensing arrangements with Perry Ellis America and Andrew Fezza in 1986. The company closed forty factories and streamlined staff, reducing LS&Co.'s payroll from 48,000 employees in 1980 to 36,000 employees by 1986.

During this period, LS&Co. restructured its organization to eliminate excess management layers. The company created three subsidiaries: LS&Co. USA—comprising the Jeanswear, Menswear, Womenswear, and Youthwear divisions—Levi Strauss International and Battery Street Enterprises (BSE). BSE focused exclusively on LS&Co.'s business in the high fashion, non-jeanswear, sportswear market. The charter for BSE was to manage the divestiture of non-jeans, non-Levi's businesses and then to focus on the Levi's Men's and Women's sportswear businesses.

LS&Co. also set out to reinvigorate the company's core products. At this time, the company faced both increased competition and shifts in fashion trends. In the early 1980s, there had been a proliferation of new products in the apparel market. Within the jeans market, competition had intensified at the same time that consumer demand began to fall. The well-defined urban image of Lee's jeans and western image of Wrangler's jeans, in addition to the high-priced, fashion image of Calvin Klein, Bill Blass, and Gloria Vanderbilt designer jeans, posed a serious threat to the loyalty of the traditional Levi's 501 jeans buyer. Moreover, LS&Co., whose historic franchise had been in the western United States, found their sales failing to meet expectations in the eastern United States, particularly in major metropolitan areas and among their key target market of 18–24 year olds. This slump in sales was due, in part, to the company's failure in product development to keep pace with changes in the jeans market. LS&Co.'s products remained "non-washed" long after designer jeans and LS&Co.'s own international markets had begun to rinse and bleach product for sale to the customer.

501 Blues

The company felt that advertising would play a key role in getting sales of its core products back on track. In keeping with the company's "back to basics" theme, LS&Co. felt the values communicated in its new ad campaign should be consistent with the desired brand image of the company. These core brand values—that Levi's jeans were honest, classic, contemporary, comfortable, approachable, universal and independent—had defined the company's philosophy through time and needed to be reflected in consumer perceptions.

The $36 million "501 Blues" advertising campaign set out to create an image for 501 jeans consistent with LS&Co.'s corporate philosophy and values. The ads featured a variety of real people "being themselves" in a series of eastern, urban settings, wearing 501s as a part of everyday life. The ads' audio focused on Levi's jeans' unique, personal "shrink-to-fit" and "button-fly" attributes and blended blues-style music with free association verbiage. The hope was that the campaign would remind existing customers of the uniqueness of 501 jeans and how comfortably they fit into their everyday lives—both in a physical and social sense—as well as introduce the company's flagship product to a new generation of adults. The award winning campaign helped 501 sales double in 1985, despite the fact that overall U.S. denim jeans sales for the year declined, and placed 501 jeans on a firmer national footing.

The "back to basics" approach had begun earlier in its overseas markets. In the early 1980s, Levi Strauss International decided to position its 501 jeans in terms of its American heritage, emphasizing how 501s represented independence, individuality, and a more casual, relaxed lifestyle. Different ads were used in different countries. Many of these ads depicted scenes where 501 wearers demonstrated their loyalty to the product in a highly unusual fashion. Often these ads featured popular rock and roll songs from the 1960s and 1970s as a backdrop to the action in the ads that focused on European and Japanese perceptions of the 1950s as the golden age of America. The ads, a mix of product and image-building ads, told stories with characters of distinctive personalities in a plot that often involved action, humor, conflict, or romance. For example, in the United Kingdom, the first 501 jeans ad, called "Launderette," showed a man stripped down to his boxer shorts while he waited for his Levi's jeans to finish drying. In Japan, ads contained the slogans "Heroes Wear Levi's" and "The Original—Levi's" and featured such American icons as James Dean and John Wayne. By 1987, international sales had risen to represent almost one-third of total sales. The prestige and cachet of 501 jeans in these markets meant that higher prices could be supported, further enhancing the company's revenues and profits.

New Challenges

By the beginning of 1986, management was confident it was on the right track. The 501 jeans campaign had proved extremely successful among its target 12- to 24-year-old urban audience. Not only had it reinvigorated jeans sales, but also had brought the Levi's brand back to its core values. Plans were to continue with the "Blues" campaign for the near future. The 1986 advertising budget was $70 million.[9]

A per-capita jeans purchases chart prepared by the LS&Co. Menswear research department, however, revealed a troubling fact: 25–49 year old U.S. males purchased an average of one to two pairs of jeans annually, as compared to an average of four to five pairs for 15–24 year olds. In 1980, there were 36.8 million men in the United States between the ages of 25 and 49; by 1990, this figure was expected to be 47.5 million, nearly half of the adult male population. Although these baby boomers had grown up with Levi's jeans and had developed tremendous loyalty to the Levi's name, they now sought a different kind of pant. Because baby boomers viewed themselves as distinct from their parents' generation in tastes and lifestyle, as they had proven by adopting jeans as kids, they wanted their clothes to be a break from tradition. Fashion assumed a far greater role for these males than for previous generations. While these men had aged chronologically, they still had a driving need to be active, involved, fashionable, and comfortable. Rejecting the artificial fabrics traditional to the menswear business in the past, they preferred more natural fibers. At the same time, in the traditionally formal work environment, many companies were relaxing their dress codes to allow employees to dress in more casual attire.

For these reasons, male baby boomers needed a pant that combined style, versatility, and comfort that would be appropriate for both professional and leisure activities. To satisfy their needs for more contemporary clothing for their varied lifestyles—both casual and dress—many of these older baby boomers had rejected the loud music and youthful ambiance of the young men's department in stores to shop at the main floor men's department. A revitalization of the main floor men's department was just beginning to take place, and the product mix was changing rapidly with an increasing emphasis on 100 percent cotton and cotton blends.

Developing a Marketing Strategy

LS&Co. recognized that the casual pant market represented an enormous opportunity. Between 1981–1985, jeans retail volume had decreased by 11 percent (25 m units) while slacks volume had increased by 19 percent (21 m units). Slacks as a percentage of bottoms sales (jeans plus slacks) grew from 33 percent in 1981 to 40 percent in 1985, and the trend was certain to continue. Between the summer of 1985 and the summer of 1986 alone, slacks sales grew by 20 percent.[10] Yet merchandising of slacks was uninspired, and consumers found the slacks department one of the most boring areas in the store. Moreover, brand fragmentation was more prevalent in the dress slacks category than with jeans, and there was no dominant brand leader. LS&Co. had been in the dress slacks market since the mid-1950s (its first non-jeans diversification effort), but the top three dress slacks brands (Levi's, Haggar, and Farah) accounted for 26 percent of the U.S. market, and the top five brands accounted for only 36 percent of the market. In contrast, the top three jeans brands (Levi's, Wrangler, and Lee) accounted for 66 percent of the U.S. men's market, and the top five brands accounted for 75 percent of the market.[11]

In addition, natural fibers and blends were replacing the traditional 100 percent polyester slacks: Research indicated that 100 percent polyester slacks were expected to account for 33 percent of sales volume in 1986—down from 59 percent in 1980—compared to 50 percent for 100 percent cotton and cotton blends. Certain designer menswear, such as Paul Smith and Ralph Lauren (Polo), did offer full-legged, tapered-bottom trousers that were cotton/cotton blend trousers.[12] Although these pants were often found in the main floor men's department, they were sold as "Better Sportswear" with a price tag of $60–$80.

LS&Co. was determined to maintain the brand loyalty of the "Levi's jeans generation"—whose members were about to enter into their peak earning years—even if they were no longer buying traditional jeans. These men had been the cornerstone of the company's success and key drivers of apparel trends for over twenty years. The company hoped to appeal to the traditional, older main floor men's customer as well as to the new, younger crossovers. As the overwhelming brand leader in the men's jeans market, LS&Co. hoped to capitalize on the changing demographics and consumer tastes in two ways: a new line of casual slacks and a new line of restyled, loose fitting jeans.

Introducing "New Casuals"

The Menswear division—led by Robert Siegel, President; Steve Schwartzbach, Vice President of Merchandising; Steve Goldstein, Director of Consumer Marketing; and Jerry Maschino, Vice President of Sales—decided to first address opportunities in the casual slacks market because it was felt that existing product lines did not sufficiently satisfy the needs of the 25–49 year old male customers. LS&Co. identified its challenge as follows:

> To increase our slacks brand share, Levi's must aggressively market and support trend-right products to create a leadership position in a market that is growing and has no category owner.[13]

The image that the Levi's brand had earned from its jeans business was thought to have already contributed in a limited way to its current slacks image—namely, that Levi's slacks were considered to be more contemporary, less conservative and more casual than other leading slacks. However, its Action Slacks line (made of 100 percent polyester) did not address the fabric shifts in the slacks market, nor did it reflect the core values that the recent 501 jeans campaign had so successfully established. As one LS&Co. executive explained: "We feel as though we've got the power of the Levi's brand, which is significant and carries with it all the mystique to be influential in the marketplace. But we recognize that we need to segment from a marketing/advertising perspective because there are so many market types."[14] LS&Co. needed a new product that motivated the customer to remain within the Levi's brand franchise but that was different from anything it had sold before. Perhaps with some reservations, LS&Co. was moving away from jeans again. In this case, however, rather than deemphasize its jeans business, the company was determined to simultaneously continue its strong core jeans focus.

To meet the needs of its customers and to establish LS&Co. as the market leader, the Menswear team believed a bold strike was necessary. They decided to create essentially a new product category—"new casuals"—that would position the new pants to men as more formal than jeans and less casual than dress slacks. To LS&Co., "new casuals" satisfied an unfulfilled need in the men's pants market. They were designed to appeal to the baby boomers' fashion demands: casual and comfortable, yet stylish; the right pant for a variety of occasions; and, of course, meeting LS&Co.'s high quality standards. The basic pants design was a 100-percent cotton, pleated, washed fabric with a "reverse silhouette" design—wider at the top and narrower at the leg opening—available in a variety of stylish colors. LS&Co. hoped that its new casuals, the first line to bring the full-leg, tapered-bottom trousers of "better sportswear" to the main floor of department stores, would give men a way to ask for a pair of loose, unfitted pants. LS&Co. wanted this new pant to become the standard for the "new casual" pant category. In an effort to make this new pant accessible and affordable, it was priced in the moderate to upper moderate price range, retailing, on average, for $32.

Branding "New Casuals"

To brand this new line of casual pants, the Menswear team needed to choose a name, logo, and other important brand elements. To attract the "baby boomer" shopper, the idea was to package the product with a memorable, trademarked name; a unique, permanent, on-garment logo; and a colorful pocket flasher. The team knew it could not simply call this new product "Levi's Pants." The strategic marketing positioning of the company's very successful 501 jeans campaign had defined Levi's as jeans. Somehow the name had to establish its independence and leverage the Levi's brand name in a way so as to maintain a link to the Levi's name and heritage but not detract from the Levi's core jeans focus. At the time the team was contemplating a name for these new pants, Sue Kilgore, a Menswear merchandiser, returned from a trip to Japan with a pair of twill pants sold by Levi Strauss Japan named Levi Docker Pants. LS&Co.'s Japanese group had adopted the moniker from a Levi's pant sold in Argentina. Both Japan and Argentina had positioned the product to their younger age consumers, but with only limited success. The team liked the Docker name but knew Americans would never say "Levi Docker Pants." The question became how to shorten the name to something Americans would say. In the end, the team decided to add an "s" to Docker and shorten the name to Levi's Dockers®. The team liked the Dockers name because although it did have some nautical connotations, for the most part it was considered a neutral empty bucket that the company could fill with imagery that was relevant to its broad target audience.

The logo that was chosen blended the Argentine and Japanese logos found on their versions of the pants and consisted of interlocked wings and anchors. In order to qualify for co-op advertising—now considered a key ingredient for establishing brand awareness—it was necessary to integrate the brand's name with its symbols. Working with a local San Francisco firm, Goldstein and the Menswear team adapted the Dockers logo and tag. The pocket flasher, attached to the back of all pants, consisted of a woman who was being led off a ship by a formally dressed man but whose attention was focused on a relaxed, casually dressed young man standing on the dock. Finally, to establish an understated association with the Levi's name, the Levi's moniker was incorporated in the Dockers' winged logo.

Introducing New Casuals to the Retail Trade

Levi's Dockers pants were marketed to the retail trade as a major fashion statement—an alternative to jeans—and the driving force in the "new casuals" category. Based on the changing demographics of the U.S. male population, Levi's projected "new casuals" to grow from 28 percent of the total bottoms business to 34 percent by 1989, with contemporary dress slacks increasing from 6 percent to 28 percent and traditional dress slacks decreasing from 38 percent to 21 percent over the same period.[15]

In an effort to establish its Dockers new casuals line, LS&Co. concentrated distribution in department stores and chains where the majority of 25- to 49-year-old men did their shopping and where one-third of all slacks were sold. The company worked closely with retailers, from J. C. Penney to Bloomingdale's, to generate excitement and support for its new pants. The company courted retailers nationwide—including those department and specialty stores that had previously curtailed business with LS&Co. in the early 1980s—with extensive presentations, sell-in brochures, and swatch books. They provided sales support in a variety of ways, including sales kits that provided a "road map" for retail-based marketing, cooperative advertising, and sales promotion programs. In addition, the company offered supplemental financial support (RAP) for advertising and promotional activities to important high-image department stores. Funds (RAP plus co-op) available to retail for 1987 totaled $1.6 m.

A critical component of the company's marketing effort to concentrate attention on the new line was the establishment of Dockers shops within main floor men's areas of major department stores. The traditional main floor men's department was changing, reducing its emphasis on dress slacks and shifting to 100 percent cotton and cotton blends that were targeted to the more youthful customer. This trend was expected to continue as the baby boomer market segment increased as a percentage of the main floor customer base. Retailers were showing greater interest in innovative merchandise techniques.

In recognition of these trends, LS&Co. introduced the first in-store concept shop for the men's main floor area. A test version was constructed for display at MAGIC (Men's Apparel Guild in California), a key trade show, to introduce Dockers casual pants to retailers. The Dockers in-store shop sought to create a friendly, accessible environment, prominently displaying the sporty Dockers logo, linking consumer advertising with point-of-sale signage and posters, and making trial as easy as possible. Fixtures and tables were installed that allowed for displaying the pants folded, similar to the experience of buying jeans and distinctly different from the rows of hanging slacks. Testing of the concept proved very successful, generating twice the sales of pants that were just hung on racks. In stores where shops were not possible due to space or financial constraints, LS&Co. planned to establish point-of-sale displays.

The company's product positioning and marketing strategy was able to overcome the initial reluctance of retailers and ultimately generated an exceptionally high level of prepromotion excitement. The company successfully placed Levi's Dockers® in all of the Menswear Division's top fifty accounts and in another fifty accounts across the country. Retailers saw Levi's Dockers as the leader in the new casuals category and moved the pants ahead of its primary competitors, including Gallery by Haggar, Savane by Farah, "M" by Bugle Boy, and Tivoli by American Trouser. With the retail trade behind it, the Menswear Division turned its attention to the development of an effective communications program focused on the consumer.

Launching Dockers To the Consumer

It quickly became apparent to the LS&Co. Menswear Division that in order to establish Levi's Dockers as a major brand in men's casual sportswear, a focused, comprehensive consumer marketing effort beyond the available resources of the Menswear

Division would be required. Given the market opportunity for casual pants, the Menswear Division believed that a high impact consumer marketing program would accelerate the growth of the Dockers line and generate consumer support that could be leveraged to effectively influence trade awareness and interest. The Menswear Division management team convinced Tom Tusher, who had established an advertising reserve for special marketing opportunities, that investment in the required marketing effort to launch Dockers would produce the requisite payback to the corporation in terms of revenues, profits, and long-term brand ownership of the crucial baby boomer segment. With the entire LS&Co. organization behind them, the Menswear Division set out to establish a clear proprietary position for Levi's Dockers in the men's bottoms market.

Advertising Strategy

The advertising challenge was to build product and brand awareness for Levi's Dockers so that they would be seen as an unpretentious alternative to traditional dressing for almost every occasion. Thus, advertising had to achieve two goals: Because there was no consumer terminology for Dockers-type pants, the ads would have to educate its audience about the new product itself and create brand awareness; and an image for the new product had to be created that leveraged the positive Levi's brand associations but also established a certain amount of autonomy or distance to signal the inherent product differences.

The target audience for their advertising was defined as follows:[16]

Demographically:	• Men 25–49
	• Higher than average education and income
	• More likely to hold white-collar job
	• Located in major metropolitan areas across the United States
Attitudinally:	• Men of the baby boom generation
	• Accomplished and interesting; interested in other people but motivated internally; self-aware; very human and down to earth
	• Fashion-aware but not fashion slaves; dress to please themselves, to feel comfortable both physically and mentally
Clothing Needs:	• Expanding wardrobes
	• More casual apparel
	• Preference for natural fibers
	• Occasion-based dressing
Purchase Behavior:	• Shops for own clothes
	• Levi's brand affinity
	• Department and specialty stores patronage

Working with Mike Koelker of Foote, Cone & Belding, LS&Co. conducted a series of focus groups with men in their target market. The men were shown pictures representing a variety of leisure situations and asked to select the pictures that best described when they were "most comfortable and relaxed." The most common scenes chosen included: a man sitting on top of a hill alone, two men walking together on a golf course, and a group of men hanging out and laughing on the beach. Even though many of the men said they did not tend to partake in these events once they were older and married, they still thought fondly in reminiscing about them.

Based on the results of the focus groups and the marketing objectives for Dockers, Koelker and LS&Co. decided that the ads should create an image for the brand based on an emotional appeal. The ads were to create a singular, appealing, and relevant image for the brand that elevated Dockers above all other possible alternatives. Given the target customer, the attitude of the advertising needed to be contemporary. It was important, however, to ensure that the styling of the pants be perceived as timeless and classic. The men wearing Dockers were to be real, approachable, and attractive, but not fashion models. The ads were to show Dockers as appropriate attire for a variety of occasions—for work and for weekends. They wanted Dockers to be seen as a way to be comfortable and casual in any setting. Therefore, the advertising was to emphasize the sociability of men wearing the pants. It was also important for the ads to convey the high quality of the Dockers pants line and maintain the link to the Levi's brand name and heritage. The Levi's name would help give the new pant credibility and capitalize on the tremendous loyalty of the target group to the Levi's brand. Finally, the ads would use the "reality-based advertising" style and imagery begun with the 501 Blues ads that LS&Co. wanted to continue. Management hoped that men would view a Dockers' commercial and say to themselves: "I like those guys. They're like me. And I like the way they look in those pants."

ADVERTISING EXECUTIONS

Based on this strategy, LS&Co. and Foote, Cone & Belding developed a $4.5 million television campaign for Dockers consisting of three 30–second ads of men in their twenties, thirties, and forties having informal conversations about life. The situations were varied to include both casual weekend and work-related settings. The audio in the ad consisted of natural, unscripted dialogue while the camera worked like an eye, moving around the group and using extreme close-ups. The ads carefully sought to exclude any "yuppie" talk or yuppie accessories (e.g., Rolex watches). The focus was on the waist down, and no faces were shown at any time. The tagline ran: "Levi's 100% Cotton Dockers. If You're Not Wearing Dockers, You're Just Wearing Pants." As Koelker explained, "using '100% cotton' provided a tangible bridge to the Levi's jeans heritage."

MEDIA STRATEGY

The company planned to introduce Dockers through a multidimensional, high-impact regional program aimed primarily at consumers and secondarily to the trade. The consumer advertising was to provide a positioning and image umbrella for both the consumer and trade markets. The Dockers ads were slotted to run in fall 1987 and winter 1988 in eleven major regional markets where Dockers pants were sold. The markets were selected on the basis of retail placement of Dockers, potential for volume growth, and geographical dispersion. The eleven markets were New York, Columbus, Cincinnati, Minneapolis, Houston, Washington D.C., L.A., Miami, Dallas, Charlotte, and Denver. Of the eleven target markets, New York City—the largest consumer market, accounting for 8 percent of the national TV viewing population—was considered the key market for a successful introduction. New York was the center of the men's apparel industry and tended to set fashion trends for the whole country. In addition, buyers from major stores across the country were influenced by what they saw placed in New York.

The Dockers media strategy used spot TV in all eleven targeted markets. Spot TV was considered the most effective medium to communicate the Dockers' "attitude" since it provided an intrusive and impactful means of delivering the message to a broad target audience quickly and efficiently. The company chose to air its commercials during selective "showcase" prime time, sports, and late night programs. To increase overall effectiveness of the effort, the company planned to show multiple commercials in a single program. In key late night shows, the commercials would be aired each night of the week. Commercials were aired in sports events that included local target market teams. In New York City, TV spots were supplemented with subway signs and mobile billboards located primarily in and around the city's garment district.

ADDITIONAL PROMOTION ACTIVITIES

In addition to TV, LS&Co. targeted consumers through co-op advertising with retailers. Dockers shops and point-of-sale displays provided in-store visibility. Sales promotion, for example, gift with purchase programs, were planned during kick-off and key seasons to create in-store excitement.

Concurrent with the initial airing of the Dockers commercials, LS&Co. organized an advertising kick-off party in New York City for buying groups, trade press, and key retail executives. In addition, a publicity campaign targeted key market influencers with talk show fashion presentations and press kits. As a follow-up to its initial marketing to retailers, LS&Co. planned a series of visits to key retail accounts by designers, merchandisers, marketing personnel, and senior management.

Discussion Questions

1. What is Levi's brand image? What makes up its brand equity? What is the role of its flagship 501 jeans product?
2. How would you characterize Levi's branding strategy in general? What are the positive aspects? Are there any negative aspects?
3. What do you think of the process by which the Dockers' brand elements or identities were chosen?
4. Analyze the Dockers' communication strategy. How does it fit in with past Levi's advertising efforts? How does it contribute to brand equity?

Notes

1. This case was made possible through the cooperation of Levi-Strauss and the assistance of Steve Goldstein, Director of Marketing, Men's Jeans, Levi-Strauss & Co. Leslie Kimerling and Gregory Tusher prepared this case under the supervision of Professor Kevin Lane Keller as the basis for class discussion.
2. *Business Week*, October 23, 1983.
3. *Business Week*, March 8, 1982.
4. *Media and Marketing Decisions*, Spring 1982.
5. *San Francisco Focus,* October 1993.
6. *Forbes*, August 11, 1986.
7. *San Francisco Focus*, October 1993.
8. In 1993, Macy's began to sell Levi's products in its stores again.
9. *Forbes*, August 11, 1986.
10. Internal company sources.
11. Internal company sources.
12. Internal company sources.
13. Internal company sources.
14. *Bobbin*, November 1990.
15. *Daily News Record*, January 6, 1988.
16. Internal company sources.

APPENDIX # Intel Corporation: Branding an Ingredient[1]

Introduction

On March 1, 1991, U.S. District Judge William Ingram ruled that the "386" designation used by Intel for its microprocessor family was a generic description and therefore did not represent a trademarkable name. Intel had been confident that the judge would rule in its favor, and the unexpected court decision effectively invalidated Intel's current branding strategy.

Within the last year, buyers of IBM-compatible personal computers had been confronted with a bewildering array of microprocessor options. A microprocessor is the central processing unit (CPU) of a computer. As the "brain" of the computer, the microprocessor, or CPU, executes all computer-program instructions.[2] Prior to 1990, consumers' choices were relatively simple: a low cost "286" computer that used Intel's older 80286 microprocessor or a more state-of-the-art "386" computer based on Intel's newer 80386 microprocessor. By 1991, however, consumers had a choice of personal computers based on one of three generations of microprocessor technology—286, 386, and 486—all available in a variety of clock speeds and bus widths,[3] made by Intel and a number of "clone" competitors. The variety of alternatives was creating significant confusion, and Intel had found it difficult to differentiate its products in the minds of the consumer. The March 1991 court ruling ensured the confusion would continue unless Intel revised its branding and communication strategy.

There was a real sense of urgency throughout the company to establish a trademarkable brand identity that would distinguish Intel products from the competition. This need was particularly acute since Intel expected to announce its next generation microprocessor, code-named "P5," in the fall of 1992. In light of the court's ruling, naming the product "586," as many people expected, would be a risky choice. Cyrix's recent introduction of its 486SLC chip—an enhanced "386" chip targeted to the notebook market—had clearly illustrated the risk of continuing to use nonprotectable numerical names for products. In addition to immediate competitive concerns, Intel also wanted to address the broader, long-term issue of how to develop brand equity in light of continuous need to introduce new products and technologies. Of specific concern was how to strike a balance between developing awareness of and image for the company as a whole versus for the individual products, which ranged from microprocessors to modems. A key question there was, would Intel, the world's leading brand of microprocessors, be able to develop a strategy that could create a premium brand image for Intel products in markets where Intel was not the clear leader?

Company Background

Intel Corporation was founded in 1968 by Robert Noyce and Gordon Moore (later to become Chairman of the Board). Soon thereafter, Andy Grove (later to become President and Chief Executive Officer) joined the firm. Intel's initial focus was the integration of large numbers of transistors into silicon chips to make semiconductor computer memory. In 1971, the company went public in the wake of two successful memory product introductions, the first LSI DRAM (large-scale integration dynamic random access memory) and the first EPROM (electronically programmable read-only memory). That year also marked the company's first profitable year, with revenues of $9 million and net income of $1 million. Growing rapidly over the next decade, the company quickly became a leading supplier of semiconductor memory for mainframes and minicomputers.

In 1974, Intel introduced the first general purpose microprocessor, the 8-bit 8080. Intel introduced the 16-bit 8086 in 1978, followed by the 8088, the 8-bit bus version of the 8086, in 1979. These microprocessors were the first of the Intel "x86" line of microprocessors. At the time, Intel faced competition from a number of companies, the most serious being Motorola with its 68000 microprocessor. In response, Intel launched a campaign to make the 8086/8088 architecture the standard in the emerging microprocessor market. A critical step in this process was IBM's selection of the 8088 in 1980 as the exclusive microprocessor architecture for its first personal computer. The success of the IBM PC placed Intel at the center of the personal computer revolution and established Intel's x86 microprocessor architecture as the de facto industry standard.

In February 1982, Intel introduced the 16-bit 80286 microprocessor, the first microprocessor to feature multitasking and on-chip security functions that ensured data would be protected. These features allowed a user to run both MS-DOS and UNIX operating systems. The 286 became the brain of the IBM AT personal computer and the AT-compatible clone computers that followed. By 1988, the installed base of 286-based PCs would grow to 15 million worldwide.

In 1985–1986, Intel suffered major setbacks, along with other U.S. semiconductor manufacturers, in face of an industry-wide recession. In 1985, Intel abandoned its DRAM business and struggled to maintain its leadership position in EPROMs. In October of that year, Intel introduced its first 32-bit microprocessor, the Intel386™ DX microprocessor. The Intel386 DX microprocessor had a top operating speed of 5 million instructions per second (MIPs), a threefold increase over the 286. The chip had memory management and multitasking features that permitted more sophisticated uses. As a 32-bit processor, the i386™ processor could process information more efficiently than the 16-bit 286 and allow for more powerful software.[4] Intel began volume shipments of this product in mid-1986. In June 1988, Intel introduced the Intel386 SX microprocessors, a lower-performance, lower-priced chip targeted to entry-level systems (for which the DX version was too expensive). The Intel386 chips became the backbone of IBM's and clone manufacturers' growing PC lines and positioned Intel for its explosive growth over the next five years.

In April 1989, the company introduced the first of its next generation microprocessor, the Intel486™ processor. The i486™, a 32-bit processor like the i386, held 1.2 million transistors on a single chip and ran typical PC programs two to three times faster than i386 processor-based machines. The i486 integrated math-processor circuits into the chip for the first time, thereby eliminating the need for a separate math co-processor. The company began volume shipments of the Intel486 processor in early 1990. In October 1990, the company introduced the Intel386™ SL processor, a slow-power consumption, highly integrated, "small" chip targeted to the burgeoning portable PC market.

In 1990, Intel sold approximately 7.5 million 386 and 486 microprocessors.[5] Intel's 1990 revenue from 386 microprocessor sales alone was estimated to be approximately $850 million.[6] As of year-end 1990, Intel was a $3.9 billion company, representing a 360 percent growth in ten years. Net income over the same period grew 570 percent to $650.3 million. Intel microprocessors were found in almost 80 percent of all IBM and IBM-compatible machines. The company, one of the largest semiconductor manufacturers in the world, was recognized as the undisputed microprocessor industry leader.

The Microprocessor Industry in 1991

Since 1986, Intel had been the only supplier of 386 technology, and since 1990, the only supplier of 486 technology. Between the second half of 1990 and the first quarter of 1991, however, a number of competitors had announced intentions to market their own versions of Intel's 386 and 486 microprocessors. The most serious threat came from Advanced Micro Devices (AMD) who in October 1990 had announced its own version of Intel's then hottest product, the i386 SX, called the AM386. Volume shipments were scheduled to begin in March 1991. In January 1991, two small semiconductors firms, Chips and Technologies and NexGen Microsystems, had announced their intentions to introduce 386-compatible chips within the year. Cyrix, a small firm who had successfully introduced a clone of Intel's 80387 math co-processor in 1989, was also actively working on development of its own 386/486 hybrid scheduled for introduction sometime in 1991. Many of these competitors claimed that their 386 microprocessors would rival certain configurations of Intel's i486 chip. Whatever their true technological capabilities, Intel knew these chips could be named "386" or "486" and that they could do nothing to prevent such naming.

As of January 1991, Intel offered over a dozen versions of their 386 and 486 microprocessors. In 1991, the company was expected to introduce six new versions of the i486 microprocessor, including an i486™ SX, a lower-priced, stripped-down version of its 80486 microprocessor. By 1992, revenues from Intel486 CPU sales were expected to surpass Intel386 CPU revenues. That year, Intel planned to announce availability of its 586-generation microprocessor, internally named "P5" until the name under which it was to be marketed was decided upon.

At the same time that competitors were introducing their own versions of 386 and 486 microprocessors, Intel was facing another long-term challenge at the high-end of its market from the makers of another type of microprocessor known as RISC (reduced-instruction-set computing) chips.[7] By the late 1980s RISC architectures dominated the workstation market, led by Sun Microsystems and MIPS Computers. In 1989, Intel had tried to sell its own RISC chip, the i860™ chip but abandoned the market one year later, refocusing its investments on its x86 line.[8] Because of recent price breaks bringing workstations into the $5,000 range, many vendors could now compete head-on with high-end PCs.[9] Historically, the presence of workstations in the desktop PC market had been limited because they were not compatible with the thousands of software programs written for PCs containing Intel processors and running Microsoft DOS and Windows operating systems. In April 1991, Compaq, Microsoft, and MIPS[10] led the creation of the ACE alliance, a consortium that intended to develop and use operating-system software that would run on both Intel's processors and MIPS's RISC chip.[11]

Branding Issues Confronting Intel

As the market and technology leader, Intel was always the first to introduce a new generation of product and to establish the name and value of the new technology in consumers' minds. With competing products carrying the same or similar names, however, it became increasingly difficult for Intel to differentiate its products from those of its competitors.

Competitors had used Intel's numerical sequencing to name their products since the introduction of the 286. In the case of the 286 and earlier generation microprocessors, Intel had licensed its technology to several vendors who manufactured Intel's technology under their own name. Intel had not licensed its 386 technology, however, so the use of the same numerical sequence did not necessarily reflect Intel's architectural standard as it had with the earlier generation microprocessors. As a result, what one competitor called a 386 chip may or may not have had the same product characteristics as an Intel microprocessor with the same name. Not only were consumers confused about who made a particular generation microprocessor, but also what level of performance to expect from a particular product. In the end, consumers were confronted with a product "alphabet soup" that made establishing a point of differentiation and a distinct brand identity for Intel products increasingly difficult.

Initial Branding Efforts

In the late 1980s, there was a significant shift in the general focus of the personal computer industry toward the mass-market, non-technical business and home PC users. Recognizing this shift, Intel moved from more of a "push" strategy to more of a "pull" strategy and began to redirect a portion of its advertising efforts away from computer manufacturers to actual computer buyers. Until this time, the consumer's choice of a personal computer was based almost exclusively on the brand image of the manufacturer, such as Compaq, Dell, or IBM. Consumers did not think about the components inside the computer. By shifting its advertising focus to the consumer, Intel hoped to create brand awareness for Intel and its microprocessors, as well as build brand preference for the microprocessor inside the PC. Intel still considered the MIS community to be its primary buyer, but also recognized the growing importance of the retail or "Circuit City"[12] buyer as a significant market segment and wanted a message that spoke directly to it.

In June 1989, the company had experimented with its first print campaign targeted to the consumer. The campaign promoted Intel microprocessors through their numbers—the 286 and 386. The initial ad was an oblique but attention-getting print ad and outdoor billboard that mimicked graffiti by spray painting over "286" and inserting "386SX." The tag line read, "Now, get 386 system performance at a 286 system performance price." The message to the consumer was to purchase a personal computer with a i386™ SX chip, a lower priced version of the i386™ DX chip, which used the latest technology for which Intel was the sole supplier, and not to purchase a computer with the older 286 chip technology, which used technology that Intel had licensed to a number of other vendors. Intel, with a $5 million promotion budget, touted the 386 SX as an investment in the future, offering both higher performance and access to new and future software.

Within months, buyers began asking for personal computers with the Intel386 SX chip, promoting computer companies to expand their production. In 1991, the 80386 SC became Intel's best-selling chip ever, shipping approximately 8 million units.[13] Intel's graffiti ad campaign had successfully introduced the microprocessor to the consumer, and market research indicated that an increasing number of consumers identified with 386 and 486 microprocessor technology.

In June 1990, Intel broadened its campaign to simultaneously promote its new 486 microprocessor as well as the Intel name. Given the recent announcements of rival chip firms, Intel wanted to make sure consumers knew to buy Intel technology. Intel continued with the graffiti type imagery it had used in its earlier ad. The first page of the two page ad showed the numbers, 486, 386, and 386SX, spray painted yellow, green, and red, respectively, on a brick wall, with the text, "The numbers outside." Upon turning the page, the reader saw a huge multicolored "Intel" spray painted across the same wall. Underneath "Intel" read the line, "The Computer Inside." The copy below the ad read: "Since buying a computer today is such a numbers game, here's a simple rule of thumb. Look for i386™ SX, i386™ DX, or i486™ on the outside to be certain that you have Intel technology on the inside . . ." At the bottom of the ad was the Intel corporate logo with the slogan, "The Computer Inside™" below it.

Evolution of the "Intel Inside" Branding Strategy

During fall 1990 and winter 1991, Intel was involved in a trademark case with AMD to prevent the use of the "386" name in a new microprocessor that AMD planned to introduce in spring 1991. Observing testimony in the "386" trademark case, Dennis

Carter, Vice President of Intel's Corporate Marketing Group (CMG), became concerned about the potential impact that a negative verdict would have on Intel's branding strategy. The proliferation of competitive products using Intel's numerical sequencing was already an issue impacting Intel's current branding strategy. A loss in the trademark case would only exacerbate the company's problems in addressing the growing market confusion among product offerings. A negative verdict would mean that in the future *any* competitor could market its products under the same marks used by Intel. It would also mean that any computer maker could call a machine "386" without regard to the manufacturer who supplied the chip. Concerned about the possible negative verdict and feeling a general need to clarify strategy, Carter began developing an alternative branding strategy, although he planned to wait until the court's ruling to decide whether to implement it.

In March 1991, Intel did in fact lose tne "386" trademark case. This ruling cleared the way for AMD to sell its new AM386 microprocessor under the "386" name when it began volume shipments later that month. Given the court's decision, it was clear to Carter that Intel needed to change its branding strategy. Knowing that AMD would begin selling its own version of the 386 microprocessor within the month, and that other competitors would soon follow, created a real sense of urgency to make the change quickly. Within a few days Carter proposed a new processor branding strategy to Intel's executive office. The strategy recognized Intel's status as an ingredient supplier to PC OEMs and consisted of three elements: (1) the use of a logo based around the words "Intel Inside" to represent Intel processors used in PCs, (2) the use of MDF funds to share PC OEM advertising expenses, and (3) an Intel advertising program to build equity in this new brand. The strategy was accepted and Carter immediately established a task force whose sole mission was to implement this new branding strategy. In the interim, Intel would refer to its microprocessor as the "i386" and "Intel386," both Intel trademarks.

The first action of the task force was the introduction of a new ad using the "Intel: The Computer Inside" slogan. This ad, focused primarily on raising awareness of the Intel name, asked the reader, "Quick, do you know the first name in microprocessor?" showing a blank line in front of the numbers 486, 386, and 386SX. Turning the page, the blanks were filled in with the word "Intel." With the ad, Intel put the company's name directly in front of the consumer. In addition, Intel486, Intel386, and Intel386 SX microprocessor were all trademarked names. The ad copy sought to assure the reader that purchasing a personal computer with an Intel microprocessor inside was a safe and technologically sound investment, providing "the power and compatibility to take you into the future." At the bottom of the ad was the Intel corporate logo with the slogan, "The Computer Inside™" below it.

Despite not having a detailed preset plan, the task force established the fundamentals of a new branding strategy within a month of the court decision. The primary focus of the new strategy was the establishment of Intel as a brand, transferring the equity of "386" and "486" microprocessors to Intel, the company. Much of the brand equity Intel had at that time was in the numbers. Given the court decision and the increasing level of product confusion, Intel rejected a product-based brand strategy in favor of a strategy that focused on establishing the company's brand image. Establishing a unique identity for Intel was considered the best way not only to distinguish Intel products, but also to communicate the depth of Intel as a corporation with respect to its competitors. Intel wanted to sell the whole company, not just microprocessors. While the majority of the company's revenues were derived from sales of microprocessors, the company offered a broad range of products for the computer industry, including microprocessor peripherals, multimedia products, microcontrollers, flash memory, OEM modules and systems, supercomputer systems and PC enhancement products. Dennis Carter explained:

> We wanted to brand the whole company, but in a way that was clearly focused on processors. An initial proposal that I rejected early on that Intel Japan was proposing to do within Japan was to brand all components. That would not, however, solve our current problem. The branding program had to carry the Intel name and image but focus on selling processors.

At the heart of the new strategy would be an advertising campaign that, according to Carter, would "cut the 'utter confusion' clones bring to the marketplace (and) drive the premium-brand message home to PC buyers."[14]

Critical to the establishment of Intel as a brand was the need to reverse perceptions of Intel as an impersonal, unfriendly technology company. If Intel was to gain the consumer's trust for its products, Intel knew the consumer had to feel good about the company itself. Intel wanted to establish a brand that offered the promise of "safety" and "technology" to the consumer. By convincing consumers that a computer with an Intel microprocessor inside was a safe investment in leading edge, software-compatible technology, Intel hoped to establish its microprocessor as the premium product and thereby command a premium price. The consumer would not necessarily need to know exactly who Intel was or what it made as long as he or she could be convinced that a personal computer powered by the "creator of microprocessors" was preferable. Intel also believed that if it could gain consumer confidence in Intel as a brand, it would be able to use the Intel name to help move the market forward into new generations of microprocessors and to transfer the equity of the Intel brand to new products and technologies.

Choosing a Logo

Since Intel's products were always inside the computer, unseen by the average purchaser of a personal computer, the company wanted to make the consumer believe that what was inside the computer was as important, if not more important, than the company that assembled the components and placed them inside a box. Intel's "The Computer Inside" campaign had not been explicit enough in linking Intel's name to the microprocessor inside the computer. The company needed a slogan, logo, or some other means that more explicitly identified an Intel microprocessor as the essential ingredient when purchasing a computer.

Carter had previously wanted to use "The Computer Inside" campaign in Japan. Intel's agency in Japan, Dentsu, believed the slogan was too complex and recommended modifying it to "Intel In It" instead, presenting it in a logo form. Japan adopted this logo and began using it for all Intel products, not just processors. Needing a logo for processors fast, Carter, as part of his recommendation to the executive office, suggested using this logo form as the basis for the new microprocessor logo. In order to keep continuity with "The Computer Inside" tag line being used elsewhere in the world, Carter changed the phrase to "Intel Inside" which clearly conveyed to the consumer that it was an Intel microprocessor in the computer. For a number of executional and trademark reasons, the Japanese logo form was modified. The new logo—a swirl with Intel Inside—placed the company and its name directly in front of the consumer.

Communications Strategy

Essential to executing its new branding strategy and establishing awareness of its Intel Inside® logo was getting the support of the OEMs who used Intel microprocessors in manufacturing their products. The most important group of OEMs were the personal computer manufacturers who purchased the vast majority of Intel's microprocessors. Intel's first priority was to get these manufacturers to include the Intel Inside logo in their print ads. In addition to this "push" strategy, the team planned Intel-sponsored advertising and promotions to build equity in the logo and create a "pull" preference among consumers for Intel products. For this pull strategy to work, however, it was also important to make it possible for consumers to easily recognize that a computer had an Intel microprocessor at the point of purchase.

ENLISTING SUPPORT OF OEMs

To enlist the support of OEMs for its Intel Inside program, Intel developed a cooperative advertising program available to all computer manufacturers who used Intel microprocessors. Intel offered computer manufacturers rebates to include the Intel Inside logo in the print ads for their products. Negotiating with a broad range of OEMs in June 1991, Intel found much positive reaction among OEMs to the idea. The smaller, third-tier manufacturers in particular loved the idea. They had no brand name of their own and promoted their products primarily on the basis of price. Print was their main medium of communications, so any advertising subsidy was considered very beneficial. In addition, adding the Intel Inside logo to their machines gave an assurance of quality to their product, and they proved eager to sign on.

The first and second tier OEMs were more skeptical. Many of these OEMs were afraid that the Intel campaign would dilute their own brand equity, weakening their points of differentiation from one another. According to Kevin Bohren, a Compaq vice-president, Intel's campaign "was leveling the playing field," thereby making Compaq's efforts to differentiate its PCs from clones harder.[15] It was this group, however, that Intel needed most to ensure the success of their strategy.

"INTEL INSIDE" PROGRAM

Intel officially announced the launch of its Intel Inside program in November 1991. Specifically, the company announced its intention to spend approximately $125 million during the next 18 months on a combination of print, billboard, and spot television advertising. Of this total, $15.2 million represented direct expenditures by Intel.[16] Intel also announced that 240 customers had agreed to participate in a cooperative advertising program and to carry the new Intel Inside logo on their packaging. For participating in the program, Intel offered to rebate 30–50 percent of the cost of any print ads that included the Intel Inside logo, up to a maximum of 3 percent of the cooperating company's Intel microprocessor volume. Dennis Carter described the program as "trying to create a brand image for products that fall under the Intel Inside umbrella."[17] As one reporter described the campaign, "The 'Intel Inside' campaign . . . is aimed at changing Intel's image from a microchip-maker to a quality standard-bearer."[18]

All advertising that included the Intel Inside logo was designed to create confidence in the consumer's mind that purchasing a personal computer with an Intel microprocessor was both a safe and technologically sound choice. All elements of the Intel Inside program focused on reinforcing those two key associations—"safety" and "technology"—whenever and wherever consumers saw the Intel Inside logo—in an Intel TV ad, a computer manufacturer's print ad, or at the point-of-purchase in a store. By successfully creating consumer "pull," the competition would not only have to create its own distinct image with consumers, but also supply some reason for an OEM to use its product in the absence of any consumer demand.

Intel planned to focus its own ad campaign on products where it was the sole supplier, such as its 80486 line. According to David House, an Intel senior vice president microprocessor products, "Intel hopes to encourage users to skip the i386™ and go right to computers using i486™ chips."[19]

OEMs AND THE INTEL INSIDE PROGRAM

IBM was the first major OEM to use the Intel Inside logo. With the introduction of its first 486-based PC in April 1991, IBM offered to use the new logo—still in draft form. Intel faxed IBM a rough drawing for its use in the ad. IBM would not tell Intel where on the ad it would be located, and all the marketing task force could do was hope for prominent, high visible placement. In fact, the Intel Inside logo was clearly visible in the ad layout. After running this ad, however, IBM did not use the Intel Inside logo again for nearly a year.

By December 1991, over 300 OEMs had signed cooperative advertising agreements with Intel, up from 240 the previous month, including first, second, and third tier manufacturers. Over 100 of these companies featured the Intel logo in their ads, including Zenith Data Systems, Everex Systems, NCR Corp., Dell Computer, and AST Research.[20] Nevertheless, at this time the largest first tier computer manufacturers—including Compaq and IBM—still were not using the Intel Inside logo in their ads.

INTEL'S AD CAMPAIGN

Simultaneous with the development of its OEM co-op advertising program, Intel developed its own Intel Inside ad campaign. The first ad using the Intel Inside logo was a print ad that ran in July 1991. This ad, affectionately called the "measles" ad, showed the Intel Inside logo splashed across a page. The headline read: "How to spot the very best computers." At the bottom of the page, was the tag line: "Intel: The Computer Inside™." The primary objective of this ad was to get the new Intel Inside logo in front of consumers and get them familiar with the Intel name. The ad text promoted

Intel as "the world's leader in microprocessor design and development" and reassured the reader that "with Intel Inside, you know you've got unquestioned compatibility and unparalleled quality. Or simply put, the very best computer technology." The ad ran in both computer trade publications and consumer magazines such as *National Geographic* and *Time.*

In November 1991, Intel launched its first TV ad, dubbed "Room for the Future." In this ad, Intel sought to move the market to i486 technology. A key consumer concern was the protection of their personal technological investment. With the i486 SX processor, consumers would be able to upgrade their computers with another new Intel product, the OverDrive® processor, due out in the first half of 1992. The ad stressed investment protection by emphasizing both the affordability of Intel486 SX technology and the added feature of "built-in upgradability." A secondary role of the ad was to fix a problem in product perception that they were experiencing in the market. The i486 SX, a stripped-down version of its i486 DX chip, had become known as the "brain-dead chip" because it did not include the math co-processing capabilities people had come to expect from 486 technology. By promoting the "built-in upgradability" of the chip, Intel hoped to overcome consumer's concerns about the i486 SX chip.

The ad, developed by Intel's ad agency, Dahlin Smith White (DSW), used special effects designed by Lucas Arts' Industrial Light and Magic Co. The ad took viewers inside the computer, giving them a whirlwind tour of the inside of a personal computer to show how the Intel486 SX chip streamlined computer upgrading. At the end of the ride, a flashing "Vacancy" sign indicated where the faster chip of the future might go—either a math co-processor or the soon-to-be introduced OverDrive processor. Careful not to use any "technospeak," a friendly voiceover said, "Something's waiting inside the powerful Intel486 SX computer. We call it . . . room for the future. Check into it. From Intel. The Computer Inside." In shooting the ad, however, the Intel Inside logo was not included. This oversight was not recognized until late in the production process, and could only be added on a coffee cup at the beginning of the spot. The TV spot ran throughout November and December on CNN and ESPN and on eleven major metropolitan stations during "Star Trek" and "Star Trek: The Next Generation."[21]

In conjunction with the TV ad, Intel also ran a print version of the Intel486 SX commercial. The two-page ad ran in *The Wall Street Journal, Business Week, Fortune, PC Week, Infoworld, PC Magazine,* and *Time.* The first page repeated the opening line of the TV ad, "Something's waiting inside the 486 SX computer." The following page displayed the inside of the computer with a "Vacancy" sign pointing to an open slot next to the Intel486 SX microprocessor. The tag line read, "Room for the future. Introducing built in upgradability." The text below the picture promised the reader that Intel would have "something" of value that would help protect the purchaser's investment. Because the new OverDrive processor was not scheduled for introduction until May 1992, the ad could not talk directly about the OverDrive processor itself. A version of this Intel486 SX processor ad was placed on billboards in Los Angeles, San Francisco, Chicago, Toronto, and seven other metropolitan markets.[22] Finally, the company prepared a small booklet describing in detail capabilities of the Intel486 SX microprocessor. Two pages of text were devoted to describing each of the following product attributes: upgradability, power, affordability, compatibility, and the experience of Intel.

The "Room for the Future" ad was Intel's first experiment with television as an advertising medium. Dennis Carter explained, "We thought it might be an interesting cost-effective way of reaching a broader audience more effectively—a more impactful way to augment the print advertising campaigns that we do."[23] Consumer research indicated that most viewers of the commercial remembered the Intel name, rather than the product, the Intel486 SX chip, being advertised. Intel's print ads, on the other hand, proved much more successful in educating the consumer on specific product attributes associated with the Intel486 SX processor.

In March 1992, Intel introduced its second television ad. The "Power Source" ad promoted the Intel486 processor as a mainstream computing solution, emphasizing its power and affordability. DSW's vice president and group account manager, David Boede, described the shift as reflecting "a combination of prices dropping for the 486 machines, as well as the complexity of Windows software."[24] As if in the cockpit of an aircraft, the viewer sweeps through the "insides" of a personal computer. Hovering briefly over the Intel486 chip itself, the voiceover said: "Want to run your windowing software fast? Then you need a real power source inside. The affordable 486. Power it up and run your software at light speed." At the end of the spot, a picture of the Intel Inside logo dramatically flashed and swirled on the TV screen, while the voiceover said: "The computer inside."

A second version of this ad was introduced in August 1992, highlighting the upgradability of Intel486 microprocessors. At the beginning of the ad, the camera zoomed towards the outside of a personal computer displaying the Intel Inside logo. The voiceover said: "Want to run all your software fast? Then look for the Intel Inside symbol on your next computer." The viewer was then taken inside the computer on a trip similar to the original "Power Source" ad. Inside the computer, the voiceover continued: "It says you have a real power source inside like the upgradable 486 microprocessor. Power it up and run your software at light speed." Like the original Power Source ad, the spot ended as a picture of the Intel Inside logo flashed and swirled on the TV screen, while the voiceover said: "The computer inside."

In developing these ads, Intel's marketing group had mixed opinions as to whether the Intel Inside logo or the company name should finish the commercial. Those who favored the use of "Intel" thought the company name was discrete and distinct from the product being advertised, and hence would be more likely remembered and could be used more effectively in advertising other Intel products in the future. Others favored using the Intel Inside logo to both motivate OEMs to join and/or remain with their co-op print ad program, as well as to enhance consumer familiarity with the Intel Inside logo. Ultimately, the Intel Inside logo was chosen and, this time, was featured prominently in the ad. The ad ran on both network and cable television, including CNN, A&E, and the Discovery Channel.

Complementing the TV campaign was a print campaign launched one week after the initial airing of the TV ad. The print ad headline read: "The affordable power source for today's software." The copy, written person-to-person to the computer buyer, described what was unique about an Intel chip: "With an Intel486 microprocessor inside, you can take full advantage of today's graphical software. In fact, where other systems get bogged down, like running Windows applications simultaneously, the Intel486 CPU powers through these kinds of challenging operations easily. Plus, the Intel486 CPU will keep generating the power you need beyond today."[25]

In October 1992, Intel began a two-month run of its third Intel Inside TV ad. The "Library" ad promoted the compatibility of Intel-equipped personal computers with leading software packages. Once again, the ad first focused on the outside of a personal computer with the Intel Inside logo. The voiceover said: "This symbol outside means you have the standard inside that an entire library of software has been written to." The ad then took the viewer inside the computer through a library of software, including Microsoft and Lotus products. The trip ended with the camera focused on a microprocessor stamped with the Intel Inside logo. The voiceover continued: "Check out computers with Intel. To run an entire library of software, look for this symbol. The Intel microprocessor . . . think of it as a library card." The ad ran on network and cable stations, including CNN. Programming choices included news, sports, and shows such as "Quantum Leap" and "Star Trek: The Next Generation." A print ad version of this ad was created, too.

Intel Inside Program in 1992

By December 1992, over 700 customers were participating in the program, up from 400 in April 1992, primarily consisting of second- and third-tier OEMs.[26] According to Dennis Carter, by July 1992, at least half the computer ads in personal computer magazines included the Intel Inside logo.[27] Participating OEMs were pleased with the results of the co-op program, and many claimed that the Intel Inside logo had boosted their advertising effectiveness.

> "The Intel Inside program has been a good program for us. It has helped add some credibility and enhancements to our messages," says Bill Saylor, manager of U.S. advertising for NCR. The advertising manager with another leading compatible maker says the logo communicates a quality message . . . "You know our product is a quality product because it has an Intel chip in it."[28]

For the first twelve to eighteen months of the Intel Inside co-op program, the first-tier OEMs remained reluctant to use the logo. Initially, they would only include the Intel name in the copy of their ads as part of their product description. As the logo became more familiar to the public from all the exposure it received from advertising by other OEMs, however, they ultimately adopted the logo into their own advertising. Their decision was partly influenced by feedback from computer resellers that people were asking for computers with Intel Inside logo. As Sally Fundakowski, a member of the marketing task force described the evolution of the OEM co-op program: "It took a long time to crack the big guys, but we did it."

In late 1992, Intel announced plans to introduce more than 25 versions of the Intel486™ microprocessor during 1993. Throughout the remainder of 1992 and into 1993, Intel planned to continue to focus its advertising message on the technological performance and software compatibility of Intel microprocessors. Most ads would highlight the company's new IntelDX2™ microprocessor, an enhanced version of its Intel486 DX microprocessor, released in March 1992. The print ads for the IntelDX2 chip would show it in the pictorial component of the ad and describe its specific bene-fits in the ad text.

Another set of ads would simply show a microprocessor with the Intel Inside logo stamped on top and describe the attributes of Intel microprocessors in general. In all the ads, the Intel Inside logo was placed to the left of the first lines of text. The slogan—"The Computer Inside"—was substituted with the Intel company logo (with the dropped "e") at the bottom right corner of each ad. In 1993, Intel planned to add the iComp® index, an internally developed rating system that indicated the relative performance among Intel microprocessors, to all its ads.

Branding "P5"

Intel had been working on its next generation processor, code named "P5" since 1989, and expected to introduce it sometime after the fall of 1992. Unlike previous proces-sors, though, it was not obvious what Intel should name the "P5" or how it should be branded in light of the developing Intel Inside program.

The Intel Inside program had generated a lot of awareness for Intel and made the company and its chip program newsworthy in the eyes of the general and business press. The existence of the Intel Inside program also meant that any branding strategy developed for the "P5" would have to work in conjunction with the Intel Inside pro-gram. The heightening of competition over the last year within the microprocessor in-dustry had generated unusually keen interest in the "P5," and both the technical and business markets were looking for information on the product—its capabilities, its ex-pected introduction date, *and* its name.

A critical event occurred on March 24, 1992 when Cyrix announced plans to in-troduce a 486SLC processor—targeted to the notebook market—in mid-April. The fi-nancial community reacted with a $2/share drop in Intel's stock price that day. Six weeks earlier, Intel had begun to market its own chip targeted to the notebook mar-ket. The Intel386™ SL chip was an integrated chip designed to minimize power con-sumption, a problem specific to the notebook market. The company had developed a series of ads designed to build brand equity in the SL name and get the SL name linked specifically to notebook computing.

Though the Cyrix chip was essentially "386" generation technology, naming it "486SLC" gave the impression that the Cyrix product was a "486" generation product and hence more advanced than Intel's own i386 SL chip. By positioning the product as "486," Cyrix negatively impacted Intel's i386 SL branding strategy and forced the company to review the possibility of altering the chip's name. After much delibera-tion, Intel concluded it could not change the i386 SL name given that the product was actually selling in the market but the episode significantly influenced Intel manage-ment's thinking concerning naming strategies.

Because of these and other events, the team knew they would have the attention of the public whenever they were ready to tell their story. However, the heightened interest in Intel and its new generation processor meant that it would be critical to manage the communications process and information flow carefully to ensure that the correct story was told.

Naming "P5"

Carter appointed Karen Alter to manage the "P5" naming process. She formed an ad hoc team whose first concern was choosing a name for this new processor. The team wanted a name that would stand on its own as well as indicate the generation of the new chip. Clearly the court's decision that numbers were not trademarkable and the recent experience with the i386 SL made the choice of "586" a risky one. In a June 1992 interview with an AP reporter, Andy Grove was quoted as saying: "Over my dead body will this new product be named 586." This quote was picked up by newspapers around the world, thus laying the issue of a numerical name to rest once and for all.

With the "586" option eliminated, the team decided to use the naming of the "P5" as an opportunity to redefine the industry language for microprocessors. Naming "P5" offered Intel the opportunity to create a new brand with a clean slate that could acquire equity of its own over time and make it more difficult for other CPU suppliers to get a "free ride" from Intel's equity.

In specifying criteria for the choice of a name for the "P5," the team decided that it was necessary that the name: (1) be difficult for competition to copy, (2) be trademarkable, (3) indicate a new generation of technology that could effectively transition from generation to generation, (4) have positive associations and work on a global basis, (5) support Intel's brand equity, and (6) sound like an ingredient so that it worked *with* Intel's partners' brand names. In selecting the name, the team's primary target audience was the retail consumer. While a key objective was to establish credibility for the new product with early adopters—industry technology experts—they knew this group did not really care that much about the actual name of a microprocessor per se.

Intel's sales force surveyed a broad range of customers during a two-month period to get their reaction to the planned naming concept (e.g., to not use a numerical name). Some customers told Intel that changing the industry language by not using "586" was not possible. They argued that the industry moved too fast, that the market was already on a level playing field, and that the product was too complicated to "reeducate" the consumer. Others, particularly the technologically sophisticated OEMs, liked the idea as a way to differentiate Intel technology. A distinctive name would allow them to distinguish their products from lower-tier manufacturers in the PC market, as well as from their competition in the workstation and server markets.

Inside of Intel the managers viewed this naming process as a major strategic move. As Karen Alter explained:

> Here we are—a company that spends $2 billion a year on capital and R&D. Every 2 to 3 weeks we would get together with the senior executives who *wanted* to be locked into a room to talk about this issue. Everyone had come to believe that technology was moving so fast that communicating to the end-users and getting them to buy the right technology was critical. It would be a huge competitive advantage for us if we got it right. Even though it's a little name, we had to get it right the first time because we wouldn't get a second chance.

Name Selection

Intel undertook the most extensive search in its history to find a name for the "P5." In addition to hundreds of names generated from the task force's own brainstorming sessions, Intel hired Lexicon—a naming firm—and ran a company-wide naming contest in which over 1200 Intel employees worldwide participated. Some of the more humorous entries submitted included, "iCUCyrix, iAmFastest, GenuIn5, and 586NOT! The company also received a number of unsolicited suggestions from many individuals around the world. A 16-year-old Australian boy submitted a detailed proposal for SWIFFT, short for Speed With Intel's Fastest Future Technology. *Computer Reseller News*, an industry trade publication, even held its own contest! In all, the selection process generated 3300 names. Karen Alter described the process that followed:

> Compared to 586, every name sounded terrible because it lacked the familiarity of the x86 naming scheme. It appeared that there were no exciting protectable names, but we knew we had to get over it. We divided the names into three concept categories: (1) closely linked to Intel; (2) technologically "cool"—e.g., naming an architecture; and (3) completely new with some generational concept embedded. We then discussed the pros and cons of each concept category and selected ten alternatives for extensive review and testing.

The company conducted a very detailed global trademark search to insure that each name on the list could not be copied, as well as a worldwide linguistic review to ensure the name would be effective in all languages. Certain that each name on the list was trademarkable and linguistically correct, the company then tested each name and its related concept with MIS and end users in the United States and Europe to determine how well each name met the established goals. In particular, the team asked the participants to evaluate each name for negative and positive associations, memorability, willingness to use, appropriateness for the product, and ability to merchandise. In addition, the team got internal input from its Asia Pacific and Japanese counterparts.

The task force discussed pros and cons for each of the ten tested names and selected one name from each of the concept categories to present to the top management executives for a final name selection. The final three name options for the respective concept categories were: InteLigence, RADAR1, and Pentium.[29] Finally, ten days before the planned announcement of the official name, the company's top executives and the members of the task force met to make the final name selection. Grove led the meeting, asking each participant to choose from the three alternatives and to tell the group what he or she liked about that name and why. Grove and Carter did not give their opinions, saying that they would make the final decision after the meeting was over. Once the meeting was over and a name was chosen, Grove told the group, the topic would never be discussed again.

Not surprisingly, the members of the task force were almost evenly split across the three names. The public relations members of the task force liked the InteLigence name because it was the easiest name for them to explain to the public. The technically oriented members liked the "techie cool" name, RADAR1. The sales/marketing-oriented members were partial to the Pentium name because it was new *and* represented the cleanest break. As a result, they felt that it would be easier to sell to OEMs and other customers. After everyone had given his or her opinion, Grove and Carter thanked them and went into Grove's office to make a final decision.

Communicating the New Name

Since the name would not be chosen until the last possible moment, the task force had to decide on a communications strategy without knowing exactly what name they would be communicating. Consequently, they developed a communications timeline for introduction of "P5"—from name announcement through products and systems launch. The task force planned to release information so as to create a "crescendo" effect by the time the product was actually introduced into the market and available for sale. A key question was how to announce the name—during a speech, press conference, television program, or what? A primary objective of the task force was to capture the attention and interest of the press so that by the time the new chip was shipped in volume, everyone would know the name of the new chip and no one would even think about "586." Even though the name would not be officially announced until October 1992, by September 1992, Intel's public relations efforts had effectively decreased mention of the "586" name in published press articles to 17 percent of press articles worldwide, from 55 percent in February.

When the naming options had been narrowed to three choices, the task force considered the impact of each name on the multiple audiences—press, OEMs/dealers, competitors, and employees—to whom they would have to communicate the decision. They knew it was critical to establish a consistent worldwide set of messages and to provide the field—sales representatives, MDMs, AMs, FSEs—with all the necessary information. Without question, many people would react negatively to any name that was not "586" and Intel wanted to counter this reaction as quickly as possible. In preparation for the name launch, the task force developed a series of presentations for customers to keep them informed of the naming process and timing of the product's introduction. The company made formal presentations explaining the company's intentions and asking for "help and understanding in launching the new name, even before it was made public."[30] Intel hoped the computer companies would market the name to users as a key product ingredient, much like Nutrasweet, Teflon, and Gortex. As one Intel spokesperson explained, "The market is changing and with other people (competing chip makers) introducing a key ingredient, you don't know what part you're getting inside."[31] Intel also hoped the computer companies would market the name to users as a way to convey the power and efficacy of its fifth-generation processor family.

Immediately prior to the name announcement—and after the final "naming" meeting—Intel wanted to communicate its decision to its top customers around the world. Karen Alter explained:

> Prior to Andy's announcement, one other person and I shipped out documents around the world so our sales force could contact our top 30 customers and tell them

Andy was going to make this announcement—this is the story, this is why we did it, this is what we are going to do to promote this thing, this is how we addressed your concerns, etc.—but without revealing the actual name.

Launching the Pentium® Processor

Intel officially announced the name of the new chip on Monday, October 20, 1992. Grove, in New York City for the tenth annual NY PC User Society convention, made the announcement during an exclusive interview on CNN at 7:30 AM eastern standard time. CNN provided Intel the ability to make a live official announcement on a world-wide basis. Andy Grove announced that the name of Intel's fifth generation micro-processor was Pentium® and said the company would begin shipping production versions of the chip in early 1993. In describing the choice of "Pentium" for the name, Grove explained, "the name should suggest an ingredient. The "Pent" of Pentium, from the Greek meaning five, alludes to the fact that the new chip is the fifth genera-tion of the family. The "ium" was added to make the chip sound like a fundamental element." The company coined the name because it conveyed the positive attributes such as quality, state-of-the-art technology, software compatibility, and performance that its OEM customers wanted their brands to be associated with. Grove explained the rationale for not using a number as a name, "We can't count on another number. It's so much cleaner to designate a name that's protectable."[32] In the interview, Grove said that the company expected to ship "hundreds of thousands" of Pentium chips in 1993 and to reach a manufacturing rate of a million Pentium processors in 1994.

The October 20th announcement was strictly limited to the Pentium name. Intel wanted to let the public know the name so that people would begin to call the new chip by its proper name, ending all the speculation that had surrounded the name since the trademark ruling 1½ years prior. Intel did not provide any product detail, explaining that it preferred to introduce the chip once production had begun so that the announcement would coincide with the introduction of computer systems using the product. At the time of the product's official introduction, Intel would provide de-tails such as price and shipment date. In the interim, Intel planned to see usage of the "P5" name curtailed and the Pentium name put in its place. In addition, while the Pentium name would be marked on the chip, the actual packaging would not be final-ized until production time.

Once the product was introduced, the company planned a huge promotion cam-paign to achieve name recognition for the Pentium processor. One executive explained:

> Branding a chip has not been done before; however, launching branded products to consumers is done routinely. Many of the Pentium microprocessor's promotional ac-tivities will be new to the semiconductor industry, but not new in consumer marketing such as with computers and software. It is very important that when our OEM cus-tomers roll out products with the Pentium microprocessor inside and when software vendors claim that their new software was tested and written to be compatible with the Pentium CPU that the Pentium microprocessor be recognized by PC users as a valuable ingredient.

Immediately following Grove's announcement on CNN, the Pentium processor marketing team launched a full-scale effort to ensure the Pentium name was quickly adopted into the everyday industry vernacular. Intel's PR department phoned all leading individuals who wrote about the industry to let them know the new name. A not uncommon response was: "I can't believe this name. This is the most ridiculous name I've ever heard." Intel's PR department carefully monitored all press for references to the Pentium processor, and if they found anyone using "586" or "P5," they immediately sent the author a letter correcting the error. Within one month after the naming launch, over 90 percent of press mentions used Pentium instead of "586."

Before Grove's announcement on CNN only six people inside Intel knew the name—Grove, Carter, Ric Giardina (the Intel attorney in charge of trademarking the name), two PR people, and Karen Alter. Alter described the scene inside Intel following Grove's announcement:

> Our microprocessor team had to convert over 20,000 documents. It wasn't like anyone really liked the name, but they just did it. We all converted everything rapidly—all the trademark documents, all the internal communications, e-mail, product material—you name it, we did it. The people preparing for Comdex had banners they were just waiting to place the name in. For two days we gave interviews non-stop. The press picked up the name more and more. Our European team loved the name because they thought it was a global name with a historical root. That got picked up favorably in the European press. The name began to grow on people. They felt better about it. We had this massive organization to handle the situation while it was still in our control.

To ensure that the Pentium mark remained protectable, the company established a set of internal and external guidelines regarding usage of the Pentium name. The guidelines included:

1. Never use the trademark as a plural or verb
   Wrong—Pentiumize your computer
2. Usage in OEM system names is not permitted
   Wrong—The CMC Pentium 50
3. OEMs may reference inclusion of Pentium processor
   Right—The CMC 500 contains the Intel Pentium microprocessor
4. ISVs may reference software applicability for Pentium processor
   Wrong—Pentium Funsheet
   Right—Funsheet for Pentium processor-based computers

The Pentium Processor Product Announcement

On March 22, 1993 Intel announced that the company had begun shipping production versions of the Pentium chip. No pricing plans were disclosed. Sales by personal computer makers would not begin until May in order to give Intel time to build up inventories of the chip to meet expected initial demand.[33] Andy Grove said Intel planned to push the Pentium processor early in its life as a mainstream microprocessor and not as an expensive high-end chip by pricing the new chip "aggressively."[34]

An extensive set of product materials was distributed on the day of the product introduction. The packet included press releases detailing the product attributes of the new chip as well as a glossy brochure that evaluated the performance of the new chip against a number of industry benchmarks. The Pentium processor ran typical software programs more than twice as fast as the Intel486 microprocessors. The chip contained over three million transistors, compared with the 486's 1.2 million, and was offered in both 60 MHz and 66 MHz versions. Its "dual-pipeline" superscalar architecture—which allowed two instructions to be performed within the same clock cycle—was specifically designed to support graphical user interface (GUI)-intensive applications, including those written for Microsoft Windows. The chip was expected initially to be used primarily by PC and workstation manufacturers to expand their server and workstation lines. According to Gary Stimack, general manager of Compaq's systems division, the chip offered the power and technology to allow PC manufacturers to "head-on address the traditional mini and mainframe markets."[35] In addition to its speed, the Pentium processor also contained circuits that made it easier for computer makers to build the Pentium processor into increasingly popular multiprocessor machines. Both Compaq Computer and AST Research said they planned to introduce "multiprocessor" Pentium processor servers—which chained together several chips for added processing power—and desktop machines in 1993.[36] According to Andy Grove, "Intel architecture in general, and the Pentium processor in particular, is the Rosetta Stone of enterprise computing." Because the Pentium processor would run operating systems ranging from OS/2 to Windows NT to the forthcoming IBM-Apple joint project, Taligent, Grove argued that the chip would be the key to multi-platform, client-server architectures.[37]

On May 10, 1993, one week before the Pentium processor-based PCs would officially be available for sale, Intel introduced its first ad for the Pentium processor. The four page magazine insert, the first in a year long "technology briefing" campaign, positioned the Pentium processor at the elitist end of the market, saying "all but the most demanding users" should use personal computers with Intel486™ chips. The insert, describing in some detail how the Pentium processor made PCs run faster, was a shift away from the simpler, consumer-style advertising Intel had done since 1989. As one Intel spokesperson explained, "In the olden days, we would do very 'techy,' spec-driven ads in engineering books, and then we got very end-user (focused) without much meat on the bones. Now we're going a little bit back to our roots."[38]

Although Intel expected to ship only "tens of thousands" of Pentium chips in 1993, the company, as with previous generation microprocessors, began advertising the new product early to create demand and stay ahead of clones of its old products.[39] "It's the eat your own children theory," explained an Intel spokesperson. "We have to do it before someone else does it to us."[40] The insert was scheduled to appear initially in computer titles and then *Business Week*. International Data Corp. estimated that 80,000 Pentium processor machines would be shipped in the United States by year-end 1993, rising to 640,000 in 1994, 2 million in 1995, and surpassing the 486 by the end of 1996.[41] The prices of Pentium processor-based desktop computers were expected to cost around $5,000 in 1994, and to drop to as little as $2,000 within three years.[42]

Indications of Success

Between 1990 and 1993, Intel had invested over $500 million in advertising and promotional programs designed to build Intel's brand equity. The Intel Inside campaign had constituted the bulk of this investment and plans were to continue with the campaign. The two pillars of the Intel brand message continued to be Intel's guarantee of safety—both in terms of software compatibility and upgradability—and providing the most advanced technology via the double-clocked i486 DX2 and Pentium processors.

Within the industry, there was considerable debate about the effectiveness of Intel's "branded ingredient" strategy. AMD, for example, had publicly rejected adoption of a similar branding strategy. As one AMD spokesman explained, "You wouldn't find an 'AMD Inside' campaign even if we had the kind of deep pockets that Intel has. We don't think it's particularly effective to try to build brand awareness."[43] In contrast, Cyrix was scheduled to introduce a print ad campaign in June 1993 for its line of 486-like chips. The ads would initially run in computer publications.

In the last two years, the Intel Inside program had won a number of advertising awards, including the Marcom Award for best TV campaign at the computer industry's premier trade show, Comdex, in 1992.[44] Also at Comdex, Dahlin Smith White, Intel's ad agency, won the "Grand Marquis" excellence award for its "Power Source" commercial. In presenting the award, Donna Tapellini, editor of *Marketing Computers* magazine, explained, "This is not just for the best marketing program or campaign, it is for a work that has raised the standard irrevocably and made a difference . . . Not only have they moved the goal posts in terms of advertising values, but this campaign is a culmination of a brilliant 'Intel Inside' branding strategy. They have done for (computer) chips what Frank Perdue has done for chickens. They have set the standard and become the ones to beat in the industry."[45] In 1993, *Financial World* rated Intel as the third most valuable brand, behind Marlboro and Coca-Cola, with an estimated worth of $17.8 billion.

Intel's own market research, both in the United States and in Europe, indicated that end-user awareness of the Intel brand name had increased significantly since the introduction of the Intel Inside program. The independent research, performed in June 1992, indicated that users worldwide viewed Intel as the technology leader versus such competitors as AMD and Cyrix and the overwhelming microprocessor of choice. Research in the United States also indicated that Intel had the strongest image on quality and compatibility attributes. Over 80 percent of those surveyed had seen the Intel Inside logo in personal computer ads and nearly half had seen the logo in store displays, product literature, or on a personal computer. Over 75 percent of those who had seen the logo said that it conveyed positive attributes, and 50 percent said they looked for the symbol in making their personal computer selection.

In Europe, two-thirds of business computer purchasers surveyed had seen the Intel Inside logo and understood that the logo indicated a CPU brand. However, among the nonsophisticated nontechnical users, the "Intel" name and Intel Inside logo were often confused. The problem was particularly acute in certain foreign languages, like character-based Chinese, that did not link the Intel Inside brand with the Intel company name.

What Next?

Looking toward the future, Carter's Corporate Marketing Group was grappling with a number of questions. First, should the Intel Inside program include the i386 processor, particularly since Intel was encouraging people to upgrade to i486 and Pentium processor-based systems? Second, should the campaign be extended to other products, particularly as Intel moved further into non-microprocessor products, such as fax modems and LAN administration software?[46] The March 1994 introduction of the PowerPC chip by Motorola, Apple, and IBM added another element of complexity to planning for Intel's branding strategy. Motorola, Apple, and IBM had directly positioned the PowerPC against Intel's Pentium processor and now Intel had to decide what would be the best response.

The broader issue facing Carter's group was the proper balance between the development of the Pentium name versus the Intel Inside logo. In particular, the research and development of the next technology "P6" chip was nearing completion, raising a difficult question: What should be the name of the soon-to-be announced new chip? Should they modify the Pentium name or come up with a new name? What should be the role of the Intel Inside logo in marketing the new and future microprocessors? Should it only apply to microprocessor? While there were no easy answers to any of these questions, decisions would need to be made.

Discussion Questions

1. Was the Intel Inside campaign worth it? What were its strengths and weaknesses? How would you characterize OEM involvement?
2. Evaluate the Pentium naming strategy. Do you think Intel arrived at the right name? What are the pros and cons?
3. What would you do now? Provide recommendations to Intel concerning the next steps in its marketing program and branding efforts.

Notes

1. This case was made possible through the cooperation of Intel and the assistance of Dennis Carter, Vice President of Marketing, Sally Fundakowski, Director of Processor Brand Marketing, and Karen Alter, Manager, Press Relations, at Intel. Leslie Kimerling prepared this case under the supervision of Professor Kevin Lane Keller as the basis for class discussion.
2. Microprocessors are also used in a wide range of consumer electronic, household, industrial, telecommunications, and military applications. Here, the term "microprocessor" refers to a microprocessor used as the central processing unit in a personal computer or workstation.
3. "Clock speed" denotes how fast a microprocessor can process data. The higher the clock speed, the faster the chip processes data. For example, a computer with a 16 MHz 286™ chip runs twice as fast as an identical computer with a 8 MHz 286™ chip. "Bus" is the electronic path by which data travel. The data bus moves data between computer memory and the microprocessor. The processor bus moves data from place to place inside the chip. A

32-bit bus can move 4 bytes of information at a time, twice as many as a 16-bit bus (from *San Jose Mercury News*, May 5, 1991).

4. While software written for a 16–bit microprocessor would run on a 32-bit chip, the reverse was not generally true.

5. *Wall Street Journal*, April 8, 1991, p. A1.

6. 386 revenues are estimates found in Morgan Stanley Analyst reports dated 4/17/90 and 4/11/91.

7. Intel chips were based on CISC (complex-instruction-set computing) technology. Microprocessor instructions are lowest level commands a processor responds to (e.g., "retrieve from memory" or "compare two numbers"). The CISC approach feeds instructions to the processor in a cluster of related operations. In contrast, RISC technology streamlines the process by using fewer instructions and imposing limits on the number of tasks contained in each instruction. The simplified instruction process ensures that tasks are performed within a split-second tick of the chips internal clock. A CISC instruction set, on the other hand, must periodically check to see that the clustered tasks are being performed in sequence. In addition, RISC processors have simpler circuits that need fewer transistors, thereby leaving extra room on the RISC chip for special, speed-enhancing circuits, such as cache memory. The speed of the RISC processor is particularly useful for computation intensive users.

8. *Wall Street Journal*, April 8, 1991, p. A1.

9. By 1990, Sun, Digital Equipment (DEC), Hewlett-Packard, and IBM all offered RISC chips and/or RISC-based workstations.

10. MIPS Computers was acquired by Silicon Graphics in 1992.

11. *Wall Street Journal*, April 8, 1991, p. A1.

12. Circuit City is a retail chain selling audio and video equipment, major household appliances, and more recently, personal computer and other technology-based products. It sells primarily to the mass market.

13. *Business Week*, April 29, 1991. In its best year with the 80286, Intel sold 4.5 million units.

14. *Business Week*, September 30, 1991.

15. *Business Week*, September 30, 1992, p. 32.

16. *Brandweek*, October 12, 1992, p. 5.

17. *The San Francisco Chronicle*, November 2, 1991, p. B1

18. *The London Sunday Times*, September 13, 1992.

19. *San Jose Mercury News*, November 1, 1991.

20. *Business Marketing*, February 1992, p. 16.

21. *Business Marketing*, February 1992, p. 19.

22. *Business Marketing*, February 1992, p. 19.

23. *Business Marketing*, October 1991, p. 48.

24. *Marketing Computers*, May 1992, p. 43.

25. Much of this description can be found in *Business Marketing*, January 1993, p. 36.

26. *Business Wire*, January 13, 1993.

27. *Advertising Age*, July 6, 1992, p. S-16.

28. *Business Marketing*, February 1992.

29. These are pseudonyms for the actual names chosen but are representative of the names chosen in each of the three concept categories.

30. Internal presentation by Intel to customer group.

31. *San Francisco Examiner*, March, 1993.

32. *Wall Street Journal*, October 20, 1992, p. B3.

33. This delay represented the Intel's second; Intel had announced in early 1992 that the Pentium-based computers would begin selling at the end of 1992. Subsequently Intel had planned to introduce Pentium in conjunction with the start of sales by PC makers by the end of March 1993. In February 1993, Intel asked computer makers to delay by two months selling of Pentium-based computers to allow Intel to build up inventories of the chip to meet the expected surge in initial demand (*Wall Street Journal*, March 22, 1993).

34. *Wall Street Journal*, March 23, 1993.

35. *Wall Street Journal*, December 21, 1992.

36. *Wall Street Journal*, December 21, 1992 and March 23, 1993.

37. *Information Week*, August 23, 1993.

38. *Advertising Age*, May 10, 1993, p. 3.

39. At the name launch in October 1992, Intel had stated it expected to ship hundreds of thousands of Pentium in 1993. This number was subsequently revised downward to tens of thousands. In 1993, Intel was expected to ship 40 million 486 microprocessors (*Information Week*, August 23, 1993).

40. *Advertising Age*, May 10, 1993, p. 3.

41. *Wall Street Journal*, May 14 1993.

42. *Wall Street Journal*, December 21, 1992, p. A1.

43. *Advertising Age*, May 10, 1993.

44. *Marketing Computers*, January 1993.

45. *Business Wire*, November 18, 1992.

46. Intel's PCED group marketed enhancements to basic PC systems under the Intel brand name. This group typically combined the Intel name with a sub-brand for a particular product area, e.g., Intel SatisFaxtion Fax Modems. The PCED group, led by Jim Johnson, marketed its products independently of Carter's Corporate Marketing Group.

APPENDIX C The California Milk Processor Board: Branding a Commodity[1]

Introduction

In February, 1993, Jeff Manning, newly appointed Executive Director of the California Milk Processor Board (CMPB), was reviewing reports on per capita U.S. consumption of milk over the last fifteen years. To anyone involved in the production and sales of milk, the numbers painted a disturbing picture. Not only had there been a steady decline in milk consumption over the previous two decades, but recently the decline was even accelerating. In the last five years, per capita milk consumption in California dropped from 26.4 gallons in 1987 to 24.8 gallons in 1992. This precipitous decrease in consumption translated to roughly a $50 million loss in profits per year.

Manning was faced with a daunting task—to revitalize sales of a product in seemingly perpetual decline. In contrast to marketing a brand, Manning was charged with marketing a commodity. His goal was therefore to increase consumption of an entire product category, not just a single brand. Yet, the CMPB had to operate on a small budget typical of most commodities, a budget that was dwarfed by other firms in the beverage industry such as Coca-Cola and Pepsi. Not only did milk have to compete with these cola giants in the beverage industry, but the recent onslaught of alternative beverages such as Snapple iced teas and Calistoga bottled waters was sure to make an already crowded industry even more competitive.

Manning realized that some of the underlying factors driving the changes in the industry also worked in his favor. The 1990s looked to be the decade of health education. Consumers cared about their health and were becoming more informed about health issues every day. Since the vast majority of consumers expressed awareness of the nutritional benefits of milk consumption, milk was well-positioned to benefit from the current trends. What puzzled Manning, however, was that even though people understood and valued the benefits of drinking milk, per capita consumption continued to decrease. With almost $2 billion in media spending annually in beverages as a category, Manning had to make the most of his $23 million budget to have milk's message heard among the noise.

The Dairy Industry

Milk has played an important role throughout American history. Milk's U.S. history began in 1611 when the first cows were brought to Jamestown, Virginia. With the prevalence of milk on supermarket shelves, it may seem as though milk has always been readily available, but that has not been the case. Milk must be refrigerated in order to be transported, and therefore requires special handling throughout the distribution process. In fact, it was not until 1841 that the first regular shipment of milk was made, from Orange County, California to New York City. Various technological advances then made mass shipment of milk a reality. In 1856, Louis Pasteur began conducting his famous experiments that led to pasteurization, the process of cleansing milk of harmful bacteria without destroying nutritional content. The milk bottle was invented by Dr. Harvey D. Thatcher in 1884, followed shortly in 1886 by the patent for the first automatic bottle filler and capper. The first tank trucks for transporting milk came along in 1914 when milk was delivered in metal cans. Finally, in 1932 the first paper milk cartons were commercially introduced and subsequently replaced by plastic milk cartons in 1964. Today milk is widely available, and sales reach upwards of $14 billion annually.

The dairy industry is comprised of a relatively short list of intermediaries separating the farmer from the consumer. Basically, there are three major groups in the dairy industry: the *farmers* who produce the milk, the *processors* who convert raw milk into whole and lower fat milks, and the *retailers* who sell the final products.

FARMERS

The number and nature of the American dairy farmer has changed quite dramatically over the years. In 1950, there were over 2 million dairy farms scattered throughout the United States. Most farms in those days were small family farms with an average herd of ten cows. Today the number of dairy farms has dwindled to a mere 150,000, primarily concentrated in a handful of states. One of the casualties of change was the small local farmer. The small dairy farmer is more the exception than the rule as the average herd now consists of 500 cows. Farmers are also more efficient than in the past. One hundred fifty years ago, the average milk production per cow was 1,500 quarts annually. Today the average cow produces over 6,600 quarts per year. Some of the small family-owned farms have been replaced by a growing number of very large farms called "factory farms." These farms are so large and technically advanced that they can turn a profit when selling their milk at $10 per 100 pounds of milk, while the family farmer usually operates with a higher breakeven of around $17.

As producers in the dairy industry, farmers in California are represented nationally by the National Dairy Public Relations Board (NDPRB) and the United Dairy Industry Association (UDIA) and locally by the California Milk Advisory Board (CMAB). Funding to support these groups comes directly from each farmer's profits. Hence, in order to raise money for a national advertising campaign, each farmer has to contribute some private funds that otherwise might have been used for personal or business activities. As a result, farmers are traditionally tight-fisted and scrutinize all program budgets carefully. For example, although milk sales had been declining for a number of years, the farmers did not fund a direct sales force to increase sales of milk within the channels of distribution.

PROCESSORS

The processors' primary function is to transform raw milk into the products that eventually hit the grocer's shelves—for example, whole, 2 percent, 1 percent, and skim milk. Raw milk is 87 percent water and 13 percent solids. The solids portion contains approximately 3.7 percent fat and the rest is nonfat solids. The milk fat portion carries the vitamins A, D, E, and K typically found in milk. The nonfat solids contain protein and carbohydrates and other vitamins and minerals. The final milk product does not matter that much to processors, who earn roughly the same amount of profit regardless of milk type. The end-product does make a difference to the farmers, who are paid on the basis of an older compensation scheme that provides royalties by percentage of milk fat sold. Whole milk is thus the most profitable product for the farmers to sell, although they do not have that much control over the final product.

There are forty processors of fluid milk in California. The relationship between the processors and the producers has historically been one of conflict due to incompatible goals. The producers ideally would like to produce milk for as little as possible and to sell it for as much as possible, while processors would obviously like to buy low and sell high. In contrast to the producers who are usually smaller farmers, the processors are generally big businesses that employ hundreds of people. For example, Lucerne, the processor for Safeway food stores in California, is a wholly owned subsidiary of Safeway. Processors typically either sell only fluid milk or reap the majority of their profits from the sale of fluid milk. Gravely concerned about lower sales, it was the processors who banded together in 1992 to allocate the funds that gave rise to the CMPB.

RETAILERS

California is dominated by two primary retailers, Safeway and Lucky food stores. Safeway obtains all of the milk sold in its stores from its Lucerne processing facility. In addition to Safeway and Lucky, there are a number of secondary grocery stores (smaller local chains) in the state. Retailers may be statewide in scope but decisions concerning shelf space and in-store promotions are made by the local store manager. Fluid milk, in all its forms, constitutes only a handful of over 50,000 products sold by most retailers. Of all these items, milk is one of the most perishable but also one of the most profitable products—commanding almost three times the profits per square foot of retail space relative to groceries. According to the Progressive Grocer's 1992 Supermarket Sales Manual, milk was the top selling supermarket product in terms of sales per shelf foot. Moreover, the dairy department racked up a total of $61.23 of sales per shelf foot, compared to $22.47 for the composite store. In fact, milk, eggs, and cottage cheese were the top three products in sales per shelf foot for all supermarket products. The news was even better in terms of direct profit return on inventory dollars, an important statistic for store managers. While the average department comes in at roughly $5, milk maintains an average of a whopping $84.83 profit.

OTHER CHANNELS OF DISTRIBUTION

Due in large part to the perishable nature of fluid milk, channels of distribution other than grocery stores did not account for a major portion of sales. Of the sales that did occur, school districts accounted for the majority, followed by foodservice establishments such as McDonald's. In California, the latest threat to milk consumption comes from the school districts. Prior to 1982, all school lunches in California included milk. Since then, school children can now choose from five items, including milk, for lunch. In other words, school children, who are traditionally heavy users of milk, are no longer a captive audience for milk. The change in school district policy certainly contributed to the 3.8 percent decline in noncommercial foodservice milk volume from 1986 to 1991. The trend is just as bad in commercial foodservice establishments such as McDonald's. Although the percentage of food dollars spent out of home is up to 33 percent in 1991 from 25 percent in 1971, milk has not enjoyed an increase in sales to these types of establishments. In fact, commercial foodservice milk volume actually dropped 23 percent from 1986 to 1991.

Dairy Promotion Groups in California

Agriculture is the largest industry in California and dairy products are the state's largest agricultural commodity, producing foods valued at approximately $3 billion annually. The consumption of milk and other dairy products in the state are promoted by six national and regional dairy groups. Each of the groups is funded either by the dairy producers—comprised of the farmers who own the herds and farms—or by the dairy processors who process fluid milk into a wide variety of dairy products.

NATIONAL DAIRY PROMOTION
AND RESEARCH BOARD (NDPRB)

The NDPRB was formed under the authority of the U.S. Department of Agriculture and chartered with the mission of coordinating a program to expand domestic and foreign markets for fluid milk and other dairy products produced in the United States. NDPRB maintains a national scope that includes advertising, promotion, and research funded by the country's dairy farmers. In California the NDPRB spends about $2 million annually on fluid milk advertising and promotions.

UNITED DAIRY INDUSTRY ASSOCIATION (UDIA)

The UDIA is a national association of dairy farmers that oversees two main divisions: the American Dairy Association (ADA) and the National Dairy Council. The ADA creates regional and national advertising, sales promotion, and public relations programs for the UDIA dairy farmer members. The National Dairy Council is the UDIA's nutrition, education, and research division that administers nutrition research grants for the NDPRB. When combined with the NDPRB, the two national boards spend approximately $55 million annually on promoting fluid milk across the country.

CALIFORNIA CHEESE AND BUTTER ASSOCIATION (CCBA)

The CCBA is a voluntary nonprofit organization that represents cheese and butter manufacturers, distributors, and brokers. The CCBA is a state-chartered organization that is dedicated to promoting and advertising the consumption of butter and cheese. The CCBA's budget is less than $5 million, none of which is used to promote fluid milk.

CALIFORNIA MILK ADVISORY BOARD (CMAB)

Funded by the state's dairy producers, the CMAB is responsible for advertising, promotions, and public relations of all dairy foods, including fluid milk. Funding assessments for the CMAB are collected by the California Department of Food and Agriculture. Currently, the CMAB spends roughly $10 million annually on promotion of fluid milk.

DAIRY COUNCIL OF CALIFORNIA (DCC)

The DCC is the nutrition education arm of the California dairy industry. Operating under the California Department of Food and Agriculture, the DCC is funded by the producers, producer-distributors, and distributors of dairy products in the state. The DCC provides programs and information designed to illustrate the role of dairy products in a balanced, healthy diet for both children and adults.

CALIFORNIA MILK PROCESSOR BOARD (CMPB)

The creation of the CMPB represents the first time that milk processors had joined together to fund advertising and public relations programs for fluid milk. The processors first became interested in the idea of a new board after consumer research revealed that per capita consumption of milk had been on a steady decline for a number of years. Sales of fluid milk is the major contributor of profits for almost all of the state's forty milk processors. In 1993, the processors displayed their commitment to reversing the downward spiral of milk by establishing the CMPB. The idea behind the CMPB was to sufficiently fund a new board whose sole purpose was to increase the sales and consumption of fluid milk. The processors agreed to sponsor legislation requiring them to contribute three cents per gallon of milk sold in the state in the first year, with slightly smaller contributions in the remaining years of an initial three year charter from the CMPB. In the first year, the CMPB is expected to raise about $23 million, all to promote fluid milk. Jeff Manning, previously a senior vice president with Ketchum advertising, was hired as executive director of the CMPB. Manning had previously worked with beef, potatoes, bananas, and eggs in commodity marketing and also brought a wealth of branded product marketing experience.

Marketing a Brand Versus Marketing a Commodity

The strategies behind marketing a commodity are not the same as those for marketing a branded product. Marketing a commodity is much more similar to marketing the product category as a whole rather than marketing a single brand within the category. One obvious difference is the lack of a brand name. Not having a brand name results in many complexities, both on the supply side—as to how the product is marketed—and on the demand side—as to how consumers perceive and value the product. Several differences in commodity marketing are highlighted below.

SUPPLY SIDE DIFFERENCES IN COMMODITY MARKETING

Perhaps the characteristic of commodity marketing most responsible for the lack of innovative programs is that each member of the industry has an input into every marketing program associated with the commodity, including the producers themselves. The fact that so many people are involved has a dramatic effect on the flexibility of the marketing programs and their ability to provide equal benefits to each group, and all programs require some extra paperwork and effort from each group in the industry. As a result, adoption of new programs is troublesome, and the industry members typically opt for the status quo, assuming that—perhaps mistakenly—"everyone needs the commodity." For example, something as "new" as couponing is extremely difficult in commodity markets because the redemption value would have to be paid by a broad range of processors, producers, and other intermediaries.

Another aspect of commodity marketing that differs from brand marketing is the budgets available for advertising, promotion, and marketing research. While a national brand may be able to draw on investment funds into the millions, funds for milk promotion budgets need to be raised either from the processors or directly from the farmers. If a farmer contributes three cents a gallon to a milk advertising campaign, that money comes directly out of that farmer's profits. If a farmer has sacrificed a family vacation to subsidize a "glitzy" new ad campaign, then the expectation is that the campaign will show some immediate results. Thus, once a budget is approved it is typically on a much smaller scale in commodity markets. To illustrate, the average $200 million brand will spend at least $5 million on advertising and another $5 million on promotions to the trade. In contrast, a commodity board usually spends about $5 million total—including advertising, promotion, marketing research, and public relations—to increase sales of a multibillion dollar category.

Not only are the budgets relatively smaller, but the commodity budgeting process itself is generally a slow moving, arduous system of approvals. Funding for budgets is accomplished through assessments—contributions from each producer or processor collected on a unit basis. These assessments are usually in the form of mandatory collections put into law and administered by a government entity. Since these budgets are decided upon in advance, they are fixed. In contrast to packaged goods companies, commodity marketers cannot raise short term capital by selling off assets or dipping into an emergency common fund.

Commodity marketing is also much different in the division of promotional funds allocated between "push" and "pull" strategies. Commodities generally spend almost all of the funds raised to generate some sort of pull with consumers. Advertising on television, on radio, in print, on billboards, and scattered public relations spots are the most common tools used to increase sales. "Pushing" product through the channels of distribution is less popular. In fact, as with most major commodities, milk does not maintain a direct sales force to build relationships with retailers. With distribution penetration levels of 100 percent and equally impressive consumer penetration levels, the belief has been that there is not a pressing need to motivate retailers to carry fluid milk.

DEMAND SIDE DIFFERENCES IN COMMODITY MARKETING

The demand side of commodity marketing is also quite different than the marketing of a traditional brand. The paramount challenge for commodity marketers is to attempt to change consumer attitudes and behaviors toward an entire category as opposed to trying to increase market share of a brand. Although difficult to change, category attitudes do evolve over time, and when they do change, the results can be quite dramatic. For example, a 1 percent increase in the consumption of milk can result in literally hundreds of millions of dollars of extra revenue to the dairy industry. Commodity marketers learned about the potentially deleterious impact of changing consumer attitudes from experiences in the beef industry. In 1950, cattlemen and meat market retailers across the country would have laughed at the notion of poultry ever coming remotely close to beef in popularity. Yet in 1990, poultry consumption passed beef in terms of per capita consumption. As the level of milk consumption has steadily declined for fifteen years, Manning feared a repeat of the beef industry.

Food commodity marketing is often closely tied to nutrition and health related issues. Nutritional issues are always "hot" items with the media, and commodity boards are frequently the target of various community activist groups. In addition, federal legislation can have a tremendous impact on the strategic options and potential market penetration of commodities, especially in global markets. The support of the medical community can also have a direct impact on sales, as demonstrated by the campaigns of oats (when oats were found to reduce cholesterol levels), eggs (when egg yolks were found to be high in cholesterol), and beef (when red meat in general was linked with high cholesterol).

Finally, demand for commodities can be dramatically influenced by other food industries. A new product in the food service industry or the consumer packaged goods industry can increase sales exponentially. For example, when Wendy's fast food restaurants introduced hot stuffed potatoes, they cleared the entire 8–12 ounce potato market almost overnight. Similarly, when McDonald's unveiled its new salads, the iceberg lettuce market boomed. The same is true of the packaged goods industry. A new ready-to-eat raisin cereal from Kellogg's can mean millions of dollars to the raisin industry. Sometimes these new products are introduced as a result of technological advancements that make them possible. Some commodity boards are capitalizing on such opportunities by investing more funds in research and development.

OTHER COMMODITY MARKETS

Recent marketing campaigns by the beef industry and the pork industry were the most relevant for the milk industry. In the late 1980s, the beef industry faced a similar situation as the milk industry faces now. Per capita beef consumption had been on the decline for a number of years. Between 1975 and 1987, per capita consumption of beef fell by over 16 percent, while per capita consumption of chicken skyrocketed by over 57 percent. In fact, the beef industry was influenced by some of the same health trends that influenced the milk industry. Consumers' concerns primarily centered around health issues, and the perception was that beef was unhealthy for the average person. Chicken, on the other hand, promoted itself as a healthy alternative to red meat. In addition to the decline in consumption and the health concerns, chicken was also putting pressure on the beef industry via innovative marketing techniques. Beef was sold in foam-packed, film-wrapped, leaky packages with fat and bones attached. Chicken unveiled new packaging that included small, convenient servings with brand names such as Tyson Foods and Holly Farms. Chicken producers also introduced boneless, skinless pieces that were low in fat and easy to cook.

In response to the decreased demand, the beef industry launched the $23 million "Real Food for Real People" campaign in 1987. Although the campaign showed early results that looked promising, it eventually proved unsuccessful, as unexpected problems arose from the spokespeople used in the advertisements. James Garner, a popular television actor, started experiencing heart trouble and underwent bypass surgery. The other main spokesperson, Cybill Shepherd—a popular television actress—was quoted that she "shuns the stuff." The negative publicity around these events resulted in the once promising campaign quickly making a turn for the worse. More recently, the beef industry has launched a new campaign entitled "Beef. It's What's for Dinner." The new campaign has seemed to strike a chord with consumers, increasing in-home purchase intent of beef by 14 percent in its first year.

The pork industry has been more effective at getting its message across to consumers. Prior to the most recent campaign, pork was a commodity with a clouded image—tasty, but full of fat and calories. Attempting to clear the confusion about its health content, the pork industry began running the campaign of "The Other White Meat." This campaign clearly positioned pork as more like chicken than beef. The campaign proved to be successful at changing consumer attitudes towards pork, and sales increased by over 17 percent from the period of 1975 to 1987.

The Beverage Category

The beverage category is characterized by intense competition and an ongoing proliferation of new products. According to a *Beverage Industry* survey, 1805 new beverages were introduced in 1991 alone. All types of beverages are included in category statistics, from beer and liquor to bottled water. Many large firms compete in the industry, spending millions of dollars on advertising and promotion. For example, media spending in the beverage category approaches $2 billion, with over half of the total accounted for by beer and soft drinks. Milk spends less than 10 percent the amount that beer spends on media. If beer and liquor sales are excluded from the totals, milk still only spends a paltry 4 percent of the total, even though its volume is three times that amount.

The beverage category has enjoyed tremendous growth in the last two decades. Since 1975, total consumption of beverages has increased by 18 percent. Although the category has increased substantially, milk is one of the few beverages to actually experience a decline in consumption over the same period. While soft drink per capita consumption increased by 80 percent from 1975 to 1991, milk consumption dropped by 10 percent and milk's market share dropped from 17 percent to 13 percent.

The winners in the nonalcoholic beverage industry have been soft drinks and more recently, bottled waters and fruit drinks. All of these beverage types are perceived to be light and refreshing by consumers. In addition, they are among the most active in new product introductions, actively pursuing opportunities in diet, decaffeinated, and clear beverages. These new products have capitalized on the latest industry trends—lighter flavors, more sophisticated "adult" flavors, less sweet, more refreshing drinks with fewer calories and natural ingredients. In terms of per capita consumption and household penetration, soft drinks are the clear leader. A brief discussion of the major beverage types follows.

SOFT DRINKS

Sales of soft drinks totaled $47 billion in 1991. Although soft drinks have posted the most impressive results over the last two decades, they have clearly lost some of their momentum. Sales increased 1.8 percent in 1991, despite previous forecasts of 5 percent. Even though per capita consumption actually decreased, it remains well above all other competitors at 47.3 gallons per year. Through innovative and creative advertising campaigns, soft drinks have managed to establish an upbeat image with consumers. Most advertising is targeted at the teenage segment and the "20-something" age group. Consumers perceive soft drinks to be trendy, active, fun, and young at heart. In contrast, milk is perceived as being dull and old fashioned. Overall sales of colas declined in 1991 while other soft drink flavors gained. Diet colas are now outperforming regular colas, and caffeine free soft drinks are the fastest growing segment.

JUICE/JUICE DRINKS

In 1991, the fruit drink segment and its companion fruit juices both grew very well, increasing sales by 5.2 percent to $10.2 billion. The rise in sales was mirrored by the first increase in per capita consumption in three years, up to 11.6 gallons per year. The growth in this segment is primarily attributable to the shift in consumer preferences for healthier beverages, the introduction of many new flavor combinations, and the extended distribution of single-serving packaging. While juices have traditionally been targeted to children or their mothers, the new campaigns have begun to sell directly to adults in the hope of appealing to their preference for healthier beverages. In addition to the nutritional, all-natural message, the new advertising focuses on taste, flavor, and excitement. The main advertising message is refreshment, presented with vibrant colors, music, and scenes of summer.

COFFEE

Sales of coffee decreased 7.5 percent in 1991 to $6.2 billion. Per capita consumption of coffee had been declining for almost a quarter of a century, but that trend has leveled off in the last four years. The current level is 26.5 gallons per individual, recently pushed up by sales of decaffeinated and specialty coffees. Decaffeinated coffees and "caffelite" (50 percent less caffeine) attract consumers concerned about health and are projected to represent one-half of all coffee sales by the year 2000. Specialty coffees have also been doing very well, appealing to consumer preference for variety and more distinct flavors. Chains such as Starbucks have been gaining popularity recently by creating a social atmosphere for drinking coffee.

Most coffees target the baby boomers in their advertising. Coffee's benefits are described as "a good way to start the day" and "fresh aroma, with a rich, flavorful taste." The imagery in coffee advertising is dominated by family situations, filled with relaxation and quiet times. Other images emphasize exotic, foreign countries that express the uniqueness of coffee as an international beverage. Specialty coffees are aimed at the upscale, college-educated segment, with ages from 25–44. The advertising for specialty coffees typically mimics the customer segment, appealing to trendiness with a bit of sophistication.

TEA

Although the overall tea market has been flat, the iced tea segment continues to grow. In 1991, iced tea represented 80 percent of total tea consumed. Iced teas are associated with attributes desired by consumers such as cool, clean, crisp, refreshing, and active. The advertising typically reflects the active and yet relaxed lifestyle of young adults. Coupled with this successful positioning, iced teas have also made giant leaps in sales as a result of new packaging that exploits the consumer's preference for convenience. New entrants, especially Snapple, have introduced easy-to-carry single servings with a variety of flavors at a point in time when these attributes are of high value to most consumers.

BOTTLED WATER

Sales of bottled water reached $2.6 billion in 1991, an increase of only 1 percent over 1990. This slow growth is in stark contrast to the double digit growth that bottled water had enjoyed for years. Attributing the slow sales to a recessive economy, projections for the future return sales growth to previous levels. Even with the disappointing results, per capita consumption reached 9.9 gallons, extending the long-term upward trend. In terms of advertising, bottled water is leading the trend for the beverage category. Bottled water is positioned as a healthier, lighter, less sweet beverage alternative. The advertising typically makes use of natural images and active lifestyles. Some products are targeted directly to health conscious adults as after exercise beverages. This positioning takes advantage of water's key attributes over soft drinks—more refreshing, easy to drink (gulpable), less sweet, and no calories.

Previous Milk Promotion Campaigns

Throughout the fifteen years of declining milk consumption there have been a number of advertising campaigns sponsored by one of the national or regional dairy boards. Milk advertising has traditionally communicated a three-tiered message to consumers:

Adults: Milk is good for you and should be a regular part of the diet.

Teens: Milk makes you beautiful and strong.

Kids: Milk is cool and fun.

Traditional milk advertising campaigns showed a member of the target group drinking a glass of milk, followed by a brief mention of the nutrients in each glass and the benefits that would accrue to the loyal milk drinker. This relatively simple formula has been a proven winner in terms of communicating the nutritional value of milk to consumers. As a result, consumer awareness represents a major strength in terms of the positive associations consumers hold for milk. A 1992 UDIA national consumer survey revealed the following:

- 80 percent agreed that "I like the taste of cold milk."
- 89 percent agreed that "Milk is a healthful drink."
- 91 percent agreed that "Milk is a good source of calcium."
- 83 percent agreed that "Milk is needed for growth."
- 74 percent agreed that "Adults should drink milk."
- 52 percent agreed that "I should drink more milk than I do."

In the early 1990s there were two dominant campaigns. The "Milk does a body good" campaign focused on the benefits of milk as part of a well balanced diet. In addition, the "Good fast food" campaign promoted milk, cheese, and other dairy products. Both campaigns were of national scope.

In recent years, conflicting reports from consumer advocates and the milk industry had created some confusion surrounding the health content of milk. First, even though prior campaigns had stressed the benefits of drinking milk, consumers remained confused about the nutritional value of whole milk, low fat milk, and even skim milk. In a Pennsylvania State University study, the majority of consumers did not know how much fat was in different types of milk. Over 40 percent and 57 percent of consumers did not know the fat content of low fat and skim milk, respectively. Over 65 percent did not know the fat content of whole milk, with most consumers believing that whole milk was 100 percent fat. The study also revealed that 30 percent of adults mistakenly believed that reducing the fat content in milk reduces the nutritional value.

In addition to the confusion about fat content, there was also widespread confusion about the effects of hormones used on dairy cows, the inability of some people to absorb calcium, whether milk causes childhood diabetes, and a new report from Dr. Spock that advised mothers not to feed their children under the age of 1 any milk at all. The milk industry had responded to these issues through press reports, but did not respond with a national advertising campaign.

Consumer Preferences for Milk in California

The per capita consumption of milk had been declining for over fifteen years before the commodity board decided to take some sort of action. Perhaps of greater concern to milk producers and processors was the trend of *accelerating* decline over the past few years. In 1987, per capita consumption of milk was 26.4 gallons per person in the state of California. By 1992, per capita consumption was down to 24.8 gallons per person. Aggregated over the state population, the decline represented a $50 million loss per year in the fluid milk industry. As a result, the charter of the CMPB was clear: Increase the sales and consumption of milk in California. In particular, Manning's primary goal was to keep the CMPB focused on getting people within the population of milk drinkers to consume the equivalent of one more eight-ounce glass of milk, in any form, per week. This seemingly modest goal was hardly an easily attainable objective. Not only was the CMPB charged with reversing the decline, but the processors wanted to actually increase consumption. If the goal of increasing consumption by one glass per week were achieved, the end result would be 3.25 incremental gallons per person, or an increase of over $100 million in profit per year.

As described above, previous advertising campaigns had been extremely effective in communicating the health benefits of milk to consumers—good news in an age of health consciousness. Whereas the 1980s witnessed the dawn of the age of health awareness, the 1990s were already proving to be the age of health education. People were not merely concerned about their health, they were now much more informed about what was good for them and how to distinguish the good from the bad. Starvation gave way to moderation. Many people now not only counted calories, but also distinguished calories from fat. Fat and cholesterol issues had even made their way into everyday news, as evident with the boom in oat bran after a medical report hailed its healthful qualities. A 1991 study by the Calorie Control Council revealed that one out of every four Americans reported that he or she was on a diet. The U.S. Department of Agriculture reported that over 50 percent of Americans were concerned about the amount of fat in their diets. The trend towards good health did not stop at mealtime. After an abundance of research extolling the virtues of regular exercise, the National Sporting Goods Association reported that sports participation was up 40 percent since 1984. Yet this trend of health consciousness also represented a point of concern. Rather than increase overall consumption of milk by virtue of its health benefits, the last ten years had marked a period of substantial cannibalization of milk sales: The gains in sales of low fat and skim milk had come at the expense of sales in whole milk.

Almost all consumers were aware of milk and its major types: whole, low fat (2 percent and 1 percent), and skim. Milk had a penetration of 66 percent of households in the United States in 1992, down from 72 percent in 1980. Total fluid milk sales in California had actually increased by 10.9 percent in the decade of the 1980s. However, that figure was misleading because the population increased by 26 percent over the same period. In 1992, the California's population was 31.3 million people. Accounting for those people who cannot or will not drink milk for various reasons such as lactose intolerance, the number of potential consumers in the state was 21.3 million people. Of those consumers, the heaviest users were under age 17. The youngest consumers drank the most milk—27.2 gallons per year—but consumption gradually declined with age, with the 60+ age group consuming only 9.4 gallons of milk per year. Indeed, these heavy milk users were of critical importance to overall consumption. Three in ten milk drinkers accounted for over 60 percent of total milk volume consumed. However, baby boomers comprised a significant segment of the population—38 percent of the California population was between the ages of 25–49, and another 25 percent was at least 50 years old. The aging California population sent both a positive and negative signal for milk sales. On the positive side, the baby boomers were now adults and should have begun to start families, bringing an influx of new children who would hopefully represent the heavy users of the future. On the other hand, as baby boomers aged, their milk consumption would continue to decrease, with a corresponding detrimental effect on per capita consumption.

Another positive trend for the CMPB was the changing ethnic composition of California. California traditionally attracted an extremely diverse population. In fact, by 2040 the white population was projected to be a minority in the state. Latinos were one of the fastest growing ethnic groups in the state, and the U.S. Census Bureau estimated that Latinos would comprise virtually half of the state's population in the year 2040. The good news for the CMPB was that Latinos also represented an important segment of heavy users. As a group, Latinos drank almost one-third more milk than the average individual. Latinos also drank significantly more whole milk than the rest of the population and usually bought larger sizes of milk.

Finally, research indicated that the family unit and home life was closely linked with milk. Of all milk volume consumed in the United States, 89 percent was consumed at home. Of the remaining milk consumption occasions, 5 percent occurred at schools, and the remainder was scattered at various other establishments. Both nostalgia and ritual helped to account for this strong link between milk and the home. "Nostalgia" refers to the long-standing heritage of milk consumption in the United States. The milkman making weekly deliveries is mentioned by consumers as one of the more vivid memories of experiences with milk. "Ritual" refers to the tendency for milk habits to be passed on from generation to generation. Many families drank milk on a regular basis at specified times—at breakfast in cereal, at lunch with a sandwich, and at dinner with the family meal. In fact, 83 percent of all milk consumption occasions were at meal time. In addition, many mothers regularly encouraged their children to drink milk. Research had shown that heavy adult users tended to have children that were also heavy users.

Nostalgia and ritual are grounded in history, however, and times were changing. The U.S. Census Bureau statistics revealed that the modern family size was shrinking. In 1970, the average family included 2.5 kids; by 1990, the average was 2.1 kids per family. In addition, there were now many more mothers in the workplace. In 1970, 49 percent of mothers with school age children kept a job as well. In 1990, the number of working mothers had increased to 74 percent. An outgrowth of the trend of working mothers was the surge in meals eaten outside of the home. According to an S&MM survey of buying power, Californians were spending substantially more money eating outside of the home. In 1982, per capita out of home consumption was $560, but by 1987 that number had risen to $760, a 36 percent increase. These trends did not bode well for milk consumption, a beverage consumed primarily by families inside their homes.

The UDIA Consumer Study

In 1992, the UDIA commissioned a marketing research study to investigate the reasons behind the perpetual decline of per capita milk consumption. The study attempted to gauge consumer preferences by taking a qualitative approach, conducting 1,252 personal interviews with consumers of all age groups to talk about milk and other beverages.

FACTORS AFFECTING CONSUMPTION

The UDIA study revealed several input factors that may have been playing a role in the decline of milk consumption. These input factors varied in the amount of direct CMPB control.

Proliferation of Other Beverages

There has never been more competition for nonalcoholic beverages. Recent trends have been towards healthier, better tasting beverages such as diet soft drinks, iced teas such as Snapple, thirst quenchers such as Gatorade, mineral and bottled waters such as Calistoga, and natural juices such as Odawalla. As evidence to the abundance of beverages, the average American family has fifteen different beverages in the refrigerator at any given moment in time.

Lack of Portability

In today's modern world, the lack of portability hurts milk consumption more than ever. Ninety percent of the consumption occasions for milk are inside the home, but over half of all of the meal occasions are outside of the home. Milk is a perishable product, and it simply does not travel well. As a result, milk stays behind when people leave their home. Yet milk is not an attractive beverage even when it is readily available outside the home. As Manning puts it, "The mother who is at home making sure that the children drink milk and only milk with all meals at home is also the same person who says 'OK' to a Coke at McDonald's when she asks them what they want to drink." Indeed, this type of behavior has begun to make its way to the bottom line. For example, milk's share of beverage transactions at the Carl's Jr. fast food chain has declined every year for the last six years. Whenever a person leaves the home, milk automatically becomes a less competitive beverage. This behavior is evident even in the heavy user segment. While the heavy users drink ten times the number of glasses of milk than light users inside the home, they only drink three times as much milk outside of the home.

Lack of Flavor Variety

To many, milk essentially comes in one flavor. The lack of variety of milk flavors is especially relevant today since other beverages are flooding the market with a myriad of flavored drinks. For example, Snapple offers over fifty different flavors of its beverages. People generally like more flavors, as they do in iced teas, specialty coffees, and soft drinks. Development of new flavors, however, could take three to five years. Moreover, even assuming new flavors could be developed, the centralized advertising budget could considerably lengthen the new product introduction process.

That is, the pooled funding of advertising would not allow any campaign to begin until all forty processors had invested in the processing equipment to be able to bring the new products to market.

Packaged goods providers have had some success with flavored milk recently. Nestle released a Butterfinger flavored milk and Borden released a root beer milk, both of which have been growing in sales. On the other hand, other Borden flavors and Hershey's flavored milk have been struggling to gain share. Nevertheless, analysts are positive on the prospects for flavored milk, and attribute the failures of Hershey on the lack of innovative flavors. Consumer opinions on the newly released flavored milks are mixed: Kids seem to love them but the parents remain skeptical of the benefits. Sales of flavored milk were up 8 percent in 1992 to reach a total of $172 million.

Not Thirst Quenching

A significant amount of those interviewed mentioned that one big problem with milk is lack of refreshment. Milk is not ice cold, it is not carbonated, it is not available in a portable bottle that is ready any place, any time, whenever they are thirsty. Consumers have noted the lack of overall refreshment, the inability to "gulp" when thirsty, and the lack of a clean, crisp taste as significant barriers to milk as a thirst-quenching beverage.

Lack of Consumer Mind Share

Milk has always been a fairly "forgettable" beverage. At specific times during the day or with specific foods, milk is irreplaceable. For example, in the morning and late at night, milk is extremely popular; with cookies, peanut butter sandwiches, cereal, or coffee, it is often seen as a must. However, beyond these particular consumption occasions, foods, or outside of the house, milk is usually forgotten.

Competitive Spending Level

In comparison to other beverages, milk lags well behind its competitors in terms of spending on advertising and promotion. Beverage companies spend a lot of money on advertising, making it more difficult than ever to get any advertising through to consumers. The total media spending was $70 million for milk nationwide in 1992. Total spending is easily dwarfed by other players in the beverage industry—beer media spending was $760 million alone, and soft drinks spent $498 million. To make matters worse, soft drinks and fruit juices both target the same segment prized by the milk industry: teenagers and children.

Shared Nature of Consumption

As mentioned previously, milk has become a part of most families through ritual and nostalgia. With such high penetration levels, virtually all people drink milk at some time during the day. Quite often, milk is a family experience. Mothers encourage children to drink milk at snack times, and fathers encourage them to drink milk at dinner. Not surprisingly, many families have more than one type of milk available in the refrigerator. Less obvious is the fact that most people are not loyal to a specific milk type. Even health conscious skim milk drinkers are apt to drink other kinds of milk. In fact, whole milk drinkers are more loyal than skim milk drinkers. The consumption of multiple milk types underscores the shared nature of milk within a household. Milk is typically a family beverage, open to anyone in need. This shared feature of milk often leads members of a family to pace themselves and "ration" milk. If there is not enough milk for their cereal in the morning, people will tend not to eat the Oreos with milk the night before. This restrained behavior could restrict the overall consumption of milk per household.

RELATIONSHIP OF MILK WITH OTHER FOODS

The research included a host of transcripts from individual customer interviews and focus groups. In these interviews consumers related their consumption experiences with milk. Below are some of the typical quotes from consumers, listed by age and sex:

> "With things like Oreos or any other kind of cookies or cake, none of these would be good without a big glass of milk."
>
> —female, mid-30s

> "At night with cereal, or for dunking Oreos."
>
> —female, mid-20s

> "It's a pain in the a— because you usually find out (that you're out of milk) just after you pour the cereal."
>
> —male, late-30s

> "Of course you get P-O'd because there's not enough (milk). You can barely dampen your cereal."
>
> —female, mid-30s

> "Even Cream-o-Wheat is a drag without milk."
>
> —female, 20s

> "What are Cheerios? They're nothing. But you add milk and it's everything."
>
> —male, late teens

These quotes highlight the close-knit relationship between milk and other types of food including cereal and cookies. Time and time again, consumers told detailed tales of milk and its close ties with other foods. These experiences emphasize the versatility of fluid milk: Milk is used as a beverage ingredient in coffee and milk shakes; as an accompaniment to sweets such as Oreos and brownies; as a staple with cereal and sandwiches; and in cooking recipes such as soups and mashed potatoes.

Indeed, beverages as a food complement was identified as one of the highly motivating forces to encourage consumers to drink beverages in general, and milk in particular. Surprisingly, nutritional requirements are only moderately motivating in beverages as a whole. Hence, the end-user benefits of milk—good for you, look and feel healthier—moderately motivate consumers to drink milk at any point in time. Some consumers felt that if a beverage must be cold to taste good or if the drink has a strong taste, these are demotivators to drinking it. For teenagers, "done something good for myself," "goes well with sweets," "satisfyingly rich," and "complements a hearty meal" were the most effective motivators.

Among the associations that were deemed highly motivating across all usage occasions of beverage consumption are "good value," "always fresh," and "perfect complement to a hearty meal." Although nutritional value was not a highly motivating attribute for milk, it was a highly motivating attribute at breakfast. Refreshing proved to be a highly motivating attribute at all meal occasions except for breakfast, where nutritional value may have overshadowed refreshment. A highly motivating attribute at dinner was the fact that "the family can enjoy milk together."

POTENTIAL CONSUMER SEGMENTS FOR MILK

The UDIA study also attempted to identify the profiles of consumer segments for milk. Many different demographic and psychographic segmentation analyses were attempted in the study. Apart from two major findings—milk consumption has an inverse relationship with both age and income level—they all failed to reveal major differences between milk consumers. Using a combination of input variables, four different adult segments and a teenage segment were identified: the "ever nourished," the "insatiables," the "occasional indulgers," the "different drummers," and the teenage segment. Each of the segments is briefly profiled in the following paragraphs.

The Ever Nourished

This segment earned its name by their ever-present desire for a healthy beverage. They prefer a beverage that "does something good for themselves" throughout the day. Even at dinner, the Ever Nourished prefer a beverage that is "full of vitamins and minerals." In some respects, this segment considers beverages as doubling for food. In terms of size, the Ever Nourished comprise 18 percent of all adult milk drinkers. 70 percent of consumers in this segment have kids.

The Insatiables

This segment was named after their "insatiable" desire for a beverage that can double as a snack throughout the day. This segment is predominantly male (60 percent) and single (60 percent). In addition, this group tends to be more blue collar and slightly less educated than the others. In terms of eating habits, the Insatiables are the least concerned about health and nutritional issues. The Insatiables seem to prefer milk for its "fillingness" rather than its health benefits.

The Occasional Indulgers

This segment is unique in its desire to balance health and nutritional needs with indulgence in various snacks. Since they enjoy indulging in unhealthy snacks to treat themselves, the Indulgers make up for their vices by primarily drinking skim milk. This segment represents 29 percent of all milk drinkers, and earn the highest income of the four segments identified.

The Different Drummers

Although they consume the fewest beverages overall, when they do seek a beverage the Different Drummers seek those that suit their individual needs and tastes or come in a variety of flavors. The most typical beverages selected are coffee and soda. Different Drummers are the largest segment, representing 30 percent of all adults. Yet they account for the smallest portion of potential sales, a meager 10 percent of the total potential sales from all segments.

Developing a Branding Strategy for Milk

Typical of most commodity markets, the milk industry had been reactive instead of proactive when it came to marketing. For years, the problems of the milk producers in terms of declining per capita consumption had been obscured by the more dominant trend of increasing population. With population growth slowing in California, the industry players could no longer afford to overlook the decline in consumption. To meet CMPB's objectives of reversing the declining trend in per capita milk consumption, Manning was considering several strategic options.

INVEST IN R&D TO EXPAND THE NUMBER OF FLAVORS AVAILABLE

A primary drawback revealed in consumer perceptions of milk was the lack of flavors. This problem was especially acute in light of the proliferation of flavors from competing beverages such as iced teas, mineral waters, and sodas. While those products are perceived as "trendy" and "cool," milk is perceived as "dull" and "boring." The flavored milks that had been introduced thus far had achieved modest success. At a time when white milk sales are slipping, flavored milk sales are up by over 8 percent in 1993. One advantage of this strategy is that it would elevate milk from the usual commodity product up to the competitive level of other beverages such as soft drinks. An industry consultant states this objective directly, "The advice that I give the dairy industry is to get out of the milk business and into beverage or snack business." A multitude of flavors would simultaneously address the lack-of-flavor issue as well as the thirst-quenching issue raised by consumers.

EXPAND THE POTENTIAL USAGE OCCASIONS

One perceived drawback for milk revealed in the UDIA consumer study was its lack of portability. If the CMPB could develop new packaging materials that made milk more portable, the potential number of usage occasions for milk could significantly increase. For example, the iced teas that have recently swamped the market have been successful in part as a result of the convenient single servings that are transportable. Milk, in contrast, typically only offers one type of packaging per container size. In fact, the packaging for milk has not changed for years with the exception of moving from bottles to containers such as cardboards and plastics, which are less expensive to ship. With most mothers in the country strongly aware of the benefits of milk and in favor of milk consumption, increasing portability could lead to increased consumption opportunities.

The distribution of milk in alternative packaging is already available in Europe. An Italian company named Parmalat, the world's leading marketer of liquid milk, has introduced a packaged, shelf-stable milk that lasts five to six months without refrigeration. This "milk in a box" allows Italian families, many who do not have big refrigerators, to store milk in the cupboard. The key lies in the ultra heat treating (UHT) process developed by Parmalat. The results are no less than stellar. Parmalat has captured almost 35 percent of the UHT market, about 50 percent of the total milk market, and the product sells for 15 percent more than pasteurized milk.

DEVELOP AN EXTENSIVE PUSH STRATEGY
VIA A DIRECT SALES FORCE

Most commodities do not support any type of direct sales force that can help push product through the channel. Although this is standard practice, milk may stand to benefit the most if a direct sales force is hired because of the enormous impact that dairy products in general and milk in particular have on supermarket sales. As noted above, the dairy department triples the performance of the average grocery department in terms of sales per shelf foot, and fluid milk is the star product in the dairy department.

Although the dairy department yields these profits, it receives little attention from store managers. Part of the problem may be due to the lack of a direct sales force for milk. Store managers are constantly bombarded with sales representatives from other categories, allowing those other categories to receive extra attention. Without a sales person to keep the store manager focused on the profitability of milk for the store, milk producers have had trouble getting cooperation from retailers in obtaining promotions for milk, in-store displays, space allocations, and so on.

EXPAND THE MARKET THROUGH OTHER CHANNELS
SUCH AS FOODSERVICE AND SCHOOL CAFETERIAS

Expanding the market for milk has always been an attractive option. Research has consistently shown that over 80 percent of all milk consumption occasions are in the home. There has been a serious communications problem with consumers in this area. Most consumers have the perception that milk is a "baby beverage" outside the home. Considering that over half of all meal occasions are outside the home, milk is losing out on a quickly growing segment of the industry. As discussed above, commodities have met with success when fast food restaurants promoted their products. In addition to restaurants, the CMPB could reemphasize sales to school cafeterias. Once dominant in this segment, milk has lost considerable share as other beverages, including soft drinks, have made their way into cafeterias.

COOPERATE WITH CONSUMER PACKAGED GOODS
AND DO JOINT PROMOTIONS

In the focus groups, consumers were openly passionate about their experiences with milk. Most frequently mentioned were those experiences that involved a relationship between milk and another food such as cookies or cereal. Since consumers seem to think of milk in relation to other foods, and since consumer packaged goods companies typically have budgets that dwarf the dairy boards, it may make sense to establish a joint marketing campaign with the packaged goods companies to leverage their products and promotional budgets. Among the ideas under consideration are offering milk coupons with purchase of cookies or cereal, offering coupons for cookies or cereal on packages of milk, establishing special sections within supermarkets for "cookies and milk," running joint advertising campaigns with packaged goods companies, and so on.

EMBARK ON A CAMPAIGN TO CLEAR THE CONFUSION ABOUT THE HEALTH CONTENT OF MILK

As mentioned above, past milk advertising had generally been effective in communicating the benefits of drinking milk. Yet other groups have worked to undermine the effectiveness of the message by introducing other concerns, such as the use of hormone injections in dairy cows, the harmfulness of whole milk, the lack of nutrition in low fat milk, and the threat to even those who are not lactose intolerant. Concerns about health issues have both increased the potential for milk and decreased current sales as a result of consumer confusion. This confusion could be particularly detrimental to sales at a time when consumers are more determined than ever to live healthy lives.

A campaign to "set the record straight" on these issues could invite many consumers to try milk again or increase their consumption of milk. Education campaigns have worked for other commodities in the past. Pork had successfully cleared the air surrounding its nutritional content with the "The Other White Meat" campaign. In addition to the pork campaign, the Australian Meat and Livestock Corporation ran a phenomenally effective campaign to boost the sales of red meat during the late 1980s. The campaign, known as Short Cuts, won the Australian advertising industry prize for best campaign of the decade. A key part of the strategy was to educate consumers and dispel two prevailing myths about the levels of fat and cholesterol in red meat and the supreme nutritional superiority of chicken over red meat. The results of this campaign were unmatched. The number of consumers holding a strong conviction that "Beef and lamb are good for you" shot up from 66 percent at the beginning of the campaign to 84 percent at the end. Perhaps even more dramatic, by 1989 butchers had become the fastest growing segment of the retailing industry in Australia!

GENERATE AN IMAGE FOR MILK THROUGH ADVERTISING

Milk has yet to try and establish an image for itself with its advertising campaigns. While previous campaigns have been extremely effective in getting their message across, per capita consumption has still declined every year. Perhaps it is time that milk developed a more vivid image that would motivate consumers to drink more milk. Bottled water, perhaps the most undifferentiated commodity, had been particularly successful by developing an image of light, refreshing beverages that are thirst quenching. Similarly, there are those occasions where milk is the beverage of choice, and those occasions could be highlighted to develop an image for milk. Image advertising has also worked for other commodities in the past. One particularly successful example is the raisin industry's "California Raisins" campaign. The campaign depicted cute, cuddly California raisins in an innovative advertising format that was among the first applications of claymation technology. The new ads were an instant hit with consumers, and sales of raisins jumped accordingly.

TARGET LATINOS AND AGING AMERICANS

Latinos have been identified as heavy users of milk with positive attitudes and supporting behaviors at the supermarket. In addition, Latinos are expected to comprise almost half of California's population by 2040. Hence, they are an important segment to target and will only grow in importance in the years to come. Some feel that it is crucial to protect these loyal users now so that the future generations will not fall prey to alternative beverages. Aging Americans, on the other hand, represent the opposite end of the spectrum. These consumers are typically light users that decrease their consumption as they age. With baby boomers representing such a large segment of the population, they also merit special attention. If these consumers change their milk drinking habits, perhaps the increased consumption will also trickle down to their children's consumption rates. Finally, another benefit of this strategy is that it targets segments of the population that are not emphasized by other beverages, hence milk advertising may obtain the most value.

Strategy Implementation

Upon reviewing each option, Manning recalled the objective of increasing consumer consumption of milk by one glass per week. Given that the CMPB was created especially for this task with only a two-year charter, Manning felt a sense of urgency to act quickly. After carefully considering all the options, Manning and representatives from his advertising agency, Goodby Silverstein and Partners in San Francisco, decided that the best strategy to increase the per capita consumption of milk was to embark on a new, innovative advertising campaign. Nobody doubted that previous milk campaigns successfully achieved positive shifts in consumer attitudes towards milk. What was missing, however, was a corresponding change in consumer behavior. Consumers knew milk was good and thought they should drink more of it, but they never thought enough about milk to be motivated to change their consumption habits. The typical milk campaign—emphasizing calcium and other vitamins—caused consumers to tune out. The recommended campaign had to break the mold for milk advertising, grab attention, and shake consumers out of their "milk malaise." Manning knew that other beverages had successfully built up strong brand images over the last decade, and he believed that milk could do the same by taking a more light-hearted approach that talked directly to consumers. Manning reflected back on the decision:

> . . . the dairy industry has taken itself too seriously. Eating is a form of entertainment . . . the most popular form of entertainment in California, the USA, and the world. Get people smiling at your advertising and they will look, listen, and, we believe, consume more milk.

Given the limited resources of the CMPB, the new campaign had to address the behavior issue directly and quickly.

CAMPAIGN OBJECTIVES

Although the new advertising campaign was not like anything ever tried before in commodity marketing, the campaign was being funded by the commodity board and had to satisfy their objectives, as follows:

1. *Change consumer behavior.* The CMPB's foremost priority was to increase milk consumption by one occasion per week. Positive attitudes towards milk failed to reverse the decline in consumption. It was felt that the new campaign should change the way consumers think about milk, which would hopefully increase the potential number of milk occasions.

2. *Make consumers think about milk.* Although so many people drink milk everyday, milk suffered from a complete lack of consumer mind share. People just did not think about milk often enough at home, and they almost never thought about milk outside of the home. In order for any campaign to be successful, this lack of mind share had to change. One way to implement the change was to get consumers to stop taking milk for granted, to take them by surprise by creating a new and different image for milk.

3. *Halt sales decline.* Obviously, sales represented the bottom line for the CMPB. The advertising campaign needed to motivate people to buy more milk and subsequently get people to drink more milk. A high awareness campaign that did not result in subsequent changes in milk consumption would not be acceptable.

TARGET MARKET

In order to generate quick results, it was decided to target "regular" users of milk who used the product several times a week or more. Regular users—70 percent of the California market—already had favorable attitudes toward drinking milk and presumably could potentially be influenced in the short-term. In contrast, nonusers or light users typically restrained from milk for actual or perceived health reasons that probably could not be changed very quickly. Manning explained:

> If the 21 million people in the state that we regard as our "marketing universe"—those people who regularly consume milk in any form, be it a glass of milk, a bowl of cereal, instant pudding, or whatever—increased consumption by just one serving a week in any form, consumption of milk would increase in California by 9–13 percent.

Since milk was a popular beverage across a wide range of demographic and psychographic groups, past segmentation strategies were of little use. Instead, regular users were segmented according to behavior. Marketing research revealed that many consumers had specific times where milk was clearly the beverage of choice. These occasions typically identified milk as the perfect complement to certain foods. For example, marketing research revealed that cereal, cookies, and peanut butter and jelly sandwiches all *needed* milk or the foods were seen as simply not the same. Regular users recognized this intimate relationship of milk with food, and they openly discussed the complementary foods in focus groups.

The behavior segmentation strategy focused attention on *when* and *where* consumers drink milk. First and foremost, almost all milk is drunk at home. The UDIA study had shown that consumers rarely drink milk outside of the home, and even when they drink milk at home it is generally during the same usage occasions. Second, as discussed above, milk is considered an essential complement to certain types of foods. The focus groups revealed that consumers talked about milk with other foods, not as a drink by itself. This was particularly revealing because although the questions typically began with a general statement about milk, the discussions almost always gravitated to milk with food. Third, consumers tended to discuss milk and these foods as though they were the same food. Oreos and milk, peanut butter and jelly sandwiches and milk, and so on was common. It became evident that not only were these foods highly associated with milk, but that these foods were the driving force behind milk consumption and the potential key to any future increase.

"GOT MILK?" CAMPAIGN CREATIVE DEVELOPMENT

Based on the market research, Manning and the Goodby Silverstein and Partners advertising agency decided to reach out to the regular users with a "deprivation strategy." The most effective way to capitalize on milk's relationship with food was to create an advertising campaign that paired the two together. Each ad in the campaign highlighted one of milk's perfect complements: cereal, chocolate chip cookies, peanut butter and jelly sandwiches, and so on. The clever creative twist, however, was to deprive the main character of milk. The end result was delicious food *without milk*—the deprivation strategy. Certain foods without milk represented "cruel and unusual punishment" to most people, and the advertising campaign would set out to drive this message home. In each of the ads, a meal or snack is essentially ruined because of the absence of milk. Manning expressed his thoughts:

> Sell milk with food. The idea is almost frighteningly simple and obvious. And yet, as we reviewed milk advertising from around the country (and from around the world), we found that food was almost totally absent. We don't know why. Perhaps in an attempt to compete against soft drinks, the dairy industry lost contact with its roots. Consumers haven't. They will tell you time and time again that food—certain foods—drive their milk decision.

The television ads gradually built the tension that was so critical to the deprivation strategy. Each television ad began with a close-up of one of the food complements such as the peanut butter and jelly sandwich. Once the desire for the food is established, the protagonist takes a big bite. While joyfully chewing the food, the protagonist casually reaches for a glass of milk. Unfortunately, there is no more milk left in the container. A desperate search for even a single drop ensues, but all efforts are in vain. At the height of anguish, the voiceover pronounces: "Got milk?"

The "Got milk?" tagline urged consumers to quickly run to the refrigerator to make sure the answer was "yes." It was felt that this deprivation strategy would bring back the consumer mind share for milk and begin to recreate a positive image for milk as a beverage. The ads were humorous and well received by focus groups. The campaign broke away from previous milk advertisements in two important ways. First, there was never any mention of how milk could benefit a healthy diet. Consumers presumably already knew about the benefits, so the new campaign instead urged them to change their behavior. Second, milk was never actually shown in the ads. Whereas in the past, milk was shown without food, in the new campaign, food was shown without milk. It was felt that the deprivation strategy would increase mind share for milk precisely because the ads hit consumers where milk (or lack thereof) hurt them the most.

ADDITIONAL COMMUNICATIONS PROGRAMS

The creative strategy lent itself to using complementary foods as promotional tools for milk. If consumers purchased more of the foods that naturally went with milk, they should also buy more milk. Joint promotions were run with many major brands including each of the types of foods featured in the advertising campaign. One of the more bold joint promotions was a Wheaties cereal box with the "Got milk?" logo in place of the brand name. Other promotions included milk coupons on many recognizable brands of complementary foods located throughout the supermarket, point of purchase displays, shelf talkers at the complementary food locations, and "Got milk?" checkout dividers. Billboards were also used extensively to reinforce the television campaign. The billboards featured the same foods as the television ads with one bite taken out. Of course, each billboard prominently displayed the key question: Got milk?

The additional communication programs complemented the television advertising by focusing on the relationship between milk and food. Breaking with the past milk campaigns, Manning and his team decided to leverage milk's relationship with food by partnering with those foods instead of relying on pulling consumers over to the dairy case. The complementary television, radio, print, and billboard campaigns all leveraged this relationship and capitalized on the advertising budgets of several major brands of cereals and cookies.

MEDIA STRATEGY

In order to maximize the impact on consumer behavior, the media strategy focused on consumers in the place where they typically used milk—in the home—and where they typically bought milk—in the supermarket. According to Manning there were three ideal times to communicate the milk message: on the way to the store, in the store, and at home where milk could be immediately consumed. The media strategy complemented the overall communications strategy to reach this goal. The advertising creative strategy motivated consumers to crave the featured food and/or check their refrigerators for availability of milk. The media strategy therefore focused primarily on television as the medium, thereby catching consumers in their homes where 90 percent of total milk is consumed. Furthermore, the media buy for the ads typically concentrated on those times of day when consumers drank the most milk, that is, mornings during breakfast, late evening snacks, and so on. It was thought that timing ads in this manner—given the "call to action" nature of the campaign—could potentially lead to more impulse uses of milk. Each usage occasion was further broken down into the type of user in order to purchase television advertising time. Children were targeted in the early morning hours as well as late afternoons, while adults were targeted at prime time and late night snack times.

In order to capitalize on the remaining communications expenditures within the store, the "Got milk?" billboards were located near supermarkets as a reminder to consumers before they entered the store. The heavy dose of outdoor advertising included a variety of billboards and signs at bus shelters. The intention was to get consumers thinking about milk before they entered the store in order to motivate them to buy milk once they were inside.

Finally, a key objective of the media strategy was to advertise at a level competitive with other beverages. The annual budget of $23 million more than doubled the previous year's spending and placed milk among the top ten advertising spenders in all of California, on par with Coca Cola and Budweiser. Hence, the campaign possessed the muscle to compete with other beverages for the first time in milk advertising history. Only one question remained: Would the deprivation strategy work?

Results

The "Got milk?" campaign was launched in November 1993. Although focus groups indicated that consumers liked the ads, the actual launch exceeded all expectations. The campaign zoomed to a 60 percent aided recall level in only three months, and surpassed the long-running "Does a Body Good" campaign in top-of-mind awareness in less than a year. The "Got milk?" campaign quickly became a consumer favorite. "Since the ad campaign began, it has reached a near-cult following," commented a reporter for the L.A. Times.

Not only did the campaign get consumers talking, it also changed their actual milk consumption. The number of consumers who reported consuming milk at least "several times a week" jumped from 72 percent at the start of the campaign to 78 percent a year later. California household consumption of milk increased every month after the launch except for the first two months that the campaign began. This performance was in sharp contrast to the rest of the country where consumption actually declined over the same period. In the year prior to the campaign launch, California milk processors experienced a decline in sales volume of 1.67 percent or $18 million. A year after the launch, sales volume increased 1.07 percent or $13 million, for a total turnaround of $31 million. On a month-to-month comparison, volume had jumped 6.08 percent by the end of the first year, with momentum increasing every month.

The unprecedented success of the "Got milk?" campaign in California led to its purchase by the national dairy board in 1995. The national board paid the California processors for the rights to the ads, much of which has been put back into media spending. The campaign was also a hit with the advertising industry, winning the coveted Effie Award in 1995 and Advertisement of the Year by several major advertising award committees. The print and billboard advertisements met with similar accolades, including best campaign awards.

With the huge success of the "Got milk?" campaign and the trend of increasing fluid milk sales in California, the question turned to how to keep up the momentum. Can the "Got milk?" campaign keep reinventing itself and keep its status as a favorite with consumers? Or should the CMPB reallocate its efforts into other projects to insure that the per capita consumption of milk never experiences another decline?

Discussion Questions

1. What are the problems or challenges faced by the CMPB?
2. What associations do consumers have for milk? What are the implications of these associations in terms of building brand equity for and increasing the consumption of milk?

3. Evaluate the CMPB marketing program. What do you see as its strengths and weaknesses? Would you do anything differently? What should be their next steps?

Note

1. This case was made possible through the cooperation of the California Milk Processor Board and the assistance of Executive Director Jeff Manning. Sanjay Sood prepared this case under the supervision of Professor Kevin Lane Keller as the basis for class discussion.

APPENDIX D   Nivea: Managing a Brand Portfolio[1]

Background

At the 1993 annual management committee planning meeting, the top managers of Beiersdorf's (BDF) Cosmed Division had gathered to plot the division's corporate strategy for the coming year. BDF was the manufacturer of Nivea skin care and personal care products. The Cosmed Division of BDF, headed by Dr. Rolf Kunisch, oversaw product development and marketing of all Nivea cosmetics and toiletries products internationally. The Nivea brand was known on a worldwide basis, although its presence was strongest in Europe where it was a leading mass market brand.

During the last two decades, BDF's Cosmed Division had successfully extended the Nivea brand from a very limited range of products—Nivea Creme, Milk, Soap, and Sun—to a full range of skin care and personal care products. Over time, these different product lines had established their own identities as "sub-brands," independent of and yet still connected to the Nivea Creme core brand. Given the breadth of products now sold under the Nivea name, however, there had become increasing debate as to how to achieve the proper synergy between the Nivea Creme core brand and the sub-brands from other product classes. In planning future developments, Cosmed management sought to define a strategy that would ensure the Nivea brand met the market needs of the 1990s while also remaining true to the heritage of Nivea, as exemplified by Nivea Creme.

In planning the division's marketing plan and communication strategy for the coming year, Cosmed management found itself grappling with a number of fundamental questions. What common brand associations should be communicated for the various sub-brands? What brand associations should be unique to specific sub-brands? Would it be possible to promote the sub-brands in conjunction with the Nivea brand and not jeopardize their independent brand identities? What should be the role of the Nivea Creme core brand in the Nivea brand franchise? How could the traditional Nivea Creme image be maintained if the company also needed to innovate and modernize it?

Cosmed management had to resolve these issues at this planning meeting. They had to leave the room with a clearly defined set of guidelines in order to provide the various product managers sufficient time to develop and implement their product marketing plans for the coming year. In particular, they had to determine the role of Nivea Creme in the brand portfolio and the supporting roles taken by other brands. Also, they needed to decide whether they should introduce corporate or umbrella brand advertising.

Development of the Nivea Brand: 1912–1970

Nivea Creme was first introduced into the German market in 1912. In the early 1900s, industrialization led to the emergence of mass markets and branded articles. Society—women in particular—began to appreciate to a greater degree physical appearance and to look for products to both care for and beautify the skin. Prior to the introduction of Nivea Creme, fat-only skin cremes were all that were available, sold primarily to upper-class women. Nivea Creme's unique water-in-oil emulsion was the first creme to offer both skin care and protection at a reasonable price. The Nivea name came from the Latin word, nives, meaning "snow"—reflecting the snow white color of Nivea Creme. As the world's first multipurpose, "universal" skin creme, Nivea Creme took skin care "out of the boudoir and onto the boulevards . . . democratizing a piece of luxury." Nivea Creme was quickly adopted for use by the entire family. Nivea Creme was introduced throughout Europe in 1912, in the United States in 1922, and in South America and other parts of the world in 1926.[2]

Recognizing the value of Nivea Creme and the need for other reasonably priced skin care products, Beiersdorf introduced over forty-eight other skin care products under the Nivea brand name between 1911 and 1970. As BDF expanded its range of product offerings, it maintained a "mono-product" philosophy—typically offering one multipurpose product in each skin care market segment and category it entered.

Throughout this period, Nivea Creme remained the company's primary product and the carrier of the Nivea brand name. The famous Nivea Creme blue tin with white lettering, standardized in 1925, was a familiar sight in millions of households worldwide. In addition to Nivea Creme, the brand's other primary products during this period were body soap and powder and two sun care products—tanning lotion and oil.[3]

Though Nivea products were sold worldwide, BDF was primarily a German company until the mid-1960s/early 1970s. Products were introduced and brands were built primarily around local German needs. This product development strategy reflected the fact that after World War II, BDF did not own the Nivea trademark in many countries where Nivea products were sold. BDF had sold or transferred these rights to its many local distributors in the early 1930s in the wake of the rise of the National Socialists to power in Germany.[4] In those countries where BDF had not trans- ferred the Nivea trademark itself, the local distributors were given trademark rights as part of the distribution of German business assets by the Allied governments at the end of World War II. As of 1945, BDF owned the Nivea trademark in only two coun- tries—Germany and Austria. Within 8 years, BDF began to repurchase trademark rights—a process that would take over 50 years to complete.

NIVEA CREME BRAND IDENTITY AND VALUES

Over the years, Nivea—primarily through Nivea Creme—had acquired a unique, widely-understood brand identity as a "caretaker" of skin. Used by the entire family, Nivea Creme had a universal, uni-sex brand image. Throughout Europe, most users were first introduced to Nivea Creme during their childhood, learning that it was a product that could be used by the entire family to satisfy all kinds of needs. Because of consumer's own personal history and brand advertising, Nivea had become strongly associated with shared family experiences—e.g., mother and child relation- ships, family vacations at the beach, etc. The childhood and family associations of Nivea users facilitated the development of a rich set of other brand associations such as "care," "mildness," "reliability," "gentleness," "protection," "high quality," "feel- ing good," and "reasonably priced." Over time, the Nivea name became synonymous with protection and caring for the skin and attained a special, almost mythical status among users. By the 1960s, Nivea Creme could be found in almost every German household and in the majority of households across Europe and was the dominant multipurpose skin creme worldwide.

EARLY NIVEA ADVERTISING

BDF first began advertising Nivea products—primarily Nivea Creme—in 1912. The company viewed advertising as a means of strengthening consumer perceptions after a Nivea product had established a quality reputation for itself. For over sixty years, Nivea advertising promoted the basic themes of skin care and protection. Ads were always simple, plain, and informative. In the 1910s and 1920s, BDF advertised three main Nivea products—cream, soap, and powder. Early ads established the image of the Nivea woman as clean, fresh, and natural. Nivea's ads in the mid-1920s introduced the "bright and shining" boys—three brothers from Hamburg—and extended the freshness and natural image to the entire family, capturing the attention of mothers throughout Germany.

Over time, Nivea ads were altered to reflect changes in self-images and lifestyles. For example, in the 1920s, when German women were becoming more ac- tive athletically, Nivea ads began to show women in more outdoor and active settings. In the 1930s, when tanning came into fashion, BDF responded by highlighting the skin protective qualities of Nivea Creme and introducing a new product—Nivea oil— to protect against sunburn. In the 1950s, following the end of World War II, Nivea ads reflected the German population's desire to enjoy life by showing Nivea products used in relaxed and happy settings, primarily outdoors in the fresh air and sunshine.

While the settings of the ads changed, the clean, fresh, and natural image of the Nivea woman remained essentially unchanged. Though she was modernized to reflect the styles of the time, she was always a face with whom the average woman could identify. Over time, Nivea ads sought to link the clean, fresh, and natural image of the Nivea user to related elements of nature—fresh air, light, and sunshine. The development of these associations was particularly strong in Nivea's sun care ads. In these ads, BDF additionally introduced special objects and symbols to strengthen the linkage of these associations. For example, in its 1932 sun care campaign, BDF introduced the Nivea weather calendar—a graph that showed the "weatherman's" predictions for the summer months—to help Germans plan their summer holidays. This weather calendar became very popular in Germany and was used for decades to come. Later, in 1964, Nivea offered a blue beach ball with the Nivea logo as part of a holiday season pack that contained a variety of skin care products. The Nivea ball was a tremendous success and could be found on beaches all over Europe, and throughout the 1960s and early 1970s, the Nivea ball was a recognizable symbol in Nivea sun care ads.

Nivea's First Competitive Challenge: The 1970s

During Nivea Creme's first fifty years, the market for multipurpose creme grew steadily. By 1970, Nivea held over 35 percent of the multipurpose cream market in Germany and majority market share in Europe. In the late 1960s and early 1970s, the multipurpose cream market changed substantially as BDF faced its first strong competition in sixty years. Henkel-Khasana, a small German toiletries company and subsidiary of Henkel, launched its own multipurpose cream—Creme 21—in 1972. A direct copy of Nivea Creme, this product was backed by extensive advertising and a distribution strategy designed to take advantage of a broader, fundamental shift in consumer purchase habits for cosmetics from specialized outlets to mass market, self-service outlets such as food stores. Also at this time, a number of manufacturers—including Ponds, Unilever, and Lingner-Fisher (now part of Procter & Gamble)—introduced a variety of specialized creams into the market, particularly moisturizing creams, designed for specific skin care uses.

Concerned with this new competition and its effect on consumer perceptions of the Nivea brand, BDF commissioned a German university marketing professor, Reinhold Bergler, to perform a study of the Nivea brand image in the German market. Bergler's study found that, among both consumers and the trade, the Nivea brand enjoyed a high degree of goodwill and confidence, representing reliability, quality, and honesty. Yet, the brand had an "older" image and was not viewed as young, dynamic, and modern, as was the case with many of the recently introduced competitive brands.

In recognition of these new competitive challenges and current consumer perceptions of the Nivea brand, BDF developed a two-pronged strategy. First, BDF sought to stabilize the strong historical market position of Nivea Creme. Second, the company sought to exploit the strength of Nivea Creme by transferring the goodwill it had created for the Nivea brand to other product classes.

REVITALIZING NIVEA CREME

To address the first objective, BDF evaluated its current Nivea Creme marketing program. Because research showed that consumers liked Nivea Creme's current product formulation and logo, no changes were made there. The company did, however, introduce larger-sized units, alter its distribution strategy by shifting from special-line out-lets to food outlets, and increase its level of promotional activities with the trade and within stores. Nevertheless, the primary means to revitalize Nivea Creme's brand image was the introduction of a very aggressive ad campaign aimed directly at the competition.

The initial campaign, launched in spring 1971, used the tag line—"Nivea, the Creme de la creme"—for which a series of ads was developed. One of seven distinct slogans was used as a headline for each ad—for example, "There is none better," "No creme is better for your skin," "For sixty years, we have produced skin-care creme," and "If there was a better one, we would make it." These ads ran in magazines across Europe, though primarily in Germany.[5]

After two years of the "Creme de la creme" campaign, Cosmed developed a new series of ads directly aimed at updating the "old" brand image. The "Only Me" campaign ran internationally and made a new brand promise: Nivea Creme meets all skin care needs. With this campaign, Cosmed wanted to preserve Nivea's reputation for skin care competence and safeguard Nivea Creme's unique historical market position while also differentiating it from the competition. Prior to Henkel's Creme 21 introduction, the name Nivea had been synonymous for the skin cream product category. This new competition now forced BDF to more directly tell consumers about Nivea Creme's actual product benefits. Previous ads had always shown Nivea Creme used in a variety of settings but had never emphasized *specific* product benefits. Each ad in this new campaign highlighted a single, but different aspect of product performance. The objective was to negate competitors' claims for special creams by positioning Nivea Creme as the best cream for every kind of special need. Taken together, these ads reinforced caring and mildness as key consumer benefits and presented Nivea as the universal skin cream that embodied all the needs of consumers in one product.

The initial set of "Only Me" ads were introduced in 1973 in both print and television form. In Germany, the campaign made an emotional appeal to the hearts of the consumer by using folk art-like cartoon drawings. Each ad showed the blue and white Nivea tin being embraced by an element of nature—day, night, wind, snow, winter, summer, spring, at holiday time, at home, and others—and highlighted a specific purpose for the use of Nivea Creme. At the bottom of each ad was the slogan, "There is no better creme." The cartoon campaign ran in Germany from 1973–1988. Over the entire fifteen-year period, the ads consistently emphasized Nivea Creme's heritage and superiority through the same fundamental brand associations of caring, mildness, protection, quality, and confidence.

EXTENDING THE NIVEA BRAND

In addition to strengthening the brand image of Nivea Creme, BDF's second objective was to use the recognition and reputation of the Nivea brand name to introduce new products—both in categories where Nivea products were currently sold as well as in related categories where Nivea did not have a product. While BDF had been selling a variety of different products under the Nivea name for years, Nivea Creme—dominating company sales—was the primary image maker for the Nivea brand. Bergler's study clearly demonstrated that the Nivea brand had a strong, positive reputation in the marketplace with a great deal of consumer loyalty. Since the market for multipurpose cream was stagnating, BDF actively targeted new and growing market segments in which to extend the Nivea brand. The company's long-term objective was to evolve Nivea from a *skin cream* brand into a *skin care* brand by providing a range of new products that would both complement Nivea Creme and broaden the meaning of the Nivea brand name.

At this time, the Nivea family of products included: Nivea Creme, Nivea Milk, Nivea Baby (oil and powder), Nivea Sun oil and milk, and regular soap (sold only in Germany). To establish Nivea as a skin care brand, the company decided to create a family of products that symbolically could be represented as the "Nivea universe." At the center of the Nivea universe was the Nivea Creme core brand. Nivea products—some already existing, some new—would function as satellites around this center. Through this universe schematic, it was easy to identify the relationship between Nivea products. For example, the more distant the product class from the Nivea Creme core brand, the weaker the image link. Certain product classes—cream and sun in particular—were close to the core of the Nivea brand image, while other products were only distantly related.

Cosmed established a set of guidelines for Nivea brand extensions. All new products had to be compatible with the Nivea brand and targeted to market segments with attractive current and potential size. While the company wanted to expand the Nivea brand to include new product classes, their "mono-product" philosophy meant that there would be only one primary product promising consumers universal application in each product category. A second version or variety of a particular product could only be introduced if it satisfied a unique need not met by the current product(s) in its product category. The company further established a set of guidelines for any possible new products. Each product must:

1. Meet a basic need: clean and/or protect
2. Offer the special care/mildness benefit of Nivea creme
3. Be simple and uncomplicated
4. Not offer to solve only a specific problem
5. Maintain a leading position in terms of quality (at a minimum, be as good as the leading product)
6. Offer the product at a reasonable price such that the consumer perceived a balanced cost-benefit relationship
7. Offer the broadest possible distribution

These criteria were established to ensure that all products reflected the desired Nivea brand image and were consistent with the philosophy of providing high quality skin care products at a reasonable price. All new products were to offer "continuity plus innovation"—that is, maintaining the essential Nivea core while offering something new through the product itself. In addition, existing products were expected to be continuously modified and improved, reflecting Cosmed's product philosophy to follow market trends and to innovate through research and development. As one long-time Cosmed executive explained:

It was like taking a teaspoon of Nivea Creme and putting it into every new Nivea product as a special benefit—as an additional amount of care. In this way the new product was really a two-in-one product: satisfying a basic need *plus* offering the care of Nivea Creme as a symbol. For example, Nivea sun care products protect the skin, but in a mild and caring way.

Positioning Strategies for Nivea Sub-Brands

Over the decade of the 1980s, the Nivea category extensions grew into distinct sub-brands. To effectively establish the individual sub-brand images, the company histori-cally had adopted separate ad campaigns for each sub-brand. Consequently, each sub-brand had built its own personality and developed its own set of brand associations that were consistent with, but independent of, the Nivea Creme core brand image. Through its own ads, each sub-brand promoted the product attributes and benefits that best satisfied the needs of its target market, although a common "Nivea" message of quality and care existed in all ads. To reinforce this continuity, the word "care" (or a word with a similar connotation) was found in all ad headlines. In addition, all ads uti-lized the Nivea logo color code of blue background with white letters. Except for these two requirements, however, each product group was allowed to develop ads as it chose.

Until 1990, each of these new product classes carried its own set of descriptive category names to easily identify what the particular Nivea products were used for. Since products had historically been launched in the national language of the coun-try—in an effort to give the brand a local character—the same product often had dif-ferent names in different countries. Given the breadth of products and the increased integration of Europe, Cosmed management redefined the products names such that each product fell into one of the following product class groupings:

- Nivea Body
- Nivea Visage
- Nivea Sun
- Nivea for Men
- Nivea Shower & Bath
- Nivea Hair Care

NIVEA BODY

The Nivea Body sub-brand was one of BDF's smallest product groups, consisting of a moisturizing milk introduced in 1963 and a moisturizing lotion introduced in 1986. Nivea Milk was a water-in-oil emulsion like Nivea Creme, but in liquid form with Neocerit to provide long-term storage of moisture for dry skin. Nivea Lotion was an oil-in-water emulsion designed for daily care of normal skin. By offering liquid skin care for dry and normal skin in addition to the classic Nivea Creme, BDF sought to provide a comprehensive range of products that met the specialized skin care needs of different skin types.[6]

Nivea Milk and Lotion were advertised together at that time. A 1989 print ad headline read: "A first choice twice." The copy continued: "Nivea milk for the dry skin. Cares creamy and intensively, penetrates gently into the skin and the skin becomes soft and supple again. Nivea lotion for normal skin. Cares with a fresh perfume and is light as a lotion, penetrates quickly into the skin and gives the skin natural moisture." The tagline read: "What your skin needs to be beautiful."

In 1990, BDF changed the packaging of Nivea Milk and Lotion to be more consistent with other Nivea product packaging. The oval-shaped bottle was replaced with a more elongated, rectangular-shaped bottle. In addition, the Nivea logo and product name was placed inside a square box with a blue background and white lettering. Finally, in an effort to differentiate the lotion from the milk on the store shelf, Nivea Lotion was placed in a white bottle, while Nivea Milk remained in the traditional dark blue bottle. A new print ad headlined: "Your skin tells you what kind of care its needs." The copy followed: "Normal skin needs Nivea lotion: It compensates the daily moisture loss quickly. Dry skin needs Nivea milk: It cares intensively and long-lastingly protects [skin] from drying out."

The "Silk and Velvet" campaign in 1992 incorporated additional elements—primarily in text lettering type and color—that promoted a common "Niveaness" to all Nivea brand advertising. Run both as a print and television campaign, the primary message of the "Silk and Velvet" ads remained unchanged from previous ads. The headline of the print ad read: "For skin like silk and velvet." The copy continued: "With dry skin, Nivea milk. It cares intensively and long-lastingly protects [skin] from drying out. With normal skin, Nivea lotion. Tender care which compensates for the daily moisture loss." At the bottom the ad read: "Nivea milk and Nivea lotion."

NIVEA VISAGE

In 1982, Cosmed introduced its first set of face care products for women on a European-wide basis. Since 1960, Nivea France had offered three face care products sold under the Nivea Visage name—a cleansing milk, tonic, and moisturizing lotion.[7] Having repurchased trademark rights for France in 1974, BDF was able to introduce this product line into other European countries. Initially, the company introduced only the cleansing milk and tonic, fearing that a moisturizer would cannibalize sales of Nivea Creme. In Germany, the face care line was called Nivea Gesicht (Nivea Face).[8] Within a year, Nivea Visage/Gesicht held leading market positions in multiple European countries. A second tonic and eye makeup remover were added in 1985.

Early Visage ads stressed the mildness of Nivea products in caring for the face. The initial ad campaign used the tagline, "The mildest way to cleanse your face." Within one year, Visage became a leading face cleanser in many European countries. For the next five years, Nivea Visage's message focused on mildness. Realizing that they would have to enter the moisturizing segment of this market to establish themselves as a specialist in the face care market, BDF introduced a beauty fluid (liquid moisturizer) in 1987 positioned directly against Oil of Olay, the only international face care brand in the mass market at the time. The product performed poorly and BDF learned that the benefit of "mildness," which had been such a successful point of difference in the cleansing segment of the market, was not as unique in the moisturizing segment of the market. Rather, consumers in this market segment were looking for proof of a product's effectiveness. Franziska Schmiedebach, Marketing Director for Nivea Visage explained:

The moisturizing segment is much more sophisticated than the cleansing segment for face care. You have to talk about anti-age benefits, specific ingredients, etc. The added value of the product in terms of packaging and claims and advertisement is much more sophisticated than what you have in the cleansing segment. The benefit of mildness in cleansing was strong enough but the benefit of mildness in moisturizing is really a standard in that category and everyone will say "so what." In our packaging, we were much too close to our cleansing product.

To effectively sell in this largest segment of the face care market, Cosmed upgraded Nivea Visage's image through a series of actions. First, Cosmed changed the packaging of its products from plastic to glass. Second, the company altered the logo for Nivea Visage. Third, the company improved its product offerings, including the introduction of a moisturizing day cream and night cream in 1989. Finally, Cosmed introduced a new series of ads that focused on highlighting specific benefits of Nivea Visage products. In this second campaign, the ads moved away from Nivea's traditional codes of simplicity and universality to develop a more sophisticated specialty image. Using a lead product strategy, Visage ads highlighted the technical functionality of the line's most sophisticated products, focusing on the specific benefits of each product to specific skin problems. A 1989 Italian TV commercial exemplified their approach. Showing a woman preparing to go out for the day, the voiceover says: "Discover the beauty of your face. Nivea Viso the new moisturizing cream rich of precious components (like jojoba oil). Nivea Viso gives your skin all the elasticity and smoothness it needs to be beautiful. Nivea Viso reveals your natural beauty."

By 1990, Nivea Visage ranked second behind L'Oreal Plentitude in European market share and generated over 100 million DM in revenue. Nivea Visage had been extended to include over a dozen products and had evolved from offering simple cleansing products to providing sophisticated, technology-based problem solving products for face care. With the addition of its first "anti-age" products in 1991, BDF introduced a third ad campaign, "Science in all confidence" that sought to blend the image of the best in face care science with the trust historically attached to the Nivea brand name. This new campaign was launched in 1991 both in print and television form. The TV commercial showed a young woman by herself as she prepared to go out for the day. The camera moved around the apartment with her as she dressed. The only skin product that she used before leaving was Nivea Visage Liposome Creme. The voiceover said: "We have just created the first Nivea Visage rejuvenating liposome range. Of course, we could tell you how fast our liposomes carry active anti-aging agents directly into your skin. We could even show you what they look like. But instead, we decided to show you the result of their efficacy. Because a woman is much prettier than a liposome. Nivea Visage. Science in all confidence." This ad ran throughout Europe.

A series of related print ads also ran, each highlighting one of three liposome products offered by Nivea Visage: youth cream with liposomes, gel cream, and eyezone gel. The layout and look of the ads remained consistent—a woman's face (usually comprising three-quarters of the page) with the product shown below her face and the ad copy in relatively small print below the product—but the copy detailed the specific attributes of whichever product was being presented and its resulting benefits. The tagline "Science in all confidence" was found at the bottom of all ads.

NIVEA SUN

Nivea Sun was one of the oldest Nivea products besides Nivea Creme and had the most extensive product range of any Nivea sub-brand. Over time, Nivea Sun had extended its oil and cream products to include lotions in a variety of SPF factors and after-sun products, among others. Nivea sun care products had a long advertising history dating back to the 1930s. Only in the early 1970s, however, did BDF consciously begin to develop Nivea Sun as an independent sub-brand. A unique logo and design was developed and a conscious decision was made to create a unique Nivea Sun "world" in its advertising where people were happy—enjoying the sun and one another—under the care and protection of Nivea Sun products. Since sun care ads only ran three months a year, they emphasized a simple, easily remembered message of good feelings, protection, and the value of the Sun products in general. By not emphasizing new Nivea Sun products in its ads, the company relied on the customer to look for them—distinguished by new packaging sizes and colors—on the shelf.

During the 1980s, BDF continually reworked its sun care advertising in an effort to upgrade the sub-brand. In 1986, there was a second relaunch of Nivea Sun—introducing both a new product formulation and new packaging, as well as a new advertising campaign. While the tone of the ads remained focused on pleasure and enjoyment, the new campaign made a stronger emotional appeal to skin protection than previous ads. The initial tag line read, "Tanning with care instead of tanning with burn. The new Nivea Sun—Your skin should be important to you." In 1988, a new ad was introduced that maintained the same tone, but with a new tag line, "Nivea Sun. Tanning Without Problems." The ad caption read: "Protect and care for your best tan." A series of television ads reinforced this same message.

In the late 1980s and early 1990s, BDF extended the Nivea Sun line to include more specialized sun care products, including a line of sensitive skin and après-ski products, further demonstrating the innovativeness of the Nivea Sun brand and its ability to fulfill specialized needs. The emphasis of Nivea Sun advertising still was on creating an image of superior care and protection, however, rather than providing detailed product information on performance. A 1991 television ad showed a woman on the beach playing with her young child. The voiceover said: "The new Nivea Sun makes sun gentle. Double protection filter, natural moisturizers, anti-free radicals, water resistant. More protection and care for a healthy, happy tan. Nivea Sun makes sun gentle." This emphasis on protection was highlighted by the addition of a large banana leaf as a symbol of protection.

NIVEA FOR MEN

In 1980, Nivea introduced its first product specifically designed for the men's skin care market—an after-shave balsam. This product was also the first Nivea product marketed on a European-wide basis that focused exclusively on care of the face. The product, an emulsion with moisturizing qualities, embodied the Nivea brand extension requirements of product innovation with brand continuity. It was the first after-shave product to provide both alcoholic water—common to other after-shave products—and a moisturizer to care for the face. From the beginning, the Nivea for Men ads emphasized the mildness and caring of Nivea as their distinguishing customer benefits. The first print ad for the after-shave balm carried the tag line, "Less alcohol, more care."

From the initial introduction of the after-shave balsam in 1980, the Nivea for Men sub-brand had grown into a full line of men's skin care products by the end of the decade, including shaving cream, gel and foam, and after-shave lotion and cream, among others. Even as Cosmed expanded the men's product line, the caring and mildness themes remained constant as ads continued to emphasize the protective and moisturizing qualities of Nivea. In the late 1980s, Cosmed ran a European television campaign called "The Couple." In this ad, after a man finished his morning shave, he was brought Nivea After-Shave Balsam to put on his face by his wife/girlfriend. As he continued to get ready for work, the voiceover said, "Nivea for Men After Shave Balsam refreshes, relaxes, and cares for the skin in a fascinating way. The After Shave with the care of Nivea—Nivea for Men."

A second television campaign that began in 1991 highlighted a new "APG" factor that ensured the mildness and caring qualities of Nivea for Men products. The "Barber" ad showed a man sitting in a chair at the barber shop with a warm towel over his face. The barber—a beautiful woman—unwrapped the towel and applied Nivea after-shave balsam to the man's face. The voiceover said: "The new After-Shave Balsam of Nivea for Men contains something others would love to have: The natural APG factor for an especially mild skin care. Nivea for Men—Once a day a man should feel so good."

NIVEA SHOWER AND BATH

Nivea Shower and Bath was Nivea's first sub-brand developed primarily for personal care, extending the Nivea brand into important skin-related personal care categories. Since their initial introduction, ads for Nivea shower and bath products promoted the high-quality, mild, caring benefits of the Nivea brand while also emphasizing the added emotional benefit of pleasure. The bath ads stressed relaxation and well-being and typically showed a woman relaxing alone, confident she was in care of Nivea bath products. The shower ads highlighted the feeling of revitalization and care experienced when showering with Nivea shower products.

A 1991 ad showed a woman washing with a new product, Nivea Creme Shower. As she washed, a pearl appeared over her body to symbolize the soft and caressing feeling of showering with Nivea. The voiceover said: "You immediately feel care that caresses your skin. Nivea Creme Shower. Delightfully gentle and creamily mild. Care you can feel. Nivea Creme Shower, the feeling of gentle care." A complementary print ad showed a woman showering—eyes closed and pearl in hand. The headline read, "When freshness becomes like a caress." The copy continued, "Feelings of freshness turning into endless pleasure like a pearl of softness caressing your body." At the bottom of the ad were pictures of two Nivea shower products: Nivea Shower and Nivea Creme Shower. The tagline read, "Nivea Shower with high valuable proteins."

NIVEA HAIR CARE

In 1983, Nivea introduced its first hair care product, a multipurpose shampoo, followed by the introduction of a conditioner a year later. The introduction of hair care products extended Nivea's presence even further in the personal care market. Unlike Nivea Bath and Shower, however, hair care was not viewed as a skin-related product line and hence was not to be closely aligned with Nivea's key association as a skin care provider. To maintain a strong link to other aspects of Nivea's core brand image, though, the two products were named (in German) "Pflege-Shampoo" and "Pflege-Spulung." By adding the word "Pflege" (Care) to the product names, it was clear that these products continued in the Nivea tradition of caring. The initial print ad headline read: "The entire care for frequently washed hair." Over the next few years, ads for Nivea Shampoo and Conditioner remained essentially unchanged. Primarily in print, they continued to emphasize the mildness and care qualities of Nivea shampoo for daily hair care.

NIVEA DEO

In 1991, BDF extended Nivea's presence in the personal care area with the introduction of a line of deodorant products called Nivea Deo. Though Cosmed had initially discussed introducing a deodorant product under the Nivea brand name since 1983, management was not convinced the time was right until 1991. Uwe Wolfer, Director of Cosmed Germany, explained:

> In the deodorant field, there is demand today for mildness and caring that wasn't there before. Ten years ago, people wanted freshness, fragrance, efficacy, and they wanted the product to be transparent. Today, even in the deodorant field, people want assurance of mildness. So we introduced a product with this caring and mildness image. If we had done the same operation ten years ago, we would not have succeeded. It is a question of timing when to enter [product] categories.

The initial Deo line included aerosol, roll-on, pump-spray, and cream products. Deo Creme was considered the real innovative product and hence was the lead product used in most advertising. In its advertising, Nivea Deo went beyond the traditional "efficacy" appeals to emphasize the additional dimension of "caring" through the introduction of a feather as a symbol of mildness and caring. The initial TV spot showed a woman placing Nivea Deo on her underarm as the voiceover said: "Now there is a deodorant that guarantees you not only secure efficacy, but also extra mildness. Because it is from Nivea. New Nivea Deodorant. The harmony of mildness and efficacy." A print campaign promoted the same theme. One ad showed a package (pack shots) of the Nivea Deo product line with the feather and the headline, "The harmony of mildness and efficacy." A second ad showed a pack shot of Deo Creme only—again with the feather—with the headline, "The deodorant that even cares for your skin."

Rationalizing the Nivea Brand

By the early 1990s, it was clear that BDF had succeeded in extending the Nivea brand from skin creme to a skin care and personal care brand. In 1992, Nivea Creme accounted for only 22 percent of total Nivea brand sales. While Nivea Creme remained the largest single contributor to total revenues, the newer product lines each made significant contributions of their own. Nivea products held strong market positions throughout Europe, especially in smaller volume markets where advertising costs were lower, as BDF was a small company relative to its competition (e.g., Unilever, Procter & Gamble, and L'Oreal) and its advertising budget was substantially lower as a result. Nivea's highest percentage market penetration was in Belgium, Switzerland, and Austria. Germany—the largest skin and personal care market in Europe—however, remained its largest volume market.

Though marketed independently, all Nivea sub-brands carried some of the brand associations established by Nivea Creme while also expanding the set of associations that consumers linked to the Nivea brand name. BDF's success in establishing Nivea as a broad skin care and personal care brand now presented the company with a new set of issues and challenges.

In the process of establishing sub-brands, everyone worried about the management and development of the Nivea brand itself. There was concern that the Nivea brand image—in particular, the Nivea Creme image—had been weakened through all of the product introductions. Moreover, there was fear that continuing to develop the sub-brands independently of one another—given the breadth of the Nivea product lines—would be complicated, risky, and could send a confusing set of messages to consumers about what Nivea represented. Currently, ad campaigns were developed independently by three different ad agencies. While there were similarities in the various campaigns, there was no consistent message strategy or standardized presentation. Because of these concerns, Cosmed management decided it was necessary to bring more consistency to the marketing of the Nivea sub-brands.

At the same time, the Cosmed Division came under new leadership. Dr. Rolf Kunisch, head of Procter & Gamble's European Division, joined BDF after twenty-two years with one of BDF's major competitors. In an effort to educate himself about the company's understanding of the Nivea brand, Kunisch joined a task force to define the Nivea brand philosophy. Years of discussions about the Nivea brand had resulted in an informal brand philosophy shared and respected by management. However, Kunisch believed that in preparation for the development of a new Nivea communications strategy, adaptation of a formalized brand philosophy would be an invaluable tool. Kunisch explained:

> Nivea is the most fascinating brand in the world, second only to Coca-Cola. The company had done a tremendous job over the last 50 years to keep the Nivea brand focused yet diversified in a very reasonable way. But at the same time there was a lack of conscientiousness of what it meant to be a brand. In the good old days, BDF had a brand relationship that was very personalized. Only three people knew how it had all been done—one retired, one left the company, and one died. When these people had gone, BDF, working with consultants, had created 12 SBUs—strategic business units—and put a chief on top of each one. In addition, there were three advertising agencies who did not talk with one another. In preparation for our first communication strategy meeting, I asked, why we did not have a logo on the wall? Someone finally came to me three days before the meeting and said Nivea did not have one clearly defined logo. I began with the basics and asked: What is Nivea? The data was all there, the feeling was there, but no one had put it on a piece of paper.

While working internally on rationalizing the Nivea brand philosophy, the company also undertook a set of market research studies. The "Inner Visuals" imagery study focused on consumer perceptions of and associations with the Nivea brand, whereas a semiological analysis of sociocultural values sought to identify general consumer trends and values for the 1990s.

LINKING THE NIVEA BRAND TO CONSUMER VALUES IN THE 1990S

The "Inner Visuals" imagery study, conducted by HTP research firm in Germany, showed consumers a variety of pictures and sequences and asked them to indicate which skin care brand the particular scene best represented. The pictures had been designed based on results from two earlier phases of the study.[9] The images with which Nivea was most often identified by consumers were those scenes that depicted the following: the traditional family ideal, communities (e.g., groups doing something together), symbols that crossed boundaries (e.g., the earth, the blue planet, symbols that evoke a feeling of community), and single properties and qualities associated with the product (e.g., scenes depicting moisture, freshness, relaxation, a classic).

The second study was a semiological analysis of consumers' sociocultural values in the 1990s, conducted by the RISC Group, that evaluated the sociocultural positioning of Nivea Creme and other major Nivea sub-brands (Nivea Body, Nivea Visage, Nivea Sun, and Nivea Bath and Shower). As part of the analysis, the study also examined the brand "territory" for each sub-brand, relative to main competitors, as conveyed by product packaging and TV and print ads. The research was primarily restricted to sociocultural attitudes in France and Germany, Nivea's two largest volume markets in Europe.

The results of these two studies showed that Nivea's brand associations fit well into the values of the 1990s consumer: The return to a more simplistic, holistic approach to life; the desire for fairness, authenticity, openness, and belonging; and integration of the past with the present were all values that were also associated with the Nivea brand and particularly Nivea Creme. Nivea's core brand associations—mildness and caring—were key needs of 1990s consumers. The results of this research clearly suggested that the 1990s presented an opportunity to grow and expand the Nivea brand.

DEVELOPING COSMED'S CORPORATE STRATEGY

Combining the results of the external research with their own internal research and discussions, the Cosmed task force developed a common brand philosophy for Nivea to be adopted by the entire company and become the basis for developing a corporate strategy that the Cosmed Division could implement at the product level.

The brand philosophy centered on maintaining the association of "universality" for Nivea products. Now that the Nivea brand represented comprehensive skin care and personal care, the company wanted to develop a marketing strategy that would continue to nurture core Nivea associations while widening their applicability and enhancing their meaning via sub-brands. Kunisch explained, "We want to build on the image of the blue tin where we are number one almost everywhere in Europe." Nivea Creme continued to represent the heart of the Nivea image, evoking the most trust and sympathy of the consumer. Even as Nivea's lines of products continued to be expanded in the 1990s, Nivea Creme was to remain the primary representative of the brand's history and myth. Though its sales share had declined some over the years, Nivea Creme was still considered the company's most important product for its role in establishing and renewing basic trust in the Nivea brand.

The role of the other sub-brands was to continue to cater to the specific skin care and personal care needs of their target market segments and contribute back their particular product class associations to reinforce and elaborate on the image of Nivea as a skin care specialist. Since facial skin care represented 75 percent of the European skin care market and was very closely related to Nivea's strong association of "general skin care" from Nivea Creme, Nivea Visage was considered the primary sub-brand to upgrade Nivea's image into the 1990s. Visage had the most sophisticated, contemporary, and specialist brand image of all Nivea sub-brands. At the same time, it benefited from the "halo" of the Nivea name that represented trust, care, mildness, and fair price. The primary challenge facing Nivea Visage was how to effectively upgrade the Nivea image as a skin care specialist while continuing to represent the universality and accessibility of the Nivea brand. As with Visage, other sub-brands were expected to offer something back to the Nivea brand. Through this combination, BDF sought to maintain Nivea's leading position in the mass market segment of the European skin care market.

While the Nivea brand was BDF's leading skin and personal care brand, the company also derived considerable revenue from other skin and personal care products sold under different brand names. The most important of these other brands were: 8x4 deodorant and bath products, Labello lip balm, and Atrix lotion.[10] In total, these other brands represented nearly 40 percent of Cosmed's sales in 1991. These brands had been developed out of the company's historical desire not to rely exclusively on one brand. While these brands would continue to be part of BDF's skin care and personal care product offerings, the company decided—with much cajoling by Dr. Kunisch—that the company's primary focus in the future would be on the further development of the Nivea brand through the introduction of new products. Only "extra" efforts and investments would be devoted to the development of these other brands.

Executing the Nivea Brand Philosophy in the 1990s

Having established corporate objectives, Cosmed now needed to design a communications strategy. Cosmed worked with its advertising agency, TBWA, to develop a set of guidelines that would communicate a certain "Niveaness" to ads and promotions for all Nivea products while also allowing the individual products to speak effectively to their specific target markets. This "Niveaness" was to be represented not only in the layout of the ads, but also in their message and image. The core brand, Nivea Creme, represented a set of desirable brand values: timelessness and agelessness, motherhood and a happy family, honesty and trustworthiness, and the product benefits of mildness and quality. Any campaign for Nivea Creme would have to incorporate these values; any campaign for a sub-brand would have to reflect elements of these values, although not necessarily only those values.

This process of creating a "Niveaness" to all products and ads had begun in 1990 when the company decided to internationalize its sub-brands by creating a universal name for each product category and common packaging on a worldwide basis. With the brand philosophy now in place, the company was able to establish additional guidelines for the ad agency to follow. These guidelines included: evoking common emotion in all ads; use of a uniform and unchangeable Nivea logo for all packaging; consistent use of lettering and typeface; incorporation of real, aspirational people in ads; and dialogue about the product in an understandable way.

THE BLUE MANIFESTO ADVERTISING CAMPAIGN

Historically, most Nivea ad campaigns had been developed from a predominantly German perspective, largely because BDF had built the Nivea brand around the local needs of the German market. With the increasing internationalization of the cosmetics and toiletries market and the international strength of its main competitors, BDF felt that it was very important in going forward to build the Nivea brand through a strong European base. Consequently, the company sought to develop a true international ad campaign. Because Nivea Creme was still the company's most important image carrier but was plagued by stagnating sales, Cosmed decided first to develop a worldwide ad campaign that presented a common brand image for Nivea Creme. As one executive explained:

> Throughout Europe, the Nivea image is really well established and is more or less the same for everyone—and this image was built by Nivea Creme. The main reason to have a more brand identity weighted campaign for Nivea Creme was to keep this heritage alive.

The "Blue Manifesto" campaign, initially introduced in January 1992, included a series of television and print ads highlighting Nivea Creme. With "Blue Manifesto," BDF believed it had captured the essence of the spirit of Nivea through Nivea Creme in a way that spoke directly to the 1990s consumer. A video introducing the "Blue Manifesto" campaign described the message behind the new campaign as follows:

> "The year is 1992. A new generation of consumers has grown up. A new consciousness had gripped the consumer of the '90's. The young generation—our new target group—is discovering family life, discovering what is really important in life, what people really need . . . less glamour, more substance, less "chic-chic" more product, less show more impact. What the new consumer is looking for is equilibrium and harmony. Again, less is more.
>
> This trend toward simplicity opens new opportunities for the Nivea brand—a new era for Nivea Creme. 1992 sees the start of a new campaign that once again shows the brand with an idea that reveals the secret of the brand and brings its fascination to life. The idea is as simple as it is brilliant and derived from the product itself . . . or to be more precise from one of the world's greatest logo's—the Nivea Creme lettering."

The campaign included five 20 second television spots and seven print ads. All television ads were shot with a blue tinted background. The first ad showed a group of seagulls flying together through the air as circus music played in the background. The headline read: "Harmony in Blue." "Harmony" was written in the Nivea logo lettering while "in Blue" was written in white cursive letters. At the end of the ad a picture of a tin of Nivea Creme flashed on the screen with the tagline "All that skin needs to live." The four other ads were identical in tone, style, and look, as follows.

> The second ad showed a moving close up of a woman with the music "You Are So Beautiful" in the background. Once the camera was close up on the woman's face the headline, "Simply Beautiful" showed on the screen. The word "Simply" was in Nivea logo lettering while the word "Beautiful" was in cursive letters. A picture of a tin of Nivea Creme was flashed on the screen with the tagline "All that skin needs to live." The print version of the ad showed the same woman in the same blue tint with the same wording and lettering. The tagline was found on the very bottom of the page next to a small tin of Nivea Creme.
>
> A third TV ad showed a couple kissing while the song, "I've Got You Babe" played in the background. The headline of this ad read, "All You Need." A print version of this ad was also run.
>
> The fourth TV ad showed a family with the headline, "Take Care." Once again "Take" was in Nivea logo lettering and "Care" was written in cursive letters. The print version of the ad was identical.
>
> The fifth TV ad showed a couple first looking at each other and then moving towards one another. The headline on this ad read, "Touch Me." Again the combination block and cursive lettering was used. In the additional print ads, the same style—blue tint, Nivea lettering, same tagline and picture of Nivea Creme at bottom—was employed but with different faces and headlines.

While the "Blue Manifesto" campaign was designed specifically for Nivea Creme, ads for other Nivea sub-brands adopted some of the design elements of the Nivea Creme ads, particularly in the use of the Nivea logo lettering—for example, the block and cursive combination. The block letters were always used to identify the product and the cursive lettering was used to highlight specific product attributes. While no other ads used the blue tinted background, most did use blue in the background of their print ads.

Strategies for the Future

As the Cosmed management team sat in their 1993 annual planning committee meeting, they reflected on all that had been accomplished in the last few years. A brand philosophy had been established and the first steps in implementing that philosophy had been taken, highlighted by their initial attempt at a truly international ad campaign with Blue Manifesto. At this point, Nivea Visage was continuing to sell extremely well, Nivea Deo had reached the number one position in Germany and was gaining market share in Europe, and Nivea for Men and Nivea Body were also faring well. Even with these accomplishments, though, many challenges and much work lay ahead as they realized the difficult issues they still needed to confront.

The first issue they had to address was how to move forward with the Blue Manifesto campaign. The campaign had been a fairly dramatic departure from their previous campaigns for Nivea Creme. How was it contributing to their brand image and equity? What changes should be made in the ad campaign to ensure that Nivea Creme was properly positioned within the Nivea brand portfolio? More generally, what role should Nivea Creme take within that portfolio? Another important issue was whether Nivea should undertake any type of an umbrella ad or corporate branding ad. An umbrella ad might emphasize the various sub-brands and how they collectively provided value to customers. A corporate branding ad might stress the key attributes or benefits found in all Nivea products. Although such ads complemented the ads for the individual sub-brands, limited funds were available and trade-offs would have to be made in terms of the relative emphasis and support individual sub-brands would receive if an umbrella or corporate branding ad were run.

The multiple opportunities and challenges had to be reconciled and directions had to be set for 1993 as to how the Nivea brand should be managed and moved forward. The Cosmed management team sat down to begin the planning meeting.

Discussion Questions

1. What is the brand image and sources of equity for the Nivea brand? Does it vary across product classes? How would you characterize its brand hierarchy?
2. What are the pros and cons of the various options available to Beiersdorf management? Should they run a corporate brand or umbrella ad for all of their products? What is the role of the Nivea skin creme advertising? Should it be changed?
3. What would you do now? What recommendations would you make to Nivea concerning next steps in its marketing program?

Notes

1. This case was made possible through the cooperation of Dr. Rolf Kunisch and Cosmed Division management for Beiersdorf AG in Hamburg, Germany. Leslie Kimerling prepared this case under the supervision of Professor Kevin Lane Keller as the basis for class discussion.
2. While Nivea Skin and Personal Care products are sold in over 140 countries worldwide, this case study focuses primarily on Nivea's European market position and brand strategy.
3. Nivea oil was introduced in the 1930s. In the 1910s and 1920s, Nivea body powder was a popular product.
4. The head of the company at that time, Oscar Tropowitz, had to leave Germany with his family after the passage of anti-Jewish legislation by the National Socialists in the early 1930s. Initially, his family moved to Amsterdam and from there, he continued to run the company in conjunction with the non-Jewish management team in Hamburg. Tropowitz later moved to Switzerland but the combination of political and personal events made it impossible for him to remain involved in the company during the war.
5. Some of BDF's competitors challenged these ads in the German courts, arguing that the ads violated German fair competition laws severely restricting comparative advertising, and in fact, "decrees" were issued against BDF to stop publication of certain motifs.
6. BDF also offered a line of problem-solving products called Nivea Body Specifics sold only in France, Belgium, and Italy.
7. A cleansing milk is a lotion-type cleaning formula used to wash the face. A tonic is used after washing as an antistringent. A moisturizing lotion is used last to replenish the skin's natural moisturizers.

8. Visage is the French word for face and carried connotations of a sophisticated product; however, in southern Germany, "visage" was an expression that translated to "slapping the face" and carried with it strong negative connotations. The same line of products was called Nivea Viso in Italy and Nivea Facial in Spain and the United Kingdom.

9. In Phase 1, HTP had developed a set of words that provoked mental images of the Nivea brand. In Phase 2, the research group had developed a series of images associated with the sight, smell, and touch of Nivea Creme. Using the output from these two research phases, the firm created a set of forty-two storyboards to show consumers and analyze their reactions.

10. Other principal brands included Basis pH, Limara and Doppeldusch, Guhl, Azea, and Solea.

APPENDIX E
Nike: Building A Global Brand[1]

In 1993, David Kottkamp, General Manager of Nike International, deliberated on how to invigorate the sluggish sales of the division. Although Nike commanded market share leadership in the U.S. athletic shoe industry—for example, controlling over half of the $1.2 billion basketball shoe business—it had experienced comparatively less success in Europe since its introduction in 1980. In an effort to regain control over the Nike brand and refocus the international effort, Kottkamp had spent the past five years repurchasing the licensing rights to Nike products from independent distributors across Europe. By 1991, Nike had obtained control over 90 percent of its European distribution, and Kottkamp was able to direct attention towards making the Nike brand the top athletic shoe in Europe. Despite intensive marketing activity surrounding the 1992 Summer Olympics in Barcelona, the Nike brand still had not achieved as much success in Europe as management had hoped. The basic question was how to best approach the European market. Should Nike attempt to duplicate its past marketing efforts in the United States that had been so successful? If so, how? Essentially, Kottkamp had to decide how to best build global brand equity for the Nike brand.

Nike's Domestic History

THE EARLY YEARS

The Nike story begins with its founder, sports enthusiast Phil Knight. Knight grew up in Oregon—a haven for the running microculture—with a deep passion for athletics in general and running in particular. In 1962, Knight started Blue Ribbon Sports, the precursor company to Nike. The idea for Blue Ribbon Sports grew out of a business plan that Knight wrote during his MBA program at Stanford University. At the time, the athletic shoe industry was dominated by two German companies, Adidas and Puma. Knight recognized a neglected segment of serious athletes that had specialized

E-1

needs that were not being addressed by the major players. The concept was simple: Provide high quality running shoes designed especially for athletes *by* athletes. Knight believed that "high-tech" shoes for runners could be manufactured at competitive prices *if* imported from abroad. After completing his degree in 1962, Knight embarked on a world tour that included a visit to Japan. During his visit, Knight contacted Onitsuka Tiger—an athletic shoe manufacturer with a reputation for high quality products—to convince them of his vision for the athletic shoe market. When asked who he represented, Knight made up a name—and Blue Ribbon Sports was born.

In December 1963, Knight received his first shipment of 200 Tiger shoes, which he promptly stored in the Blue Ribbon warehouse—his family's basement. In the initial years, Knight sold the shoes part-time while he worked full-time for an accounting firm in Portland, Oregon. In the 1960s, Oregon was filled with impassioned runners who possessed a hard-wired dedication to their sport. Although running may have failed to capture the attention of athletes in most other places, running was unquestionably respected and even revered in Oregon. Long distance runners from all over the world flocked to Oregon to hone their skills. Being a respectable runner himself during his undergraduate days at the University of Oregon, Knight had no problem understanding the needs of runners. Without much cash to do any advertising for his products, Knight crafted his "grassroots" philosophy of selling athletic shoes: Speaking to athletes in their language and on their level; sharing their true passion for running; and listening to their feedback about his products and the sport. Each weekend Knight would travel from track meet to track meet, high school and college, talking with athletes and selling Tiger shoes from the trunk of his green Plymouth Valiant.

In 1964, Knight asked Bill Bowerman, his track coach at the University of Oregon, to join him at Blue Ribbon Sports. Bowerman had a knack for designing running shoes for the track team and constantly experimented with new products. In fact, Bowerman did not like to be called "coach" by his team—he preferred the title "Professor of Competitive Response." During his running days at the university, Bowerman had used Knight and other runners as "guinea pigs" numerous times for his new shoe designs. One memorable day a teammate tried on a pair of the Bowerman sneakers and, as Knight watched, "beat a runner he had no business beating." Knight knew then that innovative, well-designed shoes could make a difference in performance, and he had always kept his mentor Bowerman in mind. Knight approached Bowerman with the concept for his business plan, and that year the Blue Ribbon Sports partnership was formed, with Knight and Bowerman each contributing $500.

In the first year of their partnership, Blue Ribbon Sports sold 1,300 Tiger running shoes totaling $8,000 in revenues. Bowerman would tinker with new shoe designs while Knight traveled to track meets refining his "grassroots" marketing approach. Many runners already knew of Bowerman and tried Blue Ribbon's shoes, providing critical feedback in the process. Unable to handle all of the business operations in a part-time capacity, Knight hired his first employee in 1965, Jeff Johnson, a middle-distance runner from Stanford with an anthropology degree. Johnson shared Knight's passion for running—he loved running more than working—and joined Blue Ribbon Sports as its first full-time salesperson, unable to resist Knight's own rationale for the company: "It is a way to continue a lifestyle *and* still make a living."

With the addition of Johnson, sales rose to $20,000 and profits rose to $3,240 in 1965. Needless to say, Knight kept his job as an accountant and Bowerman kept his job as a track coach. Johnson opened the company's first retail outlet in 1966—a small space next to a beauty parlor in Santa Monica, California—and hired more salespeople who continued the grassroots approach of selling shoes at track meets from the trunks of their cars. In 1967, Bowerman developed the Marathon, the first running shoe made with a lightweight, durable, nylon upper. Sales for Blue Ribbon began to rise as word about the innovation spread in the running community. To keep up with demand, a sales office was opened behind a mortuary in Wellesley, Massachusetts to handle East Coast distribution. The next year Bowerman developed two new products: the Cortez—Blue Ribbon's best seller—and the Boston—the first running shoe with a full-length cushioned midsole, a radical innovation in running shoe design. By 1969, sales reached $300,000, and Knight, then an Assistant Professor of Business Administration at Portland State University, resigned to dedicate himself full time to Blue Ribbon Sports, which now employed 20 workers.

THE FORMATIVE YEARS

By 1971, the company had reached $1 million in sales. In the following year, Onitsuka demanded more control over its operations so Knight decided to venture out on his own. He struck a deal with Nissho Iwai, the sixth largest Japanese trading company, to finance the contract manufacture of athletic shoes in Japan to Blue Ribbon's specifications. Manufacturing his own line of shoes required choosing a new, marketable brand name as the Blue Ribbon name seemed too cumbersome for consumers. Knight wanted to use the name "Dimension Six" to reflect the six dimensions of sports—the fan, the event, the arena, the equipment, the media, and the shoes or apparel. Other Blue Ribbon executives felt the name was too long and lobbied for something else.

Just days before the product was to go out to distributors, Jeff Johnson suggested the name Nike, the winged Greek Goddess of victory, which had come to him in a dream the night before. Although nobody else liked the name or knew what it stood for, it seemed better than Dimension Six, and thus the Nike name was accepted. Around the same time, Knight had asked a designer friend to propose some ideas for a logo for the new product. She submitted twelve proposals, none of which were liked by anybody at Blue Ribbon. Due to time constraints—the product was set to hit the shelves in days—the management team finally decided to go with the least objectionable logo, "a fat check mark." Thus, the famous Nike "swoosh" was born for a total cost of $35!

At the Olympic trials in 1972, Blue Ribbon Sports, with the Nike brand name, unveiled the Moonshoe running shoe with the patented Waffle outsole. This radical new innovation, created when Bowerman poured rubber into a kitchen waffle iron, revolutionized running by offering better traction in a lighter-weight, durable shoe. The Waffle design immediately captured the attention of athletes around the world, providing Blue Ribbon with a surge of publicity for the new Nike brand, even though the Moonshoe was not made available to the general public.

The next year, 1973, witnessed Nike's next big marketing move. University of Oregon running star Steve Prefontaine became the first athlete to be paid to wear Nike shoes. Prefontaine epitomized "the athlete against the establishment" attitude that was at the foundation of the company's irreverence and challenge to the status quo. Knight explains, "Pre(fontaine) was a rebel from a working-class background, a guy full of cockiness and pride and guts. Pre's spirit is the cornerstone of this company's soul." Knight had founded the company with the attitude to do whatever it would take to defeat established running shoe companies and "the system." Adidas was the top brand at the time. Just as Prefontaine did not care what other people thought, Knight was nurturing a corporate culture along the same lines.

Because of its grassroots marketing efforts, Blue Ribbon's close contact to customers enabled it to recruit some of the best up-and-coming runners. The endorsers typically represented more than simply athletic ability, however, as they often had distinct personalities too. Each athlete reflected a dimension of the Blue Ribbon culture. Most employees were avid runners themselves from the Oregon area. With a true love for sports, they were eager to see their athletes succeed. The athletes, in turn, were anxious to try the latest Nike innovations. In the running community, Nike quickly became the symbol of "authentic" athletic shoes, made especially for serious athletes by serious athletes. Knight explains:[2]

> We were able to get a lot of great ones under contract—people like Steve Prefontaine and Alberto Salazar—because we spent a lot of time at track events and had relationships with the runners, but mostly because we were doing interesting things with our shoes. Naturally, we thought the world stopped and started in the lab and everything revolved around the product.

Nike's first sponsorship of athletes was relatively inexpensive but, more importantly, very productive. Prefontaine never lost a race in four years at the University of Oregon and went on to set a number of U.S. running records. Jon Anderson, another long distance runner, won the Boston Marathon in a pair of Nike shoes. The early success of these Nike-sponsored runners led Knight to sign up athletes in other sports. The abundantly talented, mercurial Ilie Nastase became Nike's first tennis athletic endorser shortly before becoming the world's top-ranked tennis player. The budget was still tight, however, so only the most cost-effective athletes could be signed. In fact, Knight was so strapped financially that he had to pass on signing up one promising young tennis athlete who demanded $1,500 for his sponsorship. Jimmy Conners signed with L.K. shoes instead, a Romanian firm with shoes of questionable quality. Conners disliked the shoes so much, however, that he began to wear other shoes in spite of the contract. As fate would have it, Conners—without an endorsement contract—won the Wimbledon and U.S. Open tennis tournaments in 1974 in a pair of Nikes.

In 1974, the Waffle Trainer featuring the Waffle outsole was finally introduced to the general public. The diffusion of the Waffle Trainer benefited from the so-called "pyramid of influence" that Nike had come to believe characterized the athletic shoe marketplace—that is, the fact that product and brand choices of consumers in the mass market were influenced by the preferences and behavior of a small percentage of top athletes. The reality was that the vast majority of athletic shoes were never actually used "on the court" but rather were used in other settings, for example, for just "walking around." Nevertheless, Nike was convinced that the choices of these more casual users were affected by the choices of more serious athletes. Fueled by this "trickle-down" marketing, it quickly became the best-selling training shoe in the country.

By the end of 1974, Nike revenues had reached $4.8 million, and the company employed over 250 people. Throughout the remainder of the decade, the Nike brand experienced phenomenal growth—doubling sales and profits annually—as a running craze and health and fitness movement swept the country. Americans of all ages (and sizes!) were taking up some form of exercise to stay in shape. Blue Ribbon followed suit with a host of new innovations for shoes in a variety of sports. In 1978, the company officially changed its name from Blue Ribbon Sports to Nike, Inc., reflecting the growing recognition of the Nike brand name and the popularity of the Bowerman innovations. By 1980, the company had 2700 employees and sales of $270 million, surpassing Adidas as the number one athletic shoe company in the United States with almost 50 percent market share.

THE TROUBLED YEARS

The popularity of running, however, was beginning to give way in the early 1980s to new categories such as fitness and aerobics. The new trends were dominated by women, a market segment that had thus far remained largely unaddressed by Nike. As a result, growth for Nike started to tail off as competitors such as Reebok were better positioned to ride the aerobics wave. Around this time, Reebok made a batch of aerobic shoes with soft, garment leather instead of the traditional "tough" athletic shoe leather. The shoes caught fire in the marketplace. In the process, Reebok introduced new attribute and benefit considerations to the athletic shoe industry, namely "style," "fashion," "comfort," and "for women." Their soft leather shoes were supple, comfortable to wear, and made women's feet look smaller. Suddenly, Reebok became the industry darling. Nike's reputation for performance and innovation, its dedication to serious athletes, and its focus on the male consumer segment did not help them much in the more fashion-conscious aerobics market. Refusing to compromise on performance and failing to come to grips with a market it did not really seem to understand, Nike literally missed out on the fastest growing segment of the industry. "We wouldn't listen," says senior employee Geoff Hollister. "We wouldn't even listen to our own wives."

Market share began to drop, and warehouses became overstocked with running shoes. Nike's first layoff occurred in 1984, followed by two money-losing quarters in 1985. Finally, although Nike reached $1 billion in sales in 1986, they lost the market share lead to Reebok. By 1987, Reebok dominated the U.S. athletic shoe market, owning 30 percent of the market as compared to Nike's 18 percent. Phil Knight explains:[3]

> Reebok came out of nowhere to dominate the aerobics market, which we completely miscalculated. We made an aerobics shoe that was functionally superior to Reebok's, but we missed the styling. Reebok's shoe was sleek and attractive, while ours was sturdy and clunky. We also decided against using garment leather, as Reebok had done, because it wasn't durable. By the time we developed a leather shoe that was both strong and soft, Reebok had established a brand, won a huge chunk of sales, and gained momentum to go right by us. We were also having management problems at that time because we really hadn't adjusted to being a big company. And on top of that, we made a disastrous move into casual shoes.

THE TRANSITION YEARS

Reebok's meteoric rise forced Nike to chart a new direction with a fresh approach to the market. Nike had learned some valuable lessons. Subsequently, they would put the spotlight on the consumer—not just the product—and become more marketing-oriented as a result. Thus, they would broaden their marketing effort to embrace consumers and the brand as well as the design and manufacture of products. Rather than copy Reebok's emphasis on style, however, Nike decided to keep its focus on performance but devote more attention to basketball, which had continued its recent rise in popularity. Perhaps more importantly, Nike set out to change how it marketed new products, creating a new marketing formula that linked concepts related to shoes, colors, clothes, athletes, logos, and its first-ever widespread, mass market television advertising.

Nike had never really advertised much because it felt advertising did nothing more than possibly come between the intimate relationship that a runner had with his or her shoes. Advertising and commercialism was felt to be nothing short of heresy for the purist athlete. Nike had only advertised in peer-group running journals, which it tolerated only because they were published by runners themselves. Even then, all advertising remained performance-oriented, with no models, no gimmicks, and no hype. As part of "reinventing" Nike, however, Nike decided to take to the airwaves for a new basketball campaign. For the task of developing the campaign, Nike turned to Dan Wieden, president of Wieden and Kennedy, a little-known advertising agency just a short drive from Nike headquarters. Wieden fondly recalls Phil Knight's first word, "Hi. I'm Phil Knight, and I don't believe in advertising." Wieden and Kennedy would soon change his mind.

Applying this new marketing concept required, in particular, both new advertising *and* new technology. The product innovation was truly break-through—pressurized gas pumped into a flexible plastic membrane and placed directly into the soles of the shoe, providing cushioning unmatched by any other shoe in the industry. The technology worked because the molecules of the gas were bigger than the molecules of air, so they would be unable to escape. Consequently, the cushioning would last for the duration of the shoe. The simplicity of the technology was that consumers could actually see the air bag through a tiny window in the heel. "Visible Air" became the marketing phrase that explicitly captured this new consumer benefit.

This new technology was to be used first with the Air Max running shoes. The ad that showcased this new shoe was in its own way a bold innovation, albeit a daring and risky one. The "Revolution in Motion" spot used the heretofore untouched Beatles song as an anthem (at the cost of hundreds of thousands of dollars in licensing fees) in a TV ad that used novel black & white, 16mm, hand-held cinematography to depict professional athletes and "regular people" of all ages involved in sports. Close-up shots in the ads clearly depicted the heel of the shoe compressing and springing back after contact with the ground. Complementary print ads were run in mass market and narrowly-targeted niche publications. The campaign debuted in March 1987. Scott Bedbury, Nike's Director of Advertising at the time, recalls:

> The Revolution ad was a powerful brand statement and a massive handshake from Nike to the consumers. The ads successfully got across, both implicitly and explicitly, the product technology. It was able to communicate to a wide range of people but still

was true to the Nike brand. It reflected Nike's "soul" and a deep, almost genetic understanding of what it meant to be "Nike" and how that could and should be expressed in advertising.

Air Max was a huge success, selling $75 million at retail in its first year. Within a year, air technology was also introduced into selected higher-end shoe models in basketball, tennis, and other categories. Applying this new marketing concept to basketball required choosing a new athlete to represent the product benefits and Nike attitude. In 1985, Nike managed to sign then-rookie guard Michael Jordan to endorse Nike basketball shoes after Adidas, Jordan's first choice, refused to match Nike's offer. Although Jordan was still an up-and-coming basketball superstar, most basketball followers agreed that he was going to be something special. Nike bet on Jordan, and it paid off. His very first commercial began by showing a basketball rolling along an outdoor court towards the future superstar. As Jordan picked up the ball and drove toward the basket, the sound of jet engines roared in the background. As Jordan took flight, the engines screamed louder. The slow motion camera followed Jordan's body as he gracefully glided towards the basket for a full ten seconds. At the end of the thirty seconds, Michael Jordan became a household name and the premier superstar in basketball.

The Air Jordan line of basketball shoes literally flew off the shelves. Nike sold over $100 million of Air Jordans in the first year alone, although sales slipped when Jordan broke his foot in the following year. Considering that "successful" new product launches typically sold $20 million, Air Jordans represented one of the lone bright spots for the company as Reebok continued its surge ahead in the aerobics market in the mid-1980s. Everything about the Air Jordan line was a perfect fit. The air technology was a hit with consumers, Michael Jordan quickly became recognized as the best player in basketball, and the advertising campaign captivated Nike's target segment. Knight reflects back on the success of Air Jordans:[4]

> Basketball, unlike casual shoes, was all about performance, so it fit under the Nike umbrella. And the shoe itself was terrific. It was so colorful that the NBA banned it—which was great. . . . Michael Jordan wore the shoes despite being threatened with a fine, and of course, played like no one has ever played before. It was everything you could ask for, and sales just took off. . . . (Air Jordans) success showed us that slicing things up into digestible chunks was the wave of the future.

Nike now chose to define each sport separately, as a "category" in and of itself, and applied its successful marketing formula in different ways in different categories over the years. New categories ranged from cross-training and water sports to outdoors and walking. Within categories, sub-brands were developed to appeal to certain market segments, for example, the bold, colorful Challenge Court (endorsed by Andre Agassi) and the more subdued Supreme Court (endorsed by a now-older John McEnroe) tennis lines and the Air Force (endorsed by Charles Barkley and David Robinson) and Air Flight (endorsed by Scottie Pippin) basketball lines.

THE DOMINANT YEARS

The Air Jordan line sparked a new wave of momentum for Nike. As Michael Jordan flew through the air on his way to three championships, the image consciousness of the market gave way to a re-emphasis on performance. This time it was Reebok who got lost in the midst of a transition. Just as Nike had paid too little attention to the rise of the aerobics trend of the mid-1980s, Reebok paid too little attention to a consumer desire for performance-related products in the late 1980s. Also during this time, new competitors entered the market chasing Reebok, not Nike. Nike stayed on the fore-front of performance, while competitors such as L.A. Gear vied with Reebok for control of the fashion market.

Ironically, the difference in the values and approaches of the two market leaders was most clearly exemplified in the area Knight once loathed—advertising. As the aerobics trend began to tail off in 1988, Reebok embarked on a quirky new ad campaign with the slogan, "Reeboks Let U.B.U." The offbeat ads took a totally different approach to selling athletic shoes, showing a wide variety of often bizarre-looking and unusual-acting individuals doing all sorts of things *except* playing sports. The fast-paced, choppy-edited ads unquestionably grabbed consumers' attention, but seemed to turn off much of the market at the same time. Moreover, many sporting goods outlets just plain hated the $25 million campaign. As one retail buyer joked, "You be you. We be Nike."

While Reebok tried to breathe life into the fashion segment, Nike continued pushing the performance of its shoes. As luck would have it, literally the day after Reebok aired its first U.B.U. ads, Nike aired its first ads in their new "Just Do It" ad campaign. The $20 million month-long blitz—subtly urging Americans to participate more actively in sports—featured twelve TV spots in all. The campaign marked the launch of a category—cross-training shoes designed for athletes who played more than one sport—which was new to Nike and the athletic shoe industry as a whole. Just as Michael Jordan was the perfect professional athlete to represent air technology and basketball, the perfect professional athlete to represent cross-training was Bo Jackson. Bo had become the first modern professional athlete to excel at both baseball and football. The new ad campaign featured Jackson participating in a wide variety of other sports, excelling at anything he dared to try. For example, one ad began by showing Jackson cycling, a sport for which he was not known. As Jackson cycled up and down hills to the pounding drumbeat on the soundtrack, he appeared to get stronger and go faster. The ad ended with Jackson looking into the camera and barking, "So when is this Tour de France thing anyway?" The tag line "Just Do It" appeared as Bo rode off in the distance.

The "Just Do It" campaign challenged a generation of athletic enthusiasts to chase their goals no matter how difficult or elusive they might seem, a natural manifestation of Nike's attitude of self-empowerment through sports. "It" could refer to anything or any sport that the consumer wanted to play, and for every sport, Nike wanted consumers to believe that they had the perfect shoe. Self-empowerment reflected an attitude relevant to both celebrity and non-celebrity athletes, and the "Just Do It" advertising used both. One non-celebrity ad featured Walt Stack, an 80-year-old long distance runner, running across the Golden Gate bridge as part of his daily morning running routine. The "Just Do It" trailer appeared on the screen as the shirtless Stack made his way past the center of the bridge on a chilly San Francisco morning. Talking to the camera as it zoomed in and while still running, Stack remarked, "People ask me how I keep my teeth from chattering when it's cold." Pausing, Stack matter-of-factly replied, "I leave them in my locker."

Nike-endorsed athletes continued to embody the athletic ideals of determination, individuality, self-sacrifice, and winning through their continued successes on and off the playing field. Most importantly, Nike advertising stayed true to its obsession with high performance shoes geared towards serious athletes. Nike followed the success of cross-training with the third generation Air Jordan shoe and a follow-up to the award-winning "Just Do It" campaign for cross-training. The Air Jordan line had been launched in 1988 with a clever set of ads featuring Michael Jordan and Spike Lee reprising his Mars Blackmon character from his sleeper-hit debut movie, "She's Gotta Have It." The new ads had showcased Jordan's talent and Blackmon's love for his Air Jordan shoes—in the movie, he would not take them off for anyone or anything, including his girlfriend Lola. The second round of "Just Do It" advertising featured the highly acclaimed "Bo Knows" commercials, where Bo Jackson appeared to "know" how to play fifteen sports—to the astonishment of top athletes in each of these different sports (albeit a disbelieving Wayne Gretsky)—and even dabbled in playing the blues with Bo Diddley. The trailer for each spot always carried the "Just Do It" slogan as the definitive Nike statement on sports.

By 1990, sales had surpassed $2 billion, and Nike had reclaimed the market share lead from Reebok in the United States. Nike successfully applied its new marketing formula—blending performance and attitude through strategic product development, endorsements, and advertising—to other categories, including tennis and baseball. Nike continued to launch product innovations, with the breakthrough Air Huarache technology in 1991, which helped to revolutionize new product design, and the newly redesigned Air Max shoe in 1993, a 30 percent cushioning improvement over prior Air technology. The advertising also kept pace with its own innovations. Nike ads, reflecting the company's character, addressed controversial issues head-on. The ads ranged from Charles Barkley pronouncing that he was "Not a Role Model" to a 1995 ad showcasing a long distance runner inflicted with the AIDS virus. Finally, Nike continued to court the world's best athletes that it felt could represent some aspect of the Nike "soul" and image. Sports marketing at Nike—the sponsorship side of the business—was undeniably of huge importance. As Knight recalled:

> The whole thing happens on TV now. A few years back we were extremely proud of a novel, three-quarter-high shoe we'd developed. But we only sold 10,000 of them the first year. Then John McEnroe had ankle trouble and switched to the shoe. We sold 1½ million pairs the following year. The final game of the NCAA basketball tournament is better than any runway in Paris for launching a shoe. Kids climb up next to the screen to see what the players are wearing.

Nike kept their "finger on the pulse" of the shoe-buying public, in part, through their use of "EKINs" (Nike spelled backwards)—sports-loving employees whose job was to hit the streets to disseminate information about Nike and find out what was on the minds of retailers and consumers. Nike's "Brand Strength Monitor"—created by its marketing research and insights guru, Jerome Conlan—more formally tracked consumer perceptions three times a year to identify marketplace trends. In areas where they felt less knowledgeable, for example, outside of track and basketball, Nike was more likely to commission customized research studies. Nike's inventory control system, called "Futures," also helped Nike to better gauge consumer response and plan production accordingly. Nike required retailers to order up to 80 percent of their purchases six to eight months in advance in return for guaranteed delivery times and a discount of up to 10 percent. Nike sweetened its relationships with retailers such as Foot Locker by also giving them early looks at new lines as well as the rights to exclusively sell certain models.

Sales soared past $3 billion in 1991 as Michael Jordan took the Chicago Bulls to their first of three championships. By 1993, Nike athletes included 265 NBA basketball players, 275 NFL football players, and 290 baseball players. Half the teams that won the NCAA college basketball championships over the past ten years had worn Nike shoes. In total, Nike had arrangements with college coaches and athletic departments that resulted in over sixty top-tier "Nike schools." Many of these arrangements included apparel—an area that had grown in importance to Nike. As part of a complete overhaul in 1993, Nike decided to refocus its apparel business. Before, with the exception of track and field, apparel was mostly designed to just complement shoes. Nike decided to put more emphasis on top-of-the-line performance wear—uniforms and apparel worn in actual competition—through its Organized Team Sports group and F.I.T. lines. Although representing only a small percentage of apparel revenues, these new initiatives were thought to provide halo to other apparel lines and be consistent with broadening the Nike brand meaning to encompass "performance in sports" and not just shoes.

Nike's European History

The same year that Nike overtook Adidas as the number one athletic shoe company in the United States—1980—Phil Knight dispatched five employees to Europe to establish a presence for the U.S. shoe manufacturer there. Because of its favorable tax and business operation laws, the group set up an office in Amsterdam and began its mission to establish the Nike name and brand. Though Nike had succeeded in breaking Adidas's dominance in the United States, taking over from the leader in its home arena would be a greater challenge.

INITIAL GROWTH

In the early 1980s, the most popular sports in Europe were soccer, track and field, and tennis. If Nike wanted to have a significant presence in Europe, the company would have to establish its name in each of these sports in each of Europe's five primary markets—Germany, France, England, Italy, and Spain—which accounted for the bulk of the European sports shoe and apparel sales.

Nike's European marketing team knew it needed to attack one sport at a time. Given the company's track and field heritage, Nike initially focused on developing links in track and field whose sizable popularity in Europe was reflected by the fact that it was the second most televised sport (after soccer). Using track and field as its entry, the company sought ex-runners with the same devotion and intensity to the sport as Nike to help develop the brand. Finding such athletes to work with Nike, however, proved to be an elusive task. Of its key country accounts, only in England was Nike successful in recruiting an ex-runner, Brendan Foster—Britain's premier distance runner in the 1970s and a 1976 Olympic gold medalist—to be its local distributor. With Foster's connections and persona, Nike was able to pursue its grassroots approach to brand development there. Elsewhere in Europe, however, Nike was forced to partner with the largest local athletic shoe and apparel distributor.

Driven by a sense of urgency to establish a presence in Europe and gain shelf space, as well as a need to raise money to finance U.S. business operations during the sluggish 1980s, Nike chose to sell licensing rights to some of these local distributors. In doing so, Nike lost control over both which products found their way onto the retail shelves and how the Nike message was delivered. Each distributor—focusing on its own country and often selling a number of other athletic shoe brands—developed its own advertising, marketing and promotions, and product strategy, as a result, communicated its own interpretation of the Nike brand. Liz Dolan, V.P. of Marketing, looks back:

> The biggest problem with the independent distributors was that the product selection varied so widely from country to country. You would go into Italy and Nike would be a casual shoe brand there because the independent distributors would tend to make up their own shoes or just buy the lower end of our line. Inappropriate product selection, however, could really diminish the value of the brand. The independent distributors just didn't understand brand marketing.

The lack of cohesion evident with Nike's distributors in Europe was apparent simply from looking at their business cards—each gave the Nike brand a different look. Consequently, Nike's European team was forced to expend significant energy trying to influence each distributor's interpretation of Nike's corporate and brand philosophy.

Besides these difficulties with its marketing intermediaries, Nike faced formidable competition in Europe. Adidas, the German shoe company, dominated the European sports market. Together with Puma—a spin-off of Adidas—the two companies controlled over 75 percent of Europe's athletic shoe and apparel market. For decades, the two companies had developed the grassroots allegiance of local sports teams, particularly soccer, track and field, tennis, and rugby. They both had endorsement contracts with top European athletes in each of these sports and sponsored many local teams in cities and towns across Europe. Adidas, in particular, was respected for the quality of its shoes and had earned the reputation as the European performance brand. For any company to establish a presence in Germany—Europe's largest country market—in the face of these two companies was considered nearly impossible.

Early Nike advertising was conducted at the country level. In 1981, Nike highlighted American tennis star, John McEnroe, in a set of print ads that were run around the time of Wimbledon. These ads played on McEnroe's "nasty boy" image, showing a Nike tennis shoe and a headline underneath that read, "McEnroe Swears by Them." In another version, the headline read "McEnroe's Favorite Four-Letter Word." McEnroe's triumph at Wimbledon that year helped Nike gain some badly needed exposure as well as credibility as an authentic athletic shoe among European consumers.

FURTHER EXPANSION

For seven years, Nike struggled to build its presence in Europe. By the end of 1987, Nike's European revenues had grown to $150 million, representing 5 percent of the European athletic shoe market and a growing percentage of Nike's total revenues. Compared to its U.S. position, however, Nike's penetration of the European market was comparatively insignificant. Perhaps even more disturbing to Nike was its inability to control the growth of its brand. In most countries, the Nike distributors who controlled marketing and advertising rights were not necessarily highly motivated about selling Nike. To overcome this limitation—but still maintain its quality image—Nike restricted its product line to primarily high-end, higher-priced shoes. In doing so, the company forfeited volume and hence market share. Although the company also sold some low-end, relatively inexpensive shoes, it had no product offerings for the expansive "middle market." Moreover, as a result of this pricing policy, many European consumers saw Nike as an aggressive, expensive American brand.

Because Nike distributors controlled advertising in their local markets, each continued to develop its own interpretation of the Nike brand and identity programs. While Nike productively embarked on the "Just Do It" umbrella campaign in the United States, Grey Advertising—the agency that managed the Nike account in five countries—was developing separate, and not necessarily reinforcing, ad campaigns in each European country. Nike also did not have the same means of displaying its shoes and retailing them to customers as in the United States—athletic shoe specialty stores did not really exist in Europe.

In late 1987, Nike sent a new man to head its European operations—David Kottkamp—with a mission to focus on building the brand there. In April 1988, Kottkamp asked eight key Nike advertising and marketing executives from Portland to come to Europe to help assess Nike's position and look for ways to take control of the Nike brand. The "Beastie Boys" tour, as the trip became known, was a five-day whirlwind visit of six European countries headed by Nike's director of advertising, Scott Bedbury. One of the group's primary missions was to look at local work being done there and try to find ways to "Nike-ize" it. Soon after the Nike contingent returned to Beaverton, a follow-up trip was arranged to include Dan Weiden, head of Nike's U.S. ad agency. At the end of these two trips, it became clear to Nike that the only way to take control of the brand was to take greater control of the advertising and product strategies. To enable this to happen, Kottkamp focused on repurchasing licensing rights to Nike products from their licensed distributors in Europe.

While Kottkamp was initiating these negotiations with Nike distributors—a task that would take several years—he launched Nike's first centralized print campaign in 1988 as a means to introduce "Air" technology in that market. Despite objections from Nike's European distributors, the campaign achieved some success. As a result of its favorable response, Nike decided to develop additional pan-European advertising campaigns for both print and TV. Looking for broad appeal, Nike hoped to recreate the success of its umbrella "Revolution" ad campaign from the United States. Instead of focusing on country *differences*, however, the campaign would attempt to highlight country *similarities*. Lacking the stable of famous athletes in Europe that Nike had back home in America, the pan-European approach seemed to make the most sense. To reach this audience, the company doubled its advertising campaign from $5 million in 1987 to $10 million in 1988. In an effort to be cost effective, Nike wanted any European campaign to be broad enough to be used in multiple countries. In 1989, Nike introduced its "Gospel" campaign. This powerful, uplifting campaign was unquestionably American in its look and Nike in its attitude. Using the tag line, "True to its [Nike] soul," the campaign ran primarily on MTV Europe and Star TV in Asia, as well as various national TV networks. The print campaign developed the theme that there was air in Nike shoes because there was none in various places where well-known athletic events took place—such as Chicago Stadium, Bislett Stadium, and Ku'Damm.

REGAINING CONTROL

Over the next three years—while Kottkamp worked on repurchasing licensing rights—Nike relied heavily on advertising to promote its brand. The direction to take with that advertising, however, was not obvious. Research revealed that a 2-minute TV spot designed to portray Nike products and attitude—featuring Jimi Hendrix' adventurous rendition of the national anthem at the Woodstock rock festival and the tag line, "Play Hard. Die Old."—was seen as too aggressive and was not well received. Nike attempted to blend centralized and localized work. Thus, Nike did import some of its American heroes to promote the brand in Europe—European marketing managers could look at Wieden and Kennedy's latest creations and choose ads they felt were relevant. For example, the "Tennis Lessons" spot that spoofed Agassi and McEnroe's rebellious image was shown in Italy, Germany, and elsewhere. Ads featuring Bo Jackson, not surprisingly, were deemed as less relevant.

In 1990, Nike commissioned famous film directors from ten countries to film ads that reflected each director's vision—and presumably reflective of their European sensibilities—of the Air 180 shoes. These shoes contained Nike's latest evolution of its air-cushioning technology—the bottom of the heel held a large urethane window, bonded to the shoe by a new compound Nike developed, that afforded a 180-degree view of a greatly expanded air bag. In Nike's opinion, although not entirely unexpected, many of these ads "missed the mark," and six of the ads were literally "road killed"—that is, were never aired despite being fully produced. For example, one such ad was by the legendary French director Jean-Luc Godard, which contained the following footage:

> The Young Boy and the Young Girl skip through a field. The Witch spies them, sets down a basket, picks up a scythe. "Where are you going, children?" she screams in Latin. The Boy and Girl run. The Witch falls. Cut to a close-up of a Nike Air 180 running shoe and the sound effects of a Bronx Cheer.

Other ads were thought to dwell too much on the cushioning benefit provided by the shoe. The ads that were seen as more effective, however, were placed on the air.

As it turned out, the relative lack of success of the campaign had implications beyond Europe. One or more of the ads were intended to run in the Super Bowl in the United States in January 1991. Deciding not to air any of the ads literally days before the Super Bowl—and uncomfortable with running more typically aggressive or humorous Nike ads in the light of U.S. involvement in the Gulf War—Nike created perhaps one of its most moving and emotional ads ever. Dubbed "Heritage," the ads followed a runner as he navigated down a city's deserted streets in the dead of night. As soft, plaintive piano music played in the background, giant images of Nike's most famous athletes and most famous moments—starting with Prefontaine and moving forward—were projected on the walls of the buildings that he passed. The ad concluded with the words, "There Is No Finish Line," and the Nike swoosh and Air Max name.

That same year, the "Instant Karma" spot used John Lennon's powerful tune to introduce the "radical" new line of Air Huaraches. Interspersed with scenes of Nike's star athletic endorsers—Michael Jordan, Scottie Pippen, and Joan Benoit Samuelson—as well as everyday people working out were, in the American and English-speaking market, a series of English phrases. Overseas, stick-figure symbols designed by a Nike art director, Michael Prieve, were used instead. This creative solution—literally devising a new graphics language—allowed the ads to be run ultimately in sixty-five countries in all.

By the end of 1991, Kottkamp had successfully regained control of 90 percent of Nike's European distribution. In comparison, Adidas only controlled 65 percent and Reebok only controlled 40 percent of its European distribution. Getting European retailers, who were used to ordering whatever they wanted, whenever they wanted from the Adidas warehouse, to adopt Nike's Futures program, so successful in the United States, was a harder sell. Nevertheless, now that they had greater control over its marketing, Nike could concentrate on developing its brand in the manner that they desired.

NIKE IN 1992

Without question, Europe in 1992 represented a tremendous growth opportunity for Nike. At that time, 400 million pairs of athletic footwear were sold in the United States. Europe with 130 million *more* people than the States, bought 280 million *fewer* pairs of shoes. The largest buying group there, those in their teens and twenties, owned an average of just two pairs each (compared to an average of at least four pairs in the United States). There were several explanations for the discrepancy. First, Europeans had a different view of the role of sports and top athletes and were not as idolizing of their sports heroes as were Americans. The American workout ethic, epitomized by health and fitness clubs and a firm belief of the essential importance of exercise, was not as widely embraced in Europe. Moreover, as a general rule, Europeans were slower to embrace sneakers as off-court shoes and were more likely to wear fine leather shoes even in casual settings. Either on or off the court, Europeans just needed fewer athletic shoes.

The image of athletic shoes was changing, however, and sneakers were no longer a dead giveaway that a person was, more likely than not, an American tourist. Youth especially seem captivated by the "American" image of Nike and Reebok. As a result, some progress had been made in Europe. By 1992, Nike's European sneaker revenues were approximately $1.1 billion—nearly six times the 1987 figure! Revenues grew 100 percent between 1989 and 1990. Its European promotion budget had risen from $10 million to $50 million. Adidas—with over $1.5 billion in revenues—still had more than double the market share of Nike in Europe. Though Adidas still dominated the European market, Nike had made significant inroads in the last five years, and the German giant and its counterpart, Puma, had lost market share to Nike and Reebok. To realize its goal of being the number one sport and fitness company in the world, Nike had to dominate Europe. Its two main competitors, Adidas and Reebok, posed very different challenges:

> **Adidas.** After the death of its President, Horst Dassler in 1987, Adidas struggled with organizational and management problems and internal turmoil. Adidas had proven to be slow to adapt to the Nike and Reebok challenge in Europe. Adidas was plagued by unfocused marketing, high costs, and a glut of products. By 1991, the company sold over 1,200 different variations and styles in footwear alone—offering individual collections for each sport in each country. Nike's marketing-driven approach was new for Adidas—a company that had really only established a marketing department in 1986. Its advertising expenditures as a percentage of turnover volume were half that of Nike. Many consumers found the Adidas brand conservative and not contemporary. Though weakened, Adidas still maintained a loyal customer base, particularly among the 35-and-older generation as well as retailers. Its strong grassroots presence and entrenchment in amateur sports sponsorships—particularly soccer—had ensured Adidas's number one market position in Europe.
>
> **Reebok.** Reebok's success in the U.S. women's fitness market carried over to Europe, providing the company with the necessary inroad into the European market. Like Nike, Reebok had built its presence through local distributors. During the 1980s, individual country managers appointed their own agencies and developed their own ads. For example, the tag lines for the 1992 Reebok umbrella campaigns in France, Germany, and the United Kingdom were "Break the Rules," "Get the Feeling!," and "The Edge," respectively. By 1992, European sales were over $600 million, representing 65 percent of Reebok's international sales. Reebok owned third place in most European markets behind Adidas and Nike, although in some countries such as the United Kingdom, Sweden, and Denmark, Reebok actually held the number one position. For 1993, Reebok was in the process of launching its new campaign theme, "Planet Reebok," across Europe to replace all local campaigns. The integrated marketing communications campaign was supported by $30 million outside the United States and was intended to convey the message, "Reebok is the brand for individuals all over the world who play at the peak of their potential and live life to the fullest." The ads, targeting 12- to 24-year-old males and females, began with an image of the Earth moving toward the viewer with the caption, "What Is Life Like on Planet Reebok?" Quick cuts of exhilarating sports and fitness action followed, accompanied by fast-paced music and "negative" captions such as "No Meetings," "No Faxes," "No Phones," and ultimately, "No Slogans."

Determined to overtake Adidas and prevent Reebok from continuing to gain ground, Nike focused its attention on the 1992 Barcelona Olympics, raising its overall global advertising and promotion budget to $240 million, up from $150 million the previous year, committing $50 million to Europe. Tom Clark, Nike's VP for product marketing at the time, explained: "We're looking to increase worldwide market share by 10 percent and to grind Reebok and Adidas down."[5] With the rise in popularity of basketball as an international sport, Nike planned to lead its marketing charge with its strong stable of basketball superstars. Leading up to the Olympics, U.S. Olympic "Dream Team" members such as Charles Barkley, Michael Jordan, and others were featured in European exhibition tours (where they signed autographs and participated in basketball clinics) and in a series of ad campaigns. Nike extended its superstar endorsement approach beyond just basketball and sought to play up its endorsements of other top-flight world-class athletes who would spotlight Nike products in the Olympic games. Besides Michael Jordan, Nike concentrated its promotion efforts on U.S. sprinter Michael Johnson, Ukrainian pole vaulter Serge Bubka, and Algerian middle-distance runner, Noureddine Morceli. Lacking its own superstar stable, Reebok responded by paying millions to outfit U.S. Olympic team members—including the basketball Dream Team—and NBC announcers in Barcelona with Reebok warm-ups and attire. In many ways, the 1992 Barcelona Olympics were a great success for Nike—the publicity surrounded the U.S. basketball Dream Team's objection to wearing their Reebok warm-ups at their gold medal award ceremony, combined with the medaling of scores of Nike athletes, offered unprecedented exposure to the brand and the loyalty it instilled from the world's best athletes.

To highlight the new Air Max shoe—the latest in Nike product design—Nike launched three commercials featuring Charles Barkley, Serge Bubka, and American sprinter Quincy Watts. The $20 million pan-European TV, billboard, and posters campaign featured the athletes in mock tragi-operas: Barkley was featured in "Barkley of Seville" (for "Barber of Seville"), Bubka played in "The Magic Shoe" (for "The Magic Flute"), and Watts was featured in "Don Quincy" (for "Don Quixote"). In the spirit of Nike irreverence, the concept behind the commercials was to juxtapose a relevant European cultural item—opera—against American cultural items—superstar athletes and their shoes. The "Barkley of Seville" spot became a European sensation. Singing in Italian, Barkley pranced through a basketball cathedral, accidentally killing a referee after being called for a foul. Faced with the loss of his shoes taken away as punishment by the image of Death, Barkley's voice rises to a falsetto, "La Scarpes" ("The Shoes") as he begged, "No!" The ad concluded with Barkley dueling Death in a 1-on-1 game of basketball.

Many European consumers, however, still found the brand intimidating, aggressive, unreachable, and unattainable. Moreover, retailers bristled at the Nike's Futures program and product mix, viewing the company as arrogant. In May 1993, Nike announced to Wall Street analysts that the company's earnings projections would be lower than expected. While Knight ensured that the company would continue to grow rapidly, the numbers were not what the Street expected. The lower than expected profits were largely the result of a deepening recession in Europe—particularly in France, Germany, and Spain, three of Nike's key markets—as well as the strength of the U.S. dollar against European currencies. To reach its growth goals in Europe, Nike needed to find a way to change consumers' perceptions there of Nike as an expensive, aggressive American brand.

HITTING ITS STRIDE

Despite some successes, Nike was clearly struggling to extend its U.S. reputation for performance and innovation into the European market. In hindsight, Nike had probably overrelied on advertising and American sports heroes and had not spent enough time and money "authenticating" the brand as they had so carefully done in originally building the brand in the United States. As a result, the Nike brand image was too fashion-oriented and not performance-oriented enough. A more grassroots approach was needed that built some credibility and relevance with the Nike brand in European sports—especially soccer. As an important first step, Nike became more actively involved as a sponsor of soccer youth leagues, local clubs, and national teams. In contrast to how Nike had approached other categories, apparel—not footwear—would provide the entry point to build the consumer franchise for the Nike brand in soccer.

As had been the case in the United States, Nike also needed to first win on the true "field of sport." Winning in the stores would then follow. Authenticity required that consumers see the product used by the right athletes in the right way—winning. As luck would have it, Brazil, the only national soccer team for which Nike had any real sponsorships during the 1994 World Cup—a number of the Brazilian stars had individual contracts to wear Nike shoes—won the premiere event. Their victory provided two very different benefits for Nike: Internally, it inspired confidence and motivation; externally, it lent credibility to a soccer-crazed world. Other soccer endorsements followed, for example, leading soccer teams Borussia Dortmund in Germany, Paris Saint Germain, Boca Juniors in Argentina, and the Italian national team as well as top soccer players such as Romario, Bebetto, Paolo Maldini, Andreas Moller, Ian Wright, and Eric Cantona. A Nike ad created for the World Cup, dubbed "The Wall," showed many of these prominent players springing to life from billboards as they literally kicked a soccer ball around the world. Nike also out-bid Adidas and Reebok for the sponsorship rights to the men's and women's U.S. national team. Outside soccer, Nike tried to sign up the best athletes in other countries to push Nike products locally, for example, baseball player Hideo Nomo in Japan and Formula I race car champion Michael Schumacher in Germany.

Nike's new focus was to become seen as more culturally, geographically, and personally relevant to local consumers abroad. The challenge, however, was to find the right local country managers who would have the necessary intuitive understanding and feel for the Nike brand to understand which elements of the marketing program should stay the same and which ones should be adapted and how. In August 1992, Weiden and Kennedy had opened up an Amsterdam office, headed by creative director Susan Hoffman, to better learn and understand the local market. The first campaign that was produced there—the operatic Air Max spots that had run during the 1992 Olympics—were so successful they were even used in other markets outside Europe, including the United States.

Building on the success of its "Just Do It" campaign in the United States, Nike attempted to introduce the tag line into its European advertising in Spring 1993. Nike hoped that this campaign would successfully communicate Nike's core values of authenticity, performance, and athletics, and help establish an emotional connection with European consumers through sports. The new campaign was a nice counterpart to the flashy, Barcelona-inspired Olympic spots featuring celebrity athletes. The "Just Do It" ad campaign was adapted for the European market in 1993 by going "back to basics." Designed to make the Nike brand more approachable, understandable, and applicable to people's lives, the new campaign wrapped up an inspirational message in visuals showing common folk displaying a passion for sport. The four spots featured kids and adults running and playing soccer in the streets, wheelchair athletes climbing mountainous hills as part of a race, and two runners winding their way beside a picturesque lake.

Nike allocated $80 million to $100 million to European advertising and promotion in 1993. Four commercials showing professional athletes engaged in competitive sports also were translated and showed in fifty-two local markets. In 1994, category-specific advertising was introduced (e.g., soccer and tennis), some ads of which were run globally. By 1995, two levels of advertising existed: pan-European ads (e.g., soccer, tennis, track, and fitness) and country-specific ads (featuring local heroes and local settings). The "Just Do It" tag line was kept in English or, in some cases, did not appear at all. Sports marketing efforts were highlighted by the signing of the Brazilian and Italian national teams in soccer in 1996 to long-term deals.

To better consolidate its operations, Nike built a $138 million, 750,000-square-foot centralized distribution center in Lakdaal, Belgium. Nike's product strategy changed in Europe, too. Previously, European marketing managers had been offered a "buffet table" of products developed in the United States. In the U.S. market, however, Nike had developed a vision of a category from "top to bottom" and created products to meet those requirements, developing one category at a time. In Europe, Nike set out to do category plans by country, with the goal of finding out for each country what it meant to be the performance athletic brand there. Some products were customized for certain countries (e.g., Japanese and German running shoes) or developed, at least initially, exclusively for certain countries (e.g., cricket shoes in Australia). Nike's organized and somewhat centralized approach to managing the brand was in stark contrast to Reebok's much more decentralized approach. Reebok country managers could make deals locally, create advertising locally, and so on.

Next Steps

Throughout the 1990s, Nike's marketing and advertising program was able, in its own marketing terms, to "widen the access point" and make the brand relevant to an increasingly broader range of consumers. To meet its corporate goal of "enhancing people's lives through sports and fitness" and "keeping the magic of sport alive," Nike's unique approach creatively blended "footwear," "apparel," "advertising," "sports marketing," and "retail." While maintaining relatively constant retail distribution and premium pricing strategies, Nike's innovative product development—putting out more than one shoe style, on average, *every day*—and bold advertising demonstrated that the brand was as much about attitude and imagery as shoes and clothing. Riding the wave of increased sports participation and consumption of sports entertainment, Nike's marketing formula was characterized as, "integrating the swoosh into the cultural fabric of sports and harnessing its emotional power."

Nike continued to take chances in its marketing programs in a desire to stay fresh, unpredictable, and a step ahead of its competition, which increasingly had adopted strategies to emulate its marketing approach. Their pan-European "Nike vs.

Evil" ad campaign received heavy exposure during the June 1996 European Championships leading up to the Summer Olympic Games. With its depiction of Nike soccer endorsers from around the world battling hellish opponents, the ad played well with the Nike audience, although it received a less positive response from some other quarters such as the media. Another, equally "edgy" Olympic TV spot combined the Iggy and the Stooges punk rock anthem, "Search and Destroy," and visual images of Olympic athletes strenuously performing—including a runner vomiting—similarly evoked varied reactions. Less controversially, Nike also continued to promote P.L.A.Y. ("Participate in the Lives of America's Youth"), a multimillion dollar effort aimed at encouraging activism on the part of kids and adults to promote healthy, active lifestyles among nation's youth.

Nike's philosophical willingness to take chances is reflected, not surprisingly, by a quote from a famed sportsman—U.C.L.A.'s legendary coach John Wooden—that Nike president Tom Clarke hung in his office: "The Team That Makes the Most Mistakes Wins." Although Nike was named Advertising Age's Marketer of the Year for 1996, similar dominance on a global landscape had yet to come. In his letter to shareholders in Nike's 1995 annual report, Phil Knight laid out the company's strategic objectives for the coming years as follows:

> First, make strides toward becoming a global company, not just a company doing business internationally. Make the effort to communicate, internally and externally, on a global basis. And to manage, as one brand around the world, our opportunities:
>
> > To grow and develop the European management team
> > To establish ourselves as a real apparel company
> > To truly get "on the board" in the world's most international game—soccer
> > To establish roots in ice hockey, the fastest growing team sport in North America
> > To expand our positioning in women's sports and fitness

In that same annual report, Knight also offered the following observations concerning their pace of achievement in overseas markets:

> As to our major goal of globalization, Director Ken Ohmae said a year ago it would take ten more years. I said we do it in five. A year later, I believe Dr. Ohmae is the better forecaster. It is simply more complicated than I imagined. But one thing is certain, if we do achieve our global goals we will have something of real value. And we are making progress.

In 1996, Knight publicly set a corporate goal of growing the $6.5 billion company to $12 billion by decade's end.

Discussion Questons

1. How would you characterize Nike's brand image and sources of brand equity in the United States? How would describe Reebok's?
2. Tactically, how did they build this brand equity?
3. Should Nike attempt to create the same brand image and sources of brand equity in Europe? What should it do differently?

Notes

1. This case was made possible through the cooperation of Nike and the assistance of David Kottkamp, General Manager of Nike International; Liz Dolan, VP of Marketing; Bill Zeitz, Director, International Advertising; Steve Miller, Director, Sports Marketing; and Nelson Farris, Director, Corporate Education. Leslie Kimerling and Sanjay Sood assisted in the preparation and writing of the case.

2. Geraldine E. Willigan, "High Performance Marketing: An Interview with Nike's Phil Knight," *Harvard Business Review,* July-August 1992, pp. 91–101.

3. Geraldine E. Willigan, "High Performance Marketing: An Interview with Nike's Phil Knight," *Harvard Business Review,* July-August 1992, pp. 91–101.

4. Geraldine E. Willigan, "High Performance Marketing: An Interview with Nike's Phil Knight," *Harvard Business Review,* July-August 1992, pp. 91–101.

5. *Adweek,* April 20, 1992, p. 19.

Epilogue

When asked how he beat Jimmy Connors in the 1980 Master's tennis tournament after losing to him in their previous 16 matches, Vitas Gerulatis quipped:

"Hey, *nobody* beats Vitas Gerulatis 17 times in a row."

I guess you have to draw the line somewhere.

May all your brands be winners.

Credits

Chapter 1

Figure 1–3, p. 26. *BrandWeek,* April 1996. Reprinted by permission of ASM Communications, Inc.

Chapter 2

Figure 2–2, p. 47. From research conducted by Larry Percy, Marketing Consultant, Montgomery, Alabama.

Figure 2–5, p. 55. By permission of DDB Needham, Chicago, IL.

Branding Brief 2–3, p. 57. Adapted from a case written by John Deighton, Harvard Business School, titled "McNeil Consumer Products Company: Tylenol," published in *The Ethical Manager.* ed. Ronald M. Green, Macmillan 1994.

Figure 2–6, p. 59. Adapted from a case written by John Deighton, Harvard Business School, titled "McNeil Consumer Products Company: Tylenol," published in *The Ethical Manager.* ed. Ronald M. Green, Macmillan 1994.

Figure 2–8, p. 66. Reprinted with permission of the Coca-Cola Company.

Chapter 3

Figure 3–2, p. 94. Keller, K., "Conceptualizing, Measuring and Managing Custom-Based Brand Equity," *Jr. of Marketing,* Jan. 1993. By permission of The American Marketing Association.

Figure 3–4, p. 103. "Tried It, Liked It" in K. Brandenburg, "What's in a Brand?" *American Demographics,* May 1993, pp. 26–32. © 1993 American Demographics, Ithaca, New York. Reprinted with permission.

Figure 3–8, p. 115. "Preaching to Convertibles" in Chip Walker, "How Strong Is Your Brand?" *Marketing Tools,* Jan/Feb. 1995, p. 51. ©1995 American Demographics. Reprinted with permission.

Figure 3–9, p. 121. Reprinted with permission of Saturn Corp.

Chapter 4

Figure 4–4, p. 142. Vanden Bergh, B. K. Adler & L. Oliver, "Linguistic Distinction Among Top Brand Names," *Journal of Advertising Research,* Aug./Sept. 1987. Reprinted by permission.

Figure 4–5, p. 148. From *Brand Equity* by John Murphy. © 1990 by Prentice Hall, UK.

Figure 4–6, p. 150. Reprinted with permission by the Maytag Corp.

Chapter 5

Figure 5–3, p. 182. Reprinted from Feb./Mar. 1995 U.S. AAdvantage Newsletter with permission by American Airlines.

Figure 5–7, p. 194. Reprinted with permission of the Goodyear Tire and Rubber Company.

Figure 5–10, p. 209. Reprinted with permission by Loblaw Companies Ltd.

Chapter 6

Figure 6–6, p. 232. © 1997 V&S Vin & Spirit AB.

Figure 6–13, p. 259. Reprinted with permission of Business Week.

Chapter 7

Figure 7–4, p. 289. Reprinted with permission by the NutraSweet Company.

Figure 7–5, p. 295. Reprinted with permission of the Coca-Cola Company.

Chapter 11

Figure 11–9, pp. 418–19. Reprinted Courtesy of Ford Motor Company.

Figure 11–10, p. 425. Reprinted with permission by Toyota Motor Corp.

Figure 11–11, p. 426. Reprinted with permission of Lufthansa Airlines.

Figure 11–12, p. 427. Reprinted with permission by Chevron Corp.

Index